CW00546523

# The Collector's Guide To Heavy Metal

## by Martin Popoff

Once again, for Beth,
parents and brother:
thanks for enduring the noise!

The Collector's Guide To Heavy Metal
by Martin Popoff
Copyright CG Publishing Inc Box 62034 Burlington Ontario Canada L7R 4K2
ISBN 1-896522-32-7

# Contents

# ACKNOWLEDGMENTS

Well, ain't this a shambling mess, but here goes . . .

**Buds from like, a while back** - Fiver of course, my best man Neil Cournoyer and his best gal Morag, Geoff, Pete, Al Block, Ken, Ralph, Fraz, McDicken, Garth "Rader" McKinnon, Al Klit, Sammy, fearless leader of the band Mark Toop and the Toop parents Gerald and Gail, cousin Lawrence, Jeremy, Sandy and Paul "Cheesehead" Bergeron and the Bergeron clan, Flash, Lumpy, Myron, Terry, Craig, Peter, Mad Mike Bell, Chris "Jonesy" Jones, Drew Harris (keep painting, buddy!), Jeff Downes, Neil and Cathy Deas, Maria, Joe Camillo, O'Farrell, Browser, Doug and Lois, John and Stormy, my second family from out east (God's country!).

**Mentors, Peers, Buds in the Biz, and uh, newer buds!**- Good buddy Tim Henderson and his Brave Words & Bloody Knuckles publishing empire (baby steps!), partner in crime and inspiration Mitch Joel, Ed Balog (my Slav brother), Dean Petrovic, Kevin Julie, Stephen and John Larocque, Mike Blackburn, Robert and Jenny, Stas, Steve Warden, Joey Vendetta and the Q107 Rock Report, John Mestad, Josh Wood, Robert Christgau, whose '70s and '80s record guides are without parallel, Phil Dellio, Geoff Savage, Bob Walker, Pat Christmas, Chuck Eddy, Al, Deb, Joe, Bolle Gregmar, John Schwartz, Helen, Sandy and the band, Pye Dubois, buds in the rock journalism field: Mike Smith, Kelly Barbieri, Tomas Pascual, Brian O'Neill at Live Wire, Johnny Walker, Ed and Keith at Glass Eye, Kurt at SFK, Mike Drew, Carl VP, Borivoj, phone buds: Donald K., Shannon M., Don Bolster, Chip "Chipster" Ruggieri, Mark at CMC, Tom at Perris, Erin at Attic, Marco and Ula at Century Media (thanks for the sampler!), Gordon at Earache from Nuclear Blast, John Walters at Second Sun, Tammy at Pavement, Paula at Futurist, Paula at Hype, Tom at Alert, Greg and Liz at EMI Canada, Bruce and Tom at Hypnotic, Denon, PolyGram, and Magnetic Air, Stephanie and Brian at Metal Blade, Amber at Sony, Noise, Stephanie at MCA, Gina at TVT, Sean Palmerston and Dustin Hardman.

**Wax Dispensaries** - Thanks for the memories and/or thanks for selling Riff Kills Man!: Gord and Rock Island Tape Centre, Tweed and Kelly's, Sandy's Music, Koo's, Strawberry Jams, Magic Mushroom, Eucalyptus, Mirage, Phantasmagoria, Lyle's Place, Mezzrow's, Scratch, Collector's Cove, Cinematica, Richard's, Quintessence, Zulu, A+A, A+B Sound, Ernie's Hot Wax, Black Swan, Charles Bogle, Melissa's, Track, Cellophane Square, Cheapie's, Towers, Rave, Zap, Home Of The Hits, Sam's, Vortex, Discovery, Open City, Record Peddlar, Terry at New World, Driftwood Music, HMV, Looney Tunes, Station To Station, Sunrise, Encore, Orange Monkey, Dr. Disc, Record World, The Record Works, Second Wave, Sloth, Backstreet, Room 201, Cargo, Rock On Stock, Zap, Vinyl Museum, Sound F/X, Star, Records On Wheels, Last Gasp, Caroline, Phantom Sound & Vision, John and Garnham at Utopia Records, Peter at Fandom Paradise, Marginal Distribution, book stores too many to mention but thank you all: this new version wouldn't have happened without your help, and a hello to Roy and Jim at The World's Biggest.

**Rock Greats** - The Undone: Phil Lynott, Freddie Mercury, Jerry Garcia and Kurt Cobain
The Unstoppable: Sepultura, Pantera, Trouble, Deep Purple, Mike Watt
The Unsung: Angel, Love/Hate, Badlands, King's X, Graham Bonnet, Gillan, Budgie
The Unincludable: The Waterboys, The Grateful Dead, Little Feat, Adrian Belew and The Bears, 54-40, The Meat Puppets, The Replacements.

**Print** - (for reviewing me first time around and general good reading over many years) Access, Arena Rock, Brave Words & Bloody Knuckles, Liisa, Ed, Nada, Dan, Chris and the crew at Chart, Circus, CMJ, Creem, Danforth Report, Enrage, Exclaim, Jason at Eye, Eye Opener, From Time To Time, The Georgia Straight, The Glass Eye, Goldmine, The Hamilton Spectator, HardRadio, Hit Parader, Marco at Ill Literature, Kerrang! Live Wire, M.E.A.T., Metal Edge, Metal Forces, Metal Hammer, Metal Maniacs, Mojo, Motorbooty, Option, Pop Life, Q, RIP (thanks Janiss!), Rolling Stone, Sabre Dance, The Satellite, SFK, Spin, The Toronto Star, The Trail Times, The Vancouver Sun, Varsity, Warp.

**Radio and TV** - (for talking metal with me and/or saying a few words about Riff Kills Man!) Q107 Rock Report with Steve, Joey and Rob, CBC, CFOX, the university stations; Tanya and Teresa at MuchMusic and Power 30.

**Production** - Neil and Maria at The Perfect Page for typesetting work extraordinaire; Webcom for quality printing and bindery, Rob, Rick and Gerry at CG Publishing (and Neale, Rob and Mary at Griffin) for putting it all together.

# INTRODUCTION

So here we be, trillions of hours later, after crammin' and combin' and stuffin' tunes into every spare minute of dayspace for the past six years. This unwieldy paperweight of a book is the natural outpouring of really two lives dedicated to the world's most powerful music. The first version of **The Collector's Guide To Heavy Metal** was actually called **Riff Kills Man!: 25 Years Of Recorded Hard Rock & Heavy Metal, a** self-published jobbie which was actually started with two writers, myself and Forrest "Fiver" Toop, best bud for 25 years, the only animal on earth who has logged as many metal hours as yours truly (besides Tim, I guess!). For the first year and a half of writing this book, we had split up the alphabet, started reviewing in tandem, I in Toronto, he in Seattle. Once a week we'd get on the horn, each reading out reviews we found particularly insightful, or dare I say, brilliant. The game plan was for me to interleaf his finished half (from WordPerfect disk) with mine, which I had been keying directly into Xerox Ventura. Then, being a print broker by trade, I would half-heartedly go through the motions of trying to get published, then succumb to the reality of designing, typesetting, printing and binding the damn thing ourselves, with an initial run of about 500 copies, which we would attempt to sell on consignment through unconventional, alternative channels, hopefully picking up a major chain or two in the process (turns out I did self-publish an initial run of 2,000, and now have Rick, Rob and Neale picking up the ball three years later). This new book is pretty much an update of the initial **Riff Kills Man!**, except that a) I've rewritten much (but not all!) of the stuff I found particularly clumsy or plain illiterate the first time around and b) the old book contained 1,942 reviews, while this one counts in at about 3,650.

So anyway, along the way, Fiver became bogged with work, and probably discouraged by our shared surging then slowing enthusiasms along the way. So what results is a solo venture, all reviews written by me, less the effort because of the dozens of great records that miss inclusion here, simply because I never got to hear them, our collections, of course, not being a perfect overlap. Plus, lemme tell ya, Fiver had some hilarious lines. Maybe a point/counterpoint version of **The Collector's Guide To Heavy Metal** is still in the cards, who knows? So here's to you, Fiver. Kick back with your favorite brown beverage, and take it in. Much to my fear and trepidation, I had to do it without you, but I couldn't have done it without you!

The following 3,650 or so record reviews are the product of my past, heavy metal forming a sonic diary of cycles through a life, this book containing a generous slice of my brain's accumulated learnings. This is the only book I've ever written, a fact which may prove painfully obvious to you as a reader, as you dissect and bisect the tortured syntax that riddles my lengthy sentences and sentence fragments. Reviews were written over a span of six years, resulting in further sources of unevenness. Even I was surprised at how poor my first 300 or so reviews compared to later pieces, and although very few of these first baby steps have been completely rewritten, many are a patchwork of edit upon edit; and it probably shows. Later reviews were not so bad first time around, albeit still showing my preponderance for non-sentences, invented words, fuzzy logic, and mixed metaphor that is designed to give a sense of the topic at hand rather than concrete analysis, however much I try to deliver the goods. Finally, as with any writer, the point arrived at which I couldn't stand re-reading the thing anymore, throwing up my hands declaring "editing be damned!" For example, sloppy search and replacing has resulted in "rock 'n' roll" showing up with spaces and without, aseptic occasionally spelled with a "c", partial retention of non-words like alot and nevermind, which oughta be words as far as I'm concerned, various spellings of words I made up anyways, and a not altogether consistent mix of American English and the King's English we use here in Canada. My apologies flow freely, but I do indeed feel that at minimum, a communication of a record's worth has taken place in every instance, that insights bear some authority, and that tidbits of useful objective information have been loosed upon your wattage-crustified brain, along with much infuriating subjective dreck on my part.

Despite the rollercoaster prose, I hope that you approach **The Collector's Guide To Heavy Metal** as I intended it to be; not so much a cover-to-cover read, but as a reference guide, a place where you can look before you leap with your dollar, shiny disc in hand, a place where you might gain new insights, or otherwise enhance your enjoyment of discs you already have and ignore.

My rating system is self-evident, however I'd like to venture a few words to shape your understanding of how I arrived at the numbers. Albums are rated on a scale of 1 to 10. 0's make me miserable and actively repulsed. Ratings of 1 to about 4 can mean a few things: a scant few quality tracks by a band in which I'm generally uninterested, or quite possibly anywhere from zero to two good tunes from a band I like most of the time. Towards the **4, 5** and **6** range, the same kind of duality applies: a record may be deeply flawed, in essence half quite good, half bad; or it may be generally listenable start to finish, philosophically and stylistically dull but less characterized by peaks or valleys. And although this is less a problem in the last five years, a record's grade can be low due to bad production despite the "art" being acceptable. Thus a **6** may be completely unnecessary (or worthy only to fans of that specific genre), or quite desirable due to inclusion of a few killer tracks, or historical importance as part of a larger catalogue, movement or genre. This range may also include a wishy-washy sense of "unratedness" I might feel applies to EPs, live albums and greatest hits packs, or even something state-of-the-art that is simply not to my taste (more of an unrated **7**).

As I say, many bands I greatly admire crank out **7**'s, being pretty well minimum grade for outfits I can't fault for any reason greater than lack of personal preference of the record at hand. **7**'s also denote solid efforts from acts which haven't proven themselves yet. A band tends to grow on me over time, strengthening in grade as I begin to see patterns in an increasing body of work. Thus, **7**'s can be acceptable records from as of yet unmagical bands, or less than god-like output from god-like bands. Most **7**'s I feel are worth owning (especially the highly competitive output from the last couple years), although each fan's purchase decision should be tempered with his acceptance level of the subgenre to which the album belongs, i.e. if you loathe grindcore, definitely do not buy a grindcore **7**. To reiterate and otherwise emphasize: a **7** is a pretty good record these days!

Throughout the book, I've tried to make a conscious effort to downgrade **9**'s to **8**'s, thus leaving the top two grades for truly hallowed wax. Consequently, **8**'s are still excellent records, stuff that is either deadly important to my being, or fine, fine work of which I may be slightly missing the point. Finally, an **8** may be a near perfect record in most every way, save for two, three or maybe even four tracks that smack of filler. **9**'s are almost always killer records by killer bands, both components usually necessary for such high ranking. They usually fall short of **10** due to one to three duff tracks, tunes I begin to resent after awhile for scarring a perfectly good record.

**9**'s may also result from a vague whiff of disappointment I may feel from a truly revered act, an element of sideways drift, a record too short, too noisy, too safe, or in other ways, only slightly detectable as less than the band's greatest work.

**10**'s are quite possibly blinding perfection within the band's chosen genre, radically different from one another, but without a doubt in my obviously twisted mind, Art of the Highest Order, a designation that transcends seriousness or craft to include wondrously stupid or excruciatingly caustic, amongst a myriad of other seemingly incompatible shades of the emotional response rainbow. **10**'s can fix your pathetic life.

So enter the gates to The World's Most Powerful Music, dudes, rockettes, flannelheads, alt.slackers, church-burners and old hippies alike. I hope I'm able to turn you on to a few choice platters you may otherwise have never encountered, for indeed hundreds of records in this book would most likely never have been mentioned in print again if I hadn't dredged their memory one last time, a fact that greatly satisfies my sense of purpose. If you have any suggestions for improvements or additions next time around, write and let me know. I'll try respond to all comments, debates, issues etc. with fairness and intelligence (yeah, right!). Until then, exercise those woofers!

Oh yeah, one more thing. If you have any comments and wish to write me, use Power Chord Press, P.O. Box 65208, 358 Danforth Avenue, Toronto, Ontario M4K 2Z2. E-mailers, use martinp@inforamp.net.


*Martin Popoff*

# NOTES ON PROCESS

The following is a list of explanations and defenses of certain practices you'll see throughout this book, offered as assurance that I've considered any and all conceivable issues in terms of inclusions, omissions, focus, etc. (yeah, right!).

## EP's and Singles

Singles are not included, although I'll occasionally slide in the odd comment within an appropriate LP review. EP's are included when artistically important, when prolific in new material, and/or when deemed treatable with some minimum semblance of seriousness and value. EP's, especially in the glitzy CD age, are all too often marketing ploys, containing more graphics than guts, clogged full of extended remixes and live tracks, not to mention the obligatory inclusion of the current hit single, which is probably the one song on the album you're most likely to be sick of already. When not serving this purpose, they're most often pacifiers by bands without enough material or courage to put out a real record. And of course, EP's by nature are short, so my reviews, having little to ramble on about, should in most cases be short, with grades combing that vague middle zone, peaking at 7 or 8, given the inherent poor value enclosed.

## Greatest Hits Records

. . . which exist only for well-intentioned parents to screw up on Christmas presents. *Real* fans own all the tunes by the time such packages scar the racks, preferring to hear compositions in their intended space and time. Artistically speaking, hits are a completely random element chosen for all sorts of political and commercial reasons. A single can be the heaviest or mellowest cut on an album, the most infantile or the most ambitious, the band's choice, the record company's choice, representative or deceptive of a record's direction. As a result, greatest hits packages are almost universally and wholly externally created; bastardized collages that bear little artistic significance. In terms of rock criticism, they're usually used as vehicles to discuss the band in sweeping generalities, or wrongly as a forum to discuss songs that should have been evaluated in their proper context, i.e. back on the studio album from 1978. For the above reasons, I have never taken them too seriously. Again, I throw in a couple here and there due to some interesting anomaly, extra cuts, or self-indulgent nostalgic cravings I may feel a need to satisfy. Or I was just bored. In any event, because you shouldn't buy greatest hits records, I don't review too many, and when I do, I keep it short.

## Label and Year Of Release

Label and year are of the particular release I own, have access to, or can verify as correct, be it domestic, import, original, re-issue, CD or LP (for example, in my case, mostly Canadian editions). Label is left out if it can't be positively identified because 1) the album graphics do not make such information clear, 2) the record is being reviewed from a self-recorded tape (i.e. I have nothing to look at) and 3) none of the stores in which I did my research had a copy for me to check out. Year of release is taken from the record jacket when available, and the abbreviation "Est." for Estimate is used (i.e. "Est. '86") when I had no concrete proof of release date (or "Atlantic Est. '84" when I knew label but had to guess at year). Hopefully, I'm accurate within one year either way. I was going to simply leave such information out, but I think it's useful to have a general idea of a record's temporal context so comparisons and contrasts can be made in perspective with direct competitors. I've also made (very) scattered attempts to add distributor to the tag here and there, and to maintain integrity as to variation of name based on age, subsidiary etc. (i.e. Warner Bros. versus Warner, or CBS versus Epic, Columbia or Sony).

## Live Albums

Although some bands claim that the live venue rather than the studio LP is really their definitive artistic statement, I don't buy it, due to the same shortcomings of hits packages; mainly the fact that the songwriting (the most revealing artistic indicator) is done over time. Song selection is understandably similar to past, present, or future hits package, although cherry-picking of one's catalogue for live display usually brings out certain trends, most obvious being heaviness. In my opinion however, crowds are basically man-made ticks and pops, production is almost universally (the most revealing artistic indicator) muddier, and all the interesting bells, whistles, and other studio tricks are wrongly albeit necessarily deleted, leaving little reason to play a live record save for memories of a tour one might have seen, or on rare occasion, where versions are an improvement over some screwed-up, ancient studio mix ten years back (the "bulking up" factor). Again, because I find live albums boring, I don't spend too much energy reviewing them, leaving the odd one out if I'm feeling lazy.

## LP's versus CD's

This won't be a diatribe about how used CDs are more than twice the price of used vinyl, soundly choking risk-taking among avid rockheads. No . . . just a note about the extent to which I've reviewed came to me via LP, being of the particular generation squirming helplessly on the cusp of the format shift. Throughout this book you'll see a lot of LP lingo used, much of which I suspect will stay with the industry forever. Hopefully it won't confuse you, yet be aware of the fact that most reviews are of original releases, including original graphics, song selection, mixes, and talk of side 1 versus side 2, which was an interesting additional artistic decision in the land of LP's, in terms of song arrangement (i.e. side openers vs. closers, heavy sides vs. light sides, and the layout of concept albums). In most cases however, the mention of sides will act merely as an added way of locating tracks. Also, I'll usually bring to light material differences between original versions and their CD counterparts when possible, including alterations in packaging, added tracks, added or deleted graphics and printed lyrics, or relevant remastering information.

## Omissions Beyond My Control

Like I say, unless I borrowed it and taped it, I've at one time or another owned or still own everything in this book, which of course because I can't buy everything, means there's going to be tons of stuff missing. In my defense, however, I'm pretty confident I've caught a good 90% of everything that's unquestionably important and vital to any self-respecting metalhead's wax stack. This process is self-fulfilling in two ways. If a record is universally acclaimed as a big deal, I'll eventually hear it, in most cases agree with other critics, and explore the catalogue further. Plus really hot indie product eventually will get major label release (if the system is working!), making it that much more accessible. Very little on the majors escapes my gaze, however be cautioned that many middle tier releases don't make it north of the border, which is where almost all my buying takes place since my move to Toronto. Conversely, if somebody's '91 record sucks, I won't be racing downtown to buy the band's last four, which is a roundabout way of saying that much of what was missed in this edition was dogshit anyways, so don't worry about it, turn the page, go buy a 10 you haven't heard and crank it up. Another point: I believe my listing to be more like 97% complete for releases right from metal's formation around 1970 until about '84. If it ain't in here, chances are I've heard it and have a pretty good reason for not including it (see **Qualification For Entry**). Other probable deficiencies include local market releases, post-punk era hardcore, and the most extreme examples of thrash and grindcore, the former for obvious reasons; the latter two because I don't commit much of my buying power to the genres, and the fact that a ton of these records are indie or Euro-released only. Final point: everything that I would recommend that may be considered a borderline entry has been included, while other borderline entries I'm not crazy about, have been omitted. Translation: if one of your big league faves hasn't been included, and only a complete dickbrain could be unaware of their presence, chances are they are slightly heinous and suck. Conversely, I hope to turn you on to personal faves of mine that may not be metal strictly speaking; sorta the ulterior public service point behind this book.

## Qualification For Entry

Unlike other bullshit false alarms out there (of which there are very few), this book really *is* about hard rock and heavy metal. Being a metalhead, I know when I'm pushing the limits of acceptance under what actually constitutes Heavy Metal or Hard Rock. Having said that, there are more than a few mellow or otherwise questionable records that slide in here for the following reasons: 1) they're by bands that usually rock, 2) they're by bands that used to rock, 3) they're by bands that now rock, 4) they're of borderline heaviness sonically speaking, but generally accepted philosophically and artistically as hard rock records 5) they're sonically heavy, although not in any way considered so, artistically or philosophically, 6) they are records that are considered an important part of metal's history *and* are at least of borderline heaviness, and 7) they are solo records by dudes with previous or future heavy affiliations. And in deference to the power of metal above all, plus respect for the fact that you are reading this most probably as a metal fan first, and a general music fan second, I'll clearly warn you about a record's dodgy status and in most cases, especially when the album lacks real importance, I'll again be keeping it short. Note: since the first edition of **Riff Kills Man!** in '93, I've added "additional layers": more heavy alternative and more historically important AOR bands like Bad Company, Foreigner, Billy Squier, Night Ranger, Boston and Bon Jovi. Other more solo-related second layer additions: Phil Lynott, Tommy Bolin and Robert Plant.

## Technical Stuff

Album titles are bolded (although working titles are not), song titles italicized. Both have been rendered—major words and connectors alike—in upper and lower case for consistency's sake, except on rare occasions where it became obvious I was fooling with some form of artistic intent. As proof that this is very rarely the case, note that a good number of albums are inconsistent within themselves between front cover, spine, and or actual label (more prevalent on low budget releases and shoddy CD re-issues).

## Various Artist Albums

You'll find few "various" or soundtrack albums in this mighty tome because basically, I couldn't give a shit about various albums. Of the sixty or so that I know well, only a handful are included within (see "V"), due either to the inclusion of otherwise unreleased or rare tracks, industry trends worth commenting on, or simply cool tunes worth plugging. The point is, I consider such samplers nowhere near serious or deliberate art, thus not worthy of major comment.

## Lee Aaron - Some Girls Do (Attic '91)

One of the most pathetic circus acts in Canadian re-cording history (and we have a lot of 'em: Prism, Trooper, Triumph, Loverboy, Bryan Adams), Lee Aaron takes her ragged collection of T.O. bar circuit wipe-ups through some of the most fabulously idiotic, flakefunk clichés ever leaked on this, the woman's *sixth* album (I know . . . what kind of world would allow such misery?). A loser in her **Metal Queen** daze, and still an embarrassing example of what is wrong with Cana-dian rock. What's next, a Grammy? One of the largest mental voids I've ever peered into, perpetuating un-justly the public impression that all rock chicks are airheads.
Rating 0

## Lee Aaron - Powerline (Attic '92)

Man, I almost feel bad, given all the abuse I got for my **Some Girls Do** review first time around. But listening to this Best Of package, I think my miserable, cranky disposition was justified. I mean, even if Lee's amusing liner notes spend half the space apologizing for the utter hogswallow enclosed, it doesn't excuse the fact that this blows chunks. I'll just throw out some titles: *I Like My Rock Hard, Lady Of The Darkest Night, Rock Me All Over, Nasty Boyz*, and you figure out the rest. Mind-numbing suburban AOR rock of a most heinous, toweringly idiotic nature.
Rating 0

## Abbatoir - Vicious Attack (Roadrunner '85)

Scotch-tape yer head to the tranny of Venom's bat-tered tour bus and you'll be close to the agonizing churn of events that is an Abbatoir experience. Of no socially redeeming value. Merely another coughed up pile of bestial rust from the formative years of poverty ultra-core Americana. Record #2: '86's **The Only Safe Place**. Sure.
Rating 2

## Abomination - Abomination (Nuclear Blast '90)

Cybernetic techno-thrash like old Voivod, real greasy Destruction, or twisted and pissed Coroner, Abomina-tion do a middling job of the vortextual genre, except that I pret' near unequivocally can't stand the stuff. An awe-inspiring cyclone of dissonant clatter, ridiculously high-strung and violent. Total punishment. **2** points for

technical focus when all is flying fantastically apart unto the cradle of damnation.
Rating 2

## The Abyss - Summon The Beast (Nuclear Blast '97)

Great idea: when all the blubbery, froth-mouthed death metal losers who have no life call you a sell-out because you use yer noggin', give them a joke on which to teethe. That seems to be what Hypocrisy have done, calling themselves The Abyss, trumping up some cheesy artwork and title to match (**Summon The Beast**: stunning!), and then just blasting through eight trash-can doo-dahs of which no mudder could love. Here's three yackers for ya: *Damned, Cursed*, and *Blessed With The Wrath Of Evil*, Peter Tagtgren really out-doing himself on the creatives here. One senses joke, the diabolic fantastique of Hypocrisy's **Abducted** and his solo **Pain** purger, just laughing themselves silly at the textbook Norse-ness of this nonsense. Har har.
Rating 2

## A.C. - Top 40 Hits (Earache '95)

Punkdrunk thrashcore with a screeching wildcat for a vocalist, A.C. are not to be taken seriously, what with their 40 piffle tracks of extreme clownish terror (over 40 minutes) assaulting the senses with yelping glee. Titles like *Lives Ruined By Music* and *Don't Call Japanese Hardcore Jap Core* pretty much sum up this daredevil waste of concentration. Grating and funny for about five minutes.
Rating 3

## A.C. - 40 More Reasons To Hate Us (Earache '96)

Quite a transformation here, A.C. recording with Bruce Fairbairn and Bob Rock in Vancouver, even enlisting the likes of Jon Bon Jovi to do most of the lead vocals on this record, which is a lush cross between recent, rootsy but upbeat Mellencamp and the hair band sounds of Def Leppard. But Seth's guitar work is probably the biggest difference, the man-legend adopt-ing a blended Metheny/Holdsworth type fluidity which dovetails perfectly with studio-wiz Jim Keltner's light brushwork (Keltner plays in place of Tim Morse on three tracks here, *Harvey Korman Is Gay, I Just Saw The Gayest Guy On Earth* and *Van Full Of Retards*, which finds Seth trading vocal lines with Kate Bush and Annie Lennox over excellent guitarwork courtesy of Crim-son snob Robert Fripp). I dunno, fans may bolt for the exits, but one can't help think that the hiring of all these big names (Earache won't be releasing any more records until Spring '99) will bring in a whole new, much more discerning set of listeners. Anyways, early indications are that the ruse is paying off, A.C. set to become Page Plant's touring band on their short club tour in England this summer, while allowed a thirty minute A.C. set to open the show.

Rating                                        3

## A.C. - I Like It When You Die   (Earache '97)

More of the same over-the-top white noise, brutally truthful, brackishly Japanese. One day, the Billy Braggish limitation of it all is going to mudslide all over these guys, and they'll go straight to releasing records that are song-titles only. For this (and only here) is where A.C. triumphs. Faves this time: *Recycling Is Gay, Pottery's Gay, Your Band's In The Cut-out Bin, You Look Adopted, Your Cousin Is George Lynch, You Have Goals, You Drive An Iroc, Being A Cobbler Is Dumb, 311 Sucks, Windchimes Are Gay, You Went To See Dishwalla And Everclear (You're Gay)*, and the most hilarious by far, *I'm In A.C.*

Rating                                        2

## Accept - Accept   (Brain '79)

Accept confusingly released two self-titled "debuts", this one (the good one) otherwise known as "chick with chainsaw"; and the North American debut (some versions titled **I'm A Rebel**), which rocks limp and so inherently foreign to the Accept mindsphere, I'm suspicious it's even the same five guys. The present **Accept** is a chaotic, and sometimes brilliantly melodic, loose-bolted contraption, featuring a variety of metal styles delivered in a uniquely German, despairing manner, sounding live off the floor, hurried and unrehearsed; raw, loud and hopelessly naive in much the same manner as the Scorpions, who similarly stumbled into magnificence after a protracted search for chords Americans could understand. Only this is more **Virgin Killer** than **Lonesome Crow**, Accept wasting no time slaughtering the weak with jagged electrics. Caustic classics: *Tired Of Me* and *Sounds Of War.*

Rating                                        7

## Accept - Accept   (Passport '80)

Vacant American marketers at work, no doubt, for this the North American debut, a four-eyed, buck-tooth, cold fish sort of record like nothing else in the Accept catalogue; a type of rank, b-grade AC/DC; tired, cliché pig slop, loosely thumping along to no headbanging avail. Accept were responsible for some of the most exuberant and timeless metal ever, but next to nothing from surrounding eras could have sat here without burning a hole in the vinyl. Judging from the balance of the band's material, this record couldn't possibly have been assembled with full consent, either fashioned to please the simplistic demands of radio, or to approximate some suit's idea of what a German AC/DC could sound like. Fortunately the band abandoned this simplistic bang, storming forth in creation of the intelligent, emotional, and intricate classic '80s metal that would influence hordes of newcomers, in many ways, defining state-of-the-art for the next five years.

Rating                                        3

## Accept - Breaker   (Passport '81)

**Breaker** marks a direct progression from the band's dangerous '79 debut with the added improvement of high quality production and precision tightness, also combining mature songwriting with some of the most sincere, blood-curdling shrieks and howls from one of metal's original little Hitlers, Udo Dirkschneider. The guy's voice is a powerhouse from hell, raising the house hackles in announcement of what will become a formidable sledge of metal history. **Breaker** displays the sterling German penchant for considerable heaviness mixed with soul-vaporizing melody. And if not for

about three tunes going slightly astray stylistically (boogie, stadium rock, el boring power ballad—you find 'em), **Breaker** would be damn close to leather-lunged perfection, but hey we drank a lot of beers to it anyways!

Rating                                        8

## Accept - Restless & Wild   (Heavy Metal Worldwide '83)

An unqualified scorcher, **Restless & Wild** is where it all comes together in one searing, metallic, tour de force; without a doubt the best rock album of German descent ever. From the hell-broke-loose intro to the seminally OTT of *Fast As A Shark*, through the final strains of hypnotic and haunting classic *Princess Of The Dawn*, this wickedwerk of über-wattage pounds with the conviction of grand, fanatical masters at work. Wasted & Riled's got it all: Herr Udo's constant, relentless violence, the eminently tasteful, yet bracing twin guitar work of Hermann Frank and Wolf Hoffmann, and the kind of heat-treated rowdiness only achieved when production and percussion pound the blistering earth together in some sort of tribal war dance (must be why mine's on red vinyl). Not a single track is wasted here; all dastardly eleven raging heavy as hell and philosophically cohesive in terms of heads-down, wreck-the-place focus. **Restless & Wild**, without resorting to overkill, cheap tricks or bells and whistles, is essentially one of the meanest and proudest heavy metal albums of all time. Knock it back.

Rating                                        10

## Accept - Midnight Highway   (Passport '83)

Just a brief mention here: **Midnight Highway** is a Passport compilation of the band's first three, totally unalike records, a very roller coaster affair due to the vastly different productions all over it. Plus a real larfing boot of an album cover, featuring one tough-looking broad, a curly-maned guy in bad jeans, and a chopper. Too much.

Rating                                        7

## Accept - Balls To The Wall   (Lark '83)

Lyrically more complex, **Balls To The Wall** walks a dark and tortured terrain of oppressive authority, sexual ambiguity, despair, violent love, human misunderstanding and internal moral anguish; the record *itself* being largely misunderstood, as the plainly surprised band would spend most of their post-release interviews countering opinions that the record is homosexual in nature. Musically we find the boys formidable arsenal stripped to the basics, brilliantly but simply riffing, working within an economic framework of restraint that tends to dampen metal's inherent rowdiness, while evoking more intense blasts of emotional savagery through nuance and lyrical challenge. Everything on this thoughtfully conceived work darkens your world, yet the entire record, with the exception of the resigned album closer is decisively Heavy Metal, German-tailored. **Balls To The Wall** was to be Accept's brightest light commercially, due to the headbangers' religion status afforded the hypnotic and punishing, AC/DC-gone-ugly title track and accompanying cheeseball video. Yet sadly the band never got the lasting recognition it so richly deserved. Within metal circles however, Accept will always be remembered as one of the class acts of rock 'n'roll, hall of flamers 'til the bitter end.

Rating                                        10

## Accept - Metal Heart   (Portrait '85)

Although Accept's pivotal sixth slab (featuring the re-establishment of founding member Jörg Fischer on guitar) was a bit of a back-ratchet compared to the previous two assaults, it's still an impressive piece of '70s-bred mid-pace Euro-metal. Production values are very clean, very bright; the mood more anthemic,

upbeat, as this time around the interview circuit, the band would acknowledge, expanding on their steadfast respect for strong melodies and palatable song construction. As a result, **Metal Heart** is much more the car stereo album, propelled by powerful grooves and blazing true energies, the band's **Blackout** as it were. There's good news and bad news however, bad news being that although the entire album is unarguably heavy, three or four tunes drag lyrically and riffically, pandering too closely to AC/DC-ish American style hard rock. One suspects the label may have pushed for accessibility over art in an attempt to boost sales. The good news: **Metal Heart** contains no less than three of the most righteous and stratospheric Accept contraptions ever etched, in hero sandwich *Midnight Mover*, melodic soulstorm *Screaming For A Love Bite*, and devastating cruncher *Bound To Fail*. Soaring and fresh in its blind adherence to clarity, **Metal Heart** still regularly visits my launching pad, releasing fond memories upon take off every time.
Rating                                                          9

## Accept - Russian Roulette   (Portrait '86)

**Russian Roulette** was to be the last Acceptance with Udo on vocals, which means it should have been the last Accept record period, which unfortunately wasn't to be the case. Definitely the lost Accept album, nobody spoke or heard much about it. Yet unassumingly, **Russian Roulette** upholds a fine tradition, albeit with a loosening grasp of the band's previous sharp visions. **Russian Roulette** evokes perhaps too strongly past Accept preoccupations: OTT (in this case substandard) in *T.V. War*, loud, proud grooves in the brilliant *Monsterman* (one of my top five Accept faves ever), moody moments à la **Balls To The Wall**, and a general volatility that recalls **Breaker** or **Restless And Wild**. Given the mish-mash, **Russian Roulette** lacks cohesion, sounding more like an anti-climactic, ill-timed career retrospective. But as was the case with **Metal Heart** it's got some of the most killingly brilliant Acceptunes ever, in the aforementioned *Monsterman*, caffeine love-in *Aiming High*, and the highly strung *Man Enough To Cry*. Overall, a frustrating record that lacks enthusiasm but delivers some incendiary highs.
Rating                                                          7

## Accept - Eat The Heat   (CBS '89)

**Eat The Heat** is the first and only Accept album without the one and only Udo on microphone beratements; and of course, without Herr Udo's mischievous spark, the band is simply no longer the mighty rock 'n' Rommel juggernaut of old, although new dog David Reece has an admirable enough shriek. And it cuts me up even more that the new sound rides a hybrid of totally boring, unoriginal, teeny-bopper hard rock crossed with dumb-on-purpose metal; a forced contrivance that just drowns in a sea of L.A. teaze; resulting in a record unimaginatively designed to cash in on a great past, with no apparent understanding of the magic of metal's flame. Fortunately, the continuing lifeblood of the band could be tapped in the grooves of Udo's four solo albums which, although not quite the brilliant Accept slams of the early '80s, do a pretty spirited job of carrying the torch. So don't bother with **Eat The Heat**, as the techy, clattering drum sound alone is enough to drive you nuts. Back in '93 with **Objection Overruled**, Udo firmly at the helm once more. **Eat The Heat** one however, marked worsening problems with arthritis for drummer Stefan Kaufmann.
Rating                                                          4

## Accept - Objection Overruled   (BMG '93)

The '80s über-rockers are back, and it's frightening how few remember, and how few seem to be willing to incorporate this sort of mid to upper intensity headbang into their mental metal portfolios. Combining the chops metal of **Russian Roulette** with the fathead hypno brainshake of **Balls To The Wall**, **Objection Overruled** relives the glory days thanks to an immutable Udo, the band hitting stride with the anthemic *Bulletproof* and controlled cruise *Sick, Dirty And Mean*. But it distresses me that I don't reach for the new Accept as often as old Accept or true '90s hard music. Too close to the vest? Maybe. A little light and cheezy lyrically? Maybe. Damn close to an 8? For sure, but I gotta downgrade for some sort of lost innocence on the part of an industry that has gotten comfortable with clever. Accept may be banished from the club, fans everywhere too smart for our own good, too bombarded with quality to have the patience for something less readily apparent as remarkable.
Rating                                                          7

## Accept - Death Row   (Pavement '95)

Newly bald-shaven axe lynchpin Wolf Hoffman calls this "the first Accept record written for one guitar", which may account for the urgent, ultra-heavy barebones feel to **Death Row**, a record that stomps all over the band's first reunion outing, **Objection Overruled**. The theme is aggression, violence, injustice, but the themes matter little, Udo's face-curdling vocals overwhelming the lyrics, Hoffman's squarely metal (thank God) riffs cutting each track with a vengeance. Heaps of vintage Accept here (fifteen tracks, 71 minutes) for us oldtimers, which may be the problem, the new breed of rivethead having gone on to grungier, less obviously metal pastures. But I defy the alternative set to come up with solos like this, production like this, this kind of forward mass retain. Classic old metal, yes, wisely old for '95, Accept's traditions being trendless and timeless. If **Restless & Wild** and **Balls To The Wall** knocked you on your ass during those heady heydays of metal, believe it, **Death Row** will satisfy. As for those who weren't there, check it out, the axework positively carves.
Rating                                                          8

## Accept - Predator   (BMG '96)

Wisely adopting the trend towards shorter, fifty minute albums, Accept push forth with another proto-Acceptian gathering of clear-sailing riffsters. Now officially down to a three-piece of Peter Baltes, Wolf and Udo, the band's writing is direct and cutting, **Predator** being another "one guitar" album, a cookie-cutter of **Death Row** (for better or worse), Hoffman's riffs doing ten or twelve things Scorpions ought to think about. Bassist Baltes proves himself an excellent, dramatic vocalist on three tracks, and the pacing of the record is predictable if welcome Accept, **Predator** crammed full of those level-headed, Germanic steamrollers nobody else will touch right now. Faves: the exultatious *Take Out The Crime* and the sparse *Don't Give A Damn*. Biggest stepoff: closer *Primitive*, which does that Prince/new Leppard/Collective Soul danceclub metal thing. Three very similar, familiar records in a row . . . not sure if this is a good thing. Update: Futurist has re-released this record a year later, and after the break-up of the band to boot, members scattering to new projects in serach of some much-needed inspiration.
Rating                                                          8

## Accuser - Reflections   (Century Media '94)

Another fine sculpture of steel from the inquisitors at Century Media, **Reflections** (the band's sixth!) jerks tight the cables of the new heaviness of the mid-'90s, fusing a Metallica-style accessibility to a Machine Head-whacked pulverize factor. Accuser have established themselves masters of the power groove, while retaining snapping veins of deathness, cloaking their extreme past with a renewed power of song, solo and vocal texture (which maybe a tad often lapses into Hetfield

intonations). And producer Alex Perialis is no small part of the equation, bringing his killer sense of loud, insistent rhythm to the grindcrime, intact black and blue from work with Testament, Pro-Pain and Overkill. So suffice to say, this one's a soul crusher, moshing, grinding, and chops-level-thrashing like the vets these guys are. Adeptly poised amongst the best and brightest of the ultra-heavy sub-genre.
Rating      8

## AC/DC - High Voltage    (Atlantic '76)

This humble UK/US debut (mostly tracks from the band's second Aussie album, '75's **TNT**, not to be confused with the '74 Aussie debut also called **High Voltage**) finds Angus, Bon and the boys establishing their stripped to the very basics slouch, band steadfast on stage as Angus and his legendary schoolboy outfit (last and lasting costume after attempts at a gorilla, Superman and Zorro) provided focal point as diminutive guitar hero off the rails. **High Voltage** evokes an exposed simplicity that begs its fans to take over, and that's the magic of the band. There's open vistas galore for any half-enthused headbanger to yelp along or better still, grab a battered axe and envision being Angus for a couple of minutes. It is this oneness of party intent that is the gut of the AC/DC attraction, as these silver-tongued beer-guzzlers wrap sly entendre around concert classics like The Jack and She's Got Balls and Can I Sit Next To You Girl. Hooks, melody and beat are so obviously laid bare for all to grasp; no great sweat to walk away with four or five songs vying for attention in one's teenage head, although the whole schmooz just rides on like a medium metronome.
Rating      8

## AC/DC - Dirty Deeds Done Dirt Cheap    (Atlantic '76)

**Dirty Deeds Done Dirt Cheap** is a strange, smallish sort of record with a disarmingly warm feel that makes you want to crack a beer and quaff. Oddly, the record's got more spaces and less gel than the multi-versioned **High Voltage**, considered rushed and forced by the band, not a favorite in the harsh judgment of time. Bon Scott (first the band's driver, then the band's tattooed love boy) is all impish charm and devil dog on this collection of stripped-down boogie toons which get the simplest of points across with a spontaneous "whatever" sense of humour, banging out vanilla cone rhythms with alarming ease. Somehow, early AC/DC soundly hypnotized one's biorhythms, focusing on pure and singular sounds; an almost fanatical fascination with establishing the beat—any beat, at any speed—just as long as it succeeded in taming and restirring one's blood to the Aussie pace of life. And that's it. Guitars and drums humbly establishing a groove that would instantly take Australia by storm. And the rest was history. (Note: **Dirty Deeds** was the band's third official release in Australia, all of the first three records wrapped in different jackets from the stateside counterparts. The cover art for our version was considered in hindsight a failed stab at sophistication by design giants Hipgnosis. Trackwise, Love At First Feel and Rocker here swap places with Jailbreak and R.I.P.). The last of AC/DC's minimal, submissive records, as the band would crank it to 11 in '77, **Dirty Deeds** nevertheless turned out to be a cash cow sales-wise, inching its way to triple platinum over the years, making it one of the band's top three commercial successes.
Rating      7

## AC/DC - Let There Be Rock    (Atlantic '77)

AC/DC kick their unique, no-nonsense electric boogie into the stratosphere with heretofore unbeknownst energy levels and sizzling metallic production, **Let There Be Rock** being the album that established the band as bad-ass "metal" dudes with which to be reckoned, brandishing the classic history lessons of the title cut, twin Quo-style blasters Whole Lotta Rosie and Bad Boy Boogie, and jubilant lead single Problem Child. The band's electrically-supercharged wall of sound moves at various speeds but always with a singular devotion to the band's foot-stomping, jean-jacket groove, which is damn fine medicine by me. AC/DC takes what on paper must look like commercial suicide, death by boredom, utter simplicity or empty calories, turning the whole show into a beer-swilling rock 'n' roll housewrecker of legendary proportions. Here, less-is-more as a religion pays off handsomely, AC/DC merging relevant punk power with age-old blues anchorage like no band before. One of twenty or so historically essential hard rock documents.
Rating      10

## AC/DC - Powerage    (Atlantic '78)

Fond memories for me worrying about getting **Powerage** home unwarped, strapped to the back of my bike on a scorching summer day three miles uphill from Kelly's. The album of course (like the day it arrived) is a scorcher too; lean, mean 'n' heavy, with a decidedly southern rock feel, or at least suvvern redneck mentality, an intense party album, borrowing heavily from traditional American rock 'n' roll for its down-wind brainshake. However, the vibrant accessible production and that famous AC/DC swingbeat elevate the proceedings to new heights, bestowing upon the world such metal mainstays as Rock 'n'Roll Damnation, Riff Raff, and Sin City. Ultimately, **Powerage** is nothing more or less than scruffy teenage skidder rock at its snotty best; one of my personal favourites in terms of capturing the essence of rock 'n' roll weekends with the buds. Considered by the press a bit commercial and lax after the sheer buzz of **Let There Be Rock**, but hey, the songs are better.
Rating      10

## AC/DC - If You Want Blood    (Atlantic '78)

The obligatory live album (hastily rushed out to capitalize on the band's growing stature) comes early in the band's career, perhaps prematurely, although AC/DC are really wizened vets by now if one counts the tough Australia years. Half the tunes hail from **Let There Be Rock**, aptly so, given that record's convincing whollop-ing of previous dogwalks and indeed **Powerage**, in terms of live translatability. Personally, I don't care for live albums and there's nothing here to distinguish this one above other bands' automatic tour diaries, except maybe its refreshing brevity and an amphetamine re-tooling of The Rocker. Cool cover concept though, in which Angus gets a righteous impaling from his trusty axe.
Rating      8

## AC/DC - Highway To Hell    (Atlantic '79)

AC/DC breaks the bank commercially with **Highway To Hell**, which sadly was to be the last for vocalist Bon Scott, who will die in London, choking on his own vomit at the age of 33, while sleeping in a car after a night of alcoholic intake, February 19, 1980. **Highway To Hell** would also mark the first time AC/DC would record outside of Australia (Britain) and without the Vanda/Young team (Mutt Lange). The signature title track, no less than a religion to a whole generation of jean jackets, stands as one of the premiere hard rock anthems of all time, augmenting the sweet music of hurling on many a high school excursion, while Girls Got Rhythm, Shot Down In Flames, and Night Prowler would also register as snot-nosed, good-fer-nuthin' hits with the disgruntled and generally shiftless of the unkempt, high school set (picture a young Homer Simpson). **Highway To Hell** forever takes a lofty position in history as an exceedingly rousing, cuffs-to-the-head, guitar classic with some of the best brain-banging

grooves of AC/DC's career, driving *Touch Too Much*, *Walk All Over You*, and loopy speed rocker *Beating Around The Bush* to euphoric burstings of cranial vessels. Without a doubt, more alcohol has been consumed and subsequently returned orally to the earth to the distorted strains of this record (usually from homemade car speakers propped on trunk lids of '75 Dodge Darts) than any other release in history. *The* party album from *the* party band, one of the largest expressions of electric jubilation ever harnessed. Smells like teen freedom. Note: the record title put AC/DC squarely in the middle of the religious backlash against metal at the time, the band's explanation that it merely referred to tough slogging tours across the US, falling of deaf dimwit ears.
Rating                                                                10

### AC/DC - Back In Black   (Atlantic '80)
Huge punter anticipation and subsequent mega-stardom arrives (sales well past ten million; best selling record ever here in Canada), via one foreboding black box of self-destruction. In a bold move, the band promptly and efficiently unleashes newcomer vocalist Brian Johnson (ex of Brit barwipes Geordie), whose horrific and tortured chords draw and quarter the memory of Bon Scott's particular growl, which 'til this record was the standard for gremlin-like utterance. Nevermind, we flocked to the record stores in droves, prompted by the radio play and glorious cymbal crashing swing of mega-singles *You Shook Me All Night Long*, *Hell's Bells*, and the anthemic, lock-steppin' title cut, not to mention the visual dead calm sobriety of the record's embossed cover art. Because Johnson's vocals are so jarringly different, it's hard to compare **Back In Black** to previous efforts, but suffice to say it's similar boot-swinging grind, if slightly more bluesy, and a bit more heavy-handed in terms of pace and production. In total, I like fewer tracks on this one than on either of the last three, but the record is still great testimony to a band with a landmark sound often attempted but never convincingly duplicated. One of the most famous and infamous heavy metal records of all time; a considerably dangerous authority-bashing weapon during the opening years of the last decade. Trivia: Bon Scott had pretty well all the lyrics ready for the record at the time of his death, all of which were scrapped in his honour for new ones co-written with Johnson.
Rating                                                                10

### AC/DC - For Those About To Rock   (Atlantic '81)
Another big album commercially, **For Those About To Rock** continues to explore blues-based metal with a lot of slower, atmospheric numbers, sounding a bit tentative and automatic, marking the germination of a problem that plagues the band to this day: a total lack of anything new to say lyrically. From here-on in, AC/DC's thought process will consist of sandbagging every metal cliché in the book, snagging every last catch-phrase ever to waft past a row of high school lockers, for use as a song or album title, wrapping concepts around them, thereby continually rehashing what—even uttered *once* past about 1977—are limited, dead-predictable metal themes. Sometimes it doesn't detract from the experience, as on the superb **Flick Of The Switch** and **The Razor's Edge**, but usually, as is the case here, it's the root cause of chronic filler syndrome. This somewhat monolithic release also holds the distinction of introducing us to one of the band's few (over-used) stage props: real live cannons (well, smoke belchers with synthesizer sound effects) à la April Wine circa **Stand Back**.
Rating                                                                7

### AC/DC - Flick Of The Switch   (Atlantic '83)
This graphically-understated record got the electric chair commercially but in my opinion, **Flick Of The Switch** (originally titled I Like To Rock), represents the blinding furious peak of the Brian Johnson era, and is the rowdiest, most consistently heavy slab of kick-ass rock 'n'roll the band has ever written, if not necessarily the most endearing, given the early material's mystique of a death in the family. Bristling with metallic electricity, slow and fast ones alike are powered with that singular AC/DC conviction that make simple song structures and even simpler lyrical ideas sound brand new, liquored-up, and so incredibly high octane. And indeed that was the intent, the boys self-producing for once to recapture the raw edge lost during the Mutt Lange years. So ultimately, **Flick Of The Switch** sees AC/DC roaring back with a new lease on life, even as songs start reliving past glories. Consumed with **Highway To Hell**, **Flick Of The Switch** is the perfect left-handed chaser for the most destruction-bent of two fisted beer-swilling sessions. The ironically white dark horse of the AC/DC experience, this one was a bit of a take-stock experience, of which the band did, sacking drummer Phil Rudd during its inception, due to increasing drug problems.
Rating                                                                10

### AC/DC - '74 Jailbreak   (Atlantic '84)
A fairly lively five track EP of previously Aussie-only released old stuff (strangely all from early '75 or '76), mostly revisiting neglected material from the actual debut, the Aussie version of **High Voltage**. Nothing overly ambitious here, just tunes from the band's early Aussie LPs that would have fit comfortably and unobtrusively on any of the band's early albums. Best of the bunch: *You Ain't Got A Hold On Me* and *Soul Stripper*, which features Young and Young guitar lathers over a protracted, almost disco bass throb. The fairly boring *Jailbreak*, the advance single from the Australian **Dirty Deeds** also shows up here, having been dropped from the stateside and UK versions of the record.
Rating                                                                6

### AC/DC - Fly On The Wall   (Atlantic '85)
This confused wank of a record tries desperately to recapture wasted youth (again produced by the band), yet the material for the most part is cookie-cutter AC/DC, spewed forth with a strange lack of control that resembles a hurried, held-back jam, kinda hysterical, thrashing wildly about for something to believe in. Brian's awkward vocals are mixed quite far back, possibly because he's sounding raspier and more incoherent than ever, a trend that reaches critical mass on **The Razor's Edge** and subsides somewhat come **Ballbreaker**. Meanwhile, AC/DC continues to maintain their tie for first place with The Replacements, Anthrax, Foreigner and Faith No More for the worst album covers in rock. Somewhat charming second side, kind of the hidden half record of the band's catalogue.
Rating                                                                6

### AC/DC - Who Made Who   (Atlantic '86)
A soundtrack album from the Stephen King movie **Maximum Overdrive** (which stiffed), **Who Made Who** features a bunch of King-chosen hits plus three new tracks, the only one of any import being the title cut (understandably a band fave), one of those relentless AC/DC headshakes that adds layers over a steady bassline as it smoothly cruises towards a hero's completion. A crimson in the neck classic. The other two newies are instrumental mastadon thumpers that I imagine would sound real fine in a movie. Guess what? This sold over two million copies.
Rating                                                                6

## AC/DC - Blow Up Your Video  (Atlantic '88)

Another frustrating album that sees Angus writing strange, twisty blues metal riffs that for the most part sound like difficult, botched melody, as if the band's looking too deeply for a new enigmatic direction. I also find an irritating lack of treble in the recording, which can be construed as warm I guess, courtesy of reinstated old buds Harry Vanda and George Young. Anyway, the title track is kinda fresh and driving, although I can't believe such an awkward, pointless and ass-backwards choice of words like "blow up your video" ever made it this far off the drawing board (basically it means get off your duff and go see a live rock show). In some ways, the "lost" AC/DC album, one ripe for cyclical explorations over time. The record's subsequent tour saw Malcolm begging off to tackle his drinking problem, with nephew Stevie taking over, the band missing nary a beat in the process.
Rating     **6**

## AC/DC - The Razor's Edge  (Atco '90)

Tight, highly strung, and menacing, **The Razor's Edge** is entirely worthy of its status as the grand comeback of legendary rock 'n' roll runts. Bruce Fairbairn's production is '90s hi-tech, giving the drums a highly electronic treatment, especially the bass drum. Fortunately, however, it works, because the material is for the most part first class, mischievous, no-compromise AC/DC. The production adds a vitality to the tracks which bleed open honesty, absolutely stripped to the basics, creating electricity on the straight, tried and true. *Fire Your Guns* shows more zip than the boys have displayed in years, and *Are You Ready* (slow) and *Got You By The Balls* (slower) are mean-spirited riff-based chuggers reminiscent of **Flick Of The Switch**. I guess the best thing I can say about this album is that I've played it over fifty times and it still sounds fresh. Savour while you can; Brian Johnson may be reduced to your grandmother's shrivelled whisper on the next one. Note: for weird contractual reasons, Johnson wasn't allowed to do write the record's lyrics, not that it matters.
Rating     **8**

## AC/DC - Live  (Atco '92)

Probably not as long-awaited as rock radio might have you believe, AC/DC **Live** arrives, in two versions, "normal" and "collector's edition", the latter cramming on an extra ten cuts, least predictable being goofball oldies *Jailbreak* and *High Voltage*. On the Regular Joe version, we find pretty much energetic Ramona-romps through the anthems, with lead troll Brian Johnson dancing a valiant Joe Cocker-like squirm towards hitting the notes. Apparently super producer Bruce Fairbairn followed the band around to the various tour touchdowns to put his detailed imprint on the sound and, yes, this is headphone-quality concert footage. Having never seen the boys live (being discouraged by a perplexing mix of rave vs. bummer reviews), I can't say the prospect of this record was any big deal. I mean, somewherz around half these tunes have been flogged to death, and there ain't much window-dressing that can be (or willingly would be) done to the band's immutable, rudimentary structures to cause fresh interest. Biggest surprise: *Heatseeker*, laced here with a heavy dose of the ol' Quo. Low grade for lack of originality and yes, packaging.
Rating     **6**

## AC/DC - Ballbreaker  (Warner '95)

Like a relic that will not sleep, the venerable AC/DC arrive somewhat alive in '95, with their stoopidest, silliest slab yet. But that's not to say these guys have thrown a pooch, 'cos it just doesn't seem convincingly possible, given the dear franchise of sounds AC/DC owns. **Ballbreaker** actively, almost violently courts

lyrical terrain that is blindingly embarrassing, stunning in its inanity, and so pre-school, one bursts out laughing in confusion. And it hurts the band, but not all that much. Because wrapping such loftiness as *Cover You In Oil*, *Hard As A Rock* (first single; played at Bills games), and *Whiskey On The Rocks*, is a smooth, southern boogie slide, AC/DC's most under-stated and slyly-studied delivery, kinda what one might expect from a really good Skynyrd or Blackfoot or Quo record. Not all that heavy, **Ballbreaker** just courts the porch and rocking chair, wizened sages gathering young pups around dusk for some tales of a time when men, booze, women and trucks interparlayed their charms in a lusty wardance until hangover or twisted wreckage do us part. And all the while that soft pulse of arcane Angus boogie riffs watches over the participants, configuring and reconfiguring for three minute sculptures that deserve a hug for reasons unfathomable. Less the robust firepower of **The Razor's Edge**, but no less charmed, **Ballbreaker** is ungraspable and necessary, easily argued as offensive and worthless, but also arguably a jewel in the rough. Argue all you want, but AC/DC will just go about their business. After all, what do they care? Hell, even Phil Rudd is back behind the drum stool.
Rating     **8**

## Acid Bath - When The Kite String Pops  (Rotten '94)

Wow. Right from the John Wayne Gacy clown painting on the cover, through the putrid, torture, rape and kill lyrics, through the massive metal sounds emanating from my sorry speakers, this one's the epitome of unclean. Acid Bath brew a potent, intoxicating mix of Butthole Surfers, Melvins, Marilyn Manson, thrash and ragingly perfect doom metal into a display that just spills unchecked into the forever corrupted ears of the listener. Vocally, we get it all, Life Of Agony-style crooning sorrow through thrashing mad screams, as the band power-grooves each track through Purgatory. A minor, somewhat ignored release, **When The Kite String Pops** deserves attention, even if the heapingly hateful lyrics touch the hem of Cannibal Corpse, and then burn it with a more sadistic, purely evil emotional force.
Rating     **7**

## Acid Bath - Paegan Terrorism Tactics  (Rotten '96)

And back they come prayin', these true danger boys caustically causing another brilliant wretch of a record. Number two for these Louisiana swamp devils builds on the band's alchemical splicings of Sabbath, death, torture and psycho-delic sludge, finding Agony Column, Eyehategod and a bit of Type O in between all the excellent drumming and production work. Artwork this time is a pretty twisted Jack Kevorkian painting, the band (erroneously) by association lumping Doctor Death with actual serial killers Gacy (debut cover) and Ramirez (interim EP cover). But a rich vein of flamethrower evil is achieved, these guys truly looped like old '70s metal, scattering their throwing darts all over the hard spectrum, all the while spouting lyrics that can turn your hair white overnight. Internet newsgroup talk of the band is abundant, a surefire sign that these audio fascists are onto something real, sick and towering.
Rating     **8**

## Acrimony - the acid elephant e.p.  (Flying/Godhead '95)

Italian label Godhead is making a name for itself with its strong stable of post-death acts, not to mention its distribution deal with Lee Dorrian's Rise Above label. And I mention that because this non-Rise Above collection of bongheads sounds terminally close to the mighty Cathedral, right down to the down-tuned Sabbatherian thrust and the Ward-like cymbal bashing that permeates each solid sludgy track. Vocals-wise, there's more singing than growling, perhaps aligning this more with the St. Vitus/Obsessed camp, also an apt comparison given the raw, lapsed jammy nature to the stoned sensurround. Four swirling songs of stout riffery that work a doomy spell, not without a sense of humour, again like Dorrian's main vehicle, Cathedral. Heartily recommended.

Rating                                                                7

## Adam Bomb - Fatal Attraction   (Geffen '85)

Ex-TKO-er Adam Brenner's rock demigod aspirations make **Fatal Attraction** an upbeat and anthemic rocker, yet at the same time clunky and predictable with more than enough forced mellow stuff designed solely for pink plastic radio transmission, sorta like Bon Jovi before he started feeling guilty. Better than fellow failed brat-packer Keel, due to stronger vocals, warmer songs, the odd surprise arrangement and Adam's unswerving confidence in his craft, despite being born to lose. Riot alumni Sandy Slavin on drums, and brief Aerosmith member Jimmy Crespo on guitars. Comeback record in '90 called **Pure S.E.X.** stiffed as one might have predicted.

Rating                                                                6

## The Adverts - Crossing The Red Sea With The Adverts   (Bright '78)

Again one of only a handful of new wave entries (due to its acceptable heaviness), **Crossing** was a somewhat well-organized affair; while so obviously immersed in the depressed world of poverty punk, deserving mention if merely because it was one of a scant fifteen or so punk albums in the '70s that rocked at all. Buy not for great metal, or great punk, but for nostalgia's sake. Shortly after the record's release, T.V. Smith and crew would abandon loud guitars and fade into seas of red ink like the rest of U.K's original street scum. Modest hit: *Gary Gilmore's Eyes*.

Rating                                                                5

## Aerosmith - Aerosmith   (Columbia '73)

Aerosmith's legendary premiere was this grimy little record of loose bumpkin blues metal, an engagingly humble, backwatered first step toward establishment of perhaps America's most sizeable r'n'r institution. Sure it's the debut, but every successive release sounds light years ahead in terms of production, songcraft, maturity . . . everything, making this the mongrel mutt of the catalogue by far. Positively taken however, **Aerosmith** is raw, dirty and steeped with squalid integrity, kinda like Bad Company heavier and drunk, or the Stones, much heavier and really drunk; rumbling old as the crossroads fable, due to the strong and obscure blues feels herein enclosed. That is if you can get past the odd distraction of Tyler's voice sounding (in hindsight) uncharacteristically and uncomfortably low register. But of course, it is the band's scruff rockin' roots sincerity mixed with a penchant for heavy rock that caught the world's attention; the concept of long-haired white boys making the blues palatable, fresh and pounding enough for the ever-sophisticating masses, just like Zep. Set me up. Took Boston by storm, but did only middling business elsewhere.

Rating                                                                7

## Aerosmith - Get Your Wings   (Columbia '74)

Ahead of its time and ragingly brilliant, **Get Your Wings** (working title: **Night In The Ruts**) is a tour de force of early Yankee guitar rock, completely brand new metal ideas, and sassy r+b touches. Oddly enough, two of the record's best tracks are the mellower ones, the atmospheric, barren, darkly uncommunicative *Seasons Of Whither* and *Spaced*, a crystal-clear romp through crisp night air, sort of a one-off experiment that still sounds fresh today. *Same Old Song and Dance* and '51 rocker *Train Kept A Rollin'*

(done Yardbirds-style) offer low-slung barroom blues metal extraordinaire, while *Lord Of The Thighs* (the last song hastily written for the record) and *S.O.S. (Too Bad)* are fledgling metal greats, complex and thoughtful, well-carved and hooky. In fact everything sounds well-planned on this rich, inspired and consistently entertaining rock 'n' roller, a record far more intelligent than much metal to this point in time, both sides of the pond included. Aerosmith were alive on arrival, far outstripping their bumpy debut, defining a sound that would breath rock and the blues as one, the fusion thrown faceward by real renegade punks wanting to make it so bad, it hurt.

Rating                                                                10

## Aerosmith - Toys In The Attic   (Columbia '75)

**Get Your Wings** arrived filled with timeless rock in various styles, yet it cohered magnificently, as Aerosmith translated a complex blues/rock history into a new long-haired American pastiche. Conversely, **Toys In The Attic** breaks out and digs deep, perhaps fleshing out additional positions, while sacrificing its predecessor's cohesion. There's a multitude to devour: original speed metal wrapped and flung faceward in the bombastic, riff-mad title track, minimalist blues something-or-other in the uncharacteristically serious *Uncle Salty*, a jazz novelty tune from the '40s in *Big Ten Inch* (which would unfortunately predestine Van Halen's and solo Roth's preoccupation with joke tunes), Sabbath crunch in Whitford's *Round And Round*, and the first of many obligatory album closer wind-downs in *You See Me Crying*, a tune from Tyler's days with pre-Aero-band Chain Reaction. Last but definitely not least, **Toys In The Attic** bestows upon our hides one of the most memorable and ground-breaking funk metal riffs in the essential *Walk This Way* (what dance music *should* be) plus the classic American swaggers of *Sweet Emotion* and *No More No More*. Whereas **Get Your Wings** defined fresh accidental genius, **Toys** tells a deliberately major league, if not schizoid tale of the tape, the band turning the commercial corner with a strange new confidence. Of course growing up with the stuff makes ya kinda biased, but dammit, when metal was young, there was no precedent, no set formula for its creation, so what we heard in Sabbath, Zep, Heep, Purple, Ted, and the enigmatic Budgie came from within. Influences were merely a starting point, a base, in the formulation of such glorious noise. And Aerosmith belongs right there with them, these bands being the creators of metal, making it up with no blueprint from which to build. Little credit in terms of the essence of metal should go to The Who, Stones, Beatles, Elvis, Yardbirds, Hendrix, or really *anybody* from the '50s or '60s. Heavy metal was an entirely new species, and because of Aerosmith's contribution this side of the Atlantic, the pendulum would begin to swing stateside as we entered the era of arena rock, a goodly five U.S. institutions leading the charge.

Rating                                                                9

## Aerosmith - Rocks   (Columbia '76)

Aerosmith's always been considered a Stonesy lot, and true, they were stoned a lot, they look just as funny, got the Toxic Twins vs. Glimmer Twins, similar frontman, same instrument vs. manpower mix, both bands sharing a deep knowledge and subsequent respect for the blues. But of course, music is key, and this is where Aerosmith takes flight. Aerosmith sounds nothing like the Mick and Keef, thank God. They're miles more talented, even if both empires however sharing an attitude, sincerity, and confidence that originates with adherence to the weight of rock history. **Rocks** swaggers big time in this context, sounding like a screamin', mercury-shattering rock festival, live, overblown, decadent, and very American, as the band crashed into our consciousness so coked and doped, they could barely walk. We get nasty funk metal in *Get The Lead Out* and *Last Child*, Sabbath-based dirge metal in *Nobody's Fault* (about earthquakes), *Toys In The Attic* part II in complex speedster *Rats In The Cellar*, and the warm, stirring, Stonesy harmonies of *Sick As A Dog*, a track where the band somewhat chaotically and semi-live switched instruments back and forth in the process of recording. Tyler's classic prolonged screams on *Back In The Saddle* highlight the performance of a showboating gypsy with a three track mind: chicks, rock and piles of drugs, a primal force who's just having the time of his life blowing away a crowd and doing blow, whereas *Lick And A Promise* becomes Joe Perry's larger-than-life guitar god romp, whipping Jimmy Page at his own game. Aerosmith was ultimately no less than King Of The Hill with **Rocks**, while also plowing through a mountain of drugs. Don't know if there's any correlation there, but on **Rocks**, the band is anything but wasted.

Rating       10

## Aerosmith - Draw The Line   (Columbia '77)

Complicated, murky, and layered, **Draw The Line** comes across as the serious, distressed Aerosmith album. Reviews were mixed. Some deemed it the product of worn-out rock hogs; excessive, impenetrable and overdone; while others saw time-worn wisdom and new levels of musical maturity. There's merit in both views, **Draw The Line** being ambiguously dense, uncommunicative, and busy but in a zone only a few bands had ever seen. And hey, we're talking Aerosmith here, a band proven incapable of a lemon, even if the recording of the record was a keystone cop sort of affair, the band hoovering piles of drugs in a converted convent in upstate New York, most days rendering themselves unable to work at all. Ah, but the music that miraculously emerged. As usual, I'm not crazy about the funk like *Sight For Sore Eyes* and *Get It Up*, but *Kings And Queens* is an epic sweep, a sort of proto metal tune with more gravity than this band usually addresses, while *Draw The Line* is one of the rowdiest, most jubilant, most frenetic anthems ever plugged into this planet, thoroughly raucous and loud, driven by a brilliant, cerebral Perry riff, colourful, action-packed lyrics, and more of Tyler blowing his vocal chords like it's his last utterance before getting his gold watch (long time coming. Just ask Sony). Perry even sings (flu-like mind you), belting out lead vox on short, double-time raver *Bright Light Fright*, while *Milk Cow Blues* is a blues ditty from the '30s turned cocaine-flying and metal-heavy. All in all, a hard album to get a handle on, sounding not unlike a weary but unrelenting party blasted by three competing stereos, the unwaning vestiges of hangovers to come nagging the crowd like a smothering fog.

Rating       9

## Aerosmith - Live Bootleg   (Columbia '78)

This long-anticipated double live offering features tunes primarily from the legendary '77 and '78 crash and burn tours, also offering two old blues covers from a '73 show in hometown Beantown, tracks which capture nicely the claustrophobic bar atmosphere from whence the band originated. There's also *Come Together* (who cares) and the stirring sing-along strains of *Chip Away The Stone*, which fits the Aero-groove perfectly, although the band didn't write it. I don't play this sludge machine all that much, but there are piles of cool pictures to look at while playing the studio stuff. I guess it's also useful as a document of the band's first of two commercial primes, a heady, confrontational time when the band was so stoned out of their skulls, Perry and Tyler would scrap on stage and fall down a lot. As live offerings go, **Classics Live** excels over **Bootleg** (not the popular opinion), exuding a sort of skillful grace under pressure. But the band rightfully

takes pride in not doctoring this beast all that much, during an era when live records were usually sanitized, overdubbed and reworked to the point of pointlessness.

Rating       6

## Aerosmith - Night In The Ruts   (Columbia '79)

Critics everywhere trashed this as a washed-up band going through the motions, which is bullshit, although this and maybe **Permanent Vacation** are as close to formula rock as Aerosmith gets. Sure the drugs, the infighting, and the waning fame were taking their toll, but the album's strength is undeniable, the basic riffs and the overall songcraft behind *Three Mile Smile*, *Chiquita*, and *Cheesecake* being more intelligent than anything on **Draw The Line** (except that record's beyond classic title cut), and equal to anything on **Rocks** or **Wings**, rollicking with complicated, convoluted blues feels, with innovative Stones-heroic melodies come chorus time. Grooves are everywhere, and although some of the guitar parts are so bizarre, almost to the point of sounding forced or manufactured, most of the time it works, exuding the canny genius of years spent welding modern flash rock to the blues. It is of note that Perry was out of the band just as recording began, his contributions nobly maintained, with Jimmy Crespo and Richie Supa brought in to finish the job. Filler: obligatory ballad *Mia* and no-effort dumbo blues cover *Reefer Head Woman*, while Yardbirds cover *Think About It* somehow sounded like cold, not-so-soulful metal. No doubt about it, the circumstances surrounding **Night In The Ruts** make it a low morale release, but Aerosmith's dedication to quality elevates the proceedings to triumph amidst adversity, the band even at its least energetic, coherent and cohesive, having never denied the listener a solid record. The album's tour would find Jimmy Crespo sitting in on guitar, with even the likes of Michael Schenker being considered for Perry's hallowed throne.

Rating       9

## Aerosmith - Aerosmith's Greatest Hits   (Columbia '80)

Given the band's on-the-ropes status at the turn of the decade, '80 seemed an appropriate point to take stock of the proud legacy Aerosmith had left thus far. **Greatest Hits** demonstrates the fact that this was a rock 'n' roll band whose commercial achievements rocked loudly as often as they did quietly. As with all seriously artistic forces, hits tended to follow no pattern whatsoever. Per usual, no real fan needs this record, which offers no non-LP extras, but merely ten fine tracks sampling each fine album to date. Surprise: one of the band's biggest sellers at well over five times platinum. Where these sales come from, I certainly don't know.

Rating       6

## Aerosmith - Rock In A Hard Place   (Columbia '82)

The only Aerodisc (thus far) without the classic Tyler-Perry-Whitford-Hamilton-Kramer lineup, **Hard Place** substitutes both guitarists, Perry and Whitford with Jimmy Crespo and bad influence Rick Dufay to little discernible difference. Most of the tunes here are variations on Tyler/Crespo compositions and it's more or less a good ol' Aerosmith hootenany except that the package as a whole reads a bit patchy (no fault to the new guys), highlights being manic speed rocker *Jailbait* (outsider Perry's fave track from the record), lowrider and minor hit *Lighting Strikes*, and warm, ambitious melodic rocker *Joanie's Butterfly*, one of Tyler's loftier, more spiritual excursions. The rest comes off as variously lumbering, untuneful and forced, a type of convoluted funk riff-raff confusing the issue. I guess every Aerosmith album sports one or two pooches (except perhaps **Get Your Wings**), but here there might be upwards to four that are either below the band's high standards or probably more truthfully just not to my tastes. But still, the wild thing is that through all the rock pig slobberings, gruntings, and mudslinging, the band has never made a bad record.

Rating     **8**

## Aerosmith - Done With Mirrors  (Geffen '85)

Not since the band's debut has Aerosmith come up with such an out-of-character album, a foggy, despondent record by a band financially destitute and frail of spirit. **Done With Mirrors** has a rough, no frills, live-off-the-floor, heavy-handed blues sound, no surprise given the haste with which it was both written and recorded. For an odd comparison: while Joe Perry was away doing his solo thing (see The Joe Perry Project—both he and Whitford are back here) he wrote and recorded his barnstorming title track *Let The Music Do The Talking*. His version is the way Aerosmith would *normally* have done it in their late '70s heyday, or would do it in the '90s, while here the delivery is noisy, loose, plodding and less effective overall than Joe's. Confused yet? Well, **Done With Mirrors** generally fleshes out this comparison, although it's chock full of successes as opposed to failures; raucous, noisy, metallic boogie woogers, straight ahead, nuthin' fancy but thick with hard-fought legitimacy. Lyrically, the record's strangely farmboy, affected, and simple, sorta like metal meets Hee Haw, lending the record an off-the-handle sort of casualness. Alas, **Done With Mirrors** will probably always be the lost Aerosmith album (people regularly forget it exists), created in some sort of garage-jammin' twilight zone, no help from its sombre, backwards cover art. An uncharacteristic experiment in raw, nervy spontaneity, from a band fighting for its life, rags to riches to rags. CD and cassette include greyish, complicated blues tune *Darkness*, making a very short record, a little less short.

Rating     **8**

## Aerosmith - Classics Live  (Columbia '86)

In which the band that can do no wrong burns through some of their less live-oriented benchmarks with stirring conviction, thus *Kings And Queens*, *Sweet Emotion* and *Three Mile Smile*, plus the downright bloodthirsty *Train Kept A Rollin'* and *Lord Of The Thighs*, all wrenched through the science of electricity amidst one of those booming hockey barn recordings that keeps the game sizzling with sonic reverb, soupy mind melds and buzzing backwashes of wattage. Features one previously unreleased **Rocks**-era dittie, *Major Barbara*, an ornate psychedelic blues that accomplishes its creepy aims with typical elusive melancholy. Basically Sony exercising their option to release material by the band, this time as opposed to **Classics Live 2**, the band having no part in its assembly.

Rating     **8**

## Aerosmith - Classics Live 2  (Columbia '87)

Alright, now ol' Leber and Krebs are milkin' it (and there's nothing wrong with good capitalist values), because this one's nothing but a sad and droopy-eyed slur-speech shuffle through the tried and often trampled. Sure there's *Movin' Out* and *Let The Music Do The Talking*, but the rest is as predictable as apple pie, dimly recorded and even dimmer on inspiration. No wonder really, most of the tracks phoned in from '84, probably one of the lowest years in the band's fame trajectory.

Rating     **5**

## Aerosmith - Permanent Vacation  (Geffen '87)

Two-fisting one of rock's mightiest comebacks ever, **Permanent Vacation** (six million+ happy customers in tow) and stellar seller **Pump** (surpassing its predecessor by an additional two million units) established Aerosmith as reigning metal kings in '87-'89 similar to their heady, out-of-control success of '76-'78. **Perma-**

nent **Vacation** is Aerosmith's version of the business proposition, a record with the expressed purpose of generating hits. Vancouver career-makers Bruce Fairbairn, Bob Rock, and Mike Fraser are at the knobs (it was almost Rick Rubin!) and God knows what other creative decisions. Desmond Child and Jim Vallance are brought in to prop up the songs, and what results is a collection of successful experiments, an ambitious and lengthy opus that throws everything at the wall, banking on the fact that much of it will stick, which is exactly what happened. Embarrassing schlock ballad *Angel* (garbage worthy of Heart), became a mega-single, as did gorgeous, hooky groove-rocker *Dude (Looks Like A Lady)*, followed eventually on the charts by bumpkin shuffle *Rag Doll*. The overall result is a mixed bag of tricks that in kind words would be described as Aerosmith for everybody, best dishes being lead Panzer *Heart's Done Time*, the oddly melodic but heavy *Simoriah*, and the title track, which sports a Stones-on-coke **Rocks**-era feel, essentially the phattest groove on the record. However, a Beatles cover is unnecessary (Adrian Belew's was better), the two blues tracks come off as fake, and an instrumental is hardly good mileage for the buck. After all is said and done, **Permanent Vacation** is blatantly commercial, graciously trying so hard to please, and yet, given the talent of the band, for the most part it succeeds. However, this is not Bryan Adams or Kiss, hired song guns hardly being necessary. But nobody said Fairbairn and his chart-obsessed contingent were looking for challenges. End result: 4/5 brilliant or good, 1/5 middling or bad. Low point of career: *Angel* (what whores), possibly demonstrating what happens when such stormy creative minds get clean.

Rating     **8**

## Aerosmith - Pump  (Geffen '89)

Although Fairbairn, Fraser, Vallance and Child are still picking the band's hides like doting vultures, this time it seems like Aerosmith is pretty much back in charge. Perhaps the accountants figured they'd let the band stretch out a bit, given that Aerosmith were big shooters going into this one as opposed to washed-up nobodies prior to **Permanent Vacation**. The results are devastating, **Pump** slamming loud, obnoxious, and raucous, full of first-class hard rockers built for battlefields ranging from radio to the moshpits of metal. And the production blasts along for the ride, ripe with bass, treble, distortion and edge. **Pump** yielded no less than four smash singles, while every last track eventually found its way to radio on some semblance of regular basis. *F.I.N.E.*, *Monkey On My Back* and *The Other Side* are consummate old-style Aerosmith, full of swagger and deep, grimy grooves while *Voodoo Medicine Man* exhibits a slow insidious crunch reminiscent of *Heart's Done Time*. On the downside, *My Girl* is ditzy, *Young Lust* is just noisy, and *What It Takes* isn't noisy enough. But all told, **Pump** embodies the most vigorous qualities of Aerosmith in the '70s, the songwriting, the volatility and the Stonesy integrity, updated and upgraded for the talent-crammed '90s. As a result, **Pump** smokes when it just had to.

Rating     **10**

## Aerosmith - Livin' On The Edge  (Geffen '93)

As we all wait in wonder for the release of **Get A Grip**, the Geffen suits and the rock'n'roll gypsies called Aerosmith deem it appropriate to release this taster comprising no less than three versions of *Livin' On The Edge*, plus two non-**Grip** out-takes *Don't Stop* and *Can't Stop Messin'*, and I'm joyful at the lusty work at hand. *Livin' On The Edge* is a great tune, inspirational, ambitious, even if the alternative versions here ("acoustic" and "demo") are only slightly different, both a little more droopy than the official tale. And in the spirit of the pros that they are, Aerosmith win the day with both *Don't Stop* and *Can't Stop Messin'*, the former pumping along with major accelerated spark, the latter summing up a career of righteous marauding riffs, Stonesy sleaze, soulful choruses and blazing mastery of the game. No doubt, this teaser greased and primed distribution channels for the stunning sales to come, crowning the band as the undisputed kings of rock for 1993. Note: a **10** but a somewhat meaningless one, given its EP length and breadth.

Rating      **10**

## Aerosmith · Get A Grip   (Geffen '93)

All eyes on the prize, as a venerable rock institution gives birth to another aircraft carrier, an expansive, painstakingly-conceived record that eschews the raw bash of **Pump** for a technically intricate and sometimes sombre look at God's gracious spread. Each composition on **Get A Grip** seems the product of intense deliberation and collaboration, whether achieving filler (more often than I'd like) or grandeur, resulting in a sequence of tracks that hangs loosely as a record, more like a succession of intelligent singles, which can be both inspiring and annoying. In retro, **Pump** becomes the duke-'em-out dark horse to **Get A Grip**'s gleaming, sky-straddling, maybe too synthetic machine, a record of athletic guitar raves for '90s rock radio. Thus you gotta admire the craft, the sincerity and the very real artistic anguish that went into this fat entertaining pie. Twelve tracks (+) of Unarguable Quality, seven or eight exhibiting large doses of Aerosmith's ragtag songwriting prowess, two or three entering the Aerohall of Fame. Not one to showcase riff so much (Perry opting more for strategic placement of axe shadings amongst difficult arrangements), **Get A Grip**'s main ace is the astonishing painterly pipes of Tyler, making for the man's best full record performance, livin' well to the edges on most of **Grip**'s panoramic 62 minutes. Mixwise, Fairbairn piles on the goods (I knocked off a point just for that), the approach commercial but plausible. Three ballads, and none so braindead as *Angel*, although *Cryin'* and *Crazy* are more successful parodies of the form, while *Amazing* reaches back to *Home Tonight* with all the weariness and melodic poignancy of twenty years of hard-won wisdom. I could do without *Gotta Love It*, *Line Up* (lamely co-written by Lenny Kravitz), and Perry's somewhat phoned-in *Walk On Down*. But *Eat The Rich*, one of the band's razor-sharp rhythmic metallizers, kicks as it must, and that damn riff on *Shut Up And Dance* just sticks to my shoes like the bubblegum it is. *Fever*, *Flesh* and the bump 'n' grinding title track round out the raunchy backbone while *Livin' On The Edge* carries on its duty as this cash cow's worldly eyes and ears. Ultimately **Get A Grip** is one of those big Hollywood records that you just let roll. Not all of it brushes greatness, but there's always fertile activity: bass solos, mandolin, sampling, strange Perry solos, harmonies, harmonica, sassy lyrics. It all spells entertainment, and as Tyler says "I think the bed it's lying on is palatable enough." As with every Aerosmith record, **Get A Grip** is a bounty of mostly strong, always professional and well-intentioned mini-suites, a record with nothing resembling a central thrust, except perhaps that unforgettable Aerosmith lust for embracing life. A band too serious and worthy of respect to ever disappoint.

Rating      **9**

## Aerosmith · Pandora's Box   (Columbia '94)

A massive Thanksgiving spread of Aerosmith diary entries, **Pandora's Box** offers little in the way of serious gems, lots in the way of lesser curiosities. Over the space of three exhuberant CDs, we get a time-traveling gaggle of live tracks, including a vintage *Walkin' The Dog* from '71, a boogie cover called *On The Road Again* from '72, and boiling-over performances from the band's do-no-wrong days of roughly '76 to

'78 (*Write Me A Letter*, *Adam's Apple*, *Kings And Queens*, and a god-like *Lord Of The Thighs*). There's also an early, swampy take on *Movin' Out*, and an even earlier Steven Tyler tune from '66 called *When I Needed You*, basically yer dumb '60s bubblegum tune, but a lark all the same. In terms of actual new, real music, there ain't much to speak of: the odd short spontaneous boogie, loitered long blues, rough studio jam, intriguing early, truncated version of a later classic, and a handful of not-so-rare rarities like a *Helter Skelter* cover, Supa's inspired *Chip Away The Stone*, *Major Barbara*, and the totally out-of-place *Sharpshooter* from **Whitford/St. Holmes**, the inclusion greatly exposing how amazing Aerosmith's material was compared to regular music, like uh, *Sharpshooter*. So really, **Pandora's Box** is quite the interesting show for the seasoned fan, moderate curios coming wave by wave, made all the more fun by the excellent play-by-play liner notes of the huge CD booklet, a booklet chock full of good journalism, a few lyrics, and surprising, previously unpublished photos. Pleasantly thrilled with how this kept my attention, due in no small part to those bracing live tracks, tunes that are usually the filler on such odds and sods projects.

Rating      **8**

## Aerosmith · Big Ones   (Geffen '94)

The grandiosist foot-stompin', butt-conquerin', hair-a-flyin' boogie woogers from Boston are back for your stash of cash, conquering the crass world of commerce, givin' it up one more time for Mr. Geffen with a high-bandwidth provocation to the nation entitled **Big Ones**. If hits packs be your bag, fine, but if Aerosmith be your band, your interest will focus on the trio of newies (with *Deuces Are Wild* rendered only semifresh due to its inclusion on the **Beavis & Butt-head** soundscam). But even without the stupendous new tracks, **Big Ones** is a stellar exercise in winning the grand enchilada, Aerosmith staging the definitive comeback in showbiz, culminating in the three Geffen discs from which all these hits are culled. But alas, any true fan is extra-spicy sick of these hits: we play the records repeatedly, then get blindsided by radio, passively yet semi-OK with receiving Aero's mood-lifting emanations over crackling car FM. Great songs. Done that. One non-sonic plus: all the lyrics; my vinyl **Pump** had none (did your CD?). But then there's the fresh material. *Deuces Are Wild* is average Aero-tunage, with a gloriously warm sound segment right around that "sleeping bag" part of the big shoo. And don't forget, Toxic filler is eons further up the food chain from the work of mere mortals. Moving on, *Walk On Water* is a masterpiece; heavy, heaving, decadent, and so engrossed in hook, complexity and enthralling rhythmic mass come chorus time. *Blind Man* is equally strong, a big bag of obtuse melodic tricks; an ever-flowing river of shiny, professional blues balladry built for Luv. If mankind can wear out a CD, it's to be scientifically proven here on tracks 1 and 9. Sure it's all about Christmas presents, and maybe this would be a good time to say no to the machine. However if anybody is capable of constructing three tracks worth five bucks apiece, I'd say it'd be these guys.

Rating      **7**

## Aerosmith · Nine Lives   (Sony '97)

Gotta love it. **Nine Lives**' first seven seconds sound just like the opening moments of a better record, Max Webster's debut from 1975, and a little song we like to call *Hangover*. But enough cuteness; an Aerosmith record is serious business, especially when it's the first on a long, $34M contract for the band's old home, Columbia. A modern Aerosmith album is first and foremost, a songwriting clinic. Whoever gets in on the convoluted credits, a whole constipated batch of work has occurred: a lesson for all lazy altero-cacksters out there. So on many levels, **Nine Lives** is simply another

truly exalted, absolutely top-floor piece of work. There is just so much to digest, so many interesting nooks and crannies, a great time can be had by all. Like the last Ozzy record, the best tracks (and the worst!) are the quasi-ballads, *Kiss Your Past Good-Bye*, *Ain't That A Bitch*, and *Hole In My Soul* sounding more like the desperate emotion of *Home Tonight* than the sorry cheese of *Angel* or this record's *Full Circle*. The rockers are considerably raucous, **Nine Lives'** production in general sporting more echo, incest and crashed cymbals. Thus *Nine Lives*, *Crash* and *Taste Of India* convince, even if the latter's eastern-flavoured chorus is straight Spinal Tap. Yuck. But more importantly, that's a terrible band photo on the back, ain't it? They looked better on Saturday Night Live for God's sake. And what of Joey's chin music and long straight do? Anyways, the funny thing about this record (and maybe all good ones), is that so much activity is going on, you don't know if you're being serenaded or moshed. There are so many tracks here that are between pop and hard rock (courting psychedelia or The Beatles, or some morassed mean average), a new type of record gel has been cast, Aerosmith smearing together what? three hundred tracks of sound, until all one can do is marvel at the spectacle. And it's not Leppard studio abuse either. This army of band+consultants is trying to make it look dirty, which at minimum, doesn't make it look too excessively clean. Anyhow, loved the first single (*Falling In Love (Is Hard On The Knees)*), and swaying rhapsodically to the second one (*Ain't That A Bitch*), and may spew at the next one (remember **Get A Grip** four singles deep?). And in any event, these songs are a series of inspired ideas, usually a good six to the tune, best not viewed in isolation, best viewed, as I say, as a smug reminder of who the top seed really is.
Rating      **9**

## Afghan Whigs - Congregation    (Sub Pop '92)
Dive in and surrender. That's about the best advice I can offer for loop jams like this, which float suspended somewhere between Chameleons UK masterpiece **Strange Times**, Nudeswirl's lathered debut, and the first from Sweet Water. Early, pre-pin-up-boy Afghan Whigs are of that spacey realm, guitars out swirling, strumming, washing, feeding back, vocals slack, hurt and aimless, structures flexible and lounging. But hooks are forthcoming and ethereal, sending *Kiss The Floor*, *Congregation* and *This Is My Confession* into unkempt Soul Asylum terrain, where windmill-style power chords follow lilt and apprehension. Drop-a-tab, sensitive grunge for those who have 36 hours or so to spare. A thriving, reputable career since.
Rating      **7**

## Agent Steel - Skeptics Apocalypse    (Roadrunner '85)
More over-wrought, wall-of-sound American techno-speed-thrash with nary a new idea or reason to exist. These heinous merchants of the undeliverable (core being two guys from Abbatoir) have stuff newer than this blighted sore. So they may have improved, but I won't be sampling any of it in a paying situation.
Rating      **2**

## Age Of Electric - Ugly    (Gods Teeth Ethel '94)
Like similar Canuck success story Rusty, AOE made dents with their accomplished indie EP, the Bob Rock "executive produced" **Ugly** sparked with two hits, *Untitled* and the title track, both going to the full-length. Elsewhere, there's three more non-LP tracks, including two of the band's best, *Pin Cushion* and *Spraybomb*, which might recall Wildhearts on a good day.
Rating      **6**

## The Age Of Electric - The Age Of Electric
(Gods Teeth Ethel/Cargo '95)
The fact that one can't apply a tidy critic's label to this band might actually be a bad thing, The Age Of Electric's vaunted full-length debut sounding like so much general rock. Yes *Ugly* is a good solid hit (even sounding a bit like Sammy Hagar!), and wisely it's repeated and remastered here, and yes the record sparkles production-wise, and (one more yes) YES, performances are upbeat to the point of bursting with pride, but the sum total of the experience sounds dangerously close to all that's bad about corporate Canuck rock. I dunno, maybe it'll take the summer psyche by storm, because it's certainly sparky, but what I'm hearing is hard pop alternative recorded like poodle rock metal, a little too overkill on the Urge Overkill crossover phenom. Slick but not special. The Dahles have wisely cut their hair, got some nerdy shirts and gone alternative, now calling themselves Limblifter, while AOE is still a going concern, the prolific ones now working on another AOE record while they watch how Limblifter's pretty groovy self-titled debut does.
Rating      **6**

## Aggression - The Full Treatment    (Banzai '87)
A record really couldn't look more consumed by sewage than this, and expectations of a judicious bloodletting are unfortunately fulfilled. Features hounds like Sasquatch Barth and Dug Bugger whiplashing accelerated, Draconian thrashdrones like *Frozen Aggressor*, *Dripping Flesh*, *By The Reaping Hook*, and *Rotten By Torture*. Stunned as usual with this self-flagellating dark side of The World's Most Powerful Music. From Montreal. I just don't get it, and I don't think I ever will.
Rating      **0**

## Agony Column - God, Guns & Guts    (Big Chief '89)
Self-deemed as a "hellbilly deathmetal onslaught"; that pretty much accurately describes this cackling, sinister collection of desert tales, Agony Column crafting killer tunes borne of a hostile, twisted wilderness, driven to full reverb by cowboy representatives of Satan's minion, sent to spread the seven sins throughout the American south in full fester to the beyond. Sent with blood-curdling admonishments upon the forked tongue of one Richie Turner, reverse morality plays such as *Snakebite*, *4 X 4*, and *Cars, Sex & Violence* career along a night-shrouded, metal-flaked dirt road, choked in dust and blackened oil. But you definitely want to be along for this journey, 'cos this extremely rocking, extremely pounding death metal gorging picks up right where ZZ Top's *Tejas* threw you out of the car; chilled and alone amongst the rattlers and circling harpies disguised as vultures. But never ye mind, because Agony Column bring along jugs of the worst kind of homemade liquor, emitting a helluva grind guaranteed to melt away the evil wrought on man in distress. Or if you don't buy that, buy this record, because it kicks ass.
Rating      **9**

## Agony Column - Brave Words & Bloody Knuckles
(Big Chief '90)
Devil Chicken, Bat Lord, Crow and Redwing Viper lurch back with an expansion on the unique and barbequed concept that has become the soul-bending Agony Column. More hellbilly 'n' graveyard blues, and less flat-headed speed metal this time around, the band has assembled a wicked, chaotic and frenzied gumbo of sights and smells. From the pumping *Angel Of Def* to the suvvern death rock of *Lord Almighty*, through the laid-out sidewindin' *Big Two Hearted Sammy*, this is humorous horror at its most hopelessly hallucinogenic and hammered. Picture the Cramps crossed with old Anthrax and Alice in Chains, and you'll pretty much

ascertain that nothing this impure ever walked the earth before, the Column tapping into a rich vein of scary folklore with a blood-stained sledgehammer, rendering the world in vivid, distorted, unreal technicolour with one of the wildest deliveries in metal. Existing outside of time to warn us of the gaping hole to hell, Agony Column serve justice, faith and the 100 proof way like no other bible-whipped apparitions in the swamp. Glory be to the loudest scuzzballs in America.
Rating                                                             10

## Agressor - Symposium Of Rebirth   (Black Mark '94)

From France (and you know what FZ thinks about France), which is why this isn't any good, being about eight years behind the times, hellishly crank-thrashing through a batch of blurry semi-technical accelerated grindcore pieces that aren't so much bad, just not fresh. What is fresh however is the number of times we stop for small ensemble classical interludes. But that is of little concern, given the crudely recorded slambang enclosed. Bottom of the barrel for a usually crafty Black Mark.
Rating                                                              5

## Alaska - The Pack   (Music For Nations '85)

Bernie Marsden's half-baked Alaska leaves the sorry album purchaser raped and freezin', listening in mute disarray to this lost-in-time attempt at keyboard-piddling girlie rock by washed-up Brit blues cronies. There's no match, boys. Like the Tormés, Moores and McCoys of this world, Marsden is doomed to wallow in obscure, simplistic, '70s experimentation, playing bad catch-up ball with modern advances, made all the worse because he could never write in the first place. Get a life.
Rating                                                              2

## Alastis - The Other Side   (Century Media '97)

No, it ain't the follow-up to **Jagged Little Pill** or *Rubberband Man*, it's actually the latest and most hopeful in a royal lineage of classy, classic death metal records from Europe, this one with ties to brilliant futuro-deathsters Samael, both hailing from Switzerland. Aside from Waldemar Sorychta's (don't call him Century Media's house producer) somewhat industrial-headed drum mix, what we have is a lush, well-paced, dynamic piece of dark metal. But rather than get too frilly, Alastis veer from metal only to get sombre and funereal. No pop, dance or Celtic touches here, just churning, melancholy metal with returning mellow passages velvetted with keyboard and synth chords, roughed up by agonized, anguished vocals, just the accessible side of grind. Record #3 for the band, who have been suiciding souls since '87, and the experience shows, fouling the air like hoof dust from Four apocalyptic Horsemen. Let the tale unfold.
Rating                                                              8

## Alcatrazz - No Parole From Rock'n'Roll   (Rocshire '83)

One of my twenty favourite albums of all time, **No Parole** is a dizzying display of art metal that quietly excels in so many areas. The master of course, is Graham Bonnet whose songcraft is one of the most tasteful and innovatively subtle in music, whose lyrics work as sound as well as insightful, intelligent and compassionate views of the world. And as a voice technician, he's dead perfect. Slashing and burning through Bonnet's brilliance is one of the most inspired (and only the second, not counting an early Silver Mountain boot), recorded performance of Swede legend Yngwie Malmsteen. I'm convinced Bonnet has pushed him to his creative max here much the same way he did with Blackmore and Schenker, as there are more platinum riffs and blistering resolving solos here than on any of Malmsteen's own albums. The two

work genius here on such nimble, but heavy masterpieces as *General Hospital, Jet To Jet* and the mystical oriental shadings of *Hiroshima Mon Amour* and *Kree Nakoorie*. Aside from the pop metal *Island In The Sun* and the dirge ballad *Suffer Me*, the entire album is an elegant and searing heavy metal, yet the sense of controlled ultra-glide is phenomenal, the playing razor sharp, and the production (specifically the drum sound), all electric edge and punch, decorated by Waldo's prolific keyboard work that marries wimp rock to the grind of Jon Lord (note: Jimmy Waldo and bassist Gary Shea were previously with excellent pomp outfit New England who released a self-titled classic in '79 and **Explorer Suite** in '80). Suffice to say, **No Parole From Rock'n'Roll** is an unparalleled classic, a most confident mix of intelligence, uncompromising attention to detail, and fluidly beautiful metal guitars.
Rating                                                             10

## Alcatrazz - Live Sentence   (Rocshire '84)

Four from **No Parole**, one Bonnet solo cut, one Bach, one Malmsteen, one Rainbow and one Rainbow cover comprise this less-than-necessary and premature "live in Japan" disk. Alcatrazz sizzled with formidable science, no doubt about it, but their forté is borne more of smooth, clean, tightly precise studio metal than the fast and loose ethic of the stage. I mean, I'd like to see Steely Dan live, but I wouldn't play their live album.
Rating                                                              5

## Alcatrazz - Disturbing The Peace   (Capitol '85)

Alcatrazz dares to follow up one of the classiest debut albums ever while switching one famous and distinctive guitar god (Yngwie) for another (Steve Vai). I never liked Vai's playing; all diddling tunelessly up the fretboard and no power, a parody of man meets metal guitar; always mixed thin and always overplaying, constantly digressing from the riff, the rhythm guitar drone, the metal-ness of metal, to pull off some kind of joke fill where drums should be doing it. Nevertheless, the genius of Bonnet's intelligent songcraft shines through, making the best of Vai's odd, light-footed approach to craft, Bonnet's forceful personality driving such technical metal flash as *Mercy, Wire And Wood*, and the warm hard rock melodies of *Sons And Lovers* to new artful heights. The rest of the record finds Bonnet's veteran backing band commandeering a variety of craft-conscious embellishments, including beautiful, hook-laden choruses, complex arrangements, generous keyboard shadings, and provocative lyrics. When all is said and done, it is Bonnet's determination and fabled work ethic that lends cohesion to both Alcatrazz spreads thus far, despite fronting two stylistically very different, equally verbose and aggressive fret burners. A state-of-the-art yet playful opus of cutting integrity. Deservedly reissued in '95 by Griffin.
Rating                                                             10

## Alcatrazz - Dangerous Games   (Capitol '86)

The tragically under-rated Graham Bonnet takes one last kick at the cat with another magical, exceedingly tasteful dose of singular hard rock. Everything this guy ever touched resulted in artistic brilliance and commercial failure. The man was a big part of the best Michael Schenker and Rainbow albums, and his major vehicle, Alcatrazz was without peers. His solo stuff, Impellitteri, and Blackthorne (all lesser triumphs), also went nowhere. The man's talent cannot be denied, yet **Dangerous Games** is decidedly the least inspired of the Alcatrazz banquets, sounding hollow and scarce of soul without the stamp of a distinct guitar foil, all middling performances set to the robotic strains of over-produced drums. We do get some heavenly guitar melodies in the brilliant *Undercover, No Imagination, Ohayo, Tokyo* and *Blue Boar*. But much of the rest is an uninspiring grab-bag of fuzzy, lacklustre hard rock styles, smatterings of forced metal, and a bit of balladry, making **Dangerous Games** the man's least focused record. One fears a bit of a marketing panic. Still, the sheer quality of the good half to two thirds make **Dangerous Games** a must for fans of shiny guitar rock, of AOR before American influences smothered and snuffed those toneful European melodies.

Rating 8

## Aldo Nova - Aldo Nova (CBS '82)

Aldo Nova's debut is a marginal entry in this book, alas being fairly wimpy, corporate hard rock (the stuff **Kerrang!** lapped up in the heyday of twenty foot hairdos and red leather). I've included it partly because it *is* a hard rock album technically speaking, but mainly because his '91 return **Blood On The Bricks** (Aldo cajoled back into rock'n'roll by buddy Jon Bon Jovi) is such an amplified, guitar-drenched if somewhat calcified effort. Pause for applause, Aldo. Anyways, **Aldo Nova** is a square shot at the under-achieving Loverboy sound; simple, clear, chick-driven Journeyrock with smooth lead vox, smooth harmonies, that big beat, lotsa keyboards and dumb functionary lyrucks. Really, not much heavier than Loverboy's first or second, this record scored a few hits, most notably *Fantasy*, which was about the heaviest thing we ever got to hear when we were dragged out dancing with the gals. Things were on the up-and-up for this frost-bitten Canadian boy, the do-it-yourselfer even cracking the U.S. first time out without as much as breaking a sweat. Subsequent releases **Subject: Aldo Nova** and **Twitch** were twin turds (relying on ever-escalating wads of technology), and Aldo languished in obscurity until the kickin' **Blood On The Bricks**, which proves you're never really washed-up for good until you're six feet under, especially if you've got Jon Bon Jovi as a buddy. Also of note: in the gap, Aldo worked with both Celine Dion and Cindy Lauper.

Rating 5

## Aldo Nova - Twitch (CBS '85)

Major tech, synth, and keys as a newly cybernetic Aldo flounces his robotic way to the sorry-safe strains of the radio. **Twitch** loses the hokey, but nostalgic Camaro moves of the debut, opting for a pompous waffle of electronics, which seem to invade every potentially human element of this album, encasing performances in control room plastics. Obviously a man more in tune with the autocratic and engineering sides of making records. At least his second **Subject** covered Coney Hatch's *Hey Operator*.

Rating 2

## Alias - Alias (Capitol '90)

Two Sherriff guys, three Heart guys. That should tell you all you need to know. A dismal mess of AOR conventions; prissy vocals, lousy sounding drums, rotten keyboards, questionable motives, songs worth shooting, and the occasional tasty bit of posey guitar.

Rating 1

## Alice in Chains - Face Lift (CBS '90)

Guitars slung low, in fact everything slung low, **Facelift** is technologically harrowing metal ground to 16 rpm. One of the more promising records from the soon-to-explode Seattle scene, **Facelift** was Sub Pop grunge metal on ludes, sort of a slow, grinding, atmospheric, and at times sparse version of Black Sabbath raped and plundered by the Stooges. From day one, AiC received great press, immediately hyped as the future of metal along with bands such as Faith No More, Soundgarden and King's X. I was definitely on board—almost religiously on board—even if the record drooled a little sluggish, risking mind-rot in the process. Biggest complaint: the juvenile lyrics, a sort of celebration of squalor, shock-for-shock's-sake drivel, insulting the intelligence and towing the Sub Pop line to a T; just the usual ambiguous blood, guts and body parts dreamscapes, living hells, and "man, I'm wasted" mumblings. Ultimately though, **Facelift** was nothing less than a swift kick and wake-up call to the bloated goat of hair band metal, an accomplished but disturbing debut, vibrating in an incredibly dense, low-cycle pocket that would define the new low-tuned vibe still popular years later. Off to a fast start securing opening slot on Van Halen's '91 tour.

Rating 9

## Alice in Chains - Sap (CBS '92)

Pre-dating the whole Unplugged phenomenon in their own modest way, the eminently electric AiC delicately assemble a stealth-like EP of sombre acoustic numbers (well, *Got Me Wrong* is a bit noisy). Layne sez he was so strung-out during this time, he can't even remember doing it. Pity, 'cos there's some nice performances here, including some wailing backing vox from Chris Cornell and Mark Arm. Don't have a slot in my psyche that would welcome mellow AiC, finding the whole prospect unclean and depraved. But the band does a seedy, soiled job of going to such mental hellholes, making sense as a Roger Waters (or Roy Harper!) for the alternative set.

Rating 7

## Alice in Chains - Dirt (Sony '92)

Every so often, dirt comes rumbling down upon the sleeping innocent in waves of suffocating black. Alice in Chains' sad sod does much the same, moving with resolute calm, strength, and urge to snuff out life. **Dirt** slouches past the shackles of conventional song construction into a slower, more free-form and cerebral experience, where riffs, verses, choruses, breaks, jams and solos juxtapose with disorienting anarchy. As evil, dream-like and drugged as the debut (Layne's totally into heroin by now), **Dirt** becomes more atmospheric and detached, pushing the limits, becoming more like **Black Sabbath** or **Sabbath Bloody Sabbath** than **Master Of Reality**, while remaining stoked with sinister intelligence and bruising psychic anchors. Favourites *Them Bones*, *Sickman*, and *Godsmack* highlight Layne Staley's psychotic vocals and multiple personas, while festering sores like *Rooster* and *Would?* push **Dirt** to the precipice of paralysis, lying quivering on the edge, drowning in a quagmire of sloth, expertly stirred as the ship burns in a slick of petroleum. The quiet passages threaten to nod then pass out under first turgid spin, but song paths are so memorable (i.e. check out the chorus to *Down In A Hole*), even the low cycles become a pleasing backwards reality to a listener not averse to Alice in Chains' hungover, strung-out world. Minor complaint though, 'cos **Dirt** rules the roost as a sticky, nightmarish expulsion of metal psychedelia, laced with rat poison and ill will towards man.

Rating 10

## Alice in Chains - Jar Of Flies (Sony '93)

Somewhat more adventuresome yet just as murky as the **Sap** project, **Jar Of Flies** (seven "tracks" this time, no pun intended) was quite the success for the band, just off a major hit with their stellar cellar **Dirt**. But it's also more droney and plain sicker, *Brother* and big hit *No Excuses* being particularly brown. True death dirges through to the hollow core, **Jar Of Flies** takes the listener sewer swimming, a good prep job for the saddening sounds of Layne's Mad Season project. Note although **Sap** and **Jar Of Flies** came out as stand-alone CDs, Sony packaged both together in a gatefold double-vinyl version, last side being one of those laser-etched logo things from the '70s.

Rating 7

## Alice in Chains - Alice in Chains  (Sony '95)

Many expected Alice to die a creaking, melt-into-the-gutter death, what with Layne Staley's heroin-addled health or lack thereof constantly thwarting plans to function as a productive bad-ass band from Seattle. Well, whether they exist much longer or not, they've made the big-deal metal album of the year, this sucker being a truly haunting, unapologetically grungy pile of poison. The crossover metal of **Dirt** has been cooked up in a spoon, all edges worn off for heaviness that is apocalyptic and tired at once, and ballads that are a morbid wake for whatever. It's just a twenty-story tower of Nasty from start to bitter end; graphics-wise featuring three-legged dogs, three-legged men (there's a discussion in itself), pigs, frogs, prosthetics; one black and bloodied nightmare from page to sick page. And the music matches the visual violence, lead track and single *Grind*, just a rusty bucket of truck with loosened bolts, leading into a collapsed collection of downwound sound that is as hurtful and critically injured as it gets. Faves would include the majestic hellscapes of *Sludge Factory* and *Head Creeps*, with guiltiest pleasures being vampire campfire tunes *Heaven Beside You* and *Over Now*, but best to just let Layne howl for the full hour. OK guys, it's done, thank you, good job. Your income is guaranteed for another 24 months. Now go back to sleep.

Rating  **10**

## Alice in Chains - Unplugged  (Sony '96)

Gutted, regurgitated and declawed Alice in Chains ain't exactly my idea of frolic, so the whole premise of the light funeral music that makes up this record leaves me stone dead forever. Still, it becomes obvious that these guys write so durn good, the songs stand up as a sort of soiled swamp experience. And if this is the only way to get Layne out of his nods, so be it. *Down In A Hole* almost sounds inviting, as does the torched twang of *Angry Chair*. I'm sure it was quite a morbid little concerto, what with all those candles and people taking bets on whether this was another pre-plunk like Nirvana's similar but much more upbeat and horrific show. Simple arrangements, and truly acoustic guitar-driven, unlike some of the cheater shows of this series.

Rating  **7**

## Alien Sex Fiend - The Altered States Of America
(Anagram/Futurist '93)

Another symbolic, cursory single review for ya, of a band with lotsa records which I can't be bothered to decipher. Alien Sex Fiend are one of those dangerous, evil goth bands combining clanky industrial, Bauhaus, Christian Death, Nick Cave . . . hell, even Hawkwind, composing drugged and pummelled songs that sort of erupt then jam and drift out or just decompose, full of ranting, twisted dance moves and churning monotonous power chords. Legendary in some circles, a bunch of noise to others, but yes, an odd, integritous sort of metal, or at least awful hard music of reptilian origin. This one's live; kinda oxymoronic dontcha think?

Rating  **3**

## All - Pummel  (Interscope/Warner '95)

For years I avoided this long-suffering punk band, thinking they were a bunch of unkind noisemakers, bent on playing badly fast and snarling at life. But now I finally listen in and (I'm sure thanks to Green Day), their new record is watery, weak, panic pop punk (lowest of the low: *Million Bucks*); dumb and ditzy with a few sweet swear words to give it imagined edge. Some tasty guitarwork here and there (sorta Black Flagged), but overall, quite annoying and wimpy. Sum total: smug and commercial, a real ironic larf given the band's somewhat revered back catalogue.

Rating  **5**

## The Almighty - Soul Destruction  (PolyGram '91)

Bangin' one time much like a tougher, leather-clad rendition of Little Caesar, these rowdy Brits gained considerable media buzz with their simple biker fare. Still I can't see much real reason to check in, **Soul Destruction** running pret' near on automatic, rife with HM clichés and predictable grunt, again demonstrating the fact that U.K. metal at the time seemed out of touch with the levels of progress demanded and achieved in literally every hard rock genre. Fact being, The Almighty is little more than an up-the-ante Zodiac Mindwarp, a gravelly, growly bar band with juice to spare but mediocre songs with titles like *Free 'N' Easy*, *Praying To The Red Light* and *Hell To Pay*; asinine gutter lyrics to match. If The Almighty are after some sort of spontaneous, honest, punk-metal hybrid, then they haven't gone far enough, this project smacking of low-cal creativity and hasty disregard for quality writing. A disappointment to me, but wot the Hell, much of the rest of the world seems to groove on it. At this point, more or less a nice choice for non-threatening back-up band on someone's hockey barn sojourn.

Rating  **5**

## The Almighty - Powertrippin'  (Polydor '93)

Well, this one's about what you'd expect, dressier, trickier, grungier and down-tuned for the '90s. So it's a bit more of an urban mosh, albeit a lumbering stiff one. Circus Of Power comes to mind, drifting along the same pointless trajectory, both bands hatching good records that hold no meaning for me, confused signals, dirty rock done too clean (the damning doer here being Mark Dodson).

Rating  **6**

## The Almighty - Just Add Life  (Castle '96)

Kinda puts a damper on things when the band breaks up right after hatching a new record, Scotland's The Almighty packing it in after eight years and five records. But on this flare-out, the band goes for more of a metal-muscled Clash sound, football holler fodder with wit, charm and the benefit of experience. I hate to call it '90s punk, because it isn't, The Almighty making good use of their metal baggage and very British disposition, somewhat evoking a grimier, more street-rocked Wildhearts or at times Therapy? and even Rancid. The production and performances (especially Stumpy's drumming) are explosive and sparkling, making **Just Add Life** an oi!-ish windmiller with chops, brains and even a certain sensitivity, all those bright primary colours and nifty green plastic jewel case perhaps rose-colouring my judgment. Sell-out, sell-off, cash-in or smash hit? Hard to figure when the band is no more. Just add life and enjoy.

Rating  **7**

## Altura - Mercy  (Magna Carta '96)

Magna Carta is a label dedicated to the new wave of progressive rock. Home to acts such as Shadow Gallery, Tempest, Magellan, Cairo, World Trade and a raft of cool progressive tribute albums, the label has kept the ethic of the old prog warhorses alive and thriving. North Carolina's Altura are on the more metallic end of things. But true to their label's ethic, this comes to heaviness from prog (of a bewilderingly jazz fusion sort), rather than taking the stance of metalheads trying to be tricky. Therefore, all the metal rules are broken, resulting in fluid axework, lush piano, and overt, often frantic chops mania. Bottom line: my enjoyment of this might have much to do with optics, but the view is quite a worthy, if somewhat frosty sight.

Rating  **7**

## Amorphis - The Karelian Isthmus (Relapse '92)

Pioneers of a sound that is quite popular in underground circles, covens, and church-burnings these days, Finland's Amorphis chunder on down with a melodic, mournful and sullen grindcore churn, precision but thick, vocals quite extreme, lyrics all frost and fire fantasy. This debut (named for a historical battlefield in Finland) was a fully realized opus, the band's unique flavours intact, a dependable Sunlight Studios knobjob establishing Amorphis as a serious chunk of melodious, miserable gloom, the perfect soundtrack for seducing, expunging, or at least ice-fishing with one's demons.

Rating                                    7

## Amorphis - Tales From The Thousand Lakes
(Relapse '94)

Two long, snowy years in the making, the clumsily-titled **Tales From The Thousand Lakes** has arrived, turning heads with its ethereal heaven and hell side-drift through tundra and tide. **Tales** is a mountainous type of record, huge landslides cascading down at frequent intervals, fueled by the rumbling, down-tuned heft of these massive guitars, sporting craggier peaks and rainier valleys than the fine debut. And over the shifting earth, come delicate and occasional keyboards, really taking this into progressive tones if not prog overplaying, more a death-steeped Floyd than a Yes, Koivusaari's sandpaper scrape throwing the listener down a well of inspired sorrow, all the while extreme weather howling above the hole of hope. A perfectly pitched blend of gloom, melody, grinding grooves, and grey ambience; bruising mid-paced symphonic doom that tries harder.

Rating                                    8

## Amorphis - Black Winter Day (Relapse '94)

This saddening stopgap EP features four tracks (three previously unreleased) from the **Thousand Lakes** sessions, a record acclaimed for its doomy death drear reinforced by funereal keyboard work, something at times akin to mid-years Tiamat. As usual, vocals are at the indistinguishable end of grind, although the music's so split open and easy to digest, I don't really seem to mind. Plus there's those natty Finnish folk lyrics to twist you all up inside. Complaint: too short, and Folk Of The North's a mere mellow piano intro.

Rating                                    7

## Amorphis - Elegy (Relapse '96)

Amorphis have now spiraled headlong into sensuous musical climes, all but leaving behind the vestiges of death for a dreamy, psychedelic whirlpool of elegant classical doomtones. **Elegy** absolutely takes flight with this new chemistry, the inundation of cultures throughout the metal world over the past quarter century blending artfully and seamlessly here, crushing riffs fluttered with aristocratic twin-lead flourishes and rolling, roiling keyboards of many dimensions, grindcore vocals balanced by the self-described "clean" vocals of Pasi Koskinen, indeed even the cover art portraying the band in no particular hair or clothing style, fat concise logo in a sea of light blue, all signals far away from the band's grim, grindy past. Yet another historical Finnish text provides grist for the band's lyrics, this time Amorphis using the **Kanteletar**, an 1840 tome comprising 700 poems and ballads, many of them hundreds of years old (companion book the **Kalevala** was explored on the band's last record). The resulting lyrics are a curious blend of folk-life and its dependence on nature's bounty, all the while the band's multi-layered pageant of Scandinavian melodies rolling on with missionary zeal. Brilliance of a sort, unique without hesitation, but quite possibly limited to certain few and far between, tragically gothic moods.

Rating                                    9

## Amulance - Feel The Pain (New Renaissance '89)

Bad graphics hide this not too shabby adrenalizer that fits somewhere between Helloween, Helstar and the Bay Area thrash scene. Amulance (no, not an Italian metal band with bad proof readers), crank capable '80s Euro prog-thrash (!), complete with operatic vocals (courtesy of Rik Baez, Joan's son, just kidding) and hypergood musicianship which doesn't overwhelm the sense of song. A record that needs to be peeled layer by layer, even though I'm not sure I have the patience (read: shakey production).

Rating                                    6

## Anacrusis - Suffering Hour (Metal Blade '90)

You can tell from the bleak, black and white album cover, that Britain's Anacrusis began life as something much closer to a typical underground thrash act, **Suffering Hour** proving that these future brainy wizards grew cancerously, brilliantly if not gradually to arrive at the majesty of their mid-'90s sound. Anacrusis thank their "greatest influences: Metallica, Metal Church, Slayer, Trouble and Pink Floyd", but I'd have to pick old Metal Church and old Slayer out of that esteemed bunch to describe this everywhere and nowhere mountain of loose, ill-fitting, but technically half-way-there frash. Just leaves me an agitated rivethead, aimlessly picking out passages that point skyward, but ultimately moving on for less '80s-dated terrain. Missing in action: follow-up from '90, **Reason**.

Rating                                    5

## Anacrusis - Manic Impressions (Metal Blade '91)

Bridging Voivod and Mekong Delta in a netherworldly, new age-level thrash, Anacrusis have become cold malevolent science of the loudest order. Too accelerated and complicated to be pigeon-holed, this, the band's second, rides a frozen, gothic sort of isolation; dark, brooding and maze-like. Urgent on all fronts, and well-recorded in a mechanical sort of way, the band's biggest repelling (and attracting) factor is the depressing delivery of Kenn Nardi's generally thoughtful lyrics, turning the band into a Hawkwind for the whiplash set. Anacrusis definitely demand respect, but my academic approval of their adherence to quality and originality is tempered by the poisonous emotional slant of the whole laborious thrashcrank, start to finish. For those who like it really heavy, really alone, and really underground.

Rating                                    7

## Anacrusis - Screams And Whispers (Metal Blade '93)

Woah . . I'm freaking out. I mean, where does music like this come from? Anacrusis turn up the burners here, again pushing the frontiers of progressive metal, while offering more mature passages and alien arrangements, really blowing away their closest comparative Voivod in so many areas: heft, oddity, riffs, solidity, recording (courtesy of leader Kenn Nardi), and general pleasure principle, although the whole manic ride is one of intense psychological distress, indeed all the lyrics struggling to come to grips with the workings of the human mind. Highlights would be A Screaming Breath, with its jarring pregnant pauses, and Grateful, a complicated cranker indicative of the album as a whole. Hard to fault material as totally intellectual as this, but one does have to be blinded by science to take in the full Anacrusis experience. Worth the study, **Screams And Whispers** will unfold its wisdoms for those with patience. Well to the fore of metal's research community.

Rating                                    8

## Anathema - Serenades (Futurist '94)

Liverpudian doom lizards Anathema fry on the same rocks as early (and that's key) Paradise Lost, My Dying Bride and Cathedral, a way basic and crushing, hoarsely croaked slow-drip grind with atmospherics, pretty much boring as any number of death knells wound down to 16 RPM, except maybe for futuristic, Edge Of Sanity-styled track *Sleepless* (readily confuseable with Paradise Lost's *Sweetness*, if not King Crimson's *Sleepless*). Main problem: slow, uneventful tunes like these lose it when stripped down to these dreary basics. Note: this U.S. release comprises the **Serenades** album put out by Peaceville in '93, the five track **Crestfallen** EP from '92, and one extra Dracula rocker from the early grey days *All Faith Is Lost*, (not to mention attention).
Rating 5

## Anathema - Pentacost III (Futurist '95)

Big, earth-moving changes are afoot, Anathema digging way into their soulful sloth, becoming a slower beast but a more powerful and sullen one, evidenced by black-hearted nine minute monoliths *Kingdom* and *We, The Gods*, both mixing soft with coagulated heavy, in a sick display of evil tragi-gothic resignation unto death; vague resemblance to Viking-era Bathory. Why this works a spell (and **Serenades** didn't) is the ten foot thick wall of production expertise, loads of bass, double leads, slow-paced power drumming as per modern My Dying Bride, and lyrics that are concise in their blackness, somewhat cryptic but destructive of soul, again My Dying Bride coming to mind. 'Cept there's no violins already. Five tracks, 41 minutes, prompting the band to modestly call this an EP.
Rating 8

## Anathema - Eternity (Peaceville/Futurist '96)

UK weepsters Anathema have decided to drop the caustics, turning their black-robed backs on the lurching noises that had them crackling and cackling like a slow Godflesh or medieval Eyehategod. And I'm sure shiny boy Tony Platt in as producer had something to do with it, **Eternity** rife with fresh new textures and melodies, usually brought burnt-winged by Maiden-ish guitar and increasing waves of keyboards. Add to this many churchy effects, complex arrangements and feeling, human vocals, and this is an Anathema that becomes a much more pleasant and provocative listen. A Type O Negative for the underworld.
Rating 8

## Anesthesy - Exaltation Of The Eclipse (Black Mark '94)

This headcase starts out killer enough, but then tracks lapse into harsh speeds and peculiar, illogical constructs, no help from the sub-audible grind gargle of "Franky", who barely croaks out a discernible syllable (well, they are Belgian). The mix is downright ripping, and when the band gets up a full head of steam, clear the decks. I mean these guys power chug with the best of them. But as usual, it's the vocals that sink the listening ship for me. What a waste.
Rating 6

## Angel - Angel (Casablanca '75)

An exceedingly magical, top-flight debut, **Angel** is an album crafted and subsequently positioned like no other; grand, eventful song-stories abounding and reverberating all over this rich work, a record that swirls forth in a sort of hard progressive saintliness. On a material plane, Angel's sound evokes a divine cross between the warmly melodic, keyboard-laced elements of Queen, and the manic, fused rhythms of early Heep and Black Sabbath, resulting in long, dramatic, layered pieces with metallic interplay, supported by production that is dense, full in its scope, and confidently powerful; beautifully done, given its age. Frank

Dimino's vocals are fiercely emotive, the generous keyboard and synth work elegant, and the drumming manic, spirited, and richly recorded. On a deeper level, **Angel** embodies a timeless, epic and medieval feel, classical in proportion, yet working so firmly within the boundaries of rock'n'roll, avoiding the far-flung tangents of much progressive rock at the time. Royal and moving.
Rating 10

## Angel - Helluva Band (Casablanca '76)

The singular Angel groove is back on this the band's second, much more accessible record, dishing a sound built upon the foundations of brilliant production and mix, and of course Dimino's formidable vocal work, Giuffria's '70s synth stylings, Punky's Brian May guitarisms, and an explosive and textured rhythm section. Angel's particular hard rock palace is a seamless sonic merging of these talents; that rare and complicated old-style metal based upon that bassy, grinding keyboard/guitar duality prominent on **Machine Head**, **Uriah Heep**, and most notably **Look At Yourself**. The big difference here versus the band's unwieldy debut would be the shift from what were long epic pieces to more conventional metal and hard rock song structures, tunes truncated for easier digestibility and quicker enjoyment. And the rockers here just scorch. *Feelin' Right*, *Mirrors*, and *Pressure Point* are large scale vanguards of metal no matter what the decade, matching the royal fire of Queen, Heep or Sweet at their resoundingly heaviest, while *Fortune* and *Feelings* are emotional, dynamic builders worthy of the debut's pomp preponderances. Fleshing out this free 'n' easier sophomore are flirtations with pop metal and pioneering funk metal, possibly looking towards competitors Kiss and Aerosmith for some inclusive inspiration. All in all, an intense if less conceptually focused second effort, driven into the thinning ozone by the crushing brilliance of its metallic anchors.
Rating 10

## Angel - On Earth As It Is In Heaven (Casablanca '77)

Angel's third album brings these extraterrestrial skyhawks back to earth, wings wetted down; lacking the magical, enigmatic quality, eccentric pride, and jammin' mix of their first two trophies. More a collection of songs, **On Earth As It Is In Heaven**, strolls away from the band's previous progressive rock pretensions into the arena of hopefully hit-bound star status, Kiss producer Eddie Kramer brought in to squeeze some dollars out of this venture. The four heavy pieces are brilliant and surprisingly vintage, particularly *Cast The First Stone* (kinda Deep Purple's *Burn* slowed down), and *Can You Feel It*, a warm, lumbering chunk of **Helluva Band**-style alchemy. But the rest runs the gamut between hooky, clever hard rock and less intelligent populist rock, kinda like Aerosmith butted-up against Journey. The record's mix is sludgy and distorted, but strangely appealing, almost seamless, with boomy but midrange-heavy drums like early Zep. A mottled blessing, **On Earth** is the last of the guitar-heavy Angel albums, more jewel-studded than consistent, unfortunately the first where the accountants seemed to outnumber the creative staff in Angel's rock'n'roll boardroom.
Rating 7

## Angel - White Hot (Casablanca '77)

Angel was one of a number of hard rock marketing tragedies in the '70s. It seemed label bosses had no idea what to do with metal (talk to Buck Dharma), often conjuring illogical and divergent strategies to deal with this sonically powerful and increasingly influential genre. The few committed, clear-cut examples of metal bands that existed in the late '70s were for the most part, making money, yet labels seemed to think pop

was the better bet, so we got Starz - **Attention Shoppers**, Angel - **White Hot** and other seemingly more self-directed sell-outs from Foghat, Triumph, Nazareth, and Status Quo. In any event, **White Hot** could not have been anything but the result of nervous investors, the record stumbling through time as uncharacteristically bland, poorly written, badly arranged, all contained in a soup about as heavy and as important as Journey. Here the once regal synths just intrude and annoy, rhythm patterns are awkward, and the production is just standard corporate fodder, knobs and minds switched to suburban default. The British press liked it though, as the whole jolly empire seemed to be riding a wave of wimp rock, which this record undoubtedly was, feeding from added salable mystique as "bold new directive" from an American legend. And indeed, even many stateside thought this to be the band's finest era, eschewing the self-serious sweep of the early outings for the mundane if more psychologically adjusted underachievement herein enclosed. Go figure.
Rating 4

## Angel - Sinful (Casablanca '79)

A commendably rowdy mix is the only admirable trait afforded this low quality, early attempt at Journey/Bon Jovi/Loverboy commerciality. Angel was the wrong band for this sort of garbage, possessing more melodic ideas, more hooks, and more swirling emotion when smoking through manic rockers like *Pressure Point* and *Mirrors*, proving you didn't have to wilt or pander to write reputable, impressionable songs. A tragic last studio attempt by a band that by now couldn't be motivated to do much in a studio but spray beer at unsuspecting staff and drink a lot. Note: For a taste of what shape this album might have taken, take a look at the cover of Pet Hate's **Bad Publicity**. Both cover concept, (i.e. wrecked hotel room) and title were to be used for **Sinful**, both scrapped due to worries over tainting Angel's lily-white image. It is interesting to note that this record's persona and the band's subsequent abrupt demise may have been shaped by the near simultaneous release of the label's **Bad Girls** from Donna Summer, and **Dynasty** from Kiss (Angel's arch competitors), both records successful in a genre far away from metal. CD reissue includes two rarities: *Virginia* and soundtrack tune *20th Century Foxes*.
Rating 4

## Angel - Live Without A Net (Casablanca '80)

A representative career retrospective that samples the dramatic early material and the failed (although loved by many) later drivel. Sporting an early **Angel/Helluva Band** recording, with the crowds left in full-bore (see alter-egos Kiss and their immensely cash-generating Kiss **Alive** trio), **Live Without A Net** tends to highlight the sad fact that Angel could have been stadium gods worthy of the nifty appear/disappear act the boys were famous for live. As of '96, nothing much substantial has come from Punky et al, except the Night Ranger-ish, forgettable and short-lived Giuffria from blonde-tressed Wakeman-alike keyboardist Greg, who then moved onto the slightly more aggressive House Of Lords. Frank Dimino has also briefly come up for air, croaking miserably through a Japanese six track EP with the Paul Raymond Project called **Under The Rising Sun**.
Rating 5

## Angel - An Anthology (PolyGram '92)

76 minute, twenty song shotgun-blast at a fragmented catalogue, **An Anthology** features OK liner notes from Dave Reynolds, and only three non-LP tracks, a silly hard pop cover of *Walk Away Renee*, Giorgio Moroder-produced soundtrack pile of crap *20th Century Foxes* and nice, slightly mystical Christmas carol

*The Christmas Song*. If this sounds like fun to you, please, don't let me stop you.
Rating 6

## Angeles - We're No Angels (Mystic '84)

**We're No Angels** is nothing more than an American underground cornball, wielding a puerile pile of grim casualty rock, with occasional shafts of old Y&T circa **Struck Down**. Goofy party rock, unwillingly juxtaposed against half-hearted, ultimately botched goth, under a punishing midrange-heavy hockey barn mix; a combination only their mothers could love.
Rating 2

## The Angels - The Angels (EMI Australia '77)

A legend is born. What I assume is the debut from these long-suffering down-under scruff-rockers t'is a mere babe, faintly pulsing with backwoods charm, low-slung, barroom boogie, nowhere approaching future velocities. With imagination, one can detect future direction amongst these dunce-like wilt-rockers, songs rife with laughable corn-pone harmonica work and Jimmy Dean '50s lyricisms, but the glory to come is in scant supply indeed. Still, Angel City are like old pals, and despite this record's complete non-fit with the catalogue, it's an interesting glimpse into the hokey geminations of the band.
Rating 7

## The Angels - No Exit (EMI Australia '79)

No less than five of ten tracks from this early Aussie effort made it to the band's robust North American debut, compilation **Face To Face**. Of the five that didn't, we get a couple that could have easily fit (*Mr. Damage* and *Save Me*), one that made it to **Darkroom** (minor epic *Ivory Stairs*), and two more lyrically ambitious mellow/heavy dynamic pieces (*After Dark* and *Dawn Is Breaking*). But oddly enough, I'd have to say **Face To Face** hangs better than **No Exit**, while in isolation, **No Exit** is still a lusty good toe-tap, rarely lowering itself to less than superior, tension-ridden songcraft. No real non-domestic scorchers here, although revealing glimpses into the enigmatic mind of frontman and chief lyricist Doc Neeson keep calling me back for more. The first "professional" Angel City album. Added bonus: gatefold sleeve with lyrics.
Rating 8

## Angel City - Face To Face (Epic '80)

Angel City caused major havoc stateside with this endearing and electrifying compilation from earlier Australian releases as The Angels. At the time, AC/DC was taking the world by storm and The Angels point-blank rode their coat-tails, proposing themselves as AC/DC Part II, playing the role as a more new-wavey, more intelligent, and busier version of the same heads-down, driving backbeat that made Angus and Bon household pests. **Face To Face** is a solid barroom collection of unassuming yet infectious roots rockers, riding the line between stiff hard rock and base metal, always pleasing melodically, and heavy on memorable choruses, main virtue being its charm, its upbeat party action making **Face To Face** one of the great beer-drinking albums of our youth. Bread and butter of the bar band circuit included *Take A Long Line*, *Can't Shake It*, *Marseille*, and *After The Rain* (the latter two of which our band Torque even managed to slog through). Ultimately, **Face To Face** stands as one of the gems of fledgling hard rock, electrocuting boogie woogie into something modern and ripe for a basic headbang. A proud, historically important addition to any collection.
Rating 10

## Angel City - Darkroom (Epic '80)

Even though **Darkroom** holds major nostalgic value for me and the buds (being the sonic bible of Ken's evil

**25**

green Dodge Dart), it's a rich, amplified journey even if you didn't grow up and throw up to its smart sustain. **Darkroom** is Angel City's finest moment, no mean feat given its class predecessor. Lyrically complex, colourful, and enigmatic, **Darkroom** contains some of the best marriages between AC/DC's redneck riffery and Doc's riveting, storytelling, on such driven landscapes as *No Secrets*, *Wasted Sleepless Nights/Darkroom*, and minor hit *Face The Day*. Other livelier numbers include *Straight Jacket*, *Ivory Stairs* (first climbed on **No Exit**), and personal fave, the inverted *Night Comes Early*, which finds Doc barking out his wisdoms in an eccentric sort of monotone. Start to finish, **Darkroom** rocks gorgeously unadorned, with confidence and sly complexity, fueled by Doc Neeson's subtle flair for weaving a good creepy tale. Impossible not to appreciate.
Rating                                                    10

## Angel City - Night Attack   (Epic '82)

**Night Attack** is the mediocre, phoned-in, automatic last record of Angel City's early, commercially successful era. Yet one can't help wondering that with bolder deliveries and recordings, the record might groove on equal with its two predecessors, here the mouse-like drumming and sparseness of the mix just sapping the album of any potential it might have had. As it stands, most of the album curls up and dies, but minor hits *Fashion And Fame* and *Long Night* are at minimum, capable poppy metal, stumbling but infectious songs brought to life live, while *City Out Of Control* and *Storm The Bastille* rock appreciably, the latter perpetuating Doc Neeson's use of the French Revolution as lyrical grist. Generally speaking, **Night Attack** is an unsatisfying, uneventful spin, lacking the bite of its superficially similar predecessors, indeed lacking any reason to exist period, as I say, marking the end of an era with a meek shudder. Saw the tour: solid entertainers.
Rating                                                     7

## The Angels - Watch The Red   (CBS '83)

Huh? Anybody home? Quite surprising, but this is The Angels' worst record, pock-marked with meekly-mixed experiments in funky mood rock, replete with horns and bad barroom blues structures, for the first time since the band's hapless debut, truly assembled outside a hard rock predisposition; a crushing disappointment, because many of these tunes, given lustier arrangements, would become passable Angel City rockers (see *Shoot It Up* or *No Sleep In Hell*). You can see why this band became a hit-and-miss, logistically unmarketable commodity stateside, as **Watch The Red** becomes a very real failure of drive and ambition first, the band seemingly content with filler, at best offering slight alterations on glory riffs of old (*Stand Up*), at worst recalling the mental faculties of Men At Work. And Doc is sounding a bit strained, although he does a wheezy and charismatic job of Parisian-style Brian May-meets-Leonard Cohen ballad *Easy Prey*. Nowhere near hungry enough to maintain the fine Angel City legacy, and that's just sad.
Rating                                                     5

## Angel City - Two Minute Warning   (MCA '84)

As if **Watch The Red** never happened, **Two Minute Warning** recaptures the heads-down, shot glass raucousness of early Angel City the same way **The Razor's Edge** revived vintage AC/DC. And of course, the comparison is apt in other areas, these fellow Aussies I'm sure, caught at least once or twice, furiously taking notes while ligging a few Fosters at early Angus Co. gigs. **Two Minute Warning** finds Doc and the Brewster Bros. enjoying themselves once again, finding their pocket, stopwatching their mesmerized grooves through the brilliantly simple *Look The Other Way*, the brilliantly simple *Between The Eyes*, and the brilliantly

simple *Small Price*, while reviving other long-defanged stylings like barroom boogie, barroom balladeering and barroom Stonesiness in the funky *Sticky Little Bitch* and the cry-in-yer-beer *Be With You*, styles last seen in any convincing form way back on the debut. In the end, **Two Minute Warning** rocks and rolls with a confident pride that defies criticism at its surface simplicity and earthiness, courting timelessness through unadorned musical purity; really achieving most soulfully what AC/DC did most swillingly.
Rating                                                    10

## The Angels - The Howling   ('86)

The follow-up to one of Angel City's very best relives the band's charming boozy churn while lacking both energy and solid songs of a heavier nature. Yea and verily, this is less the clever AC/DC romp of woebegone days, as we are force-fed samples of R&B (*Can't Take Anymore*), keyboard-laced pop (*Where Do You Run*), dopey blues (*Don't Waste My Time*), and famous covers (*We Gotta Get Outta This Place*), all I might add, ironically named for the sentiments expressed when I hear them. All is not lost in a sea of lounge act sidedrift however, as *Did You Hurt Somebody* and *When The Time Comes* are classic good-time riff-rock, and *Hide Your Face* is a swaggering, lushly-outfitted Stones-type anthem. In general, kind of a laid-back, unambitious effort, loose, yet dressed-up with horns, keyboards, and acoustic touches. A little too far from home, and weary from the journey, but adequately heated to make up for the rock generalist approach.
Rating                                                     7

## The Angels - Live From Angel City   (Telegraph '88)

Just a short, beer-canned live EP, featuring five tracks repeated on the second side (this is vinyl). The goods: *Small Price*, *Don't Waste My Time*, *Standing Over You*, *Marseilles* (with long, boring mid-section), and *Take A Long Line*, all robustly laid down over an acceptable mix, begging the question of why these guys didn't succeed outside of their native homeland. Cool band shot on the back.
Rating                                                     6

## The Angels - Beyond Salvation   ('89)

Further to the theory that there are serious structural problems in Doc's barn, the long-awaited **Beyond Salvation** consists of half newies and half remakes of past glories. Of the revivals, only *City Out Of Control* offers improvement over the original, getting a major shot of adrenalin and pronounced groove. Of the Angels-for-the-'90s statements, thankfully the boys remain firmly rooted in the '70s, serving up nostalgic slabs of vintage party rock in *Dogs Are Talking*, *Let The Night Roll On*, and *I Ain't The One* (the latter two which sound suspiciously familiar yet aren't on any of the albums reviewed here: Am I missing something?). Unfortunately the crusty curmudgeonly bluesiness of **The Howling** hasn't completely been shaken as we also get low-key bumpkin shuffles like *Rhythm Rude Girl* and *Junk City*, two tracks that are just plain boring. It's a drag to see this kind of disjointed product coming from such cool chapter in hard rock's history. Let's hope Angel City can get the financial security or emotional security or whatever it is that is lacking, to complete a return to the resounding wattage they were so capable of in the early '80s.
Rating                                                     7

## The Angels - Red Back Fever/Left Hand Drive   (Mushroom '92)

I almost passed out when I saw this in the used bins, not consciously thinking the great Angels (City) were still breathing, pleased as all get out at finding this '91 record (**Red Back Fever**) and a second disc (**Left Hand Drive**), which is a fully explained, ten-track rarities collection. First, **Red Back Fever** is prime, retooled but retro Angels, sweet, unadorned AC/DC-tilted roots metal, loosely-based around an included sci-fi story about giant mutant black widows, the band suggesting more through graphic continuation throughout the lyric book, that all forms of human deceit lower the perpetrators to the level of these voracious black widows. The songs will capably zip any old fan right back to 1980, *Bedroom After Bedroom*, *Some Of That Love* and the title track built for the **Darkroom** with alarming authenticity. Ironically enough, there's also a cover of *Once Bitten Twice Shy*, The Angels covering Mott covered by Great White who make a living covering The Angels and Mott, geddit? All told, the most in-earnest return to glory years since, uh, the glory years. **Left Hand Drive** comprises either b-sides or alterno-versions, all from '84 to '92. Generally, it ain't that hot, lots of fairly tepid, laid-back riffs recorded stiffly and filler-predestined. Some fancy pants remixes dot the landscape, and *Blood On The Moon* is a robust brainshake of a tune, but all in all, just a curio for the completist fan, which, hey, count me in forever, Amen.

Rating      **8**

## Angels With Dirty Faces - Sounds Of The World Turning   (Blue Flame '94)

Hard to put trite critical labels on this one, but of course I'll try. Angels With Dirty Faces fits that fuzzy netherspace between two or three kinds of alternative and metal, given their detectably dissonant bass-driven sound over accessible, groove-laden songs, sorta like a more commercial jumbled dogpile of Gang Of Four, Wire, Therapy?, Primus, Nirvana and just the general idea of heaviness via bands like Quicksand and Wool (the catchy *Longer Than A Day* demonstrates it all). Ritzy packaging, full, action-packed lyrics: these Brits are for real.

Rating      **7**

## Angel Witch - Angel Witch   (Bronze '80)

**Angel Witch** is the New Wave Of British Heavy Metal's black metal feast of near mythic proportions, quickly becoming renowned in underground metal circles as the benchmark opus of the early '80s. Fiercely dark, messed-up and rumbling unclean, full of weighty riffs worthy of the most vintage Sabbath, **Angel Witch** is a riveting metallic blast through gothic landscapes. Everything works towards killer accomplishment here, the hurt, bleating vocals of mastermind Kevin Heybourne, the crunch recording with just the right amount of noisy uncontrolled edge, and above all, the hellishly superior songcraft which regularly lowers the boom outta nowhere with inspired British metal deviance. There's a feeling of singular pride here, an album created wholly without influences, as if the band knew damn well they were blowing anything heretofore known off the metal map. **Angel Witch** would ultimately reign as the first panoramic black metal statement of the modern era, with its mix of gothic melody, sinister surprise, and scorching dense riffery on such molten monoliths as *Atlantis*, *Confused*, and *Angel Of Death*. Unfortunately, this would be the only Angel Witch album of deep importance, as internal strife and critical derision at the band's apparently sloppy live shows would flame the band's self-doubts. After a low-key break-up in '81, the band resurfaced in an altered and less focused state for the ponderous **Screamin' n' Bleedin'**. Luckily, there are some rare, debut-era tracks floating around on various 45's and EP's such as *Flight 19*, *Hades Paradise*, *Loser*, *Suffer* and *Dr. Phibes*, all exceedingly worth whatever collectibles price you might pay.

Rating      **10**

## Angel Witch - Screamin' n' Bleedin'   (Killerwatt '85)

The coven of three is now four. Leader Heybourne and drummer Hogg have added a new bass player and, unfortunately a vocalist, and although Heybourne still writes everything on this (with a few co-writes), the effort is a definite notch below the mastery of the debut, large part due to the strained and uneven vocals of Dave Tattum, and the muddy, midrange-heavy recording. It's still bloody dark and British sounding, but there's a hint of the commonplace to the proceedings which are all too often sloppy, tired and slow. Standouts include the oddly righteous negative riffery of kick-off tune *Whose To Blame*, gothic pompster *Fatal Kiss*, and the debut-ish horror metal of *Evil Games*. Ultimately, **Screamin' n' Bleedin'** manages a blustery ill wind of deflated, fatigued depression, highlighting the sentiment that the herculean brilliance of **Angel Witch** has faded forever. Yet with a talent like Heybourne, chances are the Witch can wail again.

Rating      **6**

## Angel Witch - Live   (Metal Blade '90)

Far from their rustic home base, firmly entrenched in some L.A. snakepit, a reformed Angel Witch become stripped of their creepy mystique, demonstrating what the Brits knew all along, that the boyz in the band are yer basic grime-caked, thrashable yobs. Commandeering a listing raft of lead-headed compositions including valuable non-**Angel Witch** spectres, *Baphomet*, *Extermination Day* and the elusive *Flight 19*, Heybourne+3 sorta sell out and do the retro tour, plowing through an automatic set of sets with nary a nod to dynamic, technical synchro-mesh, production ethic or indeed vocal effort, as tunes race to resolution, white-knuckled, fragile, and relieved at the finale. Verily, Heybourne's bleat still blackens the blood, But **Live** reclines in repose as little more than a loving, after-the-buzz dedication to a band much more legendary stateside than at home. Recorded surprisingly on the band's first trip to the states, a mini-tour where Heybourne refused to play anything newer than the debut album, huffing that anything post-**Angel Witch** wasn't real Angel Witch.

Rating      **5**

## Anihilated - Created In Hate   (Metalworks '88)

Barroom death metal, horrifically amateur for its relative age. But then again, it is British, and so obviously low budget, one simply yelps in fear at the thought of enduring this hurled entity of black glue. Pea-brained in its unilevel, accelerated plod.

Rating      **3**

## Annihilator - Alice In Hell   (Roadracer '90)

After a short, silly intro, Jeff Waters and Annihilator announce their gleaming presence, leaping directly into the fray as fully-actualized metal warriors, packing riffs-a-plenty, many great ones in lead single and video *Alison Hell*, perhaps blowing their wad before the record really gets underway. But have no worries, there are sparks, flame and fire like crazy, as Waters tightens the screws on the type of precision thrash Metallica, Megadeth and the Bay Area boys honed throughout the '80s. So call this a bit dated already, but snapped airtight, aggressive and not without punk verve, vocalist Randy Rampage bringing over a rapid-fire growl from his past gig with seemingly incompatible, pioneering mosh-machine D.O.A. A Waters extravagonzo for damn sure, the boy wonder also making sure focused, economic, nimble songs are in there somewhere, even though like I say, they're firmly based in the '80s, which isn't necessarily a bad thing. Soupy mix, and Rampage's vocals are a bit over the

hardcore top, which I gather Waters thought also, sacking him before the next record.
Rating **7**

## Annihilator - Never, Neverland (Road Racer '90)

A mix between the mosh ethic of Anthrax, the innovation of Metallica, and the dynamic variation of Maiden, **Never, Neverland** is the second ambitious effort from Annihilator, the Vancouver brainchild of one Jeff Waters. Hot techno-metal, power-edge production, and piercing sharpshooter riffs (albeit too many of them) spell chops-laden quality on this technician's opus. Classics include lead single *Stonewall* (written about pollution in Vancouver—he should see Toronto!) and the anti-drinking and driving *Road To Ruin*. Waters provides brief written commentaries on his tunes which in actuality, are not as personality-damaging as they could have been; still, yet another sign that this is the Jeff Waters Show here. Aside from a slight case of Queensryche/Fates Warning syndrome here, my only complaint would be the predictable metal lyrics, which are not without humour. Minor faults though on a fairly major opus delivered with exuberant, Dave Mustaine-like pursuit of excellence. More successful overseas than in North America, **Never, Neverland** was a large part of Annihilator getting opening slot on Priest's European tour, a fond memory for Waters, and a high point of the band's existence to date.
Rating **8**

## Annihilator - Set The World On Fire (Attic '93)

A classic choppy Vancouver whitecaps riff opens this, Annihilator's ill-fated third, which will eventually see the band divorce their label. Waters is great at the exacto-chug, which belies the question: why does he stray from it so often? I mean, with the talent on board, I can see this band being another Megadeth (Waters indeed was offered the second guitarist gig for the band at one point). Instead: moody mellow passages, ballads, and tons of early '80s mistakes like *No Zone* and *Brain Dance*. too much mosh, not enough gravity. Lyrics are either too melodramatic or too flippant, the environment cropping up again amongst throwaways about crazeeness and male-female hijinx. Quality is at the helm, but the band seems caught clench-fisted between shifting market trends, very few bands being able to pull off this sort of manly munchrock with any commercial success. So lots of metalizers undermined by a sort of punk smarminess. Some welcome experiments (like catchy uptempo ballad *Sounds Good To Me*), but just not enough forward vision, Waters admitting to pressure from the label to get them sales happenin'.
Rating **7**

## Annihilator - Bag Of Tricks (Attic/Roadrunner '94)

**Bag Of Tricks** documents nine years and three records worth of quality frustration and quality tech metal from Ottawa/Vancouver's premiere, quintessentially Heavy Metal barnstormers. Closing the books on Attic's involvement (Hypnotic handled **King Of The Kill** for Canada), the record offers 75 minutes of rarities, demos and live tracks, made all the more interesting by band friend Monte Conner's excellent and detailed play-by-play liner notes which point out pieces of tunes swapped to other tracks, subtle production comparisons and full credits, most useful being the charting of vocalists along the winding road. There's also cool historical photos and of course, a slurping ladle-full of Waters' egomaniacal madman metal. Most of the previously unreleased are heart-exploding but pedestrian tech-thrashers, proving that Waters' album choices were really the right ones. But then there's a beefy cover of AC/DC's *Live Wire*, an uptempo mellow **Set The World On Fire** out-take called *Fantastic Things*, plus the illuminating '86 demos Jeff cut at home on his four track Fostex, including I

might add, his own proto-death vocals. What can I say? I've always been a fence-sitter with these guys, revelling in Waters' astonishing riffs, but dismayed at the lack of direction and average-ness of the records in totality. But judging from **King Of The Kill**, there's still some life left in this gleaming machine.
Rating **7**

## Annihilator - King Of The Kill (Hypnotic '95)

Probably Jeff Waters' lowest profile record in terms of North American exposure, **King Of The Kill** has already racked up sales of 100,000 or so in Europe and Japan in the last eight months. Add to this the fact that each of the previous albums has consistently sold in the 150,000 to 200,000 range, and Annihilator is coming up to one million records sold over the length of the catalogue. But metal is gravely out of vogue over here, and Waters seems fine with that, quietly working from his home studio in a Vancouver suburb, handling all chores here except drums. **King Of The Kill** is a return to a rawer, stripped metal sound, unrepentant in its worship of racing riffs. Even Waters admits to cliché and outdatedness, towing the precise metal line on such crunchers as *The Box*, *Second To None* and *Speed*. It's a close, almost personal record, slamming with a sort of loneliness, given its virtual solo album status and the current rarity of this sort of heavy old Megadeth-type sound and sensibility. Mellow tracks are sombre (like old Priest), and the whole thing is sort of spontaneous and speedy even while studied. Waters ain't gonna change the world with this kind of self-evident metal guitar love-in, but he will keep a dwindling tradition alive, something which needs to be done. Hail the players, especially those with their feet planted firmly on the ground.
Rating **8**

## Annihilator - Refresh The Demon (Music For Nations '96)

Better song-titles this time, and kinda catchy with that **Refresh The Demon** bit dontcha think? Anyway, Jeff had this record ready to run ages ago, even as its predecessor was finally seeing Canuck release, Waters finding it easy to make records pretty much all by himself in his home studio. And this one's a mutha, Waters making the record Megadeth and Metallica snobbily refuse to acknowledge, tapping into compressed, furtive grooves that are all hi-fidelity might and right. A glory-bound batch of riffery fer sure, Waters' niche is assured, as few others will go to his zone these days. Not much more one can say, Waters long ago tapping black waves of traditional metal that are now trickles to be cherished. Similar to the academic technician mosh of the last, which is fine by me.
Rating **8**

## Anthrax - Fistful Of Metal (Banzai '84)

Anthrax caused waves of metal consternation right from day one, due to a rage-ridden debut that was speedy as all get out, but tight, chops-laden, and well-recorded, featuring commanding, almost operatic anti-thrash vocals from the soon-to-be-ousted Neil Turbin. Anthrax was instrumental in removing the thrash tumor from speed metal's leather hide, adding an element of respectability to more uncompromising forms of metal. **Fistful Of Metal** zips along quite business-like, oscillating between fast mid-pace tenseness and double bass drum OTT, while always steamrolling in complete control, intent on blazing a path that is both palatable and punishing. Riff-wise however, **Fistful** pales compared to latter-day techno-speed from the likes of Coroner, Carcass, Anacrusis, or even the band's own second and third sonic blitzkriegs, which became catalysts for metallizers that operate today alongside the princely version of Anthrax that is well-respected in '96. But wot th' hell, **Fistful** moshed heavily for '84 putting New York back on the U.S. metal

28

map, and quality back in the books of bruising and uncompromising underground metal. **Fistful Of Metal** holds the added distinction of catching flak for the hilarious and disgusting album cover portraying a fist coming out of a mouth.
Rating                                                                6

## Anthrax - Armed And Dangerous (Megaforce '85)
This five track grab-bag of grub consists of the album-bound title track, two live and straight-faced versions of debut LP stormers, a predictably boring rendition of the Sex Pistols' God Save The Queen and an excellent mid-pace rocker Raise Hell, that despite the billing on the sleeve as "pre-release version," never made it to **Spreading The Disease**. Buy cheap or pass.
Rating                                                                4

## Anthrax - Spreading The Disease (Island '85)
Anthrax's all-important second bovine blight (originally titled Spread It, then Anthrax Kills), reigns manic, moshing and rabid, bent on kicking this band into the next pack up. The smooth but uneventful production values of the debut have been laid to waste, making way for an insidious, rats-chewing-at-the-cables aggravation; an industrial din that filters perfectly the apocalyptic punkiness of the band's deceptively chaotic songcraft. New vocalist Joey Belladonna (after the band's brief engagement of Matt Fallon), is an excellent and mischievous wailer; a perfect diminutive black-clad front-elf for a band of similar insect-like qualities. Like the jaw-breaking premiere, **Spreading The Disease** raised the stakes for speed metal, yet in entirely different directions. The thrash element is back, although more in spirit than looseness, as Anthrax single-handedly triples the amount of black coffee to ever boil and spit forth from one vigilant row of Marshalls. Twenty-flight rockers here include slashing OTT'er A.I.R. and mid-paced power drillers Lone Justice and Madhouse, which pummel with careening, urban violence, perhaps pushing the likes of Metallica to thrive for better. A shocking blast of noise from a long-haired bunch of punks that know their own business. Necessary '80s metal.
Rating                                                               10

## Anthrax - Among The Living (Island '87)
Hard to believe, but on **Among The Living**, Anthrax build on the blazing intensities of **Spreading The Disease** without sacrificing too much metallic bottom end. However, a punk ethic is lustily courted for the first time in the band's career, as witnessed on systematic mayhem such as Caught In A Mosh, Efilnikufesin (N.FL.), and One World. Superficially there's a similarity to **State** and **Persistence** here, but for some reason I was able to assimilate this one, learn it, and rise to its exploded levels of energy, whereas on the follow-ups, I was left confused at a novel sound gone on too long, feeling fed up; the blur of sound representing an ever so slightly out-of-control version of more of the same. But **Among The Living** was the first of this trio that focused on sustained manic punkiness, while retaining the band's earlier tunefulness, mid-paced elements, weight, fine grind, and reliance on more conventional song structures. Not much more to say except that for me, this was the last of the obliterating, communicating Anthrax records until **Sound Of White Noise** drop-kicked metal in '93.
Rating                                                                8

## Anthrax - State Of Euphoria (Megaforce '88)
On **State Of Euphoria**, Anthrax has taken to wearing shorts, for which they surprisingly attracted a lot of criticism. I don't know if it's the casual summer wear, the cartoon caricature of the band by **Mad**'s Mort Drucker, or the yellow album cover, but something about this album sounds less serious, flippant, punkier,

faster, less weighty, like a version of the band's own riff warehouse M.O.D. Even though the record's still heavy as hammers, dizzyingly tight, manic and techno-edged, the mosh ethic takes over, turning the proceedings into some sort of too fast, too riff-happy, and often tuneless skateboard slam. Maybe it's just the frustration at the fact that it's really just more of the familiar hi-test metal perfected last time around, while little evokes individuality, leaving the album with no point of reference. In any event, I've listened to this album tons of times and it's still just a spinning, whiny, panicky blur.
Rating                                                                7

## Anthrax - Persistence Of Time (Island '90)
Fear Of Time sees Anthrax persisting with the heads-down double-time mosh laid bare on **State Of Euphoria**. To its credit, **Persistence Of Time** seems bleaker, more cutting edge and more serious than **Euphoria**. To its detriment, it's still one very long, laborious smear of speed and riffery with the same uncompromisingly basic and industrial, yet functional and appropriate recording. This must be one of those albums you have to assimilate a track per month or something, because it's still one loud memory loss to me. Another obscure, questionable cover, here with Got The Time, as Joe Jackson, cueball head and all, is put through the Anthrax shredder. Strange what this band is up to. There's an admirable Prong/Pantera/Metallica '90s minimalism at work here, but the overall effect is just so dense and relentless that it just wears you out by hangover's end. Time for something new.
Rating                                                                7

## Anthrax - Attack Of The Killer B's (Island '91)
Obviously a collection by music fans, for music fans, **Attack** is a non-stop bus tour of Anthrax curios that stays well away from hits package status, offering few live cuts, leaving adequate moshing space for a couple a' fastballs, punky mid-pace pounders, joke toons, rap tunes, covers of Trust, Discharge, The Ventures and themselves (S.O.D.), plus a battering send-up of Kiss' Parasite, and a few otherwise unanticipated tricks. Easily worth it in terms of value, containing adequate comments, lyrics and pics, **Attack** manages to highlight the band's eclecticism, humour, and flirtation with rap which manifests itself on such fringe products as this entertaining compilation or the band's 12" product. Highlight of the hybrid: Bring The Noise, with that intoxicating whiney sound.
Rating                                                                7

## Anthrax - Sound Of White Noise (Elektra '93)
After the unceremonious sacking of long-time weak link Joey Belladonna (good pipes, wouldn't write), Anthrax mercifully puts Armored Saint to rest by absconding their predatory throat John Bush, who quickly makes his presence known on this Anthrax re-energizing for the '90s. **Sound Of White Noise**: bad cover, clever title, which captures the urban stress of a society inundated by electronic media in its chaotic yet suspended sense, while making sly commentary that metal has traditionally been noise for white guys, no racism intended, Anthrax being the last band to warrant such connotations. **White Noise** emits thick wads of wattage; boots of lead versus the boyz' previous balloons of helium, the record thumping along over a manly, guitar-drenched mix from alternative metal producer Dave Jerden, prompting from the band a performance that is grungier, greasier and more bloodthirsty, twisting the knife with delicious cast iron hooks as evidenced graciously on first track Packaged Rebellion and first single Only, particularly come chorus time, where Bush's depth and sense of drama shines through. Top flight, state-of-the-art metal, fortified by the band's usual societal concerns, here elevated to eloquent outrage at man's crumbling morality, Bush

commands the floor, inspired by a sort of constructive hate, while Benante and crew bludgeon with a slower, thicker stew. All in all, Anthrax has created an urgent and urban head-full of sounds, invading with towering stresses and shortness of breath, metal that confronts and snaps the intellect into its casing ready to fire. Anthrax is in the enviable position of potential cross-over success beyond their expectations (rumours abound about a $10 million deal). And it would be success not because of compromise, but simply by being good at what they do (through making mistakes), although much credit must go to Jerden for shaking up a band set in their ways. Pumped to slam it in the '90s, machines built to metalize, this is the band's first crank that levels without hysterics, heading out to the front lines relinquishing no heat to Metallica, Megadeth or grungier angles such as Alice In Chains and Soundgarden, bands this record seems to address with some forethought yet pride in the purity of a stricter metal.
Rating                                            10

## Anthrax - Stomp 442   (Elektra '95)

Despite liking neither the confusing title nor the confusing, albeit expensive Storm Thorgerson cover art, I happen to find **Stomp 442** a bracing blast of tried and true heavy metal, no apologies offered, none needed. The record is essentially a raft of songs that evokes and nearly equals '93's awesome and relatively under-appreciated **Sound Of White Noise**; well-crafted but not overproduced urban metal, mature lyrics, delivered via the wake-up roar of newly short-shorn John Bush. First single **Fueled** is totally like the Anthrax of old, belching chugging riffery that is all rusty hook and headbang. Elsewhere, it gets more technical, majestic, basically every welcome trick under a New York fry sky. Guitarist troubles during recording saw the ouster of Dan Spitz, with Dimebag Darrell and Paul Cook coming in to redo many of the leads. Like you or I would notice. So call this a fine, responsible collection of working man's metal, if a bit of a repetition.
Rating                                              8

## Anthrax - Live: The Island Years   (Island/Megaforce '94)

The very core definition of contractual obligation album, this combat-ready '91 live set was the last bitter puzzle piece representing Anthrax's already terminated relationship with Island. The band wasn't happy with it, but the record's no embarrassment, being both lengthy, fast, tight as a mosh, and raucously about what heavy metal hopes to evoke. Recording-wise, it's a bit too tilted towards a true live sound, very boomy in the drums, sound banging off the walls, peeling the paint, bleeding the ears. Adequate toons choice, although many tend towards the band's faster persona, but we do get Parasite and Bring The Noise, along with four live in the studio, radio show tracks from '92, funniest featuring problem member Joey Belladonna blowing through a very inadequate Metal Thrashing Mad.
Rating                                              7

## Anvil - Hard 'n' Heavy   (Attic '81)

Anvil's debut is alas, pathetic low budget club-land metal devoid of ideas, and poorly executed to boot. It's hard to believe this is even the same tower of might that fried our teenage minds to a deformed crisp on the skillful **Metal On Metal**. Lyrically the whole thing is no more than juvenile party porn and come to think of it, musically it's the same thing. Only Bedroom Game heats up at all on this lame first shot which includes a boring cover of rudimentary Stones tune Paint It Black, where the band tries valiantly to intensify the only trace of metalizable drama to be found in the vast Glimmer Twins catalogue.
Rating                                              2

## Anvil - Metal On Metal   (Attic '82)

Obliterating any thought that Anvil weren't serious contenders, **Metal On Metal** is an ultra-heavy onslaught of controlled thrash steeped in the classics. And it's even Canadian. By undercutting the sheer weight of these scorchers with two or three dumb porno tunes, Anvil lets us know they don't consider themselves super-human rock prima donnas with real feelings. This is techno-chops wollop with a healthy arterial flow of caffeine, with just enough Tank-ed Motörhead edge to keep it raucous, loose and neanderthal. This early diamond in the rough was heralded as state-of-the-art, ahead-of-its-time aggression, similar to opinions of Metallica's **Kill 'Em All**, yet Anvil became a band that never grew beyond the ideas and execution of this opus and its follow-up **Forged in Fire**, a band who does however embody the elements necessary for a breakthrough some day, possibly along the lines of a Pantera or a latter-day Metallica or Anthrax. With **Metal On Metal**, Lips and crew cemented their esteemed place within practising metal circles (i.e. up and coming powers) as respected players well to the forefront of expanding possibilities. And it didn't sound planned.
Rating                                              9

## Anvil - Forged In Fire   (Attic '83)

Lips and the boys come up with another blistering OTT opus, mixing the power, noise and chaos of one-take speed with the songcraft and control of the Priest/Scorpions/Maiden school of mid-tempo groove science. Anvil loves metal for metal's sake, inhaling deeply of its smoke and fire, and carrying on with a blow-the-speakers sincerity that is brutally evident in Lips' hysterical vocals, his blunt lyrics, and last but not least, the crazed, over-flowing chops of drummer Robb Reiner, who always manages to steal the show. **Forged In Fire** comes off as a flashier, fancier, more nimble and varied version of the boots-to-the-head **Metal On Metal**, yet it's still mega-destruction par excellence, totally manic without reprieve. Highlights include Free As The Wind and Hard Times, Fast Ladies.
Rating                                              9

## Anvil - Backwaxed   (Viper '85)

**Backwaxed** is half early greatest hits, half previously unreleased rough-hewn oddities, the best of which is the x-rated title track, a **Forged In Fire** era scorcher with that patented off-the-rails delivery we've all grown to respect. The few other newies are either commonplace, misplaced or absolutely cavemanned, making this a less than necessary grab bag of greasy grub.
Rating                                              4

## Anvil - Strength Of Steel   (Attic '87)

**Strength Of Steel** is a sad parody of what Anvil is all about, indeed a parody of metal, sort of a Canadian Spinal Tap album. The songs for the most part are slow, melodramatic and awkward, basically lacking in any strong riffs or lyrical value. The only high points (besides the manly production values) would be 9-2-5 and Cut Loose, tunes that capture the OTT mania of **Metal On Metal** or **Forged In Fire**. Lips' vocals are strained towards distraction, probably accounting for why they are so far back in the mix. Robb Reiner's wall-of-sound drumming, which enforced a bloodthirsty, painfully loud philosophy on the band's aforementioned thrash opuses, here sounds out of place, like he's the only one that came to play. Just substandard, tired, and unnecessary, definitely the odd man out in the red hot Anvil forge.
Rating                                              4

## Anvil - Pound For Pound (Metal Blade '88)

Many a fan steadfastly refused to endorse any album containing a song about hockey, so I guess it's up to me to howl the praises of this relentless and dense semi-opus. **Pound For Pound** is the slammin' Anvil of old, celebrating a work ethic that mixes rhythmic wizardry with ultra-heaviness, while retaining the chaos of OTT, Robb Reiner again pummeling his kit to a twisted mass of fibreglass and chrome. Lips takes his original line-up through weighty, well-recorded crunchers like *Senile King*, *Corporate Preacher*, and an uncharacteristically long dinosaur *Fire In The Night*, while sticking us with a couple more of his porn rockers with *Safe Sex* and a bizarre and predictably inane sexual square dance called *Toe Jam*, carrying on a tradition I think most fans wish he'd abandon. Nonetheless, **Pound For Pound** demonstrates Anvil can still be a vital force, knowing when to correct, yet in this case over-correcting to some extent, thrashing just a bit too much for my liking.
Rating     7

## Anvil - Past And Present Live (Metal Blade '89)

This lovingly bruised retro-rejoicefest for and from one of speed metal's major innovators lines up a crazy selection of tracks, which once again, are slammed home through the weltatious logs of drummer Robb Reiner, one of the coolest fillers and colliders on the planet. Major smog-belching engines like *Forged In Fire*, *Jackhammer*, and anthem-for-life *Metal On Metal* get the trench combat treatment as Lips and the band prove their might and mastery of all things leathery. San Pedro, '90s punk should heed the wrath of the Great White North.
Rating     7

## Anvil - Worth The Weight ('91)

Drawing from the band's inherent ability to combine crazy-man progressive chops, total blitz metal, and tense punk delivery, **Worth The Weight** takes charge in bone-crushing manner, offering obscene flourishes from all corners, especially the punishing skins of mad-man Robb Reiner who is the dense throb of the Anvil attack. Here we see a new approach, something akin to an otherworldly, wasted extension of Pantera, a technical feat upon high, made unpalatable, thick and loose, a looming testimony to the band's insane playing skills (skills built more often than not under a sweet cannabis haze). Most hilarious of the pain-inflicted spread would be *Bushpig*, driven by the album's most purely thrash mosh butted up against the most jarring of stop/starts. It's all a badly-crazed power metal feast, a little too scientifically nuts in places, too crammed with wall-pasting shifts, but without a doubt, this is an Anvil concerned with leaving a legacy, a wholly different outfit from the buffoon metal of **Strength Of Steel**. And nowhere else in the harsh light of heavy metal could Reiner get away with such an endless array of flaming fills, yet here it seems everybody is hostile beyond OTT, smoking the frets beneath the agile rant from Lips' guttural depth. There's no way in the world Anvil can expect to sell megagobs of albums with this dense, defiant look at life, but one gets the feeling Lips & Crew are content to sell to the connoisseur who might appreciate creative extensions of a certain '80s techno thrash sound. If that's where the man's head's at, then **Worth The Weight** is right on the money.
Rating     8

## Anvil - Plugged In Permanent (Hypnotic '96)

Like they've never been away, the over-metal legends that are Anvil (Advil?) return with a record that once more beelines it for 11, and remains in that hyper, loose-bolted, almost Mötorheaded place for the duration. By this point, the band has chucked it lyrically, just letting fly with a bunch of stuff that is often humourous, rarely poetic, and always crammed forward in futile competition with the raw, technically evil genius, instrumental barrage. So subject matter ranges from Dr. Kevorkian to mountain biking and getting a good night's sleep, to loudfast tunes in praise of masturbation and the evil weed. The overall sound of the record is caustic and frazzled like *Forged In Fire*, Reiner's drumming again blowing up the place, swooping all over Lips' lizard wizard riffs, usually at unsafe speeds, always arriving alive but loosened like jazz. Plainly nuts, but well worth the effort in deciphering, Anvil reaching back into traditional OTT (a genre which they helped invent), machine-tooling it for the '90s with a toke, swig and a larf.
Rating     8

## Apes, Pigs & Spacemen - Transfusion (Music For Nations '95)

These provocative Brits blend equal parts Galactic Cowboys, heavy Saigon Kick, heavy King's X and psychedelic grunge in construction, contusion and transfusion of a record that is aggressive and smart all at once. The big dirty difficult riffs are all over the place, driven and pounded by cool drums and loopy bits that establish these yobs as Grade-A nutters (may as well speak Kerrang!, eh?). To be stuck in a lorry with them, in search of petrol on the M1 would be truly daft. But seriously, this is good, chest-thumping, channel-flicking info-overloading thinking man's metal for the millenium, the spirit of Fishbone electrocuting the grooves of Terrorvision (see *Twice The Man*, and try stop yourself from dancing, although the spacey, boffo-bluesy sinking feeling of the tune's last movement will do it for you, as will next track *Seep*, which oscillates from sledge-size down-tuna to watery acoustic in a wink of an eye). Name refers to the band's re-engineering of Darwin's evolutionary chain.
Rating     8

## Apocalyptica - Plays Metallica By Four Cellos ('96)

These guys look like your basic mopey death metal bunch, but of course what they're doing here is using cellos to cover Metallica. Best track is *Enter Sandman*, although it's quite impressive what they do with *Creeping Death*, turning the tune into something that sounds like a swarm of locusts feasting on a swarm of common house flies. Bloody 'ell though, the cello can sound quite caustic when it wants, and what better way to hafta hear them? Here's where I say the novelty wears off after three listens.
Rating     6

## April Wine - April Wine (Aquarius '71)

And so the long, winding path commences, April Wine moving from hometown Halifax to Montreal to begin their chequered, semi-eventful career. Most tracks on this seedy debut (with the famously butt-ugly pair o' feet album cover) are Jimmy Henman compositions, the guy leaving after one record to go back to school. Raw, hippy trippy music for the dungeons. First single *Fast Train* did middling business, much like the band's next million songs.
Rating     3

## April Wine - On Record (Aquarius '72)

Reviewed here to emphasize the fact that none of the early Wine rock is worth owning except the gushy **Stand Back**, **On Record** is unbelievably backwards, nerdy, mellow, psychedelic, occasionally finding high school electric rock, the proverbial gold mine of bold heaviness passed up in search of more critically acceptable terrain. Creepy as any old music you can find under any old rock. Two big songs: semi-rawkin' *Drop Your Guns*, and non-original funkster *You Could Have Been A Lady*. Another brilliant record jacket.
Rating     3

## April Wine - Electric Jewels (Aquarius '74)

**Electric Jewels** was one of those moments of truth that seemed to fade into the distance as the band would pass on by, continuing with its stylistic meanderings into impotence, even if the Henman brothers have left, making way for the band's definitive line-up of Goodwyn, Clench, Moffet and Mercer. There's dated but advancing heavy fare such as *The Band Has Just Begun* and the semi-famous-at-the-time *Weeping Widow*, but for the most part, the band flits from one musical camp to another, glazed over with a psychedelic sheen and ponderousness that leaves them miles behind other early axe-purveyors such as Aerosmith, Purple, Sabbath, or fellow homeboys Rush. Many a fan's key April Wine fave, a debut of sorts, that shows traces of vet wisdom.
Rating **5**

## April Wine - Live (Aquarius '74)

**Live** marks a grudging acceptance on my part of this increasingly BTO-ish band of haploids. The purple acid rock flash of the album cover ushers in this clubbing, thumping record of brash, percussive semi-hits. Standouts of the sordid guitar mash: *Cat's Claw* and *The Band Has Just Begun*. Captured in full disco ball splendor at a high school in Halifax. Sounds crappy like chewed tin foil.
Rating **4**

## April Wine - Stand Back (Aquarius '75)

**Stand Back** always reminds me of the time Fiver and I were scrounging through the dump and found a foot-thick stack of psychedelic black and purple April Wine '74 tour posters. Once home with our find, we proceeded to plastered over every square inch of wall space in my basement rec room for one of our famous Grade 7 dances. Anyhoo, Wine was flying high with this album, a spot-on patch of Canuck rock including some seminal early metal in the classic *Oowatanite* (with that instantly recognizable bell-ringing intro), clod rockin' riff monsters *Victim Of Your Love*, *Don't Push Me Around*, and *Highway Hard Run*, plus melloid and harmonic radio hit *Tonite Is A Wonderful Time To Fall In Love*, somewhat of a watershed moment for the band, who would take this record on tour to their biggest crowds yet. **Stand Back** finally placed the band capable of breaking through the communication barrier, offering up warm and tasty vintage guitar rock with no more humble ambitions than to please high school shut-ins, increasingly like BTO with emotion and hue plain, fat and sequined. One of the very few high points in the bleak, chilly, embarrassing April Wine catalogue, **Stand Back** found Myles Goodwyn taking over production and most of the songwriting, very much becoming leader at the expense of Jim Clench.
Rating **7**

## April Wine - The Whole World's Going Crazy
(Aquarius '76)

In which the Winers emulate heavy Eagles, experimental BTO and Slade, to ill effect of their reputation, this first U.S. release for the band in the U.S. stiffing badly both commercially and creatively. Nothing much awake here, although the album does demonstrate a bit of backwoods, under-achieving boogie woogie fun, led down the garden path by Myles Goodwyn's smooth and marketable croon, plus underpants-achieving tracks like *Kick Willy Rd.* and the amusing, maritime apocalyptic title track, released as a single to sour, expectant faces all over Canuckland. Lone rocker: *So Bad*, although the "big hit" was high skool slowdancer *Like A Lover, Like A Song*. Subsequent tour included a big model of the troll-like dude on the nicely-embossed front cover.
Rating **4**

## April Wine - Forever For Now (Aquarius '76)

April Wine joins the burning wreckage of elevator muzak, digging under with the librarian likes of Jimmy Buffet, Barry Manilow, Elton John, Neil Sedaka, Air Supply, Down Hill, Starcastle and Firefall. But really, it's a play to Goodwyn's vanilla sensibilities, this record being hastily converted from a near-finished Goodwyn solo album called **Goody Two Shoes**. Cheese-on-purpose nostalgia tune *You Won't Dance With Me* turned into a novelty hit in Canada. Man, maybe the '70s weren't so cool after all.
Rating **0**

## April Wine - Live At The El Mocambo (Aquarius '77)

The El Mo is one of those "legendary" open-now, closed-now clubs in T.O. that hosted many a hot band throughout its '70s heyday. **Live At The El Mocambo** highlights Wine material that is marginally poppier than the catalogue as a whole and thus like many live albums, evokes a whiff of filterable playability, but is no screamin' big deal. More celebratory than the doped-out ancientisms of **Live** (Aquarius '74) and more nostalgically deep than **One For The Road** (Capitol '85). Highlight: *Don't Push Me Around*. Note: the El Mo sessions were set up as a surprise appearance of The Rolling Stones, billed as The Cockroaches. April Wine (billed as headliners) ended up the back-up band for Mick and the boys, big shot producer Eddie Kramer banging off this record, and the Stones' awful **Love You Live** in two nights.
Rating **4**

## April Wine - First Glance (Aquarius '78)

**First Glance** is one of the more advanced, modern-thinking and expertly detailed Wine outings, offering a fairly cohesive mix of styles, and probably the band's wildest, most exhuberant track ever, *Hot On The Wheels Of Love*, a super slide-guitarin' low-slung cruisin' toon that highlights the frustrating fact that this band is capable of so much more. The biggest hits on this fairly successful record were the wimpoid *Rock'n'Roll Is A Vicious Game* and the metallic but boring *Roller*, which became a radio rock staple, and perhaps April Wine's most enduring song in the U.S., oddly enough, the song going gold by accident, after launched singles *Vicious Game* and *Let Yourself Go* stiffed south of the border (even though the former propelled the record's sales at home). The first major label release for the band (now on Capitol), since the doomed London days.
Rating **6**

## April Wine - Harder . . . Faster (Aquarius '79)

Another band that never found focus after umpteen albums over 15 years or so, Halifax's only claim to hard rock fame rocked out occasionally, while scoring hits with their radio-friendly light rock fare. **Harder . . . Faster** is by far the heaviest of the catalogue, bringing back memories of road trips to Spokane in Ken's demon-green Dodge Dart during school hours on crisp autumn mornings. Full of tidy melodic rockers, sporting decent harmonies amongst the simple. characteristically bone-headed riffery, **Harder . . . Faster** (named for, you guessed it, a porn video), offers variety within a basic guitar rock framework. Highlights include the rich and dare I say, moving *Before The Dawn*, power chord classic *Babes In Arms*, and a disciplined, electric treatment of King Crimson's erratic *21st Century Schizoid Man*, soon to be a concert showstopper. It would be a stretch to say April Wine possessed metal brilliance akin to other stylistically diverse bands like Queen, Status Quo, or Uriah Heep. Nonetheless the band managed to tally a good couple dozen or so tracks that were robust, rockin' and hooky.

Could have been mega-stars if tunes congealed the right way at the right time.
Rating **8**

## April Wine - The Nature Of The Beast (Capitol '81)
**The Nature Of The Beast** (recorded in the U.K.) marked the biggest payday for this long-slogging bunch of Canadians, slowly going platinum in the U.S., hatching minor hits in *Sign Of The Gypsy Queen*, *All Over Town*, and sap prom night ballad *Just Between You And Me*, which got to 20 on the Billboard charts. But the record countered such predictable fare with the most vicious Wine track ever, the magnificent and crunching *Future Tense*, an uncharacteristic scorcher driven home by a killer doom riff, plus one other fully raging tech-monster in mechanically adept speedster *Crash And Burn*. **Nature** wins the day in its own harmless way as a likeable, inherently Canadian lite metal effort on par with occasional shafts of humanity from Triumph, well-paced and upmarket, but still within the timid April Wine modus operandi.
Rating **7**

## April Wine - Power Play (Aquarius '82)
The first of an arduous contingent of government issue AOR blights from a band that could have been stars, had they kept the amps on 11. Scored a minor hit with the mallet-headed but vanilla *Enough Is Enough*. Definitely another downturn in the band's fortunes, most of this record softened up considerably, nary a trace of the optimism and full-on urge to conquer of the last couple rounders.
Rating **3**

## April Wine - Animal Grace (Aquarius '84)
On **Animal Grace**, the band goes for a more consistent upbeat pop metal sound, complete with a zippy little delivery, and over-produced electronic drums. Obviously in search of some coin, the band comes off smelling like roses about half the time, but falls flat due to too obvious commercial pandering on the lighter hybrids. Generally dumb, but semi-innocuous fun all the same. Hell, who cares? Don't waste your money. Big trouble in the band's backrooms though. The band had been pressuring Myles for years for more input into writing the albums. Here, they submitted thirty or so songs for consideration, Myles rejecting ALL of them, then pretty much writing and producing the album, once again, by himself.
Rating **5**

## April Wine - Walking Through Fire (Capitol '85)
Slogging Through Fire is the kind of horrid, brain-negating, aseptically-produced, keyboard-laced offense that happens when old, and for the most part, untalented rock stars run out of money, and rather than fold, let record execs pick over the scraps. So here we have Myles Goodwyn (now living in the Bahamas) getting together with Brian Greenway and assorted studio musios, dragging the traveled April Wine tag through mud one last time, on what is basically a contractual obligation record. No touring ensued.
Rating **0**

## April Wine - Attitude (Flood Ross '93)
Hard to believe given the acrimonious split, but the boys are back in town, virtually intact 'cept maybe a little thinner on the top for this comeback record that sounds exactly like a comeback record. Yep, **Attitude** is probably the heaviest April Wine record, albeit in an asinine, beer (or truck) commercial sort of way, nothing too threatening, all tinged with Loverboy-era melodies above a techy Grammyjuno clatter. Fun rock'n'roll for washing your car, but quite underachieving in the usual Canuck manner, **Attitude** could have become a radio staple (especially with that ol' Cancon boost),

possessing nice guitar edge and sharp simple arrangements, i.e. something approaching hooks.
Rating **6**

## April Wine - Frigate (fre '94)
Barely even trying anymore, April Wine bulk this one up with a bunch of covers, even covering themselves with *Tonight Is A Wonderful Time To Fall In Love*. At least the title of the record is a bit o' fun, but the rest, like, forget it. A few of the originals do OK doing the three things this band does: bad heavy metal, capable pop metal, and barely capable ballads. But the clunky *I Just Want To Make Love To You* and that annoying Steve Winwood *I'm A Man* song just break up the record to the point of no repair. April Wine's blowing their chance, fueling this slow tug with fumes.
Rating **4**

## April Wine - The April Wine Collection (Aquarius '91)
This massive four CD, 67 song collection pays exhaustive homage to the April Wine legacy of broken dreams (with virtually no new material). Each CD is thematically presented as The Singles, The Rock Songs, Vintage Wine and Live respectively, with Vintage Wine really being compiler favourites, none of them particularly old. Other bonus: excellent record-by-record liner notes by Keith Brown, with lots of previously unpublished photos of this decidedly unphotogenic band. A relaxed amble through this set really does prove that any critical drubbing these guys got from me or others is entirely justified. April Wine were just not that talented.
Rating **5**

## Arcade - Arcade (Sony '93)
Stephen Pearcy's new post-Ratt showcase roared onto the scene with greater confidence and drive than the band's east coast doppelganger, Dee Snider and Widowmaker. **Arcade** works its stated purpose, bulking up a traditional, Ratt-like sound with gumwads of bass, while Pearcy gets complicatedly into his Aerosmith fixation, doing less of a sleaze metal tribute to the band, more of a celebration of Tyler & Co.'s melodic strengths (see balls-out lead tune *Dancin' With The Angels*). An under-rated talent, Pearcy is, and garnering my respect all the time, given his solid track record of records. Drums by Cinderella's Fred Coury.
Rating **7**

## Arcade - A/2 (Sony '94)
Record II for Pearcy's new vehicle was highly promoted by Sony, the label quite enthused by the band's stab at commercial hard rock in the age of blundergrunge, although this one leaned further into the '90s than the heavy, grooving AOR of the debut. And cynics quite accepted **A/2**'s slow-ish heft, fronted by a gruffer, ballsier Pearcy vocal. Ballads such as *Kidnapped* balance out piffle like *When I'm Gone*, and the rockers throb with tons of bass and open-field riffing. Perhaps taking cue from Alice in Chains, Arcade have found a victorious hybrid with the new broodiness that leaves the band squarely heavy metal yet not all that dated. Faves: lead droner *Angry* and wicked, riff-strapped street rockers *Your Only Age* and *Hot Racin'*. A celebration in relevance, which is quite a surprise given **A/2**'s conventionality. Critical path: buried in my CD collection unless I tape it for the car.
Rating **8**

## Arcturus - Aspera hiems symfonia (Century Media '96)
If you want to feel reverberating black metal magnetism, look no further than this supergroup of sorts, Arcturus demonstrating what can be unleashed when talented players descend on Norwegian grimrock with classical and progressive confidence. Arcturus is more a gathering of vets than a true band, sporting members

from Mayhem (Hellhammer!), Ulver, Ved Buens Ende and Tritonus. But I'd advise our trusted Scandinavian harpies to chuck that claptrap and focus their evil energies on this classy pile of putrid pageantry, **Aspera** really rolling out the carpet, capturing all those foreboding tones in novel musical fashion. Vocals switch off, keyboards are left to wander woefully, and the drumming is tricksville, making this probably the cleanest, clearest demonstration of smudgy Norse soot I've stumbled across.
Rating 8

## Armageddon - Armageddon (A&M '75)

Admirable more for screwy concept than actual listening value, this second string supergroup (Yardbirds, Rod Stewart, Johnny Winter, Captain Beyond, Renaissance, Steamhammer) approximates a Hawkwind/Pink Fairies/Budgie hybrid, whatever the hell that means. **Armageddon** rumbles heavy, quirky, psychedelic, and progressive, foot-faulting along with an offbeat charm that is both personable and unique. And of course, true to form, compositions are like mini epics; life and death struggles, with weird and lengthy songtitles. Basically a strange, one-off project which marries the eccentricities of all facets of "popular" music under a fairly guitar-heavy banner to questionable artistic result. The crazy uncle in the attic. Keith Relf: death by electrocution one year later.
Rating 6

## Armored Saint - March Of The Saint (Chrysalis '84)

It was hard to find anything wrong with these guys, but there was nothing resoundingly right either. Songs are faultless and adequate, the production accomplished (but dulled), and the overall collection solid, seamless yet uneventful. In a word: boring, all just too safe and self-consciously packaged in little armoured suits. Kiddie kommerce Priest.
Rating 4

## Armored Saint - Delirious Nomad (Chrysalis '85)

More of the same considerably heavy, yet safe metal, problematic in the same close to indescribable way as the band's semi-hyped premiere. Too tight, too clean, simple, and sonically fused, lacking any semblance of anarchy or edge in either Bush's vocals, Gonzo's drumming, or the production; components that must assert themselves to raise to the next plateau what here amount to pretty buoyant metal/hard rock licks. Not serious contenders for anything at this point except perhaps Kings of the Delete Bin.
Rating 4

## Armored Saint - Raising Fear (Chrysalis '87)

Heavier, a bit more growl and pain in the vocals, yet still, Exhibiting Trepidation, like the debut and **Delirious Nomad**, manages to flounder in boiling oil. Somewhere deep within the grooves there's a scared little mindset cursed with a barren psychological terrain betraying any danger or sense of adventure throughout these superficially heavy tunes. **Raising Fear** pushes 6, if only due first to my sympathy for a band carrying an unnamable curse, and second, the almost convincing zip of the title track and companion staccato chugger, *Chemical Euphoria*. A mere salamander to the Godzilla-like ground swell of '91's swansong **Symbol Of Salvation**, **Delirious Nomad** would also be the last for guitarist Dave Pritchard, who sadly is since deceased from leukemia.
Rating 5

## Armored Saint - Saints Will Conquer (Metal Blade '88)

"Hello Cleveland!" and we're off scorching the pits, on this informal live LP/EP that captures the fact that yes, as we suspected, the Saint are a much better unit live than on their head-scratchingly unrealized studio projects. Rollicking boozily, **Saints** also tacks on at the end *No Reason To Live*, a tune from the band's first demo session in '83 which had them thrusting like a blustery blue collar Queensryche. Eight tracks in total, and a legacy that never quite was.
Rating 6

## Armored Saint - Symbol Of Salvation (Metal Blade '91)

Just before Bush leaves the fold for Anthrax, the Saint seemed to be emerging from their conservative shell. **Symbol Of Salvation** is one of those smooth but powerful, purely heavy metal experiences, mixing traditional metal with a strange Bay Area thrash ethic, one more of ambition than speed or style. The record is involved, ambitious, accessible and crammed with meaty riffs. production is still a bit safe, although somehow Jerden's mix sounds more audiophile than unmetallic. But I still can't get overly excited, even as the record approaches the pride of a Metal Church. Better put to rest, although many onlookers were quite impressed with this one.
Rating 7

## Artch - Another Return To Church Hill
(Metal Blade '88)

Accomplished Norwegian power-goth that reminds one of an Yngwie-energized Vicious Rumors, a Vandenberged Metal Church, Fates Warning stripped down, or simply Maiden from 1982. Which makes perfect sense, these guys forming in that year, taking forever to bring this fine detailed gallop rocker to fruition. And Erik Hawk is a dead-ringer for Bruce Dickinson, lending these Valhalla-esque castle rockers an appropriate sense of royalty. Quality reigns.
Rating 7

## Artch - For The Sake Of Mankind (Metal Blade '91)

Artch have matured splendidly into their own, evoking a myriad of tight-ranged influences, emerging with their own slight demarcation on dramatic traditional metal. Flagship performance is once again Erik Hawk, whose newly gruff bottom end adds a dimension to his voice that parallels Dickinson's growth through the years, also evoking the thespian versatility and emotion of Kai Hansen and Rob "Cueball" Halford. The band's sound has mirrored this new depth, getting slower, chunkier, noisier like mid-speed Gamma Ray, making Artch a truly upper crust force amongst uniquely European-sounding melodic metal, mixing it up with OT-Ters, prog-minded acoustic and a general sense of confidence way beyond 1991. Solid metal, which only sounds dated in terms of the genre having flown, not the quality of the performances or penmanship.
Rating 8

## A.S.a.P. - Silver And Gold (Capitol '89)

As in Adrian Smith (ex of the mighty Maiden) and Project. I guess Smith shows his true colours here, preferring the technological hues of silver and gold over the beastly guitar whompings of black leather. And this solo work stinks to high heaven because of it, equaling a sort of headlight-stunned Shy, parlaying a ton of hours into the worst of English keyboard pop. Wimp rock through and through, **Silver And Gold** stumbles on in one boring plod to the growly, limited vocal strains of Steve himself, amidst a wash of over-worked synth pattern, tech drums, and purportedly "classy" guitar shades. The record bombed badly, no doubt a surprise to the boys in the band who were sure they were making something "commercial".
Rating 1

## Asphalt Ballet - Pigs (Virgin '93)

Quite the interesting rounder this one, combining Guns N' Roses, or maybe Skid Row with grunge and Saigon Kick, then recording the whole thing crystal

slick and assured. But it's one of those records you can't fault, but might rarely play, given its arguable creative over-extension and slightly restrained delivery. There's a hint of hair band left in this act which also causes consternation, but lyrically things are either socially conscious or colourful or both, usually way above the party rock standards of Asphalt Ballet's peers. An attempt to save hard rock from irrelevance, even if all the frills, spills and alternative thrills coalesce into a smokescreen effect.
Rating                                                                7

## Asphyx - The Rack   (Century Media '91)
Carbonic shard #1 for these Dutch tri-partite whipping boys (save for rare indie **Embrace The Death**) is a shoot 'em unholy thrashfest dealing all the punishment one can take. Featuring ex-Pestilence and future Comecon frontman Martin Van Drunen, **The Rack** is an entertaining, verbose read, as well as a better than average square-headed death metal revival. The record captures that monsterblosh bludgeon, albeit offering little above many others doing exactly the same thing. Fans of sonic festering sores will celebrate with neck-snapping reverence, because the record is medium strong for this particular corner of metal's proud domain.
Rating                                                                6

## Asphyx - Crush The Cenotaph   (Century Media '92)
This evil little five-horned EP slows and slugs Asphyx moderately to the point where they sound like a drunken cross between Celtic Frost and Unleashed, the title track, *Rite Of Shades* and *The Krusher* (the latter which will appear on their next record), chafing greatly against the two crackly brimstone live tracks from their debut record. Sinister but alive with fire.
Rating                                                                6

## Asphyx - Last One On Earth   (Century Media '92)
These spiritual heirs to Venom and Warfare are slowly coming into their own, possessing a volatile pile of evil vapors, steaming and stirring a thick brew of death, grind and old thrash into something chewable for metalheads who might take that next damnation-defining step into layers untrampled. Asphyx's ace is their spontaneous combustible delivery, really sounding quite hammered as they white-knuckle it through the scrapyard of souls. Crushing riffs, scraping production and vocals from Van Drunen that are a fiendish pleasure in light of his poor Comecon performance. One for the Frosties.
Rating                                                                8

## Asphyx - Asphyx   (Century Media '94)
This somewhat ignored last-before-reunion pales in comparison to its predecessor, being doomier, more somber and slacker, case not helped by new vocalist Ron Van Pol, who is yer basic grind gullet, less the frantic crazy-man rant of Van Drunen, the man's gruff mumblings turning Asphyx ordinary. An imposing, evil terrain for sure, but a bit sleepy, sporting too many long songs, mellow bits, slow instrumental wander-abouts and sawed-off production values.
Rating                                                                6

## Asphyx - God Cries   (Century Media '96)
After breaking up given the mass indifference to the band's self-titled trashfest from '94, two-thirds of the band are back and eviler and meloder than ever (such language!). **God Cries** is a typically blasphemous blackened blight, but as a trio, Asphyx have left themselves room to roam the crystal wilds of death's domain, leaving links to conventional songwriting tenuous at times, sharply focused and tight at others. The band's original vocalist Theo Loomans is parched, dying and quite convincing here, taking these alkaline calling

cards to a next level of rewired grindcore. Violently assembled, lovingly pierced with pain, but scarcely a half hour long.
Rating                                                                7

## Athiest - Piece Of Time   (Active/Death '90)
Somewhat blessed from the start, Florida's Athiest leaped into view with this early shard of congested mayhem, production courtesy of Scott Burns and metal impressario, writer and superfan Borivoj Krgin. **Piece Of Time** is a short piece, scarcely half an hour long, but the advanced, ebulent technical death flows convincingly, sorta like speedy Coroner or uh, Death. Tight, concise, and fraught with pointy layers.
Rating                                                                6

## Athiest - Unquestionable Presence   (Active/Death '91)
Another short record, but one could argue that there's more going down here that on both the Metallica records of the '90s, Athiest compressing lifetimes of extreme metal into carbon-hard vignettes of speed and progressive possibility. Once more Burns, Morris and Morrisound Studios have done a bang-up job translating the furious flurry to disc. Lead track *Mother Man* and its crazy-chops drum patterns prove that this is a band moving into shredded and reassembled time zones, and the rest of the record concurs. Still though, Kelly Shaefer's bark has too much bite, harshening all the fireworks until I just throw up my hands in defeat. Bassist Roger Patterson R.I.P., replaced by Tony Choy.
Rating                                                                6

## Athiest - Elements   (Active/Metal Blade '93)
Growing well into his own lyrically, Shaefer has written a quixotic, enigmatic concept record of sing-songy poetics, delightfully dancing through each tale of this highly original record, devoting tracks to an extended and adapted set of elements. Thus in total (not counting four interludes), we get convoluted, post-Rush sonics supporting songs called *Green*, *Water*, *Air*, *Animal*, *Mineral*, *Fire*, *Earth*, and *Elements*. Although convincingly flying an art rock flag, this is still heavy, harrowing work, an academic sort of underworld metal that is the grating, death equivalent of arch-band Cynic. But it's a rewarding, white-knuckle listen all the same, almost like jazz or instrumental albums, supportable and interesting just by virtue of the music. And as I say, the lyrics are highly inventive also, turning the record into an intelligent feast for all the senses.
Rating                                                                8

## Atomic Folk - Begin   (Folklore '95)
Hey clowns, I quite like this! Montreal's Atomic Folk manhandle a potent, impassioned mix of hooky hard rockers, nowhere near that alternative thing, but little to do with metal cheese, more like a quality '70s guitar smorg (Ted?) meets Drivin 'n' Cryin and The Meat Puppets, an interesting touch of fog permeating a fierce bed of solid rock. Easily one half the hooks of Green Day, plus these guys bring chops, parlaying their street-heatedness into compact rock tunes that offer mucho emotional depth with musician's substance. Comparisons have been made to Montreal's Doughboys, but that stuff's fluff compared to this smart debut. Recommended partily, although the thing sags for the last about third.
Rating                                                                7

## Atomic Opera - For Madmen Only   (Giant '94)
Atomic Opera constitute the fourth member of a family comprising The Awful Truth, Galactic Cowboys and of course King's X, each finding birth with producer/manager Sam Taylor, each fusing tech metal, melody and spacey yet warm and fuzzy lyrics for that confusing fish of a sound that refreshes and reaffirms out of the mirage magic of Texas. As you might guess,

35

I'm a sucker for these acts, given their selfless similarity, their pure pronouncement of an honest, good-willed rock'n'roll cause. King's X more or less originated the sound, and have now left the stable, Atomic Opera infusing new blood as a more groove-oriented version of Galactic, slower, chunkier, less frantic. And it works beautifully, the attention to detail up to Taylor's fine standards, harmonies swirled delicately around hooks, guitars large, stone-baked and brooding. Still, it might take a couple of records to really emanate persona, Galactic still the hands-down winner with this tight-rope of scintillating sonics, to my mind **Space In Your Face** knocking **Dogman** on its hind quarters. Vocals could use a bit more confidence, followed by an elevation in the mix, and arrangements could be a tad more eccentric, but for the most part, this is a pleasing knock-off of a jewel-size genre from the plains. Fave: the massive *War Drum*: slippery and full of bass-driven hellacious groove.

Rating                                                                8

## Atomic Rooster - Death Walks Behind You   (B&C '70)

One of those silly names you often hear batted around as originators of metal, Atomic Rooster (not to be confused with Six Ton Budgie!) certainly looked the part with all that power trio hair and ominous imagery. Formed from the blown up bits of The Crazy World Of Arthur Brown, this band's patchy, chaotic bunch of line-ups included notables like Carl Palmer and Chris Farlowe, main member being Vincent Crane who killed himself in '89. This record is widely considered the best and heaviest, although calling it metal would be a stretch, more like a German prog-type octopus with a pile of heavy Heep-ish riffs here and there, very '60s in execution, but quite Purple in arrangement with all that Lordian Hammond keyboard work from Crane (and not Paul Hammond, who was the drummer!). Kinda creeps me out really (especially that William Blake painting), but I sure like John Cann's guitar sounds, both riff and solo, which lean towards Iommi at times. Pity, if these guys would have dropped all the fancy pants noodling and wrote songs, they would have broke the bank just like every other "metal" act at the time, except, uh, Budgie. Now I suppose you want to see Amon Duul in here?

Rating                                                                6

## Atom Seed - Get In Line   (Heavy Metal '90)

Sporting unadventuresome arrangements, plus juxta-positions of styles that betray lack of finesse, Atom Seed nevertheless forge a fairly hip-hoppin' brew of early FNM and Anthrax style techno-punk, all with the rap body English of the Chili Peppers. And as you can tell from that brushstroke, it's pretty obvious that this British foursome will attract hoots of derision as derivative opportunists. More than partly right, but what the hell, more funk metal is a welcome addition to my collection, there being precious little of it out there that really rocks. Cool and capably mixed, **Get In Line** is somewhat the product of a dickin' around Anthrax; combining speed, pumping basslines and verbal assaults, even getting real quiet here and there. Good hooks, and some straight-faced rockers make it less the predictable wank-through, and all has been a good time by record's end. Kinda underground-looking, loose and personable. Post-break-up note: bassist Chris Dale has since found a home with Bruce Dickinson's valiant post-Goth outfit.

Rating                                                                6

## Atrocity - Willenskraft   (Massacre '96)

Stuck vibrating gratingly between thrash, Slayer-ish speed metal and progressive goth, Germany's Atrocity succeed due to biting, feedbacked guitar work, icy, metal drumming and a variety of vocal treatments. Quite experimental rhythmically and arrangement-wise, which might evoke vague feelings of over-extension. Similar to unhewn At The Gates and elder Edge Of Sanity.

Rating                                                                6

## Attack - Danger In The Air   (Prosound '84)

A melodious and stimulating alloy of Eurorock and classical metal, **Danger In The Air** causes one to look in awe at the reverberating palaces the mind of Ricky van Heldon hath constructed. Intricate and innovative, crystal clear and morose, Attack sings with the surety of masters at work, most notably van Helden, whose vocals are an instrumental force all their own on these exceedingly gothic collusions with pop, progressive tales of treachery, and overtly metallic jewels. O'er top the quality-obsessed proceeds come an engaging fusion of fluid axe and key patterns which again give further rise to one of the most European sounding records I've ever witnessed. Lyrics are a bit foreign, but who cares, given the signature with which they are attacked, sending weary madman epics like (don't laugh) *The Dragon From The Hill* and *Stoneway No. 3* into grimaced, medieval terrain. Weird project, but wildly successful, at least for its unique, eccentric gothics.

Rating                                                                8

## At The Gates - The Red In The Sky Is Ours   (Deaf '91)

Further inundations from the thrashcore tundra. Punky, accelerated with occasional gobs of hurried Trouble which speed by in seconds. Six guys, one with short hair. At this point (i.e. the band's debut after a crusty EP called **Gardens Of Grief**), still a pile of mess of stack of goo. But a thorny blossoming is afoot.

Rating                                                                4

## At The Gates - With Fear I Kiss The Burning Darkness   (Deaf '93)

Truly kicking into a realm of their own, At The Gates begin to carve their signature stop/start sound, soaking up the hard stuff at the core of early Cemetary, Edge Of Sanity and of course Death. Frightening and poetic, frost-bitten and fast, these guys blend goth, thrash, black metal and prog into a force worth harkening. In possession of a certain youthful enthusiasm that is lost on an obvious masterpiece like **Slaughter Of The Soul**.

Rating                                                                7

## At The Gates - Terminal Spirit Disease   (Futurist '95)

At nine tracks, three of them live, totaling 34 minutes, At The Gates' third record is a mere stopgap if an ambitious one. Ever exploring the crusty terrain of death's domain, Sweden's ATG deign fit to rise above, combining elements of chilled melody à la Sentenced, older Tiamat and those weird, horrible records from the gravest of Norwegian black metal bands. Vocals are still trad death scowlgrowls, but the riffing is progressive, fresh and difficult, racing yet with odd gallops, as Tomas Lindberg barks out lyrics that paint all shades of emotional anguish, more psychologically harrowing than death metal constrained. Heavy and unrepentant, At The Gates still manages classy exploration on par with many of their killer Swedish counterparts. The last for Peaceville (and Futurist in the U.S.), as the band moves to Earache, optimistic at new possibilities.

Rating                                                                7

## At The Gates - Slaughter Of The Soul   (Earache '95)

At long last, Gothenburg, Sweden's finest deliver their masterwerk, a record that combines the vicious anguish of past death metal platters with a searing musicality, most akin to say, Chuck Shuldiner's recent directives with Death, both bands now at the forefront of extreme, due to adherence to chops, blackhearted melody and near genius riffery colliding then burning

rubber lie a maniac, while all around the wreckage fly solos and breaks that are the ultimate in thoughtful. And vocals do the Death/Obituary thing too; thrashing mad, but not low-guttered like traditional grindcore, more hysterical and bent on chaos than just stupid. A scorched and bleakly European gold standard to which certain progressive branches of extreme metal can aspire.
Rating     **8**

## A-II-Z - The Witch Of Berkely  (Est. '83)
Similar to Witchfynde in that they were at least superficially black metal originals who had no idea what they were doing. Like Witchfynde, A-II-Z also showed major promise. But not here. This eccentric debut is a live recording of what is basically a bar band no doubt playing in a bar; pedestrian, and not at all in keeping with the sick black metal packaging of the project. Hell, I even got a sew-on patch with this. Anyways, the aforementioned promise this band exuded actually came from various professional, tuneful but heavy 45's and EP's, most notably the No Fun After Midnight EP, comprising three tidy rockers which resemble Diamond Head's early rockers and Ringside Seat (a B-side to Russ Ballard's grandly pop-directed I'm The One Who Loves You, the single featuring future AC/DC drummer Simon Wright), that kicks with a nice boogie groove and capable recording. Why this album exists is anyone's guess.
Rating     **2**

## Autopsy - Severed Survival + Retribution For The Dead  (Peaceville/Futurist '93)
A reissue of this prolific, freaky death metal band's first two EP's from '89 and '90, **Severed Survival** proves why Autopsy have been allowed to build a catalogue. And that reason would be the band's drunken crush factor, their obvious refusal to slot themselves as just death or doom or grind or thrash, busting into all these admittedly only slightly demarcated genres at will, keeping the twisted listener on the edge of his seat wondering what's next. Lyrics: total gore along the lines of Cannibal Corpse but less wordy.
Rating     **6**

## Avalanche - Pray For The Sinner  (Roadrunner '85)
Cold and clammy traditional metal from Missouri that runs together under a sloppy mix and sub-par vocals, appropriately sent to the rear of Avalanche's crumbling wall. Weird song selection that combines blockhead hard rock as per an aroused Kiss with more death metal-like blabberings reminiscent of Exciter or clueless, out-of-control emulations of Priest. Sheet metal with infectious energy and no idea what to do with it.
Rating     **4**

## Avenger - Killer Elite  (Neat '85)
Hapless British stew meat Avenger slog forth through the headbanging waiting room, doomed to a life of loitering with this painfully recorded but typical dumkopf crank from Neat. Sorta like bad Satan, Tysondog, Warfare, or really scummy Tank, **Killer Elite** is one grimefest of long forgotten metal ideas recorded fast, loose, and mission-bent, but so hopelessly below the poverty line, it rarely rises above eight-to-ten beer terrain, save for Hard Times, Face To The Ground and Sawmill, all on a seven-track side two with rousing bits of punter sweat. With tighter execution and a caring mix, this could have smoked. No, really.
Rating     **4**

## Aversion - Fall From Grace  (Doctor Dream '95)
I almost feel guilty giving records like this a wimpy little **6**, because the band do such a bang-up job. Unfortunately, what they do well is a low-brow speed metal,

packing a little bit of death and a whole lot of skatepunk, sending the whole thing back to 1985, good and bad habits of the '80s included. Ranting, die laughing lyrucks (Waco Jesus, The Weed, The Tree And Me), snotty vocals, a basket full o' fresh riffs, not inconsiderable chops, but too much anarchy on purpose for me to take it seriously. Beers would make it all better.
Rating     **6**

## Axe - Axe  (MCA '79)
This anonymous speck of dust displays a band of tuneful but grimy souls twisted and shoved into smothering, AOR radio slots, resulting in a lacklustre, emotionless, piece of false polish like early and aimless Helix if you can believe it, or that strange noise that emerges when rockers suvvern at heart enter the mainstream (38 Special, Outlaws, various Skynyrd solo abominations), which is what happens here. Originally called Babyface.
Rating     **2**

## Axe - Offering  (Atco '82)
While exhibiting none of the tasty melodic hard rock and keen eye for southern traditions displayed on **Nemesis**, **Offering** nevertheless rings a fine record of a more overt, less clever hard rock/metal hybrid. Of note, Axe pulls a class act, covering Montrose's I Got The Fire which although inferior to Iron Maiden's rendition, is still a step up on the original. Other rousing, inherently American-sounding rockers include drive-in-ready trio Rock'n'Roll Party In The Streets, Video Inspiration, and Burn The City Down, all of which would sound mighty fine on any small town main street on a hot Friday night. Overall a warm, likeable record that downplays flash or shock value for hooks and sincerity.
Rating     **7**

## Axe - Nemesis  (Atco '83)
Don't expect anyone to believe me on this one, but **Nemesis** is righteously cool, a blend of AOR and bayou-rich metal that manages to embrace roots without sacrificing sheen. Reigning kings of the delete bins, Axe serve up a hard-edged brew here that successfully bridges heavy metal, hard rock, southern rock, keyboard rock and biker rock, resulting in one heaping slab of blue collar Americana, an album paralleled by only one other I can think of, Blackfoot's masterpiece **Siogo**, which tended more towards the muscular side of the same territories. Clichéd, melodramatic, but produced smooth as silk, underdogged and capable, **Nemesis'** shining lights are profuse, oscillating mostly between groove metal (Heat In The Streets and All Through The Night) and tidy, melodic pop metal (Young Hearts and She's Had The Power). Warning: Liking this album is probably due more to some personal soft spot for this band rather than to true merits of the disc so proceed with caution. Actually don't worry about it. It'll never be more than a couple of bucks, so roll the dice. Note: vocalist Ed Riley killed in a car crash in '84, Barth briefly moving onto Blackfoot, eventually reforming Axe in '89.
Rating     **8**

## Axewitch - Visions Of The Past  (Neat '85)
This horde of messed-up, depressing Swedes play a valiant sort of frosty Euro-metal, while more often than not, tending towards murky and aimless, further marred by vocals that are thin and flat, muffling that all-important, potential human touch. As a result, Axewitch falls into my category of promising, admired, but sparingly played, reserved strictly for voracious, exploratory metal moods. A big improvement over the trashy **Lord Of The Flies** EP, at least in terms of production, **Visions** looks into the past for many mid-speed HM traditions, even if I'd sooner listen to Highway Chile, 220V, or Overdrive for my '80s

Scandinavian fix. Follow-up: '85's **Hooked On High Heels**.
Rating                                                    5

## The Awful Truth - The Awful Truth (Metal Blade '89)

Houston's The Awful Truth was none other than Monty Colvin and Alan Doss' pre-Galactic Cowboys outfit, rounded out by guitarist and chief songwriter David Von Ohlerking. In fact, the band had broken up before the record's release, Monty and Alan already ensconced in the studio building the Cowboys' zesty debut. But it would be a shame to pass over this complicated Sam Taylor-produced sound explorer, **The Awful Truth** essentially a smooth and sombre Galactic Cowboys buffet, more acoustic, way less manic, quite stand-offish, academic and alternative. Which all rolls up in a fantastical ball, the band having built this happenstance vehicle driven by Monty's dirty bass bush-roaming through a sort of '80s progressive rock ethic (Rush, Crimson, Queensryche), Ohlerking's guitarwork mixing lumbering riff with watery, texture-building chordings (like Lifeson, like Andy Summers), all the while the band introducing the heavy metal harmonies that would become the next band's imprint. Ultimately, **The Awful Truth** smells like electric jazz, sterile but in a good way, like a library or an operating room, the trio acting out with furrowed brow a respectable music school masters thesis. A head trip way out there ahead of its time, not to mention an out-of-character, forward thinking signing for the likes of Metal Blade, who would years later return with the paperwork for the Cowboys' **Machine Fish** sod-bustin' dust-up.
Rating                                                    8

# B

**Babylon A.D. - Nothing Sacred** (Arista/BMG '92)

Gee Tom Werman gets around, here producing yet another faceless pile of commercial perfection metal by a band with pret' near five yards of hair. Obviously the death of the genre was predicated by the flood of similar bands, made all the more hard to take because every last one was so laboriously well-executed. So I almost feel guilty slamming this stuff. Almost.

Rating                                                    5

**Bachman Turner Overdrive - Bachman Turner Overdrive** (Mercury '73)

Brainier and brawnier than Kiss, but dumb as a wet bag of hammers when butted-up against Sabbath, Deep Purple or Aerosmith, Buffalo Burger Overweight were pretty much the first Canadian purveyors of the lunkhead power chord. Randy Bachman (ex-of another Canadian success story, Guess Who, led by irrepressible party animal Burton Cummings) and Fred Turner ("anchor" of the band, with his unique sports broadcaster vocal stylings), are the band's two bookends, while Bachman brothers Rob and Tim round out the line-up. This the band's debut, is a pleasurable bit of '70s lard rock, weighted with chunky immovable power chords all spiced with a sort of Southern flavour, turning BTO - I into something approaching a collection of boogie woogie truck driving tunes, all fairly basic and blunted, save for jazzoid single *Blue Collar Man*. BTO's image was one of jean jackets and big bellies; lumberjack rockers with little connection to the politics of the business. Just regular guys doing their thing, which was a muscular, no bullshit batch of guitar tunes; well-recorded, well-executed, but not overly tricky. Sounds pretty rudimentary compared to the wizardry of today, but a nice memory nevertheless.

Rating                                                    6

**Bachman Turner Overdrive - II** (Mercury '73)

BTO continue on their trajectory to the top, giving us another tangled mass of guitar rock postures, most of them decidedly red in the neck, delivering mostly loud boogie rock, with touches of acoustic, jazz, psychedelia, metal and the usual obligatory pow wow beat from Turner, all with freewheeling delivery bordering on humour. Two of the band's monster hits emerge, *Let It Ride* and *Takin' Care Of Business*, the latter becoming the band's signature anthem, destined for scratchy PA Hell in every hallowed shrine from Victoria to Halifax dedicated to Canada's national sport. Still, the doofus

rock overwhelms the crunch, as BTO bash out what is more or less a hapless and pork-fisted collection of divergent but sturdy party tunes, none of which sound particularly ahead of their time.

Rating                                                    5

**Bachman Turner Overdrive - Not Fragile** (Mercury '74)

**Not Fragile** is BTO at its most self-actualized, well lowdown in that rock star groove in their country western-look sequins and satins, as they grind forth two more megahits in rhythmic flatbed rocker *Roll On Down The Highway* and *You Ain't Seen Nothing Yet* with its famous stutter chorus. Strange sort of band, in that their appeal is that it all sounds so dated, so perfect for the big '70s rawk show, lots of holler-along choruses and plain, wide-open chording, making for an effortlessly understandable gig, all chop and thunk, large on heroic without flash, working class hooks and six string bravado. Pretty well the end of the glory days, although Randy was still out there slingin' it in '93 with his "Bachman" album, **Any Road**.

Rating                                                    6

**Bachman Turner Overdrive - Four Wheel Drive** (Mercury '75)

After the massive success of **II** and **Not Fragile**, you'd think the band could afford some threads that don't make them look like Three Dog Night or Steppenwolf. Anyways, the show must go on, and here the meat truck delivers, although '75 marked the beginning of a slide in the band's heady success. **Four Wheel Drive** (recorded in six days) has that same overblown sense of drama, ludicrous '70s dynamics where the arrival of the power chords always seems like such a big deal (see *She's A Devil*), as if they were harder to play than the quiet bits. The hit this time is *Hey You*, a typical thickhead, featuring Randy's thin pipes in competition with the band's trademark old fashioned stomp, while the inane and impotent *Quick Change Artist* still infects classic rock radio from time to time. The Black Oak Arkansas of the Great White North, BTO will always be remembered as one of the heroic tales of the '70s, in which local boys from the backwoods generate an amplified ruckus that conquers the world.

Rating                                                    6

**Bachman Turner Overdrive - Head On** (Mercury '75)

Tricky little packaging concept, but the band is on its way to Dullsville, more or less abandoning their goofy metalman persona for various forays into what was

believed more expressive, more mature forms of guitar rock, concentrating on their bulky lounge hybrid, in search of a more academic rock'n'roll. Trouble is, this band was never applauded for its creativity. Thinking too much can make your wallet grow thin. So subsequent records also stiffed creatively and commercially, sounding like April Wine, maybe due in small part to the later inclusion of Jim Clench in the band. But hey, all in all a great run, with most records going at least gold in the U.S.
Rating 4

## Bachman Turner Overdrive - Freeways (PolyGram '77)
With pretty much no one but mom listening anymore, BTO dive headlong into a podunk southern heat stagger, and you know what? It ain't half bad, if you forget BTO the power chord merchants, and accept their bizarre Outlaws with a disco Who dribbling alter-ego. A very odd record indeed, the boys (classic line-up intact), sapped of both their power and intellectual faculties, but blissful in defeat. There's some almost funny things going on here, like a delete bin poltergeist sticking Jethro Tull and Max Webster in male vocal section. I mean, Easy Groove must be a joke, and Can We All Come Together . . . what is that? Stealer's Wheel? Lighthouse? Chicago? Starcastle? or merely the Stones butchering reggae? If it's a kind of All You Need Is Love, well, stop singing and we'll put down our weapons. And as usual, every last vocal is out of tune all the time in that BTO manner we've all come to love. Creeps me out. Only eight songs (all but one written by Randy), and at least four actively want to throw it all away. So bad it's . . . well, you know the routine.
Rating 6

## Bachman Turner Overdrive - Street Action
(PolyGram '78)
Randy Bachman out (onto a solo album called Survivor, two records with Ironhorse and one with Union, then a way later solo called Any Road), his replacement being April Wine stalwart Jim Clench, who has very little effect, perhaps bringing the band back to the mainstream. Takes A Lot Of People is kinda springy, and Street Action is one of those archaic ZZ Top-clogged rock plods for which this band is known, laughed at, and loved. But most of the record is happy-go-lucky Who-derived strumming; plausible, possible, likeable and dimly assembled for the lowest common denominator. And self-produced to boot. Missing in action: '84's flubbed reunion album Rock 'n' Roll Nights.
Rating 6

## Bachman Turner Overdrive - The Anthology
(PolyGram '93)
Big, eminently useful box set that offers all sorts of quarks and curios between those ham-hock rockers all Canadians have heard a million times. Highlights: an early demo called The Letter which sounds like ancient ZZ Top, I Think You Better Slow Down, a long tall one that visits everyone from the Beatles to Heep to Skynyrd, seven tracks from the band's bloodiest record Not Fragile, and four "quad" mixes (remember quad?). Booklet's a good read too, which unravels a bit of the confusing Guess Who/Brave Belt origins of the band.
Rating 6

## Bad Brains - Quickness (Caroline '89)
Bad Brains are about the strangest hybrid of diametrically-opposed worlds I've ever seen. Four black dudes, three of which are impressively dreadlocked, slurring heavily Rastafarian dogma slash dream sequences o'er-top purist metal that thrashes then grinds with heart stopping oscillations between Anthrax and Prong, wildly off-melody both musically and vocally. Makes for a perplexing ride, but one that fails to stick due to all the sonic obtuseness and jammin' chaos gumming up the processing. Kinda doom-draped, kinda Arabic, kinda funky, and really heavy, Quickness tends to disorient more than it endears, however the downright sinister yet crucially disciplined riffery of Soul Craft, No Conditions, and Voyage Into Infinity break through the rubble providing at least tentative reference points. Beautifully independent, yet frustrating and opaque.
Rating 5

## Bad Brains - Rise (Sony '93)
Sounding less the alien hybrid than Quickness in its temporal context as an '89 release, D.C.'s Bad Brains storm back with a new vocalist in the walking manifesto of Israel Joseph I. Some semblance of melody takes seed here on what is essentially a similar sound to the band's last fully-fleshed wax. Rise is still a refreshing blend of technically adept metal and loopy funk that is both minimalist and complicated at once. Outside of two near identical reggae lopes and a couple of thrash hairballs, the rest rolls like disciplined and heavy Living Colour, a bit of rap, a bit of thwappin' bass, lots of dirty, two-ton riffs, left raw and electric amongst tight arrangements. Lyrically it's a lot of challenging oppression under the watchful guidance of Jah, making for another unusual trip from one of rock's stranger philosophical contraptions. Again, hard to fault such cutting edge material, and fans of the genre will definitely not be disappointed. Personally I'm tiring of this sound, and judging from subsequent sales, so are you.
Rating 7

## Bad Brains - God Of Love (Maverick/Warner '95)
The volatile H.R. is back in the fold, but not for long, being involved in a bizarre punch-up with management, that has put the band's future in question. Anyhow, God Of Love arrives on the silent wings of freedom, the band again building their entirely own, entirely psycho world religion, rasta mass through Marshalls. But Bad Brains have developed to the point of letting their hodge podge influences hang on song one at a time. So we get basically four things here, bizarre atonal thrash, bizarre atonal reggae, bizarre atonal smokey ballads, and a highly bizarre but extremely successful sort of stutter rhythm metal, supra-intelligent riffs cascading then stopping on a dimebag. Again, Bad Brains are a type of music unto themselves, and I think most fans gravitate heavily to some of their wildly divergent styles and not others. Me too, hence my middling grade.
Rating 7

## Bad Brains - Black Dots (Caroline '96)
This pile of shite represents the very first recordings of the Bad Brains, back in 1979 D.C. before the band became the psychedelic hardcore rasta metal freaks we've all grown to respect, back when the Pistols, The Clash and the Dead Boys were hot guano. But man, it takes a caring constitution to listen to the horrible sonics of this speedy basement affair, a mess of pogo optics somewhat on non-pro par with The Beatles' bottom-scraped Anthology recordings. More bad boot than Bad Brains, Black Dots at least offers an archive trip into early punk, and punk with a rasta Clashta bent at that. But like I say, this continuous and ragged live-in-the-basement set is simply a woeful buncha crap that's going to fool a lot of consumers if word doesn't get out. You've been warned.
Rating 2

## Bad Company - Bad Company (Swan Song '74)
Like a bodacious sonic wad of chewy toffee, Bad Company's trumpeted, chest-thumpeted debut pounced chart-bound, this supergroup of long-haired thugs set to enjoy their stint as blue collar redneck

whiteboys defining red, white and blue classic rock for decades to come. Smokey-lunged Paul Rodgers led the charge fresh from his successful and similar old band Free (*All Right Now*: a Bad Co. song if there ever was). Along for the clubcrawl were three other rock luminaries/journeymen, Mick Ralphs (Mott The Hoople!), Boz Burrell (King Crimson!), and Simon Kirke (also Free!), all conspiring to form a lunkhead blues rock behemoth that would out-turgid, thwack and bunk Humble Pie or The Faces or Savoy Brown at their own butt-shake game. Fame was instant, Bad Co.'s no-frills booz-blooz reinforced by the band's rep as flagship signing of Led Zep's Swan Song Records label. So the hits were everywhere, biggest being lead calling card *Can't Get Enough* (causing single-handedly The Black Crowes and Brother Cane), others less dumb-chorded, *Ready For Love*, *Bad Company* and *Seagull* doing more of a dusky Skynyrd salute than anything sturm and drang. Stupid, effortless, and trailerpark punchdrunk, **Bad Company** is like a dim old pal that knows well enough to keep his mouth shut, letting wisdom osmose through unselfconscious and dreadfully occasional action. Dontcha think?

Rating 7

## Bad Company - Straight Shooter (Swan Song '74)

And the luv affair continues, the world in the mid-'70s quite fascinated at British bulldogs exposing the rawk faults and defaults of a core American experience, namely good ol' barroom rock'n'roll, fans subconsciously assigning higher intelligence to British pedigree, putting down as white trash those from the US of A who might write exactly the same songs as Rodgers and crew. **Straight Shooter** walks the same rusty rails as the band's lucky, worn debut, while getting grittier and a little more low-down gutsy, writin'-wise. Everything's increasingly confident, more intense; with bigger hits (*Feel Like Makin' Love*), more arcane bloozy balladry (*Weep No More* and *Call On Me*), bigger suvvern melodrama (*Shooting Star*: pre-cursor to *Jack & Diane*), and generally a bolder sound (*Wild Fire Woman*). In fact, the record truly overachieves, while swimming murkily around a genre where achievement is frowned upon. Aah liner notes in the '70s: Ron Nevison, Peter Grant (the band's and Zep's manager, R.I.P. 1995), Hipgnosis. A blues rock combo can't lose, even though losing is the chasis of the blues.

Rating 8

## Bad Company - Run With The Pack (Swan Song '76)

Only three records in, Bad Co.'s ham-fisted Humble Pie in the face begins to wane, as Rodgers and Co. grow then wander to where juvenile blues rock invariably leads. While **Run With The Pack** (nice silver embossed cover art) allows us snickering classic rock closet dwellers to take these barbarians more seriously, the whiskey chuggin' fun of it all becomes sacrificed, a pensive sort of minimalist history lesson taking over. All the old styles are here (*Honey Child* ushers in the first of many rehash brownies), but new ones emerge, including a sort of well-earned funkiness that cloaks even obvious constructs like the title track in jaded tones. However the real gems are the forays into pop and balladry; the upbeat *Silver Blue & Gold*, the almost Zen-like gospel of *Do Right By Your Woman* and *Simple Man* (nice companion piece to the beautiful Skynyrd tune of the same name), sounding peaceful, worn-out and wise like old retro rock should. But isn't failing and feeling it what the blues is all about?

Rating 8

## Bad Company - Burnin' Sky (Swan Song '76)

Bad Co.'s fatman recording values increasingly become a thing of the past, as **Burnin' Sky** sports the brightest drum sound yet. Still, performances barely pulse, all genres from gentle-picked ballads to the boys' pat-ented boom rock, thudding along to the Cozy Powell-like simplicity of Simon Kirke's heavy hand. But again, the product mix is about the same (although Mick Ralphs' guitar licks become tastier and more intrusive); spanning funk, southern rock, honky tonk, plus a couple o' BTO-dulled hard rock hamsters, designed to give the band the next fat, stupid and lazy radio hit. And like the Stones, you just kind of grow with the band at their slowpoke pace, revelling in an uneventful but resonating blues vocabulary, tapped but never brilliantly plundered; checking in, not all that intently to a comforting old sound that never claims to be more than it is. Note: the band's first relative bust at the box office.

Rating 7

## Bad Company - Desolation Angels (Swan Song '79)

Kind of a commercial and creative bright spot in Bad Company's declining fortunes, **Desolation Angels** was all affirmation and ascendance, from the fancy pants Hipgnosis artwork (which nevertheless retains the band's penchant for austere, moody graphics), through punchy hit single *rock'n'roll Fantasy* and the shimmery, almost Pagey wonderment of *Crazy Circles*. Everything spoke up on this record. The heavy tracks approached a low form of metal (fave: *Evil Wind*), and the ballads washed ashore exquisitely. But more than any specifics, **Desolation Angels** felt like a winner, like a tasty platter by one of rock's royalty. Still, the product mix persisted, while all seemed newer and separate from the foggy records before it (parallel experience: BÖC's **Mirrors**), like the band was ready to enter the '80s awake and vigorous, while remaining committed to their well-soaked and besotted roots rock vocabulary, a sentiment of copacetic hybrid perhaps best portrayed by minor, almost self-deprecating hit *Rhythm Machine*, which bridged disco, funk, new wave and southern rock like (egad!) Robert Palmer. Note: all records to this point went gold, with **Run With The Pack** and **Desolation Angels** going platinum.

Rating 8

## Bad Company - Rough Diamonds (Swan Song '82)

**Rough Diamonds**, die-cut, **The Final Cut** . . . any way you dice it, this one is the band's last gaspin' drained batteries slog through jadedness and deflatedness. Combine a disco-tinged funk with pop and depression (see the butt-end of Sweet), and this is the sort of record that slinks from darkened doorways. Probably the first Bad Co. that veers decidedly from that ol' tried tested and true formula, **Rough Diamonds** picks a directive that cloys, evoking a wasteland of broken coken dreams; a stab in the dark, big rock stars phoning it in. Welcome to the **Hotel California**, a spent junkyard of automatic r+b, lives without purpose, lives perpetuated just barely through the blood of old sounds. Sum verdict: familiar, smooth, my kind of soul music, even though no kind would suit me just fine. A **7** to a rocking chair observant like me, but hey, I guess I gotta grade responsibly. Exit Paul Rodgers for a life of misfires, so many that by the mid-'90s, he'd become a bit of a kicking post. Plus Mick Ralphs would deem it necessary to craft a stumbling, bumbling solo excursion in '84 called **Take This**.

Rating 6

## Bad Company - Fame And Fortune (Atlantic '86)

Just a sad cash-in on a pleasing enough past, **Fame And Fortune** features Nuge guy Brian Howe splitting the difference between Lou Gramm and the departed Paul Rodgers, in creation of a band that is an unexciting hybrid between, you guessed it, Foreigner and a once Bad Company. So it's really just a thumping lunkhead of an AOR record, rife with dated keyboards and dated clichés, while technically heavier than most Bad Co. rounders from the pre-corruption '70s. And that's the

41

main point here, this simmer cycle, warm water rendition of a band (that never really embraced creativity anyways), moreso stuck in a post-innocence malaise than actively getting stoopider. It's years later and you can never go back. Fans demand more, and most bands are delivering or at least making the attempt. This one just adds the '80s tricks, the big label bigshot sound, while going nowhere interesting writing-wise, just obliterating a tradition built of thick gluey songs with no pretense. Could have just as easily been a bum Nugent or Bryan Adams record really.

Rating                                                                 4

## Bad Company - Dangerous Age    (Atlantic '88)

Hmm, I wonder if the kid on the cover is the baby from Van Halen's 1984 four years later. Whatever the case, nothing on this record smokes, the band (officially just a very old looking trio at this point) thump-plodding through a raft of castaways resembling pretty much any of the hurly burly college football tunes on the last couple of regular guy rounders. Hand me that wrench, will ya?

Rating                                                                 4

## Bad Company - Holy Water    (Atlantic '90)

More of the same, which includes more of a transition into a generic stadium rock sound, Howe (with producer Terry Thomas) being chief songwriter, no old fogies gathering up the muster to interfere, defend and otherwise craft a dumb car toon like the bellbottom days of yore. And it's not like the band is completely stiffing with the formula, these cheezefests always belching up a hit or two (see If You Needed Somebody, then gag. I can picture Gene and Paul singing this tool on stools.). Again, quite guitar-adorned, in a drivelly '80s hair band, i.e. Cinderella doing retro, sort of way.

Rating                                                                 4

## Bad Company - Company Of Strangers    (eastwest '95)

Surprise, surprise, Bad Company become a company of strangers, and hopefully strangers not for long, adding a guitarist (long-time satellite member Dave "Bucket" Colwell) to trade with Mick, adding Rick Wills from Foreigner on bass and adopting ruff 'n' ready Rodgers-alike Robert Hart on vocals, all gelling for a bit of back-ratchet on four post-Rodgers records of modern excess. Still, you can never go back, fan and band alike locked in a Caught 22 gyre of nostalgia and contextual reminiscence that perhaps clouds accurate judgment of old records and old sounds. So Company Of Strangers is what we get; a bluesy, close record, eschewing all stadium stomp for various mid to low cycle Bad Company conventions, richly produced but no chrome-plated crap stuck on, left to sink or swim in the harsh light of the '90s. Styles range from laid back funk to laid back blues rock to ballads infused by the blues, ballads that are a little uncomfortably too close to new country. Hart's vocals are a kick to listen to though, the man making much better use of his wild west voice than Paul Rodgers ever did. So chalk this one up as a nice approach by a solid, worthy team. If only the songs were a little more risky and brisk.

Rating                                                                 7

## Bad 4 Good - Refugee    (Interscope/Warner '92)

2 bad these guys were forever branded a gimmick band, gimmick being that the boys in the band were in fact just that, boys; not unlike '95's entry Silverchair, yet even younger if you can believe it, barely brushing the mid-teen mark (the band shots verge on kiddie porn). But the record goes much farther than grade school, given that Steve Vai produces the thing, also writing most of the album in the over-the-top, shredking spirit of the age he was slurping up at the time. Steve makes good use of the band's choirboy harmonies, and leaves no facet of their performance compro-

mised. What results is a corporate hard rock record with charm; sly little tricks all over the place, designed to undercut the false pretense of hair band metal. Great ballads, too, especially Nothin' Great About A Heartache. Added gem: lead track Nineteen, which is of course the Phil Lynott solo toon offered in various permutations over the years.

Rating                                                                 7

## Badlands - Badlands    (Atlantic '89)

Wence upon a thyme, Jake E. Lee was just another frightening fret burner under the tyrannical tutelage of the Oz man. Badlands shatters the past and amplifies the scorching magic of a man I consider to be one of the best guitarists of all time; soulful, technically effortless, creative beyond words. Combine Lee's blinding (bad joke: Jake's eyesight is poor to the point of rendering him legally blind) axe acrobatics with the distressingly perfect croon of Ray Gillen, and you have a potent blues metal force, and one of my favourite bands ever, an act of metallic honesty I just can't rave enough about. Badlands reminds me of the high I felt jamming in basements all over my hometown, an unforgettable live rush; open, loud, surrounded by drums. Lee's riffs just kill, yet entirely without malice, charging with an uninhibited free-burning energy and love of guitar on what is more a sensitive, bluesy hard rock record than all-out metal; '70s-based, Zep and Purple-shaded, open and so devastatingly pure, as if this was a resolute struggle for our souls. Every last second of this record breathes fire, driven by the awe-inspiring rhythm section of Greg Chaisson and Eric Singer, while Gillen and Lee flare in tandem through songs borne of complex and intelligent influences both recent and ten, twenty, thirty years old; lots of mammoth bluesiness transformed by an ultimately modern metallic pair of minds. About as trustworthy a 10 I can think of, Badlands is consummate metal truth, burning free with the brilliant assimilation of all that came before, slapped down with an urgency borne of a steely determination to rock now and rock loud. Cassette features added track Ball & Chain, weak for its strangely out-of-tune quality.

Rating                                                                10

## Badlands - Voodoo Highway    (Atlantic '91)

Jake 'n' Ray take their formidable arsenal to daunting new levels on this, the follow-up to one searing, unstoppable debut, Badlands. Voodoo Highway is thankfully similar, while stretching into even bluesier, funkier, more historically academic terrain, boasting the same uncommon hearty pride, yet easing the throttle away from the debut's Whitesnake-like overtones (blowing away each and every Whitesnake record, I might add), venturing down, well, a psychological voodoo highway, shimmering with a dull heat wafting off nearby swamps. Rocking with expansive brilliance, structures simply broil and breathe, while Lee and Gillen fill the trough with doses of hundred year old blues baggage. Classics abound, but standouts would include the fiercely carnivorous Soul Stealer, lead-off groove rocker The Last Time, which displays Lee's command of nuance splendidly, James Taylor's Fire And Rain, where Gillen proceeds to shame every vocalist on the planet, and the engaging 3 Day Funk, whose chorus enters the gates of Heaven, spurs gently strafing the clouds. Out of all the disappointing commercial situations to befall rockers over the years, Badlands lack of recognition depresses me the most. Theirs was a band so sincere and so mercilessly capable within the intense realms of their chosen complex language, I can't believe the critical community didn't send the necessary word to hoist the poor sales of Badlands and Voodoo Highway. Sad, but great talent often goes un-noticed, and Badlands is one of the more tragic examples to my mind. So join me punters, in lifting a

pint to the boys in the band, will ya?... especially Mister Ray Gillen, dead December 1, '93, presumably from complications due to AIDS, although offical word was stomach cancer. Update: Sun Red Sun record out in '95 (see review) and a lost Badlands record ready for release in '96.
Rating                                                          10

## Bad Lizard - Power Of Destruction    (Roadrunner '85)
What more can you say about a band called Bad Lizard? Not much, except that it's obvious we aren't dealing with Anglo-Saxons here. Looks like Belgium is home for these down-the-middle head bangers, who mix it up to the extent of Pretty Maids or Tokyo Blade, or maybe even traces of Saxon, with nowhere near the lowest common magnetism quotient of any of the above. Nope, it's all just fists and headbands here, with little in the way of personal wit and charm to cut through the waftations of European metal that pounded ashore each day in the mid-'80s.
Rating                                                           4

## Bad Moon Rising - Bad Moon Rising    (Alfa Burnette '93)
Really, I'm amazed this kind of male root-hog in high skool rock still sees the light of day, **Bad Moon Rising** sounding like a deserved-to-be deleted commercial hard rock record without its beauty sleep. Song after turgid song trots out the hair metal clichés like a bargain basement Dokken, over scratchy bothersome production values that remind me of '90s AOR bretheren Eyewitness. Anyway, to quote the immortal Wayne, I laughed, I cried, I hurled.
Rating                                                           3

## Bad Moon Rising - Blood    (Alfa Burnette '94)
Mack is back in the producer's throne for record #2, still toying with the very uncharacteristic midrangey itch fer sound that helped destroy the band's debut. Now the songs are less the party platter, more low-munching on moody cheese, y'know, like heavier Whitesnake from fully ten years ago, for crying in a bucket! Yeah, they've branched out, but it's still an auto-walk through phoned-in metal conventions. I hope traditional metal fans don't just jump on any ol' wagon-band that stays locked in the '80s, because some of it stinks.
Rating                                                           4

## Bad Religion - Recipe For Hate    (Epitaph '93)
Nasty old punk rockers who are inching mainstream, Bad Religion dish out a sort of rudimentary melodic punk rock that combines the harmonies and hellbillies of X and the pressing, well-voiced mandate of The Clash to fiery effect. Next ace is the smooth and sympathetic lead vocal work, a refreshing unexpected croon over such a basic rock romp, a churning dish of zippy old-style punk with windmill strumming and barrelhouse drumming, a beat that gets samey and tiring after awhile. But an odd hybrid, soggy and British-like with a sort of worldly flavour. Great album cover too. The first well-distributed record of the band's grim, seven record career so far.
Rating                                                           7

## Bad Religion - Stranger Than Fiction    (Atlantic '94)
Epitaph boss Greg Graffin must be spending too much time counting his Offspring profits to write a compelling record, **Stranger Than Fiction** simply rehashing their **Recipe For Hate**, but with tangibly worse production (from Andy Wallace) and dull, simplistic '90s punk riffing, proving once again that there is no substance to this punk revival. Still a nice rainy British tarnish to the thing, but really stupid and stiff musically, although Bad Religion's lyrics are still a good read.
Rating                                                           6

## Bad Religion - The Gray Race    (Atlantic '96)
As much as the whole idea of '90s punk is a joke, Bad Religion is still your best bet, even as this articulate record is getting bad reviews for regurgitating musical ideas, those same brisk beats, those same lazy two-tone power chords. But guess what? That's all punk is these days, pretty well the most boring music imaginable, a genre based on a rigid refusal of musical ideas. If you're going to pick on Bad Religion (and yes they are in a rut, but that's punk), you might as well trash Rancid and NOFX too, because they're all dead-predictable and chops-void. Anyways, if you're going to listen to punk, you may as well get provocative packaging, Greg Graffin's sonorous, sombre vocals, and a set of lyrics that is occasionally pompous, but usually just chillingly relevant and poetic, Graffin's long-embattled, nine-record-deep punk career doing him good stead in reporting society's moral degeneration.
Rating                                                           7

## Bad Seed - Bad Seed    (Attic/Rockworld '95)
Imagine if you will, a pop-dusted Crowbar or Biohazard record with hints of Trouble-some doom and Nirvana alterno-savvy. This is where Bad Seed lives, the band's debut record living the '70s through the '90s, just like the cover art's reworking of classic '70s comedy record **Big Bambu** from Cheech & Chong. Convolutedly the product of the New York thrash scene, Bad Seed exhibit their taste and veteran skills in the record's pacing and variety, getting really heavy, sublimely catchy and even acoustically challenged throughout the record's easy-drinking brew. Lots of lyrics, lots of smart but unflashy lyrics. A double decker sandwich o' metal fun.
Rating                                                           8

## Bakers Pink - Bakers Pink    (Sony '93)
Formerly The Front, Bakers Pink shift to a sort of delicate alternative rock, mixing punchy funk monsters à la Jane's Addiction with droopy hippy ballads (some approximating the Beatles), all sterling recorded and well-planned, undermining the tender but slightly psychedelic vibe the band was shooting for. Quite an enjoyable, if somewhat unaggressive piece of work, this is the kind of record that could have been misunderstood into hatching smash singles (like Candlebox or a very different band, Offspring). But it didn't happen and the record stiffed. Simply put, a non-believable mix of the exotic and the mainstream.
Rating                                                           6

## Balaam & The Angel - The Greatest Story Ever Told    (Virgin '86)
The signal sent from across the Atlantic offered no encouragement, Balaam being more or less panned as a commercial contraption, a dull alloy of goth, pop and hard rock, skirting Sisters Of Mercy and Mission terrain, yet with less allegiance to the tenets of black. Sort of a half-baked, chimey, and considerably wimpy take on **Love**-era Cult, **The Greatest Story Ever Told** couldn't be farther from the truth. Justly ignored and/or reviled.
Rating                                                           2

## Balaam And The Angel - Days Of Madness    (Virgin '89)
Massive improvement for the three Morris' + 1, but the standing complaint remains the vocal performance of bassist Mark Morris, who keeps it fairly tight to his conservative range while still risking flats and sharps just often enough to draw attention away from already unsteady riffery. A beefing up of the axes tends to mask some of the inexpressive safeness, high point being the chorus of I Took A Little, the rumbling textures of the AC/DC-ish Two Days Of Madness, and the cool-riffed Did You Fall (Or Were You Pushed?). Yes, without a

doubt, this confusing and somewhat irritating entity is now a heavy metal band, yet one doomed to pay its dues unlearning a botched past, **Days Of Madness** sounding more like the hopeful debut of any uninteresting California combo luckily tapped into a chunky contract. Average toons tranquilized by an el boring job at the knobs.
Rating      5

## Rob Balducci - Balance   (Circumstantial '95)

The key to these instrumental albums (particularly shredmaster guitar demonstrations) appealing to more than the dreamworld of virtuoso wannabees, is to zone in on melody, tonal shading and song structure, amidst the expressed purpose, which is usually a splayed display of technical prowess. On this sparkling if only mildly innovative debut, Rob Balducci (like Gary Hoey and Joe Satriani before him), has understood and embraced this ethic, delivering an earfest of accessible tunefulness ranging from ballads to mood pieces to organ-driven full-tilt boogie, accessible that is if you give a damn (which I don't). Basically shred that doesn't overtax the senses; the first step towards any shot at mass appeal.
Rating      5

## Russ Ballard - Barnet Dogs   (Epic '79)

Ballard's known more as a tunesmith to the stars plus the not so lofty, and most of his records ride a generic and general rock everywhereness that belies inclusion in this Book of the Loud, but **Barnet Dogs** is his heaviest, waxing eloquently and whimsically like a golden years Derringer disc, full of catchy hard rock (*Rene Didn't Do It, It's Too Late* and minor hit *On The Rebound*) plus occasional metal, most notably *Riding With The Angels*, sent through the crisper on Samson's obliterating **Shock Tactics**. A nice, honest piece of unimposing, almost bashful guitar rock from a Roy Orbison-lookalike always left standing at the altar.
Rating      8

## Russ Ballard - Into The Fire   (Epic '80)

Figured I'd throw this one in here (leaving out softer projects like '78's **At The Third Stroke** and '85's **The Fire Still Burns**), **Into The Fire** being a less aggressive rehash of nostalgic fave **Barnet Dogs**, but a zippy, guitarfest all the same, something akin to boisterous Journey. But it's almost a track for track, good cop, bad cop thing, with the tunes here always losing, even if Ballard's enthusiasm shines through, songs having that new wavey bounce, that hard-edged, post-punk dance drive, dance rock still allowed to have guitars back in 1980. Fave: melodramatic arch-Ballard single *Rock & Roll Lover*.
Rating      6

## The Bambi Slam - The Bambi Slam   (WEA '88)

A lacklustre one man snooze crooze by one Ray Fielden, **The Bambi Slam** sucks wind due to blocky, stumbling erectiles, flat, whispery vocals, and either a bad but loud drum machine or ludicrously bad drumming; I think the former. Definitely a hard rock record with an underground sneer, the aforementioned, opaquely-rendered negatives hinder attempts at joyful assimilation. Ray needs collaborators real bad.
Rating      2

## Bang - Bang   (Capitol '71)

Again, we're talking holy grails of fledgling metal magic here (see Sir Lord Baltimore), Bang slouching onto the metal scene with three quite different records, which is what everybody in the '70s seemed to be about. This debut is widely considered the best (i.e. among Bang's fanbase of a dozen or so incontinent hippy headbangers), a sort of sickly anemic Sabbath trudge with excellent screechy, Ozzy Byron vocals, and handicapped

drums, more like traps (see Blue Öyster Cult's black and white era). So droopy, '60s-infected bell-bottom power chorders like *Lions, Christians, The Queen*, and *Future Shock* build up a sorry sounding mound of metal which then gets eroded by the weak production and weaker percussion. I mean, sorry to rain on nerdy collectors' parades, but after all, we already had Deep Purple, Sabbath, Budgie and Heep, so this doesn't really break a lot of new ground. Love that biker guitar sound though. That's one lo-fi convention alterno-geeks have never been able to revive and reproduce.
Rating      7

## Bang - Mother/Bow To The King   (Capitol '72)

Bang have evolved from a wrench-faced pre-metal band into something more akin to James Gang or Edgar Winter, taking trajectory from Hendrix through funk and southern rock, while occasionally visiting their duh, Sabbath power hour. Which makes this a fine, old, aged and wise guitar romp, lots of fills, licks and riffs, balanced by acoustic bits, all pleasantly recorded with more bass and greater arrangement than the doomier but deadlier debut. Side one's called **Mother**, side two, **Bow To The King**, but there's really no discernible difference in each's grab bag of unshaven unhewn rock styles. Contains a cover of the Guess Who's *No Sugar Tonight*. And speaking of covers, this one's a larf and a half, the trio looking pretty rawkin', what with that cape and sinister footwear.
Rating      6

## Bang - Music   (Capitol '73)

Officially down to a two-piece consisting of Frank Ferrara and Frank Gilcken, Bang snuff it with this unloved swansong, going for more of a glammy T. Rex sound with Beatles, flouncy little pop numbers, still bits of hair-on-chest guitar, but mostly ditzy, funtime drivel. Nice pre-hair band photo on the back, surrounded by a sea of gaudy yellow. Yuk.
Rating      3

## Bang Tango - Psycho Cafe   (MCA '89)

Promising debut from Hollyrockers with a difference, **Psycho Cafe** pumps along more conventionally than the funky follow-up, but still comes up with the hooks and excitement, in lead single *Someone Like You* and the thwappin' *Do What You're Told*. Unfortunately, Joe Lesté's Billy Idol-ish, often strained vocals are a bit of a distraction as is the noisy lack of tightness, on what are generally solid tunes. That word "frustrating" rears its head again, as this premiere succeeds in whetting an appetite more for a follow-up than the rest of itself.
Rating      6

## Bang Tango - Live Injection   (World Of Hurt '89)

The hopelessly indie **Live Injection** finds these mighty fine strut rockers blowing through six tracks in search of stardom, early in their unsatisfied career. The short biz: 27 minutes, two tracks from the debut, a cover of Hanoi Rocks' *Futurama* (bad choice: cold fish of a song), three non-LP tunes right up the band's thick funk metal alley, full lyrics, and a Joe Lesté in regal rock peacock form.
Rating      6

## Bang Tango - Dancin' On Coals   (MCA '91)

Valiantly vibrant but silken smooth funk metal from an under-rated, under-marketed band, sufficiently press-exposed yet always one step behind the pack, **Dancin' On Coals** is an engaging, bass-driven work, dressed with horns and overall dynamic, fueled by the multi-dimensional and greatly improved pipes of Joe Lesté. Nowhere near shackled to the tenets of metal, **Dancin' On Coals** throbs with an angled, concise funkiness, most graciously evidenced on melodic builder *Emotions In Gear* and the wah magic of *Big Line*;

very personable, very rich in melody and depth. Let's hope these spiritual bastard sons of **Get Your Wings** and L.A. Guns get the critical mass they deserve, 'cos this record's studded with a certain daring form of radio hit; smart, punchy rhythmic rock, brave enough to let structures breathe. Sadly overlooked but well worth an open-minded spin, Bang Tango's second reveals a band tightly focused to an artistic ethic, with talent to match.

Rating     8

## Bang Tango - Love After Death    (Music For Nations '94)

Open call-to-arms *New Generation* kinda rings hollow when the major deal has packed up and moved onto Silverchair and Bush, not to mention the raspy fact that Joe Lesté's vocals have hit the panic button, absolutely hoarse as he struggles to keep his funk metal machine on the highest possible horse. But I kinda like the down-wound acoustic break to *Live On The Moon*, and other tunes here achieve the boisterous chest-thump of the band's past work. Unfortunately, corporate rock is just rock without the corporate, which means that when the smell of money has left the building, the creaks and cracks in the confidence become caverns.

Rating     7

## Baphomet - The Dead Shall Inherit
(Peaceville/Caroline '92)

Buffalo's home for this distressed grindcore combo, who combine crushing death structures (mostly half-time double bass; few blastbeats), and all-the-way adenoidal vocal scrapes, sub-cycle, totally unintelligible. Lyrically tame compared with regional big fish Cannibal Corpse but better, heavier "music."

Rating     6

## Barbie Bones - Brake For Nobody    (Restless '90)

Irascible pop metal seen through Norwegian eyes, **Brake For Nobody** piles all sorts of electronic quirks, buzzes and keyboards onto a goodly-natured punk rock rambuction. Very weird, quite smart and enjoyable, sorta Cheap Trick meets Nine Inch Nails; power chords, Star Treknology and hooks laying claim to virgin turf really, lone partner perhaps being the utterly charming T-Ride. Whimsical but solid lyrics, production in spades, and an enthusiastically exercised imagination: it's all here. Maybe a bit stripped-down with respect to guitars, but still very inspired.

Rating     7

## Barkmarket - Lardroom    (American '95)

Following on the heels of the band's full-length debut **Gimmick**, this short, smart, sharp five track EP establishes Barkmarket as noisemakers with charm, combining Helmet or Quicksand-like mechanics with Wire, NIN without the industrial, and solid songskills. Heartwrenched vocals, Lemmy-bass and an urge to open architecture songs gel nicely, making something tuneful out of each divergent track, some laid-back, some explosive, and one called *Pushin' Air*, wholly based on distortion. **Lardroom** does what EPs are designed for, making the listener focus attention on a few strong tracks (while offering poor value). But a second function is also well-served: whetting the appetite for the impending full-length.

Rating     7

## Barkmarket - L Ron    (American '96)

. . . and **L Ron** delivers on **Lardroom**'s modest promise, expanding and expunging the band's spongy nicotine-stained uber-blues, arriving at the enigmatic elegance of Clutch, while crossing into the court of the Crimson King with all those convoluted dino-riffs. Truly alternative, truly at the edge of groovy, groovy music, Barkmarket have built a dense, moderately noisy piece of thumper lumber, a sound sculpture full of bash and

bass, songs that breathe big and then collapse. Hints of Primus, hints of Fugazi, hints of Prick but just a whole lot of steamrolled hijinx. Congrats be in order, for this is art of a most heinous nature.

Rating     8

## Baron Rojo - Larga Vita Al Rock And Roll    (Est. '81)

Probably the biggest metal band from Spain, Baron Rojo are of limited value—extremely limited value—to me personally, lyrics being in the band's mother tongue. This scruffy release, however uneven as it is, hides a good three or four fiercely rowdy AC/DC-style cuts with the added advantage of a kick-ass recording to set aflame the band's complex set of influences. Actually played it a fair bit at the time (mid '80s) as there wasn't much else around for competition.

Rating     4

## Baron Rojo - Metalmorphosis    (Chapa '83)

Many bands outside traditional metal markets seem to evoke a foreign flavour to their sound that either grossly annoys (Japan) or absolutely amazes, the latter of which is the case with five or six bizarre riffs on this semi-opus, Baron Rojo's best record on strength of music alone. Listening to **Metalmorphosis** leaves me with the same frustration I found with France's Warning's first record. Both are classic metal albums, skirting pillar-of-granite traditions spanning Priest, Purple, and blues rock, yet sung in the band's mother tongue, greatly diminishing the payoff for the Anglo punter. And to add insult to injury, both have great recordings; **Warning**'s, searing and violent, this one, muscular and full range. Go figure. I guess we Westerners can't hog it all.

Rating     6

## Baron Rojo - Volumen Brutal    (Mausoleum Est. '85)

A somewhat experimental cross between **Larga Vita Al Rock And Roll** and **Metalmorphosis**, **Volumen Brutal** emits a new urgency and roughshod grit around Baron Rojo's regal display. As usual, classy and eccentric riffs are the order of the day on this record which I owned in Spanish eight years ago, and now own in its "original English version" (which is not a heaping improvement due to hasty, fey attempts at enunciation). Still a thoroughly top-notch power release, exuding veteran confidence.

Rating .     8

## Bathory - Bathory    (Black Mark '84)

True to Quorthon's original vision of combining the music of Motörhead with the lyrics of Black Sabbath, Sweden's Bathory was belched loose upon the land, overextending and breaking on both fronts. Even though this 26 minutes blight of sound strived to be the leading edge of repellent extreme, it's amazing to hear how musical it is versus the black-hearted Norwegian acts that would cite Quorthon as a main influence. Nice voice on our boy, a kind of drooling anti-social snarl, as each track briskly trashes along, a thin, peeling wall of sound, a cruel joke but a historically poignant one. Note: for those who don't know, Bathory really *is* Quorthon, any other members being little more than inconsequential hired guns, named virtually to make this non-touring entity seem more like a band.

Rating     4

## Bathory - The Return    (Black Mark '85)

A putrid, Hellhammered belch of black smoke buries **The Return** (after a shakier cheap debut) by one orificial Bathory, pitting them in the same shallow grave as Possessed and Venom and few others. As precursors to the most thrashiest of grindcores, Bathory are of valid historical value, but smile as I may, in no way is this true "vacuum cleaner with drums" cack metal my bag. Why does it breathe? Well, apparently Quorthon wanted to reproduce "Hell on record", and with all the new studio wizardry at his hands, and a deepening interest in Satanism, I guess this is as close as it gets. To this day, one of Quorthon's fave Bathory records, along with the more panoramic **Blood Fire Death**, the last of the balls-out thrashers.

Rating 4

## Bathory - Under The Sign Of The Black Mark
(Black Mark '87)

Quorthon curses the day this record was made (by far his least favourite), due to the over-use of an overly fuzzy guitar effect popular at the time, making this sound a bit like British buffoon bards Warfare. But it doesn't much matter, this being a hard record to love by any measure, thick with all sorts of evil chemical noises, muddy, crackling drums (a machine again?), and big burning piles of the band's most unlistenable thrash to date. Lyrics are making the switch to Norse mythological themes (with Call From The Grave throwing in an out-of-place prayer to God!), even if Quorthon is mixing his Christian metaphors with his Viking metaphors, resulting in a Keystone Kop storyline where God, Satan and fallen Viking heroes all seem to be on a cross-cultural collision course, that on a mythological level, was never considered to have happened, but on a flesh and blood level, really did, with the forced arrival of Christianity. Anyhow, the sum sonic total of this gooey train wreck of snowy wattage is very similar to today's Norwegian thrash, really sanctifying Quorthon as the second coming of Odin, Burzum et al. to usher in the third.

Rating 3

## Bathory - Blood Fire Death (Black Mark '88)

The first full-blown Norsefest arrives, an isolated and singular Quorthon immersing himself in his new preoccupation with a future Viking war with the heavens, Bathory still cranking a putrid, trash thrash din, albeit with better songs (like better Venom). Musically, there's a lot more going on, and vocally, the man's belch is becoming less human. Just one intense death ray of traditional breakneck frostcore, riffs getting slightly more intricate, recording values sicker in different ways, Quorthon slogging on until the Northern battle is won.

Rating 4

## Bathory - Hammerheart (Black Mark '90)

Wot is this? Gently lapping waves, pleasant strumming, soulful crooning . . . as eleven minute epic Shores In Flames begins, soon breaking into big, smelly, chopping Manowar-type chords. Thusly **Hammerheart** commences, colossal dirt-clogged Viking metal, slowly but resolutely setting sail to pillage distant lands. Quorthon has hatched quite the feast for the gods here, his particular visions of grandeur filled over with layers of chanting, battle effects, birds, and even barking dogs, as he wisely keeps the mix trashed like the villages licked by Odin's flames. It's pretty funny, 'cos for the first time you can really hear Quorthon's thick accent, as he kind of swims awkwardly through his lyrics. But such mortal pettiness is of no concern, **Hammerheart** blasted in a blasphemous crucible, wafting forth pounding tide tales of exotic ancient Scandinavian ritual, delivered steadily, steadfast, repetitive and mesmerized. But the real reason I like it it is that it sounds like really wasted, fuzz bass-bonkers Manowar.

Rating 8

## Bathory - Twilight Of The Gods (Black Mark '91)

The second (and so far last) of Quorthon's "Viking" records, **Twilight** is a stunning departure from the unlistenable Satani-thrash for which Bathory is most renowned, and even a much softer affair than **Hammerheart**. The elusive one himself calls this phase "Manowar-type shit", which is pretty accurate, **Twilight** sounding like mellow, boring Manowar, long intros, slow acoustic stuff with boomy drums, Hell, even one of those fluttery bass solos. Quorthon sez he arrived at these sorts of themes once he discovered that Christianity and thus Satanism was all fake, the Norse mythology stuff being an attempt to get back to his nationalist roots. And really, the record works, sounding very dark, progressive and purely listenable, a true originator and proponent of a style that would come to ugly head with the Norwegian black metal bands of the mid-'90s.

Rating 7

## Bathory - Jubileum Volume I (Black Mark '94)

Part One of this well-done two part compilation plows through 72 minutes of vintage carnage Bathory tunage, displaying the band as the true contemporaries of Venom with their '83 and '84 out-takes. But the band would move on, becoming leaders in early thrash, even early originators of the atmospheric, and dare I say slow, epic sound that is rifling through death today, especially with the Nordic set. Four rarities, full lyrics, sum total of the record somewhat twistedly enjoyable in its slight wackiness, especially come vocal time.

Rating 6

## Bathory - Jubileum Volume II (Black Mark '93)

Best of Bathwater Part II is simply more of the same, once more cherry-picking tracks from all eras, this time offering three rarities, all again recalling Venom, but moreso indicative of Quorthon's aforementioned creed to fuse "the music of Motörhead with the lyrics of Black Sabbath." Also of note, his '83 Die In Fire demo sounds better than a few of his official records released years later.

Rating 6

## Bathory - Requiem (Black Mark '94)

The time seems right for a Bathory album, don't it? Much pilloried in the past, Quorthon and his macabre crew have slowly won me over, **Requiem** being a joyful record of blackness, quite musical in a Slayerish, thankfully '80s sort of way, which makes sense, given that the slab was actually recorded three years back, between **Hammerheart** and the last real album **Twilight Of The Gods**. The band knows how to punk it up, they know how to mosh, and they don't mind getting into a new headspace, having helped invent thrashin' black fumes so many awful records ago. Compared to what's spewed all over the recent retrospective, this stuff's a banging clanging funfest of heinous crimes to behold. Confuses and smokescreens nicely Bathory's sense of inverted time, especially when contrasted with Quorthon's much-maligned solo record, not to mention the still older **Blood On Ice** full-length released in '96.

Rating 7

## Bathory - Octagon (Black Mark '95)

And now the boldest record yet, as Bathory finds an upscale type of violence, by attacking new themes and new battle-ready riffs, all with a sense of alcohol that their previous alien, bizarre anti-everything-philosophy couldn't hope for. **Octagon**'s largest leap comes with Quorthon's raging lyrics (delivered with less growl), the man chewing up politics, war, psychos, the environment, and all things hateful with gallons of venom, over a soundtrack that is bruising beyond belief. Finally, Bathory is more than a novelty; finally their heaviness achieves crush, groove and deliberate pounding through an unabashed embrace of tried and true Heavy Metal. The band's **Reign In Blood**, for all the same reasons, namely the perfect mix of thrash, chaos and might. I mean, you know changes are in the wind when the band covers Deuce (note: Quorthon

began his demonic career in a Kiss cover band called KYSS.)
Rating **8**

## Bathory - Blood On Ice (Black Mark '96)

**Blood On Ice** is the piece-meal, shelved, dusted, tinkered with, and finally valiantly revived record Quorthon worked on '88, '89-ish, between **Blood Fire Death** and **Hammerheart**, giving it a swift kick in the tracks in mid-'95, mixing it in February '96, delivering it ninety days later for your lusty Viking pleasure. And it's a pretty hefty, lofty affair, beginning with the booklet, which offers five crammed pages of background narrative (part of a Bathory book the guy's working on), plus intro storylines fleshing out each track's lyrics. Musically it's a thick hammered brew, lots of almost cinematic effects, great (well, good!) singing, neato acoustic respites, and a few of Bathory's most lip-smacking tracks like *One Eyed Old Man*, *Gods Of Thunder Of Wind And Of Rain*, and *The Sword*, which rumbles crush for crush like Manowar's *Blood Of My Enemies*. I for one dig it dude, finding this pillaging epic Viking phase of the band much more palatable and plain entertaining than their wild 'n' evil fast blosh. Mix-wise, it's a bit blocky and unforgiving, but hey, it sounds more like a choice than a mistake or product of limitation, the whole phantasia-tale pounding like those thundering hooves on slo-mo, knarly, ski-able powder swirling in the pre-dawn, until the splashing blood of the vanquished makes it more like, uh, spring skiing I guess.
Rating **8**

## Baton Rouge - Baton Rouge (Eastwest '91)

This standard corporate metal release made zero waves when it showed up on the racks, and for good reason. Rough blues-metal vocals, aseptic recording values, and too much floaty wimp rock are the order of the day on this vaguely White Metal-looking release. Lead cut *Slave To The Rhythm* is kinda hot and funky but all degenerates into a morass of boring personal weakness by album's end.
Rating **3**

## Battleaxe - Burn This Town (Est. '83)

British dirt rock goes down the drain on this early headbanging error, built to cash in before talent is in place and behaving. Bad mix to boot, as if anybody would care enough to dress this up with love.
Rating **3**

## Battleaxe - Power From The Universe (Roadrunner '84)

Improvement abounds, with decent cover art and cleaner production, while a troublesome first track (*Chopper Attack*) lead the charge on this hapless sophomore gesture. Still, only of consequence if Battleaxe was one of your particular personal badges of honour back amongst the flood of similar poor releases (many of which *were* my badges of honour for no good reason). This didn't amount to much for anybody I knew.
Rating **4**

## Paul Di'anno's Battlezone - Fighting Back (Banzai '86)

Kicking off with a Tank-ful of OTT, Paul Di'anno proves he's more of a kick-ass rock'n'roll punter than the goth spook he played with Iron Maiden. As the battle wears on, we get large, marauding riffs from Paul's battalion of unknowns on such alcoholic slammers as *Warchild*, epic *The Land God Gave To Caine*, and *Voice On The Radio*. Di'anno's street-carved growl is in fine form, although mixed a bit distant throughout, this combat-ready, garagey, but powerful slice of strong-arm U.K. metal evoking the best of the NWOBHM, bands like Quartz and Chateaux, spiritually speaking. Respectable record, rowdy as hell, with occasional Lizzy-ish fret-work, yet I rarely play it, said wax falling through the cracks of my steel-enforced playlist. Di'anno's split with Maiden had to do with his dislike of touring, with the added pressure of fame arriving too quickly. I guess that's worn off, and the guy's rested, given that **Fighting Back** represents such a vigorous return to the rigors of heavy metal.
Rating **7**

## Paul Di'anno's Battlezone - Children Of Madness (Shatter/Viper '87)

New drummer and guitarist, but no difference in sound really, this second slab of blue collar metal also produced with grit by Ian Richardson, who for some reason places Di'anno's vocals distant in the mix. But I'd have to say the songs are a bit naff, stepping back in quality unto the clubs, unto 1985, unto the delete bins. Probably more interchangeable with the debut than I'll admit. Either the buzz has worn off, or I better go revisit **Fighting Back**. Nice hair, gang.
Rating **6**

## BB Rock - Make It Move! (Ewita Est. '85)

Total biker metal in every sense of the term; grimy, bluesy, rife with nods to southern rock and general contempt for all things modern. **Make It Move!** has a smooth, nostalgic, 1100cc feel to it that grooves highly and ever mindful of traditional rock flavourings, one specific being axework so close to that of Billy Gibbons, it's chilling, even though these guys are Swedes. And it's better than any Godz album, laid-back boogie rocking throughout, with nary a hokey patch of oil, above a mix that is rich with German range. No year on this one, but it sounds old as the hills, almost like Humble Pie or Savoy Brown in the '70s. Virtually alone in its function as Viking biker Live Free Or Die museum piece.
Rating **7**

## Beats The Hell Out Of Me - Beats The Hell Out Of Me (Metal Blade '94)

Wacky nutty Helmet-isms from the outbacks of Arizona, Beats The Hell Out Of Me are the Giant Sand and Royal Trux of hard alternative, slamming that tight snare drum like a merciless metronome, but also sliding off on angles that are jazzy and minor chordy like Helmet or Quicksand wishes they were allowed. Mixing awesome barks, gelatinous tunage, and dangerous mindmelts, this one captures the spirit of underground punk without being stupid. Wish there were lyrics or at least something to look at packaging-wise other than these dumb cartoons, but what the hey, the squeaky, multi-lingual axework makes up for it all.
Rating **7**

## Beats The Hell Out Of Me - Rolling Thunder Music (Metal Blade '95)

Track one is *Track*, and we're off on another bass-buzzing freakshow, stomping through Rollins-infested Quicksand. Along the way, there's lush vegetation to nap in, the odd enraged jungle animal, and lots of natives with which moshing is a must. Fave trips would be the Korn-ish face rip of *Kazooka* and the irresistible bass guitar hookery of *Oar*, which sounds like sublime Smashing Pumpkins. Again, this band with the commercially debilitating name has set themselves defiantly separate from the pack, mixing a raw, undisciplined, convincingly spontaneous psychedelia with alterno-metal sounds of the mid-'90s. One would hope this could be a smash hit (it sounds so Lollapalooza), Beats The Hell Out Of Me doing fine slippery things with their desert-cooked blend of spices and herb. But then I'm a sucker for those throbbing, gluey guitar/bass textures.
Rating **8**

## Beggars & Thieves - Beggars & Thieves (eastwest '90)

One of a preening gaggle of hard rock hopefuls, Beggars & Thieves (essentially a Phil Soussan vehicle, ex of Ozzy, Jimmy Page and Billy Idol), struck in one of the better years for hair bands. But the record blows chunks, just safe and suburban corporate swillage, which isn't surprising given the crooked claw of Desmond Child clutching and squeezing the band's creative juices dry. Gets a 4 because in ten years, all of these heavy AOR records are going to sound a major dose better than the towering piles of "alternative" records that are going to be jockeying for space in the delete bins. Today's crap is crap the likes of which we've never seen.
Rating                                                    4

## Belfegore - Belfegore (Elektra '84)

Despite the complex bank of influences that combine to create the Belfegore machine, neither the parts nor the sum total thereof, are anything I would like parked on deck. Kind of a sinister, mechanized, metallized Skinny Puppy meets Stranglers meets Billy Idol with lots of metal guitar and tribal structures, this dour trio creates something to be applauded but avoided; all too mono-droned, creepy and self-serious, not to mention crammed with synths and other cold, techy effects. Maybe an inspiration to Ministry or Killing Joke or even Jesus And The Mary Chain, but I doubt it.
Rating                                                    4

## Believer - Sanity Obscure (R.E.X./The All Blacks B.V. '90)

Pretty much as heavy a Christian act as you'll ever hear, Believer mixes scorching technical prog thrash riffery with considerable bottom end, menacing vocals, and warnings unto the pitfalls of evil pathways. So lyrically think Trouble (read: violent, threatening Christianity), musically, a flaming version of Bay Area thrash, almost towards death but just too well-executed, featuring surgical, blistering axework throughout. The printed lyrics of each track close with listings of bible passages relevant to the lyrics, Final track: a power metal version of U2's Like A Song.
Rating                                                    7

## Belladonna - Belladonna (Mausoleum/EMI '95)

Hard to get excited about this one, no one caring much when it came out in Europe a good year before. Joey Belladonna (fired from Anthrax for not writing, or for that matter caring), quixotically brings forth this tepid raft of dated Anthrax-core, creating a band he thinks is more "in-the-pocket and vocals-orientated", but really just sounds like rehashed Anthrax ideas from the mid-'80s. Not exactly terrible, the whole thing just sounds forgettable, Belladonna's vocals picking odd, anti-melodic melodies as his hard-riffing new band (all from upstate New York) churns their basic, angled ten-ton tunage fairly cold and steely like the first Fight album, frustratingly void of hooks. Even the lyrics are a fair dose like Anthrax, if a bit more vitriolic, no doubt much of it veiled jabs at the man's previous employer. So it's hard to pin what goes bad here if anything, the record just plagued with a vague case of the boredoms. Joey kinda looks like another crooning kicking post Joe Lynn Turner.
Rating                                                    6

## Benediction - The Dreams You Dread (Nuclear Blast '95)

Token review here, 'cos I'm just not a fan, too far into the loss fer words zone to speak on the band's records with eloquence. Suffice to say, these Birmingham obliterators are a death metal institution, originally including Napalm Death's Barney on vocals, who showed up only on the band's '90 debut Subconcious Terror (and later as a guest vocalist). Next up was '91's The Grand Leveller, a '92 EP called Dark Is The Season (which covered Anvil's Forged In Fire), '93's Transcend

The Rubicon, another EP in '94 called The Grotesque/Ashen Epitaph, and finally The Dreams You Dread, which was also the name of the band's '89 demo. As with Napalm Death, all the usual superlatives apply, Benediction injecting a bit of melody and a sense of settling down on the record, still an opaque wall of smoke-belched British grind, but clearer of tone and purpose.
Rating                                                    6

## Beowülf - Lost My Head . . . But I'm Back On The Right Track (Caroline '88)

A merciless gang-bang of a record, Lost My Head . . . is the soundtrack to the L.A. Riots, an intensification of fellow Hispanic-oriented slammers Suicidal Tendencies, a just and certified steel-toed comparison in a number of areas. Dale Henderson is a violent disciple of the Mike Muir school of point-and-shout, in possession of a voice that turns camp cover Cruisin' into a grizzlied wake-up call from hibernation. Henderson also writes the lyrics here, exposing the scum of the street, of which he proudly counts himself, thrasher Flare being one of the most shred-headed and accurate drinking songs to ever pound by in thirteen lines of hate. But boiling to the top is lead cut Muy Bonita, which exemplifies the caffeinated synaptic levels of this record horrifically; basically a muscling up of the Ace Of Spades school of plunder and destroy. Musically speaking, Lost My Head . . . is a loudfastrules, uni-droned version of Suicidal, lacking the latter's growing allegiance to metal, coming more from a thrash direction, yet well-recorded, almost classy, and damn intrusive given time to sew on its colours. One of those rare gems that crashes through as one large though initially opaque statement of Attitude.
Rating                                                    7

## Beowulf - 2c (Restless '95)

Well here's a succinct lesson in selling out, sliding with the trends, going for the cash etc., Beowulf basically giving up their Latino hardcore slam for a slavish emulation of Green Day. So there's all sorts of brisk, basic melodic punk making the rounds, about 1/4 the brains poured into the writing and riffery, even vocals that fake an English accent, just like Billy. The latter half redeems itself somewhat, being less pop punk and more straight punk, and the boys mix up the styles a bit. But when it comes down to it, this is bandwagon-jumping of the worst kind.
Rating                                                    5

## Beyond - Reassemble (Pavement '95)

Changing their name (and one guitarist) from Demented Ted (post-Damn Yankees '70s revivalists?), Beyond have stood their parched earth really, although making limited progress towards a self-proclaimed "mechanical aura." So predictably, this one's all about texture and a stiff, occasionally industrial non-relent, drilling heads with growling, grinding lock-step grooves, a mantra of rusted appendages, something akin to early Voivod in vanquished robot spirit, but like many over-serious U.S. thrash acts of the '90s in grey execution. Colour me blanked.
Rating                                                    5

## Big Chief - Face (Sub Pop '91)

From the demise of Detroit's Necros comes Big Chief, Barry Henssler again at the helm of a brutish and boorish guitar train wreck, only this time more at oneness with his new label Sub Pop. But disappointment abounds, given Big Chief's straight-forward, one-legged look at grunge, reaching way back to the über-genre's roots: Green River, early Mudhoney and Swallow, Henssler too often lapsing into Mark Arm impressions, riffs too often simple, unimaginative and lethargic. Tis a shame, 'cos I buy the whole "grunge grandpappies from Motor City" legitimacy. Big Chief just don't do anything with it.

Rating **6**

## Big Chief - Platinum Jive (Capitol '94)

Way more to bite into on this one, including the spiffy artwork, courtesy of the same guy that does the covers of ragingly awesome Detroit rock mag **Motorbooty** (the credits don't make clear his name!). **Platinum Jive** digs way into the band's hip-hop, '70s funk and R+B obsessions, while keeping the proceedings hard-hitting and guitar-based, again slouchingly hip like Mudhoney. There's almost a COC-type super cool at work here, Big Chief separating these slick rock talkers with odd little experiments, pushing the overall effect underground, and in no hurry to please you, the listener. So a sheen of the strange, amongst surprisingly smart funk metal feasts. I know like this band's music as much as I've always liked the band.

Rating **8**

## The Big F - The Big F (Elektra '89)

A killer California power trio that evokes the wailing walls of the beat (as in Beat) L.A. underbelly stroked with the spiritual lunging impetus of Budgie through BÖC, The Big F create arresting rhythmic dins that loft hypnotically while pummeling the gut in some sort of spacey, maze-like take on a '70s garage ethic. Serpentine riffs seem strung over constant barrages of drums like Christmas lights on an epileptic Santa, while this hushed and hunched trio of missionaries (tamed from zealots) weave a tapestry wholly their own, torn and frayed at the cusps but shimmering in waves of metallic order down an opaque and thickly double-stitched mid-section. **The Big F** is one unique and timeless ocean of alternative metal, worthy of attention, punctuated by scowling, occasionally Iggy-inflected vocals, which also pick up on Jim Dandy and points southward. No point attempting specifics here, as the record is best viewed in a totality shrouded in the fog of its thorny terrain, an underground, almost subversive and activist deconstruction of metal, bashed onto black with little in the way of restraint, resulting in blended but violent beauty borne of an urge to create without peer or precedence. Adept in the psychedelic sciences with blood coursing strongly through veins of metal, The Big F are distantly futuristic heirs to isolated noisemakers like Blue Cheer, Hawkwind, the aforementioned Budgie and BÖC, and hell, even faint heartbeats like Jane and Armageddon; heirs filtered through the discipline of modern metal and its challenging raft of fringe forces blurring the divisions of rock'n'roll in the '90s. Take a stiff belt, and realize a new dimension.

Rating **10**

## The Big F - Patience Peregrine (Chrysalis '93)

Because of the totally ass-backwards way they've run their lives so far, The Big F are being touted (by a hallowed few, mind you) as some sort of semi-grand-uncles of alternative rock, all due to their seminal and weird debut, followed by nothing but silence for four years. So finally some noise, starting with this basic Big F-cored EP that sounds like the confused three have never been away, cranking those same textured mantras, those same insistent, consistent guitar weaves, pulling along vocals that never really get to know you. Four tracks, two of which make it to **Is**, two remaining (*Three Headed Boris* and *Towed*) being intrinsic Big F journeys, cosmic but mechanically sound, ever-rising and still so isolated in rock. Grade reflects poor value.

Rating **8**

## The Big F - Is (Chrysalis "93)

I dunno, I'm kinda down and alone on this record, while still positively entranced by the whole Big F concept . . . righteous album cover, spectacular lyrics that

squeeze in so much living. But as with all sorts of eccentric anti-social professors, a good chunk of the music is difficult, awkward and unpalatable, *Fefofi* and *Lube* (the two longest tracks on a nine track record), being kinda beige, browning out with an aimless sloping jam ethic that says filler. But the band's unique soundscapes are still in ample supply, craggy peaks with snakey mule trails, sea to sky rock faces, only respite being the band's most remarkable track, brilliant and hopeful ballad *Mother Mary*, perhaps the band's brightest tale of many sharply written tales. Weird, but I don't get the same enthusiastic, play-it-through vibe from **Is** that I found so effortless with the debut, **Is** seemingly jarring in its half-tortured juxtapositions of shade and light, its thorny creative process. Maybe it's the sequencing or a nagging feeling that there's not enough of a good thing, the band perhaps holding back un-aware some of their best material, or so slack and artistically absentminded that things never gets quite finished, even after four years away, four years that saw the meteoric rise of alternative music, four years that in acceleration may have rolled right over The Big F. An engaging gallery piece nevertheless, despite the cobwebs and chill.

Rating **8**

## Big Hair - The Pickle Farm (Energy '95)

Quite unlike anything I've ever heard, Mr. Rock Writer can nevertheless have a field day conjuring warped images. Start with hard-hitting funk metal, throw in some Zappa gold, old night-crazy Crimson, Primus actually doing songs, and trashy Skyclad (cheap one that one, 'cos of the violin of course), and you begin to see why this Rochester act is such loopy fun. The sound is brisk, confident and riddled with fiddle, as "that Tod guy" mumbles a Primus-nerdy vocal track over the controlled spasms of each wicked, old hippy construct. Progressive, jamming and bassy, **The Pickle Farm** strikes me as a great place to shop for the exotic. Love that violin, love that spirit. A truly fun band for players like Zappa was circa **Joe's Garage**.

Rating **7**

## Bile - Suckpump (Energy '94)

Self-described "industrial terrorists", Bile is a ten-man, New York wrecking ball of all things seriously loud and ludicrously distorted, mixing god-awful electronics with those low stun-riffs made mainstream by White Zombie. If thorny, woofer-chomping sounds are your deal, then you'd probably like this in your small perverted way. Me, I got enough stress in my life.

Rating **4**

## Bile - Teknowhore (Energy '96)

Bile now take their grating sonics into a higher realm of aural fatigue, unleashing this lengthy, virtually continuous concept epic for your listening distaste. Once more, your tolerance for this ultimate expression of frenzied, urban sensory inundation will establish whether **Teknowhore** is something you will play of choice. Definitely not on the commercial side of electro-metal, more like a progressive rock ethic applied to the dizzy world of spiky metal riffs, samples and thirst for distortion. I can't forsee me visiting this headspace.

Rating **6**

## Bile - Biledegradeable (Energy '97)

Slowly edging over to alignment with Energy's more dance-oriented roster, Bile return somewhat diminished, Krysztoff trying a bunch of rougher, less metalized, less actualized pieces, including a scratch-slow cover of *My Generation* (double friggin' yawn). Only seven tracks here (including an old demo), and many soul-searching (destroying?) methodologies. Puts industrial back a couple of years, I should think (and so should they).

Rating    **4**

## Billion Dollar Babies - Battle Axe  (Polydor '77)

Best thing about this Alice Cooper band solo album is the so-'70s slick cover art, which looks like yummy hard candy. Otherwise, expect simpering pop boogie with guitars, tunes that recall old Alice, but the old Alice that was thin, unremarkable, and dated. A bit of Dictators in there, but really just inconsequential hard rock lite. Spiritual cousin: **Spiders From Mars**, both rare and rarely moving.

Rating    **5**

## Billy Goat - Bush Roaming Mammals  (Third Rail '92)

Quite the dizzying trip this one, along the same lines as Scatterbrain, Psychefunkepus, crossed with 24-7 Spyz and Fishbone, serving up loads of rapping and percussively-fur-lined funk. Lyrically: quite colourful, profane and humorous; accelerated like beat poetry. Best cuts are the most metallic ones (like *Clothes Off* and *Trash Can Charlie*), on a laborious jungle riot that's more like tuneful rap than hard rock. Really, in terms of richter scale rating, **Bush Roaming Mammals** is closer to Fishbone, but these guys do like their guitars, really aspiring to a hard-edged underground following versus any so grand and academic as Fishbone's multi-tiered (God bless them) psychosonic society.

Rating    **6**

## Biohazard - Biohazard  (Magnetic Air '90)

It's easy to see the germ of future success here, given the band's marriage of metal and stage-diving hardcore, here more hardcore (and fast!) than Sabbatherian. Very punked up and skate, almost California-style, even though Danny blows away anyone punk with his massive percussion skills. Strange, urgent mix, but a fairly cogent collection of songs for a debut. And that missionary spark is definitely lurking in the grooves.

Rating    **6**

## Biohazard - Urban Discipline  (Roadrunner '92)

The buzz on Biohazard is a sizeable one, but I can't help thinking how urban and bitter and NYC this whole thing is, sorta untuneful thrash/ultra/core with shouty vocals that cross into rap but from that dreary squared-off HM standpoint. And the tough inner city theme threads its way all through this punishing record with lots of lyrics straight off of **Cops** or **America's Most Wanted**. Which is my problem I guess, and not the band's, given that this kind of semi-preachy, metal mosh just doesn't float my boat. Well done, and commendable really for its altruistic philosophy by way of back door (or should I say blowing off the back door), but it's just too grouchy or something, too New York Rangers, too Spike Lee yelling like an idiot for his beloved Knicks, too grimy and smoggy, without really bringing home the bacon with focused riffs or blazing production values. Just left me kinda tired, assaulted and negative.

Rating    **6**

## Biohazard - State Of The World Address  (Warner '94)

Way fab packaging for record III, what with the neon orange jewel box featuring the zen-like Biohazard logo screened in black ink right on the plastic. The themes again are heavy-handed and heated, brainshaking the listener to stare hard at a particularly urban and violent reality of the street. Riffs again pummel square-headed-like, but songskills are improved, as is the general aggression, although the mix is still kinda live, loose and soupy. It's all pretty cool how the band's very involved and involving lyrics point to a sort of activism, this time-and-town-terror-worn posse basically barking out a state of the world address, carving metro-paranoid vignettes throughout a cracked-out set of depressing lyrics that are damn near the longest and wordiest I've ever seen. And by all accounts, the band finds this rap-metal fusion thing refreshing, looking to do more team projects similar to their tune with Onyx on the **Judgment Night** soundtrack, and *How It Is* from this record, a duet with marijuana martians Cypress Hill. But as much as **State Of The World Address** chunders along confidently, the mashing doom riff changes and slowed hardcore gangsta vibe just leaves me frigid and a bit frazzled, rather than strengthened, which is what goodly sweet nourishing metal oughta provide.

Rating    **7**

## Biohazard - Mata Leao  (Warner '96)

Internal strife (guitarist Bobby Hambel is out) has tempered this band into a machine built of a type of intensely considered finesse, each short, well-built track on **Mata Leao** thriving on stunning percussion and a half dozen or so vocal treatments. The band's pioneering hard livin' metal rap still provides the rock bed, but there are a ton of mature moves on this record, exemplified best perhaps by the intelligent change-up breaks in the increased number of hardcore punkish numbers like *Competition*. So somehow there's waves and levels of attack, undulating iron-pumped and prison-hard tides of anger, but less street raw, Dave Jerden finding a bracing balance between frequencies, like I say, the drums marching triumphantly to the fore. Without a doubt, the most serious, artistic and individualistic Biohazard record, loaded with big swooshing chord patterns that hoover like Pantera with a more forgiving mix. All this amongst quite a bit of counter-intuitive (ha!) '90s punk. Just kidding; the punk here is tattooed '80s NYHC all the way, although improved upon vastly by Biohazard's very vital ideas.

Rating    **8**

## Bitches Sin - Predator  (Heavy Metal Est. '82)

Way too early NWOBHM that lurched forth lost within bad riffs, no focus, lack of tightness and poor mix values. Great breakthru cover graphics but that's about it. File with Silverwing, Praying Mantis, Black Rose, and Wolf as third string originals. Follow-up called **Invaders**.

Rating    **3**

## Black & White - Don't Know Yet  (Atlantic '89)

Basically a joke I don't know yet, Black & White is a rap metal outfit in the purest, simplest and most superficial sense as per my limited knowledge of the Beastie Boys (i.e. *Fight For Your Right To Party*). Big riffs, heavy mix, average rap vocals . . . but all crumbles in my estimation, due to the exclusive use of drum machines, no matter how muscularly calibrated. Plus it's really set up like a novelty item, borrowing from everywhere, including *Back In Black*. Could have been much juicier, and anyways, rap is poetry, not music.

Rating    **3**

## Black Angels - Kickdown  (Gull '84)

Disturbingly loose and rickety British skank that sounds vaguely German but confused; bridging party metal, speed metal, pop, booze rock and balladry under a pub-bound self-parody that undermines the purpose of being a metal band of this straight-faced but stooped stature. Chinsy mix and cheesy keys, and way too operatic vocals as per an estrogen-pumped Klaus Meine wreck the ditzy song constructs trotted out for our amused perusal. Really just hard hitting "rock'n'roll" like Rage or an unshowered London Quireboys, Black Angels strike me as plain bad, with no delusions of fame, content to pull a few chicks, lift a few pints, and wreck a couple of hotel rooms. Anything greater would be just too much hassle. Debut way back in '81 called **Hell Machine**.

Rating 3

## Black Cat Bone - Truth (Chameleon '92)

Every so often a band comes along that just doesn't fit the grand scheme of things. Black Cat Bone have this air of the non-real, hitting hard and independent, with a streak of Bold Alone, bred of a punk, metal, Sabbath blues alloy, as it searches for **Truth** in word, deed and emotion, discovering that "the truth is you never find the truth", and subsequently such a revelation's by-product: creative self-actualization that burns bright and free. **Truth** is a more aggressive, exacting and focused stomp through pre-grunge Liquid Jesus and I Love You terrain, if comparisons can be ventured; both musically and in the soaring vocals of David Angstrom. Throw in the cranked effluent of early Sub Pop, and you've got a Kentucky power trio that spells zen-like intoxication, caving towards vortex with rhythmic riffery, large bass lines, and power drumming bent on crashing tribal eloquence. Alternative metal to the core, Black Cat Bone set the arresting officer spinning with a faint southern funk infection, raucously four-wheeling its way through *The Epic Continues*, *Be Like Me*, and *Too Cool/Shoe Shine*. Erstwhile *Truth*, the song, slinks forth in killer bass-and-drums-driven form, under chilling multi-level vocals. Classic, uncommunicative and complex, Black Cat Bone is ultimately beyond words, amply smeared with swamp muck and assigned a seat on the roller coaster through the cool desert night, somewhere along side Budgie, ZZ Top, Deep Purple and Agony Column. Confused yet? Just buy it.

Rating 8

## The Black Crowes - Shake Your Money Maker
### (Def American '90)

The Crowes' deceptively sleazy debut broke the bank, peaking at around six million copies worldwide, hatching cleverly unconventional (but conventional) hit after hit. **Shake Your Money Maker** is a fairly Stonesy piece of work above all, but imaginative and wide, looking muscular with lead track *Twice As Hard*, Aerosmith-funky with Otis cover *Hard To Handle*, and silky smooth with the haunting and intelligent *She Talks To Angels*, all three becoming huge anthems establishing the boys from Atlanta as universal beings as thick and deep as the primordial ganja-laced muck from whence they slouched. Crazy like a fox in its rounding of the roots rockin' bases, **Money Maker** is instantly likeable and full of not so much surprises, more so fresh unfoldings of things considered long forgot. Party rock with sincerity, class and spent decadence.

Rating 8

## The Black Crowes - The Southern Harmony And Musical Companion (Def American '92)

Shimmering and glimmering from the South comes this daring, deeper piece of obscure and studied blues which buries once and for all the need for comparisons with the Faces or the Stones or whoever; said release being one proud, complex and singular statement of retro bliss no matter how cleverly derivative; a record far more relevant than any of its intensely understood comparatives. A simply elegant piece of exploratory, almost gospel blues rock, this second from one fragile and ever thinning Chris Robinson and his haphazard, consumptive Crowes, **The Southern Harmony And Musical Companion** spans time and memory in reverence of times and memories past and wistful, offering forth smoothly languishing vistas of traditionally balladry, dirty well-worn blues, and searingly hot, trampled hard rock as per an intrinsic understanding as to what Foghat was after for all those years. Truly a gutsy universal gesture after the novel albeit commercially

novel release that was **Shake Your Money Maker**, The Crowes' second delves darkly in that oft-examined complexity that is the blues with a glorious desperation that behooves them beautifully. I've played this record eighty . . . ninety times, and I still can't produce simple answers to questions like how heavy it is, or specifically how many tunes I like or dislike. It's one of those cohesive concept-like records that just rolls on amorphously oblivious to its surroundings. For after all winds hugely around and down, this grand release simply sweeps in widening arcs to an astounding level of gravity. I couldn't care less as to who The Black Crowes' influences might be, because truth is, the drama is so much more real and downright gritty for all the right sordid reasons here in the '90s, it just doesn't matter about respectful links to a hokey past. **The Southern Harmony And Musical Companion** is righteous, legendary and imposing; ebbing and flowing beneath one searing, human performance from the controversial (read: asshole; a man whose antics are actually driving people away from this band) Chris Robinson and his slide-guitarin' bro Rich. A truly splendid effort, built on total honesty, that tunnels well into what the debut only hinted at, said release deserves the test of time it demands, wearing proudly in the heat of its desperado sound borne of the insecurities, hopeless futility, and inevitable lazy insanity of the deep South.

Rating 10

## Black Crowes - Amorica. (American '94)

To keep the grand statement-ness of the Crowes blessed ragtag journey on upward trajectory, this is the record the band had to make. Whether the band's wide and varied fanbase will celebrate **Amorica.** is another story, the record sprawling, cryptic and most noticeably, not very uptempo. Fact is lead single *Conspiracy* is the heaviest tune on the record, a heady hello for the heads from down under, leading a charge that is more like a stooped-shoulder shamble. But there's some beautiful, almost pastoral music on here, lush, strident, timeless ballads like *Ballad In Urgency*, *Wiser Time* and *Descending* achieving that paradox of complicated brainy rock meets southern roots simplicity. Elsewhere the band tries other forward-motioning light rock styles, all rich and moving, the band truly muse-blessed no matter where they go. But some are calling **Amorica.** boring, not buying the Crowes as the stadium-straddling Zeppelin of the '90s. Whatever your take (and this will largely stem from your pre-**Amorica.** take on the band), this is the band's pot record, striving for blunt-blowing high human art through a mellow, mellow vibe. And appropriately, the lyrics are intensely experiential but fuzzy, powerful but left to interpretation. I dunno, it's a quality piece of work which is no surprise, but it is also sort of specialized and surrendered to a laid-back ethic that may annoy some as mere laziness. Note: my Canadian version of this thing censors the crotch with pubic hair shot for a dumb looking triangle on a black background. Suggestion: if you have to change the cover, HAVE A PLAN!

Rating 9

## The Black Crowes - Three Snakes And One Charm
### (American/Warner '96)

The increasingly low profile Black Crowes are getting to be like Fishbone and Lenny Kravitz, laying on bracing, provocative levels and layers of irony and musical knowledge, some of it suspicious, much of it studied, dense and sincere, culminating in records that beg the question: where does pleasure bisect reverence? Lead single *Good Friday* is an awful way to be introduced to this rich, rewarding record. But once past this sour, droopy single, blues textures ooze out brilliantly, often too smart for their own good, but an ecstatically wel-

come sight in these days of we try larder. The instrumentation of this awkwardly titled little jewel becomes a towering testament to fifty years of rock and blues, each visceral track infused with two or three charms that don't belong, wondrous glam swirl *Nebakanezer* being one example, similar cauldron of Americana *(Only) Halfway To Everywhere* being another. So too much to assimilate? or too many gulfs bridged? or a massive spaghetti freeway of activity? Maybe so, but the super smart retro river coursing through the thing lends comfort, the listener perhaps agitated by the ambition of this band, even as he's shucked off to chuck it all and drift into an enveloping haze of dope smoke, slow-boat posted to the gumbo zone without a care in the world.
Rating                                                                9

## Black Flag - Everything Went Black   (SST '82)
This stage-diving double shot takes all sorts of old stuff, odds 'n' ends and various chuggo-fests and drops them all onto one distorted piece of vinyl pain, making for a heaping chaotic, dance of sonic violence, burnt offerings for the sleaze pits of America. Sides one through three reveal a band with a sore gut and hateful focus; really, the best punk rockers in the US of A, 24 toons of axe thrashing anarchy, delivered vivid and poisonous. Side four consists of truly amusing samples of ads for gigs, interviews and other assorted swearing and yelling. Overall, a surprisingly cohesive compilation of dense shreds from America's most upset band of lowlifes. Note: the name Blag Flag derives from, you guessed it, the bug spray!
Rating                                                                8

## Black Flag - My War   (SST '83)
The first bonafide Flag project to define the claustrophobic recording process that would become the band's trademark. Again, as uneven as all Flag records, but featuring some corrosive classics such as the paranoid title cut and manic punker *Beat My Head Against The Wall*. Another cool Pettibon cover. Swings wildly between entertaining speed and mind-numbing sloth, Rollins the tower of carbon twisting in agony above it all.
Rating                                                                6

## Black Flag - Slip It In   (SST '84)
Another one of the few fleshed-out, serious Flag projects, **Slip It In** is an angry assault of words and music that captures and shakes the moral void of all walks of American life, from the bloated establishment to the crime-minded lifestyles of drug-crazed street scum. Rollins leads the enlisted on a horrific disease-ridden charge through such sonically brutal landscapes as riffmonster *Black Coffee* (my religion), wide open, stressful cruiser *The Bars*, and the manic, scampering and unclean title track. The recording is classic Flag, that wild, up-front, live, Rubinesque(!) guitar sound of anti-melodic skronk philosopher Greg Ginn courting a stripped simplicity that makes these underground anarchists . . . yes . . . a headphone band!, the bane of Rollins' existence, I'm sure. Black Flag, when focused was an emotional ebony pit, an ultra-carbonic diamond of hatred. Unfortunately, however, the wallowing in laziness and sporadic approach to the craft of making records—the very practise of anarchy with respect to manufacturing— renders the descents into the mosh pits yawning in front of Armaggedon, few and far between. This is one of them.
Rating                                                                8

## Black Flag - Loose Nut   (SST '84)
Either named for what happens when Hank gets punched in the nethers at every slimepit the band plays, or the odd, overly loose recording of the record, **Loose Nut** is a conundrum butted up against the band's two most rock-steady records, **My War** and **Slip It In**. Garagey, chaotic and well, I guess punk, this one is a capable smear of dangerous rock styles and speeds. Nine fighting songs, all four cretins performing just that little bit more hysterical and disheveled.
Rating                                                                7

## Black Flag - Family Man   (SST '84)
Billed as a "spoken word/instrumental" album, **Family Man** is just that: one side Rollins' face-smashing poetry, the disturbing verbal equivalent to the stark Raymond Pettibon drawings that grace most of the band's cover art as well as records by Minutemen and Firehose; and another side, melted, undisciplined and mushroom-laced instrumentals that lope off-centre like early Sabbath outtakes, ultimately going nowhere fast, squashed under the thumb of God. Side one contains some pretty sobering abuse however, including *Let Your Fingers Do The Walking*, *No Deposit, No Return*, *Salt On A Slug* and of course home invasion classic *Family Man*.
Rating                                                                5

## Black Flag - In My Head   (SST '85)
**In My Head** stands as one of the more consistent and to-the-point Black Flag albums, focusing on compositions as opposed to exploration of obscure tangents. However, aside from *Drinking And Driving* and perhaps *Society's Tease*, little else can match the sheer kill factor of pressure points from **My War** and **Slip It In**. Black Flag is one of those bands that never got their shit together enough to assemble one absolute package of fear; ultimately resigning themselves to spreading their collective anger over a number of variously motivated, hopelessly mottled records. Still, one of the original catalysts for the creation of the California hardcore scene, ultimately motivating dozens of imitators, Black Flag live was jaw-smashing catharsis for the rock that is Rollins.
Rating                                                                6

## Black Flag - The Process Of Weeding Out   (SST '85)
One of those "avoid at all costs" Flag EP projects. A twisted mass of tuneless jazz-metal squawkings featuring guitarist Greg Ginn (now SST label boss) spewing forth completely out of control, succeeding in hitting everything but the right note. Shit experimentalism at its worst spread over four tortuous instrumentals, this is Ginn's deal, so read 'em and weep. Great title and cover per usual.
Rating                                                                0

## Black Flag - Annihilate This Week   (SST '86)
This three cut 12" EP features two classic fastback rockers, including one of the band's most searing scorchers *Best One Yet*, plus one of the more Sabbath-like dirges that seem to be in vogue with the boys as of late. (Rating is in comparison with other EPs; i.e. even though I give it high marks, I probably wouldn't spend the six bucks that it would take to pick up three tunes). Title track and *Best One Yet* from '84's *Loose Nut*: obviously something's out of whack here.
Rating                                                                8

## Blackfoot - No Reservations   (Island '75)
The exceedingly hard-to-find debut from amiable Floridian boys, Blackfoot is a mighty fine stew indeed, riding a muscular Skynyrd drive, dare I say, warmer, heavier and more complex than Skynyrd themselves, no surprise given that 2/4ths of Blackfoot were in an early version of the band. Lead track *Railroad Man* (reprised at the end by its writer Shorty Medlocke, Ricky's dad), is a classic; inspirational, energetic and perfectly down-home southern. Lyrics, pictures, nice package for a first album, wrapping a solid piece of this genre's puzzle, along side other lost guitarish acts like

early Point Blank, early Outlaws and early 38 Special (note the ever-present "early" qualifier).

Rating **8**

## Blackfoot - Flyin' High (Epic '76)

The even rarer **Flyin' High** somehow rings colder than the band's instantly comfortable debut, bashing along at a heavier, more frantic clip, the record's production sounding a tad thin for this kind of mushy, shoot 'em up southern metal. Fave tracks are the traditional power ballads (which always sound a bit like Free Bird), a piece like *Try A Little Harder* going down like a smooth six-pack of Bud. But generally, this record's a guitar battle, all the while Jakson Spires perhaps playing too busy for the cheap mix. Still, practically nobody out there playing southern rock this heavy, so kudos all around.

Rating **7**

## Blackfoot - Strikes (Atco '79)

Thicker and less hospitable than both its predecessors, **Strikes** embodies blockier power chords slowly shifting away from the band's traditional roots. Caught between loud southern rock and the "modern" blues metal of **Tomcattin'**, **Strikes** still finds time for the odd funky beer commercial gait on such warm rockers as *Train, Train* and *Baby Blue*. Ricky Medlocke's resonant voice is perfect for this type of rock'n'rollin' as he emotively wails his fables of backwoods goings-on to the solid colourings of Charlie Hagrett's blues metal licks. Blackfoot (named for the band's American Indian origins) can claim at least the first half of their career as one of the most comfortable and comforting purveyors of roots metal to grace the scene. One can't help but think that the lack of commercial success must have chipped away at the band's confidence, resulting in the experimentation of later efforts. Bright point: **Strikes** certified platinum in '86.

Rating **7**

## Blackfoot - Tomcattin' (Atco '80)

Blackfoot's first of the "modern era" is an endearing slice of southern metal, a genre with surprisingly few actual albums to its credit. **Tomcattin'** cuts a varied, considerably heavy swath through deep south Americana, flagshipped by two brilliant roots rockers, *Every Man Should Know (Queenie)* and fluid 'n' funky metallic boogie *Foxchase*, a rolling rock of beer-guzzler might that is probably my fave Blackfoot toon. Recording values resonate like oak, rich and full-bodied; and stylistically, we get chugging oscillations between slow and fast boogie, plus all the swaggering elements that combine to make a complete blues metal spread à la ZZ. A must for those who like their axe pickin' with a traditional down-home hospitality.

Rating **7**

## Blackfoot - Marauder (Atco '81)

**Marauder** picks up where **Tomcattin'** left off, mixing an engaging brew of metal and southern rock, confidently and time-worn, sounding more like a heavier Skynyrd with each passing year. **Marauder** kicks off with *Good Morning*, a zippy little wakeup call about fixing one's attitude, other highs including balladeering, bluesy numbers like *Searchin'*, although it can never be said that the proceedings ever get too sensitive, all corners of this record having copious loads of chunky, amplified axework. Only straight-faced boogie wooger *Rattlesnake rock'n'roller* lacks the serious gravity of Blackfoot's particular paeans to southern heritage. All in all, another fine album from a band who never reached the level of serious contender. Follow up was an inspired, UK-only live release entitled **Highway Song**.

Rating **8**

## Blackfoot - Siogo (Atco '83)

**Siogo** marks a major kick in the ass to the smooth and southern sounds so capably handled on past efforts, possibly due in part (or in whole) to the strange addition of Uriah Heep's Ken Hensley on keyboards. All fronts of this record scream power, from the punchy recording and spirited delivery, to the overall swelling nature of the tunes, barely resembling the Blackfoot of old. **Siogo** is more an energetic HR/HM album with southern inflections than any robust mix of outright metal and outright southernisms, rocking expertly with an updated agility, most evident on classic lead cruiser *Send Me An Angel*, Nazareth cover *Heart's Grown Cold* and richly warm duo *Goin' In Circles* and *Sail Away*. At the core of Blackfoot's new feel is the rejuvenated big beat of Jakson Spires' drumming (although the man himself is a long-standing 'Foot) which is a constant force throughout all the tonalities on the record. I dunno, **Siogo** just carries the day with a new exhilaration that gives it such heroic appeal; successfully fusing youthfulness with the wisdom of old medicine men. Heavy enough, perhaps the band's heaviest, yet carved with finesse and attention to details.

Rating **9**

## Blackfoot - Vertical Smiles (Atco '84)

Arguably Blackfoot's third and most convincing stylistic shift gives way to a yet a fourth on **Vertical Smiles**, a record marred by the exit of veteran axeman Charlie Hargrett, who is thanked for "fourteen years of dedication and agony." Absolute zero killer instinct on this one, as the resounding pump of Spires' percussive energy coupled with the hotter-than-hell production that slammed **Siogo** home, is scrapped for clumsy, truly sloppy drumming and a cavernous, loose, and noisy recording that makes most of **Vertical Smiles** flounder like a clubbed catfish. Only endearing moments—and not because they rock out—arise with laid-back pair *Summer Days* and *Morning Dew*, a tune that was a hit for Lynott's pre-Lizzy outfit Orphanage. Shit, the boys even cover Peter Cetera, possibly the worst excuse for a human being ever to write "rock pig" on his income tax form. Ultimately, this record fails badly, sounding slapped together and powerless, too chaotic for the pork-fisted key-laced pap it's trying to sell. No enjoyment really, just resigned loss at a heart grown cold. As it goes, leader and occasional DLR look-alike "Rattlesnake" Medlocke will be the only core member left come next record; most importantly, Hensley leaving, still shaken by the death of David Byron.

Rating **3**

## Rick Medlocke And Blackfoot - Rick Medlocke And Blackfoot (Atco '87)

Well, there's four more black feet in the fire, but all the southern fried originals are gone except the Rock himself. And the music bears out the sad revelation that this is in fact a different band, something only remotely lowdown rockin', emitting more of a funky, keyboardy, big league melodic HR din, wholly without redeeming songcraft. A real shame, first because the fine moonshine is gone, second because this could have really swung with a scrappier recording and no synths. Superficially, psychologically, but not stylistically parallels Joe Perry's strange solo career conclusions. Three or four heavy ones but who cares.

Rating **4**

## Blackfoot - After The Reign (Halli '94)

Man, Ricky Medlocke is so perfect for this type of thing, a largely acoustic-based, bluesy roots rock affair, sterling clear mix, Rick's vocals soulful and upfront. There's a Van Morrison tune, a Bonnie Raitt tune, old blues standby *Sittin' On Top Of The World* and lots of like-

minded originals. It's a damn pleasure to listen to a guy so in touch with his hobby, even if it's all pretty predictable. But as I say, he's the man that wears it well, so what we get is a nice throwback, something almost Bob Seger-ish in places, no hi-tech stuff for miles, and not a lot of fully instrumentalized rock like days of old. Still, it's smooth and easy and real, unlike Great White's flimsy **Sail Away** project.
Rating　　　　　　　　　　　　　　　　　　　7

## Black Market Flowers - Bind　(Relativity '93)

Something slid spaceward like The Big F, Black Market Flowers ride that similar alterno power trio info highway, kinda vacuum-stored beyond reach . . . dreamy melodies, eccentric bass strummings, daunting distances to travel, no particular hurry to arrive. More combat grungy and slurred than The Big F, Black Market Flowers rely more on infinite juxtapositions of bass-guitar-drums-vocals possibilities, which can be a bit much at times, **Bind**'s 60 minutes of actual music arguably a good case for the return of 40 minute albums, something that many critics seem to be calling for these days. Suggestion: play it a bunch of times before judging, for **Bind** is an odd, trippy hard music experience, art rock written for garage band. Ends with a diving competition.
Rating　　　　　　　　　　　　　　　　　　　7

## Black 'n Blue - Black 'n Blue　(Geffen '84)

Borne of considerable publicity, video play during the fledgling years of MTV, and commercial appeal during a hard rock drought, Black 'n Blue were destined to be the Next Big Thing, with their very own mini Dee Snider at the mike in Jaime St. James, and a large, forceful, corporate hard rock sound to compete with the likes of Dee's Twisted Sister, Ratt and Quiet Riot. The band's debut delivered the injected male hormone, studded with well-recorded and surprisingly heavy radio anthems, from lead single *Hold On To 18*, Sweet's *Action*, through speedster *I'm The King*. Standing tall, resolute to divide and conquer, Black 'n Blue had a stack of wacks of which to be proud, simpler than Ratt, but fatter, more groove-oriented, and simply miles above the kiddie riffs of TS and QR. Despite the wimpy pretty boy image, Black 'n Blue were accepted as serious rockers worthy of car decks everywhere. The lustre wore off quickly however, as fame waned steadily and unjustly before it could ever really take hold.
Rating　　　　　　　　　　　　　　　　　　　8

## Black 'n Blue - Without Love　(Geffen '85)

Significantly sweeter enough to be called a departure, **Without Love** took to heart the glamour image being thrust upon this young band, offering more anthemic, hooky, melodic hard rockers, kicking off splendidly with *Rockin' On Heaven's Door* and the comfortably shameless title cut. The move from producer Dieter Dierks to soap metal wimp Bruce Fairbairn (not to mention breeze-bys from a couple of Loverboy dudes, Steve Porcaro and Jim Vallance) perhaps sums up the new feel, a candy-floss extravaganza of groove and gooeyness, which in my books does a great job of establishing a carefree rock'n'roll celebration of summer. What's lost in muscle is made up in enthusiasm, minor daring, and fairly major variety. Still fat and guitar-driven, **Without Love** was seemingly a step in a lucrative direction, but soon, the general public would be starting to tune out. Strange as it may sound, this record could probably be re-issued intact and remarketed today with very different results.
Rating　　　　　　　　　　　　　　　　　　　8

## Black 'n Blue - Nasty, Nasty　(Geffen '86)

And so the dive commences, the boys misplacing their souls in a sort of striving for modern love, leaving behind the warmth and innocence of **Without Love** for a techy, tough guy clatter that dies a stiff, pre-ordained death. Basically a combination of loss of groove, and loss of rising star lustre, **Nasty, Nasty** spells lack of confidence and therefore lack of fun.
Rating　　　　　　　　　　　　　　　　　　　5

## Black 'n Blue - In Heat　(Geffen '88)

Broken-in rock pigs by this point, Black 'n Blue put their careers in the oblivious oven mitt hands of Gene Simmons, who no doubt had a part in leaning the attempted comeback in the direction of third-rate Kiss-style filler. Unwieldy, over-produced and plain slow, B'nB forego the human element for a squarehead shot at Def Leppard's stiff, technological **Pyromania**. Totally mechanical and blocky, start to finish, **In Heat** is a predictable ploy from a band on the skids, lacking in charisma and spontaneous expression on all fronts, despite the return to heavier fare, most convincing of which is Dokken-style romper *Great Guns Of Fire*. Otherwise, lazy and wholly without love.
Rating　　　　　　　　　　　　　　　　　　　4

## Blackout - Evil Game　(Roadrunner '84)

Another greasechain metal signing from the boys at Roadrunner, Blackout sounded a hell of a lot like Samain and Running Wild, with a little more tunefulness, cantankerousness and barrel-chested, alcohol-ready pride, making this the choice spin from a raft of no-name mainland European acts to slick our shores.
Rating　　　　　　　　　　　　　　　　　　　6

## Black Rose - Boys Will Be Boys　(Bullet '84)

One of the early NWOBHM releases which took to a direction of chunky hard rock in hopes of Def Leppard-type financials. Unfortunately, the mix was muddy and yellow, slowing down the fairly amateurish, and unwieldy tunes, offering the most base of melodies and the most cliché of lyrical blueprints.
Rating　　　　　　　　　　　　　　　　　　　3

## Black Rose - Walk It How You Talk It　(Neat '87)

Sad but true, this record, three long years after **Boys Will Be Boys** contains exactly the same inept cloddish high school band HR/HM that was partly excusable for a young band. Quite ridiculous really. Not nearly the level it needed to be at to compete, still rocking loosely like a third string Heavy Pettin', vacuum-packed in the low '80s.
Rating　　　　　　　　　　　　　　　　　　　3

## Black Sabbath - Black Sabbath　(Warner Bros. '70)

From the Satanic mills of working class Britain, and the ashes of a blues band called Earth, the concept of Black Sabbath was loosed upon the land, the inflammatory name derived quite simply from a 1935 horror film. Comprising chaos personified vocalist "Ossie" Osbourne, bassist Tony "Geezer" Butler, who creates something more like a subterranean vibration than conventional sound, drummer Bill Ward, the original "eighteen wheeler hits drum shop" prototype, and Tony Iommi, virtually the sole creator of heavy metal guitar (let that sink in, 'cos it's true), Black Sabbath were a new and forceful machine of horrific, complex evil, only blind-sided by Deep Purple and **In Rock** in dual invention of heavy metal, The Album. This, the landmark debut, unfortunately for the Book of Sabbath, suffers the fate of being the only transitional step towards the concept of full metal jacket. But who cares? Everybody else took longer, starting from bases far more pathetic. **Black Sabbath** still retains the psychedelic noodling and disintegrated focus of the '60s. A craggy, hurtful and inspired walk through an inhospitable, oxygen-free moonscape, **Black Sabbath** oscillates between The First Metal (*The Wizard*, *N.I.B.*, *Wicked World*) and strung-out stupor at the

thought of dark, new possibilities; long, sick, subdued jams and Satanic sleeps amongst some of the very first power chords ever etched in wax. Depraved as any Sab disc to follow, **Black Sabbath** deserves recognition as a single, cold, hard trek through depression, slogging forth to suicide beneath an oddly low-octave Ozzy, the whole shot-down affair recorded in a single day. The record cuffed a complacent rock'n'roll world in the head, and the buzz and blurred vision fortunately continues to this day.
Rating                                                                         7

## Black Sabbath - Paranoid   (Warner Bros. '70)
And the dropped jaw of the music establishment turns to crushed powder as this synergy of four disturbed audio terrorists would converge upon such enduring metal classics as War Pigs, Iron Man and the title tumbler of poison. The damp, dark underbelly of the drug culture, **Paranoid** is one nightmarish sequence after another, a battleground of the caged and weak vs. evil, and one of the original heavy metal records of all time, given its September 1970 spawning. A vinyl vortex to avoid at all cost, revealing rocks all the way down with each tortuous gaze inside, Black Sabbath's sophomore blight focuses its blazing eye on more direct hits, tightening its act, which is why this is really the first to define the band. War Pigs is the grandest back-breaker, mixing huge Iommi riffs with stop/start percussion barrages, while Paranoid is an early "new era" rocker, perhaps paralleling **In Rock**'s ground-breaking Hard Lovin' Man. On the bad trip innocently called side two, the slow drip of Hand Of Doom continues the descent into potent recreational chemistry which eventually results in salutations from fairies in boots. A record still dominated by a live, jamming feel, it is Bill Ward who rises to loudest levels, showing his chaotic skills around the swells and decays of Iommi blasts. No doubt about it, **Paranoid** emerges from a shell, yet the surroundings are still cold and clammy. As with the debut, the overall effect is ancient and heartless, and for that reason, coupled with the multiple lives of the record's best pieces, I play the record only sporadically, met at the door with fear of self-destruction, for on many levels, this is the lowest of many debilitating Sabbath lows. Certified triple platinum in '86.
Rating                                                                         8

## Black Sabbath - Master Of Reality   (Warner Bros. '71)
Constructed from pure throbbing guitar gone bad, a righteous wrecking ball that seems to just spill bass, drums and vocals out in some dense, effluent birthing, **Master Of Reality** is a masterpiece beyond words and beyond compare with other music. An expulsion of glorious thick power, this definitive Sab statement wallows in primordial energy, simply layering itself with heavier and heavier blankets of the earth's crust. The most decisive and deafening of the original four heavy metal records, above **In Rock**, above the band's own **Paranoid**, and way above **Uriah Heep**, **Master Of Reality** is a relentless and pulverizing mountain of power chords, in essence the original model for future torch bearers Trouble, and the last thing Sabbath would ever really need to say to turn rock on its broken neck forever. As with all supra-genius classics, there is no separation of band members specific tasks, no separation of art and artist, and no urge for the spectator to feel revulsion, no matter the superficially monstrous ideas of the created work at hand. Comprising a scant five battering rams, one funeral hymn, plus two short intros, all contemplation on the numeric totals becomes irrelevant, for the intros Embryo (:30) and Orchid (2:00) are introspective brilliance abbreviated, Solitude quiet and deafening, and the five all out raves filling out the purple and black, justifiably interchangeable as any thinking fan's favourites from the catalogue. Personally, I lean towards the resolute but elephantine

critical mass of Lord Of This World and Into The Void, with After Forever a mean third. Rounding out the meltdown is lead cut Sweet Leaf and concert fave Children Of The Grave; one plodding, one galloping, both weighted with cement blocks. Lyrically the band dismembers the skeletons in the closet of the hippy generation, revealing a militant, isolated and ultimately despairing side to the fight for good. There is no hope here for peace in the tangible world. Iommi does his job of counter-balancing any mistaken optimism with pools of distortion sent from his unearthly pick-ups. The only sanctuary is within one's deliberately deluded mind, which can live at best a tolerable, time-eroding existence, surrounded by shut doors and imaginary security guards. In a sense, Black Sabbath becomes the Master Of Reality, consuming the real world in flames and rebuilding it in the mind where it can be controlled by thought alone.
Rating                                                                        10

## Black Sabbath - Vol 4   (Warner Bros. '72)
Fourth philosophical shift in four albums, establishing an obstinate lack of pattern that will continue to at least the end of the wild Ozzy years, **Vol 4** offers more songs and wider reign, an ever so slightly brighter sound, and yet another form of recording so hopelessly torn open by the all-encompassing presence of Iommi's bank of amplifiers (guitar was too small a word). The cover of **Vol 4** graced my very first rock T, and in its stark lurid nothingness, lies the heat of this record's delivery, a decidedly shaggy, overwhelmed scattering of vibrations dominated by Iommi but personified by Ward's bashing struggles against suffocation by guitar. Less driven by grooves than crashing cacophonies of cymbals and war drums, pounders like Tomorrow's Dream, Supernaut and Cornucopia signaled a monster out of control; in essence, headbanging in the retina-detaching, suicidal form of the word. Thriving voraciously under a mountain of drugs by this point, the band was barreling along off-the-rails to the stunned soul-searching and uneasy delight of the throngs of listeners in its crooked path, Sabbath recording the record in an L.A. haze, an eternity from their home base both geographically and psychologically, no Roger Bain to guide the process. Consequently, the scrappiest, most wickedly bashing Sabbath of them all, considered a bit of a confused black hole by many fans. Original vinyl came with fold-out and additional four page insert of live shots.
Rating                                                                        10

## Black Sabbath - Sabbath Bloody Sabbath
(Warner Bros. '74)
Transformed forever from mortal status, Black Sabbath leave the shackles of life on the surface for a liquid, multi-dimensioned reality, recording this record in a castle in Wales, quite the change from the Record Plant in L.A., Iommi finding the means for recovery from the immense writer's block that had been plaguing him. Mesmerisingly cryptic lyrically, and stratospherically limitless musically, **Sabbath Bloody Sabbath** begins life first as an album cover, a graphically satanic ritual in full swing, yet in no way related to the intelligent but mentally anguished Ozzy inside, except perhaps acting as an extra facet, another composition of the complex whole, integral yet nowhere near defining. Drawing from rare and distant sources, none of them particularly rock'n'roll, **Sabbath Bloody Sabbath** is more a plunder and almost unimaginable projection of the band's isolated past. A different sort of bash, a different sort of acoustic, an inescapable sort of dirge, and a body of lyrics so engagingly translated from and through experiences almost exclusively seen through and from human emotions cultivated well off this planet as we know it. Overall, this makes for a less literal heavy metal than on at least either of the last two Sab statements (**SBS**

marks the first time Iommi dives headlong into the production chores), yet one more psychologically altering and unconventionally constructed, as witnessed on punishment pieces *A National Acrobat*, *Sabra Cadabra*, and the horrifically massive *Killing Yourself To Live*. Elsewhere we get traces of synth work, lavish arrangements, and for the first time (see *Looking For Today* and *Spiral Architect*), more melodic, mellower pieces dealt much more attention than previous "light" music which was so often drumless and generally simple. One could probably chalk up **SBS** and **Sabotage** as the Sab's most artistic and daring records, releases that are near indescribable, records which carry the most credence for Sabbath being viewed so seriously as creators of art on par with Zeppelin and Queen, versus more superficial comparatives Heep or Deep Purple. Definitely not pretty, or the least bit inviting on mere emotional levels, Sabbath, despite offering zero hope in humanity, challenges such company, while of course at such a level, comparisons become ludicrous and unproductive. There's an actual rock video for the title track, featuring a grinning Bill Ward quaffing a mug of beer.

Rating                                                    10

## Black Sabbath - Sabotage   (Warner Bros. '75)

One of the most formidable artistic panoramas of all time, **Sabotage** is the tour de force from a quartet fraught with the demons of genius. One giant leap beyond a universe wholly self-created, into detailed worlds fully uncomprehendable in mere language, Black Sabbath trap then emanate an unwilling and vengeful muse into the deepest, fullest, and most colourful drama of psychoses ever ventured. Punishingly lead-poisoned or punishingly dulled by ether, **Sabotage** is a frightening cascade of contrasting activities, all tied with a thread of spoken dementia from an Ozzy bent on mutually pained destruction. Far beyond evil, this is an unearthly but man-made and administered programming, focused on a slow erosion of thought processes. From *Vol 4*-style noisefest *Hole In The Sky*, one envisions fearful glimpses of the apocalypse, which then descends to roost on the neck through riff monster *Symptom Of The Universe*, relentless tirade *Megalomania*, *The Thrill Of It All*, to an awful conclusion with *The Writ*, Hell on Horse, redemption through pummeling. And *Supertzar* and *Am I Going Insane (Radio)* . . . rodents better left unexamined. The original coma of souls, **Sabotage** refuses to move as if heard outside of time, essentially personified as one piece, one moment, one nightmare; a ludicrously progressive, break-the-rules out-pouring of ideas from the complexity of human brains blown skyward. Forget loving this record, as you may do with many other of your personality's black vinyl building blocks; for love, hate, anger and indeed pedestrian human processes of any kind have no seed here. View **Sabotage** with only the cold, detached nerve ends of your intellect. All other approaches will meet certain death in collision with an unconceded, unrepentant, unimaginable collection of psychic machinery.

Rating                                                    10

## Black Sabbath - We Sold Our Soul For Rock'n'Roll
(Warner Bros. '76)

No true fan needs this retrospective double "Best Of", but hell, what a legacy of twisted thoughts to celebrate, here knarled out of intended song sequence into a legless trip through a snakepit. All I remember about elementary school homework is doing some gargantuan project to the relentless repetitions of sides 1 through 4 for hours on end. Gobs of **Black Sabbath**, **Paranoid**, **Master Of Reality** and **Vol 4** (14 of 16 cuts) blown like micromold through the fleshy head tissues becomes the birthright of any budding metalhead, and here some wicked panel of suits under the

influence of the baddest of chemistry's creations deemed it necessary to be. For an extra kick in the psyche, stare vacantly at the foldout for awhile. You won't see things quite so straight ever again.

Rating                                                    7

## Black Sabbath - Technical Ecstacy   (Warner Bros. '76)

A seedy, murky but hard-hitting display of brain-embalming depression, the brilliantly packaged **Technical Ecstacy** finds Sabbath in full descent. Emotion laid raw, and indeed, the real Sabbath world laid raw and exposed, we are taken on a detached ride akin to an outer body experience gazing down at life as *Back Street Kids*, failing relationships, trips to the *Rock'n'Roll Doctor*, finally taking solace in the bone-white arms of *Dirty Women*. Obviously this is no progressive maelstrom as per the band's previous two works, but a gutter-level look at sordid creative powers on the wane. The first "collection of songs" since **Vol 4**, **Technical Ecstacy** is unassumingly one of the band's most magnificent works, a tombstone dedicated to pain and drained batteries. Of three "ballads", two are simply Devastation, the lead-headed *You Won't Change Me*, slow and resigned to a failure in human connection, and *It's Alright*, a Beatle-esque Bill Ward-sung dittie which snickeringly became a minor pop hit for the band. *She's Gone* rounds out the light with a lonely acoustic, brain-dead creep through the dark. Metallically speaking, the band cranks it up for *Back Street Kids*, driven by an edgy Ozzy rant and massive metal groove. Surprise time, *All Moving Parts (Stand Still)* combines the Sab groan with funk, while *rock'n'roll Doctor* does the same with boogie. And rounding out each side, two classics in the atmospheric and high NRG *Gypsy*, and the wanderlust then heroically climaxed *Dirty Women*. **Technical Ecstacy** is ultimately a strange and impossible attempt at defining the real world, something Sabbath has insulated its art from since day one. And ultimately, as with many creative juggernauts, we find Black Sabbath's chemistry doesn't belong on the earth's surface, better left to the heads and cold bodies of the dismembered class.

Rating                                                    10

## Black Sabbath - Greatest Hits   (NEMS '77)

Just another botched, butchered move in the drug-ingesting, booze-imbibing life of Black Sabbath, **Greatest Hits** is the wheelchair-bound sister of **We Sold Our Soul**, both poor substitutes for what would have been a well-timed live opus of first gen doom dementia. A fright-wigged Brueghel cover wraps a tasty collection of war-torn chestnuts, but why? All headbangers worth their cheese should own the original Old Testament texts, perhaps only completists, collectors, and Christmas present-buying moms coming to the trough with any rational motivation. Buy Steven Rosen's rollicking Sabbath bio **Wheels Of Confusion** instead. *Laguna Sunrise*?

Rating                                                    7

## Black Sabbath - Never Say Die   (Warner Bros. '78)

According to Ozzy himself, it seems that the **Technical Ecstacy** through **Never Say Die** era was the lowest, most destructive period in Sabbath's tiring history, the band wallowing in depressed depravity, exhausted apathy, and broken dreams. **Never Say Die**, Ozzy's swan song, bears out such sentiment, burying the outward, very poignant anguish of its predecessor in a sludgy sea of disjointed ideas, non-personal and at the least, ambiguous tales of heavy metal oppression. Deflated, loose but tacitly disturbed, **Never Say Die** does its best to bury the band and its unstoppable knowledge of the essence of metal. But the unswerving insight remains, even on more experimental lighter numbers which as usual, are less "light" than fragmented and luded. As with its predecessor and spiritual twin,

**Never Say Die** is a collection of songs, varied in intensity, but uniformly apocalyptic. The grungy, garagey quality and the suffocated, bone-dry but creaky mix of Iommi's weapon constitute the biggest change here, with a live, off the floor (more like under the floor) feel. And the record seems everywhere at once, yet with closed eyes that do not wish to see. We get languished squalor in *Over To You* and "single" *A Hard Road*, polluted jazzy dream states in *Air Dance* and *Breakout*, Sab's first happy hard rocker in the title cut, and a few massive pounders in *Johnny Blade*, *Shock Wave* and the record's largest head plate *Swinging The Chain*. All in all, a sorry and abandoned, burnt-out sort of record, like a junk pile of wondrous recurring but tainted memories, rusting in hapless chaos with only the occasional eyes of the scavenger to adopt some particular personally-connecting scrap. Note: perhaps explaining the record's rushed feel, **Never Say Die** was recorded in Toronto in the dead of winter, Ozzy refusing to record songs written during his first break with the band when another singer was brought in for rehearsals and writing. Once a shakey patch-up was achieved, the band had to relent to Ozzy's moods and essentially rewrite the whole album in a local theater the day, with recording to commence that very evening.

Rating                                          9

### Black Sabbath - Live At Last   (Nems '80)

Not an official Sab statement, but a low key import with scant info about these sessions other than that they were recorded in Manchester and The Rainbow in London. Of course, main drawing card is the documentation of the original line-up in evil-soaked disarray, a view we were never given under the auspices of the official catalogue, which nevertheless was punctuated with the excellent Dio-led **Live Evil**. All ten enclosed boulders (*Wicked World* hides *Supernaut*) are from the first four quintessential Sabbath monuments (save for crowning achievement *Killing Yourself To Live*), and all are sent reeling via Iommi's huge unearthly drone, which just spreads over top everything like a blob of wax. Coolest relatively uncharted wells of sorrow: *Tomorrow's Dream*, aforementioned behemoth *Killing Yourself To Live*, and *Cornucopia*, all recorded with smothering psychedelic overkill, just gasping with power beneath a surprisingly straight performance from Ozzy.

Rating                                          7

### Black Sabbath - Heaven And Hell   (Warner Bros. '80)

Altering the potent chemistry of a Black Sabbath with Ozzy (who left just as the band prepared to record this opus), Tony Iommi, the emerging core of the band, manages the unimaginable, raising the mighty Sab to unforeseen heights of clarity and commerce, with the acquisition of the legendary Ronnie James Dio at the mike. From the brilliant but increasingly cryptic traumas that comprised Sabbath's late '70s output, comes a sterling, clear-headed, brightly metallic approach, most definitely in the orbit of a sort of commercial metal, yet one so beautifully melded to Iommi's unique attics of the mind. Increasingly reliant on the man's soaring, back-buckling riffs, SabbathwithDio takes it direct to the head, rather than working insidiously through tainted intravenous as per recently previous snake charmers. *Neon Knights* (the last track recorded for the record) announces the new world order, rumbling high octane, clean and proud. And the grand eloquence rarely lets up. *Children Of The Sea* and *Lady Evil* burn brightly, searingly mixed by veteran Martin Birch under lyrical gardens harvested and transported from the Rainbow's end. Yet it's the monstrously epic title cut that sets the stage for Sabbath's new era, and indeed metal in the coming decade, with a sinister angular riff, rising and falling like its moniker, racing to

something closer to blinding conclusion than mere finish. *Die Young* marks a second masterpiece, throbbing with missionary zeal on a storyteller's night, Dio in his element as magician of dreams, lightning rod of ambiguous evil, and diminutive focus of the loudest voice in metal's new surge. **Heaven And Hell** is ever so slightly coloured with the same loss of pre-marketing age innocence found on Priest's **British Steel**, but here the vision is more accurately merely altered than misplaced. Indeed, **Heaven And Hell** finds a strangely pleasing new clarity and simplicity that cements true "songs" like *Neon Knights* in the mind more than a *Johnny Blade* or *Dirty Women*. With more excitement surrounding any Sab disc in years, four very distinct individuals converge to deliver one hard-hitting work of modern alchemy, and as history would judge, **Heaven And Hell** would prove to be a classic in the true sense of the word. Bill Ward would abruptly leave the band in mid-tour due to his ever-mounting problems with booze and drugs.

Rating                                          10

### Black Sabbath - Mob Rules   (Warner Bros. '81)

Continuing to build on a surprise wave of Sabbath-mania, **Mob Rules** deepens the permanent legacy of the Dio years with a creative expansion of the **Heaven And Hell** sound. *Turn Up The Night* (incidentally sporting an uncharacteristically melodic and resolving Iommi solo), is this record's *Neon Knights*, announcing the sonic ceremony with a rapid, wreck-the-place invasion. After the manic entry, the band stretches out and opens it up with greater lulls and greater peaks than the fairly uniform predecessor. I caught the tour of this album in Vancouver, and the live expulsion of noise we experienced that night reinforces the love Sabbath has for the dense, rumbling punishment of rows of over-juiced amps. Songs were gloriously indiscernible among gobs of bass frequencies wallowing incestuously with each other, and we didn't care. **Mob Rules** dares to blast away at the convention and complacency of the old guard, laying it on thick with raw spontaneity and a somewhat warmer, more melodic make-up vs. **Heaven And Hell**. Dio is truly in sync with his muse, revealing a personal world much like Iommi's, yet one dominated by words more than imposing mountains of power chords. Classics here include the traditional Sabbath mass of *Country Girl* and the sinister *Falling Off The Edge Of The World*, both featuring the tasteful, spacious percussive attack of Vinny Appice, one of the best instinctive minds in power metal drumming. All in all, **Mob Rules** reveals greater layers of different solid, dark colours; essentially greater staying power beyond **Heaven And Hell** with an increasingly complicated approach. Yet whereas **Mob Rules** may embody the guts of the short-lived Dio era, its predecessor maintains its mystique. Both are essential pages of the heavy metal story.

Rating                                          10

### Black Sabbath - Live Evil   (Warner Bros. '82)

Sabbath's most vigorous line-up rams the living daylights out of a predictable batch of Sab classics, reliving the recent two grenades with Dio, then reaching exclusively way back, to a crunching update of selected black wind from records I through III. Killer versions of *N.I.B.*, *Children Of The Grave* and *Paranoid* lead the merciless power struggle, draped in flowing sheets of deafness under the growling, kick-ass command of the man at the mike (Dio apparently miffed at being billed as "Ronnie Dio"). And you'd never guess it, but Iommi's solo near finale of an extended *Heaven And Hell* is damn near the highlight of this powerful live feast, a display of machinery not unlike a symphony of diamond-tipped drills sent straight through the first twenty rows on the floor. It would have been a scream to have such a fortified treatment sent down some

lesser known roads from Sab's late '70s output, but on the other hand, one welcomes the expected rampage through **Heaven And Hell** and **Mob Rules**. But all in all, **Live Evil** virtually makes the band's first two records irrelevant, offering massive improvement on all fronts. A rare, necessary live document.
Rating **8**

## Black Sabbath - Born Again (Warner Bros. '83)

My high esteem for Ian Gillan as catalyst for genius grows still greater with this unsung masterpiece of devastation. Apparently of the opinion that the mix was all but botched (Geezer the supposed culprit), Sabbath creates an evil roar perfect for such a loud and obnoxious recording. Definitely my favourite non-Ozzy release, and well within the realm of the top three Sabs ever, **Born Again** is perhaps the most violent, most aggressive and simply loudest Sabbath attack, often trudging slowly, more like trashing slowly, as on *Keep It Warm*, *Disturbing The Priest* and ten ton rumbler *Zero The Hero*. Gillan is at his shriekingly most psychotic, in massive but capable struggle with the barrage crashing down around him (indeed the band had a certain pyrotechnic slant to their practical jokes on the new guy during the album's recording). Lyrically, Gillan's eccentric stamp is evident, as a hazy sort of disjointedness fogs words with a melting mix of Iommi's dark genius and the most pulverizing rhythm section in Hell's trashed acre. In general, **Born Again** is extremely surprising in its gut-wrenching intensity, surprising given the disciplined and direct approach of the Dio era, surprising in that so much anger still boils in veterans with so much unsavory bile already to their credits. Something, if not Gillan, has whipped the ol' juggernaut into a frenzied furnace blast through Purgatory, if a somewhat paralyzed and top heavy one. **Born Again**, despite being an understandable commercial disappointment, is an incredibly massive chunk of power metal, proving what can happen when Iommi is forced to his burnt creative edges. Finally, out of all the glorious Sabbath monoliths, **Born Again** left one of the darkest and deepest impressions on my dented head, and for that I humbly thank its twisted creators.
Rating **10**

## Black Sabbath Featuring Tony Iommi -Seventh Star (Warner Bros. '86)

At possibly the weakest point in Sabbath as a group concept, and after a depressingly lengthy absence, Iommi stands alone clutching his cross and namesake, steering an assortment of players towards an understanding of his imposing visions on a record that justifiably was originally intended as a solo album. Distracted by the inappropriate flouncy 'n' flirtatious signatures of vocalist Glenn Hughes, one is almost put off the rails of this quite elegant, thickly recorded collection of tracks, from OTT opener *In For The Kill* through weary death knell *No Stranger To Love* (talk about a cheesy video), to side two's awesome *Danger Zone*, featuring a melodically brooding but marauding riff from the man at the helm. Overall, this is one of the Sab's furthest departures, coloured with blues patterns, blues-sentimental lyrics, bluesy vocals and even a literal heavy blues in lengthy trudge *Heart Like A Wheel* (no relation to Steve Miller!). Again, tunes live or die on the Iommi effort, as the rest of the backing band are not Sabbath-like creatures in any form, although future Kiss and Badlands drummer Eric Singer assumes the Ward pocket with an uncanny instinct for desolate percussive moors. Definitely less the spooks and witches sellout of **Tyr** or even **Headless Cross**, **Seventh Star** retains a pride in workmanship despite foreign personnel and a lack of musical direction or intensity. Lacking in fireworks, I've got to say it still pays

my turntable (remember those?) fairly regular visits due to its digestibility.
Rating **7**

## Black Sabbath - The Eternal Idol (Warner Bros. '87)

Without no Dio to kick around no more, Iommi acquires the next best thing, vocalist and part-time troll Tony Martin, who comes with an incredibly Dio-like style and comparatively more vigorous pipes; to the effect of sounding too closely studied of the Elfin one to be taken seriously as his own man, despite his tireless defenses to the contrary. All is excused however, because Martin becomes an integral force in this, one amazing, soaring but modern Sabbath record; heavily crammed full of monster performances and beautifully powerful vistas of old guard goth. Unlike **Seventh Star**, one thinks album first, songs second, with a distinctly wide-open, intrinsically Sabbath-like attack filling the grooves, start to close. Fifth man for eternity Geoff Nichols, comes to the fore with well-placed keyboard atmospherics over what are huge, torrential hurricanes of Iommi riffs, best of which step out of the Sabbath stomp into glorious new power grooves, most notably *Hard Life To Love* and *Born To Lose*. Nothing petty or small-thinking or commercially cynical about this one, borne of a black vein of independence and artistic height of a man fortified against the pathetic trends of the rock'n'roll business. In summation, **The Eternal Idol** combines an Ozzy-era isolation, a Dio-era work ethic and raw will, and an entirely fresh blast of creativity, well-enforced by a talented though somewhat derivative vocalist. No ballads, no mercy, no more colour. Demos exist of this record with all vocals by Ray Gillen.
Rating **10**

## Black Sabbath - Headless Cross (I.R.S. '89)

Virtually a ghosts and goblins versions of **The Eternal Idol**, **Headless Cross** becomes chopped in my estimation as a cheap lyrical and graphic cop out towards what is superficially expected from a washed-up Sabbath. Comprising seven, more epic-directed cuts (plus one naff intro) with the closer being a typical Sab mellow contemplation, **Headless Cross** is a trace more infused with melody and the lighter shadings of the traditional goth sound. With titles like *Devil & Daughter*, *Call Of The Wild*, *Black Moon* and *Nightwing*, you can pretty much surmise that lyrically this is campfire tales. But sonically speaking, the fire still burns, albeit with more spaces, less consistent sledgehammering than its predecessor. Cozy Powell is in on skins and shared production chores, full-blooded on both fronts. So on a superficial but valid level, we're essentially given a scant six rockers versus **The Eternal Idol**'s no-nonsense nine, with overall quality here being down-graded riff-wise, greatly sabotaged lyrically. And the commercial and critical slide begins unabating.
Rating **7**

## Black Sabbath - Tyr (I.R.S./EMI '90)

The most sluggish of the Tony Martin-miked triptych, **Tyr** falls asleep on a bed of discarded mammoth riffs and rusted goth chunks, despite the seemingly admirable steerage away from **Headless Cross**' keyboard atmospherics. Basically bad Dio, seemingly written for the Elf's style of delivery (virtually stolen by Martin anyways), **Tyr**'s just more sell-out goth, with little purely Sabbath-like twistedness, a record smothered by the Dungeons and Dragons imagery and Manowar-style story line, rendered muddy by unsteerable riffs and cloudy drumming. With the least personality of any latter-day Sabbath release, **Tyr**'s attempt at hocus pocus pulls a dead rabbit from the hat, proving an age-old wisdom that art can't be contrived into existence.
Rating **6**

## Black Sabbath - Dehumanizer (Reprise/Warner '92)

Weathered and brutally fragmented, the re-primed legend that is The Sabs comes jackboot stomping back with a Grand Canyon of an experience; open and echoey down the middle, while rumbling masses of rock come crashing down from all sides. **Dehumanizer** (Geezer going for a name that sums up the sum total of the tracks) is an "effect" above all, a surprisingly raw, disconnected Sabbath, seemingly unconcerned with commerce (that's seemingly), a gathering of minds bent on grinding, low cycle, low lustre throb. True to their forked word, this is no re-machine of **Mob Rules**. This is a slower, more wasted and simply grungier soot factory; brutish, uncompromising and occasionally bent on implosion. The most forward-massing concepts are to my mind the best; *TV Crimes* and *Time Machine* rising quickly above the sordid sonic sloth. Yet artistically, the thick and boiling portions of the feast fill the belly with greater fire; experimental, open architectures such as *Letters From Earth*, *Sins Of The Father* and lead cut *Computer God*, slowly carving paths of electrical overload through one's circuitry. Almost as if this absolute fortress of a band is turning its back defiantly on modernity, **Dehumanizer** looms spacious, cave-like but proud; spreading in shockwaves of monster riffs and suffocating Appice cannons, under appropriately nightmarish and vague, but unadvancing Dio lyrical terrain. Sadly, while scaring them away at the box office, one can't accuse Sabbath of taking the easy road here. **Dehumanizer** is true discomfort, blistering in an inescapable ice palace erected by legendary spiral architects. But the love-in with Dio was not to last long, old spats re-emerging, and the record supposedly being excruciatingly slow in the making.
Rating                                           8

## Black Sabbath - Cross Purposes (I.R.S./EMI '94)

Sorry but Dio wins this duel, Sabbath stuck in a goth rock rut, Tony Martin too over-associated with those medieval vocal melodies and silly rock debutante posturing for anything from the riff department to overwhelm his influence. And lyrically, same alignment, Sabbath making no adjustments to their horror comic book musings, unrepentantly writing with a refusal to grow. Iommi's riffs lean towards big, stiff and scraping, very rhythmic (allowing Rainbow's Bobby Rondelli full stretch), usually a good thing, but there's an uncomfortable supply of mellow moody parts, not to mention full tracks that could be construed as dreary ballads. The record as a whole achieves that dark regal feel, that of unsociable tower trolls toiling at something gloomy and of everlasting quality. But one would hope Iommi could get over this Dungeons and Dragons stuff. I mean, at least Deep Purple can laugh at themselves. When Tony croons "The Hand That Rocks The Cradle", I feel the urge to snicker, picturing a guy in a Dracula cape or something. And *Evil Eye*, *Cross Of Thorns* . . . it's all been done before, repeatedly, even within the confines of this band that really started it all, scaring the bejesus out of us in the process. All in all, acceptably heavy I guess, just for the most part too restrained and claustrophobic, too similar to records like **Tyr** and **Headless Cross** in castle-fake tone.
Rating                                           7

## Black Sabbath - Forbidden (I.R.S./EMI '95)

Can Iommi and whoever get much lower than the watery **Cross Purposes** record of not that long ago? Yes they can, as the Coasting One enlists auto-pilot journeymen Neil Murray and Cozy Powell to prop his least inspired lineup. Ernie C. of Bodycount produces the record (adding a no-purpose Ice T sample for credibility), and thankfully the sound is nothing like those crappy early BC dives, more like a slighty rough and incestuous arrangement, slick but a bit disheveled. And the songs stink, big elephantine riffs that dunder bluesy

and spooky, fairly aimless and flaccid. Martin's voice is near shot, and Iommi is writing simpler, even approaching dumbo-head hard rock on *Rusty Angels*. Lyrics are a bit more street than castle, unremarkable songs about people problems (yawn), and the whole dull coat-tails pound just sinks in a morass of messageless mewling. It's obvious Iommi is point-blank out of ideas, proving all too sadly that what this man needs is his old band: Geezer's lyrics, Ward's barnyard bash and Ozzy's nuthouse presence demonstrating by absence their powerful contribution to the Sabbath mystique. But back to reality: **Forbidden** is just a sorry piece of crap, exposing with ruthless checkpoint efficiency all the bad characteristics of the term "dinosaur rock." Post-release: Powell out again, Rondelli back in. Like, who cares anymore?
Rating                                           5

## Black Sheep - Trouble In The Streets (Enigma '85)

More or less the domain of one Willie Basse, Black Sheep play a Velveeta-based L.A. party spread, fairly heavy, melodic metal like a dressy mozzarella Dokken or welfare Ratt. Might have liked this in '85, but then again, probably not (hey, we had David Coverdale!), although enthusiasm reigns not uncharmingly, while visions of Van Halen dance in their heads.
Rating                                           5

## Black Task - Long After Midnight (Axe '86)

American riff monsters with a dramatic sense of self-importance blowing carcinogens through speed and mid-pace constructs that do little to rise above the hammerheaded fray. Other lowlights: flat vocals, and a sorry lack of bass. Touches of Virgin Steele, Slayer, Exciter . . . a bit of anybody on a mission.
Rating                                           2

## Black Tears - Child Of The Storm (Est. '84)

Stumbling, inept, yet fairly heavy garage metal from the wasted years of the mid '80s. Extremely Mausoleum-like, i.e. painfully cheap.
Rating                                           1

## Black Train Jack - You're Not Alone (Roadrunner '94)

As I write this in November '94, Green Day and Offspring are surging for about the third time towards the top of the nutty pop charts. '90s punk rock is all the rage, and so Black Train Jack dive deeper into this fertile new terrain (we'll see how fertile it really is). Sure this is about as good as those two annoyingly catchy power punk combos, but the ploy is just all too evident, or at least I can't see past it into the crunchy sweetrock enclosed. Oh hell, give me a couple of weeks.
Rating                                           6

## Black Widow - Street Fighter (Roadrunner Est. '84)

Pig-nosed Euro grime sent into our poster-plastered bedrooms by a motherly label that loved it all equally without favourites. This butt-head biker fare hits occasional stride and is amply mixed but man, talent never enters the picture. I'm still glad most of this mid-'80s small label crap wasn't thrash, but this particular gut socker just leaves the taste of my lunch in the back of my throat.
Rating                                           4

## Blackwych - Out Of Control (Metal Masters '86)

Ireland grime rock, tinny production, crashing, bashing and disgracefully cheap. Proving there is indeed an isolation factor to Irish music, in this case to detrimental effect, **Out Of Control** rolls lopsidedly more like unstudied street rock, or the band's dim translations of sounds more capably emanating from across the shores already outmoded a good four years ago.
Rating                                           2

## Blasphemy - Gods Of War (Osmose '93)

Standard issue thrashcore torture that pastes all comers to the wall, per usual, serving no purpose far as I can surmise, than to infuriate those who must hear your stereo, be it girlfriend, wife, mother, or dog.
Rating **2**

## Blind Fury - Out Of Reach (Attic '85)

Commanding full respect for quality and complexity during the creatively blocked mid-'80s, **Out Of Reach** was a confident slice of British techno-goth from a band borne of the ashes of Satan (the band), here equipped with a new vocalist, the dour and depressing Lou Taylor. Well-crafted, well-recorded (although to specific tastes only, much like Taylor's voice), but personally rarely played, this is one heavy and commanding piece of wizardry, too doomish and European too uniformly for my liking. Hard to express my lack of interest, but there's just something too self-serious here, although when confronted track by track, it definitely kicks, full of caustic Black Metal-style riffs and basic "guitars on a mission" kill factor (witness *Dynamo (There Is A Place . . .)* and *Back Inside*). Maybe it just fades with time without the context and subsequent armchair quarterbacking afforded a large catalogue, but the Fury definitely does more sleeping than roaring in my library.
Rating **6**

## Blind Guardian - Somewhere Far Beyond (Virgin '92)

Quite a sensation in Japan and their native Germany, Blind Guardian are a fairly young and charismatic band (even though this is record #4), who sound like a frantic, high cholesterol Helloween, with a vague Sky-clad look and lyric, going places folklore-ish but with convincing aplomb. Recording values are bulky and electri-fried; thick, steamrolling drums contrasting the razor exact, arch-European speed riffery (and piercing, sky-straddling solos) of most tracks. In fact pretty much the only tunes that don't rip a strip right off ya are the straight acoustic passages, cool bagpipe instrumental *The Piper's Calling*, and the robust cover of Queen's *Spread Your Wings*. Vocals are of the operatic, traditional kind, but not way up there in the dog zone like many other German engineers. But my main complaint taints this well-respected act for me, the preponderance of hyper velocities making things samey, despite the ease with which they are handled. An **9** or **10** if this particular mystic strain of metal is your cup of mead. Hail!
Rating **8**

## Blind Guardian - Tokyo Tales (Virgin '93)

Man, I guess these guys are tired after a gig. I mean, talk about fast, the real thing, not boring old blastbeats, but a real sense of motion (no surprise they thank Iced Earth here). But of course it flies in the face of variety, each track here just blurring by, full use of Blind Guardian's German precision, gothic high octane extraordinaire. But man, wait up. So there's the rub, a cavalcade of punishing, quick rockers, very dungeons and dragons, most around the six minute mark, most like a white knuckle race down the autobahn. But as usual, strong production, scorching solos and flawless execution, with big football match choruses to boot (these Japanese know all the words. Scary.). Tons of pictures for all the kids, who I guess now have their own Iron Maiden. Ends on a rare light note with *Barbara Ann*.
Rating **7**

## Blind Melon - Blind Melon (Capitol/EMI '92)

This supra-hyped gaggle of dreamers had apparently walked away with a fat advance for this enigmatic, odd panorama of funky, folksy new age rock. Really only metal in that a strange dope smokin' attraction is in store for any punter who crosses wits with this band,

and that superficially (i.e. looks-wise), the boys could be mistaken for The Four Horsemen or mebbee even Trouble on a more cheerful day, Blind Melon possess a liquid sort of light-headed Jane's Addiction meets Zeppelin meets Pearl Jam sound (while you're at it, throw in Firehose and The Allman Brothers), all slippery and loose, frighteningly open yet insulated as their small town roots. As I emphasize, truly non-metallic, yet comfortable with a hard rocker's language, the record rolls unconcerned, and unrushed, jamming in heated funk one minute, laid back for a look at the sky the next. Leader and philosopher Shannon Hoon has been through a lot of the biz (buds with Axl, guest vox on *Don't Cry*) and a past full of booze and drugs (not to mention a future stopped by heroin), and his worn experience shows with a sort of universal, sensitivity to the fruits of navel gazing, poured forth with a younger Perry Farrell-type delivery. Spontaneous, warm and strangely comfortable, with an inclusive welcome to the outcasts of the world, the hype is justified if originality and plainspeak to the heart counts for anything anymore. Followed the Spin Doctors and Phish into Deadhead heaven, before being truncated by Hoon's demise.
Rating **7**

## Blind Melon - Soup (Capitol/EMI '95)

The record came out and most agreed this was a cold, sour, over-seasoned **Soup**, critic and fan alike frowning at the baffling contusion of sounds this loose cannon of a band had assembled amongst heated arguments in New Orleans. And then Shannon Hoon died of a heroin overdose, confirming many an opinion of the guy, that he was clearly on a downward spiral, again, all of us frowning at his frocks, eyeliner and peeing on Vancouver. And his snuffing put this befuddled record on shakier ground, the sometimes morbid, always aimless and uneasy tones sunk further in a swampy morass of confused emotions, the same darkened cloud that opens up and soaks **In Utero**. I feel pretty much alone in admiring **Soup** right out of the gate, finding the bewildered gumbo of sounds both creative and playful, filling and satisfying, despite its collapsed dogpile of yuks and rolls. It's not as weird a departure as it looks, when one remembers how engagingly odd the debut was, tracks like *2X4*, *Vernie* and *New Life* being comfortable and familiar. But lead single *Galaxie* is almost friggin' *Sails Of Charon*, *Skinned* is a psycho cannibal killer tale rendered shufflebilly, and *Lemonade* is probably the sourest thing here, save for the drowned big band intro to *Galaxie*. Yes most definitely this is an indulgent record in no hurry whatsoever, and yes, the lyrics can be obscure without resolution, bad poetry riddling the good. But it's still a brave, unique record, and unfortunately even harder enjoy given Hoon's death, even if in life he was kind of bothersome.
Rating **8**

## Blind Melon - Nico (EMI '96)

Unfortunately, it's dead impossible to look at this band the same ever again, Shannon Hoon's accidental OD casting a pall over what is essentially three records worth of giddy, creative, acoustic affirmations of living, a bunch of kaleidoscopic tracks that eggroll a whole bunch of funk and hillbilly and Zep into something unique and often a bit sour and indulgent. This odds 'n' sods has stuff from all corners of Hoon's whacked head, bookended or at least defined by an awful version of *Rain* and the poignant title track from the band's second and last love-it-hate-it abortion, **Soup**. Of course in the fruitcake spirit of that record, the song never made the final cut, so it lives here amongst many other hippie trippies like *Soul One*, Steppenwolf cover *The Pusher*, *Poor Tom*-soundalike *John Sinclair* and a tune recorded on an answering machine. Damn good stuff all in all, but haunted by the snuffing of the guy singing it. CD ROM booty also included. No CD ROM, so no review. Nico is of course the name of Hoon's daddy-less daughter.

Rating 7

## Blitzkrieg - A Time Of Changes (Neat '85)

Interwoven personnel-wise with the fates of Satan and Blind Fury, Blitzkrieg kicked around the scene floundering until this '85 debut, original Satan vocalist and reputed crazy man Brian Ross (see **Court In The Act**) at the helm. Somewhat considered a minor NWOBHM classic, **A Time Of Changes** leaves me guessing why, this record filled with fairly standard, dated, although competent riff metal. The drum sound and performance are a bit naff, and I always thought Ross' vocals were over-rated. A cross between Angel Witch, Witchfynde and Slade would sum it up for me (wait a minute, Witchfynde is a cross between Angel Witch and Slade!). Main claim to fame: rumbling signature tune *Blitzkrieg* was covered by Metallica on their now-rare **Garage Days Re-revisited** EP. Reissued on CD by Castle Communications in '92.

Rating 6

## Blitzkrieg - Unholy Trinity (Neat '95)

Yep, they've pretty much recaptured the old Blitzkrieg sound. Yet I was never much of a fan first time around, this reunion record (see parallel release from the vastly superior Savage) offering the same uncommitted, anal retentive vaguely gothic riff rock, tepid cover of *Countess Bathory* showing all the cracks that are cavernous on the originals. I don't know, it still sounds dated rather than timeless, which is I'm sure what Neat is going for with their nifty Neat Metal division, taking a kick at the old warhorses from Jolly ol' in hopes of the next Aerosmith-like comeback (yeah right!). This one however's just scrappy and kind of rusted.

Rating 6

## Blitzkrieg - Ten (Neat Metal '97)

Encouraged by underground sales of the band's **Unholy Trinity** comeback in '95, Neat Metal has seen fit to dust off, re-record and flesh out the band's '91 EP **10 Years Of Blitzkrieg**, re-doing five tracks and adding five new ones. Problems persist. Killer NWOBHM ideas do exist here, but as usual, both song execution and production values haven't improved since the early '80s, Blitzkrieg still sounding loose and midrange-murky, even signature tune *Blitzkrieg* (now *Blitzkrieg '96*) sounding like weak punk. Sorry, but in order to convince a whole new generation that '80s-derived metal is worth a looksee, the stuff's gotta shine, and this band is smudgy with fingerprints.

Rating 6

## Blitzspeer - Live (CBS '90)

Punk-o-tallic madmen from the bleary-eyed psychic heart of NYC, Blitzpeer have always lurked on the fringes, too scuzzy and punk-veneered for conventional metal and . . . well . . . there is no audience for punk rock no more. But this is what Necros should have sounded like (and where Big Chief kinda went), totally hammer-riffed and large, a reeling crunch of totally underground sentiments, learned of metal but unkempt. Still, lo and behold, it is live, and I ain't got the patience for the rougher deliveries the stage doth harbring. But convincing and leathery all the same.

Rating 7

## Bloodgood - Live Volume Two: Shakin' The World (Intense '90)

This long, boomingly recorded live album comes to us from a churchy set-up in Seattle, White Metallists Bloodgood (who look like Ratt), offering a glam-rocking fire and brimstone multi-media extravaganza, designed to alternately inspire and scare wayward teen cretins into salvation. **Live** samples sermons from the band's four records recorded from '86 to '89, **Bloodgood, Detonation, Rock In A Hard Place** and **Out Of The Darkness**, but if that ain't enough, you can get the videos, which feature two dozen actors and dancers, working in tandem with these priests of noise. The music: tedious riff metal like bad Crüe with one of those high-voiced guys with a shag at the mike.

Rating 4

## Bloodlet - Eclectic (Victory '95)

Another characteristic Victory Records band, Bloodlet grind out a hopeless, anguished, pessimistic hardcore that is usually slow, stretchy and doom-shrouded. The lyrics course with tales of souls in torment, souls resigned to a damnation as prescribed by a Christian world, making this a sort of fire and brimstone lament from the heated side of the frying pan called life. Vocals are yer basic crew-cut curdle, making this urbancore assault grating to mine ears. Recorded in various sessions between '92 and '94.

Rating 5

## Blood Money - Red Raw And Bleeding (Ebony '86)

Stormy, British poverty goth, recorded red, raw and intrinsically Ebony, mixing speed and hard liquor like a bad mistake, Blood Money gallop forth into the grime and soot of industrial mayhem like a death metal cancer. Not that I'd ever play it voluntarily, one thing is for certain, it's faster and more destructive than regular thrash, and come on, who can deny titles like *Gor, Taras Bulba*, and *Deathstiny*. Mosh babble, British-style. Stiffed, as did follow-up **Battlescarred**.

Rating 5

## Bloody Six - In The Name Of Blood (Camel '84)

Like a highly strung, underground Accept, this vicious six piece German machine chunders proudly within a characteristically German pulverizer mix, heavy on bass and treble, while the siren calls of one Peter McTanner hammer out the venom on such craggy peaks as *High Class 'n Wild, Black Eagle* and *Way Of The Hunter*. Man, there's a lot of German imports with this same derivative Accept/Scorpions wallop, yet this is one of the larger ones, extremely similar to the chug of Gravestone, both accelerated and monstrous.

Rating 6

## The Bloody Stools - Meet The Bloody Stools (Caroline '91)

About the most x-rated and profane record I've ever heard, **Meet The Bloody Stools** is the metal equivalent of the Diceman. Totally cheap looking, yet surprisingly well-recorded and seriously executed despite the ten-toon-long dirty joke, the Stools plod through some pretty cool mid-pace party metal while spewing badly-out-of-tune hilarious filth on such radio classics as *Choke The Load, Show Me Your Tits, Barnyard Love* and *Give Head Or Die*. Bangs along pretty steadily for a bunch of dudes who couldn't possibly be planning a serious assault on the Billboard charts. Guest axework from Richie Sambora and Dave "Snake" Sabo.

Rating 6

## Blu Bones - Sink (Magnetic Air '94)

Digging deep into the grung-o-rama kitchen sink and coming up fresh and rockable is London, Ontario, eight year veterans Blu Bones, who have put together a confident slab of thick, sometimes immobile, Alice in Chains-style alterno-rock. All is well-attended to here, packaging, hazy, crazy lyrics, bassy production by Paul Goss, and a creepy first video in *So Tired*, to my mind one of the weaker, more irritating tracks here. Most of **Sink** plows insistently, big, rhythmic, possibly towards Soundgarden structures of old, but choruses bolt through nicely, making tunes catchy despite their seri-

ously dark arrangements. A valid competitor for major label status, but just a mite bit simplified, recalling my complaint with the first STP, and projects like Sugartooth and Soulhat.
Rating 7

## Blue Cheer - Vincebus Eruptum (Philips '67)

Often considered by many to be America's first metal band (Get a Life.), Blue Cheer (named for a type of acid) did manage to make some pretty obnoxious guitar noises in the late sixties before anybody else. However, calling it metal is a stretch, the Blue Cheer sound equating closer to acid-washed loud 'n' slurring renditions of sixties rock, much like occasional loud moments from Cream or Hendrix, although more focused than either. Who knows? Maybe this gang did have some effect on the early shapings of Sabbath, Heep, Deep Purple and/or Budgie. On the strength of their own scant product however, really nothing revolutionary to get excited about. Scored a minor hit with the by now old standby Summertime Blues. Big deal. Chalked up no less than six records by 1971, before breaking up and reforming again for '85's NWOBHM cash-in The Beast Is Back and beyond into an undistinguished second wind.
Rating 3

## Blue Cheer - Dining With The Sharks (Nibelung '91)

A somewhat authoritative name on which to hang a band, any band. And that's all she wrote, these turgid metal pioneers, kinda reforming to cash in on the distant past. Blue Cheer '91 is nothing to write home about, just a bikerish, boorish old rock headbang, like any number of German numbskulls from '83, bands stupidly copying Krokus, occasionally trying Accept, always guzzling Heinekens. And this is supposed to be American rock (OK, throw in The Rods, The Godz, and WASP). I guess it is sort of greasechain Detroit rootsy, but no damn good all the same, strained drinking man vocals scraping forth over a garagey mix and songs stiff as a board. Only saving grace (if you must have one): a sense of humour, not unlike evil twin Pink Fairies.
Rating 6

## Blue Murder - Blue Murder (Geffen '89)

This "super trio" debut, whose memory was systematically erased by lack of a timely follow-up, is essentially the first solo effort by classic Lizzy/Whitesnake fretsman John Sykes (who also sings quite well, thank you), with support from semi-famous guys Carmine Appice and Tony Franklin. Often cluttered and opaque sounding, due in no small part to Bob Rock's echoey, drum- and treble-heavy mix, Blue Murder is nevertheless an expertly detailed, stadium quality scorcher, or, more accurately, slow-burning pounder, often massive, gothic, Zep-ish (see Jelly Roll), and occasionally funky due to some wild, ornate Sykes riffs. Quite British, quite grand, but also overly laborious. File under respectable, even revered, but sparsely chosen for action due to difficulty in deciphering what's going on. Note: Ray Gillen was almost Blue Murder's vocalist.
Rating 7

## Blue Murder - Nothin' But Trouble (Geffen/MCA '93)

In conjunction with waiting for his home studio to be completed, and replacing his entire band, John Sykes manages to spend four years piecing together this laborious follow-up to his critically acclaimed debut. And, alas it's similarly massive, unwieldy, classic rock, yet surprisingly away from metallic, looking moreso bluesy, balladic and very retro, in no hurry to get to the point. Which bothers me. As my impatience grows to see something impressive, I can't help but think Sykes is the classier, less pandering side of Mr. Big, finding the

record just too everywhere and isolated in an '80s ethic Sykes helped define. And sorry, covering Itchykoo Park smacks of novelty.
Rating 7

## Blue Murder - Screaming Blue Murder -Dedicated To Phil Lynott (Geffen '94)

It's no secret that Phil in his downward spiral found a ray of hope within his hot new guitarist John Sykes, a man who inspired the fire that seemed lost in the classy but subdued Snowy White years. They were buds, and so now Sykes puts Phil's name on the cover, yet only fleetingly into song on this Japanese live set. We get Dancin' In The Moonlight and two Sykes/Lynott compositions in stormer Cold Sweat and mournful unreleased ballad Please Don't Leave Me. Elsewhere it's a bunch of rockin' Sykes tracks plus one of the man's largest monoliths, Whitesnake's Still Of The Night. I like these Japanese packages for the love of metal, the Japanese being strong supporters of these often discarded, often British or European superplayers from the '80s. Plus as usual, there's full lyrics in both languages and a healthy amount of quality photography. Mix-wise this isn't the best of live documents, but the record serves as a nice look at the rowdy, muscular flash of Sykes and his quintessentially heavy metal band.
Rating 7

## Blue Öyster Cult - Blue Öyster Cult (Columbia '72)

Enter the orbit of the strangest Cult of them all, one monochromatic acid trip of slippery propulsions, where the weary mind becomes crammed with competing and incestuous images of The Windout, released like Chinese throwing stars from the collective imaginos of Bloom, Roeser, Bouchard, Bouchard, and Lanier, not to mention significant mental harassment from Mssrs. Krugman, Pearlman, and Meltzer, who bring a wavey "critic's parody" slant to the lunacy. Evoking nothing anyone could love, Blue Öyster Cult grafts some sort of '60s psychedelic graveyard blues to the weariest of dated hard rocks, struggling with the tiniest of guitar-driven sounds, recorded limp and lifeless, unassuming under the colourful poetic phantasm that becomes all but missed under a fog of depression. Melancholy and baffling, Blue Öyster Cult possesses the oddest of tacit performances, rock songs played by monks glaringly sabotaged by the most faint-hearted percussive display I've ever snooooooozed, simply pussy-footing through a puerile play fraught with confused genius. Tragic and beautiful BÖC compositions that fall victim to a lack of technical desire, resulting in muted bewilderment by listener and cranker alike. According to Al, crowning track Cities On Flame's lyrics were influenced by MC5's Motor City Is Burning, the riff finding its seed in Black Sabbath's The Wizard, of relevance, given that Krugman signed the band, based on the label wanting its own version of the mighty Sab.
Rating 7

## Blue Öyster Cult - Tyranny And Mutation (Columbia '73)

Satan as clown, mankind as dog, and Blue Öyster Cult as grinning court reporter to the sordid interaction, Tyranny And Mutation sets the players into mutating flirtation; molecules seeking synergy, then scattering to crusty, inhospitable terrains irritated by buzzing guitars, cheesy '70s ivories, and a submissive set of traps (no other word for it). The hallowed five come to sludgy, still frozen forms of life, parading classics like wild boars in drag; tales like The Red And The Black, 7 Screaming Diz-busters and Hot Rails To Hell, all more convincingly amplified by the live environment, here simpering and sulking in some sort of weightless orbit around an unworthy chunk of wayward meteorite, bunched up on side one around a negative blues called OD'd On Life Itself. Side two simply wings out on a tab of previously theoretical chemistry combining Edgar Allan Poe and H.P. Lovecraft with Pearlman's worst pharmaceutical nightmares. Suffocated under the psychic trappings of heaviness of every sort, Blue Öyster Cult was quickly becoming something very imposing, while the studio still cranked out a hair-balled, '60s-polluted garage clank, here picking it up ever so slightly, yet still mired in an oddly appealing maze of cobwebs. Cover art from records 1 and 2 courtesy of nutball architecture student Gawlick, buddy of Pearlman's at the Rhode Island School of Design, dreamer of futuristic city states, two views of which grace these alchemy-laced timetravels through rock.

Rating                                                      8

## Blue Öyster Cult - Secret Treaties   (Columbia '74)

The crowning blow of the band's black and white era, **Secret Treaties** is a hapless metalfest as thin and garage-like as what came before, but less psychedelic, packed with soon to be concert classics such as ME 262, Harvester Of Eyes and Astronomy. Still caught in an asthmatic hyperventilation, the mix of Munster-style keyboards, weak guitar and weak drums takes **Secret Treaties** into the land of Small, while absolutely gravity-defying storytelling steals the show, sending the listener into a cyclone of confusion along with a batch of characters no wart-covered harpie could love. As with the two previous, **Secret Treaties** is more frostbite and inner chill, similar to feelings The Stranglers would emit years later, than anything approaching modern and human rock'n'roll, cementing BÖC's reputation as demonic foreign-ness from deep beneath the earth's crust, smiling as the Apocalypse descends on the circus of man. Many a past and present BÖC member's favourite record, and significantly, the last featuring heavy literary contribution from Sandy Pearlman.

Rating                                                     10

## Blue Öyster Cult - On Your Feet Or On Your Knees
(Columbia '75)

A greasy, belching, rock showman persona begins to emerge on this seminal live document which brings the oddest raft of tales to the arena for a smoke and lights parade of fascist noises. Punctuating the end of a cold war for the band, **On Your Feet Or On Your Knees** grinds a bunch of jammin' BÖC epics through an intrinsically overblown '70s concert experience, not unlike that of Purple or Zeppelin; freewheeling, funky, and stuck with machinery-melting airplane glue. All looms way larger here than on respective chinsy origins, most notably Hot Rails To Hell, Cities On Flame, and the bashing boogie of ME 262, the band's central lightning rod for Nazi-related accusations. Much as I find this a stage classic, **On Your Feet** is permeated by an ancient melancholy due to its frightening, atonal, and unintentionally evil material. My copy still smells like incense.

Rating                                                      8

## Blue Öyster Cult - Agents Of Fortune   (Columbia '76)

Perhaps we're now experiencing what Eric Bloom sees when he takes off those mirror shades; the assorted psychic warriors haunting the BÖC kingdom becoming recognizable and even human, as the band enters its second era, marked by a modern, brighter rock universality versus the tonal wastelands of the band's first three. **Agents Of Fortune** marks a total musical transformation, borne of the fact that the band had all been set up with home recording equipment, fleshing their demos to near-song status, rendering a wealth of personable material ready for terror. The rockers are more violent and pronounced, and the rest is an all-new blast of sly accessibility, examining human issues or imagined humanity, as the lyrics still weave complex, corny-colored tales of sinuous multi-tiered evil, de-

spite candy-coated musical language. The first BÖC that actually beams, **Agents** is rich and fertile, shimmering with the new age metal of Helen Wheels' Tattoo Vampire and the semi-stolen This Ain't The Summer Of Love, the winding malevolent twin traumas of Sinful Love and Patti Smith's The Revenge Of Vera Gemini, and the luded rhapsodies of Morning Final and Tenderloin. **Agents Of Fortune** was actually considered a sell-out by a growing legion of fans weaned on the Cult's legendary live blitz, yet also predictably, new fans came on board, serenaded by (Don't Fear) The Reaper (the band's biggest hit ever, a metaphysical masterpiece that sonically pays homage to the Byrds), and the unabashed pop of True Confessions and Debbie Denise. Well now we've seen who was at that New Year's Party we all missed back on Dominance And Submission, and you can bet Times Square is still burning with the flames of psychic experiments gone wrong, flames that scorch the minds of those who linger too long, minds that well-cooked, become recorded history in the apocalyptic grooves of the Blue Öyster Cult.

Rating                                                     10

## Blue Öyster Cult - Spectres   (Columbia '77)

Call me gullible, but I always let BÖC's bitchin' cover art colour my impression of the vinyl within, and **Spectres** is no exception. All indoor fireworks (thanks Elvis), monsters and lasers, yet with a calming eye to the proceedings, **Spectres** is a smokey house of the macabre, circus-style, where apparitions display their talents on various energy planes beginning with Godzilla, closing out the parade with Nosferatu. **Spectres** fits history as the second of a two album movement, leaving the urban chill of **Agents Of Fortune** for a more insular, reflective visit to a night-shrouded place much like that depicted on its wrapping. Signature concert faves Godzilla and R. U. Ready 2 Rock are a riot, as is futuristic biker epic Golden Age Of Leather. But the record really scars the lobes within the deep wells of Death Valley Nights, the elegant Fireworks and the languished I Love The Night, all shaded by the fluid ethereals of Roeser's classy axework, lyrics entering the foggy, unsure world of dreams. All in all, **Spectres** is the usual brilliantly chaotic hodgepodge of emotive spikes and dives, more a rock-solid collection of singular masterpieces sent to live side-by-side through the unimaginable intentions of Bloom, Roeser, Lanier and the Bouchard brothers. All work a five-sided integration on this symphony of sins, leaving one apprehensive of entering the night alone with one's subconscious.

Rating                                                     10

## Blue Öyster Cult - Some Enchanted Evening
(Columbia '78)

The second of three live albums which close out defined, pronounced eras of BÖC's evolution, **Some Enchanted Evening** is somewhat of a discard, save for one of the band's coolest cover arts. Seven tracks, three worthy of attention, those being lovable basher R.U. Ready To Rock, lovable tune about a basher Godzilla, and lovable r'n'r original about bashing things Kick Out The Jams, the band's coolest live cover from a pretty unimaginative list including this record's dull We Gotta Get Out Of This Place. Gotta say here however, having seen the great ones on three different tours, BÖC are a truly smokin' live act, never losing sight of the humanity among the heavy mechanics, the fact that we're all a part of a bigger, crazy rock'n'roll revue. And of course, there's always Godzilla blowing smoke rings. Certified platinum in '88, much to the satisfaction of manager Pearlman, who had to pull teeth to get the band thinking about another live record so soon.

Rating                                                      6

## Blue Öyster Cult - Mirrors (Columbia '79)

The cleanest, brightest, most golden-tanned BÖC of them all, **Mirrors** to my mind is second only to the magnificent **Cultosaurus Erectus** in overall grandeur. Producers Krugman and Pearlman, who've done a pretty lacklustre job so far, let's face it, step aside for the crystal-brite treatment of Tom Werman, granting the Cult their first truly headphone-ready mix, full of vibrance and magic from the acoustic guitars of The Great Sun Jester, In Thee and The Vigil to the full-blooded drums of Dr. Music and I Am The Storm. In retrospect, the band considered their time with Werman pure Hell, Tom, ever the perfectionist sanitizing the band's sound way beyond what they might have preferred. But bottom line: there is unarguably more bass and treble here than on any other BÖC record. The band seems to have exorcised the demons, apparitions, monsters and depraved human wreckage that paraded through past works. Here the characters are fresh, full of positive fire, or at worst, saddled with reflections on lost love, reflections that also possess rays of hope and belief in the potential of a new day. The hard rock on **Mirrors** is positively joyful, Dr. Music and the title cut both summer rockers of the highest order, while even The Vigil, the band's grandest epic, marauds proudly (the band censoring a dirtier Patti Smith lyric for this poetic take on the Roswell legend). An amazing, surprisingly mainstream record, **Mirrors** is packed with human creative power; this time encouraged, and only subtly so, through extra-terrestrial magic from benevolent gods. Roeser, moreso here than on anything so far, supports the new exuberance with a care-free California soloing style that out-mellows The Eagles and Fleetwood Mac at their own smooth recline. But **Mirrors** miraculously remains a hard rock record, if a smooth, shiny, reflective one, driven by life-affirming forces of imagination and (heretofore unknown to BÖC) painstaking studio detail. The biggest wave of the whole BÖC story. Catch it. Question: can you spot the two (very deliberate) sperm swimming in the cover art's clouds?

Rating 10

## Blue Öyster Cult - Cultösaurus Erectus (Columbia '80)

Man, all over again like some sick synergy of paintbrush and airwave, the cover of this, my number one fave rave BÖC extravagonzo says it all. **Cultösaurus Erectus** is half scraps, half alien life-form, half desert, half alive, half approachable, goofy looking from afar but awe-inspiring from inside. Add to that doomed to extinction for the sole reason that its physical shape just does not care, and you have a grand, jovial version of altered reality, strongly evoking a slow-paced shuffle through torrid, mystery-drenched interplanetary plains, where ludicrous and horrifying testimony to the cellular folly of living pop up in random order like so many targets in a shooting gallery. Nary a remotely human experience here, except for The Marshall Plan, a bizarre, out-of-character inclusion about rock star aspirations, so laughably unwelcome here, you just gotta sit back and survey the flames as it burns like a moth at the hands of a band so perceptive and clueless at once. **Cultösaurus** is no **Mirrors**. **Cultösaurus** is Lips In The Hills, Black Blade, Monsters, Deadline, and finally Unknown Tongue, where it all unravels in a drifted pop haze unto detached apparitionals, Martin Birch edging the band back into the silvery world of metal, buoyed by his recent success with psychic Cult doppelganger Black Sabbath. Nothing is quite right here anywhere, yet it's all so comfortably as things should be, as a self-conscious but successful phantasm just pours out cornucopia-like with detached neutrality. Fraught with ambiguity, **Cultösaurus Erectus** is great

art par excellence, catalyst to multi-tiered realities, stairway to the stars, resting grounds for the extinct.

Rating 10

## Blue Öyster Cult - Fire Of Unknown Origin (Columbia '81)

Full of fireworks and over-excitement, **Fire Of Unknown Origin** is the flashiest BÖC trip, very digestible, very evidently sci-fi, and cleverly rocking, pulsing with economy and straight-forward verve. Somewhat tainted by its cutting room floor association with the **Heavy Metal** soundtrack, this, BÖC's second most commercially successful studio album, overblows its previously subtle, filtered imagery with gaudy, fantastical tales like Veterans Of The Psychic Wars, Sole Survivor, and Heavy Metal: The Black And Silver, all commendable tunes save for their touch of Cult cash-in. Classics include (desperate) monster Roeser hit Burnin' For You, energetic space race After Dark, and technicolour comedy of evil Joan Crawford. We wore the hell out of this record back in our last year of high school, eating up every buoyant moment, for the common thread throughout this day of the Cult is energy, somewhat empty and light, but optimistic energy nevertheless. What fleshes out **Fire Of Unknown Origin**, however are the unadorned, insidious elements, pieces and alien body parts; most invisible being the washing loiter of Don't Turn Your Back and the aforementioned Burnin' For You, whose chorus strikes a chord in the heart that brands forever a partitioned mass that beats only for dissolved expectation. I love the record, but that doesn't mean I have to take all of it seriously, and I don't, because I think the band was more after Art elsewhere. Still, a merciless Cult ice sends a chill from around every sonic corner in this hall of mirrors, and after too many dulling blasts, one wishes only to drift into a cryogenic sleep. I am becalmed.

Rating 9

## Blue Öyster Cult - Extraterrestrial Live (Columbia '82)

BÖC's second double live makes up for the eccentric but disposable single **Some Enchanted Evening**, concentrating on punchy, dressy performances of mostly latter-half tales of cybernetic debauchery, understandably but predictably concentrating on the hits or obvious crowd pleasers. Coolest move is the inclusion of all the lyrics, offering the listener better fish-lensed gazings into the minds of rock's strangest and arguably best writers. From the 50¢ we mailed off back in the late '70s to receive dot matrix printouts of all the lyrics up to and including **Spectres**, we were well versed with the band's surreal landscapes. **E.T. Live** demonstrates that these fiercely evolved aliens haven't let up on the literary poison (witness Joan Crawford, which is incidentally the most vital performance on the record). Still ... not the tailpipe death-trip that was **On Your Feet Or On Your Knees**, but nevertheless an acceptable and muscular testimony to one of the world's most challenging artistic forces. Could have got a bit more wild with the song selection. Features new drummer and ex-lighting engineer for the band Rick Downey, who was forced to step in after the band gave Albert the boot mid-tour in England (long story).

Rating 7

## Blue Öyster Cult - The Revolution By Night (Columbia '83)

Signalling the start of a new and inhospitable era in the BOC saga, **The Revolution By Night** (originally titled Deadman's Curb) explores murkier psychological wells through brighter, more technological, keyboard-dominated permutations on pop metal. Pre-release single Take Me Away is the lone kick-ass rocker, a classic of the catalogue punctuated by an ethereal chorus and a layered climactic finale. Shooting Shark is the literary gem, co-written with Patti Smith; vast, hypnotic and touching, yet essentially a tale of the sky written in the language of pop. Elsewhere, the emphasis on low-key dynamic continues with elusive and creeping rocker *Shadow Of California*, shaded by cascades of tribal electronic drums, a rare modern Pearlman composition linked inextricably to his complex Imaginos saga. Strange, but even though this is the usual display of baffling diversity, there's a thread of unmistakable Cult edge, characterized by provocative though sometimes gaudy lyrics, which become a metaphor for the road movie psychosis that can live amongst such works of seeming digestibility. **The Revolution By Night** ultimately becomes an inhumanly smooth and sophisticated vehicle driven by Roeser's cocktail hour soloing style weaving tasteful dialogue with Lanier's keyboard melodies. It is Roeser's persona that seems to be steering BÖC at this point, a desperately thawing mountain of emotion yearning to connect through thickening walls built of a fierce but so effortlessly self-entertaining dream world. This revolution turns out to become more of a reverse evolution back into an enveloping night, where it seems BÖC is to remain dream-locked forever.

Rating     8

## Blue Öyster Cult - Club Ninja   (Columbia '86)

**Club Ninja** is in many ways the lost record, least attached to the BÖC body of work, painfully constructed and baffling in its bad taste. While retaining the trademark limitless mix of hard rock, moody atmospherics, pop rock and interplanetary undescribables, **Club Ninja** is decidedly void of committed metal, not to mention heavily over-produced and infiltrated by non-band tunesmiths and session players, resulting in some out-of-character directives such as the slightly stupid *Beat 'Em Up* and *Make Rock Not War*, both more Bon Jovial than Bloomin' disturbed. But covering Leggat with *White Flags* speaks volumes about BÖC's depth of craft, as does *Perfect Water*, co-written with Jim Carroll, who wraps a beautifully aquatic lyric around a quintessentially submerged breezy BÖC melodica. Superficially, **Club Ninja** echoes with deflated pop defeat, yet after a few thousand spins, Roeser's wise croon wins the day, slowly filling vessels with another retrospectively necessary piece of BÖC isolation, here showcasing a band wasted on the rocks of the business, struggling down commercial avenues locked off to dinosaurs striving to update, unbeknownst to the abandoning effect their unique, unsightly vision would have on the radio-ability of the whole. Ultimately, **Club Ninja** is a Sunday afternoon, sundown, sunken sort of Cult experience, necessarily alone despite the will towards life with others.

Rating     7

## Blue Öyster Cult - Imaginos   (Columbia '88)

Never seriously warming up to this suspicious record, I've come to dismiss it as somewhat of a sell-out. Originally cast as an Albert Bouchard solo album, **Imaginos** is the band's heaviest, fulfilling many a fan's wish for sustained metal. Still, I find the whole thing perched on the edge of parody, too dressy and fantastical lyrically in a painfully self-conscious way; indeed, the band reworking Subhuman and calling it *Blue Öyster Cult* which perhaps as metaphor for the record as a whole, rehashes lyrical images from throughout the band's career, Sandy's long-winded Imaginos idea collapsing in rearranged disorder. Back on **Secret Treaties**, I could always envision the boys breathing a collective "Yeah, so what?" in the face of such amazingly wild lyrics. Here I see real awareness and second guessing; a laborious exercise in expected weird, versus an involuntary existence way off in Nightmareville. An elaborate concept album (although it's all so opaque, I've never tried to decipher the thing), I find I

just can't warm up to this creepy, brashly recorded affair, almost as if there's too much of everything we always wanted, played by a bewildering legal tangle of parties, many uncredited. Ultimately, **Imaginos** is a record I can never accurately recall tune for tune; however faves would include *Del Rio's Song* and the pulsating re-make of *Astronomy*. Lavish, lengthy and live sounding at the same time, **Imaginos** is a muscular, often plodding feast for the ears with lots of warm Roeser vocals and difficult guitar/keyboard interplay. Oddly turgid and automatic, **Imaginos** is still bright and fiery under scrutiny, perhaps offering the most baffling anti-climactic but hypnotic punctuation to this, the last BÖC studio project going on nine years now.

Rating     8

## Blue Öyster Cult - Career Of Evil: The Metal Years
(CBS '90)

The first of two CBS compilations pointless to the real fan, **Career Of Evil** is a half-stab at a greatest hits record, quite random really, spanning all the years, not just the "metal" ones, which don't actually exist by any thinking person's reliable measure. A decent but largely unremarkable essay by Arthur Levy sketchily goes over the history of the band, providing some reading material as you unexcitedly sample these tracks you've heard a zillion times before. Mostly (but not exclusively) black and white era tracks, which I guess the label execs think are the metal years.

Rating     5

## Blue Öyster Cult - Cult Classic   (Herald/Caroline '94)

An odd little record, on which the idling (but at least gigging) BÖC contrive to make some cash on songs they own, by creating versions that they will own. So **Cult Classic** finds the band (which now includes Chuck Bürgi on drums and Jon Rogers on bass) re-recording a bunch of their hits to pleasing effect. A truism on this band is that undeniably, they wrote great songs, but both deliveries and recordings often suffered. So the biggest improvements here (for various reasons) are the light party rendition of *ME 262*, the expansive, lead-textured version of *E.T.I.*, the powerful, groove-heavy version of *This Ain't The Summer Of Love* and the funkified version of *Harvester Of Eyes*. And in general, all versions here are at least equal to or better than the originals, benefiting from a warm, full spectrum mix; Bürgi's drumming especially nice, exhuberant with lots of cymbals, then softly set back in the mix. Elsewhere there's a studio version of *Buck's Boogie* and a couple of non-vocals mixes for *Reaper* and *Godzilla*. But really, you can't complain about these versions. I mean, if this was 1988 or '86 or '90, they might have been all tech-ed up like modern day ZZ Top or so much hair band metal. **Cult Classic**'s properly executed, old-style production proves BÖC's taste above trend.

Rating     8

## Blue Öyster Cult - Workshop Of The Telescopes
(Sony '95)

The long-discussed BÖC "boxed set" has arrived, sort of, **Workshop Of The Telescopes** being a double CD set of greatest hits, with a few minor curios, and quite good packaging. All eras are equally represented, amplifying the clashing quality of the band's old and new, and there's a nicely laid-out booklet with cool photos and an intelligent essay by Arthur Levy, along with full discography and a quote from ramblin' Cult fan, Mike Watt. Musically, pretty much what you'd expect, the miniscule extras being rough-shod 1972 versions of *Buck's Boogie* (from V/A album **Guitars That Destroyed The World**), *Workshop Of The Telescopes* and *The Red And The Black*, all really crusty, low and slinky. Then there's a weird, luded and deluded studio version of *Born To Be Wild* and that's all she wrote, the bigwigs at Columbia offering 28 more tracks, all from the

band's long, roller coaster catalogue of classics, **Imagi-nos** excluded. A strident haunting look at a legend, **Workshop** is actually kind of jarring given its swooping timetravels. Ultimately, one's best bet is to undulate forthrightly within the original studio slabs and leave the compilation nation to lesser beings.
Rating                                          7

## Bodine - Bodine   (Rhinoceros '81)

Who'd believe it except those already in the know, but Bodine's premiere is simply a great blues metal record, from the Netherlands no less, and from a band soon to turn decidedly more metallic. Not even remotely foreign-sounding, as one might fully expect, this is just one helluva pounding celebration of tradition and all things old, like the best of Whitesnake, like Bad Company could never be, and like ZZ Top might have been, rendered rich and muscular by an Accept-like guitar attack and parallel mix, plus the capable, full-bodied growl of vocalist Jay Van Feggelen. Grinding, marauding and steeped in blues and boogie structures, Bodine gives it all a massive metal topspin, comfortably fusing the loud and the soulful like bar-bred but missionary veterans. Unfortunately, due to its being released basically ten years before its time, this blue collar pounder could have cleaned up in the '90s, what with the retro rock buzz being ridden by bands like The Four Horsemen and The Black Crowes. But as Diamond Dave sez "that's life."
Rating                                          8

## Bodine - Bold As Brass   (Rhinoceros '82)

Trading the soulful Van Feggelen for a more metallic but equally commanding throatster in one "Mad Man Axel", and adding a second guitar for that all important Teutonic twin attack, Bodine arm themselves for the rapidly growing metal resurgence. With an arsenal of muscle and good songs similar to continental peers Accept, **Bold As Brass** is an aggressive, well-written early entry to the army of European records made in the early '80s. Retaining some of their righteous bluesiness, Bodine update confidently with such cruising rockers as the ever-intensifying *Heavy Rain* and low cycle, biker anthem *Wild Fire Queen*, both made all the more heroic by exhilarating and domineering vocal performances. Still a bit dated in terms of metal, the band may have been moving this way only recently judging from the debut's surprising history, but there's no denying the intensity of all performances despite basically pumping fist material. And that's always half the battle.
Rating                                          8

## Bodine - Three Times Running   (WEA '83)

Utterly and completely in full metallic swing, Bodine erect their first, truly modern heavy metal wall, an exceedingly classy, thundering work that retains the band's Accept-like parallels. Flagship piece *Black Star Risin'* leads the attack like a battalion of tanks through the desert, complete with massive, creaking axe work and the usual red carpet treatment from throat Axel. Other kick-ass cruisers include lead track *Shout* and the sustained sweat of *Hard Times*, fortified by waves of droning power chords in fine Black Forest fashion. One definite shortcoming in my mind is the inclusion here of two instrumentals on a record totaling eight cuts, both incidentally driven by the same galloping drum pattern. Aside from this minor annoyance however, **Three Times Running** is another large-boned Bodine statement, preserving the spirit of early Euro steel. So lift a pint in honour of the forgotten, because this may be the last place you'll ever hear about this gathering of pirates.
Rating                                          8

## Body Count - Body Count   (Sire '92)

Ice T does a commendable thing, taking Anthrax' and The Beastie Boys' lead, butting his rap arsenal up against the stronger presence of the world's most powerful music, causing a media storm over censorship in the process with the track *Cop Killer* (my two cents worth: Ice is wrong. The police have enough shit to deal with.). Unfortunately, the pig-smoking, white-baiting and mutha this and that can't bury the fact that the metal's lame, played at the simplistic, punk-predictable level of amateur novelty. Bad, no-groove drumming and dull skate riffs undermine the great idea here, which attempts to bring rap to whites and metal to blacks. Whereas the gangsta pistol-whipping lyrics are fully bracing to yer basic metal fan, the music rates a yawn with punters raised on the quality standards of Sabbath, Priest, Metallica and Megadeth. More like a video, like watching **Boyz 'n The Hood**, a foul tour of inner city cesspools: one listen, a good read, a reality we don't want to confront while we're busy acquiring assets, a tale of trash set to turgid third-rate metal, badly mixed, badly paced, Ice picking the wrong posse to show up his white brothers, all the big talk on *There Goes The Neighbourhood* being just that: empty threats, all talk no action. Still, Ice kicks. He's intense like Rollins and Mustaine, and I hope the Body Count rises. Somebody's gotta do it.
Rating                                          5

## Body Count - Born Dead   (Virgin/EMI '94)

The chill of the logically criminal mind once more stinks up the urban landscapes of Ice T's metallic alter-ego. Again irresponsibly glorifying the scumbag lifestyle, Ice does more harm to black America than good. Anyhow, it's still a good read, although less intelligent or insightful than last time around, the sparse lyrics delivered in Ice's usual tentative half sing/half rap. The music's a tad improved however, still recycled '80s riffing but occasionally finding groove (i.e. *Shallow Graves* and *Who Are You?*), y'know like an old Exciter record. So the band still can't play or write, even if the concept remains novel. Much beefier mix than the debut, so far more salvageable.
Rating                                          6

## Bogeymen - There Is No Such Thing As
(Delicious Vinyl '91)

From the ashes of the original Masters Of Reality comes Bogeymen, an outback, slidin', blues rock monster that reaches way back for a purely '70s take on timeless but hard-hitting barroom boogie. Less the metal excess of debut-era Masters, Bogeymen achieve biker rock status with well-placed shafts of the metallic allied with southern rock, Bad Company, Zep and Deep Purple, reigning as kings of a second string pile that further down the layers includes Four Horsemen, Salty Dog, Raging Slab and Rhino Bucket. But Bogeymen are perhaps the greatest purists, and the least like opportunists, honking bluesy and ancient, complete with Jon Lord keys, Bonham cannons, time-to-spare jams, and the simplest of arrangements. An over-exposed term like "unique" would definitely apply and amplify, doling Bogeymen major respect for an isolated sound, unconcerned with the hectic pace of rock in the '90s. Thoroughly detached with a High Times mind drift that says enter if you like, but we really don't care one way or another.
Rating                                          8

## Tommy Bolin - Teaser   (CBS '75)

Released more or less in conjunction with Bolin's amazing coup as "the guy who replaced Ritchie Blackmore in Deep Purple" re: the largely panned **Come Taste The Band** record, **Teaser** documents a young hotshot with all sorts of deep and divergent styles on his mind. There's fusion, ballads, funky rock and lots of Bolin's surprisingly soulful pipes. Fave would be the strident *People, People*, although the whole thing is without fault at least in terms of sincere craft. Tracks from **Teaser** even made it into Purple's set on the ill-fated tour of their last before reunion. Now somewhat a collectible, as folks peer into the short but complicated career of an instinctive guitarist dead from heroin at age 25.

Rating **8**

## Tommy Bolin - Private Eyes (CBS '76)
Released a mere couple months before Bolin's end-of-party death December 4, 1976, **Private Eyes** is an esoteric, elaborate piece of funk/jazz/soft rock created in a fog of heroin abuse, amazing given the record's ambitious arrangements and studio polish. Bolin's playing is mostly laid-back and bluesy, sparse, surprisingly scattered and intermittent as the man lets song dominate in all its melodic layering (*Post Toastee* bucks this trend, jamming up a funkwahboogie to the delirium of axe students everywhere). Weird but sincere display of free '70s indulgence from a middle America guy for which music was just music, no categories, no hangups. One of the 25 mellowest records in this book.

Rating **7**

## Tommy Bolin - The Ultimate . . . (Geffen '89)
This retrospective points to humanity's morbid curiosity with the fallen, in this case, a manchild dead from drugs at 25 way back in 1976. In this context, **The Ultimate . . .** justifies its existence, mapping Bolin's rapid and catalytic incarnations through Zephyr, James Gang (which Bolin flew in and dominated), Moxy (!), a couple of energetic fusion trips, through Deep Purple and finally his two indulgent but creative solo albums. Only 110 minutes of music over 23 tracks, this is a pretty quick survey. However the booklet is elegant, packed with great trivia and celebrity quotes, plus tons of pictures, all over 24 full-colour, 12" x 12" pages. The music's widely varied (guitarists seem to admire this in guys like Bolin and Gary Moore), ranging from blubbery psychedelia, through the buttrock of James Gang, snobby amphetamine jazz, and the thick-headed '70s funk metal of Purple's last, uncharacteristic record. Bolin is the everywhere, all-styles journeyman, revered for his intuitive, spontaneous style rather than any immediately identifiable signature. The stuff just sounded very smooth, the livelier notes left for the wankery of the jazz projects, the really wonderful soloing left for his free last days. Lovingly put together, **The Ultimate . . .** interestingly isn't all that vital musically, most of Bolin's catalogue being obtainable through a combo of vinyl and CD. But the book was real nice.

Rating **6**

## Bolt Thrower - The IVth Crusade (Earache '92)
U.K.'s Bolt Thrower are often cited as the kings of grindcore, possessing all the loathsome and repelling characteristics of this distressed but improving genre, sticking to its roots despite strayings from its contemporaries. Their fourth painful smorg erects the usual blood-caked wall of electricity, lots of OTT double-bass drums without the speed, underneath the usual grindcore gargle. As stated numerous times elsewhere, this stuff just ain't my bag, Cathedral, Entombed and Pantera (and maybe Grave and Morgoth) being about as dense as I aspire to. Female bass player if you can believe it.

Rating **4**

## Bolt Thrower - . . . For Victory (Earache '95)
Shredding, pummeling onward, the owners of "war metal" leak minor shardations of melody onto this supremely dense pile of poison tar. Still one of the most hurtful bands on record, Bolt Thrower nevertheless take it all quite seriously, attentive of quality, but still in love with all the lows and highs of thrash, grind and death. One of those "good if you can hack it (to pieces)" type of records, absolutely chaos-drenched like war itself. Note: my copy includes an entire live CD recorded in Manchester '92.

Rating **6**

## Bonham - The Disregard Of Timekeeping (CBS '89)
Badboy Jason Bonham and his lucky entourage, most notably Ontario-raised vocalist Daniel MacMaster, come fully equipped with this odd record that tugs the listener to a number of smooth and shiny worlds. Basically an imaginative, intelligent and wildly-updated corporate hard rock version of Led Zeppelin, Bonham represents the youth gone wild with the tools of the conservative. Jason builds an identical backbeat to his father's legendary approach, sounding cavernous, large and spacious beneath tricky arrangements that reflect Zep's eclecticism but builds towards a very modern sort of new monster, cool, detached, yet very commercial, due in no small part to MacMaster's personal style, which only borrows selectively from both the shrieky old Plant and rangeless, whispery new Plant. Definitely not a record that jumps into familiarity effortlessly, **The Disregard Of Timekeeping** is in many ways as artsy and ornate as its title and cover art. Fave raves would include *Cross Me And See*, one of a handful of Robert Plant solo career-style tunes on the record, and the mellow *Dreams*, which features much pleasant keyboard work from John Smithson and some very Schenker-like axe fluidity from Ian Hatton. But big, simple fills from Jason himself mark the signature sound of this intimate but lonesome record, a deceptively exploitative work that unfolds as quite brave and studied. A complicated but winning formula that deserves attention.

Rating **8**

## Bonham - Mad Hatter (Sony '92)
The long-awaited, on again/off again, one hour follow-up to **The Disregard Of Timekeeping** piques one's curiosity long before first listen, shipped in two different cover arts: one simply sporting the new Dali-inspired logo, the other, a Dali-inspired painting plus logo. **Mad Hatter** opens with *Bing*, a virtual re-telling of the debut's funky *Bringing Me Down*. As the story unfolds, Bonham's managed to reproduce their busy open architecture sound here, complete with an ever-widening vocabulary similar to Robert Plant's **Pictures At Eleven** or **Now And Zen**, although much heavier. Still, much cool-spirited homage to Zeppelin; funky **Presence**-era Zep (*Bing*), Kashmir Zep (*The Storm*), flowery Zep (*Change Of A Season*), and still daring, innovative arrangements with a "separateness" that is both attractive and cumbersome. Again, **Mad Hatter** finds the band in strangely non-committal terrain, playing sparsely, mixed loudly, coming off opaque and ornamental, somehow impenetrable before a couple o' hundred listens. Surprisingly atmospheric and moody, Bonham has created a kind of disciplined but loose studio rock almost always throbbing but rarely conventionally metallic. Well off in an admirably multi-tiered world of their own, Bonham may prove to be just beyond the grasp of the average punter, which strangely may not be bothering the band at all. Hats off for pushing the limits, Bonham II vs. Bonham I: more artistic, less immediately satisfying. Update: a whopping $800,000 to produce, **Mad Hatter** eventually stiffed, causing the band to lose their record deal, Daniel MacMaster's departure from the band, then the demise of the whole shooting match altogether.

Rating **8**

## Bon Jovi - Bon Jovi  (PolyGram Est. '83)

Yikes, the record that started it all, actually really having quite a lot to do with the birth of AOR, this feeding off that same crossover madness trumped up with Billy Idol's *Rebel Yell* (metal to new wave) and The Cult's *She Sells Sanctuary* (metal to goth). Here we find a kind of tough song like *Runaway* doing the pop fusion to metal thing, as the world becomes an oyster for this starry eyed wannabe, after all that time dreaming of stardom while sweeping up in the studio, or however the fable goes. Anyways, without much surprise, this is the rawest Bon Jovi platter, and probably the most listenable given its naivety.
Rating                                                    6

## Bon Jovi - 7800 Fahrenheit  (PolyGram '85)

Bon Jovi's sophomore effort is probably the only record in the band's catalogue considered a slight stumble (well, New Jersey kinda wore people out). Tracks are cloddish, either leaning kinda heavy or just stiff in stuck party mode, keyboards forcibly attached to structures that may not have needed them, production clinical as is expected, but almost distracting. Symptomatic of all of this: ballad *Silent Night*: gosh-awful drums, stiff all over, and those keyboards. Yuck, although as usual Richie Sambora chimes in with an eloquent solo. So consider this a bit anti-climactic and loose-fitted, given the high hopes of the pomp rockin', genre-defining debut.
Rating                                                    4

## Bon Jovi - Slippery When Wet  (PolyGram '86)

Finally this gathering of aging peacocks breaks it wide open, **Slippery When Wet** being the band's multiplatinum cash cow, the craggy peak of cheese, the hit generator of perfumigated chick rock. Everything's upratchet and uplifted here: more guitars, major multi-tracked choruses, and a springiness of step that you just knew tried so hard, they hadda win. Producer Bruce Fairbairn (with his Little Mountain studios in Vancouver) is a big part of the gang, doing what he does for the Crue, The Cult and most fabulously Aerosmith (both even use the Margarita horns; Bon Jovi here on *Social Disease*), turning Jon and posse chartable like never before. So the hits flooded radio and MTV: big, swingin' *You Give Love A Bad Name*, big swingin' *Livin' On A Prayer*, and unbelievably goofy spaghetti western tale *Wanted Dead Or Alive* doing sorta what Triumph did, stoopid anthems with as many hooks as clichés. Nice wet t-shirt shots; Warrant would be proud.
Rating                                                    6

## Bon Jovi - New Jersey  (PolyGram '88)

In homage to his roots, local boy made good Jon Bon Jovi pulls a Bruce, commemorating his home state in song. And just like Bruce, stories often surface of Jon jumping on stage with some local bar band to blow a few songs. But this gargantuan, difficult, Bruce Fairbairn/Bob Rock corporatefest was sorta too much for folks used to the clearer sentiments of **Slippery When Wet**. And when this one goes to those same stellar stadium places, it just sounds like rehash. Why, *Lay Your Hands On Me* even rips off Peter Gabriel (well, maybe). **New Jersey**'s other hits were the ultra-cheese strip mall rock of *Bad Medicine*, the ultra-cheese Mellencamp rock of *Born To Be My Baby*, and the ludicrously cheese power balladeering of *I'll Be There For You*. Hey, let's face it, Bon Jovi really deserve all the crap they get as the epitome of music for money. They are ultimately a laughing stock, even if the individual players are greater than the sum of their parts.
Rating                                                    4

## Jon Bon Jovi - Blaze Of Glory/Young Guns II  (PolyGram '90)

En route to a hobby acting career, Jon solo takes on a soundtrack project in a big way, essentially crafting a solo album around the movie **Young Guns II**. So once away from having to be pin-up commercial money boy, Jon hires a bunch of old guns to construct a fairly ambitious roots rock record, inevitable hits this time being another spaghetti western ballad *Blaze Of Glory*, and the maudlin but decent *Miracle*. Elsewhere, lots of uncharacteristic-to-Bon instrumentation (leaning Cajun), and tunes of a slightly less dressed-up nature. The list of contributors is insane, but I'll single out one guy, Jon's old bud Aldo Nova. Good to see him working. The least anal retentive Bon Jovi record, but then again, it's Jon alone, and still, very anal retentive, so much so, it belongs right here amongst the odious pack.
Rating                                                    5

## Bon Jovi - Keep The Faith  (PolyGram '92)

Jon, Richie, Tico, Dave and Alec attempt their first baby stride into the new reality, revamping and toughening their cock rock look (Jon on his way to that much ballyhooed sassy bob), and backing off on their awful hard rock priss. But it's still a mess, selling like crazy, hated by anybody with brains, the band balancing fresh new styles like *I Believe* and *Keep the Faith* with dopey casual barroom boogie like *I'll Sleep When I'm Dead* and *Blame It On The Love Of Rock & Roll*. Then there's another in a long line of dreary power ballads in *Bed Of Roses*, Bon Jovi adding to the damage Scorpions did in killing hard rock with automatic, phoned-in songwriting. I mean, this is why grunge happened. As the decade wore on, Bon Jovi survived and thrived, but it was their kind of wallpaper that wrecked the careers for dozens of other party rock mainstays.
Rating                                                    5

## Bon Jovi - Crossroad  (PolyGram '94)

Widely deserving of a hits pack, deserving for the size, smash and daunting frequency of the hits (Jon's got the golden horseshoes workin'), and for the bleak filler status of the tracks that didn't make it, Bon Jovi really are a singles band, their glossy, limp-wristed rockers really only working after repeated plays. The weather's gotta be right, the mood in rare form, otherwise, how could these sloganeering commercials compete with music actually created from the heart? But seriously, I like some of these tunes. They're so sociable. Note: *Prayer '94* does moody, mellow complicated things with moderately life-affirming, fist-pumped anthem *Livin' On A Prayer*.
Rating                                                    6

## Bon Jovi - These Days  (PolyGram '95)

The champion of the average, king of the balladeers is back with a predictable, but surprisingly soft rocking batch of songs, this time leading off with *Hey God*, one of the heavier tracks here, a third-rate Cult rip-off that would have been lambasted if it actually came from Astbury/Duffy. But Jon can do no wrong, scrapping his way to the top, becoming an embarrassing American icon of bad taste in the process. But *These Days*, the song, is passionate and sincere, arcing into the Springsteen zone to which Jon somewhat aspires, and *Something For The Pain* is a buoyant enough smash hit of AOR. But wow, the man is actually getting more maudlin and melodramatic as time goes on, *Something To Believe In* and *If That's What It Takes* combining puppy rock with world music and the Beatles respectively, Bon Jovi just getting too ambitious for their cash-filled brains. Oh whatever, I mean, sure it's built to meticulous standards, but it takes a certain dreary kind of

personality to like Bon Jovi. And there's lots of you out there.
Rating 6

## Graham Bonnet - Here Comes The Night
(President '91)
Run well the hell away, before it's too late children, as our favorite eccentric Aussie pulls a full pomp Michael Bolton, covering all sorts of tortuous, easy listening tunes from your parents' simulated wood, console 8-track, record changer hi fi. The despised Michael Bolton is the obvious comparative, but there's also the awful Forcefield situation, in which Bonnet somehow got entangled. One of those records where the man has supposedly picked some of his all-time fave old classics, and we're all supposed to care, listening intently to his "treatment", bellying up to the bar just 'cos we love his voice so much. Uh-uh. I mean, I'm as big a Bonnet fan as anybody, but this drool: no way.
Rating 0

## The Boomtown Rats - The Boomtown Rats
(Mercury '77)
Punk rock, my ass. Here came The Rats led by Irish loudmouth and future benefit concert mogul Bob Geldof, armed with a tidy pop metal sound more like BTO than The Damned. Well-recorded (by one Robert John Lange), tightly wound, and suspiciously well-written, this early bandwagon jumper fell under the gobbing guise of punk while rocking like a cleaned-up pub metal collection from time-worn vets, skirting an uncanny Springsteen on Joey's On The Street Again, and kindergarten Aerosmith on lead single Mary Of The 4th Form and (She's Gonna) Do You In. A capably well-paced gem of the naive new wave explosion, The Boomtown Rats was the first and last "heavy" Rats record (heavy for the '70s), as the boys would take their pyjamas into less limited, more fertile vistas for the excellent but purely pop Tonic For The Troops. Still, lig one back for the blushing brides of No Future in '77, who were too skilled and behaved to be reviled and elevated by a press bent on finding scuz.
Rating 8

## Boss - Step On It  (RCA '84)
Cloddish and clunky barroom metal from Down Under, built from the shards of many a defunct Aussie outfit, sorta resembling a cross between AC/DC and Dokken (whatever that means), with pretty inferior songs and a tendency towards garagey looseness and slow structures. Betrays the band's lack of thought-provoking role models in its native land. Sorta like bad Krokus with its Storace-like vocals and big drums, Step On It came and went with nary a footprint.
Rating 4

## Boston - Boston  (Epic '76)
One of the gosh-durn biggest sellers of the '70s, Boston was highly hyped as the first record made by a computer, which was grossly inaccurate of course, more of an Orwellian folk tale that made the rounds, than anything substantiated or played up in print. The liner notes allude to fresh new uses of technology, also mentioning Tom Scholz' MIT background, but really concentrate justly on the band's astonishing melodies, harmonies, guitar patterns and thrilling production. This really was an exciting record, even if we kinda hated it because it was so unabashedly hooky, not to mention the fact that those voices sounded like churchboys. Of course the monster hit was More Than A Feeling, which still is in heavy radio rotation twenty years later, even though it's got just as much prog and pomp and loud guitars as it does pop. Long Time also continues to clog classic rock waves (with its Lazy like intro), as does bouncy boogie number Smokin' and mellow More Than A Feeling-lookalike Hitch A Ride. So

Boston just kicked the stuffing out of the charts, combining Heepy keyboards with clean-burning electric guitars, lots of complexity, really sweet choruses, and a snobby sort of attention to detail not unlike Steely Dan. Funny looking guys (Barry looks like Buck Dharma!), but very, very rich. Most likely the first pop metal band proper.
Rating 8

## Boston - Don't Look Back  (CBS '78)
Nothing like a flying city shaped like a guitar to get the 'ol blood flowing, Boston bringing back their massive craft and that logo-age logo, only two years later (requisite Boston joke), for what is an even more meticulously produced record, one that prints in large letters "No Synthesizers Used, No Computers Used." Lead (and only) single Don't Look Back is once more, a cookie cutter cutout of More Than A Feeling, and just as damn good. The rest of the record however wants to explore slightly more arcane pop. There's still boogie and power chords, but also a lot more Byrdsian soft strumming, and those voices seem to be getting higher, weirder and more uh, machine-like. But you can't beat Delp and Scholz's songs for a sort of high energy, forward-massing finesse, Don't Look Back really quite entertaining, especially when those soaring, Thin Lizzy-ish guitar harmonies glide in for a little spotlight dalliance. Fun stuff, soaking in all sorts of dated but welcome back anytime '70s conventions, except maybe the glitzy stage-wear and drummer Sib Hashian's momentous afro.
Rating 8

## Boston - Third Stage  (MCA '86)
OK, it's getting a little tiring by this point, Scholz letting eight years evaporate in legal tangles and sticky tape (read the excellent liner notes), but making a record that sounds like it was made the next morning after Don't Look Back. That is, except for all the velvety balladry, over-pomp, instrumentals and general self-importance. And he sure hasn't spent the time learning anything about life, his lyrics still sounding like the vapid musings of any fourteen year old with a guitar and no dates. Lead single this time is silky sapster Amanda, OK as a song, and still superlative as a production piece, as Scholz at least doesn't opt for all the technological gizmos ruining everybody else's records in the mid '80s. So you gotta hand it to him, he still wants to make Styx and Journey and Boston records from the '70s, but just have 'em sound as good as possible. It's just that his songs are looking a little bell-bottomed, platformed and glitter-balled by this point.
Rating 6

## Boston - Walk On  (MCA '94)
Tom Scholz and the labyrinthical amalgam of technicians that is his backing org. arrive back in the '90s freeze-packed in the '70s for what is their fourth overall, first in seven years. And Walk On (I guess they didn't spend those years working on record titles, or lyrics for that matter) is probably the most lush, most melodically surrendered spread yet, layer upon layer of those patented, vaguely Queen-like guitars bedding tracks that reinforce the cushy Boston vibe, like they've never been gone. No surprise, Walk On is thick with technology, but it is technology that is designed to glue the sounds together in high calorie dreamstates (unlike say a Bon Jovi record). So the electricity is in the usual overdrive, bristling with energy as Scholz steers his vast, confusing band through compositions that sound a lot like old Boston, old Journey, selected Styx, and even Uriah Heep on the Walk On Medley, especially raging instrumental subtune Get Organ-ized. The liner notes are refreshingly free with useful information, indicating what traditional instrumentation was used, where technology has

chimed in, also including a l'il hello from the pomp legend himself, where treats with well-grounded humour the subject of his painstaking record-making habits. Plus there's full lyrics and a few pages dedicated to domestic violence and animal rights causes Tom supports. Pretty refreshing stuff, the way it harkens way back while trumpeting the cause of perfection.
Rating **7**

## Bow Wow - Bow Wow (Est. '83)

As far as I know (which ain't much), this most famous of Japanese bands in terms of local success, has never shaken its pathetic-to-western-ears Japanese musical, lyrical, and linguistic tendencies throughout countless records (at least twelve at last tally years back). Not saying that's bad, just that I would far rather listen to Loudness or Warpigs if listen to Japanese metal I must.
Rating **0**

## The Boyzz - Too Wild To Tame (Epic '78)

The Boyzz embodied a more commercially viable form of The Godz' southern-flavoured biker metal, kinda like a hard-edged version of Lynyrd Skynyrd without the depth, complete with boogie woogie ivories and pumping horns. Never heard of 'em before this record, never heard much of 'em during it, and never heard of 'em since, although three of the guys went on to form pop band B'zz. Most of **Too Wild To Tame** dopes along like the hard hitting cowpie 'n' country affairs it tries unsuccessfully to improve upon, with its more insistent guitars and only slight strayings from the laziness that gives southern rock its charm. However, two classy, more metallic numbers emerge from the corn patch, *Destined To Die*, a white line fever, cruisin' tune clocking in two seconds short of seven minutes, and *Lean 'N' Mean*, sort of a roots-fried speed rocker with shades of Deep Purple and a scrappy vocal performance by one Dirty Dan Buck. Me 'n the buds were medium-strength boosters of this band in its time, but unfortunately this is one slice of early HR that doesn't age all too finely, although its spirit lives on in relic-rockers like The Four Horsemen and Raging Slab, maybe even Brother Cane.
Rating **5**

## Brad - Shame (Sony '93)

Probably the most eccentric of the Seattle side projects (others being Hater, Temple Of The Dog, Mad Season), Brad is also the mellowest and moodiest. The main player here is Stone Gossard. I used to know who everybody else was, but I've forgotten, as has most of the world, this record barely causing a ripple with its slack, smokey, understated funk moves. Shawn Smith's vocals are a higher register, edgier take on that celebrated Vedder style, making the whole shambling, almost dream-like record very much like quiet, reflective (one-take) Pearl Jam moments. Lo-fi but high concept, pretty much conceived and slapped down in the studio over a 17 day period.
Rating **6**

## Brain Surgeons - Eponymous (Cellsum '94)

After his unceremonious and acrimonious break with the esteemed Blue Öyster Cult, Al Bouchard worked feverishly on his and Sandy Pearlman's **Imaginos** project. Once that finally saw the light of day, he and his new wife, noted rock scribe Deb Frost turned to a more unusual project, the creation of their own-home-made band. **Eponymous** became the debut, and the record does somewhat suffer the debut jitters, maybe a little too much production trickery and too many layers, the duo overcompensating for the cool idea of building this essentially from a home studio. Musically, this record is perhaps too much the stylistic smorgasbord, from jazz to thrash metal, even including covers of *I Play The Drums* (lavish, imaginative) and *Love Potion*

#9 (straight, not as good as Tygers Of Pan Tang!), on the upside coming across as playful and good-natured, on the downside, too project-like. Still, it's cool to see those cryptic, mock-literary lyrics that we've come to love from Al and his old writing parter Richard Meltzer, Deb's career in words also standing her in good stead, the sum total of the read being one of wily rock veterans who still haven't given up on people, sounding very much like Max Webster's Pye Dubois, full of image and colour and oddity.
Rating **7**

## Brain Surgeons - Trepanation (Cellsum '95)

**Trepanation** (look it up) is record #2 for the married tagteam of ex-Blue Öyster Cult drummer (and so much more) Al Bouchard and noted rock journalist Deb Frost, who buttress this home-produced, indie-released smorg of sophisticated rock songs with a full and capable band. Frost's vocals recall Patti Smith, oscillating between sweet, shrill and punk-shocking, as she commandeers a mature batch of fourteen tunes that in total, oddly recall a primetime BÖC collection, bluesy rockers next to mysterious ballads; playful versus wise and even jaded. Some amazing lyrics here (*My Civilization, Sisters Of The Precious Blood*) make these level, unflashy rockers bite through the band's cooly understated deliveries like wolves charting their way under an autumn moon. Fave: *Hansel & Gretel*: totally **Agents Of Fortune**, but then again Al was an equal amongst the deep creative wells irrigating BOC's green acres.
Rating **7**

## The Brain Surgeons - Box Of Hammers (Cellsum '96)

Glorious tall-boy power chords open this third Brain Surgeons spread in as many years, the Brain Surgeons being Blue Öyster Cult drummer Al Bouchard, his wife, noted rock scribe Deb Frost plus three efficient, tasteful rock guys, whose sense of humour and all-round well-being matches that of their leaders. Which is the crux here, **Box Of Hammers** being an almost singer-songwriter level assemblage of fourteen fully-conceived compositions by traveled and travailed pros. Style shifts are vast, playful and expertly handled, spanning blues, metal, prog, roots, balladry, through gravity-defied funk, Al even including a couple of almost-BÖC songs from the past (*Gun* and *Laura's Plastic Swords*), and a wily, cut-and-paste instrumental *Imaginos* retrospective to close things out, highlight being a set of menacing "Cappucino!" growls. All in all, more guitar textures, more bass, and a healthier band feel, despite the massive versatility enclosed.
Rating **8**

## Brighton Rock - Love Machine (Warner '91)

The last of three records for these perennial Toronto party rockers (others being '87's **Young, Wild And Free** '88's **Take A Deep Breath**) Love Machine is also the heaviest, sparked by the fireworks of Greg Fraser's raw guitar pyro and Gerry McGhee's banshee wail. Previously tagged as a ballad band, Brighton Rock reversed the trend with this collection of bright, shiny, but aggressive poodle metal ditties, tracks like *Bulletproof, Mr. Mistreater*, and the band's slippery blues metal rendition of *Cocaine* taking this straight at suntanned California rockers plying their trade just before hair metal hit the crapper. File with Haywire, Honeymoon Suite and early Harem Scarem, all descendents of Triumph, Loverboy and Coney Hatch, in search of superstardom of a particularly American nature. Why this particular proposal works: it's sparsely arranged and spontaneously produced, somewhere between Motley Crue and Van Halen, when everything else at the time was polished until blinding.
Rating **7**

## Britny Fox - Boys In Heat (CBS '89)

One of the better glam metal contenders with a stupid name, Britny Fox had a nice to-the-quick attitude, kicking off this second commercial success (working title: Fuel The Fire) with the kickin' In Motion, then playing all the angles concisely, even the ol' novelty cover game, with an unimpressive run through Nazareth's Hair Of The Dog. But the riffs are steamin' recalling the best of Cinderella, Slaughter and Poison, while Dizzy Dean Davidson's vocals screech standard tales of Sunset Strip (even if the boys are from Jersey), perhaps his voice being a bit of a weak link here, too scratchy and mixed way back. Other faves: She's So Lonely and the Balls To The Walls-y Plenty Of Love. A party to be sure, and not as wimp-rocked as you might have expected. Follow-up: '91's **Bite Down Hard**, followed by the break-up of the band in '93.
Rating                                                          7

## Brocas Helm - Into Battle (Est. '84)

Mechanically inoperable techno scuzz, entirely not on purpose, from the underground of the low income metal invasion caught speeding in the mid-'80s. Goofy like Sledgehammer, Armageddon or a heavy Hawkwind but the fun terminates just before decisions on multi-playability. '89's **Black Death** buried these SF nutters but good, after an '85 record called **Undefeated**.
Rating                                                          3

## Broken Hope - Swamped In Gore (Grind Core '91)

Combining the total gore of Cannibal Corpse and Carcass with unrepentant brutality rendered fairly state-of-the-art, Illinois' Broken Hope immediately achieved their aim to be the heaviest, baddest muthas on the scene. This very indie debut came on the heels of good press for the band's two demos, the record being a signature slice of death, solid early on in death's progression, but an awful display of punishment for those not enamoured with extreme metal. Comes with a toe tag and a first track called Borivoj's Demise, Mr. Krgin's death apparently imminent!
Rating                                                          4

## Broken Hope - The Bowels Of Repugnance
(Metal Blade '93)

Without a shred of doubt, this is the sickest, most profane record I've ever read, eclipsing Cannibal Corpse in all departments, even in terms of extremity and undecipherablility of vocal, not to mention clustered congested down-tuned riffing and blastbeats. Marks the crest of the Broken Hope conspiracy. Horrible, horrible music. The apocalypse is at hand. Note: secured deal with Metal Blade after rousing set at Milwaukee Metalfest VI.
Rating                                                          3

## Broken Hope - Repulsive Conception (Metal Blade '95)

Record III for Broken Hope finds the band sticking to their wrathful grindscrape while moving into musical (?) terrain in much the same fashion as Earache's Misery Loves Co., except not straying nearly as far from the shivering tenets of death. Production is perfect here (read: crushing), and songs span ambience to blastbeats, under vocals that are by-the-book grindgrowls; just stupid, baphometing a bloodbucket fare that crosses Carcass with Cannibal Corpse and the Diceman. Decent enough death, but far too squared-off and tuneless for my liking. Apparently that last track is Twisted Sister's Captain Howdy. Yeah, O.K.
Rating                                                          4

## Bronz - Taken By Storm (Bronze '84)

File with Shy and Chrome Molly as commercial keyed-laced Brit pop metal with generically perfect high register vocals. Probably the most annoying of the three but still heavier than you might think. Unless you're a historian of British melodic HR, there's no point in searching this one out. Lone cool move: a cover of New England's Don't Ever Wanna Lose Ya.
Rating                                                          4

## Brother Cane - Brother Cane (EMI '93)

Southerly sort of rock'n'roll that touches on all kinds of traditions while not falling prey to any of them, **Brother Cane** did pretty well at the box office on the strength of warm and fuzzy acoustic rocker Hard Act To Follow and the square Bad Co.-ishness of That Don't Satisfy Me. Perfect production and arrangements, both left over from the glory days of overly fussed over hard rock. Lots of simple ballads, plus strong soulful vocals from Damon Johnson make this miles higher than Cry Of Love but still nowhere near the masters, The Black Crowes.
Rating                                                          7

## Brother Cane - Seeds (EMI '95)

The successful little franchise that is Brother Cane continues to grow with this subtly darker, dare I say grungier slice of roots rock. There's a little more Layne Staley/Weiland in Johnson's drawl, especially on catchy gloom hit And Fools Shine On, deflating ballad Intempted or the fluid trickery of Bad Seeds. Tracks are shorter overall in comparison to the debut, pared down to the essentials of song sturdiness, then built up with more layers, resulting in full-on tunes of a grey bluesiness. More sounds, more maturity, solid harmonies fueling substantial lyrics. The acceptable face of young pups doing classic rock.
Rating                                                          8

## Brownsville Station - Motor City Connection
(Big Tree '75)

Cub Koda and his Brownsville Station were a unique but weak attempt at guitar rock during the early '70s, this astoundingly unaggressive record limping along like Humble Pie meets the Partridge Family. I always think Good Rats when I think of this hapless brown-out power trio, both bands flirting with the Rock for neither really committing their psyches to the cause. Classic moniker in drummer Henry "H-Bomb" Weck. Shakey as an entry to this tome, i.e. not much more fortified than Humble Pie's **Smokin'** or anything from Earl Slick, Grand Funk or the awesome early James Gang.
Rating                                                          5

## Brownsville - Air Special (CBS '78)

This more or less "modern" release as the abbreviated Brownsville is created with (I guess) an inevitable sense of musical awareness doubled up with a recognition of the band's semi-legendary status, being the heaviest piece of beefsteak coming late in the catalogue. Brownsville by this point were more fizzled rock dogs than artistic force; one hit wonders remembered only for Crüe-covered novelty rocker Smokin' In The Boys Room many moons back. And **Air Special** is one of the more uniform rockers of the mottled catalogue to date, rocking with a heartland, boogie woogie muscle like England's Rage or the first Ram Jam, if that's any help. Most of the record is kinda dull blues rock, thumping along with even but uneventful acceptability. One of those bands with an incredibly rare back catalogue since the turn of the '90s; a catalogue that I would definitely pick up, given halfways reasonable pricing.
Rating                                                          5

## Brujeria - Raza Odiada (Roadrunner/Attic '95)

Like some sort of wry death metal spaghetti western, **Raza Odiada** showcases a smart, Sepultura/Nailbomb like delivery of tunes entirely barked in Spanish. Re-

sponsible for one of the most gruesome album covers last time around (**Matandos Gueros**), Brujeria are elusive but not unknowns, the band rumoured to be Fear Factory's Dino Cazares and Burton C. Bell, plus FNM's Bill Gould, doing a spirited, incognito job of this genre. Yet, really, if ya don't speak Spanish . .
Rating                                                             5

## Brutality - When The Sky Turns Black
(Nuclear Blast '94)

Official record II for Florida's Brutality incorporates many of the current technical flourishes finding their way into recent death releases, while staying true to form with extreme grind vocals and doomy change-ups galore. But it's the rhythms that mark the freshest modern directive here, lots of double bass drum, halftime beats collapsing into crushing grooves and astonishingly polished and listenable guitar breaks. Tight, daunting but stuck just barely firm enough in song, Brutality just might be one of those median-dwelling acts to convert us death metal fans who accept kinder death but scoff at the loud pustule speed of extreme thrash. What I mean is, I'm slightly surprised by how listenable I find this. Bonus: a truly weighty version of Sabbath's *Electric Funeral*.
Rating                                                             7

## Brutality - In Mourning   (Nuclear Blast '96)

Gotta respect a band that still wears their black death metal t-shirts malevolently. However, **In Mourning** does little beyond a painful disembowelment, although *Died With Open Eyes* is a surreal enough precision pound. All told, this is the sum total of the median of the average of a large sample of the Florida sound, Brutality possessing all the science, most of the passion, and little of the creativity. Double bass barrages fly at all velocities, vocals bottomfeed the scrap yard, and guitars churn with disdain. Sticking with it, despite many originals wisely moving on.
Rating                                                             5

## Brutal Truth - Need To Control   (Earache '94)

This second album from the notorious chaos merchants known as Brutal Truth goes way beyond grind-core, given that even song structures collapse, melt, Melvin, or basically block shut like a cardiac arrest. Appropriately from New York, these guys are almost performance artists, or sculptures of hideous black noise. The rules have been abandoned for fresh ways to annoy. And the results are innovative but entirely in masochistic directions. There are unholy sonics you may have never heard reproduced before, sounds of an almost academically interesting nature, yet these are forbidden sounds that anyone possessed of their faculties would actively reject as pleasurable music. Gave it a **5**, but it's basically unrateable.
Rating                                                             5

## Brutal Truth - Kill Trend Suicide   (Relapse '96)

Brutal Truth press cantankerously on, jarring but dismally expected, like a collision of stone-carved sonics. Sure this is an EP (33 minutes), but it's the longest, most caffeine-buzzed half hour you'll ever experience, like an NYC jackhammer of souls. New twist: good recording. Old news: shock for shock's sake. Like a half dozen drowned inner city radios in competition for scant or nil attention from a populace too avalanched with sound.
Rating                                                             4

## B-Thong - Skinned   (Hypnotic '94)

Man, the Swedish scene is cooking these days, what with Entombed, Tiamat, Clawfinger, Meshuggah and now the awesome B-Thong gussy-ing up extreme metal. B-Thong blast through an inviting selection of power metal compositions, fairly mathematically daunting yet somehow hooky with versatile, pliably treated vocals from T. Jelencovich. **Skinned** (the debut) melts all sorts of fringe influences (only minor traces of funk, grunge, death and industrial), cramming them all into a gaping maw of flat-out, mammoth metal perfection, recalling Machine Head with even stronger songs. If Canada rewards excellence, this should compete nicely with **Jesus Christ** for top sales slot in the strong Hypnotic Records stable.
Rating                                                             8

## The Buck Pets - The Buck Pets   (Island '89)

Alternative rock that smells suspiciously like metal . . . where have we heard that one before? Yep, The Buck Pets are a dead-thick-of-it hard alternative band, a little early and geographically off-course for the mania; highly misunderstood and misplaced in a world cast towards the Pearl Jam Soundgardens of Green River, then, uh, Bush. This flat-headed riff rocker (assembled by lost punks), mixes mid-pace rockers with a plentiful spread of hangin' out, lude pieces, big on drums, sustain and lack of lustre. Plainly cool, but also often plain, without a whole lot going on, **The Buck Pets** suffers a bit from the debut blues, while rocking out like real college bands should, given the boatloads of cheap draft available.
Rating                                                             7

## The Buck Pets - Mercurotones   (Island '90)

Fairly major changes in the Buck Pets language, as things get more melodic, varied but equally heavy. Still, things are based on simple riffs although new barroom booziness adds double vision to *Pearls* and *Ave F Blues*, the latter sounding more like rockier Replacements. *Libertine* breaks the rules further, throbbing funky with horns and a tiny electronic snare sound. The blocky, unmaneuverable punk metal approach remains, and there's just too many slow, whiny trudgers for me to stay interested right through. Love the album cover, love the concept, but time to let loose.
Rating                                                             7

## The Buck Pets - To The Quick   (Restless '93)

More like to the couch for a quiet lie down, as The Pets spread more of the same ol' same ol'. Way too much slouch and not enough intense, as the band keeps to its simple garage rock concept, which given the record's variety and slick enough mix, is no concept at all. Hanging chords, lame riffs and too much downtime plague my potential enjoyment of a band I'd like to like. Continually nudged aside by more daring rock'n'roll forces.
Rating                                                             6

## Budgie - Budgie   (MCA '71)

And so it was hatched, a dynasty of enigma that would perplex for years to come. Cardiff's Burke Shelley (Geddy Lee's doppelganger if there ever was), along with Tony Bourge and Ray Phillips assumed the classic power trio pose, steeped in the dirty traditions of the growing British scene, here cranking out a murky cross between '60s psychedelia, ugly corrupt blues, and an entirely new behemoth called heavy metal, growing in tandem with Sabbath (Sab producer Rodger Bain is on board here, doing the album essentially live in the studio), yet one step behind Sabbath in the evolutionary chain, kinda like a slow, metallic version of Zep - **II** winged on acid. **Budgie** flies fat and treble-less, dominated by a wallowing bass-driven sound, low speed chunk riffs and an urge to stretch out into hippy jams. Best tracks (i.e. non-dozers) would include *Rape Of The Locks* (colour me spaced, but this one reminds me of *Hole In The Sky* for some reason), and *Homicidal Suicidal*, a clumsy but warm hard rocker, weighted with cinder blocks like all else in this luded smorgas-morgue. Too decrepit, eccentric, and simply unknown

to be considered a true cornerstone of metal, **Budgie** is nevertheless heavy, and heavy early. Shame about the pace, though. Note #1: Budgie started life as Six Ton Budgie, a moniker Ray Phillips has revived for his pub-rockin' revival act here in the '90s. Note #2: Roadracer CD reissue includes *Crash Course In Brain Surgery* and extensive liner notes.
Rating 7

## Budgie - Squawk (MCA '72)
More of the same looped, chunk funk rockers from way the hell back (funky due more to bad beats than any sort of vision), mixed with short meditations and long sludgy solos, **Squawk** brings Shelley's distinct vocals to the fore, but aside from that, it's merely yet another cranked, self-defeating gob-fest of reverberating acid rock. How else could one describe writing a carnivorous slab worthy of Iommi and calling it *Hot As A Docker's Armpit*? But sweaty this record most definitely is, sweat melted into a crusty lethargy rather than borne of furious activity. Now it's '72 boys, and it's safe to say the three deaf ones from Wales are *Stranded* in a scrapyard of riffs well past expiry date; constructs too free-form and blues-polluted to challenge the **Vol 4**'s and **Machine Head**'s of the world. Little did we know, Budgie would become a tangent too colourful and exploded to take requests.
Rating 6

## Budgie - Never Turn Your Back On A Friend (MCA '73)
The supersonic high science of Metallica-covered classic *Breadfan* sounds the alarm that Budgie has shed the shackles of old, intending to participate fully in the forging of metal. Yet the band proceeds to baffle with an enigmatic amalgam of crafted compositions, a scampering take on *Baby Please Don't Go*, a short lonely dirge, then a drum solo to introduce an older-style *You're The Biggest Thing Since Powdered Milk*. With the first quality mix of its career—headphone-quality at that—magical Yes-like Roger Dean cover art, and yet another odd collection of songs, Budgie has fully ensconced and isolated itself in the land of the unexpected; cranky, eccentric artists locked in the house on the hill, nowhere near its audience, who remain linked only by psychic story threads. Side two rolls on oblivious to reality with rocker *In The Grip Of A Tyrefitter's Hand*, classic introspective Shelley moment *Riding My Nightmare*, and eleven minutes of *Parents*. You figure it out, but the facts remain: there are no facts.
Rating 8

## Budgie - In For The Kill (MCA '74)
Like some sort of massive step back into an ugly, lethargic isolation, Budgie crawl back into the amorphous attic, taking with them their hottest, most disturbed raft of songs yet. From trademark lengthy dirges through minuscule acoustic confessions, to obscure and arcane metal classics, **In For The Kill** creates the usual unusual Budgie smokescreen. Side one is immediately here, side two has left the building. Both are dense, heat-dulled landscapes, hauled off slowly and muscularly, dragged unwillingly into the 20th century. The title track (covered by Van Halen in their bar band days), *Crash Course In Brain Surgery* (covered lovingly by Metallica on their coveted **Garage Days** EP) and *Zoom Club* are the biggest, wildest sledges, while *Hammer And Tongs* glues *Black Sabbath* to *Dazed And Confused* for what purpose, who can say? I only know it hurts like a rubber hose to the windpipe. Far out, man, what else can I say, except where we end up is no promised land, more like the land of the deaf and damned.
Rating 9

## Budgie - Bandolier (A&M '75)
**Bandolier** marks the first in-flight session for these batty birds, a new confidence and vigor, perhaps due to a new label and clarity of sound last heard on **Never Turn Your Back On A Friend**. I acquired my copy of this fiercely independent work from the original location of Magic Mushroom Records in good ol' Spokane, and the funky grooves within seemed to fit the hippy-dipped environs of my first Budgie purchase ever. Stunningly self-produced, **Bandolier** just dances from strength to strength, full of rhythmic hard rockers like *Breaking All The House Rules And Learning All The House Rules*, *I Can't See My Feelings/Rock Climbing*, plus pounding classic *Napoleon Bona-Part One/Napoleon Bona-Part Two*. Bitchin' titles, eh? Full-blooded, energetic but smooth and chock full of the unconventional, **Bandolier** is essentially the band's heartland. For once the boys exude fun and buoyancy, even party-like enthusiasm while the humour element remains subtle, complex and mind-alteringly foreign. Above all, **Bandolier** is a great mix, driven beautifully by a cutting Strat-like sound from Bourge (although I don't think he's holding a Strat on the back cover), nice bass separation, enthusiastic, clear vocals, and lots of range on Steve Williams' finely tuned drums. In concrete terms, of all Budgie sliding floors to date, this is the most solid. Six cuts: four rockers, one funky prog rock thing, and a nice mellow one. Thus **Bandolier** puts Budgie in the realm of a warmer, though still off-kilter art, one with overtones that may, after a stogie of Fruitvale Homegrown, be construed as commercially appealing. Suffice to say that when leveler heads prevailed, Budgie came nowhere near severe Rock Star coinage, punished rather than rewarded for their independence.
Rating 10

## Budgie - Best Of Budgie (MCA '75)
Most likely a contractual send-off for MCA, who probably had enough by this point (although there's **Bandolier** grist on here, which kinda blows that theory), **Best Of Budgie** does pretty good, sampling from the band's last three only vaguely similar excursions. Perhaps one of the only supporting arguments of the myth that you can't cut vinyl over an hour long, **BOB** lacks in treble, most notable on the otherwise bright **Bandolier** tunes, which are chosen with perfection here. Elsewhere, highlights include *Breadfan* and the subterranean *In For The Kill*, but who cares. For the full deal, get inside the original studio werks, where you'll find the boys layering craziness over the far corners of your mind, warts and all, for better or worse.
Rating 7

## Budgie - If I Were Brittania I'd Waive The Rules (A&M '76)
I'd say the best advice is never turn your back on this band, for the flora and fauna rapidly regroup, copulate and send forth new alien hybrids, most of which gather here for bizarre spring rituals. Perhaps the most telling metaphor for this record might be the title cut which grafts maybe Captain Beefheart onto Black Sabbath in some sort of remake of **Tyranny And Mutation**, with more effluent, perfumed and mellow studio sheen. Rockers don't simply rock (except for the out-of-place but entirely welcome *Sky High Percentage*), and ballads just won't sit still, as Budgie throws a tie-dyed wrench into anything beginning to resemble conformity until it unravels and reconstructs. To the uninitiated, this record may elicit a simple "what the hell is this?", and of course, quite predictably, prospective new fans failed to materialize (even Shelley somewhat regrets the record). But to the prepared, **If I Were Brittania** was another daunting trip into tactile, lush and inviting jungles. We get a metallic march with lead cut *Anne*

73

Neggen, an elegant piece of smooth in *You're Opening Doors*, funk rock in *Quacktors And Bureaucrats*, and a killer classic of subtlety, subversion and deception in heartbeat closer *Black Velvet Stallion*, which builds to a nervous, blinding conclusion after awesome axe solos from Bourge. In the Budgie cage of mind, one can only languish in awe; outside of it, and this is just another piece of schizoid crappola from a bunch of losers. Either/or, **If I Were Brittania** can only elicit strong responses, as only the proudly and profoundly eccentric can. Actually the first for A&M in the states, the label eventually buying **Bandolier** from MCA and releasing it after **Brittania**.

Rating                                                              9

## Budgie - Impeckable   (A&M '78)

In another of a myriad of personal linkages made throughout this book, connections that may or may not work for you, I always envisioned **Impeckable** as spiritual sister to Sab's **Never Say Die**, both released in '78, both the last before big philosophical shifts, both great works, yet having a ring of the expected and creatively hollow about them, both less alien than previous fluid states, but both still hopelessly detached in comparison to real world rock'n'roll. **Impeckable** is heavier and more straight-forward than **Brittania**, yet still the work of a twisted but happy-go-lucky hippy mindset, bemused but bonkers, multi-faceted as ever, and crammed full of interesting artistic surprise. An overall funkiness and effortless switchback ethic moves throughout this lovingly confused work as witnessed on *Pyramids* or *Love For You And Me*, both uncategorizeable but not all that strange, really, like the best of similar era BÖC. And the rockers are hard to forget; the scientifically ethereal *Melt The Ice Away*, *Smile Boy Smile* an odd but warm hard rocker with a sort of Celtic riff (?), and *I'm A Faker Too*, a large, Sabbath-like trudge peppered with the band's penchant for dopey funk moves. Comparatively speaking, **Impeckable** is an accessible update on **Bandolier**'s brightness of being, a smooth and whimsically various studio effort like a cool breeze from the sea. Recorded in Toronto as part of the band's nine month residence in Canada, a base from which the band made frequent short forays to search out markets in the states, finding only one, Texas.

Rating                                                              9

## Budgie - Power Supply   (RCA '80)

Well it's nothing new for great artists to go unloved. Budgie weren't the first, and they won't be the last. Thin Lizzy, Gamma, Badlands, King's X, and more recently Love/Hate and Last Crack (so far), have all seen commercial injustice despite critical raves, which just kills me, really. Anyways, back to the first creaks and feedbacks of the New Wave Of British Heavy Metal, on which Budgie would bandwagon—there's no other word for it. But count me along for the ride, when the bandwagon is Metal, and the jumpers are Budgie, who through convoluted and involuntary means, are one of British metal's originators, inspirations and catalysts. Significantly, key Shelly sidekick and co-author for life Tony Bourge is gone. Enter new, evidently headbanging axeman John Thomas, who cranks a convincing metallic din throughout this squarely heavy metal feast. No longer Budgie the unfathomable, this is Budgie as trench warfare rawk dudes; raw, blunted and hooked to one unrelenting supply of street-heated horsepower. Simply an accomplished, nostalgic and deeply traditional HM record, **Power Supply** bears no relation to what fluttered before, or indeed what comes after, offering a couple like AC/DC, one like AC/DC's best imitators, one **Nightflight**-style ballad, and some fierce unkempt pig iron in *Hellbender*, *Heavy Revolution* and smokin' combat classic *Secrets In My Head*, one bad mutha of a track

which could have sent *In For The Kill* through the floorboards. A sell-out through and through, **Power Supply** sadly marked the demise of something special and timeless, replacing it with something simply really cool and entertaining, but with an air of luck to it, a grudging acceptance, when in one sense, this is what we punters bitch and moan for all the time, asking a metallic "what if?" from fringe operators like Queen and Quo and Deep Purple. Well Budgie gave us The Heavy Metal Record we secretly wanted to see, and one can't help but feel some sort of loss. Well, like I say, we asked for it. The record's CD re-issue contains the long-lost **If Swallowed, Do Not Induce Vomiting** EP.

Rating                                                              8

## Budgie - If Swallowed, Do Not Induce Vomiting   (Est. '80)

Impossible to find in its virgin state, this four track EP catches up on a few tracks from the band's headbangin' **Power Supply** days, good solid hard rockers, but nuthin' special. The tracks: *Wildfire*, *High School Girls*, *Panzer Division Destroyed*, and *Lies Of Jim (The E-Type Lover)*, rounding the low income NWOBHM bases competently and with typical Budgie confidence. But no doubt, the right tracks made it to **Power Supply**.

Rating                                                              6

## Budgie - Nightflight   (RCA '81)

As if a metallic panic had worn off, Budgie settles into a similar yet more relaxed take on **Power Supply**'s gritty basics. Infused with melody and simple charm, **Nightflight** rolls on like a hundred year old bar band, plainly telling the truth and laying it down with nary an ear-splitting crack despite the full metal jacket recording and overall look to the thing. Call it an experimental, pop version of **Power Supply**, **Nightflight** offers a mix of metal, power balladry, light-headed hard rockers and atmospheric loudness; brash but not written so, in a sort of nonchalant display of working class integrity. I appreciate the album, always have, despite the sonic pull back on the ol' throttle, although this is still Budgie revelling in common man antics, well below **Impeckable** and back, yet still full of creative excellence, although lush or bizarre wouldn't enter into the vocabulary here. Faves include opening track *I Turned To Stone* (spiritual descendant of *Riding My Nightmare*), soft rocker and minor U.K. hit *Apparatus*, and heaviest blockhead on the block, *She Used Me Up*. Very brutish, almost dull but oddly heroic, **Nightflight** is in ways, for Budgie fans only, in its regression to raw delivery of seemingly inconsequential song ideas; and being a fan, I'm eminently ready year after year, to give it a wise ol' spin.

Rating                                                              8

## Budgie - Deliver Us From Evil   (RCA '82)

I'm embarrassed to say that I know nothing of Budgie past this elegant panorama of tried and true rock styles. The first with no form of budgie on the cover, **Deliver Us From Evil** marks a new phase for the band, rocking supra-intelligently, royally, and fairly metallic; the versatile array of axework alloyed with arresting, seamless pop magic. Eminently British, and layered with the multi-dimensional wisdom of experience, **Deliver Us From Evil** tells ten well-thought out stories, from opening harmonic pop rocker *Bored With Russia* to the heartfelt *Give Me The Truth*, through galloping NWOBHM rocker *Hold On To Love*. Simply a great hard rock record tempered with traditional classic nuance, technical creativity, and an overwhelming attentiveness to quality, this has always been an engaging journey, spiraling through dynamic after dynamic, like a hot BÖC or Lizzy record, enigmatic in its universal, umbrella "Rock" approach, and urge to entertain on its own intelligent terms. Unlike any other Budgie record

(which is?), **Deliver Us From Evil** enters detailed accessibility, where before, the band was either accessible but raw, or technical but bizarre. I dunno, we just played it all the time, due to its total class and independence. Respect.
Rating         10

## Bulldozer - Day Of Wrath   (Est. '84)

Mourn for the fact that human endeavour can steer so wildly off the tracks, for Italy's Bulldozer hath arrived assembling a quiltwork of dense noise no mother's son could love. And it simply cannot help the distressing situation if one's destiny is to pollute the world as some sort of visual Siamese half to the notorious St. Vitus. Five records by the turn of the decade.
Rating         4

## Bullet - No Mercy   (Arista '84)

Cheap Trick cross-pollinated with Scorpions, fronted by a shrieking Teutonic version of Dan McCafferty, Bullet don't write 'em as good as a critical stab at their influences might evoke. Tunes are schmaltzy, like bad Krokus maybe, or to be more kind, latter-day Scorpions. In any event, **No Mercy** (second record after '82's **Execution**) sounded capable and even threatening commercially at the time given that these Krauts kept it simple, with strong melodic backbone, as displayed on first two steps *Down By The Neonlights* and *I Sold My Soul To Rock N' Roll*, which both careen on home like drinking cheers. The rest finds Bullet trying all sorts of stuff one would expect of Germans who, I swear, look the most like Spinal Tap of any band I've ever seen. And about half of it works, because the concept lets it.
Rating         5

## Bulletboys - Bulletboys   (Warner Bros. '88)

Let's save the Van Halen talk for **Freakshow**, because here on the Hollyrockers' chest-thumping debut, we are pleased to receive a simply solid California hard rock album, with lots of sass, some funky hooks, but mostly straight-forward summer rockers delivered by the sometimes funny, sometimes effeminate and offensive pretty boy lungs of Marq Torien, one diminutive DLR-worshipping blondie truly in love with himself, yet somehow appropriate for such a big talkin' act from the land of walk that talk. Considerably trashier and less self-conscious live, the boys reveal themselves as punters at heart vs. businessmen, which elevates my esteem for the Bulletboys concept, much like seeing Slaughter (headliner of the same show) did for me. Maybe a **6** is a bit unkind, but hell, this record doesn't strike me as special or unique in any way, and thus I never play it; the brutal truth being that there's many a corporate HR record with more daring edge than this, the boyz own follow-up being case in point.
Rating         6

## Bulletboys - Freakshow   (Warner Bros. '91)

A major kick in the ass boots **Freakshow** in the direction of a street-heated combat attack with all the positive connotations of the Van Halen comparisons with which this band has always been plagued. DLR ego raps, lots of crash cymbals, undisciplined bluesy metal riffs, a live-feel roadmap (i.e. soloing with no underlying rhythm track), and a disdain for having to compose the perfect song before entering the studio makes **Freakshow** an exciting wild ride through corporate rock. Large, spacious, dirty, and simply the product of a band who is convinced they've won the big enchilada, this important sophomore assertion gives the band a character they lacked first time 'round. Such loopy constructs as *THC Groove* and the title track bust the norm, loitering, schmoozing, low-slung and in no particular hurry, while *Goodgirl* and *Ripping Me*, the record's two best, just smoke like VH **II** classics. A simply accomplished band has become a cool posse; wide-open and

fresh, with nothing to say, but party-hardy ways to say it. Cut after cut switches gears, offering hooks with specific history and revolutionary forward momentum under a spontaneous threat of collapse into a dogpile. Simply red-hot and overflowing with possibilities while the pretty-boy look seems to outstay its usefulness.
Rating         9

## Bulletboys - Za-Za   (Warner Bros. '93)

Whoa! Somebody put a leash on these guys, 'cos with each successive release, Bulletboys prove themselves nobody's trained puppy. On **Za-Za** (36 minutes: shame on you), the band weirds out once again, offering what is in total, a lighter record with even more nimble freedoms. In short, **Za-Za** demands respect, written with a sharper tongue, greater gravity and maturity as it looks at trends and sadly shakes its head, preferring plain deliveries of tales that are deep and colourful, sometimes ugly and graphic. The sum of the parts is anything but plain however, more like a record that plays well all over the globe, a master marauder of pacing, the rockers at times more frenetic and bent, always loud and live; mellow cuts self-assured and serious, best being *For The Damned*, although hilarious Steve Perry knock-off *Mine* is sure to raise chills of mindless Journeys taken. Funny band, increasingly isolated psychologically speaking, conjuring words like unruly, irascible, undisciplined . . . four classroom disruptions that refuse to stay still at naptime! Bitchin' band. Crank it up, dude. I mean, how can it be any simpler than that? One point short of **10** for knocking off for the day twenty minutes early.
Rating         9

## Bulletboys - Acid Monkey   (Perris '95)

Whereas a surprising number of AOR-ish bands continue to ride out grunge, punk, and now Alanis with nary an iota of change from their sugary hair stances, Bulletboys have simply wigged out. Your first clue would be the cover art and title of this manic piece of whatever. Nothing here sells out, the whole record just unzipping and blowing free. There are elements punk (*Weazel*) and of grunge (*Diss* and *Toy*), but it's all very unselfconscious, the band almost rediscovering the spirit of Van Halen II, where songs just were, falling where they may, dirty and a universe unto themselves. But that's not to say **Acid Monkey** is a work of genius, or even as enjoyable as more accessible fare like **Za-Za**. Torien under-performs (and under-dresses), the production is a bit dissonant, clattery and unexpressive, and once more we get a short, half hour record. Eccentric, spontaneous, occasionally flippant and uncaring, **Acid Monkey** is a bit of a dark, cynical and belligerent exploration for this usually optimistic band, one we rely on for uplift. Closes very appropriately with a shambling, campfire take on Don McLean classic *American Pie*.
Rating         7

## Bullet Lavolta - Swandive   (RCA '91)

Prompted by the smart Tin Machine look on the back cover, the juicy song titles, and the fact that Boston's Bullet Lavolta's been around for ages, I figured it was about time I checked in. Turns out **Swandive**'s a righteous alternative furnace blast of the guitar/bass/drums/vox format; mixing metal, Black Flag, Hüsker Dü, lots of early Seattle grunge, and a general raw bite that makes for a kick-ass independent effluence. Basically heavy underground punk metal, I'm sure Bullet Lavolta had been cranking long before Seattle touched off, drawing more from L.A. skatecore of old for its influences. Angry, occasionally minimalist yet often tricky, **Swandive** rocks beyond market segmentation, like much honest art, with an air of the intellect and discipline punching through the subversion. Smatterings of the opacity possess the same misgivings of much alternative angst metal, a preoccupation with slow, creepy, quiet passages, which thankfully move on before long. Overall . . . tough, embittered and urban aggresso-art-punk, with a slapped-to-reality anarchy that seems to set non-Seattle metalipunks apart from their blissful, isolated (and heroin-dulled) Northwest compatriots.

Rating 7

## Burn - So Far, So Bad (Formula One '93)

Weakapotomus hair band metal, the likes of which seems to be the shame of Britain, the motherland quite incapable of aspiring to anything that might look like even middle-pack status stateside. So call it a heavier but less bluesy, more synthetic Thunder, expertly detailed in all areas, but plastic underneath the paint.

Rating 4

## Jack Starr's Burning Starr - Rock The American Way (Passport '85)

Dough-brained 'n' prissy hard rock with a touch of goth as per mellow Yngwie or similar Joe Lynn Turner-affected chick rock, **Rock The American Way** is a considerable about-face from **Out Of The Darkness**, the man's heavingly committed debut. Most of this well-recorded but lifeless offering idles about the mid-pace spectrum providing the vehicle for Frank Vestry's sweet but lifeless croon. Sounds like the usually artistically-minded, and axe-focused Jack is still chained by Virgin Steele's flirtations with over-elegance. Much more the anonymous disposition in comparison with the man's angry '86 response.

Rating 4

## Jack Starr's Burning Starr -No Turning Back (Cobra '86)

Virgin Steele's Jack Starr leads the volcanic crush on this solo effort which is lifted considerably by the hot vocal prowess of one Mike Terelli. Much of **No Turning Back** is overwrought and serious goth metal, like flat-out and less mobile Virgin Steele, featuring a lot of fat, hanging chord structures, which is quite surprising given that this is a "guitar god" record. **No Turning Back** covers James Taylor's *Fire And Rain*, a tune the magnificent Badlands would brilliantly sidle through five years later, a tune that sounds wildly misplaced among these molten, uncompromising slams. Really, if this record were the backdrop for a Priest or Dio or Ozzy project, I'd probably be singing its praises to the peaks, but given what it is, it can't shake the loser complex of a third rate release. A hot record lost in "one off project" space and time. In any event, I'm starting to believe Starr's intentions and dedication, and most especially, his vehement disdain for keyboard bands.

Rating 6

## Burzum - Det Som Engang Var (Mysanthropy '94)

The shite that started it all, the notorious Burzum were arguably the originator of Norse black metal, toiling with this semi-accessible batch of cranked cockroaches, these '89 to '92 tunes not without melody beneath the ungodly churn. I mean, at least there's space for thought, chanting amongst the ranting, and occasional big, over-distorted drums like Manowar, or I guess more accurately Bathory. It would all get increasingly rank after this, each act out-soiling the last until someone like Master's Hammer would go off their rocker and create **Slagry**.

Rating 5

## Bush - Sixteen Stone (Interscope/EMI '95)

Big production credits and consequent rich 'n' chunky mix for this ambitious debut from London, England's Bush. The sound is fat and smeary grunge with delicacies; light and heavy shading re: Nirvana and Smashing Pumpkins, but a taste for beer like fellow homeboys Terrorvision. Still, there's just too much truly provocative heavy alternative on either side of the joltmeter crowding this out on my overworked and distraught CD player, even though (as a small side note of course), the record's gone on to sell three million copies, dang! I dunno, a bit too college-y and fence-sitting for my tastes, quite rough and raw, but too sensitive, although this seems to have worked magic on the singles, pin-up Gavin Rossdale connecting with his big-hearted, Cobain-smokey vocals. Whoever said grunge is dead forgot to ask the UK and Australia. April '96 re-launch contains four stretchy live tracks on a second CD. Hope similar sleeper hit Everclear gets the same treatment.

Rating 6

## Bush - Razorblade Suitcase (Interscope/MCA '96)

Obviously Bush's reckless, wanton and unselfconscious imitation of Nirvana has paid off in spades. But this is nothing to get upset over, Rossdale and Co. doing Cobain ruff, raw justice, diminished for the derivation but somehow elevated by an Oasis-like lack of self-doubt. And it is this organic, spontaneous who-cares embracement of all things Nirvanoid that makes **Razorblade Suitcase** work, Steve Albini producing with his usual crackly verve and indie snarl, the band reinforcing with a non-commercial British spin to the unhewn tracks enclosed. The hits once more are desperate alt.loving anthems, *Swallowed* smeary, phat and infectious, *Greedy Fly* likable through willful stupidity. Very garage, but somehow cooler for it, which normally isn't the case for slack sounds. This one will grow on you like like fungus, due in no small part to Rossdale's swoopy vocals. Note: the band is known as Bush X here in Canucklehead land, given the existence of a one-record (?), early '70s (?), long-forgotten (definitely!) band who claim proudly the name Bush.

Rating 8

## Jon Butcher - Pictures From The Front (Capitol '89)

Distastefully electronic, layered lite hard rock from a black axeman often considered a new Hendrix, which seems to be the fated label of all metallic axedudes of the Negro persuasion. Jon's nothing like the legendary grunge man, emoting more like any number of hi-tech 'n' shiny, nimble-fingered California blondes, with a bit of Trower and Montrose thrown in for soul quota. His record however, is subdued, waxy and keyboard-laden; sickly pale beyond reproach to the point of marginal status in this book. Reason for inclusion: the man's crunchier but equally uneventful past as The Jon Butcher Axis. Reminds me of one of those bands you occasionally see on the soaps.

Rating 1

## Butthole Surfers - Independent Worm Saloon (Capitol/EMI '93)

Texas' curmudgeonly version of The Residents finally crank intelligibly on a sustained basis for the first time in their long, masochistic recording "career", and baby, does it ever hurt so good. **Independent Worm Saloon** makes the most lethal sense when the band fires its focus, frying rock'n'roll like a magnifying glass on an ant, ridiculing all PC poseurs who think they doth rock alternatively. For in a mighty sense, Butthole Surfers are the most self-sacrificing of alternative forces, redneck, gun-totin' anti-social human mistakes, who have now made their best record. Operative here is dangerous, edgy, psychotic, and so massively rowdy when they metalize: a good four tracks here, power personified, despite the B movie sound effects and aural contusions. In between the break and enters, eccentricities five ways to Sunday fly off the handle, some hitting like hooks, many causing a kind of bad smell. Great White Zombie woofin' lead single *Who*

*Was In My Room Last Night*, which distills a lifetime of unpleasant fuzzy foundation into a banner of adrenalized subversion rock. More of this, and Gibby's going to finally bust bellies with the stars, (as if he'd want to).

Rating 7

## Butthole Surfers - Electriclarryland (EMI '96)

Butt from all angles here, Gibby, Leary, gut and butt offering (surprise: not) their most accessible sneer of sounds, a dabble of noisy snapples amongst a couple with hip-hop frames, a couple o' punkers and a whole lot of relaxed, slappy-slam-pappy grooves somewherz between Meat Puppets, Pixies and Sonic Youth. Vocals oscillate eerily from a PiL rant to a Camper Van croon, the wavy thought of spaghetti westerns swimming in and out of the alcoholic haze. But despite the plain nutters caruthers of the whole thing, it's hard to dispel the notion that there are no less than ten songs out of thirteen tracks here, only a handful linking this tuneful batch to the legendary, incendiary muck-abouts of old. What's more, the band deftly paces things almost accidentally, sorta like Hawkwind, both bands seemingly blundering through life with no idea, but you wanna watch anyways, larfing morbidly at the cruel cycle of damaged grey matter drooling out of control. Most pleasurable spacecakes: melodic punker *Ah Ha*, pretty much lone windmill rocker *L.A.*, and opening swinghammer *Birds*, but of course it's a concept album, concept of course being burn everything. Sad sack: no armor-piercing metal.

Rating 7

## Buzzcocks - Another Music In A Different Kitchen (United Artists '78)

Yeah I know, not exactly metal, yet this debut rocks quite frantically and obnoxiously, the first and last time this critically-acclaimed band would kick mouse ass before submerging themselves in quick pop. Also, one of the early truly punk efforts, coming most squarely from Britain, replete with artsy affectations and likeable eccentricities, destined to influence a whole raft of pop punksters, including Nirvana and Green Day. Heaviest numbers include *Fast Cars*, *No Reply*, *I Need*, *Love Battery* and the excellent *Fiction/Romance*; tunes that evoke images of a more clever Ramones, with an equally pleasing recording. Not the most slabbic piece of rock, but an essential piece of punk history that is fast, melodic and universally guitar-oriented. Witchfinder General's warning: the band's only remotely heavy record. Update: after their few cute but seminal records in the late '70s, the band returned with the cruddy **Trade Test Transmission** in '93, and the much better **All Set** in mid-'96. Peppered throughout were a hits pack, box set and tribute record, proving the Buzzcocks really did "arrive" at some point, not like anybody noticed. Also peppered throughout, both Pete Shelly and Howard Devoto enjoyed somewhat successful solo careers, Shelley as prissy electronic irritation, Devoto as art rocker, most triumphantly with awesome band Magazine, creators of a six record catalogue totally worth owning.

Rating 7

## Buzzoven - Sore (Roadrunner '94)

A grungy industrial death wasteland of bashing bodies, **Sore** is where all those irritating sounds your mom hates dwell drooling. Like the anti-music work ethic, kinda like Venom for the '90s, but after all the equally heavy and less distressing sounds out there these days, I'm quick to file this often slow collision of hurting riffs and misdirected samples. Trent Reznor should have snagged this one for his hobby label instead of that awful Marilyn Manson record. For those pleasant moods.

Rating 6

## James Byrd - Atlantis Rising (Shrapnel '91)

Considered more as one of the shred albums patronized by Mr. Mike Varney, **Atlantis Rising** features the two prong attack of James Byrd's smoother, mellower Malmsteen patterns and the high register, occasionally Geoff Tate-ish (or Soto) vocals of Freddy Krumins, no surprise given that these guys are from the northwest, Bellingham to be more exact, quite a hip little town with good music stores, last time I was there. So if you like your gothic, classical based metal, there's nothing wrong with coming here (Japan, ho!). For some reason, I find myself caught in the tide of rejecting this stuff as dated though, only able to go back to the mid-'80s for records like this that stuck to my circuits during my impressionable youth. Byrd followed up with **Octoglomerate**, **Son Of Man** and in '96, **The Apocalypse Chime**.

Rating 6

## The James Byrd Group - The Apocalypse Chime (Shrapnel '96)

Washington state (was Bellingham, now Kirkland?) guitar virtuoso James Byrd continues with his visceral guitar hero records, crafting vast constructions of castle-goth that is quite close to Yngwie, if recorded a bit looser and murkier, as if the close proximity of grunge was grudgingly influential in some small manner. Elsewhere there's *Death (is)*, which is like modern Hendrix or Frank Marino (who gets a thanks to), an actual Hendrix cover with *Dolly Dagger*, and tunes like *I've Got A Line On You* which is closer to vintage Deep Purple, complete with Lordsy keyboards from John Roberts. If you like technical '80s metal than by all means partake, Byrd now well-positioned to compete with Yngwie and Glenn Hughes, both quite rejuvenated on record as of late.

Rating 7

## David Byron - Take No Prisoners (Bronze '75)

This is for all intents and purposes a Uriah Heep record, given that Byron was still with the band at the time, acting and feeling very Heep, even using Lee Kerslake and Mick Box as part of his **Take No Prisoners** band. So it's no surprise things are quite heavily Heeped here, big drums, big organ work, all supporting Byron's passionate vocals, even the product mix mirroring Heep's declining years, a bit of gospel, churlish hard rock, spooky acoustic balladry and delvings into funk. Faves are the two biggest rockers, *Midnight Flyer* and *Roller Coaster*, both filled with twists and turns smartly arranged. Like a Hensley record, the hair-raising thing about this is not so much styles attempted, but the playing, singing and thick, historical production values, Byron's record successfully taking the listener back to those uniquely Heepish sounds. After this one, Byron's creative decline will match pint for pint his physical disintegration.

Rating 7

## David Byron - Baby Faced Killer (Arista '78)

Now too far from any sort of Heep-ishness, Byron frantically searches for a reason to be, **Baby Faced Killer** telling ten toneless tales given the following ten terrible treatments: disco, rockabilly, acoustic pop, disco again, ballad, gam disco pop, glam pomp rock, keyboard pop, rockabilly again, closing out with another ballad, an awful, depressing '60s sort of thing. Absolutely clueless.

Rating 2

## The Byron Band - On The Rocks (Creole '81)

As guitar-famished as many Heep ventures and each chaotic Byron solo venture before it, the aptly-titled **On The Rocks** anemically offers disjointed, shipwrecked party rock, annoyingly infected with Mel Col-

lins' horn arrangements, timidly delivered like washed-up Southside Johnny or J. Geils. Further unraveled by Robin George's frayed mix, call this third and last Byron abomination a failed, haphazard grasp for reality by a steadily faltering legend, somewhat psychically linked with early, similarly r+b-tinged purposelessness from David Coverdale. R.I.P. February 28, 1985 due to the demon alcohol. CD reissue contains three bonus tracks, all surprisingly quite good.
Rating                                                    3

# C

**Cacumen - Bad Widow**  (Boom '83)

Wasted, broke 'n' comatose Teutonic slabola to the nth degree. Most notable drivers to the Cacumen sound are the heads-down grooves and the Klaus Meine-like vox of lead mensch Claus Lebmann. Not a heapin' whole lot different than say Fisc or a whack of third rate Metal Masters or Ebony plows, albeit a bit more believable as metalheads. Still punky and basic (read: limited) with nary an original thought in their collective heads. Burns with visions of AC/DC's grandeur. Should have been on Mausoleum so nobody would make the mistake of buying it.
Rating                                                    4

**Robert Calvert - Captain Lockheed And The Starfighters**  (EMI/BGO '74)

Almost exactly fitted to the chemical brew of sounds that is an official Hawkwind album, Robert Calvert enlists the services of such Hawklinks as Lemmy, Simon King, Del Dettmar, Nik Turner, Dave Brock and Twink to create this coldish concept record mixing Hawkwind-style metal with lots of spoken word segments that are more dailogue than the band's usual freak poetry. Sound is adequate, in fact just like every other Hawkdisc at the time, kind of compressed and itchy. The true story involves the sale of American Lockheed Starfighters to the post-WWII German air force. Originally, just a light, fair weather fighter, the Germans converted them into atom bombers, in the process cutting many bureaucratic corners, turning the plane into a shoddy, unsafe, bastardized death machine, which earned the plane such nicknames as the Flying Coffin, the Widowmaker, and the Jinx Jet. Whatever you call it, the plane had been involved in 162 crashes by the time this record was made (anybody know how the story ends?). Quite a heavy record, in the not-so-heavy hierarchy of Hawkwindburns.
Rating                                                    6

**Robert Calvert - Lucky Leif And The Longships**  (EMI/BGO '87)

An exquisite little piece of eccentric prog, **Lucky Leif** is relentless here for its link to Hawkwind, not to mention Calvert's heavier **Captain Lockheed** opus. But what an endearing tale Calvert weaves, this Brian Eno-produced oddity telling in very loose, hippy-tripped terms, the story of Leif Erikson's pre-Columbus (but it had to be post-cannibis) dicovery of America (actually Newfoundland). In a sort of sub-conscious, time-straddling **Imaginos** inversion, Calvert sets his hilarious stories to musics the Americas would invent 500 years hence, offering a drop-dead hysterical Beach Boys parody with *The Lay Of The Surfers*, a fantastic Eno-slow reggae in *Volstead O Vodeo Do*, and personal fave *Moonshine In The Mountains*, which is just a rib-tickling Dixie bluegrass hoe-down singalong. Elsewhere there's scattered skirmishes with subjugated Hawkmetal and Hawkeletronic (Turner, House and Moorcock buzz the building), making this an integral or dare I say, crucial corner block of the long, looped Hawkwind journey.
Rating                                                    8

**Cancer - The Sins Of Mankind**  (Restless '93)

British death metal hairballs with a strange '80s spin, Cancer cover most of the grind bases . . . beastly growls, doomy bionic riff science perpetrated at breakneck speeds, while shuffling the deck just short of the creative levels afforded top flight pulverizers from the Sony/Earache camp. Good, loose production, but still too much Slayer-ish trigonometry, although a welcome drum-driven exuberance leaps capably from the mix. This third blight is the last of the band's death metal feasts, before a conscious shift into (surprise, no I mean it) fairly normalized heavy metal on '95's **Black Faith**.
Rating                                                    6

**Candlebox - Candlebox**  (Maverick/Warner '93)

Ah yes, Candlebox, the Hootie of grunge, flagship signing of Madonna's hobby label Maverick, the band beyond categories that can only be described by using categories. So let's begin, shall we? Wait, before we begin, I gotta say these guys bore the pants off me. OK, picture a sort of cleaned-up grunge, sort of a sterile recording of loitering light-to-heavy tunes circa Pearl Jam's **Ten**, by guys who seem like pop metal dudes, you know, nice predictable rockers, clean-cut, well-centred, not like that volatile Eddie Vedder man. Then make sure it's quiet, mellow and safe often enough for radio, just to confuse the masses, who will zig zag all over crossover town to buy the record in droves, alternative rockers, flannelheads, old AOR-leaning metalheads, classic rock retros, and ballad lickers all stunned into flopping open their wallets, not ever knowing why.
Rating                                                    4

## Candlebox - Lucy (Maverick '95)

So, triumphant marketing enigma Candlebox return with a more impassioned, powerful, grungy record, and are met with blank stares. Don't get me wrong, I still find the whole concept of this band utterly without merit (see Our Lady Peace), but **Lucy** rocks with a little more integrity. Fave is melodic buzzsaw alternative rocker *Best Friend*, flannel metal pile-up *Bothered* and sludgy lead track *Simple Lesson*, but much of the else does that tomtom meandering mellow wallow in misery that mars the worst Pearl Jam and Soundgarden songs. Pleasantly hard-hitting at times.
Rating **6**

## Candlemass - Epicus Doomicus Metallicus
(Black Dragon '86)

With a dense Sabbath throb and a purposeful grind, they pulled the burning and splintered spires down. Helpless punters with suicide brains . . . well, you get the picture and it ain't pretty. Trouble at 16 rpm (that's LP talk, kids), sent tunneling through the Swedish permafrost with a depressed groan of idolatry towards a Sabbath that trudged its muddy boots fifteen years black in thyme. And **Epicus** looms deader, weighted at six tunes, 42 minutes; lots of oases of loitered negation between thick atonal doom riffs. Killer vox, killer mix but too manic depressive too uniformly.
Rating **6**

## Candlemass - Nightfall (Metal Blade '88)

Leif Edling and his expanded line-up of executioners skulk back to centre stage, cloaked and hammered to do battle with all that moves beyond brooding crawl. Fear nowt, the increased number of demarcated song-like flowages include drear-headed instrumental intros that glue the usual Large Marge's to each other like stitched limbs on Frankenstein. Under a thick, choking cloud of purest black metal goth, **Nightfall** drones much like **Epicus**, roped to a storm-lashed Sab repast, or more specifically, brief excruciating downer ideas from it à la St. Vitus, in essence all the slowest portions from Iommi's first five years of riffs. Gotta applaud the dedication, but the bottom line is **Nightfall** ties a long unbroken string of the sleepiest moments from Trouble via Tony, the diversionary decelerated and laid-back made central, forced to carry the sorry mass alone. Sorry, wrong mass.
Rating **6**

## Candlemass - Live (Metal Blade '94)

Seventy loud and plowed minutes of the brooding ones recorded live in Stockholm is enough to invert anyone's sonic input devices, but Metal Blade has obliged, giving us twelve tracks of gluey doom. In retro, you really gotta like these guys, respecting their place in the scheme of things that has given rise to slow grind bands making a modest bit of scratch these days. Freaky bleak stuff, but lots of it, a greater amount of percolation I might add, than on any of the studio icestorms.
Rating **6**

## Cannibal Corpse - The Bleeding (Metal Blade '94)

Fourth record for Chris Barnes and his Buffalo blood-burgers who deliberately set out day one to write the most offensive and brutal lyrics in recorded music, reinforced with stomach-churning cover art that helped get their records banned all over the simpering globe. So lovers of the worst imaginables are muttering sell-out with this the most accessible Corpse spin, accessible being a relative term indeed. The lyrics are toned down, the cover art left completely vague, and even Barnes' patented grindcore gargle is lightened up, again a relative sentiment meant to be taken with a grain of Drano. So the verdict: still state-of-the-art, defining the frontal edge of the '80s version of a genre

which is mutating far beyond where Cannibal Corpse will ever go. Fact is, for all the screams of progression, this is almost regressive, compressing catalogues of patterns that are closer to amphetaphied Slayer than anything like Pantera or Entombed or Carcass. Still squarely a technically adept thrash band with a single shocking tone.
Rating **5**

## Cannibal Corpse - Vile (Metal Blade '96)

Now with Chris Barnes having left to concentrate on Six Feet Under, Cannibal Corpse have enlisted George "Corpsegrinder" Fisher (ex-Monstrosity) to lead them into the next millennium. Anyhoo, **Vile** revives the band's positively nasty cover art provocation, and lyrics are either really horrible (see *Orgasm Through Torture*) or just y'know, there. Musically, the boys are the same crappy, heard it a million times auto-death they've always been derided for, even though Scott Burns' production is tolerable on all frequencies. Just garbage, total third-rate repetition of past uh, gories.
Rating **2**

## Captain Beyond - Captain Beyond (Capricorn '72)

Of what total three Captain Beyond records, this debut is the only one that belongs our textbook of decibels, the subsequent two releases wandering into a sci-fi, hard rock Yes-type direction. **Captain Beyond** is a damnably vigorous shoe for '72, resembling an encrusted cross between Sabbath and Budgie, yet nowhere near as important and forward-thinking as either; too dated, muddily recorded, and hippie trippy to classify as a real groundbreaker, or indeed enjoyable metal listen. Fiercely riffic in spots for a total of about twelve minutes, **Captain Beyond** is one of those albums I'd like to give at least a **5** for bravery-to-rock reasons, but find just too rife with age-betraying clichés.
Rating **4**

## Carbonized - Disharmonization (Pavement '93)

Carbonized are a sort of backwater sideproject junk-pile idea warehouse for various Swede grind dignitaries, on this record, Lars from Entombed and a couple of Therion guys. Boy does it ever suck though, sort of punk, goth, psychedelic new waving it through a death metal grinder, but real demo soundcheck quality-like, rarely turning in a logical or enjoyable song. Just a lark, the kind of junk you throw on the end of your CD to get a laugh.
Rating **4**

## Carcass - Symphonies Of Sickness (Earache '89)

Record #2 after an equally stressed-out debut called **Reek Of Putrefaction**, **Symphonies** is basically the dictionary-thesaurus gross-out of **Necroticism** banged forth to a muddier, thrashier, speedier beat. Overwhelmingly sick, Carcass really give Cannibal Corpse a run for their money through sheer imagery, the stench of human mechanics cutting through the sonics with hair-raising clarity (all the blood, pus and scabbing is probably why the entire band are vegetarians!). True pioneers of extreme metal, everything full-tilt, from the look through the words through the jarring deathcore at hand. Hard to believe the maturing (some say gradual but vigorous and deliberate sell-out) that will take place over the next seven years.
Rating **3**

## Carcass - Necroticism: Descanting The Insalubrious (Earache '92)

Read 'em and weep . . . I mean the song titles, if you can call such medical insanity gone butchering, songs. And just about every disgusting, dismembering and dissectible thing that can be done to the human body in the name of weird science splatters throughout the lyrics as well, which fuel a predictable cavalcade of technically dizzy grindcore blackness. Too bad about the belched vocals though, which limit the potential pleasure within the acceptably concentric Entombed-tuned grind-gutted mondo-scrape. Gotta hand it to these Nottingham nutters though, it damn well grabs your attention. Reissued (like Entombed and select other critically acclaimed Earache titles) with two bonus tracks.

Rating    6

## Carcass - Heartwork    (Earache/Sony '94)

U.K.'s Carcass emerge as serious contenders on this bristling tech thrash opus, forsaking their scowling, monotone of old for terrain more familiar to Coroner. But Carcass' trump card is their exotic death-warmed-over, at times Cathedral-ish under-chug, a sound that Colin Richardson has made proud and powerful, sad and sorrowful. Walker's vocals are now in the tolerable mid-range of barking death, as he tumbles over all those dictionary words that are a big part of the (silly) Carcass mystique. Many speeds, many moods and chops for miles, **Heartwork** is a soaring improvement in terms of the band's thinking, an awesome example of the extremely heavy as pure bone-crushing entertainment, not to mention less the one-trick operating room joke of **Necroticism**. Look for the cover featuring freaky and sublime Giger sculpture "Life Support, 1993".

Rating    8

## Carcass - Swansong    (Earache '96)

Strange happenstance here really, the band slowly crumbling (Bill at odds with the rest of the band over musical direction), as Columbia drags their corporate butt for a year, deciding whether or not to release their growing, vital band's most commercial record yet. Fact is, **Swansong** is a fantastic, chugging metal machine just as relevant as Metallica or closer to home, Corrosion Of Conformity, tapping into those same dirt-ball grooves that would have made 3/4 of this record a blast live and even (egad!), playable on selected radio shows. Tracks like *Black Star* (the name of most of Carcass' new band), *Polarized* and percussive classic *Keep On Rotting In The Free World* catch a wave worth riding, capturing a sound that is pretty much the only kind of metal that has the potential of big sales, Carcass and those tugging the purse-strings pulling the plug at precisely the point the band could have broke big. Really a crying shame, but I'll be spending the summer freak-metalizing to this gracious bunch of bloody good songs, whether the machine cares or not. As the sun swelters, two-fist this one with Gorefest's **Soul Survivor**, both solid examples of the record Metallica's **Load** could have been, given courage and care from the boys turned suburban.

Rating    10

## Carcass - Wake Up And Smell The Carcass
(Earache '96)

'Tis a shame. Just as Carcass were creating higher class out of torture metal, the boys called it a day, slashing out their **Swansong** jewel, then spintering to parts equally creative. So it's very cool that this top-notch collectibles CD has come to pass, **Wake Up** splitting heads between crusty EP material, radio stuff, and no less than five unreleased tracks from the **Swansong** sessions. As the record wears on, tunes get older and uglier, culminating in *Exhume To Consume* from the **Grindcrusher** compilation from early '89. The stench is unbearable. But of course, the first five tunes are stunning, grimaced metal, totally amazing given the fact that these were out-takes. Booklet adds to the jolly bloodbath by giving us 29 band photos and a thorough band history by Dan Tobin. We've all lost something

special, indeed, however, maybe not quite so much as the guy on the cover . . .

Rating    8

## Carrie - Secrets    (Earthshaker '86)

Really heavy German biker fare with yelpy chick vocals that conjure nightmares of Lene Lovich or Yoko Ono getting the rotating Sabbath posting. No loss, 'cos it ain't that good anyways, stomping with acceptable Teutonic coercion, but lacking a core sound to call their own. Disadvantaged right from the word go.

Rating    3

## Castle Blak - Babes In Toyland    (Heavy Metal America '86)

Frisco's Castle Blak are the possessors of a sort of naughty sound, fusing heavy glam similar to the Crüe with booming live slur-tations of shout and reply, riffwork and reverb, and simple barroom trench rock as per the *idea* of Van Halen - **II** or Y&T's battle-ready **Struck Down**. All rumbles crashing and jamming throughout this party-time bomb brigade, which through unabashed will, slowly wins over the crowd just like they all imagined one day air-guitaring in their poster-wrapped bedrooms. Great cover of *Black Diamond*, plus crackling originals like *Crazy* and *Never Enough* make **Babes In Toyland** a studly wallop worth the price of admission. Fact is, there just aren't enough big-haired mall rats out there, and **Babes** somewhat fits the bill, being a doltish but party-intense blast of barrel-scraping styles. Slight debilitating factor: painfully brash production.

Rating    7

## Catfish - Neighbours & Dogs    (Pondslime '93)

Vancouver retro with various colourburst flavourings, Catfish have a good thing going with their unique vocabulary layering Aerosmith, alternative, balladry, bluesiness and strange funk arrangements. Although it gets a mite confused at times, skirting third-rate party metal here and there, the overall effect is one of healthy creativity, reminding me of another Canadian indie band, Soul Tattoo. Part of the charm lies with the vocals of Kevin Hemeon, who is a nice match for the band's quite new and astonishing melodies. But then the playing is a tad unintentionally loose, and the production somewhat garagey. Call it promising. Fave: *Bitter Sweet*.

Rating    6

## Cathedral - Forest Of Equilibrium    (Earache '91)

Somewhat of a genre-creator, Cathedral's first finds Lee, Gaz and the boys defining sludgy, melted death metal, more or less in reaction to the faster, louder, messier ethic of death metal to this point (a condition Lee himself was part of creating with Napalm Death). But the record sounds more intent on making this statement rather than presenting good songs, indeed most of this sounding written for mid-speed and then merely punctured and left to deflate. Plus the recording is bad, lacking treble, while Dorrian's vocals seem grudgingly delivered at low mumble. At least Dave Patchett's awesome artwork is already showing full-on inspiration. Commendable, but not a lot of good, clean fun.

Rating    6

## Cathedral - Soul Sacrifice    (Earache '92)

It's been a lengthy spell since I've heard British steel sound so festeringly Wiccan. This 24 minute long, four tune EP sends the rattled black metalhead spinning in collision with a time when the inebriated Witchfinder General were the lone Limey purveyors of eau d' Sabbath. For indeed Cathedral give reigning modern day torch bearers Trouble a run for the ruble with this pounding, powerfully recorded blast of blackest goth, indeed the band citing Trouble and St. Vitus as major

influences. Lee Dorrian's vocals are unsettlingly still borderline grindcore (although much cleaner than in his days with Napalm Death), but all disdain for tuneless pain is wiped off the faces of the onlookers below by some of the meatiest **Vol 4** turbo riffs ever to creep from the crypt. Only *Frozen Rapture* creaks too dangerously stunted while the remaining 3/4, *Soul Sacrifice* (lifted and cleaned up from the debut), *Autumn Twilight* and *Golden Blood (Flooding)* gorge themselves at the trough of Iommi-induced blight, frothing then chomping at each and every dazed megachord that stumbles into destitute view. The overall effect haemorrhages the brain with electro-magnetic jerks, and my long starvation for something convincing from the British feeds eye-glazed on the remains. The acceptable face of grind.
Rating                                                                  9

### Cathedral - The Ethereal Mirror    (Sony '93)
Pretty cool move seeing the band thank Witchfinder General "for their still unknowing influence", for here it comes again, one thieving, steaming, stinking heap of thickest distortion, establishing Cathedral as the most Sabbathy of the two best bands administering this particular kind of pain, t' other of course being Trouble. Lyrically, Cathedral are encased in a foggy sort of grindcore hell, wasting no space with word, packing heaps of insane, sky-straddling devilry into the most compact of sentence fragments, Dorrian belching out his thoughts like a lizard frying on a rock. Fantastically powerful throughout, my only reservation is the record's slower velocities, a reality that seems unavoidable under the strains of such back-buckling gravity. And without reservation, all the mid-speed stuff rocks mightily, so preposterously encased in granite, you just gotta stand back and let it burn itself out. Best track of the punishing catalogue so far: *Ride*.
Rating                                                                  9

### Cathedral - Cosmic Requiem    (Sony '94)
Cathedral are amassing a body of work that is establishing the band as the crazy professors of doom. And this curio fits the bill, a four track EP/LP clocking in at 43 minutes, dominated by 23 minute sludge epic *The Voyage Of The Homeless Sapien*. All of **Cosmic Requiem** is wondrously illogical, out-of-tune, suspended and dangerous, which works and doesn't, although the whole is a statement of the most harrowing elements of Sabbath any band has put together. We get scads of doom mixed with Hawkwind, Tull, Spinal Tap, you name it, all jumbled like a chemical-addled mind let loose. Faves would be regal disaster *Cosmic Funeral* and **Sabotage**-style scorcher *Hypnos 164*, the latter laced electric with solos that are vintage Iommi craziness. In reality (of which Cathedral has none), this makes all those other death metal bands (better ones and worse ones) look commercial and straight-forward, Dorrian and Co. refusing to buck up to convention, letting it all dump out like a steaming plate of tar. In theory at least, the most artistic dark rockers off their rocker.
Rating                                                                  9

### Cathedral - The Carnival Bizarre    (Earache '95)
Not much more can be said about the Cathedral sound that I haven't tried to articulate through previous reviews. **The Carnival Bizarre** continues the band's fine tradition of unkempt, unpredictable doom metal. The slab o' granite at hand almost didn't happen, Cathedral almost breaking up due to label, management and personnel hassles, on top of Dorrian suffering (in his own words) a severe mental breakdown. But art has triumphed, as the band comes headbanging back with their most focused, intense and purely enjoyable raft of burning wisdoms yet. I always liked the uptempo rockers of this band, because they always sounded straight off of Sabotage, and this record has at

least three like that, *Vampire Sun*, *Witchfinder General* (not a cover), and the band's crowning shining crushing achievement thus far, *Utopian Blaster*, which features a solo by Iommi himself. But the whole record flows well, unlike the occasionally turgid prog of **The Ethereal Mirror**, playing a hand built of speed, dynamic, surging sloth and even a twisted, unself-conscious psycho mellowness, recalling Monster Magnet (see *Blue Light*). Tracks are still long, but they remain stout and vigorous, always creative beyond control, escaping the madhouse of convention just like, well, **Sabbath Bloody Sabbath**. Get down with the down-tuned, and buy this crazy lump of coal. Cathedral rules.
Rating                                                                  9

### Cathedral - Hopkins (The Witchfinder General)
(Earache '96)
As has been the rule with Cathedral's EP, **Hopkins** wigs out nicely to a number of realms. First we get the title track, with added spoken word intro, but after than the experiments fly! Arthur Brown's psycho '60s standard *Fire* gets a new cinder block treatment, complete with horn section. Then there's a pretty dull slow thrash of an instrumental, an almost gothic new wave/industrial tune called *Purple Wonderland*, and a lengthy James Brown-type funk monster crammed full of horns, called (very inappropriately) *The Devil's Summit*, which Earache emphatically states is not a new direction for the band, but just a bit of fun. Both the latter leave almost too much breathing space for Dorrian's unstudied vocals, but are fairly engaging tracks nevertheless, at least loosening up for a spell on those massive doom metal reigns.
Rating                                                                  7

### Cathedral - Supernatural Birth Machine    (Earache '96)
Bottom line: if you're a Cathedral fan, you'll hum along maniacally, but if you're not, you'll wrinkle your nose at the pungent, tuneless, toneless tones enclosed, Dorrian and Co. smearing forth with more eccentric tales of sludge, wholly unsociable but for the initiated. I talked to Lee about the album, and he spoke of the spontaneous nature of the vocals, the increased use of melody, and the fact that the record was less "instant" than its predecessor, darker, heavier etc. But I *like* "instant", even if the overall crazyman vibe of this one carries its own cache, an underground, commercial-void quiltwork of motivations that sounds quite possibly older than the earliest Sabbath that crawls. After another ten Cathedralwerks, this might be the one that becomes the black hole, suitable for catalogue mining, given its strange, almost casual rockride. Passes the playability test, but I'd have to say the fireworks of **The Carnival Bizarre** burn up the soggy beard rock wallowed here.
Rating                                                                  8

### Cats In Boots - Kicked & Clawed    (EMI '89)
**Kicked & Clawed** is the Crüe doing Aerosmith, plain and simple, yet with more kick and more claw. No point reading much more into this flavour of steel. It either rocks real scuzzy-like, gives you a hard time, and promptly gets filed 'til the next locks on the block come along, or it flounders like Faster Pussycat, or worse Tora Tora. Lead cut on this, *Shot Gun Sally* is worth the scratches alone, careening along atop a bloated Perry riff that kicks you in the head from start to finish. Aerosmith should take a bow in deference and cover this song, at least live. And in fact, the whole album is blood-curdling in its rowdiness, and the recording is loud, noisy, and echoey (and kind of a hassle except on a good stereo). Musically, it's everything Crüe and Aerosmith thrown together would be: semi-wise, wild, funky, jammin', dirty, loose, boogie woogie, and emphatically big city bright lights on a Saturday night.

One of the best in a genre lacking leaders, brains, honesty or magic.
Rating **7**

## Celestial Season - Solar Lovers (Metal Blade '95)

All hail the cathedral-solid tones of Celestial Season, who slot right into the currently happening orchestral goth metal zone, maybe a bit too conveniently, depending on your will to submit. There are seven very sombre souls in this Dutch conglomerate, including two sexy female violinists, who take this right into the My Dying Bride end of the forest, weaving sad textures throughout what is a somewhat stiff and clinical death/doom hybrid, Stefan's vocals appropriately grindcore growled, although in a very relaxed, comatose manner. Possibly a bit late to market, as the novelty is wearing off but quick, even My Dying Bride having moved on to new but equally dark blue terrain.
Rating **6**

## Celtic Frost - Morbid Tales (Noise '84)

For some mold-fogged reason, only to be found festering in the dual minds of the impenetrable Martin Eric Ain and Thomas Gabriel Warrior, Hellhammer posed an amusing challenge to corrode more chemically than Venom in every direction possible. And they sure attracted a lot of press, as unsuspecting metalheads listened in and literally felt raped by a system that would unleash such obvious trash without a warning label that loudly proclaimed: "Run Away. Vacuum cleaner with drums." Well, the small appliances are back as the more accessible Celtic Frost, a sort of lobotomized Sabbath on amphetamines, where doom riffs randomly generate and fade with no apparent motivation, underneath a Venom-like but much better recorded drunken mumble that passes for the spoken word portion of our show. Suffice to say, the **Morbid Tales** EP is unpleasantly pleasant, but unredeemed by any semblance of musicality, logic, or sense of purpose that Venom hadn't already invented. The wiggling tadpole that would become grindcore, Celtic Frost would at least become a legacy as strong as Venom and Bathory in terms of early engineering of future black metals. And in many areas, the band sounded better than Cronos' cruel crew. Classic: chugging harlot *Return To The Eve*, later revamped for the **Tragic Serenades** EP.
Rating **5**

## Celtic Frost - Emperor's Return (Noise '85)

Recorded a mere six months after **Morbid Tales**, this dead similar EP begins the introduction of fantastical elements into the band's sound and artwork. Still, there's a stiffness to Celtic Frost's delivery at this point that will begin to fall away like rotting flesh come next sonic scourge. Contains arch-Frost anthem *Circle Of The Tyrants*.
Rating **6**

## Celtic Frost - To Mega Therion (Noise '85)

With Martin Ain out (briefly) part way through the protracted, chaotic recording of this disturbing black metal landmark (replaced by Dominic Steiner), Celtic Frost becomes very much the grievance domain of Tom Warrior. From the twisted, blasphemous H.R. Giger artwork (the guy was a fan!), through the trashier, thrashier grooves enclosed, the band has decided to delve more unto the extreme, inching closer to partners in slime Bathory. Indeed there are even early symphonic elements here, as the band retains its slow and mid-crush bash, creating a sludgy, intoxicating ambience, where riffs wander concussion-like (and a bit one-track minded) behind Warrior's surprisingly accomplished tales of sin-swept lands. Only the occasional fast one, and none (thankfully) containing modern-day blastbeats. Probably the most consistent

example of early death metal that exists, Celtic Frost would appropriately become the subject of a Dwell Records tribute in 1996.
Rating **7**

## Celtic Frost - Tragic Serenades (Noise '86)

This pause that retortures is a bit of a gear-up to **Into The Pandemonium**, re-oiling the band's quintessential line-up, re-tooling a handful of putrid oldies. The band's inaugural U.S. tour would ensue, deliciously teamed with label-buds Voivod. Now back to our terrible tale.
Rating **6**

## Celtic Frost - Into The Pandemonium (Noise '87)

Back to the classic line-up of Warrior, Ain and drummer Reed St. Mark, the Frosties enter once again, a German studio, dropping the Slayer-derived greasepaint, ready to do battle with Good as the latter-'80s commence. And much loopiness ensues, starting with Wall Of Voodoo cover *Mexican Radio*, a minor hit for the band, and new vocal treatments, including a haunting classical passage with female vocals (*Tristesses De La Lune*, originally left off the record), again being first off the black blocks with various flavours of death. But one couldn't say riffs are all that improved, the band still combining every minor and major chord every which way, throwing out nothing. So the signature non-structures remain, the band lurching and squeaking and creaking along, then speeding it up a bit for no apparent reason, then back again. Still in many ways, the best at what they do.
Rating **7**

## Celtic Frost - Cold Lake (Noise '88)

Laugh if you must, but your cat-calls will ring hollow, Celtic Frost despite the ridiculous transformation into a glam band, coming up with an oddly delicious stack of songs (although everybody in their right mind loathed this record). So the goods: Tom Warrior purges his entire band, subtracting two and adding three, then somewhat glamming out on their look, Tom even trying to crack a bit of a smile in the pink back-lit band photo. And gone are the black metal lyrics, substituting an almost scarier street-level sin, barked out in an out-of-tune new (York Doll) snarl that almost sounds like Cathedral's Lee Dorrian years later (and even a bit like Jess Cox from the Tygers Of Pan Tang's debut!). But the riffs are awesome, sinister (see fave *Cherry Orchards*), and not the least bit ready to party, the band feeding belching black smoke despite the visual presentation shift, maybe splitting the difference arriving at mid-to-upper quality New Wave Of British Heavy Metal. Just a twisted wreckage of motivations come awry, what falls out of **Cold Lake** is killer metal fabulously by mistake, the new guys kicking Warrior's idea-depleted band into high gear, solos achieving Accept, riffs galloping along with renewed vigor (much credit to new guitarist Curt Victor Bryant). Of course ridicule showered down upon the band like heavy rain, but in my opinion, such sentiments are superficial. This was a good record, despite the meddling of Tony Platt.
Rating **8**

## Celtic Frost - Vanity/Nemisis (Noise/BMG '90)

Now splitting the difference between the NWOBHM traditions of **Cold Lake**, and the band's previous death knells, Warrior, Bryant, drummer Stephen Priestly, and newly reinstated bassist Martin Ain construct their trickiest and smartest album yet, perhaps when all is said and done, arriving at a classic German sound that is a blacker Accept, or a simpler Rage or Coroner. But all sorts of uniquely Celtic Frost things are happening here, Warrior's smeary riffs, his retention of the expressive crooked, Cathedral-like croon from the last

record, and a twisted evil that is of this earth and earthly situations, a sort of dark poetry that is as impenetrable as it is provocative. An invitingly dark, oddly undisciplined metal experience. Note: my grading of this band flies in the face of accepted norms.
Rating     9

## Celtic Frost - 1984-1992: Parched With Thirst Am I And Dying  (Noise '92)

Probably most die-hard of hearing Frosties will disagree with my ratings of the Celtic Frost catalogue, no doubt inverting the grades, revelling in those classic black metal innovations from the mid-'80s. Hey, like, too bad. I figured they gained texture, brains, production, riffs, complexity and lyrical prowess as time marched on, but that's just me. Anyhow, here's a nice celebration of the band's unarguable legacy no matter which way you lean. There are a few recent album tracks, remixes galore, and unreleased tracks from all eras of the band, including two brand spanking new ones, Idols Of Chagrin and Under Apollyon's Sun, all clearly put in context in the extensive liner notes. An expertly arranged best of package, chock full of high quality rarities, pretty much all the eager Frostie could possibly have hoped for. Hail!
Rating     8

## Cemetary - An Evil Shade Of Grey  (Black Mark '92)

Cemetary's early years were spent far away from the slow metal sell-out of Black Vanity, strapped to a vortex of solid technical thrash that recalls early Entombed before their welcome transformation. This one's quite unique (and unlike the rest of the catalogue), full of mournfully twisted ideas that become well-travelled walls of sound, full of voracious vehement riffs and throat-ripping low gutturals that demonstrate a band going places squarely evil.
Rating     7

## Cemetary - Godless Beauty  (Black Mark '93)

The first of the band's "we try harder" era, Godless Beauty cranks up the graphics to reinforce Cemetary's newer druggie death tones, a simpler, separated sound that leaves exposed spaces in which to place Mathias Lodmalm's (still at this point) hoarse vocals. A loopy charm emerges, not unlike Unleashed, both bands welling up with a sincere, economical gothic mosh that bleeds raw with tundra-dark imagery and cloak and dagger tales of personal interaction. Basically Black Vanity without the self-conscious trendiness, a sound still evolving, the band still fresh with enthusiasm at a new, more purely tuneful possibilities. Faves: the Manowar/punk fusion of Now She Walks The Shadows, and the structure gone out of control experimentation of Sunrise (Never Again). A higher 7 than its follow-up.
Rating     7

## Cemetary - Black Vanity  (Black Mark '94)

Zounds. This one's a surprise given the personable feel of its predecessor, a sort of grindiness backwound to a simplified retro-Sabbathness, tuneful but almost dare I say too laid-back, cold fish and riffless. Which is bizarre these days, my experience usually one of being pasted to the wall by blastbeats and manic songs crammed with food. Cemetary on the other hand (note: this is essentially a Mathias Lodmalm solo band by this point), are now plainly for the Paradise Lost crowd, a decelerated sleepy-time grind that trundles from Witchfinder General, Trouble and St. Vitus through heartburst thrash to live this grey sad life, chug chugging into mid-pace anonymity with equally fence-sitting grindtune vocals. Given the splendidly twisted artwork, I'd never have thought it would be so musically simple musical and underwhelmed (basically a grindcore sell-out), but such is the new condition of death

metal as it metamorphoses into something saleable and enjoyable (Earache, are you listening?). A failure but a brave one. Oh, the wicked world we live in when a record like this isn't wild 'n' evil enough to shake our tree.
Rating     7

## Cemetary - Sundown  (Black Mark '96)

Cemetary's last marked a shakey transition from repellent death metal to a more stripped and accessible sound. The band didn't handle it well, losing respect merely for edging more commercial, then to boot, doing a bad job of the new sound. Sundown should snuff the naysayers like a cigarette butt, doing a gorgeous job of a traditional metal sound, with mournful, post-death themes and doom tones, approaching only one band I can think of at the moment, magnificent fellow Euro frostheads Sentenced. Everything's first class and lavish about this one, from the chilling, illustrated artwork to the confident fusion of chopping power chords and keyboards, Cemetary bringing solid, impressionable songs to the table, Lodmalm oxymoronically crooning rough and raw a set of lyrics that is both dark and beautiful, what he has deemed a concept album based on the coming end of the world, and people's reflections of their contributions and experiences as it all winds (sun) down. Favorite tracks are mid-paced mean machines like Elysia and Last Transmission (shades of Paradise Lost), although the band makes sure to pace things well, countering the deathly with the symphonic, the bashing with the slothful, the metallic with the band's acquired '80s gothic new wave preoccupations. Easily tied for first with Edge Of Sanity as Black Mark's flagship signing.
Rating     9

## Cemetary - Last Confessions  (Black Mark '97)

Here's supposedly one last gesture under the Cemetary moniker, Lodmalm, even as far back as a year, wanting to change the direction of the band to something more gothic and electronic, choosing the name Sundown as his new band. Well, Last Confessions is a beautiful way to blaze out, the man offering his coolest, most mainstream metal tracks, along with a half dozen or so different vocal treatments. But at 28 minutes and no lyrics, this is a slight gesture at best, even if the man's a metal genius. Let's hope he doesn't wig out and leave the genre.
Rating     9

## Paul Chain - Alkahest  (Godhead/Flying '95)

Paul Chain is a cult legend in Europe, having begun his eccentric career back in '77 with doom band Death SS, metamorphosing into experimental theatre and electronic music, all the while recording limited production run records (over ten, depending how you count) that are now collector's items, living the life of gothic metal renaissance man in his 16th century home and home studio in Italy. Alkahest is his biggest, most polished and lavish record, featuring guest contributions from long-time fan Lee Dorrian from Cathedral, culling together a raft of clear-headed, accessible doom metal tracks (middle-road Sabbath), save for the fact that a third of them are sung in no established language, although you would swear it was English. Very cool booklet, including medieval artwork, photos, the few English lyrics (which are pretty much, intense poetic black metal), and a full Chain discography. Quite a cohesive and unique artistic presentation. Highlight: Dorrian's unintelligible vocal on eleven year old track Voyage To Hell, which also features a ripping and ancient, Iommi-style axe solo.
Rating     8

## Channel Zero - Unsafe (Metal Blade '95)

Cool to hear European bands kicking ass in decidedly American genres, here Channel Zero forging perfect chemistry between the hardcore metal of Helmet, Pro-Pain, Pantera and Biohazard, and the warmer fleshtones of Seattle grunge. What falls out of this Belgian act's third record is a killer 12-pack of drinking man's metal, catchy guzzling tunes of a hard alternative '90s nature, with just enough playful punk edge to evoke that word "catchy". This arrived along with the self-titled debut from accomplished Swedish grunge-meisters Mental Hippy Blood, and both are heartening records in the fact that they soak up cool experimental ideas from these shores, and spit them back with their own Eurotones, benefitting from their distance from local scenes and hyper hypes. So this one works wonders really, all thanks to pacing and superior songwriting, resulting in a slamming spin that is neither harsh nor overbearing. Fun to eat AND digestible.
Rating 7

## Chaos UK - 100 Per Cent Two Fingers In The Air Punk Rock (Century Media '93)

So limey punk it's a parody, right down to the grainy black and white cover, the haircuts, the lunkhead lyrics, this one's kind of a snickery galloping mosh, something like bad boozy Motörhead, if you will. But even the live stuff ain't mixed half bad, achieving that no-hope, punk till you drop pogey-pogo that you would expect at this sort of gig. Funny old sod at the mike too. One of a few Century Media projects dabbling in the so-called punk resurgence (which so far has only benefited the two bands that "started" it).
Rating 5

## Chariot - The Warrior (Shades '84)

The Warrior is basically a blunt, ham-fisted traditional chugorama, sporting a Motörheaded no-frills bell-ring, albeit with less zip and less personality. English biker metal that only rarely rises above duh, which ain't necessarily a bad thing if a good headbang is the call. Something proud about it, though. High points: Evil Eye and Vigilante.
Rating 6

## Chariot - Burning Ambition (Shades Est. '85)

More blue collar brain-shaking embedded in the song-craft this time 'round, but a noisier, sloppier mix buries any advancement of intent, making Burning Ambition boozy and regressed, for completely different reasons as were the case with The Warrior. A likeable band of rogues in any event, but just a hassle to really get into, Chariot cursed with the fate of the British to lose at all costs.
Rating 5

## Chasar - Gypsy Roller (Mausoleum Est. '86)

One step beyond for Mausoleum, Chasar are a stretch 'em out, dreamy trio who show domineering heft on strident opener Destiny, then self-evaporate into wafts of cosmic metal until their title stomp mid-side two. Different from the label's usual greaseball rock, Chasar may have just picked a bad bunch of songs for this one, as the boys seem to ideate some muscular washes amidst their protracted tales. Major strivation: the almost Zeppishly mythic closer, Underground, commandeered by a twisty trilling riff and an expert gallop from skinsman Jim Marshall. Too bad, but the percentages just aren't there.
Rating 6

## Chastain - The 7th Of Never (Leviathan '87)

The third record for Cincinnati's David T. under the Chastain moniker, The 7th Of Never is merely average gruesome middle America technical metal; that is

average songs with killer soloing. Leonine female belter Leather Leone does a bitchy good job, but the production drags it all into the mud, especially those Ken Mary (ex-Alice Cooper) drum tracks, recorded by a pre-fame Terry Date. A crazy-ass metal talent, surrounded by incompetence.
Rating 4

## Chastain - The Voice Of The Cult (Leviathan '88)

Better production this time (by all the same guys), and Dave's off on another tear, crushing and cruising metal man solos, riffs that carry a whiff of Savatage and Metal Church, street screamer Leather Leone snarling out cheezy lyrics of love, sex and hocus pocus intrigue, tales built for b-market metal pits and not home listening. As usual, useful as a guitar showcase, laughable as a band recording.
Rating 5

## David T. Chastain - Movements Thru Time (Leviathan '92)

Egads, if you can believe your axe-shredded ears, Movements Thru Time is a compilation that summarizes no less than twelve records (and the oblig instructional videos) for this US guitar whiz since 1985. Chastain is one of those guys who oscillates between conventional, vocals-based metal records, instrumental fist-pumping shredding, and electric jazz metal, and all of that is evident here. As a fairly unqualified opinion, I'd say the man has full-on speed, doing very traditional shred in all its cliché glory, mixed with Schenker Eurosoul, elevating along that axis to the castle-steep runs of Yngwie. But it's all recorded in the dirty and electric fashion typical of Yankee rust belt poverty metal; thudly drums, shrieky vocals, not the best of songs. But then again, that's not where Dave's head is at.
Rating 5

## Chastain - Sick Society (Leviathan '95)

After somewherz around fifteen records spanning straight instructional shred through jazz metal through conventional mid-'80s blue collar metal, axe wunder David T. Chastain comes up with his most user-friendly slab of vocals-based metal, Sick Society featuring his best all-round packaging (he's really been pretty bad in this department), best vocalist in the low-throat howlin' Kate French, and best recording, using those down-tuned '90s tones that are all bass throb, spaces and crunch. No doubt the plan is to address a whole new audience, the one buying commercial, grunge-infected power metal, re-tooled bands like Skid Row, Fight, and even Metallica. And it's the latter to which this sounds most akin; thick, slow, un-showy riffs held fast and true by strong vocals and above-par (and above Metallica!) soloing. Of note: French is dang low-down and vicious on this, sounding like a cross between a couple of Metal Church singers and Jon Oliva of Savatage, with maybe a little Sass Jordan thrown in, 'cos they're both babes! So some will cry sell-out, this being Chastain's least David T.-like record, but hey, I for one would rather play this by a long shot, than ANY guitar solo record by anybody, except maybe Brian May or Kim Mitchell.
Rating 7

## Chastain - In Dementia (Leviathan '97)

Dave Chastain and Kate French continue their '90s metal collaboration, Kate sounding like a chain-smoking whiskey-swilling powerhouse guy vocalist, Dave chugging like Alice in Chains on slow drip. Stellar recording values do both of them justice, their chops-perfect rhythm section of bassist Kevin Kekes and drummer Dennis Lesh also getting to shine. Bio bills this as a melding of old and new Chastain, but the sound is mostly new, although a type of Zepped goth rears its head on rumblers like Tongue and Conformity. The instrumentalists get to riff often, but it is kept well in check, the grunge and hardcore derived riffs allowed to pack full steam. Dense, earth-moving, and oddly (not all goodly) dated, but a purer metal, I can't imagine.

Rating **6**

## Chateaux - Chained And Desperate  (Ebony '83)

This raw, violent record embodied all the magic and steely-eyed determination of the exploding British metal movement in the early '80s. Dense and rumbling, **Chained And Desperate** cuts a rough street-ready path of destruction, laid waste by one of Darryl Johnston's acidic trademark Ebony recordings, resulting in a record so depressingly European and so darkly arresting that it stands as one of the personally emotional and nostalgic greats of the NWOBHM. Aside from the guttural attack of the mix, **Chained And Desperate** claims further frenzied highs due to the appearance of labelmate Steve Grimmett of Grim Reaper on vocals, and some razor-sharp, metal-on-metal guitar histrionics from Tim Broughton. Riding the same mysterious mood as Reaper's first, Diamond Head, Savage, and Witchfinder General, **Chained And Desperate** combines integrity, songcraft, and grime in a way rarely seen outside the confines of these early Brit masters. A swirling cauldron of glorious noise.

Rating **9**

## Chateaux - Fire Power  (Ebony '84)

The treadmill from Hell is back, and a bit out of control. Producer Darryl Johnston delves deeper into his Ebony mindspace and pulls out an even thicker, more eclectic sound which nevertheless still makes the blood boil profusely. But the songwriting focus is lost, the singular garage din of the debut heaving forth to both OTT excursions and flirtation with AOR rock structures. Skull-flattening classics such as *Eyes Of Stone*, *Hero*, and *White Steel* make up for some of the less polished, less thought-through stuff like the meandering *Run In The Night* and the confusing *Roller Coaster*. Still a searing, filthy record sonically speaking, featuring excellent vocal work by new Grimmett sound-alike Krys Mason, **Fire Power** rocks unhewn and hurried, while burning with an intensity that melts lipsticked poseurs in their platform-booted tracks.

Rating **8**

## Chateaux - Highly Strung  (Ebony '85)

Opening with a most glorious wash of unadorned electric guitar, **Highly Strung** quickly degenerates into a slugfest of noise that obliterates the subtleties that made **Chained And Desperate** and **Fire Power** such proud records. This is Johnston's worst recording of the three, kicking ferociously on all fronts except the all-important treble. Songwise, the band follows the man at the knobs underwater, thrashing wildly, even on the more hard rocky numbers, sounding simply **Highly Strung**, the record collapsing into the punkiest, most over-the-top Chateaux in every sense of the word; scurrying, fast, loose, and indulgent. Still, you've got to admire this band, dishing out rough and mean, no-hope metal, delivered with clenched teeth and unwavering pride. Best tracks here include the staccato chug rockers which let Broughton's incredibly metallic guitar work shine, carb-cleaners like *One Too Many*, *Through The Fire*, *Turn It On*, and brilliant closer *Midnight Star*, slashing with a conviction and sense of history that seems lost with most metal today. Chateaux, over the span of three records, seemed to progressively shroud themselves in a cloak of sound that by the time **Highly Strung** hits town, leaves the proceedings dense and close to impenetrable.

Rating **7**

## Cheap Trick - Cheap Trick  (Epic '77)

There was no way this record could escape major talk around town. Here were four dudes from Chicago, two well-tailored heart throbs, lead vocalist and rhythm guitarist Robin Zander and bassist Tom Petersson, and two cartoonish hicks, lead guitarist Rick Neilsen (the original Pee Wee Herman), and drummer Bun E. Carlos, your basic bespectacled portly accountant type. Together they eventually became a short-lived institution, but first they became **Cheap Trick**, the debut record, an explosive wanderlust of axe mechanics, jangliness, grinding chords, what-the-hell experimentalism, rousing velvety pop, garage metal, ups, downs, heartfelt moments, self-deprecating humour, and general spontaneous mayhem as per my uneducated perception of vintage live Who. Neilsen turns out to be a zesty-fried little axeman, a perfect foil to Zander's torrid vocal stylings, and everybody has a blast. This was the spirit of creativity found in a lot of early hard rock. Cheap Trick slapped down whatever the tarnation popped into their collective repertoire of dementia, the surprising thing being its seductive catchiness, from the cruising chords of *He's A Whore* and the chaotic scamper of *Hot Love* through the elegant slow melodimetal of *Daddy Should Have Stayed In High School* and the prophetic pop flirtation of *Oh Candy*. Very cool, very savvy, and completely off the wall, **Cheap Trick** is testimony to an era when hard rock was way ahead of marketers' business plans, when it just sort of escaped, ran around, and defied categories. Unfortunately, Cheap Trick would eventually be recaptured, doped up with tranquilizers, and sold to the zoo.

Rating **9**

## Cheap Trick - In Color  (Epic '77)

So what might a second Cheap Trick record entail? After the non-committal oddity of the debut, nobody but the Chicago Four could have answered that one. **In Color** delivers the band to some form of mainstream as nothing on this is overtly strange on its own, while as a whole, it's still a mess of directions which manage to coalesce under some weird beach metal hybrid. '60s pop melodies, campy heartthrob hooks, good ol' '70s chuggorama, and just a trace of eccentricity combining to place Cheap Trick firmly on a path straight to the wayward hearts of all the young midwest foxes with a thin slice of bad girl in them, led of course by the siren call of drippy super hit *I Want You To Want Me*. Metallically, no question, Cheap Trick wimped out on **In Color**, surprising many of us who revelled in the controlled chaos of the band's live shows. Nevertheless, the boys knew how to entertain, and **In Color** came off as a somewhat knowing and strangely mature rendition of axe-laced ear candy.

Rating **6**

## Cheap Trick - Heaven Tonight  (Epic '78)

Cheap Trick's tendency to construct albums which juxtapose American style guitar heroics against shameless pop poodles has focused into a tendency to compose individual songs in a similar manner. The jagged, obtuse peaks and pink velour valleys have been smoothed over to create . . . well . . .*On Top Of The World*, *California Man*, and *Surrender*, the band's G-rated apocalyptic mega hit most demonstrative of their trademark sound. **Heaven Tonight** drips with a pop sheen that is critically considered Beatle-esque, a term that I think soils the Cheap Trick experience with an impression of simplistic arrangements and stupidly obvious, predictable melody or structure, something of which Cheap Trick is definitely not guilty, outside of about five tracks over the first five albums. Cheap Trick was more a self-conceived stylist, pre-dating the rise of punk's palatable offspring, power pop. That's the slant of about 3/4 of this record and most of its two follow-ups. **Heaven Tonight**'s crowning glories however, are the two metallic numbers, sassy energized riff-rocker *Stiff Competition* and legendary suicide stomper *Auf Wiedersehen*, an acerbic freight train of death, one of the band's most relentless classics. History shows that the Trick was onto something with this record, the band becoming one of the three or so big wellwisher parties of the era.

Rating      7

## Cheap Trick - At Budokan    (Epic '78)

Here we find Cheap Trick, Kings of the Teen Beat doin' that lovable duality shtick they do so well in front of teeming masses of screaming Japanese pre-pubescent foxes. The sound ain't great but who cares? This is nostalgia at work, and a pretty rockin' collection of early Tricks to boot, including *Hello There*, *Big Eyes*, and *Clock Strikes Ten* but *nothing* from the debut which I guess would be considered too "out there" for their new adoring fan base. Nonetheless it all gels into a noisy goo of hysteria like the Beatles in '64.

Rating      5

## Cheap Trick - Dream Police    (Epic '79)

**Dream Police** revives the same mixed bag that comprises **Heaven Tonight** except that everything is less convincing, over-commercialized and kinda lame. The metal, which had become a rare but god-like commodity on **Heaven Tonight** becomes shuffling, noodly and overly melodic, like a teen beat pillow fight with guitars, the straight pop, the similarly candy-coated bop rock, and the unconvinced metal, all fusing questionably. The trademark Trick pluses still abound, the rich arrangements, grooveability, and Zander's seductive lion-like roar breathing heady magic. But it's all kinda watery and edgeless. One strange aspect of this record is the inclusion of the two side closers, *Gonna Raise Hell* and the **At Budokan**-debuted *Need Your Love*, two mantra-like lumbering dinosaurs clocking in at a combined 16:53, neither being any big heaping deal. In any event, Cheap Trick seem to have settled into a comfortable persona in these their cash cow years, a persona consisting of drippy teen star melodramatics mixed with a penchant for hard rock occasionally lapsing into metal.

Rating      6

## Cheap Trick - Found All The Parts    (Epic '80)

An odds 'n' soddser that samples a track from each Cheap year so far. The spirited jangling of *Day Tripper* opens the show ('79), followed by a lethargic metal-blooz called *Can't Hold On* from the ecstatic '78 live in Japan experience. Next up, *Such A Good Girl* ('76) is a sugary if uneventful Trick popster, while closer is a loud maudlin Elvis-type '77 original called *Take Me I'm Yours*. Best tune is left for the single-sided 45 that was included in the package, a chunky bulky piece of elegant hard pop called *Everything Works If You Let It*, a proggy, perky Rundgren-type bloomer with three or four nice hooks. What more can you ask?

Rating      5

## Cheap Trick - All Shook Up    (Epic '80)

In typical industry fashion, Cheap Trick craft one of their most provocative and complex records since their debut, and no one buys it. **All Shook Up** achieves most brilliantly that hard rock cum '50s cum '60s fusion the band's always been after, variously kicking and swaggering, offering well-crafted guitar-edged timelessness in three or four innovative directions. We get lush HR hooks with the buoyant and inspired *Stop This Game* and the emotive *Can't Stop It But I'm Gonna Try*, metallic Elvis with *Just Got Back*, Stonesy lubrication with *I Love You Honey But I Hate Your Friends*, and killer state-of-the-art Trick metal with the buzzing *High Priest Of Rhythmic Noise* and *Love Comes A' Turnblin'*

*Down*, both feeding from the same well as buddy Rick Derringer. And the band is so fiercely on, playing like there's no tomorrow, which would unfortunately be the case accolades-wise. Zander's pipes righteously wail, croon, and just universally give 'er, propelling these intelligent pop metal groovers ever forth above a conservative but muscular and well-accented mix. Tragically under-rated, **All Shook Up** is one disgraced king, one bete noire, worthy of rescue from the delete bins.

Rating      8

## Cheap Trick - One On One    (Epic '82)

Here we see Cheap Trick's shameless dive into cutesy pop and my own shameless dive into humming along. **One On One** clunks and clinks along frenetically to all sorts of syrupy sweet pop hooks, achieving silly nirvana on *She's Tight*, *Time Is Runnin'* and the perky, pert title track. The thrill is gone however, and so is the potential of teeth, marked by the band's first deliberate shift away from the sounds of the '70s

Rating      5

## Cheap Trick - Next Position Please    (Epic '83)

The only truly dreamy record of Cheap Trick's latter-day pop persona finds the band focusing beatifically on the most compelling of hooks. Foremost of the spread are *I Can't Take It*, *Younger Girls*, *Heaven's Falling*, and the title cut which all glaze over in search of teen beat stardom and hot summer nights. Again, not one to shirk my responsibilities, be warned. These second half Trickster's doth not rock, but you might want to check at least this one out for that sweet tooth you might be favouring.

Rating      7

## Cheap Trick - Standing On The Edge    (Epic '85)

Post crafty pop metalists, and post cute pop obscurists, **Standing On The Edge** stands in loose alignment with latter-day Cheap Trick sellouts as a record by the beautiful people for the beautiful people. The production is big and brash, the balladry is crass and tasteless, and experimentalism is at an all time low. Besides the surprisingly complicated title track, all else on this, heavy and melloid alike, is written for the expressed purpose of radio play. The humour is gone and so is the creativity as the band tries to pass itself off as jaded rock pigs in search of *Wild Wild Women* and *Cover Girls*. Even though over half of **Standing On The Edge** technically passes as hard rock, almost all of it could pass for the cynical offspring of any band's brush with business. Corruption rules supreme, and alas, the Cheap Trick persona is up in smoke, forever groove-locked in a kinder, gentler era. Come to think of it, I guess they are jaded rock pigs.

Rating      4

## Cheap Trick - The Doctor    (Epic '86)

**The Doctor** delivers the last quirky underdog pop spread of Cheap Trick's career to date, offering a busy, highly strung, Rundgren-ish affair, full of energy and hi-tech bells and whistles, yet saddled and saddened with an edgy clattering production. Rundgren actually produced the band *last* time around, yet this one is more his timbre, full of gravity-undermining cuteness and wall of sound hyperaction. Verdict: like a trip to the circus: fun and meaningless.

Rating      5

## Cheap Trick - Lap Of Luxury    (Epic '88)

Filthy lucre takes over here as Cheap Trick picks business over pleasure, sounding like any one of the last five inane, robotic Heart records. **Lap Of Luxury** is all vanilla safeness, studio gloss, and lack of humour, bending over so far as to offer a shit novelty cover of Elvis' *Don't Be Cruel* plus an offensive power ballad as its first,

and unfortunately successful single. Three or four tolerable tracks (including the rousing *Let Go*) do make this less obviously despicable than **Busted**, but the band is tragically well on its way to full blown sellout.
Rating **3**

## Cheap Trick - Busted (Epic '90)
Sadly, on **Busted**, it's virtually impossible to even recognize this band as the belly-laughing rogues who once romped carelessly through *Elo Kiddies* and *Auf Wiedersehen*, save for Robin Zander's distinctive and pop-smooth vocals. Utmost lack of humanity and one of the most tragic yet gradual sellouts in rock makes **Busted** a sad chunk of odious fluff. And I can't see such a cool dude as Neilsen enjoying himself doing this. It's just a damn shame bands have to run out of money and sell their craft down the river. **Busted** will ever remain a useless artifact of what is terribly wrong with the corporate underside of music. An offensive rip-off.
Rating **1**

## Cheap Trick - Greatest Hits (Epic '91)
Well, the ultimate package is here for the holidays, and all the big toons are on board, including the necessary collection of hangers-on necessary to fill the record, given the band's lack of bona-fide hits of late, despite the automatic spewing of vile singles every year or so. Exceedingly pop-weighted, with little to rave about. However the novelty Beatles cover is enough to cause dry heaves. Next move: a whispy solo album for Robin Zander in '93.
Rating **4**

## Cheap Trick - Budokan II (Epic/Sony '93)
Like they've never been away wrecking their band for ten years, Cheap Trick put in their second set, cheekily counting the tracks as 11 through 22, adding onto the original ten stormers that cracked their career wide open. Yep, **Budokan II** comprises twelve vintage Trick compositions recorded on that same fateful tour (with two from '79), all different from the first album, delving deeper and weirder into the band's eccentric catalogue, even including a dose of the debut's wingnut charms. So here we get *Elo Kiddies*, *California Man*, *Oh Caroline* and the one-two metal punch of *Stiff Competition* and *Auf Wiedersehen*, the boys' slammingest axe-evil monolith. Fairly choice live album, really.
Rating **7**

## Cheap Trick - Woke Up With A Monster
(Warner Bros. '94)
Everything processed and reasoned that little bit hipper than the abysmal late '80s records, yet with the basic premise unexamined, **Woke Up With A Monster** runs the gamut of fresh guitar pop convincingly without realizing the pains that would be necessary to drag this band out of their rut. Zander is singing swell and Nielsen's guitars are heard often if not obliquely. *You're All I Wanna Do* recalls the glory years plus that whole skinny tie, pencil arms power pop movement of the early '80s, while closer *Love Me For A Minute* is almost (gasp!) tricky. It's still very glossy and gloopy and gloppy, producer Ted Templeman perhaps now tied to a different era with a kinder, gentler, sleepier treatment of the sonic palette (especially the weird synthetic drum sound here). Then there's *Never Run Out Of Love*, which is one of those unfathomable Zippo ballads this band must trashcan but quick if they expect to ever stand proud again. Like, if it's so fun to lie to the press about how this is finally the record where we're rocking out again, why not just do it? It really will work magic on both the wallet and the reputation. Nevertheless, Cheap Trick is probably the last bastion of pop metal schlock with at least half a dimension.
Rating **6**

## Cheap Trick - Sex, America, Cheap Trick
(Epic/Sony '96)
The timing somehow seems right for a box set revisitation to the small wonders of Cheap Trick. And a more than adequate job is done, **Sex, America, Cheap Trick** comprising four CDs, all the lyrics (in Japanese and English) and an excellent 40 page booklet of swanky design, stuffed with memorabilia, quotes, rare photos and detailed liner notes. Unfortunately, music-wise the set suffers from Cheap Trick's fast-waning talents as the years dragged on, so by disc four, we're summarily bored. But rarities come in all stripes. We get single, demo, live, and plain alternate versions of many Trick classics. We also find the band plowing through some dreadful covers in a live setting, best of the batch being *Down On The Bay* and *Mrs. Henry*, worst being an appropriately strung-out *Waitin' For The Man/Heroin*. Fully actualized, previously unreleased tracks total somewherez around ten, depending on what you accept as worthy, and what you dismiss as worse than filler. Truth be told, none of these knocked me slappy happy, most being turgid, gurgly, loose-fitting hard rock of meek nature, overwhelmingly underwritten and under-worked. So a vigorous and enthusiastic vault-cleaning has definitely taken place; songs are there, but those songs are kinda lame. Best of the lot: *Lovin' Money* ('77), *Born To Raise Hell* ('81), *Twisted Heart* ('83) and *A Place In France* ('85), a rare mid-years track pumped full of early years good habits. All told: call this box sincere and uncorporate, but still lacking in worthy rare material.
Rating **7**

## Chemlab - East Side Militia (Metal Blade '96)
Chemlab are a couple of nutty industrial collagists who adopt snobby airs with the best of 'em, intimidating like Ministry, The Jesus Lizard, or Killing Joke, repelling like Butthole Surfers or Foetus. Record two for the band sounds like a trip-hopped Stranglers more than anything, tracks attacking then recoiling, most trancy with fuzzy power chords, but most sorta boring me with an inescapable and lifeless detachment. But one can't escape the fact that this stuff is selling, Marilyn Manson not being too unstuck from the fork, even Bowie visiting these circuitboards with **Earthling**. Yeah it's menacing, but with all those machines, where's the blood?
Rating **4**

## Chequered Past - Chequered Past (EMI '84)
**Chequered Past** was released to almost no fanfare despite the band's interesting mix of rock pedigree in Michael Des Barres, Tony Fox Sales, Clem Burke, and Steve Jones. Toons-wise, the album is a cloddish retro-rocker which only comes out to play on booger wooger *Are You Sure Hank Done It This Way* and frightening apocalyptic riffmonster *A World Gone Wild*. Still, it's an interesting "out there" project, on the edges of acceptance, a tired, seemingly drug-worn album by some of the creepier dudes haunting the stomach walls of rock's seamier underbelly. Des Barres went on to become a respected, fairly busy and ultra-healthy T.V. actor.
Rating **4**

## Child's Play - Child's Play (Chrysalis '90)
Both negative and indifferent reviews seemed to be the order of the day for this Baltimore act's street nasty debut, a record that sounded like lazy L.A. Guns. Mean, median and average production by Howard Benson, who translates capably but not remarkably the band's quintessential rock rat vision, a scratchy buzz that approaches paid blooz dues fleetingly, before fading

into the miasma of deletion, but not before putting a drum solo on their record.
Rating 5

## China White - Run For Cover (Mausoleum Est. '83)
The front cover smells like a Savage album or something equally chiselled, but the band looks like university students. And it sucks because Brits, with very few exceptions, have no idea how to do melodic hard rock. Hazardously fragile vox and thumpy production finish it off.
Rating 2

## Chip & Donnie - Brothers (Roving Gypsies '94)
In shorthand, people call this Japan-only release the Enuff Z'nuff brothers' acoustic album, which misses the point. Actually it's a graciously produced ballads album, full of languished, plush semi-power ballads, with occasional field trips into straight unplugged folksiness, maudlin country (complete with fiddle), and hard rock, all avalanched with the boyz' love of The Beatles (there's even a cover of Lennon's *Jealous Guy*). AOR enthusiasts ate it up, and three years ago, I would have too. But I find myself getting tired of Enuff Z'nuff's sugary pop position, and I guess softer melodic hard rock in general. Call my rating an unrating. Plainest thing I can say: this is most definitely another Enuff Z'nuff record, expertly detailed, just towards the lighter side of the band's endearing catalogue. Update: pan to early '97; **Brothers** is reissued by Futurist as an Enuff Z'nuff record called **Seven**.
Rating 7

## Christ Child - Hard (Est. '78)
Another one of those long-lost, black and white indies from metal's sparsely-populated early days, Christ Child's **Hard** silently entered the scene at the height of the punk era, and as a result sounds suspiciously like the work of bar-crawling metalheads contriving to get raw and cause some controversy with a touchy band moniker. Grimy and volatile for the time, so we took it to heart in our simplistic teenage way. Fave: *Five Finger Exercise*.
Rating 5

## Christian Death - The Iron Mask (Cleopatra '92)
Consider this a sketchy, honourable mention for this long-suffering group of spooks, a band of Sabbatherian goth punks with lots of unclean evil records, many a downright hair-raising type of way underground metal. This one's a little more doped and trance-like but you know they mean well.
Rating 5

## Christian Death - Amen (Century Media '96)
Summarizing a long, deathly underground career scaring the bejeezus out of everyone, this double CD captures the band live and fright-wigged in one uninterrupted 90 minute show in Mexico City. The really cool thing is that the sound quality (digital) is on par with most of the band's studio records, so all these divergent, but mostly hard goth tunes sit together and behave, leveling out the distractions the studio record had in store like ambushes. Not exactly my cup of hemlock, but you gotta like their mystique.
Rating 6

## Chrome Molly - Angst (I.R.S. Metal '88)
These Brits sound near identical to the unremarkable Shy England, all hugely fat recording, muscularly electronic drums (a contradiction in terms), and syrupy sweet HR structures in search of admittance to the echelons of L.A. chick-magnetizing melodicism. And like Shy, Chrome Molly benefits from their position at the edge of the activity, just doing their thing, and coming up with some decent crunch among the fray, which makes tasteful use of keyboards, something rare in this genre (although it gets a bit techy in other ways, as in *Living A Lie*'s sampling confusion). Heavier than I thought it would be. Pounders include *Thanx For The Angst* and *Take It Or Leave It*.
Rating 5

## Chum - Dead To The World (Century Media '96)
Once more silvery splinters of genres peel away to reveal darn groovy bands, Huntington, West Virginia's Chum ruling another sub-sub-genre of metal's domain: power grunge. So think Crowbar meets Soundgarden, crisp clear vocals draped over some of the fattest juggernaut power chords ever recorded. But the songs are constructed with melody and spaces in mind, Chum soaking up the good habits of the alternative nation, erecting an imposing wall of sound, but using big square blocks. Catchy like a bear trap, **Dead To The World** is the kind of heavy experience that leaves no bruises, Chum delivering the hooks with the heft, tracks like *Untouchable* and the novel and Zepp ish title tune exemplifying the band's ability to mix it up into an electric ball of wonder. Closes with a highly entertaining altcore version of Prince's *Darling Nikki*.
Rating 9

## CIA - In The Red (Combat '90)
Busting eight on the richter, this intrinsically Combat noisemaker is essentially the solo domain of one Glenn Evans who plays most of the guitar and all of the drums, also handling shouty, weakly-mixed vocal duties and uneven production. Quite a spread, very heavy with '80s pacing and variances, sorta Bay Area meets New York urban metal, thrashers and Shrapnel-style groovers, technical wanks chafing against grevious bodily moshing. Dated and hodge podgy, but often well-done, side two offering the hottest tracks in *Mind Over Matter* and classic gallopfest *Turn To Stone*. Gotta admire the guy's talents.
Rating 6

## Cinderella - Night Songs (PolyGram '86)
Cinderella's rise to prominence was largely based on nothing at all, roughly paralleling Poison's sweet success, both being little more than vacant, colourful but life-affirming Crüe derivatives. On this laughably-wrapped, positively pink debut, Keifer's ragtag vocals lead the charge through weighty Kiss-like piffle such as *Shake Me* (or was that *Shock Me*) and *Push, Push*, plus more "driving" gutsy numbers such as *Once Around The Ride* and *Hell On Wheels*. Hate the indulged, noisy production, actually like the songs, which as a whole are heavier than one might expect, flying in the face of the band's teen beat image. But of course, safe, shallow and watery like the kiddie pool.
Rating 6

## Cinderella - Long Cold Winter (PolyGram '88)
Cinderella circa '88 strikes that usually annoying balance between Motley Crüe's impression of Aerosmith and L.A. metal's fake blues. What they strive to be is the real thing, a next Stones or Aerosmith, not realizing that such talents are both rare and natural, and that without the gift and conviction, the attempt reeks of imitation and crass commercialism. **Long Cold Winter** revs it up at times, achieving at least the space between fake Aerosmith and Aerosmith itself on *Gypsy Road* and *If You Don't Like It*, and simple kick-ass party action on *Fire And Ice* and *The Last Mile*. Generally though, this second offering is just piles of stoopid, doped-out boogie metal, densely recorded, featuring obligatory shriek vocals by Tommy Keifer, y'know, the kind of grit that is supposed to make us think Keifer was raised on Rod Stewart and Jack Daniels. I don't buy it. Salty Dog and Raging Slab are the only contemporaries that have been able to shamelessly profess

blues/metal integrity and get away with it, and even they both walk a fine line between brilliance and disgust. Further note of disdain: both **Night Songs** and **Long Cold Winter** quickly went double platinum in the U.S.

Rating **4**

## Cinderella - Heartbreak Station (PolyGram '90)

Very much the band's record that is the most surrendered unto the Stones, the Faces, even Status Quo, **Heartbreak Station** crosses into novelty as the boys really ask us to validate their supposed roots. So this is chock-full of creaky porch and rocking chair gumbo, led by hits *Shelter Me* and the bar bluesy title track. Then there's *One For Rock And Roll* and *Dead Man's Road* (pre-gals Fleetwood Mac meets Steve Earle at Bon Jovi's house) which really take it on down to the farm. Kinda wins me over warm all over, erasing memories of the brash, no class mishmash of corporate tones for which the band made stacks of filthy lucre. Then I wake up and get a life.

Rating **7**

## Cinderella - Still Climbing (PolyGram '94)

This '94/'95 relaunch from the embattled Keifer and Co. refuses to budge from the highball hairball rock declared dead in the '90s by armchair pundits everywhere, while learning and growing as songwriters, at least giving it a helluva go. Sticking with blues-based party metal is a bit stupid, unless of course you are true to yourself and doing what you love as I now suspect Keifer is. **Still Climbing** features a good five or so hard rock/metal tracks with strong riffs, best being *Kickstart My Heart* knock-off/update *Freewheelin*. And all three ballads are time-worn-well with the additional positive of full-on arrangements. Elsewhere there's some horns and surprisingly driving grooves from Mellenhead Kenny Aronoff (officially the band is but a three piece), and Keifer's voice is more radically grating than in the past. Trust this band to make high quality Hollyrock. I mean, after all, they're building a bit of a catalogue. Whether you want to give this time on your CD player will depend on the relative importance of Cinderella and their poodley ilk on your past. Although never really a fan, at least this time I'm not dismissing it without a fair shake, i.e. the record's just fine.

Rating **7**

## Circus Of Power - Circus Of Power (Est. '88)

American biker metal with a punk edge, a trace of Goth à la The Cult and a heeping dose of AC/DC, **Circus Of Power** is an admirable debut that falls somewhat short due to a contrived marketing sheen. On the upside: great production, solid, simple songs, and snarling vocal delivery; on the downside, predictable riffs, fake bluesiness, and lyrics that mix the same ol' tired brew of Southern rock, biker, and heavy metal clichés seen all over this beer commercial genre. One of those albums that due to the trade-offs, stands up good in theory but rarely hits the spinlist.

Rating **4**

## Circus Of Power - Vices (RCA '90)

On this surprisingly acclaimed follow-up to the middling debut, Alex Mitchell's vocals becoming increasingly seedy and desperate, sorta like a metallized George Thorogood, which is perhaps an appropriate comparison for the band as a whole, given the bluesy structures and rattlesnake shakin' lyrical terrain. **Vices** however, in comparison with **Circus Of Power**, lumbers with increased mass, moving too slowly and unadorned, boring with the beef and adopted simplistic work ethic, the record ultimately betraying itself as a lazy mix of boogie, blues, and southern rock, metalli-

cally treated although too literally translated, trying but failing to get by on heart, in place of creativity.

Rating **5**

## Circus Of Power - Magic & Madness (Sony '93)

Smacked over the head by grunge, Circus Of Power react by ingesting only what they need to turn their biker metal greasy and lethal. **Magic & Madness** works a burly brew, getting low-down grinding, even pleasantly psychedelic in a black leather sort of way, attracting the odd guest luminary contribution along the way. Judging from this record's manly rhythms and subsequent critical blessing, I'd venture to say that the new and improved Motley Crue might have bent an ear COP's way, as a possible new but compatible direction for those married to street metal. 'Cos that's what this is, a solid, low-cycle sleaze metal for the '90s, clever but still wrench-headed.

Rating **7**

## Cirith Ungol - King Of The Dead ('84)

Cybernetic warriors of the soul, Cirith Ungol, operated in a mindspace of buzzsaw guitars and equally scraping vocals, churning out albums of post nuclear wastelands, sometimes violent, often meandering and derogatorily progressive. The riffs and structures were not that enlightening, leaning towards the more ponderous and slow elements of Goth, yet the concept of the band was quite frightening. Given a real recording budget, these guys could have struck some untapped emotive dark spaces.

Rating **5**

## Fast Eddie Clarke - It Ain't Over Till It's Over (Griffin '94)

Congrats are in order to this often misguided icon of guitar, Fast Eddie finally recapturing the freight-train street scuffle of early Fastway, not to mention conjuring the spirit a few choice Motörhead patterns here and there (but maybe more accurately a synthesis of the two, like Tank). **It Ain't Over** is a true solo album, perhaps Eddie going a bit to far in doing his own vocals, which sound a lot like Ace Frehley, same unstudied holler, same sincerity. But the songs are almost all quite heavy, and over half inspiring like good whiskey (actually I hate whiskey; just sounds right here). Heck, *Laugh At The Devil* is even a Kilminster/Clarke tune, with Lemmy parachuting in for lead vocals; and it's lusty Motörhead all the way. Other faves would be *Snakebite*, *Hot Straight And Normal*, and *Naturally* (a King/Clarke credit), which both bristle with Eddie's uniquely retro riff writin'. A bit of filler here and there (heavy, but stiff Fastway-type songs), and Will Reid Dick's production is a bit muddled, but all in all, this sounds like an ass-kickin' collection of old Fastway demos, which is a tasty tonic indeed.

Rating **8**

## Gilby Clarke - Pawn Shop Guitars (Virgin '94)

Rockin' outta the blocks with snapping lead track *Cure Me . . . Or Kill Me*, **Pawn Shop Guitars** proceeds to get predictable fast, exactly what you might expect from a G'N'R guitarist, rootsy bad boy rock propped by big budgets. Not that that's all bad, many a punter pining for this sort of gritty classic rock, perhaps Clarke's offering being comparatively less cheesy and profane than Duff's, a tad more mainstream than Izzy's. Gilby is a modestly thinking man, at least sincere in his bluesology, leaning Beatlesque at times, but generally covering those honky tonk bluesy metal bases like so much G'NR filler before it. Plus I'd have to say his vocals are fairly anonymous, not exactly weak, just un-noticed. So yes, **Pawn Shop Guitars** covers well-worn terrain, while also ringing fairly solid if you like blunted-off, low risk G'NR-type groove tunes. Album oddities include a cover of *Dead Flowers* with Axl dog-whistle whining a backing track, and a totally Clash-reverential cover of fine oldie *Jail Guitar Doors*. Tough market out there, with fans so incredibly informed and, dare I say sophisticated like no generation before. And usually this sort of fun-time Stones rock would go up in flames like a rag soaked in gasoline. Whether **Pawn Shop Guitars** stiffs or not is probably not terribly important to Gilby, who like Duff and Izzy before, and probably Axl and Slash to come, is really just venting some creative ideas he may not have been able to table at the frenzied but authoritarian collective that is the Gunners. I just wished he had more provocative things to say.

Rating 6

## The Clash - The Clash (Columbia '77)

I had left The Clash out of the book first time around, for the simple (simplistic) reason that only the first two records brandished guitars to any sort of heavy effect. But of course one can't profess to handle punk strictly speaking, with any sort of closure without at least addressing **The Clash** and **Give 'Em Enough Rope**, both searing, visceral pieces of the punk puzzle. Bought this the week it came out (so mine's the green version, the later blue version swapping a bunch of tracks), and all were amazed at the sonic squalor, the sorry, underground depression that pumps from grooves often jumpy, poppy, and by virtue of their age, a large part of the definition of punk, despite a surprising lack of thrashiness. Mick Jones, Joe Strummer, Paul Simonon and and soon to be ousted Tory Crimes strangled nerves with their spot-on political commentary through a haze of squat-squalid dope-smoke and pills, these hapless, individually fizzled firecrackers somehow combining for a synergistic explosion that would cause **Time**, **Rolling Stone** and others to herald them as The World's Most Important Band, and alternately The Only Band That Matters. As with the Pistols record, The Clash benefits from fairly disciplined deliveries and mixes, letting the band's peculiar melodies torch the warehouse, Jones' naive, baby-fat croon countering Strummer's rotten-toothed bulldog bark, the record as a whole evoking deisel-choked British poverty like no other punk document. *Janie Jones*, *White Riot*, (heaviest metal) *What's My Name* and bizarre, extended reggae stroll *Police & Thieves* . . . all combined like gasoline on a gambling debtor, signalling the start of a class riot among punks, ironically placing The Clash firmly atop an aristocracy, a position which would never fall, until the band itself abdicated, leaving punk for **London Calling**, becoming part of a larger rock aristocracy in the process.

Rating 10

## The Clash - Give 'Em Enough Rope (Epic '78)

In what many saw as a strange match-up, The Clash teamed with Blue Öyster Cult, Dictators and Shakin' Street sven gali Sandy Pearlman for this brilliant, thrilling record of lasting importance. Sandy's expressed purpose was to make The Clash pallatable to American ears. In this respect he failed miserably Thank God, **Give 'Em Enough Rope** attacking with just as many buckets-ful of British black and blue blood as the tantamount debut, albeit with increased doses of metal moves, mature songwriting and general sonic layering. At the time, this record was somewhat derided for this how-dare-they American intrusion, but looking back, it's safe to say **Give 'Em Enough Rope** need take no truck from **London Calling**, the present much thornier, combat-ready slab studded with heroism like *English Civil War*, *Tommy Gun* (hey, our band played this!), honky-tonk swingtimer *Julie's In The Drug Squad* (keyboards courtesy of Allen Lanier), and *Stay Free*, a smart reggae about a friend's experience with jail. The second, last and mostest record from The Clash as angry, venomous guitar band; a masterpiece necessary to any

discerning record collection. Note: after this, the band would branch way out from their snarly, gnarly roots, and the world is better for it. Comments and grading of the the remainder of the catalogue is as follows. **London Calling** ('79): globally-recognized amazing record: **10**. **Black Market Clash** ('80): nine track EP, side one culling many of the band's inspiring b-sides, side two being filler-quality reggae: **8**. **Sandinista!** ('80): bewildering, political three-record work of Dylan-level genius, but six to eight songs too long: **10**. **Combat Rock** ('82): jabbering, confused, jaded record featuring smash hits *Should I Stay Or Should I Go?* and *Rock The Casbah*: **8**. **Cut The Crap** ('85): crap, like the Joe Strummer solo record, which this practically is: **5**. **Clash On Broadway** ('91): an incredible, three disc box set, wading deeply into unreleased tracks; excellent booklet: **10**.

Rating 10

## Clawfinger - Deaf Dumb Blind (Attic/Metal Blade '93)

Hyped and well worth it Swedish rap metalists Clawfinger had moved 400,000 copies of this catchy debut cruncher in Europe before seeing release over here over a year later. The record features strong rhythmic tracks with choruses that stick (and swear a lot), songs such as *The Truth*, *Rosegrove* (about the band's nursing home work experience) and *Wonderful World* causing that booty to move despite the large stacks of Rage Against The Machine- or Faith No More-like power riffing. Highly addictive, Mark Arm-lookalike Zak Tell and his assembled hopsters set to claw a multitude of heads in the future.

Rating 8

## Cloven Hoof - Cloven Hoof (Neat '84)

This early scary whatever-the-hell recalls Angelwitch and Iron Maiden, but the goods scamper and flip-flop around too much amongst the record's epic-based six tracks; lacking the power, conciseness and ideas to fry leather. Some sinister enough Euroriffing here coupled with substantially wicked and convincing black metal/viking image make for a minor tragedy that the metal wasn't all that toothsome and muscle-bound on a sustained basis. Produced with complementary edginess by Keith Nichol.

Rating 6

## Cloven Hoof - Dominator (Heavy Metal '88)

I dunno . . . who springs to mind . . . bad Maiden from the mid-'80s, Witchfynde, Satan . . . anything British, glued-shut, and muffled. Cloven Hoof have definitely dressed up there act this time 'round but the blocky delivery is rife with Manowar melodrama left flat with toneless production and funny vocals (courtesy of Russ North who arrives from Tony Bourge's Tredegar along with guitarist Andy Wood). Really about five years behind the times, preferring to do battle with various American leather losers prowling the delete bins in search of food after their five minutes of fame with Shrapnel and Metal Blade during the mid-'80s.

Rating 3

## Clutch - Transnational Speedway League (Atlantic '93)

Or more accurately, **Transnational Speedway League: anthems, anecdotes and undeniable truths**, one of the longer record titles going, more accurately called "Transnational whatever." But no matter one's name for it, Clutch's debut is a bruising, babbling, drunken grungefest of twisted tales, sorta the cantankerousness of Killdozer or Helmet meets the wily, wizzened story-telling skill of Blue Öyster Cult. It's a grooving low-down trip to be sure, a kind of bush-roaming lope, as Neil Fallon alternately shouts out and low-monotones some of the coolest Dr. Suess stories gone very wrong I've ever heard, sometimes

grunging like the Melvins or Tad, other times hip-hopping it like Biohazard, all glazed over with the cooling influence of a type of depraved blues. Cool titles: *A Shogun Named Marcus* and *Walking In The Great Shining Path Of Monster Trucks*, but *Ounce Epilogue* really takes the bottle, sort of mangling the Scorpions *Sails Of Charon* riff into a fortune cookie-shaped aggro-metal meal for the apocalypse.
Rating                                                                    8

**Clutch - Clutch**  (Atlantic '95)
Blowing the budget on record titling last time around, Clutch simply delivers **Clutch**, a sophomore effort that bravely digs deeper under the porch into an alien-abducted black and blue blues. Seriously (which is impossible under Clutch's mad scientific spell), *Big News I* (as opposed to the totally unrelated second track called *Big News II*) is the lustiest pirate song ever, weaving a marauding psychedelic bass riff around totally jolliest roger lyrics that sizzle and pop with storytelling vision. Then there's *Escape From The Prison Planet*, a '90s sighting of the Men In Black (see The Stranglers' **The Meninblack** or BÖC's *E.T.I.*, then don't tell anybody what you saw), also wrapped around a wayward bass headtrip, bolstered by crashing chords and admonishing, warning, heeding barks from the wrestling voice of Fallon (hey, come to think of it, there is something Mike Watt about all this). This is such a cool band really, maybe a bit crashed and luded at times, but amazing lyricists, combining the weirdness of conspiracy theories and plain old desert-baked eccentricity under a stumbling proto-metal grafting Zep - **I** to Sabbath - **I**. Remember: three men in black said "don't report this.".
Rating                                                                    9

**Coal Chamber - Coal Chamber**  (Roadrunner '97)
With **Coal Chamber** and **Karma To Burn** released about the same time (March '97), Roadrunner might find their hands full feeding the deserved buzz building for these two self-titled releases. Coal Chamber is definitely the Korn-ish hen of the two, this band of freaks (three guys, one gal), taking the aggressive tack, bolstering the sound with bigger, cholesterol-laden riffs, leaning hardcore at times, but almost always working on vital, viable new definitions for metal. It's as if Korn has been the saviour of hardcore, pulling bands away from tired ol' punk, back to grooves derived from hip-hop, but still built of metal. Bands like this may become too numerous, but for now, this is a fresh slam worthy of your miserable few rubles.
Rating                                                                    8

**Cobra - First Strike**  (Epic '83)
Not to be confused with King Kobra, although I wish both of them would slither into oncoming traffic, these guys were a nauseatingly safe and conservative lite hard rock unit that, judging from their niceboy faces on the cover, never bought into the r'n'r ethic, and went back to their day jobs.
Rating                                                                    3

**Cobra - Warriors Of The Dead**  (Ebony '85)
I've heard so much of this nervy brand of trad metal lately, I'm running out of superlatives and indeed actual enthusiasm for its cause. A great Ebony mix here, and adequate enough performances, plundering Accept, Scorpions and Priest as is usual with Teutonic destructives. Uniformly searing, but still samey on an interband basis which ain't exactly fair. Obviously not the Cobra of **First Strike**.
Rating                                                                    7

**Cold Sweat - Break Out**  (MCA '90)
Featuring the fluid and thoroughly metallic axework of Marc Ferrari and on equal footing, the borderline-intrusive double bass percussive wall of Anthony White and the perfect high-reg wail of Rory Cathey, Cold Sweat are yet another flawless corporate entry, smoked high with pyrotechnics, yet ever mindful of song concept and entertainment value. I filed it, then played it, filed it, then played it, and finally, it stuck; and even though it's just another fully crammed disc of synchro-meshed California metallic melodrama—modern stabs at early Halen as it were—it's so well constructed and professionally delivered, it possesses the class to make it a winner, these guys being serious pros, although maybe not seriously into challenging boundaries. Not too crazy about the echoey mix, but minor fault on a disc reminiscent of the vitality and hopefulness of early Ratt, Black n' Blue, Racer X or mid-years Dokken, although much noisier than all four fighting for the same hair appointment. Features yet another in a long line of enjoyable covers of *I Just Want To Make Love To You*.
Rating                                                                    6

**Cold Water Flat - Cold Water Flat**  (MCA '95)
Not all that riled by this one, a sort of lazy, faintly grungey alternative that is roughly half heavy, half unstructured, bass guitar-loping soft stuff. Three or four really nice songs here, and a general sound that gets heroic and full of meaning quite often. But gulped down in totality, too informal and slouched for my heavy metal ears.
Rating                                                                    6

**Collision - Collision**  (Sony '92)
The top flight metal just continues to flow like silvery wine in '92, with this chunky, slow-like-molasses blast of hard rock, in possession of a sound honed over thirteen years that cements our greatest expectations of Bonham, Zeppelin, and on a stranger level Liquid Jesus, The Big F, Rick Derringer and Pat Travers, although don't place too much emphasis on comparisons with that beatific smorg. Really cookin' and massively on target, this true blue traditional American power trio brew an excellent collection of power groove rockers. Searing, expressive vocals, one bludgeon of a mix (meticulously crafted in the band's own studio), and a J. Bonham-inspired rhythmic grandeur combine to make **Collision** one of the most enjoyable records in a long time; enjoyable in the sense of upbeat, free and powerful, even grungy but firmly exhilarating. On first listen, one gets distracted by the fact that most of this record moves at the same slow mid-pace boom, but personal magnetism wins the day as funky metal classics like *True Love* and *Maximum Respect* bump and grind like no other band in recent memory. Above all, really classy on all engaging facets and one of the most solid records of the year.
Rating                                                                    10

**Collision - Coarse**  (Sony '95)
Collision's '92 calling card was one of the most amazing and under-rated debuts of all history. Many in the trade saw this thrilling power trio as a mountain of timeless integrity, harbouring a sound that was "stadium" (Stasium?) rock with heft and maturity, something magical afoot, akin to those blistering premieres from Montrose and Van Halen. So this sophomore spread was highly anticipated in these parts, bound to disappoint as are such irrationally hoped-for follow-ups (see The Big F). But let me dispense with these faint elements of letdown quickly and let's party! **Coarse** has too many songs the same speed (dead-middle mid-pace) and is only 39 minutes short. Okay, now for the hysterical praise. All tracks are positively arresting, shimmering with hook-drenched deep grooves, lots of phat spaces (see *The Wheel* and *Get Up Or Get Hurt*), all swelled into tidal waves of heavy rock justice by the power-packed mixing acumen of Ed Stasium. **Coarse**

is simply a love-in of nasty, heart-wrenching vocals, of squealing guitars, of infectious song, of mountain-proud traditional metal. **Coarse** is the pinacle of power trio rock, no grungesters need apply. **Coarse** is the '70s meets the '90s like nothing else out there. Buy **Coarse!**
Rating                                                                 9

## Comecon - Megatrends In Brutality   (Century Media '92)

Temporarily astray from Entombed, L-G Petrov whacks upside the head with Comecon, for a uni-dimensional but zesty deathfest that reeks of B-grade Entombed, fast, loose and dirty; irreverence for planning, Molotov cocktail to the brain. Petrov's vox are way down the gullet, lowering himself to the boring, sawed-off grind levels of this atonal brick of a band. Better than average lyrics, and a zany, nutty delivery; sort of an underground classic with American undertones.
Rating                                                                 7

## Comecon - Converging Conspiracies   (Century Media '93)

Petrov out, Martin Van Drunen in, as Comecon shifts away from death metal to a sort of crushing hardcore punk, maybe a little old Napalm in there as riffs get both stoopider and more brilliant, as on Aerie. But Van Drunen's vocals wreck it all, his voice a sort of higher nonsense rant, like some sort of skatecore guy from California, really undermining some of the exotic arrangements put forth here. A shame, really.
Rating                                                                 5

## Company Of Wolves - Company Of Wolves
(PolyGram '90)

Company Of Wolves mix up a big, bold brew of roots metal in various well-played and well-delivered directions, led by the tasty licks of axe dude Steve Conte, whose bluesy and busy professionalism is demonstrative of this band as a whole. Hugely stadia, and not overly heavy, **Company Of Wolves** ride the less sleazy, more melodic and communicative side of roots metal, dished up with skill and adequate avoidance of cliché chord shifts, the elegant voice of one Kyf Brewer also helping the cause. Sub-standard lead tune Call Of The Wild (which sounds too close to Steve Earle's Copperhead Road) conveniently blows the band's wad of bad habits associated with the genre, but after that, it becomes easy to buy into the Company's slice of Americana. Nothing all that globe-shattering, but if you're into this down-home variety of bluesy, poppy AOR, **Company Of Wolves** is pretty well as sharply-tailored as any.
Rating                                                                 6

## Coney Hatch - Coney Hatch   (Anthem '82)

Canadian boys Coney Hatch (named for an insane asylum in England) skilfully balance exuberance with tasteful economy on this their robust debut. Produced by Kim Mitchell for Anthem (not very well, I might add), with thanks to Kim, Pye Dubois, and Mike Tilka, this is very much an in-house brew, also featuring Kim on guitar, offering perhaps his most amusingly daft, careening axe solo ever on album closer Monkey Bars. Elsewhere Coney Hatch crafts a sound that revives up-front AC/DC simplicity, the fat unadorned chords, the mindfulness of the groove potential inherent in the slow to mid-pace spectrum, sprinkled with updated hard rock trickery and strong melodic choruses. What results is a solid, memorable first effort brimming with fun and summer mischief, a heavy-handed melodic rocker delivered with self-deprecating wit and wide-eyed wonder. Unfortunately, Hatch - I represented what was to be the biggest buzz of the three Hatch outtings, spawning minor hit Hey Operator, and securing back-up slot on the Priest - **Screaming For Vengeance** tour (which Flash and I caught, then ran

the border after, in Spokane), a tour which Andy Curran considers one of the fondest of personal Hatch memories.
Rating                                                                 8

## Coney Hatch - Outa Hand   (Anthem '83)

In search of some badly needed cash, Coney Hatch over-corrects, becoming too pompous and corporate, injecting too much slow metal and too much pop, giving us yet another solid album, but one with comparatively more holes than either I or III. Consequently, the bad stuff sounds like stadium rock at 16 RPM or conversely, mellow Dokken, while the good stuff recalls the youthful drive of the debut and the funkiness of **Friction**. Raves include textured lead track Don't Say Make Me, one of Hatch's most determined marches, which features a tasty guitar dialogue between Dixon and Shelski (probably), while the Aerosmith-tinged Some Like It Hot finds the band stretching the confines of heavy AOR. Still an entertaining listen, sorta like getting another Santers album, yet still, the least focused of the Hatch trinity.
Rating                                                                 7

## Coney Hatch - Friction   (Anthem '85)

What was to be the last grab at the brass ring by these Canadian self-proclaimed poverty cases is a further exploration of the out-front, monolithic, melodic hard rock sound which first dominated on **Outa Hand,** although there, in a form comatose by comparison. Pounded by a thunderous big league recording via Max Norman, Hatch strides confidently through the proceedings here, oscillating between toothsome car stereo anthems and syrupy commercial fare which is surprisingly hooky despite its blatantly naive Canadianness. Everything's big and fat on this, and as usual the band is most convincingly in-charge when getting down to mischief, cruising through tunes like This Ain't Love, Wrong Side Of Town, and Stateline. So really, **Friction** rarely fails to entertain, as the energy level, simplicity, and sheer weight of the sound never let up, even when whining about some woman that took off. The band claims to have had close to double the toons to cherry-pick from this time around and it actually shows. A rowdy yet smoothly accomplished last effort by one of the greats of Canadian rock. Trivia note: Dream Theater's Jamie Labrie joined the band briefly for some touring in '86.
Rating                                                                 8

## Contraband - Contraband   (Impact '91)

One of those bizarre wrinkles in reality converge to form this mid-leagues supergroup, consisting of Michael Schenker, L.A. Guns' Tracii Guns, Ratt's Bobby Blotzer, Share Pedersen, and Richard Black, who is the band's vocalist as well as having the biggest hand in the songwriting credits. But there's lots of covers, all quite bracing, and forming the highlights of this fairly vanilla corporate hard rock exercise in Who Made Who. Top raves: All The Way From Memphis, Good Rockin' Tonight and especially Bowie's brisk Hang On To Yourself. Top song title goes to this little gem though: Loud Guitars, Fast Cars & Wild, Wild Livin'. Must have thrilled the Japanese, but stateside, we thought it was merely a weird, desperate hybrid of whatever crawled around L.A. that day. A nice platter full of Schenker solos for those who follow this sort of thing. Very AOR, very commercial, very phoned-in.
Rating                                                                 6

## Convict - Go Ahead . . . Make My Day   (Cobra '85)

Despite vocal credits going to one Terry "The Con" Browning, **Go Ahead . . . Make My Day** features, and is thus distinguished by, Piledriver's Pile Driver aka Gord Kirchin at the helm, who after being ripped-off as part of the contrived 'driver concept, was most

recently spotted in control of his own destiny with incorrigible outfit Dogs With Jobs. In any event, Convict is a—if you can believe—more hokey and low budget version of labelmates Piledriver. Sinister, with teeth, and stripped to the basics, the band fistfights their way through these low quality reverences to the metal gods including two hilarious attempts at melodic hard rock, *Don't Turn Away* and *When Your Dreams Are Over*, which no matter how hard our resident garbagemen try to stop the flow, still manage to drip copious amounts of blood spilled in bitter acrimony.
Rating      **5**

## Convulse - Reflections    (Relapse '94)
Wielding a gutted grind that corrodes all sorts of long-thought-lost '80s postures, Convulse are an eminently enjoyable hybrid of death and almost biker-style metal. I mean, check out that Tank riff patrolling *The Green Is Grey* or the very early, very 'umble Maidenisms of *The Rite Of Sunshine*. Strange bunch these Finns, almost Entombed in the vortex of grindcore against their will, but so comfortable in a number of pockets, all elevated by old metal traces of anthemics. Plus those crew cuts betray the band's loopy confusion.
Rating      **8**

## Alice Cooper - Pretties For You    (Straight '69)
On **Pretties For You**, five Detroit weirdoids from the sixties get together and exhume the most nightmarish 'n' stoned elements of the Beatles, placing them liquidly in the same lime-green bean-bag chair as pre-progressive Floyd, MC5 and Ted's Amboy Dukes, the latter two like Alice, also calling Detroit home. Titles like *Sing Low, Sweet Cheerio*, *10 Minutes Before The Worm*, *Apple Bush*, *No Longer Umpire*, and *Earwig To Eternity* betray the kaleidoscope fact that this is really the Munsters on acid. One of the few hilarious psychedelic albums. Witchfinder General's warning: contains no serious power chords.
Rating      **5**

## Alice Cooper - Easy Action    (Straight '70)
The cool cover on this mythic and unpalatable feast reminds me of Quo's **Piledriver**. Toons-wise, it's nowhere near inventing metal, stuck quivering in the sixties like a slab of meat without purpose, the band soon to outgrow their original premise as (freak) flagship signing on Frank Zappa's hobby label.
Rating      **4**

## Alice Cooper - Love It To Death    (Warner Bros. '71)
Alice begins (that's *begins*) to shake the strains of the psychedelic '60s on this one, thus entering his short-lived golden years. Alice's recordings were never that heavy, yet his assault on the minds of America's youth was merciless and total. The band looked heavy, lived heavy, and were certainly heavy live. And to boot, they did come up with some early metal classics. Deeming this record metal would be stretching it, however classic would not. *I'm Eighteen* was a teen anthem later metallically treated by Anthrax and *Is It My Body* is one of Vincent's most enduring sleaze hits. To be fair, this was '71, and not everyone can be first, so not surprisingly **Love It To Death** is pretty dated, keyboardy, dark and, yes, still psychedelic, yet miles ahead of the whacked out **Pretties For You**. Other overwrought early rockers include the low-slung *Ballad Of Dwight Fry* and the almost metallic *Hallowed Be My Name*. Cool 'n' ditzy album closer *Sun Arise* gives us a glimpse that from here-on in, it's all going to be pretty tongue-in-cheek.
Rating      **6**

## Alice Cooper - Killer    (Warner Bros. '71)
One of the more frightening and decadent "youth gone wild" front and back covers at the time, **Killer** invents

shock rock with the shakes, predating Kiss on vinyl by two years, lashing out with long hair, flashy clothes, make-up, and boa constrictors; basically hippies gone very, very wrong (Note: it went REALLY wrong one show in Toronto, when someone threw a chicken on stage, which Alice promptly threw back, thinking it could fly. The crowd tore it to pieces, next day's headlines blaring that Alice was sacrificing chickens on stage). The actual music was an undefined afterthought, and although rocking appreciably for the time, the sum total was more a '60s/'70s fuzz-wash hybrid, clanking and clamouring on a metro tour of hard-edged guitar rock styles, while fortunately for the dazed five, scoring a few hits of the revolution such as the Mott-ish *Under My Wheels* and the Hoople-ish *Be My Lover*. **Killer** cruises on two speeds: tight-fisted hard rock anthems vs. ever-lasting progressive symphonies of the noisy mind. The bright former is vintage ego-driven rock'n'roll, the droll latter bores. Wedged in between like a cyst is a poisonous little number, *Desperado*, which is the band's most seriously hopeless three and a half excruciating minutes ever, slithering along tucked below one of Alice's rare low register vocals. **Killer** really trots out the theatrical side of Coop's assembled trolls, which ironically was the first stuff to get File 13 live, a smooth career move, none of it being any better than pre-**In Rock** Deep Purple. God damn though, this was '71, making **Killer** state of the craft temporally, if not state-of-the-art, brutally metallic and astonishingly innovative on the psychological spectrum, if not axe-wise. Alice blew our brains all over the walls, and for that he deserves the fondest of nostalgic tributes.
Rating      **7**

## Alice Cooper - School's Out    (Warner Bros. '72)
**School's Out** is the first of the four Coop efforts widely known as historically relevant, yet rarely played aside from the hits; another one of those records incorrectly considered heavy metal, being more of a hard-edged, horror movie-ish, psychedelic stew, occasionally jazzy in a conceptually progressive manner. Some great unsung camp classics like *Gutter Cat vs. The Jets* and *Public Animal #9* make this a brighter though no less chaotic record than previous head trips. Not really all that cool or listenable, ya still gotta appreciate it because it sounds so dang decadent, twisted, indulgent, and "anything goes" '70s. Faves include the legendary groundbreaking, locker-clearing title track and mebbee *My Stars*, but on the whole, I can't say I ever play this much.
Rating      **6**

## Alice Cooper - Billion Dollar Babies    (Warner Bros. '73)
Packaging to kill for! Embossed snakeskin front cover, cardboard money clip (more embossing) hugging a big fat billion dollar bill, punch-out perforated wallet snaps, and some freaky photo collages featuring lots of long hair, white clothes, white rabbits, a little A.C. baby, and heaping stacks of cash. Now this was pentagon-level theatrics at its hawks and dovish, in direct contrast to the low-level musical theatrics, the quasi-histrionics, the gutter-level Queen, Bowie and Mott posturing, which fortunately limited itself to the contextual confines of conventional song structures. As a result, the songs breathe rather than smother, stepping out, dressed to the nines, basically raising shit from opening enchilada *Hello! Hurray!* (a moody, atmospheric piece recalling *Desperado*, dredging up the introspective second thoughts nagging those in the camera's eye), through the brilliant chunkfest title track, *Unfinished Suite* (a toon about going to the dentist), and the acoustic breakthroughs of *Generation Landslide*, before self-destructing into a trio of Hallowe'enies to end out the bittersweet affair. In between, the hits kept washing ashore, with the classic *Elected*, and the fairly lame self-parody *No More Mr. Nice Guy*. Essentially, **Billion**

**Dollar Babies** is Alice's best album, as it cuts to the chase better than any previous amorphous blobs, riding the pride, tongue firmly in cheek, making the bucks, playing to the cameras, and letting us in on the whole demented carnival rather than abusing our attentiveness and intelligence. A bright and screwy summer rocker with nostalgic mileage and palatable melodies to boot. Alice knows it's prime time and wants to shake as many hands, kiss as many babies, and grease as many palms as he can. My kind of politician.
Rating **9**

## Alice Cooper - Muscle Of Love (Warner Bros. '73)
Featuring the original **In Through The Out Door** packaging concept in actual cardboard, **Muscle Of Love** offers magical, overblown glam Bowie-isms that capture the hot and sticky summer-in-the-city decadence of vintage A.C. *Teenage Lament '74* blows away *All The Young Dudes*, *Big Apple Dreamin' (Hippo)* is brightly upbeat, and the overdrivin' title track offers another state of the nation take on early metal. Although remaining somewhat grounded due to Alice's usual disjointed experimentalism (I swear the guy just *never* knew what he was doing), **Muscle Of Love** wafts some of the danger and freeflow of early Purple and Aerosmith outings, making it yet another authentic chapter in the age of authenticity.
Rating **7**

## Alice Cooper - Alice Cooper's Greatest Hits
(Warner Bros '74)
This is one of few greatest hits albums I actually like, given its pacing as an uptempo career retrospective, highlighting a string of great singles, teen anthems and classic heavy rockers. Plus it was the first Cooper album that got heavy airplay amongst our circle of friends, the man's early studio stuff just sounding too experimental and creepy to us as young, T.V.-weaned pups.
Rating **6**

## Alice Cooper - Welcome To My Nightmare
(Atlantic '75)
**Welcome To My Nightmare** was less a bonafide attempt at studio eminence than a cheezy soundtrack to AC's feature movie—or more accurately, extended Munsters rock video—of the same name. As a result, it's a hard idea to take seriously, being Alice's first disc that is more a self-parody than the truly demented brilliance of past ghoul tools. Nonetheless, among contrived soundtrack-quality fodder like *Some Folks* and the disco era-betraying title track, there's the odd, almost magically Kiss-like party rocker, such as the kickin' *Cold Ethyl*, the hooky *Escape* and the goth-metallic *Devil's Food*, all minor classics of early metal, I'm sure in no small part responsible for Slash naming this as one of his favourite records while growing up. Still **Welcome To My Nightmare** reads too much like a bad movie script, a project, a business deal, rather than a rock'n'roll album. Harmless, although parentally-speaking, it's been derided as a mind-deforming chunk of wax. Guest star: Vincent Price.
Rating **5**

## Alice Cooper - Goes To Hell (Warner Bros. '76)
Like **Lace And Whiskey**, this Bob Ezrin-over-produced loose concept record is stylistically schizo to the max, addressing jazz, disco, progressive balladry and pomp à la Elton John; almost exclusively generic and unheavy, main exception being axe stomper *Go To Hell* and warm, upbeat hard rocker *Guilty*. Again, the abandonment of power chords deals rough justice to an icon of the '70s.
Rating **4**

## Alice Cooper - The Alice Cooper Show (Warner Bros. '77)
Not that I'd ever listen to it, but **The Alice Cooper Show** is a good career retrospective despite its muddy lacklustre feel. The only show in town that can match Kiss for sheer theatrics. Most of the major freakshows are here, including a smattering of less heralded rockers such as *Is It My Body* and *Go To Hell*. Smart move, given the man's faltering creativity.
Rating **4**

## Alice Cooper - Lace And Whiskey (Warner Bros. '77)
Recorded during Alice's fairly anonymous alcoholic daze, **Lace And Whiskey** is one of those annoying exercises in rock variety that ends up not saying much about anything. Only the hard-edged *Road Rats* and the gnarly *It's Hot Tonight* rise above the fray as Alice spins his wheels in search of the muse. Helpful cooking hint from the author: one could assemble an almost intelligently rockin' A.C. various tape out of these lost records. Long car trip stuff. Drying out and golf ensue, as Vincent works to extricate himself from Alice.
Rating **4**

## Alice Cooper - From The Inside (Warner Bros. '78)
A.C. has bestowed upon his whithered hide yet another brain-dead establishment producer in David Foster, who sadly has no hope in Hell of understanding the forces necessary for good rock'n'roll. Like its predecessor, **From The Inside** is more elevator music, funky, poppy, overblown, and schizoid, an abortion of pompous old fart noises, loosely based around Alice's experiences as an institutionalized rock star, co-written by Elton John's useless lyric boy Bernie Taupin. Obligatory lone waking moment: *Serious*. Sports a pretty cool die-cut album cover, one of those minor oddities lost forever in the CD age.
Rating **2**

## Alice Cooper - Flush The Fashion (Warner Bros. '80)
Beauty album cover, eh? This Roy Thomas Baker-produced slab marked a partial return to traces of tunefulness and the possibility of selling records, as Alice and the Lost Coopers forge some kind of Cars-ish metal alloy. Rumours of Vincent's return from the dead are substantiated as **Flush The Fashion** comes off as a confident, stylistically-adept brew of party metal, sporting innovative arrangements and hooks galore. Among the unsung gems we get the metallic *Grim Facts*, the vintage A.C. of *Model Citizen*, a (believe it or not) soulful ballad called *Pain*, the experimental and dancy *Leather Boots*, and the swaggering, Stonesy *Dance Yourself To Death*. Quite a surprising display of mobility given recent accomplishments, **Flush The Fashion** is a likeable if not earth-shattering piece of pleasureable ear candy.
Rating **7**

## Alice Cooper - Special Forces (Warner Bros. '81)
Oscillating between synth horror pop and pretty lax guitar rock, **Special Forces** is at times edgy, but for the most part goes nowhere. Even though some vitality, optimism, and actual reason to write and record quake somewhere deep in the grooves, Alice's usual stylistic wandering dissipates the energy, which is only moderate, and further masked by the lack of strong songs. Resident rocker: *Who Do We Think We Are*. Note how Alice skips the NWOBHM bandwagon-jump of so many '70s rockers (good Alice), waiting it out to ride the cheese metal thing from L.A. (bad Alice).
Rating **4**

## Alice Cooper - Da Da (Warner Bros. '83)
What a crock. Alice, apparently in his fleeting "art punk" persona comes up with a pile of dreadful, key-

board pop garbage that never would have made it to market in a million years without Alice's good name to force it in our faces. Ol' Vincent is proving himself a lost opportunist on a scale more tragic than the worst failings of Bowie, Iggy, or Neil Young (the latter who nevertheless scored a raucous return with **Ragged Glory** and is now heralded as the grandfather of grunge). Alice: more the grandmother of garish.
Rating 0

## Alice Cooper - Constrictor (MCA '86)

Finally the "give 'em what they want" record, a plain and plaintively metal pig that patronizes fans, playing to the the twelve year old in the streets and the twelve year old in all of us oldsters. Kip Winger, Kane Roberts, and producer Beau Hill are along for the cash-hopeful ride, a boardroom designed to muscle the metal chartbound. But of course, there's no real creativity here, coming off as a delete bin-delegated slickslab of warmed over Gwar. A dull, pandering, overly forced attempt at pleasing young fans.
Rating 4

## Alice Cooper - Raise Your Fist And Yell (MCA '87)

Even though this under-rated album marks a shameless corporate phase for the man, it completely flies in the face of the gutless vapors portrayed on next record **Trash**, or the stiff robot metal of its predecessor **Constrictor**, rocking most heavily, and in fact heavier (sonically, if not emotionally) than any Cooper vision to date. **Raise Your Fist And Yell** has nothing to do with Alice the demented from hazy dayz gone by, it's just a surprisingly solid and anonymous metal disc fronted by a legendary nametag. **Fist** fails to completely convince due to the miserable album title, crass packaging, shlock horror lyrics, and too perfect recording (see **Constrictor**), but it does embrace metal without the melodic pandering of **Trash**, suggesting a direction that if fleshed-out and left to squirm in filth, could someday have been delivered with authenticity. However, **Trash** proved once again that there exists panic and impatience at the A.C. purse-strings. Same sort of dil parody as Iggy's **Instinct**, really.
Rating 6

## Alice Cooper - Trash (Epic '89)

One of the biggest budget Coopers in years, the Desmond Child over-produced **Trash** has guest appearances by dudes from Aerosmith, Bon Jovi, Winger, and countless studio wizards, making it a star-studded waste of space, an insipid, lifeless, paint-by-numbers exercise in toothlessness. The metal is heartlessly candy-coated; approximating lazy Kiss, and the power ballads are predictably interchangeable with those of every other metal business deal (i.e. Heart and Cheap Trick). On **Trash**, Alice is just a withered soul-less whore selling his name to those who can't appreciate his past.
Rating 2

## Alice Cooper - Hey Stoopid (Epic '91)

Metal's wizened espouser of wastecase wisdom is back with some considerable marketing tailwind, a fresh gaggle of featured guest stars, and an ambitious one hour expulsion of effort in homage of the CD age. No matter how good **Hey Stoopid** might be, any proposal past the man's mid-'70s golden era inevitably rings hollow in its function as vehicle for corporate interests. Personality runs deeper than the mike. It would be nice to see Alice establish a band, hang out with it, introduce us to it, and write with it. **Hey Stoopid** on the other hand, is a predictable collaborative effort of a mess of pros (probably golf buds), loosely assembled under this week's hot logo. All is perfect, of course too perfect; yet as dollars-motivated rock goes, it's fairly skidsy, dishing out some well-fleshed rockers such as *Snake-*

bite, *Feed My Frankenstein*, and *Hurricane Years*. Yet heed my warning: four useless paint-by-numbers HM power ballads sap the potential sincerity from the overall collection. The partial saving grace of **Hey Stoopid**, however, is first and foremost the groovability, the backbeat raucous throughout, adding up to a good half record of car deck destructives. Many a critic's first comment on this album was that it was "more serious" and right they are. It may be asinine, big-bucks rock, but the cast of players has dealt a lot of inflection and body English into the mix, a bevy of activity for radio rock, and that's a good thing. In any event, a great excuse to hit the road with what promised to be a crass and overtly American expression of bombast.
Rating 6

## Alice Cooper - The Last Temptation (Sony '94)

The pertinent facts: a) This has the same front cover as the new Indigo Girls record. b) The Replacements already opened their **Don't Tell A Soul** album with *Sideshow*, only it was called *Talent Show*. The comic book tie-in sucks, because the story is so lame. Chuck all that though, and yes, *Sideshow* is warm and drinkable, and *Lost In America* is a pretty funny chunk of caveman logic. But still, it's a big session-type record with no cohesion, lotsa cheezy riffs from the dead hard rock era (or if the riff is acceptable, the chorus reverses the trend), and an Andy Wallace mix which is limp and corporate, working well towards Andy losing his reputation as vital power purveyor. A big, steaming plate of Who Cares? is in order here, cos unless Alice is truly ready to get psycho and unsafe, he's always going to sound like an artifact from commercial rock quarries, even if for whatever dumb reason, Chris Cornell manages to become involved. Some sort of morality play about staying off drugs threads the tunes together, and you'd be wise to stick with the lyrics vs. the disappointing comic narrative, but wiser to just visit the record academically for the piffling short look-in it requires, then move on. For those who sincerely want to check it out, **The Last Temptation** is more thoughtful and rock'n'rollishly artistic than anything since the catchy **Flush The Fashion** project from 1980, but seriously, there's so much awesome toonage out there, for most of us, why bother?
Rating 6

## Alice Cooper - Live At The Whiskey, 1969 (Boogie/Straight '94)

Like a drum-bashing, psycho-prog Mothers of Invention record, **Live At The Whiskey** might be sum fun for the acid casualty, but avoid like the plague if you didn't like the first three Cooper slabs from his preshock rock days. Not a bad mix, but also under twenty minutes short, despite the presence of seven tummy ticklers.
Rating 1

## Coroner - R.I.P. (Noize '87)

Released late for extreme music, **R.I.P.** nevertheless turned heads with its rusty crank, helping to push stale thrash into realms of death, grind and even a reversal back into traditional metal. In retrospect, many call this and its follow-up the classics, pining for those hungry, blood-craved years, suspicious of any mumblings towards growth or accessibility. Count me a fan of growth.
Rating 4

## Coroner - Punishment For Decadence (Noize '88)

Even in their fledgling years, Coroner was sunburned by science, on **Punishment For Decadence** proving themselves a speed/death metal force that rarely can be accused of thrashing out. Sure things aren't quite bolted down as per Coroner in the '90s, but the old

stuff rages, densely shredding, piling on layer upon layer of sonic strata as Tommy T. Baron, Ron Royce and Marquis Mark (love that name) detonate the waves, all chops and shifting tempos, no mercy, ill tidings to all and to all an outrageous night. Of course it's entirely hyper, 100% fire-breathing OTT, and of course it's gotta be a cold day in hell for me to whip this one out, but from a distance this is still a record at which to marvel with disbelieving reverence, capturing the charred essence of why grindcore exists, even though it's not a grindcore record per sé. I guess you'd call it grindcare.
Rating                                                          6

## Coroner - No More Color   (Noise '89)
For sheer blinding riffery, few can match the violent air assault of Coroner, a band now poised precisely on the heated knife's edge between thrashcore (which bore more heavily on the band's past) and technical maniac metal. So massively kick-ass, OTT and any other word you can conjure for heart-exploding power metal, No More Color is packed solid with high-strung goth of purest Teutonic proportions, ripping along with an evilmetal abandon under challenging precision constructs and a dangerously thrashcore vocal display. Place Coroner on the grind side of Rage, and you've pretty well come to terms; both bands courting the same gasoline-faced muse for their wildly pure riffs. But I'd call Coroner the bigger pisstank noise combobulators by a long stretch, this record catching so many insane, chaotic grooves that just wanna fly the hell out into the nuclear night like bats and pigeons at an Ozzy show. No prisoners metal. Drink heavily before handling.
Rating                                                          8

## Coroner - Mental Vortex   (Noise '91)
A sci-borg reinforcement of the No More Color concept, Mental Vortex is more acupuncture than macheté, airtight and insidious with intricate, insanely metallic riffs, constructing resolute mazes of blackest goth. Again Rage comparisons are in order, as both bands continue to combine utmost heaviness with chops and academic intelligence, stinging the nerve centres like Voivod and a host of American progressive chariots never could, by being mindful of groove, melody (of the horribly maimed variety) and restraint. Coroner occupy a space where I wish more grindcore and thrash acts would visit, many of which I know could flourish with a little mental retrenchment. Dark, doomy, cold but classy, Coroner remain fringe death purveyors to the bitter end, encased in palace walls of thickest stone, well deserving of the connoisseur rivethead's attention. Closes out with a 7:14 cover of one of a handful of Beatles songs I can tolerate: I Want You (She's So Heavy), turning it into a groovy guitar symphony worthy of Kiss or Spinal Tap.
Rating                                                          9

## Coroner - Grin   (Noise '93)
Coroner's defiant, singularly embittered traditional metal tones are back for another go, Baron, Royce and Marky chundering forward into smoke-filled streets with one of their most becalmed straight-line collections yet. Grin moves almost stealth-like, pensive in tone, strangely evoking soundtrack-type textures, like metal man's metal for atmosphere's sake. Another very strong reference point would be the angled, sci-fi melodies of Voivod, Coroner slowly and deliberately stroking the same mindspheres The Outer Limits did, both records being the bands' most accessibly recorded and intelligently restrained, Grin especially finding a level-headed balance between bass and treble which is welcome for extreme music. A very lonely,

morose sound that is futuristic, yet telling of a future with no more colour.
Rating                                                          8

## Coroner - Coroner   (Noise '95)
Closing the dungeon door on this respected rock innovator, Coroner documents the trials and tribulations of the band through samplings of the band's fine catalogue, a smattering of live and remixed curios, and a half record's worth of new songs. The new tracks are an interesting extension of the mantra-like grooves established on Grin, the band honing their riffic and melodic quality on addictive numbers like The Favorite Game and Shifter. Again (and I'm not sure why), there's a cinematic quality to the band's new sounds, a sci-fi-ishness that pops images of lonely alien worlds into the banks of my mind. A must for fans, given these fine new tracks and a running time of 73 minutes.
Rating                                                          8

## Corporal Punishment - Stonefield Of A Lifetime   (Black Mark '97)
Here's some pounding, drowning, down-tuned doom metal mastery from Finland, if you dare, Corporal Punishment on this debut record (bloody 'ell!) finding the mercury-poisoned mean between Entombed and Edge Of Sanity. Sobbing ten-ton riffs define this stonefield of the band's lifetime, most songs moved sluggishly into the mid-groove zone in which they wallow mournfully, vocalist Ali hitting us with octaves that quake foundations. And when the pace picks up, man, do the bullets fly, tunes like Justified? and Wrong Side kicking the butts of the masters Entombed with unharnessed youth. One helluva debut churnfest fer sure, delivered with authority and bone-powdered heft.
Rating                                                          9

## Corrosion Of Conformity - Eye For An Eye   (Caroline '83)
Early COC walked a dangerous line between flat-out hardcore and Black Flag's disdain for structure, scattering left and right at will causing violent sonic hangovers, often approaching the white noise of early Hüsker Dü, that is, thrash beyond coherence. Thoroughly up front, in-your-face, highly toxic on the most unpredictable of pharmaceutical accoutrements, and riddled with a vast number of brief ideas which hint at the possibility that elegantly ripping material is in ready supply for future, more thoughtful plunder. Too chaotic at this point for a pleasing mosh.
Rating                                                          3

## Corrosion Of Conformity - Animosity   (Death '86)
COC are still more a hardcore rustbucket than metal, yet this album comes up with some downright vicious power riffing peppered with eccentric, crack-headed soloing as per Greg Ginn, making it one of the more brainy early crossover scourges whether it wants to be or not (it doesn't). As usual with this sub-genre, it's distressingly simple and definitely thrash, but the recording ain't bad and a good 1/3 of the result is caustic and deafening. Shit-kicking as ever philosophically, and still ragingly opaque and vocally vile.
Rating                                                          4

## Corrosion Of Conformity - Technocracy   (Death '87)
Full-blown conversion to a thrash metal mentality (a fate in sight since record one) dogs Technocracy despite its fully realized production values. Still riffed and torn 'neath random minor chord dovetailing and the unimpressive shouts of vocalist Simon Bob. Five cuts, thirteen minutes, stunned paralysis. Time for hardcore to clue in that proving how tough you are by showing how much trashy noise you can dish out and/or take just doesn't jibe as a viable gesture past age thirteen. CD reissue is a rip-off, three of the four extra

tracks being repeats, Mike singing, different production. Total: 28 minutes.

Rating 2

## Corrosion Of Conformity - Six Songs With Mike Singing: 1985 (Caroline '88)

More seminal hardcore, frothing forth in anonymous lockstep, **Six Songs** revives, you guessed it, six cuts, all written in '83, evidently sent through the combine in '85. But never us mind, all torn tales just blurring together due to predicted destructive hypervelocities. The very definition of hardcore, a term loaded with more negatives than positives.

Rating 3

## Corrosion Of Conformity - Blind (Relativity '91)

From the ashes of a band that for eons was blurry and unambitious comes the cranium-crushing statement that was festering at the backdrop all these years. Regrouped and re-armed for the uneasy '90s with the acquisition of S.O.V.'s Karl Agell, COC finally destroy the place with this dense, violent and ill-feeling assembly of subversion metal. **Blind** deconstructs the darker, more Sabbath-like signatures from bands like Death Angel, Pantera, Metallica and yes, Trouble (who get a "t-shirt" on the back cover), poisoning their brainwashed minds with an off-balance, alternative shred of wasted disdain for the process, looming explosive but closely tense with the most evil of sounds. Lyrically, it's apocalyptic politics throughout, although the opaque sonic wall of deliberation usually triumphs in battle with Agell's warnings of collapse to come. As the juggernaut creaks to a close, Corrosion Of Conformity have carved themselves a new band, wasting probably less than five of the fifty two minutes here, rarely thrashing and never bogging to Rollins' too-oft sleep-encrusted levels. And all just swells, refusing to disperse, stuck in thick mode with its over-size, hellacious mix. Most grievous experiences: *Damned For All Time*, *Painted Smiling Face*, *Mine Are The Eyes Of God*, and cyborg-ed lead video *Vote With A Bullet*. Modern, moving and negative.

Rating 9

## Corrosion Of Conformity - Deliverance (Sony '94)

After tonnage de crap and philosophical remakes galore, North Carolina's COC are back with an scrappy new state of intent, something much more garagey in its Sabbathness, eclectic in its variety and somehow more volatile and youthful. But that's not to say the record as a whole smokes, 'cos it doesn't, many tracks here ringing dulled and nowheresy (title track, although even that one wins ya over), including haunting acoustic respites, seemingly deftly placed to make the highs seem that much more heady. From the ricketty Vol 4 bash afforded *Heaven's Not Overflowing* to the totally intentional *Balls To The Wall* drum intro to *Albatross*, this one's a puzzler, COC maybe out to regain a drunken underground feel lost on the bombastic riff rock of **Blind**. The more aggressive numbers however wail heavily at the trough of the full blood-red moon, *My Grain* and *Senor Limpio* foremost and charismatically bad to the bone. Less grandiose and critically massive, more jammy and explosive, **Deliverance** comes crammed with personality, core honesty and bewilderment, if not as many truly Large tunes as **Blind**, basically **The Skull** versus **Trouble**, more early daze rough-hewn madness, less production and arrangement acumen. Grows elegantly on the circuits. Manpower note: guitarist Pepper Keenan adds lead vocals to his repertoire after the departure of Karl Agell, proving astonishingly versatile and power-drenched.

Rating 10

## Corrosion Of Conformity - Wiseblood (Sony '96)

One of the big metal records of '96, **Wiseblood** was somewhat delayed by rumoured label disatisfaction with what they were hearing, Sony supposedly sending the band back for another go. Whatever the case, the end product is another triumph, COC delivering something very similar to **Deliverance**, if a little dirtier, relentlessly cavemanned, and psychologically harrowing. Had to knock off a single point though, for the slight element of "schtick", COC sounding almost too cool and rarified, a sense of gloat rummaging through these raggamuffin songs. As usual, the band is heat-swollen in their garage mechanic imaginations of all things Sabbatherian and motor oil-stained. And there is a sort of lumbered uniformity to most of the songs, a really crusty banging of things weighting most numbers, really only *King Of The Rotten* letting fly with a hooked moshgroove. But once again, it's a chemically-altered metal genius that makes it work, things like cranking the levels on the guitar solos giving COC that retro-edge that lends them more credence and integrity than their new "buddies" Metallica. Big things expected, COC about to do battle with labelmates Korn for short-term domination in today's diminished metal market.

Rating 9

## Count Raven - Destruction Of The Void (Hellhound '93)

Count Raven dive into the gluey thick gruel of Sabbath's past in the tradition of Candlemass and Saint Vitus, which is to say, too damn slow and chops-less, wasting a hair-raisingly exact Ozzy-style vocal on tunes that chug like a slow drip to nowhere. Cool hippy image for a trio of Scandinavians, and lyrics that do well by old Sab or Trouble, all anguish and escape from the scourge that is humanity. But as I say, it's all quite the bore, doing nothing constructive with a pretty sincere retro vibe, which disappointed me terribly, 'cos these guys are for real. Those Ozzy "yeah"s are a scream.

Rating 6

## Count Raven - Messiah Of Confusion (Hellhound '96)

Much the same mind-melted Geezer Butlered madness here, Count Raven stuck in that pocket of senior citizen sounding lug-abouts with nothing on their minds but beer and sleep. Which of course adds a certain curmudgeoned charm to the proceedings, for the same reason Dave Wyndorf somehow has Rob Zombie beat. Better recording and more riffs, but Count Raven are still doom metal's silly uncles with no teeth. Note: at least two missing here: pre-**Destruction** record **Storm Warning**, and directly post-**Destruction** record **High On Infinity**.

Rating 7

## Course Of Empire - Initiation (BMG '94)

Major display of potential here as Dallas' Course Of Empire commotion forward with this their second, an intelligent pastiche of art grunges, mixing solid lyrics, versatile throats, and a punishing but dynamic delivery. Trouble is, I never liked those tom tom-based "tribal" tracks, of which there are more than a few, and grunge dirges put me to sleep, although here pleasant surprises fall out with record-rescuing frequency. But all in all: too much bashing, squawking dissonance, too little rock'n'roll. Second half just falls apart.

Rating 6

## David Coverdale - Whitesnake/ Northwinds (Connoisseur Collection '88)

Mired in Purple-stained legal hassles, Coverdale makes his first tentative, dreary steps towards a blues-based rock that would eventually lean heavy, clear and grand. Here however, on this re-pack of the man's first two records, '77's **Whitesnake** and '78's **Northwinds**,

Coverdale is no less archaic and cloudy than arch-throat Gillan in his confounding Ian Gillan Band years, both sampling a plethora of dark and obscure blues and funk rock shadings, oscillating between honky tonkin' and barely breathing, emptying the place, and occasionally filling it for a nicotine-stained all night jam. Both Coverdale records sound very early '70s if anything, an era where aggressive rock almost always included a full range of stylings from the blues palette. The increasingly focused **Northwinds** is somewhat the bolder statement, as arrangements begin to fill in towards a subtle, more technically concerned take on Bad Company. And no mistaking Coverdale's comfortable vocal affinity for the genre, both the voice and the backing musicianship growing more metallic as the years trundled on. For a continuation of the saga, see "Whitesnake".

Rating                                                                 5

## Coverdale Page - Coverdale Page   (Geffen '93)

Surprise, surprise. Pagey returns from fossilization, collaborating with one of Plant's personal thorns, a man who for no valid reason, takes the brunt of Percy's infantile ravings that everybody is copying him (hence David Coverversion). Well, Coverdale is the one who still has his range, here using it to full capacity, adding tricks to his cat-like pipes that could only have been cajoled forth by the presence of a much bigger legend at his side. Coverdale Page is hot property, indeed. But you'd never know it after the almost Firm-stupid lead single *Pride And Joy*, which uses up at least 50% of all the Zep nods on this whole, rather lengthy and intelligent record. Page has finally recovered his riff-making prowess, spicing his traditional palette with four or five really nice guitar sounds, for once shedding the shackles of the dulled, unexpressive recording techniques that have dogged The Firm, **Outrider**, and let's face it, most of the Zeppelin records (although their age is a semi-valid defense). What results is something like a sterling clear, creative Whitesnake record, with a distinctive axeman fueling the exchange of ideas. Classy would be the operative word here, ballad and rocker alike sounding fresh and aristocratic at the same time. Faves would be the smokin' *Absolution Blues* (vague *Wearing And Tearing* feel here), surprise OTT'er *Feeling Hot*, and lumbering duo *Shake My Tree* and *Waiting On You*. One could get sneering and cynical about such a project, but let the music teach you otherwise, convincing the listener that some synergy actually does exist, that there really is a band here worth watching grow (judging from Coverdale's past relationships, that may never happen). Facts are facts. Page has proven to be a fool on his post-Zep output. Something has sparked him here to a performance with scope and wisdom, speaking a versatile language that provides a challenging new vehicle for Coverdale's larger-than-sequins persona, which here takes on a new maturity. A pleasant and unexpected piece of work, but if catty comparisons be made, I still think Plant's **Fate Of Nations** operates on a higher intellectual and artistic plane. Update: one brief tour of Japan, and Coverdale Page became long-haired history. Dave moves on to reform Whitesnake; Jimmy holds discussions with Robert Plant.

Rating                                                                 8

## Craaft - Craaft   (CBS '86)

Without the considerable upgrade afforded by **Second Honeymoon**, these useless Krauts wouldn't have even been considered a suitable inclusion to this book. Femmy and powerless without a redeeming moment amongst the cold technical clatter. A miserable walk through the most lifeless and commercial cuts Victory or Fate might have oozed had they thought only of cash.

Rating                                                                 0

## Craaft - Second Honeymoon   (BMG '88)

Not only do these Teutonic wannabe teen idols sound dead identical to **Eat The Heat**'s destroyed version of Accept, they even look like them, with the added bonus of a ghoulish Udo-like dude at the mike. The plain talk on this one: heavier and more dangerous than the shamelessly ditzy debut, more like Fate, but still too key-laced and over-produced despite the usually eardrum-shattering Michael Wagener cowering in the producer's chair.

Rating                                                                 4

## Cradle Of Filth - The Principle Of Evil Made Flesh   (Cacophonous '94)

Taking a few months to really take hold, Cradle Of Filth's debut began systematically caving skulls with its deft improvements on Norwegian metal, much headway made simply on the strength of the band being British, but doing Norwegian black metal so convincingly, perhaps edging beyond in detecting and exploiting the irony and theatrics of the whole bog-blasted proposal. But bottom line is that this is a wicked vortex of extremely dark sounds, well-recorded, whipped frostily with symphonic, crypt-plundered keyboards, not to mention monster horror chiller theatre effects inserted with panache. **Vempire** might not advance matters much, but fact is, the band already had their white-noise black-thrash philosophy welded hellbound with this hair-raising debut.

Rating                                                                 7

## Cradle Of Filth - Vempire   (Cacophonous '96)

Folks round here are hailing this forty minute EP (follow-up to debut full-length **The Principle Of Evil Made Flesh**) as a blood-stained Grail of extreme metal, and the crafty touches applied conspire to take it to this realm, U.K.'s Cradle Of Filth engineering a funeral with banquet that is hard to ignore. As with most millennial symphonic death, **Vempire** works best as theatre, all the different male and female voicings like so many players in a cyclonic whirly-dance through crust, Purgatory, and ultimately the craggy, smoke-shrouded magma formations of Lucifer's razor-trimmed lawn. **Vempire** borrows most heavily from technical Swedish deathswill, adding the queer-cut combo of Norwegian keyboard plonk and small-rat ranting (AC might spring to mind on last track *The Rape And Ruin Of Angels*), while lacing the whole unusual, sinister six-part saga with a type of British lunacy, all forms of unseemly absurdity chucked in a blender, devil may care, Venom may like. A notch above, throne aspirations way below.

Rating                                                                 8

## Cradle Of Filth - Dusk And Her Embrace   (Futurist '97)

For their most lavish assault yet, the reigning trolls of black metal have enlisted the services of Thin Lizzy and Cathedral producer Kit Woolven as supreme knob twiddler. This becomes in fact, the band's biggest trump, Cradle Of Filth sticking to their miserablizing Norse metal (via Britain), while marrying their shocking sonic blast to meticulous production and musicianship. Packaging is gorgeous (especially the British version, which also adds a bonus track), combining elegant typesetting with a myriad of band and atmosphere photos guaranteed to invert the cross. Vocals still sound exactly like Beavis in one of his nervous fits, although pure singing and female guest vocals are often utilized. But the total effect is bewitching and cinematic, orchestral and Maiden-toned, progressive and jet black. A masterpiece, lovingly and pain-stakingly assembled, proving that black metal infused with effort and creativity can result in respect and at least modest

sales (the band's two previous records have clocked 100,000 copies combined).
Rating **8**

## Crawl - Earth (Pavement '95)

Place this one cautiously within the wicked domain of industrial's heaviest, most exacting stormtroopers, Crawl emitting a din up, outside and away like Neurosis, Bile, or Skrew but with a smart and tidy Pantera sheen, somewherz closer to early Fear Factory but with clogging arteries gasping for blood. Cool photography, which makes the poignant point that anything we can capitalistically contruct pales in comparison to the ravishing ravages of nature.
Rating **7**

## Crankshaft - Crankshaft (Crankshaft '95)

Vancouver's Crankshaft have conspired to form a band that looks back to grunge's origins, dangerously close to both punk and metal, smart stop/go patterns with just enough dirt to confound the sound. One hears a bit of Helmet, a bit of old Soundgarden, Green River and Alice in Chains (especially in Slim Jacky's vocals), but as I say, more focused on the slammin' hero-stout riff. So it's the kind of stuff I love, but a little too derivative, undermining the uncontrolled creative juices of its heroes with street-level arrangements and fear of screwing up. Soundgarden never sounded afraid. Worthy, but man the competition is tough in '95.
Rating **6**

## Creepmime - Shadows (Pavement '93)

This half-English, half-Dutch amalgam has seen a few member changes since their '91 launch, arriving here with a progressive grindcore that features two-tiered harmony axes reminiscent of Carcass or even Trouble, over anti-tonal sci-fi-ish death metal melodies. Fueling this strangely warm bonfire is a convoluted but kick-ass drum performance, over which predatory riff constructs scan the scene in search of fresh kill. Vocals: aggressive but un-altered grind. Verdict: interesting, experimental but extreme to a fault.
Rating **7**

## Crimson Glory - Transcendence (Roadrunner '88)

Like an off-planet Queensryche, this Florida-based gathering of philosophers paint themselves up and journey off to the far east for this high-flown symphony of progressive metal. So by now, you can pretty much tell whether **Transcendence** is your cup of tea or vial of vile. Precise, totalitarian and flamboyantly gothic, **Transcendence** is basically the **Queensryche** EP gone full length, forever to be an imagined desired state, as Tate and Co. never did fulfil that record's vision, wandering off into various forms of inaction come LP one and beyond. But now that it's here, one may think it's no big sweat, coming from a band of androids with their heads too far in the clouds. Fact is, skill levels aside, this is extremely underground D'n'D metal for only the most gothically distressed; dark cavern grist for plotting the end of your world. Committed and heavy, but the term "kick-ass" does not apply, which is its downfall. I mean, how can you put this on in the morning if you expect to *function*, let alone conquer? Theoretically an **8**, but practically speaking a **5**, unless this genre is your thing, in which case it's well above par.
Rating **6**

## Crimson Glory - Strange And Beautiful (Atlantic '91)

No doubt prodded by cigar-chomping label beer-bellies and impatient impoverished rock wives, Crimson Glory try for a more accessible sound that subversively aims to retain some modicum of intelligent artcraft while addressing the hair-band-buying populace. So what emerges is complicated AOR, sorta like commer-cial Dream Theater with a few straight-faced ballads designed to recoup on costs; or alternatively (a dirty word in this world) Kingdom Come and Zep and Fates Warning and Dokken and TNT and Europe all mushed up in a perplexed ball of neon lightshade and gothic nightshade. Fat, heroic melodic hard rock, but you gotta buy into the band as serious artists to care. I'm hangin' in by a thread.
Rating **6**

## Crimson Jimson - Blunt Trauma (Crimson '93)

Hamilton's Crimson Jimson successfully bridge the gap between Sab-styled doom metal and grunge, loping like a sawed-off, low IQ Soundgarden or a metalizing, one-track Stone Temple Pilots. Low cycle is the operative, as all moves like boulders on the way to Stonehenge, whipmaster Scott Bell barking out vocal beratements bullhorn-style, while jagged gothmetal riffs lurch at two speeds (fairly slow and a bit slower) over six tracks of quality '90s metal, in tune with the hard pointy end of the Lollapalooza vibe but a bit stingy on arrangement or variety. No problem conceptually, indeed most of these tracks holding candle to heavier moments on **Superunknown**. Only problem is that Soundgarden envelope a good fifteen extra styles on that record, and none detracting from the band's core philosophy. Whether CJ can tap additional muses remains to be seen.
Rating **7**

## Crisis - Deathshead Extermination (Metal Blade '96)

A bizarre poison-oak-infested rock garden of angled thrash, **Deathshead Extermination** is more like a performance art piece, frontwoman Karyn Crisis (an ex-performance artist -swear to God, I pegged that one before I read the bio!) trading freaky Ono vocal phrasings with trashier male vocals over an artsy death metal knell (the band would coldly dispute this) that slashes at all speeds. But despite the cool experiment being performed here, I find the meandering riffs and floundering rhythms of this multi-national band a confused jumble of rehashed Swedish grindcore bits. And lyrically, lighten up folks. Serious, it gets to wearing and tearing the soul, all this blood, hatred, depression and self-loathing. Suggestion: get some sun.
Rating **6**

## Crisis Party - Rude Awakening (Metal Blade '89)

Moderate hopes were expressed for this one back in '89, given the record's sleazy, sassy street metal sound. Then there's Terry Date as producer and the band's G'NR bad looks to boot. Well the record kinda boots too, sounding a mite stripped and churlish like Seahags or Dangerous Toys, plain boogie metal with vocals that get out of tune occasionally despite their low octave charm. Not bad in context.
Rating **6**

## Peter Criss - Out Of Control (Casablanca '80)

Of course no self-respecting headbanger would ever think this record would rock but here's the official verdict: complete California dreamin' shit, loosely based on deleted versions of Eagles, Starcastle, Firefall, Jimmy Buffet, Down Hill, Elton John, and a host of other over-produced, boredom-steeped wimpoids from dishwater years gone by. Basically goes to show what a chore it must have been living so at-odds with an inner core so far from the Kiss koncept. Three or four ultra-lite hard rockers, most effective of which is called *In Trouble Again*. You said it, Pete, not me. Back with a new life in '92, or was that an imposter too?
Rating **1**

## Criss - Cat #1 (Tony Nicole Tony '94)

Yah, nice record label, nice logo, and finally, smashing make-up job Petey. If I can make it there, I can make it

anywhere . . . Fergeddit, Freddy. Although the record isn't as bad as the preview tracks I heard at the last Kiss Konvention (yes, I went to one: never again, you losers) would have it, fact is, **Cat #1** (it took you 14 years to come up with that?) sounds like bad Kiss in a world where good Kiss is, well, kinda bad. Pete's voice is scratchy and kind of enjoyable in its world weariness, no really. It's the thumpy glam metal that kicks the pooch, riffs so dull I coulda sworn we were back in the 1985 delete bins, surprisingly only the mellow tracks exposing the experience (both a melodic and a seedy one) of a man who has seen it all. Bottom line: the record's really unremarkable, but not as stumblingfall-over as the whole graphic presentation would have you believe.
Rating                                                                                5

## Cro-Mags - III: Alpha-Omega   (Century Media '93)
One of the premiere NYC hardcore acts of the '80s is back and slightly re-manned with full-length III. Cro-Mags are best known for their '86 classic **The Age Of Quarrel**, a record worshipped by many of my rock crit buds, a record which I've never bloody well heard myself. So I'm out of my depths here but lovin' it all the same, moshing to Harley Flanagan & Co.'s surprisingly mainstream metal crush, mixing only mid to brisk '80s HC with '80s riff metal, resulting in a sound that belies experience, given the lack of timely '90s moves you might recognize on current urbancore records by Crowbar, Life Of Agony, Helmet, Biohazard or Pro-Pain. I mean check out The Paths Of Perfection, check those unfashionable vocals, check out Victims. This stuff is outside of time, squarely inside Heavy Metal, and thankfully not the dil slam of hardcore. Big boomy cheezy metal production by Flanagan himself and I like it.
Rating                                                                                8

## Cronos - Dancing In The Fire   (Neat '90)
The esteemed and unclean Conrad Lant proves he hangs whithering on the cross as the radioactive fibres of Venom's brain trust, flagellating the earth with this decidedly Venomous slice of saw-toothed painrock. The welding torch at the ivory end of the beartrap however, is that Cronos has willed his presence on this project to exude higher degrees of technical skill, melody, dynamics, and dare we say accessibility. Dare nowt, for **Dancing In The Fire** is as violent, verbally offensive, and in a pleasant respect, thrash-acidic as any ulcerous Venom boil. It's the subtle shifts that make all the difference. Cronos' vocals are more up-front and more versatile, as are the axes in both respects. And the percentage of depraved poison is higher, as riffs are more driving and memorable, on such awesome catastrophes as the title track, Vampyr, Hell To The Unknown and delicious fave Terrorize. Both more challenging and inviting than Venom's **Prime Evil**, but not as wickedly recorded. Less OTT, less goth, less Venom.
Rating                                                                                8

## Cronos - Rock 'n' Roll Disease   (Neat Est. '92)
I guess the idea here is that Cronos can keep blasting out his firebrand of greasy, gritty street metal, and the songs will struggle through, despite the man's chosen or botched crappy production. And for the most part he's right, having assembled a batch of surly NWOBHM drinking tunes that in total recall accessible Venom once again, like Venom, chopped at the knees by a tinny, bassless mix. But it's an acceptable set of circumstances, once a few songs in, Cronos banking on us forgetting what hi-fidelity is, then bashing us with a few pints of hapless poverty metal, faves being Aphrodisiac with its tanked Tank groove and Midnight Eye, a bizarre gothic sort of thing that triumphs by showing how not to do metal.
Rating                                                                                7

## The Cross - Shove It   (Virgin '87)
I always liked Roger Taylor's wheezy voice and his playful style on his solo albums, so when this happened, I figured I was in for an off-the-cuff, percussive yet innocuous good time. **Shove It** is an interesting project that is similar to the dancier, more hi-tech Queen stuff but with more guitars; axework that is pleasantly similar to that of Brian May's. Frustratingly enough, smatterings of **Shove It** work tha grease; cutting-edge, clever, and at the same time loud and boisterous, while other parts just annoy, sounding out of place, giving the album an unfocused schizoid feel. Luckily, dance rhythms, Taylor's vocals, and May's guitar sound (even if delivered via the digits of one Clayton J. L. Moss) strike for a potent combination that just can't lose. Special killer kut of note: Love Lies Bleeding (She Was A Wicked, Wily Waitress), a fiercely weighty dance number, pummeled into glorious sonic overdrive by a devastating axe riff by May himself. Stands as the best Queen tune (and it is so exquisitely Queen) since a hallowed few studding **Jazz**. **Shove It** is worth it for this one alone, although three or four other tracks pursue this interesting alloy with some success.
Rating                                                                                7

## The Cross - Mad: Bad: and dangerous to know
(Capitol '90)
Taylor's very cool looking band is back with a very cool looking follow-up, and although it's more straight forward guitar rock than **Shove It**, it's just a bit too straight forward to cause waves of headphone madness. **Mad: Bad:** is basically a hard rock album that doesn't really say much that hasn't been said elsewhere (unlike **Shove It**), while sporting a solid proportions of good tunes, both quite heavy (Top of the world ma and Penetration guru) and mellower (Better things and Liar). Like **Shove It** however, **Mad: Bad:** is all over the bloody board. We get metal, dumb HR, dance, acoustic, hi-tech, and even a pointless cover of Hendrix's shitty Foxy Lady. Much as I like the idea of this band's existence (hell, I like the idea of any band that gets the Queen guys away from Queen), this album doesn't express anything as cutting edge as I had begun to expect from Taylor. Fun, well-produced rock'n'roll, but nothing more.
Rating                                                                                5

## Crossfire - See You In Hell   (Mausoleum Est. '83)
Righteous album covers and logo but that's about the end of it. Acute poverty crudrock desperation due to lack of talent rather than correct philosophical inclinations. Elementary hogwash.
Rating                                                                                2

## Crossfire - Second Coming   (Mausoleum '84)
Not much progress from the debut here as Crossfire drive a rusted dumptruck through life with no brakes, stopping only for discussions with God on the great white telephone. About on par with pea-brained labelmates Killer.
Rating                                                                                3

## Crowbar - Obedience Through Suffering
(Grind Core/Red Light '92)
Even though Windstein denigrates this album these days, calling the second record **Crowbar** to signal a new beginning, **Obedience Through Suffering** established the unique, turgid Crowbar sound much as it exists today. Alterations have been gradual, this record's guitars and vocals not quite as extremely low-blown, drums a little busier and more traditionally mixed. But the slow-fer-slow's-sake ethic is welded in place, as the band stumbles from one limiting idea to the next, rising out of catatonia only occasionally (i.e. Vacuum), usually just covering my eyes with pennies.

Bottom line: if you really dig Crowbar (and with this band, you really gotta want it), **Obedience Through Suffering** is near as satisfying as the newer swinghammers. Note: Pavement re-released the album in '95, adding two live tracks, live with this band being a relative term. Original band moniker: The Slugs.
Rating 6

## Crowbar - Crowbar (Pavement '93)
**Crowbar** is almost a concept record, the bastard child of hard-hitting metal realities in the '90s, combining urban American concrete with a type of British grind, Helmetpunk bruised and battered and bulked with sludgy 1994 grindcore, large scraping sounds melted by muscle fatigue. Produced by Phil Anselmo, and sounding nothing like Pantera, **Crowbar** has the metal community moderately abuzz and below, some adopting the experience as their badge, looking to the band as a multi-tiered assault of imitation, then finding no sound like it really, something between Entombed, Tool and lethargic Biohazard, but just, well, different, as if Trouble tried to write for the Lollapalooza crowd. So yes, a concept record, being one of those straight-through time-stopping cycles that sludges together in the memory banks, a brutish sound perhaps best exemplified by the band's gluecore cover of Zep's *No Quarter*, Crowbar capably turning it into 24-year-old proto-dirge *Black Sabbath*. Ugly muscle rock for ugly moods, **Crowbar** swings the club with a sort of juvenile skate underwhelm, infusing the slowburn with youth, not really energy, but young blood paralyzed by possibilities.
Rating 8

## Crowbar - Live + 1 (Pavement '94)
Crowbar churn a perfect base metal for the live forum, emitting a festering, boiling sound notable for its simple ingredients, large, straight-line, down-tuned riffs, usually delivered at a slothful pace all IQ levels can assimilate. So **Live + 1** (recorded in home-town New Orleans) sounds fab, adding just that palpable trace of chaos this band's sparse sounds can use. On the menu: five tracks from **Crowbar** plus *Numb Sensitive* which will be re-recorded for **Time Heals Nothing**.
Rating 7

## Crowbar - Time Heals Nothing (Pavement '95)
Hmm . . . weird trend I'm noticing towards short albums again. Anyhoo, Crowbar's back with their medium-highly anticipated smother mutha II. And time has indeed healed nothing, New Orleans' finest returning with another raw and chaotic sludgefest of Sabbath/Trouble-making underground metal. Sub-cycle quakings continue to pervade the Crowbar environs, while Kirk Windstein grovel-barks street-wise lyrics that push the positive through cringing cynicism, sorta like Suicidal Tendencies on 16 RPM (LP talk, sorry!). So doggedly deliberate and pugnaciously pummeling, **Time Heals Nothing** rusts solid at times, but the record taken in one black gulp ultimately converts the listener to the band's large fuzzy rhythms, even though I'm less enamoured compared to the somewhat fresher debut. So like anyways, slug it back, but then try to get some fresh air, will ya?
Rating 7

## Crowbar - Broken Glass (Pavement '96)
A mite too enamoured with doom abstraction, Crowbar seem to have grit their teeth and dug deeper into the underground, perhaps feeding off of COC talk of dirt, and Eyehategod carry-through of the same. Thus **Broken Glass** is even sludgier, more atonal, more bald-headed barked than its predecessor. I guess it's an affirmation of high-minded artistic ethics or sumthin, but man, I find myself just worn to a nub by the band's coagulated, black lung idea of fun. The alchemy is still

to be admired fer sure, that downwound fusion between doom and hardcore, but I'm finding this more of the same gesture tired and tiring. Note I: Eyehategod's guitarist Jimmy Bower joins the band *on drums*. Note 2: Paradise Lost producer Simon Efemey produces, not like it's made any difference whatsoever.
Rating 6

## Crumbsuckers - Life Of Dreams (Combat Core '86)
Standard, nippy NYC flipcore, too fast and riffically monotoned for my liking, bent on assault for fun's sake. Ain't it strange how the long ones are always slower, like they just took their boring bloshing blurs and stretched them out. Crumbsuckers is no more, having metamorphosed into mega-improved, power groove trio Pro-pain.
Rating 2

## Cry Of Love - Brother (Sony '93)
Hey man, I tried to groove with it, but I can't help but consider this a jammy, simplistic, no-risk rip-off of the Black Crowes, Kelly Holland's vocals wailing the Chris Robinson blues note-for-note, over constructs that thump along, wide-open like those dull but catchy rhythms of Bad Company. Carved perfectly for classic rock radio, **Brother** has hatched a number of timeless but unprovoking blue collar booze-alongs, *Bad Thing* being the biggest and dumbest. So far it's really only the Crowes that can pull off this sort of whiskey-soaked brawl rock because they continue to grow, obliterating the reactionary southern ethic with complex instrumentation and border-straddling writing explorations, thinking and toking well outside the box. Still, there'll always be a raft of folks who'll eat it up plain and simple, reverently citing tradition. Message for ya: why not just buy the good ol' boy vinyl itself and save yourself a few bucks?
Rating 6

## Cryptic Slaughter - Speak Your Peace (Metal Blade '90)
Cryptic Slaughter are a moderately revered staple of the hardcore scene, punching out a crushed eclair of dastardly, accomplished punk metal that would become in hindsight, an early version of what we now call urban hardcore. Brainy, sustainy, but somewhat stressful, battering one about the face, neck, head and chest. Rock solid, he-man metal recording though, which helps with digestion.
Rating 6

## Crysis - Hard As A Rock (Est. '82)
This is one of those long-lost low budget early American metal indies that is kinda likeable, sounding like it was created in a vacuum devoid of influences, kinda like Spokane's Doc Rockit or Toronto's Rapid Tears. Fairly heavy but muddy and amateurish.
Rating 3

## Cry Wolf - Crunch (Grand Slamm '90)
Something about this says "nice boys", even reminding me of the frightening Stryper at times, which is a kiss-of-death comparison taken the wrong way. To me it's just the innocent sound and maybe T. Hall's vocals, which are squeaky clean, not overly loaded with range, but likeable and exuberant like Don Dokken (avoid **Up From The Ashes** at all cost) or maybe . . . Rick Santers! Cry Wolf's got nothing up their sleeves to make you dump your shorts, but they do have a fluid, naive and wide-eyed stadium sound, very let's-make-it-in-the-city, American Dream hard rock. The production is a bit overblown but all in all it's a welcome shot of non-sensationalism and clean HR. Main complaint: a bit clunky beat-wise. Somebody control that drummer. Cool album cover.
Rating 5

## Culprit - Guilty As Charged (Shrapnel '83)

Ultra-early, pre-explosion Shrapnel product from the great Northwest, Culprit's **Guilty As Charged** developed the odd rousing, sustaining groove and hooky melody, but for the most part was an ego-enhancing exploration in techno-metal, NWOBHM-style (y'know, when there was no techno-metal); too loose, raw and undisciplined to impress. Showed promise and caused a lot of hype never to be fulfilled, 'cept for a continuation of the band's lifeblood through TKO. A spiritual kin to Queensryche.
Rating                                                                 5

## The Cult - Dreamtime ('84)

**Dreamtime** is the dullard debut from The Cult after their name trim from Southern Death Cult (and an '83 EP called **Death Cult**), their old moniker too deep for your basic illiterate goth harpie discovering hard rock. The record wanders through time as fog-clogged, psychedelic, gothic art punk, with nary a hint of future heaviness to come. About as fun as Love And Rockets, Sisters Of Mercy or other opportunistic night punk scum. Either trance-inducing or sleep-inducing depending on how easily amused or fatalistic you might be. *Spirit Walker* and *Resurrection Joe* both scored hits, sowing the seeds for the record's much more accessible follow-up.
Rating                                                                 2

## The Cult - Love (PolyGram '85)

The Cult has never been able to re-create the critical excitement **Love** generated as what was the first goth new wave/metal crossover album. Opportunists that they are (check their ultra-mutt rock pedigree), The Cult was almost certainly a state of confusion rather than a deliberate attempt at serious art, further evidenced by the fact that the title **Love** was a tongue in cheek concept from the start. Result: one half of **Love** is muddy, awkward, stumbling, psychedelic slop, both of the heavy and mellow variety; while the other half, tunes such as *Nirvana*, *Phoenix*, minor hit *Rain*, and major hit *She Sells Sanctuary* (what dance music briefly was and forever *should* be) combine Jim Morrison's mystique with deep, sizzling metal grooves emulating what The Doors might have sounded like had Jimbo lived, fired his impotent demented carnival of a band, stole Deep Purple's rhythm section and copped U2's Edge as lead axeman. Still, despite the successes, **Love** sounds suspiciously corporate and superficial, lacking a full fleshing-out of lyrical, musical, and emotional landscapes only hinted at here, resulting in a less than cohesive oddity, revealing what happens when night punk and the excesses of corporate metal collide. Obligatory Canadian connection: Ian lived in Hamilton, Ontario as a kid. Personnel trivia: Big Country's excellent Mark Brzezicki guest drums on all tracks except *She Sells Sanctuary*.
Rating                                                                 7

## The Cult - Electric (PolyGram '87)

Lo and behold, **Electric** delivers a devastating slab of crunch metal due in no small part to producer Rick Rubin and his Def sound (as it pertains to the mighty Slayer), and the all-pervading influence of that scruffy band of groove merchants from down under, AC/DC. Many classic rock platters feature well-written songs that manage to capture, for whatever reason, some classic, raucous grooves. **Electric** is unique in that it pays full homage to groove first, resulting in one of the most kick ass 'n' rowdy paeans to '70s metal ever scorched to vinyl. It ain't the heaviest slab ever, it's just got the most consistently walloping big beat of any album I can think of. **Electric** is searing hot, featuring a stripped to the basics, heads down, lean 'n' mean tour of metal's most magical grooves; a little Stones, a little Zep, a little more ZZ Top and just tons of the very guts of what makes AC/DC such a knee-slapping good time. Unbelievably stirring rockers such as *Wild Flower*, *Lil' Devil*, *Love Removal Machine* and *Outlaw* are overwhelmingly successful expressions of teamwork between a numbskullian band lacking direction and a knobmaster with a lucid vision to reproduce the gut-wrenching crunch of every '70s metal band's most molten moments. **Electric**, although superficially and predictably panned as simple clodrawk, shows a band having a blast, dropping pretensions, revealing true roots, and getting down to the glorious business of rock'n'roll.
Rating                                                                 9

## The Cult - Sonic Temple (PolyGram '89)

Ian and Billy's forever drunk pre-release hype stated that **Sonic Temple** was a hybrid of the best elements from **Love** and **Electric**. Bullshit. To my mind, this album takes a strong base of **Electric**-era song-types and waters 'em down with **Love**-era fuzziness, resulting in what is basically an apathetic and bland (albeit more varied) version of **Electric**, sadly lacking the added attraction of Rick Rubin's woofer-blowing chomp. Thanks to Bob Rock and his eye-on-the-bottom-line contingent, too much of this is just generic, commercial, washed-out metal, variously slow, noisy, clunky, or dishonest as evidenced on *American Horse*, the single *Fire Woman*, *Sweet Soul Sister*, and *Soldier Blue*. We even get two mellow ones, serving no real purpose other than to feign depth. Only *New York City*, *Sun King* and *Soul Asylum* rock with any sharp-toothed conviction. On **Sonic Temple** it seems that The Cult is trying to sound clever; in the process losing the party edge that made **Electric** so vicious and slicing, leaving us with a ponderous, unwieldy mess of sounds that just lays down and dies. Note: by this stage, the band has amassed a veritable scourge of 12" re-mixes, B-sides, live stuff and interviews (with some wild cover art). In response to the only stuff that potentially matters, i.e. the non-LP studio cuts, there are none as face-pounding as tunes from **Electric**, but there are a few that match up to middling **Sonic Temple**-era attempts, with sickly recording to match. Verdict: don't blow your cash on these overpackaged false alarms. For imaginative B-sides, buy Maiden.
Rating                                                                 5

## The Cult - Ceremony (Warner '91)

Other than having the pants sued off them for using the photo of a Sioux kid on the front cover, allegedly without the parents' permission, The Cult raised few eyebrows with this dull re-hash of old tried and true, borrowed and stolen-in-the-first-place Cult ideas. Ostensibly some sort of thematic look at the plight of the Indian (one of Ian Astbury's "spiritual" preoccupations/connections), **Ceremony** is the product of a band that's sabotaged their credibility too many times to mean anything anymore, which is why **Electric** was such a good record, having no pretensions towards political issues or indeed even serious rock star song-writing. Bash 'em out guys, and leave the thinking to Warrior Soul.
Rating                                                                 5

## The Cult - The Cult (PolyGram '94)

A sound reworking of a concept badly failing lifts **The Cult** to new heights, combining astonishing and versatile vocals from Ian Astbury punched over arrangements that ignore metal for a volatile mix of garagey psychedelia, modern cooked U2, and grunginess that often works, and often gets a little too authentic, a little too trashy. I'm respecting the hell out of this one, **The Cult** really surprising me with its musical artiness and lyrical emotion and imagery. But at the same time damn near half the record wallows in junkiness, a sickly mess of slow, no speed and quiet that bored me, while making me salivate for the next track. Some very amazing songs, best being lead tune *Gone*, which crests in something truly Woodstock-ish or Who-ish come chorus time. Hard to explain, but this one is both seriously worthy for its fine melancholy, and seriously flawed because it can't pick up much of a groove. In any event, The Cult are no longer fools.

Rating **8**

## Andy Curran - Andy Curran (Alert '90)

Andy's first post-Coney Hatch affair was much less the personable record than follow-up as Soho 69, even if both platters cranked the same sort of low, bassy, barroom throb. Here the man's just to rawk, most tracks in the belaboured zone, only slight hit *Nickels And Dimes* scoring with its Egypto Zep meets bluesy Zep hybrid, with second minor hit *Licence To Love* sounding like miserable the Robert Palmer song. Hasn't quite shaken the Canuck vestiges of Coney Hatch (which is good in a time-flipped naive push/pull way), except that the production here is just too brash and exposed, less highly lathered with guitar, more emphasis on the man's commanding bass, turning the show into stripper rock.

Rating **6**

## Curious George - Children Of A Common Mother (Nemesis '89)

More drinking man's punk from Vancouver, akin to a slurring, more fully-fleshed version of B.C. grandpappies D.O.A., Curious George kick some loose-bolted butt while raising hell in, then giving lyrical nod to all the hot spots in and around the Van area. All is left noisy and exposed, recorded sort of like Motörhead, although more committed to amusing punk tales than hauling home the decibels. Still, impressively sustained for Canadian poo; cohesive and all comfortable in its basic mid-tempo mosh factor.

Rating **6**

## Cutty Sark - Die Tonight (Mausoleum '84)

Firmly anchoring the upper quartile of the Mausoleum stable, this amusingly convincing headbang from '84's o'erflowing raft of releases pushes all the right wrist-band studs. Germanic beyond repair, sporting vocals that are everywhere, out-of-tune and apocalyptic at once, **Die Tonight** is a fine bit of underground metallic

cheez, produced with surprising muscle and constraint, again rare for this label and era. In context (I'm hearing this ten years after the fact), there's no mistaking why reviews were gracious at the time, Cutty Sark tacking into a low-to-mid-complexity groove that typifies the best of the early '80s. Classy teutonic instrumental: *October Holidays*.

Rating **7**

## Cycle Sluts From Hell - Cycle Sluts From Hell (Sony '91)

Once past the healthy she-queen band member monikers, which go something like this: Venus Penis Crusher, She-Fire Of Ice, Queen Vixen, Honey 1%er and Lord Roadkill, one is left with a surprisingly meaty basic metal record, a little bit of Motörhead 'n' Girlschool, a little European axework, a little glam, a smattering of punk, and a whole lot of heavy California metal. I immediately recall the resoundingly accomplished Phantom Blue record (chicks with attitude, chicks with chops), both it and **Cycle Sluts** being a far cry less girly than most corporate guy rock at the time. Fave: stoked metal celebration, *I Wish You Were A Beer*.

Rating **7**

## Cynic - Focus (Roadrunner '93)

Blend marinated Voivod records with 3/4 cup polyrhythms and six GIT profs on acid, and this is the sort of bionic progressive metal gorging that might splatter the walls when you take off the lid. **Focus** is just so far gone, I can't really get on board, except maybe as a gawker of the band's nutty and zany chops madness. Forget Anacrusis or Fates Warning or Mekong Delta or Death, this is as intricate a feast as you'll hear, that is if you care, given that Miami's Cynic (sporting members from Athiest, Pestilence and the aforementioned Death) play total musician's music, lacking basic punted musicality (by vaulting themselves beyond), indeed even twisting most the vocals out of reach by level heads, not to mention lyrics that fall just this side of Ulrich Roth meets Yes' **Relayer**, meets the Tibetan Book Of The Dead. Not a wet eye in the place, third eye maybe. Note: band broke up in '95, leaving a short legacy including this album and one EP.

Rating **6**

## D.A.D - No Fuel Left For The Pilgrims (Warner Bros. '89)

L.A. sleaze metal from Denmark! Sturdy, wisecracking songs, an impressive lead singer, a classy sense of humour, but also a bit of a problem with that English-as-a-second-language thing. But that's a minor complaint with this well-strategized corporate flirtation with Hollyrock; a business maneuver apparently accompanied by huge paychecks for the wide-eyed band members. All in all, a fragile virgin outing with memorable choruses and a respectable amount of snot-nosed rowdiness, yet a little too safe, which may be the result of label masters peering down from above. Actually the band's third record, but first biggie, debut being '86's **Call Of The Wild**, sophomore being '87's **Disneyland After Dark Draws A Circle**, which demonstrates what D.A.D. stands for.
Rating                                                                 6

## D.A.D - Riskin' It All (Warner Bros. '92)

Not quite riskin' it all, but Scandinavia's most promising goodtime shitkickers since Hanoi Rocks come storming back with this long-awaited follow-up to '89's solid but self-conscious major label debut, and on all fronts, the band tends to let fly with their creative urges, loosening the collective reigns for a heat-baked shuffle through roots terrain. Most prominent this time is a lazy, southern AC/DC-ish drawl; suvvern in spirit, metallic and generally up-tempo in execution, maybe like Foghat fighting for the best record of its life. The undermining factor however, as per the debut, is the Danish take on English. Only here, the boys are tackling lyrical concepts that are more info-packed, colourful, and just difficult, causing Jesper to say the darndest things. Yep, **Riskin' It All** is chock full of foreign linguistic twisters, often awkward, often truly witty and perceptive; on both extremes drawing attention to great scrutiny of the lyrics, which overall make for a knurled, obtuse experience. The production could have been a little more wild on the meters, but after the smoke clears, Binzer's juvenile Bon growl wins the day, making **Riskin' It All** a nifty little piece of kickin' cowboy metal, shiftier than AC/DC's bigger bashes, and simply wise and somehow in proper perspective as per the general philosophical solidity of Angel City. Digressions: three mellow tracks and one novelty blues.
Rating                                                                 7

## Dagger - Not Afraid Of The Night (Viper '85)

A cheap but halfways ballsy Dokken imitation with a meatier wall of sound, rough vox, and occasional keyboards, Dagger might have gone further without the ridiculous fur coats and painted faces beaming from their front cover. Actually more with-it and ready for some arena tour's support slot than most Roadrunner/Banzai dreck from '83-'85. But long gone.
Rating                                                                 4

## Damien - Stop This War (Mondo '89)

Stuck quite valiantly between grim Accept grooves and complicated blue collar melancholia, Damien were a fairly lusty trailer park metal experience, built for domination of most bands who dragged their knuckles through 1983. Problem is it's 1989, and this sort of pint-lifter sounds hollow after the headbang fare that has filled the years between. But we can all pine for a time when Crue were considered grade A childwreckers, and Damien fits those times like a fingerless leather glove. Cover depicts dog-faced WW II fighter planes dropping . . . records!
Rating                                                                 6

## Damien Thorne - The Sign Of The Jackal (Roadrunner '86)

One of a hundred hapless U.S. posses with more than enough wattage to spread around but too much ego and medieval sobriety in their cold blood, rendering the proceedings tuneless and forgettable.
Rating                                                                 3

## Dammaj - Mutiny (PAR '86)

Immediately notable for one of the most pulverizing and flawless mixes ever electronically availed, **Mutiny** puts its high production standards to the test with searing performances from a band high on class and devastatingly low cycle on the sonic register. **Mutiny** is one concrete monolith of loudness. In fact, the only thing placed above subwoofer boom on this seriously large release, are the fine operatic pipes of helmsman Greg Hill. Dammaj embody the best qualities of like Priest, Fates Warning and Virgin Steele—maybe even Savatage—emitting a shredly gothic grind as muscular as any out there. Merciless throughout its seven cuts (plus one naff instrumental send-off), **Mutiny** tends towards the weighty slow-to-mid pace spectrum, yet never gets smothered by its mass, making it highly recommended in terms of playability. In other words, not just a commendable concept, but a dense and violent, worthwhile spin.

Rating **8**

## The Damned - Damned Damned Damned (Stiff '77)

Chronologically speaking, this was the first actual punk album ever. I review a fair bit of punk in this book because let's face it punters, funny haircuts, lack of skills, bone-white pencil arms, and safety-pinned clothes aside, punk has offered us some great rock guitar mayhem. And **Damned Damned Damned** is one of the classics, offering a frenzied frash assault that stage-dives on both sides of electric anarchy. It's speedy, and the recording ain't the greatest, but the album taken as a whole is a savage swarm of beer-swilling locusts. Dave Vanian's vocals are dark and cryogenic, almost regal, and the wall-of-noise drum barrage from our man, Rat Scabies exemplifies the obliterated ethic of a way too hyper band that just doesn't give a shit. And dishing more frenetic energy than a nuclear meltdown, individual triumphs such as *New Rose*, and *Stab Your Back* (both definitive and oft-played singles at the time) are about as psychotic 'n' chaotic as heavy gets, smothered in buzzing layers of electricity turned against mankind. One of approximately seven essential punk manifestos.

Rating **9**

## The Damned - Music For Pleasure (Stiff '77)

More subdued, polished and emotionally dark versus the sugar-high-strung debut, **Music For Pleasure** is what Accept's **Balls To The Wall** is to **Restless And Wild**, a tightening of the sonic reigns, juxtaposed against chaotic disintegration of emotional and moral capacities. **Music For Pleasure** is more a crossover metal chug than a flat-out power punker, containing subversive, deflated but memorable melodies not unlike those of Golden Earring or Blue Öyster Cult, below Vanian's twisted, "tux strangles waif" view of the world and Captain Sensible's simple but expressive riffing. This clouded sky renders **Music for Pleasure** a haunting look at a very British punk phenomenon, a fiercely independent album documenting the transformation of England's youth into something rodent-like and bad for business. Possibly the finest, proudest punk record ever, and definitely the most lead-faced without resorting to shock rock. Interestingly enough, the band considers it a disaster, finding surprise producer Nick Mason from punk enemies Pink Floyd, a royal pain in the arse.

Rating **10**

## The Damned - Machine Gun Etiquette (Chiswick '79)

Third stylistic shift in three albums, **Machine Gun Etiquette** evokes a band on the verge of spectacular self-destruction, all trashy and loose, oscillating wildly between magnificently heavy punk metal, crash 'em bash 'em scrapyard punk, and humorous, new wavey self-parody. However, it's still a hulking wart-faced mass of a record, holding together like a soggy stack of job classifieds, because despite the mood swings—perhaps exemplified in *These Hands*, a swirling carousel about a demented clown—**Machine Gun Etiquette** sounds sinister, soggy, and so despondently British. But somehow, great morbid melody simmers beneath the clatter, allowing pensive twists of gut and a thoroughly flippant air of commercial suicide to permeate the proceedings as if the joke is definitely on us. Faves: *Plan 9 Channel 7* and *I Just Can't Be Happy Today*, which send ripples of bad British weather deep into my bones.

Rating **10**

## The Damned - Live Shepperton 1980 (Ace '80)

This hunk of low budget vinyl "recorded live at a special gig played for members of the damned fan club, at Shepperton, 1980" is kinda fun and trashy, focusing mainly on itchy sores from **Machine Gun Etiquette**. The recording ain't bad but the guitars are generally weak or nonexistent. Stick to the studio, it's all live anyways.

Rating **4**

## The Damned - The Black Album (IRS '80)

**The Black Album** marks a shift toward a ghoulish, psychedelic garage rock, necrotic and gothic lyrical matter bolstering that spaced underground '60s sound, while offering some rousing old-style Damned in *Therapy* and *Drinking About My Baby*; sum total being a solid, tuneful album in a shivering, haunted house sort of way. Also a meaty, "thrash" recording, with requisite cymbal crashing mayhem from drummer Rat Scabies, who is a chilling reminder of Keith Moon in all the worst possible ways. Boris Karloff or Lestat on vocals, who can tell? To be admired from a psychological and spiritual distance. The best kind of night punk.

Rating **8**

## The Damned - Strawberries (Bronze '82)

**Strawberries** and its creepy predecessor **The Black Album** portray the band leaving their punk roots for a '60s psychedelic trash rock sound, a soupy, swirling kaleidoscope ride not unlike a more forceful version of The Stranglers, heavy Lyres, or XTC side project, Dukes Of Stratosphear, somewhat going hip Anglo-goth like The Cure, Joy Division and (Southern Death) Cult. A moldy, melancholy feel permeates and dampens, driven into the ground by the band's penchant for horror style themes, artfully delivered by Vanian in all his lily-white, vampiric glory. Some interesting material (most notably the piano-driven reflective dirge *Life Goes On*), but beware headbangers, this particular era of The Damned lies three silvery moons from metallic. However, who in their rivet-headed mind could refuse snagging this for the righteous porkfruit cover concept alone?

Rating **6**

## The Damned - Phantasmagoria (MCA '85)

Grimly dark, grimly British, grimly fiendish, this classy and horrific opus is Raven Black to an extent only The Stranglers could manage during their disturbing, Satanic **Meninblack** days. Here The Damned are pale-skinned changelings; aristocratic vampires, acting more like studio professionals on heroin and cooling blood than skidsy punkers on airplane glue and warm lager. **Phantasmagoria**, like a twilight meeting with Lady Death herself, is quiet, thoughtful and damn sobering, the closest thing to sonically induced suicide ever recorded this side of John Cale's **Music For A New Society**. Faves: minor epic *Street Of Dreams* and foreboding giddy-up *Shadow Of Love*, which recalls Johnny Cash, the original man in black.

Rating **8**

## The Damned - Anything (MCA '86)

**Anything** is as upscale and well-recorded as its overcast predecessor, main difference here being the propensity towards more uptempo numbers and more thoughtful and varied arrangements. Again **Anything** is nowhere near metal in terms of instrumentation. Yet in terms of emotional terrain, this heady and potent record is as depressed, defeated and deflated as the deepest wounds Black Sabbath, Trouble or crazed scientists Mekong Delta could ever inflict, delivered by the grand masters of underground English poison, rising to manic bends of violence on the raging title cut, possibly the band's most rulebook-metallic track ever. Despite all odds to the contrary (and believe me, the press has done their fair share of the damage), Long Live The Damned.

Rating **8**

## The Damned - The Light At The End Of The Tunnel
(MCA '87)

This quite good compilation culls together the shambling, frayed catalogue of punk's favorite hapless clowns. It jumps all over the place temporally, but along the wayward way, we get a number of non-LP tracks including *Lovely Money, Thanks For The Night (Rat Mix)* and *Rabid (Over You)* (all three dreary Jam-like pop). Then there's the shmaltzy cover of Barry Ryan's '60s standard *Eloise*, which became one of those cling-to-life hits for the band, perfect for their spooky garage pop stylings of the latter years. But the only rare gem would be the brisk punk metal of '84's *Nasty*, a mean, boisterous little track that leaves us begging for the old days. Graphics-wise there's detailed liner notes by Herb Fenstein and one of Pete Frame's excellent family trees, plus good info like year of release for the mystery toons. All and all, what one could expect from a better compilation: a swinging mixed-up plow through a band's past, plus a nice supply of rock journalism shedding light on this firecracker act that screamed chaos through their very existence.
Rating 7

## The Damned - Final Damnation (Essential/Castle '89)

Billed as "The Damned Reunion Concert, London Town & Country Club 13 June 1988", this one surprisingly ain't all that different from **Live Shepperton 1980**. Same thin sound, high on treble, low on guitars, same general track situation, with almost everything hailing from either the explosive debut or the explosive **Machine Gun Etiquette**. But the sound is marginally better, and there's 17 tunes versus 10, with a rousing rendition of the Stones' *The Last Time* to close things out in touching, tearful fashion (I'm kidding). A nice testimony to the punching bags of the punk movement, but kind of braying and harsh.
Rating 6

## Damn The Diva - Damn The Diva (A&M/Plum '94)

Sorry but this one's plagued by all sorts of really annoying problems. The bedrock is yer very basic doomgrunge. The problems are thusly: weak, uncommitted recording, snickery, melodramatic self-importance, repetition of unremarkable riffs, and a stiff delivery of everything. Slow to build on almost every dull track, Damn The Diva just copy all the worst bits of bands we all like and have heard too much, and it's all so noticeable. Boring. Deflated. Vancouver: close to Seattle but really in Canada, get it?
Rating 4

## Damn The Machine - Damn The Machine (A&M '93)

A lot more than I would have expected from Megadeth discard Chris Poland, **Damn The Machine** challenges on par with **Countdown To Extinction**, while coming up timid on the power end of the spectrum. Dead similar philosophy in both lyrics and adherence to studio gloss without mercy, **Damn The Machine** is the progressive side of the modern Mustaine juggernaut, Poland constructing elaborate cyberstructures that are best viewed as moody science rather than headbanger heaven. Lyrically, titles like *Fall Of Order, Honour, Patriot, Russians, Countryside* and *Humans* ought to tell you where this one's going, the excellent purist metal pipes of Dave Clemmons called upon to clearly enunciate the Machine's often fuzzy political visions. A cerebral trip, but one that doesn't sustain its metal, often opting for quiet, demilitarized verses and breaks fraught with changeovers and those cool little synchro-fills Mustaine pioneered. A lot of drugs have come between Mustaine and Poland in the past, bringing all sorts of bitterness and resentment, but **Damn The Machine** proves the two were birds of the same frontier metal feather despite their differences. When the smoke clears however, Mustaine's is the more personable and mega-heavy outfit, more concerned with strong songs and mighty grooves than this record's labyrinth of techy behaviors. Very respect-worthy, but for academic rivetheads only.
Rating 8

## Damn Yankees - Damn Yankees (Warner Bros. '90)

This supergroup of proud-to-be American hard rockers (although canuck Mike Levine form Triumph almost joined) was a doomed concept with a goshdarn great name right from the start. **Damn Yankees** is a product of its pieces except for Ted sadly, who seems such a small part of things really, throwing in his odd hammer-on left over from **Little Miss Dangerous**. Excrutiatingly lifeless, sabotaged by stiff drumming and an obscene commerciality, like something straight off a Hollywood movie about making it in a big corporation or sumthin'. Everything Ted was always against I thought. Miserable vocals.
Rating 3

## Damn Yankees - Don't Tread (Warner Bros. '92)

Much as I wish I felt the redneck wind blowing from under the hood here, I just can't help but feel this sort of touch-all-bases hard rock won't get this truck out of the muck. Terrible Ted, Tommy Shaw, Jack Blades . . . yea, that's about what it sounds like: a heavy metal Night Ranger torn from two extremes. Too many hanging chords, vocals over solo drum patterns, surprisingly strong and varied melloid fare, and generally annoying chest-thumping metal, all kinda clattery funky and panic-stricken. Record II's a fast, shiny beast, but one without soul or direction. Too much energy expended on the Ted Nugent World Bowhunters association, I guess.
Rating 5

## Dandelion - I Think I'm Gonna Be Sick (Sony '93)

Pretty bitchin' grunge metal which courts Nirvana circa **Bleach** but with larger deconstruction, sorta like Nudeswirl, very anti-commercial, seeking no positive reinforcement, excrutiatingly slack and garagey, maybe like really old 1988 grunge. Which I guess is to the detriment of listenability, Dandelion coming off pretty bleak, brutal and basic, despite the cool premise. Gotta love spaced butthead noiseniks like this though, cos no one else will.
Rating 7

## Dandelion - Dyslexicon (Sony '95)

If the debut was **Bleach** or **Rehab Doll** without the inventive touches, just a smear-me smarmy bashfest, **Dyslexicon** at least moves this ordinary but rockin' band up to **Nevermind** and **In Utero**. Yes indeed, Philly's Dandelion is still a committed grunge act, drums flailing away at tunes that add only passing references to dynamic, briefly visiting psychedelia, alternative and the new punk, but in essence still driving their mop-top Nirvana van. Sorta lukewarm on this one, 'cos the surprises, solos and eccentricities of all those best first weird Seattle groovers just ain't here, despite better melodies. Better than the limp wrist stuff that passes for alternative these days, but still too dang slack.
Rating 7

## Jim Dandy - Ready As Hell (Heavy Metal '84)

I just damn well couldn't help myself when it came to Black Oak Arkansas records, and I now have every one, and still don't like any of 'em. Fact is, BOA were more an amusing concept than serious contenders for anything, looking pretty dangerous, decadent and dirty, which counted for a lot in the '70s. And now Diamond Dave's unspoken mentor is back, lizard breath unpacked and ready to scorch the bayou. **Ready As Hell** is more a strange twisty, ass-backwards southern rock album, eccentric and absolutely dough-brained like old BOA, with awful melodies and more almost purposely dumb moves we grew to question and live with ten times a record back in the days of dyn-O-mite. Baffling as it is, vigorously negated pleasure and playing-gone-wrong seem to dog this man everywhere he steps. Basically the modern contrivance of a painful rock curiosity whose antics were nothing less than enter-taining disaster when we were young and woefully more stupid.

Rating 3

## Danger - Danger (EMI Est. '83)

Imported Europiffle from one of those mainland coun-tries that never learned how to rock. I bought **Danger** "used import" during the great metal drought of '83-'85 because I was bored and desperate—probably paid seven bucks for it—and of course it's slop fit for chain-smoking morons, which should have been evi-dent from the naff band photo on the back. Contains a cover Gamma's immortal *Meanstreak*, which is blas-phemy coming from such blunt intellects.

Rating 1

## Danger Danger - Danger Danger (CBS '89)

It's kind of funny, but after hearing this '89 release for the first time during the crazy, hazy days of summer '91, it becomes evident how far commercial hard rock has come. Danger Danger's offensive posturing, Romper Room moves, and annoyingly buzzing key-boards just aren't tolerated these days, as fans of the teased and shiny tangents of metal have raised their standards to the point of demanding personality, soul and thought-provoking twists on a theme with their melodious hum. **Danger Danger** on the other hand's an insulting, clattering update on the no-brains Lover-boy formula, with the added attraction of timid, laven-der boy vocals. These wimps of Stryper-like proportions must press wild flowers in photo albums all day, 'cos they aren't spending any time getting a life. Worst 99 cents I ever spent.

Rating 0

## Danger Danger - Screw It! (CBS '91)

Agonizingly wicked to comprehend, but this flashy looking, big talkin' follow-up may be a worse nagging rag of an album than the debut odor, ineptly addressing party metal, funk metal, loads of whiny soft shit, even rap, in its swindling grapple for the nation's coinage. Danger Danger pull every expected commercial trick in the book, flirting with the blues, AC/DC riffs and liberal misuse of keyboards, yet all the while forgetting to climb off their lipstick tubes to hit any crunching chords. And if you think this is metal bias, forget it, **Screw It!** is also world's away from acceptable pop metal, or whatever the hell it's trying to be.

Rating 0

## Danger Danger - Cockroach (Unreleased Est. '94)

Legal and label charades, travesties and accusations conspired to stop the release of this fairly weighty AOR semi-jewel, a record widely considered D2's very best. And stop it they did, but not until two full versions of it were already in the hands of AOR tape traders the world over, one with old D2 singer Ted Poley, one with the guy that's on **Dawn**, Vancouverite Paul Laine, who puts in the more aggressive, throaty performance. The record's pretty crunchy rather than crunchy pretty, maybe a fainter version of Skid Row's intensely ignored **Subhuman Race**, tippy-toeing in the dirt of alt-rock without getting their designer black jeans musty and dusty, but self-explanatory and dim-witted all the same. Cuddly and OK, but nowhere near the holy grail, fans

of sugar-coated hard rock might lead you to believe. I mean, this is still Danger Danger.

Rating 6

## Danger Danger - Dawn (Low Dice '95)

As my AOR expert bud Mike Drew sez, if you've heard **Cockroach**, **Dawn**'s grinding gurgling grooves will come as less of a shock, D2 really gathering a head of steam, learning, progressing, updating, and making a record that builds on their strengths as pop metal semi-somebodies. The band is officially now a three piece with Paul Laine in as leonine roaring pipester, straddling quiet acoustic and freight train rumbling with capable aplomb. I never thought I'd say it, but all is rock solid confident here, D2 joining the ranks of Tyketto, and even the re-tooled Warrant as saviors of AOR, blurring the lines between hard alternative, hair band rock, roots music; basically capturing in one brush-stroke, the '70s through the '90s (six-ton blues ballad *Wide Awake And Dead* is an impassioned example of this). Well-constructed, bottom-heavy, traditional US of A rock 'n' metal, what more can you say.

Rating 8

## Dangerous Toys - Dangerous Toys (Columbia '88)

From the G'NR camp of L.A. sleezoid metal, these swillin' longhairs make up for lack of knack for inter-esting songcraft with tons of hurtin' desire and more conviction. Jason McMaster is a blast as a frontman and even though the tunes are short on ideas, following a well-traveled shitkicker rock map without insight on how to improve the journey, it does come off as a done-me-wrong good time. Diddled a little, did little, then the follow-up stiffed.

Rating 5

## Dangerous Toys - Hellacious Acres (Sony '91)

A shot of octane marks this band's brave return to a sound that's hard to get right. Still immersed in a sort of cheezy high energy boogie metal, Dangerous Toys generate some embarrassing rave waves, which undu-late into view then fast fade into the horizon. Tepid cover of Bad Company's *Feel Like Makin' Love*, but the rest does better. But what I'm getting at is, how much staying power can a stuck truck like this generate?

Rating 6

## Dangerous Toys - Pissed (dos/DMZ '94)

Losing the big label deal has knocked the bitescratchkick back into whipping boys Dangerous Toys. **Pissed** has most skeptics turned right 'round with its sprightly melodic upratchet metal. Big improvement here is strength of song and then up once more for chorus, a sound then caked with a less lethal level of the grime that saw Skid Row's **Slave To The Grind** melt party metal in its shiny shoes. The alcohol rockers steamroll, and the quiet moments genuflect at least towards a kind of Dollsy been-there-done-that sincer-ity sphere. Erstwhile, the band's decadent boogie has been muted to a hinted whiff of blues travel coating timeless hard rock, more a blasted smear of three decades than anything pinned to '80s tease-by-num-bers stripmall metal. Potentially a spirited new direc-tive for reeling and confused Hollyrockers, **Pissed** isn't so much angry as defiant.

Rating 8

## Dangerous Toys - the r-tist 4-merly known as dangerous toys (DMZ '95)

Lavish look to this commerce-corrupted about-face into an involved alt.grunge. But this band has grown and learned beyond what one might expect, tracks such as Pearl Jammy ballad *Heard It All* and melodically complex gungster *The Numb* proving that when bands from metal arrive in the new world, their work ethic holds them in good stead, kicking the stuffing out of lo-fi shoulder-stoopids through a combination of chops and hard-won road wisdoms. Redneck retros might revolt, and any thought of new fans is wishful thinking, but the record is a boisterous neu-rock excursion for those who care. I hope some day many do, and reward Jason and his cowboys (oops! alienated angry young unemployed flannelheads) with a scrap of commercial success.

Rating 8

## Danzig - Danzig (Def American '88)

Over-hyped due to affiliation with Metallica and an admirable punk pedigree, megalomaniac Glenn Danzig fails to come up with the goods here, offering instead fourth rate Cult impressions (perhaps suffering somewhat in its close temporal proximity to The Cult's best work), plus some grimy attempts at skeletal blues metal, yet with less power, imagination and studio ability than he will shortly prove capable. Nevertheless, Glenn sounds ripped out of his gourd. Just too plain a performance surrounding Glenn's black focal point, but love that logo. Album II will mark one of the most sinister, life-transforming about-faces in rock history. Yikes.

Rating 5

## Danzig - II Lucifuge (Def American '90)

Glenn Danzig (not to be confused with Tony Danza) and Rick Rubin join forces in creating one of the most unclean, brutally evil black metal albums to ever grace the racks and mean it. Judging from the videos, the reports of the band's live capabilities, and the havoc within these grooves, Glenn and his assembled harpies are going to be an unstoppable force. **Lucifuge** takes off with *Long Way Back To Hell*, a demonic rip-ride through the Black Forest, and never looks back, bridging the most depressing of metals with the most cadaverous crossroad blues in search and plunder of Satan's dominions. Other horrible visions occur within *Tired Of Being Alive*, which burns with the most blood-curdling of choruses, and *Her Black Wings*, again driven like a stake through the heart by a sinister chorus which finds Danzig's formidable voice fused to the anguished guitar work of John Christ. Throughout this truly frightening record lives the pumped up, larger than life, but eternally damned presence of Danzig himself, part post-burial Elvis, part post-burial Jim Morrison, part criminal, completely too far gone. And even though the songs rely on simple economic structures, Danzig's voice and Rubin's gut-twisting mix drag them whipped and bleeding into full-blown terror. Glenn must have sold his soul, lock, stock and barrel, and threw in those of his band, to achieve such brain-battering evil after the false alarms of his debut. **Lucifuge** definitely crosses that line.

Rating 9

## Danzig - III How The Gods Kill (Def American '92)

The meanest throat in Hell's Half Acre deems us fit to receive wench again, shifting the sands into a more atmospheric, metallic and fully-produced Exhibit A. **How The Gods Kill** cranks up on the insidious side of Glenn's evil; the man's lyrics becoming softer, deeper and blacker on an artistic level, looking to caress more intelligent souls perhaps, while the music veers away from graveyard blues metal to a more Sabbath-like and oddly "traditional black metal" assault, complete with lots of laid-back wallowing, which checkers the record with frustrating lows as well as chunk-infestinal highs. *Godless* kicks off this blackbird pie with a classic *Hole In The Sky*-style blitz, then it's four and twenty until things really kick again with the biting *Dirty Black Summer*, and on it lurches ad infinitum . . . whipping then sleep, whipping, sleep . . . Somehow **Lucifuge** struck me as having more savagery, more hunger, more swing compared to this often pensive slog through hell, a land

scarred more with terminal disease than lusty limb-severing violence. I also find the recording a bit thick and treble-less, perhaps adding to the disturbing, smothered and serious feel of the whole unpassable stone. Definitely a frightening piece of work, but also less rowdy, and less willingly taken for a spin, **How The Gods Kill** is perhaps the true manual for omnipotent taking of life, suggesting the ingestion of souls only when the urge to life fades deflated without fight.

Rating 8

## Danzig - 4 (American '94)

He of the King Diamond mutton chops and breezy black aria is back in strappling emotion-bent form for what to my mind becomes the Danzig masterwerk, **4** eschewing the inflatable munster bombast of **3**, while driving a stake through the open spiral architecture of **2**. Lo and beholden to the forked twister of word and deed, Glenn and his blacklung posse have delivered a dangerous, thought-paralyzing feast, rising below concepts of metalness into chilling all-style-encompassed scrapemarks of the soul, the most mortifying numbers being somewhat downwinded quiet pieces like *Cant-speak*, *Dominion* and *Going Down To Die*, the latter braced tall and thin with an electrifying solo that recalls ancient metal history. Sucked back tall up with the new Slayer, I'd have to say Danzig has dared to bare all with the sheerest bravery . . . scales, sores, and her black wings, melting in vampiric sunlight with astonishing authenticity. Quite simply, this is one for the critics, metal transcending, vocals pliable enough to evoke Ian Astbury, Bono and Elvis licked by the flames, songs punk-infuriated and Satan-spawned. The spirit of **2**, nothing lifted from **3**, art high concepted from the millennium, Danzig has finally lashed out a psychological soulstorm to match the bubbling-under imagery threatening to be taken seriously for the last five years. Hey, wipe that smirk off your face.

Rating 10

## Glenn Danzig - Black Aria (Caroline '92)

Classical music with no lyrics. There. That's probably the most materially relevant info out of the way, but wait, don't run! A bit dodgy not putting the interesting and cryptic disclaimer on the back cover rather than the inside, but we'll excuse this as a possible label ploy (?). Question that springs to mind is this: Is Glenn attempting to take us into a more profound evil than he can manage through the less universally accepted atmosphere of metal, or is he trying to soothe and possibly cleanse minds slated for a seat in the golds in the arena of Lucifer's domain? One suspects the former, given the track titling, which at least throws the crumb that this is a story of rebel angel triumph. So somewhat aligning himself with the English camp bringing classical into the rock world as the most potentially destructive tool of the devil, Danzig at minimum proves his foresight, along with his sincerity for art for art's sake. Even if he's an evil harpie in Satan's minion.

Rating 7

## Danzig - 5blackacidevil (Hollywood '96)

One's acceptance of L'il Glenn's latest incarnation might hinge on whether you think a complete submersion of this visceral metalman into industrial is bandwagoneering or a sincere creative exploration. So it comes down to how much patience you have, how securely you duct-tape your head to that of demonboy. Personally, I thought **4p** was a masterpiece and this one shite, to the point of depression at having a great band wiped from the face of the earth. For **5blackacidevil** is heinous, amateur, basement tape, hard industrial through and through, scratchy vocals, dil hip-hop beats, usually less than a half dozen layers of rusted goo, coagulated into bad Trent. Yeah, by most measures this is yer bald-faced sell-out, metal in the crapper,

Marilyn Manson on a high. I just didn't expect Danzig to do such a dreary, dismal, slow-drip job of it.

Rating      1

## Dare - Blood From Stone    (A&M '91)

Maybe I'm giving a couple points for being British, but this squeaky clean corp rocker somehow escapes most of those cheese connotations despite being right in the thick of the hairbrand heyday. Very brightly recorded, tasty axe licks, and somewhat new Bad Co. style vocals from Darren Wharton provide this band of semi-knowns with an arsenal. It helps to hear the record for the first time in '95, when it sounds very alien indeed.

Rating      6

## Dark Angel - Darkness Descends    (Combat '86)

Damnably powerful, but too thrash for my liking. As usual, this kind of metal sounds most sinister when avoiding the thrash-king polka, and Dark Angel slow it down only about one third of the time. Many retrials since this one.

Rating      3

## Dark Heart - Shadows In The Night    (Roadrunner '84)

Powerless pre-school goth from Britain, short-sticked by a tone-deaf vocalist, Dark Heart was one of those talentless signings from the first major flood of NWOBHM bands, when anybody with a stained Motörhead shirt could scrounge up a record contract. Just aimless, silly and slapped together.

Rating      2

## Darkstar - Darkstar    (Avatar '81)

One of the more promising NWOBHM bands crashed on the rocks of obscurity, Darkstar had an accomplished sort of '70s/Maidenish sound, replete with the usual stylistic eccentricities that resulted in a record of fragmented ideas, despite occasional diamonds of carnal knowledge. Lady Of Mars reigns smoothly evil 'n' gothic (like Trespass and Diamond Head; joining Trespass on the second Metal For Muthas compilation pak), but most else looked patchy at best. Stronger than most of the scant few platters at this early juncture in the heavy revolution.

Rating      6

## Darkthrone - Transilvanian Hunger

(Fierce/Peaceville '94)

Darkthrone are one of those jokey hokey Norse black metal beastlies wrapped up in the grim scene there, a scene that has taken to action like Blackmore to hair-weaves. But this is shite, truly and no exaggeration, recorded like an AM radio, no bass, no treble. Songs are just a uni-drone blur of weak, watery blastbeats blathered out in Norwegian. For curmudgeoned cranks who crave possession of music no one else wants.

Rating      0

## Dark Tranquility - Of chaos and eternal night

(Spinefarm '95)

This four track, nineteen minute Finnish showstopper mixes dime-on intricate metal with thrash vocals and Maiden-derived castle tones; prog but accessible, well-recorded and well-arranged like many a hip '90s Swedish act. Each ambitious track reels with goth and cool, under-utilized '80s touches, with only the title track veering into thrash. More interesting and active than similar sobbing, more rudimentary songwriting from Paradise Lost, Edge Of Sanity or Lake Of Tears.

Rating      8

## Das Damen - Triskaidekaphobe    (SST '88)

Looks like Wire, rings like a metallic Gang Of Four or Minutemen, with unwelcome grunge jangle sloppiness which sounds cool only when it collapses into good ol'

American punk, the melodic stuff like Hüsker Dü. I'm almost on board, but it's fairly beat up and schizo-eccentric, stopping and starting with the illogic of psychedelic chemistry, and an altertuned guitar-bass fusion that recalls Sonic Youth with double vision. If you haven't guessed yet, pretty damn loopy, basically along the same lines as its East Indian album cover.

Rating      5

## Dayglo Abortions - Here Today Guano Tomorrow

(Fringe '88)

My candidate for the most inhumane band in rock, B.C.'s Dayglo Abortions have actually run afoul of Canada's obscenity laws and for good reasons I don't want to go into. The wily, rude constructs kick surprising butt, especially on the scorched title cut and the humorous portrayal of the evils of Dungeons And Dragons. However, it's just too sick to play, and no, I don't own it.

Rating      0

## DBC - Dead Brain Cells    (Combat '87)

DBC thrive in an inhospitable zone known as thinking man's thrash, an emotional no man's land, cranking metallic trigonometry that no one in their right mind (except maybe Spock and Bill Gates) could ever love. Dead Brain Cells rides this continuous mono-rush, offering swelled gravity-defying spewtations that run the tireless goth-death-hardcore gamut amidst continuity-undermining rhythms rife with pointless stops and starts. Deals the necessary pain in price break volumes, but simply chills with its form of cranky cold science.

Rating      4

## DBC - Universe    (Combat '89)

Another humourless, ultimately decaf purveyor of mathematical thrash, sending wave after wave of ultra/goth/thrash structures that just sound like practice exercises, or like a lot of the Slayer breaks between verse and choruses, DBC try to wax so damn heavily, yet just confuse with their convoluted statements that neither rise or fall to the challenge. Just shows the limits and total samey-ness of ultra-heaviness when the humanity isn't there. From the album notes, presumably from Montreal. Really, no different than Dead Brain Cells except maybe even more alternative and difficult.

Rating      3

## Dead And Gone - God Loves Everyone But You

(Alternative Tentacles '97)

As with most Alternative Tentacles product, Dead And Gone strap to a punk rocket, angular visions that are thorny and unpredictable. No bio, and little in the way of liner notes, so I'm a little out of sorts on who these abrasives be. But suffice to say that this is the way punk should wind, into the netherzones of exploration, frying up a work ethic similar to that of The Jesus Lizard, NoMeansNo and old Minutemen. But this is pretty dark, serial-killed stuff, fraught with harried tribal structures, explosive power chords and vocals that sound like a belch from the soiled underbelly of some crack-addled New York hard-core lunatic. Is it nightmarish and thought-provoking? Yes. Do I find it useful or enjoyable? No.

Rating      5

## Dead Beat Honeymooners - Dead Beat Honeymooners    (Anthem '92)

When I heard lead cut and lead single Hard To Be Humble over the airwaves, I wasn't sure if it was new Keef or new Ron Wood. And much of the rest of this hyped Winnipeg debut bears out such dirty roots rock comparisons, dollopingly laid back, sparsely played and slow to wake. Sorry dudes, but I'm just plain bored with the whole schmooz, which combines corporate hard rock (very little, mind you), with heavy Mellencamp, Stones, and bending way down into the disgracefuls, Adams, the new Northern Pikes and Barney Bentall, Beer commercial rock at its most bloody awful. Immensely predictable boogie here, acoustic ballad there, traces of pedestrian Foghat . . . basically classic rock radio fodder, with great vocals and more or less exclusively sleepy, over-trampled rawk blueprints. Less than a third the IQ of The Black Crowes, and about half that of the Four Horsemen, more along the lines of the latter but stupider, duller, Canadianer, mediocre. Man, what is it about my nation's rock? Long live the Sons Of Freedom, anyways.

Rating                                                    3

## The Dead Boys - Young, Loud And Snotty   (Sire '77)
One of the first American punk Grails, **Young, Loud And Snotty** rocks chug-headed and chaotic, with a recording that is cheap yet perfectly roughshod for this sort of sonic gum wad; guitars way up front, drums sounding overwhelmed, a technique Roy Thomas Baker used on **Queen** and **Sheer Heart Attack** (not like it was planned here). Iggy-studied snarls and barks from frontman and Gilligan-lookalike Stiv (Stivin) Bators lead the charge through the ten rock-solid, mercilessly brutal drunkpunk documents that lie bleeding here like some sort of rustbelt sewer back-up. Probably the most purely committed of U.S. punkers (albeit somewhat slagged as Pistols rip-offs), The Dead Boys prowled the alleys as the dirtiest S.O.B.'s least concerned with shedding new light on world problems. A wasted and awe-inspiring furnace blast, featuring the most heroic of suicide missions *Sonic Reducer*, later covered by Overkill. Note: other bands to pay tribute with a Dead Boys cover: Green River (*Ain't Nothing To Do*), Supersuckers (*What Love Is*), Guns N' Roses (*Ain't It Fun*), and I'm sure there's more.

Rating                                                   10

## Dead Boys - We Have Come For Your Children
(Sire '78)
Felix Pappalardi (R.I.P.) produces this one, in the process remaking the band completely, **We Have Come For Your Children** being a fairly cohesive mix of tight crossover punk/metal and tight crossover punk/pop. Whereas the debut was gritty, distorted and awfully degenerate, this one seeks to entertain on a more melodic level, succeeding to some extent. Although it's all still fast guitars from start to finish, the pop embellishments are smoothing, soothing and catchy, aiming to please those beyond the bitter confines of punk, all walks of life benefiting from the added polish. As it turns out, **We Have Come For Your Children** (titled **Down To Kill** on the actual record, oddly enough) would become the second and last studio release from the Dead Boys, a damn shame, given the revelation of nefariously commercial tricks up their torn sleeves. Faves: serial killer saga *Son Of Sam* and spirited kick-off track *Third Generation Nation*. Ostrich face Stiv died years later, due to injuries incurred in a Paris car accident.

Rating                                                    8

## Deadguy - Fixation On A Coworker   (Victory/Cargo '96)
Fantabulous stuff, this Deadguy band, a bunch of New Jersey noise terrorists who wedge themselves like a cyst between artpunk like Fugazi and NoMeansNo, cranky, clanky industrial metal like Pitch Shifter, Godflesh and Fudge Tunnel and any number of drooling death metal nasties. So the thing's rough and tumble, while breaking new (arguably unmine-able) ground, stupid and oh so smart all at once. Other thing I have to mention here is the artwork, which is devilishly splendid, lots of cool graphics, typestyles, colours, a

trip in itself. Those shouty vocals might wear on you eventually, and the production is a bit loose, but the songs are a snobby, fruitful listen indeed, all those influences coalescing into something that might be akin to Helmet on crack.

Rating                                                    7

## Deadguy - Screamin' With The Deadguy Quintet
(Victory '97)
Three full-lengths into obliterating music as we know it, New Joisee's Deadguy are back with their most nightmarish statement ever, a five-track EP that answers the question: what happens when Killdozer, The Jesus Lizard and King Crimson all hit the stage simultaneously? Seriously, the last record could be construed as enjoyable in a tough love sort of way, but with this one, man, just stand back and watch 'em fry. The noise, the racket, and the god-forsaken thunder of it all is unforgivable. Dave, Pops, Crispy, Tom and Jim are crazy like a five-headed fox, carving sound sculptures that would not be out of place in a performance art gallery. So somehow the smarts show themselves, even if the band's terror-tall, hardcore crash metal hurts all over. Arm yourself with '96's **Fixation On A Coworker**, then approach '97's caustic contraption warily.

Rating                                                    6

## Dead On - Dead On   (SBK '89)
A riff-whipped variant on the Anthrax flank, **Dead On** flies double time yet controlled into doompunk crossover airspace; too extended, belaboured, complicated and monotoned, like a throbbing death metal hangover, pedal to the metal, art to the exits. As usual with this genre, the listener is inundated with too much too soon, a realization Metallica speaks of in relation to their own paths of pain. Some hearty guffaws lyrically, with rattled platitudes about young witches, being "widowed", and the plight of the matador; but all told, focus is too fragmented to really let fly with sustained power.

Rating                                                    5

## Dead Orchestra - Sounds Like Time Tastes
(Choke Hit '93)
These mid-America thrashers are gaining raves for their non-peggable whirlwind of influences, resulting in something thrashy, deathy and progressive, punked and kinda funny all at once. Chops are to the fore, as the band loops to Zappa-ville, weird flourishes everywhere, crushingly heavy but very much about creativity. Over-riding feel is one of a mad genius urbancore which doesn't take itself seriously. Refreshing, dirty and heavy. Self-released record #2 after an SPV debut called **Global Lobotomy**.

Rating                                                    7

## Deadringer - Electrocution Of The Heart   (Grudge '89)
Eminently collectible, **Electrocution Of The Heart** is a mid-star collaboration between Alice Cooper's Dennis Dunaway and Neal Smith, Ted Nugent's Charlie Huhn, Blue Öyster Cult's Joe Bouchard, and an axeman named Jay "Jesse" Johnson. Me being the raging Cult fan, key gems would be the Buck Dharma composition *Summa Cum Loud*, and the Al Bouchard/Deb Frost track *When You're In You're In*. But alas, both of these are pretty fromaged, as is the rest of the record, which in total sounds like stiff, hairspray metal, two power ballads included. Production is crisp, but the songs are all chest-beating neon rock, Huhn adding a suvvern slant to the thing, even if nothing can rescue these Quiet Riot meets Bon Jovi, meets uh, '80s Alice Cooper stinkers.

Rating                                                    4

**Deaf Dealer - Keeper Of The Flame** (Neat '86)

These Canadian boys dish out strong-arm metal like a heavy Maiden, unfortunately riddling the mayhem with the usual clichéd goth over-complexity, making this another slab of loud and overbearing sheet metal like countless American offerings throughout the mid-'80s. Improbable title: *On The Wings Of A Russian Foxbat*.
Rating                                                                 4

**Dealer - First Strike** (Ebony '86)

Like an authentic, proud underground version of Grim Reaper, Dealer take to the streets with rumbling train abandon, adding to its arsenal Grimmett-like vocalkill, while leaning more towards a blasted, down-the-middle form of power scour. Noisy and basic of instinct, but chaotic and difficult to penetrate, on many instances denying entrance to the scowling grounds.
Rating                                                                 7

**Dearly Beheaded - Temptation** (Music For Nations '96)

Hearing this minutes after the puzzling **Load** record from y'know-who, I can't help daydreaming that **Temptation** was really the new Hetfield and Revlon record, listening in glee to the oohs and aahs that might have ensued. For this bracing, faith-restoring debut from UK sensations Dearly Beheaded is an imposing cross between Metallica's black album and Machine Head's **Burn My Eyes**, Colin Richardson's electrogranite production (for Flynn & Co. applied to DB's thicker, slower, grind-tuned tunes to percolating perfection. These guys know metal, and know which cracks remain unfilled (namely as I say, positing a really heavy record Metallica might have made), inserting a fast one *We Are The Family* exactly at the point eyes would dart looking for one, then mixing various choking grooves for the record's balance, *Break My Bones* displaying expertly all of DB's many savvy new metal ideas. All the while, Alex Creamer's vocals court a clean but angered Bay Area presentation, with occasional inflections unto old Blaze Bayley. Only complaint: too many deep-dish, mid-to-slow constructs, this young band sticking too tight, constricted and conservative to their very good ideas.
Rating                                                                 9

**Death - Scream Bloody Gore** (Under One Flag/Combat '87)

Chuck Schuldiner's Death began life in Florida as Mantas, soon mutating and relocating to San Francisco, becoming this accomplished-for-the-time power trio, comprising Chuck plus two guys who will shortly get the boot, all three looking like little kids. But the debut record grabbed the band's hornet's nest of influences and ran with it, **Scream Bloody Gore** sounding like an enthusiastic amalgam of Slayer, Venom and Exciter, adequately recorded and quite fit for its fledgling, struggling origins, Schuldiner introducing a new level of convolution that will mark the beginnings of the next stage in extreme.
Rating                                                                 4

**Death - Leprosy** (Relativity/Combat '88)

Death are considered one of the unflagging progenitors of death metal, thrashing and blurring like the proverbial vacuum cleaner with drums on this, the band's second record, Chuck adopting a whole new line-up of quick-fingered trolls in Rick Rozz on second guitar, Bill Andrews on drums and Terry Butler on bass. For now, call me over and underwhelmed, this blight on the charred and sand-swept earth being a heaving, belching, skulking waste of time, unless you were seventeen, white and male to witness its unleashing in symbiotic temporal context. Translation: maybe I just don't get it.
Rating                                                                 4

**Death - Spiritual Healing** (Relativity/Combat '90)

With Rick Rozz out of the band, replaced by James Murphy (Obituary, Disincarnate, Cancer, Testament), Death deliver their last traditional (dated?), churning, riff-catalogued, frontier-agonizing monstrosity. Production has taken a leap forward, as have lyrics, which now address the usual societal gripes technical thrash usually handles with convincing aplomb, Death leaving behind the subject grist that gives them their name. The tone of this record is just too academic however, very grey and underground, Chuck still not projecting much emotion, creating worthy prototypes of a rapidly progressing genre, but still lacking in connection. This will come to pass. Note: A bizarre chapter in the Death saga occured when Chuck left the band just as they were set to conquer Europe backing Kreator. The band decided to carry on, enlisting Rotting Corpse guitarist Walter Thrashler, plus Devastation drummer Louie Carrisale for vocal chores. But this too would briefly flare, fizzle and come to pass, the band exploding, Chuck jumping in to pick up the pieces.
Rating                                                                 5

**Death - Human** (Relativity '91)

Following the previously discussed Euro-tour debacle, Chuck re-engineers his cursed albatross, enlisting two Cynic guys, drummer Sean Reinert and guitarist Paul Masvidal, also adding Steve Digiorgio from Sadus. The resulting record is Death's great vault forward, a short shocked minor masterpiece of exploratory death metal. But it is Reinert that steals the show here, putting on a super-human performance that is a whirlwind of percussive sonics, turning tales like *Secret Face* into jaw-dropped prog-feasts for those who can hack the volume. Still more of an academic exercise for other players than a gut-level emotional churn, **Human** nevertheless can thrive on this level without needing the extra kick, living well at the fringes of possibility, blowing minds of a more mathematical nature with ease. As Chuck says, "This is much more than a record to me; it is a statement, it is revenge."
Rating                                                                 7

**Death - Individual Thought Patterns** (Relativity '93)

New sinister critical mass is coming to the world of grindcore, Death appropriately being one of the trippiest explorers, having been in the dirty biz so long. Here Chuck and band (new drummer Gene Hoglan from Dark Angel and new guitarist Andy Laroque from King Diamond) truly frightens with its scarring of the metal terrain, building unyielding textures of a most demonic nature, a sad sonic commentary on the world indeed. **Individual Thought Patterns** is a mesmerizingly robotic display of death chops, often moving at such alien tempos that speed is not an issue. But before I get carried away, Death's sound is still a sickening, head-shredding experience that doesn't do a heck of a lot for me, still squatted so firmly in the annals of grindcore that its obvious skill levels are more a curiosity than a good time. But it's also one formidable opus, something to be studied, but by the initiated only, and under proper test conditions.
Rating                                                                 7

**Death - Symbolic** (Attic/Roadrunner '95)

A few personnel shuffles later, and Schuldiner is back with a further creative incantation far from the death metal he helped create. **Symbolic** is the band's most impressive and crossover-ish to date (not to mention most exquisitely mixed), combining an amphetamine but conventional metal blur circa Rage, Coroner, At The Gates and maybe even Helloween with the technical speed of unheavenly American heathens, mostly from San Fran or original homeroost Florida. Vocals still tend towards semi-expressive like Obituary, an agonized lizard-like cry of pain, but discernable and

versatile all the same, while the band razor-sharply tears through Mensa-based constructs with traces of doomy, Germanic melody and heaps 'o progressive might (see the mostly mid-speed *Without Judgement* and power ballad (!) *Crystal Mountain*). Will grow on you like a flesh-eating bacteria, or failing that, like the band's cheesy logo that will not die.
Rating 8

## Death Angel - The Ultra-Violence (Enigma '87)
A proud and spirited debut in a decidedly fast but thrashy vein, **The Ultra-Violence** delivers metal to new levels of volatility, this young band of leatherheads plagued with rifferama but cranking a flame-throwing calling card nonetheless; posse pride and solid street smarts to the fore. At this point, a bandwagon band still looking for its wings, however not without a magical, iron-pumping, kill-with-power mission. An ill-fitted bridge between the Bay sound and a frashier UK frash.
Rating 6

## Death Angel - Frolic Through The Park (Enigma '88)
The second band after Metallica to re-wire the rules of thrash, Death Angel loaded up their truck with integrity and miles of personality. Good but not remarkable material is wrenched and elevated from **Frolic's** grooves, through an innovative recording which lends the drums a furious frenetic overflow, sort of distorting the crash cymbals, cymbals which are used often as rides. Similar material to Metallica of old, but played and recorded with a hurried, violent, punk-infested feel that threatens to shatter its axis. My only complaint is the inclusion of too many fast shockers, not enough pocket constructs such as the brilliant, conquering *Bored*, which features innovative dynamics and soon-to-be-hip funk, brewing beneath a purely metallized sort of mayhem. CD reissue contains a naive but ambitious speed rocker called *Devil's Metal*. Beware!
Rating 8

## Death Angel - Fall From Grace (Enigma '90)
Deceptively packaged like a new studio record (non-live-ish title, lavish print painting), **Fall From Grace** commemorates a stoked '88 gig in Amsterdam, showcasing six from the band's **Frolic** stress test, with a few oldies like mosh machine *Mistress Of Pain* and awesome grinder *Voracious Souls*. Man these guys have chops.
Rating 7

## Death Angel - Act III (Geffen '90)
From the flood of techno-thrash bands that, after Metallica, descended beer-in-claw from the watchtowers, Death Angel is the first example of one that had progressed beyond imitation into a devastating emotional package in its own right, planting the seeds for the likes of Metal Church, Megadeth and Anthrax in overtaking the masters who choose sloth in Vancouver over progress in Purgatory. Throughout **Act III** there exists an undertone of despair that drags the record into the muck so often spread over Sabbath, and strangely enough, Suicidal Tendencies. Dealing mostly (though not often literally) with psychological trauma, Death Angel weave tales of denseness that span speed, techno, ultra-heavy, punk nihilism, innovative acoustic arrangements, only brief and unsuccessful smatterings of funkiness, and thankfully, never thrash. And the whole thing hangs together under an opaque black cloud due to the all-pervasive chunky recording that resembles blocks of granite in collision. An increasingly confident, slower, more fleshed-out album that pits Death Angel against the taunting and tormenting hellhounds of depression.
Rating 9

## Death Mask - Split The Atom (Killerwatt '86)
Exciter-like ultra-heavy with a nod to early '80s traditions and a lack thereof. Pretty basic, with vocals only dogs can hear, **Split The Atom** rocks with commendable conviction, while choosing to blast mercilessly on every last track, without the songcraft to pull off its chosen mid-to-fast power surge. How much of my indifference is chalked up to overload of this genre I'll never tell.
Rating 4

## Deathrow - Raging Steel (Noise '87)
German bloshcore with more in common with old Slayer and maybe Destruction than actual thrash. Speedy as all get out, wisely stopping just short of double time, and acceptably professional in its extreme aggression, **Raging Steel** represents to me, the shore where once traversed, becomes ridiculous noise, although as with most far-gone speed metal, I find even this too stuck in a number of ruts, flogging more than a few dead horses into dog food and glue.
Rating 4

## Deceased - The Blueprints For Madness (Relapse '95)
King Fowley and his rarified Virginia thrash machine Deceased have been around for over ten years, making demos, then finally **Luck Of The Corpse** in '90 (released in '92; 15,000 happy customers) and **The Thirteen Frightened Souls** EP in '93. So now we get **The Blueprints For Madness** which is a pretty cool piece of almost-white noise, Deceased going for a certain raw churn, with unexpected, slightly doomy twists and turns. It's still pretty extreme and unlistenable for the uninitiated. But if the music doesn't float your boat, the lyrics might, Fowley writing way above average, harrowing horror, and lots of it. Apocalyptic thrash with hints of Trouble's first.
Rating 6

## Deconstruction - Deconstruction (American '94)
Place on dusty pedestal with NIN's **The Downward Spiral**, both records belaboured, opaque, frustrating, wickedly clever, but arguably difficult beyond enjoyment. But **Deconstruction** (a one-off featuring Jane's Addiction's Eric Avery and Dave Navarro, the latter since departed for the Chili Peppers), achieves said feat with conventional instrumentation, texturizing a cool liquid slab approximating your most stand-offish 'n' slippery Jane's Addiction nightmare in nuclear fusion with Bauhaus, Julian Cope, Fripp and all things mid '70s to mid '80s psycho-delic. Lyrically it's a near infinite pageant of succinct and vivid images, a thread that overpowers the paralyzed five-fold hybrids of each arresting but uninviting track. Puts Pornos For Pyros to shame, Deconstruction strapped to a jumbo work ethic rocket Perry Farrell can't even locate with high powered binoculars. But still, demands more attention than most folks care to expend.
Rating 8

## Decoryah - Wisdom Floats (Metal Blade '95)
You may have heard funereal rumblings about a band of high school-age Finlanders creating a retro prog rock behemoth of doom, taking Tiamat's novel **Wildhoney** further unto Floyd. Well, it's arrived and yep, it's a permafrost chunk of heady **Meddle**, death-chilled via My Dying Bride moreso than relative happy meals like Cathedral or Paradise Lost. Lots of mournful howling, slowcreep dirgeable desperation . . . Hell, this could be sleepy-time tunes for Glen Benton! Or Glenn Danzig's Blacker Aria Part Too Sad. But seriously, this is damn near a new kind of music; new, slow as old age, and distressingly numbing. Polar bong rock for the expanding mindhead.
Rating 6

## Decoryah - Fall-Dark Winters (Metal Blade '96)

Maybe contrary to popular opinion, I didn't think the production was all that cruddy on the debut, or all that vastly improved here, both sporting a distracting over-abundance of treble and layers made from trebly stuff. Yes, these Finnish lads were young in '94, which doesn't make them that much older and wiser now, Decoryah still making that same plush journey to progressive death realms, death by ludicrously sub-zero Scandinavian tone if not sonics. I don't know, it was a novelty first time around but now it's getting a little ghoulish foolish, and increasingly miserable (which is the way Decoryah wishes you to feel), those female vocals and coffin-reclined keyboards beginning to sound merely quaint below Jukka Vuorinen's stoned and nocturnal nasal drift. Epic, slow but clattered full of stuff to the point of samey track by track. No longer interested.

Rating 6

## Ded Engine - Hot Shot (Black Dragon '85)

Capable American combat merchants with a convincing arsenal of seedy street metal and licks stolen from mid-years Priest. Seems to me I remember Ded Engine as the subject of a T.V. special interest story on the life of a hapless rock combo. Anyways, this record kills, chugging like a huge chrome freight train, buzzing on cheap alcohol, no prospects for advancement, yet saddled with an unquenchable desire to win the decibel war, an attitude that is this band's particular ace. An obvious love for the trappings of the metal life, Ded Engine could have gone far on fumes alone.

Rating 6

## Dedringer - Direct Line (Dindisc '81)

Had all-or-nothing expectations for this early Brit rocker that for one reason or another, escaped our grasp in the heady days of the steel revolt. No overt loss however, as Dedringer turned out to be an anemic rock machine, sorta like Rage (U.K.) or heavy Bad Company and now Thunder; simple-minded with simple concerns; more like pumped-up generalist rock than any sort of assimilator of newly dusted metal precepts. Ineffectual and common with its botched use of occasionally fine blues riffs, Direct Line ends life as a memorial to non-threatening pub rock, absorbing all the non-achieving affectations of those who slogged the wee stages before them. But call me a sucker for punishment, or a sympathizer for the underdog, I like it.

Rating 6

## Dedringer - Second Arising (Neat '83)

Dedringer seem more determined to bang thy head second time around, conjuring images of bigger beat merchants like AC/DC, Quiet Riot and Dokken, while remaining dogged by their amateur grassroots grit which is more a workable accessory this time around, given the new muscle. And the bluesy straight r'n'r influences are still erratically embedded, making this another "old time" record, firmly dated, unaware and garagey. Just a fun, low-brow record that's smooth and easy to play over and over again.

Rating 7

## Deep Purple - Book Of Taliesyn (Tetragrammaton '69)

Garbage. Psychedelic slop. Basically a no-clue contingent (previously and aptly called The Roundabouts), presently known as Deep Purple Mark I, playing exactly what was expected of them at the time, including the parading of numerous covers in search of a hit single for the suits back at the label. For the record, the band had already spawned another couple o' similar brown trouts, Shades Of Deep Purple (featuring hapless hippy hit Hush) in '68, and Deep Purple in '69, both of which I don't remotely count as Purple re-

cords, both of which reviewing would be a waste of space. What a joke, all three art-rocking along with Age Of Aquarius annoyance in demonstration of a trendoid band searching for its forté, which was to be defiantly pounced all over come In Rock, possibly the single most important record in metal. I kinda cheat by putting this in here, being totally non-metal, but I figure someone's gotta steer you clear from these pre-In Rock abortions. Thankfully, the end of the line for Rod Evans and Nicky Simper, as the gears in Blackmore's head start turning full-burn.

Rating 0

## Deep Purple - The Royal Philharmonic Orchestra Conducted By Malcolm Arnold (Harvest '70)

In which the unspeakable happens: the classical dudes play, then the psychedelic dudes play, and then the long-haired hippy sings, most everybody attending against their will, except Jon Lord who wrote it, and Malcolm Arnold who showed some interest in the possibilities. Of course it's horrible, not due to the concept, but due to the fact that Purple was the wrong band to do it, or at most the right band to do it at the wrong time. Mercyful Fate, with the King dressed to the 666's, now that would be a night at the opera.

Rating 0

## Deep Purple - In Rock (Warner Bros. '70)

In Rock was the central of three LPs instrumental in the invention of heavy metal, wrought twisted and screaming at the hands of the legendary but volatile Deep Purple Mark II, Ian Gillan, Ritchie Blackmore, Roger Glover, Jon Lord and Ian Paice. Forget Hendrix, Cream, early Zeppelin, Blue Cheer, The Who, MC5 or The Stooges. Not a real metal album among the lot, all making records which ranged (and tightly so) from loud, noisy, sloppy blues through loud, noisy, sloppy psychedelia, all sounding excruciatingly ancient, rudimentary and depressing, with not an ounce of discipline or useful metal invention anywhere. Deep Purple's In Rock, along with Sabbath's Paranoid and Heep's Uriah Heep, all in 1970, outright and triple-handedly invented Heavy Metal. In Rock may be the flashiest, freshest, and most sophisticated of the three, brimming with classic, scientific, and entirely blinding shafts of galloping guitar insight, including Hard Lovin' Man, possibly the first "staccato" chugger ever plus Bloodsucker and Speed King, dense mechanical clusters which could easily have been written for today's sophisticated punter. Indeed Child In Time, a lengthy, mellow journey with scarcely a pulse, is the only track that doesn't quite fit the bill on this otherwise brilliant opus, a record as high and mighty as its adapted Mt. Rushmore cover. Production: mid-rangy but forgivable and listenable. It's sort of strange and mildly tragic, but this legendary, 26-year-old monolith actually stood as the most focused Purple product until Perfect Strangers 14 long, tiring years later, although a good dozen individual interim tracks became crucial in shaping where metal would go in the years to come. The loftiest icebreaker in the creation of the world's sweetest sound, heavy metal.

Rating 10

## Deep Purple - Fireball (Warner Bros. '71)

Immediately after inventing and establishing a genre, Purple starts experimenting, Fireball being a proud and singular, artistic record, incorporating a number of different styles; metal, blues, psychedelia, and hillbilly, although out of seven tracks, five rock at least to some extent, lending credence to the fact that glorious walls of distortion are the foremost construct of the day. The heart-stopping, tech-metal title track and No One Came (about Gillan's fears of performing to empty halls) breathe heady fumes as metal classics demonstrating a new maturity and willingness to lean toward more

complex, almost progressive song structures, while the burly but ultimately dull *Strange Kind Of Woman* gives the band a well-deserved hit. **Fireball** establishes the Purple sound as it would exist in its Mark II heyday, while simultaneously marking the germination of an enigmatic integrity about the band similar to that of chief rivals Led Zeppelin. A riveting vintage showcase, and importantly, Ian Gillan's favourite Purple record.
Rating 9

## Deep Purple - Purple Passages (Warner Bros. '72)
How painful it is, indeed, this double disc compilation from the excruciating trio of thick black platters that comprised the total and utterly flaccid output of Mark I Purple. Useful liner notes, but that's about it.
Rating 0

## Deep Purple - Machine Head (Warner Bros. '72)
An undisputed metal classic, **Machine Head** is probably the most famous LP of Purple's roller-coaster catalogue, containing headbangin' hall of famers *Smoke On The Water* (riff of all riffs), *Highway Star* (torrid street rocker), *Lazy* (lazy), and *Space Truckin'* (novelty rocker with choice Paice embroidery). **Machine Head** as a whole is surprisingly clever, innovative metal studded with liberal use of Lord's trademark keyboards, which benefit from a mix that is a rich cathedral fusion of the unique and diverse sounds in the band; one of Martin Birch's early triumphs at the soundboard, royal pageantry at its classical best. Faves include the dark and mysterious *Pictures Of Home*, the aforementioned *Space Truckin'* and *Highway Star*, one of the most kickin' sustained grooves in metal. The rest: cool, convoluted funkster *Maybe I'm A Leo*, and the unremarkable *Never Before*, which bombed as a single. Note: For a wild version of *Smoke On The Water* check out the blistering "all-star jam" in aid of the Armenians, featuring truly wicked solos by Blackmore, Tony Iommi, Brian May and David Gilmour, plus vocal contributions from Gillan, Paul Rodgers and Bruce Dickinson, who steals the show.
Rating 9

## Deep Purple - Made In Japan (Warner Bros. '73)
If seven wandering hippy jams spread over four sides, including *Child In Time*, *Strange Kind Of Woman*, *Lazy*, and *The Mule* is your idea of a rock'n'roll show, pixie-dance on back to the '60s, man. Tokyo, Osaka, and herculean alcohol consumption '72.
Rating 3

## Deep Purple - Who Do We Think We Are!
(Warner Bros. '73)
Deep Purple's fourth non-bogus record perpetuates the philosophical underpinnings of the previous three by experimenting rhythmically and texturally under the broad banner of what was then heavy metal. However, **Who Do We Think We Are!** is still the least focused of the lot, and the weakest in terms of song quality, in effect, least possessive of reason to be. *Smooth Dancer* however (containing the odd Gillan jab at Blackmore), is one of the band's most sustained jet turbines, and *Mary Long* swaggers with wall-of-sound purpose, while much of the rest sounds loose and schizophrenic. **Who Do We Think We Are!** becomes the lost Purple disk, because aside from the pretty lame *Woman From Tokyo*, its tunes don't find their way onto the airwaves all too often. Interesting but arcane and opaque. Note: Gillan himself parallels this one with **House Of Blue Light** as records somewhat sabotaged by mounting personal disputes within the band.
Rating 8

## Deep Purple - Burn (Warner Bros. '74)
Glenn Hughes (offered huge stacks of cash) and a young, inexperienced David Coverdale take over on

vocals (bitterly competing vocals, I might add), and the change is drastically transforming, while not a complete disaster. No surprise, **Burn** is quite experimental stylistically, increasingly blues- and funk-based, while glued with a customary, all-pervading guitar ethic, if not heavy metal thread. And spirited drumming from the ever-skillful Ian Paice whips brilliant Purple romps such as *Burn* and *Lay Down, Stay Down* into huge, caustic frenzies, the proverbial beehive of activity. Unfortunately though, Ian Gillan's voice is so much a part of the Purple sound, **Burn** lacks the soul and identity of previous efforts; like the party is over and there's just a few guys left to mind the store—kind of against their will, steered by the whims of kaiser Blackmore. Over five million pancakes sold. My fondest childhood memory of this album goes back to Grade 6 when the class had to break into groups and come up with dance numbers for the whole school. While a few of us were trying to pull the chicks by doing some insane French folk dance-type thing, Fiver and Demmer donned war-paint and ran around the gym strafing the crowd with toy machine gun fire, **Burn**'s title track raging full-bore from the school "hi-fi", much to the confusion of our teachers and the rest of the school.
Rating 7

## Deep Purple - Stormbringer (Warner Bros. '74)
A bewildering stack of stinkers, **Stormbringer** features two canyon-traversing rockers in *Stormbringer* and *Lady Double Dealer*, while the rest grasps for some obscure bluesy quality that just falls flat on its face, sorta like latter-day (but pre-hiatus) Bad Company, the band diddling around thinking they're new jazzy grown-ups or somethin'. Definitely some soul-searching and personality conflicts going on with this one. I never play it, but awesome cover art nevertheless.
Rating 5

## Deep Purple - 24 Carat Purple (Warner Bros. '75)
Another butt-ugly brown record cover wraps this hits set which is almost dead identical to '80's **Deepest Purple**, in its standard run through of Mark II's finest doppel-clangers.
Rating 6

## Deep Purple - Come Taste The Band (Warner Bros. '75)
Tommy Bolin (R.I.P.) replaces Blackmore on this one, conspiring with Coverdale to pump some new life into the old machine. **Come Taste The Band** is loud, funky, bluesy, heavy and most importantly, invites us all to the party down to a bracing batch of sturdy songs. Most of this is where early Whitesnake *should* have taken us; celebratory and sassy, to-the-point within the framework of economic structures. Highlights include the rousing boogie metal of lead cut *Comin' Home* (kinda like Aerosmith's *No Surprize*), funky chopster *Gettin' Tighter*, featuring soulful Glenn Hughes vocals, and the Sab crunch of *Love Child*. My only complaint is that **Come Taste The Band** unfortunately includes a few examples of what early Whitesnake *did* sound like.
Rating 8

## Deep Purple - Made In Europe (Warner Bros. '76)
A little better on the cover art this time around, as the boys try to squeeze some blood from an exploding juggernaut, heaving their bloated loads through Europe circa '75, documenting Mark III highs, appropriately limiting the panorama to five cuts. Basically Coverdale exercising his lungs for the future.
Rating 5

## Deep Purple - Deepest Purple (Warner Bros. '80)
One heeping, solid, and lengthy greatest hits package highlighting the bountiful Mark II years, with the wise inclusion of screamin' Mark III classics *Burn* and

*Stormbringer*. Useful rarities: HeepSab sod gobbler *Black Night* and non-LP blues rocker *Demon's Eye*.
Rating 7

## Deep Purple - Perfect Strangers (Polygram '84)

Deep Purple's reunion album gracefully surpassed the hype surrounding this fragile gathering of men who after years together, still seem to be perfect strangers. **Perfect Strangers** is the work of a band that has never entered into parody of itself and as a result, is unlike any previous effort, its only nods to the '70s being its mid-pace swagger and concentration on song-craft rather than technical display. Five out of eight tunes seriously rock, Ritchie riffing and slashing all over the place, weaving textures that betray a wealth of musical knowledge beyond modern music, deep into the classics. If any band can be deemed the royal family of metal, Deep Purple would be that band, **Perfect Strangers** cruising loud and proud yet possessing the upper society weight of history that establishes Purple as the reference point of a genre in metal without categorization. Comeback classics: the silky smooth *Knocking At Your Back Door*, which swirls and climaxes towards one of the most memorable choruses in years, and the *Kashmir*-ic title track, carried by one of Gillan's trademark confusion lyrics, and an exotic riff recalling Blackmore and Dio at their most synergistic. Filler: naff ballad *Wasted Sunsets* and the almost ordinary *Mean Streak*. A fine tapestry worthy of the most dramatic room in the palace.
Rating 10

## Deep Purple - The Anthology (EMI '85)

It is on purpose that I've offered only brief commentary on Purple's various hits packages, for my usual reasoning that the officially sanctioned studio LP is the only place to view the art as the artist intended it to be viewed. This double import is of fan interest however, due to the inclusion of some previously unreleased tapes from the vault. The run down: of the four or five cuts spanning Mark I through Mark III, absolutely nothing metallic and fully-grown, although *Freedom* rides a nice ancient funk, while *When A Blind Man Cries* scores minor victory as an emotional blues. Otherwise, a bust, demonstrating that the vaults must be a pretty lonely place.
Rating 3

## Deep Purple - House Of Blue Light (Polygram '87)

A further refinement of **Perfect Strangers'** meticulous approach, yet with a closer eye to detail and keyboard-guitar interplay, **House Of Blue Light** is once again, age and wisdom combining for quiet class. Gillan's lyrics continue to stumble off the tongue with that awkward, illogical feel as if English was the man's wily adversary. It's either bad poetry or a calculated naive code, and I like to think the latter. Anyways, the man has a colourful sense of humour, refusing to say too much too clearly, which makes these legends likeable guys. Featuring nothing as effortlessly epic as *Perfect Strangers*, *A Gypsy's Kiss*, or *Knocking At Your Back Door*, **House Of Blue Light** nevertheless triumphs through its over-riding heaven-like texture, a marvel of magnificent workmanship appreciable as a brilliant whole rather than the sum of its parts. Still quite edgy while more hi-tech and stand-offish, **House Of Blue Light** is a dazzling feast of sights and sounds steered home by quite possibly the most capable helmsmen in the business. And again, Blackmore as was **Perfect Strangers**. Recorded in my beloved Stowe, Vermont, as was **Perfect Strangers**.
Rating 10

## Deep Purple - Nobody's Perfect (Polygram '88)

This pointless double live disc reveals one gracious point about rock's most elegant architects, the fact that

Gillan and the boys have a solid sense of priority, not taking themselves too seriously, hamming it up for the cameras as it were. Amongst the looseness however, we get some acceptably alternate renditions of both new and old material. It's too bad though that the romp through history wasn't a bit more creative (indeed the very evaluation of Ian Gillan himself). With so many classic unsung fables of yore to their credit such as *Speed King*, *No One Came*, *Fireball*, *Smooth Dancer*, and even *Comin' Home* and *Gettin' Tighter* just to name a few, do we really need to sit still for another *Highway Star*, *Lazy*, *Space Truckin'*, *Woman From Tokayo*, and *Child In Time*? Please, stop the madness.
Rating 5

## Deep Purple - Slaves And Masters (RCA '90)

Alas, Ian Gillan is gone (fortunately to make more Gillan albums) and enter Joe Lynn Turner, Rainboid, belladonna, and American. Worst facet of Turner's acquisition is the tacit self-doubt from a band admitting that second-string royalty is an acceptable addition to the Purple ranks, which of course isn't the case as far as the generally tradition-steeped fans are concerned. No matter how stellar the outcome may be, the gravity of the project is diminished somewhat, as was the case when Dio replaced Ozzy in Sabbath. Already a big disappointment but hey! Who knows? Well, what we find is that a class act like Deep Purple can't be destroyed, but it can be slightly damaged. **Slaves And Masters** does not rock, and it would be stretching it to say that more than four of nine tracks feature Ritchie bending his lusty Strat around them in earnest. Turner does a decent job even if his Paul Rodgers/Lou Gramm stylings are still noticeably derivative. But the major problem is the songwriting, lyrics riddled with standard HM clichés, Jon Lord carrying too much of the tune, leaving Ritchie to solo, add colour commentary, yet rarely riff like the magnificent ring leader of past cranks. And it *does* sound a bit like a latter-day Rainbow album; timidly armed, with its fanatical element of understated, elusive craft. However I really do like a good half of the record, and really, there are few obvious dogs. All in all, one of the better dinosaur LPs of the '90s thus far, but Joe Lynn Turner (really Ritchie's buddy more than anything) always seems to turn his co-workers gun-shy. Instant classic: *King Of Dreams*. Drivel: *Fortuneteller*.
Rating 8

## Deep Purple - The Battle Rages On . . . (BMG '93)

Fasten your seatbelts and prepare to encounter rock that resides levels above your pathetic station in life. For Deep Purple, unsung possessors of great tradition, formidable rock legends, return heads high and deadly serious despite flagging commercial fortunes which caused them to cancel their pre-release summer '93 tour. Only true professionals could keep the creativity so brightly aflame as we witness here, **The Battle Rages On . . .** so adept, subtle and astonishingly textured, it ranks with the best records from the band's long chequered career, three of which in my opinion are reunion era works. I'm ecstatic that Ian Gillan is back cementing the classic Mark II line-up, injecting studied and regal Purple arrangements with his swooping vocal signatures and fuzzy, irony-laden lyrical logic. And Blackmore wrenches delicately an elegant array of sounds from his traveled and travailed weaponry, dovetailing nicely with the increased quantities and qualities from Jon Lord's hungrier electric ivories. **The Battle Rages On . . .** would have to rank as the least playful from Purple; expansive, substantive, layered and surprisingly heavy in Purple's unique manner, a grand style that distracts attention from such base concerns, indeed the intro chords and chorus of *Time To Kill* and the barsy bluesy *Ramshackle Man* being the only less than chivalrous sounds on the table. No

Joe Lynn Turners here. One pictures a curmudgeonly band, defiantly distancing itself from present psycho shock rockers and their furious race into the future, a band trying to build gleaming machines using the vast vocabulary of metal's fertile past. And through **The Battle Rages On . . .**, revenge is sweet, the collection of vibes everlasting, emanating pride in craftsmanship. Sure it's infinite re-gyring through the band's recorded sights and sounds, but with a body of work so complex and divergent, Deep Purple can never be accused of re-hash. This is the glow of a distinct band experience, artists building new sculptures with a five-way personal palette, layering elements echoing a history that is worthy of re-reading. Appreciation will be passionate and educated, at least from the band's present fanbase, however diminished it may be.

Rating                                                                  8

## Deep Purple - Come Hell Or High Water    (BMG '94)

With the band once again in tatters (Blackmore is already gone as per this record's liner notes, first replaced by Joe Satriani then Steve Morse; Gillan leaves shortly thereafter, then returning), BMG pump out this live feast, essentially the band's best of a shabby live catalogue. Sporting a stellar, crystal-clear mix (with maybe too much Jon Lord), **Come Hell Or High Water**, recorded in Germany and Birmingham late in '93, benefits from a fairly imaginative track listing: *Black Night*, *Anyone's Daughter* (!), *Perfect Strangers*, two of the better **Battle**-era tunes in *Anya* and *Twist In The Tail*, plus the raging *Speed King*. Rounding out are the predictable staples (ho-hum): *Highway Star*, *Smoke On The Water* and *Child In Time*. Package-wise, there's lots of photos and good, if somewhat too effusive liner notes, helping make this one probably the most solid Purple live romp all 'round. Sidenote: got to hear a tape of the brief Satriani era. The man played more "middle-eastern" than Ritchie, proving Joe's weak self-identity. Pretty funny stuff. Face it, Blackmore's the master. Look no further than the exotic soloing artistry on the twelve minute version of *Anya* right here.

Rating                                                                  8

## Deep Purple - In Concert    (King Biscuit Flower Hour '95)

Briefly, the King Biscuit Flower Hour was a nationally syndicated radio show that taped and broadcast tons of incredible bands over the years. Tapes languished and finally, here we have it, in late '95, the first wave of releases (bonus: excellent liner notes), the most important to the story of metal being this one and Black Sabbath's. **In Concert** is quite the Purple curiosity, presenting the last rendition of the band personality clashing their way through the stadiums of the world. Tommy Bolin is acceptable if not amazing, D. Coverdale and G. Hughes trade out-of-tune vocals like there was no tomorrow, Coverdale particularly out-of-tune, scat-master Hughes particularly out-of-control, especially on *This Time Around*, a tribute to his vocal mentor Stevie Wonder. Paice is in curiously bashing form, dressing up songs more than usual, often at the expense of the groove. Of course it wouldn't be the same without everybody soloing their little booties off, probably half this two CD package dedicated to noodling. Tunes: the usual chestnuts of wisdom about burning hotels and fast cars, plus **Come Taste The Band** tracks like *Lady Luck*, *Gettin' Tighter*, *Love Child* and the aforementioned *This Time Around*. Additionally, we get two takes on soft loungester *Georgia On My Mind*, where we all get to hear why Hughes is a love/hate proposition, and old bluester *I'm Going Down*, which gets a muscle-beach *Stormbringer*-type arrangement (a tune that is also included here). So if Deep Purple live records float your boat, this is a worthy addition to the cause, adding and seldom repeating what has come before.

Rating                                                                  7

## Deep Purple - Purpendicular    (Prominent/CMC/BMG '96)

Man, it's so inspiring to hear such crowning creativity by a band so, to put it delicately, long in the tooth, Deep Purple following up their classy but a tad tired **The Battle Rages On . . .** with this bouncy, playful but unprecedentedly intelligent pageant of sounds. Interesting twist in the tale with Blackmore out, the king of weaves replaced by Dixie Dregs virtuoso Steve Morse, who chooses wisely a middle path here, not turning castle-mad, but not really being Steve Morse either, the unexpected avalanche of great songs, arrangements, lyrics, and performances from all, especially Jon Lord and Ian Gillan, making up for a new arguably non-Purpled kinda guy in the all-important axe chair. Everything pleases here, only middle rockers like *Vavoom: Ted The Mechanic* and *Somebody Stole My Guitar* descending from God-like into merely highly talented. But the most amazing pieces are mellow ones, the mystery of *Loosen My Strings* ebbing toward the charming magnetism of *Sometimes I Feel Like Screaming* (in a world of justice, that chorus would send this record multi-platinum), which eventually flows into one of the band's shining masterwerks *A Touch Away*, which combines heady, heavenly complex melodies with a concise, forceful but resigned and mature lyric about mortality. Production values are lush but muscular, Lord's very gothic keyboards on full thrust, Paice's percussion full spectrum and precisely documented, indeed the whole thing being a masterpiece of sonic separation towards a common, high performance goal. In my opinion, **Purpendicular** ranks with **Perfect Strangers**, **House Of Blue Light** and **Machine Head** as one of the band's very best records. Only this band and Aerosmith have so much left to give. Now let's hope somebody buys the damn thing. New cover art might help.

Rating                                                                 10

## Deep Throat - The Devil In Miss Jones    (Ohrwurm '82)

German porn rock that ain't no S.A.D.O. that's for sure, Deep Throat is substandard, brutish metallic fare, often speedy with double bass drum patterns (the definition of OTT ten years back), while occasionally wicked, slithering and meaty as on *Snake* and the hilarious *Dirty Party*. Weakly recorded and kinda snotty, this is more an unclean rivetheaded joke, yet fairly two-fisted for its age. Maybe Belgium's Killer crossed with the pugnacious Tank, but more pork-brained and clueless like the former.

Rating                                                                  4

## Def Leppard - On Through The Night    (PolyGram '80)

These guys were destined for fame, sounding like stadium rockers right outta the gates (not counting the useless **Rocks Off** EP), and getting adequate airplay and media buzz-dom for their efforts. The Leps' premiere was one of the most polished and savvy of the NWOBHM brigade, descending from really out of nowhere with the class and skill of the old guard firmly in grasp, even out-stripping Maiden in its evocation of the sense of British high-mindedness earned by acts like Lizzy and UFO. **On Through The Night** is blessed with a good recording (more the work of focus than good luck), universal rock'n'roll anthems, and a uniform heaviness which courted the American way with just the right amount of self-promotion. All in all, the record was a welcome breath of fresh air, in an atmosphere both sides of the Atlantic that was too often goth, thrash, imitative, or simply unskilled. Unfortunately, Def Leppard would turn out to be one of the most pathetic sell-outs in the history of the world Part I.

Rating                                                                  8

## Def Leppard - High'n'Dry (PolyGram '81)

In which the Leps continue to demonstrate their knack for catchy tunes that rage like the English hot shots that they are, primed for the road, beach and bonfire alike. **High 'n' Dry** began to reveal a penchant for space and dynamics along with a fondness for AC/DC percussive patterns amidst an ever-clarifying anthemic disposition that was simultaneously first class and so adolescent. Great sturdy riffs, however, and heeping doses of over-achieving drama help put killer croozers like the swooping *Let It Go* and speedster *No No No* on my teen playlist for months. Working class dogs on a mission to better themselves, and there's nothing wrong with that.

Rating     8

## Def Leppard - Pyromania (PolyGram '83)

Superstardom arrives, and so begins an unstoppable physical and creative degeneration. Musically, **Pyromania** is a direct evolution from its stirring predecessor, however Mutt Lange's much bally-hooed production is sabotaged (in my opinion) by a disheartening over-electrolysis of the drum sound, and an unwarranted, un-rock'n'roll, painstaking approach to detail that strips what is actually a fairly heavy album of its sweat and grit. Some more than acceptable weekend rock here, and an emphasis again on big beat and mega-huge atmosphere, while Elliott's vocals sound strained and distantly mixed as if drowning by design. Harmonies are mechanical and ultra-layered (I think the appropriate word is PHONY), and the overall sound is just too calculated and larger than life to rock, let alone breathe. Of course, somewhere around ten million fans might disagree (the record was officially seven times platinum by '88), but to me this marked the beginning of the odious decline to the abysmal muzak wretch that is **Hysteria**. However, no argument with glorious explosions like *Stagefright* and *Die Hard The Hunter*.

Rating     7

## Def Leppard - Hysteria (PolyGram '87)

Light years away from the days when the Leps were a struggling Thin Lizzy cover band backing up the likes of Pet Hate, **Hysteria**'s inane cover art painfully says it all: high tech, tasteless and devoid of all life whatsoever. **Hysteria** sucks righteously. This is by far the most pointless mountain of misused technology I've ever had arrive dismantled and disoriented at my expectant ears. It's a tragedy that such a capable band with such heart eons back can be so efficiently bombarded with cash waves that they can be fooled into believing success equals selling records. Def Leppard has soundly drooled themselves into wholesale loss of rock'n'roll humanity. Even Elliott's vocals, probably the last vestige that hasn't completely been swallowed by robots, sound like some sort of dry-wheezing mechanical lung wired to the man's deathbed, and when the spoken word portion of our show lapses into harmonies (usually spewing complete nonsense), well, it just sounds like a goddam synth, pure and simple. **Hysteria** is a major assault to anyone's intelligence. I mean just check out the crap that passes for lyrics. Twenty minutes thought, tops. The Leps manage to pull the utmost artistically contemptuous move afforded them in recording this sorry disaster. An offensive kick in the head sent straight from the rock'n'roll bored room. Oh, and ten times platinum in the space of two short years.

Rating     0

## Def Leppard - Adrenalize (PolyGram '92)

A heaping pile of chemical and bacterial hospital smells, Def Leppard's latest affront to all that walks, defecates, and pays the bills causes personal internal illness heretofore unidentified by modern science. **Adrenalize**

trudges on towards the same brain-dead stack of sorry robot parts sent corroding down our gullets with the advent of **Pyromania** nine long years back. No shit, **Adrenalize** is virtually indistinguishable from the latest Bryan Adams idiotbox. In fact it's probably even more greatly shameful, as null and void a commercial success as Bryan's vacant lyrical gaze, and actually less rock-oriented. So much technological crap has been heaped up around the feeblest of rock songs here, that I just want to cry at the systematic purging of anything vital that has taken place over this band's career. Not a riff on the whole vile, stinking mess, not a word that couldn't have come dribbling out of a ten year old, and not a stitch of the human to be found, **Adrenalize** is so dumfoundingly progressed down a synthetic, polyvinyl path I could never imagine more plundered after **Hysteria**, I'm truly aghast that Joe Elliott can even recognize himself in his mirror in the morning. Blubbering casebook ballads, rendered frozen and inanely lifeless propped against the same funk chunk crappola heard a zillion times before rolls chafed and wheezing against the occasional guitar pattern (or is it synth, Hell who knows anymore) and . . . man, forget it. Update on Joe's voice: the range is shot, but nevermind, what he's muttering way back in the mix are pre-juvenile cartoon rock sentiments that looked and sounded dismal and sadly left-fer-dead at '92's MTV Music Awards amidst searing performances from Pearl Jam, Nirvana, The Black Crowes and the Chili Peppers, essentially rock's new guard. After losing one arm and a whole guitarist, you'd think . . . man, like I said, forget it.

Rating     0

## Def Leppard - Retro Active (PolyGram '93)

A halfways decent odds 'n sods project that benefits from the smooth studio sheen added to these B-sides, covers and otherwise out-takes. Best tracks are the surprisingly hefty *Desert Song* and *Ring Of Fire*, plus a faithful cover of Sweet's *Action*. Still, too much abysmal Lep pollutes the airwaves (i.e. corporate ballads), making **Retro Active** choppy at best. Last gem: Mick Ronson's *Only After Dark*, which packs in more soul than the boys have demonstrated in ages. Yes, better than the last two crap contraptions. Cover features a nifty re-enactment of that famous "skull" optical illusion.

Rating     4

## Def Leppard - Vault: Greatest Hits (PolyGram '95)

Man, this is all I need today, all those miserable Lep "anthems" lined up along the shining path to stupidity. **Vault** does an acceptable enough job with such awful material, with detailed liner notes and credits, a big essay from Peter Mensch (it's sad how these guys still equate success with records sold: talk about having no self-respect), and one extra miserable, cold and wet puppy of a ballad just to topple the already invisibly high stacks of cash the Leps criminally generate. Said track, *When Love & Hate Collide* addresses exactly the same worthless pile of white trash that the last five softies shook down to the underwear. The rockers flop around like gasping fish left for a couple of suffocating hours on the deck of the SS '80s, only the really old ones (the band all but ignores their first two records) like *Foolin'* and *Photograph* sounding like the product of real people, and even then just barely. But whatever, I mean you, Jack Q. Public, have said Bon Jovi and Def Leppard will be allowed to exist and thrive, somehow ignoring your blinding bad taste in the process. Have a blast. See you at Wal-Mart.

Rating     0

## Def Leppard - Slang (PolyGram '96)

A spiffy new look to the band's previously moronic packaging signals that changes are afoot. And, yes, the Leps have all but buried their turgid bastardizations of

118

hair metal, for a similar stomp and wreck of hip-hop conventions, following Bon Jovi into a morass of generalist samplings from too many markets. But as before, a ton of work has gone into this mishmash of alt., world, pop metal and Inc. rock sounds, and the boys sound almost talented here and there, especially on the complicated melodies of *Turn To Dust* and bright, connecting but coy lead single *Work It Out*. Of course, there's a truckload of crap too, but it's crafty crap, modern-rocking as much as Lep's fabulously tasteless production acumen can filter through clogged hoses. And to topsy-turvey the whole thing, the boys see fit to throw in the odd dirty guitar or drum sound (both: *Gift Of Flesh*, good song), just to really pastiche the fact that there are just too many channels of nuthin' on in the late '90s. Limited edition version of **Slang** comes with the six-pack **Acoustic In Singapore**, which strips all the fancy padding from a few of their smash hit stinkers, transforming the band into Bryan Adams and the Traveling Wilburys, an overpoweringly unpleasant proposition that could only transpire on Grammy night or a Three Tenors tour (somebody shut these fat-heads up).
Rating                                      5

# D Generation - No Lunch   (Sony '96)
Just as you thought '90s punk was going to all sound dreary and identical, here comes D Generation with a markedly ragged, snarly sound that harkens more authentically and forensically back to '77 than all those sparky combos you're getting sick of but fast. Which is pretty funny, given that ol' ostrich head Ric Ocasek produces, the man able to underproduce six parking garage levels lower than anything Cars ever did. In fact, the recording is borderline too squalid, all that bloodshot distortion almost detracting from the Clash-like hollering enclosed. But this is a pretty cool band, like a pop Dead Boys or Damned with a touch of slappy happy glam, recalling a less U.S. Rancid, or my closet obsession Manic Street Preachers, but completely "in their cups" as the British are wont to say. Heck, they even got the right kinda hair and clothes, covering three eras of rudimentary rock and a couple of continents all in one.
Rating                                      8

# Deicide - Deicide   (Roadrunner '90)
Totally evil but skilful debut from Glen Benton and crew, who broke from the pack immediately due to publicity over Benton's Satanism, his branding of an inverted cross into his forehead, the band's suicide pact set for when the boys turn 33, and Benton's talk of animal sacrifice and mutilation, which has gotten him into skirmishes with animal rights groups. So he knows how to work it, also making sure his music is up to snuff, this Scott Burns-produced (who else?) bashfest worthy of similar vintage Malevolent Creation or Death or Broken Hope, which is all so much caustic turbo sewage to my ears.
Rating                                      4

# Deicide - Legion   (Roadrunner '92)
Again, I practically have to abstain from rating here, **Legion** to my ears, doing pretty much the same blast-beated mosh as the debut, violent, jarring and convincing, but man what a pain. But there's only 28 minutes of it anyway, perpetuating one of the good habits of death metal, i.e. striking, leaving no survivors, and clearing out. Benton says there was no harmonizer on his vocals here, so that bark is all his. Imagine when he chews out the kids! More or less self-produced with much better results than the debut. Wacky-ass, beyond-Slayer soloing by both Eric and Brian Hoffman.
Rating                                      5

# Deicide - Amon: Feasting The Beast   (Roadrunner '93)
Glen Benton's managed to attract a lot of press for Deicide with his overt, clearly stated Satanism, and thus his band has become somewhat famous enough for this compilation from their first two demos as "Amon", the first in '87 (remixed here) and the second in '89. And it's pretty much the band's high quality grindcore (a contradiction in terms), with the early material actually sounding better for its low budget idiosyncrasies and less extreme approach to precision noise-making. But alas, it *is* grindcore, and a bitter horsepill to boot.
Rating                                      4

# Deicide - Once Upon The Cross   (Roadrunner/Attic '95)
Unswerving in his Satanism (man does he have a bone to pick, or what?), Benton tears it up with another Christian-killing record of crushing death. But some of what I would hope to happen has. Production values are thicker but more volatile and dangerous, and blast-beats are used judiciously, as spicing to Benton's inverted tales, which usually coast along to a barrage of double-bass mid-paced structures. A love 'em/hate 'em entity to most, Deicide in my opinion is a grind machine of mild but growing interest.
Rating                                      6

# Deliverance - The Ultimate Revenge   (Griffin '94)
Wow. I'm truly spooked. This best of package culls material from this band of black metal nutters' three doomed records, '87's **Devil's Meat**, '89's **Evil Friendship**, and '90's **Book Of Lies**, while adding a couple newer numbers, best being the carbonic hate-filled genius of *Stealer Of Dreams* and the looped 'n' fried *The Church Of Deliverance*. These guys deserve a government grant. Their material is some of the most sinister, brilliant, innovative dark rock I've ever heard, totally out there in a sorta dream-like black metal hippydom, overdriven, buried under. But the production (mainly the tracks from the first two records) evokes Venom in their demo days, muffled, one mike stuff that simply sounds botched. But there's wild studio trickery everywhere, even as the basics are ignored, making this a rarity of evilmetal, recorded in a total vacuum, a void of influences. I dunno, the only vague comparative material-wise I could make would be absolutely top-form Venom, or something akin to the top five or so Witchfynde tracks. Notably, these sounds died by about 1983. Very creepy.
Rating                                      8

# Demented Ted - Promises Impure   (Pavement '93)
Thick, impenetrable and perturbable anachronistic death metal overlapped with frenetic and brilliant riffs, which unfortunately all push and shove for our attention, songs boarded-up with prog-grind flourishes until we can barely peer inside. Sound-wise, it's one of those overdriven, distortion-iced recordings that fatigues all frequencies into a midrange morass. Creative but lacking in dynamic, giving all, all the time. Only record before the name change to Beyond.
Rating                                      5

# Demilich - Nespithe   (Necropolis/Pavement '93)
A phantasmagorical, face-frying sort of death pervades this unique batch of Finns, Demilich combining manic depressive progressive thrash with an original percolating, boiling, belching vocal performance that will bend the gut with laughter. Then there's songtitles like *When The Sun Drank The Weight Of Water*, *The Sixteenth Six-Tooth Son Of Fourteen Four-Regional Dimensions (Still Unnamed)* and *Inherited Bowel Levitation - Reduced Without Any Effort*, really knocking the senses reeling past Carcass and Cynic into a carbuncled spinning turbo-dive that is a death metal demonstration unmatched. A true grindslime masterpiece, but not

**119**

something I would access again until the hoof to the forehead imprint of apocalyptic horsemen.
Rating 7

## Demon - Night Of The Demon (Carrere '81)

These anonymous NWOBHM liggers made a couple of amateurish but spirited melodic metal albums, thence switching to amateurish but spirited "thinking man's" hard rock albums, two of which I unfortunately own. **Night Of The Demon** is the gung-ho debut, basic, barroom black metal that betrays a band that has no idea what it takes to be rock stars, thus managing to sound cavernously depressed, underground, and soaked like the skin like most early nowhere-man English metal. Funny but so misguided it's sick. Sorta gave us the heebie jeebies at the time.
Rating 6

## Demon - The Unexpected Guest (Carrere '82)

**The Unexpected Guest** is Demon's second sacrifice to the Gods of the Delete Bin, a record that is more of the same rudimentary black metal, with only tolerable production and only tolerable musicianship and vocals. But believe it or not it is genuinely scary and even a bit catchy due to it's numbskullian insistence on providing hooks while serving your severed head to Satan in a gym bag. Guitarist and writer Malcolm Spooner, an asthmatic, is since deceased from pneumonia.
Rating 7

## Demon - Heart Of Our Time (Clay '85)

One of the seemingly countless post-black metal Demon albums that finds the band grunting and groaning in search of the maturity they feel results from keyboards and melodious expression. Reminds me of progressive dudes who try subvert their egos with simpler and heavier sounds, sorta like Asia, GTR, or even Genesis, thence moving on to Hologram, Magnum, Nightwing for that metal twist. Only Demon arrive at this mongrel state ass-backwards by playing to the greatest of their limited capabilities. And thankfully, Demon can't shake the poverty-ridden cellar dampness that made them such a psychological mess on their first two pleasure cruises on the Lake of Fire. Thus in the end, totally the wrong band for commercial hard rock, making **Heart Of Our Time** firmly psychotic and hopeless in practice, but strangely compelling as a concept.
Rating 4

## Demon - Breakout (Clay '87)

I own four Demon albums and combined, there isn't a single photo of the band. Talk about lack of communication. And the strange album covers are becoming interesting, this one being a pretty nifty gatefold painting of a guy with his cherished guitar, atop a scrap metal heap, looking pretty poured out, like he lost his wallet. Musically and lyrically, **Breakout** is a minuscule step up, but it's the same painful oil and water mixture of attempted sensitivity and complete British bleakness, once past the first two surprisingly classy and metallic tracks. Who knows . . . maybe these guys will punch out another twelve records and become the undisputed Residents of metal.
Rating 4

## Derringer - Derringer (Columbia '76)

In what parallels a Ted-like move, Rick attempts a new reference point from which to begin assessing his output, set to march forth with a new band and attitude (quick history: The McCoys, Johnny Winter, Edgar Winter, a handful of teen pin-up "solo" records, and later on, a ton of guest slots). **Derringer** proves, however, that the path to **Sweet Evil** is arduous and slow-brewed, falling way short of the latter's strident vistas and alchemical fireworks. **Derringer** is still mere

session man rock; funky, balladeering, unfocused and confusing. Structures are simpler and at least headed in the direction of "rock man meets guitar", but outside of the elusive and wondrously unwinding Sailor and new age Hendrix romp Beyond The Universe, nothing kicks with the conviction of a man firmly decided. Still, it's Rick, and an honest Rick at that, so one can look past the bluesy and often meandering styles to the band's obvious love of the process. Simply put: un-self-actualized, sounding uncannily like similar vintage Earl Slick Band or even Bad Company if imagination is utilized; come to think of it, pretty much a trend line from **They Only Come Out At Night**, the stellar classic from his old band, The Edgar Winter Group.
Rating 6

## Derringer - Sweet Evil (Columbia '77)

A rock-solid classic from American metal's early days. Beware hardcore dudes, **Sweet Evil** is the heaviest Derringer album, but it ain't all that heavy, although the record features a few convincing metal classics such as major guitar and percussion opus Sittin' By The Pool and early speed metal rave Let's Make It. Other beacons of studio-seasoned professionalism occur with awesome heaving popster Don't Stop Loving Me and the mysterious and mellow title track, which belts into a sinister metal riff about halfway through, fretfire worthy of vintage Tipton/Downing. I always liked the guy's bratty vocals, and his guitar work and song structures contain scads of clever inflections, setting Derringer up for his role as dependable musician to the stars. **Sweet Evil's** rife with metal, funk, pop hooks, you name it, all delivered via the unique slant on life afforded only to those considered guitar gods of the '70s. Closest thing one could compare to would be '75-'77 era Aerosmith or perhaps similarly placed Pat Travers, **Sweet Evil** containing liberal doses of that same free-flowing, sun-drenched kharma. Highly entertaining and lovingly assembled.
Rating 10

## Derringer - Live (Columbia '77)

**Live** is the first Derringer release that really stresses the hard rockin' side of our diminutive axemeister, this truncated amplified good time being a bit short on value (i.e. not enough hot rockers to keep the party going), as Rick pulls that '70s guitar wankery thing; glam boy makes good, mischievous midget makes wattage. Eight solid as oak guitar groovers (if as I say, a little poppy), including Let Me In, Teenage Love Affair and old Edgar Winter hit Still Alive And Well, covered in '95 by The Four Horsemen.
Rating 7

## Derringer - If I Weren't So Romantic I'd Shoot You (Columbia '78)

Another sumptuous classic from one of rock's unsung session men, this one's more pop-cute and light-hearted than **Sweet Evil**, but also more fun, flashy and arresting. A confident sense of humour, mixed with about four tracks of serious rock make this a warm, guitar-oriented opus, a record constructed of shorter, shimmering popsters of the highest order. Profusely gushing moments include upbeat rockers It Ain't Funny, Rocka Rolla, and Attitude plus a spirited, dressed-up cover of Warren Zevon's Lawyers, Guns And Money. Richly divergent and always full of life, this eminently finessed and tasteful display of light metal will never fail in perking up your rainy days.
Rating 9

## Derringer - Guitars And Women (Epic '79)

Derringer executes a deep dive into melodic pop hooks (save for two concave, metallic scorchers co-written by Rick Neilsen of Cheap Trick). But of course, given Derringer's well-traveled axe, all divergences

work out splendidly. And the cuteness sounds sincere on the clever comparisons of the title tune, which bounces capably amidst some amazingly effortless, sugar-coated axe-work. One complaint: Todd Rundgren's production which is characteristically midrangy and hyper, a clattery sound that is an acquired taste at best. Unbridled, nostalgic, no-worries American pop metal, simultaneously delivered with enthusiasm and a wily, tongue-in-cheek reservation as to the significance of the whole rock'n'roll game.
Rating 8

### Rick Derringer - Face To Face (CBS '80)

A real low in the Derringer saga, **Face To Face** is a mere pop record, perhaps conceived to hatch hits, but failing miserably. Rick self-produces the thing in a very Rundgren-ish manner, compressed but bassy at the same time. But the limp overlayered songs can't handle the strain, only *Burn The Midnight Oil* and the live *My My, Hey Hey* injected with any semblance of power. Sounds like an Elton John record played by a metal band, future Blue Oyster Cult drummer Jimmy Wilcox most pertinently bashing beyond what is required.
Rating 4

### Rick Derringer - Good Dirty Fun (Passport '82)

To really work, this sort of meta-and-potatoes hard rock has to emanate from a wellspring of confidence. Here, Rick lacks the killer instinct or even a sense of smug professionalism, turning it up but trying too hard, standing alone, without the consistent backing band over time to provide ballast, à la similarly flawed "organizations" Elvis Costello, Graham Parker, John Hiatt or more metallically speaking, Iggy or Alice. A bit of everything clouds the potential critical mass, while a good 3/4 of **Good Dirty Fun** is at least loosely based on the title-trumpeting geared-down 'n' dirty guitar, as evidenced most soundly on steam-rolling blaster *Party At The Hotel*, lead track *I Play Guitar*, barwipe *Hardball*, and funkster *Just Wanna Dance*, a pressure cooker reminiscent of early successful rhythmic forays by Derringer. But as **Good Dirty Fun** winds up, nothing much has happened to convert Rick to winner. All remains fuzzy, forced, corporate, project-like, and kinda diffused as Rick keeps chooglin' along without a heaping lot to say.
Rating 4

### Rick Derringer - Back To The Blues (Blues Bureau '93)

Glad to hear that voice again, and glad to hear so much smooth guitar emanate forth from one of my fave '70s dudes. But as with Pat Travers, I'm dying to hear more rock, less blues from these legends. Here Rick serves up a whole heap of Stevie Ray, with occasional bursts of manic, Foghat-style amphetamine blues, as on *Blue Suede Blues*, *Meantown Blues* and *Sink Or Swim*. The rest: not my bag.
Rating 5

### Rick Derringer - Electra Blues (Blues Bureau '94)

I dunno, maybe I'm not hip to the nuances of da blooz, but I don't see what growth this exhibits past **Back To The Blues**. More of the same slinky, swampy R+B wankery, with none of the hot rockin'. I pass respectfully but entirely uncaring.
Rating 3

### Descendents - Everything Sucks (Epitaph '96)

Hot on the heels of the Pistols reunion comes a less illustrious but more sun-tanned reformation, L.A.'s Descendents flipping back from their alter-ego ALL, into this short shocked burst of double-pumped punk. The main coup was getting punk nerd icon Milo back from a blossoming biochemistry degree. So here he is, barking out sugary chug monsters like *Sick-O-Me* and the almost Replacematted *When I Get Old*, in total 15

tracks at a mere half hour. But the band's 18 year pedigree wears well, **Everything Sucks** sporting electrifying production, firey drums and feeling vocals. Pretty much up there with Social Distortion, D Generation and Bad Religion as loudfastrules music that is (surprise!) well-written.
Rating 7

### Desire - Cry At The Sky (Rockpower '83)

Taking nod from the dedication to Jimi Hendrix and the LP's cosmic moniker, I can safely postulate about this budgetary shoestring's fluid and funky Mahogany Rush and Robin Trower inflections which flow effortlessly like a wash of good memories. For an obvious garage record, **Cry At The Sky** sounds nicely tidal, sporting tasteful, well-blended bass and drums, while hanging onto those engaging little eccentricities that bands pick up before they become jaded and aware of the fragility of fleeting fame. Old-sounding and spontaneous in a cool "power trio" sort of way; melodic, bluesy and opaque but still surrounded with an echoey sense of fun. Label says "First Pressing Limited Edition 500 Copies," and it may very well be all there were.
Rating 7

### Despair - Beyond All Reason (Century Media '91)

Germany's Despair forge one helluva tech metal furnace blast on this their second onslaught. Picture hints of greasy underground grind as per Machine Head fusing with the overlordic goth tones of Memento Mori, whipped to full tilt with a double dose of Anacrusis. But the boys can mosh a deep groove too (witness *The Day Of Desperation*), while blazing it up with their patented muscle and danger. Fresh lyrical approach too, eschewing standard death metal themes for a maturity not often found in these far-flung extremes of metal. Classy, but non-fans of speed may be over then underwhelmed. Flashfire guitarist Waldemar Sorychta has since moved on to Dave Lombardo's crushing new steamroller Grip Inc.
Rating 7

### Dessau - Dessau (Mausoleum/BMG '95)

Usually not hip to this kind of sawed-off, minimalist industrial metal, but Dessau works in enough groove, given their dance preoccupation, turning half of these tracks catchy, fave being the familiar *Isolation* by Joy Division, which gets as much lope as a robot can muster. Nice, detached, stand-offish old Killing Joke snobbery to it, which also helps. Perfect for the all-night batcaves all those chemical people with no jobs go to.
Rating 6

### Destruction - Sentence Of Death (Banzai '84)

This five track EP wins the golden hammer for the most OTT front cover in history. No mistaking what Schmier, Mike, and Tommy are all about. **Sentence Of Death** is standard-issue, adequately recorded, bleedingly frenzied frashcore, with a drummer that plays like five guys throwing their sets off the roof of a Czechoslovakian steel mill. Unless you like random punishment, keep yer coin and lock on with **Eternal Devastation**.
Rating 4

### Destruction - Infernal Overkill (Banzai '85)

Relentless and bludgeoning, **Infernal Overkill** manages to bridge thrash and techno, slamming along beneath sinister rat-like riffs and deadly, grating production values, while conjuring images of a big, black mainframe; threatening wisdom embedded beneath complex circuitry. Still, because that in almost every sense of the term, **Infernal Overkill** is brutally no-compromising OTT warfare, unless you're a mass murderer, it's not the kind of thing you'll want to spin night and day for your relatives. For hardcore Belgian waffles only.

Rating 4

## Destruction - Eternal Devastation (Metal Blade '86)

Major octane infusion. On **Eternal Devastation**, this nuclear power trio combines technical flash and complex song structures with thrashing over-profusion; OTT, with their trademark troll-like death vocals. The production is much improved, tending to highlight the almost Death Angel-like falling-apart-at-the-seams style. It's all heavier than hell and downright cacophonous, yet the leathered ones have a lot of careening and demonic ideas worth sifting from the violence. Among '80s thrash bands, Destruction have three things that put them above the "vacuum cleaner with drums" contingent: talent, production and dynamics. Absolute power-drenched classics like *Life Without Sense* and *United By Hatred* demonstrate how the sky cracks when these guys slow down and assume the power groove. Sort of like a pissed-off, late-fer-dinner Voivod, Destruction are on their way to the ultra-techno-thrash-speed hell of fame.

Rating 7

## Destruction - Release From Agony (Rock Hotel/Profile '88)

Continuing on their mission of visceral thrash in a world gone perfumed pop metal, Destruction are among a select few acts (mostly German: see Coroner, Rage, Helloween, Kreator) that have maintained the edge while pumping up the chops. For this reason, **Release From Agony** contains a myriad of sensations for the technically-minded, and a healthy dose of 100 proof alcohol for those with the head that bangs. Fast, seething and searing, although the mix is a tad compressed and mid-rangey. Plus that album cover, wow.

Rating 7

## Destruction - Live Without Sense (Noise '89)

What can I say? This is one of those blighty live banquets tapped, harnessed and reproduced from European shows we weak westerners can only imagine, Destruction blazing their way through a nice long bunch of hard-ass traditional tempered steel made dangerous through the teachings of thrash. Perfectly fine recording and good value for Destruction fans, although packaging is at a minimum, best part being the back cover illustration which reminds me of the inner sleeve to Aerosmith **Rocks**.

Rating 7

## Destruction - Cracked Brain (Steamhammer/Capitol '90)

Wouldn't say there's any change of plans here, except the loss of Schmier on bass and vocals (see band doppelganger Voivod five years later), which makes not an iota difference to the band's studied panic thrash, a sound that impresses then annoys, depending on your capacity to digest this sort of thing. Mike Sifringer remains one of the most refreshing extreme guitarists, mixing his sci-fi panzer riffery with Dali-esque Frippery come solo time. Production values slash and burn, much like the band's performance, and the new guy's vocals are back to the hysteric '80s thrash stylings Destruction pioneered five years previous. Novelty trashpunk cover of *My Sharona*, which just detracts from the furtive furrowed brow gravity of the record.

Rating 7

## Destruction - Them Not Me (Brain Butcher '95)

Destruction continue to thrive (at least creatively) through the '90s, this five track EP proving the band's prowess at thrash cum Bay Area metal, packing more thought into riffs, rhythms and solos than the likes of Metallica even care about these days. It's a similar sort of injustice to what has befallen Testament and Over-

kill, or Canuck-wise, Anvil, Voivod and Annihilator, this eminently interesting band left behind, anchored to the '80s. I guess song-titles like *Live To Start Again*, *Push Me Off The Windowsill* and *Mentally Handicapped Enterprise* sum things up. All in all, robustly recorded scientific thrash with spaces and brains. Hope they persist.

Rating 8

## Detective - Detective (Swan Song '76)

Sum total of the Detective sound wasn't all that heavy, but they do warrant entry here for links to heavy realms, the band being a Pagey-blessed signing for Led Zeppelin's Swan Song hobby label. Detective were a bit of a minor supergroup, luminaries being bassist Bobby Pickett, Yes keyboardist Tony Kaye and crashed-and-risen rockdog from Silverhead Michael Des Barres on smoky, throaty power vocals. And the boys knew heavy production, this record coming straight from the Zep books circa **Physical Graffiti**, choppy-blocked Powell/Bonham drums counterweighted by thick guitar/bass incestuousness, driving songs that fit the hard blues rock of Humble Pie, Lone Star, latter-day Mott, or I guess, fairly thwacked Zeppelin. Boomy, unbowed, and co-produced by Jimmy Page himself, under the pseudonym of Jimmy Robinson.

Rating 7

## Detective - It Takes One To Know One (Swan Song '77)

Glad that somebody made a good Firm record, heck, Detective making two of them, **It Takes One To Know One** continuing that Pagey penchant for dense, convoluted blues. And while Detective is moonlighting inventing The Firm, they also make a few Zep tracks that could have brought **Presence** to CD-age length, *Competition* and *Dynamite* standing out here as tricky chopblocks of a certain Zep quality level. But much of the rest is simply flippant party rock (*Betcha Won't Dance*), closer to old Rod Stewart in its uh, boogie with Stu. Still a nice chunk of wayward, intrinsically '70s thunk rock. And boy, are these guys snappy dressers!

Rating 6

## Detective - Live From The Atlantic Studios (Swan Song '78)

Yeah, I know, this was only a promo, but it was a pretty cool one, this Atlantic Studios thing being a pretty cool set of recordings, like the Peel, BBC One and King Biscuit sets. Here Detective are captured semi-live, giving it their sweaty best, Des Barres cranking his classy, '70s cock rock vocals bridging Plant, Steven Tyler and Paul Rodgers, while his crack band sling out the hard rockin' r+buttered hash. Nine tracks balanced between the two records, a rollicking good time if you halfways care about vintage (ahem) "classic" rock.

Rating 7

## Devilhead - Pest Control (Loosegroove/Sony '96)

Very hip and very scattered, **Pest Control** is record two for this perplexing bunch of Seattle insiders, Devilhead headed by Brian and Kevin Wood, brothers of the late Andrew Wood, leader of couldabeens Mother Love Bone. Plus they got a Satchel guy, and the band's label Loosegroove is run by Stone Gossard and Regan Hagar. One hears bassy grunge, raw funk, Lou Reed, Bowie, Pearl Jammy punk, Mudhoney, all cleverly orbiting heaviness, much like any Pearl Jam record I guess. But creativity is very much the name of the game, these guys being talented oddballs who are an unpredictable moving target, even by Seattle standards. Farthest afield: *Gay Affair*, which sounds like an even loungier *Midnight At The Oasis*, complete with breezy female vocals and sensuous sax.

Rating 7

## Buck Dharma - Flat Out   (CBS '82)

Donald "Buck Dharma" Roeser bestows upon us what to date is the only Blue Öyster Cult solo project (**Imaginos** came close, as it was going to be an Albert Bouchard record, Al also being one half of the Brain Surgeons with wife Deb Frost); and as suspected, reveals that el Buck is the smooth pop tunesmith, the eye to the charts, the refreshing, sun-dappled pool of the Bloom/Dharma fire and water BÖC dichotomy; the polished sheen of the BÖC sound. Backed by a ton of studio dudes including some past Alice Cooper guys, Roeser tip-toes his way through an album consisting mostly of unabashed mellow pop; tasteful and artfully subdued lyrically, but dangerously close to the edge of complete genericism. Only speedy hard rocker *Born To Rock* and the instrumental feature much in the way of guitar rock. Besides these two and the experimentally flip *Wind Weather And Storm*, the rest of **Flat Out** courts breezy California pop, which occurred with increasing confidence within BÖC's portfolio as the '80s wore on, yet not with such loving sincerity and musing remembrance of a simpler time that we feel here. Best of the bunch include potential BÖC hits *All Tied Up* and *Your Loving Heart*, a tragic tale about the ultimate sacrifice between two lovers. Warning: one of the mellowest albums in this book.
Rating                                                            6

## Diamond Head - Lightning To The Nations
(Woolfe '81)

Diamond Head was eminently worthy of the critical praise and legendary status heaped upon their unsuspecting shoulders, yet it's hard to articulate what lent the band's case such immediate psychological impact. This debut (originally self-financed on the band's own Happy Face label, with each copy signed by a band member) crashed headlong into the NWOBHM, offering little in the way of agility or readily identifiable personal traits throughout its hypnotic, dark and messed-up tour, except perhaps the expressive, vocal presence of Sean Harris. The product of four years as a band, **Lightning To The Nations** embodies a foreboding, bellwether sound doomed to abject failure, as if the band were creating a confused monster in a dark void, picking up none of the good *or* bad habits of the then-exploding metal scene in Britain. **Lightning** was to become the band's most squarely metallic effort, with long ugly songs rumbling on like massive chundering jam sessions nobody knew how to stop. In some ways, a decidedly unprofessional debut; in others, a serious, soul-destroying effort, all the more twisted due to its accidental, imploding nature.
Rating                                                           10

## Diamond Head - Borrowed Time   (MCA '82)

**Borrowed Time** was supposed to put Diamond Head over the top, but one listen and it's obvious why most of the record-buying public just didn't get it at all. **Borrowed Time** clunks slowly, defiantly anti-social and depressing in its defeatist, lifeless approach to musicianship and song construction, as if the band were issuing some sort of timid protest at being heralded as the new Zeppelin. Still the album absolutely hypnotizes me, evoking through willful stupidity, the dark undercurrents only hinted at on the debut's angst-ridden rockers. **Borrowed Time** comes across as a sorrowful blues record caught in the downward vortex of black metal, almost self-destructing in full knowledge of the consequences. Of the seven included tracks, two are re-carves of classics from the debut, leaving only five new, unsure, and sickly cuts to carry the heavy load. All in all, an obvious commercial disaster, but a beautiful, rainy expression of sadness; an evaluation which may be so off the mark, yet proving the adage

that one's interpretation of art may be as valid as the artist's intentions themselves.
Rating                                                            9

## Diamond Head - Canterbury   (MCA '83)

This ponderous but interesting re-wiring of the Diamond Head persona provides the band's third shift of philosophy in three albums, conjuring a mix of styles; more acoustic guitar, more complexity, more self-importance, and heaps more production. **Canterbury** (originally titled Night Of The Swords), is more the product of Diamond Head, the tireless Rush fans who could spend seemingly endless hours in soundchecks pouring over 2112. It's still an eerie Diamond Head experience; dark and sparse, while the variation makes it also the most listenable and provocative. Career-wise though, **Canterbury** became the road to nowhere, as no one but the band itself seemed to buy the line that Diamond Head would save the world from fake rock'n'roll. By '85 the band had dissolved (very close to having finished a fourth record **Flight East**), a victim of internal ego struggles and external management rip-offs, never really getting the chance to define its sound and reach its potential. Brian Tatler was good for a solo album in '91 called **World Service**. Sean Harris subsequently resurfaced with glossmeister Robin George as the somewhat INXS-ish Notorious, but has long since abandoned said ill-fated ruse for a robust and surprisingly valid Diamond Head reunion.
Rating                                                            8

## Diamond Head - Behold The Beginning
(Metal Masters '86)

Said package (one of at least four compilations) is a re-release of the band's mighty premiere with a few switched cuts wrapped by a cheesy album cover. I remember the debut having a beefier recording; otherwise, this is a great way to obtain some vintage tunes which are hard to find these days. Under-rated addition: *Waited Too Long*, a skewed pop number which would have cracked an appropriately crooked smile on **Borrowed Time**. Just a note about 'Head tunes not on LP, there being some considerably heavy, although rudimentary and obtuse, rockers to be found on such low-key releases as the **Diamond Lights** EP and the preferred **Call Me** EP. Search 'em out.
Rating                                                            7

## Diamond Head - Death And Progress   (Bronze '93)

In the same boat as Angel Witch, Diamond Head's enduring legend continually lures this band back into the biz, Diamond Head finally fulfilling the reunion rumours properly, delivering this very good if not magical spread of traditional British metal, doing a spirited job of recapturing the band's basic sound, few layers, songs that wish to achieve. The record (taking seed and song from the **Rising Up** EP project in '91) starts off strong and ends weak, while achieving victory once the ballots are counted. At the weak end, *Run*, *Wild In The Streets* and *Damnation Street* are simply sub-grade metal tunes, that unique Diamond Head fatigue overwhelming creativity. But at the front of the record, ah, pure metal heaven. *Starcrossed* (featuring additional guitars by Tony Iommi) jars the listener right back to **Lightning To The Nations**, and *Calling Your Name* finds the lush, melodic goth of **Canterbury**. But in between is the record's shining glory, maybe the band's masterpiece, *Truckin'* which features Dave Mustaine who also produces the track. This is just one of the most infectious metal riffs in eons, just a tremendous stop/start tune that could have been the centerpiece of any 'deth deal. Right in the middle, there's *Dust*, which provides an energetic respite from the cloak and dagger weight of the thing, a real party rocker that might have fit on Sean Harris' excellent Notorious AOR experiment. Best thing I can say about

this record in total, is that it sounds ten years old, usually a derision, here meant in praise, this record transporting the listener back to a rich era in metal.
Rating 8

## Diamond Rexx - Land Of The Damned (Island '86)

Mad-eyed glam from the midwest, torn and splayed onto vinyl via one raucous and crusty mix heavy on axes and drums, **Land Of The Damned** slashes predictably like high octane poverty Crüe (circa **Too Fast For Love**), unfortunately carrying the baggage of glam's simplicity and lack of mobility, a fate Crüe's debut escaped through quirky, double-vision eccentricity. Ploddish no matter what the speed, but bolstered by resolute will to destroy and conquer, Diamond Rexx are rattling enough, just not adequately equipped with the songs or brains to rise above the strip malls. Vocals tend towards flat and expressionless, but other than that wee complaint, chalk it up as merely adequate amongst tough competition. Brutal album cover.
Rating 5

## Bruce Dickinson - Tattooed Millionaire (EMI '90)

Bruce takes temporary leave from a sinking ship, coming out from his quasi-literary Maiden goth-ness to show us that he's really just one of the boys propping the bar. If this first solo album is any indication, the man likes his hard rock straight-up, tight and simple, melodic and loud. **Tattooed Millionaire** is a likeable brew of slow HR/metal (Son Of A Gun), excellent melodic hard rock (infectious title cut), wimphem (Born In '58), funky HR (Dive! Dive! Dive!) and Lickin' The Gun), and Sweet Home Alabama (Gypsy Road). Overall, the proceedings are considerably lighter-hearted, more personal, and less ornate than Maiden, both lyrically and musically, making this a smoothish car stereo album, an unpretentious one-off by one of metal's cooler characters. High points: Bruce's always expressive vocals and the soaring tunefulness of the title cut's chorus. Low points: a dull cover choice of All The Young Dudes and the all-pervading safeness of arrangement and production chores.
Rating 7

## Bruce Dickinson - Balls To Picasso (PolyGram '94)

Hats off to Bruce for knowing when to leave a snickership, Maiden by 1993 way past their relevance. **Balls To Picasso** is one of those intimidating journeys that can garner respect and blank stares at once. Dickinson goes for a sort of sparse, quietly humming metal; moody dynamics driving a serious though conventional sound. But many tracks are plain boring throughout their verses, albeit gathering anthemic steam come chorus time (see Cyclops and Gods Of War). Yes, Bruce has a hot young band (shades of Plant), the drummer evoking Dave Abbruzzese, now ex-of-Pearl Jam, and the record's production rings bright to the point of stinging. Lyrically, I don't know if Bruce has really nailed any of these themes as one would expect him to, definitely sounding a bit dated and well, Maiden-ish at times. I deem this a grudging 8 out of respect for the re-tooling of an interesting life, but I find myself a tad deflated by the record's morose gravity, which fairly often is due to a sense of isolation and entrapment in tricks used up in the mid-'80s.
Rating 8

## Bruce Dickinson - Alive In Studio A (CMC '95)

For the total Brucehead, here's a double CD set comprising essentially his second record **Balls To Picasso** done on CD#1 a little looser than the original (live performance for an aborted radio show), while CD#2 delivers pretty much the same set in a truer live format, last show of the tour, at the Marquee in London (note: no Maiden). CD#1 is quite unnecessary, but CD#2 is a helluva live album, showcasing a band of youngsters

that Dickinson is quite enthusiastic in praising. Bruce is in excellent form, but the whole thing is driven by Alex Elena's inventive percussion performance, which as I say, is not unlike the exotic, high-tuned stylings of ousted Pearl Jam drummer Dave Abbruzzese. And the recording is nicely just dirty enough, filling in the spaces of the somewhat apprehensive songs on **Balls To Picasso**. **Tattooed Millionaire** is also represented with three tracks, to my mind, tunes that carry a bit more uplift than those on **Balls**. Elsewhere: humourous liner notes and lots of pictures, making this a project not without some thought.
Rating 7

## Bruce Dickinson - Skunkworks (Castle '96)

By a country mile, the man's best record, **Skunkworks** is an elegant, cerebral metal feast that combines the hooks of Bruce Bruce's first record with the serious levity of his second. There's a sort of strong, mature metal course of life to this album, a sound that borrows from the best of Rush, Deep Purple, Diamond Head and early Maiden, Bruce usually getting right down to the business of crafting enjoyable hard rock pageantry with brains. Given his newly shorn locks, and the fact that Jack Endino has been ushered in to produce, one might think Dickinson had gone grunge like so many others. But in reality, there's a lusty, NWOBHM ethic to songs like Space Race and Inertia and personal fave Faith, which adds just a sheen of progressive rock to a marauding, war-torn riff, a riff that like so many others on this classy record, catapults into an anthemic chorus, Bruce's singing back to his projecting Air Raid Siren wails of old. Expert performances all around, this record somehow reminding me of upper crust solo contemplations like **Fate Of Nations**, while delivering Bruce's visceral, societal messages through the language of tuneful, tricky metal. Congratulations are in order. Now buy it!
Rating 9

## The Dictators - Go Girl Crazy! (Epic '75)

A zillion astute, almost universally favourable words have been written about this band, and indeed, the Dictators were in a class of their own. At a confusing and somewhat idle era in music where there was little loud rock anywhere, The Dictators were neck-deep in humanity, shattering heavy metal myths before any became solidified. **Go Girl Crazy!** isn't really all that power-packed, preferring to spit-ball its goofiness with a dose of distortion that borrows from many musical heritages, saddled with a sense of self-deprecating humour poking sticks at the seriousness of heavy metal that only Blue Öyster Cult and possibly Ted Nugent seemed to share at the time, although the Dictators were much more obviously comedians than musicians. And there's not much more to it than that. Precursors to punk? Possibly in its blasphemous use of snarling guitars but little else. Just a hook-out-of-school riot.
Rating 9

## The Dictators - Manifest Destiny (Asylum '77)

A self-effacing hybrid of subdued but complex humour, pop hooks, weirdness and struggling metal, **Manifest Destiny** never sounds old or predictable, chest-thumping through town as a lunch-bucket record that rocks (and punks) with a '70s sense of whimsy, throwbacks to both a '50s braggadocio and '50s nerd-dom included. Beware uncompromising metalheads: it ain't that heavy. But if you're looking for a glimpse at a fascinating and endearing chapter in metal's history, try this out, and become fully absorbed in plaintive teen heart rockers such as Exposed, Heartache and Hey Boys, killer punk metal classics like Young, Fast, Scientific, ambitious medical fable Disease, or a bitchin' live cover of Iggy's Search & Destroy. Immerse yourself in a simpler, stupider era where rock and marketing existed hopelessly and happily on different planes; immerse yourself in the headers-and-Hurst world of the Dictators' particular New York Mets City. As the band's manager Sandy Pearlman once told me "there are about 400,000 more people that love this record than have paid for it.". And so right he is, making **Manifest Destiny** one of the great underground classics of the our time.

Rating      10

## The Dictators - Bloodbrothers    (Asylum '78)

I'd place **Bloodbrothers** reverently amongst my top ten albums of all time. I've played it a few hundred times, and I just know I'll never tire of it, becoming an old pal of a record that will never let me down. **Bloodbrothers** is the heaviest of the three Dictators albums and by far the most vital and exuberant. The enthusiasm, pride, and urge to gather us up for a campfire tale combine for strident leaps from the record's throbbing grooves, while the gritty, street-level production of Krugman & Pearlman manages to make sure Handsome Dick (aka Richard Blum) and his fallen idols don't sound too much like rock stars. Side one's gotta be the best slab of quivering beef in rock'n'roll, sporting five absolute hall of famers in *Faster & Louder, Baby, Let's Twist, No Tomorrow, The Minnesota Strip, and Stay With Me* (I hadda name 'em all). Manitoba's quarterback-style vocals virtually assault the listener to pay attention, in melted collusion with a guitar sound that is unique, low-balled, and deeply moving; kinda at one with the pavement like a hot car. An allegory for life itself, **Bloodbrothers** invents its own environment, its own fables, and indeed its own family of characters. Years later, metal's most likeable New Yorkers were once again alive and kicking; shedding then shredding new wisdoms amongst The Del-Lords, Twisted Sister, Manowar, recently Manitoba's Wild Kingdom, and even more recently, The Dictators.

Rating      10

## Die Cheerleader - Son Of Filth    (Human Pitbull/London '95)

Britain's Die Cheerleader are the showcase signing for Henry Rollins' vanity label Human Pitbull, and it's obvious why Hank was so taken with these three gals and one guy, although this sound ain't exactly my brew. **Son Of Filth**'s main driving force is female angst, bridging new alternative noise rock like Therapy? to the sounds of X, building their songs with a vague undercurrent of older flavours from Hendrix, The Doors and '60s garage music to a sort of Cramps thing, all the while kinda beat generationed, bikered like the hogriders from the mid '60s. Where I'm getting all that is hard to say, but one thing is for sure, this reminds one heavily of X, sporting those same bleating, often wavering out-of-tune vocals like Exene and Courtney Love, and songs that somehow dig underground to a treasure trove of tradition. A bit slacked-out for my tastes, but much more accessible than the naked woman with cat head and machine gun album cover would have you believe. First deliberate record, after a full-length reissue called **Filth By Association** which culled together the band's three EPs to date.

Rating      7

## Die Krupps - A Tribute To Metallica    (Hollywood '93)

German technoids Die Krupps demonstrate ultimate fandom here, giving their medium load industrial treatment to a raft of mostly recent Metallica cuts. Leader Jurgen Engler has long been a fan of the Bay Area scene, and his band had been getting more guitarish of late, thus this record was born, or so sez the liner notes. Of course, it's more a quick spin novelty, but kinda fun once anyways, the man's vocals even sounding much like Hetfield's, the music (like I say) not terribly layered or inventive techno, low on abrasion, fairly faithful to

song. Seven different tracks plus two remixes (like, what is the point of that?).

Rating      5

## Die Toten Hosen - Learning English, Lesson One
(Atlantic '91)

Well, here's one way to learn punk, these German yobs literally wrapping themselves in the British flag and covering 21 mostly British punk anthems, including bands like UK Subs, Lurkers, Vibrators, Wreckless Eric, Eddie And The Hot Rods, The Damned, 999, and The Adverts. Awesome booklet too, including a paragraph of praise on each band and a huge scrapbook of punk paraphernalia. Solid, spicy, zesty versions with a responsible recording, something most of the originals lacked for funds.

Rating      6

## Dig - Dig    (Wasteland '93)

Classy alterna-metal along the lines of Nudeswirl meets Afghan Whigs meets Jane's Addiction, **Dig** further benefits from strong and fruitful hooks, rich vocal work and lots of surprises. Rollercoaster riding throughout, the record goes for big time dynamic, many mellow moments that break into majestic power chord washes, while the band harmonizes like their lives depended on it. Solid work; well-sequenced, well-paced, not to mention creamy production by Dave Jerden. Pushes **8**.

Rating      7

## Dig - Defenders Of The Universe    (Radioactive/MCA '96)

Perfect example of a fab alternative band before there was alternative, sliding comfortably into the current mindset, Dig already mixing power chords and pop three years previous. So it's funny seeing who I compared these guys to back then, now slapped into a different topsy-turvy world, not thinking that way at all, now aligning Dig with the likes of Bush, Tripping Daisy, and the slight glam tinge of Sponge and Manic Street Preachers. Thick, head-bashed production really sends these post-Nirvana tracks swinging, Dig making god use of whisper to roar dynamics throughout this sweet but stinging hard alternative rocker. Succeeds through arrangement above all else, **Defenders Of The Universe** leaking wisdom, even if it's not in fashion.

Rating      7

## Digger - Stronger Than Ever    (Noise '86)

This baffling but ultimately successful project finds 3/4 of the last Grave Digger line-up dropping the "Grave" from both the name and musical tone, while retaining it at the mike, through the blood-boiling wolf barks of one Chris Boltendahl. The result is both tragic and painfully hilarious, a half-hearted attempt at hard rock by extreme malletheads who exist only to bludgeon at one relentless intensity level. Digger eke out riffs that are occasionally and forcedly melodic, flavoured with forced synth shadings and updated electronic toms, while Chris desperately tries to sing, drifting in and out of his old role like Sybil in an airport during a bomb scare. What a blast. Nobody has a clue about pop rock, so what falls out approximates an oil and water Grave Digger/AOR hybrid that twists and writhes in discomfort at its own birth; most awe-stricken being the dead sinister *I Don't Need Your Love* and the Accept swing of *Stay Till The Morning*. A sort of paralyzed energy ensues, as if scanning thrash sheet music for that next anthemic chorus, the one that breaks America. Maligned and cancerous, but somehow arresting in its obvious tension, **Stronger Than Ever** is ultimately pretty damn heavy, only sporadically finding hooks, most often arriving at a rendition of Accept that's been slammed in the head with chunks of the Berlin Wall. Beautiful, so bad, and a goddam riot. Ends with one of

the band's most vicious speedballers ever, a borderline punk juggernaut that lays waste to any half-assed premise that Digger is anything but Grave Digger busted open.
Rating **8**

## Dimestore Hoods - Dimestore Hoods (MCA '96)

Finally, a band (and a truly gang-raised one at that) who really hits a funky groove that has little to do with rap, or oddly enough, other funk metal hype-machines. Some sort of unnamable spark kicks this one way above, evoking the best of RHCP and RATM, killing bands like dowset and 311, big drums, big sound courtesy of Matt Wallace, fireworks all 'round. Also just a beauty balance of rap and solid singing, both from Jim Korthe, sending these song-first songs into a slammin' zone that erases those cynical genre-damning thoughts that really jump to mine eyes around this sound. A whole wise mish-mash of elements expertly combined (including bluesy balladry into roaring altcore, no seams showing), easily making one forget that this is a debut.
Rating **8**

## Dinosaur Jr - Without A Sound (Warner '94)

Seems it's in vogue to trash poor mophead mumpster J. Mascis these days, so **Without A Sound** has gotten some unflattering reviews. Maybe it's the muddy live shows (this ain't a band I would even consider seeing live: what for?), or the anti-album covers, or the lack of J's voice in your favorite gossip rag, but people are getting a little tired with Dino Jr's insistence on no frills, no growth, low-fi record making. But not me jack, grooving this only minutely less on par with the last three, and more-so with exhilarating lead track and single Feel The Pain with its skyscraper-straddling golf video. Sure it might drag a little, but that's Mascis' reason to be, a long weezy slothful scuffle-shuffle on the music that binds and clogs and rusts with that Gen X couch potato sigh of ennui. Sign me up for the slack classes, for J Mascis is trashing Neil Young at his own game (ain't that **Sleeps With Angels** thing just the dreariest?). Note: This is what I'd call a token, representative review. I could have roll-called them all, but the combination of Dino Jr being an arguable non-entry, and the fact that all of them are pretty much the same gloriously dirty power pop, made me bow out. Probably a couple 'o **10's** there though.
Rating **8**

## Dio - Holy Diver (Warner Bros. '83)

Alas, the iron age of Dio arrives, this mighty debut being an astonishing expression of Will, whipped into office on a cartload of proud '70s conventions; bristling waves of medieval metal savagery, the product of a spectacular apprenticeship with two masters: Ritchie Blackmore and Tony Iommi. **Holy Diver** stands alone, built towering and unconquerable through muscular production, flashy but intelligent guitar wizardry from Vivian Campbell, and extremely rhythmic percussion from Vinny Appice that is perfectly suited to Ronnie's pulverizing, rolling-rock writing style. Dio's lyrics are in fine form, Ronnie sounding pained enough to shoulder the anguish and moral bleakness of a world's worth of disenchanted, self-destructive youth, yet just vague enough with his platitudes to escape direct accusations of Satanism, all the while maintaining metalli-poetic flow. All in all, **Holy Diver** is quintessential traditional metal, almost single-handedly reinventing gothic hard rock for the '80s, incorporating strong melodic hooks, and more than its share of velvety, classical-based pyrotechnics. A princely premiere from a seasoned veteran, **Holy Diver** evokes something closer to Dio's cinder block daze with Black Sabbath than his more arcane work with Rainbow, giving leather-winged birth to a number of proud classics including Straight Through

The Heart, Invisible, and melodic, infectious hit Rainbow In The Dark, which was even used for a beer commercial at the time. A raucous, roiling metal dynasty ensues.
Rating **10**

## Dio - The Last In Line (Warner Bros. '84)

A shade heavier, more complex, and livelier, **The Last In Line** is actually a stronger record than Dio's earthy debut. With more or less the same esteemed line-up, the band rocks out with greater abandon, while retaining the pulsating, rhythmic feel of the debut's guitar-bass-and-drum interplay. A few borderline mortals such as Breathless, Mystery (both almost timid), and Egypt (The Chains Are On) (yawn) make this a less than perfect album, although wildly groove-heavy golden grails such as the galloping We Rock and the ornate One Night In The City erase any ill will efficiently, while I Speed At Night blazes down the highway with a cold and calculating vampiric gaze, proving Dio a master of many intensity levels. Again, this one's muscular and meaty in a Sabbatherian space, with excellent, boulder-thrown production bolstering Dio's canny ability to dramatize the most heroic elements from early metal, zoning to the core of metal's reason to exist. An impressive and expertly-paced classic, that never fails to stir the blood. Dio rules. Scorekeeping note: **Holy Diver** certified platinum in '89; **Last In Line** by '87.
Rating **10**

## Dio - Sacred Heart (Warner Bros. '85)

I'm not as thoroughly taken with this one, the evil riffmaster shows his first signs of fallibility, Dio grab-bagging a loose collection of what are often average songs, stuffed through an irritating mid-rangey recording lends this one diminished majestic impact, the flawed mix distracting to the point of wondering if you've blown a woofer. Many of the songs seem to re-hash musical or lyrical themes from previous efforts; for the first time Dio sounding like he's either coasting or trying too hard to summons a demurring muse; definitely not screaming out of the gates, definitely not flaring with his usual other-worldly perfection. The result: less speedy, less lustful, less urgent than **Holy Diver** and **The Last In Line**, but in a way, more mournful and tragic, lumbering with a sort of sobbing lament for souls doomed to everlasting fire. Stand-outs: Just Another Day, hilarious "evil woman" tale Another Lie, and minor hit Hungry For Heaven, which is essentially Rainbow In The Dark for carnivores. Drivel: King Of Rock And Roll, which is live, no less.
Rating **8**

## Dio - Intermission (Warner Bros. '86)

This rare live EP (closer to a brief LP at approximately 32 minutes), is an acceptably hot collection of tunes including hummable slow-to-mid tempo newie Time To Burn and a medley that reaches back under Dio's Rainbow days. A truly shoddy excuse for an album cover. Contains two of my fave mental imprints by anybody in We Rock and Rainbow In The Dark. Another release from '86 was the British **Dio E.P.**: four tracks over two 45's in a nice gatefold sleeve; one tune from each LP thus far plus confident goth chunkster Hide In The Rainbow, previously unreleased but written for some movie.
Rating **6**

## Dio - Dream Evil (Warner Bros. '87)

As if **Sacred Heart** never happened, Dio is back on track with a definite progression from the druidic sights and sounds that became **The Last In Line**. **Dream Evil** rocks heavily down a dark and devilish Dio path. Apparently the record didn't do that well commercially, Ronnie in interviews stating that aside from the in-fighting (especially with keyboardist Claude

Schnell), the product itself was to blame. Which baffles me because **Dream Evil** is plainly a head-shredding wallop of quality Dio tales, tracks like flashy opener *Night People*, racing OTT'er *Overlove* and stately cruncher *When A Woman Cries* recalling the cream of the Dio crop. The band's pumped-up production values are back, driving compositions that rumble forth with renewed vigor, as Ronnie lays on those finger-pointing warnings of impending evil as thick as his power-lifting, dream team rhythm section. In total, **Dream Evil** always struck me as very similar to **The Last In Line**, almost to the extent of song-for-song match-ups, which is perfectly fine as far as I'm concerned, Dio albums always evoking that sense of being included in some sort of elitist rite. One of those records that writes some sort of unarticulated blueprint for a domineering life, much like Priest's **Hell Bent For Leather** or Megadeth's brilliant **Rust In Peace**.

Rating                                    9

## Dio - Look Up The Wolves   (Reprise '90)

A long wait for this one and I'm definitely not impressed; the over-bassed production being the first of many disorienting features, a sound way too bottom-heavy, drums cluelessly over-produced; all cannons and boulders, no crowd-strafing machine guns. Second problem: naff songwriting; tired Dio clichés tirelessly re-worked, and an astonishing number of tunes built around slow, meandering, uninspiring riffs; what proponents might call blues metal and what opponents would call excruciating boredom. Sadly, **Lock Up The Wolves** is generally quite heavy, but rarely innovative, urgent or even party-heavy, a full half sounding anaesthetized to the gills, sorely pathetic percentages given the Elf's killer track record. Two notable members of the **Lock Up The Wolves** team: Jens Johansson from Silver Mountain on keyboards, and Simon Wright from AC/DC on drums. An apt juncture at which to flee Sabbath-ward.

Rating                                    6

## Dio - Strange Highways   (Reprise '93)

Thicker and meatier than the paralyzed **Lock Up The Wolves** project three years back, Ronnie erases the unpleasantries of his uneasy reunion with Sabbath with this strapping effort of classical proportions. Still, Dio will never mesmerize metal again along the lines of **The Last In Line** or **Dream Evil**, but for the '90s, this timeless and time-locked warlock is doing fine work within his stubborn, insulated world. It is said Ronnie was after a sort of industrial metal here, and in a twisted non-Lollapalooza sense of the word, one can hear it. Both Vinnie Appice and guitarist Tracy G have brought their stone-carved mega-scrape intact from their previous **WW III** project, large, woofer-quaking sub-cycles that prove the perfect retaining wall for Ronnie's angrier growl and more intensely psychological lyrics. Still, maybe a bit much of **Strange Highways** lumbers to slumbering **Wolves** levels, but all said, variety prevails with a strong finish; eleven tracks, a good five or six dare I say, melted welts worthy of **Mob Rules** or maybe more so **Born Again**. Not doing much at the cash registers, I nevertheless find the record more relevant than arch-rival **Cross Purposes** or fellow time traveler **Motley Crüe**, all three looking to carve a semblance of validity in a tough new noisy world.

Rating                                    8

## Dio - Angry Machines   (Mayhem/Futurist '96)

Heavily awaited by most metal munchers, **Angry Machines** is an instant buzz, then a kind of quick fade, as one realizes that all is well here except for the songwriting. Dio has delivered a no-frills metal record, big on artery-blocking rhythms (what else is there with Tracy G and Vinny Appice?) but slight on memorable

riffs and majestic vistas. In place of the mini-man-legend's drama is a sort of blue collar, pig iron pigout, filling, but not one for the diary. The word "forced" comes to mind, Ronnie almost second-guessing what the fans might desire, dampening but not drowning creativity, disappointing but not devastating those who dropped jaw at those amazing mid-'80s masterpieces. It seems the man is after a sort of black-belched hypnosis, reviving some of the drear that plagued **Lock Up The Wolves**, while never really pooching any one song. Y'know how people slagged Fight's records, even when that second one on close inspection just whips a horse's ass (to quote that street person guy with all those indie CDs)? Well, that's what's happening here. Everybody's first impression has been "Dio's back! Let's wreck cars!" And then the subject changes.

Rating                                    7

## The Diodes - The Diodes   (CBS '77)

Quick mention for these original Canadian punkers, who sound suspiciously like beefed-up power popsters gone axe-endowed and scuzzy. This debut (at least two way artier records followed) was damn heavy and well-recorded for a Canadian New Wave record, sounding like a slightly smarter Ramones or Teenage Head, with guitar poses from Gonzo Ted, chugging along with fat mid-tempo grooves, amidst occasionally annoying, spoiled brat vocal croons. **The Diodes** was momentarily famous for novelty track, *Child Star*, a little dittie about Buffy, Mr. French and Uncle Bill, the record then fading into the woodwork as the band would turn timid at the sight of wattage.

Rating                                    5

## Dirty Looks - Cool From The Wire   (Atlantic '88)

Record #2 for these Frisco-via-Philadelphia street rawk raccoons (after a debut called **In Your Face**) gathered some steam, not to mention critical acclaim with their dressy AC/DC grind, large credit due to producer Max Norman who does one of his better knob jobs for these guys. However, this would be the last time anybody cared, follow-ups **Turn Of The Screw** from '89 and **One Bad Leg** doing different botched things with their low-brow idiom. But this one ain't half bad, at least excelling over similar teased beatniks Kix by keeping the grooves trashy and biting.

Rating                                    6

## Dirty Looks - One Bad Leg   (Rockworld/Attic '94)

Dirty Looks continue to stare evolution in the butt, idling in tandem with their doppelganger Rhino Bucket, producing the same AC/DC-derived bad boy hair metal for which they've become unknown. Sorry packaging here (i.e. no band info or lyrics) points to humdrum label interest for these guys, a band who seem to have just given up believin'. Suggestion: if you can't bring your classic rock self to embrace the '90s, really get down and lick the streets like L.A. Guns, who have scraped together a proud and dirty "up yours" with **Vicious Circle**. Back at the ranch however, **One Bad Leg** is just too clean, middle grounded and poorly written, except for the insightful title, that is.

Rating                                    5

## Dirty Tricks - Hit And Run   (Polydor '77)

Dirty Tricks were an early UK "metal" crowd who put out this slab of mild distinction plus two previous clogged and middling efforts, the Cro-magnon **Dirty Tricks** from '75 and the only slightly less aged **Night Man** in '76. All three went nowhere sales-wise and are impossible to find, which is just as well. Like many pretenders at the time, these guys seemed to come to metal by accident, with this depressive trilogy ranging from about 1/3 to 3/4 richter rating overall. Nothing here would get a rise from today's sophisticated punter, although riffs occasionally gather a head of

steam worthy of your attention. We bought it, because in the '70s, we bought just about anything long-haired with guitar/bass/drums listed as the instruments on the back cover, just hoping for the best, despite approximately 10% odds in our favour. In any event, **Hit And Run** is the heaviest and clearest from this opaque sort of act, despite the distractions of a claustrophobic recording and excruciatingly flat, cough syrup vocals. Pushes **5** for nostalgic reasons . . . 'cos we really tried hard to like it. Post break-up, members scattered to outfits as varied as Grand Prix, Vardis and Rogue Male.
Rating                                                                 4

## Disciples Of Power - Power Trap (Fringe '89)
I couldn't resist buying this after seeing the no-hope photos on the back cover. It just had to be psychotic metal. And for the most part **Power Trap** doesn't disappoint. Raw, ultra-heavy musically, black thrash vocally, with a really bad case of rifferama disease, Disciples Of Power is a hilariously obtuse Medicine Hat, Alberta band with all sorts of wild ideas, but an annoying disregard for structural logic. Could be killer if the band learns to distribute the product of its considerable and twisted imagination over five records, rather than trying to cram it all in here. One other complaint, too many blastbeats, which is a big problem throughout death metal sub-genres. Brutally brilliant recording, which poses the question of why the band felt the record needed remixing and re-releasing four years later.
Rating                                                                 6

## Disciples Of Power - Ominous Prophecy (Fringe '92)
Perhaps enthused with Voivod's creative triumphs, DOP wade deeper into the murky waters of sci-fi thrash, getting out the slide rules and calculators for this damp deepdive into underworld oddity. Sound like Florida death, filtered through an isolation that can only come from the band's sequestering in the wilds of western Canada or maybe Sweden. These guys should get more sun.
Rating                                                                 6

## Disincarnate - Dreams Of A Carrion Kind
(Roadrunner '93)
As the sticker sez, Disincarnate features James Murphy from Obituary, Death and Cancer. But who cares, his new band being just another up-ratchet of deafening grindcore like so much geometric wallpaper. Disincarnate's version of grind is at least well-executed, even though it's impossible to like, often so beatless it's hard to tell if it's fast or slow. Not that I'm the best judge, having never heard a grind band I liked until Entombed.
Rating                                                                 3

## Dismember - Massive Killing Capacity
(Nuclear Blast/Relapse '95)
On this long-awaited third record for Sweden's Dismember, the boys create a beat 'em up punk-infested bludgeon that does little to dispel those "baby Entombed" accusations. And who cares, there being well enough room for at least a handful of these inebriated, simplistic death juggernauts, Dismember recording with Tomas Skogsberg and Sunlight Studios for that unique bombed-out and fire-gutted buzzsaw sound. And strangely enough, it's almost a blessing that the record is barely over half an hour long, allowing for a quick sack and retreat mentality. One tough-as-nails sound, that edges away from death for a type of grimaced melody and stripped-down killing capacity, more guerilla wartorn than massive, but welcome all the same.
Rating                                                                 8

## Disrupt - Unrest (Nuclear Blast/Relapse '94)
One of those fairly illogical fusions of total blur hardcore punk unto death metal, and lyrics that lament various social injustices. Of course you'd never know unless you read the booklet, the band's two vocalists spewing out their venom in the usual post-hysterical rant tones. Thirty tracks on one disc, ten as CD bonus tracks.
Rating                                                                 1

## Dissection - Storm Of The Light's Bane
(Nuclear Blast/Relapse '95)
Dissection are another blindingly technical black metal construction from the Gothenburg, Sweden scene, sounding very much like amphetamine, frost-burned At The Gates, recording with Dan Swano in his Unisound Studio. Often insanely speedy (sounds like a drum machine), always inhumanly dime-on tight, Dissection are extreme and extremely musical, rising to the ranks of those to be taken seriously, melding daunting grind with elements of Norwegian death metal, both in terms of symphonic tones and those lizard-like vocals. Record two after a '93 indie called **The Somberlain**.
Rating                                                                 7

## Divine Sin - Winterland (Black Mark '95)
Yet one more "cool" record from the depths of Sweden, *Winterland* is a rumbling mudslide of suffocating gothic riffs, building onto a grindcore frame, everything from traditional metal to prog metal, biggest influences coming to mind being the mid-pace, double bass drum barrages of vintage Mercyful Fate and Memento Mori. And quite deliciously, vocalist Fredde Lundberg splits his duties between the sonorous cries associated with those two bands, and a gruff delivery that stops just short of a death metal rattle. But songs just storm forth no matter what, graced with a dangerous, volatile edge that puts these newcomers (first record, five years in the biz), in post position for considerable underground accolades. Ranks with Scum as the best of Black Mark's second string.
Rating                                                                 9

## Carl Dixon - One (Interplanet '93)
You're right . . . he's the guy from Coney Hatch that looked like Dennis The Menace. Well here on the man's ambitious first solo outing, weighing in at one tune over an hour, Carl dishes up some infectious hard rock Canadiana, softening Hatch's blow while remaining true to the band's power chord structures. Can't help but thinking of April Wine's inferior *Attitude* release, here Dixon mining that same rock radio vein over fifteen energetic groovesters, but with scads more purpose. It's hooks galore, but little bite, as the airtight constructs fall victim to a perky, lite-headed mix, too polished to offset the commercial fare enclosed. Could grow on me, given Dixon's voice and his attention to crafting good thoughtful intros, breaks, and guitar shadings. *More Than A Memory* would be a nice summer single, but *The Blood Rises* would have to be my fave. More perfectly pop metallic than cohort Andy Curran's solo excursion from a few years back.
Rating                                                                 7

## D'Molls - D'Molls (Atlantic '88)
Hard to gather a full-on hatred for churlish little oik bands like D'Molls, a glam-boy hairspray posse who just crank out the romper room rock and damn the faultlines to the reputation. So summin' up the goods: pretty Poison party metal, whiny Vince Neil type at the mike, total submission to the tenets of L.A. glamrock at every crease. Everybody's got a couple of these pet bands they relish with guilty pleasure, but this stiff,

unoriginal and completely non-consequential lot ain't one of mine.

Rating      4

## D'Molls - Warped    (Atlantic '90)

Still flying the neon green banner high while the stripship sinks in flames, D'Molls ease off a bit on the costumes while changing very little within their sound, maturing like Poison matured two or three records deep before they discovered crappy blues metal. A little funkier if you care, but still courtin' disaster as the market makes its wholesale shift away from twenty foot hairdo rock into stuff with a little more strange. One kind word: sophisticated metal fans I know actually like these guys, but I won't give names.

Rating      5

## DMZ - DMZ    (Sire '78)

Often considered a pre-cursor to punk, Boston's DMZ had more in common with fellow loudhairs The Dictators, but really, not much in common with anybody, resenting from day one any affiliation with punk rock. Equal part New York Dolls, Chuck Berry, the Munsters, the Stooges (the Ig version), and throwing up at the high school dance, **DMZ** is a brilliant but smoothly-swallowed enigma, and an unqualified collector's item, being both rare and magnificent, reverent to its dizzying array of influences, while also gelling into a twisty, ghoulish garage punk ride of its own persona, exuding delicious, primal fun beneath its scuzzy Cramps-like exterior. Metal quotient: about half heavy, yet nevertheless, entirely guitar-based with some cheesy keyboards thrown in for good measure. Tyrannical leader Jeff Conolly (Mono Mann) moved on after this lone studio offering to form the time-locked Lyres, a band dedicated to reviving the sounds on the mountains of obscure sixties records Conolly is legendary for collecting, a band that is unique and admirable as a study of rock influences during the '60s. But nothing can match DMZ for digging deep beneath the graveyard psyches of those eccentric tunesmiths left locked in their bedrooms throughout the formative years of rock. Minor smatterings of 45, EP, and live material exist (much of it gathered for When I Get Off) but this was it as far as concerted studio rock goes. Sorta makes you think of the Pistols, don't it?

Rating      10

## DMZ - When I Get Off    (Bomp '93)

Worth it more for the detailed recounting of the fabled DMZ story (by Mono Man himself) than the crusty, creaky punk enclosed, When I Get Off, despite an enticing 18 tracks, is no replacement for the bad-ass classic that is **DMZ**, most of it being pissed-up one-take garage rock, with recordings that range from the acceptable dirt mix of the band's Lift Up Your Hood EP to garbage recalling Metallic K.O. The first (and best) half of the record was previously released as Relics.

Rating      6

## DNA - Party Tested    (Boardwalk '83)

As in Derringer 'n' Appice. Rick's a more than decent musician, Carmine's an over-rated tin ear, and the chief dullard of percussion seems to dominate here as this seven track EPLP rides a comatose, synthesizer and keyboard-laced hard rock, 100% dull; party tested maybe, but nobody sez it passed. Sorta like Depeche Mode or New Order with guitars instead of Rice Krispies. Just intentionally stupid. It pisses me off because Derringer deserves to work with better people.

Rating      2

## D.O.A. - War On 45    (Alternative Tentacles '82)

Hot on the heels of their first two definitive records comes this 20 minute, eight tirade incitement of all things war. Faves are the Clash reggae of War In The East and chundering semi-hit cover tune War. A total, quintessentially punk affair, which demonstrates that little has changed from west coast poverty punk in '82 to west coast punk in '96. These grand-daddies deserve some credit from youse knows whose.

Rating      6

## D.O.A. - Let's Wreck The Party    (Justin Time '85)

Mista J. Keighly, better known as Joey Shithead, was kickin' ass in Vancouver right from the initial violent throes of the punk movement, spawning a few seminal and sought after punk singles before unleashing a couple of hard-hitting LP's, debut **Something Better Change**, then **Hardcore '81**, both quickly becoming collectors items as Canada's first serious punk platters (along with the Subhumans' highly professional and almost metallic **Incorrect Thoughts**). D.O.A. always scurried with chaotic speed and anarchic activist savvy, and **Let's Wreck The Party** is an authentic time-locked rave-up on par with the traditions of punk of which the band themselves had part in throwing open for revulsion. Joey became Jello Biafra of the North, with an added sense of positivism and constructive critical mass in terms of his many benefit concerts and consciousness-expanding eloquences. Aurally-bentedly, D.O.A. '85 is an exploratory, muscular chunk of chuggorama that courts the punk blast of old while infusing the D.O.A. ethic with authentic mid-pace accessibility and curiously melodic chantery. They're still in there, like the best from SST, but the boys are obviously looking to The Damned and their confused ilk for eccentric, tuneless and tuneful British fringe-ability. Great story: Murder In Hollywood, which would have been perfect for a California episode of **Cops**. Why the unimpressive grade?—a little to heavy on the hokey trappings of fledgling punk; i.e. stylistic indecision, too much politics, and too blocky a recording.

Rating      5

## D.O.A. - The Black Spot    (Essential Noise/Virgin '95)

Likely D.O.A.'s most sparks 'a flying record, **Presence**, I mean **The Black Spot** finds Joey and crew flipping the finger at all sorts of rock idioms from the last twenty years, most collapsing into a mash of airtight punk metal of various velocities. This is pretty much the most energetic whirlwind from the dismal genre known as '90s punk that has crossed my path, and it is fitting that it comes from one of the longest-suffering punk factories, one that has always sounded closest to the stuff that is selling today, most notably Rancid and Offspring. Big Guys Like D.O.A., Kill Ya Later, Cutting Time, I mean, the band means business, fueled-up and roaring like never before. But let's not forget, punk is punk is a rose is punk, pretty much the stupidest form of music going, dumb on purpose, distilled down next to nothing by philosophy, so there's only so far D.O.A. can take you without jumping ship.

Rating      7

## Doc Rockit - Azugi    (Azugi '84)

Doc Rockit are a Spokane band that have been around forever, getting weirder rather than more commercial over time. We got our hands on their indie debut when it came out fifteen years ago (as Spokane was our record-shopping Mecca), discovering an acceptable early attempt at mainstream metal. And here they are, ushering in the '90s, sounding like some sort of Hawkwind/Pink Fairies hippie hybrid, appropriately still indie and not likely to go elsewhere. Muddy, psychedelic, fiercely underground, and freeze-packed in the '70s. Conceptually esteemed but executed with only a modicum of craft.

Rating      5

## Doctor Butcher - Doctor Butcher (Gun '94)

Call this a perfect test for my theory that spirited, carefully constructed, creative records will sell steadily for hundreds of years, despite unspectacular results at the time of release. For fact is, **Doctor Butcher** is the lost Savatage album, a perfection piece of power metal built viciously to satisfy folks like me who pine for the 'tage of the mid-'80s. Four guys in the band, the chief writers and key sonic components being ex-Savatage alumni Jon Oliva on vocals and Chris Caffery on guitars, who sends chills into the riffrock hall of flame, evoking Chris Oliva's pioneering metal magic like it was 1983 again. But the record never saw proper distribution, the cover art's bootleg feel not helping either. Tis a shame, because all pressure points of reference are top notch here, production, Oliva's vocals, the focused songs, the glorious understanding of all that metal can be. Faves: *The Picture's Wild*, *The Altar*, and *Don't Talk To Me*, all three razor-sharp and totally old Savatage; groove-drenched schools of guitar wisdom on par with anything from **Sirens**. Mark my words: this one will see re-release and subsequent continuous release in some form for decades.
Rating **10**

## Dog Eat Dog - Warrant (Roadrunner '93)

Hard to believe this band of snowboarder-lookalike New Yorkers was allowed to call this EP **Warrant**, but stranger things have happened. Kind of a joke all around: picture a simpler, moshier Biohazard, or a heavy, hardcore Ugly Kid Joe with shout-rap vocals, or to keep it modern, a pedestrian version of Stuck Mojo. Picture me unimpressed, but many would disagree, the band's first full-length **All Boro Kings** doing fetching business in Europe, after the band was surprise winner of "1995 Breakthrough Artist of the Year" at the European MTV Music Awards.
Rating **4**

## Dog Eat Dog - Play Games (Roadrunner/Attic '96)

Dog Eat Dog continue to breed new mongrel musics, infusing their rap metal vibe with messages of hope and brassy horns a' plenty. **Play Games** has a fresh, sports-related look and feel to the thing, the band keeping their hip-hop light, airy and uncluttered, various rap luminaries helping out, even Ronnie James Dio showing up for a few vocal contributions to *Games*, which is a good example of the strong, good-natured tone to this strange record. Weird . . . for some reason I'm saying right on, but I respectfully decline attendance. Perhaps it's the rappy vocals, or maybe the goat-butting intrusion of punk, but I'm finding myself dismissing these guys as something for a much younger crowd.
Rating **6**

## The Dogs D'Amour - Errol Flynn (China/Polydor '89)

Somewhat likeable in an Almighty, Wildhearts, Thunder sort of English palsy way, The Dogs D'Amour are an acceptable bunch of party rock lads. But barely, **Errol Flynn** suffering from stiff, hair band production and an overt sense of wearing influences on their collective sleeves, influences like the Dolls, Hanoi Rocks, Poison, Cinderella, Bon Jovi, the Stones and maybe Mott. Which all goes to say that there are probably American bands doing this better. Too much acoustic guitar weaved into things, and like I say, the production is clinical and treble-heavy. Probably a great larf and barf if you're an insider, but the space afforded time, the death of glam, and one big cold ocean leaves me saying "So what?".
Rating **5**

## Dogs With Jobs - Shock (Fringe '90)

Bars and bikes do large and burly battle when Gord Kirchin, the legendary Pile Driver plugs in and shakes his girth. What results is usually a fight with the cops,

court, then prison making **Shock** an unaware concept record! Most of the bashing is at a level only marginally higher than old-style punk, but the band gives 'er the old penitentiary try, finding discarded Tank and Motörhead riffs amongst the scraps like cigarette butts on the highway of life. Trashy but oh so filled with wisdom.
Rating **7**

## Dogs With Jobs - Payday (Fringe '93)

Kickin' hindquarter into the low-rent zone, Gord Kirchin and his desperate, bone-chewin' dogs rock one out at large, mashing forth with an incredible stew of carnivore riffs, killer '80s-style technical metal, tinged with punk, hardcore humour and street smarts that rip-off all who lapse for a second. **Payday** rules the roost, chunking and metalizing real business-like, while Gord assaults his sorry listeners with tales of depravity. Total line-up rejuve, and Gord's got a band that reaches all over time for a feast that Exciter should kill for, an underground smear Anvil should lick, a killer grimevibe that orta sell lots of platters but probably won't. So bottom line: everybody can play, and nobody cares, which is the basis for lots of desperado rock, these guys spilling blood all over the boards with sly metal parody that betrays their love of the form. Dig down into the dogs, for again, that lovable violent vibe of the NWOBHM is at hand.
Rating **8**

## Dokken - Breakin' The Chains (Carrere '82)

Clean, emanating voice, clean, echoey sound, clean, muscular production and impressive weekending beats, **Breakin' The Chains** had stadium rocker written all over it, a major selling point at a time when most American titanium heads were clamouring to be the loudest, ugliest, and scaliest since Godzilla. Closer to American-style hard rock than heavy metal (indeed one of the mid-years definitions of the former), **Breakin' The Chains** has that balance of wailing guitars and listenability that makes it an enjoyable, elegant but booze-imbibing spin. I like this record for the hint of bar band camaraderie it retains, compared to the later business-oriented superstar albums Dokken somewhat cynically cranked out, although the actual energy level and production values seem more heavily-slammed on later efforts. A healthy start, from a guy with an ego to match his pop intellect.
Rating **7**

## Dokken - Tooth And Nail (Elektra '84)

Probably my favourite Dokken spin due to its mix of anthemic Def Leppard-ish mood metal and heavier, George Lynch guitar blasters. Only record #2, and Dapper Don sounds very accomplished, very worthy of his apparently massive ego, very in control of a sturdy and versatile crew of pop metal pyros. Faves include the AOR-ish and personal *Just Got Lucky*, plus seminal Dokken muscle-rockers *Into The Fire* and *When Heaven Comes Down*, both scorched with the heat of August pavement. As close to a new Van Halen as we've got at this point, Dokken is proving themselves capable of live-feel bombast and danger on par with the weightiest of American moving companies.
Rating **8**

## Dokken - Under Lock And Key (Elektra '84)

**Under Lock And Key** strikes me as too weighted towards Def Leppard's fat-and-open formula rock, an L.A. hairspray metal over-focus on teen/teenette problems, still fairly heavy but a bit subdued and predictable, as Don gets a little self-conscious about his weight, his hairline, and rumoured media exposure of his tyrannical nature. Lynch continues to willingly play the part of excess to success, defining the L.A. sound in his own image, banging out on his axe the frenzied soundtrack of the American dream. Note: each of the

first three Dokken records eventually reached platinum.
Rating       6

## Dokken - Back For The Attack   (Elektra '87)

Back is right. Dokken offers length, variation, and urgency as never before, hungry and heavy for critical attention. I also thought **Back For The Attack** had a pretty classy front and back cover. Cool colours. Still, a penchant for the dynamic mood piece gets a little tiresome, as Dokken grows too slowly, lapping themselves with their own tried and true formula. Yet due to its sheer length (about an hour), compared to the band's previous output, **Back For The Attack** feels like it's been about as interesting a trip on which sanitary L.A. stadium metalloids could ever take us; one of those lost records, full of brimming bravado, yet entirely lacking in something to believe in and adopt as soundtrack to any minute facet of one's life.
Rating       7

## Dokken - Beast From The East   (Elektra '88)

Dokken embodied everything loathsome about hair metal, but the depth of the band's roster put them above the common rabble, what with the rock hard tan of George Lynch providing the axe-based fireworks, and the petulant presence of Don providing the prima donna mystique of a Ritchie Blackmore from Redondo. This predictable double live opus closes the books (until '94's reunion), also predictably giving nod to Japan, where the band (and pretty well any other cheese metal act) saw its greatest glory. Twenty-one tracks of torrid Cali-fried riff rock, rumoured to be pretty touched-up after the fact. Stick with the studio records; more stylistic variety, more fidelity, less posing.
Rating       6

## Dokken - Dysfunctional   (Sony '95)

Differing quite substantially from the months-in-advance **Dokken** release in Japan, **Dysfunctional** (a title which describes the band perfectly; and the quibbles continue) is a rousing return to the slick sounds of old, even slicker, but classier, soaking up a few low rumbling textures from the '90s, proving this band can compete if it so wishes. Not really a fast friends reunion album, George's guitar tracks were added almost as an afterthought. But you'd never guess it, given the seamless conjunction of the songs to his style. Everything echoes effort here, from the harmonic balladry of The Maze to the expansive metal of Inside Looking Out. Sort of sets the standard for big beat hard rock all over again, really sticking to its guns but picking up the odd good habit. Final note: **Dysfunctional** probably displays the band's largest range of styles, the pacing and sequencing of the record resulting in an entertaining if somewhat guilty l'il headbang.
Rating       7

## Don Dokken - Up From The Ashes   (Geffen '90)

If you rave Dokken, you will find this solo album mildly pleasing, the record more or less a melodic, commercial and unaggressive Dokken release. Structures are squarely Dokken-like, but the subtle differences in delivery reflect the star status of Don's assembled international big hairs: John Norum, Billy White, Mikkey Dee and Peter Baltes making this a true journeyman's spread. Detailed yet boring.
Rating       6

## Doughboys - Whatever   (Pipeline '87)

With an axe-driven college punk wall of chords reminiscent of the Goo Goo Dolls, Montreal's Doughboys ride a melody-focused rendition of Hüsker Dü, mixed with early Replacements for dissipated convention; predictable "pained intellectual" vocals, and too little imagination. **Whatever** relies on sparse, low-budget arrangements, moving generally uni-cruised, with too much imitation of Dü's structural and lyrical psychology; Mould and crü proving to be the worst-copied band in smart-ass punk. Later releases abandoned the guitars for a limp, pseudo-sophisto sound.
Rating       4

## Doughnuts - The Age Of The Circle   (Victory '95)

My nomination for the year's biggest misnomer, Doughnuts are actually a vicious, discordant, black-hearted all-female quintet from Sweden. Call this one Trouble meets Paradise Lost meets Pyogenesis, as **The Age Of The Circle**'s seven distressed tracks over 20 minutes careen with evil, grinding aplomb, grimacing chops and deathly gothic beauty. Occasionally skirting (no pun intended) the sobering melodies of its many Swedish counterparts, Doughnuts also wallow in an arresting retro-doom throughout this lively mash of black. Doughnuts. I can see little grunge girls all over America innocently picking this up, hauling it home, and trading their flannels for black robes and twenty pound ceremonial daggers. Hide yer cats!
Rating       8

## Doughnuts - Feel Me Bleed   (Victory '96)

Not sure if I've been suckered by the EP versus full-length thing, but I find these songs just a little less weighty and charred compared to the tundra-melters of previous Doughnuts (the Doughboys, they ain't!). Either that, or this all-girl force of evil has been soaking up just a little too much American hardcore, tempering their fabulous gothic nucleus with street-ready riffs and vocals that bellow just a little suspiciously like other Victory acts. In any event, this is still a killer girl band, able to kick Courtney's frocked fannie without breaking a sweat. Monster tones achieved.
Rating       7

## Down - Nola   (Warner '95)

Metal's most current and gifted evil boys combine for this statement of hardline purity, named for the crazy hometown of the partners in crime, New Orleans, Louisiana. Pantera's satanspawn Phil Anselmo and Corrosion of Conformity's ragamuffin Pepper Keenan are the prime suspects, along with members of Eyehategod and Crowbar, all buds who came together when available to jam out these sick tales of life in the hemp metal '90s. And the songs are great ones, the sound instantly describable: the discipline of Pantera meets the wastecase creativity of COC meets the sobbing doom strains of Sabbath, end of story, cue the disc, fry in flames. Phil's vocals are more multi-faceted than on any Pantera masterpiece, really screaming, really singing, really tripping out under the influence of hallowed bud for miles. The artwork is as evil, black and grey as the band's dark metal thoughts. But **Nola**'s melancholic waves belie an undercurrent of heavenly retro riffs from ancient times, vaguely bluesy, all Sabbath, or as Pepper states, derived from the small scattering of bands who were drawing from Sabbath in the '80s, bands like Trouble, Cathedral, St. Vitus, Witchfinder General and The Obsessed. But of course this works for one reason: these are some of metal's hippest thinkers circa '95. They can do no wrong.
Rating       9

## Down By Law - Blue   (Epitaph '92)

Like mid-years Hüsker Dü product without the signature sound or advantage of being first, **Blue** is basically a traditional punk album from Pasadena, toned and trendy for the '90s. Once past the primal guitar/bass/drums approach, things actually get worse with a surprisingly vanilla-flavoured bank of lyrics. Al-

most entirely "heavy" in a miniature, college-boy way, with one lone acoustic tune, also Dü-ish and sensitive.
Rating **4**

## Downset - Lies (PolyGram '94)

L.A.'s answer to New York's Biohazard, Downset bludgeon and chop through this semi-inexcusable 30 minute exercise; semi, because the band's meaty, full-bodied lyrics make up somewhat for the temporal brevity. Downset's sermons preach to the extreme, all the profundity of man's misery wretched forth rappy and urbancore, over riffs that do the job convincingly enough; massive, mid-tempo hardcore rhythms ironically negating such exhaustive political correctness with sheer vocal and moshable aggression. If you groove to the snappy pop sounds of Pro-Pain, Prong, Life Of Agony, Crowbar, and of course Biohazard, this one will satisfy forthrightly, downset tearing open America from the sordid L.A. perspective for all to see. As usual bracing stuff, but alas, to my mind, too many records too similar in too short a timeframe.
Rating **7**

## Downset - Do We Speak A Dead Language?

### (Mercury '96)

Call this one a progressional congressional step into a creamier, more confident free-burning metal sound, Downset smoothing out those guitar tones and increasing the complexity of their riffs in construction of a hardcore album that tries harder. Vocals carry more angry heft, and those guitars are a thing of beauty, but the main reason to buy a Downset record (this is their second), is the concentrated positivism of their lyrics, sorta like Biohazard meets Rage Against The Machine, hard kernels of street poetry and politics belted in earnest. All things done right, Downset's sophomore has propelled these L.A. boys into the forefront of the urban metal moshbelt. Trivia note: an El Mocambo, Toronto gig marked the first time the band ever saw a Downset tattoo on a fan.
Rating **8**

## Dream Police - Dream Police (Sony '91)

Oh, I'm sure somebody loves this sparkling AOR band quite so muchly, and it is a good display of soft and heavier melody, funk metal riffs and general playability. But there's sure lotsa bands to choose from doing exactly this, Dream Police standing out somewhat because they are Norwegians, capturing an American genre so perfectly, it's scary. But I can't bring myself to care, and judging from sales, few of you could either. MRM (that's that new Euro term meaning melodic rock metal): you pick a few bands, weld 'em to your head with a few well-timed beers and you'll love 'em forever. Everybody's got their dozen or so faves, I guess one per brew or sumthin'. No reason this couldn't be one of them.
Rating **6**

## Dream Theater - Images And Words (Atlantic '92)

Dream Theater are making waves with their version of expertly detailed pomp rock for the '90s, a painstaking, monolithic sound approximating a Styx for the futuristic metal set. The progressive tag would also fit the bill, the band blasting into all sorts of tricky arrangements and keyboard elegances worthy of old Marillion or Magnum, yet of course ruthlessly updated for the '90s. Lead singer Jamie LaBrie (an Ontario boy) is one of those perfectionist helium throats situated somewherez between Geoff Tate and Rik Emmett, leading the charge through these high-minded concepts worthy of your respect, if not your gut emotional approval. Which is where I sit, finding absolutely no reason to care about this sound, basically bored with anything this clean, melodic, belaboured and slow to rile. I must stress: this is a perfect **10** amongst the progressive

metal pack, but personally, the record irritates me, my **7** rating an insult to how well put together this record really is. I just find the whole direction silly.
Rating **7**

## Dream Theater - Live At The Marquee

### (WEA International '93)

This might be the most studio-glitzy "live" record I've ever heard, which is testimony either to cheating or chops. But never ye mind, if you love this band (as many do), you will marvel at the godly intricacy of it all. If the Dream Theater concept causes your eyes to glaze over (like yours truly), then this might as well be another studio spread. Full-length, full on the bombast. Indulge if you like, 'cos you know they have.
Rating **6**

## Dream Theater - Awake (Atlantic '94)

Delving more into concentric progressivism, Dream Theater are beginning to buy the hype, giving the professorial fan just what he craves for cramming. No shinola, these guys are actually beginning to sound like a supra-slick 21st century schizoid U.K., stretching their artrock outlandishness over 75 minutes of unabashed ego perfection. I'll just have to defer to the slide rules and pocket protectors in the crowd and hand another **7** as if anybody cares. The lowdown: even more prog, less metal than the last, and no, not an ounce "darker" as some might have you believe. This album contains no songs. On second thought, make that a **6** for being geeks.
Rating **6**

## Dream Theater - A Change Of Seasons (Warner '95)

In typical large labour style, Dream Theater come up with an hour of music, and call it an EP. Which I guess in spirit, it is, offering one massive title track (23:06) plus a slew of gimmicky live covers. A Change Of Seasons is an old chestnut originally recorded for the **Images And Words** progslab. The song didn't make the cut, and thus languished in rarely played, slightly bootlegged status for years, until the guys decided to change much of the melody, structure and lyrics for re-recording here. It's what you would think. So much meaning and genius songwriting, I wanna cry (yeah, right). The covers are a blast to read on the back cover, and pretty cheeky keen to hear once. But there's no real reason for you to care too heavily, as this slick, clinical hard rock band basically tries to play each track or sliver thereof as closely to the original as possible. Highlights: Purple's Perfect Strangers, Zep's Achilles Last Stand, snips of Carry On My Wayward Son, and grudgingly Elton John's Funeral For A Friend. No real thrills here, unless the concept of Dream Theater playing covers gets you off. Imaginative choices, blindingly obvious execution.
Rating **6**

## D.R.I. - 4 Of A Kind (Metal Blade '88)

A junior-string version of mid to modern era Anthrax in no less than looks, lyrics and general moral sensibility, mixed with a musical melding of Metallica - **Kill 'Em All** speed riffery and more literal hardcore structures. Mostly fast, aggressive, clean, but lacking in chops and mobility, Dirty Rotten Imbeciles manage to bore before long with their uni-leveled, light-hearted skate drone, which I guess is the antithesis to bands like Prong, Suicidal Tendencies, and yes, these days Metallica themselves, who each build on basic crunch in pursuit and attainment of ever so slightly demarcated individuality. D.R.I. basically began as a hard core punk outfit (check out the vocals on this), and in actuality, **4 Of A Kind** (the band's third after **Dealing With It** and **Crossover**) smacks more of a coming-out process in search of the intricacies demanded by techno cum thrash cum ultra cum speed metal. This juvenile party trick is a long way from such necessary mastery.

Rating **3**

## D.R.I. - Thrash Zone (Metal Blade '89)

More of the same cardiac velocities and skeletal rattling from these relentless California moshkensteins, **Thrash Zone** does little to break from the steel-plated headspace of America's skate generation, a pissed-off body politic growing larger and more randomly violent every sundown. Basically fuel for the mohawk contingent, that like its audience, refuses to advance and get a job. Vague similarity to the markedly more shredly and indeed intimidating M.O.D.

Rating **4**

## Drifter - Nowhere To Hide (Front Row '89)

Fairly accomplished German (Swiss?) blosh, ultra-heaving in the Slayer/Metallica plectum, with a serious case of rifferama confusia (the dreaded Queensryche/Fate's Warning syndrome). Granted, **Nowhere To Hide** is fairly professional sounding although there definitely remains the aforementioned refusal to get to the bloody point. The packaging screams that the album features Phil Campbell of Motörhead, which doesn't make any difference whatsoever in the sound. Anyways, who cares? Lyrically, a cut above American techno-thrash, but vocals-wise, a little too melodramatic like a night at the opera. Reminds me of old Flotsam And Jetsam.

Rating **5**

## Drivin' N' Cryin' - Scarred But Smarter (Island '86)

Atlanta's Drivin' N' Cryin' are one of the newer bands in this book that could be considered questionable entries. However, in my infinite wisdom I've decided to include them for the following reasons: 1) I like them, 2) a lot of other metal types like them (so it may be worth your while to hear what they have to say), 3) they rock most righteously live, and 4) the band's newer product such as **Fly Me Courageous** and **Smoke** most definitely tip the scale towards hard rock if not heavy metal. D'N'C is the brainchild of lead guitarist/vocalist/and proud dope smoker Kevn Kinney; a band beyond categorization, somewhat to their detriment when it comes to locating an audience. Their recorded output is all over the board stylistically, yet is quite consistently accomplished and warm, whether tip-toeing through acoustic fields or trampling through loose semblances of metal. The debut is appropriately the least assured of the five to date, approximating six or seven tangents of power pop, like a slightly meaner, more erratic and less whiney version of REM (a band I've grown to loathe after worshipping them for the better part of nine records). It all adds up to a half album of classy D'N'C tunes and another half album of styles that are merely not to my liking. Warning: the least heavy of the five.

Rating **6**

## Drivin' N' Cryin' - Whisper Tames The Lion
(Island '88)

**Whisper Tames The Lion** was my introduction to this enigmatic and somewhat confusing power(?) trio who mix equal doses of cranked guitars, country folk, hippy fuzziness, and the blues (hmm . . . sounds like another band I've listened to from time to time). The heavy cuts on this drowsy classic sound more like ornery but innocent jams rather than preconceived metal tunes, giving the record an even, sensitive keel no matter what the power setting. Kinney's pent-up, claustrophobic vocals provide a further distinctive thread of continuity towards the difficult but rewarding crafting of a Drivin' N' Cryin' sound. **Whisper** is a good-time, slow-time, lazy-time record that garnered small pockets of fervent critical acclaim, but confounded market-ers in terms of figuring out who would want to own it. Definitely a timeless crossover band of some sort, a band who has no trouble being appreciated by followers of quality music despite their favoured genres. In simple terms, half folk, half rock'n'roll.

Rating **9**

## Drivin' N' Cryin' - Mystery Road (Island '89)

The boys from down south are back (plus one guitarist) with an expanded and less tentative journey through the similar and equally other-worldly peaks and valleys that comprised **Whisper Tames The Lion**. The rock is bigger as evidenced by Kinney's louder 'n' rowdier vocals, and the fireside acousticisms more lush and dreamlike. On the drivin' front we get twin cruisers *You Don't Know Me* and *Toy Never Played With*, plus the power pop thrasher *Syllables*. On the cryin' side, it's country twanger *Straight To Hell*, celtic flavoured lead cut *Ain't It Strange*, and the Zepp-ish acoustic mantra *With The People*. Again, almost total demarcation of mellow and heavy on this, yet as with **Whisper**, it's all justice true and perfect, as it could be no other way. With bands like this, it gets beyond sound to the point of being reduced and simultaneously elevated to personalities and simple honesty.

Rating **9**

## Drivin' N' Cryin' - Fly Me Courageous (Island '90)

**Fly Me Courageous** strikes me as a search for the less complex, more human and communicative truths revealed only through hard rock, and of course, only by a hallowed few. A similar excursion of failure: Iggy Pop's **Instinct**, a similar excursion of magnificent triumph: Lizzy's **Thunder And Lightning**. In Drivin' N' Cryin's case, the end result is unfortunately closer to, although not nearly as dismal as the former, in effect a loss of finesse, a step away from communication and connection. **Fly Me Courageous** moves with less agility, depth and sense of adventure than earlier outings, rocking somewhat bluntly, a frustrating record in that the structures are for the most part clumsy, simple, and unpalatable as witnessed on *Chain Reaction* and *Build A Fire*. However, the smooth cruisin' *Around The Block Again* and *Lost In The Shuffle* are pretty cool, as are the two or three mellow ones. Not really a bad album, just a bit soulless and pedestrian in comparison with its predecessors. If Drivin' N' Cryin' are going to commit fully to hard rock, they're going to have to flesh out their bag of tricks, or at least look around and quietly steal a few choice riffs.

Rating **6**

## Drivin' N' Cryin' - Smoke (Island '93)

Hard to believe it's been three years since the evolutionary ballsiness of **Fly Me Courageous**. **Smoke** continues the barroom wattage, swinging the chain more at ease with the electric side of the band. Kinney's soulful suvvern songwriting has no problem shining through the basic patterns as he weaves tales of life on the dreamy edges, leaning way over the rails for the liquid '60s acid rock of *Patron Lady Beautiful*, while for the most part sending them right down the core of rock'n'roll living as on lead track *Back Against The Wall* and the warm throb of *Eastern European Carney Man* (dedicated to Marco Sunset and Soul Asylum). So plain, yet ya gotta luv 'em, because nobody else out there wants to sound this real and simple and innocent, the band existing in an industry vacuum, creating their own good times for some kind of private party with a few close friends. Lots of big fat chords and a guitar sound sturdy as a generations-old backyard oak, yet not metal in any philosophical sense, just outside boundaries while simultaneously the stuff of regular rock. One of them secret songs tacked onto the end (jam more like it).

Rating **7**

**133**

## Drivin' N' Cryin - Wrapped In Sky (Geffen '95)

Well now I've pretty much got no truck calling this band "heavy metal" or anything thereby approximated, Kinney taking wing from his light and loving acoustic solo records, turning back the tides on his band's turned-up chordage, offering **Wrapped In Sky** instead. So doing what Soul Asylum and even Screaming Trees have done, Kevn Kinney delves deeper into his roots, offering a lush levity, recording the record in California, and becoming The Eagles! No, just kidding, the man has more cool than cranky ol' money-grubbing Joe Walsh could ever muster. But take heed, if Drivin' N' Cryin didn't belong next to Pitch Shifter, Bathory and Sepultura before, it's even less appropriate now, although I take a certain pleasure in trying to convince you they are eminently worth your while.

Rating     8

## DSK - Exploder! (Divine Industries '96)

DSK churn forth well-fraught power punk with an eye to keeping things dynamic, an effect which is achieved through an almost metallic number of riff change-ups, wise-ass vocals and lyrics to match, and lots of bass guitar verses which explode grunge-like into fresh breaks and choruses. Picture The Jesus Lizard and NoMeansNo brought back to earth by The Headstones, tricky, abrasive stuff grounded by beer tent 4/4.

Rating     6

## Dubwar - Pain (Earache '97)

Earache is doing some soul-searching as of late, trawling the waters for bands outside of the label's traditional two-middle-finger metal. Thus Wales-based Dubwar finds a strange new home, Earache fully intent on bringing the band's reggae-heavy funk metal to North American ears. I for one don't really care, having never warmed to concepts like 24-7 Spyz, Living Colour or Bad Brains (all defunct). What's worse, Dubwar is gucked up with over-production, trying to be hiphopped at the same time as funk, metal, reggae, dub and alternative (see the much smarter Fishbone). Moderately successful back home, Dubwar could break over here, given the level of competence achieved, and the trendy beats enclosed. But like I say, too wishywashy, fence-sitting, and clinical, which is why similar acts like Dan Reed Network and Bootsauce hit the crapper while FNM and the Peppers flourished.

Rating     4

## Duff - Believe In Me (Geffen '93)

Strange specimen this Duff, seemingly incapable of stringing a sentence together, but at the same time, multi-instrumentalist and apparently an all-around nice guy. But all the "talent" in the world, internal and donated, can't save this record from sounding like warmed-over G'NR; light on drama, simply sleazy and too bent by Duff's sneering NY Dollsy persona. And even though the permeating image is one of the scuzziest of street rocks, the project-like feel can't be ignored, Duff dressing up the tunes with lavish layers of rockstarstuff, as he examines all sorts of valid old-style rock genres, anything that says hard living. So despite playing the underbelly underdog, his record is really, really commercial when it's added up, Duff rounding every base G'NR ever did, with songs that just don't blow you away. And that voice gets tiring. Like I said, strange one. Likeable, but very expected.

Rating     6

## Dumpy's Rusty Nuts - Get Out On The Road (Metal Masters '87)

Blubbery bluesy biker metal with a sense of humour and history that bellows loud and clear "I've made a rock'n'roll record. I can die now." Actually more of a party souvenir, DRN aren't planning to be the next Deep Purple, they're just having a ball making a record, which, in my opinion, is as worth doing as anything else on this planet. Actually, it ain't much to listen to unless you're one of their drinking buddies, of which they probably have enough without you hanging around. This is their third (featuring guest cameos from a couple of Hawkwind guys), followed by a live record in '88.

Rating     4

## Dystopia One - Attempted Moustache (Rawkus Entertainment '96)

These NYC wiseacres play a sort of progressive garage rock, distorting full-up their Rick Wakeman keyboards and Geddy Lemmy bass so they don't need a guitarist. What results is a psychoderelict, NIN-ish stoner vibe that rants about cops, skinheads, dead insects, dates and other miscreants of the paved landscape. Call it a perplexed cross between Primus, Mr. Bungle and urban hardcore. In any event, a certain wet sandpapered terrain is achieved, even if such a world may only fit the folds of your day-to-humdrum-day reality. Profane, unique, thought-provoked but fully irritating.

Rating     5

## Earth Crisis - Destroy The Machines (Victory/Cargo '95)

Earth Crisis fuse hardcore battle ethics with the grinding chomp of the new metal, finding Biohazard, Pantera and Crowbar more often than skatepunk, while Karl Buechner's lyrics rant all over veganism, animal rights, straight-edge and wrenching personal alienation. Vocals tend towards gut-deep roaring, as a backing track of fresh, pummeling mid-pace riffs drive home Karl's PC punk points, which all combines for a healthy shot at crossover credibility. One weird thing though; the cover graphics lean dangerously close to white supremacist rock, although a careful check of the lyrics find no truck in that direction. Anyhoo, the sum total is a record that is raw, subwoofed, and groovy; totally hardcore in ambience, yet more towards the new urban metal. Quite good, really.
Rating                                                    7

## Eater - The Album (The Label '77)

Armed with one of the earliest punk albums, Eater also held the distinction of being one of the youngest bands on the British scene, apparently averaging 15 years of age between its members when this record pained its way into our necks. **The Album** is a pretty heliummy affair, zipping along like a cross between The Buzzcocks and The Ramones, with the former's wealth of ideas and exploratory ethic, and the latter's affinity for being . . . well, punks. **The Album** is a true punk up-yours; fairly loose, very British in its goofy melodies; silly, off-kilter and completely guitar-driven. Not to say that it's metal, just innocuous nostalgic new wavey gravy fun. Too rainy, however, to serve as voluntary soundtrack to one's life. Highlights: *Fifteen* (Alice Cooper's *I'm Eighteen*), *No Brains*, *Room For One*, *Get Raped*, and *Anne*, which sounds like elastics.
Rating                                                    6

## Eater - All Of Eater (Creativeman/Cargo '95)

Imagine my surprise seeing this little gem, a CD reissue of the entire first and only Eater album (1977), plus twelve tracks from various singles and whatnot. But the funny thing is the lack of liner notes, save for band personnel and song list, which effectively hides the fact that the music here is 18 years old, older than the band was when they pogo punked it together! One of THE first UK punk bands (along with the Pistols, Damned, Clash, Buzzcocks, Adverts and Vibrators), Eater were known for their perky poppy guitar briskness, their average age of 15, along with the fact that their record

was fairly clean and listenable, simple songs for simple minds. So press here for 28 truly ground-floor new wave ditties circa '77. Weird, this CD age.
Rating                                                    7

## Earthquake - 8.5 (Beserkley '76)

One look at the band photo and you know there's heaps to worry about. Mentioned here more as a laughing look back, Earthquake had at least a couple of others besides this vacuous piece of dated nonsense under their belts, although this is actually the best one, featuring shakey attempts at accessible hard rock courtesy of one of the sorry underdog labels of the '70s. ("Home of the Hits", right.) Tight, well-recorded but entirely lost in identity quandry, like a totally nerdy emulation of **Go Girl Crazy!** Well, *Motivate* Me and *Hit The Floor* anyways.
Rating                                                    2

## Earthshaker - Midnight Flight (King/Viper '84)

This accomplished Japanese act were more or less third in line to Bow Wow and Loudness, sounding right in between the two, basically Bow Wow's raw pop metal in nice collision with Loudness' European-influenced axe histrionics and general metal savvy. Too bad 90% of it is in Japanese, 'cos this would have made a nice, ragged hard rock record.
Rating                                                    6

## Econoline Crush - Purge (EMI '94)

A cacophony of technology and riffery collide to form Vancouver's Econoline Crush, a band with tenuous links to '80s embarrassments like The Cult, Zodiac, Wild and Billy Idol, with future-bound lunges into Ministry and NIN with a sweaty human touch. Fact is, EC's debut six tracker rocks smartly, much like Chicago's overlooked Mind Bomb, making technology work towards critical mass, layering the assault with lots of analogic, creating muscle-dance grooves of the future; goodly metal cashed to the cyberage. But having dished the praise, true rock pure and bludgeon-bound is far from dead, and this ain't true or pure. It's more like a welcome Canadian curio, and there's ample room for this kind of robo-mosh (I think). Whether Econoline Crush can expand on Trent Reznor's death-defying and defining contribution to this partitioned genre remains to be seen. Their level of creativity come their first full-length will have to win over the market's patience

for this trendy, almost irritating type of hybrid. **Purge** is a solid, professional and intriguing first step.
Rating 6

## Econoline Crush - Affliction (EMI '95)

Huge Canadian label push on this one, Econoline Crush criss-crossing Canada And Europe, esteemed band buddy Rhys Fulber on as full member at least for the tour. But something about **Affliction** leaves me cold, despite the worthy attempt to keep the techno at bay, concentrating on brooding staccato chugging riffs as the boys try to muster some angst. Lead single *Wicked* really reminds me of Billy Idol, as the band seems unable to pull of the evil meany tendencies of this kind of music (see front cover). Probably one of the most hyped Canadian records of '95, **Affliction** doesn't exactly come across as the bold savior of industrial in the Great White North that its pre-press trumpeted. Tried to like it, but found its nastiness fraudulent, stiff and a bit too nightclubby.
Rating 6

## Edge Of Sanity - Nothing But Death Remains
(Black Mark '91)

Thankfully, this aural turgid debut record is scarcely half an hour in length and breadth. But it's pretty cool how this young band already has their particular frosted twist on death in check and ready to rumble. Best thing one could say is that the production is crisp on top and nasty down low, low also including proto-typical death vox. Of some redeeming value, EOS already whipping up a few of their insanely guttural riffs for your wincing pleasure.
Rating 5

## Edge Of Sanity - Unorthodox (Black Mark '92)

Fledgling Edge Of Sanity demonstrates the selfsame beginnings as other Scandinavian acts which now renovate the category that is death metal, namely bands like Cemetery, Entombed, Tiamat and to an extent, Bathory, all lately arriving at strange but fresh twists on a tired and tiring sound. **Unorthodox** is your standard, sturdily erected, black metal blastarama, precursor of the grandeur to come, but only for fleeting moments between the wall-of-death bludgeon from all corners. Capable for its age, even a bit artsy and wickedly atonal, but listenable . . . no.
Rating 5

## Edge Of Sanity - The Spectral Sorrows (Black Mark '93)

Best thing about this ugly, ice-filled thrashfest is its bruising, distorted recording, Dan Swano grafting bass onto guitar like a power-mad scientist (see Entombed), turning the slower tracks like *Lost* and magnificent Manowar cover *Blood Of My Enemies* into Panzer division formations as our man Dan barks a hummable, apocalyptic grindcore tune. Picture the sum total of '94's **Purgatory Afterglow** rusted and running months and months after the prescribed oil change and tune-up, and you've pretty much entered the grinding, raw, electrified and terrified netherworld of this record. The scraping mix renders the blastbeated thrash passages inoperable, but anything below this speed is fantastic (the amount of non-blur?: exactly 20% more than the last, 20% less than the follow-up). And there are tricks galore, odd musical passages and breaks scattered like teeth to the tundra, brightest fang being Swano's vampiric Sisters Of Mercy impersonation on *Sacrificed*. A highly creative band really, and gathering might all the time, always perched wavering on the (wait for it) edge of sanity. Interim four track EP **Until Eternity Ends** contains a cover of *Invisible Sun* by The Police.
Rating 8

## Edge Of Sanity - Purgatory Afterglow (Black Mark '94)

Sweden's Edge Of Sanity are becoming genius purveyors of a futuro-thrash sound that conquers all heathens through a dead-perfect mix of melodious guitars, grind smear, blastbeats, groove, vomitvox and smooth introspective crooning, the latter brilliantly demonstrated through the emotive shine of *Black Tears*, probably the sweetest grindcore tune since Paradise Lost's *Sweetness*. What is most arresting here (here being the band's fourth full-length) is the use of breakneck speed for shade, contrast, intro and variety; rarely for verse or for long. Through all these musical choices, EOS thread the progressive mindbends of Voivod and Anacrusis, weird 2112 sci-fi excursions accompanied by the sorrow of sobbing guitar lines (see *Velvet Dreams* and vivid opener *Twilight*), very hooky but still extremely tough, underground and so Swedishly chilled. The perfect blend of crystal clear vodka, dead-blue antifreeze and snowy blow, strap on this fancy flight, drift in hellish descent, and warm to the **Purgatory Afterglow**.
Rating 9

## Edge Of Sanity - Crimson (Black Mark '96)

Dan Swano is proving himself to be weirder every year, this time taking his promising main vehicle Edge Of Sanity and crashing it on the conceptual rocks. If you want to hear what I hoped would be Swano's new record, look to Cemetery's **Sundown**, for here the guy has birthed a laborious, convoluted concept album comprising a single forty minute track. Musically, Swano has returned to his thrashy oddly ambient grindcore roots, **Crimson** leaping out of my poor speakers with a death growl and a turgid down-tuned evilblast (see early Entombed), the track then ebbing, flowing and segueing through somber but death-apparent, not all that creative acoustic passages and even messier thrash, but rarely the captivating new wavey goth that made **Purgatory Afterglow** so innovative for its time. The cover art is plainly botched, as is the production, too trebly and cymbal-crashed, somewhat unraveled by the loose performances by Dan and band. Lyrically, wow. Swano has crafted a sort of futuristic biblical tale of man's impending extinction (incapability of breeding) and rebirth at the hands of a Jesus-like figure. What results is a hazy, vague storyline pitting good against evil, kings, queens and fantasy mumbo jumbo all over the place, a complicated tale sabotaged by Swano's choppy English as second language. Conclusion: harsher and more regressed than I had expected, which puts me way out of range of having the patience to invest psychological attachment to a single forty minute track.
Rating 7

## Edge Of Sanity - Until Eternity Ends (Black Mark '94)

This four track collection of metal wonderment was a stop-gap EP for Swano & gang, comprising songs the band didn't feel would fit the record-in-progress, **Purgatory Afterglow**. Elegant and killer at once, **Until Eternity Ends** reminds one of Sentenced, especially the swingin' title track and *Eternal Eclipse*, which together are two of my fave EOS tracks bar none. Closing out: a non-Swano original called *Bleed* (boring retro-thrash), and a thick 'n' chunky cover of The Police's *Invisible Sun*, all tracks produced for iron lung headphone euphoria. Deadly stuff.
Rating 9

## Edge Of Sanity - Infernal (Black Mark '97)

This what I like to see, Swano and his assembled nutters turning in an evil little smudge of a record, one that compresses both arrangement and attack, one that ices the blood and races through the nervous system like bent staples with brains. Somehow the man has beaten to a pulp any artiness, while somehow transforming buckets of death into something listenable. This might have to do with the urgency of Peter Tagtgren's recording, the insidious melody, the versatility in Swano's vocal repertoire, and most likely, the brevity and instant hook of nigh half the tracks. Between such Sabbath Entombed alchemy as *Hell Is Where The Heart Is*, *Hollow* and *15:36* are vicious little deathpunk tracks like *The Bleakness Of It All* and *Inferno*, Swano making damn sure we never mistake EOS for Morgana Morose ever again. Call it the white hot flame of *The Spectral Sorrows* meets the tuneful heart-tug of *Purgatory Afterglow*, or just call it sharp and shocking. Whatever it is, it's sleep-deprived, hungry and in bad need of a shower.

Rating                                                    8

## EF Band - Deep Cut   (Neon '82)

Sweden's EF Band (named for the last initials of the two founding members, if you care) got their first break as an inclusion on early, legendary compilation **Metal For Muthas**. This, the band's second full-length (debut being **The Last Laughs On You**, with a third in '85 called **One Night Stands**), is a near classic chunk of royalty from the very origins of the NWOBHM. Smart, well-recorded retro-metal with just that touch of fragility that embodies spontaneity. Nicely low-budget sounding and experimental in scope, **Deep Cut** kicks off with its best cut *Love Is A Game*, a galloping romp that recalls old Quartz or old Samson. From hereon in, we get touches of pop, blues, and in the best cases, melodic hard rock, all delivered with rumbling, scrappy edge and disdain for posturing, set spinning beneath the fine, Sean Harris-style pipes of Englishman John Ridge (shortly thereafter replaced). One of those independent works that sounds like British rock vets slamming their way through a friendly, relaxed jam session, just for the fun of it. Emminently nostalgic and playable.

Rating                                                    7

## Electric Angels - Electric Angels   (Atco '90)

Street-ready HR with more than a wink and a nod to Hanoi Rocks-style glam 'n' bash, sporting requisite holler-along choruses and a likeable boozy twang. Starts moderately raucous and gets boppier as the party—dressed in pink chiffon cowboy outfit—wears long and bubbly into the night. I guess my main sentiment is just how unnecessary it all sounds: like it, don't need it.

Rating                                                    5

## Electric Boys - Funk-O-Metal Carpet Ride   (Atco '90)

This transplanted Swedish quartet raised a few eyebrows when they were taken under the wing of Bob Rock, who figured them to be the next big thing, cranking out a bass-driven funky metal carpet ride with traces of Saigon Kick and Bang Tango, plus gobs of corporate harmonic savvy and dynamic. Mix in equal doses of psychedelic sitar-ine intros, trendy wah-wah, sing-songy choruses and fairly lively riffs, and you have a ruff-disguised-as-smooth, tour-ready debut. On the negative however, too much slow dopey funk metal (probably Bob's fault) and overly techy drums (thud, rap, thud, rap, thud—see Def Leppard, but don't stare too long. The stench will make your eyes water). Pushes 7, for an untapped undercurrent of confidence.

Rating                                                    6

## Electric Boys - Groovus Maximus   (Atco '92)

Big nasty maximum grooves become the order of the day, as Sweden's Electric Boys explore with shining bombast their American party rock obsession. That undercurrent of confidence of which we spoke with regards to the debut blossoms forthrightly here, the band even self-producing, the meters red-lining all corners of the sonic spectrum, driving each phat hard rock riddim into hooky euphoria. Truly amongst the upper echelon of deservedly cocky AOR rockers, even if the record-buying public never got around to patronizing this band with zeal.

Rating                                                    7

## Electric Boys - Freewheelin'   (Music For Nations '94)

You can't scrub off star quality once it takes, **Freewheelin'** resolutely stirring the band's thick and chunky stew, convoluted, slow-brewed retro riffs wafting from the hearty meal, Electric Boys really finding their pocket, their reason to be. The operative word here is "trundle", as tracks like *Ready To Believe*, *My Knuckles Your Face* and *Not My Cross To Bear* tank forth like a tidal wave of heavy water. And it's fitting the record culminates in the final of three bonus tracks, a cover of Ram Jam's looped *Black Betty*, one of the harbingers of Electric Boys' rough-hewn, not rough-recorded, psychedelic blues stomp. Cool band, with even the likes of Hanoi Rocks, Whitesnake and fringe-dwelling Deep Purple orbiting around their rock solid centre.

Rating                                                    8

## The Electric Hellfire Club - Burn, Baby, Burn!

(Cleopatra '93)

Squarely sincere Satanic rock with a reputable industrial pedigree (My Life With The Thrill Kill Kult), the EHC mix up the Zombie culture kitsch but good, coming off as an electronified hybrid of Cramps and White Zombie with a bit of Sisters Of Mercy thrown in. But it all leaves me cold as a Siberian corpse, vocals mumbling and way back, beats stuttering and doddering, the guitar work watery and secondary to the creepy dance beats. Wisconsin souls are in grave danger, given the unmitigating evil of Thorn's lyrics, but pretty well all attempts at sonic communication are buried in night punk rave dervishness. Read it and weep, but don't bother playing it.

Rating                                                    5

## Electric Love Hogs - Electric Love Hogs   (London '92)

Electric Love Hogs travel a fairly unexplored pathway towards big, layered, metallic funk, sorta like a corporate hard rock version of Infectious Grooves, absolutely stoked riffing and slap-bass perhaps recalling Faith No More's grooved passages, but totally filled-in by Mark Dodson's over-extending production. And the band's compositions are quite elaborate, veering into prog or Jane's Addiction terrain (Stephen Perkins guests, as does Fishbone's Norwood Fisher). A total competitor, this one need not have bowed to anybody, given its attention to detail and effortless chops mania. Just too many of all types of metal bands competing for our CD dollar, most running around with major label deals. Absolutely paint-stripping axework.

Rating                                                    7

## Eleven - Thunk   (Hollywood '95)

Along with Menthol, Eleven's third opus **Thunk** was one of my main faves summer '95. Known more for being the band incorporating ex-Chili Pepper drummer Jack Irons (before his departure for slightly more recognizable pop combo Pearl Jam), Eleven is actually the brainchild of ultra-worldly duo Alain Johannes and Natasha Shneider, who trade their myriad male/female vocal personas like another great LA band, X. Exceedingly high-minded, maybe like Pearl Jam meets XTC and World Party in the Soundgarden, Thunk swirls in pop complication, drop-dead smart, yet silky smooth tracks like the catchy *Nature Wants To Kill Me* and the sensuous *Damned* forming bookends for the hip hijinx enclosed. Verdict: Sabbath and the Beatles compressed and exploded into alternative sunbursts, sorta like prog-grunge with gumdrops.

Rating                                                    8

## Elf - Elf  (Epic '72)

I used to ignore these early platters by guys that matter, knowing full well metal was nowhere to be heard. But then I found I got into pretty much any old '70s band, as long as there were guitars a' plenty. So Elf (along with Bang, Lone Star, Geordie, Sir Lord Baltimore, Mott, Humble Pie, Faces, Bad Co.) have something fine and aged to offer, besides being the first recording band of top-notch vocalist Ronnie James Dio, who sings mighty fine here, pulling the odd trick he'd never try in his next incarnation as pint-size wizard of metal. Musically, **Elf** is a pleasant, friendly display of hard-hitting pub rock, honky tonkin' boogie tunes recorded robustly and electrified, suvvern-style lyrics quite the hoot spilling from our man Ronnie. The band does manage to collapse into random heaviness here and there, a sort of Cream-derived psychedelic stew, so the record almost crosses that line into historical importance independent of Dio. Just barely, though, even if the guys looks real menacing like Trouble or Sabbath circa **Paranoid**. The band followed with **LA 59** in '74, and **Trying To Burn The Sun** in '75, with pieces of the band becoming Blackmore's first incarnation of Rainbow.
Rating                                                  6

## Elixir - The Son Of Odin  (Elixir '86)

Galloping goth from jolly ol' England, sounding more like messed-up and deluded Americans than British earthdogs, Elixir is basically Virgin Steele meets Maiden, heavily muscled and universally pounding, yet down-scale due to endless strings of frilly classical accents, and a mix low on both treble and vocals.
Rating                                                  6

## Rik Emmett - Absolutely  (Duke Street '90)

Man, don't get me started.
Rating                                                  0

## Rik Emmett - Ipso Facto  ('92)

Idiots rule again. Even more increasingly dismal. Rik's the true Peter Cetera of rock. I'm into this for almost as much as Lep's **Adrenalize**, but ground rules dictate that I can't go lower than **0**. If I could though, Rik would be my man. Wimpier and more clueless still than **Absolutely**. Back in '95 with some sort of snobby jazz rock turd.
Rating                                                  0

## Emperor - In The Nightside Eclipse  (Century Black '95)

Emperor are one of the few (phew!) for-real Norwegian black metal verminators, a list which includes Mayhem, Darkthrone, Enslaved, Mayhem, Burzum and about a dozen more with scant recordings between them. Card-carrying criminals here include Faust, jailed for killing a homosexual that came on a little heavy, and Samoth who's been sent to jail for two years for burning down an old wooden church. Make's touring a bitch. Anyhow, **In The Nightside Eclipse** is as killer as any in the genre, Emperor operating at or beyond the levels of Brits Cradle Of Filth and their own buddies Enslaved, emitting black-infected white noise, ambient thrash at inhuman holocaustical speeds, with the added rare attraction of betraying chops, which proves there must have been at least a few dark evenings when these guys were playing along to their Rush records, rather than terrorizing the countryside. I guess once you cop to the fact that this stuff is more about texture and mood than hooky choruses, it's easier to appreciate the six foot thick wall of buzzing sonics, all individual parts fried up in a gastric stew of unpleasant flavours until it just boils out of your sorry woofers. Through a filmy haze, I can almost get there theoretically, with a few more hours of conditioning to go until I can throw this on for "pleasure."
Rating                                                  6

## Empyria - Behind Closed Doors  (Dark Wings '96)

Progressive power metal in the mid-'90s has taken to heart all those complaints about bad songskills, cold vibes and long, boring wankabouts. Witness the immediate crunch 'n' cruise of Iced Earth, Nevermore, the revived Meliah Rage, and now Vancouver's Empyria. **Behind Closed Doors** is an instantly likable slab of dare I say, car deck metal! I mean, fact is, there are a ton of hooks on this record (*Seasons Of Change* would have been a hit single in the days of hard rock), Empyria coveting and developing their group chemistry, all parties obviously in control of their chops, recorded wide, trebly and bassy, over which vocalist Paul Falcon belts out dramatically confident tale after tale. A euphoric metal balance is achieved.
Rating                                                  8

## Enchantment - Dance The Marble Naked  (Century Media '94)

Jumble together the unjuxtaposable, heap them high, black and steaming and you'll begin to envision the Enchantment scarscape. Beware pixies, it ain't pretty, for this twisted Blackpool quintet combine a sort of vampiric and veiled sexuality; love poetry of a dark, sensual but awkward and not at all graphic nature, with a slow but scrappy grind doom putridplod. Cap with extremely germy grind vocals, trading pitchforks with a more "normal" type snivel, and the conundrum that is this band takes leather-winged flight. Not at all a pleasurable sort of sound, frontiersman like the plus a plethora of other curious Century Media acts are finding bold new ways to depress. Align with the Tiamat, Paradise Lost, My Dying Bride crowd (indeed Hammy, who practically defined this sound, produces), but more infested with dirt and rust. Grade reflects placement within this surreal, ambient genre. Whether you can hack this kind of dribbling, disturbing catatonia generally is up to you.
Rating                                                  7

## Jack Endino - Angle Of Attack  (Bobok '90)

The Daniel Lanois of grunge pledges forth a solo venture on which he does it all, save for minimal drums, percussion and bass by Greg Gilmore. And inside it, one can see what made the early days of the Seattle sound so mystical, **Angle Of Attack** being a spirited garage trip through all sorts of weirdness, sort of Hawkwind does Budgie does Fripp's **Exposure**, with a trace of The Edge (when he's making a racket) thrown in for good measure. Like any vanity press project, **Angle Of Attack** is a bit of a wank, but it's an eccentric and noisy one, not without intelligent scrapgrunge à la Jack's Skin Yard work. Endino tinkers, fumbles and shapes on **Angle**, indeed most song frags and realized songs alike serving some sort of architectural purpose. Highlights include *Salvation* and *Find The Key*, both tricky underground hippie metal à la mode. But after the latter, which opens side two, it's all instrumental aural terrains of various farmability, emphasizing Jack the guitarist/producer versus Jack the tunesmith. So all in all, a pretty hip trip into a grunge mind, but a surfable rock'n'roll record it ain't.
Rating                                                  6

## Engine Kid - Angel Wings  (Revelation '95)

Take a sound that evokes the blobulous, explosive guitar smear of Smashing Pumpkins and wrap it kicking and screaming around songs that only Rollins, Jesus Lizard, and our own NoMeansNo could love, and you've gotten close to the jarring Engine Kid experience. Buzzing bass, apocalyptic rhythms and angst-driven ranting usually spell odorous noise, but the Kid's version manages a sort of missionary zeal, as it creaks into songs not without hook and logic. Loud/quiet set-ups oscillate with riffs that would make a metalman

proud, as the band comes up valid, that is if this kind of scrapyard of feedbacks be your stew. My two cents: good for the genre, but it's the genre that's suspect.
Rating 6

## Engines Of Aggression - Inhuman Nature
(Priority '94)
Adding yet another shade to the rainbow blend of hard rock genres, L.A.'s EOA flourish by fusing worthy dance elements from hip-hop, buzzsaw sonics from industrial, and a sort of flat-out and understandable riff metal. What results is a boisterous and almost fun bunch of serious rock tunes from the dark/crime/street side of life (an overworked lyrical stomping ground these days), catchiest being *NYC Mass Hysteria* which recalls *Bring The Noise*. Elsewhere, elements of smeary STP riffs abound, not to mention real singing (Urge Overkill springs illogically to mind), making **Inhuman Nature** a listenable, strangely commercial piece of real heaviness, despite all of the gut-punch styles it's trying to cram in. Just ever so slightly "dance" in the most enjoyable of ways. First full-length after a self-produced indie EP called **Speak**.
Rating 7

## English Dogs - Bow To None (Century Media '94)
Bio says "learn some new tricks from old Dogs," and there's some wisdom in that, these reformed punkers doing the genre miles more justice than twirlyheads from California half their age. Better vocals 'n' riffs plus hard-fought nuggets of wisdom that come from a life like Rollins' conspire to make this a grim, soiled little mosh with brains. Cue it up and watch the cops come over!
Rating 7

## English Steel - Start 'Em Young (Griffin '94)
Very likely the worst "cheap artwork to expensive recording" ratio I've ever witnessed, this first project from the consortium known as English Steel will probably be mistaken for a sordid indie sampler, given its pencil crayon rendering straight outta 1985. But surprise: inside you'll find an exceedingly glossy melodic metal album by Fastway's Lea Hart, who is joined by (hold your breath) Maiden's Dennis Stratton (searing vocals: who'da guessed it?), Saxon's Nigel Glockler, Fast Eddie, Neil Murray, and about a dozen semi-luminaries in lesser roles, including Gary Barden on vocals for the Lizzy-proud *Don't Take These Dreams Away*, John Sloman singing piano ballad *Show Me Some Emotion*, and Paul Di'anno going back to his non-thrash, Maiden persona for *She Goes Down*. And it gels quite well, staying serious and mature, thus escaping corniness, even as it courts techy drums, lotsa keyboards, and general hi-tech pomp all around. Hats off to (mostly) Dennis and Lea for their artful, high-minded axe solos.
Rating 7

## English Steel - II: Lucky Streak (Griffin' 94)
Another braindead cover graphic, another slick record of tough-minded British AOR. Pretty much the same complicated mix of guest stars, **Lucky Streak** finds the band a tad more raw, a tad more heavy-handed, thudding through a nice stack of hard rock pancakes instead of springing lightly, which the debut seemed to managed despite all the technology. Three lead vocals by two different Girlschoolgirls, three more by by Stratton, and a couple by Di'anno mark the main contributions, and as per the debut, the solo work is veteran, traditionally-schooled and simple a joy to hear (one thinks Sykes), even if the riffs kinda plod.
Rating 7

## Enola Gay - F.O.T.H. (Shark '95)
Slot Germany's Enola Gay along Morgana Lefay as chief small label revivalists of tastefully complex, traditional metal dosed with a healthy bottom end. Skid Row and Fight meet Dream Theater and Queensryche all over this big, professional record, all with sensible attention to songwriting that makes you yearn for the day when metal didn't whack you over the head with polluted grindthrashin' Gorgon growls. Thoughtful riff metal of the highest order.
Rating 8

## Enslaved/Emperor - Hordane's Land (Century Media '94)
Out on one of those caustic, curious, disposable extremes, these two "foremost" frost bands from the comical Norwegian black metal scene mix blood-boiling satanism with ancient Norwegian themes, often in the Norwegian language, although quite honestly, I simply couldn't tell. Emperor gets the first four tracks, making me astonishingly sick to my stomach, given such a brief introduction to their dismal ways. Then Enslaved takes over, and it's more of the same dizzying noise-nasal ambience, a sort of freakish uber-thrash with scratchy, whimpering bits of melody threading each precocious trainwreck, under one of the most lizardian anti-life vocal treatments I've ever been subjected to in the nutty world of grind chords. Quite alone and ill, not to mention damaging. **5** points above **0** for that ludicrously cryogenic vibe.
Rating 5

## Enslaved - Frost (Osmose '94)
Enslaved continue to be the freakiest of Scandinavian harpies, combining a dark, blue-dead love of chill with active attacks on all things Christian and Good. This particular goat's head soup is a fumigated combo of blastbeats, funereal keyboard icings, punk-steeped anarchy, and that new breed of disgusting black metal vocal that curdles water into acid. Anti-progress but progressive, supremely destructive of light, **Frost** works an inky spell, freezing the soul before drop-kicking it into the gaping maw which is the dominion of Satan. Listen only under harsh sunlight, please, I beg of you, for the sake of the children.
Rating 6

## Enthroned - Prophecies Of Pagan Fire (Osmose '95)
Mixing the erratic bellows and iced symphonic icing of Norwegian black metal with acceptable production and a slight nod to accessibility (a very relative gesture), Belgium's Enthroned are basically an audible, hackable black beast, still entirely without value, but hey, at least they try. And those blastbeats have flipped over the top towards tame, as if these Viking hikers know they can basically forget any sort of groove when bunny-hopped into overdrive. As a result then (mainly of their cross-polination), this sounds ordinary indeed.
Rating 4

## Entombed - Left Hand Path (Earache '90)
Entombed lurched onto the scene a mere body rash of the weighty death patrol they would soon become. **Left Hand Path** sucks; a blurry photocopy of every other superfast thrash record, L-G Petrov scowling and growling by the rulebook, as his backing mechanics flip on the autopilot for a heavier-than-thou wall of rusted iron. The burning vision begins with **Clandestine**.
Rating 3

## Entombed - Clandestine (Earache '92)
The crustiest miscreant of a muse begins to tighten her leathery grip around the throats of these grand hunter-sorcerers of the death metal scene. **Clandestine** marks the temporary exit of belch belter L-G Petrov

but Johnny Dordevic does fine industrial chemical justice over an alkaline sound that is really the destructive pinnacle of total anarchy metal. The production on this record is gargantuan pure evil distortion, fat ambient bass drums and piercing cymbals amplifying the guitar attack of the damned. *Evilyn* just might be the most shoot 'em up track of the whole Entombed canon thus far, on a record that is pure hellfire, still a bit full-on, technical and confusing compared to the pared-down steel gaze of the newer stuff, but a good 80% crammed with prime death all the same. One of the ten heaviest sounds anywhere by most measures, **Clandestine** marks an inverted plateau that is a full-bodied roast of all things super-sub-sonic. Note: both **Clandestine** and its predecessor were reissued by Earache with two bonus tracks each, all four being short, swift and forgettable.
Rating                                                                9

## Entombed - Hollowman    (Earache '93)
Amplified taster for the numbing majesty to come, **Hollowman** serves up six tracks, with only the brilliantly corrosive title track to be repeated on the long play, given *Wolverine Blues* here is a type of spoken word instrumental. Erstwhile: swift kick *Serpent Speech*, swifter thrashfest *Bonehouse*, bionic metal vortex *Put Off The Scent*, and instrumental closer *Hellraiser*, bolt together a brief but thumping record of massive boots. Wake up and smell the '90s indeed.
Rating                                                                9

## Entombed - Wolverine Blues    (Earache '93)
Arcing forth with more blubbery volume than **Vol 4**, and more massive mastication than **Master Of Reality**, **Wolverine Blues** finally actualizes Entombed's potential into something heavier than chief label competitors Cathedral. After one thrashy speedball, **Wolverine Blues** lurches into undiluted Sab throb that never lets up, battered hulls crammed full with a most murderous metal, a tumultuous ringing in the ears that approaches rudimentary grunge at the edges, and underground punk through the lyrical eyes. Still, its not hard to notice the grindcore roots, what with L-G Petrov's monodrone vocals (Cathedral shows more versatility in this department) and an extremely base and gutted lo-fi attack from instruments in unholy friction. Historically speaking, **Wolverine Blues** marked an exciting new crossover phenomenon; death metal getting real, Euro-grind getting down, anarchy infesting science, for almost all of this densely packed package moves at the most profoundly perfect but loosened paces, mid, slow with change-ups, most tenacious of tracks being *Rotten Soil*, *Hollowman* and *Heavens Die*. A powerhouse of black wind, sure to buckle amplifiers the world over.
Rating                                                               10

## Entombed - Entombed    (Earache '97)
Sure the label's broken ties with this most splendid of death pioneers, but that doesn't mean they can't perform the good service of releasing a bunch of relatively rare shoot 'em ups. **Entombed** (dumb title, dumb cover) culls together tracks from the **Out Of Hand**, **Stranger Eons**, and **Crawl** EPs, while adding Roky Erikson's *Night Of The Vampire* (from a split EP with New Bomb Turks), and a couple of previously unreleased covers to close the show. From **Out Of Hand**, the band pooches Kiss' *God Of Thunder*, turning a stilted song even more awkward, while redeeming itself on Repulsion's *Black Breath*, flame-throwing decibels like Chinese death stars. *Night Of The Vampire* captures Erikson's Syd Barrettic acid sludge perfectly, while crustifying towards a Danzig of the trash heap. But fave would have to be Stiff Little Fingers' *State Of Emergency* which benefits from Entombed's back-breaking sense of panic, the band frying the melody to a crisp. All in

all, the five covers demonstrate the versatility of the band, the ability to take disparate elements and rustbucket them fabulously. Long bloody live Entombed.
Rating                                                                9

## Entropy - Transcendence    (Inazone '95)
Shaken and smeared power metal from Toronto, Entropy manage convincing heft throughout this wall of cemented chording. Consider it a fat, raw and bleeding version of Pantera, with very welcome anti-structures reminiscent of Voivod, all pressure-cooked with a perfect crush-heavy mix. Ger Schreinert's vocals are an acquired taste, sometimes too '80s, sometimes pegging the band as angsty and urban hardcore, a genre below Entropy's considerable arrangement and compositional skills.
Rating                                                                7

## Enuff Z'nuff - Enuff Z'nuff    (Atco '89)
One of very few bands to cite Cheap Trick (plus The Beatles) as a major influence, Chicago's Enuff Z'nuff rock and sway down a garden path rarely cultivated. Blasting off with the exceedingly elegant melodies of *New Thing*, this quickly likeable debut does a beautiful thing with teen dreem rock'n'roll, stepping lightly through smooth pop rockers, California metal and a host of other intelligently blended hybrids. And all sings nicely with a sort of modern pro quality, peppered with big, noisy guitars, echoey drums and the Zanderisms of Chip Z'nuff. A fine, wide-eyed leap into the bright rainbow of human emotion.
Rating                                                                8

## Enuff Z'nuff - Strength    (Atco '91)
Chip and the boyz with toyz fortify their chosen world of sweets on this full-bodied sophomore effort aptly titled **Strength**. Widening its scope into terrain that evokes the most gushing melodies of Saigon Kick (themselves via Cheap Trick and The Beatles), Enuff Z'nuff amass a huge record of torrid pop metal, from single *Mother's Eyes*, the statuesque *Holly Wood Ya*, through classy acoustic closer *Time To Let You Go*. Fourteen tunes, and all quite different though stylistically left beaming together in their own comfortable world of bright, primary colours, **Strength** has staying power, depth and effortless beauty in a rarely traveled corner of rock'n'roll. Chip's smooth pop croon simply melts the whole thing in a blinding, slow summer heat, as the band tackles deceptively banal lyrical matter with panache and honest hurt that betrays an amiable innocence at the foibles of the *In Crowd* and its ego-enhancing motivations, disarming the listener of its critical skepticism. Mixing equal touches of glam, hippy and gypsy with their Hollyrocker stance, Enuff Z'nuff ride a potent persona to full melodic shimmer with each and every dynamic level displayed here. My vote for "pop" stars of the decade.
Rating                                                                9

## Enuff Z'nuff - Animals With Human Intelligence    (Arista '93)
After a couple of years of turmoil which saw the ousting of drummer Vik Foxx (onto Vince Neil), descent into voracious drug-taking, and demoralizing label wrangling, Enuff Z'nuff wave their magic wand again, sprinkling starlight and moonbeams on the all too brutish world of hard rock, elevating our schemes and intentions at least for a brief moment in time. **Animals With Human Intelligence** (love the title, hate the cover), revisits the band's previous rolling green hills, personal faves this time being *These Days*, *One Step Closer To You*, *Right By Your Side*, and gracious Queen-like ballad *Innocence*, all shaded in delicate sentiment by Chip's candy-coated pipes. Heavier fare like *Superstitious*, *Master Of Pain* and *Rock n World* is less the treat, but even these exude elements of finesse and charm, collating unin-

trusively into the general spread of the band's scintillating landscapes. A pillar of strength in a sick world, Enuff Z'nuff recall a clearer, simpler era, an innocence that may flicker but one hopes never fracture. My respect grows.

Rating 9

## Enuff Z'nuff - 1985 (Big Deal '94)

This fulminatingly fun record captures Chip and Co. in their struggling artist phase, **1985** being the band's original, pre-debut demos. And the unabashed, unashamed, uncorrupted pop enclosed proves these guys weren't afraid to genre-bust the AOR field, exhibiting more Beatles, more Cheap Trick, and oddly enough more Elvis Costello (see Day By Day and Marie) than anybody else had or would dare to since. Nifty tabloid-style graphics are provided, plus full lyrics and an effusive, fawning essay by Howard Stern, long this band's biggest star supporter. Sound and arrangements are just fine thanks, in fact less hysterical and brash than official records #1 and #2, allowing the perfume to waft unimpeded. Man, once you get that Elvis Costello thought in yer head, it's hard to shake, Chip really going for the prolific bard's twang, even soaking up a few of those ditzy new wave arrangements for fuller effect. A very warm record, from an easy band to make your own.

Rating 8

## Enuff Z'nuff - Tweaked (Mayhem '95)

Caught in the hair band holocaust, the widely misunderstood Enuff Z'nuff has been relegated to underdog hero status, playing clubs, roaming the Net, making records, spreading their brown sugar and moonbeams through less ambitious distribution channels. **Tweaked** offers a passionate mix of love, lost love and veiled references to drugs, traveling the same lollipop road as past pageants; perhaps less effervescent, more relaxed, and more nods to the Fab Four. A thin slice of treble has been removed, adding to the thick nature of things. In fact, the first uptempo track doesn't come until the sparkly We're All Alright, which embraces the band's Cheap Trick legacy firmly with bear hug. What follows is a classic Z'nuff ballad It's Too Late, then the maudlin, luvin' it, touchin' it, squeezin' it If I Can't Have You, which reworks that great Journey vibe you all know, love or loathe. Without a doubt, Chip and Chocolate Factory's softest, sweetest record, but sugary pop wonder was always this band's forté anyways. Note: next was **Peach Fuzz** (never hoid it), then **Seven**, which is a reissue of Chip & Donnie - **Brothers** (see review).

Rating 8

## Environmental Hazzard - One Stands Alone
(Sin Klub '92)

One of the earlier releases from Toledo's Sin Klub mini-empire, run by Ed Shimborske III, who also writes, paints, illustrates and runs a mag called **Glass Eye**, **One Stands Alone** is a crisp, vivacious hunk of mosh-metal meets Metallica, coalescing into a subversive, Anthrax sort of spin as tracks build towards an epic finish with Blown Away. Picture M.O.D. with more chops and you've got this one pegged. Future put on hold due to death of a band member.

Rating 7

## Epidemic - Exit Paradise (Metal Blade '94)

Doomy, dreary, simplistic but strangely appealing California death metal, bashed out almost like mophead grunge. But such bone-mashed ditties as Deaden and the leaden title track slowly inch this band of bards into Melvins meets The Obsessed terrain, with spicy splicings from Entombed and Hawkwind circa '73. But I'm just being quaint, the crux and beyond being all about a blubbery inebriated grindcore. Track ten hides a

heat-stroked furnace blast through Ozzy's Over The Mountain, pushing this record aggressively into the gotta have zone.

Rating 7

## Epitaph - Live (Metronome/Brain '81)

When these Germans wanted to, they could rub shoulders with the best of the blues-based NWOBHMetalheads, and **Live** is all about smooth rockin' metal, made tasty with a twin guitar attack that makes this probably my favorite Wishbone Ash album. For indeed it is a churchy joy to hear twin leads sound this wonderfully aged, landing between early Lizzy's and Wishbone's **Argus**, strung over tunes that start with Rory Gallagher, Status Quo and Bad Co., and work their way through Deep Purple and Scorpions; just fine, cushily-recorded live tracks that sound suspiciously worked over, although all the power to 'em. Makes me want to hear more, although the one other record I have heard isn't nearly this direct, accessible and funtime rockin' A lost gem of metal's resurging years.

Rating 8

## Epitaph - Danger Man (Est. '82)

Main distinguishing feature of this old-as-the-hills chunk of acceptable Eurorock is a blatant rip-off of hard blues stand-by Chevrolet (covered nicely by Foghat) on opener Long Live The Children. From here on out, Epitaph work towards bridging pop and goth, sounding well outside the metal mainstream, more like a rock'n'roll band muscling-up on an outdated sound. Full recording, melodic, expertly balanced and confident, but long-lost and just slightly the wrong side of Spinal Tap. Standouts: the warm Small Town Girl and the chuggish Ain't No Liar. One of at least a few releases by the band, and quite different in tone from **Live**.

Rating 5

## Eric Steel - Infectious (Passport '87)

This Chicago act never got much recognition, lost in the power shuffle between more uncompromising flat-out metallurgists and more likeable, agile, and enthusiastic hard rockers. Eric Steel's main problem is inferior, low-finesse songcraft; riffs that move like dinosaurs, yet riffs that are depended upon to be the central attraction of these somewhat '70s-style metal stompers. Also working against the band: flat vocal delivery, and a recording that's kinda noisy. One thinks second string Riot. OK and fairly vigorous, but I just know I'll never play it, the band needing image and direction, something to project focus and persona, something to erase the bush-league feel of the band. Note I: nobody in the band called Eric Steel. Note II: this is at least the band's second of many.

Rating 4

## Eric Steel - Back For More (Leviathan '92)

I sincerely don't comprehend how this kind of turgid bar band metal sees the light of day, Eric Steel progressing not one wit from their awful early sound, which one would think could only get better, after all those wasted years slumming it around Chicago. 36 minutes of sloppy, slappy, miserably-recorded poverty metal freeze-packed in 1984, give or take a weak week. If there's something to key in on here, please tell me.

Rating 3

## Eterne - Still Dreaming ('95)

Two Brits beholden to the night make up this dreary gothdoom duo, a happy-as-clams act that borrows from Joy Division, The Mission and Sisters Of Mercy, through slow to mid-pace grindcore merchants, for a sort of drum machine march unto death; Draculan vocals leaching out the usual sentiments of batcave depression. Still, this would have kicked my ass in '85 as a Sisters Of Mercy album. Now there was a band

with so much potential, so little delivery disc after disc. Anyhow, today, Eterne merely sounds like a competent melodic ambient doom piece, utterly ruined by the absence of real drums.
Rating      4

## Ethel The Frog - Ethel The Frog    (EMI '80)

Ethel The Frog sat right in the punted thick of the first wave of NWOBHM bands, yet suffered from a lack of press, due no doubt in part to their confusing moniker (not to be confused with bathwater popsters Toad The Wet Sprocket). It all added to the mystery of this uncommunicative debut, which is essentially a well-recorded album of barroom boogie mixed with dense, traditional, and usually depressing British metal directives, rising to the challenge with more energetic numbers such as *Apple Of Your Eye* and classy rocker *Fight Back* which scored a minor hit for the band, also appearing on ultra-early compilation **Metal For Muthas**. Strange record, which mixes elements of Quo, old heavy Zep, maybe early Moxy (!), old Deep Purple, and other things old, bass-driven, laid-back and gluey. One I respect but rarely play due to its ability to depress me every time.
Rating      6

## Europe - Europe    (Epic '84)

From out of nowhere mortal, the spirits of fallen Vikings assemble miles below the permafrost to create this, one of the most stirring and heartfelt monoliths of the gothic European sound ever wrought with sword and shield. A totally baffling release from a band so perfect for this genre, yet possessive of a catalogue that will become more chick perfuminated than anything, **Europe** is a grand metallic sweep through timeless classical music-based heavy metal; chilling as it challenges the world with hurting, soulful vocals, dueling Teutonic axes, richly traditional recording values, and regal war-time percussive grooves propelling highly intelligent medieval riffs. No big haircuts, no frilly ivories, just leather and total metal fused with a sorrowful, highly proud creativity on such beautiful otherworldly pageantry as *In The Future To Come*, *Seven Doors Hotel*, *Paradize Bay*, and *Children Of This Time*, sporting a gallop so death-defyingly heroic I just wanna cry. Ultimately, **Europe** is a tragic masterpiece, a record so exquisite that it begs the tortuous thought that this band was capable of being the ruling intelligentsia of this highly esteemed subgenre of metal . . . no exaggeration, bar none.
Rating      10

## Europe - Wings Of Tomorrow    (Epic Est. '83)

With **Wings Of Tomorrow** my first visit to Europe, I became lost and perplexed, trying to zero in on the band's foreign topspin on decidedly American hard rock. But alas, this is old and not of these shores, so there's lots of wasted time as the band attempts to be sun-tanned surf gods, cranking noisy metal mixed with specious girlie rock and weird ballads. Classy for its time but right out of focus, not that there was any sort of blueprint for hard rock this far back. A crushing disappointment after the Valhalla icefields of the debut.
Rating      6

## Europe - The Final Countdown    (Epic '86)

A sort of prissy goth elegance takes shape as Europe scores an unlikely pair of hits with *The Final Countdown* (hello Styx!) and sap ballad *Carrie*, driving the record to double platinum in the U.S. And no shortage of frilly accouterments elsewhere either, as Joey Tempest et al create a Euro-goth sweetness from textured layers of keyboards and ornate axe shadings over a stiff arsenal of technological percussion. Sure it all sounds very nice, rhythmic, even modern beyond its years, but it's also gutless and shamefully commercial, which makes the awe-inspiring **Europe** debut even more the aberration.
Rating      6

## Europe - Out Of This World    (CBS '88)

Gush deeper, boys, gush way down into a world of perfume, stuffed animals and hair appointments, for this is your chosen environs. **Out Of This World** is an offensive pop rock outing, even closer to early Warrant than **The Final Countdown**, which at least had a European topspin to it, this one simply embracing stoopidly American wimp rock with the mental teeth of Stryper. How **Europe** ever came outa this band is beyond me, cause this one betrays a duncecap posse solidly in search of cash and chicks. Managed platinum, half the sales of **The Final Countdown**, but choice numbers all the same, no?
Rating      3

## Everclear - World Of Noise    (Capitol '93)

Totally one of my favourite bands for the last two years, Portland, Ore. power trio Everclear have in their clutches the good times (trial by fire: Art's seen abuse and come out the other end a poet) like no band since Paw. This rough and tumble post-grunge record is the well I go to when I just can't listen to **Sparkle And Fade** anymore. Band leader Art Alexakis sez this debut was put together for about $400, completely in the spirit and verve of that first Nirvana record. The songs straddle beautifully the crushing, punk grooves of old grunge and the complex melodies of the new, harder alt. rock. Lead vid *Fire Maple Song* is the fave, fairly tricky, light and tender then explosive, while soaring calling card *Your Genius Hands* is a steamroller, again, in fine Nirvana fashion. Great songs but Art is right, the mix and the playing can be a little junky and loose, **Sparkle And Fade** clearing all this up, and becoming far and away my favourite record of '95.
Rating      8

## Everclear - Sparkle And Fade    (Capitol '95)

Man alive, this record's on fire, as I mentioned, becoming my most deeply enjoyed album of 1995, sporting the tallest, jump up and down hooks since those roaring power punk chords of Nirvana's **Nevermind** and Paw's **Dragline** (mixed with a little Pixies). And talent is being blessed with Success, **Sparkle And Fade** slow to sell at first, but a mountain of effusive reviews slowly turning the record gold a year down the road (platinum now?), aided by constant sweat-flyin' touring, not to mention hit singles *Heroin Girl* (a bit too blustery) and the absolute thrill of *Santa Monica*, a tune that drips with emotion, poetry, simplicity and relevance, all while sounding somehow great as a mere car-deck anthem. And tracks like *Summerland* and *My Sexual Life* follow this glory road, big fat Nirvana drums, hurtful, feeling vocals and hooks for hundreds of miles. Occasionally Art and crew get too integritously punk, just blazing through churn rockers like *Chemical* and *Her Brand New Skin*, embracing a heaviness which I guess is an exercise in pacing, throwing emphasis on this record's five or six almost invisibly high peaks. **Sparkle And Fade** is the record Soul Asylum should have made (or Paw for that matter), just killing the competition with such an intelligent and emotion-drenched embrace of all that yearns in rock'n'roll. Played it easily a couple hundred times last summer and fall, which is about all the praise I can heap. Cool CD booklet, which charts through family snapshots of the three band members, the sparkle and fade nature of life, taking the innocence of babyhood through adolescence, into chemical-addled late teendom, and finally this hopefully somewhat more adjusted phase as one of the most inspirational rock'n'roll bands on earth.
Rating      10

**Evil Mothers - Pitchforks And Perverts**  (Devotion '94)

Crossing elephant-size-and-speed metal with industrial, Evil Mothers strikes curmudgeonly and uglified, sorta like Killdozer meets Pitch Shifter. Definitely loopy, eccentric and lunatic, the record nonetheless moves too sludgingly; slow, dense rhythms topped with scratchy, treated thrashing vocals that tow the industrial grind line. Truly growling, if not totally evil (although there are a couple of blasphemous religious illustrations), file this with well done, but too dour and thumpy without pep.

Rating                                                    6

**Excalibur - The Bitter End**  (Conquest Est. '86)

Faceless plasma like any number of sludgy, dragon-breathed Maiden wannabes, Excalibur aspire closer to Tokyo Blade, but mostly Hellenbach. Grand totals: Maiden - 1, for 22, Acacia Avenue-soundalike Come On And Rock; Tokyo Blade - 1, for Haunted By The Shadows; and Hellenbach -unfortunately, all the rest.

Rating                                                    4

**Excel - The Joke's On You**  (Caroline '89)

After Beowulf, I was ready to peer into another Caroline skate combo, this one obviously frequenting the same homeboy tailor as Mike and his psychout Tendencies. Yet once inside, the band's youth is exposed, as the superficially pleasing blend of urban goth, hardcore, and often tricky signatures begin to chafe and wear under a tiring, somewhat mono-grating vocal performance. Pretty hip, but somehow lacking in the Tony Robbins power of ST or the raw blitz of the more impenetrable Beowulf, although Excel's is a more heavy metal-based and therefore accessible record than the latter's. Perhaps too focused on displaying too many atonal, gloomy riffs resulting in one long emotional holler. Contains a punky cover of The Police's Message In A Bottle, which only furthers the band's frustrating guffaw status, despite the obvious work that went into this. In the end, what with a stack of albums competing for spinspace, Excel merely shows promise that only a track record of up-ratchet intensity will reward.

Rating                                                    5

**Exciter - Heavy Metal Maniac**  (Shrapnel '83)

Punishingly fast and at least moderately ground-breaking, Ottawa's Exciter made a ferocious roar during the early '80s as one of the few originators, along with Venom to the chaotic left and Metallica to the regimented right, of a new aggressive life form known as thrash or speed metal. Heavy Metal Maniac is therefore somewhat of a classic, a definite shard of hate among the more wasted at the time, garnering acclaim with its violent head of steam and cymbal-crashed disdain for subtlety. Ultimately one decade later however, it's just one loud and wailing earache-my-eye, wrought by the pummeling forces of the heavier than thou. Too uniformly brash, although if one cares to dissect it, John Ricci's solos are truly blistering quakings from the outer limits of OTT. Unique enough in its lack of compromise to transcend Canadian-ness. Definitely metalheads to the bitter, broken-toothed end.

Rating                                                    5

**Exciter - Violence & Force**  (Banzai '84)

That cover still kills me every time. The pink blood, the painted hands, the metaphysically dangling switchblade . . . it all spells violence, force and disaster, as Exciter continues to usurp Manowar's claim as heaviest on the mount. More punk-infected speed before there ever really was, Violence & Force wears the brain to a dull bubble of suspended plasma with its pedal to the floorboards ranting and raving all the way to the pis-stank. Dan Beehler's wail is almost as crazed as his one-track drum barrage, and the whole project again repels with authenticity, eliciting mumbles of "What are you looking at? I can take it." from deep beneath patched jean jackets all over suburban culverts. Only real improvement this time is that above the relentless speed din (slower '80s-style speed, that is) a lone two tracks level the place: the appropriately titled Pounding Metal, a slow, throbbing sludgefest, and grande finale War Is Hell, a mid-pace destroyer unknowingly destined to be Exciter's boldest statement thus far in a less than distinguishable career path.

Rating                                                    6

**Exciter - Long Live The Loud**  (Music For Nations '85)

The record that sabotaged a growing reputation, Long Live The Loud, outside of its righteous title and cover art (the back tries to look classy and official like Ride The Lightning) ultimately dies on the vine as one long blur of thrashy punk nowheresville, demonstrating negative growth from an irritating trio of bashers that could use more than a little finesse and dynamic. One stuck pig of a record.

Rating                                                    4

**Exciter - Unveiling The Wicked**  (Cobra '87)

Toned down just a bit from the disgraceful smear of noise that was Long Live The Loud, Unveiling The Wicked brings back the band's ghoulish, dimestore cover art, wrapped this time around something with a few more gears. But still, Exciter is stuck in a rut, belching out a trashy, '80s speed metal that unadvisedly wishes to stay unproficient. Beehler's in his same ol' hysteric mode, a cool voice that gets tiring and comical record after record, and the band just bashes out the grime crimes, uncaring and unrepentant. Totally alone in this type of metal, Exciter ought to seal its coffin altogether, and move on to more productive careers in taxidermy.

Rating                                                    5

**Exciter - Exciter**  (Maze '88)

Ottawa's Exciter finally get the picture that a drummer/lead vocalist just doesn't cut it live, hiring an OTT wailer who assumes the torch of Dan Beehler's paint-peeling howls. The band also buries the thrash ethic that aligned them with punishment rockers such as Venom, in terms of over-spontaneity, over-reliance on speed, and purposely caustic recordings. The band still suffers, however, from inferior songs and predictable musical and lyrical signatures. This is one of those records about heavy metal and nothing more, like virtually everything in the band's painful catalogue. Whereas Violence & Force amused with its exuberance (where semi-digestible), Exciter rides a persona that is old news, despite its new-ish sound. Full accolades for slowing down, cleaning up, and adding a few moves, but the redefinition, red-flagged as such by the album's simple self-titling, doesn't extend far enough into the reaches of intelligence or flash necessary to keep up with the likes of the ultra-heavy big four, not to mention Metal Church, Megadeth, or newly anointed kings of the pile Pantera. Major improvement on the last couple of horrid hounds, but now's not the time to let up on the thinking.

Rating                                                    6

**Exciter - Kill After Kill**  (Spy '92)

Well, unfortunate for some, life plods on, Exciter crawling back under the rock of their own volcanic construction, down to a two piece, Dan Beehler back on drums and vocal, John Ricci still smearing out those walls of simplistic chordage at speeds outa 1983. Sure Exciter have decided to uphold the long ago mutated version of thrash they had a big part in inventing, but they must realize that their sound is forever relegated thusly and with ear-plugs firmly crazy-glued to one's hair extensions: only thrash academics apply, curators

of crunch may view the exhibit after midnight only, professors of power leave your bullet belts at the front desk. Well, whatever. Beehler's pipes can still skin a large water mammal at fifty paces, so yes, Exciter can succeed in their twisted history lesson if they so desire. A part of me applauds and headbangs along, but man, the pain of it all.
Rating 6

### Executioner - Break The Silence (New Renaissance '87)
More cough syrup and exploding hearts as thrash's black as coal soul spits forth another industrial wall constructed of blurry speed garbage and pulverizing mid-pace potato-mashers, mixed deep and guttural in bassy, booming tonalities, with one of Cronos' many leather-lobed bat children on disgruntled, cancerous growls. So what else is new. Just another poisonous sludge in a sea of sonic pollution.
Rating 3

### Exit-13 - Ethos Musick (Relapse '94)
**Ethos Musick** is one of those ying yang sort of experiences; amazing art, provocative and studied environmental lyrics butted up ugly against semi-industrial grindcore with vomitvox to match. Throw in more than four minutes of a Phil Donahue segment, other assorted interview clips and a 28 minute last track that is quite plainly and uniformly recorded distortion (with a warning on the back stating that it might shred your speakers), and this is an excrutiatingly caustic weirdo of a record. The agonizing wrap of it all disturbs with its struggling fusion of intellectual and moral beauty, with extremely distateful metal only the most rustified can love. File with those records one must keep, simply for the awe that they elicit. I dunno, this one may slowly warm to something less than frigid and miserable, but then again, I can't see reaching for its almighty howl all that often in the course of a normal day. What a lesson in activism, though.
Rating 7

### Exit 13 Featuring Bliss Blood - Smoking Songs
(Relapse '96)
Demonstrating what happens when you lurch over the cliff and plunge like Wile E. Coyote, Exit 13 sideline their enviro-death for this juke-jazz collection of historical covers (most from the '20s, '30s and '40s), documenting a decades-old love for the bud. What results is a silly billy zoot suit toot on vaudevillian dope smokin' music from rock's rich past, Bliss Blood providing female vocals on this bloozy juke joint gangplank, turning the thing into a sort of X/Exene unplugged kind of space oddity. A hemp-olicious exposé, proving that Prince Evilweed isn't just some herb as old as all of us.
Rating 6

### Exodus - Bonded By Blood (Combat '85)
One of the original four Bay Area thrashers, big things were predicted for these polished purveyors of speed. Debuting with the disgustingly wrapped **Bonded By Blood**, Exodus already had a solid, forward-thinking record, doing what Metallica did best, and doing it with killer underground savagery. Problem is, Exodus always had this grimly grinding panic about them that rang sorta hollow despite their obvious skills; a purist lack of compromise that made them somehow toneless and haranguing compared to real personalities like Metallica or Megadeth. Aside from too much of this being too fast (but rarely thrash), I can't really say much good about Paul Baloff's harpy bellow, his characteristic thrash tendency to yell and speak his vocals, rather than ever sing. Still, **Bonded By Blood** amasses some scalding grooves, as with And Then There Were None, No Love and Deliver Us To Evil, wedged granite titans that pound much like the loudest corners of Kill 'Em All. But alas, I can't shake the Exodus curse that

caused me to visit the band only sparsely, despite such evidently advanced product.
Rating 7

### Exodus - Pleasures Of The Flesh (Combat '87)
Again well perched on the cutting edge, but nowhere near our hearts, Exodus erect a magnetron of aggression; full frontal, uncannily displayed. But new throat Steve Souza (ex-Testament) is no great shakes over Paul Baloff; no doubt hired for his similarly punishing frash qualities. And thrashin' this is, albeit with the usual tight Bay Area precision, Exodus in no way showing tendencies of easing up on the throttle. And to amplify things, the band self-produces with a trendy emphasis on mid-range for that minimalist Raw, more prevalent here in the '90s. As usual the drums of Tom Hunting rage heavily, and as usual, I'm not moved by a seemingly imposing but increasingly punky and feisty work. In some vague, indescribable way, I guess I'm just not a fan.
Rating 6

### Exodus - Fabulous Disaster (Combat '89)
In a sort of curmudgeonly act of defiance, Exodus are becoming last custodians of a manic but toneless thrash, high on allegiance low on hummability, figuring a race into oblivion justifies their existence. But Toxic Waltz, Cajun Hell and Verbal Razors are vicious and deafening, strapped to nice, meaty, no prisoners riffs forged miles under the pavement, and the cover of Low Rider is as funny as Mordred's Super Freak. But for your tormented reporter, **Fabulous Disaster** came and went with a shocking blast that barely rustled the hedges. Why? Only your meteorologist knows for sure.
Rating 6

### Exodus - Impact Is Imminent (Capitol '90)
The cool album cover, showing a big steely rolling towards a car full of Exodians on the off-ramp, perhaps personifies this record's almost meditative straight-line speed metal. Again, you gotta hand it to these razor-carved mosh fiends. **Impact Is Imminent** finds Exodus quite defiant and arguably unique in their adherence to an older, lost speed metal rant, almost to the point of me standing back and applauding. Although a low point for the band, this record nevertheless underscores the Exodus environs, perhaps forever to be the set of slammers that becomes the band's dark horse, the well to which fans return to bone up on songs briefly visited at the time, but lost amongst other pushier works.
Rating 7

### Exodus - Force Of Habit (Capitol '92)
Having been pleasantly amused by the uni-mosh of **Impact Is Imminent** (although the band regretted most of the record's material), it took little prompting to get me to fess up to a full swig of **Force Of Habit**. And without question, leaving out my emotional response for a moment, **Force Of Habit** is earth-shatteringly heavy, marking a pivotal philosophy shift for a band who as of late have been forced to regroup and reevaluate their habits. As they themselves have so eloquently put it, rather than hit you over the head a hundred times, **Force Of Habit** hits you ten times, but ten times as hard, which adds up mathematically to the benefit of all involved, believe me. All in all, this the band's sixth record is an extremely long, extremely loud sledge of sound, using a recording preference that has greatly distorted riffs drowning out the drums, resulting in ridiculous levels of power. As much as I try however, I'm still worn out by the whole opaque Exodus process, to no fault of the band really, who here construct a great record, the band's best, and a welcome shift to slowing down and bulking up to insane

proportions. To my mind, the covers suck: *Pump It Up* and *Bitch* rendered smothered and inappropriate, and 10:58 of *Architect Of Pain* is just too damn much of a loud thing. Otherwise **Force Of Habit** kills, with greatly improved vocals, lyrics . . . everything. My respect for the purity of the band's metal intent is unflagging, and with all the wild sub-genres ricocheting off the central Marshall Plan every day, there's something increasingly solid and clean about Exodus. I'm working on digesting this one, being really the first I've taken seriously since **Bonded By Blood**. And my lead count is shooting through the roof.

Rating                                                                8

## Exorcist - Nightmare Theatre   (Cobra '86)

Total and utterly surrendered death metal, Exorcist clouds the line between thrash and OTT by burying the listener beneath a congested, smothered mix at the hands of Virgin Steele's David DeFeis who should leave this one off his resumé. As is often the case with punishment metal, all is awash in painful, droning, indiscernible throbbing whether we be thrashing or plodding, crushing under its weight the spoken portion of the show which you don't want to hear anyways. A brick wall constructed only to annoy those who wish to pass.

Rating                                                                3

## Exoto - A Thousand Dreams Ago   (Black Mark '95)

Expert death metal somewhat diminished by a noisy, crackly drum mix, **A Thousand Dreams Ago** (how long is that; two, three years?) is record II for this bunch of Belgian thrashniks. But the listener is kept interested, as Floridian mayhem is mixed with the tuneful down-tuned chaos of Swedish death and old-style attention to riff, found in bands like Rage and Coroner. Lyrics are about real-life stuff (except for the bizarre treatise on whether murdering a dead person is still murder); slightly humourous due to the English as second language thing, but a sincere attempt at relevance all the same, barked out in signature death tones just this side of ludicrous. All speeds are represented (with an emphasis on the brisk gallop), and some of the axe patterns are wicked, *Behind Your Mind* and *Screams Inside* demonstrating forthrightly chops twisted intelligently around sturdy songcraft. There's about fifteen records like this in '95 comprising a bunched-up second tier. Whether you get to them depends on how many slight variances on this new (since about '93) sad death metal style you wish to adopt. Like pretty much anything on Black Mark, this one won't let you down, given that you are an eager fan of the form.

Rating                                                                7

## Export - Contraband   (Epic '84)

Vacuum-packed on a swift kick to Obscuria, Export corralled zero press and for good reason, offering nothing to really excite amongst its competent, and slightly rough melodic hard rock forays into cliché. **Contraband** wins points due to its complete inadherence to style; its essentially stoopid display of blunt guitar rock, like a '70s-locked bunch of veteran amateurs, yet rarely raising more than a "that's nice" and a polite smile. Considerably close to a **5**.

Rating                                                                4

## Export - Living In The Fear Of The Private Eye
(Epic '86)

Following a trend that is thankfully less prevalent these days, Export lighten up in a quest for cash via radio play with this unredeeming bit off hard pop fluff, featuring more keyboards, more harmonies, more bluntly faceless song skills, even more obviously a shortcoming with this band in light of the inability to project direc-

tion. Like third-rate Billy Squier, Aldo Nova, Foreigner or Loverboy, i.e. ten years old and wimpy.

Rating                                                                1

## Extreme - Extreme   (A&M '89)

If one could ever accuse Extreme of being high school butt-heads, it's here, on this stubby chunk of corporate metal, a record too overwhelmed by childish inanities like *Little Girls*, *Kid Ego*, *Teacher's Pet*, *Big Boys Don't Cry* and the ridiculous *Mutha (Don't Wanna Go To School Today)*. Musically, **Extreme** doesn't fare too much better, sounding like lacklustre and sluggish **Pornograffitti** out-takes; well-constructed, Nuno-pumped, but slightly off the mark, too anthemic, pandering and corporately predictable. But really, I'm coming down a little hard, because for a debut there's adequate sass and tantalizing hints of things to come, as witnessed on the exuberant riffs of *Teacher's Pet* and the bluesy, slashing *Smoke Signals*. Yes, there was something subtly different here, if still a bit unchanneled, difficult and claustrophobic. And people took notice, causing a groundswell of rockers who jumped all over the band's follow-up long before *More Than Words*.

Rating                                                                6

## Extreme - II Pornograffitti   (A&M '90)

On which a band with fire in their pants finally lets loose with a ballistic ballet of sight and sound, led by circus-master Nuno Bettencourt, who crams more living into ten seconds than any guitarist on the planet. **Pornograffitti** craps all over Extreme's stumbling debut from a height of several miles, enthusiastically tapping into a rich vein of songsmith heaven seemingly crafted exclusively for the boys from Boston, with a detectable pop genius wafting forth from the land of Harvard and MIT. Easily led by surprise, late-arriving smash hit *More Than Words*, followed by singalong *Hole Hearted*, the masses proceeded to be shocked out of their collective lull by such funky but blindingly scientific butt-shakin' rockers like *Decadence Dance*, *It's A Monster*), ill-fated lead single *Get The Funk Out* and fave *When I'm President*. This was a mountain of exotic spicing, peppered with good humour, sizzling hot and incredibly razor-funked, brought to full flare by the capable metallic hands of producer Michael Wagener. Billed as "a funked up fairy tale", **Pornograffitti** is lengthy enough to afford visits to questionable sorts of balladry and the occasional not-so-great chorus. But all in all, it's a lively look at life, brimming with confidence at having definitely arrived, which is half the battle in today's hectic and uncooperative world, a world which Extreme can criticize and still make light of with ambiguous provocation.

Rating                                                                9

## Extreme - III Sides To Every Story   (A&M '92)

Caressing infinitely more sides than three, Boston's Extreme stop the world with this sweeping display of artistry, extreme in its scope beyond rock boundaries into oh . . . twenty or thirty new hybrids for the '90s. Journeys freshly taken include intelligent homage to Queen, evident in both Nuno Bettencourt's searing, exacting axe solos (see *Rest In Peace*) as well as his languished, atmospheric keyboard patterns, not to mention flourishes of Freddie from Gary Cherone during quieter moments (see *Seven Sundays*), lush harmonies from all involved, plus a general high-mindedness of construction that evokes though never superficially replicates the layered magnificence of Queen's first three albums. Elsewhere, further elucidations on the band's own razor-sharp funk metal tradition established on **Pornograffitti** rule the roost, awe-struck rhythmic science such as *Politicalamity* and *Cupid's Dead* sidling sidewinded, the latter absolutely cascaded with flurries of Bettencourt's unique magic demonstrating that in many ways this ambitious record

(produced by Golden Gloves himself) is in fact The Nuno Show. Don't get me wrong however, the entire band so obviously drips with talent, assembling a full-blooded 76 minutes of mind-expanding rock'n'roll, risky from one angle, studded with singles from another, yet so killer modern head-on, evoking universal creative wells tapped by Led Zeppelin through Sweet through King's X, the latter's new age plane reflected here on the Beatles-esque *Stop The World* and ecstatic pre-release single *Rest In Peace*. One noticeable but ultimately superficial element here is **III**'s lack of metal vs. **Pornograffitti**, miraculously adding a mystique and credence over the predecessor, while simultaneously blowing it off the map artistically, Extreme **III** sculpting and nurturing many fresh and challenging new directives. Way out on a creative ledge, Extreme has partitioned the unpartitionable onto three levels, the first six cuts subtitled *Yours*, being perhaps the closest thing to **Pornograffitti** here, yet daringly expanded. The middle five cuts, deemed *Mine* are essentially indescribable as a unit, being loosely quieter, mellower and more dramatic, though still rock pieces moving at various intensities (note: no *More Than Words* here). The last act, subtitled & *The Truth* then *Everything Under The Sun* in adequately confusing prog rock fashion is exactly that: bold, intense progressive rock for the '90s, complete with full (uncredited) orchestra; lengthy, ever-widening, beautifully melodic morality plays beginning with the introspectively Zep-ish (and I mean that in the most complimentary way) *Rise 'n Shine*, followed by a similarly lush *Am I Ever Gonna Change* and finally *Who Cares?*, a whirlwind of sights and sounds like some massive Queen masterwerk; haunting, overblown, eminently larger than life, orchestra in full regalia for a finish as far away from rock as lead cut *Warheads* was close. And so it goes, Extreme -**III** brings gifts of warmest hue, texture, and vibrance, woven into intelligent, socially-conscious tales of goodwill, exquisitely constructed, effortlessly assimilated by the listener. A bold, provocative statement for the '90s and beyond. But not everybody thought so, the record marking a quick drop off in fortunes for the band.
Rating 10

## Extreme - Waiting For The Punchline (A&M '95)

You either secretly relish Extreme getting caught in the slaughter of corporate metal, or your sadness is amplified above what you might have felt for say, Kix, Crüe or even Iron Maiden. I'm kinda mixed, really, loving and occasionally and fleetingly loathing their pomp pretensions. However, this record, with its defiant, fiery, and plain jealous *Hip Today* single didn't do the band any favours, **Waiting For The Punchline** selling poorly, demonstrating that this grudgingly special band was not immune to flannel-headed market forces. Like I say, the record doesn't leap out and embrace anyways, sounding fairly arcane, stripped-down, often slow, mixing psychedelia and a slack, sleepy blues (see *Naked*, *Leave Me Alone* and *Shadow Boxing*). Of course production is clear as a crystal bell, and Bettencourt's playing is reason enough to buy it, even as the songs show a sort of predestination, a disdain for wanting to entertain, as does the stark, sad, suicidal clown artwork. But arch Extreme chestnuts exist: *No Respect* and *Evilangelist* being hot and nasty, while *Midnight Express* puts to tape a dizzying Nuno guitar solo piece that has long been a concert favourite. I don't know, Extreme still creates on a plain that is intense and sincere, but it's almost as if we're being dared to accept the band as this casual. To my mind, any bad thoughts you might have harboured for the band just come flooding through.
Rating 7

## Extreme Noise Terror - Retrobution (Earache '95)

This greatest blows package celebrated the uncelebrateable career of U.K's ENT, a band who has been annoying music in various forms for ten years now (John Peel seems to like them though). The tracks have all been re-recorded, although they still sound like precision three-chord numbskullian thrash with turgid, miserable vocals to match. Nothing special, even for fans of speedy death.
Rating 2

## Eyehategod - In The Name Of Suffering
(Century Media '92)

Eyehatedgod's notorious, eldritch, duplicitous and unholy debut is actually a slightly more musical event than the dopecrank of future stomach upsets. For at this point, the band was full into their Melvins contortions, dealing a straighter read and less eccentric mix. No question, it's still a dark cave full of bat droppings, but the muck has a purpose and a destination to which it slowly flows. Disgusting but fascinating to watch from a safe distance.
Rating 6

## Eyehategod - Take As Needed For Pain
(Century Media '93)

More bad teeth, needles, diseases and songs about the day after the week in flames. More slow-drip bass notes, more howling feedback, more vessel-splitting subversion of all that feebly exists within society's pallid clutches. And again, it's like a robust, toweringly sick stumble through lethargic Sub Pop realms, vaguely derived from the mighty Sabbath, but more a modern heat-stroked paralysis bent on stomping modern music into a thin mash. May offend some viewers.
Rating 7

## Eyehategod - Dopesick (Century Media '96)

It's (ill)-fitting that this third record by frown-tuned, tumor-brained New Orleans swamp devils Eyehategod is produced by Pepper Keenan and Billy Anderson, given that Pepper's a bud, and that Anderson has twirled dials for three other anti-social, embittered noise receptacles as of late, Neurosis, Melvins and Mr. Bungle. Eyehategod are long-suffering members of that COC, Crowbar, Down, Pantera group of incestuous down-south filth dogs, but their records are the most extreme of all, and consequently the dullenest sullenest, still sounding like Melvins without the blue cheer (band, acid, mood). Absolutely the pit of evil, **Dopesick** is also just the pits, a crappy sludgepile of ranted noise that is vaguely industrial, but more like a belching black factory, like doing the backstroke in quicksand, or Ninja moves in porridge. Promo copy came with an Eyehatedgod sewing kit, presumably to try stitch back together this slowly but consistently unraveling snake-hole constricted concept. Makes their first two records sound like Huey Lewis.
Rating 6

## Eyewitness - Eyewitness (Now & Then '95)

Something just bothers me about this heavy post-AOR-type Floridian specimen, a record that is spoiled by Scott Burns' abrasive production, no surprise given the guy's main gig is death metal (one of the band members is apparently from the band Death). So the record just hard rocks on, a dirty melodic affair with pretty cool, Euro-style soloing reminiscent of the Malmsteen school, blowing it by being such a loose, chaotic, dated affair. Weird directive, given the death of pop metal, but there you have it.
Rating 6

## Ezo - Ezo (Est. '87)

Highly touted at the time as the Japanese alternative to Kiss, Ezo played a sort of letter-perfect Amerimetal; good recording, considerably more intense than the era of Kiss the Japanese pine for, more like an aggro version of **Creatures Of The Night** or **Lick It Up**. Also like Kiss, the band looked really silly. Record #3 of at least four, the first couple **Senso** and **Esa** being Japan-only releases, with a fourth, **Fire Fire** released in '89.

Rating        6

# F

## 5 Knuckle Chuckle - Charliee Horse (Black Mark '95)

Like all '90s punk, this is boring, miserable and one dimensional; speedy, but singsongy like nursery rhymes, not to mention brief, which is a blessing in this case I guess. Not too different from fellow Black Mark odd-man-out signing Trigger Happy. Pointless and inane, but I guess every Tom, Dick and label wants a crack at the next Offspring.

Rating **0**

## Face Dancer - This World (Capitol '79)

Quick mention here for one of those unsung outfits who rocked somewhat for their era and in retrospect, had huge pop sensibility on the songs we were ignoring. **This World** crossed The Cars with BTO and got Billy Squire, spawning enjoyable minor hit *Red Shoes*, and metal chompers *The Sphinx* and *Cry Baby*. Basically choice, old pomp rock with guitars, lumbering to a full-blooded drum sound and parallel blocky recording. Follow-up **About Face**, steered the band away from the ambitious goofin' around exhibited here, into more mainstream power pop, which I nevertheless still found a heap of fun.

Rating **7**

## Facepuller - Auditory Surgical Technicians (Bang On '93)

These audio terrorists from Vancouver are a lizard hybrid of Victoria heroes NoMeansNo and the Melvins, bodyslamming around the ring with an eccentric noisepunk swirl, burying the vocals but smearing bassy their spontaneous, fungus-like songs. So without a doubt, their anti-social Killdozer disposition turns them tragically hip, even if pleasure is hard-won, distractable and stuck with pins. Like throwing gasoline on old punk standards played by a consortium of Wire and Gang Of Four snobbies.

Rating **7**

## Face To Face - Face To Face (A&M '96)

As far as these millennial punk records go, I'd slot this one as near the top, Face To Face going way up the energy pole and staying there. Speeds push the envelope too, the band never thrashing, but often playing fast mid-pace thingies that come off as real, dyed-in-the-wool anthems, Trever Keith's vocals honest, projecting, and high impact. And none of that fake English accent stuff either. Bottom line: clean, quick, melodic and full of adrenalin, all combined with a maturity that places compositions like *I Won't Lie Down* and *Handout* in the hallowed Clash zone versus the skate loafery of Face To Face's faceless contemporaries. **8** or **9** for the genre, but still a **7** in the harsh light of more thoughtful music.

Rating **7**

## Faithful Breath - Gold 'n' Glory (Mausoleum '84)

Faithful Breath are a German outfit created in the early '70s who have shelled out no less than ten records, including the expertly monikered **Back On My Hill** in '80, before entering the real world with '81's **Rock Lions** and '83's **Hard Breath**. In reference to **Gold 'n' Glory** (which is about the middle of the catalogue to date), first comparison that comes to mind is the mighty Accept; high octane, melodic, Eurometalized Accept in *Don't Feel Hate* and *Play The Game*, but more often bad renditions of slower, simpler **Balls To The Wall**- era Accept. Shows promise except for the traces of Spinal Tap syndrome in no less than looks, songwriting, and vocal ability. Still, gotta love this stuff at least in concept for its kill-with-power Viking emotion. Almost a **6**. Astutely produced by Udo and Michael Wagener.

Rating **5**

## Faith No More - We Care A Lot (Mordam '85)

As I put digit to keystroke, words fail me vis-a-vis reviews for **Introduce Yourself** and **The Real Thing**, both records being face-melting wonders of rock music magic. **We Care A Lot**, however, falls within the realm of human dialogue, sounding nothing like **The Real Thing**, while quite similar though vastly inferior to **Introduce Yourself**. Chuck Mosely is hilarious at the mike as per record II but the songs are starchy, tuneless and preoccupied with no-pay-off repetitious rhythm rather than kick-ass tribal action. Faith No More as a band became so bloody cutting edge it's ridiculous. So one might excuse the experimentalism here, the boys feeling their way through early throes of real passion in search of a sound. Recording-wise, it's a bit sparse, not unlike **Introduce Yourself**, but somehow just more cheaply clunky, lacking confidence in its juvenile rattle. And indeed, it's the mix that holds back the potential flight of tunes like *As The Worm Turns*, *The Jungle*, and the later-corrected title track. All in all, **We Care A Lot** is only the *process* of genius; a glimpse at future supercool; as a result, overtly less spinnable than future records that would briefly bring so much joy and vigor to the world of hard music. Note: word has it the odd band moniker was the name

149

of a particularly lucky dog at the races, a dog that allowed the band to continue due to a welcome respite from their abject poverty.

Rating　7

## Faith No More - Introduce Yourself (Slash '87)

Planets away from the debut in the same way in which **The Real Thing** lifts off beyond this previously defined universe, **Introduce Yourself** is an out-of-its-head classic, a record never even remotely duplicated as *its* follow-up **The Real Thing** would transform the band once more into an exceedingly more lubricated and funkier form of heaviness. In comparison, this record is funnier, warmer, more spontaneous, and less the recorded tour-de-force, which makes sense, as the band was far from being a household name at this point. **Introduce Yourself** was to be the rhythmic juggernaut to create the buzz, as FNM forged what was a chunky, funky, metal, hard rock, punk monster with hilariously ambiguous and provocative lyrics delivered via the nasal deadpan of the uncategorical Chuck Mosely, who evidently was given the boot due to his uncontrollable nature. Chuck was thoroughly perfect for FNM, but Mike's cool too, although Patton also seems to be edging towards insanity (check out the band's Saturday Night Live gig). I'm sure anything Chuck does will be worth checking out, as **Introduce Yourself** finds the man obviously in his dickbrain element. Hats off also to rasta-wigged drummer Mike Bordin, whose bang-on rhythmic intuition is really the rock-hard backbone of FNM's sometimes quite minimalist clatter. No point raving about individual tracks here, other than the slamming remake of We Care A Lot, a major (and actually dance-remixed) underground hit that was to be FNM's calling card. No, **Introduce Yourself** is an album that is to be spun as such, a craftily complex but hysterically fun opus that takes the discerning listener easily a hundred spins to fully assimilate. Totally off on its own tangent, **Introduce Yourself** may possibly be the only record ever to sound quite this way, save for a scattered third of the debut, emitting a din that is essentially an underground, unharnessed, and exuberant version of its successor's polished sheen. Would have been tragic had **The Real Thing** sucked, but hey, it doesn't. Both records are nothing less than mind-altering necessities of life.

Rating　10

## Faith No More - The Real Thing (Slash '89)

Chopping its licks and licking its chops in white noise ecstasy high above the sun comes a furnace blaster of mythic proportions, a record that slashed itself a home away from any previously self or otherwise defined genres. **The Real Thing** further expands on the band's repertoire of mind-bending acrobatics pioneered on **Introduce Yourself**, yet with greater intensities of both the funk and metal lobes of the FNM cranial matter. **The Real Thing** has Faith No More attacking like heat-swollen crackheads while caressing the high level circuitry of the studio like Steely Dan buzzing on choice biorhythms, heaping thanks to producer Matt Wallace who delivers one of the most face-melting mixes scorched to black. And of course, the songcraft the band refined here from the rumbling chaotic genius of the predecessor is now legendary, forever an essential chapter in metal's history, this fighting, arguing band delivering top-drawer dazzlers in a number of diverse but cohesive directions. First and foremost is the band's trademark funk metal, with thumping thwapping bass lines, open structures half-filled with keyboards, and the thin Prince-like whiney tendencies of new wunderbrat (and self-described "shit terrorist") Mike Patton, tendencies that often and seamlessly lapse into hard core raps. Said musical and vocal stylings are most notable on breakthrough hit *Epic*, *Falling To Pieces*, and the most purely funky *Underwater Love*.

*Surprise! You're Dead!* dishes out a tasty ultra-heavy techno thrash 3/4 time waltz which slides into an incredible 4/4 pocket come chorus time. Lead track *From Out Of Nowhere* is a flat-headed down-the-pipes rocker with cool melodic ploys throughout, while *Zombie Eaters* (5:57) and the title cut (8:10) offer funk chunk plodders riddled with obtuse corners and progressive dynamics, structures most reminiscent of **Introduce Yourself**. Throughout this record, all boils with major slam, all pieces are exquisitely conceived and delivered with utmost attention to detail, and the vast degree of experimentalism is so artfully sublimated to the righteous power of the grooves, you don't even notice the wild shit going down. **The Real Thing** is just that; the first truly ripping shotgun marriage of funk and metal that fully understands the requirements of both, coming down hard and angry in the true spirit of confidence within its own form of metallic innovation.

Rating　10

## Faith No More - Angel Dust (Slash '92)

Deep bows of respect to the mottled crew for the pursuit of art, but I'm left somewhat perplexed at this about face into tough, opaque and thorny rhythms that seems to seize onto the only briefly explored nightmare visions of **The Real Thing**, which expand obsessed for this panorama unto dark moods. **Angel Dust** seems to dwell on the gnarled and mathematic, achieving and never abandoning a sort of crushing gravity that, twinned with the daring and kaleido-poetic lyrics, tends to drown the rapt observer in a sea of competing urban noises and colours. Go-ahead-pick-one lead single *Midlife Crisis* basically captures the angular but loose mechanics of the record as a whole, holding off warmth with its telling beratements above a tribal din, to one of many heavily stylized, but often purposefully unexpressive Mike Patton vocals. I dunno, but you got to hand it to the boys for pulling a commercial "Up Yours, Big Fella" of Living Colour magnitude, 'cos this is no celebration of bright summer days as per previous wondrously molten excursions. **Angel Dust** is nevertheless, a new type of cutting edge, but the blade just hacks with quiet resolve at all our fears, rarely slicing anything close to melody in the conventional sense. With repeated plays that just may necessarily come with force (sorta like medicinal academia), I may grow into this undeniably detailed work of art, but I know it'll never blow me away for as many different reasons **The Real Thing** did. Because art or not, hitting you in the face like a baseball bat is the gut-wrenching fact that **Angel Dust** is poison.

Rating　8

## Faith No More - King For A Day, Fool For A Lifetime (Warner '95)

Resembling no other fantastical FNM opus, **King For A Day** is nevertheless a return of sorts to conventionally instrumentalized rock songs, back to (oxymoronic) progfunk basics, chugging guitars, manic grooves, melody-pegging keys, swirling and thrashing smartly beneath a suave, unsettled and stellar Mike Patton performance. And suave is definitely the set-up on such smarmy, r+b-tinged complexi-ballads as *Take This Bottle*, *Just A Man* and the melancholic title track, songs that are easy to love, their certain drinkability carrying into the itchy, perky, bombastic rock numbers too, solidifying a record with an intellectual but toned-down character, peaceable agitation, busy buzz on neurotic simmer. The crazy professors have hatched an enigmatic one here, in remission from the insanity of **Angel Dust**, rediscovering **The Real Thing**, but sawing off the edges to load up the layers, a kind of world-weary loungey maturity when mellow and introspective, which is nearly half the record. And when heavy, the band moshes on pins and needles, churning out the decibels only inches from Anthrax, finding punkfunk that manifests itself as sturdy face-flung-forward songs. Executive summary: artists off-the-rails harnessing the mania for something altogether rational.

Rating 9

## Fallen Angels - Fallen Angels (Quality '84)

This novelty project led by Knox of original punkers The Vibrators plus three members of Hanoi Rocks is a historical rock ride luv affair with The Stooges, NY Dolls, Lou Reed, Mott, doo-wop, and the snarling poverty-ridden sounds of early British punk; what The Lyres would sound like if they were more strung out, enamoured with the rock star life, and heavier. **Fallen Angels** would be a screamin' '50s/'60s/metal classic if the dense blitz of the first few tunes prevailed throughout. However side two deflates, sounding a bit too stoned and lackadaisical, predictable and all too derivative. Still, **Fallen Angels** is just the kind of noisy, sax-laced, drug-hooverin' booze-cruisin' that Aerosmith would kill for, if they didn't have so much responsibility as world's coolest band.

Rating 8

## The Fallen Angels - Wheel Of Fortune (Jungle '89)

Knox still sounds like a shakey, snakey Lou Reed, but unfortunately his Hanoi Rocks backing band is long gone, Knox adopting an entirely new set of wastecases to hopefully recreate the spark. Dream on, 'cos this one's a stiff, sounding like a tentative, sterile demo of the fab concept that Knox had whipped up. Basically New York Dolls versus Johnny Thunders, or Hanoi Rocks versus Mike Monroe, **Wheel Of Fortune** creaking and collapsing like a lazy solo album, barely walking this earth, perhaps most compromised by the cracked production and the sleepy percussion performance. A mere shell of a great rock'n'roll presence.

Rating 5

## Faster Pussycat - Faster Pussycat (Elektra '87)

Marketing was way ahead of chops on this one, a package that looked like GN'R, smelled like GN'R, and could have rode GN'R's rocket, given the fact that paying homage to Aerosmith was still basically a fresh idea in '87. Unfortunately, however, Faster Pussycat deemed it sufficient to spend less than a quarter the time Axl n' Co. did refining their direction, planning their played ace. Everybody I know, and every critic I read, trashed this record when it plunked itself on the racks, and as a result, I didn't even check it out until '90. And y'know what? It's pretty cool. Taime Downe and his assembled training wheel gypsies deliver a cogent enough Junkyard/Seahags/Dangerous Toys bar boogie, slimed with believable deference to the New York Dolls, coming up with an admirably wasted brew of decadent, no-brains party weenies. In effect, **Faster Pussycat** came out before it was fashionable to rock bare bones, thus the slagging by the press was partially because they just didn't get it. In my opinion, **Faster Pussycat** achieves the boozy troublemaker status to which it aspires, and the recording ain't bad, just appropriately low key.

Rating 7

## Faster Pussycat - Wake Me When It's Over (Elektra '89)

Two years hence, Faster Pussycat add the frills, arrangements, and arguably, depth that Guns N' Roses brought to the genre. Yet, **Wake Me When It's Over** falls short of carving a persona, abstaining from any show of purpose, the boyz mucking about like disoriented bed-heads, cynically mixing slavish Crüe-level plunder of the Toxic Twins with stripper blues, California-style. Added boner: grunge recording that sounds like the album cover, psychedelic, blunt and muzzled. This is stoned and stupid L.A. metal, void of sincerity,

gratuitously hopeless, while still managing to be a fairly kick-ass shmeer when skipping dipshit boogie like *Cryin' Shame* and *Poison Ivy*, and sticking to the attack of righteous grooves like shuffle doo-wop *Little Dove*, mid-tempo rocker *Ain't No Way Around It* and lead track *Where There's A Whip There's A Way* which rivals (but loses to) lead cartoon on sister album **Kicked & Clawed** by Cats In Boots, as steamiest Aerosmith sass the '90s. Half raucous, half senile doper blues.

Rating 6

## Faster Pussycat - Whipped! (Elektra '92)

A most excellent 50 ft. woman album cover graces this funkiest, most relaxed, most well-adjusted of Faster Pussycat scratches. The band is down with Bang Tango, not to mention more flippant, good-natured GN'R on such Jack-drinkin' smoothies as *Nonstop To Nowhere* and *Mr. Lovedog*. The boyz so cogently want to please, really throwing themselves into their relevant street sleaze, as Taime Downe's cackle gets rough like sandpaper. Highly arranged, highly enjoyable like a choice Califried party, **Whipped!** proves these guys to be one of the better acts sticking to their Aerosmith guns, scattering like chestnuts of wisdom, image-packed lyrics that Steven Tyler or David Lee Roth would be proud of. Shame it all went bust. Sequel to Devo's biggest hit single.

Rating 8

## Fast Kutz - Burnin' (Ebony '87)

Too much the Ebony ethic, **Burnin'** gets buried underneath its own critical mass, rendered fossilized even as it's clipping along at the upper end of mid-pace. No big loss anyways, as the riffs don't exactly crumble the plaster. This down 'n' dirty wall of sound stuff really rips if recorded evenly and delivered with conviction. Here the latter may be true, but the recording is all bluntness, no edge. With the mess of European crap from '83 to '87 that actually made it to vinyl (Mausoleum getting the lion's share), **Burnin'** crawls its way into the upper percentile, heavy like a hammer, but dumb like a rock. A beer swillin' slab if anything.

Rating 5

## Fastway - Fastway (Columbia '83)

A classic debut from a band comprising Fast Eddie Clarke, ex of Motörhead, seasoned ex-Humble Pie drummer Jerry Shirley, and 19-year-old wonder throat Dave King, whose most bodacious shriek resembles early Plant, while stylistically blazing a trail that has soaked up ideas from the recent rising of metal. Legendary ex-UFO souse Pete Way was of course supposed to be on board (hence, Fastway), but the guy up and left the band shortly after conception for an illfated liaison with Ozzy, who sacked the man after one tour. Nonetheless, **Fastway** became a consistently smokin' album of traditional metal, traditional less in a British or European sense, more in the spirit of heady American highs, like updated and inspired Ted Nugent or Aerosmith; big, weighty, proud, rumbling and clean. Other elements flirting the edges included adapted blues, Zep style (another Zeppism: Bonham's echoey drum sound), as on minor hit *Say What You Will*, plus traces of Sabbath in the brooding *Heft!* and *We Become One*. And throughout each rich metal hybrid, the delivery is kept spontaneous and warm, somewhat hard rock versus actual metal, with missionary, starry-eyed focus that is singular and intense. Right out of the blocks, Fastway makes its shrill presence known, with a lusty debut that was a timeless slice of intrusive guitar machinery on par with the hallowed reputations of its many influences. Close to gold in the U.S.

Rating 10

**Fastway - All Fired Up**   (Columbia '84)

**All Fired Up**'s title track revs up the old Harley where the debut left off, slamming into gear as King harkens us to listen up to this unit screaming with so much potential. But unfortunately it's all downhill from here, **All Fired Up** committing all sorts of gaffs: too much boring, blues-based material such as *Telephone* and *Hurtin' Me*, too many sleepy, failed, hard rock riffs, most notable being the painful, almost Scottish-sounding boogie(?) of *Station* and lead single *Tell Me* (basically an inferior copy *Say What You Will*). There's even traces of insipid balladry, pointing to a discernible element of commercial panic. The recording and delivery swagger much like the debut, but here we simply get bad songs, almost as if the first two albums were recorded in one session and somebody said "keep this half, throw the rest out", the discards becoming **All Fired Up**. But hey, it's Fastway and there are other salvageables, the metallic *If You Could See* and Zep-quality bloozer *Misunderstood* propping the record at least to the point that it aligns with the debut, not the rest of the crappy catalogue.

Rating                                                                6

**Fastway - Waiting For The Roar**   (Columbia '85)

In the meantime, a sickly mewing. Nary a trace of the debut's glory left here as the band takes a vague, half-baked stab at corporate commercial rock, replete with unwelcome keyboard poison and cold fish techno-production. Rather than producing upbeat pop metal, Fast Eddie and the boys sound awkward, clunky, and time-worn, abandoning their not inconsiderable charm for sonic anonymity, in effect subjugating the British-ness for imagined greener pastures in the land of AOR.

Rating                                                                3

**Fastway - Trick Or Treat: Original Motion Picture Soundtrack**   (CBS '86)

Technically a soundtrack album, yet not resembling one in any way, **Trick Or Treat** comprises nine Fastway metalbunnies, the worst seven brand new for the movie (yeah right), and one each from the band's first two records, *Heft* and *If You Could See*, both excellent songs and better than anything pooped out here. I never saw the movie, but I'm sure it's a larf, sort of a cautionary sell your heavy metal soul to the devil tale, featuring Ozzy and Gene Simmons. But these new Fastway tunes (which are probably only incidentally and sparingly used), seem written for the lowest common denominator, sounding like stripped power chord rock'n'roll akin to Great White, thankfully no keyboards, but super dull all the same, even screecher Dave King sounding hideously like Jack Russell. Totally and legitimately a Fastway record, but one past the band's brief, brilliant prime.

Rating                                                                4

**Fastway - On Target**   (GWR '88)

Hard to believe this was the same scraper that belched fire from his fretboards on all those silly Motörhead spreads. File this one with all those other prissy pop metal deletes, nothing on here rising above total clattery swill, all killed by keys, although of course, there's no keyboardist in the band (the "band" being pretty much Eddie and his buddy Lea Hart). Seals its doom with a hyper, compressed, and simply awful mix. Fastway's just bought their one way ticket to the delete bin.

Rating                                                                0

**Fastway - Bad Bad Girls**   (Legacy/Enigma '90)

Kinda the same dang thing here, albeit with a tad more zippy guitar. But Eddie doesn't exactly burn rubber here, barely even getting in on the writing credits. And when he does solo, it's that fairly uninspiring trad-meets-'80s-pyro sound that could be anybody. Hard-edged commercial metal with electronic drums, and a bad bad cover.

Rating                                                                3

**Fate - Fate**   (Capitol Est. '85)

Hank Shermann always struck me as a frightened lamb in the midst of Mercyful Fate's heaping Satanic slaughter. Here he crawls out from beneath King Diamond's festered leather wing as a redeemed party-time rocker, after a spell of becoming increasingly at odds with the Kingster's Satanimastications, steadily distancing himself from the Mercyful metal community. Breaking off half the name of his old homeland, Hank makes Fate, playing up every lyrical and musical hook in the book as tastefully as the limited genre of commercial hard rock allows. Titles like *Love On The Rox*, *Fallen Angel*, *Rip It Up*, and *Danger Zone* should be your first clue that this isn't going to redefine the parameters of rock'n'roll. But as hard AOR goes, this is pretty heady stuff, with more than its share of fast ones, packed full of confidence and rich Euro inflections from one of the EC's masters. More life and agility than parallel career-jumper Herman Frank from Accept, and his near-identical band Victory.

Rating                                                                7

**Fate - A Matter Of Attitude**   (EMI '86)

A dissipation of focus and smoothing of edges marks Fate's second gesture of commercial sheen. Melodies are gushier, production values are busier, and to the dismay of metalheads everywhere, the keyboards and synths are at the fore, resulting in a less heavy, more Bon Jovi-ish sound. Nevertheless, Fate remains a likeable band even in this silky smooth state, due to the capable vocal performances and largesse of appetite, coming off as very professional and sorta wise.

Rating                                                                5

**Fates Warning - Night On Bröcken**   (Roadrunner '84)

Like its cover, **Night On Bröcken** is a tackier, low-budget version of the weighty, labour-intensive bombast to follow. Not as bottom heavy and a bit more off-the-cuff, this critically acclaimed debut has a sense of unharnessed spontaneity that the later epic material lacks. Surprise, surprise: in '94 the record was reissued on CD with different (still bad) cover, but more importantly, a remix by Eddy Schreyer. My appreciation for what this band was doing grows. Original grade: 4.

Rating                                                                6

**Fates Warning - The Spectre Within**   (Banzai '85)

Fates Warning is the band you will see mentioned in this tome as a part of the derogatory label: "Fates Warning/Queensryche syndrome", otherwise known as rifferama disease. The ailment's symptoms include the pointless cramming of as many riffs and time changes as possible under the unwarranted guise of a "song". Three or four perfectly plausible structures on which to base metal tunes may wander by before the first vocal utterance, and six or seven more may intrude by epic's end. Can be written on drugs yet cannot be played live on drugs. Its cause is the confused state that exists when whole bands learn to play from bitter, washed-up jazz musicians who refuse to teach them metal. Its cure is blank stares of confusion from their buddies, teachers they're trying to impress, and other influentials such as label bosses and agitated concert-goers. Another cure is no sales and subsequent abject poverty. The only known survivor has been Rush, although the patient has languished in a state of ill health for more than fifteen years. As with the debut, **The Spectre Within** has been remixed and reissued on

CD, somehow converting me to wary fan. Original grade: **4**.

Rating     **7**

## Fates Warning - Awaken The Guardian
(Metal Blade '86)

More riff-mad fungi and bombast from the heavy alter-ego of Queensryche, so much more, that if you relent and accept the Fates Warning premise, this may be the only sustenance you need all year. Fates Warning is the quintessential heavy metal progressive rock band, a modern day actualization of vintage Rush, but much heavier, o'erflowing with long tunes, signature changes, operatic vocals, and dungeons and dragons lyrics. There are no less than about sixty completely viable riffs on this unwieldy slab, and even some more succinct self-contained songs, one clocking a mere 5:21! But seriously, this band kills when they get down to headbangin', even evoking images of the mighty Trouble's earth-moving magnificence. Alas, Fates Warning would have crushed many of its contemporaries if only the band had learned to focus its considerable bludgeon into less pointlessly amorphous chunks of graphite. Never happened.

Rating     **6**

## Fates Warning - No Exit  (Metal Blade '88)

**No Exit** finds the band de-progging their record covers while continuing the chugging heavy art rock that has established them in second place after Queensryche, the last two bands of any stature doing this stuff until Dream Theater arrives. Quite mid-riffed and almost Priesty when mellow, **No Exit** blows it all open with a 21 minute track on this brief 39 minute album. Absolutely no difference from records II and III. If you wilfully lost yourself in the band's previous headtrips, and reveled in the escapist qualities of their elaborately planned decibel mazes, then you will wilfully burn your map back to reality here.

Rating     **6**

## Fates Warning - Perfect Symmetry  (Metal Blade '89)

And now the shift into a more esoteric, fusiony, arrangement-crazy prog rock begins. Already with track I, the riffs are oblique and sublime, with new drummer Mark Zonder expanding this band's mandate with the trickiest drumming of the entire catalogue to date. He is the man. As Zonder propels the band into its present supra-planetary terrain, the rest of the boys get less doomy, more purely musical, colouring each track, while somehow very unfathomably getting busier! Go figure. So Fates Warning is somehow more fantastical and academic while also crafting better songs. Front cover is a precursor to **Countdown To Extinction** (or maybe the *Teen Spirit* video?).

Rating     **7**

## Fates Warning - Parallels  (Metal Blade '91)

Oh dear, there's that old guy again. Hope he gets better. But his band is doing just fine thanks, adding stronger tunes, catchier choruses amidst even loopier progressive diddling, led once again by the trigonometrical calculus-defying sliderule beats of Mark Zonder (over-player extraordinaire, but he is the Man). Forget really rocking out. That's not why we come here anymore. We come for the fluid beauty, the dynamic, the over-extending Herculean task, whether it's all successful or not. Most tracks creep into existence with quiet, uneventful passages but we no longer complain. This is simply and wonderfully an infinitely fidgety Marillion with guitars, axes that no longer crunch, but flow like shimmering wine. They vanquish Queensryche at this game, and they kill Dream Theater (the Kenny G of the movement), but prog metal in itself is an acquired taste, one that I'm only occasionally interested in. I mean, I come here from fatigue caused by

grunge, punk and death, to hear something executed well, even though the raw material might be suspect. In this light, I hold up this particular record as one of the best of a questionable genre.

Rating     **8**

## Fates Warning - Inside Out  (Metal Blade '94)

Picture fine Rush albums like **Hemispheres** or **Moving Pictures** with even less power chords and you'll somewhat surmise where the elusive Fates Warning is going. This is metal for those environmental stores in the mall, almost easy listening new age hyper mathematics, multi-instrumentalized progressive sci-fi stuff with smooth melodies and noticeably little cranked guitar. Queensryche never played so convoluted, but Queensryche is about this dynamically low-key these days, both bands bespectacled and intellectual, after similar audiences, both working in earnest with challenging rock, again main difference being Queensryche's pop song preponderance as of late. So file with the admired, almost pined-for in the occasional '80s fog, but really of little value beyond those who study craft for fun, or professionally 'cos they wanna be rock stars.

Rating     **7**

## Fates Warning - Chasing Time  (Metal Blade/MCA '95)

**Chasing Time** isn't exactly a celebratory retro (Closing Time?), given the band's continuing lack of recognition despite constructing increasingly elegant prog metal feasts year after year. Rush built this bastard son of the metal world, and then it was really Queensryche and Fates Warning who have piled up the plastic, with latecomers Dream Theater now reviving the genre. But Fates Warning were always the more unrepentant, heads-in-the-clouds metal fantasists, able to stare egomaniacal time signatures in the face and laugh at cheese while they confused all, except maybe fellow Mozart-ists of metaldom aiming to score jazz-like respect and chicks alike. **Chasing Time** is a retrospective that leaps time as it tracks forward, mixing the harsh early stuff and the slinky new stuff in a complex brew, great blow-by-blow liner notes, lots of band pics and a couple of unreleased ditties in *At Fates Fingers* and *Circles*. A fine peer-in at a band alone, but a compilation album all the same, which chafes against prog rock's solid sense of concept and continuity (i.e. treat as sampler, then swim into the band's full-lengths once satisfied that you're ready).

Rating     **6**

## Fear Factory - Soul Of A New Machine  (Roadrunner '92)

Fear Factory have attracted magnetic shards of kinetic respect for their otherworldly ubergrind, a massive technical strain of kill that sits somewhere between Death, Sepultura, Cynic and Anacrusis. Yes, discordant and dry lung describe this bionic progressive thrash perfectly, the listener forced pasted to his Lazyboy, paralyzed with reverence to the wall of perfection that hovers and hoovers before the masses. Almost hard-won and hard-wired for its complete adherence to the soft grey emotions of the most digitals-twisting tenets of disciplined thrash, Fear Factory have carved a hole in the blow-zone that is theirs alone. Fear nowt and submit completely.

Rating     **8**

## Fear Factory - Fear Is The Mindkiller
(Roadrunner/Attic '93)

Proving in so many ways that they are the cutting razor tip of industrial metal, Fear Factory take four different tracks from their pioneering debut, and sculpt a total of five new mixes totalling just over half an hour (*Self Immolation* also offered in its virgin state). If I cared, I'd go into all the oxymoronic sledgehammer subtleties here, but suffice to say it's a percolating, dance-club hellsmell akin to NIN's heavier trips, mutated at the hands of cyber-metal journeyman Rhys Fulber at homebase back in Vancouver. To me, this is craft, not art.

Rating     **5**

### Fear Factory - Demanufacture   (MCA '95)

Fear Factory's debut **Soul Of A New Machine** raised eyebrows as one of a handful of potent and viable industrial/metal marriages. Brutally heavy, technical as a shuttle flight, and smartly slick, the record held major promise. Well, **Demanufacture** arrives, after a few difficult studio delays, mounting bills and subsequent label pressure, and the record has proven worth the effort. **Demanufacture** furthers this intelligent L.A. band's helmsmanship of extreme metal through the use of warm melodies, haunting tonalities, well-positioned keyboard fortification, and various vocal dimensions ranging from growls to real gosh-darn singing. Think of the record as a heady mix of catchy Pantera riffing, subtle industrial postures, and deep-seated, well-adjusted writing absolutely cutting edge for mid-'95. Kind of a death metal ambience (the band plays down this connection) with accessible, uncluttered deliveries, **Demanufacture** puts Fear Factory amongst the leaders of the new breed (Machine Head and Sepultura would have to be in there), specifically carving their place in the industrial-tinted metal genre by showing restraint and emphasis on song, easing the info-overload throttle of their frantic debut. Classy artwork by Dave McKean, who was also responsible for Machine Head's **Burn My Eyes** and Front Line Assembly's latest (although he's getting dangerously close to repeating himself!).

Rating     **9**

### Fear Disorder - In A Rage   (Fear Disorder '96)

Hard to tell an indie from the real thing these days, **In A Rage** jack-booting to centre stage fit for fight, competent packaging and crushing production values in tow. Fear Disorder's sound is primal, percussive hardcore metal, leaning into Machine Head at times, which can only mean good things. Slamming, grooves, angry, urbancore vocals and crushing rhythms combine for a powerful, aggressive and totally pro piece of power metal polish, dirtier than Pantera but often along those lines. Group with Tribal Stomp, Gutsonic, and Twelfth Hour as cold Toronto steel embracing the '90s.

Rating     **7**

### Fifth Angel - Time Will Tell   (Epic '89)

A noisier version of Dokken (i.e. closer to Lynch Mob), with those same predictable anthemic choruses and guitar histrionics, **Time Will Tell** is accomplished and flawless, except for the fact that it is forgettable and devoid of personality. This is one of those albums that painfully demonstrates that you have to be more than just competent to break from the pack, **Time Will Tell** lacking that certain something. Commendable and hip cover: UFO's *Lights Out*.

Rating     **4**

### Fight - War Of Words   (Sony '93)

So here's the story; Halfie abruptly leaves Priest after one last, ill-fated and anti-climactic gig with the band in Toronto, communicating with his old pals only by fax, as he schemes to create an aggravated new act Fight, fresh meat for players, calling hometown Phoenix headquarters for new world domination. And for the most part, **War Of Words** is up to the challenge, albeit a lot closer to super heavy '80s metal (i.e. **Painkiller**) than the nutty alternative Pantera riffing one might have expected. Nifty packaging (black and white cover art smeared with "assaultive" words, cool photo, old-time metal logo), but the mania enclosed is of a surprisingly simplistic nature, more plain and obvious

riff-wise than I would have liked. No question, the record has edge . . . careening solos, clusterbomb drumming from last Priest pounder Scott Travis, and a performance from Halford that is, to quote the chrome-domed gnome himself, a *Little Crazy*. But overall, the psychological make-up of **War Of Words** is very close to **Metallica** in a lot of ways, most crucial comparative being stiff, often lumbering riffing, others being production values and general lyric feel. Pretty cool, but futuristic brainiac metal like contemporaries **Vulgar Display Of Power, Countdown To Extinction** or **Sound Of White Noise**, it ain't. The pace picks up towards the end with *Kill It, Vicious*, and trashy but sublime punkster *Jesus Saves* (?) (tacked on the end as a secret track), which all play to this record's melodic strength come chorus time. Not the record to re-wire metal that I was looking for, but a solid grunt rocker all the same.

Rating     **7**

### Fight - A Small Deadly Space   (Sony '95)

The consummate metallion is back with record II before his ex-leathermates even pump a single statement (with rumours of Priest's demise swirling in the Birmingham fog). And "Lifer" Halford is up for the game, taking his unruly gang of rivetheads through a thick, meltatious celebration of all things squarely and unashamedly Heavy Metal. Only one ballad here (more like a hammerhead dirge), while the rest of the record burns its way through a wider bandwidth, more muscular and brooding brew of tunes that leave the minimalist Metallica Ari-zone sound of **War Of Words** for a boomy '90s assault, Rob ever the stylist, playing like Lawrence Olivier a good half-dozen vocal roles that skirt everything from Ozzy Bloody Sabbath (*I Am Alive*), to AiC grunge (*Blowout In The Radio Room*) to Grinder groove Hell (*Never Again*) to noisy '80s low-fi thrash (*Psycho Suicide*). Simply a solid, thoughtful collection of traditional heavy metal, **A Small Deadly Space** (a better description of the debut, emphasis on Small) bows to no particular trend, combining metal's premiere vocalist with an increasingly talented and multi-dimensional ambitious band, pounded into action by one mutha of a mix.

Rating     **8**

### Filter - Short Bus   (Reprise '95)

This Nine Inch Nails offshoot band, comprising Richard Patrick and Brian Liesegang did fairly brisk business with this abrasive debut, fueling the fire with really cool lead single *Hey Man Nice Shot*. And once you've heard the single, you'll have the gist of the record, this cyber-duo using technology in measured doses, butting-up the electronics against chundering, angry grunge riffs, usually slow and poisonous, usually marked by stealth-like verses breaking into cascading waves of dirty black guitars as tracks wear on. Vocals are a bit too textbook industrial, but the overall quality of the songs wins the day, especially the odd men out, like soft and silky dirge *Stuck In Here*, and slightly more melodic gut churners like *It's Over*. Too hip and current? Maybe, and if so, with all the good and bad connotations thereof.

Rating     **7**

### Firehouse - Hold Your Fire   (Sony '92)

Well the debut was O.K., even inspiring, but here the well-behaved from North Carolina take us way down into a mediocrity full of funky HR metal, below average ballads and sleepy hard rock structures, sorta like third-rate Slaughter. Lots of harmonies and general preening, but nothing to distinguish the band above other chick rock combos. A sound on its way out.

Rating     **4**

## Firehouse - 3  (Sony '95)

Same thing as last time, Firehouse going beyond dull into an unapologetically mainstream, beyond hard rock, and way beyond anything "hip today" into total soapstar vanilla. Very clean, somewhat simple but again, funk metal mixed with sweet balladry like Extreme II without the sparkling enthusiasm. What's the point?

Rating                                                                    2

## Firehouse - Good Acoustics  (Sony '96)

Never thought much of these smug, smudgy hair rock oiks, and **Good Acoustics** certainly won't change that watery feeling I get, Firehouse going shiny, treble and acoustic for three new tracks, a bunch of their semihits, and an Eagles cover. What year is this? Anyways, I'm sure someone cares, 'cos this is the umpteenth AOR band to try this sick ruse. Positive point: the Eagles track, *Seven Bridges Road* sounds like the Ozark Mountain Daredevils!

Rating                                                                    4

## The Firm - The Firm  (Atlantic '85)

Highly hyped supergroup The Firm don't even pick up the ball on this worn-out scrapyard of failed blues-rock ideas from the early '70s. It is fitting that Paul Rodgers is Jimmy Page's chief foil here, Page being perfectly suited for the droopy thud blues sounds Rodgers was pooping out during the final sad days of Bad Company, and on his **Cut Loose** solo record. Both just meld into a morass of cloudy sounds, so fatigued and boring, even Tony Franklin's novel-at-the-time fretless bass playing can't drag this record out of bed. *Radioactive* was kind of an annoying hit single; so bad, so instinctively erroneous, it works through perversion of taste.

Rating                                                                    3

## The Firm - Mean Business  (Atlantic '86)

Swanky, but appropriately dark and morose cover graphics wrap this second and thankfully final artistically void Firm project, the band still stuck in a bass-throbbing glue that gets these songs nowhere. Sure Page is front row centre, but what he bends out of his axe is the same floundering, slidey riffs that even as they suck, are quite unique to him, academically of interest, but off-base as enjoyable music. Faves are minor mellow hit *All The Kings Horses*, melancholic ballad *Live In Peace* (revived from Rodgers' **Cut Loose**), and tricky R+B funkster *Dreaming*. But man, is this the living sound of grey.

Rating                                                                    5

## Fisc - Tracker  (Mausoleum '84)

Fisc is one of those talentless bands of boulder people that locks into a rough-shod groove once they've discovered what they consider a suitable manifestation of song. After staying for three or four minutes, they switch gears and do it all over again; zero mobility, zero reason to be. Mausoleum turns monotony to 11 once again in quest of a near perfect track record of stunning incompetence.

Rating                                                                    2

## Fist - Round One  (Fist '79)

Over-wrought progressive pop rock garbage, so naive it's embarrassing to the Canadian flag. Something fabulously inconsistent is born.

Rating                                                                    0

## Fist - Hot Spikes  (A&M '80)

Looks like a metal album, so of course we were sucked into buying it. Sounds like a minor improvement on the debut which was basically bad Max Webster. Surveying the back cover, is it my imagination or is there some unhealthy tension between the pretty boys and the bikers in this band? The only decent tune herein enclosed is the title churn, which would fit right in on dirt opus **Fleet Street**.

Rating                                                                    2

## Fist - Fleet Street  (A&M '81)

The gods of metal smile upon Fist for one brief instance, producing a brutal and ugly record of innocent brilliance. Battle-worn Ron Chenier is definitely the dominating personality as **Fleet Street** is blunt rumbling metal; very basic and keyboard-laced but definitely bottom heavy; straight-forward, reminiscent of the primal naive feel of Diamond Head's debut or other early '80s fledgling Brit rock. This however risks reading too much into Fist's capabilities, for **Fleet Street** is a turbulent, visceral record most likely by accident. It's either deceptively dumb or plainly dumb; and in either case very Canadian. Yet **Fleet Street** has a value built of a singular, cranky mood. And whether you give a shit or not, this is obviously the only Fist album with focus, built around the economic riffs of the heavier cuts such as *Double or Nothin'*, *Evil Cold*, and *Open The Gates*. Not exactly talented but kinda hypnotic and depressing. Beer written and spilled all over it, preferably 50, Ex or Black Label before it became hip.

Rating                                                                    9

## Fist - In The Red  (A&M '83)

One album after the black noise of **Fleet Street**, Fist again has no identity, **In The Red** being a collection of bad hard rock and badder heavy metal that could be anybody's. Somewherz about four good songs squirm to life amongst the sheet metal that abounds here. Although the recording is good and the arrangements tight, this ploy toward mainstream commercial acceptance comes off as faceless, stiff and dull. And we're also back to weakapotamus vocals, unfortunately **In The Red** demonstrating that **Fleet Street** was indeed a brilliant spot of luck.

Rating                                                                    5

## Fist - Danger Zone  (Cobra '85)

**Danger Zone** can be commended for being dirtier, lustier and louder than the last, but it's actually a worse album due to the mind-numbing garbage being passed off as songs. All the hands this must have passed through to become product should be soundly severed with an industrial-sized paper cutter. Hard to understand how such obviously incorrect music could ever make the long, convoluted journey to our shelves. Gotta love Canada.

Rating                                                                    1

## Fist - Reign Of Terror  (MaGaDa '93)

Chenier keeps churning, obviously with no idea how far metal has progressed in the last ten years. **Reign Of Terror**'s album cover alone should freeze any prospective buyer in his tracks with a snicker as he reaches for the new Anthrax or Mindfunk instead. And inside, if he chooses to be curious? Plodding, one dimensional riff pigs, ugly, out-of-style drum sound, Chenier's big growl wrapped around lyrics so inane, this must be something of a sly parody of warriors guarding the delete bins. Like, dig *God Damn* or *Good Hard Rock*. Like, where does that come from anyways?

Rating                                                                    3

## Fist - Turn The Hell On  (Est. '81)

Fist's debut album (UK band, not the Canadians) rocked with an attitude and pride that put most of these fighting tunes over the top in the spirit of boastfully delivered rough 'n' roll, if not in terms of originality or recording finesse. Not as life-sustaining as the follow-up, **Turn The Hell On** nevertheless sports some choice no-frills hard rock such as lead track *Hole In The Wall Gang* and minor hit in Britain, *Forever Amber*. Fist

was another example of the fact that among the amateur metal that polluted the early '80s, the British stuff held up much better over time versus the stroke-inducing, faddish stateside product. Don't know why, but I think it's got something to do with the fact that there was simply less of it, and that the Brits were slower to leap all over the sword and sorcery, violence and leather clichés that ruined so much Shrapnel and Metal Blade flak. In any event, Fist evokes the basement, while still offering something personable and pintable in these times of complete metal profusion.
Rating **5**

## Fist - Back With A Vengeance  (Neat '82)
Britain's answer to metal's foremost concert gesture was an original NWOBHM gutter rock combo that combined low-budget punkiness with traditional '70s metal songcraft and edgy growling vocals from leader Keith Satchfield. **Back With A Vengeance** is a fairly solid bump and grinder, holding up like an early Samson record with hooks. Fave raves include the title track, *The Feeling's Right*, and *All I Can Do*, dirty-faced little cookers that reveal a band that wants to kick ass but don't have enough leg room. Although **Back With A Vengeance** rolls pretty loose and lo-fi, it's got a bar-room, paid-our-dues integrity that makes it somewhat of a listen with ambiance, steeped from endless tours of boozy, dark dungeons and occasional moments of glory culled from a memorable jaunt with the mighty UFO.
Rating **7**

## Flesh - Flesh  (Colorblind '94)
This is a cool collector's item for Extreme fans, given that it is on Nuno's vanity label, also featuring Nuno's little brother Paulo on vocals (apparently someone else here is Gary's li'l brother). And the sound is heavy metal funkin' much like more metallic Extreme, capably recorded and played, only cheap thing about it being the very indie looking front cover. Definitely deserving of the "Son Of Extreme" tag they've been given. Went nowhere, even if it's a briskly circulating gem amongst AOR fanatics.
Rating **7**

## Fleshcrawl - Descend Into The Absurd  (Black Mark '92)
Fleshy bits #1 and #2 are pretty much the same impenetrable fortress of dime-perfect techtonic death-thrash, perhaps even awe-causing in some camps, perhaps one day looked upon as top-quality demonstrations of a tired type, textbook-executed death, no more or less creativity than others sticking to tradition. But I couldn't care less.
Rating **4**

## Fleshcrawl - Impurity  (Black Mark '94)
By-the-book perfection grindcore that might float your boat if you relish every minuscule variance found in this limiting genre. For alas, Fleshcrawl's sophomore blight is the real thing, brutal bass drum barrages, vocals that quake, belch, croak and generally annoy, and patterns that some consider "fast" and those in the know consider double time, or more accurately, heavy metal polka beats, which suspend speed rather than represent it. If you like this stuff, then Germany's Fleshcrawl can thrash scientifically as well as any, blitzing the audio spectrum with lightning dexterity towards destruction. But after about ten of these dead-identical Euro-bloshes, who cares?
Rating **5**

## Fleshcrawl - Bloodsoul  (Black Mark '96)
Now when a band plays unoriginal grindcore, it's called traditional, pure and authentic, which is where **Bloodsoul** lies bleeding. And you can't really fault what Fleshcrawl is doing on this their third, an eminently

freezing cold robotic thrash, exquisitely over-produced to dent the music industry. Killer drums and smoked riffs from the creaky pits of Beelzebub's barbecue, good in this grimacing subset of the genre.
Rating **6**

## Fleshpaint - Imitate Yourself  (Sour Music '96)
Definitely not pleased with that *Cigarette Religion* single clogging classic rock radio (file with Dishwalla, Tripping Daisy and Pluto), I nevertheless approached this as a no-name indie making waves; that is, predisposed to acceptance. However (disregarding a somewhat cheap shot), the Ottawa Alanis connection springs to mind, Fleshpaint fusing those same miserable hip-hop, industrial, pop and metallic power chord elements with lack slack. So the slickness smothers, layers of de rigueur sounds killing any thoughts of freshness, turning this into Age Of Electric does Def Leppard's *Slang* one step trendier. Those who recognize and like this pastiche of motivations (really started with Prince's *When Doves Cry*, Billy Idol and Dan Reed Network if you want to be archaeological about it), might get on board. But IMHO, the uncountable levels of irony just kill this record in its tracks.
Rating **5**

## Flies On Fire - Flies On Fire  (Atlantic '89)
California rockers with a name way too cool for the timid roots rock enclosed, Flies On Fire are yer basic amalgam of Chuck Berry and Stones riffs on the rockers, while writing something more akin to campfire tales on the acoustic numbers. Simply simple, and recorded way too cleanly for such traditional (read predictable) fare to really breathe.
Rating **4**

## Flipper - American Grafishy  (Def American '93)
Lodged like a cyst between Melvins and Butthole Surfers, Flipper are a band with legend and history, four longhair misfits on a dangerous collision course with punk, possessors of a potent magic that a rabid few, including executive producer Rick Rubin have come to love. Seriously, this is the only record I know that reminds me of that hectic Richard Hell - **Blank Generation** album from the late '70s, a record that swam and swam then drowned due to a hysterical hemorrhage of power. Only **American Grafishy** (the band's biggest grasp for the brass ring) is fraught with furtive buzzing bass, and a stumbling inefficiency that eventually drags one under unto the band's demonic undulations. The lyrics are cool too, fusing perfectly with the boyz' mantra-like art chaos; live, pointless and chartless, sorta between Black Flag's songs and their instrumental experiments. Really, really stupid but hey, it somehow sounds like a bar gig loaded with meaning. Spiritual squid: Butthole Surfers and The Jesus Lizard.
Rating **8**

## Floodgate - Penalty  (Roadrunner/Attic '96)
Floodgate dredges the vestiges of thrashers Exhorder, (classical!) singer Kyle Thomas hauling along his old band's metal hate, while jumping head-long into the world of angsty, flannel, scowls and chin-hair grunge: for better and worse. Perhaps the band has adopted too many GenX signatures, but I'm finding myself "up to here" with this sound right now, Floodgate doing the whole Alice in Chains crossed with Pantera bit, kinda what Anthrax has been doing (artistically but not commercially) successfully. See review of I'M'L's **Instigating The Loud** for a band that gets the mix right, more by dropping the depression more than anything. Both singers sound like John Bush!.
Rating **6**

## Flotsam And Jetsam - Doomsday For The Deceiver
(Metal Blade '86)

This debut pile of speed spewage was actually quite well-received back in the metal daze, the band combining the fancy pants riffery and speed of Bay Area thrash with a self-made scrapiness of tone and delivery. Add to that totally dated helium yelps and a one-track minded urge to obliterate, and what emerges gets forgettable fast. But the band's cult following was immediately established, F&J hitting hard that poverty metal underground sound with their erratically displayed and splayed chops. For those metalheads exactly the right age, this is considered a minor classic.
Rating                                                                4

## Flotsam And Jetsam - No Place For Disgrace
(Elektra '88)

F&J plug on, delving deeper into their murky visions of blood, sweat and gears, a type of intrinsically American gothic headbang that wears the listener to a bloody stump by record's end. Again, it's a type of loose, inebriated Bay Area thrash, sounding like a million acts on much tinier and tinnier labels. Most tracks are long for no reason, just clogged up with intros and musical passages that just throw it all out to see what sticks. Very little stuck for anybody. Contains a ludicrous novelty cover of Elton's Saturday Night's Alright For Fighting. This band gets on my nerves.
Rating                                                                4

## Flotsam And Jetsam - When The Storm Comes Down   (MCA '90)

Migraine music of the highest order, one of those unwieldy, relentless efforts lacking any point of reference as it careens from one dark goth riff to another. Like a cross between Death Angel, Anthrax, Vicious Rumors and Metal Church, yet nowhere as listenable, **When The Storm Comes Down** blurs and bores its way to the depressing techno-metal scrap heap. Jason Newsted did well to jump ship, real well obviously, given this band's bad business luck, and his new one's massive good fortune (born of hard work, of course). But these guys need a major dose of lightening up, and a pronounced dislodging from their '80s metal cocoons.
Rating                                                                4

## Flotsam And Jetsam - Cuatro   (MCA '92)

Obviously still preoccupied with science, F&J amass another ambitious but for once, accessible collection of sounds, working oddly and somewhat tragic-heroically in a creative vein much akin to Metallica's **Ride The Lightning** and **Master Of Puppets** era. Seemingly frozen in time, **Cuatro** is a breath-taking but ultimately cold assemblage of tight thrash, slow Sabbath, heavy Queensryche, Death Angel (lyrically) and inspired Hetfield trips. Best performance comes from the Vedder-intense lungs of vocalist Eric A.K., who throws a cloak of goth over all spectrums of the F&J psyche, one that has always been complex, defiant and isolated, but only now, master of its squalid metalman genre. Faves would include the chunk-riffed Swatting At Flies and the punk-direct Hypodermic Midnight Snack. Still, the rock'n'rollin' peaks are separated by distressing valleys marked by long builds and unproductive progressive passages, lending this long-suffering band growing respect at least as obstinate '80s purists, bent on an academic, mechanical kind of headbang, seemingly long forgotten with the latest trend towards simultaneous simplification and intensification (Symphony Of Destruction, need I say any goddamn more). Sure, tracks are shorter, and more swing a shovel to the cranial sphere, but busy minds will play. The trend however, is there, the band increasingly

focusing its talents. Stay tuned, 'cos things just gotta turn around someday.
Rating                                                                7

## Flotsam And Jetsam - Drift   (MCA '95)

F&J have finally produced their statement of being, their record that shows the band in full, battered bloom, their words of wisdom spoken with the weight of various personal and professional tragedies that have befallen the band (including the death of bassist Jason Ward's brother Jeff: see driving, emotional metal track Missing). Compositions in general, are simpler, spacier and crushingly wrought with the wry observations of Eric A.K., who belts out his tales in a fashion that is both technically superb and dramatic. Still, I do believe this band to be one that you had to get early in their career and follow, at this point feeling I've missed the boat on really investing in them on a personal basis. Faves: intro freight train Me, which really tells the truth, and psychedelic metalized ballad Destructive Signs which is a sort of Ramble On for the moshers.
Rating                                                                8

## Fluffy - Black Eye   (Virgin/EMI '96)

Quite logic-defying, but even the Rolling Stone crowd seem to think this all-female U.K. "punk" band is all that and more. Plus they toured with the Pistols, and Pat Smear likes them blah blah blah. But in the cold harsh light of reality, all I hear is commercially produced, third-rate, third-chord Stooges, Dolls and Ramones. And I do mean third-rate, Fluffy's turgid middle of the road hard rock sounding like The Cult when they sucked, or a Steve Jones solo album, or worse, the mean average of the Gunners' solo records with flat, snarling chick vocals. Wake up, public. This isn't punk, it's Girlschool and the Runaways without the ambition or imagination. I mean, these gals look and sound like the band Pamela Lee will eventually make with Tommy when when she decides she too is Bruce Willis. There is nothing here. Now go home. Fluff note #1: **Black Eye** is the band's debut album after a CBGBs-recorded live EP called **5 Live**. Fluff note #2: cool heavy metal cover art!
Rating                                                                3

## The Fluid - Roadmouth   (Sub Pop '89)

**Roadmouth** is the first Sub Pop product that smacks of cash in, even though competitors Swallow seem to be the ones locally accused of being rip-offs so early on in Seattle's rise. To me, Denver's The Fluid sound like wise-ass college boy Stooges fans who have contrived an unpowerful merger of aseptic punk and stolen Green River riffs, reeking of insincerity and lack of metallic knowledge unlike true grungsters. **Roadmouth** holds some strong individual tracks, but I've always had a hard time respecting bands who sound like they're straight-out copying authentic, early years Sub Pop (Green River, Soundgarden, Nirvana, Swallow), or for that matter, bands who copy The Replacements, Hüsker Dü and REM, to the paranoid point of imagining it happening when it ain't. In any event, here it's painful and puerile.
Rating                                                                4

## The Fluid - Purplemetalflakemusic   (Hollywood '93)

Outside of the album moniker, this one didn't impress too many flannelheads, the band drifting into the woodwork shortly thereafter. I still find it an improvement on the flanilla debut, a sort of blurring of the line between grunge, garage, and hard-edged '60s conventions. Again, something akin to The Stooges, which is rarely found, although it's no great shakes here. Low-blow stun bass, some nice harmonies, lots of caterwaul performances; sorta the accessible face of Mudhoney.
Rating                                                                7

**FN Guns - Nightmare** (Mausoleum Est. '84)

Ailing, pedestrian Brit metal sporting a cover of *Living Loving Maid*. Amateurish but spirited scumdog holler fodder. Not the worst circus act on earth, just not overly necessary. Flanked by '83's self-titled debut and **Burnin' Out** in '88.

Rating      4

**Foghat - Foghat** (Bearsville '72)

Closer to guitar-based blues than the blues metal thud of the band's inspired mid-years, **Foghat** is neverthe-less endearing and close in much the same manner as early ZZ Top material relates to **Tres Hombres** and the studio half of **Fandango**. Full up with various forms of literal blues: slow, fast, funky, bluegrass, etc., **Foghat** is reverent to all, going a step further in covering old standbys *Maybelline* (who cares) and *I Just Want To Make Love To You* (blistering). Just updated, energized, and varied enough to be entertaining versus the mind crushing boredom of "real" blues, delivered by a sou-ped-up but pedigreed band of perspective-steeped Brits (essentially most of Savoy Brown gone commer-cially viable). A truly likeable amalgam of new and old is born, produced oddly enough by a young Dave Edmunds.

Rating      6

**Foghat - Foghat (Rock And Roll)** (Bearsville '73)

Like the debut, **Rock And Roll** strides confidently and lazily (or more appropriately, confident in its laziness) through the encyclopedia of hard-edged guitar blues, rocking at times with the boogie woogie abandon that would soon become the band's trademark, most evi-denced on such backwoods, under-achieving ditties as *Road Fever*, *Ride, Ride, Ride* and *Long Way To Go*. This is one of those warm, resonant albums that lounges comfortably at tailgate parties beside pre-stardom ZZ Top, speaking in ancient tongues in fine reverence of tradition. Better than anything by band-buds Humble Pie.

Rating      7

**Foghat - Energized** (Bearsville '74)

**Energized** is the first of the best five Foghat albums recorded one after another from '74 to '78, and im-portantly the first from the band to go gold stateside. It's also the first where the blues/metal alloy spells heat-stroked magic, where the band could be said to match stride-for-stride ZZ Top or Status Quo at their heads-down grooviest. The literal fast metal boogie of *Wild Cherry* and *Honey Hush* (a revved-up, red-line adaptation of the *Train Kept a' Rollin* riff) lead the attack, while *Home In My Hand* and *Golden Arrow* take a warmer, homegrown boogie approach, infusing a gen-eralist pop into a traditional music that can begin to sound samey. This is what country music *should* sound like; real redneck and loud, with a bit of outlaw, goofin' off dope haze thrown in for lack of hope. So Foghat's blues heritage and chops combined with an obvious love of their job, make Lonesome Dave and the boyz a band for the good times as well as the wailin' bad. Trivia note: the band wasn't altogether pleased with the production but hey, sounds mighty fine to me.

Rating      8

**Foghat - Rock And Roll Outlaws** (Bearsville '74)

As Steve Martin used to say, you can't stay in a bad mood listening to banjo music. Much the same thing can be mused in wistful reference to early Foghat. **Rock And Roll Outlaws**, however, is the nearest thing to a lapse in the band's golden era, studded with funkier (shades of James Gang?), more experimental takes on the classic Foghat sound with such Travers-quality two steppers as *Eight Days On The Road*, *Hate To See You Go*, the bright, more straight-forward title track, and my fave, the bubbling *Blue Spruce Woman*.

Definitely in the boogie rock camp as opposed to metal, or even the '70s hard rock of the band's sta-dium-packing peers, **Rock And Roll Outlaws** is nev-ertheless a truckin', hot-blooded good time, balancing innocence and wisdom in a way that takes the snob-bery and exclusivity out of traditional blues and boogie. Did not go gold until much later, due perhaps to its more pronounced return to blues traditions, versus the revved stadium-conquering spirit of **Energized**. Exit Tony Stevens.

Rating      7

**Foghat - Fool For The City** (Bearsville '75)

One of the cool things about Foghat was that it was hard to tell whether the boys were genuine shit-kickin' rednecks or actually the kind of good-for-nothing hippy bums rednecks would sooner stomp all over than talk to. Regardless of their stars and stripes or deliberate lack thereof, along with Quo's **Quo**, and ZZ Top's **Tejas** and **Tres Hombres** duo, **Fool For The City** ranks as one of the four most consistently brilliant blues metal albums of all time. And of the bunch, it's defi-nitely the most crazy from the heat, a near unanimous band fave, and second biggest seller after **Live**. We were damn near raised on this record and it still sounds fresh to me today. Aside from the reflective *Take It Or Leave It*, the entire album sizzles with guitar party action, proudly driving home kick-ass summer rockers like *My Babe*, *Drive Me Home* and the long-striding, glorious title cut; plus chunky slide guitar monoliths *Terraplane Blues* and the band's biggest, most timeless classic *Slow Ride*. Hot rockin' and brimming with con-fidence, **Fool For The City** is a non-stop road trip of southern fried licks, the essential beer-stained 8-track soundtrack for your next Tijuana bender. Ride on . . .

Rating      10

**Foghat - Night Shift** (Bearsville '76)

More gritty barroom blues metal from one of the genre's greats, **Night Shift's** first side is Foghat's best half album, while side two pales immeasurably save for the straight-ahead, eerily-riffed title track. Still, it's classic heartland guitar booger, featuring yet another lengthy but plush and hypnotic classic in *Don't Run Me Down*, which features a rousing build to the finish, plus two more friendly, boogie rumblers in minor hit *Drivin' Wheel* and the side-stepping *Burnin' The Midnight Oil*. Again, Foghat manages perfect summer cruising rock, full of personal warmth and the weight of rock'n'roll heritage, used wisely with heated frets and cool per-spective. Trivia note: the sleeve lists a missing track, *New Place To Call Home*, a Dan Hartman composition which was dropped from the record at the last minute.

Rating      8

**Foghat - Live** (Bearsville '77)

One of the great kickin' live albums for all time, cranked out in the bluesy funky metal spirit of tourmate Pat Travers' **Go For What You Know**, **Live** succeeds due simply to song selection that strikes the molten core of what Foghat is all about, hot roots rockers like *Fool For The City*, *Slow Ride*, *Honey Hush*, and successful, live-beefed single, *I Just Wanna Make Love To You*, delivered in serious planetarily-aligned homage to the wavy heat of a midwest summer, further accented by the fact that this was the band's only double platinum seller. A fine ride through gutsy heartland metal from the glory days of pork rind American rock. One of a nostalgic few die-cut record covers, so like I had to buy two.

Rating      8

**Foghat - Stone Blue** (Bearsville '78)

**Night Shift** and more so **Stone Blue** mark Foghat's gradual shift to more straight-forward HR boogie, mar-bled with various forms of moody mellow exploration,

as opposed to the band's vintage period blues/metal grit. However, for all the variety, the majority of these compositions are the aural, non-threatening equivalent of your favourite old blue jeans, most notably the lazy Stonesiness of cover It Hurts Me Too (Lonesome Dave's professed "signature track"), the rhythmic bashing of expert speed rocker Easy Money, and the heavy metal he-manhandling of oldie Chevrolet. **Stone Blue** leans dangerously close to schizoid, scattered and aimless, staying just this side of chaotic due to the rock'n'blues current flowing righteously and dependably beneath the surface. Nice homemade feel, even if straying a little far from home.
Rating     7

## Foghat - Boogie Motel   (Bearsville '79)
The decline towards lounge status continues, but with fewer lights still on at the inn, Foghat exploring successfully some of their simpler, guitar-edged boogie structures, albeit without the creative acumen to do much more. But side two is choice blues-fried pickin's, offering forth the hard rockin' travellin' man's title track, the melodically arresting Love In Motion and the git goin' Nervous Release. Side one's mellower fare adds to the enjoyable rootsy din making this the one solid latter-day Foghat project devoid of metal, save for the manic Nervous Release. A vivacious and capable steering of old American traditions. Ballad Third Time Lucky, a minor hit in the states, turned out to be one of Dave's proudest mellow faves from the band's entire catalogue.
Rating     7

## Foghat - Tight Shoes   (Bearsville '80)
**Tight Shoes** is as close to harmless boppy guitar rock as Foghat gets, reflecting Peverett's attentiveness to the era's new wave explosion and its subsequent shift towards power pop. All of **Tight Shoes** clips along at a tidy medium pace; nothing too heavy, all upbeat, and supposedly contemporary with boogie shadings, all simple entertainment, all empty and lightly delivered, Foghat thereby continuing its slide from seriously talented rock contender to innocuous mainstream light rockers. **Tight Shoes** gets decent marks here because even though this is soulless fluff, each and every cut holds at least a trace of luke-warm party mentality.
Rating     4

## Foghat - Girls To Chat & Boys To Bounce
(Bearsville '81)
A bit grittier, bluesier, and rollicking than '80's **Tight Shoes**, **Girls To Chat** is like a collection of the less inspired tunes from the **Stone Blue/ Night Shift** era. Nothing remotely heavy here, just well-chapeau'ed boogie and blues-based rock tunes, with thankfully little in the way of **Tight Shoes'** dishwater rock. Again though, decent marks for fresh, consistent, yet not earth-shattering default rock, leaning again to the new wave with added nod to the pub rock traditions of a Dave Edmunds or early Graham Parker. **Girls To Chat** accentuates Foghat's and Status Quo's striking career similarities as they shuffle through time. Both produced god-like blues metal three or four albums into their catalogues and then inexplicably opted for tireless, exhaustive re-creations of the middle-of-the-road boogie tune. I guess all we can do is lament the loss of past grandeur, and either abandon later product out of frustration, or derive what scant enjoyment we can from the strange muses these kin have decided to follow. Lonesome Dave's favorite post-**Boogie Motel** experiment.
Rating     5

## Foghat - In The Mood For Something Rude
(Bearsville '82)
Another piss-poor release that loiters around various rock, pop and blues bus stations, **In The Mood** continues Foghat's all too comfortable slide into the mediocrity of middle age. In contrast to previous non-events, the record's funkier, while still the same mindless, semi-entertaining goo, like an ever so slightly more dangerous Huey Lewis or J. Geils Band. Survives complete pasting only by virtue of the likeability of the band, and definitely not the quality of the music.
Rating     4

## Foghat - Zig-Zag Walk   (Bearsville '83)
Minimalist electronic boogie-woogie. If those three terms mashed together don't send you into dry heaves, I don't know what will, **Zig-Zag Walk** being some tortured soul's idea of a new direction for the band, about the worst advice they could have taken. Ten cartoons, five covers. A most embarrassing pile of confused, concept record rockabilly, after which, in '84, the band would break up, only to be revived as two fragile touring units (Dave vs. Roger) early in the '90s, and then of course, the vanilla, middling comeback record of eleven years hence.
Rating     1

## Foghat - The Best Of   (Rhino '89)
A warm, respectful package of finer moments, including Ubangi Stomp, a charming little micro-boogie from the **Foghat** sessions. Sixteen cuts highlighting a frustrating, rollercoastin', rags to riches to rags career. Sidenote: Rhino has done surprisingly well with the catalogue on CD as a whole, after purchasing the rights from Bearsville, focusing moreso on the label's Rundgren catalogue during negotiations, but finding Foghat sales a pleasant by-product.
Rating     7

## Foghat - The Best Of - Volume 2   (Rhino '92)
Grasping at straws for more of those finer moments, **Volume 2** proves that sixteen cuts is pret' near enough. Trad and timeless newie: All I Want For Christmas Is You proves that bred-in-the-bone blues never leaves the bloodstream. Excellent liner notes on this fairly ignored bunch of blokes who basically created their own close and memorable time and place, owning hard rock in the '70s along with a handful of other brave, axe-slinging souls.
Rating     5

## Foghat - Return Of The Boogie Men   (Modern '94)
When I heard that Rick Rubin was bringing Foghat back from the dead, I was floored, fathomed, foaming. Rick eventually was dropped from the fray due to mutual scheduling difficulties, but he had planted the seed in terms of a straight blues direction for the band. God love the boys for pulling it together after the squabbles. However, even though that magical sound simmers somewhere in these grooves, alas the record's faults are many. **Boogie Men** features the classic Foghat lineage with no substitutions, Peverett, Price, Stevens and Earl rocking through a divided record highlighting a few old-style, slide-axein' originals amongst too many covers, four getting the tired-by-now unplugged treatment (yawn). Oh, and two of these are I Just Want To Make Love To You and Take Me To The River, both tired, trampled and unproductive in terms of establishing this record as a purposeful comeback. Still, despite the haphazard assemblage and the middling, stiff quality of the new tracks, I still gotta crack a smile at hearing Peverett wail the blues over Price's profuse slide. Too many pleasurable hours to deny this record a sincere looksee, and really it's got a merit and tone only Foghat can provide. A faint air of wasted opportunity, perhaps?

**159**

I'd say so, given that there are another ten finished tracks that were ready for possible inclusion.
Rating 6

## Foo Fighters - Foo Fighters (EMI '95)
The hype machine is on, Foo Fighters (a U.S. nickname for UFO's being sighted over Germany circa WWII) being the first post-Nirvana project for multi-talented skinsman Dave Grohl (if one doesn't count his contribution to the ramblin', gamblin' Mike Watt album). So Dave turns his tables, donning axe, clutching microphone, giving up the drums (although Grohl played everything on the album), metamorphosing into hip, churlish frontman of a new gung-ho, guitars-slung-lo generation. And his record's fun and furious, very Nirvana (in their rare upbeat moments), a thick, smeary mess of lush pop hooks pounded home track after purple track. Simple and coy, **Foo Fighters** exudes au courant almost to a fault, but slowly those blustery hooks will pull you Grohl-ward and you will be pogo-ing up a storm. Trust me. Faves: *This Is A Call* and the sublimely floaty *Floaty*. Printing the lyrics would have been a good thing.
Rating 8

## Forbidden - Forbidden Evil (Combat '88)
Forbidden fall into the camp of the over-juiced, like Exodus, Overkill and Testament, slamming out an ultra-heavy speed metal that is coldly disciplined, classy but ultimately hyper and harder to pass than fresh lava. Great vocals but too much too often. Turned out to be a great farm team for the fortification of other bands, latest transaction being the defection of their drummer to Slayer.
Rating 7

## Forbidden - Raw Evil: Live At The Dynamo
(Combat/Relativity '89)
Four track EP of primetime Forbidden fried up and served almost imploded, three from **Forbidden Evil** (actually the original name of the band), and one being a clusterbomb cover of Priest's *Victims Of Changes*. Crappy sound but adequate length (for four songs) at 26 minutes.
Rating 5

## Forbidden - Twisted Into Form (Combat/Relativity '90)
New guitarist, but the definitive Bay Area song remains the same, Forbidden vaulting themselves into the Exodus and Testament frame of mind through their first precision delivery-mix combo. Plus these guys are way more complicated, **Twisted Into Form** occasionally evoking Coroner, Athiest or Anacrusis with its rapid-fire chicanery. Excellent vocals from Russ Anderson, the man able to growl and swirl like Halford on steroids. Missing in action: '94's **Distortion**, released on German label Gun.
Rating 7

## Forbidden - Point Of No Return: The Best Of
(Relativity '92)
Ten tracks of high-minded power thrash, documenting a short but esteemed career by one of the Bay Area's best second-tier acts. Alternates between songs from the debut and record #2, with *Victim Of Changes* closing the show.
Rating 6

## Forcefield - Forcefield (President '87)
Cozy Powell, the world's second dullest drummer after Carmine Appice, gangs up with an assortment of talentless and aging British knobs to stiffly blow covers of already tortuous and over-plundered rock standards, in some sort of hugely counter-productive homage to their barren roots. Thus we get *Whole Lotta Love*, *Sunshine Of Your Love*, *White Room* and *You Really*

Got Me (now that's thinkin' with yer arse) amongst a fabulously numbskullian set of sleepers that in total comprises nine covers and three equally dil originals. The most stunned example of out-of-touch I've ever heard. And there's at least one other Forcefield project that somehow ropes in Graham Bonnet, but I ain't biting, unless the next one features Tortelvis from Dread Zeppelin.
Rating 0

## Forcefield - II: The Talisman (President '88)
The baffling, violently tasteless proposal that is Forcefield improves on their game here, peppering **The Talisman** with seven originals out of eleven tracks, mirroring the similar English Steel project both with a novel (but not all that bright) revolving door concept featuring questionable rock caricatures. Here the leader is definitely Ray Fenwick, who is backed by Cozy Powell, Jan Akkerman, Neil Murray, Tony Martin and others, for a raft of heavy-handed AOR tracks that fail, but not as miserably as the awful covers on the first Forceflu. Very bad chemistry all in all, potential good chemistry being the only reason to do something like this. Horrible reworkings of *Black Night* and *Strange Kind Of Woman* included for your wretching displeasure.
Rating 4

## Forcefield - Three: To Oz And Back (President '89)
Uh, great, here comes Graham Bonnet, who valiantly tries to prop an additional raft of moldy covers and Fenwick originals to no avail. Once more, it's a thick as a brick collection of cloggy, foggy, vaguely r+b-ish (fill in the blanks) AOR, pummeled like a bloody lamb by Powell's lockstep decibels, and merciless bad keyboard technology from the pits of the '80s. Title refers to the fact that the record was recorded in London, but Bonnet's vocals were added in Australia. Talk about separation.
Rating 4

## Forcefield - IV: Let The Wild Run Free (President '90)
The boys are back (like anybody asked), once again bringing mostly covers, although a bit of imagination has miraculously flown in, Powell, Fenwick and Bonnet this time butchering *Can't Get Enough Of Your Love*, *The Wind Cries Mary*, *Ball Of Confusion* and Henley's excellent *I Will Not Go Quietly*, layering the record up and out with the usual process cheese toppings until it's a pizza that vigorously arrests the heart. By a longshot, my favourite Forcefailed.
Rating 5

## Lita Ford - Dangerous Curves (BMG '91)
Abysmally similar to Lee Aaron, Lita, the second most successful ex-Runaway so far after Joan Jett, again sets the women's movement back twenty years with this vapid display of duff commercial jelly. Roughly one third middle-of-the-road metal, one third bubblegum hard rock, and one third crass, chick-style balladry, **Dangerous Curves** represents the mental capacities of an ox wrapped in the guise of a leather-swathed major fox. It's becoming readily obvious that the gals with creativity (i.e. Kate Bush, Jane Siberry, Exene Cervenka, early Heart) steer clear of metal almost exclusively. Somewherz around her fourth record. Married a drooling Chris Holmes from W.A.S.P. in '89.
Rating 0

## Foreigner - Foreigner (Atlantic '77)
The smug bane of AOR critics, Foreigner burst onto the charts for seven year stay, wielding this fabulously received debut record, led by the two-fisted smash punch of *Feels Like The First Time* and massive pomp single *Cold As Ice*. Way up there with the worst string of album covers in rock (Go look. Yuck.), Foreigner

wove a deceptively pointless fabric of sounds, finding hooks pointing to Journey, big boisterous arena rock vocals from Lou Gramm, thick, slow-brewed hard rock outta Bad Company, even smatterings of Queen, Zep, Beatles and space rock. Fave tracks though are smart moderately metal duo *Long, Long Way From Home* and *Woman Oh Woman*, which betray these guys as the veterans they are (Mick Jones was ex-Spooky Tooth and Leslie West, Ian McDonald, ex-King Crimson, Lou Gramm(atico) ex-Black Sheep), chest-thumping like Ted Nugent, while clear, unabashed keyboards pierce the traveled hard rock murk. Y'know as young metalheads we used to hate these guys, finding it just too watery and often stupid (I think their secret weapon was writing for the lowest common denominator), not to mention that they stole all the thunder from who we thought were worthier acts. But time heals all wounds, and after a dizzying decade and a half of bands that tried so hard to sound as professional and produced as possible, these old Foreigner records (and only the old ones) sound astoundingly real and homemade, and quite unduplicated by bands that followed, even if Foreigner's early AOR spawned an entire genre of corporate metal.
Rating                                                                7

## Foreigner - Double Vision  (Atlantic '78)
Talk about a Bad Company classic, *Hot Blooded* lurching out of the '70s like any number of perfect Bad Co. monoliths on a hot summer night. **Double Vision** further emphasized Foreigner's canny knack for songs that stick, the band diving deeper into their previously latent Beatles influences on *I Have Waited So Long* and *You're All I Am*, also dabbling in their odd space pop (for the last time) on basic instrumental *Tramontane*. But it's the blunted rockers that give this record its richness, *Hot Blooded*, *Double Vision* and the rumbling *Blue Morning, Blue Day* reinforcing the hook-making ability of Jones, a plain, no-frills delivery that finds support in the boring drumming of Dennis Elliot. But this one's a definite guilty pleasure for me, memories still etched in my mind of hearing it on 8-track, over and over again, against my will (along with Boston's smash debut), in Howard's classic, violently souped-up, dark blue Mustang on the way to school (often with changed plans) circa 1979. An exercise in making unimpressive rock work, and work it did, selling eight million copies and still counting.
Rating                                                                8

## Foreigner - Head Games  (Atlantic '79)
The tradition continues, and the sales roll in, Foreigner half-causing the sexist traditions of '80s metal with another set of dumb male lyrics, wrapped in an album cover which features a pained-looking bad girl erasing graffiti off the wall of the men's can (**Head Games**, geddit?). But the irresistible pop hooks continue unabated, on this record that is arguably the band's most guitar-pervading; certainly side one being the band's heaviest half-shell, kicking off with the good-time gallop of *Dirty White Boy*, through the blustery, almost goth AOR of *Love On The Telephone*, the twangy boogie rock of *Women*, the Steve Miller-sweet hooks of *I'll Get Even With You*, and flat-line riff rocker *Seventeen*. But side two gave the band one of their biggest hits ever in the moody and broody *Head Games*, which gives way to *The Modern Day*, a lively pop classic, again finding the highest high of melodic hard rock heavens, something again akin to Steve Miller's smash hits from the '70s. Roy Thomas Baker's production is only marginally more electric or busier than Keith Olsen's last time around, both more or less maintaining the band's Keep It Simple Stupid philosophy, to fab commercial success. Many a fan's favorite Foreigner chestnut, including mine.
Rating                                                                8

## Foreigner - 4  (Atlantic '81)
The world's favourite luv 'em hate 'em, quintessentially song-based band hatches their fourth hit record in a row, this time around, enlisting the services of Robert "Mutt" Lange, who previews with Foreigner, that Def Leppard drum sound, all electro-boom and fade, on this imaginatively titled fourth opus. And as usual, there's hits, hits and more hits, three biggest being *Waiting For A Girl Like You* (surprisingly the first chartable ballad for the band), John Cougar (as opposed to Mellencamp) schmaltz *Juke Box Hero*, and hot 'n' nasty dance number *Urgent*, with its famous, blow-yer-lungs-out Jr. Walker sax solo. But there's something stiff and post-marketing age about this one, the band sounding formulaic, the tracks not hanging together as well as on past efforts, many here phoned-in rehashes of past, more enthusiastic experiments. Maybe it's Mutt, and maybe it's the fact that the band has been pared down from six to four members, guys like Thomas Dolby and Larry Fast brought in to prop things up electronically. Who knows? Anyways, after *Urgent*, side two pretty much wilts, for the first time, curly locks Gramm and an increasingly professorial Jones encountering empty creative wells (uh, again, eight million sold).
Rating                                                                6

## Foreigner - Records  (Atlantic '82)
I guess your run-of-the-mill Foreigner fan might be one of the least adventurous of the rock species, so sheep bought this in droves, **Records** culling together a blinding, all-star ten pack of hits for those who just want want society has approved for consumption, another miserable album cover, no lauding, elucidating essay or nuthin'. Sole surprise: a smartly headbanging, live, seven minute version of *Hot Blooded*.
Rating                                                                6

## Foreigner - Agent Provocateur  (Atlantic '84)
Well, if kind words can be mustered, at least the formula has been shattered, Foreigner writing either some of their smartest, textured rockers, or horrible, synthesizer-polluted ballads, with very little middle ground. So no matter how you slice it, this is a bit of a dark, uncommunicative album, the quiet stuff sounding deflated and the heavy stuff on the angry side. Only one hit single here, but it's a big one, *I Want To Know What Love Is*, a contemplative, somber ballad that seeped into American homes not unlike sewer gas (just kidding, it ain't all that bad). The best track is tricky (even gated!) opener *Tooth And Nail*, one of the band's zippiest metal highballs, bolstered by cool soloing from a usually dozy Jones. Other fairly chunkified hard rockers: *Reaction To Action*, *Stranger In My House*, and closer *She's Too Tough*, all throwing in more noisy layers than earlier heavy bones by the band. Strange one, deserving of a quiet respect, but half packed with crap.
Rating                                                                6

## Foreigner - Inside Information  (Atlantic '87)
Just as **4** kind of rehashes **Head Games**, **Inside Information** rehashes **Agent Provocateur**, offering the same grab bag of brash but tuneful hard rock (five songs) and droopy, vitamin-deficient softies. Only difference here is that nobody's listening, this being the band's first of three bombs at the box office, the non-Lou Gramm **Unusual Heat** and the reunion **Mr. Moonlight** continuing the band's bad streak into the mid-'90s. But even the rockers have soft centres (or if they don't, they panic), the band almost becoming a has-been storehouse of expired AOR ideas, like synthesizers as lead, for example. Man, nice album cover guys.
Rating                                                                4

161

### Foreigner - Unusual Heat (Atlantic '91)

Thus far the only Foreigner record without spunky Lou Gramm at the mike, **Unusual Heat** enlists Johnny Edwards (Diamond Head's Sean Harris was offered the job!), in the process taking this so close to '80s Bad Company, the bands become indistinguishable, Edwards' pipes blending Gramm, Howe and Rodgers like some sort of ruthless mathematical leveling. But oddly enough, Foreigner managed to sell even less plastic than Bad Co. with this one, nobody much giving a toss (cozy British lingo) about this straight-faced band anymore, especially without that theatrical voice. Not that **Unusual Heat** doesn't try, most of the record guitar-packed, Jones and Thomas writing thumpy, slow heft rockers whose heart beat is often single thumping bass notes (see Bad Co.). Pretty dull, but nicely devoid of keyboards or idiosyncratic ballads.
Rating                                                            6

### Foreigner - The Very Best . . . And Beyond
(Atlantic '92)

This one's a Foreigner hits pack for the CD age, offering up fourteen of the band's silly rock boy smashes plus three bracing "Gramm is back" calling cards. The three new ones act almost as a senior management-level resumé, the band dedicating a track each to what they do best, *Soul Doctor* rocking expansively and with muscle, *Prisoner Of Love* doing that pomp *Cold As Ice* thing but with muscle, *With Heaven On Our Side* being a quality arch-Foreigner ballad, no muscle required, Gramm putting in a strange but provocative vocal. Our fave conservative rockers are definitely back. Too bad the spunk waned by the time **Mr. Moonlight** rolled along. Detailed liner notes, essay, lyrics to the new ones.
Rating                                                            7

### Foreigner - Classic Hits Live (Atlantic '93)

Done up just about as right as it could have been, **Classic Hits Live** displays 74 minutes of passionately delivered Foreigner hits, lots of pictures, extensive track by track liner notes, and a historical essay by the band's manager. Tunes were selected from individual shows over an eight year period, and renditions are explosive and entertaining, this from a band with a bad live reputation (I saw them once in '94. They were pretty good). Includes dynamic covers of *Not Fade Away* and *Love Maker*, Gramm as usual stealing the show with his blue collar, everyman pipes.
Rating                                                            7

### Foreigner - Mr. Moonlight (Rhythm Safari/Attic '95)

The not exactly highly trumpeted return of Foreigner, major parties intact, rides a surprisingly mellow tide, while for the most part turning down the synths, replaced here by glossy acoustic arrangements. A couple of the upbeat numbers, *Under The Gun* and *White Lie* (this one reminds me of Lou Gramm's solo hit *Midnight Blue*), scored minor hits, but the record as a whole caused nary a ripple. One dim scrap of hope: the soft rockers like *All I Need To Know* and *Hole In My Soul* almost approach close and personal (if somewhat depressed), something this band never even attempted in the past. But it's pretty much obvious, given Foreigner's latter half career plus the Jones and Gramm solo records, that songwriting has not progressed a wit over the years. Saw them live in '94: a rollicking good time really, although that new bass player with the monstrous ego (the guy spent the evening striking poses and locking eyes with the night's potential sexual conquest) really doesn't do the band's aura of maturity any favours.
Rating                                                            5

### Rhett Forrester - Gone With The Wind (Bernett '84)

Sounds like there's some decent metal buried behind the disgraceful clatter of electronic drums, which single-handedly ruins any semblance of listenability this disc could have had. The writing sounds like the heavy stuff from Rhett's days with Riot but the drums are so bloody awful, clunking and banging like amplified metronomes, that nothing much else can even be heard. Huge mixing mistake on what could have been a TKO-ish barnburner.
Rating                                                            4

### Rhett Forrester - Even The Score (Rampage/Rhino '88)

Pretty much the same stiff and sterile treatment of third-rate cock rock, **Even The Score** finds Forrester truly acting washed-up, drifting into rust belt bush-league type compositions from the worst mid-'80s metal disasters. A whole lot of mixing and crap goes into each song, but you can't fix bad songs, and all that mixing is done poorly anyways. Sorta looks like Coverdale, don't he? Contains a cover of Bad Co.'s *Ready For Love*. Note: Forrester is now dead (see below).
Rating                                                            4

### Rhett Forrester - Hell Or Highwater
(Digital Force/TCE '96)

You couldn't ask for a better tribute album, this lengthy compilation of known and unknown Forrester tracks paying homage to the golden-tressed consumate front man, who was shot dead in his car at an intersection in Atlanta 1994, in what looked to be some sort of robbery or car-jacking. **Hell Or Highwater** culls together tunes from his Riot career, and also work with Thrasher, Jack Starr, solo stuff and his last band, Dr. Dirty out of Calgary (pretty crappy stuff). Add to this a ton of pictures both personal and professional, quotes and testimonials, explanatory and biographical notes, and like I say, you couldn't do much better. Except fact is, most of the material Forrester was part of was substandard, no one really making good use of the man's powerful, bluesy pipes, most collaborations focusing on the man's '80s cock rock presence and not his hurtin' feeling potential. Some of this is Forrester's fault, and part is the nature of the times in which he flourished. In any event, a great vocalist has been lost, one whose most artistically lasting legacy will be his years with Riot, a second-stringer who at least adopted a bit of a cowboy slant to things during Forrester's reign. Horrible front cover, which is another Forrester legacy. Note: ends with a chilling, hidden 18th track which is a rainy recording of Forrester accompanying the organ to *Amazing Grace* at his grandmother's funeral, six weeks before he was shot.
Rating                                                            6

### Fortnox - Fortnox (Est. '78)

Pressed of the era when anything heavy was viewed with at least cursory awe, this unassuming very American, somewhat biker-ish power trio didn't disappoint. However, it didn't exactly cause us to put lighter fluid to our copies of **Sad Wings Of Destiny** or even our scratched-up **Free For Alls**. Speaking of the Motor City Madman, **Fortnox** could be said to be circling about Ted's intensity level and emotive plane, but a bit bereft of the Whackmaster's grand flash musically. Still, one of those "wish I had's" now. Almost entirely heavy but '70s heavy which means pretty subdued and conservatively mixed.
Rating                                                            5

### 454 Big Block - Your Jesus (Century Media '95)

Beantown's 454 Big Block (hail all car buffs) stomp forth with an expansive urbanized doomcore, much more esoteric and dreamlike than the band's previous incarnation as Wrecking Crew, who had one record a few years back called **Balance Of Terror. Your Jesus** on the other hand, is sort of a commercial Eyehategod, leaving clear the floundering, exploratory riff collusions, while Elgin James wrenches out tales of bleak life from the drilled inside of his besieged skull (no really, that's what it sounds like). Hurtful little pile of these creative, millennium-strangling grunge bands at hand, many of the best ones oddly enough, finding homes on Century Media. Whether any of them make a dent remains to be seen.

Rating                                                                 7

## The Four Horsemen - Nobody Said It Was Easy
(Def American '91)

Hard to side-step the concept or novelty feel of a band so shamelessly vacuum-sealed in the '70s as this distilled version of AC/DC's minimal dressing crossed with Foghat's countrified urge to boogie all night long. No mistaking that Rick Rubin was wallowing in his past with this one, and for the most part, critics seem to agree that the record has those simple, honest elements that make for a committed piece of radio-defined classic rock. However much I buy into it though, it still seems contrived; too accurate in its direct re-telling of the '70s, somewhat air-filled and lacking in any improvement over the bands we loved back then. Worst tendencies for offering absolutely nothing to hold attention fall within automatic fluff like *Wanted Man* and *Can't Stop Rockin'*, two boogers on different energy waves, yet totally similar in their fate as exceedingly boring. However, the title track and Angus-twanging lead single/vid *Rockin' Is Ma Business* are prime biker metal, while the slide-axin' *Tired Wings* actually swoops with finesse, 'neath the emotively bluesy vocals of the versatile and just all-around cool Frank C. Starr. All in all, one of those great background music records, wholly unchallenging, but pleasing nonetheless given that all the jobs are done well except songwriting. Very little of substance, compared to less metallic but equally time-locked labelmates Black Crowes, whose emotional palette makes for a less juvenile, one-track set of gestures. Still hard rockers, almost alone in their purist faith, yet nearly roots rock, boogie-woogie-ing pret' near non-stop. And man, do they look the part.

Rating                                                                 7

## The Four Horsemen - Gettin' Pretty Good At Barely Gettin' By (Magnetic Air '95)

Be the band, Billy, then disappear due to a drug-related death in the family (drummer Dimwit), label wranglings (with American: see Trouble), and band tension (Starr in, Starr out). And after a four year absence (one per Horseman), become dang near a holy grail, at least here in Canada, where the band's debut did better 'n anywhere else, going gold (300,000 worldwide), becoming a classic rock radio staple in the process. So it's apt that Toronto indie Magnetic Air has picked up this fetching sophomore effort, **Gettin' Pretty Good** expanding intelligently on the debut's straight-no-chaser boogie euphoria, acting downright zesty through and through, kicking off delectably with a searing, sparkling cover of Derringer's *Still Alive And Well*. Then there's the *Riff Raff*-in' AC/DC of *Hot Rod*, the spacious southern slide of *What The Hell Went Wrong*, the perfect metal Skynyrd of the title track . . . just loads of proud, party-high boogie metal, acoustic closeness, and big-hearted fun, the writing vastly improved to the point of sounding like a fifteen record band. Gingerly side-stepping the pitfalls of hair metal bands gone blues (Cinderella, Poison and Thunder come to mind), The Four Horsemen now deserve side-by-side ranking with the the Black Crowes or certainly Brother Cane, if not a few '70s bands like Foghat or AC/DC themselves. What a beauty fer sure, brightly, perfectly recorded, delivered with so much ungodly,

whiskey-swilling verve, ya just gotta join in. Low note: as I write this Frank Starr lies in a coma, the victim of a bad motorcycle accident, with Little Caesar's Ron Young stepping in so the band can tour.

Rating                                                                 9

## 4 Non Blondes - Bigger, Better, Faster, More!
(Interscope/Atlantic '92)

Somewhat accepted into hard rock circles, though more of a swampy roots rock act awash in acoustic guitars, 4 Non Blondes garnered smatterings of success with their passionate but annoying *What's Up* ballad, a tune indicative of the record's lush mechanics, due in large part to the overwrought, almost blood-curdlingly powerful vocals of leader Linda Perry. Really off the wall, like Melissa Etheridge meets Zep meets the Chili Peppers, each directive infused with a strange hair band sheen. Three gals, one guy; one ultimately airy, unsatisfying record.

Rating                                                                 5

## Freak Of Nature - Freak Of Nature (Music For Nations '93)

So what are ya going to do next time if the band you left had already set high standard for intelligent, guitar-driven AOR? Well, White Lion's Mike Tramp does the expected, but in this case, also the best case scenario for a guy with his talents. So his new band Freak Of Nature inches the White Lion sound just a bit forward, a shade heavier, still (luckily for us) mixing tricky, smooth but steely guitar work with strong commercial metal songs (I hear the funk of Skid Row or Spread Eagle in here, but with a more polite disposition). There's nothing '90s or alternative about this, Tramp deciding to work within a system he helped raise in stature. So folks liked White Lion, lamented their demise, then lied eagerly in wait, this next logical step satiating most just fine.

Rating                                                                 8

## Freak Of Nature - Gathering Of Freaks
(Music For Nations '94)

Uh, I guess **Gathering Of Freaks** brings to fruition the other thing we might have expected first time around, fusing slick commercial metal chops to excursions into, out of, then into again, alternative circa Seattle, Tramp even inflecting a considerable dose towards Sir Vedder, as his band trips up the time signatures and downtunes like Soundgarden (see and soak up the irony of *Big Black Hole*). But these guys are pros, and whatever the slight lean west, they do a killer job marrying two worlds (à la Skid Row and yes, Ugly Kid Joe), proving that it helps knowing what you're doing if you are going to play slightly psychedelic, exploratory heavy metal. Passionate, if a little opportunistic, but like I say, these guys find ways to produce the goods. Faves: strident grunge epic *The Tree* and frantic rhythm machine *Powerless*, anything but.

Rating                                                                 8

## Ace Frehley - Frehley's Comet (Megaforce '87)

Hapless Ace's debut is an extremely likeable hard rock/metal album right from the opening strains of the humorous and autobiographical *Rock Soldiers*, through Russ Ballard's *Into The Night*, the moving *Something Moved*, and the chunky *Stranger In A Strange Land*. Solid, well-produced, big league, but warm and varied, **Frehley's Comet** is an admirable, spacebooted first step back into the limelight, and a weighty enough return to the crazy and often unforgiving world of rock'n'roll. Anything but tentative.

Rating                                                                 7

## Frehley's Comet - Live + 1 (Megaforce '88)

This five track EP offers five Ace classics, 4 live + 1, including vamp-Acer *Rip It Out*, Kiss' heaviest pre-loss-of-innocence-days cut, *Rocket Ride*, and the most rau-

cous Cometcut to date *Something Moved*. Lone studio track, *Words Are Not Enough* is a warm keyboardy hard rocker driven home by a catchy chorus, recorded with that great Comet live feel with which we've grown to groove.
Rating  **7**

### Frehley's Comet - Second Sighting  (Megaforce '88)
More of the same uplifting hard rock, mixing slower mood pieces such as *Separate* with more mid-paced groove stuff like *Loser In A Fight*, *Insane*, and the sinister *Dancin' With Danger*. Again another album which, had it been recorded by Ace's ex-greasemates, would be considered one of the best Kiss albums of the past ten years. And perhaps this is its greatest testimony. While Kiss stagnates, Ace is out exploring the oft-overlooked subtleties of rock structures, albeit within the tight framework of American-style hard rock. Ace's form of self-deprecating humour at his life's ups and downs reveals a guy without pretensions, a simple man who just wants to communicate through his music. Good intentions all around.
Rating  **7**

### Ace Frehley - Trouble Walkin'  (Megaforce Worldwide '89)
Press talk seemed to indicate that Space Ace was the biggest medicine chest renegade in Kiss and if true, it might account for the extra effort and levity Ace pours into his projects compared to the automatic, rip-off-the-fans callousness of latter-day Kiss. So **Trouble Walkin'** is basically an ambitious, high quality version of Kiss, replete with party hardy anthems delivered via Ace's rag-tag band grinding away behind the charm of the circus master's can't-sing-who-cares vocals. Oddities include *Hide Your Heart*, featured here *and* on Molly Hatchet's **Lightning Strikes Twice**, roughly the same time Kiss released it as a single, and a cover of ELO's *Do Ya*. In general, look for a lot of the memorable emotive high points of Kiss, yet with greater complexity, warmth and self-deprecating humour, if not a bit of Joe Perry and Keef thrown in for good measure.
Rating  **8**

### Ace Frehley - 12 Picks  (Megaforce '97)
Hopefully cashing in all all things Kiss-able in '97, Megaforce have conceived this compilation sampling Ace's four releases, while adding no less than six live nuggets on which to chew nostalgically. And full advantage is used here, the vaults coughing up *Breakout* (yawn), plus the chummy *Rip It Out*, and four Kiss classics, including what is possibly that band's best song, *Rocket Ride*. The mix is killer, chops on full throttle, and the band's inter-track banter amusing in its overpowering fromage. *Shock Me* includes an exhausting solo from the damaged one that is C.C. Devillian in the extreme, and all go away pleased at having touched the hem of rock history. Or something like that. Nice essay by executive producer and Comet bassist John Regan.
Rating  **6**

### The Front - The Front  (CBS '89)
Right off the bat I have big problems with this garishly packaged sliver of imitation rock, The Front's lead vocalist being such a painfully accurate knock-off of Billy Idol that the concept just disintegrates into a cheap novelty act before mine eyes; second all too clear influence being The Cult, with the big beat simplicity, traces of U2's Edge, and the short "mystical" song titles such as *Fire*, *Sunshine Girl*, *Pain*, *Ritual* and *Sister Moon*. It ain't necessarily a recipe for disaster when bands overtly draw on one or two major influences, but the gesture's got to offer something more; an improvement, either in emotional intensity, technicality, musical supercharge, or even humour . . . just something to make us care. Here we're subjected to cliché and powerless-to-boot Cult filler, rendering **The Front** all

tried and tired, toothless and annoying, idea-void and contrived. This Kansas City act needed a major kick in the ass if they ever aspired to replacing The Cult, not an insurmountable feat given the comatose deliveries on then-current dishtowels like **Sonic Temple** and **Ceremony**. Renamed Bakers Pink for a self-titled release in '93, not that it makes any difference.
Rating  **3**

### Front Line Assembly - Millennium  (Attic/Roadrunner '94)
On what is incredibly this Vancouver duo's seventh full-length album, Front Line Assembly layer industrial metal loud and spacious, offering yet another in a series of records in the '90s that leap past Ministry's ground-breaking **Psalm 69** in terms of tech advancement. **Millennium** is a bunch of long tracks crammed with samples, dance repetition and strong riffs. But the monotony of tone and time wins over and loses me, while those vocals and hate-steeped lyrics just wear me down. As wild a ride as any industrial out there but I guess I'm just not a fan (drummer's grudge?).
Rating  **6**

### Fudge Tunnel - Creep Diets  (Earache '91)
Record two for these turgid U.K. badboys (after the pretty dumb **Hate Songs In E Minor** debut in '91, the **Teeth** EP in '92, and a bunch of singles) finds the band magnifying and solidifying their novel-for-Europe, dangerous punk metal sound, more accurately known as grunge. Which is (I think) why critics embraced the band, finding in them an explosive, caustic machine that used only rudimentary tools to create a metal din that would rattle around in one's head for days. Problem is, it all gets a little tiring after a few plays, this anti-social crap factor, repelling listenability, y'know, sounding uh, anti-social, like Butthole Surfers, cool but maybe later. So anyhow, the boys are pretty young. Things will and do improve.
Rating  **6**

### Fudge Tunnel - The Complicated Futility Of Ignorance  (Earache '94)
Fudge Tunnel's previous work suffered by its Melvins-like disdain for quality finish, but this third full-length bulks up and smells the roar, "chug advisor" Max Cavalera of Sepultura (who with Alex Newport was one half of Nailbomb) rubbing off a bit of Brazilian fudge on the young but putridly prolific from Nottingham. The record's bass cycles are stereophonically destructive, and there's more of that ol' metal touch, even a sort of Helmet-like economy of word and riff, although Fudge Tunnel likes it slow and thick, maybe a bit too simple for info-addled minds; lots of way-back-in-the-mix shoutiness, but also some innovative arrangements amongst all the tiring but sincere noise. Cantankerous, hateful of many things and themes, and I guess the band's best, although I for one am still looking for more musical stuff packed in, less uni-modal throb.
Rating  **7**

### Fudge Tunnel - In A Word  (Earache '95)
And the scowling noise that was Fudge Tunnel is no more, the band calling it quits after this scraps 'n' scrapes project, culling together nasty live tracks, b-sides, demos and the odd curio like a heavy Sabbathy version of Sabbath's *Changes*, which was of course a piano ballad in its original form. But as usual, Newport's hoarse bark is recorded distant in the mix, letting the band's stinky riffs overpower, pollute and seize-up each pleasant composition. Almost Ministry-like in emotional tone (although with no industrial elements whatsoever), Fudge Tunnel managed to grimace their way to an almost hallowed position amongst renegade rockers, lovers of uncompromised noise, daylight-shunning wallowers of the underground. Stand tall a

moment and hail these sewer-dwelling Nottingham nutters.

Rating **7**

## Full Circle - Negative  (Leviathan '95)

Calling this one Pantera-esque would be an understatement, Full Circle adopting that same futuristic guitar sound and punchy electro-bass drum recording, as lead barker Doug Carter (formerly of pretty fab labelmates Simple Aggression) belts out tales of steadfast human will. But like Paul Di'anno's latest Killers project, one can never quite get away from the derivation, which might also include Prong and Pro-Pain. So despite the quality of the music (if a little basic), **Negative** is plagued by this one big negative, even though it's damn near an **8**, despite. Beware the vaguely White Metal cover art. Behaved this ain't.

Rating **7**

## Fu Manchu - In Search Of . . .  (Mammoth/Attic '96)

This kitschy slog through '70s stuff is getting outa hand, Fu Manchu giving us hot cars, a '70s babe, the typestyles, the devil dolls, **In Search Of . . .**, and of course the big liquid Sabbath riffs last heard by the defunct Kyuss. So even if this looks a little like a **Dukes Of Hazzard** episode, it would be a mistake to write this hoover groover off, Fu Manchu conjurin' up massive overdriven riff monsters that arrive fuel-injected with equal but minute doses of alternative and grunge. Vocalist Scott Hill possesses the perfect half-Ozzy, half-Iggy, all-1971 mop-head drawl, which he just tosses overtop a sludgy, slurring barrage of concrete guitars and drums, made only less impressive by the fact that Kyuss thought of it first. Which is the bottom line: if you miss Kyuss, pay a visit to Fu Manchu.

Rating **8**

## Funhouse - Generation Generator  (Caroline '90)

Strange little album this one, and I do mean little, clocking in at under 33 minutes, which in the CD age is brief, fleeting, and inexcusable. Funhouse is a dead ringer for Mother Love Bone on the first five cuts here, while a sloppy hard rock band on the last three, toons which are further distinguished as being live, making this a short, screwed-up ying and yang platter not without flashes of admirable funkiness. Brings to mind GN'R, Aerosmith and most definitely dead Bone vocalist Andrew Wood. Too disjointed to establish flesh and blood, but promising in its minor decadence.

Rating **4**

## Furbowl - The Autumn Years  (Blackmark '94)

A bewildering slapdash of U.S. skatepunk, grindcore, and straight-forward metal, Furbowl end up as a sort of bruising punk rock ride with chops, mixing their myriad of influences into a misbegotten, three-legged mash of sounds, totally illogical but kinda fun, like Swedish grindcore by party animals who just can't take themselves seriously, like an underground death metal take on U.K.'s Terrorvision. Vocals lean towards the out-of-tune but tuneful adnoidal scrape of Paradise Lost (not like it's planned that way), although real singing infects some of the normal rock'n'roll parts. **The Autumn Years** (the band's second) will definitely confuse, bother and provoke (witness the country-goth Mission-ary Cramps of closer *Still Breathing*). Still, it's cool to see someone breaking the rules (or more like not knowing them). Anyways, I hope the record somehow worms its way to an audience, whoever it might be. Good sense of alcohol.

Rating **7**

# G

## Galactic Cowboys - Galactic Cowboys (Geffen '91)

The only band to my knowledge that feeds from the same trough as the legendary King's X, Galactic Cowboys portray a trippy and technical whirlwind of sights, smells, tastes and sounds; borne of King's X' self-same Sam Taylor/ Wilde Silas umbilicals, borne of interstellar liaisons from the plains of outback Texas, and borne of daunting creativity and fluid imagination. Dead similar harmonies and guitar sound to the big X, the record is also a delimited fragmentation to further extremes, be they metallic as on *Sea Of Tranquility*, or wallowingly lush as on the sanguine *Someone For Everyone*. A wild experimentation takes over this ride through colour, that if not for the obvious derivation, would make **Galactic Cowboys** so soaringly wonderful and alone on a specified near empty plane. Slippery, agile and not above good humour, **Galactic Cowboys** is intellectual grist for the discerning dreamer amongst the metallic set. Underground with its head in the clouds.
Rating                                                                      8

## Galactic Cowboys - Space In Your Face (Geffen '93)

Pristine but jagged, maniacal but clear-thinking, **Space In Your Face** offers further delvations into the machinations of Colvin, Doss, Huggins and Sonnier, only this time passing on the bean sprouts for a sixteen ounce slab of bleeding cow flesh. From controversial (pro life?) lead single *If I Were A Killer* through the thrashin' *Circles In The Field* (I still prefer Mike Scott's *Corn Circles*) and well beyond, **Space** is indeed in your face, a much meatier record than Galactic One. Harmonies swirl in and swirl out rather than provide platform, and riffs find Metallica more often than spiritual twins King's X, making for less of a college band odor, more sonic wallop. Exhilarating and perfect alternative art metal for the nanosecond '90s, nimble enough for those entertained by elegance and chops, but irreverent and spontaneous enough for the grunge set, Galactic Cowboys are indeed food for thought, composing challenging rock tunes that will crack a smile, if not floor you, still caught somewhere between commitment to power and commitment to melody. Nine cuts, then a long silence, another track, another long silence and yet another track, all designed to crash the processors of your CD player I guess. The crystal cogent balance between might and flight. A mesmerizing feast for the senses, not unlike the metallic distillation of **Sgt. Pepper** through Extreme's **III Sides To Every Story**.
Rating                                                                     10

## Galactic Cowboys - Machine Fish (Metal Blade '95)

After a swirl of break-up rumours, Galactic Cowboys emerge intact (well, Wally Farkas replaces Dane Sonnier on guitar), thanks in large part to metal mover 'n' shaker, and rabid Cowboy fan Brian Slagel. And **Machine Fish** scores the band a hat trick, this third delivering a gutsy dose of bottom end, lots of drums (skinsman Alan Doss produces), and a coat of gritty grime to reintensify this gloriously creative band's circular trick metal visions. The record as a whole is heavier (and yikes! a slight shade grungier) than the classic **Space In Your Face**, and even a trace more direct and he-manhandled. But those Beatle-esque harmonies (the Fish) glossed over some of the most inventive and uplifting power metal around (the Machine) . . . why it's all still so fantabulously there, ya gotta thank Slagel for keeping the dream alive. And the Houston supernauts haven't ignored their penchant for beautious, gushing ballads either, *Easy To Love* and *Arrow* taking the blessed listener to places only Saigon Kick have seen. All in all, a gorgeous, colourful, and deceptively hard-hitting album, **Machine Fish** is neither the best nor the worst from the band, for such comparitives are useless and crass when the catalogue is this daunting. It's simply the third. Just be thankful it's actually arrived; here to add sense and wisdom to your dreary existence, here to uh, rock you like a hurricane.
Rating                                                                      9

## Galactic Cowboys - Feel The Rage (Metal Blade '96)

Cover art of this odds and sods, sorta Helloweenie EP (out first in Europe) features another one of Colvin's bright and lively paintings (two were used on the inner sleeve of **Machine Fish**). And the music enclosed is similarly explosive, beginning with the excellent *Feel The Rage* from the last record, a bursting piece of power popped metal, catchy as a cold. Next up: a long powerful ballad called *Paradigm Shift*, followed by *I Want You*, the best Kiss kover I've ever heard, the Cowboys mixing up tempos like a blender full of crunchy frogs. Track four is Wings cover *Junior's Farm*, again, well done with loving reverence of hearty harmonies. Closing things out: a couple of fairly pointless live tracks from **Machine Fish**, both a l'il worse than the studio renditions. But hey, one can only enjoy this groovy half hour session with this most likable and refreshing of metal combos. In fact as music goes, quite indispensable.
Rating                                                                      8

## The Eric Gales Band - The Eric Gales Band
(Elektra '91)
Initiating a degree of buzz with this confident debut, EGB go on to become somewhat a guitarist's study, what with Eric's soulful trad stylings fusing the blues, dinosaur funk, metal and Hendrix, somewhere within the galaxies of Frank Marino and even Pat Travers. Songs are eminently digestible, even a bit too easily assimilated, all political (Hootie?) correctness, good intentions and buoyancy, with little in the way of edge or emotional force. Still, a plausible act with a nice niche addressed by only a handful of acts.
Rating                                                    6

## The Eric Gales Band - Picture Of A Thousand Faces
(Elektra '93)
The Eric Gales Band return with this highly credible second effort, which marries hopeful morality pieces to bright funk metal and acoustic structures (more here than on the debut) à la King's X (Eric's vocals definitely recall Doug's expressive phrasings) and Living Colour (Eric's axework, like Vernon Reid's paying homage to Hendrix with well-rationed flourishes of unbridled noisiness). Squeaky clean and brightly recorded, **Picture Of A Thousand Faces** is a pleasing spin first and foremost, challenging as a whole with its well-paced variety, well within the realm of polite (each of the trio thanks God before all else). Professional, funky hard rock that is shoe-in for crossover success, expressing a maturity that sidesteps the trappings of metal in every respect, arriving at heft through energy, not riffs. Not sure if anything passed between, but '96 saw the release of **Left Hand Brand** on boutique label House Of Blues, a crisp and vibrant electric blues record, credited to "The Gales Bros."
Rating                                                    7

## Rory Gallagher - Top Priority   (Chrysalis '79)
This Irish hard rockin' blues marksman (since deceased from chronic alcoholism) constitutes a marginal entry in this volume. His early material is more literal blues, his later stuff I haven't heard, but his mid-years product was often technically hard rock, and at times smokin' metallic, as on this record's *Just Hit Town* and to some extent *Follow Me*. **Top Priority** is the classiest, most accessible Gallagher of the five or six I've heard, scoring the aforementioned top notch rockers, plus the soulful *Philby* and *Bad Penny*. Another excellent although less consistently loud Gallagher effort is '78's **Photo Finish**, featuring the emotive builder *Shadow Play*. And one I wouldn't qualify as excellent, but simply a good barroom boogie blues record nevertheless, would be '82's **Jinx**. In any event, if you're into '70s style British, bluesy hard rock, (I know, he's Irish), latch onto **Top Priority** or **Photo Finish**.
Rating                                                    7

## Gamma - 1   (Elektra '79)
Gamma - **1** and **2** are the finest moments of Ronnie Montrose's recording portfolio, a roller coaster catalogue of mixed successes including Gamma, early and latter-day Montrose, various experimental solo explorations, and production credits. Gamma - **1** is a tour de force of hard rock styles, brilliant, dark, and ever so first class, offering comfortable but large keyboard-based hard rockers such as *Thunder And Lightning* and *I'm Alive*, stormy metal in the classic *Razor King* and epic builder *Fight To The Finish*, plus bluesy, heartfelt, acoustic balladeering in *Wish I Was*. The qualities that make Gamma formidable are many: the progressive arrangements, the synth and keyboard stylings, the timeless riffs, the variety, and maybe most importantly, the talented, emotive vocals of Davey Pattison (later joining Robin Trower) who evokes a wiser, more confident and feeling version of Lou Gramm or Paul Rodgers.

Pattison also figures prominently in the songwriting, lending more credence to his words. All in all, Gamma - **1** rocks with joy; a gorgeous and princely record, entertaining on many levels; a dynamically complex classic of innovative hard rock.
Rating                                                    10

## Gamma - 2   (Elektra '80)
The masterpiece of the Gamma tryst, **2** rages also the heaviest and most focused, easily establishing itself as one of my 25 favourite albums of all time, a vibrant heavy record that featured more of Pattison's bluesy but fortified vocal work trading licks with layers of up-front tradition-steeped guitar work from a short-shorn Montrose. More than half the record is truly ground-breaking, yet subtly so, traits like the elegant hard rock treatment of '60s anthem *Something In The Air*, the wit and slow prowl of *Skin And Bone* and the lowdown bluesiness of *Voyager* and *Cat On A Leash* working seamlessly a combination of brains, chops and power. Ultimately, Gamma - **2** is one of those magical releases with nary a wasted moment, a smooth spin with a vaguely modern-day Deep Purple ethic, in its all pervasive high quality, and its effortless and believable marrying of diverse influences under a heavy metal banner. In the final analysis, Gamma was a band beyond comparisons, a band that created self-assured and timeless art out of below-the-surface flowings of '70s extravagance. Sadly missed. Speaking of art, this record's worth it for the hilarious front cover alone, which features a couple of sharks tearing through someone's back yard.
Rating                                                    10

## Gamma - 3   (Elektra '82)
An earthly disappointment from a god-like band, **3** abandons Montrose's innovative hard rock class for an experimental, razor sharp, and technically skyward foray into synthesizer rock, albeit of a heavier nature. Standouts: fairly metallic duo *Moving Violation* and *No Way Out*, plus *Modern Girl* and poppy minor hit *Right The First Time*, while all in all less of the devastating magic of **1** and **2**, and basically no guitars, the band switching gears, perpetuating Montrose's musical eclecticism. Still, **3** is rich, complex, well-recorded, and up to **1** and **2**'s quality standards, while demonstrating a surgical substitution of keyboards for guitars, something Montrose wanted to try with this band all along, given his recent embracing of synthesizer technology. Strange direction but still very much cutting edge. In a pique of frustration, Montrose would leave the band mid-tour in Europe (backing up Foreigner), just as the record was starting to break back home in the U.S.
Rating                                                    8

## Gamma Ray - Heading For Tomorrow   (Noise/BMG '90)
And Helloween begat Gamma Ray, an equal partner in European sophistication, led by departed axe maestro Kai Hansen, who surrounds himself with a classy thinking entourage of like-minded alchemists bent on a clamorous metal for the '90s. **Heading For Tomorrow** rocks proudly with time-honoured tradition recalling Priest, Accept and a general purity of mind that echoed so resoundingly inside the chosen cranial casement of Pumpkinhead. And speaking of the esteemed Priest, Ralf Scheepers sends chills down the middle of these goodwill crunchers, similar to the commanding slice of Halford's circa **Sad Wings** or **Sin After Sin**, while the capable ones at his back crank something closer to inspired, speedy and spontaneous **British Steel**. Hell, there's even Queen come *Money*, a hyper speed demon that even sports a short Abba rip-off, and *The Silence*, which sounds like a full-on Queen ballad, resplendent in piano, May-inspired axework and epic **Sheer Heart Attack** breaks. But enough comparisons, 'cos Gamma Ray are no derivative, creating me-

lodic peaks of their own occupation, woven with a lyrical fabric of a thoughtful band so comfortably, unselfconsciously and unparadoxically resolved to a life of metal, a life spiced with bright technological edge, as tasteful keyboard passages collide with booming techy drums in creation of energy personified. A fine, fine metal band with none of the fantastical componentry of other way cool '90s acts, but all of the charm and class, under a framework so simply stated, yet convincingly delivered at face level. Ends with a bombastic, theatrical cover of Look At Yourself.
Rating                                                              8

## Gamma Ray - Sigh No More   (Noise/BMG '91)

Gamma Ray adds a guitarist and changes drummers, but as long as the core of Kai Hansen and the gosh-darn hardest working voice in rock, Ralf Scheepers remains, this band will always be a potent force. **Sigh No More** hunkers down, the band stripping some of the extreme frilliness out of **Heading For Tomorrow**, tracks like One With The World and genius closer The Spirit sparkling with effervescent drama, Scheepers sending them spiralling home like Shakespeare. Also gone is some of the more eccentric, football chanting that recalled Helloween, **Sigh No More** absolutely cruising with urgent, metal intent. Just such a classy band really, Gamma Ray strike at the heart of classical-based, European metal, melody of a steely, regal nature welded to the metal frame of this band with so much intelligence and discipline.
Rating                                                              9

## Gamma Ray - Insanity And Genius   (Noise/Rough Trade '93)

Gamma Ray fall prey to the syndrome that saw Helloween lapse in the '90s, branching too far out, believing their own press, and filling out their sound with too many tricks. But where Helloween really tripped into odd realms of acoustic thrash prog pop metal (whatever that means), Gamma Ray just write too dressy, staying into gothic speed metal, but getting a bit too smart for their own good. Eccentricity reigns, even Scheepers sounding a bit of a twangy, tangy crank, playing too many roles, while Hansen over-fills each song, allowing no breathing room for the vocal and guitar majesty the band used to tap with ease. Still loads of upper crust German metal here, but just too much too often.
Rating                                                              8

## Gamma Ray - Land Of The Free   (Noise '95)

Onwards upwards with layers and speed, as an increasingly Kai-controlled vehicle belts out an expected but daunting display of German engineering. Things are heavier and lighter here, balaboured, balladic passages broken by precision speed metal more insistent and persistent than in the past. Back dime-on overlapped with Helloween like never before, and I really don't care. Pass the Pantera.
Rating                                                              7

## Gaskin - End Of The World   (Rondelet Est. '81)

Hapless NWOBHMetallers who weren't in the least ready to record. Cheap production, amateurish execution and barwipe song skills make this clunky oldster dull and forgettable.
Rating                                                              3

## Gaskin - No Way Out   (Rondelet '82)

Almost cavalier improvement, but **No Way Out** still suffers from mediocre songcraft, treble-weak production, and strained, unexpressive vocals. Heavy and well-paced for early metal but still no big woop. Exceptions: kick-ass rockers, High Crime Zone and the roaring riff-from-Hellbound title track, which recalls the desperate black wind of labelmates Witchfynde.
Rating                                                              5

## The Gathering - Always   (Pavement '93)

**Always** is the debut from this much ballyhoo-ed Dutch act, recorded in late '91, originally released on Foundation 2000 Records. The record shows the band already crafting their doomy, deathy, symphonic sound, but in a cloistered manner, exposing stiffness and inexperience not unlike the vibe found on Decoryah's debut. The spooky melodies draped over the simple but effective grind tracks sound almost forcefully inserted and maudlin, like a horror movie from the '30s, as Bart Smits' anachronistic grind vocals do little to lift the cause (he's gone by record #2, the mellower **Almost A Dance**). A worthy debut, if only for the attempts made and the curiosity seeded, not to mention surprise sales of over 20,000 copies.
Rating                                                              6

## The Gathering - Mandylion   (Century Media '95)

Century Media continues to lead when it comes to new transformations of death metal into a heaviness of hope. Towards this end, the label gave us the latest classic from Tiamat, and now **Mandylion**, like Tiamat's **Wildhoney**, produced by Despair/Grip Inc. master Waldemar Sorychta (with Siggi Bemm). Panoramic, and for the first time, almost twistedly warm, The Gathering's atmospheric type of leaden metal is a thought-provoking beauty to behold, still moody and mysterious but so tastefully delivered and well-recorded, you almost forget the metalness, the Century Media-ness, and the long-haired hellions within the band, not to mention their grindcore pasts. Goldenthroated Bjork-alike Anneke van Giersbergen soars o'ertop the fat smeary lushness of her backing band, slow-noted, sure-footed and mixed clear as a bell, making this one somewhat of a benchmark in this odd, mesmerizing genre. Vampiric, black and in love with dying, or heavenly and life-affirming, you decide.
Rating                                                              8

## GBH - A Fridge Too Far   (Fringe '89)

An accelerated, 45 RPM casualty from Britain's poverty punk scene, GBH clobber their throng with a high energy, California skatepunk assault; smeared, electric and futile. Dead Kennedys without the convincing manifesto.
Rating                                                              3

## Generation - Brutal Reality   (Metal Blade '93)

Trouble guitarist Bruce Franklin teams up with a couple of more "current" fellow Chicagoans for this pummelling exercise in white industrial metal, offering intelligent and concise spiritual lyrics, slick computer-y graphics and a stiff belt of oddly distant riffery. What makes the record somewhat uncommunicative is the infrequency of the lyrics, their reduced volume and their predictable cyborg-ed treatment. But I can't help embracing the concept even though the whole brash thing rolls like a square wheel, thick and ugly just like most industrial. Chemkill's pretty funny though, what with its mangled pop melody and somewhat playfully espousing chemical dependence, but otherwise frankly, it's a bit irritating. Bible reading at track (psalm) 69 makes metal acceptable in the eyes of God.
Rating                                                              6

## Genetic Wisdom - Humanity On Parole   (Pavement '94)

This dutch act has deemed themselves powercore, a term that pretty much describes Genetic Wisdom's sweat-slam delivery (metalcore would also do), the band toasting their grind and metal-tooled craft with the flame of urban hardcore. Pretty addictive headbang to the thing, leading one to a mosh-pitted death, the barking rants of vocalist Mike Lucarelli keeping the record violent and fast-paced. All in all, a cool, hoover-riffed loopiness ensues, sparse, street metal arrangements kept urgent through a snappy drum mix, most

noticeably one of the highest-tuned snares I've ever heard.
Rating 7

## Brian Johnson And Geordie - Brian Johnson And Geordie (MCA '81)

Yobbish, likeable AC/DC belter Brian Johnson has proven his integrity by slamming MCA for regurgitating this sample pak from Johnson's biggest pre-Angus band. Cash-in that it is, this compilation sheds light on the fact that the ignored Geordie was a viable fusion between pub rock like the Alex Harvey Band and a sharp, blues-based metal, tracks like *Natural Born Loser*, *Goin' Down*, *Rockin' With The Boys* and *Fire Queen* thumping along spare and vital, sorta like really early Sweet, Slade, or even The Guess Who. It's also cool to see where that hair-raising shriek originated. And hell's bells, this record leads one to surmise that the short Youngs probably got a performance much more reptilian and extreme out of Johnson than they might have expected. For here the guy is merely a powerful singer with massive, booze-fortified lungs, a rock monster who nevertheless sounds much more human than we're used to. Probably some of the guy's best singing, although he seems pretty embarrassed by the whole thing. But hey, if you approach this record prepared for hard-hitting, nostalgic yet eccentric pub fare by a minor act, and not some sort of pre-AC/DC sensation, you'll be just fine, you hear?
Rating 7

## Georgia Satellites - Georgia Satellites (Elektra '86)

Dan Baird and his ragtag gang of hard boogie roadies stumbled over bar-room rock success right from day one with sludgy, beer-drinking blues anthem *Keep Your Hands To Yourself*. Basically the bastard sons of George Thorogood and his Destroyers, Georgia Satellites crank that same hard-hitting boogie-in-yer-bourbon din, most of this sounding like roots rock meets Status Quo at Tom Petty's place. It's all quite full-up, thick and chunky like Texas chili, right through to a closing cover of Rod Stewart's kharmic *Every Picture Tells A Story*. Frat-housed, rednecked and hillbilly, but in a polite, popular, all-are-invited way.
Rating 6

## Georgia Satellites - Open All Night (Elektra '88)

Yer formula's showing, **Open All Night** slinky slidin' into gunsight with its title track, pretty much a knock-off of *Keep Your Hands To Yourself* (as is side two's *Mon Cheri*). But I guess the band stretches a bit, *Sheila* almost hair-banding it, and *Cool Inside* more of a scowling blues metal. And the covers zip like Speedy Gonzales, both *Whole Lotta Shakin'* and *Don't Pass Me By* buoyed by the tinkling, honky tonk ivories of Ian McLagan. Baird's occasionally Dwight Yoakam-sublime twang is in fine yarn-spinning form, as the band's big beat boogie one-ups ol' *Bad To The Bone* George Thorogood, who hasn't done much for anybody lately. Stiffed at the cash counter.
Rating 6

## Georgia Satellites - In The Land Of Salvation And Sin (Elektra '89)

Producer Jeff Glixman and his boomy, musclebound drums are out, replaced by Joe Hardy (ZZ Top, Kim Mitchell), and his lighter, snapping snare drum sound, recording this first "smart" record in Joe's home territory of Memphis. And changes are afoot, Rick Richards' freight-train geeetar licks propelled through shorter, more numerous snappers in fine, four-wheel-drive fashion. And the band's previous, quite exclusively drooly boogie wooger flavours have given way to forays into funk, roots music, balladry, bluegrass, new country and disciplined harmonies (*Games People Play*'s

gotta go). So this progresses exactly as one would expect, if a whiskey-soaked batch of bumpkins decides to progress at all. And Baird's crew most noticeably does, soaking up and spitting out their dues-paying blues vocabulary, working themselves into a lathered integrity somewheres akin to John Mellencamp or Bruce. I mean, you could have just looked at these records and knew where this band would go when ready. But I played 'em, trust me. Good, solid, family values type of band.
Rating 7

## G-Force - G-Force (Jet '78)

Gary Moore's brief foray into bandishness, G-Force actually smokes and slides with more boozy desperation than his other cold records, although the bookish metal riffs aren't all that prevalent, leaving way for a comfortable, no pretensions pop lilt, completely at odds with the record's hot sweaty delivery. I mean *She's Got You* is club rockin' warfare, with a closing solo that is wonky and one of Moore's most liberated and free, aided and abetted by an extremely fuzzy Chris Tsangarides guitar mix, the man obviously turning it way up every time Moore blazes into his weapon. Weird one but oddly one of the most engaging, having none of that doomed stadium posturing which I'm afraid the Moore concept has never been able to live up to.
Rating 7

## Ghostorm - Frozen In Fire (Black Mark '95)

Despite the poor album cover, this Lithuanian monstrosity sidesteps the unimagination of rote death metal, probably by festering well outside of the scene's hotspots. What initially leaps forth is the band's scorched drumming, good in the pocket, complicated and capable of twisted time (shades of Meshuggah?). But the vocals are traditionally untoneful, as "Marius" stumbles over hilarious lyrics written in second, third or fourth language English. Saved by novel song assembly and an Entombed/Gorefest-like springiness of step. Produced unremarkably by Edge Of Sanity's Dan Swano.
Rating 7

## Giant - Last Of The Runaways (A&M '89)

Bolton the hatches, a weak form of Thunder hath been wrought upon your soapstar soul, Giant plagued with those same annoying, he-man in middle America vanilla tones, even though both bands are quixotically British. But whereas Thunder are just vacant stare bad, these guys are actively, proactively horrible. AO dribbly R.
Rating 0

## Giant's Causeway - New Light (Massacre '96)

Less doom metal and more goth new wave, this second record from Germany's Giant Causeway sounds like a metal-buffed Killing Joke or Sisters Of Mercy, morose as all hell, but less apt to slay with power chords than slow-dripped guitar textures. Actually, it's kinda dull.
Rating 4

## g//z/r - Plastic Planet (TVT '95)

I haven't taken to this like I thought I would, Sabbath's Geezer Butler (more than just the band's bassist. He also wrote the lyrics.) enlisting the services of Fear Factory's Burton C. Bell in construction of an aggressively heavy, '90s anger-filled record crossing the raw metal of Machine Head and Fight with the tighter technical sheen of Bell's influential band. Maybe a bit too '90s, at a point when a scattering of voices are calling for a return to the artistry and restraint of the '80s again, **Plastic Planet** just hits you over the head with rumbling, tumbling low register rock demons, riff after churning riff, as Burton belts out his trademark oscillations between thrash and operatic, Life Of Agony (via Ozzy's)-type singing. Extremely single-minded, **Plastic Planet** is tight as a drum, yet a moshfest all the same, very grey, hard-hitting and almost berating in an unenjoyable way. In some respects, this is more Bell's record than Geezer's, due to voice, nature of the music and even lyrics, which may account for the cold steel vision of the thing. Obviously good, but unobviously stiff and stifling.

Rating      **7**

### Ian Gillan Band - Child In Time    (Oyster '76)

Side one crosses uninformed, unrestrained hard rock with electric jazz and funk, while side two mixes bad Pink Floyd with Wetton-era King Crimson. One guesses Gillan is trying to establish a direction after Purple. Keep looking. As the title suggests, the present wandering wax revives *Child In Time* from **In Rock**, a track over which both bands seemed to be hypnotized with studious awe. Woe to be that it wasn't *Smooth Dancer* or *Bloodsucker*.

Rating      **0**

### Ian Gillan Band - Scarabus    (Island '77)

Comprising more dreadful fusion jazz boogie woogie hard rock whatever, which nevertheless sports some loopy bass and drumming acrobatics, **Scarabus** is ultimately a collaboration of serious musicians with no songs. For professors of rock only. After this third kick at the can, Gillan would retire the whole IGB mess, admitting his lack of control at the band's progressive direction, one at odds with his personal predilection for the hard stuff, straight and simple.

Rating      **2**

### Ian Gillan & Roger Glover - Accidentally On Purpose    (Virgin '88)

I gather Ian and Roger have stayed pretty close buddies through all the emotional turmoil the Purple experience has caused, the two often vacationing together, which seems to have elicited the celebratory vibe of this scattered, personable collaboration. **Accidentally On Purpose** is a vehicle for many fruit-flavoured styles not acceptable with Purple, including electric funk, honky tonk boogie, low, creepy blues, jokey pop, calypso and the occasional masterpiece of atmospheric balladry, opener *Clouds And Rain* worth the price of admission all by its proud self. The boys really dress this record up, despite the casual nature of many of the songs, using a phalanx of strong players and layers of tracking, turning irresistible tunes like *She Took My Breath Away* and *Evil Eye* into lush jungles of world music. Only one rocker on the whole thing, *I Can't Dance To That*, perhaps explaining why there is only one rocker on the whole thing. An entertaining, light meal for the fans, and a logical companion piece to Glover's even more tropical '84 solo record, **Mask**.

Rating      **7**

### Ian Gillan - Naked Thunder    (Teldec '90)

Obviously hurtin' for a hit, Gillan glosses it up but good for this fairly awful collection of studio-strangled pop metal, a record that goes all over the place: Grammy-style ballads, unambitious popular blues, cheezy low-California hairspray metal, trashy hyper rock, all hospitalized by synths everywhere, the odd horn and overall performances that seem terrified of living. Sorry, but any supposed humour or playfulness on Gillan's part is just suffocated by the lack of direction and the out of control, adult contemporary production job. Forget it.

Rating      **4**

### Gillan - Mr. Universe    (Fame '79)

An accomplished display of '70s metal styles which manages to sound innovative due to superior, heaven-sent songcraft and grating but extensive keyboard embellishments. We get speed rockers in *Secret Of The Dance*, *Roller*, and *Message In A Bottle*; plus driving, powerful, mid-pace classics in head-throbber *Dead Of Night* and the ambitious title track (the first of three, sky-high, philosophical, sociological, state-of-the-nation addresses from the man's catalogue), only weak partners being out-of-place lunkhead rocker *Vengeance*, and comatose blues paraplegic *Puget Sound*. **Mr. Universe** features Gillan's typical low-budget-on-purpose production values; loose, noisy, and somewhat low on treble, yet strangely no hindrance to listenability in the least. Excellent traditional metal reminiscent of Gillan's work with Purple at its most focused. A masterpiece of spontaneous, artfully controlled scatter-brained genius, a record welcoming a legend back to the smokin' and drinkin', hard working basics of heavy metal.

Rating      **10**

### Gillan - Glory Road    (Virgin '80)

Gillan's follow-up to the confident **Mr. Universe** contains a similar mix of AOR-ish hard rock, fast, mid-pace and slowpoke metal, and more than a touch of distressed greaser blues. So although **Glory Road** is a rock-solid, axe-laden grinder, soaking up quickly good habits from the exploding metal scene, two blues-by-the-book slowpokes, *If You Believe Me* and *Time And Again*, coupled with the snail-paced trudgemetal of *Nervous*, make it less a percentage winner than **Mr. Universe**, albeit still deserving of high marks due to the dazzling quality of the two perkiest numbers, *Unchain Your Brain* and *Running, White Face, City Boy*, while *On The Rocks*, the record's atmospheric, key-swirled epic, becomes soul sister to *Mr. Universe* and **Double Trouble**'s *Born To Kill*, the three working a tri-partite concept that eloquently explains Ian's peculiar outlook on life. All in all, distinctive and thoughtful keyboard metal replete with Ian Gillan's strange and gnarled lyrical style, **Glory Road** offering state-of-the-art Brit metal that is just a touch too obscure and wilfully opaque to be considered mainstream, exposing the sense of offbeat humour Gillan always felt to be an integral part of his crazy, hard-drinking life.

Rating      **9**

### Gillan - For Gillan Fans Only    (Virgin '80)

This non-official studio album "for no money" and "for Gillan fans only" comes in plain white cardboard with a hole for the label like a disco 12", sporting four serious Gillan tunes plus assorted sound effects, spoken comments, instrumentals, lounge act blues, and general joking around. Two of the four real tunes, *Higher And Higher* and *Your Mother Was Right*, were excellent heavy B-sides. A full-length album, but basically just a fun one-off. Van Halen made a record like this, only they sold it as the real thing, calling it **Diver Down**, I believe.

Rating      **4**

### Gillan - Future Shock    (Virgin '81)

Something about this caustic, confident work sounds detached and subdued; very British and rainy, especially side two, which somehow reminds me of the wasteland encountered exactly halfway through Nazareth's **Hair Of The Dog**. Again the composition is similar to the first two blaze kings; manic, almost punky speed metal, mid-paced rockers, hard, bitter blues mixed with moody mellow fare. Almost all of **Future Shock** is finely-wrought, experimental, aristocratic metal, but there really aren't too many mind-altering landscapes (save for from the driving and philosophical title cut), to match the three or four flagship tracks consistently studding Gillan's other fine works. Solid, but a notch below the inspired songcraft elsewhere in the catalogue. The first 60,000 British copies came with an elegant 16 page booklet saddle-stitched into the gatefold featuring great shots of the band, historical snapshots, full lyrics, and three additional paintings similar in theme to the cover art. And if that ain't enough, the CD reissue contains no less than ten extra tracks, known B-sides and other oddities, including classic branding irons like *One For The Road* and *Higher And Higher*, plus funkier, bloozy bangers like *Your Sister's On My List*, *Handles On Her Hips*, and *Bad News*, among other less-finished divergences. Very scattered, very cool. Ian Gillan's favourite Gillan record.

Rating 8

## Gillan - Double Trouble  (Virgin '81)

Here we get one studio and one live disc, the live one being less than useless, for the same reasons all three DP live offerings smelled badly. I'm not sure I've even played it right through once. Six murky tracks, two covers, no neck-snappers, el boring. The studio LP however is classic Gillan, maybe the band's most esteemed record, full of strange but intelligent keyboard-laced fringe metal, encrusted with a loose, driving, somewhat awkward and weighty recording. The metallicuts, most notably *I'll Rip Your Spine Out*, *Sunbeam*, and the killer-riffed *Life Goes On* are powerful and ambitious, soaring through rock fifty feet under the earth's crust; and *Born To Kill* is simply the band's proudest lofty epic, espousing a somewhat brutish and inescapable philosophy for mankind. **Double Trouble** is yet another inspired but stylistically perplexing Gillan gem where arrangement and songcraft, rather than anyone's particular musical skills, stand out, because indeed none really do, rendering Gillan albums creations from a vacuum, where none of the individual players seem to draw on any technical influences from the outside world. Nonetheless, despite this or because of this, riveting stuff.

Rating 10

## Gillan - Magic  (Virgin '82)

Gillan's last-before-hiatus is also Gillan's heaviest, most complex, and maybe the band's brightest in terms of human connectivity. **Magic** is full of Gillan's usual obscure but dazzling arrangements, overt keyboards, unique metal made all the more assertive by Ian Gillan's vocal and lyrical charm. Gillan, the band thrived on breaking all the house rules, gracing us with intelligent metal that was never cliché; approximating an experimental, yet punky version of reunion-era Deep Purple, complete with surprise mood and tempo shifts throughout. Highlights here include speed rocker *What's The Matter*, the Sabbath/blues hybrid of *Bluesy Blue Sea*, and the ponderous melodic ballad *Living A Lie*. We also get a metallized version of Stevie Wonder's *Living For The City*, where the subtleties of Wonder's keyboard jazzisms have been miraculously retained. Gillan was one of the classiest of exploratory chapters in metal, a collection of divergent and often bickering talents, friction and intensity fuelling fine rock, evoking the constant wars that marked Ian's glory years with Purple. And now many moons later, after the soul-searching, often playful, often disastrous material that comprised **Accidentally On Purpose**, **Naked Thunder** and **Toolbox**, the battle rages on.

Rating 10

## Gillan - Toolbox  (eastwest '91)

Salivating at the concept of another Gillan record, I eagerly opened **Toolbox**, only to find that the eccentric soul of "the band" had been eradicated for the lifeless studio sheen of Ian Gillan's adjacent **Naked Thunder** solo album. And as far as I'm concerned, this record's the same sound, the same low-end writing, except in a heavy metal context. Yes things are improved, spirited rockers coming in the form of *Candy Horizon* and the title track, but the playing is stiff and clinical, which

Gillan of old was anything but. And still too much in that stripper tune guise, a sort of DLR funky blues metal that undermines (or perhaps betrays) Gillan's casual approach to rock'n'roll. Frustrating, 'cos yes it rocks, but no it ain't Gillan.

Rating 6

## Gillan - The Best Of  (Griffin '95)

An adequate survey of Gillan's expansive, quirk-ridden catalogue to date, **The Best Of** offers a lengthy 16 tracks, the goofy (*Trouble, New Orleans, No Laughing In Heaven, Dislocated*), doing battle with the visceral (*Fighting Man, Mr. Universe* and *Born To Kill*). Peppered throughout, there's the odd gem I haven't had the pleasure of encountering yet (Ian sez that Gillan recorded constantly, given that Ian had his own studio at the time), including *Smoke On The Water* live (ho-hum), an innovative *Helter Skelter* and a tidy speedster called *Purple Sky*. Like I say, a decent sample-pak, but given how amazing the body of work is, my suggestion is save up your shekels and get all of it, although records like this are the only way to find many of the b-sides and non-LP tracks.

Rating 7

## Brad Gillis - Gilrock Ranch  (Guitar Recordings '93)

Looks sort of like a Hee Haw record, sounds like a fret-burning, mostly instrumental spread for axemen. Gillis (he of Night Ranger and Ozzy) proves that he's the ideal choice for Roth guitarist if the sorry showman ever comes back, blazing his way through sunny riffs and contortions philosophically in Vai-land, but thicker and more musical. Greg Allman appears on the odd vocal track but the songs all suck as songs. For guitar students only.

Rating 3

## Gin On The Rocks - Coolest Groove  (Steamhammer '90)

After eight minute opener *Dawn*, a jazzy, light-footed ballad-type thing, Gin On The Rocks get down to business, with their confident mix of blues, boogie and funk styles, half filled-up with metal moves, sorta like GN'R unplugged. And like the Gunners, this cuts deep, perhaps these guys being Dutch, shielding them from too many L.A. rawk clichés that collapsed bluesy metal into corporate fodder. Quite enigmatic. In fact there's three very relaxed, un-noisy and charming tracks in a row: southern rocker *Trip To The Red Lite*, sincere ballad *Times*, and happy *Jump*-like syth-rocker *Sign In The Streets*, making this a no-borders, instantly personable type of roots rocker. Tasty, tasty guitar work.

Rating 7

## Girl - Sheer Greed  (Jet '80)

Girl was a band ahead of its time, precursors to the rafts of glam bop metal that were blowing into L.A. bars everyday from America's heartland. **Sheer Greed** is a solid and well-paced hard rock record, not outstanding, yet a pleasing listen throughout, sporting a cover of Kiss' *Do You Love Me* and a general display of stripped, hard-edged AOR that at times borders on the temptress danger of fringe Hanoi Rocks. Although **Sheer Greed** feels more like a business venture, it succeeds by avoiding the play-by-numbers safety of later, modern-day Girls, who unfortunately had to play the game with increasing rigidity, intense levels of micro-categorization eventually imploding the genre. First recording band for a press-maligned Phil Lewis, before his bitter forsaking of ol' Blighty in favour of LA (Guns).

Rating 7

## Girl - Wasted Youth  (CBS '81)

Scrappier and punkier, with increasingly desperate songs and a honed sense of survival, **Wasted Youth** marked a shift from the Poison penthouse to the GN'R

bunker, gritty, stark production and exposed architecture to match. However, Girl's only lasting contributions would be guitarist Phil Collen to Def Leppard and Lewis to LA Guns, as the rumoured lack of direction (made all the more obvious at the band's confused live gigs), sabotaged the band's potential shot at success.
Rating     7

## Girlschool - Demolition    (Bronze '80)

Loud and ringing garage metal mark this U.K. debut by Britain's female scuz rock survivors. Sticking closely to a sustained Motörhead stomp, Girlschool dish up a spirited performance, especially drummer Denise Dufort, who dominates the mix with trashcan resolve. Oddly, the most urgent record of the bunch, featuring logical, Lemmy-like extensions such as *Not For Sale* (rightfully re-cut for **Hit And Run**), *Breakdown*, and *Midnight Ride*. First and last of the band's classy cover graphics.
Rating     4

## Girlschool - Hit And Run    (Solid Gold '81)

This all girl band's stateside premiere sounds like mid-level Motörhead through the amps, and like The Go-Gos through the mikes, although cute and Californian they most definitely weren't. Punky, rough, basic, but bloody straight-shooting like a revved-up Ramones, Girlschool were a walloping attempt at a dirtier, smellier version of The Runaways, a concept basically doomed from the word go, until of course L7 and Hole.
Rating     4

## Girlschool - Screaming Blue Murder    (Solid Gold '82)

The biker metal of the debut caves way to a cleaner, commercial sound and no idea how to use it. Similar to skeletal Saxon, or low-grade Tank (at least with the title cut), **Screaming Blue Murder** collapses into naff experiments with economical new wave structures versus the band's previous walls of metal, in an effort to clean it up so we all can hear. Very British and well-recorded, but it's still chicks doing metal: outta there! Features *It Turns Your Head Around*, an awesome *Killed By Death*-style greaseball, and a weird cover of *Tush*, sabotaged by an odd hiccup beat.
Rating     2

## Girlschool - Play Dirty    (Solid Gold '83)

With the writing on the wall, Kim and the gang go somewhere new, arriving at this over-produced pop metal ploy, packed and frozen with tons of stiff Rick Allen-style drum patterns, which here, due to volume, drag all toons caught in its vortex down to a dull stomp. Still some pleasant experimentation, traces of cleverness, and a welcome taming of the band's usual yelp into studied harmonies, but the general drift is into jack-off studio rock.
Rating     3

## Glory Bell's Band - Dressed In Black    (SOS '82)

Right radical vocals fuel this wildly frozen layer of the Scandinavian north, which bristles with searing Euro-metal energy start to finish. All is so pointedly steel-hearted about this magnificently skewed opus, it's hard to nail any one factor that causes it to wrench the heartstrings with metallic despair. Glory North's vocals are just insane with lack of discipline, as are the percussive shadings of Peter Udd, whose touch just sings above the massively exacting and absolutely clear-thundered production values of Bosse Waldersten. Constructs ebb and flow, switching gears, coasting then revving, and simply knocking the shit out of previously held convictions as to realized blue levels to which Goth can fall. Very underground and bleak in terms of emotional pinpoints, like a far-gone case of **Sad Wings Of Destiny**, and only recommended for

the most metallic of moods. Actually *better* for the fact that the English is so mangled.
Rating     9

## Glory Bells - Century Rendezvous    (SOS '84)

Flushed from the innocent crystal vacuum that created **Dressed In Black**, a maturing Glory Bells looks to experiment, losing focus with the risk it takes, swelling forth a new pounding hard rock, amidst a couple of too laid-back dynamics pieces, and a curious pair of sloppy fast ones further chopped short by a scrappy midrange recording, oddly used only on these two throwaways. Fer damn sure, the rest of this grand work is pummelled with the same woofer-chomping mix that caused **Dressed In Black** to yelp in pain. The best stuff here courts a fresh, level-headed hard rock feel, tunes such as *Five Foxes* and *In The Attic* swimming with heady party-down emotion. **Century Rendezvous** still is the work of metal genius, purely European in nature, not unlike the emotional highs of Accept, Torch or Europe during the highly punishing, highly uncharacteristic Europe album. Most masochistic of the whole axe-ground mess would have to be painful, confessional ballad *My Life*, which contains one of the sickest, most psychopathic, yet depressingly human vocal performances I've ever had chill my spine. Glory North is emotionally wrapped like no other voice on earth. As usual, with the exception of the two "OTT'ers", all benefits from one truly remarkable, and thankfully faithfully documented rhythm section and an over-riding commitment and vision that's simply awe-inspiring. Unfortunately a step back for this isolated gem of a band, but nevertheless full of lumbering kick-ass Euroblight, and if you know what I'm talking about, you can understand that such push-pull sentiments aren't contradictions in terms when steeped in the ice caves of the North.
Rating     8

## Roger Glover - Mask    (PolyGram '84)

Really stretching it, including this light pop experiment in our mighty tome, so call this one discussable due to its metal link, Deep Purple's Roger Glover enlisting other rock notables like Chuck Burgi and David Rosenthal in creation of an electronic pop/world music hybrid that is entertaining for its sounds, more than its songs. But the title track is a masterpiece, even becoming a radio hit, *The Mask* being a lengthy, happy and intelligent precursor to Peter Gabriel's *Sledgehammer*, *Big Time* and *Steam*. Elsewhere it's pretty much fancypants technology applied to reggae, funk and lush balladry, so loaded with cutting edge verve that one thinks Howard Jones and Robert Palmer before Purple. So call it the work of Roger as enthusiastic, studious and ultimately creative producer rather than blubbery metal bassist, and you'll be just fine.
Rating     6

## Goddo - Goddo    (Polydor '77)

Ex-Fludd dude Greg Godovitz and gang lived their rock'n'roll lives as the ultimate rock pigs, although after much substance and human abuse, they've cleaned up their act, and lo and behold, came back in '92 with a new record which works in a twisted old man sort of way. The heaviest Goddo album, however, was this doltish but decent debut, roughly 3/4 courting weighty '70s metal. **Goddo** is clean, self-deprecating guitar rock, accomplished and raucous for its time, doin' the nasty with contemporaries like Moxy's **Ridin' High** and Teaze's **On The Loose**, while looking pretty pale given what's out there today, lacking any lovable idiosyncrasies or all out magic to carry that all important nostalgic value. Full credit to the band for early Ted-head loudness their robust mix and decent quality of the rockers, m.. ' of which showed up in rising Canuck bar band setlists th'oughout the late '70s. Contains a song about driving a schoolbus, and another that mentions O.H.I.P.

Rating     **7**

## Goddo - Who Cares  (Polydor '78)

Cleaner with less metal, more hard rock, more mellow stuff, and more humour, **Who Cares** displays the identity crisis of much early metal. Guitars are set to stun for exactly half of this, meaning that unless Goddo's a band that can write well outta both sides of their brains, no one is going to be completely happy with the resulting product. Half an album, no matter which slice you ingest. Not that the band gave a shit what was going on by this point, prematurely depressed about their status as yet another stalled Canadian career. Big, heart valve-clogging hangover tune: *Too Much Carousing*. Moderately big, high school dance hit: *Sweet Thing*.

Rating     **5**

## Goddo - Act Of Goddo  (PolyGram '79)

Three heavy tracks, the rest various types of non-metal, **Act of Goddo** is the second act of a thus far three part tragedy portraying a band without direction or any inkling of how to carry on the business half of the rock'n'roll spectrum. Forgettable.

Rating     **3**

## Goddo - Lighve-Best Seat In The House  (Attic '81)

This double live disk is (unsurprisingly) considerably heavier than the catalogue as a whole, thus a good look at a more focused, electricity-churning direction Goddo could have pursued, had the bankers any clue how big metal would break over the next couple years. Still a chest-thumping headbang for this time and this barsy band, documenting an influential-to-Canucks career with zero U.S. exposure.

Rating     **4**

## Goddo - Pretty Bad Boys  (Attic '81)

Possessing more life than anything previous, this was considered to be the enchilada that would break the band commercially. **Pretty Bad Boys** is heavier and more confident than past confusions but is still replete with only average songs, many bordering on non-steerable clod rock (i.e. *Forget About Forgetting*), exception being the hard rock, honky tonk Warren Zevon-isms of the title cut. Goddo no longer has an excuse for substandard output, as **Pretty Bad Boys** is more or less a modern era release. Maybe Greg just couldn't write.

Rating     **4**

## Goddo - King Of Broken Hearts  (MCA '92)

So why not reform? What the hell else you gonna do? To feed the legend and a pretty healthy overseas appetite for Goddo, Greg, Doug 'n' Gino get it together for the bonafide studio elpee. One hour and fourteen cuts later, what hath transpired is a nostalgic Canadian experience, a sort of thick, time-locked rock'n'roll, surprisingly fat and warm, simple, but more "experienced" than washed-up without ideas. And even the ballads, of which there are many, are somewhat fully instrumentalized and hooky, best being the bluesy *Quicksand* and *It's Good To be Alive*, the latter a truly heartfelt sentiment for Greg I'm sure. A humbly resonating return, which could have pulled a Triumph-like heavy metal sell-out, but stuck to its guns and worn ideals instead. Ultimately, **King Of Broken Hearts** is completely unchallenging but also completely unself-conscious and '70s-celebratory, making rumbling tracks like *Egypt*, *You Must Fight Back* and *Mirror Mirror* feel right at home amongst the first dough-headed records I ever bought. No '90s savvy here, as subsequent sales figures would attest, but man, Goddo still has their integrity.

Rating     **7**

## Godflesh - Streetcleaner  (Earache '89)

Thick, navy blue depression guaranteed to turn your cranial cavity into a diseased pail of pus, **Streetcleaner** just cracks, creaks and falls over with the weightiest of pioneering industrial clangbangs, real industrial, like working Britain's satanic mills circa 1910, feeding some smoke-belching machine until your twelve hours were up for the day and you could go back to being a ten-year-old. Gruesome, bothersome dreck.

Rating     **4**

## Godflesh - Pure  (Earache '91)

Godflesh's duo of devilboys are back at it paining and poking their way into your spinal fjord, this time pushing the snappy, almost epileptic, slo dance rhythms to the fore, while their craggy, hate-drenched utterances become less intelligible. The sound is still built around numbing repetition, lulling you to sleep despite the deafening din bouncing off the cave walls, driving the bats dervishly devilish. Once more, a handful of points for impression fulfilled.

Rating     **4**

## Godflesh - Selfless  (Earache '94)

Surprise, a front cover with colour, for this most colour-challenged of bands (appropriately, it's some sort of germ or virus). Now you know where Ministry got the idea to skip real songs and just make machine-tooled turd sculptures, Godflesh not letting up an inch on their pointless, powder-burned hitting of things. File with old Fudge Tunnel and old Pitch Shifter as cranky caustics that would rather not be bothered.

Rating     **4**

## Godflesh - Songs Of Love And Hate  (Earache '96)

A slight shift towards industrial electrics has infused this band with a tad more reason to be, even if a similar shift has ruined Prong. But still the monotone monotony of the band's crowbar-creaked terrorvisions just raises cynical chemistries all over my skull-encased lobes, an effect in full bloom without further sonic prompting. Sounds vaguely like the backtracks of a devil-domed danceclub, although I can't imagine what such an establishment would en-"tail." It's almost as if Godflesh exists to further blacken black moods, a pretty pointless exercise, dontcha think?

Rating     **5**

## godheadSilo - Skyward In Triumph  (Sub Pop '96)

Don't know much about these simpering idiots, and I don't think I want to, godheadSilo being an Inbreds-type arrangement of two guys, a drummer and a bassist. What slumps into the room and onto the couch for a snooze is a dense, gluey, wholly undisciplined arch Sub Pop bash that lapses into Melvins or Kyuss or Sons Of Otis terrain, a complete bore, all "spontaneous" (read: lazy and slack), thoroughly and relentlessly noisy and smashed. I guess if you want to hear a band recording the writing, rehearsing and aimless jamming of their songs, sign up here. But given that I'm a sucker for loud, dangerous, un-hewn grunge, I'd have to offer at least a modicum of praise.

Rating     **5**

## God Lives Underwater - God Lives Underwater  (American '95)

I'm a firm believer that anything on American deserves a good long listen, and even if GLU's debut 6 track EP falls squarely under the industrial banner, as usual, the label has picked an act with depth. GLU's trump cards are a combination of buzzing, punk-distorted guitars that weave unintrusive but intricate riffs (see lead track *Drag Me Down*), and sounds that converge eventually on melodies, the smooth vocals adding to the limited humanity of anything industrial. More like a trickier, more electronic Econoline Crush for this reason, the proceedings filling up with ticks, buzzes and pops peppering very legitimate songs. Fine industrial, if you care at all, which I fundamentally don't.

Rating    6

## The God Machine - Scenes From The Second Storey
(Fiction '92)

A psycho alternative pig metal ride from over and under seas, The God Machine take it through the eyelids in globs, emitting slow-to-rile waves of riff not unlike Kyuss crossed with The Cure. Lots of strange samples, snippets of eccentric instrumentation, and chilled chanting, driving it like a stake into alienated Ministry terrain. Yet this is something more Sabbathy via Seattle; repetition, distortion, trudging evil sludge and more than the occasional droop from attention as de-militarized sections seem to drone on forever resulting in welcome but miniscule oases between sand-spitting treks through the harsh, godless sun of reality. Spooky and soul-parched as a Joy Division lynching but leaning heavily an all too often into an anaesthetic fog that obscures most of my reasons for listening to music.

Rating    7

## The Godz - The Godz  (Millenium '78)

Southern-fried biker metal produced by Grand Funk's Don Brewer, featuring an amorphous, lumbering cover of Golden Earring's freight train epic Candy's Going Bad. Lowbrow, amusingly-wrapped boogie guitar piffle from the lunchbox '70s, featuring a gruff and sleazy Jim Dandy soundalike on vocals, The Godz stumble humbly through good ol' American mechanic-with-beer heartland rock, with a red eye to redneck science. Best bangers: lusty rumbler Under The Table and autobiographical kick-butt anthem, Gotta Keep A Runnin', which is one of the biggest dust-storms in southern rock. Round-bellied and robust.

Rating    8

## The Godz - Nothing Is Sacred  (Millenium '79)

Great album cover, dumkopf record. The metal's gone the way of the platform boot, and all that's left is dipshit country booger hard rock; all affectatious style, no woofer-destroying substance. Closer to lobotomized southern rock than southern metal, although they might be from Cleveland. Another metal marketing tragedy of the '70s? Hard to tell because The Godz never got much press, but rumour has it this band's troubles emanated from the fact that various band members couldn't stay out of jail. Righteous back cover too.

Rating    4

## The Godz - I'll Get You Rockin'  (Heavy Metal America '85)

Well, one cool thing about this project is that the immortal bad boyz didn't cheap out, said record being fairly polished and well-recorded, on its way to a simplex boogie metal strip mall near you. More straight gargle-throated, biker har-har'd rock than anything else, I'll Get You Rockin's sends forth a few decent trucker toons, close to no metal, and little in the way of distinct hooks. The sell-out metal alternative to Skynyrd, I guess, or maybe The Outlaws. Contains previously released Godz tunes and covers. Not a lot of new territory being explored here to say the least.

Rating    4

## The Godz - Mongolians  (Cobra '87)

Heavier than the second but not as heavy as the first, Mongolians lacks the soul of either, speaking less than eloquently through the no-brains drawl of the third, establishing the band's seeming state of laziness in the cynical marketing era of the 80's versus the take-on-the-world enthusiasm of the band's naive less calculat-

ing '70s. An unnecessary attempt to cash in on legendary status that never really was.

Rating    3

## David Gogo - David Gogo  (EMI '94)

Vancouver blues sensation David Gogo is a heavier, less commercial and plainly more creative piece of the Canuck hard blues puzzle, other two components being Jeff Healy and Colin James. Gogo's definitely the more electric and integritous, becoming a moderate darling of classic rock stations at least here in Canada with Hendrixed hit single Deep End. Quite a punchy record, chock full 'o riffs, wailing solos and a grumbling, phlegmatic, porch-squatted vocal from the man himself, taking this to the Mahogany Rush zone but fast. Not a comfy fit to the tag "metal" by any stretch, but this would definitely be deemed a hard rocker in say, 1975.

Rating    7

## Craig Goldy's Ritual - Hidden In Plain Sight
(Grand Slamm '91)

Goldy's known as the guy who wielded the crucial instrument on Dio's rippingest record **Dream Evil**. Here he assembles a band to go into that same classic goth netherworld, although not so attacking, more like middle-intensity Yngwie, but with bigger drums. Vocal chores are split between Mike Stone and David Glen Eisley, who both do that aristocratic pomp metal thang o'ertop Goldy's inventive, very Sykes-like pyro. Some of it's insipid, but other moments, like Eye For An Eye and Hard Times Comin' have that same authority as old Dio or Ozzy, Rainbow or even Whitesnake, which, combined with its rarity, make this quite a cool record to own. Graham Bonnet should have sung the thing.

Rating    7

## Craig Goldy - Insufficient Therapy  (Shrapnel '93)

Trust Goldy to make an interesting, half-instrumental, guitar-guy record, the man gathering a steam of eccentric, bendy-squeally sounds almost to the point of Steve Vai and his Nitro-ish, Racer Xed parody of metal routine. All the odd-numbered tracks are Goldy-penned instrumentals, while all the even-numbered tracks are vocals tracks, sung robustly by Dokken guy Jeff Pilson, writing credits given as Goldy/Pilson. For the non axe mechanic, these are of course the potential jewels, all four being loose, raw, creative takes on Dio-style goth metal, a healthy spell of interrogation and exploration, cogent recording, fun for all purist metalheads. One highly interesting guitarist, and Pilson really gives 'er as frontman.

Rating    7

## Gomorrah - Reflections Of Inanimate Matter
(Black Mark '95)

Textbook precision death from Britain, with well-written lyrics but well-trampled themes. And unfortunately, riffs, vocal non-style and the band's Slaytanic drum-driven atonal death constructs have all been done way too many times and places before. Really, this is where death begins and has began, metamorphosing into four or five subgenres, most well-addressed by Scandinavian acts, thank you. Guest vocals on Human Trophies by prog bard Fish!

Rating    4

## Gomorrah - Caress The Grotesque  (Black Mark '96)

Very enthused how these guys have gotten musical, melodic and very Venom-historic (Perfection Dies = Harmony Dies?), melding their stirring Euro-tones with layers of Maiden, Manowar and Slayer. Sure, an ATG/EOS frost-scurry still persists, but Gomorrah have acquired persona, fusing their progressive death with a restrained level of Raw, rocking in a decidedly metal vein throughout these dark metaphysical num-

**175**

bers. Sven Olafson sports a nice Cronos/Obituary croak, adding an angsty spin to these careening grind tracks, tunes which are sequenced for maximum variation in velocity, attention to entertainment firmly pasted to the band's circuitry.

Rating 7

## Myles Goodwyn - Myles Goodwyn (Est. '85)

Listening to this, it becomes obvious loser-leader Goodwyn is the elevator musician in the ill-fated April Wine. **Myles Goodwyn** heaves the most reeking, comatose slab of keyboard dance fluff, fit for every Aisle 13 of your local supermarket. Truly offensive in its stupefying baseness in a way only Rik Emmett could appreciate.

Rating 0

## Goo Goo Dolls - Jed (Metal Blade '89)

These Buffalo, N.Y. modern-day punkers go for that wise-ass blend of early Replacements and later Hüsker Dü in quest of cool college band status. Boozy send-ups of CCR and the Stones highlight the lowly fact that what's lacking is original brilliance of the band's own, unlike the magnificent Soul Asylum who gulp at the same turbulent Minneapolis waters, albeit from closer proximity. And the Mould/Westerberg vocal postures just annoy immediately (worst on *James Dean*); the band only stepping into a chaotic fray of their own making on the thrashier numbers, where they finally sound like the likeable brats they want to be. Rumour has it that the critically-accepted follow-up smooths out the edges a bit, meaning it's just been relegated to my "under 4$" purchase threshold, given that I only like bands like this when they bulk up. Became a big, irritating, Gin Blossoms-type hit in '95.

Rating 5

## Gorefest - Mindloss (Foundation 2000 '91)

Gorefest's initial offering of black-hearted rot was pretty much a standard blast of perky grindcore, **Mindloss** only sporadically revealing the melodic shards of mourning that will come full bloom on the magnificent **Erase** four years hence. Stunned, harrowing, and firey for its time, but sounding pretty average years later.

Rating 5

## Gorefest - False (Nuclear Blast '93)

This first for Nuclear Blast is hailed in death pentagrams as somewhat of a magical marriage between opaque, depraved grind science and advancing human connection between claw and clawed. Colin Richardson takes over full production duties here (he only mixed the debut), working a tag-team of terror with esteemed, new drummer Ed Warby. Even if it's too sonically sickening for my trembly tastes, **False** most definitely put these lizardian malforms on the map.

Rating 6

## Gorefest - The Eindhoven Insanity (Nuclear Blast '93)

Riding high on the hog with their **False** record, Gorefest are included as part of the huge Dynamo festival in Holland, the band calling this a career highlight, getting to play in front of 40,000 metalheads in a Donnington-like atmosphere. Drummer Ed Warby had just had surgery on his right hand the day before, but you'd never know it, Gorefest frying the place with their unyielding, youth-fuelled death metal. Came to fruition because a radio station was recording the show on 24 tracks anyways, the station graciously saying, hey, here's the tapes, do what you want.

Rating 6

## Gorefest - Erase (Nuclear Blast '95)

I'm always amazed at the feverish maniacal following a chosen few of these extreme acts attract. Gorefest is building quite a legion, following up studio record II

False with this almost musical and sorrowful shining shard of death perplexity. Raining blood and body parts from the nether Netherlands, Gorefest combine deep-slashing mid-pace grind with the relative (!) musicality of Entombed and Sepultura. The melody (that only a trained professional can extract) bubbles through the tracks like cheap paint, leaving the glory-bound thickness of death intact, while hooking us into the Gorefest vulturevibe, hellish '90s-osity skewed and crispy-fried unto delirium. They do it well, constructing something this whole death underworld can consider some sort of coagulational masterpiece as the huge stream of humanity merely walks on by oblivious of the Sound. Woe begotten.

Rating 8

## Gorefest - Soul Survivor (Nuclear Blast '96)

The bio calls **Erase** a transitional record, which now makes some sense, **Soul Survivor** taking Gorefest into elegant power metal terrain, something akin to Amorphis crossed with Metallica's **Load** crossed with old Sabbath. Faves are the chunder crunch of *Electric Poet*, the death metal Rainbow tones of *River*, and the title track's simple melodic chug, but these guys have awesome metal surprises everywhere, having pretty much left death metal for new twisted vistas on a multi-variate metal. A perfect, almost regal metal for these times, taking gruff grindcore into easily accessible realms, addictive, hard-rolling songs to the fore, warming the innovations of **Erase**, leaping into competitive rings with rock-solid maturity. Call it extreme metal heaven for those approaching from the light, while perhaps a guilty, tuneful pleasure for those chained in the dark.

Rating 9

## Gorelust - Reign Of Lunacy (New World/UMG '95)

Turbine-accelerated caustic thrash from Quebec, where gory grindcore (not to mention treason and sedition) thrives. Bottom of the barrel, but sure to please "traditional" death metal fans.

Rating 0

## Gorguts - The Erosion Of Sanity (Roadrunner '93)

Whether it's thrash metal, speed metal (too flattering), or all out grindcore, I'll never tell, but despite your take on this graphic pile of cack, it's definitely grindcore gargle coming from the throat of lead band-wrecker Luc Lemay so I'm immediately tuning out.

Rating 3

## Gothic Slam - Just A Face In The Crowd (Epic '89)

New Jersey ultra-heavy hardcore similar to Metallica, Testament, or Overkill with an emphasis on straight-laid, face-eroding riff work; i.e. mid-pace vs. speed or thrash songcraft, and little in the way of artistic or technical embellishment. Power production provided by Rob "Wacko" Hunter, Raven's drummer. Overall, quite pulverizing due to its non-thrash, trench-level ethic, this opaque pasting from this long-defunct quintet definitely has a bad case of rifferama syndrome, an ailment which seems to dog this genre. Lyrically it's sick world morality and depression stuff as per contemporaries Suicidal Tendencies, Anthrax or Megadeth; politically correct with no hope. No wonder the bleakness, they are from Jersey. Classy cover: Thin Lizzy's *Thunder And Lightning*.

Rating 7

## Gouds Thumb - Gouds Thumb (Critique/BMG '96)

Not so much indie as indie-minded, this rawk-rollerizing alterno masher is quite the entertaining spin. Moving like nomads from Portland to Boston to New York, Gouds Thumb (named for a friend's woodshop-severed hitch-hiking machine) set then spark a whole bunch of butch textures, evoking Fugazi, Nirvana, heavy XTC, Sponge and on the more accessible end of things, Stone Temple Pilots and Alice in Chains. It is of note that the Boston stop on Gouds' journey was to brush up at the Berklee College of Music, which might account for the general braininess of the band's blustered brawn. Rhythmic, touched by the psychedelic, but confident.

Rating         **7**

## Grave - Into The Grave   (Century Media '91)

Early Grave was a bleak, sliced and gutted machine of whirlwake sonics, a handily recorded slash of built-to-code death metal. If you liked all the other grind-heavy Century Media records from '91, '92, then this one will fit your silly putty psyche just fine. Nice artwork. Hey, I mean it!

Rating         **3**

## Grave - You'll Never See . . .   (Century Media '92)

Warts this? More bludgeoning bathcore from the phase-shifted depths of Scandinavian grind. Grave are still about as extreme as the oversized genre gets, bricking us over with a sort of cryptified Edge Of Sanity à la Entombed, matching much of the speed with muscleplod, then rendering the pie gravel-caked and corroded. First clue as per usual would be the outrageous cover art and juvenile, unreadable logo. Leave the hell alone.

Rating         **3**

## Grave - . . . And Here I Die . . . Satisfied
(Century Media '93)

. . . And now a certain artfulness, a Voivodian dissonance begins to permeate this encrusted and entombed grindcore mainstay, the three new tracks on this EP distinguishing themselves from the three old ones (from '90) with thie exposed looped spaces. But make no mistake, it's still a fairly tightly defined thing this band does.

Rating         **4**

## Grave - Soulless   (Century Media '94)

Grave have come into considerable acceptance with this much more battle-torn record, one that makes a wholesale adoption of the drilled Entombed guitar sound and requisite apocalyptic production values; no surprise given the same production team of Mr. Tomas Skogsberg and Mr. Sunlight Studios. Even Sandström's vocals have inched towards hardcore, turning this into a harsh, brutal but valid type of trainwreck, moving forward in blackwind time, away from the trappings of middle-ground death. A grindcore bloodfeast worthy of your attention and praise.

Rating         **8**

## Grave - Hating Life   (Century Media '96)

Now officially a mere two piece (Sandström has departed for Entombed), Grave finds guitarist Ola Lindgren resuming vocal duties (really no difference), joining drummer Jensa Paulsson for this crashing, bashing cruel-fest of eldritch, malignant proportions. Warning: some are unimpressed with this record, but I'd have to disagree, finding it ever as much appropriately balanced between stress and song as Soulless, if a bit more raw and dissembled. A shoot 'em up cry-and-die stirfry of deathly gloomery, or something like that.

Rating         **8**

## Grave Digger - Heavy Metal Breakdown   (Banzai '84)

Merciless jackboot Germans Grave Digger burst onto the scene unsmiling and bestial with this violent and relentless bludgeon that combines the classic OTT vocal performances of one Chris Boltendahl (next in line after Klaus and Udo), and the killer, wall of guitar bash of Peter Masson, wedging them like a powderkeg into a corrosive and boiling cauldron of Euro-death.

Grave Digger epitomizes all the power and anger of OTT slowed down to expose the furnace-blast steel from which it is composed. What results is an incredibly weighty and obnoxious wall of def, yet a sound uniform, tightly-wound, and well-recorded; a head-banging, anti-social drinking feast of distortion and overdrive. On **Heavy Metal Breakdown**, Grave Digger carves a niche of this flat-out, plaintive heaviness, raising ire and fire on such mid-pace cardiac arrests as We Wanna Rock You, Legions Of The Lost, and the wrenching Back From The War, all delivered below ze growling German accent of said Boltendahl. Magnificent noise with a direct cranial vessel to Dave Mustaine.

Rating         **9**

## Grave Digger - Witch Hunter   (Banzai '85)

The world's most unwelcome Black Forest migraine is back and coked-up as ever with **Heavy Metal Breakdown** - Mark II. **Witch Hunter** is equally caustic, equally brash, but splits the difference cut-wise, offering two or three more pedestrian fast ones but at the same time, three of the band's most searing metallic classics in the twisted and pissed Shoot Her Down, sonic builder Friends Of Mine, and the almost melodic groover Here I Stand. **Witch Hunter** closes the books on this particular class of the Grave Digger sound; a merciless crunch that earned the band critical billing as successors to Accept, up-ratcheting as a denser, faster, and more intense version of Udo's oddballs, a throne Grave Digger would abandon before the seat even got warm as **War Games** would ever so slightly stray from the brick-to-the-head approach portrayed here. Note: my reviews of **Witch Hunter** and the debut are of Canadian versions which contain different and interchanged cuts from American and other releases. Not of grave consequence either way.

Rating         **8**

## Grave Digger - War Games   (Combat '86)

**War Games** is superficially more of the great sustained mayhem as on the first two, but something is lacking. There's a dirgy ballad, a waste of space called The End, plus hints of misplaced hard rockiness, not to mention a couple of uninspired speedy numbers. Production values are still excruciatingly glorious, but the band's delivery is a tad loose, slapdash and lackadaisical. I don't know what it is, but this is one of those records that cuffs you in the head upon close inspection, even though I never play it, personally being somewhat annoyed at a band I perceive to be resting on its laurels. Admirably fierce but a trace sluggish, **War Games** still manages to kick harder emotionally than a lot of the aggro of the '90s. See Digger - **Stronger Than Ever** for a few words on the band's next, bewildered incarnation.

Rating         **6**

## Gravestone - Victim Of Chains   (Scratch '84)

Searing, stirring Euro-metal similar to 220V; devastatingly recorded, as is most stuff on Scratch Records. Melodic and heavy-as-hell in the grand tradition of messed-up early Germania, **Victim Of Chains** is for the most part, high-octane riff rock with electric but gritty vocal signatures, permeated with that usual depressing quality that causes me to avoid it like the plague, despite its power and pride.

Rating         **7**

## Gravestone - Back To Attack   (Banzai '85)

**Back To Attack** bears an uncanny (but most likely unintentional) resemblance to Accept's **Restless and Wild**, the production (midrange-heavy guitar sound, boomy but raucous drums) even the riffs echoing for the most part R+W's speedy fare like Flash Rockin' Man and Demon's Night. Very heavy, solid Eurometal,

**177**

traditionally speaking, that is much tighter and flashier while also more in-your-face than the rough-hewn debut. If you like the hero metal of 220V or Accept, check this out. Although Gravestone went nowhere stateside, the band sounds neither naive or low budget versus countless other Euro or Brit metal no-names from this era one unfortunately stumbles upon in the delete/cheapo import racks. Rowdy, aggressive and shredly, with a nod to the classics.
Rating                                                                8

## Graveyard Rodeo - On The Verge   (Century Media '94)

Conjested, body-blow hardcore that jackboots the line between thrash metal and urbancore, Graveyard Rodeo deliver ten tales of total no-hope depression, sounding like a bunch of other similar torture chambers, including about a half dozen on this label, Century Media deliberately building a stable of brain-bashing, gutter-dwelling tattoo'ed hateboys. I got enough stress.
Rating                                                                5

## Graveyard Train - Graveyard Train   (Geffen '93)

Slick, synthetic sad sack bluesy hard rock produced by big shot Tom Werman. Sorta, like (ennui sets in) . . . Tattoo Rodeo, Cinderella, Thunder: strip-mall boogie, shakin' them locks until last call. Passed by unnoticed. Earth to Graveyard: nobody buys this stuff anymore.
Rating                                                                4

## Gravityhead - Dropped!   (Wonderland '94)

Gravityhead play a sort of pro-level slacker melodic grunge, high on anthemic emotion, benefitting from a solid mix (courtesy big cheese Don Gilmore) and confident, exacting guitarwork from Brian Larney. If you're into Wool, Therapy?, Collective Soul or for that matter, Our Lady Peace, this could be your bag, although there's something more poppy, well-wishing and almost progressive about the Gravityhead delivery. **Dropped!** is billed as the 5 track preview EP and bodes well for the full-length due soon, given the loopy dynamics and variety of the thing. Still, a bit melodramatic, listless and twenty-something whiney for my liking.
Rating                                                                5

## Great White - Great White   (Aegean Est. '83)

Great White's calling card was this five track EP, sporting three tunes that made it (re-recorded) to the debut album, and two that didn't, one of which is the heaviest cruncher Kendall and Co. ever built, mid-pace chunderhead No Way. **Great White** is a well-carved label shopper, showcasing a serious contender, much the way Ratt's EP did, featuring loud 'n' proud production by Don Dokken and Michael Wagener, and a Van Halen timelessness and confidence that spells success. Same five cuts on both sides. Go figure.
Rating                                                                8

## Great White - Great White   (EMI '84)

Great White's official major label debut picks up where the band's professional EP left off, missing nary a beat as the White machine establish themselves middling and average amongst a million other California metal acts. Thick-headed and heavy '70s riff rock cascades all over this, kinda like power-Dokken with the bass turned way up. Great grooves, some slow, some fast, and a couple of low-key OTTers mix it up well, carving what is generally a solid, traditional car stereo blast-off with spirited, cat-shrill vocals courtesy of convict Jack Russell, whose voice is a potent cross between a more ballsy early Plant shriek and Vince Neil's spoiled whine. Dumb cover: The Who's Substitute. The first and last firm and forward-thinking record before the great white regression.
Rating                                                                7

## Great White - Shot In The Dark   (Capitol '86)

Garbage. About a quarter of this great white void evokes images of writer's-block Judas Priest circa **Point Of Entry** and the bad half of **Screaming For Vengeance** in both song calibre and over-production. The rest is worse; stultifyingly clunky "dynamics" metal, like lobotomized, granite-brained Dokken or Poison. Awkward, slow, and ever so pedestrian, **Shot In The Dark** rides a formula that Great White would adopt from hereon in: the novelty cover as hit single, a direction that would inexplicably make them tiny mounds of money. In actuality, fame flowed in spite of this direction, covers such as Substitute from the first, Once Bitten Twice Shy from the fourth, and this record's double duty of Gimme Some Lovin and Angel City's Face The Day proving the tall stupidity of the record-buying public at large. The bulk of my paltry grade goes to the band's uncharacteristically intelligent choice of Angel City as fertile cover ground. Otherwise, a wasteland of manufactured metal.
Rating                                                                4

## Great White - Recovery: Live!   (Enigma '87)

A rags, sags 'n' shags project that demonstrates two of Great White's real or imagined saving graces: their covers and their old songs. Side one is a no-overdubs session featuring a clumsy Immigrant Song, a smooth more interpretive Rock And Roll, and three more insipid, old fogie choices. Side two reaches way back to '83 (although this sounds suspiciously clean), for live renditions of some of the band's best tracks (i.e. Streetkiller and Stick It), exposing once again this band's steady decline from Ratt-quality origins. Lone rarity: chummy metal cheeseball Hard And Cold.
Rating                                                                6

## Great White - Once Bitten   (Capitol '87)

More brutally talentless metal that once again at its most virile, sounds like Priest's You've Got Another Thing Comin' and at its worst, bad substance-embalmed Crüe circa **Theatre Of Pain**. The songwriting on **Once Bitten** is just so ass-backwards, so idea-void, that one wonders how throngs of no-job-big-hairs get sucked into patronizing Great White year after year. The big bucks production, complete with deep snare, scant high hat, and zero spontaneity dooms any saving grace that improved delivery could have brought to these tunes. Quite unbelievable, **Once Bitten** finds premature exhausted rock star syndrome exposing the most cynical face of rock for dollars.
Rating                                                                2

## Great White - . . . Twice Shy   (Capitol '89)

Great White claims to have discovered the blues here. What the hell, such ploys were fashionable during the dying days of hair metal; and I guess it does give the band at least a semblance of a reason to ask for our paychecks. But alas, . . . **Twice Shy**'s still very similar, piss-poor posturing to the last two turds, with maybe a trace more soul in the axework and the band's traditionally anemic drum sound. Song-wise it's a veritable suburban wasteland, but Move It does face the day as one of the band's better highway anthems, and Once Bitten Twice Shy is such a great boogie bloozer, try as they may, even Great White can't wreck it. Note: this one somehow scraped its way to double platinum, on the heels of its predecessor's single platinum status.
Rating                                                                4

## Great White - Hooked   (Capitol '91)

Best thing here is the cover art, flipped over, showing a great white shark making off with the "bait." But the sounds inside are sorry and simpering, just more of the same squeaky-clean watered-down AC/DC meets old, tired and ready for the farm blooz. What a joke, even coughing up another Angel City cover in Can't Shake

*It*, sufficiently de-clawed for the American masses. Went gold, surprisingly a considerable let-down for this band, perhaps their incredibly moronic public catching on as to the predictability of the band's shucks 'n' roll ruse.
Rating                                                                    4

### Great White - Psycho City   (Capitol '92)
Hoped to be the comeback record after the disappointing sales of '91's **Hooked**, **Psycho City** takes the band even further into a schizoid existence between fairly accomplished, laid-back blues and Kiss-meets-Hagar nerd rock; the very sound that has driven me away since record III. **Psycho City** is a puzzler no question, but less from a stupidity point of view, more from a continued awe at the band's simplistic approach to a simplistic music; basically dressed-down versions of old trampled riffs from the '70s dulled with the ether of blues inaction. And dulled is the operative language here, as Russell and his time-worn posse simply do their thing, with zero flash and zero thought at rising above a sort of booger wooger bar mentality. But at least the sound is filled up this time, with more going on in terms of layered axes and what not. Still, one strangely heavy-lidded bunch of dudes.
Rating                                                                    6

### Great White - The Best Of: 1986 - 1992   (Capitol '93)
As the erroneously effusive CD booklet essay states, Great White are a live band first and foremost. And I'll reserve judgement on that having never seen them. I mean, I can half-ways believe it. But the aimless inclusions here do two more things: 1) demonstrate that the boys did have a stream of often-heard semi hits, and 2) that they really pooched their time in the studio, just making all the mistakes available to hair bands at the time; dull, dull, dull. Sum gain: no non-LP tracks, no real direction, doing the band's automatic walk between the most obvious blues and even more obvious Cali-fried party rock.
Rating                                                                    4

### Great White - Sail Away   (BMG '94)
Great White stand at the crossroads battered by the wholesale rejection of '80s-style street rock, LA glam, party metal, poodle metal . . . you name it, it's dead. So what to do now? After Jack Russell emphatically promising this band will never fly the flannel, the virtually unplugged **Sail Away** seems one of a limited few avenues (after which some kind of supercharged comeback is no doubt planned). From a doofus bunch who were forever champions of the most butthead of rocks, this collection of dreary, turned-down blues ballads (and mild boogie woogers) offers really just more of the same, just no pedals, metals, Marshalls or derivative Plant shrieks. Fans of a kinder, gentler classic rock past may choose to live in it here. Also included: a second CD featuring seven live tracks spanning the band's quizzling career. Have a blast. See you when you grow up.
Rating                                                                    4

### Great White - Let It Rock   (Imago '96)
Well, they're back in that groove that, ahem, either lifts your spirits or gets treated with blank stares, me being in the latter camp, finding myself unmoved and almost unbelieving at this collection of vaguely bluesy, vaguely heavy, vaguely rootsy, vaguely funky, vague rock tunes, none with so much as a pulse. The occasionally heartfelt riff slinks forth (there's a really nice, if brief one in *My World*), but for the most part, this is just stiff and sterile demo-quality stripper rock from 1984. I mean, I really wanted to see Great White save hard rock (while never thinking it possible), but Jack Russell just has his thing, and for many it's a really, really *dull* thing.
Rating                                                                    5

### Green - The Pop Tarts   (Futurist '92)
A smart short shock of glorious Hanoi Rocks-style plush velour retro-crush greets you at the door of Green's **The Pop Tarts**. I eat this stuff up (no pun intended), especially when it's this authentic and obscurist, crossing way past NY Dolls into Lyres and Del Lords terrain. Granted, a tight fit into the realm of metal, but really punchy and wholly concerned with fun, kinda like a poorboy Urge Overkill.
Rating                                                                    6

### Green Day - Dookie   (Reprise '94)
What's left to be uttered in scorn and giddy love of Billy and his smash hit trio of good-for-everything punks? Green Day along with Offspring have of course led the charge of something not quite a movement called '90s punk rock. Of course dozens of U.S. grade punk albums of superficially this ilk have been pooped every year since about 1982, 'cept few have had the ridiculously catchy pop hooks of this sizzling little spunkfest. No, Green Day are like a harmless guitar-crazy take on early '60s Beatlemania, absolutely daft with heady harmonies, choruses from starry Shangrila, hapless humour and ten-story pogo grooves. Green Day somehow gleans all the golden, pure, skinny tie happiness from that lost power pop movement from the early '80s, bands like The Knack, The dbs and especially The Records, while boiling the concoction fresh and urgent with windmill chords and garage bash drum patterns until we just can't stand it and gotta dance like fools. But seriously kids, the one thing about this record is the valour and horror of its radio-ness: you gotta love it, and it drives you bonkers! You're addicted and mad about the whole thing! They're Green Day and they're mad about you! '90s punk rock is driving me mad! This is a great driving tape! Tape my hands so I stop playing this!
Rating                                                                    8

### Green Day - Insomniac   (Reprise '95)
Okay, the bloom's worn off me, and to some extent all of you, Green Day now just coasting with this rushed collection of songs (opportunity knocks), sporting half the hooks, twists, and vivacious turn of events we all cuddled up to last record. The hit *Geek Stink Breath* sounds nothing like Green Day, moving slow, sludgy and almost hi-fi, but the rest sounds too much like Green Day, which we're all learning can be a bad thing. Lyrics court more meaning than one might expect but those fake British vocals are getting more fake, and man, musically this thing coasts more than it pogos. The title **Insomniac** is a reference to Billy's new fatherly role, and the lack of sleep afforded those who must care for even smaller punks than themselves.
Rating                                                                    6

### Green Jelly - Cereal Killer Soundtrack   (BMG '93)
If you don't know the scoop already, I'm not going to tell ya, but in short, Green Jelly (originally Green Jello before General Foods caught wind) are a video project and costume machine first, punk/thrash/funk comedy rock combo second, sorta the kiddie version of Gwar, lots of bright colours, simple Ugly Kid Joe riffs and amusing vocal rantings, the whole mess pretty funny if you're thirteen or under. Sorta early Tubes gone Disney. Just silly.
Rating                                                                    3

### Green Jelly - 333   (BMG '94)
Back in semi-Satanic grey for '94 is the surprisingly successful novelty act from last year Green Jelly, primed to turn their technicolour yawn into the premiere and most exhausting multi-media act of the cartoon millenium. This one's more of the same with a thrashier bent (witness *Fight*), amidst lots of mid-chuggin caveghoul riffs and stories from the creases of

life. But yet again, the cereal leaves me empty and unenergized, not exactly predisposed to partake in fun punk metal antics. All the power to 'em, 'cos for a brash bit of volume, the jelly can satisfy. Just leave me out of it.

Rating 5

## Green River - Come On Down (Homestead '85)

The most devastating wax from the Sub Pop invasion came early, and the most righteous of the lot was Green River's **Rehab Doll**, the only LP the band ever did. **Come On Down** is the innocuous debut trump card, a 26 minute EP which captures a now legendary sound in its formative, luded-out punk stages. The feel is loose and slushy, like a pissed-up Sabbath playing in a cold cell block, and Arm's vocals are appropriately out-of-tune, flu-like, infected and droning. Besides an early half-screwed version of Swallow My Pride, the other five tracks never saw the light of day in any souped-up form after this EP, which could have turned some of these festering wounds into classics. More a collective blight than a package of individual triumphs, the sound revs then wallows mercilessly and often, ever churning out thick wads of goo. All in all, a dark and wasted debut that sludges towards Seattle to be born.

Rating 7

## Green River - Dry As A Bone (Sub Pop '86)

As metal kept getting cleaner, more business-like, and well-planned, shit-kickers like Green River, Soundgarden, Melvins and Nirvana were holed up in Seattle reworking the monoliths of the '70s, twisting and ripping into their carcasses, regalvanizing the shreds with a '77 punk glue, reviving a long-dead hybrid of metal, muck, and depravity which first and last reared its leather skullmask on the Stooges' **Raw Power**. Green River was uncompromising and unclassifiable in its slithering existence as Sabbath and Aerosmith and The Damned vibrating and shaking in diseased flux. Mark Arm singlehandedly defines "bedhead vocalist" on this five cut sucker punch, and Bruce and Stone's axework melds diametrically opposed doom-goth and blues camps within a decidedly garage metal context, establishing a chaotic exercise in distortion-based time travel. Most righteous blows come from Joe Perry-on-Thunderbird Wine lead cut Unwind and funeral dirge Baby Takes; but, as with **Come On Over**, **Dry As A Bone** is best experienced in its rough-hewn, uncut totality, although in comparison, the songs do fly further on their own, being light years ahead lyrically, vocally, riff-wise, production-wise and in terms of overall acidity. An essential of pre-commercial Sub Pop, and in fact, one of a surprisingly few cornerstones of the label's success.

Rating 10

## Green River - Rehab Doll (Sub Pop '88)

How could a record be crafted with such uncanny perfection and class, and still sound like a head-exploding case of the bends? Ask Green River, who in my opinion are responsible for the single most important artifact of the Sub Pop sound. **Rehab Doll** is a further refinement of the brew that kills. Sick blues via Zeppelin (although not so much as with formative Soundgarden), sick riffs via Sabbath (ditto), sick variations on the guitar god via messengers Perry, Nugent, Bloom, and Roeser, sick lyrics via the dementia of one Mark Arm, and overall depressed angst via any number of tragic rock dogs who ever picked up a bottle or needle in boredom. Everything hurts on this, but instead of curling up and doing the deep sleep, **Rehab Doll** pops a few uppers and downers and heads into town packing an all-consuming, all-confusing random hatred. Although the speed shifts and innovative arrangements keep you off balance and interested throughout, the

two constants seem to be the uncompromising and relentless moral hopelessness of Arm's wild ideas, and the resolving loopy fluidity of the riffs, as evidenced most brilliantly on Smiling & Dyin', Porkfist, and Forever Means, the latter, one of the most venomous statements of intent laid to wax. Although Soundgarden's highest highs may strike with more sheer ferocity than Green River's (witness Head Injury and Jesus Christ Pose), no single Sub Pop album can match **Rehab Doll** for consistently banging off classic after classic of groundbreaking chaos-metal grunge-ified ugliness. After this first and last full-length opus, the band fragmented, metamorphosing into experimental torch-bearers Mudhoney and cautious pretenders Mother Love Bone, whose Green River alumni Stone Gossard and Jeff Ament would eventually make their way to forming Pearl Jam. Note: **Dry As A Bone** and **Rehab Doll** would be combined for the CD reissue, adding three more tracks, Searchin', Dead Boys cover Ain't Nothing To Do, and Bowie's Queen Bitch.

Rating 10

## Greenway - Serious Business (Atlantic '88)

What is basically a flagrant commercial ploy by Canadian music establishment losers here, comes off as a kind of catchy, smooth product of wimp metal, à la Bryan Adams, Foreigner, Loverboy et al. Ex-April Winer Brian Greenway actually writes all of this keyboard-laden dross, which in itself, counts for something on odious projects such as these. I mean, usually it's rivetting storytellers such as Jim Vallance, David Foster and Desmond Child (check out Sebastian Bach's bang-on attitude on these guys). Overall however, a good half of **Serious Business** is anything but; healthy harmless fun delivered flawlessly albeit rigidly.

Rating 5

## Gregory's Funhouse - Obey (Big Chief '88)

One glance at the cover screams comedy rock and this is correct, Gregory's Funhouse loping through a sort of stiff Ramones metal, pepped-up 'n' hardrocked Lyres or 10%-creative Dictators. Which all would have worked, given real singing, **Obey** instead opting for a spoken word vocal track too prominent in the mix, which gets tiring fast.

Rating 4

## Greta - No Biting (PolyGram '93)

For some vague reason, I instinctively think Candlebox, Our Lady Peace, even Collective Soul when I hear this fuzzy melding of alternative and metal, not particularly due to the music, more because of the unslottable presentation of the whole package. But Greta has thorns, and is not for the faint of heart, more often wallowing on the unshowered, poison ivy, profane side of grunge (see fat redneck song Off The Slug and the slamming psychedelic speed of Fathom). The whole creative bombshell is based on whisper-to-roar dynamics, either between tracks or within them, and most times it works great, suspiciously easy, like this is an ex-metal band gone alternative. Lots of fireworks, but no one had any idea who was to go buy the record. Produced by Sylvia Massy.

Rating 7

## Greta - This Is Greta! (PolyGram '95)

Big changes here as the angsty drop-kicks of **No Biting** are eschewed for a more serendipitous and creamy alternative smear, a kind of power chord Beatles, elegantly produced to sound like Nirvana's **Nevermind**, complete with ringing, crashing, swinging cymbals. So the whole thing is a bit of a foppish, British-sounding tuff love, velvety songs rendered with rockin' tools. I find it a bit opportunistic though, a kind of less creative and sincere set of songs, basically nicer and more accomodating to little grunge girls.

Rating         **6**

## Grief - Miserably Ever After (Pessimer/Theologian '96)

Oh the stuff we'll listen to. We metalheads can be sick individuals, producing and patronizing such coagulated, clogged, plainly sick music, Boston's Grief making sure the exits are boarded shut before their dense, Eyehate-Godly thud wallows and tremblulates like a stuck rhino. Think A.C. musically realized, or Napalm Death and old-age Melvins with arsenic poisoning, and you're crashed on the rocks of Grief's corpse-ridden shores. A long-bong sludge metal mistake (possibly) worth making.

Rating         **5**

## Griffin - Flight Of The Griffin (Shrapnel '84)

A fairly solid traditional metal effort with a couple of smokers in Hawk The Slayer and Heavy Metal Attack, but also three dog turds and some other less than inspired material. **Flight** features kick-ass vocals from "William Rodrick McKay", rowdy drumming, and hot production (for Shrapnel), fitting the much imitated Priest/Dio/Scorpions sense of song, albeit delivering their tales a bit more low-budget and punky than its mentors. All in all, a decent and well-varied debut if not a bit lyrically self-serious.

Rating         **5**

## Grim Reaper - See You In Hell (RCA '84)

A grand and impressive debut, **See You In Hell** exudes confidence and an uncanny talent for purity of metal essence. Rich and full-up with integrity, this album features one in a long line of excellent Darryl Johnston/Ebony Records recordings, this particular one boomy and loose, perfect for the band's brand of tunnel-visored chaos. Another shaft of brilliance is Steve Grimmett's voice, an expressive and chivalrous wail that leads the Reaper's rumbling and careening juggernaut with class, sincerity, and capable control. Hard to pin down the genius behind this album. It's a mix of the aforementioned heroic vocals, production and songcraft, but maybe most importantly, the absolutely focused delivery of these straight-forward, metallic, but richly melodic tunes, like a bus out of control, like Diamond Head. Classic, magical, and timeless British metal with a mystique that did not go unnoticed by punters both sides of the Atlantic.

Rating         **10**

## Grim Reaper - Fear No Evil (RCA '85)

The self-proclaimed "ugliest band in metal" is back with **See You In Hell** - Part 2, in hopes of re-creating the considerable media buzz that enveloped said rollicking premiere. **Fear No Evil** is another dose of solid, distinctive raucous roll, even heavier and generally faster than the debut. However, the record takes no chances with a proven brew and because of its safeness, falls short songcraft-wise due to its self-conscious emulation of its predecessor; too many here-to-rock-you macho metal clichés evidenced in titles such as Fight For The Last, Lay It On The Line, Let The Thunder Roar, and Final Scream. Still a great album, but just a bit forced, a bit of a Grim Reaper parody of the debut which seemed effortlessly well-written in comparison. **Fear No Evil** seems to be preoccupied with the trappings of metal, rather than metal itself, signalling a loss of fresh, innocent wonder at the awesomeness of metallic power. Anyways, on a basic headbangin' level, it's still pretty cool. Another raging plus: same recording as the first.

Rating         **7**

## Grim Reaper - Rock You To Hell (RCA '87)

As with **Fear No Evil**, it's hard to fault the exuberant delivery or the plain heaviness of this follow-up, it's just that the band once again sounds like a camp version of a once great band called Grim Reaper. No progression. Not only does the album title evoke the erroneous second-rate English characteristic of Scorpions, it's a virtual repeat of the debut's moniker. And although **Rock You To Hell** and **Fear No Evil** are direct copies of **See You In Hell**, both lack the debut's spontaneity, wide-eyed wonder, grit and innocence. Frustrating, 'cos this is a band one could learn to believe in. Per usual, power and talent electrify the grooves, thus the shortcomings are more philosophical and unwritten than overtly musical. In any event, **Rock You To Hell** just manages to tip the scales on the right side of kiddie horror metal, leaving Grim Reaper an empty shell of a once disturbing metal machine.

Rating         **6**

## Grim Skunk - Grim Skunk (Cargo '95)

Searing production values collide with exuberant Jon Lord keyboard honkin' grunge all over this acclaimed sophomore effort from Montreal's pungently-monikered Grim Skunk. And the results wail, shimmy, mosh and grind, the band layering cool '70s influences (indeed faithfully covering Heep's Look At Yourself) with that playful wot th' hell ethic that made early Soul Asylum such a fab mess of wires. Lyrics built of weed, graphics built of vibrant greens and browns, and a record built by skimming the cream of three decades of guitar crunch, flung '90s-bound with a def sense of fun. What more can you ask? Smokin' major play for action, from a band that has prided itself on professionalism right from the start.

Rating         **8**

## Grim Skunk - Meltdown (Cargo '96)

This hotly anticipated second serious record (third overall) for Montreal's hottest alt.rock property perpetuates the band's unique Hammond flavours, while veering deliberately into a manic punk thrill, eschewing much of the metalli-grunge of its predecessor for a textured slam that is more consistent, while less enjoyable. Also not crazy about the loose-knit deliveries, the shouting, the overall noise and the unsupportive production values, causing the bloom to wear off somewhat, **Meltdown** lacking the peaks and valleys of **Grim Skunk**, while nevertheless intensifying the middle eastern tonalities, demonstrating that these guys are still a serious force to be reckoned with, probably the most vital and creative descendant of Faith No More going. Told me a year ago they were all moving to Texas. Looks like that ain't happened yet. Swanky, gold-stamped packaging, way outside for an indie, proving that like I say, Grim Skunk are serious about craft, if not a bit enamoured with this new punk scourge.

Rating         **7**

## Grip Inc. - Power Of Inner Strength (Metal Blade '95)

The word "hard" applies splendiferously here, steely and cold unlike the breathing human chaos of Slayer (wardrummer Dave Lombardo's last band); hard and unsentimental like Machine Head and the technical Florida-to-San Fran underworld metal this embraces. The record packs pride and sense of mission, leaping from crunchful track to track, often undressing Slayer at their own vein-busting game through leaden, unflinching contemplation of precision slam. Chambers' vocals get a little tiring, punkish and shouty, but minor complaint. The closest thing to Slayer you'll probably hear from 1995 AD, surgically removing the hysterics for heartless, robotic intent and a tad more versatility. Note: although this record was touted as the return of Dave Lombardo, in reality it is more ex-Despair gui-

tarist Waldemar Sorychta's band, who unlike Dave, figures in all the songwriting, also producing with stinging aplomb.
Rating                                                    8

## Grip Inc. - Nemesis (Metal Blade '97)
This is quite the scorch about the head, neck, arms and face, **Nemesis** really stomping all over Grip Inc.'s stiff, cold, but squarely competent debut from two years back. Personalities are beginning to gel fabulously. Ex-Slayer drum tornado Dave Lombardo is front, centre, and vicious, Gus Chambers has become less punk-ranted and more Kerry King-like (this is a good thing), and German metal guru Waldemar Sorychta has added a bevy of new tones. What occurs is a face-frying collection of professional metal tracks, not unlike Machine Head meets **Reign In Blood** (Let's face it. War Between Blood is carbon-copy Slayer), breathing, organic metal that harkens to the very best of Lombardo's ex-experience. Reviews thus far have been insanely positive. Look for Grip Inc. to enter metal's middle tier with this one, that 100,000 to 250,000 sales zone where all the best product has lived for the last few years.
Rating                                                    8

## Groovezilla - Groovezilla (Mausoleum '94)
Thick and steamy funk/rap metal from Kentucky, as good as any in the genre (kinda like Pavement's L.U.N.G.S.), with lots of poppin' bass and complicated power riffing. Can't get too excited about it though, basically deciding that the record we always wanted from the Chili Peppers is an unremarkable thing unless it comes from the Peppers themselves. Nice touch with the sax though.
Rating                                                    6

## Groovy Aardvark - Vacuum (M.P.V. '96)
Trying single-handedly to merge Canada's two solitudes, Montreal's Groovy Aardvark sing half of this firecracker in French, half in English. Another great Montreal act, Grim Skunk also mixed its heritages, and that isn't the only comparative between these bands. For both are tight, irreverent hard alternative machines, both with a touch of ska and middle eastern world swirl immersed within often fantastical structures (see Human Candles and Dormitory). Groovy Aardvark is (by a shade) the more accessible of the two, given their functional, flawless production values, but the writing is zesty enough to keep the listener guessing.
Rating                                                    7

## Grotus - Mass (London '96)
This third full-length for SF's favourite noise squeaker conundrums finds the band's industrial quorum lumbering down a bassy, jammy, bluesy pathway, sort of if Butthole Surfers cared about record-making. Sampling and transfiguring sounds is still priority one, but most everything here is stuffed-up with a relentless, slow funk swing, somewhere between hip-hop, NIN, Led's When The Levee Breaks and Zep's Four Sticks, and Led Zeppelin's Boogie With Stu, sorta where I Mother Earth might have been had they gone industrial rather than alternative. A buzzing marvel of tangled cables, and a damn good read, even though as strictly pleasurable listening, it's a hassle like waking up with the flu.
Rating                                                    7

## Groundhogs - Groundhog Night (Griffin '94)
I've had a few rock historians (i.e. buddies Paul Surdin and Mike Blackburn), tell me these fogies ought to be given at minimum an honourable mention. So call this a token review for this band's protracted up-and-down 33 years (!) as an underground pleasure, Tony McPhee and various Hog assemblages cranking out a very elec-

tric hard blues fer ages, often laspsing into power chordage that was definitely heavy in the early '70s. This double live set is an appropriate survey, offering eighteen tracks elevated in heaviness through the live experience. Kinda like Hawkwind meets Savoy Brown, or Trower meets early Rory Gallagher, sheened over with a bit of live Dead. Bottom line: not metal, but if you like hard bluesy guitar, McPhee's the ticket. About nineteen records beginning in '68 (that number includes six compilations), definitive wax being '70's **Thank Christ For The Bomb** and '71's **Split**.
Rating                                                    7

## Gruntruck - Inside Yours (The All Blacks B.V. '91)
My world of rock trends is torn asunder, having heard this record for the first time in mid-'96, years after grooving to Tribe, wondering wherefore at the demise of grunge except for but a few (Soundgarden, Pearl Jam, STP and AiC). Fact is, early Gruntruck was a cogent example of the format, getting in on the ground floor, much less embarrassing than Mother Love Bone, welded directly into the heavy part of the pipeline, well worthy of your attention. So riffs trundle with metallic betrayance, as Ben often out-Cornells Navarro, Hammett and Chris combined. They look pretty metal too, '91 being just before the barbers got out their Marine handbooks.
Rating                                                    7

## Gruntruck - Push (Roadrunner '92)
I'd have to put Gruntruck at the top of the second (and completely derivative) tier of Seattle sonics, ahead of such noisemaking hybrids as Stone Temple Pilots and Tool (but beneath Helmet), due to greater busy-ness and technical stroll-about of a metallic nature. Vocalist Ben is signature Sub, and the riffs are volcanic (check out the hair-raising opening to Tribe), out-working those more enamoured with slouch and slack than sweat. Not quite so inquisitive as Alice in Chains but I can imagine greater things to come under mutual influence of a few cocktails. After all is said and done, **Push** and **Inside Yours** represent a fine chapter of what unfortunately has become a sound that has to look over its shoulder at cynics, lamenting the commercialization of the grunge community.
Rating                                                    8

## Gunjah - Heredity (Noise/Futurist '93)
Frantic, technical punk thrash with a sense of humour, massive energy and a bunch of cool ideas, **Heredity** kicks off with a recording of the boys enjoying a good toke, perhaps the source of the band's verve and swerve. Gunjah pile on the moves, taking the listener through a ripping rock ride encompassing Bay Area frash, through hardcore and traces of funk and hip hop, all the while barking out urban tales of crime, violence and drugs, in that usual spit-it-out manner that comes across as scathing beratement. Cool band, lotsa layers, lotsa ambition, although they'd probably rather be known as just regular losers with no prospects.
Rating                                                    7

## Guns N' Roses - Appetite For Destruction (Geffen '87)
The legend built of bad press and Herculean substance abuse would be yesterday's news without this fairly ambitious, complete album to back up the biggest hype in L.A. (second biggest: Jane's Addiction). Turns out that it would have to have the legs to run four years, and for the most part it's up to the task, going eight times platinum by the early '90s. But **Appetite** is full of contradictions. GN'R put across as certified street scum yet their record is scrubbed clean, professional, well-recorded and tight, in a word, commercial. And when Axl swears on It's So Easy and Night Train, he actually sounds insincere, embarrassed, like the brat he is. And if this is supposed to be the "real thing", i.e. a

'90s version of previous generation badboys Aerosmith, why does it sound so calculated? But enough slaggin'. Questionable sincerity is more than likely a bad read on my part, the band definitely convincing me of their deep love for rock'n'roll with the **Illusion** projects, not to mention the fact that dues had been paid on the moral-numbing L.A. club scene. So **Appetite** is entertaining if not ground-breaking grit rock, spanning many American rock traditions, sizzling and partaaaying with an intensity that makes you want to lay waste to a few brain cells. *Welcome to the Jungle*, *Paradise City* and *My Michelle* sport classic metal riffs, and elements of emotive soul and funk intersperse with the sleaze amongst Skynyrdy hit *Sweet Child O' Mine* and the totally bitchin', Hanoi Roxy *Mr. Brownstone*. Overall there's lots going on to hold one's interest and due to the entire project's pervasive "no mistakes" philosophy, it's damn listenable. And the rest is history, as they say. CD reissue sports a different cover, basically a collage of band photos.

Rating       8

## Guns N' Roses - G N' R Lies    (Geffen '88)

Incapable of producing a bonafide follow-up to **Appetite For Destruction** going on four years, **GN'R Lies** was released to capitalize on the intoxicated commercial juggernaut that Slash and Axl built. One side is doped-out street-dead acoustic tunes, the other, live non-**Appetite** cuts from '86 including an inconsequential take on Aerosmith's *Mama Kin*. All in all, not too bad in a screwed, half-baked sort of way. The acoustic stuff, particularly *Patience*, is sincere and bleak, further distinguished by Axl's abrasive vocals, and the live fare is at least rowdy, albeit in total, below **Appetite's** compositional standards. GN'R cemented their place in history as bad boy wastecases with the overt racism and homophobia of *One In A Million*. Bet Axl wishes he could have that one back. Or since he became king of the world, does he care? As the jacket sez, this record contains previously released material from indie-released EP **Live Like A Suicide**, pumped out to wild local success, shortly *after* the band's signing with Geffen.

Rating       6

## Guns N' Roses - Use Your Illusion I    (Geffen '91)

## Guns N' Roses - Use Your Illusion II    (Geffen '91)

Stateside, half a million copies sold in two hours. Triple platinum in Canada in three days, and that's each record. Destined to reign as one of the largest recorded statements of the '90s, **Use Your Illusion I** and **Use Your Illusion II** (in case you're from another planet, two simultaneously released studio albums), speak tragically and eloquently as the true and trampled Voice of America. Operating on polluted blood, three day old sweat, and a life-battered lack of tears, Guns N' Roses have transcended metal to embrace and essentially shelter all that is seedy and beaten by life in America, through an all-encompassing walk through the gutters of traditional musical genres, spanning punk, hard rock, r+b, the blues, boogie woogie, balladry, metal itself, and numerous self-styled hybrids that claim a universality where U2's reflective sprawl **Rattle And Hum** could not. Comprising 30 tracks totalling 152 minutes, this novel expulsion is really no less than three records worth of material, even four if translated to vinyl, making up for the four years since **Appetite For Destruction**, and the two years of rumour-fuelled delays. Packed with verbal venom, sonic anarchy, quiet hopelessness, and violent desperation, **Use Your Illusion I** and **II** sadly and artfully document the psychological skid rows infecting the brains of America's filthiest generation, the scum floating to the top of the slackers. On a purely musical level, GN'R's sound has expanded magnificently, accepting both the responsibility and tooling to speak the language of an audience much larger than metal. Of the roughly one half of the two records that is metal (**Illusion I** is heavier, but who's counting), GN'R sounds uglier and punkier, Axl crawling further up his ass, slurring and mumbling his words, over rough-shod and often uncharacteristically fast structures that sound like they were recorded in one drug-accelerated take. No secret that Slash and the boys groove on punk both philosophically and sonically, having recorded their **Spaghetti Incident?** record of hot punk covers during the **Illusion** sessions. Conversely, the mellower offerings, such as the both pre-released *Civil War* and Dylan's *Knockin' On Heaven's Door*, debut post-release single *Don't Cry* and the sprawling *November Rain*, sound like fully conceived masterpieces, emitting wads of pain amidst some of Slash's finest axework on the record; absolutely wasting other anonymous light moments such as the bloody awful *Estranged* (9:20) and *So Fine*. In betwixt, we get a dense array of GN'R Aerosmith-isms, rock 'n' bluesy, funky, boogie woogie metal plus occasional smatterings of melloid moments approaching bluegrass, tunes further coloured by sixth member Dizzy Reed's honky tonk ivories which elevate the quieter moments, and painfully intrude on the heavier numbers. It's hard to make generalizations about such a far-reaching package, except that perhaps GN'R have gotten both more violent and more resigned to inaction, but rarely warm and likeable. A mesmerising sleaze, not to mention railing doses of swearing, reigns throughout both the rock and the roll, although personal faves such as my #1, *Breakdown*, plus *Bad Apples*, *Dead Horse* and *Back Off Bitch* seem to break through the complication and urban muck to communicate on a more inclusive and tuneful level. No doubt, given such a large selection of targets, critics will be flying out of each others butts to whine about supposed filler and offense, yet really there ain't much that isn't attention-grabbing in one crazy direction or another. The nastiest end of the heavy spectrum may be unenjoyably dense, and the aforementioned two ballads suck, but the rest of **Illusion I** and **II** succeeds in its exhaustive search for, and ultimate resolve with the confusion and pain which is life in the '90s for so many who have fallen or crammed themselves through the cracks. It is this ultimate resolve and even celebration of grime and dysfunction that makes this package such an arresting and emotionally assaultive listen throughout its panoramic rock ride, variously provoking swinging spectrums of aggression and mental destruction ranging from resigned decay to active abuse. **Use Your Illusion I** and **Use Your Illusion II**, not to mention the equally corrupt **Slave To The Grind**, the diametrically positive **Metallica**, and the out-of-the-blue **Nevermind** are testimony to the fact that the upper echelons of rock'n'roll can still be infiltrated upon by those that shred heavily, perhaps carrying with the aggression the added responsibility as lightning rod to society's cancers.

Rating       10

## Guns N' Roses - The Spaghetti Incident?    (Geffen '93)

Forthrightly a cool idea, covering many spider-webbed thangs we'd all relish in sound by the most dangerous band in rock. But all get that uniform Gunners treatment, put through a middling shredder that is Axl, Slash and Matt, the three comprising the Gun ilk, goodly L.A. beats driving a sneer and a scrape. *New Rose* sounded way more manic in original state, Rat Scabies suiciding Matt's delivery, but *Raw Power* is fine here, as is Nazareth's solid *Hair Of The Dog*. Elsewhere, too much of that Johnny Thunders influence, making **Spaghetti** sound like a slick Heartbreakers album, too slummy and laconic, which is I guess where GN'R live their turbulent anti-lives. But like all covers experiences, this one wears out fast, hanging together as badly as one would think. Total record highlight: the Dead Boys' *Ain't It Fun*, on which Axl captures and explodes all of Stiv's shattered depression, creating squalid bombast on par with anything from Axl's own twisted deliberations, which as I write in mid-'94 seem ready to blow to pieces the band. Update: Okay, gents and gals, it's now early '97. So far, Slash wants to rock similarly, and Axl wants to trip-hop into the future. Factions are fractioned with rumblings of work going ahead with that really talented guy, Steve Jones of The Sex Pistols. By the time you read this, maybe the smoke will have cleared and we'll have product. But please, no more solo albums.

Rating　　　　　　　　　　　　　　　　7

## Gutsonic - Impetus 23　(Second Sun '96)

One strident and confident serving of rhythm-drunk '90s metal, Gutsonic's **Impetus 23** floppy boot stomps like the most intensely heaving of Faith No More ideas, all slamming, concave riffery, and headphone-ready drums, under a vocal performance from Andrew Sanger that emulates Mike Patton's ethic unto fragmented personality. But the vocals don't stop there, the band's other four members also credited with voice, chiming in with harmonies and jazzy scat touches that recall magic little Zappa moments, driving hook-heavy tracks like *Metamorph*, *Instant Excuses* and closing vista-galore epic *Scumbag Intersection* to new, super-smart, quite subtle, prog rock dynamics. I dunno, just a whole lotta finesse-able things going on here, all of them really heavy; quirky breaks, fire-breathing riffs, solos that rock one second, then flip into Belew, Fripp and Holdsworth the next, without batting an eye, the band full-on mission-bent, cutting a path to the next surprise. You gotta respect the work that went into this thing, and the weird pastiche of many rock eras that grind together, then emerge as soberingly up to date. Thick '90s aggro-metal that reverberates with about five resurfacing subplots.

Rating　　　　　　　　　　　　　　　　8

## Gwar - Scumdogs Of The Universe　(Metal Blade '90)

**Scumdogs** was the big, fetid, feet-first splash for Gwar, a band based on filth, taking theatrics to new buggering extremes, combining slasher horror with sci-fi disease, mutant body parts a' flyin', fluids a' squirtin', hard tech-thrash a slammin'. **Scumdogs** rocks '70s punky, rocks '80s hard rocky, and rocks with the brisk, shouty vocals of the '90s. But the band can play, and even arrange (see all that soloing stuff in *Maggots*), although the above average but somewhat rote exercise in metallic styles makes the whole up-tempo monster mash feel like a parody of hard rock's history, like an X-rated Dictators or Tubes circa '75. It's dirty comedy first and foremost, theatre pros arranging

an entertainment package that kaleido-brutalizes decaying American culture. Love them bagpipes.

Rating　　　　　　　　　　　　　　　　6

## Gwar - America Must Be Destroyed　(Metal Blade '92)

Faster, higher, rougher on the skin, Gwar upratchets the aggression and loose violence, while also gussying up the always thoughtful breaks, prog-punking the whole hyperparody, channel-surfing through U.S. societal Hells until the wide-screen monitor blows. Also more looking unto the conceptual Gwarness of Gwar and the band's effect on mankind, what with *The Morality Squad* and the sample-strewn title track. Slowly making the shift from harmless to harmful, still sickening and offensive to just about everybody, but surprising wholesale with spare but catchy songskill.

Rating　　　　　　　　　　　　　　　　7

## Gwar - This Toilet Earth　(Metal Blade '94)

Forever degenerates been sayin' there's a smokin' rock band beneath those Barney costumes. **This Toilet Earth** might perplex those sentiments however, leaning increasingly whimsical, abstract, rushed, thrashed and punked, but at the same time somewhat sucked clinical by an unremarkable mix, undermining the band's crazy-like-a-fox chaos. But minor complaint on an expansive record that can be hilarious, filthy, and sonically challenging at once, like a proto-obscene metalized Zappa from space. Sure, the band will never avoid accusations of novelty or even a sort of inverse commercialism, but open your mind and Gwar will gladly jump right in and wreck it. Lots to chew on, even if you might want to spit most of it out. Increasingly evil through intelligence.

Rating　　　　　　　　　　　　　　　　7

## Gwar - Ragnarok　(Metal Blade '95)

And the moral bad apple crumble of mankind accelerates, prompted by the impending arrival of an earth-destroying comet, **Ragnarok**, the Twilight Of The Gods, as told in Norse legend. So this is the latest reason Gwar has put forth to party insanely unto death, for the end is near, drink lotsa beer! As usual, it's a greatly involved read, and those refrains of "everybody rip everybody else off!" are chillingly relevant. Musically, the band is full into a sort of raw, progressive punk metal meets street rock, almost like the Dictators at times. So if you can get past the overpowering, comic book from hell persona of this most unique and persistent of bands, **Ragnarok** can be a visit to the theatre like no other. I mean, this really works best as a soundtrack album, so where's the screenplay?

Rating　　　　　　　　　　　　　　　　7

## Sammy Hagar - Nine On A Ten Scale   (Capitol '76)

Here, oddly enough on the man's debut, Hagar puts on his most creative hard hat, serving up some of his most complex and expertly fleshed-out ideas, mixing his hard rock and acoustical non-committals with shades of psychedelia and melancholy. Best of the lot—and really best ever for Sam—are the obtusely progressive but balanced *Urban Guerilla* and epic-like acid trip *Silver Lights*. Although this debut was ironically Sam's most mature effort (maybe not so ironic given its temporal proximity to Montrose) , its somewhat muffled and claustrophobic recording limits its playability but only slightly. Still, pretty impressive as Sam and his band out-do themselves for one immediate and brief instant.

Rating   **7**

## Sammy Hagar - Sammy Hagar   (Capitol '77)

Sam's sophomore effort is a much mellower piece of general and generic rock versus the fairly kickin' and complicated **Nine On A Ten Scale**. Absolutely nothing impresses on this variously hard rock, acoustic, R+B, poppy finger food platter, but at least it's sincere and kind of funny in its age-betraying clichés and regular guy entertainer stance. Two lonely rockers in a sea of soap: *Rock'n'Roll Weekend* and *Love Has Found Me*.

Rating   **3**

## Sammy Hagar - Musical Chairs   (Capitol '77)

Sam's third album is one of Mr. Rogers' more enjoyable documents of fragmented styles, offering brief smatterings of metal (*Reckless, Crack In The World*, and *Don't Stop Me Now*) amongst the innocuous and semi-fun HR, acoustic rock and mellowisms. As per all of Sam's first five albums, the lack of focus leaves you wondering if Hagar has any clue of where he wants to go, which was much the case with Montrose after the molten debut. I guess at this point Sam sees himself as a tunesmith and album maker unhindered by categories. Unfortunately he and his band are just not intellectually imposing enough to be Zeppelin or even Purple, a most nagging reality that will dog Sam forever as he searches in vain for his special purpose.

Rating   **5**

## Sammy Hagar - All Night Long   (Capitol '78)

The rock dude most vehemently supportive of a colour (get a life) puts on a halfways convincing performance here of a middle-of-the-road nature, raising the corpses of his greatest walking dullards including *Red, Rock'n'Roll Weekend* and *Turn Up The Music*. We always subconsciously compared this record to Derringer - **Live**, but in retrospect, it's no contest which rocked with greater creativity, wit and intelligence. Includes the sun-baked 'n' slippery *Bad Motor Scooter* from **Montrose**, Sam's last resumé maker until Van Halen's **For Unlawful Carnal Knowledge** eighteen long years later.

Rating   **4**

## Sammy Hagar - Street Machine   (Capitol '79)

My fave rave Hagar disc, which nevertheless despite such ranking, places it stax of wax below desert island status. Metallically speaking, **Street Machine** is on par with **Nine On A Ten Scale** and **Danger Zone**, which is to say 60% rockin'. Sam was a somewhat medium-scale, B-hall rock entity by this point, coming up with a steady one hit per album or so, in this case one of his most celebrated, *Plain Jane*, another dumb but uplifting and summery piece of common man fluff which I bought into heavily enough at the time. **Street Machine** also includes two of Sam's four or five truly rousing rockers in *This Planet's On Fire* and Guido hit *Trans Am (Highway Wonderland)*. Even mellower fare such as *Child To Man* and *Never Say Die* connect emotively in a rare-fer-Sam moment of artistic lucidity. Recommendation: snag this one and its two heavy equivalents at a maximum total expenditure not exceeding 12$ or so.

Rating   **7**

## Sammy Hagar - Danger Zone   (Capitol '80)

Although a somewhat slammin' side one drags this record from complete meltation, the all-pervading dullard infecting the mind of Sam-I-am begins to emerge and cloud the collective visions of his already fairly idea-void back-up band come side two. Rockwise, the red one deals up aseptic but driven automotives in *Love Or Money, 20th Century Man, Miles Of Boredom*, and the sorta ambitious (read: simple by any other band's standards except The Ramones and Quo) *In The Night (Entering The Danger Zone)*. That's it for crunch however, as the balance of this mildly successful ruse offers up uneventful variations on vacated, occasionally comical guitar-laced pop. Really the last of the pre-lobotomy outings.

Rating   **6**

## Sammy Hagar - Standing Hampton (Geffen '81)

Chinks in the man's fire engine-red plastic begin to weaken the minuscule amounts of credibility Sam has acquired over time with this still somewhat shiny record, featuring the upbeat pop of *I'll Fall In Love Again*, pea-brained dinosaur *Heavy Metal* and a tolerable cover of *Piece Of My Heart*. The artsy cover graphic is about the only fresh ploy up Sam's sleeve however, as a laconic simp-rock muse begins to smother the life out of this particular B-market machine. Beneath the offense however, I can't help think there might have been a direction here with the more ornate, keyboardy, and somehow Cheap Trick-like playfulness exhibited throughout, but most notably on the sparkling *Can't Get Loose*. Confusing but not without comfortable merit.
Rating                                                          5

## Sammy Hagar - Rematch (Capitol '82)

Ten tune greatest hits record. Still, not the gathering of power chords that could have conceivably been constructed to sidestep the sea of drivel breaking wind amongst Sam's sprawling suburban repertoire.
Rating                                                          4

## Sammy Hagar - Three Lock Box (Geffen '82)

**Three Lock Box** begins Hagar's descent into the most stroke-inducing of boredoms. From hereon in, heavy or not, Sammy becomes self-doomed with his image as mental and emotional lightweight, an image that dogs him to this day, five albums into his unjust and eventually ill-fated Cinderella story with the mighty Van Halen, who seem to have been creatively bludgeoned by the marriage. **Three Lock Box** is a surprisingly poppy, infantile effort which achieves some sense of cotton candy whimsy due to half-hearted attempts at dynamics as witnessed on the lumbering title track, *Remote Love*, and minor hit *Your Love Is Driving Me Crazy*. I'm embarrassed to reveal that I actually liked this record for a good six month period about seven years back. Where the hell my head was at, I can't remember.
Rating                                                          4

## Sammy Hagar - Live 1980 (Capitol '83)

The scarlet gumball pulls a complete headbang on this one (within his mental capabilities), demonstrating how Sam could have been a thoroughly average metal guy if he committed his limited arsenal to the cause. Extra score: Montrose's *Space Station #5*.
Rating                                                          5

## Sammy Hagar - VOA (Geffen '84)

Similar talk show rock to '87's **Sammy Hagar**, **VOA** is an improvement volume-wise to **Three Lock Box**, while even more robotic, going through its lacklustre motions with brain-dead precision. Most noted (in fact, only noted) for welterweight hit *I Can't Drive 55*, which sucks just like all else on this corporate pap, Sam's attempt at fist-pumping identification with the teen masses falling flat on its crimson face. Huey Lewis in red tights. A horrid thought. Even more horrid: Van Halen now features *I Can't Drive 55* live. Ooo Nellie, break out the beers. Sad commentary: **VOA** somehow went platinum, with its two studio predecessors reaching gold.
Rating                                                          1

## Sammy Hagar - Sammy Hagar (Geffen '87)

When this sonic pudding quietly blemished its way onto the racks, there was some dim hope Sammy might be finished with Van Halen. Too bad, probably just a contractual obligation thing, which doesn't excuse the offensive gutlessness of Sammy's vanilla persona or total lack of conviction. Sam's lot in life has been a continual spiral from frontman of the shot-from-a-

rocket Montrose through to this, his blandest personal statement ever, a mirror to the man himself. Sam's problem is that he has zero empathy or identification with his market, having no inkling of magic, danger, rowdiness, mischief, depression, love, hate . . . nothing but blueprints handed to him. Thus Sam stumbles on blindly, knee-jerking through brutally trampled rock clichés such as *When The Hammer Falls*, *Boys Night Out*, ultra-generic power ballad *Give To Live* and *Radar Love* rip-off *Privacy*. You've been warned. Lay down and avoid, and don't worry it won't jump up and bite back. This rock'n'roll corpse has been sucked dry years ago.
Rating                                                          0

## Sammy Hagar - Unboxed (Geffen '94)

It's always a marvel how greatest hits packages sell, given that logic would imply that fans already bought the music as it transpired. So it's no surprise Sam gets one now, smearing like peanut butter time's wand over one stultifyingly boring solo career, a career that did modest business before Hagar's departure for his illustrious gig with Van Halen. Hits from the latter half of Sam's pop poop domain are displayed here, along with two nice newies, *High Hopes*, a grinding enough summer rocker, and *Buying My Way Into Heaven*, a kind of quirky pop metal speedster. Strange wrinkle: tracks from **I Never Said Goodbye**, which I'm surprised to read is the record I coulda sworn was just called **Sammy Hagar** (number II, the one from '87.)
Rating                                                          6

## Hagar, Schon, Aaronson, Shrieve - Through The Fire (Geffen '84)

Hagar further underscores his existence as loser generalist, ganging up with a bunch of like-minded identity crises, and not a leader among 'em, in creation of this not altogether awful slice of corporate boredom, monikered imaginatively like an accounting firm. And **Through The Fire**. Great title. Ekes out a **6** 'cos it's sort of heavy, sort of adventuresome in terms of Schon's vibrant, sparkly axework (see the hot clockin' *My Home Town*), and for the slightly bulbous cover of *Whiter Shade Of Pale*. Recorded live, then heavily doctored, during an eight date tour of the San Fran area. Reissued on CD in '95.
Rating                                                          6

## Hall Aflame - Guaranteed Forever (I.R.S. '91)

Sideline band for main Metal Church muse Kurt Vanderhoof, Hall Aflame bring a welcome honest rural clarity to the tough urban sounds of heavy metal. Vanderhoof has called this band a reflection of its members' identity as small town boys from outback Washington state (see Nirvana). Whatever the motivation, **Guaranteed Forever** holds gutsy purity of purpose, rocking economically in four wheel drive as it bushwacks through such riff-blown terrain as *Shake The Pain*, *The Money*, *One Time Winner*, *Pirate's Life* and personal fave, the immensely uplifting *No How, No Way*. And the acoustic is just as smooth, beginning with *Cold Wind* and closer *Country Angel*, both warmly southern-tinged, both brought to truth by the rich vocals of Ron Lowd. What's best about **Guaranteed Forever** is that each of the twelve tracks enclosed are enveloped in their own tones and imagery, while reinforcing the love of music, the integrity of the whole unpretentious, ass-kickin' display, the laid-back bar band Raw. I hope we hear more from these guys, because as much as I love the majesty of Metal Church, it's great to see a little primal undressing of pure, no pretense wattage once in a while.
Rating                                                          9

## Hallows Eve - Tales Of Terror (Metal Blade '85)

Don't really remember much about this long-ago-cashed-in chunk of bile, except that it was ridiculously

overwrought, ultra-heavy white noise, and I hated it. Basically the U.S. equivalent of Exciter's yelpy amphetamine gallop, with solid recording values by metal guru Brian Slagel.
Rating                                                                      3

## Hallows Eve - Monument   (Metal Blade '88)

L.A.'s Hallows Eve have honed their act considerably since their useless debut (and follow-up **Death And Insanity**) a few loud years hence, creating one well-carved but unnecessary block of ice, evoking the more aggressive and philosophically claustrophobic and moshing elements of the Overkill, Sanctuary, Testament, Exodus, Mordred, or Anthrax camps of technical, pounding, ultra-heaviness, much of which leaves me frozen for dead. **Monument's** got a Fates Warning look to it, and indeed Hallows Eve seems saddled with Fates' lack of dynamic and profusion of illogical constructs, although not so riffically-plundering. **Monument** is considerably molten, but I don't think I'll ever internalize it, due to the record's all too dour lapses into emotive monotone and lack of compelling reason to exist. Hard to warm up to a machine.
Rating                                                                      5

## Hammerschmitt - Hammerschmitt   (Rockport '85)

Yet another Germanic monolith full of galloping gothic broodery that stirs the soul to suicide. Too shambling and broken up to gather major steam like kharmic bro's on Scratch or out-of-bounds soulmates from melancholy Scandinavian shores, Hammerschmitt's biggest transgression is lack of groove, lapsing into Maiden-ish progressive passages all too often, wandering the moors in search of dragons and Holy Grails and what not. In other words, too soupy and grandiose, forgetting to net it out and roll.
Rating                                                                      6

## Hammersmith - It's For You   (Polydor '76)

Goofy and powerless Canadian hard rock that briefly attracted our gaze as young pups, having caught the band in concert at the illustrious Nelson Civic Centre. Sounds like a dull Moxy, boneheaded guitar-conscious Styx, or blunted variant on the hapless Lynx or even Streetheart, wanking off the odd power chord amidst its embarrassing '70s mealy-mindedness. Second record after a self-titled debut one year earlier.
Rating                                                                      1

## Handsome - Handsome   (Sony '97)

Wow, this is the kind of record Tool's **Aenima** professes to be, only a lot more fun. By the Tool reference, I mean the preponderance of rainy guitar layers, the insistent forward mass, the stellar but conservative production designed to emphasize hard-won greatness. And it's no accident, members of this thinking man's NYC hardcore act having done time with respected collectives such as Helmet, Quicksand and Cro-Mags. But what makes Handsome so handsome are the olive branches to sounds less stifling and aggro, starting with Jeremy Chatelain's emotive, almost sweet vocals, through Peter Mengede's chimy, versatile guitar work, both providing a framework on which to build true anthems, tracks that sound like the best of heavy Pumpkins, connecting Helmet, or on occasion, harrowing Jesus Lizard. An amazing exploration of various hard musics, dripping with star quality start to finish. Almost Crimsonian!
Rating                                                                      9

## The Hangmen - The Hangmen   (Capitol '89)

Slushy, garagey commercial blues metal that fits the Dangerous Toys, Johnny Crash, Junkyard vein with a particular edge towards polluted punkiness and Stoogemania, albeit cleanly mixed and rawk radio friendly. And not much more comes to mind, **The Hangmen** being kinda catchy but only 'til the novelty of having a new CD wanes. Whiney, out of tune vocals and a cover of cool Dictators covers, *Slow Death* are about this band's only distinguishing factors. Verdict: forgettable.
Rating                                                                      5

## Hanoi Rocks - Bangkok Shocks Saigon Shakes   (Mercury '81)

Potent party rock from new sensations Hanoi Rocks comes in the form of this headphone-quality slice of hyper boogie thump, a record so confident, optimistic, upbeat and under-achievingly kickin', it turned the world on with memories of shooting stars New York Dolls, also evoking traces of Mott, Aerosmith and the Stones. Best of the bunch are raucous rabble-rousers *Tragedy*, *Stop Cryin'* and *Pretender*, all propelled by sassy, old time grooves under a nice cruise metal pummel. Michael Monroe is instant stage presence, edgy chaos personified as he takes his assembled gypsies through the backstreets of life in search of a little guilty pleasure and pain. But Hanoi Rocks is essentially the Andy McCoy show, the axe victim more or less responsible for all the songwriting, not to mention a slidin' guitar language reverent of things past. All in all, a classy presentation of what is an endearing garage rock, fully bent on fun through pop metal showboating.
Rating                                                                      8

## Hanoi Rocks - Oriental Beat   (Lick '83)

More the collapse quotient of **Self Destruction Blues**, **Oriental Beat** lacks the songs and overall desperate gel of both **SDB** and the debut, sounding more toothless glam than street-diseased. Still, Hanoi Rocks are always jumping around my mental void, this record being no exception. Amongst three or four clankers, which are less bad than simply unstirred, we get true gems like the Clash reggae of *No Law Or Order*, slushy booze cover *Lightnin' Bar Blues* and melancholy piano closer (more like life terminator) *Fallen Star*. My least fave of the HR collective, **Oriental Beat** nevertheless made my playlist a couple a' hundred times during my mid '80s university days. A rumbling caboose of care-free bashables that just adds to the hapless mystique of one singular band of rogues.
Rating                                                                      7

## Hanoi Rocks - Self Destruction Blues   (Lick '83)

Always my fave Hanoi highball, **Self Destruction Blues** is also in my opinion the trashiest, most chaotic, most squalid and real, tearing away the metallic pretensions of much else HR for an honest, irreversible skid through garage life. Urgent in a losing battle for street survival, **Self Destruction Blues** is the closest thing to the *idea* of The Dolls or Stooges one can get, careening with a sort of beat generation aimlessness, celebration of inebriation and ability to find life in the examination of ailment, brought to full slide on such ragtag rockers as *Kill City Kills*, *Beer And A Cigarette*, and the charming *Dead By X-Mas*. Totally JD and Johnny Thunders, and totally nightclubbing in a shabby '60s sort of way, **Self Destruction Blues** is strangely the band's most cohesive, all points of the compass leading to thin, desperate and rock'n'roll heroic.
Rating                                                                      9

## Hanoi Rocks - Back To Mystery City   (Quality '84)

Emanating the most convincing grafting of loud guitars onto '60s doo-wop traditions of all the Hanoi projects, **Back To Mystery City** thereby best approximates the pre-punk party groove of the New York Dolls' **Too Much Too Soon**, accomplished through guttersnipe blues invaded by swigs of cabaret sax, harmonica, and nicotine wheeze. Thus, *Malibu Beach Nightmare*, *Mental Beat*, *Tragedy* and the Bo Diddley-beat title cut. No question, this band was the product of demented gene splicing, 'cos you gotta be brave and even careless to

strip down, chill out, reach back and embrace the garage like this band did, especially given the new attention to craft permeating the business at the time. Essentially, you luv 'em or hate 'em on their own terms, because HR were the ultimate moving targets, defying marketing definition, which was ultimately the band's downfall.
Rating 8

### Hanoi Rocks - Two Steps From The Move (CBS '84)

And finally, the wheels of commerce catch up with our fave gaggle of erratic Finns, bestowing upon the band The Big Record Deal, some press (much of it unfortunately doing with Vince Neil's drunk driving death of drummer Razzle), and a new life as muscle car rockers extraordinaire. What the newly commercial Hanoi Rocks lacks in weirdness, it makes up for in sonic fullness and completion of ideas; professionalism basically, nurtured by big production (and songwriting services) from Bob Ezrin of Kiss fame. And the hamfisted approach wears well on the boys, as the lyrical streetisms bring the whole thing back to party scuz in a way that is truly unique like the first Crüe but with less corruption. Hats off to **Kerrang!**, who'd been dreaming for years about this band getting a break, Hanoi Rocks no question in possession of an inebriated psychic baggage that puts them so comfortably in the driver's seat of barroom rock'n'roll. Faves include CCR cover Up Around The Bend, always one of that band's best tunes, the re-padded ballad's ballad Don't You Ever Leave Me, the fish and chips Boiler, and the dour Cutting Corners, but it's all choice, timeless r'n'r, stroked with the best from the '50s, '60s and '70s strapped onto a thudly sort of glam metal, essentially the band's heaviest album even if you don't really notice. Wish it was as commercially big as the hype, but a sort of opacity cloaks the record in a doomed world, left to reflect on a life of spills on the boulevard of broken dreams.
Rating 9

### Hanoi Rocks - "All those wasted years" (Lick '85)

Slippery, ancient and boozy like my imagined impressions of the Dolls kickin' towards heat stroke in some N.Y. cave, **"All those wasted years"** is a swell-recorded document of a legendary party outfit captured live at the Marquee. Comprising great and plain goofy tracks from the band's first four plus some unimaginative covers, most remarkable of the lot being A.C's Under My Wheels, this mildly entertaining but unintrusive double rolls thoroughly loose but full-range through its pub-brewed tales of the street. A nice curiosity but no real drawing power over the oh-so-cool studio smorg. This is as good a place as any for an honourable mention of another double: compilation, Castle's **Dead By Christmas**, which lifts tunes from all the studio records adding three live ones. Hey, buy this band however you can get it.
Rating 6

### Hanover - Hungry Eyes (Est. '83)

My dim recollection of said corporate-wannabe dross is further clouded by the fact that I cashed it in quickly and efficiently, finding the naive, thudly attempts at early Helix pointless in theory, botched in execution. Overall, about 40% axe-insistent, 10% convincing of anything.
Rating 3

### Hans Naughty - Paint The Town Red (Iron Works '88)

Living blissfully in vacuum land, Hans Naughty fully embrace everything that was laughable about mid-'80s metal, looking something like Quiet Riot crossed with debut-era DLR, over-the-top Hollyrock all the way, squinting desperately for that Van Halen - **Van Halen** magic, finding only scurrying, unfocused U.S. poverty

metal like a Metal Blade casualty from the pits of '84. Gotta love the aspirations. Even Don Dokken gets involved.
Rating 4

### Hanson Brothers - Sudden Death (Essential/Virgin '96)

Yet another NoMeansNo incarnation, Hanson Brothers are the hockey branch of the org., punkin' and puckin' their way through sweet pogo anthems to Canada's national sport. So it's apt that this loudfast celebration kicks off with a decibelled version of Stompin' Tom Connors' The Hockey Song, and that the main reason for the record to exist is to aid in the cause of getting Dave "Tiger" Williams inducted in the Hockey Hall of Fame. Tiger of course was the Vancouver Canucks' most famous enforcer, and also the NHL's all-time penalty minute leader. And he looked a bit like Tom Jones. Anyways, **Sudden Death** is the product of punk vets, one with a wicked rhythm section at that. All in all, it's a bit like explosive, energetic, entertaining Dead Kennedys or Ramones, (what with all those count-ins), perhaps demonstrating the fact that the Wright Bros. punk blueprints are from the '80s and not the less creative '90s.
Rating 7

### Hardline - Double Eclipse (MCA '92)

Reliving the collaboration with Hagar way back, Journey's Neal Schon creates a second tougher rock project, Hardline rollicking with a drop-dead ordinary batch of songs, expertly executed in hair band fashion. But **Double Eclipse** is of course of some value just to hear Schon, who burns through riffs like John Sykes, and solos like Satriani, to be somewhat simplistic about things. Schon isn't exactly known for an obviously distinctive style, but when he writes riffs, they do come out thick and melodic, the man being in part responsible for schlocky soapy rock due to his legacy with Journey, a veritable heaven for AOR fanatics. Those same sappy folks would do well to flick their Bics at **Double Eclipse**.
Rating 6

### Hardware - Third Eye Open (Black Arc/Ryko '92)

Not sure the drill on this, but I believe Black Arc is some sort of niche label designed to promote black musicians. In any event, Hardware is a barnstormer of an electric blues project, Stevie Salas, Bootsy Collins and Buddy Miles forming a legendary and chemically-volatile power trio that spans three generations of metal-lifunk. And to boot (no pun intended), there are no covers, just ten tasty guitar-bass-drum-driven chunks of, uh, hardware that entertain much more lubricatedly than traditional blues, sorta like Living Colour meets Stevie Ray. A joy to behold, at least for fans of hard rocking, commercially viable blues.
Rating 7

### Harem Scarem - Harem Scarem (Warner '91)

Harem Scarem began life as just another slick AOR band with a bad name; awful songs with lush harmonies and a promising bit of dual lead guitar texture. After winning Toronto's Q107 sponsored Homegrown contest, Warner took quick notice, releasing this Night Ranger-ish pile of poo, which nevertheless did good business in Canada and abroad (but not the U.S.) with pomp hits like Love Reaction and insipid, housewifey ballad Honestly. Wouldn't be in this book, if not for the big philosophical changes afoot.
Rating 3

### Harem Scarem - Mood Swings (Warner '93)

Learning to confound by their second record, Ontario's Harem Scarem get funky and raw, really pushing the guitars up front over arrangements that are sparse but often still stuck in poodle town. Again nice servings of guitar of both a riff-based and solo nature, on a record that is much more spontaneous, Harem Scarem growing in integrity while retaining their hair band sweetness. I guess it's worked, given the band's growing foreign fanbase, the boys finding their product positioned somewheres in that Dream Theater zone, even though this sounds a heck of a lot more like Journey than Queensryche. Fave: nasty razor-sharp rocker *Empty Promises*.

Rating 6

## Harem Scarem - Live And Acoustic (Warner '94)

You know you're on your way when you can do the unplugged thing, this 29 minute, seven track EP (basically designed for the Japanese), splitting it down the middle between live and acoustic and/or lightly arranged. *Jealousy* and *Honestly* get the biggest geardown, whereas **Mood Swings** hit *No Justice* sounds most enjoyably maudlin, with that big Survivor-bound chorus. For real fans only, which (ahem) may not include me.

Rating 4

## Harem Scarem - Voice Of Reason (Warner '95)

Jeez, who put the kerosene in Harem Scarem's cornflakes? I mean, something heavy, brooding and severely agitated has taken over this band, propelling them to new creative heights, or more accurately completely retooling the thing into a sort of down-tuned King's X. Even when sounding sugary (as on *Candle*'s chorus), the band swings the sledge with new authority, really soaking in '90s influences like Soundgarden and Alice in Chains (no wussy Pearl Jam for these guys), even approaching Saigon Kick and Enuff Z'nuff at times (Hess can sound like Chip). And judging from fan response, this tantamount horseshoe band has emerged unscathed by any utterance of sell-out (Sven Gali, Slik Toxik and yes, even Skid Row: take notes). To my mind, it's the dual passion of Hess' big vocals and Peter Lesperance's carving, chunky guitar that makes this about-face work, the band as a whole learning hook through their earlier sillier "Alanis before Alanis" records, now getting to apply their knowledge to real music. Applause please.

Rating 8

## Michael Harris - Ego Decimation Profile
(Leviathan '96)

Yet another highly inventive instrumental prog metalfest from niche label Leviathan, **Ego Decimation Profile** is truly one of those you wish took the next step and added vocals. For the tracks enclosed play wonderfully to Harris' stated influences such as Schenker (melodic and slightly gothic but not overwrought), Steve Morse (versatile, upbeat), and Rush (the newer, bratty instrumentals). The second solo from Harris, even though he's circled Chastain's orbit repeatedly, recording records with Leather, Arch Rival and Chastain Harris. And all get to play their toned butts off, making this as much a treat for drummers and bassists as well as drop-jaw axe aspirers.

Rating 6

## Harter Attack - Human Hell (I.R.S. Metal '90)

Three streetcleaners presumably from Jersey spew thrash versions of morality plays like a bush-league Anthrax, lots of simple, noisy degenerations into blastbeats from promising chunk intros, and that's it, game over, like a zillion other thrash comboids. Harter Attack fails to realize that speed becomes double time when played too fast, falling prey to all the additional baggage double time entails, such as paint by numbers riffery, impatient shouting, and loss of both beat and heaviness due to thrash's thinning nature.

Rating 3

## Hash - Hash (Elektra '93)

This alterna-funk campfire record apparently contains guys from even funkier, bigger-sounding juggernaut White Trash. But I'd have to say Hash is the better band, rattling their way through a close but garagey and percussive collection of fruit loopsters, perhaps like an, ahem, cigarette-smoking Camper van Beethoven. Quite trite, cute and in love with the alternative nation, Hash is nevertheless fun, fun, fun with springy, punky ideas, sent into the world really jangly, like. Goofy, actually.

Rating 6

## Hater - Hater (A&M '93)

Throw this one in the same curio bin as Brad (worst), Mad Season (better) and Temple Of The Dog (best), and Three Fish (undecided), Hater being another off-the-cuff dog-pile of Northwest luminaries, featuring bed-headed Soundgarden rhythm section Ben Shepherd and Matt Cameron plus three buds, for a half hour of mid to upper quartile garage rock, ten tracks, half an hour, one hangover right out of 1965. But these are real songs, not just sludge, open and loose-fitting but with some modicum of sock-hop hook, as vocalist Brian Wood kind of slack-jaw warbles over a simple, historically accurate Lyres/Mudhoney din. A '60s bad boy grunge perhaps slacker and gruesomely poppier than Mudhoney.

Rating 7

## Hatrik - The Beast (Roadrunner '85)

Leopard prints, eyeliner, headbands, ripped fishnet, it's all here, hanging off of another glammy, overplaying fromage metal act (home: Chicago) hoping to be the next Quiet Ratt. Yelpy vocals, drummer with ego, really, really funny looking.

Rating 2

## Haunted Garage - Possession Park (Metal Blade '91)

In a move once relegated to indie drunk punk, Haunted Garage produce a blood-soaked splatter metal feast with such carnival creep shows as *967-Kill*, *Party In The Graveyard* and *Little Green Men* (with little green tans and great big brains). It's all moderately amusing, stroking the dead somewhere between Anthrax, The Cramps, Black Flag and Gwar with messed-up lead growls from one Dukey Flyswatter. Getting-wasted-party-trash for Halloween, and not intended to be anything more. Exactly as it looks. The genre's only real success thus far: Green Jelly.

Rating 5

## Havana Black - Indian Warrior (Capitol '89)

Odd little record here. Totally like an inspired, only slightly updated version of Bad Company meets Blackfoot, yet the guys are from Finland! Thrown in are modern power elements from Thunder through Whitesnake, making this a somewhat more hard rockin' effort versus its follow-up. Firmly written songs, solid and hooky, simple and full of energy; no doubt sounding timeless due to no real attachment to any scene, plus this really does sound like all the best Bad Company singles from the mid '70s.

Rating 7

## Havana Black - Exiles In Mainstream (Hollywood '91)

Havana Black never struck me as a rock band of any sort . . . more like a book, a parade of characters like a tough love Del Lords, a band with tales to tell and an all too frustrating medium in which to tell them. The heartwarmingly acoustic *Faceless Days* opens this curious roots rock record, which features blasting honky tonk boogie, marauding blues rock, Zep-ish funk metal, and swampy acoustic ballads all wrapped in a sort of southern literary integrity, despite Scandinavian

189

roots. **Exiles In Mainstream** essentially lives up to its moniker, working in an odd, indecipherable isolation with what are very common blues-based licks, ticks and roadpops, somehow painting new shades of an old trick, walking fresh down over-trampled musical paths, glossed up just a bit through the production expertise of Eddie Kramer. Quite mentally distant from metal, but still a welcome oasis of comfortable twilight rock for the punter pining for escape into a clearer, simpler past.
Rating                                              8

**Havoc - The Grip**   (Auburn '85)
With an invitation to "Aarrgghh! . . . Blow Your Doors!", and track names like *Blazes* and *Bullets Of Blood* (think about it), this one's firmly and psychically linked to 1985 like many a poor man's metal breakfast. Singer looks like David Hasselhoff (?), but hey, at least he's got a skull t-shirt. Middle of the pack power metal, not thrash, not glam, just perched leather-clad in the Shrapnel zone.
Rating                                              5

**Hawaii - One Nation Underground**   (Shrapnel '83)
Pre-empting what could have been another sloganeering Warrior Soul record title, Hawaii also pre-empt life in general by cranking out one of the better early Shrapnel piss-ups, a record full of manic speed, blurring ideas, personable conceits and sharded steel shavings to disrupt one's blood flow through the anonymous early '80s. Hawaii had something, but gave it to a world that couldn't digest the spontaneous mania and general alcoholic genius of metal flown off the rails. Nursery band for Megadeth's Marty Friedman.
Rating                                              6

**Hawaii - Loud Wild And Heavy**   (Important '84)
Sure it's poverty metal, and granted they begat life merely a matchbox of what they are here, but Hawaii were always one of the crazier, more likeable chunks of early muscle metal. On this four track 12" it gets downright dizzy and nicely punk-like on such Anthrax-ish digs as *Bad Boys Of Metal* and the sleazy scientific title track. An uncompromising, hard-edged intoxicant.
Rating                                              7

**Hawkwind - Hawkwind**   (Liberty '70)
The baffling consortium of tangled cables that is Hawkwind metamorphosed out of the most mindblown corners of the '60s, pre-Hawks like Famous Cure, Mobile Freakout, Group X and Hawkwind Zoo finally becoming the far-out-man gathering of freaks that made this salamandered debut. But **Hawkwind** the record bears little resemblance to any of the million pointy hats the band would wear over the next truckload of records, being a true psychedelic casualty, very little in the way of loud noises, much almost unplugged noodling of an almost folky nature. Oddly enough, it ain't that bad a recording either, better than most until modern times. But this would be partially because of the relaxed unlayering of the thing, the lack of crazy guitars and/or synths. Still quite the trip though, given that few bands actually had the courage to be this weird all over their studio albums.
Rating                                              5

**Hawkwind - In Search Of Space**   (Liberty '71)
More line-up shuffles ensue as the band quietly begins to shape their tweedle-dee sound, *In Search Of Space* being widely considered one of the better Hawkwind trips, if only for the fact that it's a twisty sort of easy listening, courting pre-Pink Floyd meets chilly Nick Drake-type acoustic on such pretzels as *We Took The Wrong Step Years Ago* and *Children Of The Sun*. Del Dettmar and Dik Mik coalesce into crazy uncle electrics no matter what the main fare on plate happens to

be, sprinkling like crop dust original synth experiments (read: anything they can coax from their plugged contraptions) little blips and percolates that define Hawkwind to this day. Only *Master Of The Universe* "rocks", Hawkwind's widely veering attention span (either too long or too short), converging into an oxymoronically meekly-recorded Sabbath riff, while fifteen minute lead blow-out *You Shouldn't Do That* really crumples the fenders of this Beetle but good. As I say, somewhat digestible.
Rating                                              5

**Hawkwind - Greasy Truckers Party**   ('72)
It's a whole world, this Hawkind stuff, here the band captured white-knuckle live along with a bunch of other space cadets (mainly Brinsley Schwarz and Man), on what really isn't an official Hawkwind record, but an indie double-dose in benefit of, uh, truckers? But it's a key Hawkwind performance, offering *Born To Go* for the first time, plus one other lone track, pie-eyed proto-metal epic *Master Of The Universe*, combining for a 21 minute mind-churn unto oblivion. Recorded live at the Roundhouse, 1972, as is another similar indie live nutcase called **Glastonbury Fayre**.
Rating                                              4

**Hawkwind - Doremi Fasol Latido**   (United Artists '72)
Ladies, fish and gentlemen, here we have it, the world's only three chord progressive rock band. Hawkwind loiter absentmindedly in alternative space, churning forth like butter this slurring mess of rumbling, repetitive bong metal chords studded with nightmarish little synthesizer and acoustic asteroids; drug jams of psychedelic space junk impenetrable to the human ear. The band carved its name forever in the ship's log by playing incubator to incubus, Lemmy, who here subjects us to an early, buried alive version of *The Watcher*. This record ultimately ends its sorry life oscillating quite rigidly and shamelessly between paralyzed Sabbath and pre-**Meddle** Floyd, offering no hope for humanity in its wake. Clear goo or sludgy goo, in the boiling pots of Hawkwinds collective skulls, it's still goo.
Rating                                              3

**Hawkwind - Space Ritual**   (United Artists '73)
Only in Hawkwind's corner of the Quantum (or perhaps Venom's), can one find live records that are better recorded than studio records, which is the case with **Space Ritual** versus **Doremi**. You'd simply have to be fried to a shaking crisp to ever consider going to the two concerts that comprise this long, tortuous flood of distorted chords, feedback, and synth bleeding, a document most akin in whimpering spirit to Lou's **Metal Machine Music**. To break the droning oneness, we are sent bits of spoken poetry and an odd three minutes here and there that approach the compositional complexity of a basic rock song. But for the most part, **Space Ritual** is just a wall of brain-blistering boredom, promoting suicide by chemical ingestion, which apparently can only be avoided by careful study of the naked hippy chick on the inside cover, in conjunction with the acid-sautéed writings linking past civilizations, eastern religions, man's future, and molecular science. The cover art folds out to no less than six square feet, like some sort of roadmap to Hell. But don't mind me: **Space Ritual** is actually considered one of the band's classics. This is troubling.
Rating                                              2

**Hawkwind - Hall Of The Mountain Grill**
(United Artists '74)
Proving the band is hopelessly locked on autopilot, **Hall Of The Mountain Grill** (named for the band's favourite Notting Hill eatery) offers little to lull the senses from catatonia other than the frightening piano

melody of the title track and a filmy, mud-caked version of future Motörhead monolith *Lost Johnny*. Another trippy album cover, another ditch digger of a record, although lead epic *Psychedelic Warlords* holds promise with its unfolding daymare dreamscape. I'm not sure what comprises a Hawkwind fan, but here's hoping whatever subterranean life form he may be, stays locked in the basement with his comic books and conspiracy theories.

Rating **5**

## Hawkwind - Warrior On The Edge Of Time
(United Artists '75)

Somewhat akin to floating in a warm, salt water marsh (the Dead Sea will do), **Warrior On The Edge Of Time** finds new ways to embalm, sending forth undulating waves of synthesizer madness, but with less silly layers and evolved production. And what accompanies the somewhat pleasant Kraut-rockish mind-drift swings two ways; one, into android poetry bits courtesy Michael Moorcock (*The Wizard Blew His Horn* and *Warriors*), and two, into an increasingly creamy, eccentric Hawkwind metal (i.e. *Magnu* or *Dying Seas*). But around track eleven, everybody wakes up from their plush nod, Hawkwind turning into a type of affected and slightly deaf biker gang (400cc max) for two rumbling rockers, *Kings Of Speed* and an early wiggling wormy version of *Motorhead* (CD reissue only), stun violin solo included, Simon House considered to have tamed the band's earlier, accidentally heavy metal sound. Completely nuts, but when you get right down to it, actually a form of music. And slowly the archhippy trappings are being shed for a deeper dive into a self-consciously wide, pulpy tour of sci-fi's past, present and future, feeding judiciously off of various authors' works for the band's pretty cool, perfectly opaque lyrics.

Rating **6**

## Hawkwind - Astounding Sounds, Amazing Music
(Charisma '76)

In which some semblance of discernible instrumentation begins to rise out of the swamp, and lo and behold, the instrumentation at hand is jazzy, blasting horns, like some sort of amorphous German prog rock orchestra (perhaps a makeover in keeping with their move to Charisma, a label known for its snobby sounds). Otherwise, a song list like *Reefer Madness*, *Steppenwolf*, *City Of Lagoons*, *The Aubergine That Ate Rangoon*, *Kerb Crawler*, *Kadu Flyer*, and *Chromoglide Skyway*, I believe, captures the confused multivariate reality in which the band now operates, bestowing on our spangled hides a bank of lyrics only Blue Öyster Cult could decode. But hey, snazzy production and a surfeit of texture make this a colourburst of all things that make Hawkwind such a befuddling stack 'o fun. Calvert back in after a short absence, writing like crazy, frontmanning like crazy, singing like a crazy man.

Rating **7**

## Hawkwind - Quark Strangeness And Charm
(Sire '77)

Sifting and sorting, I'd have to recommend three Hawkwind albums above all, one being this present **Quark**, the others being Hawklords - **25 Years On** (trust me, it's a Hawkwind album) and **Space Bandits**, the rest being really fantabulous variations on logic-defied and defiled noodling, despite the way greato cover graphics. **Quark Strangeness And Charm** (the first without Nik Turner), compared to noisefests of old, is a more disciplined Floyd-ish effort that finds futuro new wave, even getting a little Pere Ubu-ish (especially with respect to the yelpy vocal delivery), and downright gleeful, as witnessed on the title toon which finally sees the band lightening up and offering hooks, for once really projecting through one of their dunce-cap

boogies. Other treats include psychotic Krishna/Egyptian-type sculptures like *Hassan I Sabha* (kingpin of a hash-eating Muslim sect) and the autobiographical *Days Of The Underground*. Eclectic but neither hysterically over-crammed with freakey styleys, nor dead like a cold fish, forged in the spirit of funky folky backwater hippies who might move out to the coolest place in the world, Nelson, B.C., as Del the keyboardist had managed.

Rating **8**

## Hawklords - 25 Years On   (Charisma '78)

And we're off on another frenzied, off-kilter trip through the medicine cabinet, courtesy this time of the *Flying Doctor* (not to be confused with *Doctor Doctor*), a rare metal cruise for Brock, Calvert and new crew. About one third of **25 Years On** (actually more than on **Quark**), is either psychedelic metal or either similarly hippy-fried hard rock. The other 2/3 is the usual display of beeps and buzzes characteristic of latter-day Hawkwind, i.e. Floydian underwater mellowisms mixed with the subtle electro-hyperness of early Gary Numan. Strangely enough, HW '77 and '78 are two of the more subdued (more like unagitated) Hawkwind efforts, yet they're quite possibly the most entertaining and most balanced. So I guess **25 Years On** is thoroughly lude-lidded, while still a drowsy voyage worth taking. The new name was to coincide with yet another personnel shuffle and a supposed new direction for the band.

Rating **7**

## Hawkwind - PXR5   (Charisma '79)

Tight and economical like **Quark**, **PXR5** was in fact recorded just after said pleasing slab, and released just after **Hawklords**. So there's no surprise in the record's compressed, punk-with-keyboards sound (especially *Death Trap*). And just to add confusion, there's malformed, transformed, transmogrified live stuff involved, making **PXR5** one of those amorphous and sticky era-bridgers for the band. End of relations with Charisma.

Rating **6**

## Hawkwind - Live Seventy Nine   (Bronze '80)

This winter gigging collection of seven tracks is adequately recorded, finding the band full-on their punk inflected mantra, pogo-progging through a bunch of very recognizable Hawkclassics, all delivered with fervent compulsive zeal to a crowd of equally compulsive fans, head-trippin' archivists of the highest order. Accessible as any Hawkwind record, from a band whose live stuff is often considered more relevant and plain real than the uneven studio excursions. The return of Huw Lloyd Langton.

Rating **6**

## Hawkwind - Levitation   (Bronze '80)

A nice three-legged Egypto-metal fuzzball opens the circus, *Levitation* (the song) being somewhat of a bright Hawk moment, **Levitation** (the album) actually the return of good sound, even though key member Calvert was again cast into space. Probably my favorite Hawk instrumental in *World Of Tiers*, propped by a nice Ginger Baker (!) hep hop (even if the track cops part of *Oh Well*). And then *Space Chase* isn't so bad for a bit of almost chopsy prog filler. Problem is the filler's better than the songs, most of which stumble forward in a fog of tin foil hat schiz fits. More line-up shuffles and more way greato cover art. Pretty together, man.

Rating **6**

## Hawkwind - Sonic Attack   (RCA '81)

It's all academic at this point. Another metallic album graphic, more psychedelic synth jams and paranoid mumblings (Moorcock's back after a six year silence),

amidst four menacing heavy rockers in *Angel Of Death, Streets of Fear, Disintegration,* and *Rocky Paths,* the latter of which represents the band's finest moment, a complex melodic, confident metal scorcher that demonstrates how all the cybernetic trappings and electronic chaos can be used to comparative advantage if applied. Even though there exist a good six, fairly disciplined song structures, the proceedings too often lapse into Pere Ubu-ish skronk and baffling extended "breaks", causing blurred vision and aural fatigue. One of the heavier, more mainstream, and believe it or not, almost enjoyable Hawkwind voyages. A low-flying **7**.
Rating　　　　　　　　　　　　　　　　　　　**7**

## Hawkwind · Church Of Hawkwind　(RCA '82)
Long considered one of the more baffling, love it/hate it, Hawk pieces of the errant '80s, **Church** reverts to the optic fishbowl after the quasi-metalness of **Levitation** and **Sonic Attack** (the latter suspiciously soaking up the good habits of the surrounding and stifling NWOBHM). Loads of electronic bleeps and creeps cut a terrain that is seriously back to the soggy womb circa '72, all mashed to a milky pulp by three dozen or so of the band's worst recording tips and tricks. Bizarre lane change into derange; extremely unhinged, ancient and unmusical, but a cogent escape all the same. Three bonus tracks on the Griffin reissue, sounding very much like the Brock solo album this was meant to be.
Rating　　　　　　　　　　　　　　　　　　　**5**

## Hawkwind · Choose Your Masques　(RCA '82)
And it's back to a happy, humpy glassy-eyed medium, the band making one of those defining Hawkwind records for better or worse, perhaps personified by yet another fairly lucid version of the band's one hit *Silver Machine*. So in what can be construed as typical fashion, **Choose Your Masques** gets a pretty good recording, between cyborgotron mantras to old synth ideas, offering old pick-up truck punk numbers like *Farenheit 451* (a Ray Bradbury book) and the overlordic and metallic *Waiting For Tomorrow,* both somehow evoking the hands-on-the-wheel lockstep of old Quo, despite the Hawks' blasted philosophical dishevelment. Lots of loud everythings and quiet vacancies, Hawkwind making sure the listener is always on edge, ready for robed and spangled alien abduction. Close to what can be called an all-star Hawkwind line-up, if you include the "guests," one being Nik Turner, back after a six-year floatation.
Rating　　　　　　　　　　　　　　　　　　　**6**

## Hawkwind · Zones　(Flicknife '83)
Not the kind of zone Hawkwind could afford to enter, the mid-'80s were a bit of a creative and commercial wasteland for the band, this first for indie Flicknife being a chaotic mix of old live chestnuts and droopy new tunes. All mind-melds into a sort of somber, lukewarm like bathwater hasty assemblage, even the cover art failing the band's usual high standards. Too creepy and German sounding; and the guitars have all but been caged, tamed and starved of their aggression, buried under a tangle of wires and fuzzy motivations.
Rating　　　　　　　　　　　　　　　　　　　**4**

## Hawkwind · This Is Hawkwind Do Not Panic
(Flicknife '84)
Finally a live set that culls and captures the band's mercury-poisoned metal in one place, one recording, one tightly defined set of arrangements. Which, me being an impatient metalhead, is heady heaven indeed, **This Is Hawkwind** (the tag **Stonehenge** also being added to the title, sometimes at front, sometimes at back), giving us almost prog-smart live renditions of *Psy Power* (honky tonk!), *Levitation, Circles* and *Angels Of Death* (kind of a skiffle-Sabbath version), among other well-dressed, forward-moving bongwaters, perhaps

climaxing with the almost hummable zip metal of *Shot Down In The Night.* Original vinyl version was gatefold, comprising a full-length record with a 12" EP, tapping into transmissions from '80 and '84. Interstellar proof that with these freaks, waiting for an agreeable live version can be jolly fun indeed.
Rating　　　　　　　　　　　　　　　　　　　**8**

## Hawkwind · The Chronicle Of The Black Sword
(Flicknife '85)
Snapped back onto track, Hawkwind piece together this unashamed concept album, entirely based on Michael Moorcock's Elric stories, Elric of Melnibone being a recurring character who gains power from an enchanted black sword (BÖC's *Black Blade* is a Moorcock lyric with the same theme). The record oscillates with typical Hawklogic from plaintive unglued melodic metal (bordering on lazy punk) to soft keyboard pieces to spoken hocus pocus. And even though the production is a bit compressed, both bass and treble disconcertingly absent, the band keeps it together with their surprisingly accessible music (see the almost happy time *Needle Gun*). CD reissue contains three bonus tracks. You gotta hand it to this band. Whether they planned it or not, they've kind of weathered or muddled in or transformed pretty well every rock'n'roll genre through time, building a psychedelic base from which to make rape-and-plunder trips into metal, punk, progressive, world, jazz, folk, spoken word . . . you name it, they've been there, dropped a tab and dabbled. Whether they have a clue what they're doing is another question.
Rating　　　　　　　　　　　　　　　　　　　**6**

## Hawkwind · Live Chronicles　(GWR '86)
Almost a complete Hawkwind show, **Live Chronicles** splices and dices the whole **Chronicle Of The Black Sword** tale with a bunch of Hawkwind classics plus new stuff in no logical fashion, forcing the listener to cop to Brock's multi-tiered reality, Moorcock also added for creepy colour commentary. Hawk expert Rob Godwin surmises that this record might surpass **Space Ritual** as the band's best live record. Whatever your opinion, it is certainly one of the most expansive and expensive, the band full-on prog detailed, giving up a show that really reinforces how much Spinal Tapped work all this lunacy is (although I find the recording here a bit lackadaisical and muddy, lessening the power of the weighty numbers). Griffin reissue includes full lyrics plus a 48 page booklet containing **The Dreaming City**, the Elric piece that is key to Hawkwind's version of the story.
Rating　　　　　　　　　　　　　　　　　　　**7**

## Hawkwind · Out & Intake　(Flicknife '87)
An apt title for this scooped collection of space junk, featuring new beeps and blurps, some live moshing, some reinvention (*Hassan I Sahba* transmogrified!) and a gaggling vortex of Hawk personnel hitting, wailing and blowing an assortment of sounds that would never make it market if not for the critical mass that has landed before. One of those black holes (dumpsters) from which the damaged and escapist alike can feed when the more cohesive records begin to make too much rational sense.
Rating　　　　　　　　　　　　　　　　　　　**6**

## Hawkwind · The Xenon Codex　(GWR '88)
More hippy math from our favourite progressive band who forgot to learn how to play, **The Xenon Codex** fades so deeply into drug-induced psi-fi coma to the point where the starship Hawkwind essentially no longer belongs in our hallowed anthology of pain. The band's chemically pickled guitars are all but banished to the swirling poisonous gases of Saturn, as layers of bent keyboards, synths, and voice boxes attack de-

fenseless, unwilling ears like a hail of gamma rays, proving that the '60s are forever. And this from the first full-fledged studio attempt in three years. A harsh, cold jumble.

Rating     4

## Hawkwind - Space Bandits   (GWR '90)

Vital in its Hawkwindedness, **Space Bandits** kicks off with a melodic eight-minute hard rocker called *Images*, which implodes a couple minutes in for a trip to La La Land, triumphantly returning to its mousy 4/4 electroglide for a spirited send-off. All in all an excellent display of Hawkwind's many angled angels, including one new one here in the band's first female vocalist, ex-Hippy Slags singer Bridgett Wishart. From here-on in, the record's a swoopy, dart-eyed schizoid affair, reflecting the hypno-swell of the rave culture gaining ground in Britain at the time. So we get spoken word, lots of jungle warfare between bits and bytes, heck, even one more jammy power chord oscillation come *Out Of The Shadows*, a consistent rocker that brings the band out of the primordial trance muck, only to slide oozily back under, never to recover. Almost feels like an EP, which is a good thing, boding well for the record's pacing. Stand-out track for most fans: *Black Elk Speaks*, which is a spoken word sculpture featuring anthropologist John Neihardt reading from his book of the same name, the testimony of Black Elk, one of the survivors of the Wounded Knee massacre. Also of note: **Space Bandits** featured the band's ninth drummer in Richard Chadwick, who performs the same meek function as all who came before.

Rating     7

## Hawkwind - Palace Springs   (GWR '91)

Yet another live record, this one recorded at the Hollywood Palace then I suspect totally tinkered, proving that live versus studio is a seamless continuum for this band, both used to full (lazy?) effect in quiltworking a musical experience that can be ironic miles of rehash and resucitation. Which brings us to continuum #2: the fact that the included versions of mouldy oldies here are so twisted and redressed, proving that a written song for the Hawks is never a finished piece of ear candy. Players and layers will forever conspire to blotter new blobs of quirks and quarks, which will cause most people to throw their hands up in anguish and defeat, all but a few failing to unravel the root system of songs, let alone the family tree of folks. Slot me with the baffled bunch. Both Bainbridge and Wishart evaporate from the Hawkwind dogdish after this tour.

Rating     6

## Hawkwind - Electric Tepee   (Essential/Castle '92)

Even though the band is down to a three piece, comprising Dave Brock, Alan Davey and Richard Chadwick, **Electric Tepee** is an extensive but focused piece of work, driving at the crux of this band's '70s psychedelic sound, quite close to a Pink Floyd record, even recorded quite capably at Dave's home studio. At this point Hawkwind has owned the franchise on this sort of unhewn space rock for years now, and Brock is sounding more like the reigning king of Anglo eccentricity ever day, almost crossing into Julian Cope's dreamworld, the two combining for a body of work that dares to explore challenging realms, dim mental faculties notwithstanding. So **Electric Tepee** races its ship with pride and an arguably stupid lack of fear, lots of synth-textured space music, collapsed into jams (battles?), just a whole lotta fun for those wishing to fly, most tracks clomping by with an authoritative gallop that belies a knowledge of the fantastical worlds ahead. The first "mature", self-actualized Hawkwind record.

Rating     8

## Hawkwind - It Is The Business Of The Future To Be Dangerous   (Griffin '94)

Clearly farther off their rockers than previously imagined, Hawkwind-as-trio is back for another of their confounding loitered messes, this time the instrumentals taking centre stage. So we get fairly hi-fi hijinx like the spooky and smart title track, and *Space Is (Their Palestine)* showing up weirdo floundered vocals toons like *Letting In The Past*, a bizarre Stranglers-infected reggae called *The Camera That Couldn't Lie* and a drowned synthesized version of the Stones' *Gimme Shelter*. They should have left the whole thing instrumental, given the welcome levels of accomplishment mustered, managing a trippy new age feel that could rub shoulders with the snobbiest of Enos and Gabriels. Could have been a cool soundtrack album.

Rating     5

## Hawkwind - The Business Trip   (Griffin '94)

On Hawkwind's 78th live record, our favourite time-trampling "trio" (yeah, right) wade through a bunch of their more eccentric, non-anthemic stone tunes, all recorded with as much attention as any studio spread, probably because they have no idea if and when new writing might take place. Cutest li'l dittie is the easy listening version of *Quark Strangeness And Charm*. Fifteen tracks of dissipating electronic rock that can't hide the fact that these guys somewhere along the line, learned to play their instruments, something which a quarter decade in the biz will eventually bring about.

Rating     5

## Hawkwind - 25 Years On   (Griffin '95)

Hapless space travelers Hawkwind probably have the most complicated, incestuous re-hashed catalogue on Neptune, given all the legal hijinks that has marked their long bong, utterly ludicrous career. So it's nice to see something like this that really works at making sense of the band's labyrinthical discography. **25 Years On** is an amazing box set, more than an introduction to the band, more like a roadmap with a start and a destination, pretty much all you might need from these frustrating noisemakers. Here's the goods: five hours over four CDs laid out chronologically, with the lyrics to all included tracks, plus excellent reference notes as to which songs showed up on which album officially (that's a loaded word with this band), including a photo of each album cover. Then there's liner notes by Michael Moorcock and a couple of pretty cheesy comic books. Add six previously unreleased tracks and a bunch of new artwork, and this is one set that goes further. Oh and the music? Quite pleasurable in a twisted Hawkwind sort of way, selecting more bright, relatively commercial tracks that leave out all that excrutiating ambient jamming and punk chaos nonsense (blanga) that plague the catalogue like a virus. And of course there's vintage Lemmy. So like, fire up the furnace and let's generate some sweet smoke.

Rating     8

## Hawkwind - Alien 4   (The Emergency Broadcast System '96)

Hard to believe, but Hawkwind press on, dishing out buckets of the same brisk textured metal separated, lift and tuck by an avalanche of psycho sounds and mad man rantings. Breaking it down, **Alien 4**'s fourteen tracks work thusly: six jammy metal things of virtually the same speed (fave being the punk, almost awake, sinister and unwasteful *Death Trap*), and only one other kitchen sink fried egg that might be construed as a "song" (*Beam Me Up*), all interwoven with seven laborious, usually interesting mostly instrumental pieces, really druggy, ravey, and unsettling. Quite amazing really, that there can be so much similarity with a dozen other Hawkdiscs, and glad all over for it really, there being nobody else able to create this perfect mix of serious, bumbling, mysterious and larfable all at once, this world of elusive frivolity, this guilty escape into wishful unreality, this much crap and have us all back for more!

Rating 8

## Haywire - Private Hell (New Beginning Est. '88)

California whiplash punk that consumes with a healthy monotone and curdling shouts from lead vox "Billy", **Private Hell** has a kind of cool, powerfully fused recording with simple, boring loudfastsongs, including a cover of Motörhead's *Bomber*. Dil, useless frash with the usual amusing "outsider-lookin'-in" lyrics which are still in no way substitute for a halfways serious approach to life and the making of records. Not to be confused with the considerably more polite east coast Canadian band.

Rating 3

## Hazzard - Hazzard (Mausoleum '84)

Accept's Herman Frank offers somewhat of a solo venture here, an eminently professional HR/HM display; muscular, well-executed, not particularly territorial, and potentially bank-breakable compared to much other mid-'80s trop. Rockers like *Moonlight*, melodic singalongs *Nothing At All*, *We Are The Band* and *Tonight* plus the speedy, swashbuckling *Satisfied* lead the charge into metalhead heaven, sorta like early 220V or suitably, Accept. A perfect mix of hard-edged party destruction, heroic metal and doom 'n' gloom for the time, **Hazzard** wears well, suffering only from occasional flat vocals and forgotten isolation in recorded history, to no fault of the band. But truth be known, this is respectable, classy stuff, even as it fades into the woodwork with the passing years.

Rating 7

## Headcleaner - Head Of The Next One (Big Deal '94)

Apparently making an appreciable level of squawky noise in the U.K., Headcleaner occupy a slightly acidic left-of-centre roost between Wool, Nirvana and Helmet, with a sort of collapsed mix that is a bit scratchy and sickly, the perfect translator for the band's jazzy rhythmic punk twang. A butt-ugly sort of ballet between word, deed and visage, the band definitely has that subversive, dangerous aura about its stubbly presence. More ornery than metal, which may be its shortcoming, the record sounding like drugs and rain and mistakes and scumbags.

Rating 6

## Headlock - It Found Me (Hypnotic/Pavement '94)

Heavy, dense and rhythmic much like Biohazard, Headlock are making de rigeur sounds, while grinding me down with all that shouty, quick change perfection slamming. Here's where it gets mundane journalizing a metal band: the record is as good as anything in punishing, urban-assault metal, and if that's your thing, you should buy this. I mean, few band's make objectively poor product these days, Headlock being no exception, but I'm just not going to play this all that much. **It Found Me** maybe just found me overloaded, saddled and burdened with too many berating metal experiences.

Rating 7

## Heads Or Tails - Eternity Becomes A Lie (Black Mark '95)

Hot on the heels of critically successful Black Mark bands like Tad Morose and Morgana Lefay comes this staccato prog fest, all craggy metal peaks and no valleys, fairly highly strung from start to finish, in a Rush or Dream Theater (or Fates Warning or Cynic blah blah blah) sort of way. Robert Forse's vocals take a middle ground, no low gutturals here and very little high wailing, as his band courts all the tricky time

signatures in the book of snob. But it's fast becoming a genre filled to the brim, all that machine gun precision going to waste on a metal public becoming too accustomed to brilliant chops. But still, it's these records that will retain their staying power, the listener not likely to soak it all in after just a few plays. And it's musical enough that it's worth repeated visits.

Rating 7

## Heathen - Breaking The Silence (Combat '87)

Hard to get a line on these Ronnie Montrose-produced thunderheads, churning a backbreaker of a release combining well-mixed pedestrian thrash with hints of Grave Digger-style clang factor. Professional, speedy death metal, **Breaking The Silence** is yer basic controlled mosh, lyrically naff, vocally fine, but uncomfortably mired in an early '80s metal mentality, machine-gunning over a rumbling race to the finish; zero variation, and that includes Sweet's *Set Me Free*, that sits sandwiched into this OTT blur practically unnoticed. Unimaginative, but well done for mallethead metal.

Rating 5

## Heaven - Bent (CBS '82)

Seems like every band of scuzzies from down under pined to be the next AC/DC (appropriately Heaven includes the band's old bassist Mark Evans); understandable in a land with few metallic role models. Heaven follows this same simple bang-thy-head, cranking out road mechanic renditions of the famous Aussie backbeat, sounding admirably grimy, lowbrow, and amateurish, much like early Krokus, yet with less deviation from the norm and more consistent crunch, making this a pretty solid and relaxed plod if an uneventful one, with a weighty mix and feeling vocals. Kinda the third diminishing wave after the reign of wave II, Angel City.

Rating 6

## Heaven - Where Angels Fear To Tread (CBS '83)

The dirt merchants with little to say but an entertaining way to churn it are back wielding more inter-cut dynamics, causing sad mediumrock on half of this, countered with equal amounts of their most ambitious whipsaws thus far on the other half, most notably the major slammin' title track, the e-z cruising *You*, and high-tensile riff-romper *Sleeping Dogs*. Again, nothing to rewrite the books here, merely pre-commercialism barroom metal, simplistic and cohesive with real grit, an unfinished sound that would have been brushed aside in the business-like environment of today's metal. Token backing vocals by Glenn Hughes and Lita Ford.

Rating 6

## Heaven - Knockin' On Heaven's Door (CBS '85)

Here the boys somehow exceed our low expectations, self-creating a sound not entirely their own, but perfectly mongrelized for their crusted veins, an unadorned, up-front AC/DC blast, more like mature, mid-years Krokus; a combination of **Headhunter**'s somewhat intricate metal and **One Vice At A Time**'s blunted wall. All rings proud to be stupid on this, making for a fat and rolling headbang, cool metallic characters like *Last Laugh*, *Burn*, and *Show On The Road* butted-up against successful melloid fare like *Keep The Fire* and ho-hum centerpiece, Dylan's *Knockin' On Heaven's Door*. Above all the clanking and used motor oil, this record works a dumb charm, providing one of which are actually few, old-days alternatives to AC/DC.

Rating 7

## Heaven's Cry - Food For Thought Substitute (Hypnotic '97)

First thing that hits you about this quite stunning progressive metal feast from Montreal is the highly interesting album cover, graphics and type combining to signal that this is not average fare. And once inside, expectations are exceeded, Heaven's Cry finding the golden mean between chaotic crunch and art rock wizardry, shooting up the east side of town while erecting cathedrals in the west. One thinks Nevermore or Iced Earth here, rather than the silkiness of Queensryche or Fates Warning, Heaven's Cry buzzing with activity and aggression, while urgent, painterly vocals espouse hope and good will, something rare in metal lyrics these days. Truly and wholeheartedly recommended for those who lament the de-clawing of Rush.

Rating 8

## Heavenwood - Diva (Massacre '96)

Following in the wake of Moonspell's modest success, Portugal's Heavenwood carve a similarly enigmatic melodic death, Diva taking the listener on a trip into foreboding darkness, painful melodies and frequent grooves similar to recent Cemetary and peak-performance Paradise Lost. Layers work as one, velvet and steel merge, and the knowledgeable doomster comes away satisfied. A tantalizing debut.

Rating 8

## Heavy Load - Metal Conquest (Thunderload '81)

Load fried my brain in the psyche-bruising daze of metal's early '80s resurgence, wielding the cast-iron frying pan that was '82's Death Or Glory. These power-crazed Swedes were so stupefyingly OTT in terms of emotional backbone, one marveled at their ridiculous band photos in a haze, wondering from whence the mighty Load's twisted and clandestine hatred emerged. Metal Conquest is the earliest quizzling we've been privileged to plunder, having never heard nor seen the elusive debut Full Speed At High Level. This meter-melting five track descendence from the shredded tundra lifts splinters of bone from Sabbath and the most forbidden corners of old Priest in creation of a proudly Scandinavian killing machine, a total mess of tangled buzzing nerves; resigned to failure, steeped and drowned in metallic depression; downright system-threatening in its throaty, bottom-ruled 45 RPM mix. Most cascaded with medieval torture: You've Got The Power and the underestimatedly-titled Hey. A tragic, sub-freezing sea of sorrow.

Rating 9

## Heavy Load - Death Or Glory (Thunderload '82)

Pints to Metal Gord in Victoria for letting me tape this massive classic of tundra metal, a record so hilariously Manowar, I had visions of Beowulf trashing the mead house 'n snapping soldiers in half for years after its inebriated buzz froze my circuitry. Well I eventually bought it, being none to easy to find, and the Great White Fire God now rules the "H"'s in my library along side Highway Chile's Storybook Heroes. Tale after Load tale simply waste the place, sent above the clouds by soaring vocals and incredible dueling axework, backed by a rhythm section that threatens to collapse at every gut-wrenching turn, speeding up, laying back, everything you're not supposed to do. Built on total Euro riffs and unstoppable grooves, Death Or Glory is all melody and might, sterling metallic to an alloy forged of the darkest, most isolated metal mentality (again see the delusions of Manowar). Faves include kick off cut Heavy Metal Angels, the echoey, secluded Traveller, and Daybreak Ecstacy, demented genius in full riff-torn battle, and the heaviest of Load poisons. Rock out, dudes. The blizzard of ice await.

Rating 10

## Heavy Load - Stronger Than Evil (Thunderload '83)

Sadly, Stronger Than Evil loses the conciseness of the band's classic predecessor, stretching out into ponderous, open structure Valhalla metal with a strange looseness found both in the playing and mix, not to mention Wahlquist's distinctive vocals. Things sound a bit sloppy overall, as witnessed on the clattery Singing Swords, although anthem Free is one of the band's stronger moments ever, propelled by smooth crescendos come chorus time. Uneven and choppy, Stronger Than Evil logically fits somewherz before Metal Conquest, with its fragile, almost amateur deliveries, while showing flashes of complexity that point to a brighter future. Still a totally subversive (and submersive) Scandinavian rock experience that behooves bloodshed on a northern storyteller's night.

Rating 8

## Heavy Pettin' - Heavy Pettin' (PolyGram '83)

Highly touted as the next Def Leppard, Britain's Heavy Pottin' were an ass-kickin', pretty boy entry to the American hard rock fray, landing somewhere between On Through The Night and High 'n' Dry, all dueling axes, big grooves, gargantuan luv songs and overblown tramp vocals from our man Hamie. And on this debut (which came out with various song lists, cover arts, titles, etc.), it all works a well-oiled magic, injecting a loose, irreverent and urgent heavy metal-ness that the Leps never had. Choruses usually build to soaring harmony, as on In And Out Of Love, Love On The Run and Devil In Her Eyes, and the whole palace ball sustains that feel of better-than-average anthemic, basically top of a second string heap, relegated there-so by the band's obvious derivation. Most importantly, it holds up a decade later, due to its missionary zeal for world domination.

Rating 8

## Heavy Pettin' - Rock Ain't Dead (PolyGram '85)

What happens here mirrors Highway Chile's fate, both bands casting aspersions towards a Pyromania-like tech drum-driven plod, cutting the groove out from under what were once energetic, vibrant song types. Rock Ain't Dead has Heavy Pettin' barely breathing as it slogs through one anti-climactic dirge to the next, heavy lids opening only for decent harmony-driven choruses (see China Boy and Heart Attack) and the occasional muscle riff (see Northwinds). And Hamie sounds nasal to the point of distraction, sabotaging any commercial appeal this record may have attracted through random luck. Thoroughly and single-handedly wrecked by the drum sound, which in turn handcuffs and ossifies the songwriting, Rock Ain't Dead is a sorry decision clouded by the success of Mutt Lange's ground-breaking torch job on Pyromania. Follow-up Big Bang wasn't even heavy.

Rating 6

## Hecate Enthroned - Upon Promeathean Shores (Blackend/IRS '96)

Forged in the Cradle Of Filth and all things raccoon-faced in Norwegian flame, England's Hecate Enthroned perform the usual crank call vocal assaults over a mix of keyboard-toned blastbeats and beyond. But their mix is almost pleasant, like old Motörhead or Venom, kinda sludgy and uncaustic. Songs? Can't really say there are any . . . just a bunch of curmudgeoned belching over atonal death prog scampers that illogically fly, fry and die. But as usual, the English are improving on Norse black coffee through texture, respite, hue and a deep (almost buried) sense of the theatrical. Hence, Cradle Of Filth's relative success.

Rating 6

## Heist - High Heel Heaven   (I.R.S. '89)

If I can make it in Hollyrock, I can make it anywhere! So here swaggers the 4H club, ready to Ratt it up, sleaze it down, oh spare me the details. OK the beers are flowing, but as I slog through all these self-serious jarring grindcore records, I can't help but think irresponsible fun (and cowboy boots) just might return to the fold one day. Don't expect these guys to be there however. Maybe Arcade or Van Halen, but Heist? . . . no. Ronnie Montrose on two tracks.

Rating                                                        5

## Helix - Breaking Loose   (H&S '79)

Another band born in a time when metal was still partially an accidental revelation by and for the few, Helix were isolated Canadian boys, lost to say the least, looking much rougher than the recorded output that would stand as their calling card. **Breaking Loose** is an up and down, confusing road map through various loosely r'n'r styles, sampling hard rock, pop metal, hippy rock, country, barroom boogie and balladeering. Descending piping hot from no more distant than the heavens, however, comes a truly breathtaking tour de force in Billy Oxygen, an imposing and mesmerizing brew of hard rock, heavy metal, exacting chops, limitless funk, progressive mobility and, yes, humour all wrapped up in one surprisingly concise piece of brilliantly out-of-character songcraft. Really, one album that is worth it for one lone, stuffed-full track. **Breaking Loose** as an entirety however, is a Helix before commercial pressures or cliché, but unfortunately for most of its stunned wanderings, also a Helix before merit or purpose.

Rating                                                        4

## Helix - White Lace & Black Leather   (H&S '81)

More of the same pre-identity shotgunning that says little about direction, although a notch up in vitality. Another thoroughly cool cut with Breaking Loose, which like the other-worldly Billy Oxygen, displays major groove. Otherwise, mostly mellow and ass-backwoods countrified hard rock.

Rating                                                        3

## Helix - No Rest For The Wicked   (Capitol '83)

Helix takes their giant leap into the real world with this, their first party metal rocker, a lacklustre but enthusiastic attempt at an American sound, with that unavoidable feel of Canadian isolation from trends or competitive pressures. Really basic, sparse, and downwritten to the young ones, **No Rest For The Wicked** nevertheless hits the bottle on such candy years Twisted Sister-style anthems as slight hit Heavy Metal Love, driver Dirty Dog and big beat hard rocker Let's All Do It Tonight. Possesses the spirit of Helix's best, **Wild In The Streets**, but not the flash and domineering attitude, containing too many predictable riffs and celebrations/demonstrations of stupidity. In fact most of it wouldn't make it as filler these days. Basically a band waiting to happen, learning a new genre while making records we're presumably expected to buy.

Rating                                                        5

## Helix - Walkin' The Razor's Edge   (Capitol '84)

Not nearly the manic whomp dealt firmly with backhand on **Wild In The Streets**, Walkin' The Razor's Edge nevertheless slaughters its unsure predecessor and its philosophically stunned follow-up. The first fully hopped-up muscle car from a band with a hot urge to rhythmically beef up the commercial side of Priest, Helix's fourth swaggers deep but firmly lite-hearted, offering nary an inkling of cerebral aspersions amidst its teen-gone-off-the-rocker mayhem. Spikiest of the brew would be flat-head rocker When The Hammer Falls, warmly chuggin' tour fuel You Keep Me Rockin', and richter scale grinder Six Strings, Nine Lives.

Throughout the kitchen party, optimism reigns supreme, as all negative emotional baggage gets chucked for a night of dumbshit headbanging. Again, you either buy into it or you don't. And for me, Vollmer and his crew of road rats are the band of choice time and again when I ain't taking my obsession too seriously.

Rating                                                        7

## Helix - Live At The Marquee   (Capitol '85)

This rare and rarely seen indie-looking six track live EP celebrates what sounds like a characteristically cookin' British gig for the good-time veterans known as Helix. In robust thrust and reply fashion, the band converts into touchdowns five tunes from their current **Walkin' The Razor's Edge** partyfest, plus live staple Heavy Metal Love. The sound is muscular and very live. Grab a brew. Everybody wins.

Rating                                                        7

## Helix - Long Way To Heaven   (Capitol '85)

The simplest and most by-the-book attempt at teen dreem hard rock to blemish the band's catalogue, **Long Way To Heaven** reads like a dictionary to all that is cliché with rock'n'roll, one of those records that was obviously made under pressure from the suits or possibly a set of impatient rock wives. Just plods lifelessly to the metronomic deep-treated snare beneath fat anthemic choruses, much to the absolute disposal of the band's already questionable integrity. I seem to remember talk of creeping religious influences on the band surrounding this album, but I may be mistaken.

Rating                                                        3

## Helix - Wild In The Streets   (Capitol '87)

Hell-bent on a mission to re-create the highly credible **Walkin' The Razor's Edge**, Helix walks in with a brash collection of inebriation rock, fully filled to the brim with the elixir of positive rowdiness. All roars with self-assured power on this sustained chunk of party metal, celebrations such as Never Gonna Stop The Rock, High Voltage Kids, and Shot Full Of Love cruising with caffeinated alcohol consumption. Not intent on changing the world, Helix gets down to what they do best, littering their brand of simplistic retro hard rock with welcome but worn-out '70s moves and newer nimble embellishments, lending the record that touch of veteran wisdom necessary to convince the listener that this is the deep woods bonfire to be at tonight. Even the balladry is bold and corny, as witnessed with the clod-oid Dream On. Ya gotta like the band to buy into this basically unambitious genre with any conviction, and Helix fits the bill as rock dogs from the fringes of acceptability, who've kept their heads in their beers despite the long haul.

Rating                                                        8

## Helix - Over 60 Minutes With . . .   (Est. '89)

This 21 cut, 72:12 career retro is essentially a thorough "best of" from the band's first three Capitol releases, while including three previously unreleased chompers, with Give It To You eventually winding up on **Back For Another Taste**. Of the remaining two, we get Jaws Of The Tiger, a characteristic Helix rocker, stripped, speedy and AC/DC-tilted, with an anti-climactic melodi-chorus, and Everybody Pays The Price, another metal moment, this time reminiscent of slow, pounding Kiss. Both demonstrate Helix's drive and enthusiasm for dressing up the commonplace 'til it works.

Rating                                                        7

## Helix - Back For Another Taste   (Capitol '90)

Helix's first of the '90s kicks off with a serious snapper demonstrating that Volmer's crew is dead set on slurping the decade as contenders, armed with an updated edge, big on drums and exuberance, (although the band in retrospect was not happy with the production).

For the most part, **Back For Another Taste** is up to the challenge, brewing a large and looming display of low IQ party favours reminiscent of the stirring **Walkin' The Razor's Edge**, yet newly adorned with a '90s mix and adherence to space and riffic economy. Most effective tracks include aforementioned kick-off *The Storm*, the driving *Heavy Metal Cowboys*, and the gnarly retro-Helix title track, punctuated by that trustworthy leonine Vollmer roar. After the smoke clears, what remains is a solid Helix record large on largesse, yet not without middling commercial filler. Fortunately this is a band for which I've always had a soft spot, having been won over by the smokin', high energy, Priest-like live extravaganza. Despite a fairly large percentage of substandard material, Helix remains an unpretentious, ambitious, and viable purveyor of all that parties. Sadly, **Back For Another Taste** would be the last for guitarist Paul Hackman, who in '92 was killed in a car crash while returning from tourdates in B.C. Big changes planned way ahead of time for the next record.
Rating                                                    7

## Helix - It's A Business Doing Pleasure   (Aquarius '93)
After a short break to get their heads together, Helix re-emerge with their most pop-oriented, solidly commercial-friendly record to date, a richly-produced effort that finds the band forsaking their metal edge for a round of ballad-like tales, roots rockers, acoustic-based hard rockers and every smooth and likeable posture in between; basically perky campfire songs. Featuring a few notable Canadian guest performances, and a heartfelt farewell to Paul Hackman, **It's A Business Doing Pleasure** can't be faulted for its gravity and courage to remake the band. But I don't know . . . it's not like this is my cup of tea, being something quite close to Bon Jovi (or modern Cinderella/Poison) in most places; traditional light hard rock; guitar, bass and drums wrapped around simple general and generic rock structures, with only *Sleepin' In The Dog House Again* sounding anything like romps of old. Well-assembled and sincere, but a little too relaxed and conservative for my liking.
Rating                                                    6

## Hellanbach - Now Hear This   (Neat '84)
A cheap and rickety approach to the vinyl excursion scars this larger-than-their-minds outfit of American wannabes. The Van Halen comparisons came out in droves, yet it's hard to fathom, given the immense and plentiful layers of talent between the real Big H and this mouse-like band of boastful British rogues. Still, gotta give 'em credit for raising ire. If they weren't worth getting upset over, then it wouldn't happen. Fact is, these guys have ideas, and fact is, we'd really never get to hear them fully matured.
Rating                                                    4

## Hellanbach - The Big H   (Neat '84)
Slightly interesting early U.K. product that always seemed to inspire hefty praise or equally intense ridicule at the time. The press considered Hellanbach some sort of Van Halen rip-off for no good reason I can ascertain, except perhaps the big talk at the mike and traces of Eddie-like picking. Believe it or not, given a massively beefed recording, this might have been a pretty cool disc, sporting some fluid axe-driven melodic HR. But alas, the mix is dreadfully scuzzy and thin, rendering the overall experience more like hemorrhoids. Contains a punky, no-results cover of Elton John hit *Saturday Night*.
Rating                                                    5

## Hellhammer - Apocalyptic Raids   (Banzai '82)
The blistering, raw, ragingly awful on puerile purpose precursor to the considerably more musical Celtic Frost, Hellhammer were the definition of extreme, quickly garnering luv 'em hate 'em reviews the likes of which music had never seen. And this rudimentary mental EP is the lone official anti-art artifact (save for three demos), Warrior and his Baphometamine bastards quickly realizing that there was little left to say, given the harsh one-trick vocabulary of the band's far-flung Satani-thrash. The original seed of sonic sedition tucked into those sunken Norse noggins.
Rating                                                    1

## Helloween - Helloween   (Banzai '85)
Commanding instant respect with this debut five track EP, Helloween was well on their way to a successful career, which to this day hasn't carried over to North American markets. Right off the bat, we're experiencing a coked-up, ravished version of Iron Maiden, an already tight speed metal force with a cold commitment to Valhalla metal; frost-bitten goth science, sprayed with machine-gun axe flurries and double bass drum intensity. Only shortcoming here is an inconsistent albeit acrobatic vocal performance from key pumpkin Kai Hansen, who will show noticeable improvement come **Walls Of Jericho**. Fave: *Warrior*.
Rating                                                    6

## Helloween - Walls Of Jericho   (Banzai '85)
Like piranhas in a feeding frenzy, *Ride The Sky* opens Helloween's first full-length record with merciless speed and even greater surgeon's precision, in demonstration of a band on a mission to be the proudly European version of the heaviest band in metal. One mountain of vibrating riffs later, ears are left buzzing at the flurry of activity that's transpired. Favourite face-melts however, are the less moshables like the awesome *Phantoms Of Death*, which rides an ever-intensifying mid-pace groove, and *Gorgar*, yer basic thumping monster tune. Much of the rest is quintessential Pumpkin pie, all sorta samey, albeit super-humanly speed-shifted.
Rating                                                    7

## Helloween - Keeper Of The Seven Keys Part I
(Noise '87)
With the addition of Michael Kiske on impossible vocals, Helloween crank it up a notch, eliminating the previously tentative delivery in the vocal department, Kiske easily hitting any and every note necessary to match the sonic swarm from chief songsmiths Hansen, Weikath and the rest of the band. And indeed Kiske's own inspiring *A Little Time* is one of the highlights of this perfectly executed mass of techno metal circuitry. **Seven Keys Part I** expands the Helloween hyperspace, mixing in more mid-pace chug and loud/quiet dynamic, to almost progressive metal levels while all remains razor-sharp and glory-bound. An axe ballet to the molten core, all comes to a head with *Halloween*, clocking in at a labour-intensive 13:18, much of it traveling at decipherable velocities, making the record one solid mass of twisted riffery from start to finish, despite the usually debilitating inclusion of a long tune. **Close To The Edge** this ain't.
Rating                                                    8

## Helloween - Keeper Of The Seven Keys Part II
(Noise '88)
A continuation of Helloween's uniquely high-strung mega-goth, with increasing use of different gears, in side one's excellent soccer holler *Rise And Fall*, *Dr. Stein*, and deceptive ballad *We Got The Right*, and really, most of side two. Nine tunes here versus six on **Part I**, however really marks the biggest improvement, offering tons of variety and unswerving class, as the boys erect a buzzing wall of pain atop from which they cast oppressors, aggressors and any who stray from what is morally correct. Easily a 10 within the confines

**197**

of classical music-based metal, but personally an **8** due to the heavy European element that still after all these years, feels cold and foreign to my ears.
Rating                                                                 8

## Helloween - I Want Out - Live   (RCA '89)

Proving how incredibly vital and valid these perennial favourites are to Gothic metal, **I Want Out - Live** twists and dives with killer aplomb, pumping the band's surging amphetaMaiden anthems through to Odin's dominion, cruising tightly beneath the soaring calls to battle of the immutable Michael Kiske. Likeable liggers and legends both, Helloween simply and without distraction, tear through these protracted tales of netherworlds loud and lordly. Massively hot and effortlessly pro, **Live** demonstrates that demanding, progressive metal tackled with guts, sweat, and carnivorous mosh does not necessarily have to be confined to the studio. Helloween can smoke where-ever there's a crowd to level. The downside: **Live** is full length, yet only comprises six cuts, which necessarily takes our juvenile surgeons on their more elaborate voyages, side-stepping probably their best five statements in the process. In any event, classic band with loads of integrity and at least a European base of admirers to match.
Rating                                                                 7

## Helloween - The Best The Rest The Rare   (Noise '91)

Man, you listen to the expanse of metal on this thing, and you really get to appreciating what a cool Priest-for-the-'80s this band was, wasn't and now is again. Main point of interest here are the non-LP tracks (culled from 7" and 12" EP sources), quick, zesty German jabs like *Judas, Savage, Don't Run For Cover* and *Livin' Ain't No Crime* only a notch below the majesty of the band's official output. Elsewhere lots of those Helloween calling cards that have become high tech mosh highlights of the band's stout-hearted live shows. Provides closure, as the band would begin indulging their creative fancies.
Rating                                                                 8

## Helloween - Pink Bubbles Go Ape   (EMI '91)

I cringe to think how many prospects were turned away by this curious, artsy packaging of what amounts to a near brilliant, flat-out metal album, on exploded trajectory way past Helloween's previously all quite similar output. The title thematically works its way through the expensive surreal graphics that comprise the CD booklet, plus a flip, brief acoustic intro, and that's it. Otherwise, **Pink Bubbles Go Ape** (I'm still confused) is your basic although steadily intellectualizing Helloween techno-feast. May as well be Hitler's beloved Wagner, for the deeply European identity boils under every painstaking construction, hitting glory ride on *Number One, Goin' Home* and lead speedster *Kids Of The Century*, while overall things are less hyper, simpler and wider in scope. Lyrically Kiske and Grapow are still seeking human understanding and honest connection, maturing beyond metal in tandem with Kai Hansen's Gamma Ray, indeed the amicable splintering producing two quality bands, both emerging as frontrunners of a specific, scholarly, Euro-melodic speed genre rarely experienced in North America anymore. As I write, **Pink Bubbles** is still an import in the States, only becoming widely available in Canada more than a year after its release in Europe, the band being well on its way to the record's follow-up. As Kiske himself observes, Americans aren't used to this sort of sound anymore, and it will always be a challenge to educate the masses on such uniquely melodic yet still totally metallic goth displays. So hoist a hearty brew to the pumpkins, and may their craftsmanship and sense of higher mission never wane.
Rating                                                                 8

## Helloween - Chameleon   (EMI '93)

So now all the grumbling and conjecture comes to full head, as the confused organization that is Helloween looks for a new set of flavours to explore. Strange, understated cover, strange rainbow of thoughts, as Kiske and Co. go for a labyrinth of sounds, manly goth, crammed tight with horns, keyboards and a sort of power folk, amidst the usual spanking fresh batch of lyric concerns (put to paper peppered with the band's patented pumpkin cartoons). Makes you wanna reminisce, as Helloween delivers their most acoustic, most down-throttled album yet, full of sensuous challenges, new avenues, new ideas you wouldn't dare try stateside (same trebly, open hi-hat mix as last time). Time elapsed: 71: 26. Faves: *Stay Out Of Hell* and the Maiden/Ozzy-ish *I Believe*. Doesn't exactly float my boat, but one nods in approval just the same.
Rating                                                                 7

## Helloween - Master Of The Rings   (Castle '94)

After five years of drift, resulting in two records only I seemed to like (!), Helloween have returned to the large symphonic classical-based speed and precision for which they've become semi-legendary, big personnel shifts afoot with Pink Cream 69's Andi Deris replacing Michael Kiske on Valhalla bellows, drummer Uli Kusch coming over from Gamma Ray after the shocking suicide of Ingo Schwichtenberg. Vague enough to possibly fit the unremarkable "Rings" storyline, yet probably not conceptual in the least, **Master Of The Rings** rocks smartly from start to finish, Helloween still able to inter-weave pan-world melodies that sound like a quiltwork of national anthems. So the classical tunefulness is back in full flight, as Weikath and Grapow put on a gothic guitar clinic, surgical, exacting Wagnerian castle-grey riffs propelling each brisk or faster track into signature Helloween hinterlands. I dunno, it's starting to blur for me, **Master** just maybe a little too much of a good thing. The real treat is disc #2, 35 minutes of hi-jinx, kicking off with *Grapowski's Malmsuite 1001*, which is just that, a Malmsteen clinic by Grapow. Elsewhere, more originals plus a few covers including Lizzy's *Cold Sweat*, Grand Funk ballad *Closer To Home* and *I Stole Your Love* from **Love Gun** (erroneously called *I Stole Your Heart*).
Rating                                                                 8

## Helloween - The Time Of The Oath   (Castle '96)

Time to get workin' on some new record titles guys, these swords and sorcery ones getting a little tired and samey, dontcha think? Anyhow fresh from their reportedly one million worldwide sales of **Master Of The Rings**, Maiden's living, breathing hellspawn return with a very similar shoot 'em up spread of technical speed metal. This time around, the concept is renaissance seer and spooky Frenchman Nostradamus and his prophecies (a guy on which I did a book report project in Grade 7). But you can quickly forget all the hocus pocus and dwell within the stormy Germanic agility here, a sound that harkens us back to those early Helloween records, records which dampened our disappointment at Maiden losing their minds as the '80s wore on. A marginally better record that its predecessor, due to a detectable dressing-down, letting riffs breathe with added fire. How many records we all need that sound like this is another question.
Rating                                                                 8

## Helloween - High Live   (Castle '96)

For a long-time fan who is feeling overwhelmed at the frequency and the intensity of Helloween product in the '90s, this is just too much. Music overload, picture overload, lyric overload . . . heck, I'm in the Maiden zone! Sixteen tracks over two discs is heart attack material. I'd rather have a quiet lie-down with the studio stuff, one complex composition at a time, slowly, than tackle this horsepill of speed science. I'm sure some are in heady euphoria at the whole Castle-perfect package of the thing, but count me daunted by the challenge.

Rating       7

## Hell's Kitchen - If You Can't Take The Heat . . .
(Boner '89)

One always risks getting it all wrong reviewing records like this, where we know nothing of the band's history, other recorded product if any, and fate since the one artifact that's crossed our paths. I guess that shouldn't stop me from diving into the vinyl evidence at hand however, which is what I gotta do here. This way-too-cool punk metal band reminds me of a more talented Necros, coming through with vicious metal riffs and completely hammered good humour on such slams as Brake Check, Guns, Guts And God, Spiral Staircase, and Spinal Tap's Tonight I'm Gonna Rock You Tonight. Lyrically it's all a joke along the lines of countless hardcore albums, but for once, the music comes through with a perfectly unadorned, occasionally unfast, and always unthrashy high level of entertainment, including horrendously savage, pre-conceived axe solos driven by the spirit of Greg Ginn but the fingers of George Lynch. Quite simply a hardcore band who loves '70s metal, recorded poisonous, stinging and true.

Rating       8

## Helmet - Strap It On   (Interscope '90)

Strap It On (nine tracks, 31 minutes) went a long ways towards establishing Helmet as a band to track, what with its grunge poison and insane athletic tension, a vocabulary that will expand and tighten come the mastery of Meantime. Here it's a sort of drowned exasperation, an underground wallow that threatens burial under a mountain of cheap indie guitars, which slam then shut up with that patented Helmet arrangement; cascades of noise, then jarring respite. And ain't that the tightest snare drum ever, sounding hopelessly out-gunned by the spreading spawn of Vol 4 riffs colliding with the urgent hip hop rhythms of the '90s. Quite a spectacle.

Rating       7

## Helmet - Meantime   (Interscope '92)

Toil, sweat and New York, New York fight it out in the grooves of Helmet, a band with a buzz, a good barber, a fat contract, and hulking doses of base aggression. One of those cancerous hybrids of bad feeling and sick, confused musical root canals, Meantime collides into earshot with In The Meantime's slashing, punch-drunk power gristle announcing the rave. Tight, rhythmic and uncompromising, Meantime exploits the power of tall, crackhead simplicity, sorta like Sub Pop meets Sons Of Freedom. Page Hamilton's vocals are of exactly two species: smooth slacker rock bewilderment, and gruff, rap-like barks. Both crack a smile. What captivates is the neurotic sort of repetition, a constant manic itch; anxiety attacking empty minds, total punk exasperation. Throw in a taint of the Sab, and the brew gets even more crunchy, a record for "the room", the mosh pits of the mind. Falling somewhere between Generation X (not the band) and the apocalypse, Meantime is an appropriate psychic scalpel with which to carve sharp the senses. For whatever you need to cope with and conquer, this lid's for you.

Rating       9

## Helmet - Betty   (Interscope '94)

Helmet pull a weird one with record III, somehow expanding on the shoe-gazing super-slack psyche of the band, while getting more complex. Less the amphetamine bass-scrape of old, Betty taps into an insidious, incestuous groove that wallows in its Helmetness, Page carpet-shedding his compressed lyrics in that sad, sad softspeak while the rhythmic mantra smears on in slightly more technical, but slightly less aggressive manner than was the case with Meantime. And industry folks are kinda lukewarm on it, given its lessened bite, the whole thing roundly recorded and mid-to-slow to quake. But again, I think there's an increased sophistication here, Helmet creating unique environments, a truer fusion of vacant Sabbath and injured hip hop, a depressing metallic pimp roll that can be heard nowhere else on the planet. One becomes surprised at how short this record's compositions actually are (and the record AGAIN as a whole), because they feel long and laboured, the listener perhaps sucked into the band's thick grey non-textures as a sort of harnessed and exhausted anti-speed indoctrination. So on roll Helmet, layered over and reflecting upon itself, more Helmety, less enthusiastic, more quietly disturbing.

Rating       9

## Helmet - Aftertaste   (MCA '97)

If in retrospect, Helmet's last record Betty felt a tad snobby, all has been corrected here, Helmet adjusting after a near break-up with an almost self-deprecating record, one that rings more human, live, volatile and less suffocatingly aggro. Funny hearing this the same week as Handsome, a record and band featuring ex-Helmeteer Peter Mengede. For both acts zero in on song, Helmet perhaps the punkier and more likely to lock on the minimal (please see Birth Defect). But both triumph, Helmet making sure an aftertaste is achieved, welcoming back the listener for another dose of their easily digestible arena rock songs. So the relaxed, ever so slightly lo-fi vibe works, even if Helmet's form of relaxation is always fraught with white-knuckle twists and turns, all parties bent on creating a percussive din that must be awesome live. Note: recorded as a trio, Page and Co. adding former Orange 9mm axeman Chris Traynor post-taste. Note II: virtually finished since September '96, but launched March '97, delay due to remixing with Terry Date in Seattle in December, the switching of a couple tracks, the re-doing of some vocals, and finally, the label not wanting to release the record right at Christmas.

Rating       8

## Helstar - Burning Star   (Combat '84)

Who can deny the hellion that is Burning Star, one classic of mid '80s American goth metal, which in itself is a genre to which I ascribe a certain degree of humour, its purveyors, like Helstar, bent on a metal mission that is both pure and ludicrous, both noble and so distressingly doomed. Burning Star is such an unstoppable sort of Manowar meets Maiden meets Virgin Steele force, brightly recorded by The Rods' Carl Canedy, driven by great yelping vocal work and quintessential mid '80s metal drumming, heavy on tom fills and trumpeted gallops. One of those records that only becomes clear after five or six beers in the company of other hopeless metalheads, all in reverent, slightly embarrassed contemplation on cheezy ol' days.

Rating       7

## Helstar - Remnants Of War   (Combat '86)

Our fave Texan metali-Mexicalis are back with a less dated, more combat-ready sound, not to mention greatly improved cover art. Outside of a vastly different, "tougher" recording and (apparently) a new vocalist, Remnants Of War is much the same sort of chuggin' half-serious medieval death metal, yet somehow with a bit more integrity and aggression; dirtier and crammed full of mental OTT thought patterns. Respectable as an artifact of a lost and deservedly buried tentacle of metal.

Rating       7

## Helstar - Nosferatu (Metal Blade '89)

Delving deeper into technical precision rock, Helstar are now a cross between Bay Area thrash, grim rust belt metal, and Germanic engineering like Coroner, Rage and most completely, Helloween, with a little crusty old Metallica thrown in to keep the boys traditionally rooted. But the big, almost distracting show is the wealth of guitarwork, from machine gun riffing to harmony solos (all a bit like lusty Yngwie), sent six guns blazing behind an operatic but not crazy-high vocal performance from James Riviera. '89 was sort of a transition point for this sort of snobby speed metal, nobody paying much attention, so it was no surprise **Nosferatu** was uh, coffin-bound by daylight.

Rating                                                         7

## Jimi Hendrix - The Cry Of Love (Reprise '71)

I realize it was a travesty not paying at least cursory homage to the inventor of rock guitar in the previous edition of this book, leaving ol' Jimi out because I really wanted to draw quite strictly the line between metal and not metal. So here's the compromise, the "token review" thing. Live with it. Hendrix is of course the raging monster of heavy guitar, taking his left-handed, upside-down otherworldly chops way beyond previous conventions, the man unfortunately for the progress of music and mankind as we know it, dying a drug-related demise in 1970 after inspiring more people since the Beatles to "pick up my guitar and play". Through three records (**Are You Experienced?**, **Axis: Bold As Love** and **Electric Ladyland**), The Jimi Hendrix Experience gave us such crucial rock staples as *Foxy Lady*, *Little Wing*, *Hey Joe*, *Crosstown Traffic*, *Voodoo Child*, *Fire*, his tortured version of *Star Spangled Banner*, his curvy take on Dylan's *All Along The Watchtower*, and of course *Purple Haze*, tracks covered reverently by many a metal band, Jimi providing the spark to so many, in fact Frank Marino, Robin Trower, Uli Jon Roth and Randy California practically trying to become their hero, record after record built as a neverending tribute to Jimi's lusty stomped wah-wah. **The Cry Of Love** is the record Hendrix was finishing when he died, and is an almost hi-fidelity piece of shambling '60s rock, offering loads of unique Hendrix mannerisms texturing ballads, blues, funk and yes, even fledgling metal in *Ezy Rider* (to which Alice Cooper owes a debt of gratitude). And although Hendrix was definitely more '60s rock, psychedelia, funk and blues than metal, it is still a pleasure to hear both the man's expressive vocals and shimmering, fluid guitar prowess, Hendrix probably the most effortless and free-flowing axe wizard we'll likely ever hear.

Rating                                                         8

## Ken Hensley - Proud Words On A Dusty Shelf
(Bronze '73)

Again the warnings go out: this is a very mellow album, included for its link to Uriah Heep, Hensley of course being chief songwriter during the band's golden era and the uh, less golden era that followed. Here, right in the thick of things, he put out this brooding, ancient soft rock record, leaden and serious with the man's somber slow songs, lent additional gravity by his pastoral vocals, closest comparison being that of his teammate David Byron. **Proud Words** is surprisingly acoustic guitar-ish (Ken's a keyboardist), tunes such as *From Time To Time*, *The Last Time*, and *Black Hearted Lady* being delicate, rootsy affairs, nicely recorded, benefiting greatly from Hensley's knack for song. Oddly enough, there's a detectable dirgy patina to this record, as many of these songs might sound fine as Black Sabbath ballads, especially *When Evening Comes* and *Fortune*, both heavy-handed in that soaring and crashing Heep fashion. When it all winds down, this record just sounds like really cool, really subversive underground '70s soft rock, seemingly plain, but all tied up in all sorts of influences from both the '70s and the '60s. Hard to pin it . . . I'd just have to say the record has a vaguely depressing sort of weight. Rhythm section: Gary Thain and Lee Kerslake.

Rating                                                         7

## Ken Hensley - Eager To Please (Bronze '75)

The prolific Heep organ grinder is back with more dark yet cleansing spillovers from his main gig, **Eager To Please** offering more full production numbers than his sparse record from '73. I totally love this stuff, because it sounds so old yet well-produced, but I can see how some might just think it's crap, I really can. Old Heep bassist Mark Clarke is on board here, as is a drummer, but there's no question the real show again is Hensley's plush vocals, his spooky keyboard vocabulary and his laid-back slide guitar. The man is just this unpeggable kind of talent, writing soft, sinking psychedelic-laced balladry that never bores, just heavy, heavy music, for the most part tooled with light precision instrumentation. Faves of this ilk would be *Eager To Please*, *Take And Take*, and *How Shall I Know*, many of his lighter moments welling over into a kind of gospel mania, while heavier moments are almost best viewed as reservoirs of really cool old sounds doing medieval battle for what purpose, we'll never know. Inspirational in the same, not altogether healthy, despondently escapist way Pink Floyd is inspirational.

Rating                                                         8

## Ken Hensley - Free Spirit (Bronze '81)

**Free Spirit** finds Hensley doing the stylistic shotgun thing that marred so many Heep and Byron records, the man experimenting with various types of percolating disco and new wave beats (see *Inside The Mystery*, *The System* and *Do You Feel Alright*), while kicking out his coolest solo rocker yet in the driving *Brown Eyed Boy*, groove-laden backbeat courtesy of Ian Paice, even *Telephone* coming off as a good-time blast of pop-tinged power chords. In betwixt all this brighter, future-tense fare, Hensley pastes in a couple of his characteristic towering grey ballads in *Woman* and *No More*, further demarcating this record's fun-time highs and pensive lows. Still, it's Hensley and the treatments are what count, even if the record forgets to cohere, the man going through a re-evaluation of his life and work, something that was bound to hit full-on sooner or later.

Rating                                                         7

## Ken Hensley - From Time To Time (Viceroy '94)

Who'd have thought Ken Hensley would warrant a rarities, demos and alternates record, but I'm glad it's happened, oddities label Viceroy stepping up to the plate for what plays like a cohesive Hensley solo record from the '70s. Thankfully, the record contains a long letter from Hensley himself putting the record in context (not that it really has one), the man then going on to explain the origins of each of the sixteen tracks one-by-one, also providing full lyrics. The recordings are all solid as an oak, as those weighty ballads ebb and flow into view, punctuated by more throbbing, slightly uptempo numbers like *I Don't Wanna Wait*, *Love At First Sight* and *The Name Of The Game*, a killer track which features most of Bad Company pounding out the rhythms (note: there's all sorts of '70s legends on various tracks). Sum total: an elegant, stirring collection of Hensley tunes (indeed some of these actually being Heep tunes in waiting, never to be realized until now). Great songwriter's songs, little filler if any, and overall, solid value for Hensley fans both in terms of words, music and pictures.

Rating                                                         8

## Heresy - Face Up To It (Still Thinking '88)

So degenerately thrash that it truly sounds recorded at 78 RPM with vocals mixed in at 33 1/3. The usual wall of noise and assaultive shouts, best part is the lyric sheet which includes long explanations/justifications for each buzzing bee. Stupid and unlistenable even once.
Rating 0

## Hericane Alice - Tear The House Down (Atlantic '90)

From the band's pouty faces to their putrid name, this California quartet emits a half dozen signals that spell out why hair metal went bald. But if you can sweep aside the lyrics and the look, these forgotten records are going to sound a lot better in twenty years versus all the lo-fi jangly alternative crap that is clogging the market these days. Between street and glam, sorta like modern Kiss. Oh what's the difference. Are you even reading this?
Rating 5

## Herman Ze German And Friends - Herman Ze German And Friends (Est. '83)

A star-studded exercise in shiny-as-a-dime metal à la Dokken (Don cameos on guest vocals), further demonstrating that Scorpions' Rarebell is primarily a groove-oriented drummer, satisfied in living life the keeper of the bottom end, no frills, all power. Still just a very professional, obvious one-off with all the fragmentation afforded "project" records.
Rating 5

## Hexx - Morbid Reality (Century Media '91)

I'm sure somebody somewhere thinks this is a classic, California's Hexx thrashing maniacally yet not without twisted gothic passages and lyrics that are provocative, positions well-stated sorta like Lovecraft (see the eldritch and unholy Fire Mushrooms). High-strung frashcore vocals personify the scampery techno-blur enclosed, but not before Hexx escape with a modicum of respectability.
Rating 6

## Heyday - Heyday (Room '94)

Sorry Ross (The Boss, that is), but no Dice (despite your resemblance), this one's dead and rotting in the hairspray era; generic Kiss-quality party rock mixed with predictable covers (Brown Eyed Girl and Search And Destroy) rendered aseptic and dullsville. Smatterings of blues, acoustic strummers and stripper funk like a million records like this straddling 1990 by a couple o' years either way. Absolutely dick-all in terms of charisma, or the inclusion of other venerable Dictators types that might have fumbled the stew into something savory. Handsome Dick, save us now!
Rating 4

## Highway Chile - Storybook Heroes (21 '83)

One of the crowning classics of early '80s glory metal, **Storybook Heroes** broke all the house rules afforded Scandinavian steel by cranking a brightly brash but ethereal blast of American stadium rock, perched on the cusp of chaos while creating massive grooves that rolled the whole shaggy masterwerk over town and country alike; loud, proud, grandly perfect but dangerously unstable. **Storybook Heroes** is everything Lep's **On Through The Night**, **High'n'Dry** or Heavy Pettin's debut could only dream about; a fusion of party metal and cold European metallic instinct that rained from the skies with merciless focus and control. All is blindingly face-melting here: the July '83 remix—big on cymbals and sizzle, Armand Vander Stigchel's erratic vocal emotion, and a slew of songs so perfectly ass-kickin', they produce a totality two feet thick and ready to pound back beers in earnest. Jesse James, Headbang-

ers, Run, Run . . . I could name 'em all and I should, but just buy the record, if you love spirit, power, and layers of dueling guitars whiplashing some of the tastiest hard rock ever to scorch the sphere.
Rating 10

## Highway Chile - For The Wild And Lonely (Mirus '84)

Like any unmistakably gifted gathering of minds, Highway Chile display a willingness to experiment, altering their core sound with a strangely mechanical delivery, like slow dance metal, where riffs weave tacit magic over blocky techno-drums. Recipe for disaster? Not on your life, as **For The Wild And Lonely** is one of the greatest EP's ever crafted; six metallic cuts of gut-wrenching heart and conviction using an odd language, but proven intelligence coupled with the vocal majesty of Vander Stigchel. The word for this is infectious, a release so effortlessly assimilated and respectable, one to wear out and curse for the fact that it wasn't full-length (see **Kim Mitchell** and Mudhoney's **Superfuzz Bigmuff**) Power And The Force and Custers Last Stand work incredible grooves from slow simple beats, utilizing dynamic, tasteful Euro axe work, and rousing breaks to complete the ruse, while fave Pale Blue Eyes (different and better on the EP's European version), and The Omerta (Lucky No More) ride tragic, melancholy atmospheres over similarly low-key rhythms. Rounding out are Brand-New Star and Horses And Shields, two more conventional HM highballs, both buoyed by thoughtfully melodic intricacies come chorus time, resulting in all six tracks being sturdy and memorable; all quite different, all successful while taking risks.
Rating 10

## Highway Chile - Rockarama (21 '85)

Disappointing though still not without charm, **Rockarama** extends the band's brilliant '83 EP's penchant for electronic treatment, while assimilating much of the pop affectations of American hard rock, in calculated search for commercial success. A key personnel change to vocalist Sav Pearce is less distressing than one might surmise; the new guy possessing a similar set of pipes and similar drive to Armand's, while dealing with a wimpier, less dressy set of tunes. Yes indeed, **Rockarama** really takes sparseness to heart, squarely relying on **Pyromania**-style pre-school drumming ("digital" if you really care), to carry the weight of submissive guitars, in turn so easily overpowered by vocals and too many keyboard parts. But occasional tracks here shine and shimmer with the fire of old, dishing warm melodies borne of guitar, most notably You Took My Heart and Broken Promises, both somewhat fitting the lighter facets of the **Wild And Lonely** EP. Much else just goes clunk, clunk, clunk, leaving one to wonder how this clumsy foray could have been imagined as a cash-generator. As the record trudges to conclusion, anger reigns once more as the band teases the onlooker with one of their best tunes ever in the metallic, heart-breaking machinery of On The Rox, lending the record a sort of Golden Earring-like mystique as enigma off the rails.
Rating 7

## Hinge - Accidental Meeting Of Minds (Pavement '94)

I found this really annoying after awhile, Michigan's Hinge looking for that twee zone between heavy underground cool quotient, and wayward creativity for creativity's sake, hoping we can hear Faith No More, Saigon Kick, RHCP, Soundgarden, Pearl Jam, maybe even Grateful Dead and the Spin Doctors. Give 'em credit, this baffled and baffling debut is an exploded pastiche of sounds, considerably imaginative, resulting in an ambiance which can be admired without argument. But it just tries to hard, ending up sounding like a way-indulged, pre-editing Bush demo or a smarmy

Nixons album; too much showiness, not enough emphasis on song. The pinched, panicky recording doesn't help either.
Rating 5

## Holland - Early Warning (Ebony '84)

This one stood above the fray, garnering patches of positive press for its savvy, controlled, but looming chaos and Americanly competent vocals (from a guy named Doggy) which vaguely inflect towards Glenn Hughes. Closest approximation I can think of would be early Tokyo Blade, with an ever so slight shift towards boozy grime like Savage or Grim Reaper; appropriate given the label's trademark sound. Simply warm, blue collar barroom metal with nice, time-worn touches on such tracks as the melodic title cut, chomper Do It, the phase-shifted Kicking Back, and lead rouser Shout It Out, **Early Warning** harkens back to all that was honourable and universal about the NWOBHM. Trench rockin' but sensitive to strong, working class hooks.
Rating 7

## Holocaust - The Nightcomers (Phoenix '81)

And what better way to celebrate the New Wave Of Heavy Metal than under the dumb decibels of hapless bashers Holocaust, perennial undermutt favourites of an exploding genre characterized by acts that in most cases could both play their instruments and sing. **The Nightcomers** is legendary more for what it can't do rather than what it can, kickin' ass on guts and patched jean jacket alone, as it variously rips, plods and slogs through a set of bar band compositions so perfectly attuned to the metal mentality as it exists after a dozen or so brown bottles deep into the night and two feet of snow, most of it in your sneakers (least that's how we experienced it). Smokin Valves, Cryin Shame and the definitive Heavy Metal Mania . . . what better soundtrack to hypothermia. So wence again, foist ye drafts on high for the geezers in the band, for **The Nightcomers** hath come and gone, leaving only a distant ringing memory of crashing cymbals in its polluted wake.
Rating 10

## Holocaust - Live (hot curry and wine) (Phoenix '83)

The live document of the walking dead, **Live** was recorded in front of about twelve people way back in '81, at least ten of which sounded like they were being burned at the stake. This record's major claim to fame is that Metallica lifted a tune from it, the previously unavailable The Small Hours for Lars and Co.'s nifty covers EP. Other than its understandably low budget recording, there's lots worth grooving over on this thoroughly Spinal Tap-ish swillfest, most notably the fact that five of eight cuts are non-**Nightcomers** tracks wholly worthy of said attitudinally-forensic opus. Simple, screwed rock by the Ramones of the NWOBHM, **Live** kills scores of brain cells by example, blowing its arsenal in a mid-paced mosh of morons. Nobody said rock'n'roll was pretty.
Rating 7

## Holocaust - No Mans Land (Phoenix '84)

One of the big disappointments of the NWOBHM, Holocaust proudly flew their tattered metal banner on high with **The Nightcomers**, a perfect tangle of wires for the times, only to degenerate into jokeweights with wimp rock project Hologram, and this sordid mess that simply defies understanding, a record that sounds like it was recorded under the garage. Where to start . . . anywhere and nowhere . . . which is where this awful one-take lives; the product of major depressed swilling no doubt, given the no-talent playing, out-of-tune vocal chores and absolutely loaded attempts at song construction. If you're thinking, sure, but that's why **The**

**Nightcomers** was such a blast, forget it, this ain't even remotely in the same piss tank.
Rating 0

## Holy Moses - Finished With The Dogs (Aaarrg/SPV Est. '86)

Cool album title, eh? I thought so. Anyways, the record's quite the sterling pound also, these Teutons putting together a record of manic '80s thrash that falls between Voivod and Destruction, lots of cut up top and fire down below, technical but clearly bonkers. Access in place of coffee and crack.
Rating 7

## Holy Terror - Terror And Submission (Under One Flag '86)

Of a sort of cringing academic interest, this cannily-assembled wall of thrash is demonstrative of the line between Slayer and Exciter-derived speed metal and the newer death (see Tomorrow's End). So it's really heavy, kinda black, well-arranged but leaning thick into the '90s; musical but quite extreme, landing squarely on the professional side of the somewhat overplaying, musically untalented bands characteristic of American thrash in the mid '80s. Competes handily with the better Euro acts of the day, which I guess is why it belongs on a mid-size British label known for at least minimal levels of quality (follow-up: **Mind Wars**).
Rating 6

## The Honeydrippers - Volume One (Es Paranza '84)

Yeah, I know, not remotely loud rockin', but a Zeppelin curio (just an EP) all the same, given that this is Plant and Page (and even Jeff Beck) incognito, doing old soul and r+b covers. Hit tune and video for Sea Of Love. Orchestration, the whole bit.
Rating 5

## Hostility - Brick (Century Media '95)

Occupying the mid-zone between Crowbar and Pantera, sorta like the earth-shaking grooves of **Chaos A.D.**-era Sepultura or Entombed, Hostility (from Kansas!) doth rock mighty fine. The bio sez the band tuned their guitars as low as they could without going out of tune all the time, which is pretty much the clobbering sound **Brick** makes, something caught between European death metal and the Melvins, Phil 'n' Pepper's Down and downer and dirtier. Ten tracks of truck-crash torment (save for dirge Goodbye, which is a tribute to the Book brothers' deceased father, and unlisted eleventh tune, Kiss cover Black Diamond), **Brick** sounds like a dozen or so other bands, main point being though, that all the comparatives are great bands head-carving deep, often grave, psychological impressions. Sounds German or Swedish, which I guess means they've found that blackened element that usually only comes from over frigid seas.
Rating 8

## Hounds - Unleashed (Columbia '78)

Chewy '70s hard rock with a twang of the Hoople (or more accurately Mott, sans Hunter), with so much street-level soul you just gotta take it homeward, **Unleashed** is the unsung product of a band lost like countless others at the time in an identity crisis between the boppers and the rockers, further complicated by the decisively incorrect punk rock graphics of the front cover art. Balladry so convincing, peppered with great '70s rock moves including sprinkles of Bowie, the Stones, rockier Roxy Music and on the louder tilt, The Nuge, Aerosmith, and Derringer, co-exist to make this a bombastic piece of humility worthy of a genuine look back. One either embraces these sorts of scratchy old records (see Piper and Lonestar) or lets them lie in psychic obsolescence. And indeed you can go either way here. I dunno, I'm just into it, even though it ain't that heavy. Colour me marinated in its smorg of hard rock sounds and pop metal preening, while sipping from a few of my old Tubes albums. Rumbling near classic: *Portrait Of A Dead Man*.

Rating     **7**

## Hounds - Puttin' On The Dog   (Columbia '79)

Wire your heads for guilty pleasure No. 2 from nowherz. **Puttin' On The Dog** takes the full implication of the Hounds' line-up and production transitions, sounding more like Max Webster's **A Million Vacations** than anything as raw and lovingly misguided as the debut. This scintillating headphone escape keeps the songwriting buoyant, Cars-driven but non-exclusive, dipping into the world's backtrax for a technical and techy past blast through *Do Wah Diddy* Diddy and *Under My Thumb* (really, the two low points on the disc). Elsewhere, bloomin' wisdom par excellence caresses the monitors with killer metallized slowie *Angel Of Fire*, progressive, piano-beautified partytoon *Workin' On My Cool*, and machine gunning Kinks kover *Who'll Be The Next In Line*. Just glittery as the crown jewels, as this press-less, commercial assemblage of musical wonders whips together one fine piece of pop metal; vintage and cutting edge all at once, with a sense of humour and solid mental acuity firmly to the fore. A real oddity, created and creative in a void, unnoticed and tossed aside by a cruel, Eagles' **Long Run**-lovin' world.

Rating     **8**

## House Of Lords - House Of Lords   (BMG '88)

At the height of hair heaven, House Of Lords bring their long blonde animal rock (to quote the immortal Golden Earring) to the world, standard, silky, soaring vocals from James Christian, other notables by Chuck Wright on bass, and of course Greg Giuffria from Angel and Giuffria on keyboards. But this is probably the most over-produced album I've ever heard, so drenched with treble and echo, bugging out way past anything Night Ranger would ever dream of, that I just wanna turn it off. So I will. One of Gene Simmons' pet projects, just another diversion to keep his mind off of making bad Kiss records.

Rating     **4**

## House Of Lords - Sahara   (BMG '90)

Surprisingly more guitarish than the insipid debut, **Sahara** nevertheless comes stiff and glossed-up almost as much as the hilariously air-brushed band photo included here for your oggling pleasure. The usual bunch of big names orbit by for requisite backing vocals chores, notably Zander and Neilsen from Cheap Trick who are no doubt buried somewhere on Neilsen's *Heart On The Line* (other visitors include Ron Keel, Mike Tramp and David Glenn Eisley). Also as usual for the genre, molten but smooth leads from new guitarist Michael Guy and even more gosh-darn visitors who picked up axes for a quick shred.

Rating     **6**

## H.P. Zinker - Mountains Of Madness   (Energy '94)

I don't know if the bio's comparisons to Lou Reed, Fripp and Shaft hold much water. I'd be more inclined to lichen Zinker's 'shroom rumble to a cross between Masters Of Reality, Firehose and Wire, embodying a sound that is heavy on loose compelling rhythm, lots of prominent bass guitar prodding a retro glueyness that becomes alive and refreshing through polar exploration. Loop in some Primus, Soundgarden, Hawkwind, and The Cure, and H.P. Zinker's on some sort of twisted, sub-street sewer roll, illuminating through blown manhole covers the human rot of hometown Manhattan. But it's an enigmatic and quirky exam for this trio, not the tiring tire iron angst everybody else is expunging. Liquid and cratchety, lolligagging and sly,

**Mountains Of Madness** (named for an H.P. Lovecraft novel) is a smart piece of alternative alternative, alternately slamming and sleeping with an integrity steeped from completely vacuum-sealed music manufacture, a sound quite beyond influences. Fave rave: the seething *Fortress Of Fear*, at 9:10, this record's *A Light In The Black*. **Mountains Of Madness** is this band's fifth record, my first, my, my, my.

Rating     **8**

## Hughes Thrall - Hughes Thrall   (CBS '82)

Your perfect companion to another brown CBS twosome release **Whitford/St. Holmes**, **Hughes Thrall** is a predictably pop-oriented affair between cult legend Glenn Hughes and ex-Pat Travers axeman Pat Thrall. Well assembled and rare as hell, the record has verve and keyboards, enthusiasm and overproduction, stadium level guitar work from Thrall, and those luv 'em or hate 'em vocals of journeyman (in more ways than one) Glenn Hughes, who despite his spotty recording record, is studied and pontificated over by those still enamoured by the major musical chairs musicians of the '80s. Conclusion: lightweight curio for collectors.

Rating     **6**

## Glenn Hughes - Play Me Out   (Safari/Deep Purple '77)

When I lifted **Play Me Out** from the used bins in surprise, I thought there might be a chance it could sound like y'know who. But then of course market forces would have conspired over the years to make it much more visible. Alas and alack, **Play Me Out** delves swimmingly into Hughes' not-so-closet addiction: r+b in all its funked-up glory, from slow blues through jazz-funk and disco, liberal doses of horns and strings accompanying the man himself howling like a stuck pig. Lots of middle rankers here, many of who make and have made that Gillan, Whitesnake, and otherwise solo Purple circuit. Recognizables: Mel Galley, Pat Travers, Dave Holland, Terry Rowley and Mark Nauseef.

Rating     **4**

## Glenn Hughes - Blues   (Blues Bureau '92)

Glenn Hughes adopts a snappy Graham Bonnet/James Dean look for this under-titled sizzler commissioned for Mike Varney's interesting Blues Bureau label, steering his way through some considerably hard rocking "blues" tracks contrasting traditional blues and Stevie Ray-style funk blues. Along for the ride come a good ten or so famous axe-handlers, including Europe's John Norum, Ratt's Warren DeMartini, the Crue's Mick Mars, Richie Kotzen, and Great White's Mark Kendall. **Blues** sounds like the record Coverdale would kill to make, souping up the past with the language of metal, carving a companion record to Pat Travers' output in the '90s. Entertaining, well-paced and a veritable heaven of sounds for those fanatical Hughes fans out there who expressed interest in hearing Glenn's unhinged stylings exactly where they belong.

Rating     **7**

## Glenn Hughes - From Now On . . .   (Empire/Attic '94)

Esteemed journeyman belter Glenn Hughes has essentially constructed a record similar to **Blues**, this one perhaps going a bit more AOR-ish, definitely slick to his usual standards, always leaning to blues directives (starting to remind me of John Sykes these days), giving equal stagetime to guitar, keyboards and his acquired taste vocals. Lyrically, **From Now On . . .** mixes the man's deep religious convictions with songs of love, Hughes these days being entirely about life affirmation, perhaps love in this world, and in the next being interdependent. Whatever the case, bonus track *Burn* leaps out like a hot spark from the barbecue pit (strange that Riot covered this song in the same year),

making the rest of the record sound limp in the process. Very smooth AOR from one of the genre's kings; not saying I care a whole lot.
Rating 7

## Glenn Hughes - Burning Japan Live (Zero '94)

Now this is the way to kick back and enjoy Glenn Hughes, the man giving it his all for 76 minutes of Hughes solo and lesser-known Deep Purple classics. As usual, Hughes surrounds himself with players, creating a vital, musicianly band experience, an art that only seems to be appreciated in Japan and Germany these days. Purple-wise we get such barnstormers as Burn, Lady Double Dealer and Stormbringer, amongst more Hughesy bluesy fare like This Time Around and Gettin' Tighter. And the Hughes stuff belies the man's turbulent many faces and age-lines thereof, reaching back and forward, left and right, mixing the record nicely between nimble, spacious metal and icy AOR. Nice production too, but what did you expect?
Rating 8

## Humble Gods - Humble Gods (Tacklebox '95)

This big bad (old!) punk band is a minor supergroup, gigging quite successfully around the LA area. Significant God for me would be all round cool guy Spike from Mind Over Four, the guy in fact more enthused about this band's prospects than his long suffering mainstay. But hey, even though this first swift kick is in possession of a vicious guitar sound and wise guy vocals fer miles, punk as a rule is a raging bore. Humble Gods do their valiant, Clash-bloodied best to visit Detroit and NY circa the '70s, so it's not all burn your textbook mosh, coming across somewhat like Rancid and Dead Kennedys weighted by an understanding of metal. A whiff of hard-won wisdom pervades, but punk still stinks.
Rating 7

## The Hunt - Back On The Hunt (Daffodil '80)

To keep it appropriately Canadian, first comparisons that come to mind would include Wireless, Moxy, heavy Max Webster, early Triumph, early Helix, and stretching it, early Santers. The Hunt were perennial frost-bitten losers from my homeland; an isolated power trio sending confused signals ranging from metal to clueless melodic guitar rock, landing in the wrong pile more often than not in terms of focus. Chunky, funky, and studio-dressed in that usual '70s manner, where the band seemed more concerned with crafting a clean project, than addressing a particular form of music. Tidy, disciplined barroom rock more than anything "heavy", yet nevertheless perfectly at home in this book, being basically axe-driven all over.
Rating 5

## Hunter - Sign Of The Hunter (Bacillus '85)

Greasy Germans who barely got their English together before stumbling into the studio, laboriously attempting to get their ideas across as if they mattered anyways. Hunter machine gun-riff it through the usual Teutonic bleakscapes with evil aplomb. Swear to God, German bands seem to be stuck quivering with the essence of metal more deeply than anyone else, seemingly driving any number of rock dogs into an emotive shreddability with dead-eye effortlessness. So, characteristically, Sign Of The Hunter smokes foot-long TNT, yet like many who travel this well-defined path, lack a personal stamp to establish useful pathos.
Rating 6

## Hurricane - Over The Edge (Enigma '88)

Kind of a nice, open and aerated pop metal sound to this one, Mike Clink letting the garage seep into his meticulous control room, taking a quartet of pin-ups and leaving them urgent and hungry as I'm sure they were at the time. Coolest thing here is sequencing their blues ballad version of I'm Eighteen as second track, shaking up one's perceptions right from the start. Kind of the pre-cursor to Slaughter and Kik Tracee in the light, fluffy and weirdly loose AOR sweepstakes (which Zep oddly enough flirted with from time to time). Oozing personality probably by mistake, Hurricane bashing passionately their way through songs that often evoke a whiff of white metal.
Rating 7

## Hurricane - Slave To The Thrill (Enigma '90)

Stylish but faltering AOR from journeymen Kelly Hansen, Jay Schellen, Tony Cavazo, and Doug Aldrich (who replaces Robert Sarzo), Slave To The Thrill displays a band with clear, projecting chemistry but an unexpected dearth of good songs. Yep, L.A. was full of great bands chasing the poodle rock formula, feeding off of two or three of the best years for American as apple pie metal, kicked off with the success of GN'R's Appetite For Destruction. But call this one dropping the ball, shampooed, conditioned, manicured and pedicured compared to Rose n' Bros, Hurricane going for that distinctly Bon Jovi-ish type of fanbase, much more dissipated in spirit versus the anxious debut. Colour me unimpressed 'cept for the vocals and guitar solos.
Rating 5

## Hüsker Dü - Land Speed Record (SST '81)

Man alive . . . hard to imagine that the invincible Hüsker Dü (apparently named for a Swedish board game) could have entered this wicked world kicking such a horribly loud, messed-up, and thoroughly opaque thrashpunk. I have no idea what the band could possibly have been getting at on this four-alarm blaze. The recording sucks, the playing sucks, the vocals suck. All is drowned, droning and blurred like no other piece of carnal corepunk known to man. Really, defies all logic, much like the Meat Puppets dumb and dumber debut.
Rating 0

## Hüsker Dü - Metal Circus (SST '83)

Hints of flaming genius begin to take root on this seven track EP which mixes the breakneck thrash of Land Speed Record with dim mindshafts of melody, in establishment of the patented Dü sound, albeit still in its primal stages. Real World and First Of The Last Calls manage to slam intensely, slashing and scorching beneath Bob Mould's trademark roar and frenzied riffery while insidious infusions of human connection freeze you in your tracks. Brilliant, sludgy, and mercilessly assaulting, Metal Circus is the most uncompromising and punk-steeped of intrinsically Dü experiences.
Rating 7

## Hüsker Dü - Zen Arcade (SST '84)

Messily palpitating through an inelegant labyrinth of distortion pedals comes Zen Arcade, a sprawled double dose of carnivorous anarchy which revs like poison start to collapse, most of the reinforced thrash oddly pleasing, and all of the hinted tints of genius ferociously euphoric. Think of Zen Arcade as a desert with oases; the heat never letting up but the will to live receding and rising with each colourful improvement in environs. Double Nickels On The Dime it ain't (It's OK. Dü's got Warehouse), but Zen has a few thorny blooms that evoke mindrot like no other fevered trio can. Kick-off slammer Something I Learned Today, the jagged What's Going On (Inside My Head), way cool wake Pink Turns To Blue, and most notably rumbling destroyer Turn On The News all crush the Clash and all their high-flown ideals. Dü sound drowning, clawing for rope, ready and willing to drag the whole despicable world under for one last slo mo struggle before bloat. Patched forlornly in mostly single takes, Zen

Arcade is still too hypertensile and un-pruned to shine the light, but there's always some sort of earthly pleasure in working up a claustrophobic fever in search of mental reinforcement against the blatherings of the frail.

Rating      7

## Hüsker Dü - New Day Rising   (SST '84)

The rawest, most spontaneous, and most eclectic of post-thrash Dü discs, **New Day Rising** seems to have the most enthusiasm and adrenaline; unselfconscious with its imperfections and roll-the-dice anarchy. For those who might have found Dü in its last throes too preachy, or too melodically sweet, **New Day Rising** provides the antidote, with blood-curdling links to a nihilistic punk past, as punishingly displayed through the double-time title cut, opening the record with one of the most powerful and roaring blasts of ferocity ever almost harnessed. The whole lengthy quest evokes an inhospitable, rocky terrain crashed by freezing tidal waves, with warming emotional respites such as master piece Celebrated Summer and the lonely Books About UFOs which both endear while retaining the band's sonic meltdown which tears through the whole mountainous mosh. **New Day Rising** ultimately stands as the pinnacle of Hüsker Dü's art, a record where an exploded thrash unit was dragged kicking and screaming into the realms of human interaction, forced to face the inner wells of their collective, often inhospitable psyches. One of my favourite works of cascading distortion ever sandblasted to wax, **New Day Rising** manages to reveal human truths behind its blinding blizzard of ice, perfection buried in deafening chaos.

Rating      10

## Hüsker Dü - Flip Your Wig   (SST '85)

A merciless sun in which to fry to a lesion-popping crisp, **Flip Your Wig** is the Hüsker's most wilful and effortless deception between pleasure and pain. Axes flying like wounded bats at an Ozzy show, Dü rocks out like a technicolour wall of the brightest, hardest glass, infusing greater ebbs of complicated melody than ever previously ventured, creating the Dü "pop" album, only surpassed in crowd-descension by **Candy Apple Grey**. Witness the absolute sweet of Makes No Sense At All, Green Eyes and Flexible Flyer which all take the last drops of life from the conventional world and build gleaming new machines. But grab a chair and swim upstream with Games and more so the triumphant Divide And Conquer, both containing that strenuous intensity of emotion that just somehow soars o'ertop the manacles of metal for a brief suspended moment. Just a huge and emotionally sophisticated guitar, bass and drums orgy, crammed overfull with sonic muscle, bleeding at the edges with uncontrollable descents into angular white noise.

Rating      9

## Hüsker Dü - Candy Apple Grey   (Warner Bros. '86)

The disorienting dichotomy of this masterpiece is summed up exquisitely within its title, which accurately evokes the band's acidic lyrical thorniness tightly wound beneath the bright stinging tones of the sonic Dü avalanche. **Candy Apple Grey** is essentially an introduction to the seething and frenzied production values which guard **Warehouse**: from intruders; cuts such as the brilliant and caustic Crystal, and the gushingly warm cum deafeningly loud Eiffel Tower High; vignettes interchangeable with the componentry of Dü's swan song. Main distinguishing mark, however, is the band's descent into no less than three acoustic pastiches, dour and moving, yet still managing the band's strange buzzing quality which lends a sense of urgent panic akin to a near death experience. Lyrically, both Hart and Mould are eloquent and poignant, swelling forth with emotion, wisdom, and purpose, in ex-

amination of life's courses, obstacles, traumas, and resolutions—in retrospect, in fear of the future, in confusion at the now. And aside from these three quieter out-of-body driftings, all is set spinning sparks a' flying beneath layers of painful buzz-saw axe piercings, coalescing into the most heroic of metallic melodics, as only Hüsker Dü has a clue how to construct. Wildly important, yet possibly the most wondrously deflated of Dü statements.

Rating      10

## Hüsker Dü - Warehouse: Songs And Stories
(Warner Bros. '87)

In some frightfully abstract way, **New Day Rising**, warts and all, froths to the brim as Hüsker Dü's most important record to my way of thinking. They all rule, and **Warehouse**: rules too; the last before the implosion, the crowning double opus, the culmination of mind and matter by a band universally looked upon as legendary. And just defying flesh-gone-softs to tune in, such disturbing truths come wrapped in an ever-masochistic swarm of wasps wired to attack through a series of electric jolts. Mould just denies his melodic ego an upper hand, kicking up the usual storm of axe-slashings far above an ever-clarifying lyric and vocal vision. **Warehouse: Songs And Stories** is a walk through my town, your town, a telling panorama of life's perils assembled like deafening poetry so convincingly driven in both directions. Lots of crank-ups (sorry, Grant), lots of hot rays through breaking clouds, shards of stultifying noise, and welcome deliberate breezes of brutal honesty weave a complex texture through no less than twenty loud vignettes, charting a geography that encompasses breathless variation. Most mentally imprinting pieces to me would pretty much have to include all of sides one and four, most splendidly These Important Years, Turn It Around, and Up In The Air, but really, why bother pulling it apart? Treated as an intellectually intense, heat-swelled stroll through the world, **Warehouse**: is a construct that reveals despair, while oscillating between its acceptance and its joyful destruction. Plus it kicks ass and never stops. Post-Dü note: Mould went on to create two very cool solo records **Workbook** (mellow and refreshing) and **Black Sheets Of Rain** (loud and depressing), then moving on to form power trio Sugar (similar to Dü but the magic is gone), now back again as angry solo guy.

Rating      10

## Hüsker Dü - Everything Falls Apart And More
(Rykodisc '93)

After one stinging and abstract piece of live white noise, the Hüskers' entered an actual studio to record this first real record, also a whip of a thing, 45 RPM, too much revolution, then     And trust Ryko to lovingly reassemble it, remastering the shambling mess and adding a bunch of rarities. The astonishing thing is how close these firebrands were to being a straighteighthate hardcore band, how when recording values were elevated, the blockchop of it all flared through. Only the title track and maybe Gravity hint at future pop gush, the rest of the time Mould and Crew just bashing all about the head violently like crazed killer bees drunk on Minutemen. For the record, the twelve tracks that were **Everything Falls Apart** were recorded summer '82, released Jan. '83, and the seven rarities span the years '80 to '82. Enjoyment? It barely occurs or matters.

Rating      5

## Hypocrisy - Penetralia   (Nuclear Blast '92)

The band's bio recounts how Hypcrisy began as a promise to Phil of Malevolent Creation, that next time Peter Tagtgren returned to the U.S., he would have a killer band and a recording contract. So back in Sweden

Tagtgren worked steadily, eventually making this blistering death abomination in his own studio, **Penetralia** featuring awesome production for a debut, and a cogent enough, blasphemously-black death onslaught for fans of the form (you might be able to tell that I'm not exactly of that ilk). But fer damn sure, this is firmly upper crust for the genre, Tagtgren proving his capabilities as a renaissance demon-troll of sorts.

Rating 6

## Hypocrisy - Osculum Obscenum (Nuclear Blast '93)

**Osculum Obscenum** can be classified as merely more of the same visceral, eye-watering death blosh as its predecessor, once again Tagtgren offering no printed lyrics, although we pretty much know he ain't crooning about saving the whales. If anything, the recording this time is a touch weaker, while the music makes up for it, offering a few more slow groove penetrations amongst the usual kiln-fired blastbeats. A distinct and palpable Swedish air to it, which helps immensely, but bottom line: a continuation without advance.

Rating 5

## Hypocrisy - The Fourth Dimension (Nuclear Blast '94)

Peter Tagtgren's death metal machine Hipocrisy has evolved into a more powerful, less hysterical experience over four punishing, hypo-death releases. While not quite blazing the new terrain of Swedish cohorts like Entombed and Tiamat, Hypocrisy nevertheless has ground out something more musical than past scrapes yet equally aggressive, a sound more epic and patient, dynamic yet still grounded in Tagtgren's ever-luvin' deathcore. It's the type of record that can grow on you over time, as you disassemble and reassemble the logic of the thing, barely crossing that line into creative rather than just stupid and loud. Too bad there's no lyric sheet, because this trio looks half-smart.

Rating 7

## Hypocrisy - Abducted (Nuclear Blast '96)

Hard not to draw comparisons with Voivod here, fantastical, computer-generated cover art and the whole UFO/conspiracy concept of the thing (including the Roswell incident: see BÖC's The Vigil and Megadeth's Hangar 18), making for a punishing sci-fi excursion of pleasing proportions. The record was a total pain to make, even though it was recorded in Tagtgren's thriving home studio, the band having to discard four complete songs in the process. **Abducted** is still a brutal assault of death, but greater textures are infused, including those creamy sublime grindcore melodies you only hear way up north. Vocals tone it down just a bit, entering the range of a Quorthon, still distressingly croaked but slightly human. Extreme metal that can serve as one's introduction to the more brutal sounds within the genre, **Abducted** is sorta like old Voivod meets geared-up Swedish thrash of the '90s, caustic, twistedly and opaquely tuneful, yet not afraid to borrow from the '80s.

Rating 8

# I

## Iced Earth - Iced Earth (Century Media '91)

Eschewing one of many usual grading patterns, I'd have to say Iced Earth's debut beats all until **The Dark Saga**, finding the band less exaggerated and eccentric than on their middle spreads. I mean, this album is almost NWOBHM, truly expert gothic metal, somewhere between Gamma Ray, early Maiden, and even Angel Witch. And the axework of Schaffer and Shawver positively shreds like no twin attack I know. Songs are to-the-quick headbangers and really retro in a cool way. Plus like I say, if you like high octane Germanic guitar (via Florida!), you'll probably find this a heady lesson indeed. Surprisingly decent sales, for a far-flung debut.
Rating     8

## Iced Earth - Night Of The Stormrider
(Century Media '92)

Florida's Iced Earth are an oddity in these slobbering times, parlaying their considerable chops into a speedy tech metal ballet worthy of mid-'80s Helloween or Rage or other things post-Maiden and serious. Explosive delivery, but a mite dated, and not particularly in a good way, as was the case with the debut's charming lead-foot rockers. But the artful ones prop it up, introducing to their sound very imaginative, almost new-agey riffs; very classical and freeze-packed in castle blacks, which like I say leaves me a bit blue. Getting too fancy.
Rating     6

## Iced Earth - Burnt Offerings (Century Media '95)

In these times of death, industrial and grunge, there are still light-sensitive trolls who cower dungeon-deep in pursuit of gothic tech-metal à la early Maiden, Fates Warning, Queensryche, and strangely enough here, **Sad Wings**-era Priest. Yea and verily, Florida's Iced Earth still sound extremely ancient and wise, which is what they want, evoking all those grey sour emotions that snuffed our souls in metal's NWOBHM dawning. All is executed with precision here, the band adding for the first time just a tad of death heft to distant themselves from anything too prog or wimpy, getting really dark then staying there until the castle burns brightly. Still, three records deep, of limited appeal I would think, but somewhat a boon to those who like spooky perfection metal.
Rating     7

## Iced Earth - The Dark Saga (Century Media '96)

Funny this world, Iced Earth's earlier records being met with indifference for all the band's dated gothic bluster. But now, well, if this isn't alternative, I don't know what is. **The Dark Saga** is a menacing, power-prog concept record, based on guitarist Jon Schaffer's favourite comic book, **Spawn**, Schaffer even securing **Spawn** artwork for the album cover (of which posters and even a double gatefold vinyl version have been produced). But it's easy to forget this is a concept record, with all the biting, aggressive power metal at hand, tracks like *The Last Laugh* and *Violate* leaving the mark of earlier Iced Earth for Testament (and even Nevermore) terrain. Elsewhere the band's canny gothic grooves return, aided by a crystal-clear Morrisound Studios mix, Schaffer writing tracks with stripped rhythms and pregnant pauses, competing breastplate-to-armor with the Morgana Lefays and Blind Guardians of the world, netting out the Maidenisms for a new marauding urgency.
Rating     8

## Icon - Icon (Capitol '84)

Icon (formerly The Schoolboys), have the distinction of being the only band (besides Quiet Riot for the rest of their sorry career) to attempt to duplicate **Metal Health**. The production is dead identical (for better or worse), the vocals are similar to Chivon DuBlouse's, and the songcraft is admirably thick and anthemic, like the best send-ups from QR's U.S. debut. A direction worth pursuing, yet abandoned, no doubt due to the lack of interest as QR crashed in flames, spewing debris all over the delete bins. The boys back at head office, however, apparently had raging hopes for these Phoenix phoenix's. Easy come, easy go.
Rating     6

## Icon - Night Of The Crime (Capitol '85)

Second time around, Icon winds its way through the vampy, lady killer stylings of Dokken, slowly, atmospherically, but also predictably and melodramatically. In one sense, this style of soap metal was five years ahead of its time, but unfortunately the band hadn't struck its stride yet in terms of carving a persona, which is crucial in this genre of polished radio-motivated gloss, given the necessary sacrifice of edge or danger.
Rating     4

## Icon - Right Between The Eyes  (Megaforce '89)

Icon have become one of those minor Holy Grails in the world of commercial hard rock, their sound rounding many of the hair band bases with considerable skill. So years later, AOR fans look back with some semblance of fondness on their scant and somewhat rare output. Here Wexler and his leathered, lathered angels still retain that Pasha mix of old, while finessing it through conservative but lively songs that sound like Whitesnake meets Ratt, with a touch of the ol' sensitive softy. So rhythms do that stiff metal march, as Coverdaled vocals and vocal harmonies fill up the spaces. Of course none of this stands up in the '90s really, unless you are an AOR archivist and activist, in which instance a case could be made for calling this equal to much of Ratt's output of any era. Second stringers who never really scaled the hump, no thanks to their carbon-dating illustrated cover arts.
Rating                                                              6

## I Found God - Lure  (Outcast '95)

Don't know much about these guys + one gal (vocalist "Christy"), but their sound is worth knowing, a disciplined yet psychedelic deep dish grunge bolstered by a robust guitarist in "Stress" (luv them names). Classy and controlled solos rifle their way through the record while strong, soulful riffs support tracks like Junkie and personal fave Go To Hell, aided and abetted by cannily balanced, punchy yet raw production values. Sorta Soundgarden and RATM meets Zeppelin (Heart!?), with snarling rock chick vocals. Trippy, freaky styleys galore!
Rating                                                              6

## I Love You - I Love You  (Geffen '91)

One of the hottest debut albums in recent years, **I Love You** is yet another of a growing number of releases demonstrating that in the fiercely competitive '90s, you don't have to be veterans to create complicated and mature metal. This gorgeous and haunting roller coaster rock ride mixes stream of consciousness lyrics, where verbs, nouns, and adjectives become each other frequently and chaotically, with sounds as varied as Zeppelin, Sabbath, Soundgarden, The Cult, Danzig, Masters Of Reality, Jane's Addiction, Warrior Soul, and Salty Dog. And that, my friends, is probably the longest list of comparatives in this book, highlighting the fact that I Love You is really a sound unto itself. A psychedelic treatment of straight ahead blues-based metal, I Love You manages to keep it innovative and buoyant, kicking off an ambitious start to what I hope is a long and prolific career. If we must label, this band would be one of a growing legion of spectacular bands operating under the psychedelic metal banner which includes Warrior Soul, Liquid Jesus, Last Crack, Alice in Chains, Mindfunk and to some extent Jane's Addiction and Pearl Jam, all unique creative forces in their own right, beyond and above simple categorization. Suffice to say **I Love You** is bent and nightmarish, yet above ground, full of low-slung grooves, hook-laden in a twisted bluesy metallic way; indeterminable and other-worldly.
Rating                                                              8

## I Love You - All Of Us  (Geffen '94)

In the soaring spirit of true creative souls, I Love You wing out on a tab of euphoric melody, kindred producer Chris Goss accompanying them to netherworlds of hook occupied by the Beatles, Cheap Trick, Saigon Kick and Jellyfish, more often fat and acoustic than the convoluted metal componentry of the debut; all in all, less dark, more fun, funky and unabashedly arranged. This record is just too smart for the masses, plain and simple, **All Of Us** just too full up with sensation, although stunning tracks like Blood, Want Something and especially ecstatic closer 2011 could have as sin-

gles, broken the band big. I get the feeling this is something Blind Melon was after with their maligned and misunderstood **Soup**, a verdant plush collection of sounds that individually are the easiest to digest, yet bunched-up and over-flowing, just confuse those without the patience to persist with a mentalsonic challenge. Remember these guys when combing the delete bins: they are the very essence of under-ratedness.
Rating                                                              9

## I'M'L - Instigating The Mean & Loud  (DeRock '96)

Don't let the cartoony cover art fool you, this is no hardcore harassment. What you will get is a thoroughly funtime powerful blast of metal that crosses Korn, Anthrax and the aggro of Downset. The Korn is in the spaces, the guard let down, the goofin', the slight trace of hip-hopped stoop, the Anthrax is in Dan's awesome Bush-heavy vocal prowess, and the Downset is in the commanding guitar-overdrove street-heat of the thing. I don't know, for a debut from a bunch of Montreal college guys, this one can get its hooks deep within the blood, track after track doing a controlled, riff-perfect mosh that balances heft with lockable melodies. One of the first conventional releases for new imprint DeRock (the band are longtime acquaintances of labelmaker Steve Fazio), and in terms of picking a project with all the musical ducks in a row, the man has picked well.
Rating                                                              8

## Immolation - Dawn Of Possession  (The All Blacks B.V. '91)

Trash thrash that could only come from America's rustbelt, NYC or Florida, Immolation are proto-anachronistic to the bitter poisoned core, wedged betwixt the Broken Hopes and Cannibal Corpses of the world, complex and worldy yet left on 'til burnt and smoking out the place. Beauty cover shot portraying a battle of angels, good and bad, plus of course requisite unreadable logo, like we all care enough to squint, concentrate and bug out, just to be subjected to this dreck.
Rating                                                              3

## Immolation - Here In After  (Metal Blade '95)

I've got about thirty or so of these identical death metal cowpies, rendered useless through suffocation by cheap blastbeats and anti-melodic, sour-faced riffs that smear into songs that smear into full albums that smear into waste-of-space catalogues and careers. Short snappers: utter Satanic death metal from New York; the band's second after '91's **Dawn Of Possession**. Almost a type of hellish jazz or deafening ambient, this stuff goes to very odd, very scorched musical locales, none of which are much use to anybody who isn't going to be in jail soon.
Rating                                                              4

## I Mother Earth - Dig  (Capitol '93)

Lead track The Mothers (also the band's nickname) reminds me of The End from The Doors, and so does the next one even though Jane's Addiction and Soundgarden join the wake, making for one helluva distorted mindbender. Yep, Toronto's I Mother Earth is a wobbly and galactic entity, one of Canada's hippest acts since Sons Of Freedom, something like next generation alternative, lotsa jammin' grunge, psychedelia, funkiness and general lack of concern for the passage of time, which moves with a trajectory similar to January molasses spoon flung at popping popcorn. Head tunes fer sure, very multi-rhythmed and spacey, but when all is said and done, it's too much loitering for my liking, the record jarring in its juxtaposition of hyperlicks with mundane, loungey Floydjazz, sounding something like Jane's **Nothing's Shocking**, but less entertaining on the whackers and not entertaining at all on the quiet bits. I'm always glad to see a band from my homeland that doesn't worship at the red leather altar of Loverboy (see Triumph, Honeymoon Suite, Brighton Rock, Slik Toxik, Harem Scarem, etc.), and apparently it took a lot of chemicals to get the Mothers this "cool", but as much as **Dig** flips all the right philosophical switches in my head, large patches of the record bore me to tears, these of course being the aimless Santana-like noodlings. Granted, the record's 68 minutes long, but it sounds longer, the band's acid haze just crying out for a bit more crack caffeine. Big U.S. buzz, and I wish them well, but I'll be hangin' with Mindfunk or Alice in Chains when I'm looking for a bowl of this type of greenish gruel.

Rating **7**

## I Mother Earth - Scenery And Fish    (EMI '96)

It was pretty easy to peg the Mothers' celebrated debut. They mixed the heavy Jane's Addiction thing with the Santana thing; novel, fresh but easy to demystify. **Scenery And Fish** (dumb title) re-cranks the mystery machine, I Mother Earth dishing up their Blind Melon - **Soup**, perfectly willing to psychedelic down to size their alternative metal tag to alternative. Slinky bass patterns explode reliably into big windmill chords, like a Nirvana with lush, plush and sensual arrangements, very much like Smashing Pumpkins, no qualifiers needed. *Three Days Old* shows us what '90s punk could do with brains, whereas *One More Astronaut* remodels grunge in much the same manner, nice lyric about the weariness of being an astronaut included, no charge. So yes it's true, I Mother Earth are now one of many alternative bands. But their chops and past interest in metal have given them an edge, writing and recording meticulously in this wide, lazy genre, something which the Mothers and the Pumpkins stand pretty much alone. Really has it all within the grooves to break it big, impressionist, infinite colours, lyrics for pleasurable miles, and a plethora of caring sounds arranged so as not to bore, keeping the many circus rings alive with showmanship and suspense. And Santana isn't back until the last song. Why only an **8**? My general weariness with the preciousness of alternative rock, even though this is as healthy as it gets.

Rating **8**

## Impaled Nazarene - Suomi Finland Perkele
(Osmose '94)

Melted shut but sporadically musical, Impaled Nazarene (guys from Impaler and Nazareth?) are yet another grimetime traveller on the hellcome wagon that is the enigmatic, productive (like cancer), and extremely smelly Scandinavian death metal scene. Lots of spewing in Finnish, lots of distressed superfast horror, all peppered with those morose keyboard chords that are all the vogue. All is evidently not well in Reindeerville. Run, hide, repent.

Rating **2**

## Impaled Nazarene - Latex Cult    (Osmose '96)

Making a shift into sexual perversion, Impaled Nazarene also delve into a past rickety thrash metal that becomes almost punk and disassembled at times. So it's just a bunch of noise of a different nature, less overtly evil, more grating. The deathly amongst ye might find humanity here; others, repulsion and annoyance.

Rating **3**

## Imperium - Too Short A Season    (Leviathan '93)

Screw Solitude Aeturnus and Memento Mori, man. I'd rather listen to Imperium (from Holland) for my fix of lumbering prog metal anyday. At least this has bite and direction, **Too Short A Season** benefiting splendidly from stellar but properly raw production and a repertoire of riffs that is fresh as well as aggressive. And vocally, André Vuurboom is a quintessential prog metal voice, clear and operatic but not too high pitched or

theatrical, preferring a cool, understated delivery as his band smokes the song structures to traditional gothic perfection. Probably passed over in favour of better-promoted sonic wizards, Imperium undeniably deserves to join the snobby pack, and maybe lead it, given their wily balance of the violent with the virtuoso.

Rating **8**

## Impaler - If We Had Brains . . .We'd Be Dangerous
(Combat '86)

These Minneapolis moshmorons had a chance at cult status which they inevitably blew, because lo and behold, they're losers. Sense of humour, a novelty cover in Iggy's *Search And Destroy*, some pre-press hype, and crossover production (read: bad) from half-famous guy Bob Mould couldn't help this shit-thrash, which was really meant to be techno or speed.

Rating **3**

## Impellitteri - Stand In Line    (Relativity '88)

Graham Bonnet makes the first less than god like artistic move of his career, finding another egomaniac axe diddler to co-host Alcatrazz - Mark II. **Stand In Line** shines decent, yet could have been another stellar Bonnet project if not for the inanely dil *Somewhere Over The Rainbow* (yes, the same one), another unnecessary remake of *Since You've Been Gone*, a second instrumental, and the overt use of the complete catalogue of Bonnetisms, which in well-placed doses, can be as regal as music gets. One other negative: a brash, clattering recording with too much emphasis on keyboards and techy drums, while on the upside, some quintessential Bonnet rock in *Tonight I Fly, White And Perfect, Secret Lover*, and the title track. Bonnet seems stuck in a rut on this opaque pile, left brooding too deeply in the same gothic, classical, emotive harshness that is also plaguing ex-cohort Malmsteen. I hope someday this guy gets the credit and the backing band he deserves.

Rating **6**

## Impellitteri - Victim Of The System    (Victor '93)

No more Bonnet for fingers-flyin' Chris, as he teams up with Rob Rock for a five track, 18 minute EP that is unsurprisingly state-of-the-art Yngwie with high AOR harmonies (*Cross To Bear* and *The Young And The Ruthless*) and a ton of artful shred (please see "Mozart, Bach and Paganini"-influenced egowank *Glory*. Nice touch: Chris offers a few words on the music and Rob does the same with the lyrics.

Rating **6**

## Incantation - Mortal Throne Of Nazarene
(Relapse '94)

Completely ambient thrashdeathgrind way past the point of ludicrousness. Lyrics are provided, but seriously, I can't even tell when the words begin. Even with printed lyrics, I could not follow a single word in at least six of eight tracks, much less any of the drum "beats." I guess you could call this traditional thrash taken to new heights of brutality, but man, why? Really this is as bad as that Norwegian stuff, but I guess it still gets made because bad is good or something like that.

Rating **0**

## The Incredible Shrinking Dickies - The Incredible Shrinking Dickies    (A&M '79)

An early attempt at cashing in on the punk movement (which we all learned was a logical impossibility), The Dickies were a considerably manic, guitar-based version of The Dead Milkmen crossed with The Buzzcocks (sonically speaking only), with a hint of The Ramones. This mosquito rock debut is a blur of fast plastic guitars; all too often poppy and comical. And the annoyingly yappy helium vocals don't help. Sports a

couple of caustic punk ravers including *Curb Job* and a cover of *Paranoid*. Note: also from the band, **Dawn Of The Dickies** (A&M '80) which is much less the guitar romp, thus, in conjunction with being from the New Wave realm, a bit too much of a stretch to be officially reviewed in our hallowed volume.
Rating 4

### Incubus - To The Devil A Daughter (Guardian '84)

Like, do these guys think they're Demon or what? Thoroughly quizzling goo goo goth, drained of any semblance of power or misty mood by a hands-tied delivery and crusty-tone knob job. Manacled and laughable to the point of exhaustion. Lucifer betwixt.
Rating 0

### Incubus - Enjoy Incubus (Immortal/Sony '97)

Geez, for a somewhat dismissed band, Faith No More sure seem to have inspired many followers, including California hard-hoppers Incubus, who commence their big label career with this modest odds 'n' sods EP. The six tracks enclosed attack with explosive deliberation, sounding like a fired-up Peppers 'n' Primus with the Bloodhound Gang's sense of culture shock. So there's meat on them thar bones, the band's nasty, razor-funked grooves filled up with all sorts of novel sounds, few samples really, more like a smorg of production tips and tricks. Performances of note: Patton-miked Brandon Of The Jungle on vine-swinging vocals, and Dirk Lance, billed as bass and adult entertainment. Very recommended, if over-the-top mid-years Peppers be your thing.
Rating 7

### Infectious Grooves - The Plague That Makes Your Booty Move . . . It's The Infectious Grooves (Sony '91)

Essentially a solo project from Mike Muir, lead throat of ever-tightening crossover thrashers Suicidal Tendencies, and self-proclaimed, sky-straddling philosopher of a disintegrating America, Infectious Grooves explores the more intensely fwapping, funky, bass-driven thang in Muir's cluttered and anxious head. To my mind, the infectious grooves that fill this whirlwind of urban reckoning represent the highest, most enjoyable points of the Suicidal experience, while respecting the modern rock fan's short attention span, appreciation of risky arrangements, and sophisticated sense of humour. Lots of cuts, and hilarious inter-toon dialogues featuring one "Sarsippius Sulemanagic Jackson The Third", central but intrusive third man out in some kind of reptilian recording session that forms the sub-plot of this dynamic funk metal fest. Some bad and indifferent reviews in the music press due to its supposed exploitation of a hot genre, yet to be fair, it never pretends to mimic any particular other band. Fact is, there really isn't much out there to imitate, the limited numbers making up the genre possessing wildly different sounds. Just kick back, assume the attitude, and strut the funky ass beat reverberating through this technically adept mosh. Eminently worth it, if only for an additional trip at Muir's life-obsessed brain, set to a disciplined ballet of edgy street mechanics. Notable publics include Jane's Addiction drummer Stephen Perkins (who actually gets equal billing in the ads), Suicidal's Rocky George, and Ozzy, who took the band on his **No More Tears** tour.
Rating 8

### Infectious Grooves - Sarsippius' Ark (Sony '93)

More of the same hot-blooded sticky jams and I'm in deep dish, groove fish heaven. Y'know, it's kinda like this: I rarely play this band (indeed no one does), but dang it when I do, if I'm not in awe at the slamming large power grooves Mike and Co. squeeze from these songs. Main dif here: more of Sarsippius and his raps

(again fine by me), and a couple of covers, Bowie's *Fame*, and the best rendition of Zep's difficult to perfect *Immigrant Song* I've ever heard, driven into the concrete by a recurring wah wah mantra and phat drums fer miles. Face it, Mike's a cool guy, even if his singing style is more about speak than croon.
Rating 8

### Infectious Grooves - Groove Family Cyco (Sony '94)

The Grooves regroup and rethink the increasing novelty feel of their act, storming back with this feast of stun guitar set to crystal-strung bass flippers, going dis way and dat for a sound that delves deeper into hybridness and intellect. Gone are those inter-raps, laying plain a bunch of big, bad songs, stretchy punkfunk ravers that profess and succeed in funk metal dominion, while others are running from the genre on the heels of the Faith No More guys who created it. Easy to do when you have two totally different vehicles at your behest. So the verdict: seriously hung, seriously funky by way of pollution. And Muir's lyrical vision has sharpened, his tales both focused and colourful, hard-hitting and crammed with energy. So the band wars continue. Who shall triumph, this intensified Grooves or the flat out-of-control Suicidal of '94? Well, neither, both fizzling like a dud firecracker, Muir moving onto an anemic solo career.
Rating 8

### In Flames - The Jester Race (Nuclear Blast '96)

Folks of the metal ilk everywhere are diggin' this semi-veteran band of thoughtful Swedes. For wedged between the banalities of purely anti-social death metal and more commercial forms, In Flames carve their niche, combining harmonic, surgically steely twin-riffing with the caustic scrape of frostcore. Almost a backlash against dangerously commercial bands like Cemetary and Sentenced (not to mention the gone-full-alt. of Pyogenesis), In Flames have said enough is enough, drawing the line well within the zone of grind. But the magic comes with the fact that they have embraced musicianship, careful arrangements and meticulous, (thought brutish) production, arriving at a type of snobby gothic form of Entombed, less the mess-abouts, more aspired to classical greatness. Lyrics also aspire to a level not unlike poetry, even if it gets a little awkward of idiom at times. Nevertheless, quite a refreshing read. But it is all those smarter than Maiden twin leads that really usher us along red carpet-like, visions of Sykes and Gorham and Robertson floating by like mist in the night. Reminds me of the excitement of those mid-years Edge Of Sanity and At The Gates records, In Flames tapping that vein, figuring out how to deliver just enough sweet nectar with their blightful, hurtful death metal.
Rating 9

### Inner Thought - Worldly Separation (Witchhunt '94)

Toronto legend Bob Sadzak and his grim, dead-serious death metal band Inner Thought have done quite well with this first sojourn, attracting the attention of Dwell Records in California, who breathed second life into sales despite the band not touring. The record is dedicated to the victims of the war in Yugoslavia, grinding forth a peculiar and exacting industrial death, emphasis on the grind but sent modern with samples and tastefully applied electronic drums. All in all, a daunting success, even though it's misery through and through, the effect hair-raisingly bolstered by the decayed face medical shots throughout the booklet.
Rating 6

### Inner Thought - Perspectives (Witchhunt '95)

Bobby Sadzak's cathedrals of pain loom larger on this skull-frying and obtuse death metal headtrip (once again crushingly recorded at Metalworks in Missis-

sauga, Ont.), getting both more caustic and progressive at once, taking the listener on a journey into the depths of political and personal agony. Almost scared to listen to it, finding this industrial-based labyrinth of undercrust metal just too somber and detached to prove pleasurable. Once again, sales have been modestly brisk, demonstrating that there are a ton of sick metal puppies out there. Essentially a two-man band at this point.
Rating 7

## Integrity - Systems Overload (Victory '95)

These urbancore crewcuts are gathering a bit of a history, prolifically pumping out a capable metallic hardcore street punk that whacks the listener upside the skinhead. **Systems Overload** is a bit of a chore to listen to, but for fans, is a bane of pain, offering tracks from '86 and '89 demos for your huffing pleasure. An unmistakable sheen of cool, even if it's a bunch of racket.
Rating 5

## Integrity - Humanity Is The Devil (Victory '96)

Man, Dwid's hollering can grate the nerves after awhile, but his backing clan churns out an elevated din that is edging closer to metal every sermon. And if that don't float your goat, there's always the Pushead cover art, the little Charles Manson boy riding a flying fish, and the little matchbook pamphlet warning that in fact "humanity is the devil", and there ain't a damn thing you can do about it. A shocking blast of rough-hewn, straight-edge scarface punk that dents the head with thoughts that all is not well.
Rating 7

## Internal Bleeding - Voracious Contempt
(Pavement '95)

Blasphemous grimcore of a tormentous and shivering nature, **Voracious Contempt** teams New York's Internal Bleeding with cracked brain producer Scott Burns for a low-groveled, down-toned death surge of cruel, mechani-Hell proportions. Brutally bashed beyond recognition except to the trained and tortured of ear, call this one kinda like Cannibal Corpse meets the blast furnaces of Florida. What's a **3** anyways?
Rating 3

## Into Another - Seemless (Hollywood '95)

Recipe for success in '96: look pasty, thin and British with stringy problem hair like Alanis, but play heavy metal (just don't call it that), or more accurately good ol' grunge. Well, it's working for Into Another, this '95 record released for real in June '96, attracting lots of talk with its smart, tidy, upscale Soundgarden vibe, good alternative lyrics (the one department where alt. often thrives) crooned Cornell-like by Richie Birkenhead over a catchy, slightly pop-blended version of lusty Seattle sonics, this record recoincidentally recorded by Rick Parashar in the rainy city. Despite dumb band and record name, plus dumb cover art, word is deservedly getting out. Like I say, just don't call it metal. Similar situations: Howlin' Maggie, Imperial Drag, The Verve Pipe, Tripping Daisy and Seven Mary Three, all ever so slightly too mellow for the Guide.
Rating 8

## Intricate - [va:l] (Century Media '93)

This artsy, inhospitable little piece of German thrash terror makes quite a dent, demarcating yet another sliverish subgenre in extreme metal, Intricate blasting out a sort of ragged, unhewn technical goth, somehow capturing the creative ethic of prime Faith No More while sounding nothing like Patton and co. Quite nightmarish and drowned, one thinks of bands like Anacrusis and Mekong Delta, although Intricate go for more of a crushing, simple and effective vibe, creating escape

scapes of a considerably intellectual nature. Like I say, it makes an impression fer sure.
Rating 8

## Iron Angel - Hellish Crossfire (Banzai '85)

Iron Angel wane through life as Helloween with the flu; a dense wall of speed, with simpler heads-down riffs and muttering vocals mixed way back in a manner that says with a thick German accent: "our music is so loud, you can't hear me sing." **Hellish Crossfire** is OTT-level intense, but so drearily uniform in its sonic assault that it wears the listener to a withered mass of sludge by album's end. German metal in every non-flattering sense of the term.
Rating 3

## Iron Angel - Winds Of War (Banzai '86)

More of the same relentless, humourless, mechanical clatter as per **Hellish Crossfire**. I take it this type of heavy machinery is crafted for those filthy Belgian poverty-metal slugfests you read about in **Kerrang!**, which are usually visited by massive rainstorms and amusing reports of crushed fans.
Rating 3

## Iron Maiden - Iron Maiden (EMI '80)

The spraypaint was on the wall for Maiden to acquire intense coin with this simplest of approaches. Maiden were one of the first NWOBHM bands to get their act together enough to put out a decent album, after a good three years as the original princes of the poverty line, while simultaneously filling a theatrical void in music at a time more accustomed to punk nihilism, packing Eddie, their large green dude, and a recognizable logo ready for the marketing age. Maiden also had Attitude, the punter work ethic, headbangin' along side and never above the growing legion of rivetheads worldwide. Maiden just seemed to have it all together, as underdogs with hugely upward momentum; well-regarded liggers who were fans first, respecting of their metal precursors, working with an obsessed enthusiasm for creation. **Iron Maiden** was a fitting debut, setting the mood for the historical, neon horror concept that mutates Eddie to this day. The record's decidedly gothic, based firmly in the ghoulish metal camp with such Euro-tinged mania as *Prowler, Phantom Of The Opera*, and *Charlotte The Harlot*, all emphasizing the album's hurried, energetic delivery, the record as a whole representing a souped-up although less ground-breaking version of Priest or Rainbow, textured with a newer, more metallized version of harmony-based soloing made famous first by Wishbone Ash then Lizzy. An admirable, if not musically earth-shattering first step that goes a long way towards establishing a base on which to build empires. Brooding ballad *Remember Tomorrow* is apparently written for Di'anno's grandfather. Note: In '95, Castle Communications reissued the entire catalogue up to **Fear Of The Dark**, as double picture disc CD sets, exhaustively and methodically providing Maiden's wealth of b-sides, rarities etc., on each second provided disc. See end of each respective review for brief run-down. Disc at hand, Iron Maiden, offered *Drifter* (live), silly 1980 pop metal tune *Burning Ambition*, and a live Di'anno-era take on *I've Got The Fire*.
Rating 7

## Iron Maiden - Killers (EMI '81)

We young punters went absolutely nutters when this ghoulish beast feast first hit the racks, and many still thinks it's Maiden's best ever. I on the other hand marvel at the concept, the recording, the power and the energy, but find it a bit flawed in terms of consistency. But hard denying the righteous ground-breaking metal here, driving classics like *Wrathchild, Murders In The Rue Morgue, Innocent Exile*, and the galloping

proto-speed title tune to new plateaus. But there is one instrumental and, yea and verily, *Twilight Zone* and *Drifter* suck. Still, minor drawbacks on an early NWOBHM cornerstone with so many innovative ideas, emotive riffs and confident technical touches. And **Killers** is worlds ahead of the band's debut in class and maturity, Maiden no longer being denied star status given this huge, exuberant leap into respectability. Still fairly speedy and rough, **Killers** offers all sorts of twists on goth themes and other still fresh '70s traditions, while Di'anno (who would shortly leave, apparently at odds with Maiden's rapidly changing fortunes) proves himself an enigmatic voice at the mike. **Killers** found Maiden poised nicely to take over the Brit metal throne so willingly vacated by Judas Priest, and in subsequent years, the band would prove worthy of the position as kings of the genre. That is, until Priest stormed the palace and raped its subjects wielding *Painkiller*, their awe-inspiring battle royal for the '90s, while Maiden would sit mired in complex impotence. Castle reissue bonus tracks: catchy beefed-up Skyhooks number *Women In Uniform*, third-rate Maiden scamper *Invasion*, *Phantom* (live), and all of **Maiden Japan**.
Rating                                                                 9

# Iron Maiden - Maiden Japan   (EMI '81)
This live 5-track EP slices and dices tracks from **Iron Maiden** and **Killers**, serving as a decent swan song for founding vocalist Paul Di'anno who would shortly hereafter be replaced by manic Samson troll, Bruce Dickinson. Highlights: *Wrathchild* and *Killers*. Included in entirety with the Castle reissue of **Killers**.
Rating                                                                 6

# Iron Maiden - The Number Of The Beast   (EMI '82)
Maiden albums seem to make or break on how convincingly the percussive attack carries the momentum. On **The Number Of The Beast**, Clive Burr's drumming and indeed the overall sound is loose, midrange and clumsy, which tends to bury ditties like the pointless *Run To The Hills*, *Gangland*, and to some extent, the much feared title track. It's as if the tunes were too fast for a band scurrying along, trying to keep up with faster metal from overseas, and thrashier vibes from the likes of Venom. However, the odd, open recording lends a more successful chaos to the more imposing tracks such as *Invaders*, *The Prisoner*, and top fave, furious *Charlotte The Harlot* sequel *22, Acacia Avenue*. Strange that after the accomplished, sure-footed whomp of **Killers**, Maiden would make such a punk-drunk disc, one that has more in common with the debut's hurried tone. In any event, **The Number Of The Beast** is generally solid (taken with a heaping dose of nostalgia), as we watched the ludicrous scorn heaped upon Eddie's green-skinned shoulders by the religious right. Bruce Dickinson puts in a maniacal performance here as he convincing slides into the driver's seat as both vocal hellion and circus master (Note: Bruce was a proven screamer. Check out his awesome performance on Samson's fierce **Shock Tactics** and earlier, less impressive works by Paul's doomed assemblage). Even though this album was undeniably and unfortunately taken to heart by busloads of messed-up little teenage Satanic dudes, those of us who kept it in perspective rocked to a celebratory, drinkin' at the pub, Up The Hammers! record, a spontaneous mean little slab, exuding the freshness of a band on their way to bigger and better wallets. Castle reissue bonus tracks (not much of which to speak): awesome Maiden original *Total Eclipse* and a live *Remember Tomorrow*.
Rating                                                                 8

# Iron Maiden - Piece Of Mind   (EMI '83)
Eddie's pissed, and so we have it, Maiden's finest hour, a heaping slab of molten sullen gothic death that wastes all pretenders with a single unstoppable offensive of doom. **Piece Of Mind** rages most heavily, due in no small part to two elements: Martin Birch's most purely punishing recording anywhere, and Nicko's most convincing kick-ass percussive performance ever stamped with the Maiden seal of approval. The two work a rhythmic whirlwind of fear, caging and expressing the core element of the Maiden persona for really the first time, a devastating backbone that carries some of the weightiest grooves forged in metallic fire (even Harris and his over-active bass find synergy). Bruce lays waste a healthy piece of his own mind, belting out truly interesting tales of deceit and intrigue over well-written riff rockers such as the percussively complex *Where Eagles Dare*, the heads-down *Die With Your Boots On*, and Maiden catalogue centerpiece *The Trooper*, which features the single most remembered and celebrated Murray/Smith death-from-the-skies twin-lead riff. Only the filler-ish *Quest For Fire* falls short, as the band has never sounded so steadfast, driven and focused towards war-torn battle. **Piece Of Mind** becomes the thickest, most uncompromising chapter in the sometimes disjointed Iron Maiden catalogue, garnering further distinction as a metal disc that inspired and drove other musicians towards getting into the bars and kicking some Marshall ass. A stirring display of triumph for players and listeners alike. Castle reissue bonus tracks: raging studio covers of Montrose's *I've Got The Fire* and Jethro Tull's *Cross Eyed Mary*, both rendered top-flight by a **Piece Of Mind**-inspired performance and mix.
Rating                                                                 10

# Iron Maiden - Powerslave   (EMI '84)
**Powerslave** is what **No Prayer For The Dying** attempts to be. Lacking the coherent brilliance and emotional focus of **Piece Of Mind**, **Powerslave** is nevertheless full of fierce metal, recorded with considerably more spontaneous edge and danger than any previous Maiden slab (indeed, the band's quickest assembled record to date), as witnessed on no-frills classic *2 Minutes To Midnight*, one of the band's most passionate and powerful, yet least characteristic tracks ever. Main shortcoming though: stylistically and lyrically, **Powerslave** is a chaotic disjointed ride through time. Concepts are too cute and encapsulated, as we get a World War II story, a tune about dueling, and an all too simple sketch re-telling of *Rime Of The Ancient Mariner*, only *2 Minutes To Midnight* rising above schlock, offering a poetic apocalyptic vision that exceeds the pretentious story-telling slant of the rest of the album. Luckily, the screaming live-feel metal tends to deafen the conceptual shortness as rockers like *Aces High*, *Flash Of The Blade*, and the epic crunching title toon kick with a conviction that matches at least the crystalline intent of **Piece Of Mind**. So even if **Powerslave** is musically up to snuff, for the first time we witness writer's block, as the toys, trinkets, and novelty ideations crowd the foreground where amps once stood alone. Castle reissue bonus tracks (a classic batch): two very good covers, *Rainbow's Gold* and *King Of Twilight*, a live tune, plus the covert recording of that hilarious, legendary backstage band dust-up, Nicko all upset over a roadie trying to get him a message during his drum solo. Absolutely eye-watering. Don't miss it.
Rating                                                                 9

# Iron Maiden - Live After Death   (EMI '85)
**Live After Death** is one of the better live records around due to great tunes and the meticulous attention paid to the recording process. Packaging-wise we get stacks of desirable extras: muchos live and backstage shots (over 150), production notes from Martin Birch, equipment lists, all the tour dates, and even lyrics to the included tunes to catch up on a few that didn't come with the studio stuff. Good value from a band that prides itself on coming through with the goods.

CD version clipped off all of side four of the double vinyl, so the thing could fit on a single CD (a rare victory for wax!). Castle reissue bonus tracks (surprise and yawn): three live tunes not on the original vinyl or CD. Also of note, the reissue also lops off all of side four (five tracks) from the original vinyl release.

Rating 7

## Iron Maiden - Somewhere In Time (EMI '86)

A major letdown after the metallic depth of **Powerslave**, **Somewhere In Time** is exactly half an album's worth of good material. The general feel is of a record that did not need to be written, of stories that did not need to be told. On the positive, we get the trademark Maiden gallop of *Caught Somewhere In Time*, emotive but percussively clumsy lead single *Wasted Years*, the weighty and innovative *Sea Of Madness*, and the mysterious *Stranger In A Strange Land*. As for scrap metal, we get the ridiculous melodies of *Heaven Can Wait*, straight filler *Deja Vu*, another trite history lesson in *Alexander The Great*, and a song about long distance running fer chrisake! And that's it. Four good (not even all great) Maiden tunes and four losers, most too long, mucking about and melodramatic, totaling a hefty bag 51:18. The worst Maiden album so far, sporting a collection of rehashed ideas that are too topical, overwrought and forced, while at the same time lazy. Album cover contains a good 75 or so "in jokes", making this a better view than listen. Castle reissue bonus tracks: three solid covers (by whom, I don't know), and one humourous, heavy and likeable original called *Sheriff Of Huddersfield*.

Rating 6

## Iron Maiden - Seventh Son Of A Seventh Son
(EMI '88)

This album sucks, sort of, track for track there being some fair to middling Maiden rockers. But I, and nobody I know, ever plays it. Faults are numerous and thinly veiled: boring simplistic manifestations of the trademark harmony solo sound, unnecessary and profuse riff changes, pointless breaks, obnoxious yet pointless lyrics steeped in hocus pocus, and general middle-age (and middle ages) malaise. **Seventh Son** slogs along competently enough, even rocking out somewhat on *The Evil That Men Do, Only The Good Die Young*, and *Moonchild*. But generally, tunes take too long to build, polluted with strange sprawling instrumental sections that go nowhere, based on oxymoronically untuneful melodic riffs. Idea-wise the band is grasping for whatever they can fashion into a "Maiden" song, absolutely forcing the concept, in general, **Seventh Son** finding Maiden painting by numbers in exploration of the most dubious of hair-brained schemes, as the muse stays home for the second album in a row. Hell, even Eddie's got one foot in the grave. Castle reissue bonus tracks: chunky retro original *Black Bart Blues*, stirring Lizzy cover *Massacre*, remakes of *Prowler* and *Charlotte The Harlot*, and five catalogue-spanning live tracks.

Rating 5

## Iron Maiden - No Prayer For The Dying (EMI '90)

Maiden was left for dead, lost somewhere in time, doomed to repeat the seventh song of the same song in the eternal scrap heap in the sky when from out of nowhere comes the realization that there will be truly no prayer for the dying. Maybe it was the departure of Adrian Smith (see A.S.A.P.), the Bruce solo excursion, the long layoff, or maybe the tired slop that passed for the last two vinyl disasters, but **No Prayer For The Dying** marks a more than partial return to the days with teeth. Full hell-bent merits for aggression and power from all camps, especially Bruce, Nicko, and the knobmeisters. And judging from interviews, new axeman Janick Gers apparently deserves much credit for

the renewed vigor. The problem however is a two-fold continued lapse in the riff and lyrical departments. Riff-wise, a good third of this is old as the hills, almost reactionary, sounding as if the tattooed millionaires are panicking for ideas. Lyrically, we get the same disjointed mix of history lessons, war stories, morality pieces, tales of horror and laughable attempts at controversy in the lame x-ratedness of *Bring Your Daughter . . . To The Slaughter* and *Hooks In You*. And the inter-album, cut-for-cut comparisons are beginning to show with painful clarity (You figure them out. It ain't hard). Hell, enough whining though. I actually like this flawed, never brilliant, but often kick-ass effort more than I had expected. And it actually gets better with repeated headbangs. Despite three or four shit-box clunkers, much of **No Prayer** shows a band of vets having a blast for the first time in a long time. Smokers such as *Tailgunner*, the previously maligned *Bring Your Daughter . . . To The Slaughter* and *Hooks In You*, and lead single *Holy Smoke* have timeless feels and knock 'em dead deliveries, propelled by Bruce's most venomous and insistent vocal efforts laid to wax. Yet **No Prayer For The Dying** is not without problems: *The Assassin* is dull and clunky, *Mother Russia* could be the centerpiece of the next Spinal Tap tour, much of the record indicative of a band with pride forced to try harder. Sadly, follow-ups will prove **No Prayer** to be a mere blip in Maiden's creative collapse. Castle reissue bonus tracks: four covers, *All In Your Mind (?)*, *Kill Me Ce Soir* (Golden Earring), *I'm A Mover* (Free), and *Communication Breakdown* (duh), all mere cute curiosities than anything synergistic with the Maiden sound.

Rating 7

## Iron Maiden - Fear Of The Dark (EMI '92)

Obviously completely out of touch with reality, Maiden come limping back with this sad relapse, sporting another brutal album cover, on which Eddie is portrayed as a doddering old crumbler fused to a tree, an apt metaphor to say the least. Minds obviously not on their work, the boys in the band simply sleepwalk through this tiring, surprisingly mellow journey that harkens back to the worst of progressive Maiden mistakes. And Bruce's lyrics are *still* going downhill, along with the musicianship, arrangements and mix, again too lite-weighted towards 'arry's strangely rickety, null 'n' void bass sound. Too bad, because I'd like to have some kind words for such an influential lot, but **Fear Of The Dark** proves **No Prayer For The Dying** was more a snarling fluke than a conscious realization of what's sliding where. What can these guys be thinking? I don't know . . . but one is simply led to cringe at the awful choruses, confusing breaks, lame twin leads, and hasty assemblage at work in these shiftless tunes. And there's no point in getting specific about it, because even the best efforts like lead taste *Be Quick Or Be Dead* envelope annoying failed experiments that betray a band furiously combing their back catalogue for that lost spark. Sadly uniform and dull, and surprisingly lacking in direction relentless composition after composition, Maiden seems on the verge of losing all semblance of respect for good, truly and grimly exemplifying the term washed-up. Fear of the dark . . . hot issue, that one. . . definitely worth examination. Castle reissue bonus tracks: a real hodge podge including three live tracks, a jokey acoustic boogie, two electric boogies, and an uncharacteristically lacklustre performance on Montrose's *Space Station No.5* and Budgie's *I Can't See My Feelings*.

Rating 4

## Iron Maiden - Live At Donnington 1992 (EMI '93)

Recorded at Maiden's choice domain, home of the biggest metalfests in the world, **Live At Donnington** is one of *three* concurrent live releases for this long-standing bunch of yobs. Weird. Mix of old and new, inspired and insipid. Designed to look like a bootleg. Ho-hum and hum-drum.

Rating     6

## Iron Maiden - A Real Live One  (EMI '93)

With a title that leaks droll sarcasm, Maiden's fourth live release proves that mainland Europeans will cheer at anything, not to mention sing along, as if they knew what the words meant. As if subjecting us to even hastier renditions of the band's last few and most disastrous years is supposed to revive a flagging career, I mean, some reality pie here, please. Actually, it's more of a tombstone, because **A Real Live One** was being discussed (even before release) as one last nail before Bruce leaves for a solo career, the only honourable move from the Maiden camp in metal eons. Shit tunes, save for *Be Quick Or Be Dead* (Bruce's range is shot), *Bring Your Daughter . . . To The Slaughter* and *Tailgunner*, with laughable emphasis on Harris' bass (Steve, it's not that interesting an instrument). File with the onslaught of Genesis and Tull live showstoppers as stupefyingly unnecessary.

Rating     4

## Iron Maiden - A Real Dead One  (EMI '93)

Eminently more enjoyable than its shovel-to-the-head twin, **A Real Dead One** only mangles old songs, exhibiting and vilifying a rhythm section that is not so much cookin', but boiled over and burning up, staining the stove. Cool things about this waste of space: one of those family trees by Frame and Carver which illuminates much, and a couple moldy oldies like *Prowler* and *Transylvania* that had yet to make it to record live. Bruce sounds so bored though, as if he's daydreaming about his writing career or something, self-reflecting on the ludicrousness of his lyrics. I dunno, Maiden's tantamount career screw-up just creeps me, melting my respect for the human race. I mean, these guys really worked hard to find out how to suck. An **8** without Steve Harris on bass.

Rating     6

## Iron Maiden - The X Factor  (EMI '95)

Pathetic. You'd think with all eyes on the band, a new singer "chosen from thousands" and three years to think about it, Steve Harris and his stooges would come up with something with a pulse. First Blaze: obvious choice, likeable Limey bloke, looks like Bruce, can do a weak impression of Bruce. Safe as milk. Good job Steve. Why rock a sinking tugboat. Somehow, Blaze's spirited performances on those robust Wolfsbane albums is erased from his memory banks. Here the man is unbelievably cheesy (what else can you be given these lyrucks), poorly doing Bruce, occasionally out of tune, always asleep and thankfully mixed way back, no treble, no bass, no authority whatsoever. Great. Then there's the songs: long for no reason (it's called cellulose), boring as, well, Maiden's last five records, lame bass intros, outros, insidetros, tacos . . . songs about movies (again), war (five of them: all worse than the one before it, grade eight literacy level at best), being depressed and monks (complete with three-times-removed ripped-off chanting). The production is awful: noisy drums (which evidently have never met a click track), too much bass as usual (both the frequency and the instrument), lame guitars, and ah, Blaze. And speaking of guitars: slow aimless trademark Maiden solos leaping out at the most inopportune times, and riffs seriously, not worthy of the band's debut album back in '80. Gers is a joke. He hasn't contributed a thing to this band since he's arrived. These are barely even riffs at all, more like brainless strumming. And then there's the dismal soccer chants handed over to Blaze (Steve's a football fanatic. Evidently what he hears in the stadium is worthy of his records). It's now (and always was) painfully obvious

why Bruce flew the coop, and it's the same reason Halford disturbed the Priest: to avoid being buried under an avalanche of CHEESE, or in kinder terms to get out before the band became an out-dated, outmoded, caricature of the worst cartoon abuses of the tired term heavy metal. You know what? Creativity can just dry up. It happened with Scorpions, it happened with Priest, it happened with Ted, and it's happened to Tony Iommi. Steve, it's happened to you.

Rating     2

## Iron Maiden - Best Of The Beast  (Castle '96)

This is pret' near a book review, any self-respecting Maiden fan already in possession of 95% of the musical nuggets enclosed. The rarities are: a humdrum new track called *Virus*, and pioneering, bluesy Soundhouse takes on *Strange World* and *Iron Maiden*, circa '78, featuring the elegant Paul Sam(p)son on guitar, the rest being a collection of the band's hits assembled in reverse chronological order over two long CDs, present metal senility to blessed birth. But the packaging is remarkable, a hardcover book in box, featuring a ton of photos, lyrics to all enclosed tracks, and most notably, every Eddie illustration ever used, including some that have never seen the light of day. Also included, the updated Maiden family tree by Pete Frame. Verdict: a must-have for collectors and Eddie fans, less so for catalogue miners, although a fond time-travel is magically achieved come the earlier disc two. Important note: EMI version is a single CD with a 20 page book crammed with much the same stuff. Jolly Roger!

Rating     7

## It Bites - The Big Lad In The Windmill  (Virgin '86)

Impeccable musicheads who have come full circle from the progressive meadows grafted by U.K. and replanted by Marillion, It Bites always put on a great spread, as evidenced by this rich and varied debut. Rivethead's warning: this record contains no metal, and really very little in terms of guitar-dominated rock. Conversely, it's a cool, upbeat and forward-marching, progressive rock record that overflows with arrangement cleverness. It Bites would eventually discover the wisdom embedded in loud guitars, but for now, the present piece garners some degree of admiration in its heavily adorned attention to craft.

Rating     6

## It Bites - Once Around The World  (Virgin '88)

Coming to the band's first two records after introduction via **St. Louis**, it's easy to track the progression from the dizzying prog rock love-in of the first, through the smart clatter and edge of **Once Around The World** to the guitar-based rhythmic machine of the third. And that's about it. In comparison to the debut, less straight-faced reverence of Genesis (as per modern manifestation Marillion) as a growing use of rock'n'roll idioms grace this gushingly enjoyable and indulgent work of very British pomp rock. Again, in defense of including It Bites in this book at all, they're the sort of band the adventuresome metal fan and indeed the practicing musician among our legions may appreciate, and may not otherwise ever hear about. Worth checking out for lovers of the musical process or merely followers of melodious contusion.

Rating     7

## It Bites - Eat Me In St. Louis  (Virgin '89)

This third album by these enigmatic northern Englanders wails on its predecessors rock-wise yet still isn't overly heavy. But it looks the part, what with all the long hair and cool Roger Dean graphics, so if you are the uncompromising sort, consider yourself saved from disappointment. The best way to describe It Bites '89 is as a modern day Gentle Giant, yet simultaneously much more guitar-edged (shades of Brian May?), dan-

cier, more electronic, and somehow metal-like although only occasionally heavy metal. Vocally, Peter Gabriel comes to mind all too immediately, complete with Pete's latter-day yelping, a too sincere rendering yet not so slavish to the point of parody. I only like about half of this album, finding the hi-techiness and dance rhythms a bit cold, but the half that I do like is just so heady and beautiful, so extremely rich in melodic choruses, I just want to play it over and over, and slide into a deep blue, inescapable melancholy. **Eat Me In St. Louis** is unique in so many areas that it deserves respect at least as a studio tour de force and fusion-ethic groundbreaker. It may not be your style, but check it out, if only for the admiration of its inherent stand-alone quality. Guitarist and leader Francis Dunnery moved on to join Robert Plant's band for the **Fate Of Nations** album and tour, after which he hatched two under-rated, vastly divergent solo albums.
Rating    8

## It Is I - Evolve    (Dwell '94)

A young Dwell Records has picked It Is I to be one of their first signings, and it is with excrutiating pain that I wade into this odd sound-destroying experience. San Jose's It Is I thunder forth with a dazed, sludgey retro-grind characterized by deliberately crashy, trashy slow drum beats. The entire delivery is thoughtfully rough-hewn, wastey and jammy, lending the band an anti-commercial integrity, even as it squashes the listener's face against the exit door, waves of black tar filling the room with stench, heat and utter darkness. Imagine Trouble, Penance and Candlemass driven further underground, left smothering, gasping, slowly slowing. Love the conceptual fumes, verdict's still out on the pragmatic, demonstrated, realized death knells.
Rating    7

## Jackyl - Jackyl (Geffen '92)

At long, lizardly last, a shambling band of mischief makers wicked this way comes, packing a rare shakedown of party metal sounds most akin to '70s-obsessed rumbling train Salty Dog. Jackyl reign from the South, and the isolation in the land of heat and stuck pigs does the party proud, this debut just cookin' with sterling crisp recordings of open wide, strong-arm hard rock structures, evoking images of Bon Scott and the emotional legacy of **Highway To Hell**. Simply a splendid blunt rock album, **Jackyl** is a perfect blend of past values and present levels of quality, mustached maniac Jesse Dupree considered by some to have revived the dormant spirit of the Motor City Madman himself. Faves would include the memorable *Down On Me*, *Back Off Brother*, and lead cut *I Stand Alone*, all emphasizing the band's excellent harmony vocals come chorus time. There's no reason these mildly X-rated rock dogs can't be big news on the strip. The attitude's dead on, keeping the proceedings well within the finest intentions of simple rock'n'roll. One of the best power chord party records of the year, one that put deceptively better acts like Slaughter and Rhino Bucket in a curiously bad light. Became notorious for their chainsaw solo in boogie buzzard hit *The Lumberjack*, and solidly respected for their support slot success on Aerosmith's **Get A Grip** tour.
Rating                                                      8

## Jackyl - Push Comes To Shove (Geffen '94)

Coming from a band with so much forward thrust, a band touted as the next Aerosmith, **Push Comes To Shove**'s a bit of a limp one, and it ain't just me sayin' it. Jackyl's important second surprisingly lacks the bite, the hunger, the rhythmic aggression of the debut. Dupree and his leather lungs are in shrieking fine form, but riffs meander and smear rather than slice, over lukewarm production that is up to Bruce Fairbairn's usual clueless standards. True, the record has a strange charm to it, definitely shambling less commercial, more authentically southern, engaging some truly cool melodies as on *I Want It* and *I Am The I Am*, but it's hard to believe nobody picked up on how lackadaisical the songwriting was here. I'm distressed, 'cos somebody has to save party rock.
Rating                                                      6

## Jackyl - Night Of The Living Dead (Music For Nations '96)

Jackyl's a band that's done surprisingly brisk business with their redneck roots metal, so it's only a bit stupid to be making this live record after only two slabs. I caught the band live in T.O., backing up Aerosmith, and they are pretty good at their shtick (let's face it, these are easy songs to play live). So here we have it, a record manufactured in England, distributed by Futurist at regular price, celebrating a New Year's Eve gig in Dallas ushering in '95. The sound is solid, pure concert bottom end, and Jesse's Jesse, circus-mastering the band through eight album highlights plus two newies, *Mental Masturbation*, a no-brains booger, and *Deeper In Darkness*, one of those Hagar hang-fer-verse then cut in with a mean riff thangs. Some photos, a dirty little letter from Dupree, and a hair band with a quarter ounce of integrity good time.
Rating                                                      6

## Jag Panzer - Ample Destruction (Azra '84)

Mechanically sound upon its unleashing, **Ample Destruction** had actually been repackaged and shipped in ample supply seven years after the fact, demonstrating that a band's kill factor alone can keep the torch flaming for Olympic level competition with the formidable vanguard of the '90s. **Ample Destruction** was a kick-ass chunk of polished steel; gothic, but more in lust with the idea of metallic glory than anything squarely medieval, chugging through the black and silver like a combat zone Priest, bridging Oz, Heavy Load, Torch, Exciter, Anvil, and anyone else who focused their sonic fryer on metal for metal's sake. **Ample Destruction** was about both quality and dirt; hurried control, vocal overload and operatic reverence; metal-plowing finesse from the mouths of madmen. However not so premeditated as all that (more likely benefiting from having to get through recording under budget), Jag Panzer has built one destructive piece of machinery. After the smoke clears, **Ample Destruction** was simply a kick-ass record—no better term for it—that holds up over the years, and hence is still around, charring the remains of those who did not witness it in its temporal space during the years of The Metal Inundation. Collector's note: Metalcore CD reissue adds three extra tracks (plus intro) at the end: *Black Sunday*, *Eyes Of The Night*, and *Fallen Angel*, making a weltatious metal gorging, that much more

217

lusty and complete, given that all three blaze brightly. Different, cheesier cover art also.

Rating **9**

## Jag Panzer - Dissident Alliance   (Rising Sun/Pavement '94)

Like ten years of shrapnel have never floated under the bridge, Jag Panzer are back with their patented crunch metal, somehow still cranking a type of mechanical metal that is theirs and theirs alone. Musically, this is cryogenically packed in their version of '84, Briody, Tetley and a bunch of new guys still able to churn songs that excel in riffery, and triumph despite very raw production, raw in the sense of simplicity, even though there is enough bass and treble to keep headphones hopping. Not too crazy about Daniel Conca's sort of spoken word vocals, the guy not knowing if he's a Bay Area frasher or a Priesty kinda guy. But it's pretty cool that the boys can construct tunes like Forsaken Child (power metal unplugged) and Eve Of Penance, which combines a brainshake groove with a really weird arrangement, really demonstrating that there is a river of creativity flowing through this band.

Rating **8**

## Jaguar - Power Games   (Banzai '83)

Simple British headbanging fare from a wildly swinging gang of restless punters, **Power Games** reconciles the guts of Motörhead and early Saxon with the compositional over-extension of Tokyo Blade, making Jaguar one of the better pent-up, messed-up and impatient of British bombs; one with soul, punky emotional drive, and competent metal vocals from Paul Merrell, all delivered feet firmly planted knee-deep in reality's mundane, daily struggles. Highlights include Ain't No Fantasy and Raw Deal. A forgiving **7**.

Rating **7**

## Jaguar - This Time   (Roadrunner '84)

**This Time** amounts to a concerted ideological shift from the scruff rockin' punk metal of **Power Games** to what was hoped to be a cash-generating melodic hard rock sound; "Muppet metal" to "dance metal", in the band's own words. Well, the production is annoying enough, but the zero buoyancy keeps even the most earnestly lite metal crooners on **This Time** sounding like nothing more than lazy, toned-down heavy metal. Contributing to the lack of sweetness in Jaguar's commercial ploy is the fact that the drums are too damn loud, exuberant, and overwhelmingly steeped in the ways of metal. It's always been said that Brits can't do hard rock, and Jaguar again continues the strained and ultimately unsuccessful forays into such tunefulness, even though this record is a kind of nostalgic blast for those with a greater interest in the NWOBHM. Considering **Power Games** and **This Time**, the steelier moments on the latter did demonstrate a general maturing that could have raised Jaguar out of the bush leagues, given a shot of life from the former. In any event, **This Time** reflects the band's admitted widening tastes for acts like U2 and Big Country.

Rating **6**

## Jag Wire - Made In Heaven   (Banzai/PolyGram '85)

Average hair band metal that tries harder, **Made In Heaven** gets too frilly for the blue collar metal tunes enclosed, most of the record being pop metal with too much drums, loud vocals, and a metal approach to ditzy songs that just can't take the stress. Loose bolts production tops it off, making this sound more rust belt indie than the distribution deal with PolyGram would imply. Hey, they oughta sue Queen for that record title, no?

Rating **4**

## Jane's Addiction - Jane's Addiction   (Triple X '87)

As the liner notes sez "Jane's Addiction was bread and spread in Los Angeles", and the spirit of lost angels permeates the beatnik funk punk that comprises this shambling live debut album, a well-recorded first peek, from label showcase gigs at The Roxy and The Edge, at a time when hype for Perry Farrell and crew was so virulent, the boys decided a quick indie was the way to give the hype some solid rocket fuel. Songs are trippier than on **Nothing's Shocking**; rougher, unfinished in idea and deed, yet still bleeding the band's unique bitter taste and bratty grasp of rhythm, scattering forth into a number of bastard hybrids, indeed the band performing full-on rockin' gigs next to proto-unplugged shows. Two covers: Lou Reed's Rock'n'Roll and the Stones' Sympathy For The Devil, both dull tunes rendered with shabby but intimate hippy chaos, more babbled than ranted. Fave originals: the acoustic My Time, with its Porno-style harmonica angles, and Jane Says, the latter being the only track here that makes it to **Nothing Shocking**, becoming something of a suicide/angst anthem. Otherwise: jumpy, nervy, excitable or soundly comatose, as Jane at least succeeds in demonstrating its regard for art above artifice, exploration of the edges. A band to watch like a hawk; one lapse and they'll mutate beyond recognition. The name Jane's Addiction is apparently homage to a prostitute who took a shine to the band, becoming somewhat of an early financial benefactor.

Rating **7**

## Jane's Addiction - Nothing's Shocking
(Warner Bros. '88)

The masterpiece of the erratic and uncompromising Jane's Addiction legacy, **Nothing's Shocking** is also its anchor, its centre of gravity, an awe-inspiring and disturbing blast of hopelessness that champions the splendor and excitement in watching a civilization's inhabitants crumble. **Nothing's Shocking** stands like a defiant criminal at the stake, carving and shaping its own style of grunge, forged of a carnival craziness that is missing from the best of the Seattle slews. Controversy followed this volatile band everywhere. Perry's front cover "sculpture" of his wife Casey as a nude, on fire, Siamese twin caused chains all over the U.S. to refuses stocking the record. Plus Farrell insisted on producing the record himself, something Warner hadn't let happen for a debut since Prince. A then unknown Dave Jerden was brought in as engineer, but he was such help, Farrell ended up sharing production credits with him. So with a blood-shot eye towards mangling the metal exploding all around their scene, Jane piled up ocean-size riffs, amphetamine funk, distressed feedback and tribal war toms, setting the whole infected package afire with the flames of Perry Farrell's sad damnations. **Nothing's Shocking** seems melted in an urban summer's haze, demobilized by a cocktail of exhaust fumes, sweat, garbage and stormclouds that just wait stubborn and stupid. But the band's co-production with Jerden assures that Stephen Perkins' manic percussive imagination and Eric A.'s snakey bass lines see no domination from the wayward axe slashings of Dave Navarro, each instrumentalist allowed to yowl, breathing deeply of the fumes, expunging whatever heaving groans he might feel at the hassle that is life (including a treatise on yet another controversial song, Ted, Just Admit It . . ., Ted being serial killer Ted Bundy). Thus **Nothing's Shocking** is a four-way tour de force full of ebb and flow, never in control, whether ready to snap or be snapped, stumbling into raging metal, stumbling into noisy funk anarchy, stumbling into unclean meditations, all like a five course meal wolfed down back to front. When it all crashes, the bruises on the moral centres of the brain are tender and unhealing, the sonic stew leaving an impression of impending

doom and collapse, like there's no point acquiring assets. CD contained bonus track *Pigs In Zen*.
Rating      **10**

## Jane's Addiction - Ritual De Lo Habitual
(Warner Bros. '90)
For those who were quite rightly disturbed by Jane's brain-straining studio premiere, yet held reservations at the record's ironic rawk self-assurance, **Ritual De Lo Habitual** deconstructs the music to match Farrell's psychological (and heroin-induced) chaos. Adopting modus operandi for many a great band, Jane's Addiction mutates beyond recognition, scattering its sound, breaking it into something more akin to Minutemen than Megadeth, if I may be so inexact. **Ritual** is of two minds, intense nervousness and intense sloth, novel constructions like *Stop* and amusing ode to shoplifting *Been Caught Stealing* stringing hyper jazzpunk chords over apocalyptic rhythms, about the least comforting thing one would want haunting your acid trip. Then the record descends into a swirling, hypnotic haze, the band following Farrell's lead into active inaction, *more* than the last half of the album (*Three Days, Then She Did, Of Course* and *Classic Girl*), squandering their sorry lives, becoming shiftless jams, albeit jams that achieve a degree of moral depravity that is our addiction with Jane. No question **Ritual** is an elusive pleasure, repugnant and cacophonous upon first brutal introduction, all electrocution and drop-dead coma, but as the record wears down one's resistance, a certain bravery emerges, the band trumpeting the integrity of filth, oblivious to the passage of time or the pressures towards perfection. The spontaneous expulsion of slack anger and angst becomes a thing of ugly beauty, rather than a rip-off, as previous conceptions of what constitute Jane become stripped away by harsh angles and sonic degradation. Easy comparisons to Zep become deeper and more maniacal ones, something found in soul rather than soundwave. Censorship note: Exhibiting typical puritanical ludicrousness, Canada banned the cover art of **Ritual** (nudity and witchcraft heavily kitsched), resulting in the default black and white no-brainer I happen to own, a look that is oddly appropriate for the stop/go nature of the mayhem enclosed.
Rating      **9**

## Jerk - Scream Against Walls (Major '95)
Presumably Swiss, Jerk sound like a top-flight aggrometal band from the U.S., only the riffs are better, more like inspired Megadeth or Anthrax, as vocalist Fri Rieder barks out hilarious, semi-literate, profanity-strewn complaints on man's humanity to his fellow cretin. There's even a hint of Pantera or Prong in there, as these bad-ass lookin' dudes would rather lean to the dangerous, guitar-jammed side of accessible. Total masters of groove, Jerk would do well to land an American deal and hit the tour circuit, 'cos this is probably the best-selling kind of metal in these dog days of the genre, basically the record Megadeth could have made if Mustaine were still "tippling".
Rating      **8**

## Jesus Christ - Jesus Christ (Hypnotic '94)
Lucifer betwixt, this raging Toronto act is on a mission of salvation, cranking up the jets, crushing popular conceptions of Canada's music scene as the crucible of mainstream sameyness. This sucker packs a wallop, the record approximating a psycho-heavy cross-stitch between loud, abrasive grunge and straight-ahead crushing doom metal, kind of an alternatively slanted version of new cranium crushers Machine Head, or maybe Entombed meets Soundgarden. Monstrously heavy, **Jesus Christ** does everything in grand, smokin' style, from the wailing, crazy man vocals of Andy Hoyle (occasionally overlapping with the best of Cornell),

through the thick, '90s-sickoid riffing of A.J. McCready. And the production rules, putrid where it counts, full throttle, woofer-chomping, dirty, black and loud. Aside of an out-of-place cover of *Ace Of Spades*, and one or two dirgy numbers, this one's on the cutting edge of all metal rusty, corroding, and sick of lethargy. Jesus Christ stomps grunge dead, while furiously thrashing at the front of metal's new pack of mangy mutts. Spread his message of peace and love. Best Canadian record of the decade thus far.
Rating      **9**

## The Jesus Lizard - Liar (Touch and Go '92)
From the angular netherworld of Sin that spawned NoMeansNo and Fugazi, comes an intensified evil of jarring, bothersome collisions, basically establishing The Jesus Lizard as kings of kaleidoscopic noise. Lyrically, Chicago's Lizard, borne from the ashes of Cargo Cult and the appropriately named Scratch Acid, fuse the profane and the nightmarish, spinning tales of fragmented light over an intense jazzpunk assault. Heavier, less disjointed, and more caustic than Fugazi, *Liar* (the band's third following the **Pure** EP, **Head** and **Goat**) provides the missing link between NoMeansNo's **Wrong** and **0+2=1**, combining the former's studied metal, and the latter's disintegration, amidst a great mix and a haunting, affected muffle vocal from one bad pig David Yow. You can't help but be disappointed when cuts 1 & 2 (*Boilermaker* and *Gladiator*) are your faves, but other barbed gems arrive. Truly a unique and wicked outfit, but still too chaotic and noisy for my tastes. Wary respect at best.
Rating      **7**

## The Jesus Lizard - Down (Touch and Go '94)
Once more, The Jesus Lizard take the listener unarmed and pretty much freezing in their underwear, into a disturbing and unique world, lyrics and graphics (cool falling cow) combining with a volatile mix of artistic punk metal peaks, vales, values and valleys. Their shaggy, collapsed, then burning free sound is a vehicle of perfection for Yow's visions, even if once more, fave tracks are the first few, particularly *Fly On The Wall* and the southern rock speed metal of *Mistletoe*. But as usual the band's anti-social, misanthropic streak results in songs that repel through (still arguably accessible) white noise (Minutemen on heroin?), Yow throwing out broken glass on which to cut our tentative steps through his cackling, tin-foil schizo domain. Totally hard art.
Rating      **8**

## The Jesus Lizard - Shot (Capitol/EMI '96)
Now legendary cranks of the alternative nation, Jesus Lizard press on to arrive in '96 with the same scrapyard of pointy art metal compositions that has made Yow and crew shining couriers of pain worthy of six digit sales across a very sick nation. But **Shot** is downright rock'n'roll, songs like *Churl* and *Now Then* displaying that rollicking riffwork these guys are so good at, dangerous, rough-hewn metal monsters that coast along, well off the rails but in love with the drift into rainy smoke-choked bushes. Yow's lyrics are the most crushingly vivid and imagistic of his tortured canon, a helluva read even by poetry's standards, the eccentric bard delivering with his usual crazy man yell. All told though, cool band, really psychopathic but getting more cunningly musical all the time. Sort of in that same struggle as Rollins, but winning.
Rating      **8**

## Jetboy - Damned Nation (MCA '90)
Total weakapotamus hair band rock from Frisco. Again, hard to muster any sort of words of praise or disdain for such a tired, vanilla-mixed, vaguely glam display of

loitered chords and rehashed silliness. Passed without a ripple.

Rating **3**

## Johnny Crash - Neighbourhood Threat (CBS '90)

One of the more flagrant and committed of golden era AC/DC understudies rewriting **Powerage** and **Highway To Hell**, Johnny Crash make no apologies for shooting straight at Bon's growl (courtesy ex-Tokyo Blade vocalist Vicki James Wright) and the patented Angus 'n' Malcolm twin axe burn. Adding a little '90s zip, a few frills, and a lot of off-colour clichés, Johnny Crash climbs on and stays bucking for the duration, with lean and mean bangers like *Sink Or Swim, No Bones About It,* and *Trigger Happy,* which would have held mighty fine on AC/DC's boldest wax statements. Hard not to let the fact that these guys are just a bunch of under-achieving '90s scuzzball imitators hinder total surrender to the good times herein enclosed, however with a few maybe forced spins early on, the tunes start to achieve mass and roll. Nothing here that's going to re-arrange your personal make-up, but if you buy into it, the goods will back it up, unlike Hangmen, Seahags or Junkyard.

Rating **6**

## Johnny Law - Johnny Law (Metal Blade '91)

Surprisingly toothless roots metal that draws heavily the breath of more universal, more accessible, and less defining roots rock à la The Tragically Hip (who still suck five albums deep, except for *Fifty Mission Cap*) or The Del-Lords (who rule with greater dominion with each passing sunset). Still, **Johnny Law** postures itself like metal, in terms of imagery, recording, vocal inflection and road-map riffs. Took me nowhere slowly and without incident.

Rating **4**

## Steve Jones - Fire And Gasoline (MCA '89)

This fairly plodding, no-frills riff rocker features our fave delinquent Sex Pistol gone long-hair L.A. rawk rat and kinda corporate. **Fire And Gasoline** tries to please, with its big production wrapped around slap 'em down, sturdy guitar anthems, but the sum total of the thing is kinda stiff and sterile; simple bar fare dressed-up too far unto L.A. Fave is boogie-ish Pistols cover *Did U No Wrong,* which finds Ian Astbury and Axl Rose trading vocals with our exiled ex-thug. Main point: nobody thought much of this record.

Rating **5**

## The Joneses - Keeping Up With The Jones (Dr. Dream '86)

Messy, slippery glam rock with little California cheez, lotsa New York Dolls and Hanoi Rocks boozery, not to mention a cool album cover. Well-oiled for an indie. Sizzling cover of *Chip Away At The Stone,* painful cover of *Crocodile Rock.*

Rating **6**

## Judas Priest - Rocka Rolla (Gull '74)

A strange, bitter record that no one could love, **Rocka Rolla** announced the recording career of a band that would transform metal like no other, catapulting the category to new levels of distinction during its '76 to '79 run of genius. Here vocalist "Bob" Halford, budding axe gods Glenn Tipton and K.K. Downing, invisible bassist Ian Hill, and soon to be sacked sticksman John Hinch come up with a proud but confused work drawing from Purple, Heep and fellow Birmingham bashers Sabbath, but only vaguely, and not much else, finding a unique sound that is medieval, dark and blurry with a hint of psychedelia. Its best track, *Rocka Rolla,* courts a style never to be repeated (until the '80s, where the comparison becomes futile), a sort of elephantine and sinister hard rock lope, finding a magnetic hook right

out of the gates. Long cuts, short cuts, snakey dinosaur blues riffs, all wrapped in a dull, mysterious dream state, superficially constructed like **Black Sabbath** or **The Magician's Birthday**, spiritually somewhere in that vicinity also, but somehow more exhausted with respect to riff. Hints of **Sad Wings Of Destiny** in *Never Satisfied* and *Cheater* but in general, a subdued and non-commercial enigma.

Rating **7**

## Judas Priest - Sad Wings Of Destiny (Janus '76)

This record scared the crap out of us, entering our systems as wide-eyed thirteen year-olds, a time when our ability to process malevolent imagery was being honed by slowly increasing ingestions of this new (for us) raging entity called heavy metal. And **Sad Wings Of Destiny** carved a new plateau for the fledgling form; an intensifying of darkness (more uncertainty than evil), an invasion of the imagination with abstract but disturbing flurries of torment, the only distant relative to its frightful vibe being perhaps **Sabotage** or oddly enough, **Vol 4**, Priest however offering a vastly more futuristic type of heavy metal than either Sabfest. **Sad Wings** marks no less than the second of three landmark events in the history of metal. Five years earlier, we have the in earnest invention of the form, with **Uriah Heep, In Rock** and **Paranoid**. **Sad Wings** (and incredibly Priest's next three in a row), amazingly bereft of challengers from '76 to '80, marked the first spike in an established genre, raising metal to new, mind-expanding, technically impeccable levels, second spike being the intensified, majestic speed metal of Metallica's **Ride The Lightning** in '84. Comprising six visceral metal classics and two extremely delicate funeral dirges, **Sad Wings** proceeded to rewire hard rock with legendary masterworks like strident prog metal opener *Victim Of Changes,* seminal slasher tale *Ripper,* and rampant mind-grind *Tyrant,* all working a sort of becalmed night, guarded monks toiling in rapt seclusion, mediums receiving an avalanche of seismic, sobbing and sobering riffery, puzzle-pieced into sturdy towers of previously unknown medieval metallics. Lyrics tend towards the darker corners of the brain; religion in conflict, moral and material struggles, death and other concerns above time, concerns never rendered flashy or even colourful, evoking the subdued but rock-solid tones within the monster cathedrals of Britain. And the record's bass-bedded production supports such earthy and ancient engineering with trustworthy strength, all players reverent of the record's pulse, each offering his wisdom with restraint and recognition of the massive grooves at work, a restraint that will fly out the window come the blinding fury of **Sin After Sin**. Unquestionably, this is a record that established Priest's enviable reputation, even if any degree of commercial success would elude the band for another four years or so, **Sad Wings Of Destiny** becoming a pioneer of a new and versatile type of gothic riffery, and as history would show, a woodshed record for all sorts of metalizers gaining their sea legs in the late '70s. Grave and serious metal innovation, tragically unnoticed in its time.

Rating **10**

## Judas Priest - Sin After Sin (Columbia '77)

After blinding the world (or at least six or seven of its inhabitants) with the metallic supra-intelligence of **Sad Wings Of Destiny**, Priest nonchalantly lay down this magnificent storm of a record, the first for a major label, the first to feature mind-bending musical acrobatics along with the leaden seriousness of the band's rejuvenation of the genre one short year previous. **Sin After Sin** injects an intoxicating flash that is wholly new for heavy metal, cementing the band's status as the constructors of the first techno-metal. The record flies at a multitude of altitudes. *Let Us Prey* is speed

obliterato par excellence, propelled by uncanny performances on all fronts, particularly the inhuman percussion machine that is Simon Phillips and supreme operatic commander Rob Halford, who proves his love of shattering glass. *Sinner* (perfect here or on **Sad Wings**) and *Starbreaker* redefine brisk cruising brilliance, while *Call For The Priest/Raw Deal* deconstructs for a bit of maze-like metallic back-throttle. A galloping rendition of Joan Baez' *Diamonds And Rust* becomes the band's first hit (albeit a tiny one), and *Dissident Aggressor* (later reverently covered by Slayer) displays a powerful ability to pulverize the mind while standing steadfast in concrete paralysis, crunching bone and body under a daring mountain of immutable riffery. Ultimately, **Sin After Sin** is metal's first intellectual and technological classic, raising the genre's reputation, as the world was forced to realize the levels of quality purveyors of the loud were intent on seeking. The record introduced a new language, constructed of blinding chops and a willingness to exploit them at ludicrous energy levels. And in '77, it all seemed a bit much for a world tiring of heavy metal, a world either sedated by the California casual wear of Fleetwood Mac and The Eagles, or forsaking all for a leap into the slampits of punk. Whatever the reason, Priest would incredibly cause little more than critical sneers and commercial anonymity at this preview to the British metallic flood of '79.
Rating     10

## Judas Priest - Stained Class   (Columbia '78)

Probably the classiest album of the Priest repertoire (no pun intended), **Stained Class** hones and perfects the **Sin After Sin** maelstrom, a feat one would think unimaginable. But here it is: sterling crisp production that amplifies Simon Phillips' percussive greatness while the Downing/Tipton axe dialogue becomes understated and stealth-like, fully confident in its ability to weave silvery silk within a mix rather than above it. More songs, and more of them packing a metallic knowledge light years ahead of the band's closest competitors; nine tracks and fully eight rockers, only *Beyond The Realms Of Death* approaching ballad (dirge), a composition that would become the accused in the teenage suicide pact case against the band a decade later. No metal academic would deny the importance of this record in terms of sheer quality and intellect. **Stained Class** is the type of experience that either made you put down the guitar in frustration forever, or practice twice as hard in hopes of catching up. It was the new reference point for the metal frontier, and years later it still sounds cutting edge, testimony to the effort on the part of the whole band to get everything just perfect. These are hallowed sounds, all nine tales way above the weak conceits of humankind, carved with laser-exact technical care and a level of metallic understanding that won't even exist outside of the Priest realm for another six years following. Ultimately, **Stained Class**' ancestral lineage is untraceable. It is the product of original thought, and it is as important a record that exists in the long, raging history of hard rock. The third of four extremely influential records, comprising the single most remarkable creative streak in the evolution of the form. An additional quirky, hithero unrecognizable cover in Spooky Tooth's *Better By You Better Than Me*, written by that *Dream Weaver* guy!
Rating     10

## Judas Priest - The Best Of Judas Priest   (Gull '78)

The sharks at Gull repackage selections from Priest's inauspicious debut and landmark follow-up, offering nothing new except the concise but conspiring lyrics from four cuts and a great album cover. Lend your moral support to the band and pass on this Gull cash grab.
Rating     7

## Judas Priest - Hell Bent For Leather   (Columbia '79)

Declaring a holy day in Trail, B.C., Fiver cruised home wielding Judas Priest's **Killing Machine**, the advance British version of the monolith that stateside would be re-monikered **Hell Bent For Leather**, the North American version also adding *The Green Manalishi (With The Two-Pronged Crown)*, a head-stomping re-shred of an old Fleetwood Mac tune. And Priest was firing on all sixes, replacing the sophisticated fabrics of **Stained Class** with the tough-as-nails thickness of black leather. Priest usher in a new era of metal as get-dirty participants versus lofty academics, shaking their airtight metal architecture with a new combat ethic, finding vibration, bottom end, and an ever so slight propensity for wayward, uncontrollable wattage. Thus tracks become more primal and simultaneously more commercial, Halford's lyrical visions more universal and forceful, thus grinding opener *Delivering The Goods*, rudimentary thumper *Take On The World* (the first in a line of often dreary battle anthems), searing, rhythmic metal funkster *Burnin' Up*, plus lumbering duo *Killing Machine* and *Evil Fantasies*. And further up the electro-glide scale come *Rock Forever*, *Running Wild* and early OTT classic *Hell Bent For Leather*, all combining **Stained Class**' high technology with increased aggression levels for the '80s. So Priest finally makes the shift that brings them mainstream, putting might back into their metal (not really the case since **Sad Wings**), while building a well-programmed record with all sorts of speed and intensity levels, not to mention various basic arrangements; chops well to the fore but comfortably so, Halford more guttural and bloodthirsty in places, more skillfully dramatic in others, definitely more versatile. And once again, Priest prove themselves the most vital creative metal force of the day, Sabbath on the wane, Rainbow on the rocks, Scorpions full of momentum, but more commercial in approach, Maiden (doomed to diminished impact by default of its placement in a more marketing-oriented age for metal), still lying in imitative wait.
Rating     10

## Judas Priest - Unleashed In The East (Live In Japan)   (Columbia '79)

Smoked with a formidable line-up of compositions like no other, **Unleashed** is one of the killer live albums of all time. Only *Diamonds And Rust* falls behind the pack here, as Halfie and the leathered ones blaze through such maniacal shards as *Exciter*, *Ripper* and *Tyrant*, with top flight performances from Rob and producer Tom Allom. Not a particularly heart-stopping paste overall, just an awesome raft of tunage, the cream of a rock-solid catalogue. Collector's note: Japanese CD version of the record adds four soaring tracks: *Rock Forever*, *Delivering The Goods*, *Hell Bent For Leather*, and the under-utilized *Starbreaker*, along with dubiously transcribed lyrics, *Delivering The Goods* being particularly amusing.
Rating     9

## Judas Priest - British Steel   (Columbia '80)

Proving the impossibility of upstaging a legendary document like **Hell Bent For Leather**, Priest step back into an intensifying spotlight wielding their first less than God-like record since their debut, a commendable yet surprisingly no-frills offering of well above average stadium metal. All flash and no finesse, **British Steel** was a classic muscle car rocker, the quintessential school-wrecking soundtrack record to teenage mischief and backseat alcoholic ODs. Built around simple, bone-crushing riffery, headbanging classics like *Grinder*, *Metal Gods* and *Breaking The Law*

221

defined a golden age in metal, while surprise hit *Living After Midnight* brought the band new, stupider fans, with a suspiciously dim-witted hard rock sound, a decidedly mediocre addition to Priest's bulging bag of tricks, also rearing its zit face on *Don't Have To Be Old To Be Wise*, both tracks more or less pandering, simplistic paeans to high school rebellion (Oh, the irony of it all). First words that come to mind would be solid but commercial, marking the first time the band would write down to its fans, a strategy that would work tremendously in the coming glory years. Fortunately there's little wasted time and no ballads, but there are also no tunes that would unequivocally rank with the band's top ten or so, as everything contains a debilitating, deflating sheen of economy.
Rating           **9**

## Judas Priest - Hero, Hero    (Gull/Attic '81)

Nicely appointed double vinyl gatefold reissue of **Rocka Rolla** in its entirety, most of **Sad Wings**, and straggler *Diamonds And Rust*. Only true newie is a short instrumental called *Prelude*, which sports a Queen-like mix of tympany, piano and light guitar. Frazetta-like cover art by "Melvyn", Warhol-like band illustration (sans drummer) by Alan Morrison, and remix of the **Rocka Rolla** tracks by Rodger Bain.
Rating           **7**

## Judas Priest - Point Of Entry    (Columbia '81)

Perhaps caught in the headlights of **British Steel**'s success, Priest piddle out with this timid re-make, which is all pandering, netted-out hard rock power chords, little in the way of the band's astonishing intricacy so prominent only two records back. *Breaking The Law*, *Don't Have To Be Old To Be Wise*, and *Living After Midnight* are sequelled all over **Point Of Entry**, two best being intro anthem *Heading Out To The Highway*, guilty headbanger *Hot Rockin'*, and high-strung "boogie" closer *On The Run*, worst being the disgraceful *You Say Yes*, *All The Way*, *Troubleshooter* and to a lesser extent, *Turning Circles*, the latter at least striking a moody melodic chord seldom seen with this most metal-encased of acts. **Point Of Entry** is definitely a Priest for the masses, the recently turned teen masses at that, a serious blow to the band's reputation as the thirst for rock'n'roll stardom overtakes the band's artistic integrity. Still, **Point Of Entry** succeeds in finding simple hard rock hookery, avoiding complete wash-out by trying with typical enthusiasm to learn a new, stoopider corner of the idiom.
Rating           **7**

## Judas Priest - Screaming For Vengeance    (Columbia '82)

Aptly monikered for Priest '82, **Screaming For Vengeance** has the band scrapping (for the most part), the simple, down-wind hard rock of **Point Of Entry** for a return to marauding riffery, evidenced in brilliant kick-off *Electric Eye* and the following two, *Riding On The Wind* and *Bloodstone*, all three heavier than anything on **Point Of Entry**. Yet of the remaining six, only the '80s OTT title track is balls-out metallic, the rest of this "comeback" doing only moderately well with various stoopider speed and intensity levels. *Pleasure And Pain*, *Fever*, and minor hit *(Take These) Chains* take a sort of pork-fisted bluesy chunk metal approach while the band's unexpectedly huge chest-thumper of a hit *You've Got Another Thing Comin'* and closer *Devil's Child* are meat-head hard rockers to the fist-pumping core, blue collar volume machines which once and for all establish a suspected penchant for netting out the brainy complexity for a shot at some major coinage. But throw all the analysis out the window, 'cos fact be, all of us long-time fans grooved heavily to the new market-savvy Priest, 'cos now we had a top echelon metal force *and* a party band, all of this record working a co-operative concert buzz despite the variation.

Priest was back in the driver's seat, and bringing 'em in in droves, as punters around the world declared the band a major player. Warm, thick and likeable, **Screaming For Vengeance** was car deck Priest once again, even if the band would never show their insane mastery of brainiac metal ever again.
Rating           **8**

## Judas Priest - Defenders Of The Faith    (Columbia '84)

In attempted duplication of **Screaming For Vengeance**'s breakthrough success, Priest once again goes for an unwieldy collection of metal pounders, good songs so over-clogged by the dual sabotage of long-time producer Tom Allom and drummer Dave Holland, who combine for the dullest of rhythm section displays: boring drumming rendered technologically lifeless and overblown. Swear to god, Tom Allom is the worst thing to happen to Priest, basically wrecking their sound for no less than seven albums in a row, in spite of the band's successful efforts (for the most part) to overpower Allom's lack of both production restraint and metal acuity. **Defenders Of The Faith** is the record most destroyed by his touch, a treatment marked by a turgid snare sound and lack of hi-hat. Anyways, the record rocks, combining moody, atmospheric but thumpy thud rockers like *Rock Hard Ride Free* and *Some Heads Are Gonna Roll* with speedy axe-rabid ravers like *Freewheel Burning* and *Eat Me Alive* (which Halfie amusingly defends as being written under the influence of too many recreational beverages). Faves *Love Bites* and *The Sentinel* work a metallic violence towards making this a tougher album than its psychologically paired though brighter predecessor. Ultimately **Defenders Of The Faith** benefits from Priest's growing reputation as the tour to see, giving major tailwind to acceptance of the band's increasing reliance on predictable metal imagery. Long since losing their immortal status, Priest succeed in cranking some fairly uncompromising corporate metal. There's still some power left in them grooves. The dynasty lives on.
Rating           **8**

## Judas Priest - Turbo    (Columbia '86)

Most probably nagged by traces of self-doubt, Priest pull a reversal on their bigger, louder, faster trajectory, introducing a strangely sparse, electronic-driven sound (digital recording and lots of "synthesizer guitar"), with this career back-ratchet, their second after **Point Of Entry**. **Turbo** attempts to trumpet the cause of technology, restraint and melody above metal raving, getting right down to business with the most excellent *Turbo Lover*, a cruising, thoughtful combination of atmosphere and hard rock. Things get really stupid for the painfully Scorpions-like *Rock You All Around The World* and minor hit *Parental Guidance*, an offensive kiddie rock turd better left to Twisted Sister. Elsewhere, the spirit of renewal props up questionable hard rockers like *Locked In* and *Wild Nights, Hot & Crazy Days*, the latter which begs the question: who let Rudy and Klaus back into the building? A strangely pedestrian record, one you could love to hate, although really the strength of the melodies, particularly come chorus time, was a welcome cerebral addition to the stagnating Priest identity. What was sacrificed in metallic purity doesn't lack for significance however, Priest continually distancing itself from the state-of-the-art status it completely owned from '76 through '79. And the famed Priest solos (always specifically credited in the liner notes) certainly didn't suffer, as *Turbo Lover* and *Hot For Love* demonstrate some of the tastiest Tipton/Downing fretfulness of the band's career. Closing out, the perfect marriage of new and old, fave track on the record: *Reckless*, which contains both heft and hook, showing that perhaps the band was onto

something pursuable here. Pursue, they didn't. Not great, but fine, after the initial hostility wanes.
Rating 7

## Judas Priest - Priest . . . Live! (Columbia '87)

Taking a rare minute off from debating the artistic relevance behind **Priest . . . Live!**'s strange, yukky brown album cover, one need only to dive head-long into the grooves of said double boiler for a rousing albeit safely calculated stomp through Priest's "commercial" years (all tracks post-**Hell Bent For Leather**). Lots of flathead classics here, adorned only to the ceiling afforded Dave Holland's limited percussive skills; influential signature bang-thy-head anthems such as *Heading Out To The Highway*, *Metal Gods*, *Electric Eye*, *Living After Midnight* and of course *You've Got Another Thing Comin'*, an awkward dumbo of endearment, and a dubious concert closer, here offered in extended version. On a weightier level, we get *Love Bites*, *The Sentinel*, and *Freewheel Burning* from the under-rated but over-cosmetized **Defenders Of The Faith**. A muscular but automatic drive nevertheless, with a spotless mix (often better than studio), and a characteristically show-boating performance from "Lifer", who proves that his range is genuine and effortlessly summoned hockey barn after barn. Cool record, but no competition for the searing and succinct **Unleashed In The East**, one of the world's more explosive live experiences.
Rating 6

## Judas Priest - Ram It Down (Columbia '88)

Abandoning the admirable but failed experimentation of **Turbo**, Priest step back into trajectory from **Defenders Of The Faith**, unfortunately on full coast as they turn it up but flip on the auto-pilot with this pandering, T-shirt-ready metal feast. **Ram It Down** sends conflicting signals. On the positive, it's lively, heavy and intensely constructed, but on the negative: total kiddie metal lyrically, and a commercially-motivated re-hash of metal ideas musically. Tom Allom's recording is standard dull techno-metal, doing adequate but expected things with the axes, but loud, boomy, interfering things with Holland's unimaginative backbeats. All-time low: a novelty cover of *Johnny B. Goode*, a total transformation that may have been tolerable had an original not existed. I dunno, not bad, but a throwaway nevertheless, in temporal and positional comparison to the rest of the vast Priest repertoire; sort of dull and too content to rest on a reputation in full dive, seemingly unnoticed by the band itself. Uncomfortable parallels to the disgraceful misfortunes of both Scorpions and Maiden. No hits.
Rating 6

## Judas Priest - Painkiller (Columbia '90)

And so the Priest finally returns with a mighty, razor-sharp roar, *All Guns Blazing*, bent on *Metal Meltdown*. In parallel with the catalyst effect virtuoso jazz-based drummer Simon Phillips had on smokers like **Sin After Sin** and **Stained Class**, Priest acquire skins maniac Scott Travis, who's your basic fully-up-to-speed, meticulously studied metal man, patching the band's self-admitted limiting factor on the percussion riser. **Painkiller** summarily destroys the notion that this band had gone the way of grandchildren Maiden or granddaddies Sabbath into toothless retirement, kicking with a fury and aggression the band never had, even when they were a better band for other reasons. The biggest surprise is that Tipton and Downing are totally juiced and primed for Travis' 90s percussive challenge, simply tearing an axe-acrobatic swath through such OTT mindbenders as the ludicrously caffeinated title cut, *Leather Rebel* and *All Guns Blazing*. And the armor-

plating of the Priest tank continues unabated with an edgy, sterling clear mix from vet Chris Tsangarides and extreme vocal command from our man Halford, one of the most dedicated performers in metal to this day. One negative remains. Priest can't shake their ingrained opinion that metal is entertainment for teenagers and nothing greater, so lyrically the band is getting increasingly embarrassing and behind the times. I mean, *Hell Patrol*, *Night Crawler*, *Between The Hammer & The Anvil*, *Battle Hymn* . . . butt that up against provocative lyrical work from equally metallic forces like Pantera, Megadeth, Metallica (lesser so, these days), or fringe acts like Warrior Soul, King's X and Soundgarden, and **Painkiller** looks pretty laughable indeed. Halford's intentions are good, but his writing down to "the kids who come to our shows" (always "the kids"), is getting a little out of control. His respect for the genre will grow even greater, I'm sure, when he realizes he's been wasting the lyrical side of the vehicle for upwards to ten years now. Of course, Halford had indeed realized it was time to move on, jumping ship to form heinous power metal act Fight (two records: **War Of Words** and **A Small Deadly Space**), in his hometown of Phoenix, recently shelved in place of a new solo project called Halford.
Rating 9

## Juggernaut - Trouble Within (Metal Blade '87)

A frenzied, scientific acceleration test from Texas that swirls with wild technicality like Fates Warning, Forbidden or Flotsam And Jetsam, **Trouble Within** is one of those unfortunate records that would be tagged as thrash, the bane of this band's existence, I'm sure. Still, to me, who cares? It's just another extreme and lengthy checklist of riffs, an assemblage of around 200 ideas which inundate the brain's processing centres until overload causes alienation and ultimate reversal of the charges. Sorry, just not my bag. Dull album cover for such a details-obsessed band.
Rating 3

## Jughead's Revenge - Elimination (BYO '94)

Good ole fashioned punk rock slams forth from this, the band's fourth stage-diving record. Solid, mosh rock sound, recalling early '80s California stuff like Black Flag, colleged up a bit with Soul Asylum, Necros and Hell's Kitchen. But what carries it is the glue-throated bark of vocalist Joe D, who's got one of those perfect skatecore whines, propping up what are tried and true loudpusrules structures, lots of heroic windmill chords, mixed with lager and ale. Inane t' be sure, but a craptankerous blaze through the genre all the same. Might turn themselves into the next Offspring if they aren't too careless.
Rating 7

## Junkyard - Junkyard (Geffen '89)

Yer basic boogie metal support band . . . least that's the way I sized 'em on the Lynyrd Skynyrd's mighty fine '91 tour. **Junkyard** rolls through a pretty potent mix of scuzzola roots metal postures; lotsa boogie (both speeds), high energy Tedhead '70s rock, some southern balladry (a tune called *Simple Man*, hence the connection?), and a general flathead Ford, all-systems-go simplicity, making Junkyard perhaps one of the best of this not so challenging catch-all, a genre badly damaged by the fact that everything is heavily, faithfully and reverently borrowed, leaving little room for personal stamping. Side one totally walks all over side two, perhaps prophesizing the lack of growth that would become the band's disappointing second album.
Rating 6

## Kamelot - Eternity (Noise '95)

Looks like some sort of pansy air-brushed white metal thing, sounds like a fairly aggressive, pro-rated Queensryche with a purpose, those overwrought thespian vocals of Mark Vanderbilt taking this Florida anomaly unto Virgin Steele and Crimson Glory. But songs are kept logical, making the record more a dramatic, hair band progressive than anything fingers flying. Kinda fresh and shortly marvelous in these alternative times.
Rating 7

## Karma To Burn - Karma To Burn (Roadrunner '97)

There are some elusive ironies at work here, Karma To Burn faking us out with their smart suits, short hair, demented Tool-like graphics, and kaleidoscopic song-titles straight off of old Jane's Addiction records. No metal there, right? Dead wrong, man. This is explosive stadium metal at its lusty best, a sort of glossy Alice in Chains (imagine that!), or Helmet meets the Screamin' Cheetah Wheelies, super-duper dynamics, drums a' poundin', vocals a' hurtin', this band of hotshot upstarts tuning heads all over alt.dom. And that's turning them back to well-planned, well-written, overachieving metal, KTB hoping y'all won't notice that some of your generation are actually working at something. Causes twinges not unlike the feeling we all got when The Cult made their AC/DC record, or Masters Of Reality made their Cult record that was their AC/DC record. A light went on, know what I mean?
Rating 9

## Karroll Brothers - Karroll Brothers (KB '78)

Had to mention these dudes. The Karroll Brothers were an early Canadian power trio (well, three bro's plus an aberrant keyboardist) that we saw live about six or seven times as young metalheads in and around our hometown of Trail, B.C. The Karroll Brothers inflamed our blood live, cranking out rockers like *Goin' Downtown* and covering weird stuff like Uriah Heep's *The Wizard* (which I proudly still possess on 45). The band decked themselves in black (we thought it was leather, turned out it was corduroy), whipped their guitars whenever the urge came over them, and used smoke bombs and strobe lights to impressionable effect. Then they took the brilliant decision to construct two bush-league, barely audible lite rock albums, this debut and **Baby Get Down**, neither containing a mere thimbleful of the band's potent live fury, defying all logic

and marketing acumen in the process. No less than a crushing let-down, because this was our band.
Rating 3

## Kataklysm - Sorcery (Nuclear Blast '95)

**Sorcery** marks the full-length debut from Montreal's Kataklysm, who turned heads right 'round with their extreme **The Mystical Gate Of Reincarnation** in '94. Ferocious and thrashgrind to the extreme, the band still manages technicality with their rotted crustified sound, rising to Bolt Thrower levels, riding the balance between wrathbent repugnance and virtual musicality. Not my bag, but not bad. A somewhat important release for the legions of the damned. What a twisted world we weave.
Rating 6

## Kataklysm - Temple Of Knowledge (Nuclear Blast '96)

Kataklysm continue their in-grown shaggy, scraggy white-knuckle thrash unto phantasia, sounding like a symphony of abominable snowmen barking, cursing and smashing rocks together. And it all makes for quite the jaw-dropped expression on uncommerciality, a sort of ricketty, noisecore spewage with grand progressive rock aspirations, math-defying riffs zig-zagging the temple while a coterie of vocal tracks just complain loudly, vociferously and subjectless. Sorta Norwegian black mixed with Florida death, the subsequent implosion leaving a battered, boomy, echo-plagued husk.
Rating 5

## Katmandu - Katmandu (CBS '90)

Rather than pointlessly update, Dave King, skinny, carrot-topped wunder-throat, ex-of-Fastway, leads a newly assembled crack band through some of the more magical directives of traditional '70s metal and indeed vintage Fastway itself. Katmandu carries itself with boyish exuberance through this whirlwind of strong and varied anthems (including a hip, metallized version of U2's *God Part II*), projecting about as complete and as human a persona as possible with just one record. There's a bit of Zep in this, especially in folksy acoustic numbers like *Sometime Again* and *Heart & Soul*, a dedication due less to the fact that King's voice resembles Plant's, more to the fact that Zep was a big, impressionable part of the '70s. Yet there's also inklings of Purple, Dio, Whitesnake (witness blues killer *When The Rain Comes*), and sun-warmed American stadium rock like *Only The Good Die Young* and *Love Hurts*. This record reminds me of all those good feelings we de-

rived from fledgling late '70s/early '80s hard rock, yet **Katmandu** doesn't date itself, the value of such early metal being borne of its own timelessness, variety, vitality, and disdain for formula. **Katmandu** stands tall as a proud and ever-entertaining display of fierce independence in the face of modern short-term values and sensory overload, choosing a universality that spans blues, metal, hard rock, pop and acoustic intimacy, delivered with intelligence and naive charm.
Rating                                              8

### Keel - The Right To Rock   (A&M '85)

Keel's second rounder (after a bebut that proposes to **Lay Down The Law**) is actually the guy's most stirring record, due to its mix of fun but toothy heavy metal and ready acceptance on my part of the man's beak-nosed ego, which hasn't started to sound tripped-up and desperate yet, although his voice mirrors that of desperation personified, QR hair-weave dustmop Kevin DuBrow. Features stiff, ham-fisted production by Gene Simmons, widening businessman ever on the lookout for the next Van Halen.
Rating                                              6

### Keel - The Final Frontier   (MCA '86)

Ron Keel, attitudinally aligned with early entrepreneurial types like Ratt, Black'n'Blue, and Adam Bomb, **Kerrang!** darling, over-achiever and proud of it, has unfortunately got a spiel bigger than his collective band's talent. **The Final Frontier** resembles a rough, low quality, clod-rocking version of Dokken, grandiose on heart, but clogged and weighted with cavernous over-production and blunt attempts at dynamics. Wasn't quite enough vim, vigor or lyrical insight to propel themselves into the corporate echelons to which they aspired.
Rating                                              4

### Keel - Keel   (MCA '87)

Featuring tighter arrangements, more bells and whistles, more keyboards, and even more anthems, the all-important, reaffirming, self-titled release nevertheless did nothing to further Ron's drive for world domination, due to his band's badly clichéd songwriting and production-line riff patterns. Unfortunately, Keel's got little else to say except how ready he is to rock, sounding like the embarrassing and panicky self-assurances of latter-day Black'n'Blue.
Rating                                              4

### Keel - Larger Than Live   (Gold Castle/SPV '89)

This guilty pleasure features six new studio trax and six live tunes all recorded in '89. The studio stuff lightens up, revels in its hard rockiness, and generally breathes, Keel and crew obviously unconcerned about saving the world of recorded music. So it's surprisingly non-metal, more like party hardy Helix, with insidious ounces of soul. The live side's another matter, one of two new tracks here, **Hard As Hell** blowing the casings off with a dose of bad-smelling OTT. Then it's on through some of Ron's deathly unremarkable Great White impressions until the bar-belting bashfest closes with moldy old classic **Cold Day In Hell**, the single that with the help of Yngwie, got Ron his small part in the crazy heavy metal circus in the first place.
Rating                                              6

### Keen Hue - Ogre King   (Criminal Response '85)

Probably one of the hottest and darkest of underground Euro offerings, **Ogre King** rides that classic messed-up twin lead heaviness beneath wickedly capable early Klaus Meine-style vocals, with just that added street-level urgency to keep it loose and lethal (although judging from the overall sense of solitary confinement, I don't know if these dudes have ever seen a street). Keen Hue tunnels six feet into the frozen Swedish sub-strata to resonate the pain of the most choice and suicidal Ebony or Scratch Records poverty lowlifes, even 220V, rumbling ever downward like disoriented victims of a world gone wrong. So **Ogre King** thoroughly pounds, that is save for three half-hearted attempts at happy hard rock. Of the earth, for the wired.
Rating                                              8

### Kerbdog - Kerbdog   (PolyGram '94)

England's Kerbdog slide their way through a fairly charismatic grunge sex type thing, indeed enlisting Jack Endino for production duties. Riffs and arrangements are snakey but infectious, with vocals from Cormac Battle that sound like James Hetfield's most tuneful singing voice. And tuneful's the operative here, most tracks coming across as catchy metal-cozies-up-to-alternative, despite many hiccup beats, rising to groovy singalong choruses in quest of cementing an impression in these competitive times. Only shortcoming: a pervading sameyness, which will probably clear right up after ten or twenty applications.
Rating                                              7

### Kick Axe - Vices   (Pasha '84)

A rich and powerful masterpiece of hard rock songcraft, **Vices** is a celebration of living on par with the most cherished highs from Van Halen, Kiss and Aerosmith. The elements that make **Vices** brilliant are many, first and foremost being the king-of-the-world vocal prowess of George Criston who soars, screams, yelps, and croons all over this, a performance so sincere and inspired, that the band can't help but be lifted to new heights in the process. And the playing is awesome, bottom-heavy, chunky, sparse and tasteful. Solos are metallic and resolvingly melodic, drumming is manic but level-headed, production is hi-tech, overtreated but warm. Musically **Vices** occupies the space between simple, economic, mischievous metal and melodically complex hard rock pageantry. Just about everything rages on this, the smooth cruising riffs of *Cause For Alarm* and *All The Right Moves*, the otherworldly philosophizing of *Just Passin' Through*, and the anthemic bad boy stomps of minor hit *Heavy Metal Shuffle* through the autobiographical title track. **Vices** remains a devastating and enduring piece of metal history after the passing years, the drift, and the ultimate break-up of Kick Axe. It's unfortunate that the overflowing talent on this album had not been recognized and nurtured. After all, this is the label and production team that brought us the obscenely successful debut from Quiet Riot. Instead, it seems that someone had prematurely pushed the panic button, causing the subsequent stylistic shifts that would be **Welcome To The Club** and **Rock The World**, albums that tended to cloud the band's obvious knack for spirited songcraft. **Vices** on the other hand, is a necessity of life.
Rating                                             10

### Kick Axe - Welcome To The Club   (Pasha '85)

Awaiting this important second album with eager anticipation, alas we find it's fairly fine, even though the knob twiddlers have definitely altered the Kick Axe sound, which is rendered loose, echoey and boomy; drums taking centre stage, resulting in an overall effect of rowdiness but lack of instrumental cohesion, sounding not unlike a stadium venue soundcheck. Second disappointment: inconsistent, cold-fish songs. Overall, the package is less metallic, awkwardly and sporadically studded with forced, uninspired rockers that too often exist for no other reason but to rave about how heavy they are. Highlights include the southern-tinged, optimistic title tirade, the mellow, morose and ponderous *Never Let Go* and flat-out rocker *Hellraisers*. Kinda frustrating because even though the record grows on

you over time, and even though the emotive charm and exuberance of frontman George Criston shines ever so brightly, songcraft is far below the effortless penmanship of the debut, finding Kick Axe clamoring for philosophical focus.
Rating 8

## Kick Axe - Rock The World (Epic '86)

With titles like *Medusa*, *The Dark Crusade*, *Magic Man*, *Devachan* and *Warriors*, Kick Axe drift even further away from what made them impressive in the beginning: a Diamond Dave affirmation of all that parties, delivered with an incredible array of ideas and small town soul. **Rock The World** is a slickly produced yet curiously low-powered "serious" metal album wholly without heart; predictable and thematically old news, especially in '90s retrospect. Whereas **Vices** bestowed upon us one of the best hard AOR albums ever conceived, **Rock The World** is just another forgettable piece of cliché clunk rock, awash in misguided melodies and technical busy-ness, devoid of good feeling and indeed lyrical grist that even embodies the *potential* of good feeling. **Rock The World** is basically a bad business move, a direction that brought out mediocrity in a band with an uncanny gift for delivering proud r'n'r anthems. Let's hope Criston finds himself at his rightful throne once again. He deserves the chance.
Rating 5

## Kik Tracee - No Rules (BMG '91)

Strange as it seems, Kik Tracee was my path to acceptance of Slaughter, the band acting as mentors here, with Dana himself offering his unique brand of spontaneous, shambling combustible production values. And fact is, **No Rules** out-brains, out-brawns and yes, out-parties Slaughter on all fronts, while inhaling heavily on Slaughter's trademark loose volatility. When Stephen Shareaux (billed as Voice and Vision), belts out that he don't need rules, you believe it, and for that matter everything else he croons on this blazing chunk of corporate hard rock, a rounder not unlike the blazing sun. Slippery, slurring and irascible, **No Rules** is studded with engaging, sensitive modern tales, faves being the dynamic *You're So Strange*, party maker *Hard Time*, and the simply correct *Big Western Sky*, which gives the word ballad a fresh new perspective. Unfortunately **No Rules** disappointed at the box office where it should have flourished, yet again exposing the fickle nature of fame. And I can't help but think following it up with an EP, **Field Trip** echoes a sort of dissipation of purpose. Indeed Kik Tracee is worth believing in, as demonstrated by Shareaux turning down lead mike chores for Motley Crüe. Thoroughly exciting California metal, brimming with life and an off-kilter sense of urgency, Kik Tracee was the cream of the corporate metal crop, not afraid to break with convention, not afraid to sound frayed, exposed, or laid back to the point of collapse; all accomplished with a guns-ablaze mission to become reigning lords of the loud.
Rating 9

## Kik Tracee - Field Trip (BMG '92)

C'mon people now, get on the **Field Trip**, and make Kik Tracee a household name. They deserve it but they will need your help, given their penchant for lovingly eccentric rock'n'roll that can astonish but confuse lesser beings. **Field Trip** is a long (34 minute), six song EP that follows the band's excellent debut after much too long an absence. And the band has grown and flown, offering a loopy jaunt through many a provocative posture; unraveled, groovy and unconcerned with appearances. As the band sez in the liner notes (the record's production coinciding with the L.A. riots, affecting the band deeply): "These songs were recorded with the intention of taking you to another

place -Hopefully a better place. So sit back - relax . . . & enjoy the field trip." Can't improve on that. Let the record speak for itself with its rollercoaster mix of metal, funk explorations and endearing acoustics (faves: the marshmallow-roasting title track and the Zepp-ish bluegrass *Drop In The Ocean*), and you will be improved indeed, by witnessing an ethic towards life and art that embraces experience with energy. Not a duff track anywhere, Kik Tracee quietly building a reputation for spontaneity, edgy, accentual, sensuous and concentric vocals, and a guitar sound that evokes the biker roar of Jake E. Lee's Badlands work. "Additional Arrangements" credits go to Chris Goss, and his influence to my mind is in evidence, **Field Trip** spilling over with the same deconstructed verve that makes **Sunrise On The Sufferbus** such a weirdo. Two bus trips with the same idealistic, kaleidoscopic view of the road ahead.
Rating 10

## Killdozer - Little Baby Buntin' (Touch And Go '87)

Alternative to say the least, **Little Baby Buntin'** is one of a number of vile Killdozer clankers, featuring drunken old man vocals, absolutely enraged every minute of every day with having to deal with the idiotic itch called mankind. Sonically, imagine Skinny Puppy with guitars, or Sons Of Freedom cryogenically slowed, rendered opaque, stumbling wholly amnesiatic with respect to human emotional blueprints, or indeed, musical dexterity. This exquisitely disgusting, sneering pile of smell could have been a brilliant chunderous torture, 'cos I laughed my head off at some of the antisocial lyrics scattered with gravel-lunged intent, yet unfortunately all reverbs with a vessel-popping din brought crashing aground like a pre-animated scrap metal heap pushing match. Actually thoroughly metallic, but like jazzy, free-form Sabbath, or punk mechanically de-revolved to Sabbath's tempos (see Melvins), a doom version of bad NoMeansNo, **Little Baby Buntin'**'s pretty bloody amusing, but just too industrial (a hip deal these days) for voluntary consumption.
Rating 4

## Killdozer - Uncompromising War On Art Under The Dictatorship Of The Proletariat (Touch And Go '94)

Hilarious track-by-track explanations champion the workers' struggle against capitalism, as Killdozer craps forth with their gutted Melvins metal, as or more musical than on other Kills. Basically growly grizzly-on-heroin metal by the unruliest bunch of curmudgeonly comrades to ever record. A menace to society. Includes the **Burl** EP from '86.
Rating 6

## Killer - Thriller (Bellaphon '82)

**Thriller** displays a band bent on scooping the crumbs of Krokus' growing entourage, stealing the whole schmooz, the Bon Scott growl, the boogie woogie Angus riffs, and the general party ethic of blue collar take-out everywhere. Broman's vocals suck however, a man most likely in possession of a voice absolutely unsuited for Bonisms, yet jammed so painfully into the image by a band so focused on the success of the local Swiss derivatives. Barring Broman's muted gasp however, **Thriller**'s basically a solid if uneventful Krokus record.
Rating 4

## Killer - Stronger Than Ever (Rockport '84)

Not the talentless grime-rockers from Belgium, these guys are a much cleaner, polished, hard rocky bunch of Swiss nobodies sporting that demented Visigoth look. This great improvement on '82's smothered **Thriller** causes increased frustration with its stellar production, strong vocals, and three or so devastating rockers (especially *Blood On The Black Flag*, where everything

comes off god-like), the rest of the disc running the gamut from mediocre to boring or downright repellent. Good mixed with bad. As a result, with better songs, plus general lyrical updating, these guys could be kicking some butt on future boogie bangs.
Rating 5

## Killer - Ready For Hell (Est. '81)
Greasy-haired rock from Belgium! Occasional Motörhead-driven lust for life, but generally awful songs and even worse production.
Rating 2

## Killer - Wall Of Sound (Mausoleum '82)
Wall Of Sound improves upon Ready For Hell in most areas and arenas: production, aggression, tightness, yet it's still pretty forgettable stuff, drooling forth bemused at getting to play rock star. Gotta give 'em an A for effort. They've at least graduated from the garage to the scummiest of drinking establishments.
Rating 4

## Killer - Shock Waves (Mausoleum '83)
Even more overcast and leaden than the bruising Wall Of Sound, Shock Waves is similarly mean, gritty, growly, and despicably hard to handle. Here they come. Hide!
Rating 4

## The Killer Dwarfs - The Killer Dwarfs (Attic '83)
If these diminutive Canucks never make it "big", it won't be because of the belittling short act, Russ Dwarf's somersaults, or the man's on stage tricycle rides, it will be because of the almost breath-taking lack of ideas, both lyrically and musically. KD's debut is stripped and clinically clean retro-metal, professional for its time, but only in theory, as the lack of edge, danger, and originality combine to form a smothering conformity of sound.
Rating 4

## Killer Dwarfs - Stand Tall (Maze '86)
The generic metal of the debut heaves way to a generic melodic hard rock sound, replete with wimpy choruses and poseur structures. Da Dwarfs try to go for that Triumph "you're a loser, be proud of it", morale-building philosophy on this one to no great success.
Rating 3

## Killer Dwarfs - Big Deal (CBS '88)
Not sure if it was intentional or not, but the album title is the wittiest thing about this acne-faced teen slop, as the short ones finally land one with CBS. Wide-eyed and drooling, ready to sell their souls, KD dive in hook, line and sinker, generating like spores this radio-friendly blemish of Dokken and Keel out-takes. Harmless, demonstrating an alarming shortage of backbone (huh-huh).
Rating 3

## Killer Dwarfs - Dirty Weapons (CBS '90)
Similarly aimless songcraft to all that preceded it, Plugged Barrels revives the stultifyingly anonymous metal-steeped hard rock the Dwarfs have sleepwalked through time and time again, granted a bit heavier of stature. A few good riffs, considerable rowdiness, yet to this day, nothing identifiable as a personal sound. Most chomp arrives with Comin' Through, Nothin' Gets Nothin', and stop/go closer Want It Bad, on a record with lots of energy, lots more than on any previous plodder, but nothing that red-flags the world to take another look; just a flawless, simply detailed and sincere delivery of nothing. Basically no innovation and no magic on this disappointing gesture away from the band's patented humour.
Rating 5

## Killer Dwarfs - Method To The Madness (Sony '92)
Doing heroic battle with a self-inflicted reputation for weak rock'n'roll, Russ and Co. come bounding back with what is easily their most ambitious, unified chunk of product to date. Kicking off with lead single Hard Luck Town, a thumpy, blues metal stomper marbled with complex melodies, hilariously preambled by a foul-mouthed miner doing a little whiskey-soaked reminiscing, Method To The Madness goes for value, the '90s thing to do, filling 'er up full of old ham-fisted riffery, Zep allusions, fleshy ballads and a few pooches to boot. "Full" is the operative word here, as KD do a strident job battling a track record none too impressive. Again, the humour is left for the stage, as the business-like mass of this record dominates everything, including the vocals (which are mixed way back) and the melodies which snooze to generic levels on some of the hard apples, metallic numbers strangely being the weak links, songcraft-wise. All in all, the best heavy tracks churn slowly, and the best ballads possess that shambling GN'R quality, instrumented up to but not beyond the time-worn levels that are required. Not really a problem at all throwing this in the car and letting it play. Recommended Canuck cuts: Just As Well, Give And Take, and the pulverizing title track.
Rating 7

## Killers - Murder One (BMG '92)
Quite the pooch, Di'anno doing little more than re-naming and re-staffing Battlezone and then hoping it will work in the '90s. But it's no go, given the usual rusted nuts and bolts, a grab bag of bruising mid-riffs, clunky ballads and scampered old OTT, adding up to a whole lot of bluster, but not much in the way of vision. You can see why the shift in style had to happen, Killers being stuck spinning in the '80s like so many British metal units that don't know when to quit. I mean, next to this, Menace To Society looks like a work of art.
Rating 4

## Paul Di'anno & Killers - South American Assault Live (Magnetic Air '94)
This semi-worthy live document finds Di'anno and crew reliving the past, headbanging through Brazil, Argentina and Venezuela, packing a bunch of solo tracks and Maiden compositions, with a We Will Rock You/Smoke On The Water medley closing the show. The band is full-on, the sound acceptable, and Di'anno in fine form. Of course the value for most fans derives from the Maiden tracks (all from Iron Maiden or Killers of course), highlights being Murders In The Rue Morgue, Remember Tomorrow, Phantom Of The Opera and the swift hooks of Sanctuary. Rock-solid live record, if a bit contextually sad.
Rating 6

## Killers - Menace To Society (Bleeding Hearts/Metal Blade '94)
The fairly unproductive Paul Di'anno's Killers (one poor debut and one poor live album following the underwhelming Battlezone incarnation) is back with something of a cheap ruse that works better than the alternative. For the band has discovered Pantera in a big way, emulating them wholly on about 65% of this solid but imitative sledge. The other influence would be slow Sabbathy grunge, making for a record that shamelessly and somewhat purposefully updates, even Di'anno's distinct pipes givin' it all up for growl. I mean, it doesn't even sound like the same guy. So consider this one you might file unless you're some sort of garrish Maiden watcher. But maybe we should be allowing these guys complete makeovers and not just dismissing them. It's just that this one even cops Pantera's tough guy lyrics, not to mention the look, really making the transformation that much more embarrassing. Oh well, if they can't make it on their own,

maybe Killers can be the scrapyard of Dimebag Darrell riffs, the storage shed from which he will construct his next pink-goateed opus.
Rating **7**

## Kill For Thrills - Dynamite From Nightmareland
(MCA '90)

Something suspicious about the packaging and the songtitles told me this was just too cute and opportunistic to speak eloquently on man's fried condition, but for $4.99, I laid out my coin. Oh that it weren't so. Kill For Thrills embody a Cult/L.A. sleeze rock combination full of low-slung guitars, simple arrangements, weak attempts at groove, and even pop jangliness. Problem is, nothing really shakes the brain here lyrically, sonically, or emotionally, coming off as too white, clean and neat, nowhere innovative enough to become slab of choice for any particular occasion, exercise or pressure point on the emotive spectrum. Follow-up material seems poised to take the band further askance from metal which is just as well. Claim to fame: a guitarist to GN'R commencing with the Gunners' globetrotting '92 tour.
Rating **4**

## Killingculture - Killingculture  (Edel America '97)

A bunch of bands are going for this futuristic, mutated metal sound these days, a sound that somehow manages an industrial din without much electronics. Amongst the realm are the likes of Fear Factory, Machine Head, Grip Inc. and now hot new upstarts Killingculture. Talk about stressed. Killingculture evoke some sort of inexorable mechanized march, carving harsh, harsh, rhythm-dense metal, over which vocalist Marcus Peyton ratches his lungs until all culture is killed. No surprise that drummer Pat Magrath was considered for the Slayer throne, for it is his Lombardo-eyed onslaught that drives each detailed, pummel-head track. Cue-bald producer Scott Ian (of Anthrax, of bloody course) does a cleanly caustic (if necessarily cold) job, sprinkling in fifty or so very novel electronic flourishes and/or samples and/or effects, which all wrapped up in the band's obvious single-mindedness, makes for a package of resolute star quality. The lump this gets lumped with can sometimes be a hard one to swallow (aggro is pretty much the only emotion attempted), but amongst this quite successful metal subgenre, almost all the bands are of unarguable quality, Killingculture wallopingly included.
Rating **8**

## Killing Joke - Extremities Dirt And Various Repressed Emotions  (Noise/Futurist '90)

Killing Joke (named for a Monty Python skit) enter the '90s on edge, still clanging their neurotic structures very much the way they had through the '80s, inventing and expanding upon industrial music through guitar, bass, drums and vocals pushed to the crumbling precipice of humanity. I much prefer this era of the band to any other, finding the old stuff too raw and tribal, and the newer records stiff and clinical. **Extremities** strikes the perfect snooty balance between noise, art and discipline, all personified quite well in lead track and Joke staple *Money Is Not Our God*, which is rife with the fluid, lurid, Crimsonian guitar contortions that make this record sound so itchy and psychotic, but smart and acidic at the same time.
Rating **7**

## Killing Joke - Pandemonium  (BMG '94)

Dandy fractal-laced package to this one, seminal U.K. frownlanders Killing Joke reforming across great geographical distances (some of this was recorded in an Egyptian pyramid) for a mesmerizing but characteristically repetitive tarot foretelling cataclysms of the millennium. Practically inventing industrial by fusing crushing, caustic riffs with square electronic beats, Killing Joke garnered insider and outside respect with their poisonous electro-metal fusions. Here the aging trio (Youth once again joining Jaz and Geordie after a twelve year hiatus) is in fine royal form, weaving middle eastern tonalities through ten tales of the apocalypse, high thespian British vocals (Stranglers anyone?), high-minded attention to literary standards, but lots of curmudgeonly ugliness music-wise, patterns that incite boredom, the band well-known for landing on a texture and staying there arguably too long. Anyways, **Pandemonium** just feels like one you want to keep, surpassing that fine gothic chalkmark between self-important and important.
Rating **6**

## Killing Joke - Democracy  (BMG '96)

With **Pandemonium** being the band's most successful US release yet, the serious souls in Killing Joke are back relatively soon with this intelligent, political look at America and its institutions. Songs are characteristically thick, blocky and choppy, using acoustic instruments to create a vaguely industrial vibe, steamrolling challenging concepts whiskey-throated in anguish, turning the band into cynical professors of doom, despite statements by Youth that this is a stripped-down and even optimistic Killing Joke. So all in all, the band remains quite heavy, rumbling down the causeway with its industrial ethic intact and a pervading leaden importance, recalling heavier U2 songs from Bono and Co.'s first five or so records. Undying respect, even reverence from my camp, even if the music still sounds poisoned, sullen and deflating. Fave: *Prozac People*, which sounds like watery ennui exploding into a Prozac buzz, something which Coleman became acquainted with during his eighteen month battle with depression.
Rating **7**

## King Diamond - Fatal Portrait  (Roadrunner '86)

The legendary King Diamond has always suffered for refusal to pull his Satanic punches. King Diamond, the band, is the first result of such controversy, Mercyful Fate just proving to be too intensely hateful for the masses and indeed some of its own band members. **Fatal Portrait** perpetuates the King's twisted, religion-inverting world, offering a record that would very much approximate what we would have seen as Fate's next step. I'm not sure why I never bought into this band as heavily as I did the Fate. Perhaps it's the relentless, insensitive flood of riffs over the coven's career thus far, or the Hallowe'enie concept album lyrics, but despite such soberingly obvious black metal class, all points of the wicked one's output just blur into a Satanic fog in my over-inundated memory banks. **Fatal Portrait** is of course, supremely professional, well-produced gothic black metal, albeit less adventurous in comparison to **Don't Break The Oath**, exhibiting too much preponderance on galloping, wall of sound structures. Call me an idiot, but outside of the deeply carved *Charon*, I rarely remember much of what goes on here. Hats off to the Kingster for his exterminate-the-weak quality levels, but I'm just not on board.
Rating **7**

## King Diamond - Abigail  (Roadrunner '87)

The demonic Dane returns with his first elaborate concept record slithered forth on forked tongue, a morbid but colourful tale of psychotropic childbirth and rebirth, set to blistering gothic elevations, cut after putrefied cut. Like its predecessor, **Abigail** is metallic perfection in every direction; horrific, doom-soaked poison snapped to life by the trademark alternating falsettos and growls of the King's twisted set of pipes, definitely an acquired taste at best, eliciting love it/hate it response all over punter terrains. As I say, metallic excellence, yet the whole damp 'n' creepy package tends to snuff out any positive emotion one might be able to conjure, despite the criminal attention to detail the man embodies. No doubt a 10 in many circles, but chalk my 7 up to lyrics incompatible with my headspace.

Rating 7

### King Diamond - Them (Roadrunner '88)

Grandma, blood-laced tea and "them." Throw in the King, Missy and their mother and you have another macabre tale of hellish apparition and life's thrills and spills in the house on the hill. And as per the King's usual high standards, the whole disturbing story is set to wickedly cutting edge goth-metal, constructed of adept, purely-metallic performances from Yngwie-influenced axe-attackers Andy La Rocque and new disciple Pete Blakk, not to mention fierce exactments from percussionist Mikky Dee. Another sheer, formidable 10, if Satanic Eurogoth is your teapot, but unlike Venom, King Diamond's world can actually infect the moral centres with some level of gravity. Dark, sick secluded genius. Follow-up, **Conspiracy** (sorry, not reviewed!) would mark the band's first welcome retooling with the addition of keyboards to the cannibal stew, not to mention new makeup after getting given the legal boots from Gene Simmons.

Rating 8

### King Diamond - The Eye (Roadrunner '90)

Once again I become overwhelmed then smothered by the unrepentant übergoth tones of the King Diamond organization. I feel I must forfeit my pulpit as commentator on the mighty King, having not the patience to penetrate these elaborately assembled castleblaks, epic phantom fortresses that focus the best talents from Eurogoth to wicked perfection. Our story finds the King of morality exposing wicked deeds perpetrated in the name of religion circa the mid-1600s. And you thought metal couldn't stay current. Here's the part where I say conceivably a 10 in your particular basement or dungeon-like death chamber.

Rating 7

### King Diamond/Mercyful Fate - A Dangerous Meeting (Roadrunner '92)

This pleasant 16 track career retro combines the two phases of the King, beginning with a couple pre-**Melissa** tracks (available on **The Beginning**), wending its way through Dr. Diamond's salacious evil, stopping for one more non-LP tune No Presents For Christmas. But the package has been lovingly constructed, with an informative essay on the man (with talk of the King's early bands: Brainstorm, Black Rose and The Brats) including lots of photos, and a full explanation of track origins. A leather-winged legacy is assured.

Rating 8

### King Diamond - The Spider's Lullaby (Metal Blade '95)

Ever the champion of quality, however black and twisted his impression might be, King Diamond is a prolific talent who keeps delivering the goods. Nevertheless, his eerie falsetto, and increasingly his elegant phantom operations are an acquired taste, sort of a lost art that only he and his more urgently guitarish alter-band Mercyful Fate seem to want to address. **The Spider's Lullaby** upholds this tradition, combining hyper, double-bass-style structures with dressy keyboards, while the King crafts a record that is half concept and half not, always progressive and well-heeled, but a bit brash production-wise. Probably the man's most aggressive and doomy outing, with some pretty chilling character vocals to boot. Drink heavily from the trough of night if you must, however I think I prefer the Fate.

Rating 7

### King Diamond - The Graveyard (Metal Blade '96)

As can be quickly ascertained, I'm much more enamoured by Mercyful Fate than King Diamond, finding the King imprint too horror-movied, conceptual and for some reason, always quite mid-rangey. The Kingster told me that this record was originally going to be about graveyards, the inhabitants thereof, and the society of the dead that comes to life when the living are safe in bed. But as circumstances go, Mr. D. altered the plot, feeding off of stories of child abduction in his native Texas. So full applause should flow to the man's sense of service, to his exposing and discussing the ugly subject of child abuse. But as usual, King's alter-band seems stuck in a B-movie rut, leaving very little personal warmth anywhere on this record. And a straw poll of metal critics I know confirmed these sentiments. Hands-down victory to Mercyful Fate.

Rating 7

### Kingdom Come - Kingdom Come (PolyGram '88)

You can't blame Lenny Wolf for having a voice like Robert Plant, but you can give him the gears for ripping off ol' Percy's singing styles. So Kingdom Come deserves the bashing and subsequent pigeon-holing they received for imitating Zep here. Wolf emulates Plant 100% of the time on this, with three tracks being unabashed sonic forgeries from the mighty Zep catalogue, Get It On (Kashmir), Loving You (Zep acoustic), and What Love Can Be (Zep blues). Otherwise what we get is an adequate range of hard rock styles, with tasteful soloing and nice riffs, although a few cuts are a bit Dokken-ishly melodramatic and pretty-buoyed. Still the novelty aspect of this disc cheapens the band, making serious listening next to impossible. In a twist of fate, Kingdom Come would take the criticism to heart and forge their own identity, yet in their wake, leave a minor wave of similar pretenders to the Zep throne.

Rating 6

### Kingdom Come - In Your Face (PolyGram '89)

The man with the quality '60s bouffant is back and haulin' ass. **In Your Face** thrusts forth a telling album cover (a woofer on a plain white background), with a soundly stated attitude to match. The band has explained that the album title represents a confrontation with those who thought the band had no personal backbone or identity, and in demonstration, the ponderousness, and most importantly the Zep tricks are long gone. **In Your Face** pulls off this "coming out" famously. If you took all the hottest tracks from the mostly boring catalogue of Great White and put them on one record, this would be it, **In Your Face** running the course from good ol' American hard rock and traditional '70s metal to a healthy dose of brooding, Sabbatherian metal-blues. Riffs are innovative while traditional, and the soft/loud dynamic works due to honesty, unlike the rough-shod Dokken-isms of the debut, all cohering due to a consistent, sonically big league recording that manages not to sap the humanity from the endeavour. Contrary to what eventually happened, these dudes deserved to make big coin. Mising in action: ignored follow-up **Hands Of Time**.

Rating 8

### Kingdom Come - Bad Image (Warner Music Germany '93)

It's a multi-tiered exercise in reality that this band even exists any more, Lenny Wolf weathering the Zepclone accusations, the rise and fall of his band and the death of AOR to create a record that is at minimum a vital chunk of light-footed hair band metal, and if words be kind, a dramatic, dynamic collection of well-engineered pop metal sculptures. Almost reminds one of the Leps' **Slang** situation, Wolf (and pretty much Wolf alone) lathering each of these cold, not all that heavy tunes with a slick layer of electronics. But it's not like

this is even written for us, AOR being a language we North Americans barely understand anymore. So I'm sure Wolf does bracing business in Germany or Japan, fully resigned to the fact that we're going to find the record a joke. Well, it ain't a joke, but it also ain't all that lively or warm or urgent, only tracks like the mysterious *Can't Resist* or the surprise pop connection of *Little Wild Thing* rising above the record's overbearing aseptic snobbiness. Still, I marvel at and almost crave the craft enclosed, but then I come to my senses.
Rating        6

### King Kobra - Ready To Strike    (Pasha '84)

I'll grudgingly admit that this is at least heavy, but durn it all if this isn't the silliest looking bunch of bleached big hairs I've ever seen walk the runway. Of course Carmine kept his bouffant black, to distinguish the old no-talents from the young ones, our man Appice phoning in his usual sand-fer-brains performance on what are, again grudgingly, acceptable party rock anthems, suspended for view by some sweet Lizzy-ish soloing from Philips and Sweda. Re-issued (at least in Germany) in '94 by EMI.
Rating        5

### King Kobra - Thrill Of A Lifetime    (Capitol '86)

Carmine Appice just has no idea. And if this simply sad piece of work isn't primarily his doing, then his very presence has surely dragged it towards its homogeneous drivel quotient, as it has everywhere else he's been. Absolutely hollow, keyboard puppy complaisance, as stiff as a warm glass of skim milk, King Kobra have gotten staggeringly worse, dishing forth the most offensive, corporately pandering, deafeningly toneless wimp rock, devoid of any inkling of brains. So monumentally cheesed and indeed dead-bottom of even its turgid genre, **Thrill Of A Lifetime** laboriously and methodically blows every category of characteristic: faceless drumming, generic vocals, useless, passé early '80s pop metal moves, over-cluttered, metallically clueless production, and the most distressing of predictable song constructs; dreadfully painful, robotic tune after tune. The laughing stock of the scene, I'm sure. Please, please just go away.
Rating        0

### King Of The Hill - King Of The Hill    (SBK '91)

Swirling somewhere within the wheels of confusion and aspirations borne of the funk metal conspiracy, with all its overt commercialism and questionable intentions, pimp-rolls another loose-hipped gang of crossovers; white boys from St. Louis with black blood via white translations of black music, most notably Red Hot Chili Peppers, Aerosmith, and Pat Travers, plus more minor traces of the Stones, Zep, GN'R, and funky Ted. Don't know if you're confused, 'cos I sure am, given that once you think the groove thang has taken your butt, the Kings ease into straight-faced acousticisms, which come comfortably, melodiously, and too often for formulaic slagging. **King Of The Hill** has a definite alternative feel to it, more with its exploded identity than any overt sonic eccentricities. Once the rock 'n' throb of *Electric Riot* bops to a stop, it becomes apparent that a party hath occurred, yet one that is both intimate, awkward, and strangely vulnerable. Definitely on edge and convincingly true to their funk dogma, **King Of The Hill** lays a fine foundation for future, more confident brilliance. Miles more interesting than the aseptic and guitar-shy Dan Reed Network, yet still miles beneath the dazzling violence of Faith No More, King Of The Hill do one better than contemporaries Lock Up in keeping it light and entirely about living with rock'n'roll ambition.
Rating        7

### Kings Of The Sun - Kings Of The Sun    (RCA '88)

These Australian dudes are an affable bunch of unpretentious roots rockers, hard-hittin' cowboys, who despite their down-under address, serve up a hot slice of Americana here that resembles a turned-up, black-eyed version of Jason and the Scorchers, a recipe for a brawl if there ever was one. Replete with hooky sagas, barroom raucousness, snarling vocals and damn loud drumming, anthems like *Serpentine*, *Get On Up* and *Hot To Trot* strike an arresting balance between pie-eyed AC/DC, the determined grit of mid-westers like J.C. Mellencamp, and the traditional values of legendary bad boys of the south, Lynyrd Skynyrd. **Kings Of The Sun** is the real enchilada; highly recommended for the car deck or summer beer spillage, infectious redneck rock'n'roll that wakes the senses to the Aussie way of life.
Rating        8

### Kings Of The Sun - Full Frontal Attack    (RCA '90)

The Kings' second hot slab picks up right where the debut left off, smokin' it home with more of the same rip-roarin' redneck metal, tearin' along behind one of the rowdiest displays of drumming ever thrashed out in the name of roots rock, a raging percussive flood that always insists upon being heard. Whereas the debut may score points in terms of simple unassuming charm, **Full Frontal Attack** makes up for its inherent busy-ness in the delivery department, kickin' with an unabashed barroom intensity most eloquently put on killers such as *Crazy*, *Drop The Gun* and *Rescue Me*. The slower tunes here possess the same bluesy soul as on the debut, highlighting the capabilities of this band to mix it up and still sound like they have the pedigree of the Stones. Again, *serious* car tunes.
Rating        9

### King's X - Out Of The Silent Planet    (Megaforce '88)

Houston's King's X are one of the more highly esteemed bands of the '90s, positioned by others (and modestly, never themselves) as intellectual vanguards of new creativity in metal, along with Faith No More and the defunct Jane's Addiction, atop contemporary oddities like Warrior Soul, Last Crack, and Soundgarden, plus a good five or six other outfits with only debut albums as of '93, Rage Against The Machine and Stone Temple Pilots springing to mind. King's X contribution to metal is a delicate maelstrom fusing Sabbath-like riffery and mass, flawless harmonies, Beatle-esque melodies, and alternative tunings. Lyrically, the title of the band's third masterpiece **Faith Hope Love** succinctly captures the essence of the panoramic but intimate vistas the band explores, offering a bright, exhilarating and cleansing examination of man's relationship with himself and the collective soul, a philosophy no doubt linked to two-thirds of the trio's origins with seminal Christian rock band Petra. And, unlike many musical enigmas that arrive almost unwillingly, or accidentally into full blossom, King's X (veterans by this time; leader Pirner being 37 years old here) wastes no time in unlocking the gates, as this, the band's debut is essentially interchangeable in time with the band's next three records (or at minimum, **Gretchen**), offering fully matured visions set within beautifully dressed landscapes of both lush warmth, as in lone ballad *Goldilox*, and the inspiring *Shot Of Love*, and more blunt, lumbering displays of power such as *Visions* and *What Is This?*. My only complaint with **Out Of The Silent Planet** is its preponderance with slow to mid-tempo structures, a shortcoming which glares somewhat due to the singular nature of King's X's self-defining craft. Indeed this is the only area in which the newer product can be said to be improvements, as follow-ups seem to progressively stretch and experiment with increasing confidence. The catalogue as a whole, however, is a must-own, King's X no less than single-handedly

**231**

fashioning a genre which I predict few will ever be so audacious as to try duplicate (save for mates Galactic Cowboys, who in total are plain weirder and more manic), a situation that was and still is the case with the world's greatest band Queen.

Rating           9

### King's X - Gretchen Goes To Nebraska    (Megaforce '89)

Lead single and video from this opulent masterpiece *Over My Head* addresses the universality of good music, and indeed universality is something **Gretchen Goes To Nebraska** is wholly capable of, as the swirling guitars, comforting wisdoms, and hypnotic melodies take the willing, the open-minded, and thus the privileged into the vortex of complex religion that is this band's train of thought. **Gretchen** perpetuates this trio's timeless guitar chimings and innovative mantra-like structures, while stepping out with greater flair, as on the aforementioned minor hit (a rare straight ahead rocker), the folky acoustic washes of *The Difference*, the Hendrix via Mahogany Rush via Pat Travers funkster *Fall On Me*, and fave rave, the vaguely Max Webster-ish *Send A Message*. As per the debut, the harmonies are ethereal and dead-perfect (all three members get equal "vocals" billing), and the guitarwork is front, centre, psychedelic and loopy. This is one of those records that took about 150 listens before slipping from my regular playlist, and even now, a sort of renewed awe washes over me when I throw it on. King's X is a sonic entity unto itself, a sound that in interviews, the band modestly discounts as simply the product of the individual members' diverse musical heritages; nothing to get all that worked-up about. In any event, the hybrid is refreshing and brilliant, to which critics, fans, and the band's own musical contemporaries will almost universally attest. If you haven't already checked in, rush forth, abscond and ingest this band's body of work for a journey that is the antithesis to the almost exclusively destructive sentiments of most modern-day metal (thanks to grunge!); a journey along an optimistic and hopeful high road towards at minimum glimpses of inner peace, if not shafts of greater truths.

Rating           10

### King's X - Faith Hope Love    (Megaforce '90)

King's X eagerly awaited follow-up to the fully brilliant but ineptly marketed **Gretchen Goes To Nebraska** takes the band into deeper and more mind-bending explorations of their captivating core sound. **Faith Hope Love**'s peaks and valleys are more multi-altitudinal than the steadying guitar drone of the previous two offerings; the instrumentation more regal, the arrangements more mathematical. Two of the band's finest funk metal feasts kick off this one-hour opus, the harmonic *We Are Finding Who We Are* and lead single, a most Beatle-esque and most metallic charmer, *Its Love*. Other more "out there" events take place with the speed metal *Moanjam*, kaleidoscopic road movie *Six Broken Soldiers*, the acoustic purity of *Legal Kill*, the rhythmic high science of *Talk To You*, and the KX mantra of all mantras *Faith Hope Love*, a psychedelic bluesy escape clocking in at a healthy 9:23. The rich textures and blinding beauty of this record unfold relentlessly with each impending and successive listen, capping off a further elevation of a sound that was lofty and full since its recorded inception back in '88. King's X continues to expand the limits of guitar-oriented rock into more musically demanding, life-affirming and philosophically complex vistas, making this unassuming Texas trio one of the most challenging catalysts of the new music.

Rating           10

### King's X - King's X    (Atlantic '92)

Suffering from the condition of not being sufficiently deprived in wait of an important release (rare these days), I found myself strangely unmoved at the prospect of a new King's X album, which in my opinion comes too soon on the wings of the ambitious and unjustly ignored **Faith Hope Love**. And **King's X**, possibly due to its hasty release, marks only a seamlessly slight progression to the trio's long-enchanted, singular refrain. Temporally and philosophically similar to the fortitudinous platitudes of its predecessor, if any distinction can be ventured at all, one might surmise that the present release is a little more wistful, soulful, ponderous, less forceful, although at the same time, less protracted, more spontaneous, closer maybe, humble and even more infused with the band's trademark cascades of shimmering melody. It cuts me up how critically valued this band is now four albums deep in accomplishment, yet, commercially, the band is nowhere. Such are the crimes of art, much like that committed on Badlands and Alcatrazz of old, King's X and Love/Hate to date. Anyhowz, coolest tracks here include cold steel cruiser *The World Around Me*, bemused tour fable *Lost In Germany*, and playful lead vid *Black Flag*, the latter two making the slight repositioning towards a strange, spontaneous, but slower containment. Rich and pastoral as usual, but possibly time for bolder strides towards a new concoction, one which I'm sure would revolutionize metal once again.

Rating           9

### King's X - Dogman    (Atlantic '94)

Time marches on indifferent, for whatever reason King's X still stuck in cult band underdrive, gods to an industry that doesn't always find ways to reward their heroes, dogmen of a perplexed marketplace. So only a slight shift, borne of less slight internal and external exasperation. Longtime manager and fifth King Sam Taylor is out, enter enthusiastic Ray Daniels of Rush fame. Also please welcome new "successful" producer (for what it matters) Brendan O'Brien, who brings a dirtier, incestuous low-end, muscling up the drums, swelling the slow, generally brutalizing the delicate King's X ecosystem. But the new foot-stomping mix causes only slight distraction from another raft of fine but urgent and open-structured tunes highlighting a unique triple alchemy, and lyrics which confuse and frustrate me to no end. Still despite being strangely less commercial than its predecessor, I believe great singles hide in potential wait, ready to soar if chosen, personal faves being lush mellowscape *Fool You*, and heavier pageant *Pretend*. But when it gets both ballad-like and really slow, the record can drag, and *Manic Depression*: three-legged novelty I can live without. So, life trudges forth and good fortune continues to elude the deserving, and victory again is bittersweet.

Rating           9

### King's X - Ear Candy    (Atlantic '96)

Why this stately trio of venerable veterans can't rule the alternative roost 'long side Soudgarden is a mystery to all in the critical community, **Ear Candy** delivering another God-gracious amalgam of beautiful music. But I say alternative for a purpose, Pinnick, Tabor and Gaskill retaining all that made them kings, while muddying and loosening their deliveries in warm fashion (and un-coding, not decoding their sometimes frustrating, unfocused lyrics), resulting in a record that with a squint and a headshake, could conceivably be the next from Cornell and crew, not exactly as dirty but as thick, echoey and purely genius. Take 'em on tour fer crissake! Anyhow, the time is right and the record is right, King's X probably making its boldest shift with Arnold Lanni's production blending torridly the band's new, wide-open, often tribal tunes. Fave raves are the melodic wonders like *A Box*, *Mississippi Moon* and *Picture*,

all three blowing free love with choruses that give me faith in music as healing. Other serious masterpieces: *Run*, with its thick, aggressive heaviness and plaintive, understated vocal, and *Fathers*, sparse power and wisdom interwove unto the stars, the band's age-old skill of marrying the Beatles to shimmering power chords displayed for all to marvel. A bitter triumph, reviewing this on the eve of its release, hoping against hope that this long-suffering champion of the under-rated will break, like Soul Asylum, like Meat Puppets, avoiding the hollow responses afforded the likes of Paul Westerberg, Bob Mould, and closer to metal base, Kyuss and Overkill. Unreal, but I think this is my favourite King's X (and that's saying more than I have space for).
Rating                                                                     10

## Kiss - Kiss (Casablanca '74)

Out of nowhere comes an album and more importantly a proto-multimedia extravaganza that combined the overblown excesses of the psychedelic '60s with the prima-donna glam stylings of the early '70s as per T. Rex, Bowie and Alice Cooper, all supercharged through the world of comics. Kiss took stage theatrics beyond previously established limits, igniting all-out warfare between musical puritans and glitzy, campy drag merchants who felt r'n'r could use some dressing up. Listening to **Kiss**, I get the feeling this is not a band that wore their hands to bloodied stumps playing at Berkeley. Although this historically tantamount debut is infectiously hooky, and yes, completely unprecedented in American music, it sure ain't rocket science. And Kiss never professed it to be so. This is a band that knew what they were chasing: screaming legions of horror fans, those who loved it loud and shocking; chicks, guys, whoever would be crazy enough to strap themselves in for the ride. And ride they did, in droves, as Kiss would up the ante considerably for showmanship and commercial audacity, while churning out nothing more than power chords in primary colours. So **Kiss** is a likeable enough debut, giving leather-winged birth to a number of meat-and-potato rock standards such as *Strutter*, *Firehouse*, *Cold Gin* (competently but uneventfully covered by Death Angel), and *Black Diamond* (drunkenly and eventfully covered by The Replacements). Innocuously fun as this album is, **Kiss** was more a vehicle for the band's righteous stage onslaught rather than any attempt at toppling Zeppelin from the critical mount. Still, taken in context, it's a suitable calling card to the ranks of everything your mother ever warned you about.
Rating                                                                      8

## Kiss - Hotter Than Hell (Casablanca '74)

**Hotter Than Hell** sees the moral majority's Kings In Satan's Service delving deeper into the four-part Kiss psyche than perhaps was evident on the band's lightheaded debut. Darker, slower and more tantalizingly decadent than **Kiss**, Pucker II gave us some of the more overtly metallic Kiss classics, tracks like *Got To Choose*, *Parasite*, *Watchin' You* and Ace's *Strange Ways* plodding perturbably down pathways of stoopid evil. With a muddy (although not unpleasantly so) recording that leans more to the debut rather than **Dressed To Kill**, **Hotter Than Hell** puts Kiss more squarely in the metal camp, clearly among the first in U.S. rock. Still though, despite the seriousness here, it's definitely clod rock, unwieldy, even Sabbath-like at times, fun due to its ham-fisted delivery and simple we-just-learned-how-to-play structures (in comparison, remember that Aerosmith unleashed **Get Your Wings** the same year). So **Hotter Than Hell** doesn't forget to relax, *Comin' Home* and *Let Me Go, Rock 'n Roll* becoming long-simmering and under-rated cornerstones in the long, likeable Kiss saga.)
Rating                                                                      8

## Kiss - Dressed To Kill (Casablanca '75)

Kiss' third play for world domination marks a stylistic shift towards greater buoyancy and brightness, **Dressed To Kill** being poppier, cleaner, more upbeat and straight-forward than its excellent but lethargic predecessor. Back in the old days, we never realized how much Kiss relied on simple boogie structures (or sexual double entendres) but they are definitely front and foremost here as Kiss pioneers the simple, communicative, intrinsically American hard rock sound that would literally make them cartoon heroes one day. Hummables such as *Anything For My Baby*, *Room Service*, *C'mon And Love Me* and Ace's *Getaway* zip along tightly, lightly, and economically, the riffs often backed-up with spirited acoustic strumming. Another nice touch here that is more a characteristic of early rock'n'roll in general, is that the bass guitar carries its own riff independent of the rhythm guitar, colouring the main riff rather than mimicking it or doing the one-note thing. Gene's no John Paul Jones, but his input does add to the ensemble feel of the proceedings. All in all, an enjoyable early hard rock album, full of all the naiveties of fledgling metal that make one crack a smile nostalgically.
Rating                                                                      8

## Kiss - Alive (Casablanca '75)

**Alive** was the album that turned Kiss into an insane rock'n'roll phenomenon eliciting a level of sheer noise, ecstasy and controversy unparalleled since The Beatles. By blowing to pieces any semblance of restraint, Kiss shocked the world with their ultra-excessive mixture of black leather, high heels, white greasepaint, bombs, fire, sex and violence, the band taking their "Oakland Raiders on acid" circus show to a drop-jaw contingent of fans whose minds will blow as they rock and roll all night. **Alive** gives what were economical and low-key hard rock ditties larger-than-life status, enveloping the fire-breathing mayhem in screaming, hysterical crowds, exploding smoke bombs; total and utter chaos (although it is rumoured that the record was not all that "live" in execution). It's hard to believe how nuts we all were about Kiss in the mid-'70s, vaguely recalling that **Alive**'s arrival at the hands of Bobby Davidson ruined a Grade 7 dance for all our girlfriends when the guys suspended the operation to give the album its full due, crowding around my parents' stereophonic hi-fi console like voracious fire ants. No question, **Alive** would have been blaring in glorious distortion from our car decks had we been old enough to drive. **Alive** was the scruffy teenager's bible, foisted for protection against age, any time responsibility would threaten a night of beers. And **Alive** wholly deserved the accolades and stacks of filthy lucre it generated because really, Kiss was the first of the truly American Metal Bands, the first U.S. purveyors of no-frills squarehead power rock. And even though Kiss couldn't play or write as good as Aerosmith, **Alive** - The Event was their statement that no one else would dare question. After **Alive**, mere music wasn't going to be good enough any more.
Rating                                                                     10

## Kiss - Destroyer (Casablanca '76)

Kiss has been pretty uniformly hard rock or heavy metal to this point. Three studio albums and one stellar live monument to mark the end of an era and Kiss is ready to stretch out, **Destroyer** striding to centre stage with a bunch of Kiss firsts. We get the band's lone ambitious epic in highway classic *Detroit Rock City*, startlingly mellow piffle in *Great Expectations* and *Beth* (both throwaways, *Beth* a massive, Criss-featuring hit), Sabbath-like psycho mud in *God Of Thunder*, and in general terms, fancier instrumentation including an array of sound effects, as new bigshot producer Bob Ezrin blows the budget on party favours. And, try as it

**233**

does to sock-hop to our hearts (see *Flaming Youth* and *Shout It Out Loud*), **Destroyer** is no party album, looming dark, ponderous, almost haunting at times; basically uncommunicative and puzzling due to its stylistic over-extension, an album as apocalyptic and excessive as its album cover. Still it's a sort of camp serious, not the real thing, sort of like what Alice Cooper might have done if he were heavier in his **Billion Dollar Babies/Killer** heyday, a kind of wry look at the life of a circus freak, all the while laughing and skipping on repeated trips to the bank. Overall, a success of early no-chops metal, a record which as much as any other, defined an unabashedly superficial age full of **Wayne's World** rejects like us.

Rating                                                              8

## Kiss - Rock And Roll Over   (Casablanca '76)

A disappointment after the amusing ambitions of **Destroyer**, said platter returns to the wee dumb hard rock cartoons of the early albums, but with more dollar-chasing clichés, less power, less sincerity and less creative acumen, something always in short supply with these brilliant numbskulls. Lyrically we've heard it all before, and outside of catchy stompers *I Want You*, *Makin' Love* and Peter Criss' pulsating *Baby Driver*, the rest is fairly lifeless, awkward, ditzy, self-aggrandizing pop metal that signals a band on the edge of self-parody. Tied with **Love Gun** (incidentally also produced by Eddie Kramer) as the most childish Kiss album. Note: San Francisco bud Shannon Mehaffey said he's kick my ass if I didn't raise my Kiss ratings, so thank him for setting me straight!

Rating                                                              7

## Kiss - Love Gun   (Casablanca '77)

**Love Gun** finds the novelty filler starting to outweigh the gettin' down to business. Who cares though when you get a cardboard "love gun" inside? Boppy, pandering gumwad pop like *Tomorrow And Tonight* and the innocuous *Plaster Caster* (written for a pair of talented historians with a love of erotic sculpture), stains this phoned-in proposition like a virus transmitted by tainted cotton candy, while the odd statements of Kissitude still abound, anthems like the scampering *I Stole Your Love*, Ace's appropriately slammin' *Shock Me*, and the impassioned title track, a Stanley ravefest of silly proportions sending us oohing and aahing for our air guitars. It was a blast to see a band getting so incredibly huge as Kiss, the music being only one insignificant cog in the capitalist juggernaut at this point, a career that culminated in this record *shipping* platinum, no mean feat in the symbiotic, less-populated '70s. Ya still have to laugh. Didn't the '70s just rule?

Rating                                                              7

## Kiss - Alive II   (Casablanca '77)

**Alive II** marks the pinnacle of Kiss' success of excess. Coming off a huge tour with a show that was one of the, if not *the*, grandest, most expensive pyrotechnical maelstroms to date (I experienced it in Montreal with Cheap Trick as back up, and I remember it as mega, but certainly no **Steel Wheels**), **Alive II** harnesses the same magic as **Alive**, comprising three live sides of all post-**Alive** toons, and one studio side featuring three throwaways and two killer kuts in Stanley's cock-rock-in' *All American Man* and Ace's virulent metal opus *Rocket Ride*. On the live side, the teeming masses are left screaming full-bore throughout the proceedings making this sound like the Beatles (talentless losers) in '64. And of course we also get explosions, lots of explosions, lots and lots of explosions, again a necessary part of any Kiss blowout, pretty much more important than the chummy chapped songs trotted out almost inconsequentially. A loud 'n' proud chapter in the history of live rock'n'roll, the whole technical she-

bang trotted-out once again in '96, for the retro cash-in to crush even the likes of The Eagles.

Rating                                                              6

## Kiss - Peter Criss   (Casablanca '78)

Four solo platters, and we didn't even have to ask! I always figured Ringo, I mean Peter had the least to say of the four damn lucky Kiss dudes. This, the biggest commercial bomb of the novel solo fourplex, shows he doesn't even speak the same language.

Rating                                                              2

## Kiss - Ace Frehley   (Casablanca '78)

Space Ace comes through with the least pretentious, heaviest, and best-selling platter of Kiss' solo album quartet, combining warm simplistic hard rock like *Rip It Out* and *Speedin' Back To My Baby* with more serious, slow and moody metal in *Snowblind* and *Wiped Out*, yielding a good, well-rounded simplified '70s metal album, if a somewhat flip and experimental one. No surprise that Ace stays closest of the four to Kiss' hard rock core, complete with wot-the-hell-give-er delivery and good-ol'-college-try vocals. And no surprise the producer is recent Kiss mainstay Eddie Kramer. Evidence of lasting power: Ace (including much of this record) was the subject of a tribute record in '96.

Rating                                                              8

## Kiss - Gene Simmons   (Casablanca '78)

Gene's is the second worst of the four simultaneously released Kiss solo albums (God bless the '70s!), generally comprising stumbling, powerless, watery hard rock, like the worst mechanically de-boned luncheon meat from **Love Gun** or **Rock And Roll Over**. The over-production and use of about 18 million quite impressive guest stars greatly overstates the mediocre songcraft here. Surprisingly disappointing, really. I had hoped Gene was a rocker, but I guess he's just another cheesy Vegas diva.

Rating                                                              3

## Kiss - Paul Stanley   (Casablanca '78)

Stanley, the supposedly "sensitive one", predictably offers forth hooky hard rock butted-up against cheezy love-hungry ballads. Side one generally sucks but side two scores three strong Kiss-intrinsic pop rockers out of four tracks in *It's Alright*, *Love In Chains*, and *Goodbye*. An observation on the solo excursion in general: whenever any of these guys stray from simple hard rock, it's a disaster in synthetics. It's not surprising that one or more of these wily nutters had a predilection for some form of non-metal, but it is surprising how unfocused, indiscernible, wishy-washy, and poorly-written any of these leanings show themselves to be. It tends to prove that the only creation of value Kiss can claim is the concept of Kiss itself, and that individually the band is lost like David Lee Roth at Lollapalooza. Years later, only Ace has released solo stuff of any substance, and even then, it sounds much like puffed-up Kiss.

Rating                                                              4

## Kiss - Best Of Solo Albums   (Casablanca '78)

Must have got help from Scorpions on that album title. Anyhoo, this is a bit of a Kiss rarity, basically culling three tracks from each cartoonman's solo stab. Tracks are fairly random, not theming and scheming to any obvious purpose. No new artwork, no new tracks, nuthin' doing. Mine's German.

Rating                                                              4

## Kiss - Double Platinum   (Casablanca '78)

An automatic and thoughtless career synopsis proudly displayed in a nifty and expensive embossed silver gatefold sleeve. Nothing more except a re-recorded *Strutter*. Get the original elpees for the complete goo on the painted ones psychologies and pass on such disjointed displays of crass commerce.

Rating **5**

## Kiss - Dynasty (Casablanca '79)

Critics called this the puckered ones' stab at the disco cat, however, besides disgraceful world hit *I Was Made For Lovin' You*, of which this is true, **Dynasty** is basically low quality, low batteries hard rock that finds Kiss spinning their wheels. One cool happenin' here was Kiss' warming rendition of unsung Stones gem *2,000 Man*, complete with ragged Ace vocal. But alas, for collectors only, of which a multitude exists, nearing Star Trek proportions. Produced and co-written to some extent by Vini Poncia, who the band would have back wrecking things come **Unmasked**.

Rating **4**

## Kiss - Unmasked (Casablanca '80)

**Unmasked** marks a further decline into aimlessness, sounding like a contrived mess of the most gutless and badly written tracks from the boys' middling solo albums. Actually features studio rock Anton Fig on drums. A smattering of luded-out hard rock rescues **Unmasked** from total disaster, although millions of former Kiss fans might well up into armies and agree or disagree, debating long into the night. Resident kool kut: *Is That You*.

Rating **4**

## Kiss - Music From The Elder (Casablanca '81)

This weird, forgotten little record is admirable in that it contains the odd metal bolt-from-blue that surprises in its musical quality (witness the obligatory lead-off stomper and Ace's quirky *Dark Light*), while lacking relevance due to the maligned concept album precept. Much of the rest of the platter is experimental or just bad Kiss, again worse off in that it is wrapped around what is some sort of unrealized soundtrack album, which hangs like **Welcome To My Nightmare** Act II.

Rating **5**

## Kiss - Killers (Phonogram '82)

This European-only compilation culls together an eccentric batch of Kiss from all eras thus far, while splaying four new tracks (*I'm A Legend Tonight, Down On Your Knees, Nowhere To Run* and *Partners In Crime*) which wouldn't make any official Kiss record state-side. All of them are middling to horrible, lethargically delivered, recorded raw and unbecoming of the band's star status. True garage band filler, from a band not unacquainted with the concept. Two would eventually show up on the **Forever** EP, but if you care you are either a collector or have no taste.

Rating **5**

## Kiss - Creatures Of The Night (Casablanca '82)

On **Creatures Of The Night**, Kiss return to metal from the dicking around that was **Dynasty** and **Unmasked**. Alas, whilst they were away, metal has progressed drastically and as hard as **Creatures** tries, it pales greatly in enthusiasm and talent in comparison to new rock-hog wannabes concurrently washing ashore in droves from the U.K. A few highpoints: the cutting-edge title track (Kiss' fleeting shot at the new metal) and funky, infectious Stanley rave *Keep Me Comin'*. Generally though, Kiss' attempt at remaining vital fails, sounding humourless, mediocre and lick-less. And Gene sounds like an idiot too, accentuating the fact that **Creatures Of The Night** is a parody, weighing too heavily on the idea of Kiss, rather than the idea of the heavy rock'n'roll the band somewhat anemically pioneered ten years back. Leads performed by new nutcase Vinnie Vincent (new indie EP in '96), despite Ace

retaining official member status during the record's low-key release.

Rating **7**

## Kiss - Lick It Up (PolyGram '83)

The much-hyped removal of the band's makeup is paralleled by another gesture of honesty, a realization that the Kiss persona is one of a nuthin' fancy, decisively unserious, quintessentially American attitude over substance; that the music must be allowed to crank second to the walk, talk, strut and stroll. This is why the boys can write cartoons so stultifyingly stripped as *Lick It Up* and get away with it. Stanley's philosophy of live and love, and Gene's philosophy of divide and conquer work an amiable dichotomy here and the party's quite the blast. Gene as evil, stumbling metalhead comes up with the city-slick rockers in *Not For The Innocent* and *Young And Wasted*, while Stanley brings in the hooky choruses on *A Million To One* and Kiss' most assertive, autobiographical stomper, *All Hell's Breakin' Loose*, the two imposing personas together carving their own synergistic twinning, something inherent in most great bands of the '60s and '70s. So on **Lick It Up**, Kiss is back in spades and most importantly, they know it oh so well.

Rating **8**

## Kiss - Animalize (PolyGram '84)

As with **Lick It Up**, a healthy quantity of strong Kiss vignettes stud **Animalize**. On the richter scale, it clocks in about the same, that is, really heavy for Kiss, offering speed rockers such as *I've Had Enough (Into The Fire)* and *Under The Gun* (which lean a bit close to formula), plus two more Stanley meets Diamond Dave classics in smash hit *Heaven's On Fire* and meaty, greedy funkster *Get All You Can Take*. Gene is still the likeable buffoon, as self-proclaimed master of all things, and together he and Paul are about the best old-man tag-team party bulldozers in the seedy, contrived world of corporate metal. Conclusion: very similar to **Lick It Up**; on the downside, *too* similar, equally bland and more formulaic; on the upside, a bit more technically adept. Lone record for guitarist Mark St. John, who is replaced after contracting a rare form of arthritis, which put him temporarily out of action.

Rating **8**

## Kiss - Asylum (PolyGram '85)

Although it can't be said that any of the latter-day Kiss discs leave any sort of lasting mark, given that they all sound the same, are all basically stoopid, and that they seem to come out with greater frequency than is warranted, **Asylum** seems to possess a heightened aura of being unjustly lost in the shuffle. Nevertheless, it's one of the better collections of anthemic Kissitude, with rockers like *King Of The Mountain* and somewhat formulaic OTT'er *Love's A Deadly Weapon*, choice Stanley melodicisms like *Who Wants To Be Lonely* and *Tears Are Falling*, and *Lick It Up*-soundalike *Trial By Fire*. As usual, nothing earth-shattering here, **Asylum** nonetheless qualifying as one of the strongest rounders of the four basically identical '80s LPs Kiss cranked out after the **Lick It Up** exposé.

Rating **7**

## Kiss - Crazy Nights (PolyGram '87)

Don't know what in tarnation happened on this one. Take weirdly unpowerful melodrama like **Hot In The Shade**'s *Hide Your Heart*, completely wreck it and that's what **Crazy Nights** does for the profuse like fungus Kiss catalogue. A totally coasting case of mind rot. Strange twist, possibly owing to Gene's admitted-in-retrospect drift from the band into other projects.

Rating **3**

### Kiss - Smashes, Thrashes & Hits  (PolyGram '88)

Your basic hits potluck with four, count 'em four, distinctions: two new weenie rockers, in the vampy, campy but dullard *Let's Put The X In Sex* and the bubbling and acceptable *(You Make Me) Rock Hard*, lyrics to the whole schmooz, demonstrating once and for all that you haven't missed a damn thing, and last but not least, a new hair-do for *Beth*, appropriately featuring vocals by drummer Eric Carr (Criss sang the first one, as he'll be sure to remind you).

Rating 6

### Kiss - Hot In The Shade  (PolyGram '89)

Finally, Kiss is starting to wear on me like the Ramones (alright, I'm easily amused). **Hot In The Shade** (working title: Crimes Of Passion), like the Ramones, proves that if you've heard one, you've heard 'em all. Brains on auto-pilot, our favorite NYNY capitalists dish forth assembly line commercials for the wearing-thin Kiss philosophy, annoying heavily here like the houseguest from hell that wouldn't leave. Gotta give 'em credit for value though (thank the CD age). Lots of tunes, and given the sheer volume, we do get a fair number of post-greasepaint era successes such as *Rise To It*, *Silver Spoon* and *Hide Your Heart*. Lots of shit filler though coagulates to make this another smug côrporate project devoid of personality, by a duo rumoured to be just a little caught up by the success thing. It's time for the Vegas circuit, or possibly gracious heading status on some travelling '70s revival (note: I wrote that four years ago, and dang nab it, in '96 it happened!).

Rating 4

### Kiss - Revenge  (PolyGram '92)

Nice to see the grizzled ones taking the act of record-making seriously for once, on this well-crafted come-back, dedicated to the memory of recently deceased, long-time drummer Eric Carr, who succumbed to complications from brain cancer November '91 within days of Freddie Mercury's death. **Revenge** is so psychopathically the Gene 'n' Paul show once again, but Kiss '92 is undeniably raised to new levels of intricacy and surprise metalodies, most intelligently shaded in personal faves *Tough Love*, second video *I Just Wanna*, hellbound thumper *Thou Shalt Not*, and hip (!) Gene funk-up *Spit*. Bob Ezrin takes the whole modestly ambitious shmeer and gives it a slow, thick spin not unlike **Creatures Of The Night**, only with a little more modern-day sizzle. Lots of harmonies and multi-tracking of the Grimmer Twins' most sincere vocals in years adds muscle everywhere, with the new-found work ethic proving luck follows hard work. And to underscore the forever commercial, kinda perpetually ridiculous sheen of Kissworld, the humour and ham-headed intimacy of things makes **Revenge** one dumb party like the best of Kiss efforts; the warmest possible chunk of American Everyman steel for the surprise club tour that preceded the record's release, a gesture that Stanley considered a telling indication of the band's ability to engage in trench warfare like veterans still in touch with the street. A welcome upping of the ante, putting Kiss squarely back in charge of their particular brand of doofus metal.

Rating 8

### Kiss - Alive III  (PolyGram '93)

A big steaming plate of WHO CARES all around for Kiss' latest live opus, **Alive III**, a record that ain't half bad really, nice and long (fifteen party faves plus *Star Spangled Banner*; 67 minutes), and well-endowed, particularly with respect to Eric Singer's drum sound, which overwhelms despite its clarity, making for a shoot-'em-up trashfest, rock'n'roll with no grand purpose as Stanley slavishly emphasizes, a celebration, something to get our minds off the recession. A bunch of generally comfy but ditzy rock tunes from every era,

highlighting a career that was never less than percolating on simmer, never less than bubbling under, more often than not, ecstatically blessed with good luck. Most interesting part of the package: one of those band family trees, letting us in on a few pre-Kiss band monikers like Uncle Joe, Cathedral, Bullfrog Beer, Lips (Hey, just like Anvil!), The Muff Divers and Wicked Lester. And damn it if the second half (i.e. *Lick It Up*, *Forever*, *I Love It Loud*, *Detroit Rock City* and *God Gave Rock'n'Roll To You II*) doesn't send star-spangled tingles up my spine.

Rating 7

### Kiss - MTV Unplugged  (MTV/PolyGram '96)

You can't make this stuff up, Kiss setting 'em up for the millennium by calling Ace and Peter back, first for this six-man tag team (Eric and Bruce remain grudgingly intact), then a full make-up and stage show reunion tour using the bombastic and plastic **Love Gun** set. And **MTV Unplugged** is a loving look back at the band's spacious gracious catalogue, sounding like a *Rock And Roll All Nite* party in the seat, due to great, retro-maudlin vocal performances, the inclusion of full drums (no wimpy brushwork here, Mr. Grohl), and marauding bass to back the vigorous acoustic strumming. It's no surprise songs like *2,000 Man* (rogueish vocal performance by Ace), *Do You Love Me*, *Rock Bottom* and *Nothin' To Lose* (sung appropriately by Criss, who also obliges with *Beth*) sound campfire comfy done this way, the unplugged format exposing the no-brains all-heart pop craft of these songs. But the crowning glory is opener *Comin' Home* which takes on a life and puffy-eyed poignancy I never would have thought possible. Heck, even *Plaster Caster* rises above its doltishness, all those politically-correct guitars turning the song positively sweet. But you didn't expect Kiss to screw up, now did you?

Rating 7

### Kiss - You Wanted The Best, You Got The Best!!
(PolyGram '96)

Second live-type piffle in a row, when all we want is the new studio record (tapes are starting to circulate), **You Wanted The Best** is a sort of reminder of what the reunion tour is all about. So we get a bunch of tunes from **Alive** and **Alive II**, plus some really steamy, unreleased, remastered live tracks in *Room Service*, *Two Timer*, *Let Me Know* and a very thumpered *Take Me*. Tacked on the end is a typically inane, propagandizing, agrandizing, bombastible, rock-pigged 17 minute interview with the band by the Sam Hagar of the talk circuit, Jay Leno. Average at best. Still kinda trippy to hear these most uptempo of Kiss koncepts all shuffled up and sent into the CD age. But for a band who sez it ain't about money, this is pretty pompous pablum-pushing indeed.

Rating 6

### Kix - Kix  (Atlantic '81)

This one looked heavy way back in '81, so of course we forked over our cabbage. Mistake at the time, yet **Kix** wore well with age as these D.C. (Baltimore, whatever) underdudes have an unmistakable Attitude that locates them admirably in Kiss or Cheap Trick mindscapes. Still can't help think that the recording deal came a bit before the maturity to compete. **Kix**, however, caused me not to check into the Hotel K until **Blow My Fuse** popped up at my favourite wax emporium for a single buck. I'd have to say I'd now fork it over again as the interim product happens to cross my gaze. Heavier than the oddball follow-up.

Rating 5

### Kix - Cool Kids  (Atlantic '83)

Kix serve it up for a second time with heat and enthusiasm. However, what *it* is, ain't much this time; basic kiddie metal, with an undercurrent of in-earnest realization that it's only rock'n'roll, but at the same time, something the boyz in the band can't live without. Like The Dictators, living the rock life is in this band's blood; comfortable, clean, and well-intentioned rock'n'roll you can bring home to mother, without her noticing that it's all just a joke. The recording is warm, well-rounded and rich, sorta cheap and fully realized at the same time, which is the perfect environs for such goofy guitar rock as Kix so modestly spills. And because this is '83, or possibly because the guys are just a bit weird, there's poppy little intrusions that add a spaghetti western/B-grade horror movie feel to the proceeds. Decidedly less raw and metallic than Kix #1, **Cool Kids** can be adequately described as fringe metal, but fringe towards teeny bopper in a way that bypasses commercial cynicism.

Rating                                                                 7

## Kix - Midnite Dynamite   (Atlantic '85)

The first Kix record to successfully bridge Kiss and the not too distant Helix, **Midnite Dynamite** wells up with thundering, limited, '70s hard rock; slow, stupid, and quite aware of its chutzpah, lumbering through the basics wholly comfortable with the process and its small-time, backwards lot in life. **Midnite Dynamite** sounds nicely old, but doesn't really rev up too often, waiting until speed rocker *Layin' Rubber*, which rivals anything from **Blow My Fuse**, the band's liveliest. Then it's back down to a crawl for an expectedly above-par ballad, *Walkin' Away*, after which we return full-circle to the usual well-worn, drum-driven clod rockers—fine by me, but a little sparse after a few plays. So seemingly mainstream, but as usual, so oddly on the sidelines, always five years back of current trends and swinging wildly at balls sent right to them.

Rating                                                                 6

## Kix - Blow My Fuse   (Atlantic '88)

These guys have been around for awhile and it shows. **Blow My Fuse** is well-recorded, high-calibre party metal, heavier than most melodic hard rock, but simple, to the point and effective; with hints of AC/DC and L.A. cheeze (although they're east coast dudes), vocals with that great Helix or Metal Church rebel yell, and strong, infectious choruses. Hot city rockers include the heads-down *Dirty Boys*, lead cut *Red Lite, Green Lite, TNT* and the tribal drivin' *No Ring Around Rosie*. Actually come to think of it, **Blow My Fuse** sounds like a collection of all the most kick-ass Helix cuts on one record, sort of a supercharged **Walkin' The Razor's Edge**. A rockin', sassy celebration of summer featuring melodramatically brilliant hit ballad *Don't Close Your Eyes*, **Blow My Fuse** brought Kix a modicum of success that was long overdue.

Rating                                                                 7

## Kix - Hot Wire   (Attic '91)

The record that should have endeared this band to the hearts of America once and forever, basically drops the ball of grand gestures, opting for a sound that, I suppose, tries to carve its own unambitious niche within the framework of economic, AC/DC-style blues metal, with its lackadaisical slow limpers, party metal hard rockers, occasional forays into high-octane metal, and an all-pervading layer of roots authenticity. Either that, or the boys are plain lazy and out of good songs; only sporadically pushing the envelope inside the band's chosen but well-traveled path. Gone are the melodic surprises, the Spinal Tap puffery, and the general goofy explorations we've come to expect. Instead . . . unarmed, low-down, barroom axe slingin', which is nice, albeit better done elsewhere. Basically silenced the growing buzz on the band.

Rating                                                                 6

## Kix - Live   (Atlantic '93)

Fun permeates the room as Kix sleaze rocks it through a sampling of their party favours, most of which sound straight off of **Powerage**, played like Helix with harmonica. But the best are the tracks from **Blow My Fuse**, culminating in the band's cinematic power ballad *Don't Close Your Eyes*.

Rating                                                                 6

## Kix - Show Business   (CMC '95)

I guess once you cop to the Kix beat, you can appreciate where they're going here. **Show Business** finds the band bluesy, glam, even pop at times, while perfect duplicates of AC/DC songs well up when the urge overtakes the band (*Put My Money Where Your Mouth Is = Riff Raff*). But risks are taken. *She Loves Me Not* is a sort of grey, three-legged quiet one, and generally speaking, compositions don't lean towards trends, the band just trying to write good, laid-back party rock, kinda like third-rate Aerosmith if there was such a thing. Quite panned critically, caught in that whole backlash against CMC's not dissimilar, early stable of '80s throwbacks.

Rating                                                                 7

## Konkhra - Sexual Affective Disorder   (Nuclear Blast '94)

Joining the rabid legion of grindcore/thrash bands emerging from the frozen Swedish tundra, Konkhra have scraped together a solid, if limiting death release, heavy on half-speed intensities and low-cycle riffs lifted smartly from mid-years Entombed, or originally Slayer. Definitely stuck deep within the genre, Konkhra nevertheless mix up the velocities well, while the band's two vocalists alternately spew and bark out lyrics that run the usual gamut from fantasy through brutal psychology and of course, heaps of physical pain; fairly self-assured wordplay for a bunch of non-Anglos. Peg SAD as a fairly typical death metal release, more listenable and technical than most, but nowhere near as eccentric or crossoverable as bright creative lights like Entombed, Carcass, At The Gates or Sepultura.

Rating                                                                 7

## Korn - Korn   (Immortal/Sony '94)

Body-slam Kalifornia's Korn next to Pantera, B-Thong, Tool, and Machine Head as full-flare aggro-metal relevant in the '90s. Korn's particular claim to legitimacy is the band's freaky arrangements, more percussive and hard-hitting than Helmet, while often grooving real tuneful-like, maybe recalling Nirvana circa **In Utero**. Vocal assault specialist Jonathan Davis packs a formidable punch, beating Phil Anselmo at his own game by mixing up the deliveries, adding to batty filibustering constructions that sprinkle squawking jazznoise and bass-as-lead buzz-riffing over violent, driven rhythms which defy gravity by pounding a stake through it. Drilled, shrill, thrilling and sick, Korn's a stress-soaked bag of basketcases worth watching. Run away! Update I: this record's novel sound had an effect on the outcome of Sepultura's **Roots**, Max being a big fan of the band, even bringing in Davis to guest-vocal on a track. Update II: the record began selling like crazy, months after its original release, legions of metalheads copping to the band's peculiar hip-hopped, tragi-metal rhythms.

Rating                                                                 8

## Korn - Life Is Peachy   (Sony '96)

The first one saw exhaustive touring, a sort of second wind, and subsequent steady insistent rise to sales of 800,000 hambones. Now **Life Is Peachy** has attracted scads of press, white rasta-head Jonathan Davis and his skatish, skiddish ensemble basking in the attention, just ready to work this one to death. Davis told me, possibly with lack of anything better to say, that this one's just way more mature, more about adult issues. But to

my mind, it's dead-on more of the same and thank you dudes, **Life Is Peachy** perhaps digging more into the Korn-ness of Korn, really underscoring the definition built of Fieldy's squeezy bass, Davis' over-insane vocal fretfulness, and Ross Robinson's distinct, disassembled, stressed and stretched production values. The record opens with an alien invasion of vocals and drums hoovering in big gulps all in sight, and just never lets up, Korn's futuristic hip-hop metal shagwag sucking the listener into a hypnotic pimp roll that rearranges and deranges brain cells like late night channel-surfing. Should do well, given the lack of hard music competition and a very legitimate product-positioning with the likes of Rage Against The Machine and Soundgarden, all three hyphen/slash/hyphen hybrids of genre-bursting deliciousness.
Rating                                                                 9

## Richie Kotzen - Richie Kotzen   (Shrapnel '89)
Recorded analog, **Richie Kotzen** is a fairly down 'n' dirty batch of blue collar axe workouts. But the wonder manchild at least gets in the ring, combining shred and schlock metal, serving it thick and exceedingly distorted. Not much else to say: tuneful, dirty metal, but boring without vocals!
Rating                                                                 4

## Richie Kotzen - Fever Dream   (Shrapnel '90)
On record II, Kotzen does the smokin' power trio thing, adding vocals for a smartly assembled traditional metal record, a bit dated, a modicum of funk and a modicum of blues. Good mix, soloing with feet firmly planted, a solid job all around. Richie's pipes are appropriate enough, somewhat derived from Coverdale, comfy if unremarkable, and the record is well-paced; again, professional but fairly unnecessary unless you hang on Kotzen's every note.
Rating                                                                 6

## Richie Kotzen - Electric Joy   (Shrapnel '91)
Probably Richie's brightest showcase, **Electric Joy** finds the guy fluid, exuberant and revealing of the man's traditional electric blues influences, Hendrix, Clapton, and Stevie Ray Vaughan springing to mind. Prog, jumpy, jazzy and slick. A joy to those who study this sort of thing (usually to improve their own skills).
Rating                                                                 6

## Richie Kotzen - Mother Head's Family Reunion
(Geffen '94)
Press statements make note that Richie Kotzen had clocked 500 club dates by the time he was eighteen. Now a scant five years later, he has three solo records to his name, a doomed stint in Poison (girlfriend stuff!), and now a fourth spread which dives deeply and loosely into a funky retro blues similar to that of soul brother Zakk Wylde and his Pride & Glory project. And like Zakk, Richie is blessed with a quirky, cough-syrupy blues-bent set of pipes, which complement the fluid '70s-style axework enclosed. Aside from yucky '60s cover Reach Out I'll Be There, I'm in tune with the childman's internal vibe, easing into this one quicker than Zakk's oblong feast, despite the more pedestrian arrangements used here. Fact is, this not only sounds old, it sounds a tad indie or at least long-lost and buried, like a big-hearted, schlocky attempt at heavy rock from 1973 (please, no loitering at Grand Funk, BTO, Humble Pie, Lone Star, Earl Slick and Hunter-less Mott). Sure all that talk of soul is valid, but really this is more what the mainstream was trying to do, and much more tuneful and beer-liggin' welcome for it. Turf in a little Skynyrd and Hendrix and you've got a whirlwind flash through the past, quite importantly, with players who can bang off nice fills that don't trundle all over the necessarily fragile constructs. If you crave this sort of thing, call it a **9**. If you prefer the old stuff, or simply

like too many other types of music to care about sincere reworkings of the much maligned classic rock genre, pass respectfully.
Rating                                                                 7

## Krakatoa - White Heat   (21 '83)
Clean, gutless hard rock with gibberish English for lyrics, painfully printed and enclosed for our eternal wincing. Simple and bouncy, **White Heat** has a kind of shuffling wimpy mindset that makes these technically "heavy" tunes sound like campfire tales for girl guides. I guess it's some unfathomable and twisted European notion of American hard rock that motivates these ornamental humans, but the sound coming out the other end is more like toned-down, lifeless metal, which ultimately jams simplified and purposely retarded. But the lyrics are a downright scream, sorta like the Chinese English you get for instructions with electronic gizmos from Hong Kong.
Rating                                                                 2

## Wayne Kramer - The Hard Stuff   (Epitaph '95)
Somewhat a surprise, this first since the MC5 days for Wayne Kramer, crawled from the gutter, the man wrestling with his demons, finally deciding to teach those punks how to really pack a piece, as he was wont to explain in the many engaging interviews he did for the record. **The Hard Stuff** was therefore a bitter, icy spin, wrapping up three or four eras of hard music (all except the obvious: metal), in a kind of apocalyptic, burn-the-bar history lesson. So it came out kinda Stoogie, not quite so smart as Bowie or Lou Reed, but definitely alluding to a sort of sublimated artiness. For this reason, signals seemed crossed, the listening public confused, and all wondering how old you should be to be a fan.
Rating                                                                 7

## Wayne Kramer - Citizen Wayne   (Epitaph '97)
Wayne's debut **The Hard Stuff** garnered much acclaim for its gritty, strangely old-ish punk metal snarl, something Kramer had developed after years of hard living, not to mention his legendary status as guitarist for sonic terrorists MC5. Here, the energy is somewhat dissipated, Kramer opting for a rootsy flavour, mixing equal parts Velvet Underground, Sheryl Crow and Gary Lucas, resulting in a record that is a metaphor for the city itself, a bastardized hybrid of many motivations. So we get lots of cerebral guitar wailing over trip-hop beats, snobby jazz ethic as applied to barroom squalor, funk pawed by grease monkey hands. And Wayne's got hair this time too, going for the bleach-blonde thug look. Almost too smart to belong in a book on metal, this is more a singer-songwriter type thing, something like loud, corrupted John Hiatt. Whatever, it's good stuff, if no longer hard stuff.
Rating                                                                 8

## Krank - Hideous   (Metal Blade '86)
Major black 'n' red leather 'n' studs theme to this livin' 'n' breathin' it gang of American bar rats. Besides the fact that they look like idiots and probably realize it by now, Krank's got attitude and even chops, while losing it on riffs past expiration date and lack of groove; too many stops and starts, too much accentuation. And I'm not overly amused by the thrashy street-scum screaming of one Frank Tyson, whose kill-with-power stylings are a bit too OTT for his own band's good. Krank just seem to have too much wild metal shit they wanna cram in, in the healthy spirit of American excess, and not enough taste to cruise where cruise is due, rendering the proceedings not unlike a hyper joy ride through every metal move of the '70s. Top raves: Rented Heat and Head Like A Rock. Not nearly enough bass.
Rating                                                                 4

## Kreator - Pleasure To Kill (Noise '86)

This early steaming cowpie (rounder #2) from the German quintet known as Kreator is little more than a complete racket, fit for the most effluent of sewers, much ranting and much blastbeatery clogging the passing lanes. But the band are considered originators of such tech-thrash ugliness, and for that some applause is in order.

Rating 4

## Kreator - Renewal (Noise/Futurist '92)

Kreator are one of those bands whose red, raw and bleeding past has made way for a smarter, more provocative mid-metal beastliness that manages to retain spontaneity while writing somewhere between Slayer (Renewal) and Voivod (Reflection). What results is a classy, mature record, one that succeeds in exposing pedigree and experience, the band also not afraid to go for basic arrangements, fairly clean vocals and high snappy snare, again, all pointing to a type of urgent Voivodian creativity. The hurried feel works, and this band in which I've never really invested, has become a pleasurable revisitation.

Rating 8

## Kreator - Cause For Conflict (Noise '95)

It's a minor sin that I've missed well on nigh five Kreator offerings in my reviewing travels, coming to the supposition that had I followed these grim reapers from day one, I'd probably have had an excellent lesson in extreme metal's evolution. Cause For Conflict is a back to roots affair, and back heavily into Slayer, riffs, vocals, tornado drums (courtesy new guy and key catalyst Joe Cangelossi), controlled blastbeats, everything. Great graphics can't hide the fact that these guys are still searching after all these years for their table in the morgue. I'd still rather listen to this kind of level-headed mega-metal than all-out thrash any day, but the engaging imaginativeness of Renewal has evaporated here, for something a little grimier and built for speed, not beauty. I'm probably against the tide on this one, but then again, I liked The Outer Limits better than Negatron.

Rating 7

## Kreator - Scenarios Of Violence (Noise '96)

Lo and behorned, Kreator have hung up their leather booties, Noise announcing the wake with this live plus greatest smacks pack, not making it to clear what's what (Coroner was done better). What emerges is the tale of a band comprising regular German punters, enamoured equally with NWOBHM thrash and their tighter American counterparts, mainly Slayer. And despite the cheapo thrash graphics throughout the early years, this was always a capable, chopsy, caring band, forever in punted psyches as a leader of thrash's second wave. Vocals were always a bit of an acquired taste, oscillating between Quorthon's nervous diabolical bray and more ordinary growls. But riffs more often than not stuck hot pins into flesh aching for metal. Hail! Not the band's first record, previous material finding the band in surprise progressive rock mode. Yipes.

Rating 6

## Krokus - Pay It In Metal (Phonogram '78)

Mainland European bands always needed to be dragged kicking and screaming into the twentieth century, and Krokus was no exception, Pay It In Metal being hokey, barroom boogie woogie hard rock, stumbling over the odd Angus riff by default as it struggles its way out of the garage, wide-eyed, in search of America. Ultimately it would take Krokus two more gestures, until Hardware, to really establish its unam-

bitious poverty gutrock sound, and as many more again, to lose it entirely.

Rating 4

## Krokus - Metal Rendez-vous (Ariola '80)

Metal Rendez-vous was the official North American debut for Krokus, ready-set-go graphically for the assault; logo in place, nifty "metal rendez-vous" car crash album cover, but nowhere near musically up to snuff, merely a minor improvement on the dipshit guitar boogie of the previous half-cooked enchilada. A classic case of a band from a non-traditional metal market, here the land of chocolate, watches and suspicious banking practices, operating way behind the times, illogically combing their Chuck Berry catalogues for modern inspiration. Best tracks prophetic of future identity (as someone else): Back Seat Rock'n'Roll, which revives Whole Lotta Rosie, and Heatstrokes, which revives Riff Raff.

Rating 5

## Krokus - Hardware (Ariola '81)

Krokus aren't going to win any awards for redefining metal, or even coming up with reworks that achieve minimum doses of eyebrow-raising nirvana. Nope, when Krokus is turned on, the best we're going to get is animated party rock; drinking metal set squarely and sonically in the gutter, cliché-ridden and G-rated generic. Hardware somewhat achieves this buzz, evoking a laid-back version of One Vice At A Time, while less obviously grafted from AC/DC, mixing in other uneventful and simplistic rock fingerprints (most from early American AOR) as on Easy Rocker and She's Got Everything. Still very backwoods and garagey, the band's grooves start to gain a grim, grudgingly-earned lustre, Mark Storace's now full-blown, poor-man Bon Scott wails beginning to command the floor, Krokus riding those same Aussie coattails as their smarter, more talented doppelganger, Angel City. Laughable but listenable from start to finish.

Rating 6

## Krokus - One Vice At A Time (Arista '82)

On One Vice At A Time, after years on the highway to Hell, Krokus finally completes the journey, achieving the sustained high voltage previous outings merely craved. Vice is a consistently loud and slavishly flagrant ride through every down 'n' dirty AC/DC riff in the book, a concentrated chunk of granite that champions the cause of the big beat, shaking its foundations, letting it worm its way through nine barn-burning flathead rockers. From one angle, this is a wholesale ripoff of AC/DC's craft, yet from another, it's merely another solid and consistent AC/DC album—something of which there can never be enough—just played by taller guys, worthy replacements with really old amps. You can either dismiss it or ride along on the sideboards. We rode along, fueled by such soiled rockers as lengthy, building mood piece Long Stick Goes Boom (minor hit), heads-down groovers Bad Boys - Rag Dolls and To The Top, plus the Guess Who's American Woman (again a minor hit). For me, Vice served its intended function as a beer-soaked, simplistic but grungy, consistently mean adaptation of a classic sound from a classic band (and I don't mean Krokus).

Rating 8

## Krokus - Headhunter (Arista '83)

On Headhunter, Swiss wannabes Krokus make the major leap from their lifted lowball, down 'n' dirty AC/DC metal to a plausible early '80s version of state-of-the-art. Headhunter still stands today as Krokus' best album, offering an admirable array of kick-ass mid-pacers, a couple of bonehead boogie 'eadbangers for old-time sake, and a bevy of techno-speed rockers which capture the magic and optimism of a band on

their way to bigger and better Spandex. Nothing too earth-shattering here, just a batch of ever so slightly elevated hi-jinx, with some memorable Accept-style choruses (*Russian Winter, Screaming In The Night*), all springy beyond previous work, somehow evoking the excitement of heavy Ted Nugent. **Headhunter** remains the trickiest and heaviest Krokus album, and one of the shining lights amongst early Eurometal in general, a movement which eventually outgrew the band as Krokus lurched their records into reverse, blowing their reputation as serious contenders.
Rating                                                             8

### Krokus - The Blitz   (Arista '84)

What a difference a year can make if you let people boss you around, **The Blitz**'s dismally aseptic kiddie metal surprising those reveling in the jagged riffs of **Headhunter**, offering little more than safely candy-coated corporate rock, lacking in life on all facets, including novelty cover #3 in Sweet's *Ballroom Blitz*, here ineptly portrayed on par with Saxon's phoned-in *Set Me Free*. **The Blitz** is more than a partial about-face on last year's technical **Headhunter** back to the band's blue-jean, bangin' brew, yet in a manner unrecognizably tired, slow, glossed-up and pinched, no doubt some stiff at the label wanting to see some cash in the till. Shudders of Twisted Sister come to mind, both bands matching wits with a decidedly younger, pre-teen batch of headbangers, leaving in the lurch those that thought metal could mature.
Rating                                                             3

### Krokus - Change Of Address   (Arista '86)

Novelty cover #4 in Alice Cooper's *School's Out* stands out like an IQ over 100 at a Rik Emmett gig, on this continued spiral descent into L.A. glam, all femmy, dolled-up and keyboard-frilled with predictable clatters of electronic drums and unbelievably idiotic poser clichés. Chains Of A Dress once more finds big bucks upset at the continued flow of no bucks.
Rating                                                             3

### Krokus - Alive And Screamin'   (Arista '86)

Good ol' Krokus material here (raise your fist and yell!), but a surprisingly soupy mix by Tony Platt, cutting off this nine cartoon record below the knees. Still very nice to hear *Long Stick Goes Boom* opening the show, plus *Eat The Rich*, minor hit from **The Blitz**, *Midnite Maniac*, and non-LPer *Lay Me Down*, which sounds like a lighter, more pop metal excerpt from **One Vice At A Time**. **Headhunter** closes things out in fine OTT fashion, but the overall impression is ultimately no impression at all, this landing squarely below average, due mainly to the bad production job but also to the band's cheesy metal presence on stage. Out a mere six months after the dismal **Change Of Address**.
Rating                                                             5

### Krokus - Heart Attack   (MCA '88)

At long last, Krokus embarks on a partial return from the funeral home, as the boys look deep within their souls to what lent them credence in the first place: greasy adaptations of heavy AC/DC. Gone is the Krokus logo. Gone are the feeble and predictable cover versions that were turning Krokus into a Swiss Great White. Also gone: the band's comfortable but sparse, street-ready production, although the electronic percussive treatments and the polished backing vocals are offset somewhat by loose 'n' dirty playing, not to mention a renewed Skid Roses vigor writing-wise. But who cares really, it's still Krokus, an irreversibly tainted band, opportunists who always seemed to lack the sincerity or the ideas necessary to really impress. Because they'll never shake this loser aura due to their slow rise, momentary acceptance and quick embarrassing fall, it's going to take more than a

moderately good record to win hearts as well as ears. Still, **Heart Attack** is a decent re-focus towards gut-check rock. Who knows, given new management or an internally-bred kick in the ass, Krokus may still have it in them to build another neck-snapping release some day, if age and disillusion don't ground them first.
Rating                                                             5

### Krokus - Stampede   (Krokus/MCA '91)

Fernando von Arb is the only original guy left, main change of all being the addition of Peter Tanner on vocals, Krokus pulling an AC/DC at about 1/150th the level of importance. So out spills the sad-sack sounds of **Stampede**, combining lobotomized Scorpions with thinking-real-hard Twisted Sister, or in simpler terms, sleep-walked Krokus, about as dullard as any of the band's always stupid records but at least heavy and minimally glazed over with commercial conventions.
Rating                                                             5

### Krokus - To Rock Or Not To Be   (Phonag '95)

Very cool. The band is for all intents and purposes back to their original line-up, and only a little worse for wear, von Arb looking like Jimmy Dale Gilmour, Storace like Joe Peschi, this comeback roiling like a hot, bluesy stormtrooper of **One Vice At A Time** proportions. Once past the dumb **Fly On The Wall** cover art and the dumber Scorpions-level record moniker, any old Krokusoid can revel in these only slightly clever AC/DC grooves, recorded open and fat with bass child. Slow ones, fast ones . . . all pulse with the beat of a band renewed. And the reason this works is that Krokus was never about brains, **To Rock Or Not To Be** basking in blissful volume without aspirations toward wily skill. Nice to see these wrench-heads make it back full circle. Only question is, how come they ain't on Angus and crew's **Ballbreaker** tour?
Rating                                                             8

### Krokus - The Dirty Dozen   (BMG Ariola '93)

That's the way (uh huh, uh huh) we like it, BMG digging back into the glory days of dirty rock'n'roll for this swaggering greatest hits pack, **The Dirty Dozen** (logically!) providing seventeen tracks from the band's best years, 1979 - 1983. What's more, the band has decided to remaster each tooth, fang, and claw, wrapping the whole thing in swanky packaging, including a few light-hearted vintage band pics. The tracks are the ones you wanted, the ones you bought, the ones you drank your first beers to, the ones highlighted throughout my reviews of those brief few sparked, stoked and smoked Krokus records from long ago. Foist ye drafts!
Rating                                                             8

### Kyuss - Blues For The Red Sun   (Dali/Elektra '92)

Deservedly slated to be the next big thing, Arizona's Kyuss sludged through with this near masterpiece of melted grunge, a record that takes the woofer-distorting sub-cycles from seminal Seattle recordings like Nirvana's **Bleach** and Mudhoney's **Superfuzz Big-muff**, and applies them to hopelessly bomb-blasted riff monsters from deep beneath Sabbath-dredged caverns. The band plays down the Seattle connection, and fair enough, this is record III. But the greasy facts are that Kyuss is an excellent old Sub Pop-type band, and there's no shame in that. Stated influences run the range from old metal, the desert and isolation from influence all together, all three sentiments justifiable as this is one rare head-shredder of a record, made all the more harrowing by John Garcia's molten vocal wake-up calls. Produced in conjunction with Chris Goss of Masters Of Reality, **Blues For The Red Sun** takes bass to the extreme, flat-out woofer-chomping bass, as everything wallows in opaque riffs and backing throb on such powerful old Sab send-ups like *Thumb, Green Machine, Allen's Wrench* and the insane *Thong Song*.

Only complaint: long, disintegrated passages of aural mud; independently named cuts or yawning, extended intros which turn the record to undulating infinities of sand punctuated with hell-bent rants through oases. Anyhow, the mega-metal makes up for it, sounding like the *Hole In The Sky* opened up over Arizona's outback frying Kyuss to a hardened crisp, forever fused to unending banks of the sludgiest of amplifiers, destination: burial. At least that's how the Meat Puppets would see it.

Rating                                                          9

## Kyuss - Sky Valley   (Elektra '94)

After a long, frustrating bake-break that saw their record delayed by the demise of their label and the desertion of their drummer, Kyuss return to the desert to lay their particular brand of buzzing bassrock on the bloodthirsty buzzards that comprise their heat-crazed fanbase. Originally titled Pools Of Mercury, **Sky Valley** was put on slow simmer, allowing the record's languid structures to bury themselves even further under the cracked earth. Split into three gooey chunks of song (hindering your urge to search), the record celebrates an unwillingness for treble and all things bright and shiny, less bent on song than its predecessor, more enamoured with jammy excursion. This is the entire bass spectrum in all its '70s glory; neon orange, lemon yellow, lime green, all awash with burnt sienna, slopped down on canvas with healthy huffs of Mexican paint thinner. It's a masterful dirtslide, billows of choking dust rising from the awesome forward mass of *Gardenia, Demon Cleaner* (plus its unfathomable video),

and *Odyssey*. Kyuss are the Ones for those who get it, and an aural retro mess for those who don't. But if thick is your stew, commandeer your dune-buggy over the next mound of sound and feel the vibes ripple our most fleshy bits. And as it sez in the instructions: listen without distraction.

Rating                                                          9

## Kyuss - . . . And The Circus Leaves Town   (Elektra '95)

No surprise really that this record is out so quickly, given that **Sky Valley** languished finished and unemployed for somewherz about a year before seeing release. **Circus Leaves Town** veers the band a good sort of psychedelic-ward, finding the cultural mishmashes of a confused Monster Magnet feast, dipping unto Hawkwind, as the band rolls out their patented quakeable sludge. Opener *Hurricane* is quintessential Kyuss brilliance, but from there things get weirdly contemplative, almost substituting the band's U.S. desert psyche for one African and exotic. More twisty, eastern-flavoured high notes permeate the heat waves, pulling the record into a vortex of the enigmatic, as the listener's rhythms are sent into synch with the stoned bongbeats of the band at hand. Primal, raw, and more of-the-earth than the last two, **Circus Leaves Town** is the crazy uncle on both ludes and acid, unpredictable and sloth-like, bound to surprise, even amongst all the buzzing subcycles. I prefer more bang-on rock, but ya just gotta love this band no matter what. Dissolved in low-key fashion by the end of the year.

Rating                                                          8

## Laaz Rocket - City's Gonna Burn (Target '84)

Cut-rate American pig iron from the early wave of post-NWOBHM crap to hit the racks stateside, **City's Gonna Burn** chunders heavy, humourless, and self-gratifying without a hook or nimble move of which to speak. Porkfisted, dense and forgettable, despite critics predicting big things on the leather horizon.
Rating **2**

## Laaz Rocket - No Stranger To Danger (Target '85)

Choice threads, even choicer drum sound, and the choicest vocals to ever grace the delete bins in metallic valor. Hair for miles. Every last mistake of the vacuous mid-'80s is in tow as these boys seriously limit their prospects. Metal of the lowest common denominator. Four records total as of late '91.
Rating **1**

## L.A. Guns - L.A. Guns (PolyGram Est. '87)

Offering no great shakes over any other wild-maned bar dogs, Tracii Guns (from which Guns N' Roses get their name) and hiz boyz (notably ex-pat Brit Phil Lewis, who had done time with Girl and Tormé) emerged on the scene with their basic, appealing brand of dirty rock'n'roll. Essentially a street version of Kiss or a glossy version of the Crüe, L.A. Guns garnered moderate acclaim for this ready-steady-go batch of grit rock. Plausible, no frills California metal which sidestepped the trappings of glam or shlock rock trends in pursuit of credibility.
Rating **6**

## L.A. Guns - Cocked & Loaded (PolyGram '89)

Unsung heroes of the Hollyrock underbelly, L.A. Guns finally really crank their stuff with this rumbling career careener which drops the icing for a downwind intensity applied to the basic party metal format. All rocks with a Crüe-style inebriation here, yet with a strange, almost indiscernible cloak of mystery, a sort of loneliness in crowds as capable helmsman Phil Lewis lays his pillaged soul all over plain jane rumbling trains like raucous rat *Rip And Tear*, layered opener *Slap In The Face*, and the elusive *Magdalaine* which perhaps best exemplifies the touch of night enveloping this superficially party-primed slab. **Cocked & Loaded** will probably remain the band's best, as it still retains a sense of fiery hope at the possibilities of filthy lucre to be had. Even if the original Gunners never hit the pot, this

record will stand as a proud piece of street-desperate combat rock.
Rating **8**

## L.A. Guns - Hollywood Vampires (PolyGram '91)

Perhaps clouded by ongoing internal strife and the inevitable, soul-destroying swirlings of break-up rumours, L.A. Guns misfire with this lengthy, laborious and ultimately less charismatic collection of rock ideas. Twelve cuts, 52 minutes and overall, far less life, as the band seem to sleepwalk through various blues metals, lethargic Zep-isms, Aero-funk, prostituted boogie and subdued party rock styles, amongst some genuine ballads of the heart. I dunno, hard to say it's any less in total than **Cocked & Loaded**, given its scope and breadth, but percentage-wise, this is a band on idle, destitute for a rousing reason to bat one home. Much fault goes to the cleaned-up production and general good behaviour of the players as really, much of this is the grungier, unruly **Cocked & Loaded** on luke-warm simmer. Sad, but for a record that could have kicked the band into a lustrous, vibrant force for the CD age, all corners seem to emanate a tired pessimism looking straight down the barrel at a career in decline. Still, salvageable as an honest piece of work by a band for which I have a forgiving soft spot.
Rating **7**

## L.A. Guns - Cuts (PolyGram '92)

**Cuts** is one of those innocuous little catch-all EPs that seems to leak out of the woodwork when a band is shivering on the ropes of survival (how's that for badly mixed metaphor?). Two dull, knocking originals and three even duller covers, worst being an absolutely pointless *Suffragette City*, just an automatic walk-through that epitomizes this band's barely clinging status. This is no way to assert one's existence.
Rating **3**

## L.A. Guns - Vicious Circle (PolyGram '95)

Always one of the unsungs who carried a modicum of integrity, L.A. Guns bite back with their trainwreck record, the big crash-in-flames, streetfightin', go ahead make my day sledge, a remarkably seedy slice of their addled minds. The loud trashthrashers sound like crack, the mellow dirge-ables like high-grade junk, establishing **Vicious Circle** as the second coming of Johnny Thunders after soaking up a few cheeseball riffs from a stint with the Crue. Garage rock at various hungover speeds, some licks sorry and sadly dated,

others slamming and happily dated, all caked with the guilty pleasure of committing the ultimate grimecrime. But then again I liked the Corabi Crue record.
Rating 7

## The L.A. Guns - American Hardcore (CMC '96)
Choked, chuggy and clogged, **American Hardcore** intensifies the dirty rawk sounds that made **Vicious Circle** such a bash, so much so that enjoyment flies out the window. This cantankerous submersion in all things polluted comes in conjunction with a couple of personnel changes, most jarring being the loss of Phil Lewis on vocals, the belcher/belter replaced by Boneyard's Chris Van Dahl, who does nothing for me. Yes, **American Hardcore** is volatile, punky, grungy, unshowered and credibly street, but recording these dour, depressing caveman metal mopefests live in the studio has really made for a sordid affair, and I don't mean that in a good way. A bit like a somewhat purposeful Johnny Thunders record (see Hey World, but watch for the nods), which just ain't enough creativity for a band this long in the tooth.
Rating 4

## Paul Laine - Stick It In Your Ear (Long Island '95)
This is a re-issue (with bonus tracks) of a record that is now six years old, **Stick It In Your Ear** being a Bruce Fairbairn-produced pop metal spin, trumpeting the arrival of a promising west-coasting unknown. But I don't see what all the fuss is about, this just stuffing the hole between Bryan Adams and Keel, sort of Bon Jovi of the Great White North, a little on the rudimentary, blue collar side of town. Re-issue corresponds nicely with Paul Laine's stout-of-heart arrival at the helm of a newly re-tooled and re-focused Danger Danger. Mix sound like a Doug & The Slugs album! Maybe not. I just felt like saying Doug & The Slugs.
Rating 5

## Lake Of Tears - Greater Art (Black Mark '94)
It's no wonder this sounds like slow basic Cemetary, given that Cemetary frontman Mathias Lodmalm co-produces with Thomas Skogsberg. But the sound is one of the problems here, an unexciting mix that is low on treble, making these often trudging and self-evident doom pieces fade into the icy plains of the north. Still all told, this short 35 minute debut is a somewhat inspired flowing river of sadness, Lake Of Tears attaching themselves to a really effective form of poison-melodious doom, one that will find splendid wing-span on the self-actualized follow-through record one year hence.
Rating 7

## Lake Of Tears - Headstones (Black Mark '95)
Swede doom fantasists Lake Of Tears dive further under the waves of melancholic goth, adding more vocal shade, grey melody, keys and acoustic work than was found on their lauded but raw debut **Greater Art**. Daniel Brennare's voice evokes Paradise Lost, Hetfield and three or four styles closer to real singing (!), but his Euro accent remains, distracting from the majestic if enigmatically fuzzed power goth enclosed. But I eat this stuff up, excited at seeing bands already taking Paradise Lost's lead (arguably via Entombed, Pyogenesis, Tiamat, Cemetary and even Edge Of Sanity) and running with it. Many looming death ballads, at the expense of all-out rockers like the exquisite Burn Fire Burn, but a perfect existential metal for these times all the same, balancing entertainment and indulged depression with more class than any number of pencil-necked alterno-geeks.
Rating 9

## Lake Of Tears - A Crimson Cosmos (Black Mark '97)
Kind words have been uttered about this newish melodic death metal band, making Lake Of Tears plausible grist for moderate success come this bold new directive called **A Crimson Cosmos**. The present record lightens up considerably on the heft, using gothic, pop, progressive and Celtic tones for its overall experimental vibe, while retaining for the most part, smeary power chords and middle-aggressive vocals (read: Hetfield and Paradise Lost). But the songs are absolutely gripping, Lake Of Tears melding Hawkwind and Floyd with grinding but commercial metal. Over this undulating, sunny metal bed flow fantasy lyrics of a more colourful and forgiving nature, the band offering such playful titles as Boogie Bubble, Cosmic Weed, Lady Rosenred and Raistlin And The Rose to keep us thinking splendiferously. Fantastic moods are achieved, the languished power of a simple tune like When My Sun Comes Down showing so much class, restraint and wily song skills, you just gotta stand back and smile. Acts like Skyclad, Cathedral and Cemetary come to mind, all able to make us forget extremity and find well-wishing within still quite heavy metal. This is one for the history books.
Rating 10

## Larva - Waiting For Daybreak (Energy '94)
Larva grow an arresting concoction of dreamy epic psychedelia à la Warrior Soul or Jane's Addiction, topping the tumbler with the entertaining slambam of grunge, turning most every track into a boomy tractor pull celebrating Zepriffs while attending to the hard-nosed demands of life in the '90s. Vocally I think of Saigon Kick, Kik Tracee and Law & Order, which just means I like Roger's soaring anthemic style. Fully entertaining although a bit too in love with mud.
Rating 7

## Last Crack - Sinister Funkhouse #17 (Roadrunner '89)
You gotta give credit to a front man who appears buck-screamin'-naked on the front and back covers of his inaugural outing. Meet Buddo, wise sage, philosopher, and prolific elf of a band who is a religion unto themselves. **Sinister Funkhouse #17** takes off on an acid-laced, swashbuckling trip through jerky push-pull chunkfests reminiscent of the undermining dreammares of Sabbath's **Paranoid**. Buddo's world is a frenzied crowded cage of mythology, love, anarchy, sex, violence, God, naturalism, and wild animals, existing in cacophonous harmony, and his crack band's soundtrack is appropriately earthy, tribal, and gut-wrenching, acting as a reference base, pounding with metallic funk; choppy, exacting, complex, yet mindful of groove. Last Crack operates on a plane of which they alone are aware, one, in fact, of their own creation, a plane echoing with the brutish shrieks of the jungle, and the reassuring words of the sanctuary. A must-own for those not content with the status quo. Lacks the linguistic surgical tooling of **Burning Time** yet nevertheless makes grand embracements of its own imperfections.
Rating 9

## Last Crack - Burning Time (Roadracer '91)
Last Crack, one of the most enigmatic and hopeful of new bands is back with the ambitious follow-up to '89's searing hot **Sinister Funkhouse #17**, and this time the tone is more insidious, slithering and covert. **Burning Time** marks a refinement and intensification of the polydecibel mindspheres penetrated on the debut. Dave Jerden's production and the boggling arrangements spell crackling state of the art, causing both heavy and mellow extremes of the Last Crack totality to shine and shimmer like infinitely-faceted diamonds. The ever-soaring funkiness flows like so much mathematical nirvana, sublimated beautifully within the supe-

rior songcraft of the masterpieces that abound here, stripping them of any possible ill effects of their inherent complexity. **Burning Time** rises and crashes like a long, perilous and bliss-studded dream sequence. Metallic and again vaguely Sabbath-souled classics like *Wicked Sandbox*, *Down Beat Dirt Messiah*, and *My Burning Time* weave weight and nimbleness into dense artillery barrages which stop and start on a dime at will. Mellower cuts like *Mini Toboggan* and *Blue Fly*, *Fish Sky* wander dazed through deserts of mirages, ringing guitars, and buzzing sun, completing the circle, cementing the overall effect of stifling heat throughout. And the all-pervading constant is the presence of Buddo, whose voice commands rapt attention to his frontier-invading lyrics, lyrics that fuse reality and myth effortlessly the way religion is supposed to, recalling the ethic of one of the band's few professed influences, U2. Major art from one of the few assembled musical forces pushing the limits of perception.

Rating　　　　　　　　　　　　　　　　　　　　**10**

## Law And Order - Guilty Of Innocence　(MCA '89)

Having heard record II before finding this debut, I was pleasantly prepared for the lush, Kik Tracee-style vocals of "Shane", plus the acoustic hooks of the band's hybrid stylings. But as predicted, N.Y.'s Law Order's debut also blow through a fair bit of third-rate hair metal amongst the engaging blues rockers, which include a barroom cover of Skynyrd's *The Needle And The Spoon*. But it's Shane's silky rock gawd vox that make the day, linking each divergent tune with that Spread Eagle, Saigon Kickin' thread of creative dancery. Full-range rock production from the pliable, unidentifiable Joe Hardy, who's knob-twiddled for many of the best. Fine campfire ballad: *In The Shelter*.

Rating　　　　　　　　　　　　　　　　　　　　　**7**

## Law And Order - Rites Of Passage　(MCA '91)

Metal in the early '90s was right on schedule rising to new levels of sophistication and diversity, a myriad of new directives taking place, Law And Order the latest addition to blur the distinctions between previous rough demarcations. First and foremost, **Rites Of Passage**, the band's second record, isn't that heavy, offering more than hard rock's usual share of acoustic guitar, aimed at the blues, pop metal, and elements of '60s folk. In terms of influences, one can hear Zeppelin, Angel, Warrior Soul, and Masters Of Reality/Bogeymen to name a confusing few, winding up as Cheap Trick meets Saigon Kick (!). Spiritual, political and otherwise cerebral, the band's concerns are mostly moral and societal along the lines of the aforementioned Warrior Soul (but nowhere as paranoid). Musically, things are well-produced but fairly basic and raw: garage-delivered from a posh studio environs, making for a decidedly human feel to these strange and divergent tunes that are a little well-behaved, low on octane in total, but authentic in their aims overall. Maybe the pop antithesis to Loudhouse, around a Warrior Soul axis, lacking both the sonic and verbal aggression of either band, although closer in disposition to the latter. Above all the platitudes however, it's passed my test of repeated playability for whatever reasons.

Rating　　　　　　　　　　　　　　　　　　　　　**7**

## Lawnmower Deth - Ooh Crikey It's . . .　(Earache '91)

These U.K. nutters are a sort of toned-down AC or Gwar (no costumes), blazing through an astounding 35 compositions here, mixing beer-guzzling punk with thrash, lyrically barking forth a naughty, good-natured comedy schtick, sending up most kinds of metal with culturally astute aplomb. Pretty much unlistenable more than a few times (like any comedy record), **Ooh Crikey** is best consumed with full due attention one time and one time only, reading along with the spinning,

abbreviated thrashin' show, yuk-yukking it with the flipped out boys in the band, pint in hand.

Rating　　　　　　　　　　　　　　　　　　　　　**6**

## Lawnmower Deth - Return Of The Fabulous Metal Bozo Clowns　(Earache '92)

Only a scant 22 cartoons this time around, this record's title pretty much says it all, Lawnmower Deth giving another buzzcut to metal conventions of all sort, funny as Ritchie Blackmore's hair weave, but funny once or twice, given the band's forced and transferable attention span. A little more seriously metal this time. Fave track: the Osmonds' *Crazy Horses*, also covered by Tank years ago. Full lyrics supplied once again, which is about half this record's fleeting value.

Rating　　　　　　　　　　　　　　　　　　　　　**6**

## Leatherwolf - Leatherwolf　(Island '87)

These big-haired Californians are a less ethereal Fates Warning, wanking and clanking along below a three guitar attack (that sounds like half of one guitar), a barrage of drums, and the over-profusion of riffs, tempo shifts and lengthy intros indicative of a progressive metal experience. For confusion sake, there's a bit of balladry, some anthemic soccer chant choruses, and a metal throwaway cover of the inappropriate *Bad Moon Rising*. The grooves suck, which is the combined fault of the fluffy arrangements, busy, no-class drumming, and cavernous recording by Kevin Beamish, who's known for a similar but cleaner sound he pioneered for Y&T. Really, a pointless mix of genres that mucks around and never leaves the runway. Big things were predicted, given the buzz in L.A.

Rating　　　　　　　　　　　　　　　　　　　　　**4**

## Leatherwolf - Street Ready　(Island '89)

**Street Ready**'s overall sound contains more bite than the debut, but the drums are even more cyborg-ed, reminiscent of the annoying din from Quiet Riot's **Metal Health**. No improvement in the songwriting. Similar goth riffery, mellow passages, ego-enhancing breaks in praise of Yngwie the fire god, and general leather 'n' dragons self-importance. Street ready? No. Dope smokin' in the bedroom, trying to play the bass ready? Maybe.

Rating　　　　　　　　　　　　　　　　　　　　　**4**

## Led Zeppelin - Led Zeppelin　(Atlantic '69)

In which two seasoned studio vets team up with a couple of greenhorns, the loudest drummer in London and an anonymous young wailer with blues-ridden blood to form the ultimate rock monolith. **Led Zeppelin**, although much heralded historically as one of the first metal albums, is not a record that actually delivers anything resembling the heavy metal of today, existing as a hybrid of loud, obnoxious blues, adapted blues, breath-taking acoustic work, and '60s hippy sentiments. No, **Zep** the record and Zep the band were more a catalyst. Just as The Beatles and Elvis fired the souls of our '60s and '70s rock heroes (note: there are no worthy '60s heroes), **Led Zeppelin**, Led Zeppelin - **II** and their hallowed creators, with their aggression, indulgence, long-haired prima dinero'd delivery, and hints at hocus pocus propelled later generations to discover hard rock and heavy metal. It is the *idea* of Led Zeppelin that is the Zep contribution, not the early recorded output itself. And Zep, although prominent and artistically more esteemed than its loud contemporaries, was by no means alone. Quite simply, **In Rock** and **Paranoid** (although insignificantly newer albums) laid waste to any inkling of a thought that Zep knew metal. These records were from Hell, while **Led Zeppelin** was merely from England via the crossroads of the American south. While Led Zeppelin was chasing and angering the blues, creating by process, and growing as writers and explorers, Sabbath was sending

**245**

terrified youth to the exits with black sheets of wind, blowing the casings off conventional opinion as to the extremes of power. It was Led Zeppelin as a movement that was more responsible for shaking life back into rock'n'roll and in particular American rock'n'roll. **Led Zeppelin**, the record offered a mix of old musical tendencies and really little new, except this catalytic ability and renewed vigor. We get two sincere and ancient blues re-makes, both Willie Dixon covers, which accentuate so forcefully Robert Plant's obviously heaven-sent vocal chords, two cuts that approach the new music, *Good Times Bad Times* and *Communication Breakdown*, plus two monolithic dirges, *Dazed And Confused* and *How Many More Times*, hinting at both the future majesty and horror of Sabbath. And rounding it out, we get some of that introspective, beautiful, and soon-to-be-trademark Page acoustic picking that just mellows with age in *Black Mountain Side* and the haunting *Babe I'm Gonna Leave You*. In retrospect, I really don't give a shit about this record, and in fact to my mind it's the second worst Zep album after Zep - **II**. The blues are boring, the fey attempts at metal rudimentary, and the entire package, so morosely frozen in the '60s. Sure, **Led Zeppelin** is of historical significance, yet the muddy old-ness and lack of cohesion to the thing just puts me to sleep. However, time would be kinder to this record, as we would learn to put it in context as merely the first tentative steps in the legendary Zeppelin creative process and exploratory zeal, the first heaving sighs of a breathing and ever-advancing monster that would later reward us with **Physical Graffiti**.

Rating                                                              6

## Led Zeppelin - II   (Atlantic '69)

Percy, Page and Co. continue their exploration of hard-edged, unwieldy blues structures which randomly take the band into metallic territory with *Whole Lotta Love* and *Living Loving Maid (She's Just A Woman)*, which although both being pretty mediocre, become instant classics almost by default. Does Zeppelin do anything to be heralded as gods of the new music here? The answer is no. More of the same dreary blues jamming make this album for the most part as dated and comatose as the rolling English countryside, even more wishy-washy, psychedelic and meandering than the debut. Again however, the process is what counts. Zeppelin never professed to write in any particular direction. The greats create for themselves, create what they want to hear, and on **II** they succeed in climbing deep within the rib cage of the blues, once there, making a lot of basic, rumbling, tribal noise. Almost non-existent are the acoustic elements of the debut, and still nowhere to be seen is any semblance of sunlight. To me, these are still the formative Zep years, the band still trying to shake the cobwebs of, or at least subjugate and control, past influences by playing directly to them, in order to shape and expose their complex collective soul in its own right. Led Zeppelin - **II** is considered a classic rock'n'roll cornerstone by millions around the world, and, due both to its formidable history and undeniable sincerity, is really above criticism. Suffice to say that in my humble opinion, it bores the hell out of me and exposes all that was lazy and unfocused with pre-'70s hard rock.

Rating                                                              6

## Led Zeppelin - III   (Atlantic '70)

On **III**, Led Zeppelin commence the enigmatic journey that will captivate listeners throughout the remainder of the band's legendary catalogue. **III** is a rich, mesmerizing album with exactly two sentiments: intimate, delicate, though occasionally dark acoustic sunrises with the muse, and surprisingly innovative and complex rockers; both sides cloaked in an uncommunicative alone-ness that locates the proceedings in the sort of magical forested landscapes of myth that would become the mindset over the next three, and arguably five albums. Side one is dominated by the three heavy tracks, the classic and tense *Immigrant Song*, really the first modern metal tune of Zep's career, featuring ominous Plant siren calls, *Celebration Day*, a good time groove tune, sort of a pre-cursor to Aerosmith, and *Out On The Tiles*, another upbeat hard rocker, funky and heavy with some choice chops from Bonzo. Completing the first side is one of only two (the other being *Hats Off To (Roy) Harper*) direct blues tunes, the ultraslow *Since I've Been Loving You*, and *Friends*, a brilliantly dark and apocalyptic acoustic dirge which sounds as if it was recorded in a cave. Side two has Zep confounding the critics as these supposed heavyweights of the new order record an entire side of acoustic pageantry, drawing on the blues, bluegrass, simple balladry, and a hint of psychedelia. Warmest of the five are *Tangerine* and *That's The Way* while *Bron-y-aur Stomp* and *Gallow's Pole* take us out into the backwoods for an edgy appointment with some questionable moonshine. It is important to note here that much can be learned about the motivations behind the Zep records from the excellent biography **Hammer Of The Gods**, which examines lyrical origins, procedure, emotional situations, and outside influences that give birth to the confusing product that is a Zep record. Get the book. It's a must read, one of the better rock tomes ever assembled. In any event, taken as a whole, Led Zeppelin - **III** is a gorgeous work that all but buries the loud, mallethead blues approach of the last two; an album that perplexed the public but nevertheless became accepted after the initial shock as part of the trip. **III** remains a testimony to a multi-faceted band with freshness and vitality, a band with a sense of dynamic and a sense of danger. From here-on in, Led Zeppelin would be operating on the fringes of reality, and in doing so, carve some of the most purely artistic, unique, and enduring pieces in rock history. Plus if you don't like the record, you can always play with the twirly disc album cover (LP only).

Rating                                                             10

## Led Zeppelin - Led Zeppelin (IV)   (Atlantic '71)

All is cosmic and perfect on **IV** except for the fact that these mini-galaxies chafe when placed side by side, which I guess is the point of Zep anyways as the sum total, drawing from infinite wells, invariably spells enigma. The brash and unfeeling production tries but does little to diminish the enjoyment of these mostly heavy rock and blues classics. The downright punky, heat-treated *Rock And Roll* (the definitive statement on the subject), drunken riffmonster of all rampages, *Black Dog*, and monolithic psychological epic *Stairway To Heaven*, are literally three of the most famous and influential rock songs ever recorded. One re-energized a world crashing after the summer of love, one helped invent metal, and one redefined the level of hysteria and mental dependence rock'n'roll could generate among youth in turmoil, not to mention the well-known war story concerning New Year's Day rock radio countdowns, where *Stairway* has, from the day it hit the streets to the present, dominated top slot as #1 rock song ever. Aside from these staples however, Zep ferociously shakes the foundations of the blues, going both bright and kharmic as on *Misty Mountain Hop* and dense and demonic as on rumblers *When The Levee Breaks* and *Four Sticks*. Rounding it off, as even more proof that the charmed four are so turned on here they didn't even have to name the album, we are blessed with two of the band's warmest acoustic fires in the new age *Going To California* and the newer and older age *Battle Of Evermore*. Still, my appreciation of this predominately loud and brutish record goes further than its playability. And in defense, it's hard to get freshly excited about songs that have been crammed down my throat since I was eight. But the less played gems are just as rich and innovative as the multiple ultra-famed cornerstones of rock here-in enclosed. If only the production didn't suck. Nevertheless, minor complaints on another Zep opus beyond criticism.

Rating      8

## Led Zeppelin - Houses Of The Holy    (Atlantic '73)

The follow-up to the hugely influential Zep - **IV** finds the band in more obscure, experimental, and equally raw territory. The Zep exploratory creative process is in full swing here as this unassuming record, tentatively held fast by naturalist hippiedom, embarks on a kaleidoscopic journey through rock idioms, transforming them in the process. Two gems right out on the fringes of previously established limits of white r'n'r set the tone for this latest rock ride through the enigmatic Zep psyche, the lumbering reggae strains of *D'yer Mak'er* and the bizarre percussive jazz trippiness of *The Crunge* floating Zep firmly to the outside looking down. Metal-wise, we get **Physical Graffiti** pre-cursor *Dancing Days*, the prog-rockin' title cut, plus dinosaur stomper *The Ocean*, while on the more subdued front it's the beautiful acoustic-then-rocking *Over The Hills And Far Away*, acid trip dirge *No Quarter*, and the smooth and homey *The Rain Song*. Not that warmth is something Zeppelin material is said to exude in consistent supply anyways, **Houses Of The Holy** is nevertheless one of the chillier offerings, never really allowing the listener the key to the gates of camaraderie. As a result, for me, **Houses**, along with IV to some extent, will remain one of my lesser played Zep discs, a brash and unwieldy record full of unique songcraft, yet lacking point of reference as far as encompassing concept goes.

Rating      7

## Led Zeppelin - Physical Graffiti    (Swan Song '75)

**Physical Graffiti** is the Grand Dame of rock'n'roll albums, possibly the richest and most rewarding record ever crafted across the music spectrum, the Zeppelin zodiacs aligning with ethereal divinity for four sides of sonic astonishment. First off, the production is Zeppelin's best, equal to **In Through The Out Door**'s, fuller, more complex, and more palatable than all others in the somewhat clanky Zep repertoire, featuring Bonham's most volcanic, fat and cavernous sound documented to wax, driven home by one of the man's most complex performances. Second, this, Zep's only double studio release, has less material approaching either filler or too literal interpretations of other life forms (i.e. the blues) than Zep's single albums. Third, it coheres on a tonal and energetic level, despite its violent sonic shifts from all-out metal to acoustic experiments, bluegrass (deZeptively configured), hard rock, prophetic keyboard rock, hippy meditation, hippy celebration, and dizzying epic soundscapes. Fourth, **Physical Graffiti**'s classics are truly such, infused with more innovation and danger than the over-rated six or eight ultra-hits from past offerings. Here Zeppelin blooms into a creative maelstrom, crafting incredible music all over the sonic terrain. **Physical Graffiti** is meticulously assembled in the spirit of scientific breakthrough; an obsession with not only exploring, but solving the unknown. Whereas other monuments of rock open fruitful dialogue with the muse, here Zeppelin ingests her wisdoms, devouring voraciously, letting her influence emanate through the band. It's sort of ridiculous to highlight what our preferred moments might be on a record that is such a well-integrated, metropolitan puzzle, but my humble list would include my favorite Zepcut ever, pre-eminent metal opus of all time *Kashmir*, close second *In My Time Of Dying*, a blown, progressive chunk that could have conceivably held its own on Sabbath's **Sabotage**, low-slung rocker *The Rover*, the mellow 'n' spacey side

three in its entirety, the good feeling *Night Flight*, and metal mudfest *Sick Again*. If you're from Mars and don't own this masterpiece already, get the hell out on the tiles and snag both the LP for the cool die-cut cover and the CD for a graciously-hosted sonic cruise on the Concorde of all records.

Rating      10

## Led Zeppelin - The Soundtrack From The Film The Song Remains The Same    (Swan Song '76)

The companion disk to the legendary if not slow and self-dating movie is less an actual soundtrack album than a conventional, sprawling '70's live record. After hearing this amorphous blob of superlative indulgence, I never felt deprived having not seen the mighty Zep live. Worse than Deep Purple or offspring Rainbow, Zep manages to stretch nine tunes over four sides, and risk being arrested for loitering in the process. Only side one even attempts to entertain, comprising four cuts including the under-rated *Celebration Day*. Otherwise, the song selection is dead predictable, relying appropriately on hits, but hits that are among the band's least shimmering and most rambling (i.e. *Whole Lotta Love*, *Moby Dick*, *Dazed And Confused*), and the delivery is as laid back, smug and self-centred as bombast gets. Plant treats his vocal responsibilities with nearly the same lax contempt as alter-ego Jagger does; and the rest of the band seems so bored, they rarely arrive back at the beat together, cocooned in their own little interpretive worlds as if Bob 'n' Jerry had just poured the boys into *Sugar Magnolia*. Not knocking the Dead (one of my all-time favorite bands), but this is supposed to be heavy metal. You'd have to be ripped out of your mind to enjoy this wake.

Rating      3

## Led Zeppelin - Presence    (Swan Song '76)

**Presence** is Zeppelin's opaque mess; a rough-hewn brew where the band stands aside and looks back at itself with detached boredom, morally and physically spent. Zep seems transfixed by the heat, sleepwalking after years of fruitless road-weary amusement through territory well traveled on previous efforts, r+b, hard rock, funk, heavy metal, and the blues; sounding loopy, foreign, choppy, and strained; arresting but uncommunicative and cold, loose but jaded. Superficially hottest is epic *Achilles Last Stand*, weighing in at 10:26, which upon repeated listens, becomes formulaic with respect to a formula Zep practically invented, or at least pioneered with considerable aplomb, a short year previous (in defense, it still rages as the lustiest post-**Physical Graffiti** track ever). And besides the depression-worn album closer, *Tea For One*, a morose blues, the rest of the album rides a twisty theme of flip and choolin' Page mathematics, funky axe-weighted shufflers that work splendidly but never reach out with reassurance. And Plant is losing his range. Hard to pin, but everybody who know this record says the same thing: great record, but I'll be damned if I remember anything past *Nobody's Fault But Mine* and *Achilles Last Stand*. **Presence** meanders, browses and does the two-step, wrinkling its brow as a record that did not need to be, even if it's somehow one of the more consistent Zep records sticking to a tight spectrum of unique and dense hard rockin' r+b, delivered via an instinctive back hand, setting the ball spinning and disoriented deep to the back court. A fine and again fiercely independent, if emotionally barren chapter in the Zep saga. And it really could have been no other way during this ponderous and crashed point in the collective Zep psyche.

Rating      8

## Led Zeppelin - In Through The Out Door
(Swan Song '79)

Like an incredible wash of good feelings, the radio debut of **In Through The Out Door** drifted from KREM - FM, Spokane as I taped along on a newly acquired blaster. It was late summer, and I and the rest of the world was surprised at the freshness and vitality of the new Zeppelin sound. Here was a breakthrough in communication, a letting down of one's guard, and a warm receptive oneness of performer and fan. **In Through The Out Door** arrived on the shelves in the now legendary packaging of brown paper bag guarding six (?) different album covers plus a black and white inner sleeve that turned various different primary colours with the application of water. The music was comfortably less tricky, offering a surprisingly human, keyboard-laden sound that approximated an amusing retrospective smile at what through the ages had been seen as a very serious band. The plaintive beauty of this record is everywhere. Rather than spoil the unassuming grandeur and pageantry of this masterpiece with unnecessarily detailed analysis, it is best to just live within the vibrance of the grooves. This record wasn't heavy in the least, and no one cared. **In Through The Out Door** mirrored the mature state of modern music as it bristled for another decade threatened by punk; as it cushioned itself against an unsure future, as it rose above the ugliness of the street and reveled in the complex bliss borne of Caribbean rhythms, American blues, soul-penetrating balladry, self-deprecating country hoe-downs, swaggering metal, and general appreciation of living. A deeply rhythmic record where the less celebrated half of the band comes to the fore, **In Through The Out Door** placed John Paul Jones' keyboards and John Bonham's drumming as pre-eminent pattern makers, leaving Plant and Page to colour and augment, providing additional dimension to the considerably vital force of the album. **In Through The Out Door** will be fondly remembered as the last of many Zep surprises, a refreshing about-face that grandly capped a career of mythic proportions, a record that will always be placed in time, and universally re-celebrated, as a blast of humanity that re-focused rock'n'roll's efforts at the end of a decade, towards the pursuance of spirit above all trends. A grand and fitting finale to one of the world's finest musical traditions, finale due of course to the Jimi Hendrix-style death of John Bonham after a night of monumental drinking. Note: the band had fleetingly considered both Cozy Powell and Phil Collins as replacements, but then decided the circle had been irreparably broken. Also in the works but scuttled: XYZ with Chris Squire and Alan White.

Rating    10

## Led Zeppelin - Coda (Swan Song '82)

This posthumous compilation of out-takes spanning nine years provides the listener with further glimpses behind the scenes of Zep's thought process, bringing to the fore some interesting "what ifs" in terms of album composition and directions the hallowed four might have taken. Dispensing with the pointless inclusions, two boring ol' blues covers and the drum solo, what remains are all decent to downright god-like Zep ravers, which ever so slightly tip towards Zep's harder rocking persona. Lone acoustic number *Poor Tom* ('70) is a stylish bluegrass dittie with an interesting Bonham shuffle. *Walter's Walk* ('72), an early metal romp features a cool an' chaotic Page riff, some emotive Plant wails, and a rousing race to the finish. Side two features three cuts, all recorded November '78 from the **In Through The Out Door** sessions, that together demonstrate how Zep's last studio extravaganza could have been rockier, earthier, less exotic. *Ozone Baby* is a fresh, complicated but almost Stonesy guitar rocker,

while *Darlene* offers a less desirable vampy boogie tune, nevertheless still a notch livelier, though less classic than the final construct of **In Through The Out Door**. Album closer *Wearing And Tearing* offers a full metal rip-ride with a vaguely boogie and even somewhat country western feel to the basic riff, which would have easily blown the doors off of any Page rumblings on the band's swansong. **Coda's** well worth the money for Zep followers and indeed serious music fans in general, offering for the most part fully fleshed-out ideas, bonafide and completed high quality tunes, from one of rock's most innovative band of explorers. A capsulated examination of post-Zep solo output: John Paul Jones has been more of a behind-the-scenes guy, mostly producing. Jimmy Page did a soundtrack album, ill-received solo album **Outrider**, two iller-received records with Paul Rodgers as The Firm, then of course was half of Coverdale-Page. Plus as a "mystery" band, there's The Honeydrippers' E.P. Unarguably, Robert Plant has had the biggest effect on the post-Zep world, with six solo albums as of '96. Capping it off: Page Plant and their **Unledded** revivalist road show.

Rating    7

## Leeway - Adult Crash (Futurist '94)

Wacky how time flies. But I almost forgot how to irresponsibly label music as critics must. So it was both refreshing and confusing to hear a square-jawed grunge record, Leeway only fleetingly addressing punk, satisfied to shoot holes in metal with a rushed edgy delivery that skirts urbancore, oddly enough Life Of Agony coming to mind, even if the sum total is something closer to grunge grandpappies Green River. Solid, heavy garage rock, nothing more, nothing less, just nicely retro and underground enough to lick the gutter with pride.

Rating    7

## Leeway - Open Mouth Kiss (Fierce '95)

The harder, grindy grooves here prove that the youthful, bashy grunge of **Adult Crash** was likely a limitation of production and chops, this time 'round, Leeway going for a heavier, brighter batch of street tales, really indulging those skatecore influences unto Biohazard and Life Of Agony (Eddie's vocals are sonorous like Keith's), while still remaining simply and solidly metal-bent at heart. Pete Shelley tune *I Believe* is a melodious rock respite however, showing these guys don't need to thwack the listener over the head all the time. Mounds of integrity, from wence I know not, making this a low **8**, commendable for its blurring of genres, but a bit mono.

Rating    8

## Legend - Death In The Nursery (Workshop '82)

A long lost—and I do mean lost—early NWOBProgressiveM squeaker along the lines of the lovably stunned Saracen, or an axe-loving Marillion, Pallas, or IQ. Really sinister, approaching Angel Witch tone-wise for about six minutes total, but hilariously low budget and queer. Legend just had no idea, and for that I salute them.

Rating    3

## Legs Diamond - Legs Diamond (Mercury '77)

Legs Diamond has been lurking around ever since the early days of American heavy metal, yet their only decent output to date has been their first two and a half records light years ago, which emitted a controlled din resembling at various times Deep Purple, Moxy, early Rush, The Nuge etc. ad infinitum. **Legs Diamond** is surprisingly slick and cock-sure, oscillating between very modern metal and light-to-medium intensity hard rock, best of the lot being fledgling speed rockers, *Deadly Dancer* and *Satin Peacock*. Pretty listenable given

the solid tunes, accomplished production, and excellent vocal work of one Rick Sanford.
Rating 7

## Legs Diamond - A Diamond Is A Hard Rock
(Polygram '77)
Record #2 builds confidently on the modern metal of the band's debut. Less stylistically scattered, and more uniformly forearm-smashin' over a greater number of tracks, **Hard Rock** is a solid listen virtually from start to finish, led fabulously by the smart Purple-ish title tune. I mean, here's a band ready for the hockey barns, complete with yards of long hair, that unkempt Aerosmith look, clear simple communicative metal, and consistently great production. With so few metal bands around at the time, and such obvious demand, it's beyond me why Legs never made the big coin.
Rating 8

## Legs Diamond - Fire Power (Cream '78)
This is where the Diamond's light begins to fragment, **Fire Power** going out on a limb, but failing on every stylistic foray that strays from the band's traditional hard rock core. We get boogie, mellowness, dynamics pieces, even a cover of You've Lost That Lovin' Feelin', a song I've always despised. Yet perplexingly, we find two of the fiercest compositions of the Legs catalogue in early metal showcase Underworld King, a hot Deep Purple-style classic, and Midnight Lady, a slide guitarin' AeroFoghat jammer that actually reveals a new, trickier facet to the band, further highlighting the chaos of this failed effort, a record on which the band is said to have had dismally low levels of artistic control compared to the executives at the label. **Fire Power** remains one of those frustrating records of never to be realized potential, most notable for its soaring peaks and depressing valleys. To coin deadly Don, this is the end of the innocence.
Rating 6

## Legs Diamond - Land Of The Gun (Music For Nations '86)
This follow-up to the apparently excellent **Out On Bail** EP from '84, is the kind of American wimphem that **Kerrang!** circa the '80s ate up seemingly without any discrimination whatsoever. **Land Of The Gun**, however, may make fans of the earlier flashes of brilliance turn the ol' 44 Magnum on themselves, given the enclosed anonymous wash of tired keyboard/synth rock, with nary an intelligent thing to say. This blatant attempt at teeny bop stardom shouldn't even carry the Legs moniker, given that only two of five original guys remain, one being vocalist Sanford who fortunately can still belt it out high upon high. Anyways, don't look to this band for any kind of comeback. Aerosmith Legs ain't.
Rating 2

## Legs Diamond - Town Bad Girl (Metal Blade '90)
Band significantly intact from the old days, Legs Diamond prove themselves back and somewhat relevant, at least to the hair band standards of 1990. **Town Bad Girl** comprises twelve all original tracks (including a nice remake of Legs oldie Stage Fright), most kind of slow, open and plodding (can you say Keel?), none exhibiting any particular pedigree or old soul wisdoms, even Sanford's voice sounding raspy and strained, like any number of shaggy-maned west coast metal mooch. Not all that heavy really, the band going for melody and melodrama, Michael Prince's keyboards fairly prominent in the mix, everything drop-dead predictable so it doesn't upset your day. Kinda proves once and for all, the band's self-assured hard rock exercises from the '70s were a fluke. Uh, nice album cover.
Rating 5

## Lemans - On The Street (Shrapnel Ent. '84)
Lemans was one of the few American indie label outfits from the barren early '80s who steered clear of the hordes spending their time figuring out how to out-race Judas Priest and steal their clothes at the same time. Consequently, **On The Street** stood out somewhat as a self-confident effort, with hooks, subjects one could relate to (i.e. nuthin' fancy, just hard rock stuff as opposed to slasher movie stuff), and a sturdy recording from Mista Metal Mike Varney. One of the better offerings at the time, but pales greatly in the perfectionist '90s.
Rating 5

## Lethal - Poison Seed (Massacre '96)
A record like this can take you back to a time when craftsmanship was revered, Kentucky's Lethal hatching a heavy-ended progressive metal banquet of sounds of which they can be quite proud. Song is kept to the fore (Bruce Dickinson's **Skunkworks** comes to mind), as the band weave tales of moody, Gothic beauty, all the while a very electro drum mix adding distinction and exaggerated treble, which somehow gels with all these magical tunes afoot. In addition, the band isn't afraid to make tall work of their softer tunes, everything benefitting from nice attention to detail that tones along the lines of Fates Warning while staying more focused.
Rating 8

## Liege Lord - Freedom's Rise (Black Dragon/Banzai '85)
Typical mid-'80s speed metal, rife with laughable dungeons and dragons overtones and mushed-up mix. The usual roll call of influences, usually starting with Priest collapsed into scampering Maiden on no sleep. Overplaying everywhere, just like f'rinstance other sad franchises such as Virgin Steele, Laaz Rocket or Iron Angel. Had a bit of a following, and for some reason, other records, two being **Burn To My Touch** and **Master Control**. Yo, delete bin!
Rating 4

## Life Of Agony - River Runs Red (Roadrunner '93)
Life Of Agony's fine **River Runs Red** fried more than a few brains with its brand of therapeutic homewrecked depression metal, a sound that melds lyrical hardcore with modern Metallica deflationary heft, all draped with the Wagnerian operizing of lead psychoanalyst Keith Caputo. What results is a tricky, mostly mid-tempo guitarfest whipped and emotionally scarred, fed up with the present, burning all bridges to the future. And the whole thing moves smartly, each track offering new hard music hooks along with a lyrical window into souls on fire. Life Of Agony's Type O Negative connection is an apt pairing, both bands hung low and grey with an urban toughness that makes for a cold, unfriendly but engaging rapworld environment. Cool answering machine messages too.
Rating 8

## Life Of Agony - Ugly (Roadrunner '95)
Life Of Agony's **River Runs Red** debut blew a lot of minds with its distressing flood of emotions, fueled and reinforced by a musical backtrack mixing urbancore and Sabbath via Trouble. And now **Ugly** continues the tradition, getting more intricate, more arcane with its doom riffery, and stronger of song, emulating a Stone Temple Pilots-type sturdiness of hook. And the fragile frame of Keith Caputo is anything but small here, belting out his sobbing, operatic apocalyptic strains with charismatic authority, again visiting the whole spectrum of depression and interpersonal relations and the inevitable breakdowns thereof. Crisp production and just tricky enough arrangements complete the circle of doom, welding Life Of Agony in place as a genre unto itself, demarcated by its subtle mix of metal

goth grey and a more multi-hued knack for musicality. Dumb cover of *Don't You (Forget About Me)*.

Rating **8**

## Life Sex & Death - The Silent Majority (Reprise '92)

Whether it was a publicity ploy or not, the fact that this band claimed a lead vocalist called Stanley, who was described as a certifiably crazy bum who hasn't washed in a year (he looked and apparently smelled the part), actually hurt the band's chances more than helped, even though it was good for a press angle. Too bad, because the guy's vocals are deep, sonorous and unique, leading a metal attack that is fresh and guitar-drenched, venturing off into a pretty exciting artsy glaminess at regular intervals. Add to that provocative lyrics and a great drummer, and it becomes a damn shame everybody was creeped out by Stanley. Cos that's what happened, LSD becoming a novelty act that would constantly be on the verge of breaking up due to Stanley's lack of fitness for regular work. Hey, I was turned off too.

Rating **7**

## Likwid - Likwid (MCA '96)

A competent, promising debut of dynamic "modern rock" (read: grunge with feelings), **Likwid** cavorts through many useful and valid grunge conventions, this young Montreal band most evoking Pearl Jam or softer AiC. The record's driving force is the loose and fairly frontal drumming, sending rhythmic rockers and lighter arrangements alike compellingly forward. The umbrella'ed derivation of the thing sends me away somewhat, but if adventuresome hard alternative be your drug, this works with the best of 'em. Trouble is, the pack it runs with ain't exactly all that ambitious these days, Bush being the gosh-darn luckiest band since Motley Crue.

Rating **6**

## Lillian Axe - Lillian Axe (MCA '88)

Lillian Axe's first kick at the cat sounds close enough to a buzzing party but as the evening wears on, it becomes all too apparent that the proceedings are more preening and prissing as per a gaggle of high school chicks. **Lillian Axe** is produced by Robbin Crosby which might lead one to assume Ratt-like qualities, and one would assume correct, except that the gooey sweetness overpowers the might. Noisy enough but too prima donna'd to cause much commotion. High point: *Inside Out* which almost sounds real. Personnel notes: Stevie Blaze, based in New Orleans, formed this band by absorbing vocalist Ron Taylor and his Dallas band Stiff.

Rating **5**

## Lillian Axe - Love And War (MCA '89)

Plush, lush and beautiful things have happened to this band since last time we checked in, Lillian Axe finding an exquisite cache of pop hooks that have less to do with poodle rock, than '70s glam, The Beatles, '80s new wave and Cheap Trick. Tony Platt produces with razor-sharp discipline, approaching Mutt-level Def Leppard, although his working material is miles above the crap spewed by the Defs. Lead track *All's Fair In Love And War* is the record's tour de force, a sort of AOR meets European aristocracy piece that's just chest-high with entertainment value, while *Diana* is the most sublime piece of silly pop balladry I've heard since 1974. A very smart melodic hard rock record for 1989 indeed, **Love And War** is the product of a band who will dare to do more with their chosen perfume rock corner of metal, lifting themselves from the ranks of the obvious and uncreative. Missing in action: '92's **Poetic Justice**.

Rating **8**

## Lillian Axe - Psychoschizophrenia (Music For Nations '93)

An elegant example of what was right with commercial hard rock, Lillian Axe now lives in the exalted company of bands like Extreme, Saigon Kick and Tesla, combining their smooth jet aeroplane hooks with brave battling axes, while bracing European-inspired harmonies soar above the heavy tapestries. **Psychoschizophrenia** displays the talents of a vastly evolved Lillian Axe, Ron Taylor leading his charge through expertly engineered AOR like lead rocker *Crucified*, the forward-massing *Sign Of The Times*, and the Extreme-ly explosive *Deepfreeze*. And ballads like *The Needle And Your Pain* demonstrate an effortless versatility (big Crosby, Stills and Nash moments in this one), leaning nicely into '70s pomp rather than '80s power balladry for their soft rock influences. Pretty cool, this act with an incredibly stupid name quietly carrying out their business, amassing a reputation through sheer talent, propping up the prospects of this embattled squeaky clean genre, somehow giving an American twist to sounds that are the cream of European AOR, like good 220V or Europe when heavy, ocean-straddling prog, pomp and folk when treading lightly.

Rating **9**

## Lionsheart - Lionsheart (Music For Nations '92)

Elegant belter Steve Grimmett moves onto band and genre #3, first bestowing upon us the roiling NWOBHM sounds of Grim Reaper, then the tech-thrash of Onslaught, and now, accomplished heavy AOR. Steve is joined by a four-piece band including the Owers twins who would both leave before this record even came out. **Lionsheart** is a sprited, seasoned example of hair metal, way above other British acts attempting this difficult American genre, awesome production, roaring vocals, big harmonies and fluid, musical, Yngwieeny guitar solos all over the place, the band bounding in with purpose, a crucial element to making this stuff work. Chopsy, riff-mad, funky and lightly Gothic like mainland Euro hard rock. AORists will be pleased. Followed by **Pride In Tact** in '94.

Rating **7**

## Liquid Jesus - Liquid Jesus (Triple X '90)

This loopy, eccentric premiere from Liquid Jesus happens to be live, but don't let that stick in your craw, because loose, dirty and uninhibited define the band's texture anyways. Compared to its follow-up, **Liquid Jesus** is perhaps a bit junkier, offering both busier, more conventional rockers, and mellower, less dressed respites, establishing the quirky, enigmatic look to these California granola cases, who come to full bloom one short year away. On its own, I wouldn't say **Liquid Jesus** reveals genius, but as an interspersed exploratory companion piece to **Pour In The Sky**, the record provides telling commentary on the band's weird but ultimately human origins.

Rating **6**

## Liquid Jesus - Pour In The Sky (MCA '91)

Record II cracks it wide open as the boys from Mars bring to ethereal fruition their funky '70s brew of blended influences, ranging from Zep to Queen (Brian May anyways), demonstrating what happens when acid punks run full steam into ornate riffery and superfluous gobules of garage sludgery. Paste on a vocalist who evokes the emotional palette of Diamond Head's Sean Harris, and you've got one engaging, time-traveling mess of wires, a comfortable hippy thickness for the bust generation. Better than I Love You, for its warm, fat melodies and basic humanity, Liquid Jesus have a throbbing masterpiece on their hands, a record so hard to nail down as it drifts in wavy heat from metal jam to bluegrass acoustic and bluesy psychedelic like a heavy metal Dead; slow, dense and stumbling, but groovy and experimental, and above all, thoroughly in love with the six string religion. And thoughtful but invitingly fuzzy lyrics, tasteful playing and a cavernous old-time mix accentuate the laid-back festival feel of the record with an almost ironic creative zeal. The end effect is something rare and honest to behold. Let's hope they don't liquify and disperse.

Rating                                                                  9

## Little Angels - Young Gods   (Polydor '91)

The geeky inability of the British to present themselves as pouting poster children underscores this weak puff of radio cack. All the stereotypical California moves are crammed onto this record, amidst song after pathetic song of pop metal worthy of early Warrant, Firehouse or a rash of hugely clueless Canadian pretty boys. Lots of over-playing, layered production, choruses of Angels, synths, pianos, real or fake horns, and general swishiness make **Young Gods** an automatic exercise in airhead rock. No delusions of artistic purpose here.

Rating                                                                  1

## Little Caesar - Little Caesar   (Geffen '90)

I dunno, luck and attitude maybe teamed up to give Little Caesar the buzz they needed to turn the fairly ordinary Chain Of Fools and this Bob Rock-blessed album into minor hard rock success stories. **Little Caesar**, the record, works without trying to save the world as it shambles through a tough, unambitious bar set of tales designed to sound good through a nasty, unpredictable P.A. Faves oddly would have to include the bright lights of Midtown and old cover I Wish It Would Rain, both showing an enigmatically sensitive side to these embattled urban survivors. Right down the middle, and I guess that's the record's attraction, as everything is immediately digestible; simple, flatheaded rock'n'roll for the man in the street intent on obliterating any memories of the working week.

Rating                                                                  7

## Little Caesar - Influence   (Geffen '92)

One of the world's many bar bands made real by a vocalist's willpower, Little Caesar writes simple, honest blue collar rock with guts, dynamic and hook. Definitely a chicken wings and draft kinda ride, **Influence** picks up where the commercially successful (near gold) debut got off, offering more of the same, with about the same ruff 'n' tumble results, buoyed by Ron Young's expressive attack at the mike. Nothing as memorable as **Little Caesar**'s Midtown, but Rum And Coke and Pray For Me are kickin', urban but personable, given the band's obvious disdain for frills and fancy. One just can't get too excited about this band in this present, non-improving state. You just kinda keep coming back to the record in narrowing arcs, hopefully adopting three or four cuts as personal anthems of some sort, not intense ones, but playable, non-threatening car stereo fuel, because underscoring the possibility of buying into the Little Caesar generic rock, beer commercial experience is the fact that the band's capable at cool, despite what you may think of the constructs they figure pass for camera ready art. To me, this acceptance happens more so with the debut, even though **Influence** still has that undeniable smell of trouble-bound America. New resident guitar legend: Earl Slick, who's begun contributing immediately in terms of axe texture and songwriting. Update: Ron Young has moved on to the Four Horsemen, replacing Frank Starr, who lies in an irreversible coma.

Rating                                                                  7

## Living Colour - Vivid   (Epic '88)

Living Colour's debut injected a new twist to the world of rock'n'roll, offering a unique hybrid of wide-open funk, loud garagey guitars, and the overt black vocal stylings of Corey Glover, a complex brew that came stage-diving off the speakers with clattering spontane-

ity and obvious second nature chops. There's no denying Living Colour won novelty points right off the blocks, benefiting from the sorry fact that black dudes rarely rock out. But unlike previous unknown metalheads Sound Barrier, rasta-thrash Martians Bad Brains and even the over-rated Hendrix, Living Colour can swing and groove melodically while keeping it fairly rowdy throughout. Lyrically, the band is Spike Lee on 11, anger personified, almost wholly concerned with black issues, or the plight of the poor, which in Living Colour's urban nightmare are one and the same. Sonically speaking, **Vivid** embodies a Van Halen-ish ethic, sounding live and jammin', with Vernon Reid's solos screeching and squealing alone, without rhythm guitar back-up. And elevating the dissonance is William Calhoun's drumming, which swells and crashes all over the kit, again in the spirit of one-take rock. As a whole, the album's surprisingly not that heavy, yet it's a stirring listen, offering such classic morality pieces as big hits Cult Of Personality and my fave Open Letter (To A Landlord). Much of the rest is a searing hot, sun drenched good time (although that sentiment somewhat belittles the weight of the message), only stumbling when it gets too purely funky or r+b, or when Reid (who really likes noise), roars in with one of his painfully untuneful axe solos. **Vivid** stands proud as a precursor to the metal/funk fusion happening today and is a thinking, feeling, socially conscious record to boot. A lot of energy, heat and anger went into putting this record together and it shows, although history would prove **Vivid** to be the band's most behaved rock walk.

Rating                                                                  9

## Living Colour - Time's Up   (Epic '90)

Gotta give these shit disturbers credit. **Time's Up** is the follow-up from Hell, rattling the bones with its jarring juxtapositions. Not content to milk a formula they alone monopolized, Living Colour puts their amps where their mouths are, delivering a slamming, loud, and downright cacophonous explosion of thrashing guitars and drums, not for the weak at heart, who might have wanted to shake their tight butts around the dance floor to Glamour Boys one more time. Lyrically, **Time's Up** speaks less predominately about black issues, widening its scope to include the environment, the stresses of urban life, drugs, relationships, and over-reliance on Elvis. Corey Glover sounds equally venomous as on **Vivid**—when he can be heard above the uncompromising din howling from the loud three behind him. As much as I admire the concept of pissing off everybody who was willingly poised to provide the world on a silver platter, this record is at times so brutish and untunefully obscured by white noise, it lacks the consistency of **Vivid**, serving up brilliant anarchist rockers like Type, Pride, New Jack Theme, and Information Overload, among bad thrash in Time's Up, dopey, joke r+b in Love Rears Its Ugly Head, and chaotic, unwieldy funk in Under Cover Of Darkness. Ultimately, **Time's Up**'s defining feature is dissonance, while somehow not that heavy, soaring and crashing nearly on par with 247-Spyz' shambling, headache-inducing landscapes. Gotta give 'em a hand though. If Living Colour want to remain true to the urban hardcore, **Time's Up** is the piece they should be packing.

Rating                                                                  7

## Living Colour - Biscuits   (Sony '91)

**Biscuits** is a half hour of Living Colour odds 'n' sods comprising covers of James Brown's dopey funk loiter Talkin' Loud And Sayin' Nothing, even greater waste of space, Green/Hodge number Love And Happiness, and Hendrix's Burning Of The Midnight Lamp, again shambling, irritating crap. Then there's two fierce, chopscrazy live tracks, and the previously unreleased Money Talks, closing the record with a perfect six for six loud, jammy, cacophonous tracks, firmly establishing Living Colour as an anti-social pain in the ass.

Rating 6

## Living Colour - Stain (Sony '93)

Seeing their light somewhat flicker and wane, Living Colour betray their mortal shackles in production of another spontaneous hodge podge of brutish hybrid rock. Falling between **Vivid**'s convention and **Time's Up**'s chaos, **Stain** bumps and thumps through a variety of competencies, roughly rendered vital and base, due mostly to axeman Reid and skinsman Calhoun, who flail their meathooks through a scattered live wall of fills and flurries, wandering spirits in search of jazzoid deconstruction. Representing more punk qualities than anything, **Stain** rips and roars with unharnessed weirdness, landscapes such as *Mind Your Own Business*, *Autländer*, *WTFF* and *Hemp* acting as disturbed oases within the meat of the record. Erstwhile, a pleasing enough funk heft is in the house, *Ignorance Is Bliss* and *Never Satisfied* recalling the digestibility of **Vivid**, while *Nothingness* goes ethereal and again, sort of tragic and disturbing, like a sensitive soul trapped in the projects, being slammed over the head with a kitchen sink. Fave metallirockers: *Go Away*, *Postman* and the manic *This Little Pig*. Yet overall, **Stain** is a case of rock drift, one of those "collections of songs", unsure and panicky with no central plan, sort of lax and slouching compared to the frontier-expanding pack the band once led, caught in an urban web of gnarly guitar, politically correct samples, cooking bass lines (courtesy respected new guy Doug Wimbish) and tough anti-social melodies. I play it, try warm to it, but I can't deny being affected by the record's critical drubbing, and the band's exposed bitterness at society's treatment of blacks, the poor and Living Colour. Best cut on the whole enchilada comes with *17 Days* on the included "limited edition" EP, a flat-line mid-pacer with a nice Glover vocal melody.

Rating 7

## Living Colour - Pride (Sony '95)

After the slow fizzle of a band turned bassy, bluesy and unenjoyable, Sony provides this well-deserved, lengthy retrospective sampling of Living Colour's three albums and one EP. And the sum total is curiously indicative of why the band ran their course, butting up against the patience of the public. Living Colour became increasingly skronky, textured, melancholic and jammy as it limped towards its difficult **Stain** swansong, and the four included newer, unreleased tracks from late '94 continue that trajectory, indeed none of them standing out as particularly likeable, even though integrity is there in bucketloads. But that sincerity and uniqueness make this record a must-have for fans, and serious students of tunes alike. No one sounded much like Living Colour, and their social indignation rang true, biting with that added forcefulness that can only come from metal (i.e. rap all you want over a synth drum pattern and a few samples. It ain't ever going to suckerpunch like Sepultura.).

Rating 7

## Living Death - Vengeance Of Hell (Mausoleum '84)

One of the early German one-trick ponies attempting to clean up the image of thrash by tightening its act while retaining the speed, Living Death attracted the obligatory high accolades for such a postulate still fresh in '84. Yet giving it the old college spin in the '90s will invariably result in amusing grins at the zero mobility and simple moshdom beneath the delusions of grandeur. Supremely heavy, and occasionally hurtful in its chug, but ultimately doomed through lack of originality and Thorsten Bergman's toneless vocals.

Rating 4

## Living Death - Metal Revolution (Banzai '85)

Humourless German mustard gas, combining basic, clean, but really boring speed metal with about the same cut-rate quality mid-tempo groove stuff, kinda like early Running Wild. Can't think of any reason to own this. Second record, more or less dead identical to the first.

Rating 4

## Lizzy Borden - Love You To Pieces (Metal Blade '85)

One of a rash of American loser bands that mixed identical amounts of leather, smoke, blood, flesh wounds, violence, goth, razor blades, speed, fire, techno, doom, and ultra-heaviness in order to emulate their multiple ideals of a re-intensified Judas Priest. Lizzy Bord'em (form Hollywood of course) adds in shades of Alice and W.A.S.P. to complete the trip to the wax museum, managing to stir the brew even more unwelcome and crass. Luckily the band would become a little less stiff on subsequent spins.

Rating 3

## Lizzy Borden - Visual Lies (Metal Blade '87)

And well (writer scratches head), Frizzy's getting somewhat more listenable, sounding like a hair metal band coming from good influences. There's pocket, groove, European-style melodies, something approaching bad Scorpions or bad Priest, good Twisted Sister or good Quiet Riot, and I mean all that in a good way! Strong production, theatrical, Geoff Tate-ish vocals and some under-stated axework (both solo and riff) from the team of Allen and Holmes combine for an acceptable trip to the way metal was in the mid-'80s. Sure, here in the modern day it's total cheese (with eyeliner), but live with it.

Rating 6

## Lizzy Borden - Master Of Disguise (Metal Blade '90)

And the show must go on, Lizzy bringing his higher and higher vocals to a new raft of trickier, dressier songs that nevertheless are still framed around party metal headbang riffs. Slightly conceptual towards Lizzy heroes Alice Cooper and Kiss, **Master Of Disguise** is more of the same fully capable but dated metal, leather 'n' lace guitars churning vibrantly through the record (although it's two different guys this time, Lizzy essentially firing his whole band and doing this as a solo record with hired guns). Laugh if you must, but you won't be laughing in joy, because they did a lousy job of it, bringing in horns, a 40 piece orchestra and a belaboured pain concept on par with Blackie Lawless.

Rating 7

## Lock Up - Something Bitchin' This Way Comes (Geffen '90)

Lock Up was one of a number of early '90s funk metal outfits, possessing a general non-image exoticism, a sound that approximates a groove-locked Living Colour, yet without the sizzling grit, which becomes the central shortcoming with Lock Up's noteworthy guitar-driven sound. Saddled with a picture-perfect mix that lacks character (believe it or not, at the hands of the usually rad Matt Wallace), and vocals from Brad Grillo that are a tad safe, Lock Up smells like self-serious Australian new wave, whatever that means. It's all too funk-o-rama pimp roll speed-wise; spinning ever so slight variations of mid-pace with relentless duck and cover riffing. The songs are commendable, but they could, and should pulverize. Seriously, if this were a Red Hot Chili Peppers album, I'd probably be blown away, because Flea'd punk it up to a manic degree where the grooves would just fly. All Lock Up needed was a dose of sleaze (heroin would do it), bad attitude or killer instinct, and their stuff might have slammed with the ragged edge of life. But alas, not to be, as the

band would break up, stonewalled by their label in attempts to make record II. Guitarist Morello now with Rage Against The Machine.
Rating     6

### Lone Star - Lone Star  (CBS '76)
Not to be confused with similarly rare and slightly more revered Alex Chilton vehicle Big Star, six-piece Lone Star were a hapless bunch of British semi-some-bodies making their own confused brand of hard-hit-ting rock'n'roll. Chucked and stirred into the band's belaboured brew: the bash of Bad Co. and Humble Pie, the loose booze of latterday Mott (without the Hoople), the trendy key-wizardry of Styx, the good ol' boy booger riffs of failed Southern rock acts, and the pomp and circus pants of prog rock. It all kind of flounders and flips, while communicating a raw '70s sincerity through a hammy, dough-fisted mix. Vocals: Kenny Driscoll; guitarist (one of them): Paul Chapman, later to join UFO. One of those minor collector's items amongst us desperate hoarders of '70s guitar rock.
Rating     6

### Lone Star - Firing On All Six  (CBS '77)
A much more high-brow sort of record, **Firing On All Six** kicks off with the Styx-y Magnum seven minute pomp of The Bells Of Berlin and never looks back, rocking very creatively through tricky metal, tricky funk and all points in between, no doubt the influence of rock universalist John Sloman (now Lone Star's vocalist) taking the band to intricate new places. Faves are elegant, technical rockers The Ballad Of Crafty Jack and surprise heft closer All Of Us To All Of You. Heck boys, this is the sort of record that ought to be rere-corded, because the combination of less dressy drums and way more guitar would make this quite an inter-esting, textural record indeed. As it stands though, it's a schizophrenic, half failed, half highly successful pro-posal.
Rating     7

### Lord Belial - Kiss The Goat  (No Fashion/House Of Kicks '95)
Awestruck demonic metal with frightwig packaging, graphics and lyrics, **Kiss The Goat** certainly makes a point with its frozen death metal perturbance, Dark's Norse-trampled vocals just a gnawing chaw that bites the soul and never releases. Probably wouldn't even had paid attention to it, had the record been wrapped in standard black with unreadable logo, but all purple points conspire to make this an imposing monolith to evil forces. And in truth, there are some almost proggy, Edge Of Sanity-like grooves between the blistering blastbeats, aided by upscale production and of course the band-members names, Bloodlord, Sin, Dark, Lilith and Vassago, I'm sure nice once you get to know them.
Rating     6

### The Lords Of The New Church - The Lords Of The New Church  (I.R.S. '82)
The Dead Boys' Stiv Bators and The Damned's Brian James are the somewhat contrived masterminds be-hind this (small c) cultish, early Goth outfit that mixed punk and tribal structures (like a garage Killing Joke), with general clangyness cloaked in black. Of the three bonafide albums, this debut is the most raucous, sounding like medium-grade Damned, heavy Stran-glers or heavy Gang Of Four about three quarters of the time, and like medium-intensity Stranglers for the remainder. The recording is a bit skeletal, but the overall effect is quite chilling, British and chemically sinister. Not metal, rather noisy post-punk punk, rife with that British knack for unwelcome, skewed melo-dies. Rave cat-sacrificing cuts include Portobello (the heaviest), Holy War, and Li'l Boys Play With Dolls which strings a story from N.Y. Dolls' songtitles. Clever, huh?
Rating     7

### The Lords Of The New Church - Is Nothing Sacred?  (I.R.S. '83)
The most thorny, shrill and unwelcome component of the ever-blackening Lords persona, **Is Nothing Sa-cred?** is also the least metallic, garbage-loping again through elements of the Stranglers and The Damned but also teetering into the vat of frail depravity in which swims thankfully The Cure and even Magazine (wit-ness Bad Timing). **Is Nothing Sacred?**, if nothing more, is another odd, fringe experiment for this grimy, sordid outfit not afraid of risk. Kind of a NYC sort of late night out, with a tangle of complex roots mixing r+b, The Cramps, David Johansen, Syl Sylvain and of course Stiv's hero Iggy, along with the aforementioned pack of pale-skinned Brits.
Rating     6

### The Lords Of The New Church - The Method To Our Madness  (I.R.S. '84)
About as accessible as the Lords get, **Method** still lies so desperately cellar-bound, joints creaking in damp collusion with a Stiv more intent on exploring the dark side of his Iggy fixation (coupled with a sketchy Satanic side) over the band's least murky delivery which mixes cheesy keys, acoustic guitar and surprising metal into a sort of poisoned re-run of latter-day Damned. Again tribal and depraved in a death dance not unlike a post-mortem probing of Johnny Thunders exotically embalmed skull casing. Anthems thoroughly worthy of reverent cover status someday: Dollsy necro-party S.F.&T., and smartly whipped metal rave Kiss Of Death.
Rating     7

### Lord Tracy - Deaf Gods Of Babylon  (Uni '89)
Simplistic corporate hard rock with a touch of the blues, **Deaf Gods Of Babylon** (stupid title) does nothing to distinguish itself amongst a corral of hun-grier, more daring acts. It revs pretty handsomely come Rats Motel and joke OTT'er Piranha, but for the most part, it's a grab bag of airhead weekend rock, radio ballads, and underachieving boogie metal, not without a sense of fun.
Rating     5

### The Lost - The Lost  (Epic '91)
This wild little bronco takes the listener to the same underground blues metal backlots as Badlands, yet without the obvious avalanche of finesse and wisdom. A whole tangled mass of often incompatible philoso-phies come swelling forth including those of ZZ Top, NY Dolls, Smack, Meat Puppets, Hanoi Rocks, Gonzo Ted, The Stones, George Thorogood, Kings Of The Sun and Budgie (well, at least ZZ and The Nuge then). It's more to the effect of a youthful, kaleidoscopic garage weirdness, that spins a web throughout these wicked little roots metal romps. Most righteously kick-in' of the dozen dramas here include a stunning and brief melodi-metallic instrumental Solid Body, sly hard rocker I Want Some Fun, and cruisin' boogie-metal scorcher Bijou Dreams, which wraps a totally Ted riff package, and even the man's difficult guitar sound, around a diamond-hard Texas power twister. **The Lost** reverberates and twangs with warmth, cooking with a charm that hooked me right away with its integrity and total lack of commercial bullshit, much in the same manner as Badlands' debut, Hall Aflame's debut, and Metal Church's **The Human Factor** did; all classics that carved their own space in the collective psyche without resorting to overt shock (which has nevertheless proven to be a resoundingly fertile vehi-cle in itself). Anyways, check this out for its uplifting freshness and innocence, for its ability to court punk with manners and get along, and its inherent listenabil-ity as a smoothly cruising '70s guitar trip.
Rating     7

## Lost Breed - Save Yourself (Noise '94)

Man, maybe after the imminent demise of '90s punk rock, L.A.'s long-coming Lost Breed will lead the next wave with their revival of deleted, one record metal bands from 1984. **Save Yourself** is truly surprising, smearing old metal lo-fi over arrangements that are just barely too dressy to be called grunge or even retro-Sab like bud Wino and The Obsessed. No, this is twistedly welcome, not to mention downright at risk at being totally misunderstood as laughably amateur, which it ain't, Lost Breed riding that Obsessed/Monster Magnet undercave cache a little bit further into metal cheez. Which is why I like it. It's freaky, totally old, but inventive like a hapless but under-rated NWOBHM posse cut from its moorings, drifting on acid and forlornly without cash. Nothing pegs its time-frame, which lends the record an integrity that makes me snicker at the upside-down cake that is the music industry. So like trust me and buy it, for the the love of unrepentant leather rock.

Rating 8

## Lost City - Watching You (Scotti Bros./BMG '92)

The usual raft of L.A. rawk folk filling up the credits (and to some extent the band shot) would lead one to believe this is a hair band incognito, but once inside their weird, frustrating record, one will find a sort of progressive, world music slant to Lost City's nimble hard rock. There's everything in here, a slightly repulsive corporate sheen, smatterings of Zeppelin, a type of establishment easy listening, and a voice on Rue Phillips which is a polite and restrained big rock roar, like Kevin DuBrow in one of his cheezy straightjackets. Lots of playing by everybody, perhaps most obtuseness emanating from drummer Kofi Baker. Interesting record, I mean, I almost hear the great Collision in some of this, but again, something really Hootie holds me away.

Rating 6

## Loudness - Disillusion (Music For Nations '84)

Japan's most savvy shot at success in the West (forget the ludicrous Bow Wow or wimpoids Earthshaker) serves up a fairly accomplished slab of variously brilliant, nerve-shattering metal and thoroughly tortuous hard rock that betrays the band's Japanese roots with painful lucidity, **Disillusion** sporting better and worse material than the more uniform and Western follow-up. Obviously a band that has cut its musical teeth on current technical wizards like Yngwie and Priest, Loudness is an outfit that could rage, given success in communicating Westernisms vocally and lyrically. As it is, it's just foreign and weird, but man, do the heavy tracks kill.

Rating 5

## Loudness - Thunder In The East (Atco '85)

**Thunder In The East** marks the great Loudness leap into considerable synch with traditional metal markets. Musically the voyage across the ocean is more than complete, skipping the Americas completely, offering up a tasteful chunk of Eurometal à la Accept, with mid-years Priest embellishments riff-wise, Yngwie embellishments solo-wise. Through both sides, the execution is flawless, the production big beat and more than adequate. As usual though, the English as second language thing remains painfully obvious, relegating Loudness yet again into novelty act status. The lyrics suck like old Scorpions, and the Japanese enunciation and idiomatic gaffs expose the band's all too frequent discomfort with the official language of business and metal. And for these reasons, Loudness still remains a joke at least to these Western ears, lyrics being the most insurmountable offense to intelligence. With some dirtbag L.A. vocalist, Loudness could be a major force with which to be reckoned, given the band's technical

skills and canny ability for tuneful songcraft and groove. Right now, they still remind me of Bruce Lee and Godzilla movies. Pushes **5**.

Rating 4

## Loudness - Lightning Strikes (Est. '87)

Basically, **Thunder In The East** - Part II with a slightly more pronounced hard rock sheen. Very accomplished, axe-precise, and effortlessly brush-stroked with inventive riffs, yet at the same time, still asinine lyrically, yelpy vocally and utterly soul-less. Again pushes **5**.

Rating 4

## Loudness - Soldier Of Fortune (Atlantic '89)

I guess the writing was on the wall, Loudness adopting Mike Vescera on cat-like American vocals, while Takasaki has retained his Japanese guy for recording and touring back home in the earthquake zone. **Soldier Of Fortune** continues dishing those clean, precise Accept meets Europe type compositions, exhibiting real growth on mellower numbers like Danger Of Love. Main trouble keeping this from being deemed a classic of Euro hard rock would be the stiff, often non-grooving drumwork of Higuchi, no doubt stifled by Max Norman's unexpressive mix. But Takasaki's guitars are afire with passion, the man's vocabulary, texture and shade astonishing in its metaldom, and the addition of Vescera has softened this to Anglo ears, even if the lyrics are still a joke.

Rating 7

## Loudness - On The Prowl (Atlantic '91)

Well, count on a pushy American to project his presence, Vescera now taking over on lyrics as well, in the process somehow pulling Takasaki's riffs in a bolder, brasher party rock direction. The results are just fine though, because this has always been one studied and emotional guitarist, a master of riffs and a soloist with brains. I like the fact that the cover art is a step back, sort of prog metal meets the early '80s, the steely logo and freaky sci-fi illustration helping with the exotica of this long-standing Japanese band with the scuzz-rock vocalist. Faultless yet cliché-infested and heavily AOR, Loudness still retaining its Euro-tones, despite an increasingly suntanned L.A. disposition.

Rating 7

## Love Chain - Burn (MCA '94)

Ottawa's Love Chain join the legion of savvy Canadian acts making solid, uncheesy records, fairly grunged up, looking cool, sounding appropriately alternative, dark and thudly. Trouble being, **Burn**, as competent as it is, doesn't add to the plethora of dirty '90s rock records in any appreciable manner, perhaps the band's differing directions over the last five years betraying a second guessing of the rock environment. Reminds me of another debut released roughly the same week by Sugartooth, both records maybe diving too deeply into what many imagine the '90s to be about. Not without its charms, but easily lost in the shuffle as everybody starts slagging the concept of alternative. Could warm on you, given a few carbon cleanings on the ol' car deck.

Rating 7

## Love/Hate - Blackout In The Red Room (CBS '90)

There's something huge, brash and smothering about this record that gives it major die-hard conviction and resounding, ultra-toothsome kick among the thieves, poseurs, talentless gypsies, and occasional rock icons that coalesce to attempt wastecase metal, Californ-I-A-style. Sure the lifestyle persona (and Jizzy Pearl's rat-like whine to some extent) is lifted wholesale from GN'R, yet the sound pounding Love/Hate deals out summarily wails the shit out of Axl and crew. **Blackout**

**In The Red Room** rocks heavily due to a dramatically powerful mix via knob veteran Tom Werman, and a seething delivery from all four corners of the Love/Hate cage match, churning a most skidsy din, one helluva party record beyond compare, even though its sales unjustly peaked around the 250,000 mark in the U.S., making it a treasure for the few. **Blackout** thoroughly smokes. Although the album never even hints of relaxing for a second anyways, the most potent of highs come with the percussive *One More Round*, the driving yet melodic *She's An Angel*, and slammin' last call *Hell, CA., Pop. 4*. In the dog-eat-dog jungle of American hard rock/metal, with its myriad of philosophies and sonic tweakings, a sorry majority of all releases lose it on intensity alone. **Blackout In The Red Room** slams with such pride, leaving the party early never even crosses one's mind. I look forward to the follow-up. If anybody can kick some snot back into a scene that is too often gutless, inauthentic and contrived, it's these livin' it, breathin' it rock dogs. Lock up your medicine chests, there's gonna be a showdown.
Rating                                                    10

## Love/Hate - Wasted In America   (Sony '92)

Def'ning urgency and apocalyptic terror, plain and simple, **Wasted In America** is a disorienting freefall into a depths ruled by excess for the sheer, gleeful self-destruction of it all. Played to a neon collage of killer progressive Punk so painstakingly scientific in its rapid-fire violence, said Statement has quickly and ruthlessly become my favorite record of the decade so far. **Wasted In America** just destroys previously held conventions as to the cerebral and consequently damaging possibilities of sleaze metal, a term that whimpers into total denigration at the spiraling heights of evil wisdom this record caresses. The ultimate ironic travesty of this glittering palace of automatic vice is the manner in which the band slings such hopeless tales of trash gone wild over some of the classiest, most daring metal arrangements in years, the record apparently set spinning by the band's immersion in the New York scene, complete with different emotional baggage, as opposed to their native L.A. roost. Exquisite melodies reverently draped over bass-driven verses, muscle-cruise courting odd time twists, surprise neck-snapping breaks encasing downright crazy riffs, and above all, pummeling metallic force breathing deeply through chemical energy, coalesce to create an effortlessly fluid but imposingly ornate construction that's well to the edges of both Heaven and Hell. **Wasted In America** is one of the most invitingly stressful works in years, a record for the veins, a record to replace blood. Toonswise, had the first four maneuvers on the disc not fried me skyclad, I never would have been shaking and willing for the trilogy of competitive fire to follow in three of the most unhuman, nervy chunks of steel ever placed one after another in *Yucca Man*, *Happy Hour*, and *Tranquillizer*, no shit, about the three best rock songs in a row forever in time, Amen. And so the inhumanity of this wretched planet spews onward, and Love/Hate are firmly in love/hate with it, or at least glad to be participants in the whole thieving, steaming mess. But the solid beauty of the story is that the band just play their collective asses off in elitist determination towards wrecking the few minds left to wreck, taking leave of the immoral for a turgid, closed eyelid, nod to the eternal amoral. If you gotta go, go state of the art, go with the baddest, meanest slab of wax strapped to your chests. Do it for the band, because in the end, achieving a masterpiece like this is all that matters. Something wicked to believe in. Note: four track **Wasted In America** EP contains one non-LP tune called *Castles From Sand*, while four track **Evil Twin** EP contains another newie, *I Am The Snake*, plus a live track and a "schizo" mix of *Evil Twin*.
Rating                                                    10

## Love/Hate - Let's Rumble   (BMG Records (UK) '93)

Booted by Sony, Love/Hate refuse to die, cranking the jets on this visceral brash rocker of classic proportions, again blowing the doors off with the first few tracks, then becoming merely one of the best bands in the world for the back half. So *Let's Rumble* opens the show with an expansive boom, *Spinning Wheel* gets headbanged and tribal, *The Boozer* gets technical, then *Wrong Side Of The Grape* enters friggin' metal Valhalla, offering one of the band's odd-timed hiccup beats, a nasty riff from new guitarist Darren Housholder (*Jon E. Love* is back on **I'm Not Happy**), and a fab Love/Hate chorus that is all hook, fang and finger. Only a couple are less than inspiring to start fires (*Devil's Squaw* and *Sexical*), with the record as a whole sounding a bit more morose, less flashy and truly genius, somehow closer and more combat-hungry. Other fave: *Beer Money*, doing that frantic but artful thing these metal masters can crank at will, and *If You Believe In Miracles*, which is an edgy, metaphysical blues ballad with a clouds-breaking chorus that builds to a morally bankrupt conclusion that seduces the listener into bitter grey angst with more authority than any number of ranting alterno-geeks. Oh, and I'd say *Here's To You* gets pretty much the same soul-crushing result, through more of a hard-hitting, yet still bluesy assault. Downstroke: **Let's Rumble** is only 33 minutes brief. Man, it just ain't enough.
Rating                                                     9

## Love/Hate - I'm Not Happy   (Mayhem/Futurist '95)

Ecstatically glad to see these rudest of Cali-fried rawk rats are still grinding out the goods. After two brilliant major label sleaze rock records (**Wasted In America** is ludicrously essential), and low-key release **Let's Rumble**, Love/Hate changes labels again for this sneering, snarling paean to all emotions corrupted. There are amazing songs here as usual (the bluesy and covert *Cutting Chain* and the insanely butt-shaking *Ola Mola* come to mind), but the record as the whole goes everywhere exquisitely, slow and quiet, simple and riff-mad, celebratory and sick, all recorded with a potent balance of grit and fidelity, all driven home by the paint-peeling vocals of Jizzy Pearl, newly short-shorn, still able to crumble good with a glance. Embattled but always mindful of producing superior product, Love/Hate are a bit of a best kept secret, certainly the best band to do anything remotely close to Guns N' Roses. But in ways, Skid, Jizzy and crew better Axl's fragmenting rats by wallowing deeper in the gutter and remaining heavier and way more inventive musically. In a genre gone way south, this dirt-faced posse still deserves to exist and thrive. They are the saviours of cheese, the messiahs of mozza . . . well, you get the picture.
Rating                                                     8

## Lucifer - Big Gun   (Lucifer '72)

This is quite possibly the coolest metal collectible I've ever encountered, and it ain't exactly for the music, but the whole Spinal Tapped presentation to the thing. Remember, the year's '72 (that's important), and metal is just breaking. Well, Lucifer are twenty years ahead of their time, doing Black Sabbath's first album unplugged, a bit of Butler bass here and there, mad hippy vocals, some fledgling synth skronks, and a percussion display that crosses mellow Santana with beat bongos. The record cover? Completely black both sides, just like Spinal Tap's **Smell The Glove**. But the boys throw in a sheet with awesome metal photos (swear to God, the drummer looks just like Dave Wyndorf), especially the bass player, who is shown backdropped against a stormy sky, hair blowin' free, machine heads glowing with fright (this stellar shot is also used as the record's centrepiece). Brief typed missive sez, "Lucifer is English but we have this cave in Arizona where we record

255

a lot of our stuff." Which about sums up this unique toss-off: Kyuss, on mushrooms, in a cave, with a bass and not much else.
Rating 5

## Lucifer's Friend - Lucifer's Friend (Philips '70)

Man, did these German wonkoids exhibit big ugly metal promise. **Lucifer's Friend** is a scary cross between **Uriah Heep**, **Look At Yourself**, **Black Sabbath**, hippy rock and the progressive noodling that will ruin all of this band's other records. Future Heepster John Lawton's pipes are clear and powerful, and the recording is one of the best I've heard on a record this vintage. The very Iommi-ish guitar sound melds seamlessly with those honking Lord-ian keys as the boys sludge through, unaware that they were acting an integral part to metal's conception. But hold those bell-bottomed hellhounds, this is still merely a roaring loud hippy record, more concerned with acidy illogical jams than riff-mapping our cerebral cortexes. As an opener however, Ride The Sky certainly makes a dent (so much so I guess that the band found it fit for re-make on '94's **Sumo Grip**), and as I say, the whole smashy mash is pleasantly mixed, bringing to the fore sounds that would roam all over **Machine Head** in a couple of years. But it really is unanimous, the rest of the records went everywhere fancypants and rarely heavy, the four records reviewed here being the heaviest, all points in between being creepy progressive, often brassy fusion of various snobby persuasions.
Rating 7

## Lucifer's Friend - Mind Exploding (Janus '76)

I guess you can call this semi-committed look at Lucifer's Friend (I'm doing about half their records here), a public service announcement, given that metalheads the world over have wondered how heavy this band with the evil name and evil record jackets to match, ever was. Answer is not very, the record at hand, a sort of middle era rounder that begins to get commercial sounding like lost years Heep, often jazz-inflected but usually a sort of loose and flighty hard rock, recorded like prog (Ian Gillan's **Scarabus** comes to mind). Still, lost of guitars, Lawton and somber sounds, even if these elements are jumbled dogpile-like in a sort of confused tangle that wants to crossover like crazy.
Rating 6

## Lucifer's Friend - Mean Machine (Elektra '81)

With Lawton gone and now back, Lucifer's Friend crank their heaviest record, a tension-filled no frills rocker finding Lawton's soaring vocals and Hecht's pomp keys doing battle with a refreshingly dirty guitar attack that even lapses into Motörheaded speed metal on Cool Hand Killer. If you can get past the obvious NWOBHM cash-in of the thing (see fellow longball catalogue wankers Heep and Budgie), cool things from the band's circuitous past creep in, most notably those Heep and Purple sounds, regal tones that give the band weight of history, arriving at comfortably aged Gillan and White Spirit through the back door.
Rating 7

## Lucifer's Friend - Sumo Grip (Castle '94)

Lawton is again on board for yet another wholesale shift, this time into hard-hitting pop metal in a myriad of failing directives. Cool that the band re-do their Ride The Sky of 23 years ago, even if the record around it is a sorry example of fragmentation, stiffly arranged, just silly, like your least favorite Heep record meets deleted British wimp rock from the mid-'80s. A perfect case of a band that should have changed their name long ago, this Lucifer's Friend moniker being an albatross around this confounding band's neck from the word go.
Rating 4

## L.U.N.G.S. - Better Class Of Losers (Pavement '96)

Florida's L.U.N.G.S. hit the rock road in '94 as Collapsing Lungs, more of an industrial act, releasing only one ill-fated EP called **Colorblind**. After a bad tour experience with a demon RV, infighting, and label hassles, the band imploded, now reforming as a seven piece rap metal tour de force, hip-hopping their way through chunky, chopping riffs, bad-mouthin' like a gangland army their tales of crime and depravity, basically berating the listener like that's what we want. All the comparatives apply, Stuck Mojo, Biohazard, 311, Infectious Grooves, Murphy's Law (the drummer's ex-band), this big assault on the senses fitting in well, holding their own. But like all rap (with or without guitars), this is a better read than a listen, given that the aural experience is not unlike getting mugged by a bunch of low-life scumbags. Not my idea of fun.
Rating 6

## The Lurkers - Fulham Fallout (Beggars Banquet '78)

Largely ignored and largely ignorable during the heyday of punk, **Fulham Fallout** shagged along like a garage version of the Ramones, with occasional mistakes of metallic riffery (sinister loud punk, anyways), all so depressingly conveying a complete lack of financial prospects or artistic future. Kinda like a pissed-up, rain-soaked soccer match, rife with the most famous of Europe's ardent hooligans, **Fulham Fallout** is grimy trench punk at its least inviting. As a result, it's a sort of dumb blast, like a clueless vandalism of guitar rock's silliest moves. Basically aimless unemployment rock, wholly and vacantly concerned with bashing things.
Rating 5

## The Lurkers - God's Lonely Men (Beggars Banquet '79)

Flowing through the pipes deep beneath the overcast skies of The Lurkers polluted punk wheeze comes increased dexterity amidst a good five rockers that crash and bang willfully, with classy crossover riffs and determined, plow-ahead maturity. Only a third of **God's Lonely Men** evokes the juvenile garage new wave of the debut, and even that becomes transformed into buzzing punk mania via a killer, wasted mix. What's left divies the cake, leaning towards gracious, loose metal (Out In The Dark, Room 309, and the title cut), or getting downright subtle while steadfastly retaining the turned up guitar/bass/drums format for stabs at loud pop, as is the case with Whatever Happened To Mary, Non-Contender, and minor hit Sleep On Diamonds. Occasionally The Lurkers emit flashes of supremely authentic punk, as if they were the heavy alter-ego of The Clash, despite having no agenda. Unique chaos really, as the whole mess sounds like it's locked in some sort of merciless fight for survival. Performance of note: Esso on drums.
Rating 8

## George Lynch - Sacred Groove (Elektra '93)

Exacto George is back with his latest razor-sharp rendition of a groove gone by, sending forth a somewhat metal-physical exercise in stiff '80s sheen, better than a similar shmeer from parallel technician Stevie Vai, for its chunky love of the riff, lacing a number of these guitar wankers with vocals from Glen Hughes, the mangy Mandy Lion and the god-like Ray Gillen. Still, it's a relic of times much brighter (so the economists tell us—I remember just as much bitching about the economy in the '80s as I hear now), and George squanders precious minutes here, despite a few first rate Dokken-style chugfests. You and Ray, George, rockin', raw and pissed . . . one take, no instrumentals . . . now that's a band I could believe in.
Rating 6

## Lynch Mob - Wicked Sensation (Elektra '90)

Shove **Wicked Sensation** up against Don Dokken's **Up From The Ashes** and it becomes readily apparent who cranked Dokken when they cranked. Why, George Lynch of course, who takes his newly assembled paratroopers through high-octane send-ups of the Dokken core. **Wicked Sensation** rocks smartly, high on the hog and full of commercial savvy. Lynch proves his mettle, playing the axe like a woman (I don't know any other way of putting it), the man being in possession of a natural feel not unlike that of Extreme's virtuoso fret burner Nuno Bettencourt. Still, the overall approach is a little cliché and overly based on riffs circa the '80s. Vocals are fine but ultimately void of personality and tunes seem to exist to prop up the shine, almost as if George is intent on making a kickin' electric Dokken record and little more. Competent, highly groove-based but in reactionary avoidance of the creative.

Rating 7

## Philip Lynott - Solo In Soho (PolyGram '80)

Ever the dabbler and experimentalist (which basically killed him), Lynott found himself at the turn of the decade, restless, reinvigorated by the energy of punk, in other moods soulful and reflective, in yet others, delving deeper into his black heritage. So along comes the magnificent and universal **Solo In Soho**, which finds the man exploring his frazzled world, much in the same manner Pete Townshend's gorgeous **Empty Glass** and **All The Best Cowboys Have Chinese Eyes** found Pete fantastically out-leaping the constraints of his main gig. So, a bit of a catch-all for ideas Lizzy couldn't dare use, we get torridly moving pop ballads like ode to Elvis, *King's Call* (a classic, musical Phil lyric), *Dear Miss Lonely Hearts* (shades of Nathanael West?) and *Girls*, the latter two welling up with the fairer sex's sensuality, something with which Phil was well-versed. *Yellow Pearl* offers somewhat of a failed experiment with early techno, as friend Midge Ure from Ultravox (and Lizzy's touring band) makes his presence known. Articulating racial themes, the record switches to the tumbling boogie of *Ode To A Black Man*, the calypso of *Jamaican Rum*, the Clash-like reggae of the title track and the orchestrated r+b of *Tattoo (Giving It All Up For Love)*. May as well name 'em all: *A Child's Lullaby*, one of my faves, previews the passionate, spiritual balladry of Phil's second and last solo album, and closer *Talk In '79* features an amazing percussion blitz by Mark Nauseef, over which Phil expertly roll-calls the history of punk, and its inevitable crashing, one band at a time. So when the sun goes down, remember this record as one that went many places valiantly, the mark of a true creative force, Phil surrounding himself with fierce players, all working an aristocratically British execution of ideas that betray the breadth and width of Lynott's vision.

Rating 9

## Philip Lynott - The Philip Lynott Album (Warner '82)

Man, if **Solo In Soho** didn't surprise and amaze, taking Phil to realms far beyond Lizzy, this one finishes the job, Lynott crafting a masterpiece of lush, confessional sonics, shatteringly inspirational on many levels. **The Philip Lynott Album** is very much a spirit-cleansing, very visceral and intelligent record of the soul, from the gorgeous pageantry of opener *Fatalistic Attitude*, with its *Renegade*-type soft lilt and evangelist sampling, through no less than three of Phil's very best ballads in *Old Town*, *Cathleen* and *Growing Up*, to shining jewel of the record, *Little Bit Of Water*, which manages a professorial reggae with the lightest of instrumental touches. And the production on the record is sympathetic and yielding, a large task given the talent involved, pros like Midge Ure, Darren Wharton, Mark Knopfler (who kicks in a great solo), Mel Collins,

Gorham, Bain, Downey and Nauseef turning this towering sweeping statement into nothing less than a mission, blending their expertise with Phil's diamond-bright songs with the greatest of ease. I don't think it's an exaggerating to call this ultimately expression of solo self Phil's greatest achievement inclusive of the Lizzy catalogue, much the same way one might surmise that Jerry Garcia's **Cats Under The Stars** is the best Grateful Dead record to ever walk this planet. Both are Art blessed by the most gracious of muses. So run along now, you've got some shopping to do.

Rating 10

## Philip Lynott - The Man And His Music: Vol. 1: The Early Years (Nightlife Est. '93)

Don Bolster's a raving Lizzy lunatic who runs a Lizzy paraphernalia business out of Illinois called Wild One. From what I gather, he's probably one of the most knowledgeable Lizzy aficionados anywhere, keeping tabs on all the past members and their recordings. Well, probably his biggest accomplishment (at least to fans of big Phil) has been distributing these **The Man And His Music** CDs which seemingly sweep the vaults clean of all sorts of Lizzy 'n Lynott gems spanning fifteen or so years. Each disc features massively useful but excrutiatingly short and typo-ridden liner notes pinpointing the origins of each track. This first one is predictably the least interesting, finding a bunch of wide-eyed kids seeking their sea legs. The first half is typical flip America-enamoured hippie rock, lighthearted, loopy but serious about the search for song. Following, we get a batch of unnecessary (and quietly mixed) live tracks (with a laid-back boogie version of *Suicide*), then the most-known version of *Little Darling*, followed by perhaps the record's coolest soundbite, *A Song For Jimi*, a fairly tricky, percussive track featuring Phil, Eric Bell and Brian Robertson together again for a few laughs in 1980.

Rating 7

## Philip Lynott - The Man And His Music: Vol. 2: The Sun Goes Down (Nightlife Est. '93)

Phildisk 2 heats into the Lizzy career proper, opening with *Halfcaste*, a warm reggae shuffle from '74 that might have held ground on The Clash's **London Calling**. Following is a fairly uneventful bevy of **Nightlife**-era live tracks, plus a live B-side from the golden years entitled *Me And The Boys*, which sucks basically. But far and away classic here is *Just The Two Of Us* from the **Black Rose** sessions, a sort of well-rhymed barroom rocker; nice hook, energy and Lizzy class despite its blue collarness. Second biggest treat: *Don't Play Around* from the **Chinatown** sessions, a muscular hard rocker again gorged with sumptuous six-string hookery. Elsewhere, a grandiose treatment for *Dublin*, and an ill-advised foray into a rockabilly image with Dave Edmunds' excellent *Trouble Boys*, here half-baked but still, y'know . . . Lizzy. Backing this marketing-minded single was *Memory Pain*, which is a slow, blocky blues, a thrill to hear due to its rarity, but still filler. Again, whoevr made these records has managed a surprisingly solid package here, with sound quality just fine if not justifiably different from track to track. There are the occasional irritants like vinyl tics and pops, and the odd bit of distortion from high recording levels, but all in all it's absolutely acceptable. No ghetto-blaster bootleg stuff here as one would imagine, Someone must have really jumped some hoops to gather such an array of material spanning so many years. Hats off to the world's biggest Lizzy fan, whereever you are.

Rating 8

## Philip Lynott - The Man And His Music: Vol. 3: Solo And Sessions (Nightlife Est. '93)

The third installment in the wonderful tribute-to-Phil series from Nightlife focuses on Lynott's often sporadic, experimental and introspective solo "career". Throughout and after the Lizzy experience Phil basically dabbled in a daze, searching somewhat aimlessly for new voices. However, **Vol. 3** is to my mind the best of the trio. Highlights would include masterful *Together* B-side *Somebody Else's Dream*, *A Tribute To Sandy Denny* and the hilarious *Tennessee Stud*. There's also a novelty Christmas tune, a seedy track with Johnny Thunders, and the best of many versions of Gary Moore's *Spanish Guitar*. Closing out, we get what are probably Phil's last recorded works ever, in three middling commercial tracks recorded with members of Huey Lewis And The News, long-time buddies of Lizzy. Phil was dead two months later. One last mention: a cushy warm singalong version of long-lost Lizzy hit *Whisky In The Jar*, which demonstrates both how catchy the tune was, and why the band was somewhat embarrassed by it. Throughout **Vol. 3**, one really begins to sense how Phil was looking desperately for new musical terrain outside of what was supposedly allowable within Lizzy, a band as versatile as any. Maybe had he found this non-Lizzy identity, he may still be buzzing today.
Rating **8**

## Philip Lynott - The Man And His Music: Vol 4: Don't Let Him Slip Away (Nightlife '94)

Don Bolster manages to eke out one more of these exciting archive objects, this time scraping the residue of the vaults for mere scraps compared to the awesome tracks all over the previous trio of discs. The only real revelation here is the title track, offered in two versions, a long moody number reminiscent of *Renegade*. While quite raw and stripped, '82's *Don't Let Him Slip Away* might have really shone if cleaned up and filled in with a couple of breaks. Otherwise, it's really a bunch of abysmally recorded live and demo stuff, only '73's *Going Down* and '82's *Hate* being previously unreleased. *Hate* is kinda fun, a sort of power punk pop rocker with neat sound effects and a spirited rhyming frolic from Phil. Of historical importance are the trio of tracks from Lizzy's last show ever (Germany, August '83), *Jailbreak*, *Thunder And Lightning*, the band finally crashing off with *Rosalie*. Hats off again for finding all this, although we all wish the mixes might have been a little better. Ah well.
Rating **6**

## Philip Lynott - The Man And His Music: Vol. V: 1978 (Nightlife '95)

Well, OK, ONE MORE TIME, as a few that slipped between the cracks come to you damaged but willing. The theme here is 1978, the band basically limbering up to make **Black Rose**, 7 of 11 tracks here coming from one February session at Goodearth Studios, three the previous month at Ramport, and a bunch unknown. The Goodearth tracks are considerably injured by a warbling, slowing down, speeding up of the guitar tracks. Aside from this sad occurence, the overall sound is demo quality, raw but not horrible. Dispensing with the total wastes of time, we get a non-surprising trio of slow depressors in alternate versions of *A Night In The Life Of An Old Blues Singer*, *Parisienne Walkways* and *Spanish Guitar*. Snoozers one and all. Then there's a very basic version of *Waiting For An Alibi*, plus spirited rumbling demo run-throughs of *Ode To A Black Man* (later on **Solo In Soho**) and *Fanatical Fascists* (later on Gary Moore's **Back On The Streets**). Another cool oddity is a shakey studio version of *Are You Ready* with different, equally dolt-ish lyrics. Then there's the new tracks: *Rocklila* (probably a typo: *Rockula*?), a Jimmy Bain number with a hum-

mable hard rock lilt, *Cold Black Night*, basically the *Dancing In The Moonlight* riff turned into a blues, and *Black Mail*, a typically third-rate riff rocker that the band was always smart enough to keep off their stunning official releases. But the real wild ride is left for the end. With the liner notes and the track listing running out at 11 with *Leaving Town*, a nice, high quality Lynott ballad, the counter goes clear through to 16, offering various acoustic tunes (including yet another turn at *Dublin*), finding Lynott close and intimate with folksy blues. It's a chiller, like you're just sitting in the studio with him, picking away at some heartfelt oldies. Pretty cool surprise, which I guess I've blown for y'all, not like you are going to track these collector's items down too easily.
Rating **6**

## Phil Lynott's Grand Slam - Live & Demos (Bondage '94)

Grand Slam was to be Phil's rock'n'roll salvation as he sunk deeper into drug-steeped surrender. All involved knew Phil couldn't really handle the pressures and responsibilities of assembling a new upstart rock posse, but 21-year-old Laurence Archer, Mark Stanway and Co. gave it the ol' pub try anyways, notching a few gigs and demos along the way. This disc however is horribly assembled. Like a bad boot, we get a single page, single-sided b&w cover shot, plus one more photo and the track listings. The only other info provided: tracks 1 - 8 are from an '84 gig in Glasgow and tracks 9 - 13 are '84 demos. The sound quality is quite awful, but the playing is surprisingly solid, making one quickly forget the muddy mix. A heady cauldron of classy keyboards, muscular guitar playing and fine vocal work from Phil make the live gig truly well worth it. *Nineteen* is full-on metallic, *Sisters Of Mercy* is a rousing mellow/heavy Lizzy-ish epic with an amazing blazing Archer solo, *Harlem* features astonishing Lizzy axe harmonies, and *Breakdown* is a beautifully melodic uptempo rocker again, a potentially proud addition to any Lizzy record. Rounding out, it's *Yellow Pearl*, *Parisienne Walkways*, boring blues *Crime Rate Is Going Up* and affable skinhead-ish punker *Here We Go*. Onto the demos, we get *Dancing In The Moonlight*-soundalike *Gay Boys*, sappy lounge rocker *Can't Get Away*, *Military Man*, another version of *Crime Rate* plus another run-through of that punchy *Breakdown* track, better represented by the live version. Pity about the recording, but of deathly importance just the same, these tracks portray Grand Slam as possibly a more adventurous, keyboardy version of Lizzy, still quite guitar-propelled but perhaps a bit more cognizant of power pop. In addition, it seems Phil really did use the band as a catch-all of Lizzy and solo rejects and outtakes over many years, a forum to exercise ideas that didn't fit the definition of Lizzy. Not like any of it was overtly planned that way, given Phil's distressed state of mind. The man was basically searching for a way to keep it all from crumbling and slipping away. If anything, this collection proves that the Grand Slam vehicle was something any Lizzy fan could have taken seriously. Note: other tracks that would typically flesh out a Grand Slam gig: *Cold Sweat*, *I Don't Need This*, *Dear Miss Lonely Hearts*, *Dedication*, *Sarah* and a handful of humourous covers.
Rating **7**

## Lynx - Missing Lynx (Quality '76)

Stack this lost pancake (and then cover with syrup) with similar dopey Canuck "hard" rock as Streetheart, Hammersmith, Wireless, Madcats, The Hunt and Teaze-lite, this churlish debut coming logo-ready and mean-looking, what with those yellowy eyes and songs like *Lucifer* and *Goodbye Education, Hello Rock & Roll*. So retro-geeks (you know who you are) probably revere this as they desperately try to bury themselves in a kinder gentler rock'n'roll era when nobody expected much. But **Missing Lynx** was this band's only sorta heavy record, subsequent attempts at brainier fare ('78's even heavier-looking **Sneak Attack**), then pop fare ('79's **We Are The People**) locating the pet cemetary but fast. Note: The entire band is replaced, except for Tony Caputo, on each of records #2 and #3. Take that, David Coverdale!

Rating        **6**

# M

## M80 - Maniac's Revenge  (Roadrunner '85)

Rowdy but budget-minded U.S. tour grind from a
power trio led by Niki Buzz (ex-Vendetta), **Maniac's
Revenge** annoys the senses when either too OTT or
too geared-down, while managing a decent swing
when clipping along at around 70 M.P.H An album
suffering from lacklustre production, rough mix, and
overuse/misuse of electronic tom fills, this record becomes a tentative keeper due to innovative guitarwork
and choice "black guy" vocals. Shows promise.
Rating                                                                  4

## MacAlpine - Eyes Of The World  (PolyGram '90)

Side one's a pooch, but side two starts to insinuate
MacAlpine's strange brand of California meets Europe
hard rock into one's heart. Falling like apples from a
tree are traces of Leppard and Dokken, but also Vandenberg, TNT, keyboard-infected Helix and Christian
metal, every other song stabbing through with somewhat hooky choruses and big harmonies. Tony MacAlpine is best known for his guitar shred records, and no
doubt, this one was the most deliberate grab at commercial crossover. Not the worst shamelessly AOR
record I've ever heard, this one's trump being MacAlpine's tasteful Yngwie-style runs, and an odd under-ar-
rangement to the whole thing, even though it's
produced for miles.
Rating                                                                  6

## Tony MacAlpine - Freedom To Fly  (Shrapnel '92)

Pretty much a card-carrying metal shred record, mixing hard funk with melodic OTT and all points in
between. And not a whole lot to hold one's interest,
circulating a few good riffs and soloing that is no better
technically or emotionally than thirty or so other twee-
dle dumbers. Better off in a band.
Rating                                                                  4

## McCoy - Mini Album  (Legacy '83)

It never ceases to amaze me how Gillan's particular
circle of wizened veterans managed to sound like such
talent show drop-outs on their own. McCoy's four
track EP comprises three very basic metallic originals,
one mellow anaesthetic, and a cover of Fleetwood
Mac's awesome *Oh Well*, the inclusion of which was
my sole reason for buying this. Of course McCoy
screws it up, giving it a biker-ish speed metal spin, still
leaving the only brilliant rendition that I can recall as
one by The Rockets, which I haven't heard in eight

years. **Mini Album** features the immensely talented
Paul Samson on guitar but you wouldn't know it.
Rating                                                                  3

## McCoy - Think Hard  (Mausoleum '85)

Doesn't strike me as too different from Mammoth,
Alaska, or Tormé for that matter, **Think Hard** finds Big
Bald John (think Chris Slade or April Wine's drummer)
doing just that, thinking too hard in hopes of someday
becoming a songwriter, stifling the visceral Paul Samson in the process. And it's going to take the man a few
more years to achieve his goal, judging from these
simple but ineffective fragments of ideas.
Rating                                                                  4

## MC5 - Kick Out The Jams  (Elektra '68)

Verging on heavy metal, but more a loud, bashing blast
of wasted anarchy rock '60s-style, **Kick Out The
Jams** is an unexpected cornerstone of early heavy
metal, questionable due to the two shakey studio
follow-ups, records crammed with noodly, back to the
bong activist banter and deconstructed hysterics, not
to mention straight-faced '50s rock. Not the reply we
looked for following the clanging flare that was **Kick
Out The Jams**. Along with medicinal buds the
Stooges, MC5 (house band for the White Panther
party) were a new, volatile needlemark on rock'n'roll,
embracing a life of drugs, free love and the occasional
terrorist action. And **Kick Out The Jams**, recorded
Hallowe'en '68 in Detroit, is amusing given that backdrop, truly an early distortion rock classic, if not built
like a convincing heavy metal pig. The performance is
intense, bordering on edgy collapse, capturing the heat
of the hawks versus doves era. Faves would include the
smothering *Rocket Reducer No. 62 (Rama Lama Fa Fa
Fa)*, the Sabslow *I Want You Right Now* and the hep title
cut, but really the whole magically dated mess is just a
tangle of crusty, rusted wires, led by Rob Tyner's (R.I.P.)
call to arms. One of the main claimed influences of the
'70s punk set, although more in buzzard spirit than in
substance.
Rating                                                                  8

## MC5 - Back In The USA  (Atlantic '70)

With high-powered rose-coloured glasses, I can almost
visualize what all the fuss was about. On this first studio
(and I use the term loosely) record for the band, MC5
pre-date The Dictators, The Lyres and The Ramones
more than metal or punk, **Back In The USA** being a
hazy, crazy mania rocker; '60s biker grit and grease

261

with scrapyard doggies like *Teenage Lust, Looking At You* and *Call Me Animal* for songs. Really, really funny for its hapless ancientness, far and away more tiny than chemical cohorts The Stooges. Pret' near the thinnest recording I've ever heard, tweeters and tweezers is about all you'll require for an accurate portrayal of MC5's unique Flintstones flavourings. But there's something hip amongst all the erroneous rock'n'roll here, real reasons for MC5's alleged historical significance as prime and primal purveyors of all that is smelly about rock music. Turned-up '60s pop with a leather jacket. Interesting, and as Bobby Vinton is wont to say of his own music: so far out, it's in.

Rating      7

## MC5 - High Time    (Atlantic '71)

The third and last from Detroit's second baddest is also the band's third completely whacked-out departure (as if this band ever possessed a conscious centre), only overt constant in the brief fireball of a catalogue being Tyner's splendid speech-making abilities. **High Time** adopts psychedelic era packaging, putting an "everything Owsley but the kitchen sink" spin on the carnival of sights and sounds inside. And quite a spectacle it is, kicking off with the warmed-over choogling funky sweat of *Sister Anne* and *Baby Won't Ya*. The cool thing about **High Time** is its unrestrained monster instrumentation of what is basically slack-minded hippy music; better for the busy-ness, for the brashness and raw dressed-up, like a big be-in where everybody is given a brownie to munch on, then something/anything to play or hit. And the bed tracks are robust and rockin', a sort of jumpy guitar sockhop, not quite metal but riding that fine line between universal love and vandalism, primitive and nervous, culminating in the distress of *Poison*, '60s rock truly aflame. Just the swirling confusion of it all is something to gawk at, a statement of oatmeal more in tune with the mind-blowing wattage associated with the revolution than the revolution itself. Just those darn kids misbehavin'. Update: Rob Tyner and Fred "Sonic" Smith (husband of Patti Smith) are now dead. Chrome-domed Wayne Kramer is back kicking at the '90s with his venomous record **The Hard Stuff** and a follow-up in '95.

Rating      8

## McQueen Street - McQueen Street    (SBK '91)

Not a poodle band, not exactly vicious rock by urban pit bulls, McQueen Street is more like Main Street for a sound gone by, kinda reminding me of snappier Canadian boys Sven Gali before grunge. Still, there's no good reason to glom onto something this unremarkable. Crispy, tight production and leonine roars from lead muscle beach Derek Welsh are about all that raise eyebrows here. Competent but destroyed by a premise that is dead in the water.

Rating      6

## Machine Head - Burn My Eyes    (Roadrunner '94)

For those who mutter to themselves (damn deep green with envy) that Pantera is somehow too clean or too produced and therefore, less heavy, here comes SF's Machine Head (bruisechild of former Violence axeman Robb Flynn), again a band who can arguably be deemed the heaviest mutha on the planet. Eagerly anticipated in underground circles, **Burn My Eyes** lives up to the hype, turning up the burners on metal's inherent violence, smacking tight, technical metal with a backhand built blasted by the likes of Entombed, another buzz band right up there in terms of raucousness. Machine Head scorches big-time, combining scraping production values, accessible grindcore vocals (see Paradise Lost) and big, well-planned uber-anthem-epics built as mean as they come, lyrics bridging Biohazard's urban jungle with Trouble's inner, introspective torment. Hopefully more of this really pulver-

izing, rhythmic, loose-circuited stuff is going to flourish in the coming years, many calling the long-anticipated Slayer Fall '94 release a sort of litmus test for the world's acceptance of this heart-bursting extreme of the genre. Machine Head are wasting no time gaining massive respect, sitting poised to contend, no prisoners, no apologies. Killer chops colliding with an uncanny grasp of chaos. Drenched with star quality, no small credit to wunder producer Colin Richardson.

Rating      9

## Machine Head - The More Things Change
(Roadrunner/Attic '97)

Many hair-whitening experiences later, Robb Flynn and crew return, a little worse for wear. After touring for fifteen months, selling well nigh 500,000 copies of **Burn My Eyes** in the process (half in North America, half in Europe), the assembly of **The More Things Change** commenced. Many delays ensued, due to botched mixes, accidentally erased guitar parts and vocals, car accidents, and burglaries of the band's gear. The record has finally arrived, and reviews are mixed, moreso from the standard set by the debut, this one being a bit of a repeater. Positively speaking, new drummer Dave McClain (from Sacred Reich) steals the show, tornado-moshing through each aggressive track, recalling the best of Dave Lombardo and Vinnie Paul. Also, Flynn's vocals are more versatile, the man's singing being more soulful, his bark more bitten, an effect which mirrors the record's arrangements, which demonstrate greater peaks and valleys than the debut. The bottom line is this: Machine Head are a great metal band, true top-flight creators, but this over-the-top anger stuff can fatigue, adding a hint of soul-lessness or emptiness or antagonism between band and fan. It's the Fear Factory syndrome all over again: efficient machine or fallible humans? Is the record forced, overwritten musically, but lyrically under-conceived? Maybe. Or is this just the case of a jaded, overwhelmed, consumer of too much metal merely needing something to complain about? Why do I agonize? Because I care. Here's an **8**, a damn solid grade, but I almost feel guilty . . .

Rating      8

## Machines Of Loving Grace - Gilt    (Mammoth/Attic '95)

Yeah, y'know it's heavy but it's humanless and humourless, not to mention so buzzed-up with itchy sound that my eyes just glaze. **Gilt** is like a dour, sour, creepy Killing Joke record, stiff with dull, knobby vocals, invitingly psycho like NIN but just overworked like similar industrial contraptions like Prick, Dink and even Stabbing Westward. Five tunes here could be coasty, wastey-type things on a White Zombie spread, but what would be the point of that? Produced by Sylvia Massey, who stopped Tool from making records.

Rating      6

## Madball - Ball Of Destruction    (Century Media '96)

Madball has been considered a baby Agnostic Front, due to Madball's leader being Freddy Cricien, little bro of AF's Roger Miret. The band's sound is typical crankcase hardcore punk with welcome metal overtones, very smeared, geared and primed for mosh-pit destruction. First record **Set It Off** climbed to sales of 50,000 copies, setting the stage for this reissue of the band's highly-prized first single and a bunch of live tracks plus odds 'n' sods (including three Agnostic Front covers). Buncha noise really, even if these guys matter amongst this hope-void genre.

Rating      4

## Madball - Demonstrating My Style    (Roadrunner/Attic '96)

Yeesh, stand back, as Madball injects the venom, kicking off with a title track that is a big metal hairball, honed through hardcore and rap, but triumphant metal all the same. Then *Live Or Die* unleashes more of the same, establishing these former oi-ish oiks as something beyond Biohazard. Even the hammer-hearted fast ones are looped metal science, *Streets Of Hate* moshing with prog rock rhythms and tempo shifts, all the while Matt Henderson's guitars sounding like rolling boulders, an uppercut of doom brought to the sewers of the city. Big hoovering improvements all around (that is, if you crave metal and not hardcore!), Madball finally glueing disparate hard music elements into something with a life of its own, something that makes you forget the base building blocks, all the while the band shotgun-blasting solid, confident songs.

Rating                                                                 8

## Mad Max - Mad Max   (Roof Est. '82)

Mad Max's inauspicious debut contains nary a hint of the Teutonic metal professionalism to come on albums II and III; for reasons not the least of which is the fact that present vocalist Andrea Baesler doesn't deserve to lick the leather booties of future wunder-throat Michael Voss. Hidden beneath the dime-store production lie traces of the stirring headiness of **Rollin' Thunder**, if only in basic structure, but it's far from enough to ever warrant spinning this for actual pleasure. Rough around the edges with fairly purposeless edges, **Mad Max** is a predictably premature first effort.

Rating                                                                 4

## Mad Max - Rollin' Thunder   (Roadrunner '84)

One of the more palatable and tidy metal outfits from Germany allowed to make repeated recorded overtures to Lady Fame (to no avail). **Rollin' Thunder** contains a lot of stops and starts, chugging riffery, intensely Euro melodies, and engaging vocal work from new guy Michael Voss, leaving the listener in considerable but unremarkable admiration of most of the album, most notably the mid-paced Acceptisms such as *Fly Fly Away*, *Riding Through The Night* and frosty, dejected cruiser *Losing You*, which all evolve seamlessly into melting and memorable choruses of utmost classicism. However, all is not rolling boulders, as Mad Max pursues more than its formulaic share of diversity here including headache-inducing (but fragile) speed metal and one long, dreary power ballad, rendering **Rollin' Thunder** a strong and projecting record, yet disorienting in its multiple power levels. Really stood out at the time, and still rocks with its own unassuming pride.

Rating                                                                 7

## Mad Max - Stormchild   (Roadrunner '85)

Even when trying to reach out and touch someone, this icy Euro-gloss always manages to sound medieval and creepy. **Stormchild** sees Mad Max raising the stakes on quality, details, and complexity while remaining molten and Teutonically melodic. Proud and chrome-plated yet still tragic, **Stormchild** embodies that push/pull philosophy that ices the veins with emotional paralysis while superficially courting human connection. Thus, admired but often avoided.

Rating                                                                 8

## Mad Season - Above   (Sony '95)

If yer looking for trouble, then Layne Staley's your man these days, rumours abounding of the AiC vocalist's continuing heroin problems and the on/off demise of the Grinch/grunge powerhouse that he charismatically leads. So here, the man creates a Temple of The Dog-type side project for '95, collaborating with notable Mike McCready from Pearl Jam and other assorted Seattle semi-somebodies for this muted, depressing but more uptempo version of AiC's unplugged **Sap/Jar Of Flies** freaky styley. Even the recording is somewhat treble-challenged, as the band shuffles through tuneful, bluesy but entirely drooped and stooped low-cruise/no-cruise numbers that are almost exclusively

toe-tagged "OD: combination of horse, downers, bad attitude and death-warmed squalor." Like I say, mellow, trippy and defeated like the EPs but more fully-instrumentalized, even rising to lobotomy metal twice or thrice. Scary as all get out, so I guess it works, even if it's just too sunny outside and in my head for me to wanna know.

Rating                                                                 7

## Mahogany Rush - Maxoom   (20th Century '73)

Rather than spend pages waxing poetically over the Mahogany Rush repertoire, I've chucked in a few reviews of representative records (old, middle, new, all blue) for your displeasure. Suffice to say, Frank's vast catalogue represents a hugely Hendrix-based scourge of loudness; rarely heavy metal, always dense, soupy, and wrought with painful, dog whistle guitar solos, all blurring and segueing into Jimi-jonesing etherealism, occasionally and wondrously emitting wads of welting metal briefly at the rate of one or two cuts per record (makes a great various tape). But this debut is pretty trippy. Sure it's Hendrix-based, but there's real drugs flowing through this. The boys are on fire when rocking (*All In Your Mind* and *Back On Home*), and freaky when freakin' (*Maxoom* and exquisite southern rocker *Boardwalk Lady*), dancing through this lively electricfest way better than Amboy Dukes could ever dream. Lots of tangents, way more than on future morose mud.

Rating                                                                 6

## Mahogany Rush - Child Of The Novelty
(20th Century '74)

Montreal's voodoo children are back with another groovy, psychedelic album cover wrapping another groovy, psychedelic batch of power trio trips that refuse to believe the '70s are in full swing. Whether you can stomach the dirty funk blues metal of the whole thing can be immaterial if you just focus on where that axe is going, not to mention James Ayoub's light progressive percussion touch and Paul Harwood's spider-fingered bass licks. Faves: tasty ballad *Chains Of (S)pace* and the wonky weirdness of *Changing*, but the thing to get hip to here is the space-walking versatility, even if it's totally, almost miserably old.

Rating                                                                 6

## Mahogany Rush - Strange Universe   (20th Century '75)

Strange indeed, as Frank and his time-locked wizards pull their Jimi job until the link is thin and ready to snap. The heaviest tracks here are *Tryin' Anyway* and *Dear Music*, with much of the rest winging out on a pharmaceutica tab, courting blues, pseudo jazz, wild prog and general kick back and drift. Eccentric recording too, with loads of cavernous echo. Cool CD note: these first three records were reissued on one double CD set by UK company Big Beat. Cool, given how these records have been firmly in the rarity category since the late '70s.

Rating                                                                 5

## Frank Marino & Mahogany Rush - World Anthem
(CBS '77)

Said album featured is no exception to Frank's fret-fired rule, hatching the righteously snakey *Requiem For A Sinner*, an evil *Kashmir*-ic number demonstrating subjugated genius behind Marino's misplaced obsession. After the feedback has settled however, this one offers the usual range of comatose to scorch-osity, all points north and south designed to enthrall the Trower-ites and Hendrix-onians amongst ye. Beware: **World Anthem** actually attempts to write and *explain* an actual world anthem.

Rating                                                                 5

## Frank Marino & Mahogany Rush - Tales Of The Unexpected (CBS '79)

One of the poorer post-Uli Jon Roth wankfests from our man Frankie, **Tales** is one half sloppy studio foray, and one half sloppy live deci-ball. And it's the studio side that features *All Along The Watchtower* and *Norwegian Wood*. Break out the party hats. And if you're still with us, the tinny, scratchy mix of the whole bluesy funk feedback fest will send you into the wings but quick.
Rating **4**

## Frank Marino & Mahogany Rush - What's Next (CBS '80)

And the answer is anything but this, Frankie subjecting us to his junkiest, funkiest batch of noise sculptures yet, **What's Next** being technically one of the man's "heaviest" records, if only for the fact that it's so unclean and loose. Fave part? Why, the extra wrench on the back cover, of course, pretty much everything else about this fatigued body shop of psychedelic biker noodling just annoying the senses like a howling dog. The cover of *Roadhouse Blues* actually made it to radio now and again, but doesn't one always? Self-produced into the toilet.
Rating **5**

## Frank Marino - From The Hip (Par Excellence/Vision '93)

Pretty wild (not in a good or bad way, if that's possible) to hear Marino really nailing his roots, driving the soup back to Hendrix again, or old Mahogany Rush, perhaps deciding a boutique, cottage industry career is just fine, if I gets to play da blues da way Jimi heard 'em. So consider this one straddling commercial songs and those Mike Varney-produced guitar showcases, being accessible yet full of noodling. Even the mix sounds straight outta the baby boomer era to which the record might appeal (at least the closet axe warriors), oddly cloudy when it comes to the guitar and Marino's Uli Jon Roth vocal stylings. Fave: resplendent psychedelic blues ballad *Rise Above*, which steps outside the box, and at 11:37 stays out there for a friggin' long time. Otherwise, pretty heavy, at least in Marino's slinky '60s frame of reference. Note: big gaps in Marino story here, skipping "solo" records like **The Power Of Rock'n'Roll**, **Juggernaut** (killer sped metal title track!), and **Full Circle**. Older ones missed include **IV** and **Live**, and that may be all of them.
Rating **6**

## Maineeaxe - Shout It Out (Banzai '84)

One of those weird situations where the debut exhibits more polish than the follow-up, **Shout It Out** straddles more conservative production values and indeed more conservative riffing, which is basic, kinda uneventful but still palatable. Vocals are flat although strangely arresting, and side two shows major slam. Trying too hard to express calm maturity.
Rating **6**

## Maineeaxe - Going For Gold (Banzai '85)

A quintet of perennial losers for no justifiable reason, Maineeaxe suffered commercial inattention probably due to off-base marketing; a cheezy name, all too cheery looking band photos, and inappropriate graphics. The whole presentation of the band flies soundly in the face of the punky, energetic, Grim Reaper-ish assault of this surprisingly fiery, violently recorded slab of Brit metal, a record that lays treadmarks to the metallic face of hard rock 'neath a rowdy, Ebony-like buzzsaw of a mix (although not so heavily committed), not to mention the wailing lead vox which evoke a fluid combination of throats from the same Ebony stable. Again, it's so easy to be psyched away by the deleted nature of Maineeaxe's uninspiring half-life. Put the

prejudices aside, slap down yer 99¢ and immerse yourself in this fairly kickin', raucous display of sonic boozery. No matter what town you call home, it's gotta be worth the asking price.
Rating **7**

## Malevolent Creation - Retribution (The All Blacks B.V. '92)

Early Malevolent Creation sounds much like early Death, both carrying the stamp of Scott Burns' powerful but somewhat congested recording values, both vocalized somewhere between thrash and grindcore, both creating walls of technical sound at many speeds. Fortunately, both improved as time went on, perhaps fuelled and rebirthed by a similar situation in terms of near dissolution, Malevolent Creation's due to label hassles, Death's due to personnel hassles.
Rating **5**

## Malevolent Creation - Eternal (Pavement '95)

If you're ready to wade into the deeper, darker, shark-infested waters of extreme metal, Florida's Malevolent Creation will greet you at the door with a tumbler of whiskey and a foot-long spliff, quickly initiating you into their surprisingly listenable but vicious grindcore madness. Why it works is beyond me, possibly the electrocuted production, the twisted death-prog drumming, the whacked-out soloing, or the many speeds and anti-speeds. Not saying I have the steadiness to reach for this on many occasions, but as far as the slammiest stuff goes, this is a drill to the head that releases some degree of pressure. The band's fourth.
Rating **7**

## Malevolent Creation - Joe Black (Pavement '96)

Malevolent Creation continue to burn holes in the stale corpse of death metal, some of their experiments working, some of them not. **Joe Black** (brilliant title, brilliant, non-death artwork) is an odds 'n' sods project offers ten track of terrorism, three being trendy remixes from **Eternal**, but three being absolute scorched earth non-album tunes, recorded during the **Eternal** sessions but left vaulted and screaming until now. All are gravity-defying shards of precious radio-active metal, in my opinion, better than most that made the record. Elsewhere, a demo version from '94's **Stillborn**, a couple of '90 demos that got them their first deal, and a wicked cover of Slayer's *Raining Blood*. Disjointed of course, but this stereophonic pop combo is quickly becoming a top-flight force in the halls of death.
Rating **7**

## Malformed Earthborn - Defiance Of The Ugly By The Merely Repulsive (Relapse '95)

More of a Project Joke by a trio of noisecore pros, **Defiance** is one way-too-long tangle of crusty, caustic industrial grind, laced with and corroded by more extreme pure distortion as per Jap crap like Merzbow. Twelve sick soundscapes, twelve visions of music as disemboweling agent, which means of course that any hardy, logical soul will race this through to the end but quick, and then file as oddity never to be revisited for any conceivable reason. Utter hogswallow.
Rating **2**

## Malice - In The Beginning . . . (Atlantic '85)

Malice was a solid, American outfit that seemed set for accolades, yet sadly never reached major recognition, suffering much the same frustration as parallel band Armored Saint. **In The Beginning . . .** riffed its way through chest-thumping, clear-headed metal like a cross between **British Steel** and **Point Of Entry**; nice, fat guitar sound, simple, mid-paced beats, and totally Halford-influenced vocals from James Neal. A capable, confident record, easy to strap on, which was the intention, this band pre-packed 'n ready with logo,

label, big name producer and even laughable tour wear which made them look like the L.A. Raiders of the headbangers ball. Detrimental hints of its era and its hope, but for the most part, still makes the grade.
Rating 7

## Malice - License To Kill (Atlantic '87)

More of the same Winnebago-riffed chunk metal, low on frills, carried by the versatile vocals of James Neal, the metal acumen of Jay Reynolds, and the power of the band's convictions. But still a little corporate, laid-back and well-groomed, as if the boys in the band are already looked upon as boardroom darlings, first predictable outcome of such treatment being stifled drumming and arrangements. **License To Kill** thumps and chugs start to finish but with uniform, sweatless energy, lacking the peaks and valleys of stars versus dogs, which to my mind is almost the preferred state of a good if not great album. Here Malice has located its groove, really having no external or internal inclination to stray from it, leaving the listener level rather than leveled. Long since long gone, last release being posthumous four song EP **Crazy In The Night**.
Rating 7

## Malicious Intent - Shades Of Black (Resistance '89)

Riffs worthy of Celtic Frost whipped into a frenzied speed inferno to the usual artistic non-avail. When will this genre learn that all its heavier-than-thou intentions fly out the window when all points of the compass flail their limbs at a hopped-up 78 RPM, doomed to come across like blasphemed munchkins on nitrous oxide? Simply put, speed becomes double time, and double time hath no groove. Standard thrash garbage wrecked by twisted misunderstanding of the word speed. Sounds identical to about thirty other flying crapola ships.
Rating 0

## Mallet-Head - Mallet-Head (Frontier '88)

C'mon, you've seen this one in the delete bins a hundred times. Well I finally bit for a buck and it ain't half bad. College metal sturdy and simple, but verging on polite punk, **Mallet-Head** has wisecrack written all over it, although the power chords are loud and clear, as are the grooves, even though it's engineering student rock all the way, with all the usual detrimental connotations afforded indie product. Almost a **5**.
Rating 4

## Yngwie J. Malmsteen's Rising Force -Yngwie J. Malmsteen's Rising Force (Polydor '84)

Record one, and the wonder Swede fashions himself a guitar god. Well, as much as his childish petulance would have you deny it, he *is* one, recognized far before this first solo outing as a ferociously talented fret burner complete with his very own, classical music-based ideas, complex scale runs and thoughtfully conceived solos. But I never paid much attention to this one, 'cos it's mostly instrumental, and in '90s retrospect, totally unnecessary, given the swack of great solos on his "vocals" albums.
Rating 4

## Yngwie J. Malmsteen's Rising Force -Marching Out (PolyGram '85)

The state-of-the-art gothic metal record arrives on the burning wings of a bona fide axe god, one arrogant Swede with unswerving Nietzschean visions of immortal grandeur, built of fierce talent, obsession for the guitar and desire towards fusing classical music (the stateliness of Bach and the devilishness of Paganini) with uncompromising but scientifically disciplined heavy metal. The successful fulfillment of such goals bring Yngwie to this masterpiece of the genre, a record that necessarily taps into influences such as Rainbow and Priest and really little else, catapulting itself way beyond into totally focused classical-based metal, intense and timeless expressions of goth. Within the realms of a single record, one can't do it all, but on **Marching Out**, Malmsteen is clearly agonizing towards being the very best at what he does, painstakingly constructing this monument to Valhalla; brooding castle rock, blazing with Yngwie's feverishly intelligent (and much copied) soloing style and deadly heroic riffs, while demanding peak performances from his band of ultimately disposable mortals. The end result is a dead serious work of art, an elaborate palace of lightning-fast auditory inundation, an exacting but scorching piece of achievement metal full of pride and bombast, but totally to the point, aggressive and wisely anchored by the rules of song construction, a necessary factor in raising this above academic into such uncouth realms as kick-ass. Obscenely elegant, but always metallic in the extreme.
Rating 10

## Yngwie J. Malmsteen - Trilogy (PolyGram '86)

Riding the razor's edge between gothic metal and Euro hard rock is a risky proposition, the latter comparatively lacking depth of possibility, often sounding incompatible with the standard dungeons and dragons imagery so associated with goth. Here the fusion works, although the results are often cold and clammy, like a mist on the moors, driving **Trilogy** to a sort of alternative fate, an isolated feel, still fanatically gothic, yet almost dainty but dead, like an apparition in a tattered wedding gown. New throat Mark Boals completes the circle with his Dio-ish soars and growls, playing right into the hands of the typical medieval connotations. Fave would be *Magic Mirror*, one of the dirtier, less prim rockers on this dark and mysterious journey. A concept of increasingly limited personal appeal.
Rating 8

## Yngwie J. Malmsteen's Rising Force -Odyssey (PolyGram '88)

Less the underground seclusion of **Trilogy**, **Odyssey** warms up with the totally appropriate acquisition of Joe Lynn Turner for revolving microphone duties. Of course, Turner is Mr. Goth Pin-up himself, the perfect reinforcement for Malmsteen's increasingly hard rock direction, a fusion that works well on *Crystal Ball*, the strange *Now Is The Time* and lead single *Heaven Tonight*. Elsewhere, the harpsichord-like keyboards tend to intrude, even though there's still a hefty number of trademark OTT speed rockers here, fastidious as they may be. Solid, bombastic, self-important metal, but any semblance of humanity is grudgingly offered, Malmsteen for better or worse, still barricading himself in a castle without heat or lighting.
Rating 7

## Yngwie Malmsteen - Eclipse (PolyGram '90)

The first major collapse of the Malmsteen mission, **Eclipse** is definitely more prissy goth-pop than metal; bad, dishwater parodies of past grandeur with too many keyboard parts and a thin drum sound. And new vocalist Goran Edman is fairly expressionless while of course, smooth and competent. Best moments: the funky *Bedroom Eyes* and the racing *Motherless Child*. Otherwise, bloated and relaxed, as Yngwie buries himself in his deluded rut.
Rating 6

## Yngwie Malmsteen - Fire & Ice (Elektra '92)

The path established one record back is traveled into the sewers of poseur rock. Yngwie is long gone into forced sensitivity of which he has none. Candy-assed pop metal with the usual unshakeable gothic twingings. And critically reviled to boot.

Rating 3

## Yngwie Malmsteen - The Seventh Sign (BMG '94)

Largely a welcome correction, Yngwie possibly noting the demise of poodle rock, cranks back to what he does best, complete metal craftsmanship, isolated deep within a belief of what is pure and noble of cause. There will always be a market of some sort for Yngwie's marvelous metal acumen, even if the songwriting pines for days gone by, becoming dated and politically incorrect: nobody is supposed to show off to this hair-raising extent. And of course YJM gives his fans what they crave, hopelessly gothic ornament of many speeds, a few moody massive ballads, lightning digitized instrumentals and a fiercely energized blues called I Don't Know (oh yes he does). Faves would include Never Die, Meant To Be and the golden cheez of the title track. But suffice to say, now after all the misdirection, Yngwie can be applauded for staying with a club of which he is lone remaining member or more accurately, a leader of ten or twelve goneby '80s virtuosos, all making records that are appreciated with fanatical zeal in Japan if nowhere else. A bit of everything, and some of it so out-of-touch with reality, but isn't that where eccentric genius lives? Oh, and by the way, the velocities are unparalleled anywhere in the catalogue, and probably anywhere on the planet.

Rating 7

## Yngwie Malmsteen - Magnum Opus

(Music For Nations '95)

Same core band as the last is back (Yngwie, Mike Vescera on vocals and Matts Olausson on keyboards), for a record that is dead identical and loving it, graphically even using the exact same greens, purples and blacks, the band kicking out a glorious batch of technically high-minded mini-suites that cannot be matched in the unreal speed-goth realm of things. One ballad, a couple of inhuman instrumentals, and eight tall Viking hikes turn **Magnum Opus** elegant and majestic indeed; if filters are working, pretty well indistinguishable from the ten-year-old Yngwie records that were such an over-achieving part of my young punted life. Production is of course blended to perfection, rapid-fire keyboards and axes doing interwoven battle 'neath Vescera's gruff goth operatics. Just a whole heap of roiling Valhalla clouds, making the spirit sing in sword-swinging ecstasy. Foist ye draft up high and hail the metal gods!

Rating 8

## Yngwie Malmsteen - Inspiration (Music For Nations '96)

Cool to see one of metal's purported bigger egos devoting a record to songs he didn't write, Yngwie paying homage to his influences in typical clinical fashion. Of course this sounds razor-chopped as all get out, similar to those second tier tribute records (Priest, Purple, Rush, Stevie Ray, Cream) that sound less impressive with each subsequent release. Average song selection, most vapid, insipid and pointless being Mistreated, Child In Time and Manic Depression, most thrilling being Carry On My Wayward Son, The Sails Of Charon, Pictures Of Home (lots of cymbals!) and hands-down winner, U.K.'s In The Dead Of Night, probably the only really surprising choice on the whole mildly interesting project.

Rating 7

## Maltese Falcon - Metal Rush (Est. '85)

A sliver above average for that rash of Euro bands getting releases in the mid '80s against all logic. Nice biker grime to it, despite its addressing the world of technically sound goth metal. Ah, youth.

Rating 5

## Mama's Boys - Mama's Boys (Jive '84)

Zero excitement left for this hyped trio of Brit (Irish?) brothers, who garnered acclaim more for fiddle solos and above average professionalism than great songs. Big bucks production, perfect harmonies and a warm inclusive hard rock sound made this safe, amiable and above all, accessible, something rare among early overseas metallic warriors. So it stood above the fray, looking down its nose with an appropriate ironic humility as underdogs making good. But years later, it's just barroom rock'n'roll like bad Santers or Goddo. Yeah, kinda Canadian.

Rating 5

## Mama's Boys - Power And Passion (Jive '85)

Same thing . . . polite, easygoing rock'n'roll you can bring home to mama, vanilla American fare from overseas, aseptically and unremarkably captured by Chris Tsangarides; ever so slightly more annoying in terms of song mix, particularly come chorus time with harmonies a bit too frequent and ingratiating (not to mention thin). Just no real urge to blow anyone away.

Rating 4

## Mama's Boys - Growing Up The Hard Way (Jive '87)

Never really a serious contender stateside, England's squeaky clean and capable Mama's Boys (three brothers + 1, hence the name) seal their doom with this awful commercial piece of panic pop, burying their previously-tame-anyways axes beneath layers of percussive electronics and keyboard tricks. Simply terrible sit-com rock aimed squarely at raising some cash, a ploy so sadly resigned to failure due to the total boredom that has always cloaked this band's nerdy output, no matter how loud. Contains a comatose delivery of Stevie Wonder's Higher Ground.

Rating 1

## Mammoth - Mammoth (BMG '89)

It's public and painful knowledge that fat guys in a band spell doom for commercial acceptance (exception: Meatloaf's 25 million seller **Bat Out Of Hell**). So what happens when you corral four washed-up, fleshy chunks in one place, form a novelty band called Mammoth, and pen a tune called Fatman? You sink four times as fast. Two of the blobs I'm not familiar with, however we all know bassist John McCoy, whose best days were spent with Gillan, and lead throat Nicky Moore, who tried to make a bluesy go of it on two classy Samson records. **Mammoth** topples more towards the simple and stupid bass-driven rock that becomes a McCoy project; unpleasant, unlistenable, wimpy retro-rock with intrusive keyboards, wildly inappropriate melodic choruses, and laughable attempts at mystery, y'know . . . clunky, clattery slow stuff that sound like tunes written for rolly-polly middle-aged rock vets to play live. Tasty axe solos, otherwise miserable.

Rating 3

## Manhole - All Is Not Well (Noise '96)

First there was Hole, now there's Manhole, lead rapper/vocalist Tairrie B. going way beyond C. Love's wastecase meander into one freaky, slamming demonstration of gangsta rap metal, very political and angry like RATM, Biohazard and Downset, and just as musically sharp. But rap metal ain't to my taste, as ain't rap, both making me feel like the short end of a mugging, or at least a chewing out. And this doesn't improve on the genre either.

Rating 6

## Maniac - Maniac (Hot Blood '85)

Hot Blood continues to act as second tier stable for uncompromising strains of Germanic zeal through the

premature signing of bands still in training for their iron crosses. Maniac fits the bill, captured well before the minimum command of English necessary to divert attention towards the power chords. A bit cheezy and dirty compared to usual German adherences to quality.
Rating 4

## Manic Street Preachers - Gold Against The Soul
(Sony '93)
Weird hybrid this one, sounding like a souped-up and considerably metallic melodic new wave/general rock-type band with great songs. The look is quite non-specific also, sorta glammy and unwashed at the same time, and the overall package is very British indeed, going for that healthy ideal of musicians just trying to write natural music, no influences, no sleazy agenda. And I'd say they've done a good job of it, sounding truly heroic and uplifting throughout, almost a Clash or U2 ethic with loud guitars, featuring vocals from James Dean Bradfield that inflect heavily towards Freddie Mercury, a comparative one doesn't find too often. Choruses are usually soaring and heartfelt, in direct contrast to the fairly distressed and druggy nature of the well-written lyric bank. Most of Gold rocks up-rightly, perhaps mirroring U.K. brethren Terrorvision at their heavier, less pop-panderable moments. I can see how this record might be rejected by some, definitely riding that "self-important" vibe for some intangible reason. But to my mind, the band makes that fine transition to actually important, these rich and varied guitar-drenched tales propped with stirring hooks and thoughtful arrangements, despite in no way behaving like the songs of other bands this electric. In the end, Gold Against The Soul soaks up all things English like a sponge, letting deluge through the sounds of a talented band blessed with golden ears for quality hard rock hookery. Refreshing fer sure.
Rating 9

## Manic Street Preachers - The Holy Bible (Sony '94)
Having guitarist Richey James vanish without a trace casts a mysterious pall over this vibrant, sparkling but tragically cynical fist of a record. The Holy Bible revives the same axe fireworks found on its predecessor, but lyrically Wire and James have built a flaring, condemning shrine to the ideals of poison British punk, spitting out a daring, intellectual treatise on society's eye-watering stench, while those superhero power chords slash and crash through titles like Of Walking Abortion and Die In The Summertime, both weighted unto the earth's baked metal centre with the hairiest of depressions. And it's that chemistry between daggers for words and silky, seductive vocals, tough, contortioned, embattled verse riffs and big pay-off choruses, that makes the Preachers' sermon so insidious, grinning from ear to ear as the muzzle jabs deep up the ribs. All comes to a head with Revol, the band's paean to Communist leaders and their sexual deviances, a song delivered over a steamrolling punk metal blast that is pure hard music euphoria. Bloody 'ell!
Rating 9

## Manic Street Preachers - Everything Must Go
(Sony '96)
Beginning life as a yukky, plainly deflating album cover, Everything Must Go finds this somewhat severed but blessed band softening their textures and their core song decisions, perhaps the disappeared taking with him those amps that go to eleven. But I still find these guys a criminally engaging concept. Personal faves are not surprisingly the stout of volume explosions (of which there are few), Interiors really taking the golden cake, rocking the fillings come chorus time, those black clouds breaking like they did five times on the last couple records. Elsewhere, it's thoughtful, pensive,

and fatigued of texture, flirting with fussy British things like The Jam, XTC, and The Smiths, while really arriving at the mauve of the cover art. Crooked smiles all around. Crucial crucible rock for the thinking man, even if drained of colour.
Rating 8

## Manilla Road - The Deluge (Black Dragon '86)
If I could shake the visions of Spock's creepy relatives giving me that neck thing every time I hear the over-lordic strains of vocalist Mark W. Shelton, I might learn to groove on this band's shakey but chemically volatile demonic death goth. For indeed, all is sceptres and entrails on this progressive flesh feast, ambitiously assembled and thoughtfully riffed, amongst such tasty-frozen power tools as Hammer Of The Witches, Morbid Tabernacle, and Friction In Mass. From Kansas, yet so deadly German smelling.
Rating 6

## Manitoba's Wild Kingdom - . . . And You? (MCA '90)
The handsome one steps back to the mike after "taking the '80s off to get my head together", dragging into the pit with him old soulmates Andy Shernoff and Ross The Boss, recently vacated from Manowar. And what we have is a tough-as-nails, heavy metal Dick, armed with ten sawed-off highballs (totalling an inexcusable 26:32), low on frills, high on metro NRG, and steeped in the traditional, affable Dictators' philosophy which basically espouses survival of the coolest for anybody stupid enough to live in NYC. Caught the tour, the band was smokin', and Dick seemed bent on loud revenge, as he tore through blinding, almost punk ravers like Fired Up and Speedball, which brings me to my only complaint with this record (outside of brevity): the baffling similarity between no less than the last five cuts, half this record, all fast, simple, ranting and low on lustre. But never ye fret, because lead single The Party Starts Now, New York, New York and especially D.W.I. (the best '50s/Dictators/'60s/Elvis/'70s toon ever), rank right up their with heavies from Bloodbrothers and Manifest Destiny, perfect timeless anthems of bravado, sweat and selfless humour. Surprisingly far from the Dictators, Wild Kingdom is fast, to-the-point, economical, almost urgent and built for the bar. Metal all the way, . . . And You? is worthy of your mixed reaction, a record almost too straight-forward for its own good and definitely below ambitious, if at the same time, totally inspiring, as Dick berates a complacent humanity to keep up with him. And no doubt about it, Dick's actions portray a man racing with time.
Rating 8

## Mannequin Beach - Don't Laugh, You're Next
(Mordam '88)
Nebraskan hardcore with vague NoMeansNo-like tendencies; an almost slippery drone that thankfully enters full polka mosh only occasionally, opting for simply accelerated traditional punk, which to my mind, achieves violence more convincingly than the usual thrash tempos. Kinda crungeabilly and white-noise jazzoid at times; dissonant and drowned in its hopeless, way-underground, scumbag anarchy. Tasteless cover graphics featuring dissected lab animals (least I hope they're from a lab).
Rating 4

## Manninya Blade - Merchants In Metal (Killerwatt '86)
Eminently more cagey to pronounce than Tokyo Blade or Jack Blades, Manninya Blade slashes to the fore, causing wretching on par with the blackest of the unclean. Punkin' out with raging sickness, I've come to know and love this record as a wedge of anger, tweaked plain and despaired. Merchants In Metal smokes forth in a quizzling habitat of reptilian anguish, conjuring a terminal Tank, a talented Motörhead, and

god-awful rackets there-placed ensconced as tunes trundle on towards climactic destroy. Then again, I only listen to it once in a black moon.

Rating       7

## Manowar - Battle Hymns   (Liberty '82)

And so it is conceived, the Manowar kingdom, borne of U.S. muscle and might, trash-talking confrontation with those who pose and oppose, spiritual descendants of The Nuge (especially on *Shell Shock*), embracing the new power genre in full combat fatigue. Never mind that the music won't catch up to the spiel until **Hail To England**, vocalist Eric Adams is Attitude on full throttle (fave singers: Ian Gillan and Geoff Tate), and the trademark trashy bass and drums foundation is articulated albeit in somewhat primitive form. Still, while the claims to heaviest on the hill ring a little premature, **Battle Hymns** is chock full o' anthemic punter nuggets, tastiest being *Manowar*, a soccer chant of a tune rendered greasy and trustworthy by Adams' killer delivery. Also our first of many insect-like bass solos with the hyper *William's Tale* (*William Tell Overture* on uppers). Immediately rowdy, outcast alcohol metal with vacuum-packed isolation from current overseas trends, Manowar's debut tends to leak melody like old American metal, an important factor in making this one of the more accessible Manowar mental tattoos, uniformly moving it along into glory ride.

Rating       8

## Manowar - Into Glory Ride   (Megaforce '83)

Parallel this to Trouble's **The Skull**, both following up by slowing it down and crawling under in the name of establishing band psyche; metallic backdrop over which to future play. **Into Glory Ride** is even more crusty and archaic than the debut, smashing and hitting and beating on songs in no way strong enough to take the battery. However, the Manowar religion becomes firmly transcribed with three "of" songs in a row, *Secret Of Steel*, *Gloves Of Metal*, and *Gates Of Valhalla*, which basically sum up (along with the album covers) the band's unstoppable, delusional mission to conquer. Trashy, grungy, and weighted with Viking swords, **Into Glory Ride** is the lost Manowar record, a transition between first life and one of a kind, fur-lined fantasia.

Rating       6

## Manowar - Hail To England   (Music For Nations '84)

Ross The Boss, Eric Adams, Joey DeMaio and Scott Columbus come bone-breaking back with their strongest to date, a record that is my sentimental favorite, arriving at the peak of my metallic dependence. Monikered to thank Manowar's mighty fan base in the U.K. versus a noticeably smaller following stateside, **Hail To England** was a heroic, over-blown facemelt of a record, filled with excessive, mercilessly recorded metal gems, clocked at various welcome velocities, each bloody tale a beacon of stone thumping victoriously on its own. Side one, *Blood Of My Enemies*, *Each Dawn I Die*, *Kill With Power* and the title track is the most solid side of Manowar to date, highlighted by cut three, one face-pasting OTT shredder that became for a good six months my catalyst to rise and move forward each morning. **Hail To England** triumphantly made audible the buzz that metal was capable of installing in one's brain, using typical Manowar language fused to the band's trademark distortion levels to drive the point home like a ruby-encrusted dagger through the heart, all four corners of the attack pulverizing with over-the top beatings of their chosen weapons. In the end, **Hail To England** kills with power because of its unquenchable will to power, a knowledge that its blackened but unbowed spirit cannot be compromised.

Rating       10

## Manowar - Sign Of the Hammer   (10 '84)

And the roaring poseur bonfire finds more vindictive petrol, as the Immovable Four follow up a head-strafing classic with yet another, in a metal year that is owned by the band, at least in terms of respect, underground buzz and European media coverage. Steadfast and resolute in their calling to be the loudest, heaviest, bad-ass force on stage, **Sign Of The Hammer** has that same chaotic, hysterical production sound, a grinding, buzzing battle between pumped-up man and machine, which even infects near ballad *Mountains* (strummed sensitively on bass), a surprisingly catchy piece of dynamic bravado. Top it all off with *Guyana (Cult Of The Damned)*, a tribute to the good reverend Jim and a few hundred dead chosen ones, and you've got one appalling, harrowing trip down Manowar's Nordic coastline in the sky. Perhaps more frenetic and thrashy than its confident predecessor, **Sign Of The Hammer** is nevertheless a power-hungry feast on which to gorge, a journey on which the music nor the lyrics can be taken seriously on their own, only the resulting death tones of their fused attack. Truly a panic of a record for whatever reason.

Rating       8

## Manowar - Fighting The World   (Atlantic '87)

Having been pasted to the wall by Manowar live and in concert, I now can begin to understand the dismally unjust reasons for the band's lack of commercial glory, for fact is, the band's fanbase has been systematically driven to deafness by the unholy wrenching of cavernous howling that is Manowar in the flesh. Yea and verily, mine interest might have waned in these later lean years, were it not for the insane conviction of the band's on and off stage dedication to annihilation. **Fighting The World**, although largely "unheard" if you get my drift, is a fine pageant of ageless lore, a feast of godly strength, recalling the band's finest fistfuls of rage. That tell-tale Manowar sound has been brilliantly fine-aged 'til it rumbles and destroys with more grating fear than henceforth willed, still encrusted with the distorted gutturals of Joey Demaio's bass and Scott Columbus' killer percussive machinations. All of side one is thunderously perfect Manowar, offering one half glory-bound anthems, one half metal-encased statements of war. Side two upholds the band's brave tradition of epic, lumbering into being with the previously released, Orson Welles-narrated *Defender*, then the Valhalla-entombed dynamics of *Holy War*, which comes as a bit of a ponderous lull compared to merciless closer *Black Wind, Fire and Steel*, a characteristic explosion of speed done in typical Manowar disdain for the weak, chafing with raw collisions of bass and vocal will from the supreme and unwielding Eric Adams. After the smoke melts, what hath just occurred is another characteristically muscular offering, one side fully great, one side, sprawling and maybe 1/3 or 1/2 as direct as one might want, spending much time strenuously re-establishing the "Death To False Metal" doctrine and accompanying fur-lined image already labouriously and relentlessly enforced at every lull in the violence. However, despite such sermons which we've grown to love and live for, Manowar is the reigning human bullet of uncompromise, no question. Long live.

Rating       9

## Manowar - Kings Of Metal   (Atlantic '88)

Deeming this band a parody is a futile pursuit in infinite ironic layering, for Manowar is a philosophy of interconnecting unbelievables that just disintegrates into mass ludicrousness under too serious scrutiny. Having said that, **Kings Of Metal** comes along and for once, this band that finds, record after record, impressive and bludgeoning terrain while unrepentantly repeating itself, finally begins to stumble over its past, curmudg-

eoning itself into a dim reflection of the spiel it until now pulled off with impressive weight and authority. Not that **Kings Of Metal** is a waste of space, but it most definitely is chock full of traditional but usually limited Manowar flaws such as bad thrash, lots of silly instrumental interludes, slow, boring sections, extravagant arrangements, and above all one of the poorer mixes in years, something known on the back cover as "full digital recording" which more or less exposes the band's sonic holes, here sounding all clattering and noisy, little in the way of full range or bottom-end muscle (perplexing to me, Eric Adams proudly deemed this closest to the band's live sound). And only now, do the lyrics echo with empty threats. High points: the dramatic and tuneful *Kingdom Come* and the OTT cheeze of *Hail And Kill*. All in all, merely a low calibre collection of songs, blown away at the knees by one uninviting and clanky mix.
Rating                                              6

## Manowar - The Triumph Of Steel   (Atlantic '92)
Manowar's return despite humbling (never!), almost mortal (never!) trials and tribulations embraces the CD age with one endless epic tale about, you guessed it, muscle-beaches with swords, unassumingly deemed *Achilles, Agony And Ecstacy In Eight Parts*, which at 28:37 is destined to throw in every Manowar excess ever mustered under the flag of megaton mastery. Builds, ebbs, flows, mini-songs, ravings, mini-suites and an awe-inspiring, quintessentially metallic drum solo (plus cymbal solo intro) from new boot Rhino, all combine to cut a landscape that is the ultimate Manowar profile, for better and worse; gut-turning textures but, well, long. Anyhow, strapped on the back end, we get no less than seven more caterwauls, all pressing the band to even further extremes; extremes of speed, anger, sloth, quiet seclusion, noise, panic, experimentation, sound effects, solo frenetics and production fanaticism, which is damn near equal to the band's insane live mix. New drummer Rhino and new axeman David Shankle are forces to behold out of necessity, as they assume their respective thrones in a band that manages to showcase everybody all the time. Without a doubt, the most lavish, psychologically forceful Manowar project yet; to use a volatile term, progressive, as the men on the mount define their world in intense vividness within and away from their music towards aural narrative (Orson, can you hear us?). Big, blinding and overblown (not to mention six more "of" songs), **The Triumph Of Steel** is unswerving ambition filling the confines of the long established Manowar world of ancient heroics. Whether it spills into your world is a question of personal taste. In my world, Manowar now goes even further beyond discussion of good vs. bad metal, into one of mental landscaping, as I seem to become less concerned with counting good riffs and choruses, more blasted by the welded vibes.
Rating                                              9

## Manowar - Louder Than Hell   (MCA '96)
After a veritable firestorm of false trends, weak-tea rock personalities, and the passages thereof, Joey Demaio and Manowar return from their fertile European stomping grounds, to the land of alternative, to the recording and small-scale launch of another manifesto. Yea and wisely, the band has done well across the pond, particularly in Germany, and it is probably this continuing "volume" that makes such a full-scale, committed, enthusiastic record like this possible. **Louder Than Hell** gathers all the sage-like ingredients our tinctured blood crave, delivering the proud, the predictable, the pathologically fabulous. Unlike its predecessor, **Louder Than Hell** hits us fast with the brethren anthems, *Return Of The Warlord*, *Brothers Of Metal Pt. 1* and *The Gods Made Heavy Metal* succinctly inviting us to the hall of the Marshall king. But after this, the band

stretches, statistically taking the listener to all Manowarian places samples of fans either approach with disgust, boredom, indifference, acceptance or lusty embrace. Like I say, it's all here, the pipsqueaked, the speedy, and all attention spans in between. What is admirable is the adherence to the band's meticulously intended rustbucket sound, all players (including new guitarist Karl Logan, incidentally Joey's only writing partner), sticking to the decade-old Manowar pudding, unique sounds and performances melded four-way into a brewage slewage stewage of decibel glory. All is well with the world, course is stayed, and mankind gets another chance to pursue the best.
Rating                                              9

## Mantas - Winds Of Change   (Neat '84)
The ol' Venom rogue fancies a bit of a change evidently, assembling this prissy keyboard-tainted project to show his serious side. Despite the record's heart-palpitating pace, nothing's all that aggressive here, although Mantas absolutely shines on axe, surprising wholesale with licks, riffs and solo excursions that are variously exact and fluid, very often creative and enjoyable. The rest of the show's piffle though, flat-on-its-face pop metal with theatrically British vocals from one Pete Harrison, band on hi-tech overdrive, songs stuck in climate-controlled commercial comfort. Verdict: now two bands are a waste of this man's talents.
Rating                                              4

## Mapknea - Mapknea   (BTMO '90)
**Mapknea** (Sorry, Ventura doesn't have Russian characters) is Soviet metal with chick vocals, sounding like Scorpions, not surprising given that Klaus and his assembled chrome-going domes were the most righteous celebs in the now defunct Union of Fewer and Fewer Republics. Faves: the more steel-riffic numbers like the aptly-titled *220 BONBT*, which sounds alien in a good way. Downside: more enamoured with Scorpions' pathetic power ballads than their rockers.
Rating                                              1

## Marduk - Heaven Shall Burn When We Are Created
(Osmose '96)
And **Heaven Shall Burn**, so Marduk deems their ashen selves fit to take head-exploding Norse black-thrash into the latter '90s, adequate dentist drill mix, a totally sand-blasted batch of "songs". Fact is, these aren't even really blastbeats, more like single-stroke rolls with anemic little cymbal decays and quite possibly, bass drums too! Signature Norse belch also, a little up-octave and reptilian, scowled and achieving of a certain otherworldly drool. But boil it down to a thick, syrupy coagulate, and what you've got is simply a tight, well thought-out, sanely-produced averaging of five or so other bands with which Marduk rubs scaley shoulders; baby steps forward, sounding I guess like '96 versus '93.
Rating                                              6

## Marduk - Glorification   (Osmose '96)
Black metal mainstays Marduk do the tribute bit with this 18 minute EP featuring one of their own tracks, one Destruction ditty, one Bathory track and two thrashers from Canadian legends Piledriver. The whole thing gels quite putridly, just going to show how clubbing, gutting and frying can make anything taste like fast food.
Rating                                              5

## Marilyn Manson - Portrait Of An American Family
(Interscope '94)
I dunno man, this proves to me that even an advanced humanoid like Trent Reznor gets wax in his ears, picking these cretins as his proteges, plopping them onto his anti-label, and hauling their vacant trashpunk asses

out on tour, along with the indestructible Jim Rose. Hype, hype, hype. Sure the Manson family's werdz are sick, profane and colourfully depressing, amphetamizing the debauchery that was considerably but artfully veiled within the canon of predecessors Jane's Addiction. My problem with this is the plodding, unimaginative riffs that break each tired track's back. The predictably dramatic industrial vox and electronic drumming (not to mention those irritating tom tom beats) are enough to grind enjoyment to a mucked-up halt, but it's the underlying song structure that is usually the lamest act, the sort of cheez metal I would think Trent usually snickers at. Trashy, truly unclean and repulsive, **Portrait** relies on shock factor (including the band's drug clown looks), to carry the tune. But if the tune is stiff, blocky, over-layered and ultimately tiring, who cares? These jokers forgot about the songs. Here's what you do: read the lyrics once through, then cash it in. Slow, did I mention slow?
Rating                                                          3

## Marilyn Manson - Smells Like Children
(Interscope '96)
Yeah, we get it, already. We are reality, we are a reflection of how sick society has become, we are your children, blah blah blah. So since the first album has sold OK, we the public get subjected to a second assaultive espousal of the unremarkable Manson reason to be. Not a new album mind you, but 54 minutes of remixes, scary little spoken/effect bits, and surprisingly thoughtful covers. All work towards rotting the mind, slowly corrupting until what poops out the other end is a cynical crank ready to enjoy the kill. In this respect, as a once-through, it's a trip and a half. But repeated listens are pointless, the band's caustic over-the-top industrial blast, wholly without ideas, wearing thin fast. Half saved by those covers: Sweet Dreams (Are Made Of This), I Put A Spell On You, and a vicious metalized blaze through old Patti Smith anthem Rock'n'Roll Nigger. Sum total: bad theater wholly without purpose.
Rating                                                          4

## Marilyn Manson - Antichrist Superstar   (Interscope '96)
Count me in the camp that still thinks Manson's a wastecase joke, his thoughts barely formed, his convictions as permanent as the lifespan of flies, his schtick only a crack generation upratchet on Alice, Kiss, Slayer and Trent. And the Rolling Stone cover story didn't help sway that view, my impression remaining of a bent, self-mutilating, mixed-up guy who outside of what he does to himself visually, is miserably uninteresting. That's not to say this record isn't a wolloping improvement over the debut crudpie, this one being closer to Nine Inch Nails but with enough human instruments involved to breathe. And those graphics are without a doubt, the most over-the-top disturbed I've ever seen. Lyrics are profuse, provocative, and expressive of youth rage, although really, only minutely above the aspirations of any pimply death metal band of five years ago. Modern fer sure, but still, no really new messages, not to mention millennial or futuristic or clairvoyant ones. I dunno, maybe it's the clanky, cranky industrial prog-wank of it all, but I'd rather read this record than hear it. And read it once, I did. So the guy can't cope, all things need inversion to expose the evil of it all, and our parents need to wake up. Got it. Now shut off those damn drum machines.
Rating                                                          6

## Marseille - Marseille   (RCA '79)
Fitting nowhere in the history of metal, Marseille were a fully-actualized British hard rock act, pre-dating Def Leppard by a year with this smooth, professional HR meal, a little light on riffery but definitely no worse in many departments than the Leps' landmark debut, rocking with the same blinkered pre-NWOBHM nod

to '70s rockers like Riot, the Nuge, Starz or Legs Diamond, if a little towards the bar songcraft-wise. Yeah, definitely a little isolated and naive, but remarkably well put together, with nostalgic hip-shaking moves which tend to evoke the fortunes and mainly misfortunes of UFO and Quo.
Rating                                                          6

## Marseille - Touch The Night   (Ultra Noise '84)
A very promising debut dissipates into this awkward pop metal sellout, a record too wide open production-wise to have such skeletal and airy structures carry the weight. Marks a general English tendency to either bulk up on the metal or court the sickly sweet affections of the Americans. Here it's the latter, as Marseille and countless others fed off a **Kerrang!**-fuelled appetite for weedy wimphem.
Rating                                                          4

## Martyr - For The Universe   (Megaton '85)
One heavy Dutch Maiden with nowhere near Eddie's sense of song, melody, restraint, and bottom end, this five track, two write-off short LP sends all the illogical frills further into incomprehension with a treble-low mix which is the kiss of death for difficult rock.
Rating                                                          1

## Mary Beats Jane - Mary Beats Jane   (MVG/MCA '94)
This one looks innocuous enough, like some lame and watery alternative thing from Chicago, but the goods inside pack a punch like watt-smoked firewater, moshing real vicious like a cross between Pantera and Black Flag. And they're a bunch of Swedes no less, skirting that thriving death metal scene through bizarre arrangements and progressions, smartening the band's smarting sound with Helmet-like chunks of think for lyrics, and a real grungy stubble to intelligent constructions like Old and Grind. Jittery, assaultive and damn well-done, **MBJ** should have been the new Rollins record, given its ferociously believable punk chaos. Only 35 minutes but it's so packed with activity, ya don't even notice.
Rating                                                          8

## Masi - Fire In The Rain   (Metal Blade '87)
Swear to Yngwie, these blue collar U.S. guitar showcases never have the songs, **Fire In The Rain** (what kind of weather is that?), being no exception. Here Alex Masi (originally from Venice, Italy) writes an old Talas record, over which he laces his fluid, Eddie/Yngwie/Holdsworth/Vai doodles, decent enough stuff, varied, adequately produced with Brian Slagel overseeing things. I guess these records really are guitar instruction pieces, so the purpose is served, Daybreak being the record's most rippin' piece of prime Malmsteen. Ten marks for chops, six taken away for copious cheez.
Rating                                                          4

## Masquerade - Surface Of Pain   (Metal Blade '95)
Just being truthful. Listened to this after three Century Media pre-releases, Hostility, Merauder and My Own Victim. all vigorous and true, but all haranguing and angry in that grimacing '90s metal manner. And I'm throwing out the 7's and 8's, thinking 8's and 9's if not for the fact that I can't see myself caring enough to actually psychologically graft myself to any of those bands on a personal level. Which I probably won't do with this one either. But I windbag for a purpose, purpose being that Masquerade's clear operatic vocals and frilly progressive snobbiness has become the true alternative metal, the three aforementioned weighty sledges somehow becoming the mainstream sound. A dramatic band like Masquerade finds itself defiant, wanting to be superhuman, reveling in the high class, wanting to be better than the rest of us. And that's a cool motivation for artists, making me warm to what

the band is trying to say, willing to give it a listen. Only comparative I can think of would be fellow Swedish countrymen Tad Morose, Masquerade (on this second record), combining the same heavy guttural riffing with progressive, melodic metal touches, under vocals from one Tony Yoanson who twangs and tangs much like Geoff Tate. So call this one of a limited few bands doing what Queensryche forgot to do, that is rock out. Towards that end, the guitars spill forth with that war-torn Swedish sound, and the rhythm section is recorded like an arena show, all other window dressing draped over the metal core meticulously, Masquerade balancing loftiness and mosh perfectly (at least for those beginning to tire of aggro-metal). Sorta like theatre.
Rating                                    8

## Mass - Swiss Connection  (Strand '81)

Cross Krokus with Colonel Klink and Lemmy, and you pretty much got the idea of this grimly criminal outfit. Credit due however for being in on the steel revolution early, and outside mainstream markets to boot. However credit revoked for the piss-poor holler fodder and general nose-picking on this stoopid pile of pub rags.
Rating                                    0

## Mass - War Law  (Macho '84)

Comparisons with Mausoleum's hapless Killer come wincingly home to roost on this bothersome and powerless speck of dirt rock which scoots along punishingly with absolutely no point. Moronic.
Rating                                    0

## Mass - New Birth  (RCA '85)

Often annoying U.S. Christian metal with an interesting mix of influences that foam to the brim as some sort of slurring, half-drunk, heavy metal Babys. **New Birth** lets loose and carouses on close to half of this strange but proud AOR hard rocker, most notably with the rumbling Too Far Gone (no, not the Babys this time) and the mechanically chaotic title track. Much of the rest rolls nicely along like medium-grade, sludgly hard rock designed not to offend anyone, again sort of like latter-day Babys, chugging with tension beneath the smooth, generic strains of lead mike Louie St. August, whose wimpy, librarian-like disposition gels perfectly with the simplistic, robotic dogma of all White Metalists.
Rating                                    7

## Mass - Voices In The Night  (Enigma '89)

Either I was ascribing too much nostalgic value to **New Birth**, or this band has gotten worse, **Voices In The Night** just chugging out the riffs with little of the spontaneous edge that made **New Birth** a fortunate accident. Still, songs are melodic and fresh, raw but just more conservative, the band perhaps soaking up too many influences along the way (hopefully) to a Stryper-size congregation. Still a good Christian AOR band that balances those sweet harmonies against considerably dirty guitars and scrappy drums.
Rating                                    6

## Massacra - Final Holocaust  (Shark '90)

Hugely impetuous, bile-soaked thrash from France, recorded in the worst of German spirits. Infested, rank with evil abomination and thoroughly gluttonous on noise, wretched albums like this seem to be recorded to make people just go away, and I can guarantee that once the exterminatee is gone, the exterminator shuts it off.
Rating                                    0

## Master's Hammer - Ritual  (Osmose '95)

Standard, tedious death metal with ever so slightly raised production values and executed clarity, **Ritual** is ultimately banal and fraudulent, riffs that work be-

cause they've worked in a thousand deathly tight spots before, structures that started with Slayer and clobbered their way through Sweden and Norway a decade late. Not in English, but who can tell?
Rating                                    4

## Master's Hammer - Slagry  (Osmose '96)

Woah, this death realm is getting freaky, Master's Hammer skipping town on black metal completely, and I do mean all the way. **Slagry** is mostly electronic effects, synths, horn ensembles and far-flung weirdness that sounds like experimental, instrumental Zappa crossed with German prog in Aleister Crowley's swimming pool. The evil is so thick you can cut it with a knife, which I guess is the plan, this previously grim blast-beated behemoth doing the Danzig **Black Aria** thing, but taking a horrible left turn into a convention of crazy clowns, tent-trapped and on fire. Unarguably unique and even aesthetically pleasing, but to a whole different class of people.
Rating                                    6

## Masters Of Reality - Masters Of Reality
(Def American '88)

Pair this one with The Cult's **Electric** as ultimate '70s metal pounders of the '80s, both produced significantly by Rick Rubin, who takes his headphone-pulverizing whomp to these modern purveyors of the old and hand-made. **Masters Of Reality** is the more complex record of the two, although a lot of what one might deem mysterious or literary here seems a might bit contrived for ambiance sake; i.e. the creepy, paranormal lyrics, the road movie elements, the cheezy keyboards, the occasional Morrison-rich vocals. But I'm splitting skulls here, because one can live ecstatically isolated within this record while accepting its strange commerciality and surface translations of classic metal. **Masters Of Reality** is ultimately so hot if you're a '70s kinda animal, cranked full of Sabbath meets ZZ Top biker riff collisions, large and bluesy bayou folk tales looming luminously, powered by Rubin's crystal-clear, back-cracking mix and the relaxed, unaffected vocals of Chris Goss. Putting on a great spread start to finish, **Masters Of Reality** moves at a few different, heaven-sent slows, resulting in a sort of redneck Southern rock hippy brew that sips on Jack all day then kicks back with a doobie, come the cool, crisp shades of evening. An arresting, sterling-brite marriage of styles throughout, **Masters** moves like a leather-clad mirage through the desert, ultimately alone and resigned to a harsh external world's trashing of traditions, a time-worn feeling of self-inflicted alienation borne of a simpler life. Probably the best of the Kyuss/Bogeymen/Masters landscape due to a stunning, wide open lazy love of the guitar in all its reclining moods.
Rating                                   10

## Masters Of Reality - Sunrise On The Sufferbus
(Chrysalis '92)

Well damn the safety nets . . . insomniac Chris Goss (thus the touring-inspired record moniker), a well-aged Ginger Baker (see Bill Ward) and something called Gooch come refloating surreptitiously into view with a crazyman, daydream record of mathematic risk and back-behind-the-chickenshack mysticism. Ethereal gristle, tip-toeing twirly smoke kharma and backwatery poesy collide in construction of surprise worlds of Cream-like blues, tribal minimalism and Syd Barrett sidetrips, making for an about-face on **Masters Of Reality** into a gloopy, fish-eyed alter reality; double helix twistables that roam through the '60s and '70s, dredging trace elements of every decade since 1310. Hawkwind comes to mind, and Radar Love, and Peter Hammill, as the Masters confound the internal alarm clocks of a rock audience thirsting for something fastidious, frugal and in no hurry. Rolling Green, Jody Sings, and *The Moon In Your Pocket* . . . if only all were so delicious. But it ain't, with stretches of the journey courting tedium, wait, linger and snooze, albeit idleness that is more a pleasurable fog than anything mustering impatience. In the end, **Sunrise On The Sufferbus** engages the mind more as a process, as a long, thin thought, losing me periodically while my respect remains feathered in the aimless winds of Goss' strange, peacefulnightride. Exquisitely mixed and respectfully retro-baked.

Rating                                                                 9

## Max Havoc - Max Havoc   (Triple Platinum '83)

Brutal, low-budget Manowar graphics encasing duff generalist metal, which draws on no-frills Priest, Scorpions and Van Halen in creation of a mock-TKO. All performances on **Max Havoc** are overstated far beyond the production capabilities afforded this debut, not to mention the paper-thin credibility of the song constructs. A California band of blow-hards who could have grown into a respectable HR/metal task force given the patience to hang tough while things are lean. For now, cheap product through and through.

Rating                                                                 3

## Max Webster - Max Webster   (Anthem '75)

Of course, Max Webster was the be all and end all. Descended from planet Sarnia to emanate revolutionary wisdoms of heretofore undiscovered creases of the brain, lead artisan and spiritual guide Kim Mitchell, lyricist Pye Dubois, bassist Mike Tilka, and soon to be ex-drummer Paul Kersey wailed on our senses and sensibilities with this cosmic good luck talisman of provocative thought, major chops, and self-diagnosed schizophrenia. Like wise sages from the past and seekers of the new, Max Webster infused a molten core of then contemporary hard rock with a pure-intentioned, mankind-embracing Zappa-esque insight, and ambitious, fresh melody-laced arrangements which took progressive rock beyond its pretensions into crystal blue waters. And this was a debut record. Max Webster lived on the edge no matter where they built camp, be it tech metal (*Hangover*), straight up HR (*Only Your Nose Knows*), prog metal (*Coming Off The Moon*), wistful eccentricity (*Toronto Tontos*) or lush melodic pastures (*Summer Turning Blue*). The wild thing about this record is that it floats miles beyond any simple comparisons. It rocks on many tangents, stirs the soul on many more, yet never throughout its multiple directives, sounds like any other band. Max Webster wasn't wisdom beyond its years, it was wisdom beyond *anyone's* years, while somehow managing to dive right into the pool of everyday human endeavour, imperfections and all, never acting exclusive or above folly. Eminently confusing but effortlessly enjoyed, Max played its hand, quickly establishing itself as a challenge to tried and true rock conventions with an ironically strong statement on ambiguity and disorientation. One of the greatest under-rated artistic achievements from the musical fringes.

Rating                                                                10

## Max Webster - High Class In Borrowed Shoes
(Anthem '77)

The one unifying factor coursing through Max Webster's magnificent premiere was a rural warmth that evoked images of . . . I dunno . . . carved cherry wood. In comparison, **High Class In Borrowed Shoes**, although no heavier, evokes a sheen of polished aluminum, with its bright, uncompromising headphone-ready drum sound, everlite keys, and painstakingly perfect execution. **High Class** sails the same passionate seas of non-committal, offering arguably four metal or hard rock works, most proud being classic scorcher *America's Veins* and the intricate manic swing of the title cut. Lyricist Pye Dubois, although not

an official noise-making member of the band (in the great tradition of The Dead's Robert Hunter), continues to be the band's philosophical engine and perfect soulmate to Kim Mitchell's musical challenges and fluid guitar mathematics, offering truly memorable yet cryptic slants on society's ills and man's monologue with respect to his allotted space. And as per the debut, all points of the compass lead to the heart no matter what the action level, whipped clean and chiming via elegant keyboard work, and absolutely top-of-the-line pride in craftsmanship. It seems almost a mixed symbol that the band would so plainly embrace controversy with the gender-bending weirdness of the cover art, given that all parties involved, including producer Terry Brown, worked so hard to make Max's challenges so warmly inviting and simultaneously so state-of-the-art. It basically stands as more evidence that the complexities of both the Max message and medium were beyond marketing comprehension, and unfortunately beyond the market.

Rating                                                                10

## Max Webster - Mutiny Up My Sleeve   (Anthem '78)

The Max machine just keeps ascending further into the bright blue with this cooler, darker, and mellower release, fashioned sorta like a dry Martini intravenous. The boys are sounding more like a Steely Dan entombed in ice, Kim's Strat coming out to play less often and less inflamed, preferring quieter, intimate moments within the listener's mind. Of the more aggressive cuts, *The Party* finds the band in free-form, progressive heaven, closest in acerbic kinship with Zappa, while *Lip Service* rides a jagged funk edge through to its bluesy finale, both tunes becoming concert faves. Of the melloid material, *Astonish Me* is the most heartening; small and jewel-like with Watkinson's Mercury-toned piano stylings. Overall, another fine and disturbed Max project that is aware of its oddity yet comfortable with it, never alienating despite its total trippiness. An integral piece of the band's moonscaped psyche.

Rating                                                                 9

## Max Webster - A Million Vacations   (Anthem '79)

All is silky, ethereal, and crisp as winter snow on Max's most polished piece of studio jewellery. Max's lightest excursion, **A Million Vacations** chimes clear as a bell, layered with keyboards, buoyant with bright guitars and lush, letter-perfect harmonies. Highlight of the collection comes with what proved to be the band's biggest hit *Paradise Skies*, a masterwerk of dynamics and uncompromising professionalism with one of the most gushingly enjoyable drum sounds ever tweaked from the airwaves. Other tunes that spot Max's moving target of offbeat inversion include the whacked-out *Rascal Houdi*, the live and unkempt *Research (At Beach Resorts)*, the spring water-pure *Charmonium*, and last but not least, the good feeling boogie rockin' title cut. The sounds on this truly awesome head trip just ebb and flow as if the band were wrapped in a dream, all the while firmly rooted in an earthly and knowing pride in its obvious accomplishment, creating on high, working with a shared love of quality craftsmanship. The final result is evident in the grooves, which just sing with enthusiasm, no small thanks to the state-of-the-art Maxmix. **A Million Vacations** is largely considered Max Webster's quintessential, defining work, most likely due to its maturity, accessibility, and seemingly elliptical but somehow comfortable cohesion; merely another masterpiece of a body of knowledge necessary to assimilate for divine survival in the 20th century.

Rating                                                                10

## Max Webster - Live Magnetic Air   (Anthem '79)

The closest me an' the buds ever came to viewing Max in the flesh (until '96!) was being denied entrance

(underage) at one of their near final shows at some bar in Nelson, B.C. We obviously missed a legend, a classic circus act, who cut their collective fangs on the cornerstones of technical brilliance, humour, self-control and attention to detail. **Live Magnetic Air** is a well-recorded and well-executed romp through some of Max's more celebratory moments, a veritable love-in of sound and galactic obtusion. Max will forever rule their own particular corner of the universe, always unfolding and revealing new possibilities amongst the seven sparkling works so fortunately preserved for coming generations drawn to the fringes.
Rating                                                              8

## Max Webster - Universal Juveniles  (Anthem '80)
Max's slightly anti-climactic last tornado extends its scope with more trickery, more speed, more heaviness, more humour and more colour than on any previous outing, yet still manages a stiff, less communicative feel, a less forgiving winter chill, due to some mute foreboding of the end evidenced by a frenzied, moth-to-the-fire terminal expulsion of talent and power. Kick-off trip *In The World Of Giants* drives home with technical tragedy the point that the band will henceforth engage in blowing its mind all over the carpet in deliverance of some of its most dazzling, chaotic, jagged, and inherently Maxoid numbers. For me, **Universal Juveniles** embodies melancholy, partly due to a strong association with the winter of its tiring birth; yet the seeming darkness goes beyond personal skewing, due to a definite sense that on this awesome display of complex hard rock, Max has lost its innocence, its boyish wonder at the trappings of fame, in mute smugness of the impossibility of obtaining such riches. **Universal Juveniles**, although curiously lacking in warmth or honest, human art, makes up for it in cold, hard talent, offering spirited mathematical ravers such as the aforementioned opener, the high strung 'n' riffic *Check*, and the stadium roar of *Drive And Desire*. Also featured is *Battle Scar*, a tag team with buddies Rush, which lumbers slowly and resolutely between dinosaur blues and dinosaur metal, with unmistakable traces of progressive bombast to confound the issue. On further experimental fronts, *April In Toledo* and *Chalkers* marry funk and new age in formation of some Zen high circuitry, and in terms of balladry, *Blue River Liquor Shine* rises grandly to the discriminating levels achieved on each and every Max predecessor. When all is said and done, **Universal Juveniles** exudes calculated class, if not gushing levels of spontaneous charm, in effect parading around a bit too aggressively. Yet Max's level of high preparedness still originates arrestingly from the rubber rooms of the misaligned artist, as if the right hands have molded a wicked and amorphous sculpture with the wrong intentions. **Universal Juveniles**, thus stands for me as a perplexing record of almost contrived, controlled chaos, one that takes its place in history as the flaming finale to one of rock's most enigmatic and provocative tales.
Rating                                                              9

## Max Webster - Diamonds, Diamonds  (Anthem '81)
Max was a revered entity throughout Canada and amongst small pockets of discerning rockheads throughout the States and Europe, and thusly speaking, there was no way in Cabbagetown the boys would be allowed to exit stage left without tribute. **Diamonds, Diamonds** is such a record, a greatest hits package (more like a "most preferred after a few tokes" package) that revives all sorts of ethereal mania including *High Class In Borrowed Shoes*, *A Million Vacations*, *Hangover*, and the immortal *Paradise Skies*. Of particular note however, are two previously unreleased rockers which occupy that straight-faced hard rock ground the band seldom addressed. *Hot Spots* rolls like your basic beer commercial boogie, complete with honky tonk ivories

and barroom choruses while *Overnight Sensation* takes basic power chords down a simplistic, time-worn but nostalgic path of '70s metallic postures. Neither cut is up to the standards of the band's fine studio catalogue and such intelligent beings obviously knew it, leaving them for this afterthought. A stunning career retro, yet aside from the two newies, unnecessary for the true fan. Update: the band reassembled in late '95 for a few enthusiastically received, absolutely ripping Ontario (and Buffalo) live dates, all intact except for a new bassist in none other than Peter Fredette, stellar professional, effortless bass monster, soaring vocalist and Kim Mitchell band sidekick extraordinaire.
Rating                                                              7

## Brian May & Friends - Star Fleet Project  (Capitol '83)
Becoming somewhat rare, this three track, 31 minute EP is the product of May and some friends, namely Eddie Van Halen, Alan Gratzer, Phil Chen and Fred Mandel, holding an impromptu jam during a trip by May to I A Very raw, one takish, and overall quite dull, the record nevertheless features a lot of (fairly average) Eddie and a good dose of a sublime May. Best track is *Star Fleet*, May's springy, hopeful hard rock treatment of the British sci-fi show theme tune. *Let Me Out* is the other actual song, a May composition that is a sort of cabaret blues, made all the funnier by May's shakey vocals. *Blues Breaker* is just an uninspired blues jam. Yahoo. Just had to own it though, 'cos this is the world's most talented all-round axe purveyor.
Rating                                                              5

## Brian May - Back To The Light  (Hollywood '93)
Queen's reserved master, re-embraces the world of rock'n'roll with a new set of reflections on life's journey. Less the criminally artistic masterwerk it could have been, **Back To The Light** is an extremely poignant, human work that is well-built but ultimately stingy on pyrotechnics, opting for the bare emotion of May's shakey vocal stylings over strong melodies and conventional rock'n'roll turns in the road. Pure, fresh and enthusiastic, **Back To The Light** benefits from the relaxed atmosphere that I hope is May's life now, envisioning an ordinary sort of emotional palette extended but never exploded by an extraordinary career path, culminating in no less than the death of May's father, the break-up of his marriage, and the passing of co-worker Freddie Mercury. And as a result, when layered in the protection of Big Rock such as the title track, *Driven By You*, and personal fave *I'm Scared*, May is inspirational and sanctified by pain, fortified by weighty chords, slashing solos and ethereal Queen-style harmonies. And when left alone with his thoughts, some of that fragility of which he speaks comes to the fore, giving quiet moments such as *Too Much Love Will Kill You* and *Just One Life* an eccentric and isolated quality, the work of a huge star who as of yet has never really revealed himself. Over the course of this record, the variety and overall good-natured tone keeps it interesting if not the potential tire-screeching blowout I might have preferred. It's almost as if May is asserting his participation in the web of life to combat his God-like status, being largely misunderstood in the same spirit as similarly mysterious regular bloke Dave Gilmour. Odd one, with the close, scattered quality of a debut record crossed with the explorations of a guitar great gone solo, all encased in a down-to-earth love of spinning a solid entertaining yarn. Also a bit of a career rejuvenator for Cozy Powell, who was recovering from a bad pelvis injury.
Rating                                                              8

## Brian May - Live At The Brixton Academy  (EMI '94)
A bit dodgy (appropriate Brit word) shelling out a live album so quick, but the world's best guitarist makes sure to find reason, biggest of which is the sonic

consistency of this big band effort. This UK only record (also available on double vinyl), documents the first show in hometown London (not the first show of the tour overall), offering no less than seven Queen songs, a bunch from May's record, plus a warm rendition of *Since You've Been Gone*. Saw the band in Toronto and they were smoking; no surprise given the veterans involved. May's voice live is of course, just that little bit more fragile, but the wall of hi-fi sound behind him makes you forget but fast, and then there's all that soloing. Lukewarm grade due to the fact that these are not my fave Queen tunes, nor my faves from **Back To The Light**, and that Spinal Tapped drum solo from our man Cozy's got to go.

Rating     **7**

## Mayhem - Burned Alive    (Black Dragon '87)

Lead throat from Wild Dogs, Matt McCourt is back and chillin', on this speed metal hairball, also calling Portland, Oregon home. Mayhem centre themselves around thrash, punk and hardcore tendencies on this technically-advanced, aggressive, and almost exclusively really fast headache. It's a dense shroud of noise, but a violent and convincing one, that, although pretty unlistenable, rarely degenerates into double time, preferring a constant OTT din to conventional, no-beat thrash constructs. But too damn relentless for too long. Highlights: creepy and thus successful anti-drug title cut and a shredly version of Motörhead's *Ace Of Spades*.

Rating     **5**

## Mayhem - De Mysteriis Dom Sathanas
(Century Media '94)

Don't care to know how they do it, but all of this Norwegian black metal manages to be totally unlistenable, yet damn near the most evil sounding thing ever recorded at the same time. This tribute to band leader and murdered Satanist Euronymous, features the most guttural, depressing, somber, hateful vocal I think I've ever heard (courtesy Atilla Csihar), without lapsing into typical grind-retch vocals, sounding like some sort of tortured, spiteful reptile that I just had to exterminate before I lost my mind. Musically (and I use that term loosely), it's breakneck hyperthrash barely recorded, more or less ambient distortion, sorry to exist, much like the band's first vocalist "Dead", who committed suicide in '91. Slap it on, run and hide, and watch the fireworks. Symphonic yet sickening, and I can't even begin to discern the lyrics. Chances are you just don't want to know, given this band's commitment to Satanic Jihad under the auspices of The Inner Circle. Grade reflects the very active inversion of values this supra-evil communion of anti-souls embraced.

Rating     **0**

## MD.45 - The Craving    (EMI '96)

I found myself pulling for this record pre-release and virgin spin, but lo and behold, my enthusiasm just fell off riff after stale 1986 riff, MD.45 (essentially Dave Mustaine gone solo, with Fear's Lee Ving on vocals) sounding like the mid-enthusiasm of recent Megadeth toughened up but not intensified. Which is why I'm left a but non-plussed, **The Craving** going for a rumbling, sorta thrash, sorta punk, sorta '80s metal hybrid with weak, demo-quality songs. The riffs just ain't there, and this is from a guy who is unarguably riff royalty, Mustaine stuck in a sullen, non-melodic, non-impressive zone of average metal mayhem. So track after track rolled on then dropped off, never grafting to my head for imagined car deck euphoria, no hatred applied, no marked appreciation welling up, just a sort of detached neutrality. Oh well, there's always **Rust In Peace** to salve those wounds. BTW: Bio sez MD = Mustaine Dave, and 45 in roman numerals is LV for Lee Ving, but isn't LV 55? Get back to me.

Rating     **6**

## Meathook Seed - Embedded    (Earache '95)

Typical gruesome, bloody ugliness from Earache, **Embedded** crams its fist into that space between Fudge Tunnel, Pitch Shifter and Godflesh, assaulting the sorry onlooker with an urban, opaque, contra-social industrial throb that comes lathered with healthy layers of guitars gone serial killer. Does for me what rap does, which is makes me feel like I'm in the middle of a mugging (I live in the city, and don't need to be reminded).

Rating     **5**

## Megadeth - Killing is my business . . . and business is good!    (Combat '85)

Much anticipated in stage-diving circles, the arrival of Megadeth brings to fruition the rise of Dave Mustaine after the fall, the fall being his unceremonious booting from Metallica, the invincible (more from Dave on that later). Driven from the band by a volatile mix of booze, drugs and ego, Mustaine resolves to work out his depression, aggression and creativity with a concept of which he alone is master. Thus . . . Megadeth, whose first record is a battle between chops and fierce imagination on one front, obstinate, untuneful difficulty and noise on another. With clearly more to offer than Metallica imitators Exodus, **Killing is my business** is a sort of rebellious but academic speed metal sculpture, never thrash but somewhat cacophonous, a sentiment reinforced by the blunt, atonal midrange-y mix, a sound that I imagine was deliberately chosen with trademark Mustaine sneer rather than being a mistake or the result of an affordability issue. Often lumped in with thrash due to its violent velocities (witness *Rattlehead* and corroded Nancy Sinatra cover *These Boots*), **Killing is my business** is best understood as exploded wattage from a pissed off, pissed-up metallic genius, definitely a man with something to prove. In any event, Megadeth's debut proves a lot of things, much of which are barely filtered through the primal mix and parallel acrimonious delivery. And Mustaine's battle to really communicate ideas with force would not be won easily or quickly.

Rating     **7**

## Megadeth - Peace Sells . . . But Who's Buying?
(Capitol '86)

Much the same opaque, ultra-heavy landscapes and distant, codger-like mumblings as on the debut calling card, **Peace Sells** establishes Mustaine as a subversive shit-kicker with a mission, working with a difficult, uncompromising and tough underground language; lots of riff change-ups, full speed raves outta nowhere, and ugly, cantankerous lyrics. But *Peace Sells*, the song, is really a precursor to *Symphony Of Destruction*, a glimpse that Mustaine loves a regular grind as much as the next punter. Still, despite the band's four-tiered chops perfection, **Peace Sells** is torn and frayed with a crusty sort of punk anarchy, among such chaos Mustaine busily working towards showcasing rather than art, technical exercise rather than emotion and shade. Bleak and bludgeoning but not everlasting; a product of major, life-threatening drug abuse.

Rating     **7**

## Megadeth - so far, so good . . . so what!    (Capitol '87)

More serious chemical dependence, new drummer, new co-guitarist, new mix . . . new fame and fortune! With everybody watching, Mustaine takes his first tentative steps towards the insane, heart-exploding grandeur that is Megadeth in the '90s. With more memorable riffs and a cleaner sound, *so far, so good* is the band's first big league metal feast, marred only by an instrumental, an ill-chosen cover of *Anarchy In The U.K.* (a hit, mind you), and a questionable techy snare sound. Elsewhere, this is Megadeth set to cruise,

502, In My Darkest Hour and especially Liar and Hook In Mouth kicking ass without being hysterical and panicky, making side two the first easily enjoyable half slab from the band so far. Never really aligning itself with the Bay Area bashers anyways, Megadeth are really beginning to demarcate, pulling away into full contention for universal acceptance with this record's new strength of song.
Rating 8

## Megadeth - Rust In Peace  (Capitol '90)

The band rocked mightily . . . the band rocked hard. These were at times the immortal words of Joe Cole in response to the Black Flag and Rollins Band gigs he roadied for before his murder in '92. But it's Megadeth I think of when I read those words, not to mention the sobering written works of Rollins himself. Nothing conquers like Megadeth in the '90s, nothing typifies the pain, the obsession to make mind and body hard like the first two records Mustaine has delivered this decade. Rust In Peace finds Mustaine cementing the Mega-force into a seething tower of perfection, adding Marty Friedman and Nick Menza to the Mustaine/Ellefson core. What results is blinding metal at the very edge of human achievement, killer chops wrapped around constructs that go for the throat while making sure logic and intellect reign over riff. Thus a blitz of mighty sonics that sets your pulse for you, whether you can keep up or not. Thus Holy Wars . . . The Punishment Due, Hangar 18 (dumb video), and Lucretia, impressionable monsters of steel establishing Megadeth as the band way out in front, able to assimilate years of speed metal histrionics, letting fly like Chinese throwing darts only when something bigger and bloodier won't do.
Rating 10

## Megadeth - Countdown To Extinction  (Capitol '92)

Being my second favorite album of the decade so far (after Trouble's hell-hammering Manic Frustration) and within my top ten of all time, it's hard to put keystroke to keyboard the effect this record has had on my psyche. Countdown To Extinction perches Megadeth firmly amongst the leaders of the heavy metal heap, exercising an economy of riff that is devastating in its effect, all made lucid and mercilessly exact under a production job by Mustaine and Max Norman that is perhaps the best I've ever heard. At this level there's only different. Nothing could sound punchier or more suitable to the Megadeth assault. Flagship track here is of course Symphony Of Destruction, a song which pretty well elicits a response of some sort from anyone who hears it; if he or she be a denigrator of metal, it's always paralysis and then revulsion, assuring me that there's something very special about what that riff coupled with that one note bass line does to people. No doubt about it, building this record must have been painstakingly arduous, because everything is so dead-on synchro-meshed, it's almost robotic, although nothing sounds stiff. Other shuddering classics include lead track Skin O' My Teeth, This Was My Life, High Speed Dirt, and Foreclosure Of A Dream, written in response to Ellefson's father's farm being foreclosed upon by the bank. All eyes are focused on making the strongest collection of metallic sounds ever, fulfilling Mustaine's mission to be state-of-the-art in every possible facet, not the least being lyrically, as Mustaine lets his moral beliefs (and his humour) filter through a quintessentially metallic vocabulary, avoiding preachiness with sarcasm and brevity. I can't say enough, and I'm not half the writer to say it even if I could shape my thoughts, but this is a record that has the capability to improve people through its pursuit and demonstration of excellence. Strap it on.
Rating 10

## Megadeth - Youthanasia  (Capitol '94)

After the twin brilliance of Mustaine and Co.'s last two celebrations of excellence, it was with staggering anticipation I first cracked open Youthanasia. Interviews spoke of the open, unconventional recording process, the rejuvenated band-iness of the posse, the wild clean-vs.-dirty last few years of the enigma clutching the mike. Surprise and wary acceptance was my result of the new opus, finding enclosed a package that is unflashy, melodic and old-time song-based, recalling the smooth chug of vintage Rainbow, Scorpions, Dio and Priest. No return to Rust's combat as many figured was going to happen, and much less the studio shine of Countdown, Youthanasia pays major heed to catchiness of an astonishingly square metal nature. Mustaine's vocals take a backseat to the rolling fat grooves, mixed somewhat back, the boy also more in synch with his mumbling style of old, all laced within a sound that leaves less jarring spaces than Countdown (especially drum-wise), while not exactly getting heavier, exuding shade, texture and cohesion and sturdiness of hook. Standouts are Reckoning Day and Elysian Fields, both bolstered by infectious but conventional riffing, again right in there with a sort of top-tier Euro '80s-ness perhaps recalling Accept. Solid, extremely playable record, but one that somehow lives outside of the Megadeth identity.
Rating 8

## Megadeth - Hidden Treasures  (EMI '95)

Youthanasia was, well, sour; kind of there but not there, riddled with failed ambitions, but ambitious failures. So hot on the heels of this commercially successful/artistically questionable opus comes a longish EP that gathers together all those killer tracks Megadeth lent to various soundtrack projects, adding their tight-as-a-drum Sab-cover Paranoid and fairly anticlimactic Pistols cover Problems to the brew for a total of eight tracks at a brisk half hour. But I always thought Breakpoint, Go To Hell, Angry Again, and 99 Ways To Die were classic 'deth, freezing the band between their frenzied volatile Rust In Peace spark and fire, and their studied low-level mosh of the last two records. Would have liked a few more goodies, fleshing this out to full-length, but still, this is groovy prime-time sustainable Mustaine. Catch the flame before it flickered pensive.
Rating 8

## Megadeth - Cryptic Writings  (EMI '97)

Comprising this review months before scheduled release, unnerstan' that things may change. But I'm glad to be working out my car deck with Deth '97, Dave and Co. becoming comfortable and even playful with their persona as mainstream metalists. Spicing things with interesting sound effects and reflective respites, the band has hatched a number of quality riff rockers here, most of this rock-dogging it all over Youthanasia's unsure semi-cheese ride. There's an MD45-ish punky tune, a couple of tributes to perfection NWOBHM (including what amounts to a Maiden quote on guitar), plus four or so classic tracks, distinguished by their composition as simply great songs. Dave's reflective lyrics are getting a little past due-date, and his vocals are increasingly inflective and distracting, but this is a record chock full of personality. Nice to hear people really thinking about riffs again. For once, mainstream is not a dirty word.
Rating 9

## Mekong Delta - Mekong Delta  (GWR '89)

Nowhere in the rulebooks is there a recipe for cooking ordered chaos like Mekong Delta, an alien force so steeped in Warp Nine reality, far beyond the reaches of Voivod or Anacrusis, sent via the Hawkwind jet stream into a space commanded by jarring, brainiac

techno-metal barrages, riffs theorized by hippy math, waves of striped light, disorienting acceleration masking comprehension. My utmost respect and deferential reverence, but it's all too much to cope with in one lifetime, the spinning of **Mekong Delta** causing much concern for my already over-stressed heart. I can bite down hard (like tin foil on a filling) on *Heroes Grief* and the amusing celebration *Black Sabbath*, but much of the rest just hurts my brain, rendering me inoperable.
Rating                                                                 7

## Meliah Rage - Kill To Survive   (CBS '88)

Top-flight power metal, leaping over similar proudly metal act Vicious Rumors, Boston's Meliah Rage were a short-lived (until reforming for '96), considerably-praised entity that knew how to assume the power groove when absolutely necessary. The album covers were a joke though, which probably scared 'em away at the box office. Pity, because this was one of a handful of acts that finally figured out how to rock the house like Metal Church.
Rating                                                                 7

## Meliah Rage - Live Kill   (CBS '89)

Recorded blood-caked and live in Detroit, Meliah Rage blow through five lethal doses of rivethead/earthdog metal, creating an experience we might not ever experience again, that being a band built of chops galore slugging it out real gleaming metal-like at some urban dive. Now it's just slack-jawed, slack-jeaned alternative airheads. But I guess the lyrics are better these days, which counts for sumthin'.
Rating                                                                 6

## Meliah Rage - Solitary Solitude   (CBS '90)

This is what happens when that heavy, gothic, Priest/Maiden-meets-thrash-derived metal from the mid-'80s is allowed to sneak into the '90s. Songs increase in crush factor, structures tighten and grooves leap from muscular mixes. Which is where **Solitary Solitude** lives (no better or worse than **Kill To Survive**), still stuck in the '80s in terms of spooky, cheese factor, but musically moving it up like modern Exodus, Testament, Overkill, splintering unto the commercial riff magic of Megadeth. Chops-driven thrash not without magic moments. A few brown pops at a sweaty club gig and I'd probably care.
Rating                                                                 7

## Meliah Rage - Death Valley Dream   (Backstreet '96)

First couple of tracks, *Death Valley Dream* and *Stranger*, demonstrate hypnotic-headbangedly that Meliah Rage soak up the slack dishwatered by modern music, sending it straight to metaldom but good. Fact be, there are crushing, cruising grooves on this record, bridging such dichotomous acts as Helloween and Manowar, clashing on a battleground most trampled by Metal Church and Metallica. Serious metal grooves are a-hoof, these guys building on their rabid if compact reputation as Bay Area-style thrashers who never quite made the second tier. But too many fairly brisk ones decay the heft, this retooled act not sure whether they be fast, technical warriors or large chugging belchmen. A bit cold and serious, but all in all, impressively defiant of trends.
Rating                                                                 7

## Melidian - Lost In The Wild   (CBS '89)

Aside from the melodious axe solos, there's nothing positive about this grossly erroneous N.Y. hard rock outfit that combines panty-waisting retro-'80s keyboards worthy of Loverboy and grievously toneless gravel vocals amidst generic cock rock gestures. Production is appropriately over-electronic à la Accept's **Eat The Heat**, as all swims in a distorted sea of circuitry while the hairdressed ones pomp rock their way through various chick-potentiating flounces. Features things like digital mixing, digital mastering, tracking engineering, assistant engineering, additional keyboards, and drum programming, yet nobody but the overstudied thespian at the mike takes any credit for songwriting. Stand aside Melidian, here come the Melvins.
Rating                                                                 I

## Melvins - Houdini   (Atlantic '93)

The history lesson: Washington's Melvins are the grandfathers of the grunge sound, cranking a bunch of slow, beat-up records way back, truly underground, hopelessly uncommercial expressions of lethargic ugliness, a young Kurt Cobain attending with awe, virtually a groupie (actually a roadie) to the already mythic Buzz Osbourne and Crew. **Houdini** is the major label debut, and one of the band's "livelier" outings, although the uninitiated wouldn't think as much given **Houdini**'s trashy recording, loose musicianship and ground-down anti-velocities. Gotta admit though, there's something real and dangerous about the Melvins sound, something that becomes wonder personified when they manage a head of steam (see Butthole Surfers). And they've got to be the funniest looking band on earth. The cover of Kiss' *Going Blind* pretty well captures the turtle rock directive, oft-heard comparisons to Sabbath also somewhat justified, although this is a one-take, chemically impaired Sabbath at best. So **Houdini** works a modest charm, or more like lots of charm without much substance, Melvins' lunatic world mashing the listener into a sort of volatile paralysis, rusted joints refusing oil, oncoming train welcome with open arms.
Rating                                                                 7

## Melvins - Stoner Witch   (Atlantic '94)

Trapped by rush hour one broiling T.O. day, this record lowered my blood pressure, slowing me down to the heatwave crawl of steel surrounding my melting chariot. **Stoner Witch** is more of the Melvins' patented crashdrone, all frequencies recorded with hollow point distortion. Saw 'em live backing up White Zombie and surprise, this is the one band out there who sounds clearer and more cogent live than on record, the trio of disease cutting out all the broiled collapses into bassnote lunacy this record seems to love with grinding teeth. Still, the walking definition of a certain rare cool, and extremely dirty while exuding their airs. With the weird side projects floating in the river like, well, floaters, a Melvins record is achingly becoming this twisted posse's most accessible suckerpunch of all their goopy output. Scary.
Rating                                                                 7

## Melvins - Stag   (Atlantic '96)

**Stag** knocks the stuffing out of all things Melvinian previously spawned, simply by poking us with songs. I mean *Black Bock* is positively REM meets Beck, and *Skin Horse* is a lily-livered, melodic alt.rock foray, elsewhere the band making up for brief white noise excursions by trying out a dozen or so new hi-fidelity sounds, many applied to the drums. So even if **Stag** is more psychedelic, it is also more complicated and listenable, Melvins becoming a forbidden woodshed of hilarious sonics, tracks like *Goggles* and *Soup* being an example of total trash made at least academically viable. The rock is rare (and ironically well-done), providing horse-hoofed apocalyptic awe briefly and convincingly, before another low-lidded lapse into mad scientist tinkering. I mean things are getting weird into the Mr. Bungle zone (and that's saying much), Melvins truly establishing themselves as complete nutters with a ton of talent. Just eclipsed Butthole Surfers as my favourite dangerous, unpredictable band; way brainier, way more esoteric, way more serious about crinkling the edges.

Missing in action: '86's **Gluey Porch Treatments**, '87's **Ozma**, '91's **Bullhead**, and '92's **Lysol**.
Rating                                                                9

## Memento Mori - Rhymes Of Lunacy   (Black Mark '93)

Messiah Marcolin is back on the throne, glowing Danzig III shirt draped across his heartless torso, ready to do demonic damage to poseurs, grungers and thrashers alike, all who dare question the superiority of thick, black and exquisitely artful Gothic ornament that upholds craftsmanship above all as its central tenet. Yeah and verily, taking cue more from the mastery of Mercyful Fate than his own scrapped bulldozer Candlemass, Marcolin and his distressed pipes steer this flamboyant masterwerk, a crystal-perfect, punishing sledge of dark European power metal that adds to a thick base of M. Fate, Grave Digger, Trouble and Cathedral, doses of skillfully-controlled progressive metal. But in reality, Memento Mori is guitarist Mike Wead's baby, conceiving the band's direction after his departure, along with drummer Snowy Shaw from King Diamond's band (also credited drummer on the M. Fate comeback record **In The Shadows**, although he doesn't play a thing on it). As a result, **Rhymes Of Lunacy** is a foreboding cloud of black rain, often slow but astonishingly fresh and intelligent at every speed, massive cover of Schenker's mega-classic *Lost Horizons* being indicative of the tone; complex, emotional but outside of speed and time. Memento Mori deserves to be the next supergroup with such elegant power flowing proudly from its hands, if its total adherence to pure metal doesn't scare 'em away at the box office. I hope this type of revisitation becomes metal's next trend. Welcome to the mass.
Rating                                                                8

## Memento Mori - Life, Death And Other Morbid Tales   (Black Mark '94)

The thing that unglues this follow-slow to the solid and sick **Rhymes Of Lunacy** is a seemingly incidental thing as drum sound, Snowy Shaw overwhelming these epic plunderers with infinite sloth and goth. Record II gets so sludgingly psycho that I no longer have the patience, envisioning a Candlemass that can play, but can't get out of bed like Oblomov (requisite Russian literature reference). It's almost as if the band wants to wallow in ambience, in a time gone yellow and frayed, in a world where temporal progress is ravaged and tamed by evil. Cool move with the Munsters typestyle, but I can't escape the fact that Memento Mori is carving a deep dark niche that will only appeal to a patient, fog-enshrouded few. Bless their stone-carved hollow hearts and damn them to cash-starved underground Hell.
Rating                                                                6

## Memento Mori - La Danse Macabre   (Black Mark '96)

Despite the introduction of Kristian Andrén on vocals, Memento Mori's dreary sound hasn't changed a bit, save for a noticeable improvement in production, **La Danse Macabre** being cleaner but still solid, stolid and conservative. So you'll either love this, hate it, or respect and reject it, which is where I stand, simply bored by such extremely classical, gothic monotones, draped like a cloak of monkish gloom over different all-slow progressive sounds. Definitely not one for summer swilling, **La Danse Macabre** is an impressive enough banquet of funereal keyboards, long, textured instrumental passages, and objectively good music. But man, what a mudslide of depression, Memento Mori really becoming the supreme storehouse of all things medievally metal. If that sounds good to you (and I'm surprised it doesn't to me), then by all means, partake.
Rating                                                                7

## Mental Hippie Blood - Pounds   (Metal Blade '95)

Do a little time-travel with me here. **Pounds**, from Sweden's oddly-named Mental Hippie Blood is essentially what Silverchair are going to sound like six or seven records from now, **Pounds** actually pre-dating **Frogstomp** (so they aren't ripping 'em off), having been out since '94 in Europe. But that's pretty much it, Mental Hippie Blood being like a way better Silverchair record, an excellent rolling thunder of psychedelic grunge, finely recorded, slow and methodical like heavy Soundgarden, an eminently enjoyable record. And what kicks it to the next level are the vocals of Michael Oran, which swing two ways, one back to the low, crooning blues tones of David Coverdale circa 1980, the other into the present towards the Cherokee banshee of Chris Cornell (I told you we were time-traveling). And lyrically, the band is a poetic ride through many worlds and emotions, displaying a maturity that makes this sound like a totally veteran offering, like, uh, Silverchair in 2005. Note: these guys toured with Accept all through Europe last year, and Wolf Hoffman thought they were awesome. So do I.
Rating                                                                8

## Merauder - Master Killer   (Century Media '95)

Clobbering and clamoring through the New York hardcore scene, Merauder have paid their dues with six years of grueling clubwork, not to mention their roots in Brooklyn and requisite gang involvement. But their sound is gratefully closer to groove-ridden grindcore than urban punk metal, occasionally sounding like early-to-mid years Sepultura and a looser, lower, more street-savvy Slayer, with just a touch of urban grit. An American tour with Fear Factory plus a stint in Europe saw the band off to a quick, post-release start, reversing the tide on the years of hardship. Hard, heavy and hammered, **Master Killer** deserves to sell a few pancakes, as a pretty hoppin' example of a type of relevant, aggressive metal that may be the only saving grace of the genre. Waffling towards **8**, but I just know I'm not going to play it much. Don't hold that against it.
Rating                                                                7

## Mercy - Witchburner   (Eurorecords Est. '84)

Pre-Candlemass band for Messiah Marcolin, who shows up here in full-on facepaint which makes him look like a frightened Satanic raccoon. Plus the understated priest garb hasn't given way yet to the grim monk's habit of his Candlemass heyday, perhaps personifying the sonics enclosed, Mercy being a loose, weakly delivered, more mainstream version of Candlemass' lethargic doom, albeit pretty much the same sort of underground frost heave. A palpable sense of youth pervades, the band perhaps well aware of the pioneering nature of their fledgling sound.
Rating                                                                6

## Mercyful Fate - Melissa   (Roadrunner '83)

The King is dead, long live the King . . . Diamond, that is, one mutha of a metal despot, the great horn-ed Dane himself, feared hellhound of Copenhagen, mastermind behind the legendary Mercyful Fate, the first dead serious, letter-perfect black metal band. **Melissa** commands the mystique of a **Sad Wings Of Destiny** or **Sirens**, records that crashed into our psyches like surgical steel sledges, leaving voracious devourers of metal everywhere babbling at having to recalibrate their expectations. This was music from Satan's sunroom: played with the force and wisdom of two thousand years in the fire. And in front of such scientific anti-mayhem, stood the King; black and white greasepaint, upside-down crosses; bones, leather, mutton chops 'n' mirror shades equipped for no-holds-barred animal sacrifice right there at his mike, an instrument punished by the most hair-raising of vocal bruisings, low guttural damnations layered with an other-worldly

**277**

falsetto that either paralyzed you with fear or sent you snickering for the exits. For us, the former, after all with a band this good, where's the joke? Nowhere, as we all became genuinely concerned about endorsing metal this brazenly evil, this maniacal in its state-of-the-art construction, as if the lead guitars of Shermann and Denner were being manipulated by unseen forces of diabolical origins. Only complaint: a few over-frilly progressive tendencies on the longer cuts, i.e. *Satan's Fall*: all dressed up, and no coven meeting scheduled 'til the King gets back from the FA Cup final. Faves: triumphant lead track *Evil* and *Curse Of The Pharaohs*.
Rating                                                        9

## Mercyful Fate - Don't Break The Oath   (Roadrunner '84)

Broken open by the band's largest masterpiece, *A Dangerous Meeting*, **Don't Break The Oath** erects another tower in the Fate's kingdom of respect. Severely limited in its sales potential by King Diamond's disturbing satanic beliefs, Mercyful's second is nevertheless universally recognized as a huge record in the history of metal, revered the world over by committed followers of the form, drinking deeply of its doom goth ornament, searing solos, violent but exacting drumming and That Voice. The record is just a shining wedge of black coal, firmly knocking off all who pretend to the throne, including Maiden, who are pummeled into a mash by *The Oath*, a tune that up-ratchets on the most vain-glorious of Maiden statements, and Dio, who gets an adequate thrashing at the hands of *Gypsy*, one monster tune bedecked in gleaming riffery that intoxicates, hypnotizes then eradicates. But **Don't Break The Oath**'s biggest advance is in the pacing of the band's infinite array of song ideas, keeping the sequence of riffs logical and dynamic, carving discernible waves through the lake of fire. Black, blazing and delicious, Mercyful Fate were just too much to handle, shriveling to a close like the wicked witch under the house. But wait, nine years have passed . . . what's that I hear?
Rating                                                       10

## Mercyful Fate - The Beginning   (Roadrunner '87)

A hearty mug of poison for the discerning fan, **The Beginning** plays catch-up ball with some lost gems. The liner notes explain it all perfectly, but here's the rundown: side one is the band's pre-**Melissa** EP, a steaming cauldron of professional metal, for which the band modestly apologizes, noting the haste in which it was slapped down. No apologies required. These tracks smoke, best being *Doomed By The Living Dead* and *Nuns Have No Fun*, but all four demonstrating the band's awesome grasp of complicated, full-frontal metal despite their inexperience. Side two: three from **Melissa**, recorded for a live radio show, months before their reworking for the debut record. Scorching version of *Evil*, fer damn sure. And to break the circle, a **Melissa** sessions B-side, *Black Masses*, a sinister piece of witchcraft rock albeit sub par compared to the majesty of what made the record. Stunning how wickedly first-rate this band was so early on in their career. Some still chalk it up to Luciferian guidance.
Rating                                                        8

## Mercyful Fate - In The Shadows   (Metal Blade '93)

Yes it has been nine years, and it really is like they've never been away, for better or worse. When these guys get down to work, man, do they work, **In The Shadows** sporting some of the most innovative arrangements ever carved in metal. But despite M. Fate being damn near the best at what they do, large parts of the '80s nag this comeback opus: dumb cover, forceless title, and lyrics that show no advance, basically the same evilhorror of old, lacking the soul destruction of disciples like Danzig. Last complaint: two long ones and one instrumental, with much of the

remainder also stretching and cramming near the point of chaos. But per usual with challenging metal (and musically, this is a doctorate thesis), one has to approach with order and calm, biting into each black apple one at a time. And thereout falls the brutal beauty of this record's solid tragi-goth sound, much more guitar-heavy than the King's solo output, truly a Fate show. Faves would be intelligent opener *Egypt*, retro-Fate axe stomp *Shadows*, and the totally headbangin' *A Gruesome Time*. But as I say, this is a chilling return to a genre owned by Fate in the early '80s, stunning creativity and obsession with perfection, at the time only Yngwie skirting the majesty of goth this proud, today only Memento Mori reaching the standard this record upholds. Alas, nothing will rekindle those flames we felt for Fate in our early twenties. Metal and its fans have grown away from this sort of sound, *matured* past these lyrics, while musically, things have simply changed, arguably for the worse, definitely in many cases less ambitious and careful. A frothy mug of mead for battles well fought.
Rating                                                        8

## Mercyful Fate - The Bell Witch   (Metal Blade '94)

An EP comprising two studio tracks from **In The Shadows** and four live tracks from L.A., all top-tier Fate compositions: *Curse Of The Pharoahs*, *Egypt* (also a newie), *Come To The Sabbath* and the immortal *Black Funeral*. The Kingster doesn't hit the notes as he does ensconced in his studio lair, but the man can still entertain, whirling through his vocal characters with Vegas showmanship. Great recording, killer demon-bent chops.
Rating                                                        6

## Mercyful Fate - Time   (Metal Blade '94)

Really cranking the burners where it counts, King Diamond and Co. carve into **Time** with an urgency and consistency that matches those shorter, guitar-laden masterwerks that highlight both **In The Shadows** and **Don't Break The Oath**. Kicking forth with two strappling highballs in *Nightmare Be Thy Name* and *Angel Of Light*, **Time** shows just enough adherence to the short attention span of the '90s headbanger to keep us online and enraptured. Vocals kick in quickly, and riffs steam along briskly, despite their often (and expected) huge goth tones. If classical metal be your poison, Mercyful Fate are about the only ones left to fill your cup (well, there's Morgana Lefay and Iced Earth), **Time** layered with visitations to the book of old Fate, not to mention Yngwie, Rainbow and Priest in the '70s. Still, the horror tale mosaics threading every last Fate and King Diamond record just draw a blank with me after awhile, tending to fade in importance compared to all that fine progressive metal riff and arrangement expertise. And the guitar work here is exquisite, biggest surprise being in the solos, which step outside goth into something truly artistic without tag (witness the title track), or if I might offer some sort of comparative, take the king of all axework: Brian May. Very produced, very progressive, but also lots of tracks, and loads of fascinating guitars. With gothic metal all but dead (the new Momento Mori blows chunks), trust the King to reach right in and ingest its steaming heart, for the Fate will always be the blinding vortex of this narrowing, harrowing corner of metal. Whether the genre can offer you anything in the '90s is another question.
Rating                                                        8

## Mercyful Fate - Into The Unknown   (Metal Blade '96)

Finally all reservations melt away like glacier ice in Satan's swimming pool, the King and crew dropping all epic pretensions for a perfect old-style metal movement that is heady euphoria for all us frustrated Kingsters indeed. Glory-bound grooves are everywhere, *The Uninvited Guest*, *Listen To The Bell*, *Into The Un-*

known and *Under The Spell* especially black and delicious, fusing old M. Fate with mid-pace magic straight out of Accept. And that is the beauty of this record, really the first that makes a certain clear break with the King Diamond material (apparently his new solo record is pretty bad), **Into The Unknown**, despite its faceless and powerless title, being a controlled and deliberate display of subtly arranged guitar songs, no hyper overload, no lace-laced goth. Indeed, many in the metal community are abuzz over this record, and I happen to think that despite the September sun, this just might be worthy of automotive play, something I have rarely considered as of late with this once-mighty.

Rating 9

## Mercyless - Coloured Funeral (Century Media '93)

This short exercise in meat and potatoes thrash clocks in at nine thorned horned tales, 36 minutes, France's Mercyless mixing blastbeats with Slayer triadinal grooves to competent if unremarkable effect. Sounds east coast American (and a bit German), which is quite a compliment for a French band.

Rating 6

## Meshuggah - None (Nuclear Blast '94)

One of the most inventive, extremely hard music records of 1994, Meshuggah's **None** EP (distressingly, a scant five tracks, and only the band's third release in seven years, including just one full-length) rewires the whole grindcore scene once more, offering a damn near indescribable hybrid between stuttering, dynamic-crammed, mathematical Pantera and a sort of percussive psychosis last witnessed on early Soundgarden, seminal Death Angel, or even within Anvil's raving Robb Reiner, an ahead-of-the-beat aggression that propels these zig-zagging, heart-stopping constructs of utter rhythm into insanely high-strung terrain. While **None** may look industrial, with songtags that suggest standard thrash, passing on this glimpse into hardcore's bombastic future would be a grave mistake, for Meshuggah deserves to provoke along with those who have graduated to major labels, reputations intact. With grunge getting pedestrian and slack, and standard death metal forced to metamorphose or perish, it is this type of fresh, ambient heaviness that should prevail. Sign 'em up and let 'em take a run at Pantera, for with songwriting this searing, over the course of a full record, Meshuggah will have to bow to no sound-carving presence on earth. Note: interim **Self-Caged** EP contains two from **None**, two from the forthcoming full-length, and a flame-broiled live take on *Gods Of Rapture*.

Rating 9

## Meshuggah - Destroy Erase Improve (Nuclear Blast '95)

Take a virtual virtuoso who sounds like Allan Holdsworth (rainy, sublime, jazzily new age), butt him up against rapid fire machine gun death riffs that approximate . . . **And Justice For All**-era Metallica on crack, and then slam the whole explosive mash in a pressure cooker, and you'll begin to appreciate the insane grindcore majesty of Meshuggah. The band's **None** EP from last year knocked me on my ass, the brains of Soundgarden shotgunned all over a sound kicking and howling out of the Swedish permafrost. And this plainly nuts full-length debut don't disappoint. The patented stutter riffs spark and fire relentlessly, fueled by the hippie math trigonometric polyrhythms of drummer Tomas Haake, who Is the edgy heart and soul of the highly innovative, astonishingly jarring Meshuggah sound. The record just doesn't let up, embracing hyperactivity through a highly poisonous, perfectly blended concoction of dime-on prog-thrash and canny raw production. And the production has a lot to play with, Jens Kidman's maddening gutturals sparring chaotically with Haake's

distressed, abused cymbals, crash as ride, metal alloy as material conducive to intense battering. Hell, I'm worn out just writing about this. I mean, ultimately **Destroy Erase Improve** is unique in the world of all musics, extremely heavy, dauntingly technical, yet somehow hammered into smooth-drinking compositions of enjoyable heavy metal. One of the most creative metal discs you'll see all year.

Rating 10

## Messiah - Underground (Noise '95)

Messiah's twisted past reaches way back into uncomely Swiss-made death, but you'd never know it here, on this fabulously entertaining shard of stripped but swimmingly catchy regular grind. New vocalist Christofer Johnsson can take credit for the transformation, still growly but humanized, taking the band loud but multi-utilitarian, into Unleashed, Entombed or Gorefest terrain, a slow edge into an evil, underfrost Metallica. Messiah represent the fine face of death metal, willing to search out new fans through musicality and focus on song, which is something a ton of Swedish acts have discovered, opening the doors of extreme heaviness to the many.

Rating 8

## Metal Church - Metal Church (Banzai '84)

Seattle's Metal Church were right in the punted thick of it, ranked as one of the fast-rising metal acts championing chops and total reverence of metal, aligning them with the Bay Area thrashers, while leaning a tad more goth, traditional and progressive. Which didn't help, saddling the band with a lack of identity, most the tunes here trying to do all things at once (Shrapnel, anyone?), sounding dressy and loose, save for the mega-riff that strafes title track *Metal Church*, probably the only tune on here that could rival the intensity levels commonplace on **Ride The Lightning**. Sure, we didn't shitcan it ten years ago. Hell, we even learned songs from it, but now after the mountain of metal madness that hath transpired, it shows its age: dumb cover, dumb lyrics and too much frantic playing. Includes an unraveling cover of *Highway Star*, not fooling anyone.

Rating 6

## Metal Church - The Dark (Elektra '86)

Big label, big changes as David Wayne takes his bratty belt to a new raft of chest thumpers, this time tightening the delivery befitting the band's second tier star status. But like the debut, **The Dark** is marred by too many by-the-book speed metal hairballs. I mean as far as I'm concerned, *Psycho*, *Line Of Death*, and *Western Alliance* are just garbage. It's like a heavier-than-thou ethic the band cannot or will not shake. I saw Metal Church tour this record backing Metallica who had just released **Puppets**, and they just seemed to race through their set like they wanted to get the hell off the stage but fast. Suffice to say Metallica just scorched the place (Maple Leaf Gardens). Power that valiant and awesome is something everybody oughta try absorb once. But enough. **The Dark** does have some cool tracks, *Ton Of Bricks*, *Start The Fire*, *Method To Your Madness* and the title track sporting Class A arrangements and groove to move Mount Ranier. Still, this is a band without a specific cohesive factor, all the while making solid, cutting-edge metal that invariably sounds harsh, bitter and self-defeated by defiance of tone, dynamic and melody, an avoidance of passion that is all too pronounced. One half a very good record, one half filler.

Rating 7

## Metal Church - Blessing In Disguise (Elektra '89)

Time for a little musical pews, as thorn in the ass David Wayne gets replaced by diminutive belter Mike Howe;

and band leader Kurt Vanderhoof by John Marshall, even though tunes are essentially Vanderhoof/Wells compositions, Kurt also being credited with additional guitars (the weird part: Vanderhoof also co-writes and co-arranges most of **The Human Factor**, even though he's out as an official member of the band). **Blessing In Disguise** rages, producer Terry Date leaching all the pleasantries out of the mix, leaving a toxic spill that fries the red earth to a crisp. Howe does for the Church what Bush is doing for Anthrax: amplification, G-Force and projection, turning the band into a tower of strength, a guitar-driven machine set to stun. Faves would be *Badlands* and *Fake Healer* (to be chased with Ozzy's *Miracle Man*), both oscillating between agility and flesh-tearing gravity, looming riffs aflame, hook in mouth as Mustaine is wont to say. Still the brashness takes its toll as side two peels off, tires squealing in search of Inter-thrash I-90. Alas, I lose interest as the band again expresses disdain for pleasure. Tough as a tumbler full of battery acid, but just as destructive on the internal circuitry, **Blessing In Disguise** feels like a stiff belt of the best until your stomach decides to leak from all the poison.
Rating      **8**

## Metal Church - The Human Factor    (Sony '91)
The esteemed Church finally deliver the masterwerk of metallic artistry **Blessing In Disguise** almost was one short record back. One thundering blast of intelligent wattage, **The Human Factor** delivers Metal Church to the lofty heights of no less than Dave Mustaine and Megadeth, as metal perfection personified: amazing songs in collision with ballsy production and killer chops. No one else compares (within this tight definition) as of 07/25/96, although Love/Hate, Last Crack, and Trouble have done equally beautiful things albeit in three other worlds (the five together in my opinion accounting for the best records of the '90s thus far). Conversely, Metal Church and Megadeth speak the same language, blazing with the core essence of metal, exhibiting supra-intelligence in expert control of the form. Lyrically, the Church tackle civil rights, the tragic side of the Ozzy/Priest lawsuits, lack of humanity in music, child abuse, the frailty of world peace, and alcoholism, along with refreshingly amusing rants on poverty and going nuts, all handled with appropriate maturity and sensitivity above bone-crushing riffs commandeered with exquisite technical skill that pays homage to strength of song first, and believe me, the songs are without exception, infectious and unstoppable. And to complete the concrete ballet, leaving no stone uncarved, is Mark Dodson's hulking, eighteen wheeler production, which finds the bass/guitar/drums attack fueling and fusing with Mike Howe's top-flight vocal performance in power-drenched mid-rangey labrynthical madness. It's a crime that this band doesn't share the commercial and critical booty with Metallica and Megadeth, for in the '90s, the **Human Factor** craps all over the former, and barely drops a final round decision with the latter. Powerful medicine, and no justice, having been dropped by their label in late '93.
Rating      **10**

## Metal Church - Hanging In The Balance
(Blackheart '93)
Now relegated to Joan Jett's home label, and seriously messing with their credibility with that "humourous" cover graphic, Metal Church seem isolated and isolating. The sound this time is thankfully similar to the last, except songs brood and breathe, thundering along with dangerous edge, cracks in the hull, top-flight metal to the fore. So the mood is grim, although the grooves are grinding and everlasting, the band setting a less hurried and concerned stage with curiously unhewn, bass-heavy opener *Gods Of Second Chance*, which almost serves as a deflator, next to classic Church romps

like *Losers In The Game* and chugulator *No Friend Of Mine*. Lyrics are of course passionate, smart and at times self-deprecating, most songs still penned by the Howe/Vanderhoof team plus variations thereof, How belting out the tunes in his usual hair-raising rebel yell. I don't know man, it becomes hollow and stinging to keep calling these guys under-rated, Metal Church carrying themselves with such authority and relevance beyond trend, you gotta just chalk it up to a series of business misfortunes. Call this one every bit as imposing and power-hungry as the **The Human Factor**, if just a bit more opaque, less flashy, and less eager to please a dwindling fanbase.
Rating      **9**

## Metallica - Kill 'Em All    (Music For Nations '83)
A hearty metal up yer ass! as Metallica used to expound, sums up **Kill 'Em All**'s core meltdown, as this monumentally profound debut from Hell (the gold seats right behind the bench) sends in electrified wave after wave of insatiable riffery, beginning life as a collection of insane asylum soundtracks, growing into an anthill of red frenzy by record's heart-stopping close. **Kill 'Em All** was a feast to be inhaled like the last Happy Meal before the apocalypse. Nowhere previous had a band made such a beeline for 11 and just stayed there, riffs relentlessly carving and cramming full all the spaces once reserved for respites like filler, ballads, epics or party rockers. No, as the first true fans of the NWOBHM who dreamed of an improved animal *and* delivered, Metallica put action to their word, concentrating the mosh, the lig, the punt and the bang-thy-head from overseas and in the gutter beneath their battered sneakers, into the premier speed metal opus, extricating the thrash from the brew, tightening its grip on a rocket sent straight up the arse of a complacent metal community. And amongst the well-executed speed such as *Metal Militia*, *Hit The Lights* and *Whiplash*, Metallica was the first to truly internalize and expunge the obsessed fan's love of grinding, mow 'em down groove, the grandeur of a mid-pace attack, pushing such classic caffeinators as *The Four Horsemen*, *No Remorse* and personal pressure point *Seek & Destroy* to the foreground of metal's resurgence, finding, as Pantera would later so eloquently put it (while now trashing Metallica at their own game) "a new level of confidence and power." Which again brings us to our original premise: **Kill 'Em All**, although a bit rushed, raw and unrealized, reached new heights of six string fury. Nobody ever tried quite this hard to wake us up. Nobody had ever sent such a swift kick to the heads of its competitors. A hearty metal up yer ass indeed. Only Metallica could make it both a blessing and a punishment.
Rating      **9**

## Metallica - Ride The Lightning    (Music For Nations '84)
**Kill 'Em All** was the call to load the muskets, but **Ride The Lightning** finished the job, pounding all comers into a pulpy mash of tangled limbs. This was purity of thought, purity of Metal. Forget *Justice* or **Metallica**; by 1984 Metallica were already kings of the heap where it counted: within their own highly discerning, mercilessly metallizing imaginations of how accomplished and crushing metal could become; within hearts and within those of the most ardent students of the genre, which importantly were one and the same. If a denigrator of the form could possess an inkling of truth in deeming **Kill 'Em All** a borderline thrash record, he would find no truck here, **Ride The Lightning**'s biggest potential thrasher, *Fight Fire With Fire* busting the record open with the most mesmerizing of precision speeds, mayhem unhinged with frightening technicality. Really, it takes about sixty seconds to realize **Lightning** had established a third plateau in the history of metal, following its invention in the early '70s

with **In Rock**, **Paranoid** and **Uriah Heep** and the reinvention in '76 with **Sad Wings Of Destiny**: invention, reinvention, re-intensification. Not once did I see a review that didn't realize the changes this record would cause. **Ride The Lightning** just kept coming at you with opus after opus, sledge after sledge, *For Whom The Bell Tolls*, *Escape* and *Creeping Death* all insanely power-packed . . . bounders, stompers and destructors sent right to the exploding heart of why metal must be. Spokesmen? Damn rights, Metallica taking the responsibility on behalf of an entire industry of mopheads; setting the bar, soaring over it, and then whacking upside the head with its triangular point all who aspire to mediocrity. One of the massive corner blocks in the house of pain that Gibson and Les Paul hath wrought.
Rating                                                                 10

## Metallica - Master Of Puppets   (Elektra '86)
No pause that refreshes here as Metallica returns to the monolithic storehouse of riffs that built **Ride The Lighting**. Similar in awesome power and effect, **Puppets** is no remake, more like a repeat of a championship drive, deadly metal thick as the sun and twice as heavy over its spacious, brain-frying quake. Kirk and King James prove once more their at the time unrivaled mastery of the blackest of riffs, logically arranged for maximum heft and destruction. Most women *hate* this record so it must be right. **Puppets** invades with one of my favourite Metalli-thrashers of all time, *Battery*, the essence of sleepless, nervous speed. Then it's onward electric soldiers to the lengthy title track, then an ambitious slow one, then the teenager-slaying power ballad. Sound familiar? Yep . . . the same skeletal blueprint for side one of **Lightning**, but again points of reference are almost welcome, there being just so much jaw-breaking genius a punter can assimilate in one day. Three eight minute tracks on the record and they all smoke, a feat in its own right, best being *Disposable Heroes* which mines speed, thrash and monster chunks of mid-pace shrapnel like the smartest of virtual reality computers. Then there's *Leper Messiah*, huge power chord turbines roaming the bush at a forlorn sideways lope . . . *Orion*, then *Damage, Inc.*, damn near the heaviest musical artifact in the world . . . so beautiful, ya just wanna cry. Tragically, **Master Of Puppets** would be the last for bass king Cliff Burton who was killed on tour in Sweden, having been thrown from the band's tour bus as it tumbled out of control, crushing him in the process. Cliff was Metallica to the core, no bullshit, no pretensions, his death understandably a major blow to the band. However, nothing stops metal of this magnitude, and the band plays on.
Rating                                                                 10

## Metallica - The $5.98 EP - Garage Days Re-revisited   (Elektra '87)
Now we were positive Metallica came from the same zitspace as us, if a little more punk-tilted. No Zep or Stones or Beatles for these boys. It's back to the NWOBHM for Diamond Head's *Helpless* (medium to poor DH choice. *Am I Evil?* was better), Holocaust's *The Small Hours* (excellent and obscure choice), and farther back for Budgie's *Crash Course In Brain Surgery* (again, excellent choice). On the skate side, *Last Caress/Green Hell* from Glenn Danzig and the Misfits, and on the seminal industrial goth punk side, Killing Joke's *The Wait*. All pound with that new minimalist, pure metal sound the band would take in and dress up for **Justice**, although here definitely more spontaneous. More than anything, this EP simply cements the case that Metallica picks the best covers, and they do. And the sound quality is just fine.
Rating                                                                 7

## Metallica - . . . And Justice For All   (Elektra '88)
The first full-bore Metalliprod featuring new bassist Jason Newsted (ex of Flotsam & Jetsam) finds the band exploring the vast possibilities of metal, beginning with an awesome mix, standout characteristic being Lars Ulrich's minimalist electro (gated?) drum sound, all punch and cyberpunk edge, setting the stage for acrobatic rhythms which make this record both noble and exhausting. The facts: double record, nine tracks, two under six minutes and those just barely. Many of the band's steeliest riffs are on this record, often buried in over-wanked labyrinths, but there for you to discover nevertheless. As it turned out, the band would grow tired of reproducing this record's songs live given the concentration levels required, further stating that in some respects **Justice** was an ego jerk, the boys somehow feeling they had to prove their chops, something no punter or critic I ever heard question. But it's a phase that had to happen, and at minimum it's a record that will always unfold with new pleasures, as I return to it in widening arcs, **Justice** living everlasting as the band's never fully plundered treasure trove of elusive sonics. Some tracks are instant head-treaders: *Blackened*, *Eye Of The Beholder*, and *The Frayed Ends Of Sanity* truly going beyond the cardiac hells of old into new and unimaginable electric purity, rendered cold and perfect by Rasmussen's strange mix. And *One* was the band's breakthrough hit, pushed in the public's face by its frightening and critically acclaimed video. I dunno, the song's both awkward and lame as far as I'm concerned. All in all, what's left to say about this opus beyond bombast? It's hard to believe the record sold so well really, there being little on board that really grunts like an animal (although Hetfield's bark yields no mercy). Off on a tangent? Hell, it's all tangent, not to mention hyperbole, hippy math, riff maps, inversions, diversions, theorized, applied then crammed through a meat grinder that squeals with metal cogwork that just makes you cringe. Industrial terrorism par excellence.
Rating                                                                 9

## Metallica - Metallica   (Elektra '91)
Bob Rock brings out the hidden Canadian mediocrity in a band who replies by over-correcting on their criminally complicated predecessor. Fact is, no matter what it sounded like within reason, Metallica's next step was going to sell a zillion pancake, and **Metallica** didn't need to be that record. Lars talks of simplicity and groove. *Enter Sandman*, *Holier Than Thou* and *The Struggle Within* work both to acceptable success. *Sad But True*, *Wherever I May Roam*, and *Through The Never* are for the most part, simple to the point of dumb or at least unfinished, and beyond groove towards turgid. In one word: over-correction. Sub-par riffs left to struggle alone with the new Metallica ethic. I don't know . . . it's basically come to this: a band that was so cutting edge their whole career has fallen behind creatively, coincidental with insane commercial success. Case in point: *Enter Sandman*, the supposed flagship of the record, is no screamin' reinvention of anything. Metallica had a ton of similarly-paced, similarly-dressed classics, examples being *Escape* and *Leper Messiah*, both actually catchier but born out of time. Conversely, Mustaine's *Symphony Of Destruction* craps all over anything on **Metallica** from a height of several miles; simple, modern, grooved like nothing on earth, exactly what the band wanted but couldn't achieve here. **Metallica** is simply less flashy, but almost dated, which conceptually could have made this the band's best record except that percentage-wise, the riffs just sound like the band was strapped for ideas. Full points for in many ways, making it acceptable to dress it down, indeed possibly having some effect on Mustaine's creation of **Countdown To Extinction**, the masterpiece of the '90s so far. But at the same time, a band with legendary status seems to have leveled their

sound, while exhibiting no growth lyrically, inexcusable in an area that has seen such huge strides in recent years. Ultimately, the record's slower but to no advantage, not gaining any of Lars' coveted "groove" or "pocket" over say **Lightning** or **Puppets**. There isn't particularly more melody, although we get two coma-inducing ballads, direct rip-offs of the band's previous acoustic dirges. It's more simplistic than simple, and it isn't even noticeably less heavy metal, just more ham-fisted, like a third-rate Sabbath. I hope that this band that has done so much for the advancement of metal doesn't become chart-obsessed at the mass commercial success of **Metallica**, for artistically, the record is a failure, even to the band's admitted goals and intentions, sadly showed up by a good five or six recent bands playing similar purist metal. For a band built on creative integrity, **Metallica** is indeed cold, vacuous and dull, a lacklustre and deflating disappointment. I do however, defend my **8** rating, because compared to the rest of an often idiotic music industry, **Metallica** is still a strong piece of work. Go figure.

Rating                                                                        8

## Metallica - Live Shit: Binge & Purge   (Elektra '93)

Woe to you, the theme here is definitely binge, OD and purge, as Metallica stomp all over the live record concept with what is billed as "almost 9 hours of live Metallica". We get three CDs capturing the band incinerating Mexico City, three videos covering two complete concerts in San Diego and Seattle, a full-colour 72 page booklet, and two cheezy pieces called snakepit pass and scary guy stencil. Starting with the videos: somewhat a disappointment, all the jittery quick angles getting on one's nerves after awhile. Not enough variety in direction here. A pain in the ass to watch. The booklet gives the Metallifan all the band photos one would care for, although most are stage shots. Scattered throughout are internal memos and faxes which give us all a rare glimpse into the workings of such an awesome machine, from the interesting to the mundane, much of it the latter. And finally one overall complaint: way too much overlap between the CDs and the videos. Yes this is Metallica Live, but the set lists are too close, and I for one might have liked some ol' Cliff footage or some behind the scenes goofing off. This is just all too by-the-book. But over to the music. It's a triumph of both sound quality and projected power. The band indeed sounds very live, bounding purposefully through a wattage smearage of some of metal's biggest classics. Hetfield is in robust form, provoking the crowd, goodnatured and badmouthing all at once. And fills spill over drenched with power and confidence, everybody in the house lapping up one of metal's greatest bands enjoying the crest of platinum success, damn amazed I'm sure at being able to sell this kind of brutal mayhem to such a thick mass of humanity. So, hey, chalk it up as a groundbreaking offering of the mostest ever witnessed under one catalogue number, although the imagination that went into what filled the spaces leaves something to be desired. However, once you get right down to business with the actual CDs, you're in for one inspiring stack of goods. Highlights: *Am I Evil*, *Battery*, *Seek And Destroy* (without the inane crowd participation portion) and *For Whom The Bell Tolls*, which all really bring out the watery nature of the tunes from **Metallica**, I'm sorry.

Rating                                                                        8

## Metallica - Load   (Warner '96)

Yeah, of course I'm disappointed. Isn't everybody? But as I've said before, like Aerosmith and like Ozzy, this machine's just too big to punch out a lemon, so **Load** is mildly amusing at worst, a well-constructed, well-written record at best. No question, the band now look like idiots, big, egomaniacal rock stars what with all the eyeliner, piercing, goatees, danceclub fashion,

and general bloated self-importance. It really is more than enough to cloud one's judgment of the music, Metallica really letting us know that they won't be identifying with the fans any longer, please don't touch me, don't mess my hair, guard, please remove him. It's U2 all over again. What next, a duet with Pavarotti? And the interviews didn't help, the band just blabbering out the usual dreary, sanitized platitudes expected from polished rock star airheads. To the music: as expected by a group who have lost touch, it's taken five years to make **Metallica** Part II. But I'd say the songs are better, braver, and at 78 minutes, there's lots to keep one occupied. Hammet's riffs are a notch above those on **Metallica**, but his soloing textures have advanced greatly, using a number of effects to augment his new bluesy sound. Hetfield also branches out, turning a few tracks here almost southern rocking. Wise not printing the lyrics, because they are a Spinal Tapped joke. But you might not care given all the hypnotic slow grooves afoot, many like lead track *Ain't My Bitch* a triumph of style over substance, some like *2 X 4*, just an insipid, cheese metal mistake. And Lars should have a blast on tour, able to phone in his performance when hangovers strike, his rhythms being the most simplistic of his career, sparsely keeping time, Ulrich adding his unique punctuation first heard on **Justice**, but generally letting the riffs breathe, even when they suck. A very general rock record, but a big, steamy one, effective in its basic distillation of traditional metal, thankfully not in the least alternative, but often unshowy to the point of boredom (case in point: advance single *Until It Sleeps*, which sounds like The Damned stumbling through a Crue ballad), taking this dramatic dynamic thing a bit too seriously. But with fourteen long tracks, it is still possible to chew on this for hours, Metallica upgrading the quality of their ballads (*Mama Said*), while churning out at least a half dozen quality, level-headed heft rockers, all amplified nicely by Bob Rock's lusty and powerful mix. Uh, nice hair though, you morons.

Rating                                                                        7

## Mezzrow - Then Came The Killing   (Active '90)

Sweden's Mezzrow blaze through a sort of sturdy ultra-heavy à la Bay Area thrash meets old Anthrax, guitars souped like a '60s muscle car, riffs straight down the gullet, if not a bit stiff and one dimensional. Still, the vocals are rough and ready, and the overall effect is of a band that could be contenders, mixing goth, thrash and mid-pace mayhem to swillaging results, maybe recalling the heady enthusiasm of Metallica's **Kill 'Em All**. Thick and pro-level, if not a bit dated.

Rating                                                                        6

## Michelin Slave - Poised To Meet The Maker   (MaGaDa '96)

At this point, these guys are just a lowly indie band from Stoney Creek, Ontario, but they deserve to be duking it out with the cream of hard alternative sounds, **Poised To Meet The Maker** galloping quixotically with a whole raft of spicy sonics, influences ranging from AiC to Soundgarden to Faith No More to Saigon Kick, although these guys are really a genre unto themselves, thickening their innovative structures with dirty production and doses of mastodon-tuned traditional metal. Add to this plainly wrecked description a myriad of actorly, painterly, thespian, dramatic vocal styles (Halford re: Fight comes to mind) and each song builds on the last until a minor work of alternative metal genius emerges at the other end. If you've heard a band called Schubert from Austria, you might get a taste of the edgy creatives rustling under these cliff-edge compositions. Anyhoo, just a big grungy, brainy cathedral of metal. Get these guys a label deal. Band moniker is the name of a Dali sculpture.

Rating                                                                        9

## Midnight Darkness - Midnight Darkness
(Hot Blood Est. '85)

A nicely over-gliding German grimefest with a Steve Grimmett-like high reg hero at the mike, Midnight Darkness commandeer that well-trodden Gravestone/Tyran Pace pathology, bringing ample energy and sizzling if cumbersome riffs to the table, while lacking that Goth conquering over-extension of personal will to blow it wide open. Competent as always with this niche but unremarkable.

Rating 6

## Mind Bomb - Mind Bomb (PolyGram '93)

Brandishing this chunk of electrician school metal like a ten foot soldering iron, Chicago's Mind Bomb have successfully wedged themselves between the industrial, the artsy and the leather-winged. Sort of grunge with a dance beat, **Mind Bomb** is a deftly computerized clap trap of scintillating carnage, propelled by fresh '90s technologies, yet always cognizant of killer chords and the immutable tenets of metal, leaning warmly human-ward versus the sonic mental gashes afforded acts like Nine Inch Nails and Ministry (both more notably industrial than the present wax). Vague, disjointed lyrics recall the more sensitive of the grungers leaning pharmaceutical and daydreamy in spots, vocals are versatile and dynamic, and the overall effect is truly pleasing, energetically heavy, and frontier-expanding to a modest extent. Faves would be chilling ballads *Almost There* and *Goodbye Everything* although this is one to just let 'er ride, due to the record's unselfconscious diversity. Only complaint: maybe a bit too slicked-up by producer Max Norman. Contains one of those hidden bonus tracks that threatens to paralyze your CD player.

Rating 8

## MindBomb - Do You Need Some? (PolyGram '93)

Looks better than it sounds, this five track EP on ten-inch vinyl taking over half an hour to do the Fear Factory thing. So we get the album version of *Prepare Yourself!*, a weird pastiche of frenzied sounds called *Barry White's Hell*, and three remixes of boring album track *Do You Need Some?* which combined, take about 25 minutes to make the point that this song sucks and can't be fixed.

Rating 4

## Mind Funk - Mind Funk (Sony '91)

Big buzz on Mind Funk, in the heady, shifting daze of early '90s metal, this, the band's debut being one of those enlightened records which willfully forms a pastiche of metal styles, mostly quite heavy and underground. Yet all is cloaked in a sort of tough, urban mean-ness that's downright venomous at times, but always uncomfortable, edgy and ever so slightly loose feeling, like a riot about to explode. **Mind Funk** is the dark side of new agey metal, with minor chord structures sandwiched between funky metal, loping Sabbath, and even elements of Black Flag; more draining than inspiring (in retrospect, band leader Dubar himself has expressed a certain dislike for the record). Even ballad *Sister Blue* feels like trouble brewing, and the overall emanation is one of spitefulness and an imagination to make revenge complicated and sweet. Under the cold gaze of reality, **Mind Funk** bears gifts cut after cut, but as I scan my CDs for something to play, my eye avoids this record for more forgiving, human fare. Fave: fiery lead single *Big House Burning*.

Rating 7

## Mindfunk - Dropped (Megaforce '93)

Proudly wearing the concept of being "dropped" by Sony becomes a badge of honour in ways beyond this record's clever moniker, even though the ousting almost broke the band's will to carry on. Mindfunk (now one word) actively embrace the underground here, seemingly unconcerned with accessibility, unless the record's increased grunge factor is a ploy for cash, which I somehow doubt, more like additional shadings brought by new guitarist Jason Everman, who was part of Nirvana for the band's awesome **Bleach** opus. **Dropped** finds Mindfunk shifting gears, going for more of an exotic, psychedelic metal sound, something more like Nudeswirl (from the band's own home scene) or Tool crossed with the rumblings of confused old Sabbath circa **Black Sabbath** or **Paranoid**, the incomprehensible vocals of Patrick Dubar, with his lower octave Ozzy-isms being no small part of the analogy. More a multi-hued acid trip this time than a collection of rockers, **Dropped** continues the philosophical shift with exotic songtitles like *In The Way Eye*, *Zootiehead*, *Wisteria*, *11 Ton Butterfly* and *Hogwallow* (fave track), and freaky cover art sans band name or record title. My heartfelt respect and good tidings flow freely, as much thought and self-belief must have went into this difficult, opaque and bleak work. Hope it works, 'cos the soupy sludge rock of **Dropped** seems to be a natural environment for this collection of fried souls, this record's crunge being only a slight shift from the loose metallic mayhem of the debut. Cohesive, but as is the case with most nightmare rock, recommended for sporadic and measured consumption only.

Rating 8

## Mindfunk - People Who Fell From The Sky
(Music For Nations '95)

Mindfunk marginalizes themselves further unto mire, knocked down a notch label-wise, jostled into a sort of exaggerated lethargy all over this somewhat nobly conceptual album of plainly boring dirge metal. Using the same cover concept as Queensryche's latest, **People Who Fell** simply mucks around slow muddy and psychedelic, the band's most sustained defiance of commerciality so far. To boot, even the playing is loose and garagey, the band rarely sounding less than unkempt and deflated. Still heaps of integrity, but man, wake up.

Rating 6

## Mind Over Four - The Goddess (Caroline '90)

Spike Xavier and Mike Jensen's Mind Over Four has always been a strange, roller-coaster ride. **The Goddess** (the band's third) is a sort of loose progressive meta-punk-metal, like Queensryche meets Prong, raw but going all places at all time, which left me confused and eventually bored (no help from the non-committal cover graphics), this L.A. band's ideals of hodgepodgey ornament more like lots of ordinary change-ups stuffed together in a meat grinder; quantity over quality. But in many ways, that is Spike's point, given the punk roots, the jazz sensibility and the metal actuality of the band's confounded sound.

Rating 5

## Mind Over Four - Half Way Down (Restless '93)

Many feel **The Goddess** was this band's high point (commercially it was), But if you care, **Half Way Down** is Spike's fave, a record that carves deep into alternative terrain while using the tools of metal, establishing a different, non-dragon-breathing kind of progressive metal, one that leans more towards Soundgarden; early, tribal, bashing, sorrowful Soundgarden from way back when grunge was a fresh commodity. So **Half Way Down** thrashes about with an almost controlled powwow type mantra, the band working in a vacuum, weaving an alchemy that is theirs alone, a driven, sometimes dissonant metalpunk with no rules. Demanding, maybe too full-up with creativity, but definitely ahead of its time.

Rating 7

## Mind Over Four - Empty Hands   (Futurist '95)

Mind Over Four has been on a strange, bitter, delightful journey through recorded music since 1982. This sixth mental mindbend finds the band leaving the chains of their difficult metal, charting yet another exploration into uniques-ville, trampling and stomping often stealth-like and elephantine through oddly mesmerizing compositions built around Xavier's sublime basswork. Tracks like Paralyzed, Quick Bright Things and Phobos Y Damos are elegantly simple mantras that stir the heart of alternative metal. Feeding the insistent river of rhythms all over this record are elements of hiphop, grunge, and psychedelia, tinctures that blend with the life-affirming, earthy mud flowing down this river of a release. Lyrics are cryptic but about real things, enigmatic and attention-grabbing due to the close, personal nature of the sparse arrangements. An arresting sort of stand-alone band, growing more formidably creative with each passing year.
Rating   8

## Mindrot - Forlorn   (Nuclear Blast/Relapse '95)

My-o-my, talk about intense. Forlorn is the first real baby step for this California-based death behemoth, an epic three track EP called a taster for the forthcoming Dawning full-length. Picture the crustiest of charged grinds, deliveries slowed and grossly complicated at once, main genius being the cyclonic drumming of Evan Kilbourne. Then there's the brain-shaking drum mix, which captures the man's daunting chops in all their sweeping fury. Lyrics are appropriately sky-shattering and apocalyptic, as the band lurches through a trio of HEAVY, HEAVY prog crawlers that prove there are new emotions and shades under the crushing death rays of the sun. Sorta like a way extreme version of Paradise Lost, insanely muscled-up, blood-caked and seething with violence. Kinda blisters a path through one's expectations. Bio sez the bass player wants to do mail interviews from prison, busted on drug charges.
Rating   7

## Mindrot - Dawning   (Nuclear Blast/Relapse '95)

The steaming opacity that is Mindrot finally makes itself known and notorious for a full-length slab o' pain. Dawning takes two tracks from the band's Forlorn EP, and adds four more plus an intro in assemblage of this dense, ultra-heavy grindcore stressball, that nearly buckles under its own sludgy mass. But melody worms through like a stunned virus, causing at least a semblance of morbid enjoyment for lovers of sound's darker permutations. Stands out for its ambience and spaces, many peppered by intelligent drum fills from Hell. Long, tortuous tracks as sick, destructive and brutal as it gets, sorta like My Dying Bride with no women, violins, or other politically correct pollutants.
Rating   8

## Ministry - The Land Of Rape And Honey   (Sire '88)

Actually crammed with more nifty sounds than the band's fully-actualized breakthrough record of '92, this, Ministry's transformer record from dil dance band to ugly electrical storm is an interesting spin on an academic level, but tedious once past the tech. Lead tracks Stigmata and The Missing are acceptable hyperventilations, but much of the rest courts the electrodirge punk of the U.K., excuses for taking heroin and nothing more. Still, it's cool to see the germinations of Psalm 69, not to mention a whole new hybrid between computers and metal. A swift kick in the ass for synthesizer bands.
Rating   6

## Ministry - Psalm 69   (Sire '92)

Jourgensen and Barker a.k.a. Ministry, blaze into town packing one of the most lethal state of the nation addresses of our time, a record that finally brings to soul-destroying fruition a career that started eons away from metal, and has now come to devour it. After stealing the show at Lollapalooza II, more people were led into head-on collision with this record, a truly disturbing wall of no repentance that marries industrial sampling to repetitive but hypnotic slam-riffing that knocks you off yer chair, forcing submission, resulting in unpredictable heart palpitations, agitation and eventually nervous action, whatever form that may take. From the mind-melting yelps of N.W.O., one quickly surmises this is no picnic in the woods, Ministry intent on wearing down your resolve through metronomic wave after wave of dense, subversive metal. Onto Hero and first video Jesus Built My Hot Rod (lead vocal by lead Butthole Surfer) for intensified speed coddling the same unclean aims. And things morally degenerate after that, my friends, after one tortuous dirge, which snakes way for the title cut (sort of), on which the duo and its partners in urban decay tan the hides of the wicked and chosen alike. Then disintegration, machinery, suffering and distortion spread their scourge over two final cuts, closing the door, demonstrating a vehement disdain for communication on any level other than truck-size pain. Brilliant, disgusting and truly alarming, Psalm 69 ultimately pastes society on a rocket to Hell, while miraculously uttering only a handful of decipherable words, preferring to let its message fester in washes of layered aural horror. Congregation be damned.
Rating   9

## Ministry - Filth Pig   (Warner '96)

It's almost a mantra to cite Nine Inch Nails and Ministry as the only two pioneers of industrial metal, and really, Ministry's Psalm 69 from a long four years ago still sounds fresh and flesh-tearing today, packed with manic riff-meets-machine mayhem, becoming the standard for this widening genre. Well, much has evolved since then, all the while and Ministry joining the ranks of Boston, Def Leppard, Metallica, Rage Against The Machine and Tool in the game of "uh, where's that record?" Well, in Ministry's case the wasting away of time is probably due to reported ongoing dalliances with heroin, one surefire way to delay a record. And the other reason I perhaps, with nastiness, bring up the big H, is that the record sucks, Ministry cranking a big boring lazy mess of irritating sounds, repetitive, slow, all gucked-up with raw, slack scratches and pops. Got to hand it to them for one thing though, they know when they've eroded their ability to compete, staying fairly away from the onward and upward trajectory of technology practiced by Trent, other industrial acts, and many hip-hop and rap sculptors of sound. And Al's vocals are somewhat versatile and untreated, again, staying away from tech clichés. So the record qualifies as a "surprise", even if it's a dribbling, drooling mess of bashing, foggily-recorded crap that is going to be a joke live. I mean, it took me until the sixth track to find a half-ways constructed tune on this strung-out wasteland. And I don't care really, what it's called, the packaging making it none to easy to promote identification through learning names (no listing on the back cover, no lyrics, just a hard to read rundown on a booklet you have to unfold to read). Maybe people will buy this record, but the only ones who will play it are sorry, miserable cretins, and the type of death metal fan who grits his teeth and claims to really play for pleasure extreme, blast-beated grindcore, both it and this Filth Pig being lousy listening, except for maybe gas-huffing teens bugging their parents. The polluted, unremarkable product of hard drugs.
Rating   5

## Mirage - . . . And The Earth Shall Crumble
(Metal Masters '86)

Yet another bad painting graces . . . **And The Earth Shall Crumble**, as Mirage offers their unique vision of the apocalypse, which apparently will be visited by Flying V's with swords for necks. The guys in this presumably Danish outfit look eminently more extreme than the tight keyboard-laced melodigoth herein crafted; Euro-ice that simply depresses with its hokey lyrics and un-toothy arrangements on such staples of humanity as *Lords In Space & Time* and *Killer Dwarf Shorty*. Too self-important and dramatic.
Rating                                                        4

## Misery Loves Co. - Misery Loves Co.   (Earache '95)

Maybe it sounds done before, but this really hasn't, Misery Loves Co. somehow newly fusing grindcore and industrial, breathing humanity into the clank, loose power into the very remarkable songs, terror into enjoyment. The vibe is something fresh and deep, almost hip, which has never been the domain of extreme thrash, a genre that usually crowds into a rathole of its own filth, never exuding the charm that this scraping, weighty and depressive tome flings faceward. A wall of reckoning worthy of the push Earache will be affording it in the coming months, **Misery Loves Co.** suffers only from a bit of the plods, almost smothering the listener with its pound and pounds of layering. Still, one of the dearest of Earache hammerheads. Messed-up and caustic.
Rating                                                        8

## Misery Loves Co. - happy?   (Earache '96)

**happy?** is a bit of a stopgap follow-up to MLC's much-vaunted debut, hot on the heels of the promo-only **Need Another One** EP, which featured the single, one new track and three remixes of *Kiss Your Boots*. Here there's much more to chew on. Track one is a multimedia CD ROM thing which I can't report on (except that there's bio stuff and a full-length video for *My Mind Still Speaks*), followed by forty minutes of miserably delicious scratchy crunch metal. Main gem is brand new dragonslayer *Strain Of Frustration*, which gives way to four live tracks from the band's tour with Paradise Lost. Closing the show is a caustic (could it be anything else?) remix of *Sonic Attack*. Just call 'em the likeable noise doctors, but don't call 'em late for dinner.
Rating                                                        7

## Kim Mitchell - Kim Mitchell   (Anthem '82)

Canada's veins come snapping back after the frustrating demise of the legendary Max Webster with this superlative five track EP, a collection of masterful hard rockers which stride confidently and artfully through deep and diverse directions, comprising classics second to nothing. **Kim Mitchell** is the hottest EP ever assembled, containing fully conceived mini suites that far surpass the limits of conventional songcraft. Fueling the considerable tour de force is the ever-meldous twining of Kim's hugely rhythmic riff work, shadings, solo excursions, and other alien body English, with Paul DeLong's percussive magnificence. The melodic guitar rock absolutely flies, as beatifically evidenced on the regal and complex *Kids In Action*, sharp-shooting boogie-structured cruiser *Tennessee Water*, and buoyant, perspective-building anthem *Big Best Summer*. And techy hard rock segues into scientific metal on *Chain Of Events*, a stomper that reduces boy meets girl to its neanderthal motivations o'er top a hypnotizing, negating riff mantra, axework that by tune's end rides sonic obtuseness to extremes on one of Kim's crazier, mind-blowing solos. Only breather of the five (energy-wise) resides with *Miss Demeanor*, a swooping, bluesy ballad that manages to endear warmly, without compromising in the least, dishing liberal and loose doses of Kim's complex funkiness and chops wizardy. **Kim Mitchell** climbs and dives often, attaining altitude changes that are breath-taking and bold, all capably handled with time-steeped skill and feather-light finesse, unbelievably surpassing the sky-high expectations one would have for the man after Max. Ultimately, the record heaves and tugs between metal and hard rock, redefining both with a sort of Zappa-esque jazz-level snobbery and work ethic as wily undertow, while also reclining with effortless glide. After such masterful workings, all eyes were on Kim and his virtually anonymous band of virtuosos to set the world alight. Mixed results ensued. Note: (criminally) never re-issued on CD.
Rating                                                       10

## Kim Mitchell - Akimbo Alogo   (Alert '84)

Kim Mitchell reasserts his inherent grasp of human nature, descending from the dizzying heights of his slashing and innovative EP to produce merely a great record. This first full-length LP from Canada's singlemost eventful axeman holds as a somewhat checkered collection of excellent, melodically innovative, but for the most part, mechanically simple rock songs. The focused magnificence of **Kim Mitchell** fragments into three or four camps on the present release, offering HR/metal in minor hit and MADD theme song *Go For Soda*, wrench-head crunchers *Diary For Rock'n'Roll Men* and *Lager & Ale*, and the razor-sharp *Rumour Has It*, perhaps the only tune wicked enough to rub shoulders with the debut EP's smorg of smokers. Kim's penchant for melloid theatrics and skewed melancholy drifts skyward with second hit *All We Are* and the Strat-ified ballad *Feel It Burn*, while *Love Ties*, *That's A Man*, *Called Off*, and *Caroline* round out the show scrambling for the rock'n'roll edges in perhaps unwitting establishment of confusion. Throughout **Akimbo Alogo**, Pye Dubois' sense of fun and wizened rock dog sarcasm combine with Kim's obvious penchant for quality to produce these variously weighted, plainly enjoyable rock songs, with twisted, sly undercurrents which disorient and alarm, yet only semi-consciously in comparison to the debut's four alarm blaze. Classy and upbeat, yet somewhat a disappointment in both guitar histrionics and overall arranged complexity, **Akimbo Alogo** remains an impressive full-bodied work by one of Canada's pre-eminent rock thinkers. Original cover art quickly scrapped for something more accessible.
Rating                                                        9

## Kim Mitchell - Shakin' Like A Human Being
(Alert '86)

Destined to infuriate lovers of Max, or for that matter, fans of Kim Mitchell product to date, **Shakin' Like A Human Being** dove headlong into mellowness, sheen, simplicity, and truly committed doses of G-rated innocence rock with the inane paean to golden youth, *Patio Lanterns*. No denying the major affront to discerning music fans that permeates most facets of this record, however one can't deny the superb flavourings that add the words subtlety and grace to Kim's large and obscure vocabulary. Really not much lighter than the just plain miserable **Rockland** (and, really, how less rock'n'roll can one possibly get?), **Shakin'** nevertheless triumphs graciously on the most shamelessly simple of levels, as witnessed on triple masterpieces *Hitting The Ground*, *Cameo Spirit* and *Alana Loves Me*, and to a less ethereal extent, *Easy To Tame* and *In Your Arms*. The rockier directives such as *In My Shoes*, *Get Lucky (Boys & Girls)*, and *That's The Hold*, on first listen, seem to be written well below Kim's sky-high standards, rife with almost satirical predictability and party-time goofiness, yet on repeated radio-delivered listens, even these shine with understated well-being, swimming through one's head for months. An easy album to throw up over and just toss, **Shakin' Like A**

**285**

**Human Being** does, without question, all but obliterate the hard rockin', heavily pyrotechnic persona from Kim Mitchell's convoluted make-up, but it also manages to replace the mad axeman with some less thrilling, but equally engaging subdued soloing and simple human finesse. And throughout this record, the melodies and confident vocal work from both Kim and straight man Peter Fredette are as strong as ever, crooning forth some of long-time literary partner Pye Dubois's subtler lyrical statements. **Shakin'** is a bit of a piss-off as we place a personality who always talked the big rebel story essentially selling out. But luckily, much immense talent still filters through, richly and quietly, which is not the case with the deadpan commercial offenses that are **Rockland** and **Aural Fixations**, which find the humour, songcraft, stylish axework, and the simple humanity of the man and his impressive band savaged, choked off, and unceremoniously discarded.

Rating      8

## Kim Mitchell - Rockland    (Alert '89)

Listen to my guitar? More like listen to the hum of my elevator. Listen to my once great drummer replaced by the mindless simplicity of a robot raised on metronomes and electronic clatter. Listen to my AOR predictability, listen to my faceless keyboard pap, listen to my inane melodramatics, and listen to what happens when even Pye Dubois becomes smothered by the creaking, boring ordinary-ness of his impending old age. Listen to my guitar. Listen hard but you won't find it, as Kim becomes so obsessed, distracted, by who knows what, money, hits, paying for kids, middle age, some peace and quiet, something that lets him sleep, trading up digs in the expensive Toronto housing market? I so much wanted to like this record, expecting another masterpiece soon, from a man who always seemed to have a grasp of greatness, but there's just so miserably little life, danger, class; indeed, any facet or minuscule sound bite on this that isn't the definition of utter genericism, all from a pair of minds that used to be first commanders of the outer limits of possibility. Of course, Canada couldn't give a shit what's actually on the record, as MuchMusic, the magazines, and radio drooled swimming pools in honour of one of our few remaining favourite sons. Well, I think Kim's become a national embarrassment on par with Triumph, Jeff Healey, the Cowboy Junkies and Barenaked Ladies and I'm sincerely astonished—no, floored—that no one else has noticed what a huge corporate screw-over **Rockland** is. The embracing of this record by the Canadian press and public strips the last shred of respect I may have had for our scene here in Canada. Kim's spiral is so tragic for so many reasons, first and foremost being the man's amazing guitar playing, which he's simply abandoned. Second, his skewed and wonderful songwriting, and the magic he conjured with Pye, which could be commercial and still provoke, as witnessed on his last, is snuffed in favour of weak and watery radio fodder. History. Third, his fiercely cool band: dismembered, most notable omission being the mega-talented Paul DeLong on drums. Fourth, Kim used to rock, more than occasionally, and when he didn't, he was rewriting the books on whatever directive he was courting. All gone, replaced by some sort of ice cold, technical, soap opera, "sophisticated" loungy clatter. Hard to believe how stunning Kim's debut EP was, and how robotic, brain-dead, wimpy, paint-by-numbers, cynically yuppified, and just plain stoopid **Rockland** is. Nowhere does Kim give a shit about art here and no doubt I'll buy the next one. What could be worse. Seriously.

Rating      3

## Kim Mitchell - I Am A Wild Party (Live)    (Alert '90)

Its title as empty a threat as "listen to my guitar," brief live LP **I Am A Wild Party (Live)** demonstrates that the band still flexes its iron on stage, cranking out musician's music—loud musician's music—beneath a G-rated sense of clowning that is anything but wild. Said release is a frustratingly strong collection of Kim's rockers sporting a couple of newies, the ditzy title track (a dino-riffed percussive storm with a cornball chorus), plus the heavy but dullard *Deep Dive*; the entire grab bag frustrating in that the general weightiness reveals a band that still grooves highly live, but whose studio track record, culminating in the disastrous **Rockland**, has forever been increasingly weak and toothless. As usual, what are billed as "assorted" drummers steal the show here, with terrifying, soaring fills delivered with trademark sixth sense for rhythm, only problem is none of them are Paul DeLong, who I had the title cut pegged as until I got to read the credits. Definitely not metal, but likeable bozo rock from Canada just the same.

Rating      6

## Kim Mitchell - Aural Fixations    (Alert '92)

Confirmed. He's lost it. Too embarrassed to even print the lyrics (of which Pye Dubois was no part), Canada's imploding icon has been reduced to a slick, scatter-brained MOR songsmith, who occasionally pulls out his axe for the odd hockey barn hard rocker (on just three of twelve occasions to be exact), despite his incessant, hollow talk of rock. Any personal style from any of Kim's players are muted in favour of an insipid radio blandness dealt emotionlessly and without discrimination to each of maybe six or seven divergent but all unimaginative styles on this all-business release. And again, more praise, and not an utterance of dissent from the Canadian music press because Kim is such a nice, important guy. Despite my extreme disappointment at the loss of Kim Mitchell, **Aural Fixations** is an acceptable piece of background music, which I throw on fairly often when I'm mentally busy with other things. The guitar toons are mildly catchy, and two of the mellower offerings are clean and true: *Some Folks*, sort of a country ballad, and *There's A Story*, the brainiest composition on the record, still totally commercial and instrumentally docile yet for the only instance on the album, sounding special, creative and fresh, much like most of the also deceptively mainstream **Shakin' Like A Human Being**. The rest of the record could have been erected by anybody with an over-used mechanical inclination and an obsession with being accepted. I mean forget metal, the last time Mitchell even wrote a truly committed *hard rocker* was on **Akimbo Alogo**, and there, no less than three or four times. If I could just ignore my total disgust and just listen, I can mildly enjoy about half of this laboriously assembled record, but still, in no way due to any revelation of who this person actually once was, because as I've lamented earlier, Kim's just lost it. He doesn't care.

Rating      4

## Kim Mitchell - Itch    (Alert '94)

Canada's favorite axemeister is backscratched and amplified, reversing the tide of aimlessness that destroyed his last two outings, launching what many are calling Kim's most colourful and cranked record since **Akimbo Alogo**. And no small part of this is Kim's rejuvenated partnership with Pye Dubois, who paints elegant enigmatic lyrical strokes through such magical Maxoid throwbacks as funky lead single *Acrimony*, silky bluester *U.S. Of Ache* and crazy cousin *Human Condition*. **Itch**'s guitar voices are many, Kim shading and texturizing at every opportunity, and although all-out scorchers are kept to a minimum (this still is Canada, y'understand), every last track overspills with tasty

licks, leads and solos, while Memphis drummer Greg Morrow adds brightness of being, attacking his cymbals in fine Alex Van Halen form. The occasional simple party tune emerges and smirks at the Kingswood crowd, but all in all, creativity is at a heady high, oddness running free, Kim 'n' Pye putting on a kaleidoscopic reminder of why those Max Webster albums stand so proud after all these years. Faves would include highly strung, Zappa dance freakout *Lemon Wedge*, and the record's rockiest track *Wonder Where & Why*, somewhat of a send-up of another Van Halen bro. **Itch** blossoms into a well-rounded goodtime rocker fer sure, but for those who want to delve deeper, an artful display of both story-telling and six-string virtuosity unfolds, both aspects separate shows coursing through one, highly enjoyable record, both academic studies on what is superficially a round-the-bases, radio accessible rock'n'roll show. Which to me is a greatly utilitarian kind of record, one approachable from many angles. And I keep swinging back with this in mind, because even though a good four of the compositions can be safely classified as mainstream or intellectually flighty, all the tracks have lyrics and guitar going for them in a big blinding bright way. Congrats on a rippling fine piece of rock magic.
Rating **8**

## Kim Mitchell - Greatest Hits   (Alert '95)

Canny timing here, as Canada's consumate summer rocker returns with a deserved "best of" package, just in time for those sizzling Canadian days and nights, drinking up the good times and good tunes. Last summer's vastly under-rated **Itch** album (probably my fave after the debut EP and **Akimbo Alogo**) failed to sell the number of pancakes it should have, so here we have **Greatest Hits**, which exhibits the depth of the Kim catalogue, while spicing the proceedings with a few surprises. Again, I'm not a fan of hits packages (I'd rather own the catalogue of bands I dig), so I'm kinda yawning at all these big Canuck radio staples, faves o' mine here being the gee shucks *That's The Hold*, infectious axe rocker *Go For Soda*, and brilliant **Itch** experiments *Acrimony* and *Lemon Wedge*. To me the gems are the newies (nice touch giving us lyrics), mid-temperature love toon *No More Walking Away* and rhythmic pumpbeast *Rainbow*, the record's tallest ace. There's also a remake of amusing lunkhead rocker *Lager And Ale* (slightly worse than the sure-footed original) and Kim's biggest hit *Patio Lanterns* (way better: informal, acoustic, wise). So as a celebratory retro: good job, although it would be nice to hear more of Mitchell's amazing guitar technique. As for making a wise Mitchell purchase, y'know what, get out there and keep buying **Itch**.
Rating **7**

## M.O.D. - U.S.A. For M.O.D.   (Megaforce '87)

Chief vehicle for the mind of Billy Milano, Method Of Destruction are a hard core version of buddies Anthrax, fiercely produced, magnificently riffed, and explosively brief. Only problem is, M.O.D., sharing the all-important Anthrax grind, tend to turn left to thrash (or more accurately tight hardcore), where Anthrax turn right into ambitious, song-serious metal. Basically the same band otherwise, with the same approach to recording, hollering choruses, and concrete, monster riffery. So why is Anthrax the better band? M.O.D.'s aforementioned predilection for chaotic passages, more riff changes for no reason, and obvious goof-up ethic in terms of a lack of drive for perfection and artistic recognition. Kinda like the farm team for Anthrax riffs, most of them quite amazing, yet unfortunately set up like a catalogue.
Rating **5**

## M.O.D. - Rhythm Of Fear   (Megaforce '92)

The Milano mosh is back, considerably hairier with a record that fleshes more towards band status with a thoughtful collection of brutal punk metal. More an advancement of song than sound, M.O.D. are still a toneless gut metal experience, all urban grime, shouting and trashing. Fairly advanced for the genre, but still a sort of dough-headed Anthrax garage of unused parts.
Rating **6**

## M.O.D. - Devolution   (Energy '95)

Three years since the last record, six since playing the U.S., and M.O.D. are in combat mode, cranking these gritty, stripped and screamin' punk tunes apparently in quest of a younger audience. Written mostly on the road, these "new" tracks are bleak, aggressive but to my cultured (!) ears, boring, like really old M.O.D., like debut-era Biohazard. Sordid sound overall, so clubbin', rock-ratted and street, this is a throwback to the indie days, with irritating production by Raven's Rob "Whacko" Hunter lining right up for the slamdance. I dunno, maybe if I didn't live downtown with all the noise, this might sound refreshing like an oil barrel full of coffee, but hey, as it stands, I just want to turn it off.
Rating **5**

## M.O.D. - Dictated Aggression   (Futurist '96)

Back once more, this time self-producing just fine thanks, Billy brings an upscale raft of political and war-related tomahawks. pretty much staying the course. M.O.D. rise to new heights here and there, as on the canyon-deep grooves of *Silence Your Sin* and the hilarious *Shot Glass*, which coulda been Anvil. Stupid excuse, but call me perennially fatigued by the hardcore harangue of it all, even though the munchy riffs here strike at the spleen of metaldom. Missing in action: the band's second and third records: '88's **Surfin' M.O.D.** and '89's **Gross Misconduct,** plus '95 compilation **Loved By Thousands, Hated By Millions.**
Rating **6**

## Moho Pack - Flesh To The Dream   (Fun After All '87)

Hey kids, it's Adam And The Ants doin' The Cult doin' **Dances With Wolves** and guess what? . . . nobody can play or sing! So you can imagine the comical Keystone confusion. All beatless and distressingly inconsequential, as simple tribal drums tom tom monotonous patterns o'er which to string homely riffs and laughable Indian chantery. Ludicrous from initial conception.
Rating **0**

## Michael Monroe - Not Fakin' It   (PolyGram '89)

Mike "Marilyn" Monroe's kick at the can after the untimely disintegration of Hanoi Rocks (who were perched to save the world) turns a stiff one, suffering from culture shock as the unwashed and wasted run head on into lifeboats full of studio guns, who colour these simple rockers dead and unfeeling as a lily white porcelain foot wash. Stripped rock'n'roll sagas rendered all too slick and one dimensional, although a few tunes manage to ingratiate with their street-heated hookery. And Nazareth's *Not Fakin' It* always was a tall cool one. Parallel cadavers: Iggy's **Instinct,** Jagger's **She's The Boss** and Billy Idol's **Whiplash Smile.**
Rating **6**

## Monster Magnet - Spine Of God   (Caroline '92)

Devil dog Dave Wyndorf's professed love of comic books, sci-fi, scratchy records and dark basements comes through fuzz and clear on this huggable enough collection of Monster Mag swampslogs. The entire catalogue thus far is fairly interchangeable really, which ain't a slight on the newer stuff, but merely a comment

that these psychedelic revisionists were quite enter-taining even as far back as this rattling, buzzing space-feast. It's no wonder the band is an entirely welcome topic on the Net's BÖC/Hawkwind newsgroup.
Rating 7

## Monster Magnet - Superjudge (A&M '93)

Everybody's grungin' these days, even the fashion in-dustry, even these noisy NYC lunkheads. **Superjudge** is one of the better chunks of rubble, going for a sound that bombards Mudhoney from two angles: a soupy, warm sort of psychedelia via Hawkwind's quarks and charms, and a fortified Sabbath throb, best evidenced by *Evil Is Going On* which has Danzig rolling in the mud with *War Pigs*. But the scuzzy Seattle influence is most headache-inducing, making cuts like *Cyclops Revolution* and *Elephant Bell* the vital goop that Staley & Co. would be proud to serve. As with much second generation Seattle-isms however, much of **Superjudge** takes too long to get revved, and once arrived, struggles with lazy riffs, forcing the magic man vocals of old bongster Dave Wyndorf to pay the piper at the gates of dawn. Overall, a cigarette-burned pastiche of personas, even tainted with a touch of White Zombie as it blobs and crashes through a world gone dreamy and pharmaceutical. Where's Magma, Jane and Lucifer's Friend when you need 'em?
Rating 7

## Monster Magnet - Dopes To Infinity (A&M '95)

Dave Wyndorf's world circa '95 swirls real interplane-tary-like, images floating, gazing, changing channels, emitting heat, emotion and car parts, as the sound of alien rapture builds to a 1974 roar. Dave's new black box recordings of such netherworldly shenanigans be-come sweet tunetalk to the pointy ears of elation's nations, dripping into gluey view fun, freaky and retro-generated. It appears Hawkwind, Budgie and Sabbath still echo through this colour collage void, colliding with asteroids of chemicals earthlings used for mind expan-sion deep way back wence. Dave then pastes the gleaming mash on pressed aluminum, stomps it hard and tells us about the exponential experiential delirium of the time-suspended task. And it is good to listen, as he whispers, roars, rants, demon-croons and trips us out all real home-spun, y'understand, taking us ele-phant-loping guitar-weary and heaving of soul into the land of amplified nod. Wise, thick, and uncomfortably warm, ten thousand years old, twenty years old, and new for 1995.
Rating 8

## Monster Voodoo Machine - Suffersystem (PolyGram '94)

**Suffersystem** (artwork by Pushead, for the band's second time) marks MVM's major label debut after a couple of well-received EPs. This is six Canadians making more noise than the entire Canuck industry put together save for blastface saviors Jesus Christ. But MVM are more of a high production smear of big chords, industrial touches and treat vocals (mixed way too far back), making for a bit of a tiring, non-stop Sabbatherian wall of metal; no spaces, too much too toppling tall. Really heavy stuff, but it all kinda blurs together after awhile. Promising, but for a mix of tricks that really strokes the circuits, I'd lean towards Claw-finger or even Skrew. Off to a promising start with a Juno award and opening slot on the Fight tour. Update: label deal is now toast; band back with an indie EP.
Rating 6

## Monster Voodoo Machine - Pirate Radio (45 Revolutions Groove '96)

After the unceremonious split with their big shot label (various versions abound), Monster Voodoo Machine consider themselves renewed and re-wired to the street, whether by choice or not. So this 23:00, five track EP is supposed to be their reintroduction, new, lighter industrial sound in place. Whether it stays is another question, MVM still wracked with metallic guitars and angsty vocals, despite their trendier, clois-tered, dance-affected, hip-hopped drum sound. Many in the know are crying foul, but one thing is for sure, these guys know how to manufacture tricky, techy sounds that please the ear. Whether these dour, some-what drab songs live up to the production values is another question. Update: it all turned out to be bull, the band calling it quits weeks after release.
Rating 6

## Montrose - Montrose (Warner Bros.' 73)

Ted Templeman blazes onto our radar screens in much the same fashion as he would with another legendary Warner debut, **Van Halen**, five years later, Van Halen hiring him largely in quest of capturing the sound on this legendary record. Well here the heat is indeed intense, as the man parlays a ton of energy from Montroids Denny Carmassi, Bill Church, Ronnie him-self (ex-Van Morrison, Boz Scaggs, Edgar Winter) and a lead vocalist called Sammy Hagar, four clashing egos that would eventually burn the band out. And a classic was born, one screeching, defiant, capable debut re-cord which put American metal on the map with guitar masterpieces like the revvin' *Bad Motor Scooter*, the chewy *Rock Candy*, and state-of-the-art metalizers *Rock The Nation* and *Space Station #5*. Hagar's voice is scorching (the man has not yet become the Sammy we love to loathe on his own and with Van Halen), and Ronnie proves to be a versatile axe alchemist captured in full grind by Templeman's awesome mix, all the more amazing given the record's age. Other killer stadium rockers would include *One Thing On My Mind* and personal fave *Make It Last*, pure guitar and thump. I have no idea how well this record sold. All I know is that everybody I looked up to was still playing it two or three years after its release, and for good reason. It's timeless, searing guitar rock, sounding not a day older than anything that came out anywhere before 1980 at least (well, of course there's Priest). Fast, slow, tricky or straight up, **Montrose** is an excellent hard rock record, well ahead of its time, and insanely crammed with talent for a debut offering. And others would agree: Toronto's The Pursuit Of Happiness, not a metal band by any stretch, used to start out their show by blasting *Space Station #5* in its entirety, full P.A., lights off, before they sauntered on to start their set. Respect.
Rating 10

## Montrose - Paper Money (Warner Bros. '74)

The second and last with Sammy Hagar at the mike finds the band sabotaging a stellar future for strange progressive noodlings, funky-ass hard rock, drippy bal-ladry and only the occasional irascible rocker, the title track being very occasional, *I've Got The Fire* kickin' major irascible butt, a complicated, much-covered classic that is arguably the band's most profound blast ever. And it was all down hill after this. A bizarre second effort after one of the hottest early metal albums of all time.
Rating 5

## Montrose - Warner Bros. Presents (Warner Bros. '75)

**Warner Bros. Presents** marks a partial return to the convincing metal of the debut, but without the distinc-tive pipes of Hagar, and more importantly, possessing a sort of cold, creepy feel as genuine rockers like Purple-ish cruiser *Matriarch* and the funky *Twenty Flight Rock* are mixed in with spacier, more progressive mo-ments left over from **Paper Money**'s mindbend. Sadly, the fire is not recaptured as this fairly heavy release is enjoyable in theory only, shrouded in a sort of loser fog of a personnel-altered band out of focus with human connectivity. Ronnie regretted self-producing the album, largely blaming himself for the record's cold feel.

Rating 6

## Montrose - Jump On It (Warner Bros. '76)

Doing much the same mixed experimental bag as **Paper Money**, the controversially jacketed **Jump On It** follows Ronnie's whims as he flies through his art rock clouds. In essence garnering respect for creativity and daring in the face of certain superstardom had he made **Montrose** II. Like **Paper Money**, one technical, state-of-the-art speed rocker sticks out like King Diamond, Diamond Dave and Diamond Darrell at a Neil Diamond show, the title cut, an agile memorable classic that just amplifies my pain at the directions this band could have taken. Elsewhere Ronnie does a nice job really, of making this a vocals record by a guitar player, no other way to describe it, except verging on the academic.

Rating 6

## Montrose - Mean (Enigma '87)

Strangely a bit like metallic Hagar, in its low maneuverability, lack of tricks, and one-off approach to recording, **Mean** features a completely out-of-character Ronnie and his assembled no-names swaggering through dense metallic hard rockers which fully evoke the bluntness (although not the wimpy manners) of reunion-era Foreigner and Bad Company; which also stands to reason with the inclusion of Johnny Edwards (singer on Foreigner's **Unusual Heat**, also doing time with King Kobra), at the mike. Sure it's weighted and simpli-fried, but it's also kinda fresh and spontaneous in its unexpected garage ethic. Includes a smoky rendition of old classic *Game Of Love*. Note: drummer James Kottak will move on to Kingdom Come.

Rating 6

## Ronnie Montrose - Open Fire (Warner Bros. '78)

Ronnie indulging in a bit of art away from his real responsibilities of cranking out choice, bluesy, innovative metal, **Open Fire** is a fresh, instrumental jazz rock foray of fluid guitarisms which around the jazz precept, includes acoustic segments, classical, hard rock, funk and new age blues. If delving deeper into the mind that created Gamma and Montrose appeals to you, then by all means partake, because this is a hell of a lot nicer a ride than similar stuff by Jeff Beck (although I do have a soft spot for **There And Back**) or any of the new metal types like Vinnie Moore, Satriani or that weird but amiable violin guy, Mark Wood.

Rating 5

## Ronnie Montrose - The Speed Of Sound (Enigma '88)

Ronnie gets more electric and rocky here, as really his non-style shows through, or in more positive terms, his traditional approach. A bit o' blues, lots of square soloing, and a fairly dirty electric sound pervade these fairly uptempo instrumental tracks, all named futuristically, lending the album a sort of propulsive space flight feel. Still, very close to songs, which makes Montrose's particular brand of instrumental record at least potentially enjoyable to the non-axe guy, even if Ronnie later derided the album as too stiff.

Rating 5

## Ronnie Montrose - The Diva Station (Enigma '90)

The reclusive axeman strolls tacitly onto life's stage once more with this cerebral, mostly instrumental collection of hard rock experiments, highlighting Montrose's skill less as a riff mapper or soloist (both of which the words icy, bluesy and detached might apply), more as an arranger or engineer of thoughts. Something almost Belew-like about tracks *Little Demons* and *Solitaire*, and in essence the whole intellectual exercise.

It's a drag really, that such rock legends possess this penchant for the instrumental, although thankfully we get two vocals here from Gamma sidekick Davey Pattison, one of which is wasted on the nth cover of *Stay With Me*. Fresh for instrumental music, but I gotta say, for almost any occasion, I would simply pass. Nevertheless, it all seems sorta highbrow and important.

Rating 5

## Moonspell - Wolfheart (Century Media '95)

Gothic doom metal from Portugal. But before you snicker, realize that these guys have quietly sat by and soaked up only the good habits from the genre, proving themselves ardent students of the form, injecting fascinating melodies into the brew that could only come from their unique cultural heritage. Other positives include the dual vocal style adopted by Edge Of Sanity, lots of keyboards, killer drumming like Sentenced and amazing songs, most irresistibly hookiest being *Love Crimes* and *Alma Mater*. Above all, Paradise Lost is the band that bounds strongly to mind, Moonspell carrying itself with just that much class. Headphone-ready production by Waldemar Sorychta.

Rating 8

## Moonspell - Irreligious (Century Media '96)

**Wolfheart** established these guys as a band to watch warily. So now comes **Irreligious**, Moonspell really leaping into the new goth fray, losing all vestiges of their Portuguese imprint, for a sound that is slick, British and well, Type O Negative. So call this one slightly downratchet in terms of heaviness, much more gothic and commercially spooky (i.e. not spooky) in every way, like an entertaining My Dying Bride set, many layers of keyboards and other exotic sounds, bent and tempered by expansive, slow-to-mid structures with cannonating double bass drums. And the vocals visit all the vampiric crypts, again, a big black cape cloaking the proceedings, as Moonspell do as good a job as any of a genre getting a little silly. Bottom line: liked the more naive, enthusiastic and raw debut a shade of grey better.

Rating 7

## Gary Moore - Grinding Stone (CBS '73)

Guitar legend Gary Moore's first real post-Skid Row (and pre-Thin Lizzy) output is this large, jammy progressive blues feast, not altogether unenjoyable, sorta crossing Allman Brothers with Yes and the borderless extravagance of psychedelia. Fat, rolling recording and lots of guitar, including Lizzy-ish (via Allmans I guess) dual dueling. A power trio: Moore, Pearce Kelly and John Curtis, the record produced by Martin Birch.

Rating 7

## Gary Moore - Back On The Streets (Grand Slamm '79)

Early Claptonian slumming from the prolific Mr. Moore, **Back On The Streets** is quite the rarity, even given this reissue (my copy reads 1989). And it's actually quite cool to hear Moore's earlier solo era (record II after a bluesy affair in '73), sliding all over the place; pub rock, ballads, smart hard rock and lotsa electric funk jazz competing for reason to be. Features a rousing Lynott-penned rocker called *Fanatical Fascists*, plus a slow blues version of Lizzy great *Don't Believe A Word* (with Phil trading verses with Gary). More or less the sum total spells progressive guitar wank meets shabby recording, but Moore does make significant stabs at entertaining the layman.

Rating 5

## Gary Moore - Corridors Of Power (Virgin '82)

As you'll see elsewhere if you deem it necessary to swim through this raft of Moore reviews, I'll accept the world's universal judgment of Moore as an important guitar figure, a man who is master of many styles; blues, metal, pop, and fusion which is the case with his trying Colloseum records. Here once again, the songs are a pain in the neck, but Moore manages to inflect chunky metal flourishes, solo, fill and otherwise into what are dull pop metal incidentals, and horrible ballads. The band this time around features Moore, Ian Paice, Neil Murray and Tommy Eyre, an esteemed line-up to be sure. Unfortunately, Moore does all the singing.

Rating      5

## Gary Moore - Victims Of The Future    (Mirage '84)

I know many a serious axe aficionado who will swear by this particular ex-Lizzy guitarist, yet in my opinion, Moore's soloing, although moderately tasteful and re-solving, is completely run-of-the-mill, and hell, the man couldn't write an original riff if his life depended on it. I dunno, maybe he's one of those cases akin to Clapton, who sounds like dog whistle shit unless you're some-how connected to some club of ethereal six string divinity (seriously, if I hear the acoustic version of *Layla* one more time, I'm gonna blow chunks). **Victims Of The Future** stumbles through various hard rock and metal terrains, going nowhere, saying nothing. Mellow-est cut, *Empty Rooms* was a minor British hit and a major personal annoyance, and *Murder In The Skies* rides a fairly menacing metallic romp. The rest? As dull-minded as any loud rock format gets, courtesy of a cast which draws heavily from the more lacklustre elements in the musical chairs department of the Brit-ish metal aristocracy. Hell, even Ozzy's on here some-where, Ozzy having auditioned Moore for his band way back when, generating tapes that are said to have escaped the cutting floor.

Rating      5

## Gary Moore - Run For Cover    (Virgin '85)

Another reason I'm no fan of the Moore concept lies with Gary's vampy vocal stylings, a yelp which resem-bles the over-extension of Glenn Hughes, who appears on this album, probably for reasons of said similarity. More abject poverty riffs, clunky metal, soapy wimp rock; a veritable profusion of futile ideas. By far the utmost coolest point to this record is sweeping, Phil Lynott-penned opus *Military Man*, on which the great one also sings lead vocals. *Military Man* is a minor epic; a heart-felt, precision metal lament against war that builds steadily over its 5:40 lifespan towards a swirling, climactic finish. Other prime cuts include the quick *Out In The Fields*, where Lynott and Moore trade off vocal chores, and the menacing *All Messed Up*, on which Hughes preens heavily at the mike. Again, overall, Moore puts forth a record of second-rate retro-metal juxtaposed against loser hard rock, even going so far as to include another stab at *Empty Rooms*, proving that Moore's songwriting book has all too high a vacancy rate.

Rating      4

## Gary Moore - Dirty Fingers    (Castle Communications '87)

Probably the most accessible Moore record for those who don't understand what all the fuss is about, **Dirty Fingers** is a tight, considerably heavy record with flawless performances all around, an album actually recorded in 1980 as the first for Jet, shelved until Moore's European success in '87. Pumping away val-iantly are a crack team that includes Charlie Huhn, Don Airey, Jimmy Bain and none other than Tommy Aldridge. But Moore also shines with his spirited heavy metal solo work here, despite his conventional riffs and cheezy lyrics, blazing through crunchy fretboard runs that sound composed . . . y'know, thought about . . . finest piece being *Really Gonna Rock* (great title, eh?). The band also shows a penchant for those rhythmic gallop structures (i.e. *Nuclear Attack*, which was a hit for Moore's working buddy Greg Lake). I guess I'll

grudgingly accept Moore as a quality metal soloist, even though his songwriting sucks, and I really can't take that tweedle-dee blues stuff he's on about. Clever pop metal cover of *Don't Let Me Be Misunderstood* though.

Rating      7

## Gary Moore - Live At The Marquee
### (Castle Communications '87)

Nice hearing *Back On The Streets* tear **Live At The Marquee** open, a record that zips along nicely, lots of dueling chops from Moore and wonder drummer Tommy Aldridge. Better mix of songs than most of his schizophrenic studio efforts, **Live** is an appropriate showcase for Moore's alternately sizzling and under-stated axe carvings. Slight lack of treble.

Rating      6

## Gary Moore - Wild Frontier    (Virgin '87)

**Wild Frontier** is yet another ambitious yet boring example of the old British guard going stale, failing to keep pace with the professionalism, emotional inten-sity and innovation demanded today of even the base common denominator. Two standout cuts here in the Irish-influenced *Over The Hills And Far Away* (featuring vocals by a chilling Pete Townshend-soundalike) and the very Lizzy-ish *Thunder Rising* (Phil's death was still on Moore's mind during this record's conception), and then again virtually nothing to drag Moore from the swamps of obscurity. Granted, in comparison to pre-vious outings, it's a bit more zippy with not altogether poor use of electronic drums. But per usual, bad riffs and smothering predictability smear the show as Moore just does not update quickly or fully enough. Anyway, nowadays the man thinks he's Clapton or Robert Cray, writing superficially within the trendy blues rock genre, where songwriting is hardly re-quired. Best way to land a beer commercial when you're broke, I guess.

Rating      4

## Gary Moore - After The War    (Virgin '88)

Moore's last rock record before its switchover to the blues is a thumpy affair (what else could it be with Cozy Powell on drums?), still plagued with anemic middle-of-the-fence songs, highlight being the hilariously *Kash-mir*-ic *Led Clones*, featuring Ozzy on vocals, a tune apparently taking jab at the whole Kingdom Come phenomenon happening at the time. Plus there's *Blood Of Emeralds*, a not all that moving throwback to *Black Rose* and Phil in general. Slick production, slick graph-ics, and tasteful axework, but boring riffs and arrange-ments.

Rating      6

## Gary Moore - Still Got The Blues    (Virgin '90)

Gary Moore finally finds his niche, eschewing his flirta-tions with generalist metal for a jumpy, spring-loaded working man blues, half originals, half covers, all quite electric and awake. And the record was a commercial success of sorts, a whole new fanbase detecting and rewarding Moore's enthusiastic axe and vocal play. It's insane the dozens of talent years that guest star on this record (including Albert King, Nicky Hopkins, Albert Collins, George Harrison, Don Airey, Bob Daisley, Brian Downey), Moore instantly in good company, **Still Got The Blues** delivering crisp high notes, sparse and steely production and well-timed horn blasts, do-ing well by its dozen or so creators, establishing Moore as a Clapton coat-tailer wilfully accepted by commer-cial blues markets the world over.

Rating      6

## Gary Moore - After Hours    (Virgin '92)

More originals this time, even if the record mirrors quite closely the electric sizzle of **Still Got The Blues**.

But small adjustments occur, Moore adding more horns, and really coming into his own as a vocalist quite suitable for this genre, burying his twang in an energetic but reverent performance. But not my bag really, so like, see ya later.
Rating **6**

## Gary Moore - Blues For Greeny (Virgin '95)

As smotheringly dull as any Eric Clapton Grammy garbage, **Blues For Greeny** is Gary Moore's tribute to legendary Fleetwood Mac guitarist from the early, pre-gals days, Peter Green(baum). Moore writes a laudatory essay on the guy, leaving out the part about Green going completely off his rocker and walking away from rock much like Syd Barrett, becoming a religious nut, a bum, and finally just a weird recluse, while praising Green's soulful, instinctive, golden-toned blues playing. The two had become friends when Moore's Skid Row had backed up Fleetwood around '74, culminating years later in Green "swapping" his '59 Gibson Les Paul with Moore, who has used it on this record. And the record itself? Well, as with Clapton, I'm sure there's something mere mortals can't hear, but to me, this is just a drag; straight-faced blues that takes me nowhere, axe-play included.
Rating **5**

## Gary Moore - Ballads & Blues 1982 - 1994 (Virgin '94)

Sounds kinda like something Scorpions would poop out. Just what you'd expect, Moore bestowing on his populace a bunch of his failed, cold-fish ballads and his conservative blues numbers, all pierced with his howling, unmusical solo non-style. But that's just me, many an axe afficianado holding Moore wistfully as the grand sage grail water buffalo exalted wizard of white-boy blooz. A couple of unreleased tracks, a bunch of "single" versions and the rest album tracks, totalling 71 minutes, all lyrics included.
Rating **4**

## Vinnie Moore - Out Of Nowhere (Mayhem '96)s

The fact that Moore (known for his stint with Alice Cooper) does it all on this, his fourth guitar star record, makes **Out Of Nowhere** move along with a modicum of interest for the non-guitarists out there, sorta like a walk through Satriani's many phases. The best stuff is the funk, which packages riff and fluid soloing in a seamless set of circumstances, while the mellow acoustic material is also novel and enjoyable, one-upping Pagey in sublime Zepp-ishness. The best tune-by-tune liner notes for one of these yet, spiced with Moore's humour and inspiring quotes from famous achievers.
Rating **7**

## Morbid Angel - Domination (Giant '95)

With grindy gurgly vocals that slash to the bone (most gruesomely notable on Where The Slime Live), **Domination** points to new patterns and riff configs for traditional death metal, without selling out or otherwise twisting the beast beyond recognition. The record leaps and crackles with cryogenic freshness, punishing power metal rearing its majestic head with heartening regularity. Eyes To See, Ears To Hear is a chemical classic, and Nothing But Fear is so sonically twisted, it defines new emotional shades of anti-social heaviness. Ultimately, amongst the eviler-than-thou (and believe me, David Vincent is in the Creator's bad books), this kills Deicide through innovation and caring, although both band's '95 records still have too many trashy blastbeats for my liking, velocities where few creative advances can transpire, where possibilities are imprisoned by speed. Still, on the cutting sortilege of

American death, which at this level differs very little from the curdled cream of Scandinavian-based gore.
Rating **7**

## Mordred - Fool's Game (Noise '89)

Yet another trumped-up Bay Area-style gathering of ultra-metal virtuosos (à la Exodus, Testament, Overkill, Metallica and especially Death Angel), who through no shortcoming of theirs, evade permanence in my mental metal banks. I'm sure it takes tons of concentration to re-make **Master Of Puppets** in one's own image, but for some reason, this is one of the main forms of mimicry I have no time for, somehow not "needing" any more bands of this genre to reinforce my mental arsenal. Mordred are definitely promising, with their traces of funk and high regard for song over the usual multi-tiered riff labyrinths, but it takes skill and character to really ingratiate, given the insane competition always waiting in the wings.
Rating **6**

## Mordred - In This Life (Noise '91)

Basically surrendering themselves to the funk gods, Mordred dive headlong into a hyper brew of Infectious Grooves, Chili Peppers and stop-on-a-dime technical thrash, bass acrobatics pretty much taking over lead spot, putting this band way to the side of metal, in their own wise guy holding pen, a genre seemingly more about shocking and perplexing metalheads than about true art. But maybe I'm wrong, and maybe Mordred is sincerely chasing a muse with this highly strung, hung-up compressed funky stew. I guess I respect the process, but am agitated and mildly repelled by the results.
Rating **6**

## Mordred - Vision (Noise '92)

As is usual with EPs, this six tracker psyches the listener into thinking these chosen tunes are somewhat blessed, focusing the gullible rawk dude on a scant few tracks, which is to Mordred's advantage for sure, given their busy funk metal vignettes. So the art funk metal of In Time and Close Minded sound like inspired Faith No More, bolstered by a snappy, perfect mix, and the band's usual enthused playing (special mention for Scott Holderby's emotive The Organization-like vocals). More guitars again, and less hyperactive songs, resulting in greater dynamics.
Rating **7**

## Mordred - The Next Room (Noise '95)

Creative metal that looks to new frontiers for a purpose, Mordred have evolved (naturally, I guess) from a bracing Bay Area sound through fairly literal funk, to an act that incorporates hip-hop, fierce, angled funk, and prog, rising to an odd underground aloofness like Flotsam And Jetsam, The (now defunct) Organization or Saigon Kick. But this can spell a coldness, a lack of purpose, a lack of fun, as the forced identity search occasionally overwhelms the songs. And like these other bands, Mordred has slipped between the cracks while trying to instill in the genre a standard of intelligence. Still, this is classy, thoughtfully conceived stuff that enters many exotic lands (see Shut, woah!). Applaud the bravery, the brawn and the brains. Hell, just clap.
Rating **8**

## More - Warhead (Atlantic '81)

More quietly and without warning fell out of the NWOBHM pack onto a major label, but alas to no avail, as for reasons unbeknownst to me, the record bombed, as did the gravity-defying follow-up. Both, at least on the merit of music alone, were well-paced, smoothly-assembled hard rock contenders. **Warhead** benefits from the ready-for-prime-time belt of soon-to-depart vocalist Paul Mario Day (Iron Maiden's first vocalist back in '76!), and the underwhelming but solid production of Henry (H-Bomb) Weck, who adds his southern flavour to this considerably riff-packed record. But no matter how academically proud **War-head** stacks up, I never play it, due to a pervasive sense of restraint borne of a rhythm section and supporting mix that forces the songs to live on riff alone. Strange one to pin, but I immediately think early Armored Saint crossed with heavy Blackfoot or Boyzz, whatever that means. Definitely ahead of its time but sabotaged by a '70s tendency to remove the edges from metal.

Rating    **6**

## More - Blood & Thunder  (Atlantic '82)

Totally gutting a gutless line-up, Kenny Cox retains only ligger-lookalike Brian Day on bass while adding two exquisite talents in drummer A. J. Burton and vocalist Mick Stratton, whose pipes blow this record into a rare level of rock'n'roll euphoria. No bull man, **Blood & Thunder** has no trouble carrying its own with the likes of Quartz' **Stand Up And Fight**, Diamond Head's **Lightning To The Nations** and Witchfinder General's **Friends Of Hell** as seminal wedges of the U.K. metal resurgence, while taking a decidedly more mainstream metal directive; flashy, tuneful, polished and intelligent rockers of all speeds, gleaming with strong choruses racing in and out of tasteful riffs and lofty ambitions. When it blazes it blazes, as on the killer title cut, *Traitors Gate* and instrumental *The Eye*, and when it explores hard rock, it triumphs with elegance as on *I Just Can't Believe It* and *Rock And Roll*. And above all, it's just vintage metal to the bone, solid track after track, in the proudest of metal traditions, Kenny Cox proving his mercurial talent for synthesizing UFO, Priest and Purple with the barrage of recent talents competing along side him, carving technical but effortlessly enjoyable anthems at will. Supreme metal magic in the making, More deserved to be rock royalty, having that star quality borne of being blessed with four distinct personalities whose talents can be attended to in isolation, yet who combine for such strong songs, versus so many acts that were off on flights of fancy. One of a hallowed few task forces to which this book is dedicated.

Rating    **10**

## Morgana Lefay - Knowing Just As I  (Black Mark '93)

Just to keep things on the up-and-up, this is the band's second record after a rare indie debut called **Symphony For The Damned**. And **Knowing** doesn't smack the least of the debut jitters, diving right into precision power metal, a sound that differs from future fantastical forays, here the band (and especially Rytkonen's vocals) rocking down a decidedly Savatage-ian left hand path to the shrine of the Metal Church. Which is probably why this is my fave, giving no truck production and engineering-wise to the bombastic plastics of the future, even lightening up enough to cover Nazareth's *Razamanaz*. And man, does Rytkonen sound like Jon Oliva, recalling all that great, heavy but hook-laden muscleman metal from Savatage's early records. Huge, gleaming, crystal-blue chunks of traditional metal. Done up right.

Rating    **9**

## Morgana Lefay - The Secret Doctrine  (Black Mark '93)

Hearing this one out of sequence, after **Sanctified**, it's pretty much impossible to distinguish the sounds and philosophies of any of the band's output. Which is a good thing, good because it's cool to see that the quality has always been there, **The Secret Doctrine** full of that triumphantly perfect, sparklingly recorded (hear that snare drum snap!) power goth that is usually reserved for German bands (Helloween, Gamma Ray, Blind Guardian, and all those searing Scratch and Bonebreaker Records released in the mid-'80s). Lead singer

Charles Rytkonen looks and sings a bit like Sebastian Bach, but this is no sleaze metal affair, more like a keeper of the flame, built ambitiously to uphold or elevate or at least revive the form. Lyrics tend towards fantasy themes (count the "of" songs: *Rooms Of Sleep*, *Alleys Of Oaks*, *Soldiers Of The Holy Empire*, *State Of Intoxication*, *Lord Of The Rings*), but this just reinforces the godly aspirations of this particular metal machine, carving a precision sound that is above human concerns.

Rating    **8**

## Morgana Lefay - Sanctified  (Black Mark '95)

Again, genres collide and spit out what can only be described as a sort of traditional goth metal, a smattering of prog, a touch of death, maybe a heavy, no-nonsense Fates Warning (i.e. Nevermore or Iced Earth?). Riffs are large, complex but pummeling and dirty, crunching through a raw '90s mix, as Charles Rytkonen's old-style metal man vocals place this backwards, amongst the tried and true, if somewhat melodramatic strains of snickery '80s sentiments. A potent mix of thoughtful arrangement and jugular attack, **Sanctified** (record #4) proudly upholds a tradition that might be better dead, as even this truly rock hard record fails only in areas that are *too* heavy metal. Better than Fight, while in that same ring, call this one an updated love-in with the core tenets of traditional gothic metal, a rare foray into this realm for a Swedish band. Only a shade more advancing than **The Secret Doctrine**, perhaps steered more aggressively down a doom-dark path.

Rating    **8**

## Morgana Lefay - Past Present Future  (Black Mark '95)

If you are prone to find complaint with Morgana Lefay's chivalrous sound, this compilation will gladly feed you ammunition. Because what you'll find is a bunch of songs from three elaborate studio albums that are to a man, all quite slow, fairly mellow and acoustic-based, progressive power ballads one and all. Which is a misrepresentation, given that much of the studio slabs rock. But it is a bit of a pained point with me, watching these often boring songs that take ages to work themselves into a lather. To break up the "greatest hits" nature of the thing though, Morgana offers two "new" originals *Sculptures Of Pain* and *Symphony Of The Damned* (two of five "of" songs here), the latter being a ten minute remix from the basically unattainable first record, a belaboured opus that does just what I talked about above. Then there's a pointless cover of Crimson Glory ballad *Lost Reflection*, and the record's far-and-away gem, Abba's *Voulez Vous*, which is turned into a razor-sharp power slam, one of the band's coolest tracks ever. But like I say, this compilation dwells on Morgana Lefay's sole weakness: too much dicking around.

Rating    **7**

## Morgana Lefay - Maleficium  (Black Mark '96)

**Maleficium** finds our favourite castle-dwelling Swedes spinning a concept yarn of torture and forced confession at the hands of a remorseless Inquisition. It's the band's usual highly engineered gothic power metal, which is both a curse and blessing, given that **Maleficium** is great music, albeit possibly too close in temporal proximity to only recently previous Morgana slabs. But all is well, for this is probably the heaviest, most immediate record by the band, especially the latter half, tracks like *Master Of The Masquerade* and *Creatures Of The Hierarchy* sounding like golden era Priest and Rainbow. So per usual, call me systematically impressed but emotionally uninvested.

Rating    **8**

## Morgion - Among Majestic Ruin (Relapse '97)

Morgion have been kicking about California for six years, doing demos and a 7 inch, before appearing on the Celtic Frost tribute. And even this 34 minute, five track EP was recorded in '94, the band well on its way to a new record while we speak, major line-up changes included. **Among Majestic Ruins** is adequate if unremarkable shaggy doom metal, quite laudable for its retro uncommerciality, and its no-hurries, no-worries steamroll. Vocals are textweight death, but drums, riffs and occasional spooky keyboards are firmly in the underworld doom doldrums; slow, chewy and finally successful in creating an eyes-sewn-shut darkness, the whole tone even approaching psychedelic in wandering nature. Eagerly awaiting the new material, for an enriched alchemy is present and accounted for.
Rating                                                                  6

## Morgoth - The Eternal Fall/Resurrection Absurd
(Century Media '91)

Quickly making roiling black waves with their vicious but controlled proto-death metal attack, Germany's Morgoth have vaulted themselves into the legions of the first tier. Which is not to say I can hack them at these early stages, although the heft coupled with their nasty edge is something to behold, given that this dual EP-ish type release harkens back to 1990. Evokes anguished battle through turgid, smoking choke.
Rating                                                                  6

## Morgoth - Cursed (Century Media '91)

If anything, these hare-brains have gotten thrashier, smooshing everything together come blast-beat time, only assuming grooves fleetingly, while vocal terror Mark Grewe rants out his death tales in those tones you either love or hate. Nice artwork though, all fancy-pants metallic gold, looking like a goth new wave thang. You still gotta appreciate this band's grasp of the words "over the top", Morgoth really lighting a match to the tired concept of death, again, especially for 1991.
Rating                                                                  6

## Morgoth - Odium (Century Media '93)

Again here I stand (to quote the immortal Grave Digger), outta my depths, confronted with what is one of the bigger, long-awaited grindcore releases of the year, from Germany's Morgoth. **Odium** blisters the walls in heaving blasts, up-intensifying on the old Entombed catalogue and not really their own (while looking like Slayer) with fistfuls of outrageous riffs moving at speeds I can live with; lots of bottom and mid-level grindpunk grooves, unfortunately punctuated with thrashy vocals from bleach gullet Marc Grewe, although the man does often cross that line from machine to tortured bloodbag (almost like Cronos), driving these chaotic wunderthrashers to insane levels of buried deep heft, much cleaner than on previous Morgoth spins, if you can believe it. At the upper register of grindcore output, due to dynamic, inspired riffs and an urge towards musicality, joining the ranks of Death, At The Gates and Grave as some of my wall-pasting favourites.
Rating                                                                  8

## Morgoth - Feel Sorry For The Fanatic
(Century Media '96)

Venturing down an enlightened path travelled by many (Amorphis, Carcass and Samael spring elegantly to mind), Morgoth return after a three year absence (abcess?) with a shockingly forward-thinking but accessible mainstream metal record. Riffs are king, grooves command attention (there's a bit of prime Killing Joke in those tribal drums), and arrangements stab straight at the heart of why metal causes rapture to the initiated. This Fantastic Decade, Forgotten Days, A New Start and the humourous Cash can stand proud with anything

from the '70s, '80s, or '90s material from the likes of Sentenced or Carcass' **Swansong**. The brief and fleeting techno touches to the thing seem to be an afterthought, not really possessive of purpose, given songs that are this solid, memorable and melodic. However, it has read well in suckered reviews, allowing Morgoth entry past death metal into the supposedly more intelligent cliques. But don't be fooled, this one's right in there with the Metallicas, Dearly Beheadeds, and Cemetarys of the world, that is for lack of a better term, mainstream metal, even if Morgoth has retained fabulously their sense of stand-offish underground cool.
Rating                                                                  9

## Steve Morse Band - Stressfest (Windham Hill '96)

For those who've taken as much of a shine to the new Deep Purple opus as I have, The Steve Morse Band's new record (where does he find the time?) **Stressfest** might be a pleasing, if academic listen. Morse has made countless records with the Dixie Dregs, also crafting solo records plus odd-logging time with Kansas for a spell. But **Stressfest** is definitely the man's heaviest metal, leaving behind his Pat Metheny-icy southern licks for the chunky rhythms driving **Purpendicular**. Joining Morse are bassist Dave LaRue and drummer Van Romaine, who help turn the record 4/5 rockin', 1/5 jazzy inflection, LaRue throwing in choice bits of slap bass, Van Romaine offering blistering mathematical acumen on lead title track Stressfest. All the while, Morse is very electric, running the vast range of his talents, always musical, light-hearted, and never dull. A perfect instrumental companion piece to **Purpendicular**.
Rating                                                                  7

## Mortal Remains - No Cash Flow (Tender Stone '97)

Not a fan of NY hardcore at its best, I found myself fatigued quickly by this raucous angst-ridden act, up to here with all the aggro, and reaching for more convincing art from (as usual) Sweden. Something about the drums-dominated live mix that betrays a garageness that ultimately depresses, **No Cash Flow** sounding like just that, something recorded on the cheap. All the frequencies are there, but a claustrophobic spontaneity distracts. Like I can feel the water dripping down the basement walls, the swinging light bulb, the sweat. And I've always hated that wound-too-tight snare sound, another distraction. Sorry, just does nothing for me, even though I somewhat recommend these guys to fans of Agnostic Front, M.O.D., Sacred Reich and Downset.
Rating                                                                  4

## Mortal Sin - Face Of Despair (Phonogram '89)

Wielding a sort of tight 'n' taut Bay Area-style techthrash, Australia's (?) Mortal Sin crank stack all over this well-produced, well-sequenced powerfest. Vocally, kinda shout-based like Exodus, which gets tiring (for him as well as me). Fans of the genre should be impressed, sort of in your **8** zone.
Rating                                                                  6

## Motherland - Peace For Me (Sony '94)

**Peace For Me** (peace designated by a peace sign), came and went without much of a stir, even though it was a '90s vehicle for (almost unrecognizable) drummer Jason Bonham, also featuring Brother Cane producer and extensive co-writer Marti Frederiksen on guitar and lead vocals. The record itself is a tad bandwagonesque, coming off as an interesting hybrid of Collision, Extreme, Soundgarden and Pearl Jam, big, angular rhythmic canyons, brooding, dynamic vocals and that ever so slight Zep-based bombast that Bonham brings to any project. Pretty cool, spontaneous and jammy, retaining just enough old hard, charmingly southern rock to lend respect.

Rating 7

## Mother Love Bone - Apple (PolyGram '90)

If you're from Mars and don't already know the story, Mother Love Bone were considered one of the more promising Seattle acts until front man Andrew Wood bit the big one from a particularly nasty encounter with heroin, giving the scene its first martyr, spawning the Temple Of The Dog project (Dog being Wood), and the immense Pearl Jam, not to mention more than a few tribute tunes and a further compilation record, **Stardog Champion**, long after this already posthumous release. So what's inside? Not what I would consider the crème de la scene by any stretch, but a fairly derivative drug metal exercise, often deflated and/or funky, often really cool. I guess I'm the odd flannelhead out, because even though I happily inhale grunge, this one always struck me as sorta hyped and commercial, and I never warmed to the production, especially on the heavy ones. Faves for me thus become the more liquid tracks like Come Bite The Apple, Stargazer, and Man Of Golden Words. Pretty accomplished and varied (if it didn't push the envelope, it wouldn't be Northwest), but almost too much to digest, and too laid-back, making it rudimentary in the armchair arts to see where Pearl Jam gets its languid recline. And surprising as it seems, despite all that's gone on, this sounds pretty establishment when butted up against Mudhoney and Soundgarden. Still solid as it disrobes of its emotional layers, but gotta say it, definitely behind a formidable pack of geographic comparatives.

Rating 7

## Mother Tongue - Mother Tongue (Sony '94)

It don't look like grunge, but it sure sounds like the real thing, mixing Pearl Jam, Soundgarden and Mother Love Bone to pleasing effect. Cool thing about this one is its undisciplined, unrefined, sort of un-tampered with rock lolligag through isolated worlds. Lots of punky psychedelia, retro grooves and slinky guitar sounds that borrow from Hendrix through Masters Of Reality through the Black Crowes (well, that's what I hear anyways). The good kind of bed-headed mess.

Rating 7

## Mötley Crüe - Too Fast For Love (Elektra '81)

**Too Fast For Love** was a record on fire, mixing elements that had no business being together for an effect that was electrifying and terrifying in its sleaze. This is supposed to be some kind of glam rock record, but somewhere it just went so bad, Vince Neil's twangy whine wrapping itself around tales grimy from living on the streets, caged 'n' drooling somewhere between erroneous and brilliant; guitars gutted and hopeless, drums booming and unrestrained, gongs, bells, muted cymbals all hit at exactly the wrong and exactly the right time. Under the crustified electrocution, there are glam tunes, tracks like Starry Eyes and Public Enemy #1, but something goes horribly wrong along the way, their hulks twisted beyond recognition by the most inebriated of performances, not to mention the ear-splitting soloing style (or is that non-style) of Mick Mars, who turns the record into the rattiest of bar gigs, all sweat and blood and beer. So **Too Fast For Love** is one deadly debut, absolutely locked on powerdrive whether it's at the wheel of one of its trashy rockers or attempting some sort of sick power ballad (of which Merry-Go-Round is a classic, probably my favorite track here). And that's the ugly beauty of this record, a total lack of dynamic, a performance threatening to implode from the heat, driven by the totally blitzing drum attack of Tommy Lee, who really goes downhill after this (due in no small part to the band's choice of producers). A real shit-kicker. Later remixed and re-launched.

Rating 10

## Mötley Crüe - Shout At The Devil (Elektra '83)

Talk about crass marketing. The Crüe, after making probably the most hilarious strip mall record of all time, come bounding back as baby-eating Satanists! Well, at least as the cover art is concerned (plain upside down pentagram) and one naff throwaway track called God Bless The Children Of The Beast. And it pays off big, as headless teens everywhere mixed their blood together after a few beers and banged their heads to rippin' hits like Looks That Kill and Too Young To Fall In Love, two tracks every respecting bar band had to learn. But on a deeper level, this really was a wild 'n' evil record, celebrating all things destructive to the soul while the band bashed us over the head with moronic riffs and caveman-level percussion work, a half-calculated, half by mistake sound that just did something to the morality centres of the brain. Metal didn't come any stupider than **Shout At The Devil**, sounding frozen in its tracks as it bulldozed its way through one rehashed power chord after another, really doing a lot of damage to the world's perception of heavy metal: dumb music with the ability to corrupt our youth at the same time. I must say I bought right into the Crüe at the time along with everybody else, more for the reason that it was all so bad and so heavily gone, kinda like Manowar, even if this album began to wear thin real fast, with tracks like Bastard and Red Hot being the ultimate in lobotomy metal. Compared with its predecessor, **Shout At The Devil** is a bust; totally immobilized by blunt retarded power, but the overall mystique of the band leaked through like a sore, somewhat fortifying the experience. Just unclean in every sense of the word.

Rating 8

## Mötley Crüe - Theatre Of Pain (Elektra '85)

After building the perfectly flawed beast for both bars and graveyards, Crüe blow it big time with this follow-up, a record that opens with gusto, packing City Boy Blues, an interesting ether-dulled Aerosmith-style stomp which really puts the toxic in the twins; all things equal, a rumbling, stumbling, likeable mess of a tune. Then it's one surgical dismantling of cranial matter after another, like Smokin' In The Boys Room (cheap Quiet Riot ploy), like Louder Than Hell, like Save Our Souls, and the list bloats on in nauseating waves. Stiff, awkward, thick with boredom and immersed in a pile of mud by one of the blockiest recordings I've ever heard: something like punching loaves of day-old bread. Really, about as dumbo-eared as metal gets, and given the Crüe's largely undeserved commercial success, one of the shining examples of the silliness of metal, in effect, the #1 band for which metal gets a bad name. If the Crüe have their spandex pulse on the state of America's youth, then this world is a stinking mess indeed.

Rating 4

## Mötley Crüe - Girls, Girls, Girls (Elektra '87)

Dumped into our sewers at the lowest of low points in the harrowing Crüe saga, **Girls, Girls, Girls** is the band's second dumbest records (after the inexcusable **Theatre Of Pain**), a deflated chunk of bubble gum sleeze, full of doped and dopey thumpers that like its predecessor, exposes the boys' sorry lack of technical expertise. Side one ain't half bad, highlight being kick-off sweat hog Wild Side, but side two is moronic, truly high school skidder at its most mentally class-skipping. No, this is a band on chemically-induced auto-pilot, shamelessly stepping up to the podium with a raft of pooches that must have been written during raging hangovers: one weekend of work max. Like Vince sez: "leave the money where it's easy to see."

Rating 5

## Mötley Crüe - Dr. Feelgood (Elektra '89)

**Dr. Feelgood** has the beleaguered Crüe assembling all their faculties, working to the best of their abilities, gathering their best ideas, working really, really, really hard, really wanting it this time. But when the band has all the brains of a welding bench, and the musical ability of a spring roll, one can't expect too much, even if career rejuvenator Bob Rock is cracking the whip. But call me animal, I've got a soft spot for the Crüe, and my ears were open. And the luckiest band in rock come through, sort of, with what one can imagine the product of a really dumb band trying really hard. Maybe the sorry fact that I buy into the Crüe $tory accounts for my liking the hits, the rowdy, Radar Lovin' *Kickstart My Heart*, good-time ballad *Don't Go Away Mad (Just Go Away)*, and the almost ambitious title cut, with its infectious, respiratory riff. Elsewhere there's still some staggeringly inept Hollyrock, but definitely less of it, as Rock drowns out all the rough spots with all varieties of sprinkles and coloured icing. And damn it if the Crüe didn't do it again, selling a mountain of acetate, ribbon and pressed tinfoil, confounding us naysayers who thought the youth was reclaiming its brains. And at the end of the day, I guess that's why I'm on board.

Rating 7

## Mötley Crüe - Decade Of Decadence (Elektra '91)

This lively and entertaining career retro packs major value in offering some appropriately stoopid but fun new cuts from a legendary band of decadent pigs, bent wiggling over the frying pan of obsolescence with the sacking of blonde bad boy Vince Neil. Worth it for the brilliant *Primal Scream* alone, a scorching, haunted metal force way above the band's usual primary cream, **Decade Of Decadence** mixes a brew of memories with new directives and odds 'n' sods, including a rowdy *Anarchy In The U.K.*, a live smoke through **Dr. Feelgood**'s best moment, major hit *Kickstart My Heart*, and a couple of OK-ish soundtrack tunes. Plus there's a l'il rah-rah essay by metal dignitary Lonn Friend, and lyrics to the new stuff. With a growing soft spot for Crüe, borne of **Dr. Feelgood**'s sincere attempt to reverse the odorous effluent that comprised the brain-dead **Theatre Of Pain** and **Girls, Girls, Girls**, I strongly buy into this cool look back at the notorious sleezoids called the Crüe. So for now, my CD player reeks with guilty leather, defiant at sensitive college rock and the lark that is '90s punk.

Rating 8

## Motley Crue - Motley Crue (Elektra '94)

The long-awaited, long-feared Crue-without-Vince has finally pulled up to the curb in dire need of a shower and shave. Yep, **Motley Crue** (band and record sans ümlauts) carries with it a heavy layer of dirt, as John Corabi's snakebelly-level growls personify the new scraping, scrapping slow-burn sound. The record lumbers open with a basic but bold scratch of a tune that poses the question "Who said music's dead in the streets?" with a soul-searching irony that is perhaps lost on Nikki and the boys. But **Motley Crue** is no slouch, despite its adherence to remedial skidder metal, updating with a noisy grunge mix that is borderline hard to listen to. Lead single *Hooligan's Holiday* (working LP title I) continues the elephantine lope, at first listen just dumb, on second spin greasy with hook. And on and on the sordid fun continues, pleasant surprise being the gravity and maturity of the softer numbers, which are somehow lavish and still gutter-bound. Again hooks walk by, creepiest and most appetizing being *Til Death Do Us Part* (working LP title II). So in a way, not remotely Crüe-like; too slow, cavernous, echoey, itchy and scratchy, but by the same stretch, still of the street, for the street, Crue eradicating many of the embarrassing '80s elements past records lived by, while retaining a few less disparaging ones that succeed due to marginally elevated playing, marginally elevated lyrics, and a bad mutha of a mix. A guilty pleasure, and of course nowhere near creative or brainiac, **Motley Crue** nevertheless becomes the perfect tonic when slumming it for a day. So in a way, Crue is still Crüe, although this record hit the tanks but fast.

Rating 8

## Motley Crue - Quaternary (Warner '94)

**Quaternary** is the five-track EP that was offered for sale through mail, with the **Motley Crue** album, comprising one solo track from each member (hence the title) and a rousing new-Crue style band track called *Babykills*. Lots of profane, funny and idiotic rock star grunting goes on between the tracks which can be summed up as follows. Tommy Lee's *Planet Boom* and Nikki Sixx's *Father* are both big, layered, rustified and dirty industrial hip hoppin' metal tunes. Mick Mars offers *Bittersuite*, a thick and steamy blues, while John Corabi surprises with *Friends*, a nice Beatle-esque piano ballad. Apparently a slightly different version occurs in Japan, but ain't that always the case? Curio value only.

Rating 6

## Motley Crue - Generation Swine (Warner '97)

Prepare for the summer record of '97 (I'm writing this three months before scheduled release), Crue doing daring things with sound, combining noise metal with Cheap Trick, complexity with melody, the Beatles with Alice in Chains, basically Warrant without showering (that's a good thing!). Vince is back and well on track, singing his heart out way back behind the din, a din hugely dominated by trashcan drums and very distorted guitars. A sublime sludge squelches forth, but the songs are diamonds, many speeds periodically collapsing into gosh-crazy memorable choruses, until Nikki and Tommy barrage it all once again. I mention daring and I mean it, **Generation Swine** not exactly being easily decipherble or indeed slottable, the Crue taking us very rambunctiously into something that erases that metal tag but still rocks, much like the under-rated **Motley Crue** record. So congrats are in resounding order. And I hope the damn thing sells, because these guys are no trip down memory lane, turning in what is by far their most intelligent and tricky record, as I say, incorporating new elements while still slapping us sleazy. A happy consolation reunion, after the dreary dog show surrounding Van Halen.

Rating 9

## Motörhead - Motörhead (Chiswick '77)

Collapsed to form a metal band so scuzzy the punks thought they were the ones being serenaded, wizened rock pigs Fast Eddie Clarke, Filthy Animal Taylor and the warted wizard Ian "Lemmy" Kilminster (ex-Hendrix roadie, ex-Hawkwind bass guy) converged upon a world unprepared for the brutish bashing to come. Motörhead were big, bad and loud, recorded rank and putrid as they slogged their way through shabby pounder after shabby pounder. And **Motörhead**, the bonafide studio (yeah, right) debut is the dirtiest of them all, as the bikers in the band create a unified, uniform distorto-drone through all eight enclosed. Motörhead were instantly recognizable as the first metal band who weren't trying to look good, play good or record good, which resulted in the ultimate deception of punks who were embracing the most fossilized of hippies, and critics who generally despised the tenets of metal. The record had tons of crowd favourites, if not musical art works, faves being *Keep Us On The Road*, *Lost Johnny* and *The Watcher*. Above dissection, **Motörhead** stands more as an influence towards more purposefully polluted metal; faint echoes of the Stooges, but really occupying space as the original

grunge rockers, being the first who could actually play, but rather chose to stink up the place. A crass act all the way.
Rating 7

## Motörhead - Overkill (Bronze '79)

With a raging cover like this one . . . looking totally bitchin' in full four-colour flare, blue ink on schoolbook, or black felt pen on jean jacket, how can you lose? Overkill was tattooed on our life in much that manner during our high school daze, as one obnoxious crank of a rocker, sticking its finger in the eye of punk and shaking up a bloated metal aristocracy with one vile mess of decibel lunacy. Lemmy in full flak throat leads the charge, croaking through such bashable jems as I'll Be Your Sister, Stay Clean, and ultimately No Class with its slaughtering of Tush's classic riff amidst WWII (the big one) axe solos from one pillaging Fast Eddie. The ultimate power trio, Motörhead as a recorded experience was pure unharnessed wattage, unrelenting underground destruction, playing the soldier, the hapless underdog with the loudest toys and drunken vision to stomp the blues, psychedelia and punk rock under a tarnished metal mash that lives to subjugate under spreading rust. Thus Overkill becomes the first Motörhead masterwerk, where the band forms a ripped and bleedin' ball of rock, bowing to no trace of melody, cleanliness or respectability.
Rating 9

## Motörhead - Bomber (Bronze '79)

And the mental harassment drags ever on, as Fast Eddie Clarke, Philthy Animal Taylor and "Lemme a fiver" explore further corrosion between conspiring aged hippies, doing battle with the forces of sensible music. Overkill, Bomber . . . what's the difference, it all rocks proud and scarred, strafing the crowd with the likes of new classics Poison and All The Aces, plus the catchy, automotive, speed-riffed title track. If anything, Bomber is even more imploded than its turf-busting predecessor, downright diseased as Philthy buries every attempt at pattern under layers of crashing trash can lids and power shuffles too fast for the creaking digits of his frontmen. A crazy weenie roast to behold, from a one-of-a-kind metal experience.
Rating 8

## Motörhead - On Parole (United Artists '79)

Comprising mostly timid takes on greaseballers that would rage full fester on the Motörhead debut, On Parole is like a demo, B-side, barrel-scraping trip through the formative stages of a concept. Kinda behaved and dopey and fraught with production inconsistencies, this pre-Philthy look back is a weak collection of calling cards indeed, what with City Kids, a low juice Vibrator, totally bumbling The Watcher and a guitar-void Lost Johnny wandering about the acetate looking for amps that go to 11. Old classic Leaving Here is kinda funny though, totally punky and brainless like a good Motörhead B-side should be. Still, one mangy mutt of a record from the ultimate "wot th' hell" gang.
Rating 6

## Motörhead - Ace Of Spades (Bronze '80)

Man, it doesn't get any better than this. With a headsdown conviction fortified by frothing mugs of battery acid, Motörhead reach their peak, strangling the gullet of rock'n'roll with this four alarm fire, their best collection of survival tales yet, packed full of buzzing bass, crazy old hippy guitar noises, and totally blitzed drumming, while Lemmy spits like nails his truth, the only truth, the hard truth. Heavy as hell throughout, Ace Of Spades is a raging demolition derby of tortuous battle-torn sounds, from the frantic opening title cut through Love Me Like A Reptile, Fast And Loose and finally after one sledge of a hangover, The Hammer, closing

the wound with as much terminal velocity as the opener. Ultimately Ace Of Spades buries once and for all any catatonic jamming qualities that occasionally frayed the edges of past tunes, moving either farther away into inhospitable terrains into the seediest of seething metals, wrestling twelve foot alligators with frenetic sheer force, all the while tightening up their three part disharmony o'er top a traditional Motörmasochist mix. Rumbling, corrosive machinery from the masters of formidable noise. Pass me another and make it black.
Rating 10

## Motörhead - No Sleep 'til Hammersmith (Bronze '81)

Power trio is the ultimate understatement here, as the three blighted ones, Lemmy in classic stance bellowing northward into a mike tilted down at eye level, belt out highlights from record I through IV, most letting fly with thrashy abandon, best being the oddly melodic Bomber and greatly improved closer Motörhead. After this record however, I don't know why I would ever go see this legendary band live, the word dynamics nowhere to be seen within twenty miles of the stage (audible radius). An adequately recorded testimony to a force with loads of no compromise integrity, and a record considered to be a live classic in many punter circles. Reality pie, anyone?
Rating 6

## Motörhead - Iron Fist (Mercury '82)

After punctuating massive English success with a "cheers, mates!" sort of live tunes, Motörhead make perhaps an ill-timed trip back to the studio with this most thoughtful 'head case, a record which steps aside from the ever-intensifying head-exploding frenzy of the band's output thus far, with an ever so slight riff and dynamic upgrade, not to mention a barely detectable smoothing of production edges. Although there's better quality metal here, most notably America, the complex and meaty (Don't Let 'Em) Grind Ya Down and finally (Don't Need) Religion, a tune that demonstrates Lemmy's colourful and independent grasp of living, there's also a liberal dose of mindless headbanging, like Speedfreak and the rehashing title cut. It all makes for another good Motörhead whipping, if somewhat uneven, as half the record becomes the new anthems of the year, and half begin what will by '92 comprise a sizeable scrap pile of filler based mostly on repetitive, progressively self-deprecating and comical reiterations of the Lemmy philosophy over punk-unquality speed riffs. Verdict: hazy memories of good loud mileage.
Rating 8

## Motörhead - Another Perfect Day (Mercury '83)

Sure Lizzy's elegant stringsmith Brian Robertson is the wrong man for the job, but what results (in my very lonely opinion) is an interesting new lease on life for a concept that was beginning to wear through the scalp. What we get are fully melodious fragments of finesse woven throughout the usual celebration of noise, and a slightly more reverent attention to song, albeit still of crippled and scowling disposition. No question, Robbo causes no wholesale paradigm shift, most likely dragged into playing as much like Eddie as possible, which may have been cause for his speedy exit. Anyhoo, Another Perfect Day versus Iron Fist manages to sound drunker and more mature at the same time. Faves would include the hot/cold lead single I Got Mine and the even more eccentric Dancing On Your Grave, both cantankerous grunge rockers with tasty Robbo fills from outta nowhere, plus total punk rave closer Die You Bastard, a tune pumped full of bullets but defiant of death. Motörhead seems back to making a hell of a din, capturing the blinding ozone blur of past

records like **Ace Of Spades**, almost over-compensation for acquiring a guy that can play so dog-gone good.
Rating 9

## Motörhead - No Remorse (Bronze '84)

My kinda compilation, one with buying incentive even for actual fans, if you can believe it. **No Remorse** is a hits package that goes the extra mile: a detailed history of the band to date, amusing notes from Lemmy on each included cut, lyrics to everything, plus a beefy ten cuts previously unreleased on LP. Besides a bunch of classics, (too many pulled from **No Sleep**), there's three punky scroungers done with liggin' partners Girlschool, a couple of oldies, including an endearing version of *Louie Louie*, some B-sides, best being marauding riffster *Too Late Too Late*, and four brand new hot rods, sustained wall *Steal Your Face*, two OTT thrashers, and one of the grooviest survival tales of the band's vast and greasy repertoire, *Killed By Death*, an almost Stonesy low-slung distortion piece, the highlight of the record. A well-conceived, if not premature history of a legend, with lots to stimulate the pistons, **No Remorse** just may be flashy enough to fill your Motörhead fix more often than the official studio booty. Notable omission: the boozier of the two totally different *Under The Knife*'s.
Rating 7

## Motörhead - Orgasmatron (GWR '86)

**Orgasmatron** features Motörhead as a four piece with Lemmy as sole original membrain, which is more a moral defeat than one causing any damage to the Motörcore. But the low tide in the Motörhead sense of family marks a hazy sense of death that coincides with metal making great strides year after year, leaving old Motörhead legendary, nostalgic and almost mythical, while the new stuff seems to be choking in the dust. **Orgasmatron** rants and raves way beyond its gravity in a sort of hysterical imitation of Motörhead's glory days. It also sets an unfortunate pattern where the gulf between dogs and classics will widen even further to the point of tearing apart the very concept of long-play. Bluntly, *Deaf Forever*, *Built For Speed* and *Orgasmatron*, three of Lemmy's grandest, grimiest monstrosities ever are the only material reasons for this record to exist, the title cut being one unstoppable and intelligent piece of work on man's condition, set to a throbbing, bitter cold riff which eloquently charts man's meaningless trudge through this world. And the rest? . . . neurotic flying crapola, screaming to be heard amongst a metal community that is saving what's left of its ears for something far less brash, simple and punishingly angular.
Rating 6

## Motörhead - Rock'N'Roll (GWR '87)

Lemmy continues to play the incurable ham, desperately and unwittingly stuck in a groove, undercutting the Motörhead tonic with self-defeating lyrical rehashes and an obstinate and obsolete urge to trash the place, blow the amps and take no prisoners. **Rock'n'Roll** for me becomes the lost release, having the least number of memorable cuts, faves being *Dogs* (nicely built like *I'll Be Your Sister*) and the truly melodic (close to a first) *All For You*, which becomes almost sensitive come chorus time. **Rock'n'Roll** is also the least serious, to no admirable advantage, with soupy, unambitious tracks like *Eat The Rich* and *Boogeyman*, two different velocities, one lacklustre boogie premise. Weird, but I'd say Motörhead are now fully transformed into a Motörhead tribute act, endlessly cranking permutations and alterations on a lifestream long exhausted. Notable improvements to come, but I can't help but think a surprisingly literary mind like Lemmy's has so much more to say, tales that would best be served on a higher and more technical metal plane,

which, as the band has aspired to sporadically in the past, can be flown under the usual highly distorted circumstances.
Rating 6

## Motörhead - No Sleep At All (GWR '88)

Lemmy go, enough already. Motörhead as a studio experience is dirt-faced and drano-dragged as it is, making these live infections non-events of the bloodiest order. Solid tracks, nice thought throwing in the lyrics, inspiring stage raps from Reverend Kilminster, but awful recording with no bass.
Rating 5

## Motörhead - 1916 (Sony '91)

For all the talk of significant departure, 1916 is yer basic Motörhead crank-up, a good solid punk metal blaze, led by the record's three best cuts, riffster *The One To Sing The Blues*, traditional 'head speedster *I'm So Bad (Baby I Don't Care)*, and laid-back single *No Voices In The Sky*. Then a boogie, then a bass scape, then a ballad, another scuzzy boogie, and three sub-par moshes, followed by closer *1916*, another of Lemmy's thoughtful and vivid anti-war tunes, set to a feel not unlike Pink Floyd's **The Wall** (Yeah, all of it. What do you want from me?). In total, a bit on the weak and automatic side, falling together like a disjointed stack of ideas, sometimes symbiotic sometimes not, put through the 'head shredder with numbing lack of forethought. And I don't think this is the band to be writing tributes to the Ramones.
Rating 7

## Motörhead - March Or Die (Sony '92)

Pretty damn easy to miss this one in the racks, given the cover's similarity to **Motörhead, No Remorse** and various other compilation-style output. Verdict: not a great cover. Anyways, King Diamond's capable Mikkey Dee sits in on skins, and that combined with some deeper arrangements and up-town production makes this the most polished Motörhead yet. Even Slash and long-time bud Ozzy contribute, as we get *Hellraiser*, the same dopey chunk rocker that was on **No More Tears**. Riffs are upscale too, but not too tricky, as Lemmy's usual welfare case ethic remains dog-eared but intact. Weird record by a seemingly tired old ship; one of the best in a long time, with an ever-pontificating Lemmy showing his wit and colour, yet still a record by a band sadly losing its necessity, or its sense of personal mission. Low points: novelty cover of *Cat Scratch Fever*, and another war dirge title track to wind things down. Solid but still sounding assembled rather than smeared.
Rating 7

## Motörhead - Bastards (ZYX '93)

Bloodrust waves of torrential torrent mark the raucous return to form that we were all craving from Kilminster and Co. Woe be it to beast and bike, **Bastards** has arrived, coked to the nines, grinding steel grooves, grease and fire, lunatic wattage raised skyclad in rage. You'd never guess the face-pasting internals from yet another bored and toothless, black and white album cover, but **Bastards** reaches right into the oil-stained intestinals of Lemmy's golden glories and pulls out steaming iron dogtags like *I Am The Sword*, *Bad Woman*, and stunning amplified mantra *We Bring The Shake*, all absolutely thrilled with a twin-terror guitar sound that is all bite, chew and spew. And Lemmy's vocals are dead-on, crunching through an awesome stretch of provoking lyrics while his band pumps a performance that is all lift and separate the men from the boys. Quite simply, masterful and recorded with large scraping heroics, all corners of the Motörmachine forced full-on in reverence to edge, mass and bad-ass biker metal. Other fave raves: *Liar* with its *Orgasmatron*

297

bass pulse, and lead track *On Your Feet Or On Your Knees* (Eric Bloom would be proudly shaking that cheesy afro in reverent accordance). Best advice would be to sink your teeth into this deafening feast, for Motörhead has hatched a headbangin' beauty, perfectly fused to the most admirable tenets of the philosophical core of why this band stands alone.

Rating                                                                10

## Motörhead - Fistful Of Aces: The Best Of Motörhead   (Griffin '94)

Sporting twenty unshaven tales of mayhem from the one and only, **Fistful Of Aces** offers more than enough knock-knock jokes from the first two-thirds of the band's tarnished time on this planet. Just goes to show how little things change within this crusty institution. Good to see oddities from **No Remorse** (three beers for *Snaggletooth!*) but bad to see blighties from the band's worst live album, **No Sleep At All**. Pictures, credits, but no liner notes.

Rating                                                                 6

## Motörhead - Sacrifice   (CMC/MCA '95)

And it's down to an explosive three piece again for what is Motörhead's second best album since the old days. And I say that almost in spite, 'cos really those old "classics" are viewed with heaps of nostalgia, and in reality, there's a good case to be made for **Bastards** and **Sacrifice** being stronger statements than **Ace Of Spades**, **Another Perfect Day**, and quite certainly **Overkill** and **Bomber**. All this is to argue that Lemmy really knows the grease of metal, his vocals more raked and urgent than ever; his songs a volatile mix of dirty, metal anarchy and the best poison of punk. Eleven good to awe-inspiring songs (*Dog-Face Boy* moshes beyond belief, as does octane freight train *In Another Time*) make up for the fact that this record is only 36 minutes vicious. Ya just don't care when these guys straddle the cannons and light the fuse. BTW, Wurzel's out, but the rest of da mechanics build a noisy grunting beast, Mikkey Dee and Phil "Zoom" Campbell quite surprisingly and increasingly perfect for the Lemmy scrapyard, their more arty pasts beat out of them by the blast of Motörhead's rich boozy heritage. Bloody but unbowed, this is the band that really captures the energy of punk rock, without having to write songs as dull as the Ramones, one of the Lemster's favorite bands. Killer, carnivorous and raw.

Rating                                                                 8

## Motörhead - Overnight Sensation   (CMC/BMG '96)

People are luvin' the last three Motörhead records, but after this trio of tasty treats, most are starting to choose favourites. Well, I like 'em all, the band really bursting with bustle and pride all over '93's **Bastards** and '95's **Sacrifice**, Lemmy serving notice that greasy bear meat metal ain't dead. Fact is, the textures are fantastic, Lemmy's buzz bass well nigh overshadowed by Mickey Dee's punchy, beer-blasted percussion and the overall explosiveness of another Howard Benson mix. The grooves are killer, really deep-pocketed, especially on chuggin' rockers like *Love Can't Buy You Money*, *Broken* and *Murder Show*, pretty much locked in time with your headiest headbangs from the NWOBHM, trickier and smarter than old Motörhead (which really doesn't stand up to these new songs, let's face it), more like the best from Tank or Saxon sent way up the power spectrum. Also quite thankfully, no token ballad, although there's a sort of campfire acoustic rocker that works quite well. So how much longer does Lemmy have to deliver such respectful records and not get the sales?

Rating                                                                 9

## Mourning Sign - Mourning Sign   (Godhead/Flying '95)

The Swedes strike again, and the hitting is hard, heavy and high-flying. **Mourning Sign** is an insane patchwork of tricky death metal, Sentenced-style trad metal, Sepultura heart and soul, and searing progressive arrangements circa Fear Factory. The end result is a bombastic assault that sounds like three Pantera songs playing at once, adding a thin, sophisticated industrial shine on top to blow the thing so ragingly skyward, the jaw drops in awe. Riffs, solos and those swirling, complex arrangements perform a ballet of extreme beauty all over this long, laboured earfest, while Robert Porschke's exquisitely death vocals bark out harsh sentiments that have become the staple of the Swede scene, no better, no worse than the band's contemporaries. Hard to play, hard as nails, and so easy to suck one in, Mourning Sign may mark the next intensifying wave of excellent Swedish acts, fusing the best elements of groove, guts and glory from Meshuggah to Entombed. Who would have thought that it could get heavier and more sonically intelligent at once? Ultratop flight extremism. Buy it.

Rating                                                                 9

## Movida - Movida   (Spell/Dig It '95)

No one's going to know what the hell I'm talking about here, but let's give it a shot. This enigmatic Movida thingie is a pretty cool, sickly sweet sort of underground metal record, carving itself a sub-sub-niche which is basically this: Nirvana meets melodic death metal, the absolutely brand-new stuff played by Paradise Lost and Lake Of Tears and Pyogenesis. And you know how they do it? By being from a weird place, in this case Italy, out of the rush and hype of traditional metal markets, off to the side where a band can really whip up some fresh tonalities, *Against It All* and *Distant Plains* sporting absolutely fabulous hooks. Call it pop death metal or sumthin', I don't know. All I can tell is that this is lavishly produced melodic rock with more than a touch of death, made by standard issue longhaired freaks, with a very nice and costly looking CD booklet to boot. Sum total, Movida makes a strong case for multi-culturalism, given its fine example of the cool, catchy but mainly unique tunes and melodies that can emerge from non-Anglophone markets (incidentally all the lyrics are English, and very good). But to boil it right down, this is pretty much an alternative, pop version of Paradise Lost, a damn fine proposal indeed.

Rating                                                                 8

## Moxy - Moxy   (Polydor '75)

This confident Canuck debut reveals an innovative band raised on Zeppelin and Deep Purple, ready to turn it up. Considerably heavy, ham-fisted and Neanderthal for the time, **Moxy** is an exercise in slow, unwieldy metal, glued with one of those dense '70s recording that sounds created of the packed soil itself. The guitars slouch forth with determination, maneuvering like an eighteen wheeler, and so does the one and only Buzz on molten vocals. So what if it's a little boring and derived, it's history in the making, one of a handful of records this heavy, this far back.

Rating                                                                 6

## Moxy - II   (Polydor '76)

In which we find the band in transition, adding complexity, yet stretching experimentation too far from the metallic homebase. **II** is mellower and funkier, even more dated, than both its predecessor and its follow-up, and not all that entertaining anywhere outside of two of the four louder metal gestures. Great. Sounds like a subdued version of **Ridin' High**'s unproductive low points. A band in search of metal, with few role models to light the way.

Rating                                                                 4

## Moxy - Ridin' High  (Polydor '77)

One of a small fistful of heavy rock records to come out of Canada in the '70s, **Ridin' High** rocks appreciably, stumbling amidst its short list of influences, bobbing to the surface with a sound not unlike early Nuge meets BTO, or early Teaze mixed with Angel's funkier moments. Technically speaking, there's only one ballad on the whole shmooze, the rest oscillating 'twixt loud barroom rock and uncharacteristically advanced metal, as on the galloping, ambient and ambitious *Sweet Reputation (Symphony For Margaret)* and the beefy *Are You Ready*. Still, it's all kinda blunt and lowbrow, hanging desperately to each merely acceptable riff, showing its age, as early metallic tinkerers Eddie Leonetti and Jack Douglas work on their sea legs, coming up with a fairly uninteresting, toneless mix. In conclusion this is easily the band's shining moment; a work constructed at the band's creative threshold, lifted by the fiery growl of Buzz Shearman and little else, aside from a few long-lost and amusing hard rock poses.
Rating                                                                     7

## Moxy - Under The Lights  (Polydor '78)

Like screaming in a nightmare, no sound emerges from these lifeless general rock toons, despite their periodic attempts to be heard. Moxy is sadly on full idle, Mike Rynoski at the helm—better known as Mike Reno of Loverboy—replacing the irreplaceable Buzz Shearman, whose violent throat (if hindsight be permitted) was the heart and soul of a band slow to fire, a band who burned brightly for one lonely well-hung record. Here it's just a pathetic embarrassment, like clueless first steps by any number of delete-fated Canucks.
Rating                                                                     2

## Moxy - A Tribute To Buzz Shearman  (Ahed Est. '80)

This compilation tracks the stunted but influential career of these early Canadian leadfoots in the form of a memorial to the deceased Buzz Shearman, vocalist on all but the last and worst Moxy outing, who would die in a motorcycle crash after a short career plagued by booze and drugs. The album isn't that important, juxtaposing many styles and recording values, nonetheless serving as a testimonial to one of the earlier bands who weren't afraid to attack with aggression and carve fresh gashes in the new sound. Sez they were big in Texas.
Rating                                                                     4

## Moxy - Self-Destruction  (Pacemaker '94)

This fifteen track CD compilation relives the Moxy legacy, a brief, mildly metallic spark on the sleepy Canadian scene. **Self-Destruction** samples (not all that intelligently) the first three records, then adds *Trouble*, a 45-only simple-chorded rock burger with cheese, and *Feed The Fire*, a watery, mild-on-the-hands, Buddy Caine Band rocker. Doesn't much do this band much justice, given the already handicapped catalogue.
Rating                                                                     6

## Mozart - Mozart  (Bachoven Musicwerks '93)

Played this a whole bunch of times and nothing's sticking, yet the record's elusive illusion comes as no detriment, these boastfully-named musical vortextbooks sending in a hyperactive performance of agile technical metal with more that a couple o' nods to Queen, no surprise given the operatic production treatment of Roy Thomas Baker. Rumour is that Gene Simmons was quite taken by the band, getting them signed, so that you can see Mozart's sensuous rock pastiche. Lead vocalist and period piece pianist "Adam", can project like Freddy, as guitars howl like Brian May, the whole fast-paced snobby hodge podge bolstered by huge harmonies, and a detectably playful chaotic edge, taking the band into the satire of Extreme or Saigon Kick. Often perfumed with finesse, often indulged with

cheesy results. I mean, what other kind of band would think of covering Sting's *Fortress Around Your Heart*?
Rating                                                                     7

## Mr. Big - Mr. Big  (Atlantic '89)

All traces of cleverness are left to the colour commentary on this debut by this assembly of speedy minds. No waves were made due to a brevity of brains when it comes to songwriting, the most vital part of a rock record, no matter what the talent translating the game into action. Really, only kick-off track *Addicted To That Rush* has any sort of liveliness to it, the rest running the gamut from bad Kiss, bad Whitesnake, medium quality Y&T and generally dopey hard rock glued shut with derivative funk and blues. Point is, **Mr. Big** and its considerably successful follow-up both have that downwound, out of touch feel, like a dazed hard rock record trying to be all things to all people with nary a core sound, save for Eric Martin's scat-brained rambunctiousness and Sheehan's piccolo bass protrusions. All in all, on the right side of acceptable due to conviction without basis, and an over-emphasized isolation. In a word: nerdy; but somehow backwardly acceptable.
Rating                                                                     6

## Mr. Big - Lean Into It  (Atlantic '91)

The meeting of unlike minds that became Mr. Big's blunted and limp debut gives way to a semblance of symbiosis as this supergroup of modern day hotshots, leader and bass whiz Billy Sheehan, solo artist and songsmith in his own right Eric Martin, Racer X fretburner Paul Gilbert (who was also an instructor at GIT at 17 years of age!), and appropriately wicked drummer Pat Torpey, reach frequent levels of pleasant connectivity that the nerdish debut so frustratingly lacked. There's still something loose-fitting, out-of-date, and unnecessary about this merger, but passing years have bonded the individuals in question to the point where one thinks band first, technicians second. One hears interesting melds of emotion on a number of levels, reverberating throughout such diversities as bluesy kick-off speedster *Daddy, Brother, Lover, Little Boy (The Electric Drill Song)*, soupy slow-brewed *CDFF-Lucky This Time*, totally bright, beautifully-voiced smash hit ballad *To Be With You*, and the hugely connecting lead-off single *Green-Tinted Sixties Mind*, a rare Paul Gilbert-penned sidewinder. Mr. Big has evolved into a comfortably soulful chunk of corporate metal, fuelled by Eric Martin's skilful, bluesy wail, and overall attention to detail and showmanship that nevertheless leaves centre stage to the message. The sloth and simple riffs that made the debut such an inept sleeper are still apparent, only now the mediocre is uniquely hard-wired; retro-'70s to the point of absorbing only the decade's bad habits, yet saved by instrumental dressy-ness, simple hooky choruses, and Martin's youthful but confident vocals. Seemingly resigned to understate, Mr. Big reminds one of Asia, in the sense of majorly verbose artistes playing down their skills forcefully and somewhat unwillingly. Again though, best thing I can say is, I play it a lot and it still sounds good. And like Extreme with the annoying *More Than Words*, major belated buzz rose to a roar on the wings of the mellowest of singles, aforementioned silky ballad *To Be With You*.
Rating                                                                     7

## Mr. Big - Bump Ahead  (Atlantic '93)

Well, sorry . . . I'm pretty disinterested at this point, with so much massively more mind-blowing product out there. Mr. Big's third finds the band perfectly intact, with a blueprint collection of mainstream rockers with which to assault your El Lay senses. Heaps more sterling playing, watery-like in its mass profusion, collectively focused in its chartable aspirations, **Bump**

**Ahead** (cool cover) does an iron-pumping wake-up call all over **Lean Into It**, but rides the line so judiciously, one can't discern any sort of step ahead, 'cept maybe for an admirable Whitesnake-like versatility to Eric Martin's soul-stirring pipes. Churlish and Lynchable, '80s and quenchable, **Bump Ahead** is for those who seek a more straight-forward piece of living, a thick steak, and some pale ale, steered down a regular path by irregular players. Craft: yes, creativity: no.
Rating                                                                  6

## Mr. Big - Japandemonium   (Atlantic '94)

Predictably so, Japan loves these guys, given their four-way shred abilities. And this is no less than the fourth live record built for the Land of the Rising Sun, previous slabs like **Live! Raw Like Sushi** ('90), **Raw Like Sushi II** ('92), and **Live** ('92), pretty much exhausting the scheme in my eyes. This set happens just before **Bump Ahead**, offering all the hits and then some (including Gilbert and Sheehan solos) in a surprisingly bashy, trashy, shoot 'em up format. As usual, lots of nice packaging. Two studio tracks: *Seven Impossible Days* (probably the band's best ballad), and *I've Learned My Lesson*, a slack metal funkster.
Rating                                                                  6

## Mr. Big - Hey Man   (Atlantic '96)

. . . and Mr. Big press blithely on, creating in a much more positive spirit than alterno rock to be sure, but very caught, wrapped and dropped cement-shoed in a realm of uncool, so much that judgment is clouded, even though tunes be quite good. The bridge mix is much the same, if a tad bluesier, funkier, and psychedelic all in one (!), coming off like the baby Van Halen these guys always were, at least latently, capturing just that slight bright spark of spontaneous boombash and quiet cool found within ripping players who don't over-extend. Of course, nobody much cared, and Mr. Big became unceremoniously axed from their label deal along with King's X, who had just launched the criminally swell **Ear Candy** opus.
Rating                                                                  7

## Mr. Bungle - Mr. Bungle   (Warner '91)

It's taken me years to finally hear this fascinating record, years of people telling me with blank, confused stares that they weren't even sure if there's music on **Mr. Bungle**. Well, music exists in cornucopian, flowing gumwads, a music that is an exploded King Crimson for the '90s, really old Crimson from '69, '70 (you can see the sax smoke) made really new, nightmarish and overblown of sense, channel-changin' with spastic, compressed delight through twenty or so rock style offshoots. Mr. Bungle is best known as the overcluttered side project of Faith No More freak Mike Patton, but it is the entire band that out-fishes Fishbone here; every large, funky, heavy, twistedly prog-rockin' compost heap of a song being full-up with playing fer miles. Lyrically it's all about nasty, circus-coloured perversion, adding to the collage of sonics, taking this record way to the alternative like no sorry Cranberries or Oasis dribble could ever manage. Genius in the name of crazy evil.
Rating                                                                  8

## Mr. Bungle - Disco Volante   (Warner '95)

Call this one a **Trout Mask Replica** for the '90s, Patton and his triumphant schizofriends twirling the late night radio dial, stopping nowhere, laughing maniacally, committing crimes, feeding their faces, then burning down a barn at midnight. **Disco Volante** might possibly be the weirdest timeless hour plus I've ever heard, dropkicking the debut way beyond into the mental institution hall of sonic flame. One hears everything you ever learned in a three mile pile of pop culture; B-grade horror film music, spaghetti western scores, old Crim-

son (again), Hammond organ, experimental, almost Japanese grindcore, steaming cowpies of Mothers Of Invention, visits through all of Zappa, two phases of Beefheart and a stupifyingly disturbed jadedness with all things regular. The crazy person artwork presses the issue, taking the viewer/listener/purger further into morphed exotica, all green and gooey, distressingly wigged-out to places and planets unknown. Unlike the eventually understandable debut, **Disco Volante** contains very little that could be called conventional, the record being more a collage of loud, cardiac arrested alarms separated by confused loiterings in a bus depot, quiet as a church mouse, brain on fire, miles out of one's gourd, waiting for the next night-time neuron fry. Lyrics, let's not even start with the lyrics. Knocked a point off for its towering inaccessibility.
Rating                                                                  7

## Mucky Pup - Act Of Faith   (Century Media '92)

Kind of a cool band here, and a novel signing for demonic metal flamethrowers Century Media, Mucky Pup being more of a grind-tinged Red Hot Chili Peppers or Faith No More, funking along on a set of fratboy rockers under a recording straight out of frozen grim Sweden. Pretty heavy I guess, even crossing into hip-hop urbancore like the moderate side of say, Biohazard. Kind of amusing, but not everlasting.
Rating                                                                  6

## Mucky Pup - Lemonade   (Century Media '93)

Less yuk-yukking it up, as Mucky Pup gets considerably heavier, diving into slamming grooves often on this (opportunistically?) more alternative affair, tighter songs, focused angst, just a real authority to the thing. Mellow, psychedelic and broodingly slow stuff breaks up the big power chord swingsets, **Lemonade** as a result being paced like a funtime show to behold. Faves: *Mountain Song* and opener *Own Up For What You Say* which sound like '70s metal. Almost an **8**.
Rating                                                                  7

## Mudhoney - Superfuzz Bigmuff   (Sub Pop '88)

Dan, Steve, Mark and Matt emerge full flannel as the fumbling heroes of the Seattle sound, here cranking what is probably its most flammable document, the baddest, crustiest miscreant of a record ever to carry the Sub Pop dogtag. Only Green River's **Rehab Doll** and Nirvana's **Bleach** come close to the majestic plaque-encrusted placard that is Mudhoney's debut, a record that pounds the Cramps and The Lyres under a jolting metal monster mash, all creaky and cobwebbed, as our favourite big-nosed waif unhinges all over the battlefield. Paid a single dollar to see the "tour" of **Superfuzz** at Club Soda in Vancouver, and I will never forget how proficiently frenetic the band played, sprawling to grab every deranged power chord in the hall, just levelling the place, chaos be proud. Alas, in the end, **Superfuzz Bigmuff** is without reserve, a thing of beauty, six tracks all mud, sweat and tears, total annihilation, absolute Grunge in probably the truest sense of the term, with that patented guitar rot that lives most robustedly in the guts of Kyuss, and to a lesser extent, the mod-ish '60s austerity of modern day (yeah right) Mudhoney itself. Major facemelt. Note: **Mudhoney** was a Russ Meyer film.
Rating                                                                 10

## Mudhoney - Mudhoney   (Sub Pop '89)

Tube amps the world over were on tenderhook alert for Mudhoney's full-length debut, and the results are best described as confounding and anti-social, as Arm and Co. dig underneath their roots to find the wormiest of influences, something diseased and labrynthical as '60s garageability, The Stooges, and The Munsters. So **Mudhoney** becomes an even more academic and historical examination of mental music through the ages, even more dreamland-browned than the debut, aligning its curmudgeonly self with Jeff Connolly of The Lyres as a sort of scrapyard of 25 years of garbage rock, but of course much more shit-kickin' and brutal. Yet really, **Mudhoney** disappointed, with its broken beats, luded retro-escapes and flat-out flea-bitten illness, relying more on atmosphere (which it achieves with alarming odor), versus **Superfuzz**, which worked a sound trashing more in tune with the metallic grafting of Green River. Still **Mudhoney** is a work to be stared at, if mainly for its sheer hideousness of sound, perhaps Jack Endino's most repugnant aural pustule to date. Totally important in the formulation of Seattle's integrity as sonic hotbed, but damn near commercial suicide at the same time.

Rating                                                8

## Mudhoney - Every Good Boy Deserves Fudge
(Sub Pop '91)
Ever at threat of giving up rock'n'droll and going back to skool, Mudhoney proceeds to lock the toolshed, tolling everybody to just go away with this impenetrable hubba hubba dyn-O-mite celebration of bad engineering, fraught with mystical overabundances of midrange and splendidly numbskullian guitar solo excursionables. You've just got to laugh at a record this vacuum-packed in an imagined time and space. Because fact is, the '60s never sounded this extremely rusty, and the '70s never really tried outside of **Funhouse**, and even *that* was accidentally on purpose. A rumbling blur of under-the-hood rock, primed for lime-green Gremlins everywhere.

Rating                                                8

## Mudhoney - Piece Of Cake (Reprise/Warner '92)
Much the same bruising basement rock as its melted predecessor, **Piece Of Cake** (tastefully named for those white discs at the bottom of men's urinals) intersperses a gaggle of disheveled punk rants with snippets of cheezy sound effects like some sort of off-the-rails, '60s variety show, complete with wide lapels, three-legged tap dancers and lava lamps. Compression and depression collide with the most sincere trip into another era I've ever heard; basically Detroit circa '69, the worst the stinking city had to offer, abysmal gigs by various vermin flaunting their inexcusable dearth of talent, rendered increasingly garish and ugly by mountains of cheap, unreliable drugs. Quite the spectacle, but bordering on novelty at this stage in the game, almost stuck with a sound, however noble it may be, that inherent in its nature, shuns progress. Thus Mudhoney sits, bent and wheezing on Seattle's porch, waving its cane at mischievous young 'uns who wander onto the property, punctuating the mad charade with occasional blasts from the salt gun.

Rating                                                8

## Mudhoney - Five Dollar Bob's Mock Cooter Stew
(Reprise/Warner '93)
Critics panned this lazy EP, basically losing patience with Mudhoney's refusal to grow or more pertinently, *desire* to grow. So here we have it, seven more tracks of vile recording mistakes, crafty craftlessness, mayhem harkening to an underneath vibe, silliness fusing with academic snobbery, Mudhoney doing what they do best, by default, because nobody else would touch their moldy obsession with a ten-foot hangover. Crawling further into their ivory crawlspace with the potatoes and mom's canning, Mudhoney still do it for me, carving that ghastly little unswept niche that is a marvel to visit when time's creases touch and overlap at the centre.

Rating                                                7

## Mudhoney - My Brother The Cow (Reprise '94)
I read the favourable reviews, slapped it in, noted the 74 minute playing time, then realized this was a ruse, the band closing out their 1969-remake 1995 with 31 minutes of LA Blues (see **Funhouse**: you either know or you don't), and some backwards diddling. But that's it for the lark, elsewhere the band getting inside their gravely sincere, '60s garage clank and staying there for the Lyres-like duration. Yep, the godfogies of grunge scowl on like beatniks snorting rust, creeping Munster-like wence again, while rocking out on F.D.K. and Execution Style, guitars oozing out like used motor oil, the Muds' reputation as cholic alcoholic Seattle eccentrics unchallenged for another couple of belted, welted years. The world's losing patience, though.

Rating                                                7

## Mumbleskinny - Head Above Water (Sector 2 '95)
A Texan indie that crossed my path (no bio, putting me somewhat in the dark), Mumbleskinny reminds me of Alice in Chains played with the subtle, stealth arrangements of Pearl Jam's **Ten**. Pretty lowdown and spacey, sparse and depresso, **Head Above Water** manages to sound veteran enough to convince, despite its negative grunge swallow wallow. Rating reflects somewhat slouchy songs

Rating                                                6

## Mundane - Seed (Raw Energy/Black Mark '94)
Considerably ahead of their time, Toronto's Mundane lashed out with a forearm smash of a sound that mixes Pantera with a stiff belt of industrial. Songs tend towards sawed-off mantras, heaviness through hypnosis, the Rebelo Bros. and crew creating a rustscape worth visiting, occasionally lacing the thing with I Mother Earth-style percussion, but usually slamming with huge whacks of precision power-riffs. Sort of an anti-social, misanthropic Killing Joke integrity to the thing, while thankfully cranking mountains of metal.

Rating                                                8

## Murder Inc. - Murder Inc. (Futurist '93)
Good reason this sounds like lusty, agitated, tribal old Killing Joke, this six-man team of terrorists including Joke alumni like Martin Atkins, Paul Raven and Geordie Walker. Upper crust crusties carving the visceral soundscapes include none other than Paul Barker, Jim Thirlwell and "recorder" Steve Albini, who keeps it in his pants, allowing the band a relatively traditional sound on which to scatter their very untraditional perplexing stew of instrumentation sensations, finding that floodly wave of apocalyptic tones that are all over early Killing Joke documents. Definitely a return to roots, **Murder Inc.** satisfies, preaching from a well-earned pulpit the nascent fact that industrial planks can be hammered with bare, bloody hands.

Rating                                                8

## Murphy's Law - Murphy's Law/Back With A Bong
(Profile '94)
This nicely packaged reissue combines this smarmy skatepunk band's first two records, **Murphy's Law** from '86, and **Back With A Bong** (and a 3/4 brand new line-up) from '89. The band's keg party sound is a shoot 'em up combo of NY hardcore, college boy reggae and jokey stuff, kinda like warmed-over and very old Soul Asylum. Managed to get on some snooty tours, not to mention securing a major label deal for their third, **The Best Of Times**. For the adolescent in us all, or something like that.

Rating                                                5

## Mutha's Day Out - My Soul Is Wet (Chrysalis '93)
Young band from down south, slamming out an explosive, dynamic post-grunge metal, leaping wide-eyed

into the world of alternative, perhaps a couple years ahead of themselves (this kills Bush, Nixons, and Seven Mary Three). Fact be, Mutha's Day Out is overflowing with ideas, and the boys love rockin' out, as Get A Clue, Blank Page and Breakfast First Please will fully attest. As you wade deeper into this enjoyable record. expect quality, emotion and great change-ups track to track, which more often than not, are welded to frames of willfully bashed drums, vigorous rap-inflected vocals and an engaging display of guitar voices, from slinky funk grunge riffs (Mother Love Bone, even Spread Eagle) to bluesy solos, all blended with a properly dirty mix. The kind of record that if re-released, could be a hit, **My Soul Is Wet** just may have been too multi-layered for 1993, a true alternative metal jem sadly passed by at the time of its '93 launch.

Rating                                                              8

## Muzza Chunka - Fishy Pants   (Rowdy '93)

Firey, irreverent punk-bred metal, in the spirit of Detroit redneck rockers like Necros, Big Chief and the pappies of it all, the Stooges, California's Muzza Chunka are one of those bands you have to call grunge for lack of a better, fully complimentary term. But it's the old, crusty stuff this record evokes, the grunge of Green River, loud and snotty, punk-infested slashing chords lounging around metal structures. Anarchy anthem: Feed Me, which is just broken power chord euphoria, possibly touching the hem of DMZ or even the Dictators on a particularly nasty tear. Smoke-choking garage rock slapped down with purpose.

Rating                                                              7

## My Dying Bride - As The Flower Whithers
(Peaceville '92)

Imagine an unsure, club-footed version of the horribly magnificent **Turn Loose The Swans** sophomore, and you've pretty much nailed this debut full-length from one of the oddest, most refreshingly unfresh of doom gangs. **Flower** is more the "rock" record of the two, stunned in the headlights between its slow-brewed ultragoth, and its increasingly dramatic directive, **Swans** moving into an almost soundtrack-type classical mentality. Outside of a couple well-heeled thrashers with lots of change-ups, **Flower** pretty much waits patiently for the cement to dry. Expertly crafted ('cept for a weak drum sound), but less the eccentric and repulsive genius of record II.

Rating                                                              7

## My Dying Bride - Turn Loose The Swans
(Peaceville '93)

The word masterpiece would not be unwarranted here, but what kind and for whom is another miserable, downward spiraling question. Nothing sounds like My Dying Bride, and few would exhibit such aspirations, this record being perhaps the slowest and most depressing thing of beauty ever proposed for destruction of mind, body and soul. Those who bask beneath the soil on deep driven Floyd trips, yet who love the growling scowls of death metal's turgid vocabulary might gleefully sever their jugulars to this weeks-long monument to agony. Steep, engorging builds constructed of the doomiest of classical elements usually make way for lyrics that can be imagined as an evangelist, manic depressive heroin addict's description of Hell. These wisdoms in turn arrive etched over droning thick gothriffs that turn to black powder all the twisted violin and keyboard parts that wander lobotomized into the fray. A fascinating thing to behold, **Turn Loose The Swans** might very well trick your beating heart into a dead stop through a sort of merciless hypnosis, cutting the oxygen to the brain, collapsing the lungs, as it slugs off in victory, a trail of venomous ooze the only clue to the crime. Some mutter that Paradise Lost has copped a few ideas from these boys,

both bands finding ways to make palatable and interesting, the slow and unemotional. But whatever the case, Paradise Lost got the better end of this shtick, My Dying Bride doomed to be an extreme, maybe coveted joy, limited to but a few (my **8** rating is probably the highest in this book for a record I'll probably only play once a year). Burn it before it burns you.

Rating                                                              8

## My Dying Bride - Trinity   (Fierce '95)

Cool move here, making sense of the band's confusing recorded history by combining three pricey import EPs into one U.S. release full-length howl of pain. All has been remastered, full lyrics are provided, and there's an extra dry lump of poison in typical paralyzer Sexuality Of Bereavement. 1991-1993 AD are represented through nine powerful brain embalmers, but this music has more in common with Gregorian chants and other things medieval and evil than say, Collective Soul. Note: the band's truly disturbed **The Angel And The Dark River** ultra-opus saw European release before this compilation, but U.S. release after it. But like I say, time is irrelevant.

Rating                                                              7

## My Dying Bride - The Angel And The Dark River
(Peaceville '95)

The seething crusty majestic sloth that was past My Dying Bride juggernauts has made way for a closer examination of grey-to-black solitude. And given the clear, less extreme recording values, the toweringly painful long bong songs enclosed drill straight to the heart. Lyrically, Aaron hasn't veered too far. His world is still a liquid realm of torture, vague goings-on that wallow and dissipate due to evil, a type of Hell on earth that is amplified by solitude and boredom let loose unto mania; just intense, drooling, cancerous emotion spreading unchecked like a blob of pin-pricked soul. Musically, My Dying Bride is no longer an exercise in novelty. The band's writing can be enjoyed on a less perverse level, but one that is still at the heart of pleasure in being down, likened to one's experience of Pink Floyd's **The Wall**, Joy Division, Bauhaus, NIN and of course the dozen or so bands dipping their forked hooves into this sort of symphonic, funereal goth, My Dying Bride still probably one of the furthest committed. I mean, lead dirge The Cry Of Mankind is wicked beyond belief, very likely the most depressing thing I've ever heard, a melting terrain that just seeps into the ground half-way through, collapsed into an eerie keyboard mantra and . . . that foghorn. But it's vocally where this record really distinguishes itself, Aaron swelling forth with a crooked, cranky eccentric whine kind of like Roger Waters, or even Howard Devoto of Magazine or Peter Hammill, giving the whole thing a dank retro chill that arrives maybe at prime Stranglers. Combine this listenable and hearable croak with the band's most active and purely progressive deathly death metal meal, then deliver it all with high fidelity separation (all being the usual cavalcade of keys, violins and down-tuned power chords), and you've got a My Dying Bride for a thousands-strong mass suicide pack. A limited run of 5,000 includes a second (pretty dull) live CD recorded at Dynamo, proving that this band really is designed for intense home use.

Rating                                                              9

## My Dying Bride - Like Gods Of The Sun   (Peaceville '96)

My Dying Bride press ever onward, rolling their thunderous, apocalyptic black cloud of doom over mind and body, this time making small adjustments only, adding an immediacy and primal metal energy to their signature slow burn. The overall effect is one of timelessness, one almost envisioning this type of gravely gothic heft as the soundtrack to medieval British wars, an almost continuous power chord rumble flanked by

wailing violins and the band's best drum performance yet. So the main advance would be the record's relatively quick involvement in verse and vocal, coupled with an upgrade in riff, turning the still morbid landscape into more of a mosh of the damned, fan and blackhearted musicmaker alike itching with anticipation of millennial flameout, less in search of escape, more lip-smacking at the crackle of self-barbecue.
Rating                                                                    9

## My Little Funhouse - Standunder   (Geffen '92)

Strange one to stand under here, sorta like a loud rock'n'rollin' bar band, metallic in a simple, hanging chord manner; low cal, garagey like Smack (if that helps) or The Buck Pets but stupider and tending towards loose. Weird seeing this on the dynamic Geffen, because first word that comes to mind is amateur, then plain, then (horrors!) safe, despite the psychotic looks of the band. Fair number of ballads too, which lean towards roots rock. Blended, sludgy, but quite ineffectual.
Rating                                                                    5

## My Own Victim - Burning Inside   (Century Media '96)

Kentucky's My Own Victim have been mucking about for six years now, doing demos and an EP, but it is only with Burning Inside that their sound flows and explodes. Fact is, this fills the void between power metal, alternative and urban hardcore, essentially leaching the rappy elements out of urbancore and melting huge wads of riffery in gooey chunks, resulting in a powerful sweep that works better than anything by Biohazard or Downset. Century Media is racking up a few of these kinds of acts (Chum, Hostility and Only Living Witness coming to mind), and it's a pretty cool thing that they do, because there is a conspicuous lack of really heavy grungy stuff out there right now, most bands beyond the top five, opting for limp-wristed grunge lite. Let's hope there's a trend there.
Rating                                                                    8

## My Own Victim - No Voice, No Rights, No Freedom
(Century Media '97)

PDQ with a new wad of wampum, My Own Victim following up a solid debut with this slightly more erratic work. All the usual elements are there, if not a bit more punk and shades of Korn, bolstering what are thick, carving stresscore riffs. Faves are the catchy Make A Change and the assaultive Walls Apart, while From The

Bottom throws in the trickery. Doing what an unknown should do, My Own Victim are working on a catalogue of personality-determining signatures. Could do with less hep-hep fast parts, but such is coffee. And all those cliff-edge pauses help the game immensely, even if the genre itself is becoming well trampled.
Rating                                                                    8

## My Sister's Machine - Diva   (Caroline '92)

After huge initial buzz, hassles with Caroline cooled the heels of My Sister's Machine's ascendance to power, no fault to this bitchin' display of psychedelic grunge metal, combining the alienation of Ten-era Pearl Jam with the steamrolling riffs of Alice in Chains. And for once a vocalist who owns his own pipes, Nick Pollock still occasionally slipping into his native Seattle phrasings, but for the most part proving himself a voice to be reckoned with. Diva's first half just blisters; Hands And Feet, Pain, I Hate You and especially Love At High Speed all wattage machines of the highest order, with twists and turns that have become the hallmark of frontier metalists. As the record weighs in however, much of the remainder wallows wholly unconcerned with categories, lulling the listener with melloid verses that convert to major poundage, then back again, all bound by a sort of lazy chill. The overall feel is one of isolation, a seemingly rulebook record somehow pushed to the edges of the grunge world, almost too adult for the scene to absorb. A confidently textured first statement ruled by large, cantankerous bass strings.
Rating                                                                    8

## My Sister's Machine - Wallflower   (Chameleon/Elektra '93)

Inside Of Me finds MSM back in heat-soaked business, slamming into town with a killer grunge metal riff that is one of this band's most memorable. Again, hard to believe these guys weren't grunge success #5 (you know the big four), what with those unconventional breaks throughout their mature futuristic metal compositions. First word that comes to mind is "cool", as lead growler Nick Pollock and gang just seem to have mastered the meaning of low-slung metal, something vaguely Kyuss-like in approach but still closest to early Alice in Chains in actual sound, or perhaps Mindfunk's under-rated Dropped contusion. My appreciation grows with the passing years, where in most cases, it wanes.
Rating                                                                    8

## Nailbomb - Point Blank (Attic/Roadrunner '94)

Sepultura's Max Cavalera and Fudge Tunnel's Alex Newport team up for what is fortunately more like an eclectic, panicky and futuristic Sepultura record than anything like the square deliveries of Fudge Tunnel. Both rock dogs belt their vox in their inimitable style over caustic riffs bracketed by industrial stabbings, an area Max finds interesting these days. Many tracks blur by at thrashpunk velocities, while the few plodding numbers clutter up tastefully, strafed by exacting chuggery that keeps the whole slaughtering smear well-paced and moving along. Nothing gets too seriously arranged here, most tracks living or dying on how good the riff weathers the incessant repetition, a repetition broken by cool samples and stressfully barked out sloganeering disguised as verses. Probably one of the toughest, most hyper and impenetrable releases of the year, **Point Blank** (no relation to the beefy Southern rock act), is a creative storehouse of ideas from two guys truly collaborating, honing their industrial languages, and moshing away a few braincells at the same time.
Rating 8

## Nailbomb - Proud To Commit Commercial Suicide
(Attic/Roadrunner '95)

A nasty chunk of bleeding carcass, this live record documents the chaos of Nailbomb's "second and last show", sent down yer throat at the Dynamo festival, June 3, '95. It's a no-holds-barred riprock through the tracks on **Point Blank** (adding the Dead Kennedys' Police Truck), plus a couple of studio abominations, While You Sleep, I Destroy Your World and Zero Tolerance, which are both long, extreme, industrial hiphops. Max and Alex rationalize closing the dirty books on Nailbomb by reiterating that the whole thing was meant to be quick and intense, get in, get out, stare into the crater. Mission accomplished.
Rating 7

## Naked Planet - Naked Planet (Naked Planet '96)

I love Faith No More's sound now, but but I also liked it then. Well, Naked Planet grab and shake that "then" with such conviction, you'd never guess that this wasn't a multi-million dollar signing with Mike Wallace ushered in to produce the smash savior of hardmusik '96. Fact is, this fairly unknown Toronto act has done a bang-up job of spicing FNM's angular funk metal with potent injections of today's rap, hip-hop and industrial

moves. And the mix is sizzling, the band having no problem slipping and sliding from dynamic to dynamic, Vic Branco matching his hot backing band beat for beat, eliciting a Mike Patton one moment, an Anthony Kiedis the next. Derivation fer sure, but a derivation that can fill a void heavily and heartily.
Rating 7

## Napalm Death - Harmony Corruption (Earache '90)

Even semi-early on (this is the fourth), these decibellian goonies were bellicose veining the most hyper-tense thrash sounds on the planet, loud, lathered crap-traptions that served no other purpose than to define the fried edge of music. Of course on the edges, there is no enjoyment, as is the def case here, even though this is the band's most "commercial", least punked record to date, Greenway (ex-Benediction) & Co. slashing through garbage piles as thick as a sewage treatment plant's receive ducts. But folks apparently love Napalm Death, and I know who they are. Why they are is another story. Partial saving grace: the treble-forsaken production of Scott Burns and Mick Harris' ludicrously Lombardo-OD'ed percussion panzer.
Rating 5

## Napalm Death - Utopia Banished (Relativity '92)

Excruciating UK blight merchants who lay it on thrash-acidic, loud and trembling year after year, Napalm Death '92 evokes a cross between thrashcore and auto-Slayer; thorny sheet metal and math, with trademark By-tor vocal etchings. Fairly state of the grind-core, which is no surprise as these Brit destructos have become more or less the kings of the genre, building to crescendo going on five records deep, guttural, and unutterable now. The fast here simply negatizes and the slow constructs the same calculus proof as argued many a mosh pit past, new drummer Danny Herrera upholding the band's rock hard back-bludgeon. Not a fan of the species to say the least, so for further critical demarcation of such industrial walls, go elsewhere and far away.
Rating 4

## Napalm Death - The World Keeps Turning
(Earache '92)

Compilation. Japanese import. Way past blindcore into ludicrously unlistenable and plain banal. I mean what is the point? Total turd. No way out.
Rating 0

## Napalm Death - Fear, Emptiness, Despair
(Earache '94)

Napalm Death have found a grueling golden mean between grind and absolute heaviness here, lashing out into an almost experimental thickness, sort of the Sonic Youth of death metal. But the impact is skull-frying, especially on deep grooves like *Twist The Knife (Slowly)*, *Hung* and *Plague Remains*, bass guitar, bassy production and down-tuned madness combining for something that can only sound like war. And oddly enough, that snappy small snare sound amplifies the electric juggernaut of the thankfully more controlled riffs. Also a welcome sight: lyrics, photography and graphics are up to snuff for the first time, subliminally flinging these trolls of terror into the art zone. A fantastical battlefield of sound, like I say, really biting into the crux of heaviness.
Rating                                                                8

## Napalm Death - Greed Killing  (Earache '95)

This strike-and-recoil seven track EP served as a taster for Napalm Death's **Diatribes** opus, showcasing the record's two most distinguished tracks, *Greed Killing* and *My Own Worst Enemy*, then adding four more that didn't make the cut, plus one live track. Of the new head-cuffs, *Self Betrayal* and *Finer Truths, White Lies* are grooved enough slams, but *Antibody* and *All Links Severed* are abbreviated blastbeated jokes, short, bitter and broken. But hey, this is undoubtedly a band still learning new things.
Rating                                                                6

## Napalm Death - Diatribes  (Earache '95)

Perhaps the original purveyors of pure black death, Napalm Death have progressed (and sometimes stumbled) through fantastical belches of noise not for the weak of heart. Many arguably unlisteneable slabs 'o pain have converged on this new, and frankly stunning shard of post-modern grindcore. You know something is right with the world when a death metal riff hits you like Green Day, sticking to and moshing upon yer frontal lobe, which is the case with *Greed Killing* and especially *My Own Worst Enemy*. And you figure the folks at Earache know this, because these are the flagship tracks of the pre-release **Greed Killing** EP. But really, the whole record achieves a twisted, perverted sort of hookery, dense walls of sound made palatable by an evil addicted strain of melody, as Barney and crew grovel, hovel, and burrow through raw constructs at all speeds, from groove to the band's patented dissonant thrash. Not elegant and technical like At The Gates or Death; in fact very, very ugly, but Napalm Death have succeeded in letting their long unlikeable experience burn through like battery acid.
Rating                                                                8

## Napalm Death & Coalesce - Split EP  (Earache '97)

Stylish packaging afoot for the first split EP of Napalm Death's career, the band sending off Barney (replaced by Extreme Noise Terror's Phil Vane) in short, sharp, cardiac fashion. The Napalm tracks: a demo version of lousy oldie *Upward And Uninterested*, and a great recent composition entitled *Food Chains*. Coalesce mirrors things with a turgid trasher called *A Safe Place*, and a really cool, metal coagulator deemed *Harvest Of Maturity*. In total, 12:19 of subliminal, painful electrocuted enjoyment!?! Update: Barney is now back in the band.
Rating                                                                7

## Nasty Savage - Nasty Savage  (Metal Blade '85)

No, this was something different, something with brains and a wicked propensity to misuse them. The premiere from Florida's Nasty Savage was death metal at its doom-laden best, exploded with the obsession and trappings of its own mission, pounding with higher determination, completely lost in violent unreality and soaked in confused, unpredictable energy. Nasty Ronnie out-blasts Manowar on all philosophical tenets, constructing a verbal campaign of terror swathed in his backing arsenal's horrendously gothic display of power metal evoking Mercyful Fate, the heaviest from Maiden, the blackest from old Priest, and all things leather-clad and pissed. Just a sustained wall of attitude technically documented with unhealthy aplomb. So drilled with the will to beat the crap out of anything in its path, it's ridiculous.
Rating                                                                9

## Nasty Savage - Indulgence  (Metal Blade '87)

The singular carbonic soul of this band heavily overslurps at the trough of night on this fortress of gothic surgery. Nasty Ronnie and his crazed sonic mercenaries overdo everything and kick copious amounts of ass doing it, **Indulgence** raising a hilariously blown, percussive wall of sound, blasting truck-size chunks of concrete in its wake. The playing is manic, tight, fast and varied, yet all becomes underscored with an OTT attitude that threatens to crack open chaos amidst effortless binding ties. The rabies infecting this band continues to spread as Ronnie shreds his way past most death purveyors of the day with a combination of versatility and a soul forged of purest medieval blue blood. Only complaint: too many constructs based on double bass drum patterns, with the usual accompanying elevated levels of speed and noise. The debut accomplished the same with more restraint.
Rating                                                                8

## Nasty Savage - Abstract Reality  (Metal Blade '88)

Four tracks of prime Nasty Ronnie, kicking off with title track: quick-gallop mercenary metal par excellence. What follows is even more lethal; piledriving mayhem from one of the best, bleakest, obliterating-est underground bands in the biz. All told: four of the band's strongest destructors, cramming in all sorts of '80s metal know-how like there's no tomorrow.
Rating                                                                9

## Nasty Savage - Penetration Point  (Rotten '89)

More algebraic insanity from one of my favorite butcher metal acts, a band so obviously nuts, their sandblast riffery can't be seen as anything but pure demented genius. But it really is a case of total slobbering metal inundation (the best kind, mind you), a scrapping, gut-level OTT that works most all the time, due to an anti-life punk disposition, leaking like used motor oil from what is a formidable piece of aggressive engineering. Vocalist Nasty Ronnie crams major over-Will into every desperate blazefest, in construction of one dense demonstration of Florida carjack metal. Shame about the cover though. Call it death metal, speed metal . . . definitely doom metal built for the apocalypse, but don't call it thrash; something more like the big four on amphetamine horsepills.
Rating                                                                8

## Nazareth - Nazareth  (A&M '72)

Given the dream-like states attempted on **Exercises**, one would never suspect that the puzzling ones would offer such a diverse and more than occasionally rocking affair as their first foray into vinyl jungles. **Nazareth** contains roughly the same stylistic mix that constructed the first two Zep records; bluesy metal, blues, dinosaur metal, '60s psychedelia, and acoustic rock, rendering this debut full of interesting peaks and valleys, amidst a surprisingly full mix, which may have something to do with Roy Thomas Baker in as "engineer." This is the chunk of oak from which **Razamanaz** is a plausible progression, as if **Exercises** never existed. Could have easily been psychedelic slop through and through given this band's fragile identity

and the early date from which it lurches. Sporting a good four rockers, best being the almost Sab-like *Witchdoctor Woman*, **Nazareth** is surprisingly self-assured, securing these Scots a modest chapter in the preliminary construction of metal. Fairly high grade because it's not nearly as creepy as one might think.
Rating 6

## Nazareth - Exercises (A&M '72)

Nazareth's second album is a surprisingly mellow, almost completely acoustic (unplugged!) offering, demonstrating that even from its conception, the band had no idea who they were. Lo and behold, **Exercises** is actually kinda decent and warm, when it could have creaked and groaned with the dying ideals of the '60s, **Exercises** running the gamut from blues, balladry, country, blue grass, and minor rock but comes off more cohesive than a lot of Naz offerings. **Exercises** also brings to fruition one of the band's first of many interesting cover art concepts. Maybe a coffee table book is in the cards.
Rating 4

## Nazareth - Razamanaz (A&M '73)

Damn near the definitive band of our youth, Nazareth jolted our ten-year-old brains with the manic cavalcade of distortion that is **Razamanaz**. Hard to tell what was more grating, Manny Charlton's sizzling power chords, or Dan McCafferty's infernal sandpaper yowlings. In any event, this was sheer contortion, a new level of metallic lunge that defined our exploding mania for riff rock with a hearty "That's it, world. Keep making *that sound*, and you can have my allowance money." Nazareth were a righteous entity, this along with **Loud 'N' Proud** comprising the band's glory days. *Razamanaz*, with all its crazed grinding may have been this record's heaviest track, but other more gloomy pieces also blew our minds, most notably *Alcatraz, Woke Up This Morning*, and *Too Bad, Too Sad*, which even to this day have an air of rock aristocracy to them, a sort of melding of American and British styles brewed clammy and cold in Scottish isolation. And the mellow stuff is almost creepier, tunes of hell and brimstone like *Vigilante Man, Sold My Soul* and *Broken Down Angel* rendered shrill and desperate by McCafferty's canine bark. Kings of the heath and moor, even in such far away lands as our Trail, B.C., Nazareth were the Dudes of metal, a band above the circus antics of Kiss, and as we later found out, not above leaving their metal roots for bewildering muses.
Rating 8

## Nazareth - Loud 'N' Proud (A&M '73)

**Loud 'N' Proud** had that same hair-raising appeal as its paired companion in pain, **Razamanaz**, while mining deeper psychological disintegration with its awesome and expansive cover of Bob Dylan's *The Ballad Of Hollis Brown*. Better known for a galloping send-up of Joni Mitchell's *This Flight Tonight*, pret' near the band's most recognized song, **Loud 'N' Proud** is an elusive and perplexed sort of guitar rocker due to *Hollis Brown*'s hypnotic and suicidal nine minute undertones, which grinds side two into the pavement under the blood-soaked thumb of God, leaving one to question the perky punk metal rockers of side one. Other faves would include the mop-top boogie of *Go Down Fighting*, metallized Little Feat cover *Teenage Nervous Breakdown* and heir to *Razamanaz*, the sinister *Not Faking It*. All in all, a high school, hockey barn sort of guitar feast; bashing, crowing, sweating, thumping like the best of the simpletoon '70s.
Rating 8

## Nazareth - Rampant (A&M '74)

I'm sorry man, but this whole record makes me feel like Hollis Brown himself, no matter what kind of smiley faces are painted on the music herein enclosed. Chinks in the armor begin to crack the facade, as the tunes get moodier, more reflective and explorative of American rock styles, like exhausted road warriors who just want out. The rockers are longer and more fanciful, thus *Silver Dollar Forger, Shanghai'd In Shanghai* and the strangely haunting *Jet Lag*. And the rest, well, it's Nazareth at its quintessentially anti-social, destroying its reputation as the lovable hard rockin' lads from Scotland. Always loved the album cover, which put an odd, uncommunicative twist on the record, seemingly draping inappropriate colours on a doomful collection of unintegrated tales. Anyways, **Rampant**'s blues, acoustic, and psychedelic tendencies were quickly minimized by our forgiving psyches as we rocked to exactly one half the record, steadfast in our convictions that *next time* we'll get the barnstormer. Next time never came, as the band would eventually slide into vanilla psycho-synch with such Canadian conundrums as April Wine and BTO.
Rating 6

## Nazareth - Hair Of The Dog (A&M '75)

**Hair Of The Dog** lurks darkly as one of those bleak, gloomy records that manages to ooze evil without any overt intention of doing so, pacing itself as a vinyl suicide pill that assaults the senses on side one, and then degenerates into Floyd-ian nightmares as it worms through side two. **Hair Of The Dog** has the further distinction of offering three of the wildest whipped and chained Naz flare-ups ever, with the Sab-like *Miss Misery, Black Dog* dark horse *Changin' Times*, and the funky sub-woofin' title cut, while also scoring Nazareth's largest hit to date with quasi-tender Everly Bros. ballad *Love Hurts*, further confusing the nature of this dog's spots. **Hair Of The Dog** is one of those depressing, half-defeated, black marks on rock'n'roll, a record that sounds so perfectly like its album art. Check it out; if you survive, you'll be stronger for it. An uncharacteristically pained release from a band whose only outstanding characteristic since this last mental penetrator has been an inability to jar listeners to any sort of response at all.
Rating 7

## Nazareth - Greatest Hits (A&M '75)

Contains the endearing pop verve of *My White Bicycle*, a cover featuring Dan McCafferty's best Monkees' impression. The rest? Like the title sez, a compilation from the band's glorious heyday. Twenty years on, you'd think the boys would wise up and re-visit their strengths.
Rating 5

## Nazareth - Close Enough For Rock'n'Roll (A&M '76)

Weird, hurtful, misguided and bleak, **Close Enough For Rock'n'Roll** grinds on with the same time-weariness as **Hair Of The Dog**, while riding a more superficially accessible plane, yet one that is depressingly botched, confused and so degenerately '70s in the spirit of the Eagles' **Hotel California**. Moral defeat lies everywhere on this, as does plain fatigue, especially amongst marsh-sunken heavy tracks such as *Loretta, Lift The Lid*, and *You're The Violin*. No mistaking the classy and effortless acidic lounging on this strange, stand-offish release. Much less metal than variously funky, acoustic and bluesy hard rock mixed with a more pronounced penchant to fragment, **Close Enough** will never win praise for focus, yet the record most definitely evokes the fogged over-indulgence and unguided moral loitering that dogged the '70s into listless myopia.
Rating 6

## Nazareth - Play 'N' The Game (A&M '76)

More exasperated and restrained experiments in diversity as per its predecessor, **Play 'N' The Game** emerges somewhat from the cloud of negation, while still distancing itself from hard rock, offering only two, arguably three, forays of axe mechanics, preferring the simpletoon, funky bluesiness in fashion throughout the no-worries late '70s. Somebody To Roll and Born To Love pretty well end the attempts at hard rock, both percussively self-defeating, whilst the rest enters a cauldron brewed of intense sloth, which becomes both likeable and terribly tragic, as four flaming pariahs transform themselves into lazily ascending wisps of dope smoke.
Rating 5

## Nazareth - Expect No Mercy (A&M '77)

Expect No Money is yet another spot of Nazareth piddle that coughs and wheezes to plausibility exactly half the time: on the lazy warm boogie of Shot Me Down, the funky Gimme What's Mine, the smooth Place Your Heart, and the bleak, minimalist metallic title track, featuring our man Dan struggling on the ropes of hope. Again it's all total aimlessness in the name of imagined universality, and on this particular outing, a more pronounced lack of power chords and woofer food.
Rating 5

## Nazareth - No Mean City (A&M '79)

Finally, the ballsiest Naz disc since the manic heyday of **Razamanaz** and **Loud 'n' Proud**, **No Mean City** makes a fairly convincing return to guitar rock with the speedy Just To Get Into It, slow clunker Claim To Fame, the bluesy title cut and the morally bleak, near classic Simple Solution (Parts 1+2), which mixes a line dancing-style cornpone riff with an evil, null 'n' void coda, break, whatever; Cafferty barking in hair-raising desperation through to the bitter end. Much as I'd like to recommend this disc due to its attempts at metal, I can't, because for the most part, it's basically simplistic, boring, and muzzled by a noisy, compressed Manny Charlton recording. It's too bad, but Nazareth just can't seem to write more than half an album of strong rock'n'roll using any of their profuse stylistic leanings. However, they do have drained and depressing down pat. Striking Frazetta-like graphics from Rodney Matthews.
Rating 6

## Nazareth - Malice In Wonderland (A&M '80)

**Malice In Wonderland** marks the first and fleeting occasion where the baffling Nazareth waft convincing fumes of comfort in their self-afflicted role as nothing in particular, as hollow shell of emotion. Perhaps the addition of first new blood ever in Alex Harvey's Zal Cleminson and forceful producer Jeff "Skunk" Baxter upped the ante in terms of humanity and acerbic wit here, but something is definitely livelier, yet squarely morose sounding about the new disposition, as discovered bleeding on the cool and edgy Talkin' To One Of The Boys, Fast Cars, and the Spanish and snakey Ship Of Dreams. Weird. As if the band has come to acceptance, when they tragically have not, **Malice In Wonderland** courts California as the invited, yet in reality working the chosen ones awkwardly, spending and wasting the time of the enchanted as the embarrassing colour of the crowd. Brilliant and sad, painfully exposing all the imperfections of the race. Hanging on with bleeding fingernails in full pursuit of tension. Immortal Aryan cover art.
Rating 7

## Nazareth - The Fool Circle (A&M '80)

The lull in the overcast conditions that was the quivering and insistent **Malice In Wonderland** is eradicated as Nazareth enters their trampled and awfully incon-

sequential era that persists to this day. **The Fool Circle**'s simple, disorienting cover art establishes the mood of dead ennui that will persist from this day hence as Nazareth drives eons away from hard rock, courting nothing more than half-conceived acoustic rock in various mealy directions, causing no stirrances of life, in fact, no potentiality of energy, in resigned defeat unleashed from the hand of an industry increasingly abrupt in its silence towards any prospective Nazareth contribution. Intimate yet completely asocial in its embracing of nothing and its indifference towards playing the game.
Rating 6

## Nazareth - 'Snaz (A&M '81)

A double live set with a surprisingly kick-ass recording which unfortunately suffers from the band's painful and protracted catalogue, demonstrating the fact that these wizened Scots actually like all that geriatric rock they've been cranking out over the previous six years or so. Really, a grand total of six lonely tunes of twenty that could be described as classic Nazareth. Too bad. Judging from the easy crowd mania created here with generally flighty material, this could have been another **Strangers In The Night**, given a preponderance of the band's nasty rockers of old.
Rating 4

## Nazareth - 2XS (A&M '82)

And thus we slide full-scale into Nazareth's anonymous period, much more unsuccessful and dull than parallel straight-line EKG's by Status Quo, Foghat, Sweet, Deep Purple or Uriah Heep. All is not lost however. In an attempt to embrace the newly adopted MOR universality, we kinda bought into **2XS**, reveling in its warm explorations of roots rock, honky tonk, funk, lazy balladry, mellow boogie, and remaining vestiges of metal, which assert themselves with surprising weight on the almost OTT Boys In The Band and the tricky Back To The Trenches. McCafferty's reptilian wail sounds great, and the overall effect is one of exploded sophistication, with some of the simple ones' more tasty and innovative arrangements. The last that seems to show the boys excited about their new vistas.
Rating 6

## Nazareth - Sound Elixir (A&M '83)

Again, continued examinations of watery soft rock, which this time stumbles blindly with little beat and even less melody, exploring slow and clumsy renditions of the blues, funk, boogie, and general lite rock morass. Not a single metallic shard, and very little soft stuff that reflects any warmth.
Rating 3

## Nazareth - The Catch (A&M '86)

And the boys plod ever on, in search of some new and elusive muse, in search of something to believe in, offering doped up and malignant bass-driven dirges that only their mothers could love. Appropriately, the new stylistic disasters include stuff that smells like slow disco or R+B plus other never enjoyable forms of music.
Rating 3

## Nazareth - Cinema (Vertigo '86)

Slightly heavier or maybe just more active, **Cinema** contains additional amounts of smoky lounge tunes, sprinkled with what can loosely be described as rock, which tries to lift off but crashes due to wrong instrumentation and loss of killer instinct. I dunno, all this latter-day ear food from Nazareth has a sort of comfortable, non-threatening generic sound to it which makes for decent background music. Hard to actually come out and hate it, but also impossible to get ripped over. Brutal album cover. The question remains: why

the mindless wandering? Obviously an element of frustrated battles with the moving targets of art, yet also possibly the culmination of the effects of old age, simple burnout, or both.
Rating 4

## Nazareth - No Jive  (Attic '92)
Still touring after all these years, and still looking for that elusive muse in the moors, Nazareth slink back with a bit of volume albeit delivered with the usual lack of urge overkill. Billy Rankin gets in a few nasty licks, but structures usually plod, Nazareth proving that smarter doesn't necessarily follow older. Yeah, so it's an attempt at a harder rockin' sound, but performances are so subdued, the increased riffery gets lost in a conservative mix built for lighter fare, like warm popster Keeping Our Love Alive for example. Hard-edged but cold, alone and exhausted.
Rating 5

## Nazareth - Move Me  (Mayhem/Polydor '94)
In the Welcome Back Kotter '70s, when Nazareth or Queen lashed out out with a heavy song, you know they had metal on the brains, for however long it lasted. Here the increasingly distinguished looking ones dish more of that phoned-in starchy "guitar rock", pretty much all of it written by lone youngster Billy Rankin, who I guess is just a lousy writer. Structures trade dreary eights between slow (Let Me Be Your Dog: okay, you're a dog) and a sort of beer commercial boogie (simplistic, slidy, and insipid), occasionally evoking sophistication with a few invertedly hooky choruses, but moreso just zero muse. And finally we get the attempt at rehashing the cash: an orchestral version of Love Hurts, and unplugged versions of Razamanaz (a plugged song if there ever was one), My White Bicycle and This Flight Tonight. Break out the M+M's.
Rating 4

## Necrophobic - The Nocturnal Silence  (Black Mark '93)
Frost-blue black metal from the young and damned at heart, The Nocturnal Silence gallops forthrightly like early At The Gates, Cemetery or Edge Of Sanity, all bitter, pinched and twisted, offering an adequate if grim glimpse into the anguished, ashen souls of scarred Scandinavian metalheads. I hate to keep harping on the same harpies of thrash, but so many of these second stringers are mere imtensifications of early Slayer, worthy, even relevant, but proliferous like cockroaches. May carve a presence one day, just as many Black Markers have after a couple o' slabs.
Rating 6

## Necrophobic - Spawned By Evil  (Black Mark '96)
This grim-looking bunch of death metal overlords are somewhat respected despite only one official album since forming in '89. This four tracker is kinda swingin', containing one caustic but unremarkable original (most on the debut were better; hmmm.) plus a thorned, horned cover each from Slayer, Venom and Bathory, all witheringly black-blooded and eroding of soul.
Rating 6

## Necrophobic - Darkside  (Black Mark '97)
Darkside's retro-death cover graphics might be your first clue that Necrophobic might prefer sticking to their blackened roots. And indeed the record, harkens back to the frigid sounds of Scandinavian thrash circa '92, phenomena like early Edge Of Sanity, early Cemetary and early At The Gates. But a sense of Filth-Cradled melody pervades these speedy, harshly recorded tracks, both bands doing well by their cancerous updating of Maiden-ish goth-tones. For all those black metal morons who tirelessly complain that all their bands are moving South Of Heaven, here's one that remains crustified, proud and briskly snarled. Personnel note: major change in loss of co-founder David Parland, replaced by Sebastian Ramstedt, who is only featured on the odd guitar solo, due to him joining only a week before recording commenced.
Rating 6

## Necros - Tangled Up  (Restless '87)
Well, I guess it was inevitable that I absconded heavily of more Necros product sooner or later after experiencing the smokin' bludgeon of the live one. Tangled Up tears along much like Live Or Else, with mostly the same selection of vicious, punked up simpletoons, including the most kickin' cuts Gun and Blizzard Of Glass. The whole ornery car crash is bemusing to say the least, one of those ramrodding, idiotic records you huck on when pissed off, merely to reinforce that choice mood, rather than to challenge heavily one's sense of musicality, or hammer out new revelations. I placed a few of the more pertinent thorns from this along side some Skin Yard, Hell's Kitchen, and Mudhoney on a tape exclusively for automotive use. I highly recommended fuel for executing those freeway, fast lane brakechecks.
Rating 7

## Necros - Live Or Else  (Medusa '90)
One of the goddam funniest albums I've ever read, Live Or Else comes with excerpts from lead singer Barry Henssler's tour diary, written during their booze up/back up of Megadeth's '87 tour, the selfsame source of the sonic slamdance herein enclosed. Don't know these guys from Barclay James Harvest, Horslips or Hot Tuna, but judging from this well-recorded live disc, they're worth knowing. Necros roll roughshod with a kind of stripped-down mid to fast metal/punk chug that manages to retain some sort of sonic manifest destiny. Nothing mind-scarring, just rowdy, diamond-brutal, mischievous kick ass r'n'r battery. Also features a Ted Nugent medley which disappoints heavily, being a half-ass, straight-faced walk-through of Stranglehold, Great White Buffalo, and Cat Scratch Fever. Sominex City. But again, this disc is totally worth it ("it" being seven bucks, tops) for the hilarious tour notes, which chronicle backstage "nutcracker" sessions with Mustaine and the boys, plus some cool anecdotes about hanging with the Nuge himself, as Henssler's and Ted's families are old friends. Henssler marches on in the '90s with Big Chief.
Rating 7

## Necrosis - Acta Sanctorum  (Black Mark '95)
Funny how all of these seizure-causing death gorgings are all half an hour short, like it's all anybody can hack in one adult serving. Necrosis is dreadfully far-gone stuff, full-on craziness, corrosive, mixed and played in smeary proportions no matter what the velocity. Probably the most annoying thing from Rhode Island, musical or otherwise. I got no time for this.
Rating 3

## Vince Neil - Exposed  (Warner Bros. '93)
After the unceremonious split with the Crüe, Neil takes time off for a few laps around the racetrack, where he runs headlong into brand new gleaming rock'n'roll reasons to live. Exposed is the fruits of his labour, a record which revs the red line thanks to the razor-sharp stylings of near legend Steve Stevens, who puts in his purest metal performance ever. Exposed clips smartly like the best of early '80s metal; Dio, Y&T, and the very best of Crüe, best exemplified in the stinging riffs of Look In Her Eyes and lead single You're Invited (But You're Friend Can't Come), which both percolate with a new metal pride with an eye to the past. Also included is the best cover of Sweet's Set Me Free I've ever encountered, the song like all others on this expansive effort benefiting from snappy pyrotech-

nics from Stevie and the rest of the band, sorta re-writing metal circa ten years ago, re-energizing it for the level of competition characteristic of the '90s. Very convincing, very serious, but party metal all the same, **Exposed** is a powerful rebuttal to the mealy output of the Crüe over the last three albums. The ball's in their court. Let's hope everybody wins. Update: the battle turned out to be a two-way tie for last, Tommy at least getting Pamela.

Rating 7

## Vince Neil - Carved In Stone (Warner '95)

Of course this had to stiff, but you can't help applauding Neil's artistically somewhat successful attempt at joining the alt.rock fray. But there's just too much ambition here, **Carved In Stone** sampling from the whole buffet: grunge, psychedelia, hip-hop-inspired industrial, things close to hair band metal, and of course *Skylar's Song*, Vince's heartfelt dedication to his deceased daughter. The record as a whole satisfied no one, being ignored by new rockers, and reviled by those who liked both the old Crue and the new Crue. But the record's quite heavy, in a doomy, lethargic AiC frame of mind, so it ain't a complete wash-out. And there's lots of production prowess employed, making the record one with brains as well as brawn. Any distaste for the project can only come from the complex concept of trends, and your perception of Neil's slavishness or lack thereof, in the face of some big ones.

Rating 7

## Neolithic - The Personal Fragments Of Life
(Adipocere '95)

Best part about this quite worldly half hour Polish doomscape is the broken English essay from lead Neolith, Piotr, who runs down the band's stumbling history, getting the point across that the Polish metal world runs as bad as all other metal worlds, and worse than all other things Polish. Anyways, the melodic deathtones enclosed are confident enough, sounding Swedish, like early Tiamat, usually slow and growly, cold and grinding. Fave larf title: *Wickedness Of The Objects*.

Rating 6

## Neurosis - Enemy Of The Sun (Alternative Tentacles '93)

Well, again, I'd have to hand it to Sabbath for the germination of the idea Neurosis finds exhaustingly explorable. Yes, **Enemy** (unfathomably the band's fourth) is the hyper-distressed '90s actuality of *Supertzar*, **Sabotage**'s goth metal soundscape, Neurosis adding long industrial builds, breaking forth with a sort of deconstructed **Vol 4** bashing once arrived at the thick mess we are to believe hides a song. The band punishes aural canals wormwide through layer upon layer of music interleafing noise, non-melodic death overlapping chaos. Demanding to say the least, fearful for most, dull through sonic inundation, **Enemy Of The Sun** becomes your enemy, glueing shut with bass-bottomed dirge tones all that you call pleasure, sinking the sorry construct under a burning oil slick fiery and choked at once. Yeah, in a way, the record is a sick masterpiece, lyrics razor-sharp and deathly, but forget approaching this one with any sort of joy. Best to drill holes pentagramatically through your skull roof, and pour in slowly after five minutes on rapid boil. 6 grade represents wild oscillation between **9** and **3**. For fans of punishing, industrial, experimental toxins only.

Rating 6

## Neurosis - Through Silver In Blood (Relapse '96)

Well if you're looking for the sound of ruler-width apocalyptic hooves thundering by in digital slow mo, dust-busting terror, look no further, **Through Silver In Blood** taking Neurosis way beyond the arch-industrial jarrings of its predecessor of three years back, into an expansive, cerebral-frying black-hearted melt. And the sound within almost approaches a sort of theatrical tire-burning stench, Neurosis achieving the widest of evil fidelities, letting their unbelievably muscular structures breath rather than get gunked-up with layers of samples or noise for noise sake. Vague, unjust comparisons might be Pitch Shifter, Eyehategod or selected rumblings from the Melvins, but this is just way closer to art than all of the above noise plumbers combined (indeed the band plans to expand into books, film, visual art and multi-media in the near future). One pretty impressive display of frightening aural disgust, somehow accessible (with a bit of work on your part), given it's adherence to detail. Possibly a masterpiece of sorts.

Rating 7

## Nevada Beach - Zero Day (Metal Blade/Warner '90)

Harmless, unarmed and spineless commercial hard rock, leaning towards the simple riffs of AC/DC (one of about five allowed directions for poodle rock). Ruff-house vocals reinforce the unremarkable deal, as Slagel glosses this one up to fit the band strategically in the middle of a pack of bands whose hard rock style would die at the hands of first grunge, then that hated, borderless enigma called alternative. Sounds vaguely D.A.D. or even War Babies, but nowhere near as impressionable as either (unless you are the four guys' moms).

Rating 5

## Nevermore - Nevermore (Century Media '95)

Nevermore's a bit of a second string Seattle supergroup, main selling point being Sanctuary's proto-metal pipist Warrell Dane in on fist-pump vocals. Featuring eight unwieldy techno-liths rolling thunder like Testament meets Memento Mori and Candlemass, Nevermore makes a loud, large and proud metalli-goth statement, even ballad *The Sanity Assassin* hooking in Manowar-like pestilence. Slow mixes with fast, growls offset shrieks, and the metal roars like a lion, secure in its love of committed '80s conventions, not the ones that fell so embarrassingly out of vogue, but the ones that never sold in the first place. Mighty fine wine for us old rivetheads but only in that queasy mid-'80s mood. Admiration and respect but still a record only infrequently useable.

Rating 7

## Nevermore - In Memory (Century Media '96)

Authoritative progressive power metal act Nevermore return with this long-awaited taste of new music, a limited edition, 5000 copy, five track EP that blisters paint with its elegant, emotional rumblings. Sorta like **Sad Wings Of Destiny** soaking up a measured dose of grindcore bile, **In Memory** is distinguished by its ancient heroics, brooding mellow passages flanked by columns of gritty gothic granite, faves being thespian terrain like *Matricide* and *In Memory*. The mix is perfect, fluid Steve Morse-coded guitar work foiling Warrell Dane's vocals which are cut back a bit versus the debut. It's a morose, heavier sound, even if there are frequent balladic moments. Gorgeous stuff. Track #4 *Silent Hedges/Double Dare* is a Bauhaus cover.

Rating 8

## Nevermore - The Politics Of Ecstasy (Century Media '96)

Seattle's finest keep coming back with undulating waves of vista-fantastic metal, **The Politics Of Ecstasy** striking quickly on the heels of the long and frightening **In Memory** EP, which gathered a backlog of more morose numbers for forbidden consumption. Now we're back to snorting horses hoofing and battering the history of metal until a hypnotic headbang is achieved. Picture a toss between Dickinson-Maiden and Solitude Aeturnus, and the curve that Nevermore

has thrown becomes euphorically understood. It is a battering, medieval march that takes hold of most every track, a pure and robust sort of restrained chaos, accompanied by vibes and moods straight out of **Stained Class** and Rainbow's **Rising**. Drums are recorded for combat, and Warrell Dane plays the tormented wizard, taking the band's sound somewhat raw and underground, while obvious musicianship and cathedral-tall melodies drag it back to centre. This one's for all those collectors pining for the days of quality German fare (a cheery salute to Stephen and John LaRocque, Euro-metal authorities extraordinaire!), for those looking for toil in their music. Except thankfully, Nevermore has learned the lessons of grunge, and have recorded stormily, Van Williams double-bass barrage particularly immediate and viciously squared off. Oh and one other thing, ain't read a bad review of any of Nevermore's three releases.
Rating                                                        9

## The New Adventures - Crusade   (Topanga/PolyGram '82)
Spine says New Adventurers which makes more sense but who cares? I'll be brief, 'cos this one is a delete bin special (which I think I've owned three times). Rollicking biker-themed boogie metal probably from Holland. Heavier than Spider and Dumpy's Rusty Nuts, but not BB Rock or harder Quo. One cover, but they all sound like covers. More importantly, surprisingly useful.
Rating                                                        6

## New Idol Sun - Reach   (Pavement '94)
'Tis a shame this record didn't part some waves, New Idol Sun scoring a legitimate post-grunge strike. Their quilted sound is is only partly grunge however (grunge itself, I guess, is only a sum of its parts), finding a cleaner slow-burn which like Mindfunk and to some extent Soundgarden, mixes equal part psychedelic blues and psychedelic doom, under clear vocals that project for a country mile. But the amount of wallowed, near paralysis on **Reach** just might prevent me from getting involved, the record really hitting the bog on tunes like *Past The Point Of God* and *Embrace*. Heck, then it gets grooved and stout of riff wence again, so I dunno, check it out if you like the gooey retro stuff. **Reach** just might stick to your ribs.
Rating                                                        7

## New York Dolls - New York Dolls   (Phonogram '73)
Linking MC5, The Stooges and The Velvet Underground with The Dictators, Kiss and Aerosmith, David Johansen and the New York Dolls carried on the fine tradition of depraved and excessive underground rock until punk would take over in '76. But underlying the band's decadent glam and drag mystique was a band that could rock, whipping up a muscular Stonesy brew, rounding many obscure '60s bases while embracing and aiding in the invention of the new guitar rock. In essence, the Dolls are one of the few "legendary" acts that deserved the tag on raw, documented recorded work alone (unlike The Doors or Velvet Underground), even though the band's historical importance is as solid as The Stooges'. No, unlike a bevy of wastecases, this was strong material. From the seminal cruise metal of *Frankenstein* and *Jet Boy* through freight train boogie rockers like *Bad Girl* and *Looking For A Kiss* and all stops in between, **New York Dolls** is a respectful celebration of American music through the years, powered down the boulevards of broken dreams by the twin turbines of Syl Sylvain (aka Syl Mizrahi) and Johnny Thunders, who serve both the romance and reality of the street, the drudgery of clubbing and the glittering dreams of superstardom.
Rating                                                        10

## New York Dolls - Too Much Too Soon   (Phonogram '74)
The Dolls follow their cocksure debut with a record that finds the band more at ease with their role as archivists, offering less raunchy metal rock stuff, more clever evocations of the '50s and '60s, and many not their own, covers *Bad Detective*, *(There's Gonna Be A) Showdown* and *Don't Start Me Talkin'* rendered punky and clashable, finding tragedy and nostalgia in the collision of cultures; comfortable, no-worry, no-hurry classics dragged against their will into a decade moving too fast for the Dolls themselves. As all grows slick around them (except of course for Johansen's mentor Mick Jagger and his Stones, whose spiritual and material planes are not so sordidly close together as the Dolls'), Dave, Syl, Johnny, Killer and Jerry are digging in, back and under, perhaps in search of a purity and simplicity of living that they had so convincingly lost. So much of **Too Much Too Soon** is a nostalgic but bracing club rock, delivered with punk snarl and time-worn wisdoms, feet in the gutter, shooting for the surreal, excessive world of rock's upper echelon. Still, it sounds creepy, ancient and dark, kinda like a party but a morbid and apocalyptic one, and the record accomplishes this by being so outside of time, going way back for its influences. A classic band in the true sense of the word, almost mythical, definitely burning out before they faded away. Johansen went on to make five fine, playful solo albums (fave: **In Style**) before his transformation into comic character Buster Pointdexter.
Rating                                                        10

## New York Dolls - Red Patent Leather   (Fan Club '84)
I always heard these guys were a pathetic sham live, combining booze and drugs with zero ability, trashing through their sets with stupefying ineptitude. Well, I'd say this poorly recorded semi-boot catches them on a good night, because the delivery is merely awful, something akin to Iggy's **Metallic K.O.** in dour dank dampness. The songs are an even split between predictable covers and Dolls originals, many of which aren't from the band's two stellar studio feasts. The non-LP originals (*Red Patent Leather*, *On Fire*, *Down Down Downtown*, *Pirate Love* and *Teenage News*) ride the standard shoot 'em up boogie wooger freight train that marks the band's less adventuresome output, thereby steering the entire sordid show into this one very retro direction. Dull. My copy's on red vinyl in an unmarked white jacket, although I believe I've seen more upscale versions.
Rating                                                        4

## Niagara - Now Or Never   (Killerwatt '88)
Smartly dressed keyboard metal with amazingly American momentum for a Spanish band, Niagara resemble a heavy and ornate Dokken forced into the streets with an electric yet scrapling production. Classy yet still spontaneous with cocksure vocals from Tony Cuevas, one could imagine these boys as big 'merican stars with nary a trace of their mainland European roots.
Rating                                                        7

## Nightingale - The Breathing Shadow   (Black Mark '95)
Nightingale is a solo project from busy Edge Of Sanity frontman Dan Swano. "Written, recorded and mixed" in seven days, with all instruments and programming by Swano, **The Breathing Shadow** is predictably close and personal, Swano remaining beyond the realms of death psychologically while delivering his message through understated, singing-style vocals and small keyboard/computer structures. So call it soft industrial death, axes wandering dazed through the slow cold tundra, as Swano indulges in his Sisters Of Mercy cum Floyd cum stoner Queensryche complex. But he's an interesting guy, and his Scandinavian chill shudders the spine, even if the music is spacey, sub-

dued, and probably designed to comfort. So call this one a creepy success.
Rating 7

## Nightingale - The Closing Chronicles (Black Mark '96)
Swano takes a different tack on this second solo project, stating that **The Breathing Shadow** purged him of his Gothic influences, this one "reflecting more of the music I really listen to, like Marillion, Kansas, a specific period of Santana, U.K., and Asia. And that pretty much sums it up, **The Closing Chronicles** sideswiping erudite prog rock, occasionally electric jazz-inflected, but for the most part lying somewhere within old Genesis and lush and layered U.K. Second cool thing is that the record is all real drums, and when the guitars kick in, it almost sounds like a mellow, progressive Priest from the late '70s meets early synthesized Rush, morose, brooding songs full up with drama, ready to compete with any pomp rock from any era.
Rating 8

## Night Ranger - Dawn Patrol (Boardwalk/CBS '82)
More like fromage patrol, San Fran's Night Ranger arriving on the scene, finding immediate if modest success with their brand of girlie keyboard pop metal. So here we had it, the slick debut from Jack Blades (future Damn Yankees, Shaw Blades), Brad Gillis (brief Ozzy henchman, solo) and crew, really kicking some life into a genre that had always been quite small and fuzzy up until now, different, disparate bands like Journey, Boston, Loverboy, Foreigner, Styx and even Kansas stacked together to describe the pomp, perfumed side of hard rock. But Night Ranger takes as much from Sammy Hagar and Triumph to form their tuneful, guitar-driven alloy, a hybrid softened by Blades' crystal clear, basically bland vocals, and hardened by Gillis' moderately shredded solo style, guitar sound, but not really his sleepy riffing. Creatively, a pretty average band, even if their place in AOR archives is assured. Best track on the album, *Don't Tell Me You Love Me*, was also the band's first hit.
Rating 5

## Night Ranger - Midnight Madness (MCA '83)
Fave commercialite fashion plates Night Ranger (funniest looking guy is still the Supertrampled Alan "Fitz" Gerald) stormed back with what is widely considered their best album, **Midnight Madness** also marking the quintet's commercial peak. Gillis is all silk and steel, producer Pat Glasser layering his constrained axes with feminique sermons from Fitz's synthesizer handbook, all the while the band's four part harmonies sending it on home like the pomp experts they have become. Hits this time out are *(You Can Still) Rock In America* (basically white trash's *Born In The USA*), monster smash Elton Joel ballad *Sister Christian* (the band's biggest meal ticket), and *When You Close Your Eyes*, an eminently hummable popster in the time (!?) Toto tradition. Yes folks, this is the band's best record, quintessential warm pop metal, dare I say a historically pertinent piece of the AOR puzzle.
Rating 7

## Night Ranger - 7 Wishes (MCA '84)
And here comes the flood, the flood of insipid, pinkish AOR melodies that is, Blades and Gillis barely breaking a sweat on this first Night Ranger platter that points down. Basically the band is taken over by producer Pat Glasser and nerdy looking keyboardist, even drummer Kelly Keagy falling prey to hi-tech wizardry, his drum sound all gucked-up with fake plogs and drogs. I guess this is the textured, serious record, but it just comes off lifeless, the band abdicating their

delicate alchemy of heft and hook. Pretty much like '80s Styx.
Rating 4

## Night Ranger - Big Life (MCA '87)
Still fairly tech'ed to the teeth, Night Ranger (that logo-era logo proudly remains!) adopt a new producer, Kevin Elson, who somehow reconciles the keyboards and Gillis' exacting guitarwork, turning everything up equally for a rejuvenated pomp sound from these likeable purveyors of puff. **Big Life** didn't make any more of a dent than **7 Wishes**, but soundtrack hit *The Secret Of My Success* defined the '80s perfectly (see Queen's *I Want It All*), percolating along like uh, Queen's *Radio Ga Ga* as Blades overextends himself nicely on polite white boy vocals. Generally, an ambitious, over-the-top buffet of gloss pop that crosses the line into prog (*Better Let It Go*), foreshadowing a direction that might have given these shiny merchants of goodness a new, big life. Even the ballads flick the ceremonious lighter upon high.
Rating 7

## Night Ranger - Man In Motion (MCA '88)
Once again, a producer change, this time to hair band guru Keith Olsen, who loads up the hi-fidelity while letting all corners of the Night Ranger chemistry sing their inspiring sentiments. So it's a pleasure just to listen to the arranged interplay, still the only thing botched being the drums, which are too synthetic and stiff as usual. Blades' voice has gotten more rock'n'roll weary and it sounds great, as he and Gillis trade licks throughout some solid Ranger rockers like *Woman In Love* and *Right On You*. Pretty much my fave of the whole catalogue is this record's *Reason To Be* (and maybe the band's), which marries Zeppelin to Kansas to Cali-fried hard rock, miraculously sounding genuine in the process, possibly a harbringer of the most excellent Shaw Blades record of '95. Too bad about this band. Really, the decline came at no fault to the records, which methodically ushered in increasing levels of tasteful sophistication, making up for the loss of youthful exuberance.
Rating 7

## Night Ranger - Greatest Hits (MCA '89)
Long gone and acrimonious by this time, Night Ranger had seen their dreams somewhat fulfilled, somewhat dashed, rising to a level most six stringers would give their brain for (sold as new). MCA reportedly pushed the band to get soft and mushy, and relations deteriorated. So out comes this posthumous slapdash affair (the band wasn't even consulted), no new tracks, scant liner notes, really bad job all around. The shame: Night Ranger only had enough hits for about half of this twelve ton tuna. Update: the band has reformed for a record in '97.
Rating 4

## Nightstick - Blotter (Relapse '96)
With a smudgy line descended from A.C., you might guess that the wattage enclosed doth reek. What Nightstick is on about is acid sludge, or as they call it, psychedeli-core, sounding like raped, pillaged and valium-hoovered Napalm Death, or a kind of tone-deaf Eyehategod. But even if the space boulder jams make you sleepy in a bad way, the boys give good read, explaining each turgid assemblage in detail, pointing out where answering machines were used, guitars broken, old amps provoked with a plastic bag, and where we're supposed to imaging spacemen dying as they get sucked into the sun, or a blanket of German fighter planes surveying bombed-out Britain. Plainly acid-scorched, with the whole trip faithfully documented by noisecore guitars frozen in blocks of tenement cement, undiscriminating wrecking ball

rubble-izing player, weapon and listener alike, unenjoyable except under pharmaceutical brain-embalmage.
Rating      5

## Nightwing - Something In The Air   (Ovation '80)

Ahead of their time in terms of scary album covers and even their thin attempts at metal, Nightwing (used to be Strife, putting out two records), perennial losers due to their own delusions of grandeur, get off to a pretty weak stride early on with this plain jane record of bad mellow-to-HR Heep, in an ill-fated and unprepared crusade towards mature and less technically adorned progressive rock. Softest offering from a band who rarely punted booty anyways.
Rating      2

## Nightwing - Black Summer   (Attic '82)

For the only time in its near anonymous existence, Nightwing dish out a concentrated dose of their Heep Purple visions, zippy but hokey melodic metal flying everywhere like picks at a guitar clinic, achieving Magnum filler on full throttle. As a self-produced effort, **Black Summer** ain't half bad, trodding forth with an incestuous "hockey barn soundcheck" audio leakage, blending together the band's not so compatible mix of barroom mucking about with a predilection for expensive electronics. Only the eerie title track commands any sort of notice, evoking vintage Jon Lord grafted onto any number of third string NWOBHMetallers. The best of Nightwing, but avoid nevertheless, despite there being no ballads.
Rating      6

## Nightwing - My Kingdom Come   (Gull '84)

The flirtation with progressive rock continues and elevates on this dressing up of the eminently Anglo Nightwing sound. Steve Hackett provides one song (*Cell 151* from his **Highly Strung** LP), some production and some axework, Max Bacon is in on yelpy vocals fresh from Bronz, and spaceman Roger Dean comes up with one of his classiest cover concepts yet. Musically things are quite busy and over-produced as one might expect, although ideas remain dumb as a bag of wet hammers. **My Kingdom Come** ultimately closes its existence sleepwalking through various keyboard-laced pomp rock styles which betray a surprising continuance of regressed song skills, again like the worst of Heep from the unexplainable middle 2/3 of their career. Why must the pain continue?
Rating      4

## Nine Inch Nails - Pretty Hate Machine   (TVT '89)

Although this first piece of bit-mapped sculpture from Trent immediately put the boy-brooder on the map to alt.stardom, **Pretty Hate Machine** is little more than angsty dance percolation. Lyrically, Trent has arrived alive and writhing, primed for a shocking ice-water dive into vortextual depression, but musically, he's all-electronic, offering many innovations, but none of the metallic body-blows that would begin wholesale with **Broken**. Resident chart-bound calling card: *Head Like A Hole*, the track being the first of what will be a scant few intense anthems of the hippest, snobbiest sliver of the alternative set.
Rating      5

## Nine Inch Nails - Broken   (Interscope '92)

Reznor's early days were spent highly regarded by musicians and fans alike as one of the mixmasters to the stars, transformer of the metallic into the frenzied, frowner to all humanity. Squarely more industrial, introspective and basement-sealed than Ministry, Reznor's own work is well known for its caustic manic depressive soundscapes, both lyrics and bells 'n' whistles alike covered in buckets of blood. **Broken** kicks

and shatters; truly a carnivorous sort of animal, technology gone very nasty, the ultimate revenge on dance music I guess. A six tune EP officially, with two "secret" tracks tacked on the end, one being Adam And The Ants hit *Physical*, carved up and left to limp into the bush and die. Cool packaging and an interesting project, best ingested with a tall mug of amino acids.
Rating      7

## Nine Inch Nails - The Downward Spiral
(Interscope '94)

A masterpiece no one can listen to, a baffling, bubbling, blistering volcano of sound, a body of lyrics that placidically screams with pain, a record that doesn't rock. It's all been muttered (always in hushed tones) about the stultifying piece of sonic mayhem that is **The Downward Spiral**. Rolling Stone went on about how you couldn't get straight your volume levels, others lamented the lack of guitars, but no matter what, I'd have to stick with my own bewildered utterance: I love it, and I can't play it. If ever a record demanded your undivided attention, this is it, for better or worse, a seemingly endless undulation of electronic killskill, sequencing that in fact doesn't reveal its scabbard-drawn pleasures until an elongated second half. Trent Reznor is indeed the magnet of tech, the actualization of all that is possible and exploitable in the electronic cottage age we are all told is at hand. **The Downward Spiral** erects an impenetrable wall for sure. It is a difficult record like no other, something you envy academically and dismiss as rock fan from outside. The marriage of Trent's stunning, futuristic arrangements and his bare-all bloody lyrics is more than either alone, musically the record chopping block along, limping like a robot hacked by machetes, lyrically seven Sundays waze to trauma. And therein lies a bit of my sandpaper disgust, me basically unsympathetic for a whole raft of characters (I'm being kind: I don't think they're all Trent) who can't cope. Yea, too much whining or brutalizing from a lack of whine-ability, but squalidly overall, too depressing and defeated, which is not Trent at all, who is I gather (he was my first interview ever) impressively wise beyond his years, but no, not the mucous-enshrouded mental captive of his songs. So whereto and wherefore with this elegant thorn? I'll tell you wherefore: wherefore being the perch on which certain (none before this) CDs sit leering at the piffle that passes for rock'n'roll, that fancy pants packaging of **The Downward Spiral** saying "I'm the Syd Barrett record your parents never imagined", the bruising chunk of techchain that splatters oil at all that is not well. And so this treatise shudders to a halt.
Rating      9

## Nine Inch Nails - Further Down The Spiral
(TVT/Interscope '95)

As if **The Downward Spiral** wasn't psychically harrowing enough, Trent chides us into donning schizophrenic tin foil hats, sending us into a bush plain locust storm to receive buzzing buzzed radio signals as the plague sings its winged symphony around our info-and-sound-inundated headspaces. In Reznor's frenzied world, a song is just static long enough to get recorded, the very nature of industrial bonks, squonks and squeaks residing in the living mutating, almost meditative nature of such shiftable instruments as computers. So **Further Down** we go, Trent re-carving half of his last opus deafening then inaudible, forgiving then homicidal, as each track sees renaming, reworking, new life. No EP this one (at 63 minutes), but a new cracklingly electric and manic revisitation of one thorny record, along with a few new poison ivy bouquets. Plainspeak: quite interchangeable with the "official" record really, because both are equally impenetrable, showering down so many unique sonic laser beads, you never quite get a handle on more than a couple tracks at a

time. Verdict: worshipable more as art for sound-hounds (or sculpture in real time) than entertainment, but important all the same.
Rating 7

## 9.0 - Too Far Gone (Shrapnel '90)

Sure, roll your eyes in hair band disgust when you see this, but with a sweep of your flannel hand, you will have missed a fairly blazing piece of heavy AOR, 9.0 often getting up a head of steam that stabs the crux of Van Halen, or at least the Bullet Boys or Spread Eagle (please proceed to *First Of My Generation* and *Little Sister*, but don't feed the animals). Then there's the spiritual Perry riff that sends *Gypsy Queen* a' flyin', Craig Small chomping down on street metal conventions like a rabid bulldog, while moonlighting in three or four Van Halen zones simultaneously. But there's also a plethora of sparse, funky metal clunkers, making this a peaks and valleys affair, upper quartile but not the dike to spike grunge's tidal wave. Could do worse.
Rating 7

## Nirvana - Bleach (Sub Pop '89)

The grungiest grungester of them all, **Bleach** is perhaps the crowning Sub Pop artifact, somewherz three-way-tied with Green River's **Rehab Doll** and Mudhoney's **Superfuzz Bigmuff** for Seattle sound encrusted and personified. **Bleach** is total sonic basswallow (does anybody remember 16 RPM?), brutal collisions of primal, depraved riffery, often finding a dazed and amnesiatic sort of Sabbath turned onto Motörhead, often finding an astonishing but shredded grasp of hook that hints at the largess of **Nevermind** (see *About A Girl* and *Love Buzz*). **Bleach**-era Nirvana is a sordid, guitar-heavy affair, indeed the band being a four-piece, with now-deleted axe dude Jason Everman (since moved to Mindfunk), who with (K)obain works supreme gravel mix dementia on this classic recorded by Jack Endino for $600. I don't know . . . this is just the slackest and loudest migraine headache on God's green earth; bleak metallized gruntpunk that strips out all the pleasantries, leaving only fatigued steel and rust, only scrape and frame, a frame that will get bright new aluminum siding come **Nevermind**. The backbone of grunge. Note: CD adds two tracks, *Big Cheese* and *Downer*, the latter also showing up on **Incesticide**.
Rating 10

## Nirvana - Nevermind (Geffen '91)

How this record broke is a case study of how the rock biz in the '90s has become a healthier, universally more intelligent and creative juggernaut. Suffice to say **Nevermind** was the first dangerous record in the '90s to infiltrate the slumbering mass market, a potent gathering of toxins that seeped into the collective, almost through hypnosis, deafening subconscious trauma like *Come As You Are* and the immortal *Smells Like Teen Spirit* somehow unraveling the wallets of the weak, who will take their first wild ride sleepless in Seattle. **Nevermind** was the ultimate marriage of chaos and order, bruising power chords and sexy hooks, Cobain captured in all his slack apocalyptic grandeur, from whisper to full roar, transformed into fragile, disheveled and contemptuous superstar via the gut-level sonics of Butch Vig and Andy Wallace, who accent the contrasts with supreme finesse. And indeed that's how most tracks on this one hour opus are written, mebbee a sturdy bass line and a sweet (but babbling) vocal, strapped to a sinful churning drone come chorus time, the band unapologetic for their respect of simple pop, although such sentiments underplay the startling maneuvers that this record entails. Ultimately **Nevermind** is the most rock-solid and chartable chunk of Seattle; simple, immediately likeable, the '90s version of power pop, which like everything else these days is intensified beyond recognition,

an entirely fresh hybrid of melody, metal and punk, totally nuts, but less psychologically malevolent than Alice in Chains, Soundgarden and yes, even Pearl Jam's **Ten**, which eclipses **Nevermind** on brains (and commercial staying power), but simpers off to the corner on brawn. It restores your faith in brainkind, seeing a record this eccentric and "alternative" sell; and judging from the fallout, **Nevermind** had marked somewhat of a paradigm shift, exposing the dinosaur mentality of the old guard, while opening the doors for a whole raft of weirdos, kinda what the Sex Pistols were supposed to do.
Rating 10

## Nirvana - Incesticide (Geffen '92)

Proving his anti-social, anti-commercial disposition, Cobain deems it fit to release a record of hurried, harried, wasted B-sides, covers and other gutter swill experiments. Hope nobody was misled into thinking this was **Nevermind**'s bonafide follow-up, because unfortunately, **Incesticide** is neither the caustic blitz of **Bleach**, nor the lush, melodic grunge of the band's logic-defying breakthrough. It's somewhere in between; a goofy, off-the-cuff collection of simple, new wavey tunes put through the punishing grunge shredder, many under two minutes, most rusting out for dear life, drowning out a distant and mumbling Cobain who sounds like he's munching on a major, brain-frying buffet of industrial cleansers. Best cuts are *Sliver*, *Stain*, *Mexican Seafood* and *Aero Zeppelin*, but even these sound less wisely-considered than similar pollution from **Bleach**. And the covers are simply songs that may make Kurt giddy but don't fit the Nirvana crank in the least. Lots of stuff, but it's all pretty rude, raw and fast-fading, just enough to reassure us that Nirvana (and especially Kurt) is still a mess fit to crash. So now starts all the bullshit about a Nirvana backlash.
Rating 7

## Nirvana - In Utero (Geffen '93)

Having read three or four cryptic and universally effusive reviews of **In Utero** even before the record hit the racks, once September 21 finally arrived, I ran at breaksweat speed to acquire my personal piece of the Nirvana rocket. And after all the Hype, all the controversy about producer Steve Albini and his desire to make the record bracingly caustic, apparently more so than Geffen (where Nirvana fits in all this has been skillfully obscured), what falls out of the Cobain complex of complication is a record that bows to no god. In base terms (of which I've read none), **In Utero** is like an **Incesticide** of acceptably crafty and crafted originals. Albini's (tampered?) mix is nothing worth talking about, just a grungy, snarling gathering of sounds, not really thrashy or poor, just dirtier than **Nevermind**, cleaner than **Bleach** (nice touch providing "suggested bass and treble positions." It actually helps, although why didn't they just provide enough treble to begin with?). Cobain's lyrics are sensual and ugly, sort of an intense but rambling poetry of nasty colours; brief, packed thick with images. The record is also crammed with lots of old-style grunge guitar pain, yowling, howling feedback which nevertheless yields to the almighty power of song. Mellow tracks come off as clanky, deflated and rushed, as do the rockers, which is a preferred state of garage anyways, but the overall effect is one of the gifted shiftless in urgent and desperate battle with electricity, solid punk rock songwriting with a thin pop veil. And I don't want to get any deeper than that, because even if Cobain's exotic weirdscapes are arguably heavy scenery, musically, these boys are trashing it up, bashing cymbals and patch cord carnage everywhere, definitely more free and easy and smelly than **Nevermind**'s studied grandeur. Fewer lovable hooks than its obscenely successful predecessor, way more mind and body distortion, and a good three or four duff tracks. Probably the best raft of songtitles though since BÖC's **Secret Treaties**. Oh yeah, and then Cobain went and killed himself April 7, 1994.

Rating                                                                    10

## Nirvana - Unplugged In New York   (Geffen '94)

I thought the concept of squeezing the uproarious, loud-luvin' Nirvana into an MTV unplugged situation would be utterly without point. Watching Grohl with those brushes was painful bad. But painful good was peering into the paralyzing, despairing presence of Kurt Cobain bringing fresh horror to misunderstood **In Utero** tracks like All Apologies, Dumb, and the apocalyptically bitter Pennyroyal Tea. For me, that damn show (and the man's grunge-shattering, gunshot suicide) elevated **In Utero** to hysterical levels of soul-incinerating brilliance. **Unplugged In New York**'s usefulness needed no further confirmation. But then, Kurt splays his professorial intelligence and impeccable taste by covering three supra-haunting little-known nuggets of insightful melancholia (from Bowie, The Vaselines, and Leadbelly), plus darn near my favorite trio of Meat Puppets tracks (mangled, albeit) all from the seminal **II** album, virtually single-handedly rejuvenating the Kirkwoods' career (although a fine record like **Too High To Die** didn't hurt). Ultimately, **Unplugged In New York** is an agonizing wake, producing additional acidic bile we might have thought unconjurable after the gut-wrenching, exhausting dry heaves of **In Utero**. We see deeper into the physical and psychic pain that any of us ever imagined we could. Whether writing for himself, or unearthing others' pain, Cobain will ultimately be remembered as one of the saddest, perfect students of song, a mere and fragile fan at heart. Released in conjunction with a retrospective video entitled **Live! Tonight! Sold Out!**

Rating                                                                     8

## Nirvana - From The Muddy Banks Of The Wishkah
(Geffen '96)

No doubt this was a necessary coda to Nirvana's legacy, Geffen assembling sixteen tracks of whack spanning five years of sluggin' and slammin'. And the record proves the band was explosive punk when on, and a cynical, weary ruse when off. Which is no surprise given Cobain's love/hate purge/pain relationship with the live experience. But even when Kurt's voice drags and wanes, the fierce percussion talent that is Dave Grohl lifts the spirit of all, including Spirit, which is a mite rickety all-told. Krist Novoselic's liner notes have a curious, naive, outsider quality to them: they read like his face and physique. But all in all, quite good mixes, fairly elevated performances, and a time-trippin' song selection (Negative Creep: yeah!). Nevertheless, I'd still rather hear the flamethrown blast of **Bleach** or the creamy pioneering grunge of **Nevermind** than this bumpy ride. Sold like freakin' hotcakes.

Rating                                                                     6

## Nitro - O.F.R.   (Rampage/Rhino '89)

These dudes were kind of (twistedly) accepted by metalheads in the know, because their glam metal sheen was so over the top, you had to break down in tearful laughter until gut was fully bust, Nitro's particular gleanings from glam being shimmering wafer-thin production, super-smooth but dog-whistle-pierced vocal harmonies, and songs that sizzle with the WAY over the top axe carvings of Michael Angelo (pictured here with a ludicrous four-neck guitar). Basically a dueling duo of Angelo and highly strung vocalist Jim "Jimmy Dean" Gillette, who is a cross between Geoff Tate and Dave Defeis of Virgin Steele, a guy absolutely winged-out on the high notes (check out the beginning of Machine Gunn Eddie. Yeesh!). So consider this one an impossibly pink poodle rocker so far gone into tiny treble, it's a viable parody of the form, basically the kind of band you'd hire for a silly movie.

Rating                                                                     3

## Nitro - II: Hot Wet Drippin' With Sweat
(Rampage/Rhino '91)

Surprisingly enjoyable for a few reasons, vocals, axes, almost relevant songs, even if the Cat Scratch Fever cover is a bit dopey butted up against the rest of this still hyper-tense record. So maybe glam's the wrong word this time around, Nitro **II** more like totally alive, totally blitzed hair band metal (Slaughter, Kik Tracee?), by a seething posse who have settled down the histrionics, while still remaining as much a guitar hero showcase as anything. Nice to hear that Jimmy Gillette now inflects a bit more towards Graham Bonnet than the shrill chick yelps of the debut.

Rating                                                                     7

## The Nixons - Foma   (MCA '95)

Grunge will not die, because, as the old joke goes about pizza and sex, even when it's bad, it's pretty good. So The Nixons are here to nestle that cash spot between Stone Temple Pilots and latest raves Bush, who have quietly built sales of over three million copies for their insipid, opportunistic debut. Yeah, it's all pretty much angsty and over-dramatic here (oy! you got problems?), but it's also much more smeary and heavy than you'd think (with good, almost half-sincere vocals), these guys sleepers in many ways, even now sniffing out radio play (PJ smarmy ballad Sister) a good year after the record limped out of the gates. Produced with three day stubble by Mark Dodson. A grudging acceptance is proffered, if partially because Glenn Tipton rips off some solos on Drink The Fear.

Rating                                                                     7

## Nocturnus - The Key   (Earache '90)

Highly evil and tangled looking, **The Key** has that foreboding waft of sin to it, like something heavy this way comes. And man, is this a mathematically metallic maze, overwhelming fellow brutish Floridians Nasty Savage with molten, blood-caked abandon. Not that it does much for me, the absolutely mechanized layers of overkill just pounding any semblance of pleasure into a wee pebble. It's basically one of those records that really is as mercilessly distraught as metal gets, yet lies crushed under its own lack of compromise, riffic multitude, and tempo switchbacks. Flagrantly overdriven, yet 100% power-drenched. Weird band, and about the most aggressive progressive metal act I've ever heard. I mean, these guys even have a full time keyboardist, albeit one whose mealy mews can be deciphered only sparingly amongst the smoked convolutory den of serpents. Fiercely professional evil genius, twistedly misdirected.

Rating                                                                     6

## Nocturnus - Thresholds   (Earache '92)

Things get a tad more discernible this time as Nocturnus proves in an entirely different way that they were ahead of their time. This one's more a low-down death metal thingie, a little more squalid and scampering, more trench-ready, signaled by the aggro-bark of new vocalist Dan Izzo. Still tastefully prog at times, almost ambient at others, while occasionally thrashy unto modern-day Bay Area or technical Slayer, **Thresholds** was a creative piece of textured extremism that just never quite caught on, no fault to the music.

Rating                                                                     6

## NOFX - I Heard They Suck Live!   (Fat Wreck Chords '95)

The funny liner notes to this record (sample: "We would like to thank a bunch of people, but I'm kinda busy right now, so forget it.") sez that the record exists because there are too many boots around with crappy sound quality, so like, here's our response. **I Heard They Suck Live!** caps off a decade of pioneering SoCal punk, not to mention a ton of records like '86's **Liberal Animation**, '89's **S&M Airlines**, '91's **Ribbed**, '93's **Two Heebs & A Bean** and '94's **Punk In Drublic**. The NOFX sound is down-the-middle '90s punk really, fairly light-headed and tuneful, nowhere near the urbancore sounds of the NYC scene; just good vocals and windmill chords. Consider these guys the grandpappies of the scene, along with Bad Religion, and in terms of buying their product, if you like Green Day, you won't be disappointed.

Rating    **5**

## NOFX - Heavy Petting Zoo   (Epitaph '96)

Leave it to punk royalty to provoke new flavours amongst all the speedy three chord crap '90s punk has been feeding us, NOFX smelling the coffin, and mixing their brisk biscuits with Rancid-like reggae and tons o' pop (*Bleeding Heart Disease* even sounds like a Cheap Trick track off their first record, the title of which I can't recall). Cool packaging also (won't touch that cover!), including vastly entertaining lyrics written over all sorts of body parts, dollar bills, t-shirts, pillows and pieces of cardboard. Very few bands that don't put me to sleep in this over-rated genre, and this is one of them, finding NOFX's sunny, wind 'em up disposition a kick in the keester that is a larf rather than the usual mugging, the band (liner notes: "same as last album but older and fatter (Eric's up to 178 lbs)") fully prepared to belt out inspired harmonies, while surgical punk chords run the realm of irreverent rock history up and down the strip until all are entertained and sweaty.

Rating    **7**

## Noisy Mama - Everybody Has One   (Atco '91)

One of the statistically better offerings from the corporate genre, **Everybody Has One** has at least one of everything which seems to be the case with all packages of slick, mainstream American hard rock these days. So it runs the predicted range: a ballad, a couple of cabaret blues, some uptempo anthems, two fast ones, some weighted sledges, and lots of inflections to Bon and Angus. But even though there's zero innovation here, there are a number of hot, flawlessly displayed rockers such as Stonesy lead cut *Heart Of Stone*, racer *Dave's Brain*, plain, low-slung strutter *It's You*, and yes, ballad *Long Way Home*. Cerebrally speaking, Noisy Mama are yer basic drinking man's, blues-via-AC/DC metal, with the usual awful lyrics, merely stringing cliché after cliché until the allotted space is filled. Still it's well over half party-hardy, unlike a number who try so sadly.

Rating    **5**

## NoMeansNo - The Day Everything Became Isolated And Destroyed   (Virus '88)

Have no fear, the above cumbersome title of this CD represents a twinning of the band's six track EP **The Day Everything Became Nothing** with first (?) full length blight **Small Parts Isolated And Destroyed**, which makes sense, the whole fourteen-cut festering sore sounding like one large, rusting collection of like-minded mental music. Ultimately alarming and so life-like in its anarchy, this fledgling poison from one of Vancouver's most enigmatic duos just flies in the face of convention, at the same time destroying pleasure with its severe marriage of violent atonal frequencies, finding much more in common with the pretty hate machine that is **0 + 2 = 1** than the focused, bright silver insanity of **Wrong**. Sorta Zappa meets the Stranglers without keyboards, early NoMeansNo wore its contempt for melodious harmony on its sleeve. Where, when and why would anybody voluntarily play this sort of sonic implosion? Beats me, the whole monstrous mash sounding like a manifesto for the

abolition of music, a kind of Beat ethic punk gnawing that berates over an ugly jazz metal bed of barbed wire that only Rollins and Beefheart could imagine. And damn near none of it's enjoyable, tunes disintegrating into heavy-lidded basslines and drug-induced mumbles just as you think riff has met rhythm. Admirable as a concept, but ugly and masochistic.

Rating    **5**

## NoMeansNo - Wrong   (Cargo '89)

Simply put, **Wrong** was the mightiest merger between the hateful aggression of punk and the discipline of heavy metal; Rollins' word put to deed with an intensity and will to conquer to which Black Flag or Rollins Band rarely rise. And to this day, **Wrong** upholds this quasi-band's reputation, all records before and after finding dissipation and dissolution more often than **Wrong**'s towering fury. It's *Catching Up* is this record's *Tom Sawyer*, initiating the carnage with an exacting onslaught of precision progpunk, all distortion and blood-caked glory, hyper metal mania at its finest. And the pain keeps coming, *The Tower*, *Stocktaking* and *Rags And Bones* blowing away any and all comers on the band's other records. Foremost but thoughtfully dovetailed into the song's tricky constructions is Rob Wright's marauding bass work, handled with tons more restraint than Primus, Maiden or even Rush, in hand-to-bayonet combat with the uncredited guitarist's wickedly distorted guitar riffs. Finalizing NoMeansNo's unified front is brother John Wright's drumming, which is dead-perfect here, angry, tribal, quick to explode, while Rob delivers an impressive rant for hate with total impatience and disgust for mediocrity. Tragically, **Wrong** is proving to be a flash in the pan, sunlight magnified to a burning pinpoint, one strong cordial, one stiff belt, one brave blast of wattage, but alas, alone in NoMeansNo's negative time and space, and indeed the wider universe. Read the blitz or you're dead.

Rating    **10**

## NoMeansNo - 0 + 2 = 1   (Cargo '91)

Gotta hand it to NoMeansNo. They are utterly alone in this world. After the disemboweling that was '89's **Wrong**, who could ever ingest the band's tongue-lashing and amplified whipping yet again? **Wrong** was nothing like any record before it, savagely tearing at life at levels Black Flag couldn't even dream about. And sonically, this was no Black Flag; more like Rush on crack, hating themselves; all bones, too fast for blood. So in fear of synaptic destruction, **0 + 2 = 1** was lifted piously from its molded bed of coals. At first . . . tragic disappointment . . . sentiments which sadly still hold true, at least on a superficial musical level, for NoMeansNo has shattered their killing wall; left buzzing and clanking and vibrating and colliding in confused stupor among the ruins. All is chaos, caveman sounds, jagged, clunky jazzy scurrying, imploded ensembles of Lemmybass and drums (the latter term used loosely), with unbelievably few riffic slashings emanating from John Wright's axe (he also plays drums, bassist and brother Rob Wright completing the band's sin-wrapped duo). In simple terms, this is the sparse, tribal, timeless, thorn-poked, junky, and instrumentally powerless (except esoterically speaking) NoMeansNo of old; a punky and frenzied improvement on Gang Of Four or Fugazi, yet nevertheless an often unlistenable experiment in noise, and never approaching the expert mosh or disciplined metal of **Wrong**. Yet after many repelling then attracting listens, the most structured pieces step forth first to reveal, if you can believe it, elevated levels of poison surpassing **Wrong**, when swallowed whole: intellectual, sickening poetics and all. Gotta smile at NoMeansNo. They are still utterly alone, yet now further removed from reality. Taken as one long, loud, sad mess, start to finish, this record is post-Satan-rule, as only the fiercest minds among the tormented

learned could imagine. Simply put, it conquers **Wrong** lyrically speaking; and for that, it deserves cautious but serious courting, even if musically the band seems wrecked, doped-up, basically dismantled, in symbolic repulsion of life. Utterly, utterly alone, and also just damn near impossible to listen to. A low **8**.
Rating                                                                                          8

## NoMeansNo - Why Do They Call Me Mr.Happy?
(Alternative Tentacles '93)
Another bust as far as I'm concerned, as the **Wrong** Bros. carve more hard grey angles built of bass lines and non-beats, rashers of negative melodies, sloth and boredom. **Mr. Happy** is somewhat more produced than its cacophonous predecessor, but the tunes have lost their edge, their carnivorous bite as the punk Rush is back, only this time it's not **Moving Pictures** on angel dust, it's more like **Hold The Fire** or **Roll The Bones** on warm sherry, as tunes rumble and ramble on far too long, the record's ten tracks weighing in close to an hour. Pissed-off hugely I be, 'cos this is a cool band from so many angles. The lyrics just fry, and the whole concept of the band is merciless. I just wish the music kicked as per **Wrong**, but again it's mostly bent progressive rock with a big ugly wart on its nose. A low **7**.
Rating                                                                                          7

## NoMeansNo - Mr. Right & Mr. Wrong   (Wrong '95)
Not really a NoMeansNo record, not even really a record but a "musical magazine", **Mr. Right & Mr. Wrong** culls together all sorts of bass-buzzing, hitting-things nuttiness from Victoria's chaospunks (a band Mike Watt called "Minutemen's doppelganger"). The songs almost exclusively suck, whether they're the recent tracks from '92, '93, and '94 sessions or the oldies from '79 and '80. Nice rollicking version of The Kinks' *Victoria*, re-phrased as a paean to the bros. sleepy hometown, and of course the lyrics are wily, wise, lucid and twisted. Please boys, come back from that devil-may-care attitude and weld us some heavy music. Nice touch: extensive semi-fake liner notes, plus the Alternative Track Listings, which tongue-in-cheek helpfully rearrange the tunes by song type, age, and alphabetically.
Rating                                                                                          5

## NoMeansNo - The Worldhood Of The World (as such)   (Alternative Tentacles '95)
Rumblings by the cool pre-rumoured this as a return to form, form being hard-wired progressive punk, driven insane by bass and the apocalyptic wisdoms of the brothers Wright. And **Worldhood** roars back with class, after the stumbling last two official records and the three or so bad jokes under varied monikers. I've always described these mad professors as Rush on crack, and the tag flies in flame here forthrightly. Add a bit of Firehose to that, and a manic dose of hardcore via Dead Kennedys, and the NoMeansNo dangerous marriage of quality chaos-debauched qualities whips this one stinging and true. The record opens like Hüsker Dü's **New Day Rising** with *Joy*, after which the hooky songs (they forgot that word for a few years) take over. The headbanging punk metal hooks of *Humans*, the progressive angst of *Angel Or Devil*, and the grand textures of two long closers *State Of Grace* and *The Jungle* (total Mike Watt here) bookend the record splendidly. If you want a properly viable form of punk in the '90s, here it is, the buzz to blacken all your green days; wily, jaded veterans with chops, actively choosing to shred up the underground. Buy it.
Rating                                                                                          9

## Nomind - Tales Of Ordinary Madness   (Lone Wolf '88)
Nomind (Canadians, no less) grinds Sabbath for punkers with chronic nods to the grimiest of Stooges riffs circa **Raw Power**. Things cook and swell on this bonecrushing mosh to the death not unlike drunk 'n' dulled Green River. Sounds blistered off the wall of some stagediving barn, with pulverizing basslines and a general no tomorrow, here and now, survivalist immediacy. Crammed with noise, tunes shake tall then destruct, with dramatic regularity, making this one of the coolest hunks of wasted power punk to cross my gaze. Classic of total hangoverkill, the totally obliterated *Nomind (To Lose)*, the deepest slash of metal on the record fusing hot riffs and gutter rock with choice sensitivity.
Rating                                                                                          7

## Non-Fiction - In The Know   (Grand Slamm/IRS '92)
A truly engaging band this one, Non-Fiction sounding nothing like its slick album cover, more like Trouble meets Dream Theater or Corrosion Of Conformity meets Skid Row. **In The Know** is one of those record's with a faintly progressive, conceptual flow, making the demarcation of songs difficult and ultimately pointless, the band's precision doomgoth being a shining pleasure to behold, especially Alan Tecchio's Eric Wagnerian vocals, an impassioned cry of metal valor that kicks this band into the upper echelons of the sadly under-rated. Peg this one as a Sabbath-riffed oddity with hair band production and discipline, Non-Fiction thereby carving a niche no-one else has considered, really. Occasionally things get languid and too spaced like Mindfunk, but usually it's a castle royale of sturdy grey glory, tunes like *First And Lasting Impressions* cruising along loud and proud. Geez, what a cool band.
Rating                                                                                          9

## John Norum - Total Control   (CBS '87)
Searing axeman from Europe gone solo (leaving due to the band's increasingly keyboardy sound), John Norum dishes a surprisingly heavy rocking affair, despite a gothpop sheen that coats most tracks. **Total Control** fits that ultra-commercial mindset found within a lot of CBS signings in the late '80s, flawless soap graphics, clattery high end production, and a general waft of hairspray to the whole project. But Norum wants to strafe his fretboards, which he does in fine Euro fashion, recalling Fate, Victory, and latter-day 220V (whose drummer plays on this record). Sorta like a conservative, sold-out Yngwie record; posturing filler, staggeringly large balladry, occasional killer metal. Castle cruncher: *Eternal Flame*, which thankfully gallops mighty like old 220V, and exquisitely tasteful rendition of obscure Lizzy track *Wild One*. One for the followers of craft.
Rating                                                                                          7

## John Norum - Face The Truth   (Sony '92)
And further unto craft we go, as Norum enlists a drummer named Hempo (?), Peter Baltes from Accept and vocal icon Glenn Hughes to create a superstar slick metal opus for the AOR in all of us. Keeping up his tradition of offering a Lizzy cover with each solo release, we get the regal *Opium Trail*, faithful rendition if not earth-shattering, canny understated vocal included. Elsewhere, it's much pop and exacto axework (stinging, clear, reverent of song), as Norum indulges his love for lush hard rock harmonies and all things "just so".
Rating                                                                                          7

## John Norum - Another Destination   (Shrapnel '95)
No Lizzy this time, but it's easy to forget, given all the bracing originals here, Norum steamrolling out of this record like a robust John Sykes, resulting in an athletic guitar monster that parks its leather butt somewhere between vintage MSG, Blue Murder and Whitesnake. Highlights would be the daunting, intelligent metal finesse of *Inside* and *Whose Side Are You On?*,

both snakecharmers of gargantuan proportions. Low points of the record: the two covers, one a Steve Marriot-penned blues, the other a Sabbath-fried version of *Sunshine Of Your Love* (please everybody, leave Cream in the carton where they belong). But the fantabulous rest bristles with luminous six-string pride, Norum (whose looking like Blaze Bayley!) combining artful guitar and enjoyable songs in expected veteran fashion.

Rating **8**

## Nothingface - Pacifier (DCide '96)

This new DC act worships bloodthirstingly at the altar of Korn, which is still a good thing, given that as of yet, Nothingface are only about the third or fourth band in this headspace right now. But place them kick-assed on the metal axis of Korn-dom, many of these turbo riffs recalling Downset or Pantera without the production. A plethora of swingin' ideas keep the ball rolling, bouncing and stinging, vocalist Matt Holt making sure all are disturbed in the process. Also, an amazing drummer in Chris Houck, a powerhouse of fills, grooves and crashed attacks. Rank with I'M'L, Downset and the newly splendid Madball as surprisingly creative new ways to metalize, while still retaining hardcore credibility.

Rating **8**

## Notorious - Notorious (Bronze/WEA '90)

Land sakes and mercy, this record's an AOR fan's dream. But that didn't stop everybody from trashing it, punters just not ready for Diamond Head's Sean Harris in a pop metal outfit, the man teaming up with producer, player and journeyman Robin George (ex-David Byron, Magnum, Robert Plant and solo) for a heavenly slice of music magic that rounded the most exalted of melodic rock bases exquisitely and with towering passion. Lead single and minor hit *The Swalk* stole heavily from INXS, as did stealth popster *Arianne*, both working gorgeously of course. Other influences seem to be Queen and Billy Squier (or that space between the two), *Eyes Of The World* being most Queen-ie (their scant heavy rock of the mid-'80s), with tunes like *Radio Silence* and *This Night* also taking the guitars to streets paved with sugar. Sean Harris is of course in fine form, very breathy, dramatic and believable, while Robin George fires off those session-standard licks and fills he has given to so many. Heck, I may be pretty much in the minority on this record, but swear to God, the first six tracks I played into the ground, just soaking up the AOR passion that this duo so astonishingly taps. *You Need More* is a ballad that has to be heard to be believed. Harmonies, soloing like Brian May, it's just incredible. I gotta sit down. Note: deleted within mere weeks, the duo at odds with the label's insistence that they get a band and tour.

Rating **10**

## No Trouble - Looking For Trouble (Hot Blood Est. '85)

Again, one of many European wedgies that causes a twisted smile when spun, yet is rarely encountered due to a colourless depression to the whole package, **Looking For Trouble** is edgy, heavy hard rock; tight and energetic but still very foreign and uncommunicative. Kinda highly strung and mischievous but strangely uninviting. Most painful pressure point: *Highway Hunter*, a thoroughly rabid, twenty flight rocker reminiscent of Accept.

Rating **6**

## Nuclear Assault - Game Over (Under One Flag '86)

Close to the pits of thrash, but more enamoured with supremely accelerated speed metal as per a young and fast Metallica, **Game Over** erects a huge, stinging wall of sound, buzzing noisily but almost exclusively at breakneck tempos, with welcome high-reg vocals in

the spirit of Bay Area metal, in one of the more obvious departures from the standard dog barks that accompany ultra-heavy death forms. One of the more hypertense records ever carved, and fairly scientific for its age.

Rating **5**

## Nuclear Assault - The Plague (Under One Flag '87)

One of those catch-up EP's with a mish mash of metals. Here the deaf are blessed with a cranially-imploding instrumental, a joke mosh, a serious mosh to end all moshes, and three chunks of cardiac castle rock. Connelly's range seems to be under a bit of strain, but other than that it's all just more really heavy and stressed-out underground metal; good, but riding the fine line between energetically-leaden Attitude and noisy, fatigue-generating defense.

Rating **5**

## Nuclear Assault - Survive (I.R.S. '88)

One guy gets tired, but lo and behold, the band discovers that their other guitarist can sing, so in steps Anthony Bramante on pipes, or so we're led to believe, because it still sounds like Connely's thinning wail. But never thee mind, because the most pounding of improvements comes with the vastly focused production, coupled with a mental shift to more mid-paced forward mass, like a cross between Dan Lilker's old band Anthrax, Metallica, and the more manic of technical Bay Area speedballs. Pure sound and pure blazing glory bestow a new gravity to the Nuclear Assault train off the rails. It's still too obsessed with screaming velocities, but for once, the Assault can be considered modern day heavyweights, save for the awful rendition of the out-of-character *Good Times, Bad Times*, in which the band's stiffness and lack of vocal range are painfully betrayed as the record winds to a close.

Rating **8**

## Nuclear Assault - Good Times, Bad Times
(Under One Flag '89)

More or less a cruel punk rip-off with the truly inept Zep cover, three OTT mushes totalling 2:17, and a thrash cover of the *Happy Days* theme, funnier in concept than execution. Total elapsed time: about seven minutes.

Rating **0**

## Nuclear Assault - Handle With Care (Under One Flag '89)

A rattling regression to the rumbling, noisy speed metal that caused nervous frenzy on all but '88's compelling **Survive**. Conelly's back on vocals, and things sound kind of loose and on the cheap again on this strange return below ground, away from the clarity that caused **Survive** to shimmer so righteously, even though both were produced by Randy Burns. Still massive and steadfast in its high degree of energy and sheer power, I can't help but feel this band could become a favorite with multiple soakings, given its integrity and old-time love of the loud.

Rating **7**

## Nudeswirl - Nudeswirl (Megaforce '93)

One of the better "slow to grow" records of the '90s thus far, **Nudeswirl**'s rough slurtations construct a record far from the discipline of any branch of the alternative metal tree, rubbing a pink pearl eraser through a restless subconscious in slumber. Oddest factor on the 'Swirling soundscape would have to be Green's edgy vocals, which evoke Ozzy's low register days circa **Black Sabbath** and **Paranoid** (yeah I know, I said the same thing about Mindfunk), a from-the-depths bleat for help that grafts alarmingly onto the loose tangle of wires that comprise this Jersey band's slouch of decibels. Creamy-like-butter metal which owes much to no one in particular, although the oldest

and crustiest of the Seattle sound cut ever widening arcs through the dense foliage clouding all understanding. Gotta love Dogfood, When I'm Dead and Buffalo though, which begin to clog the brain's circuitry after a few almost laborious spins. Seemingly endless portions of this record leave me in wait, but I keep coming back, marveling at Nudeswirl's lack of tangible ties to convention, their *really* underground shock waves, making this debut something you set aside when you need a trip away. Thick liquid far from the shores of reality, and really in no hurry to reach land.
Rating                                                                          9

## The Amboy Dukes - The Amboy Dukes
(Mainstream '67/Repertoire '91)
The earliest wigglings of Ted "The Duck" Nugent (age 19) and his wigged out band (a few of which are now dead). Basically psychedelic garage punk like the Mothers Of Invention or prehistoric Alice Cooper, featuring their first hit Baby, Please Don't Go. Go. Please go.
Rating                                                                          0

## The Amboy Dukes - Journey To The Centre Of The Mind   (Mainstream '68/Repertoire '91)
If you listen closely (and I don't expect you to), this one's a bit heavier, more urgent, exploded and elaborate than the total creeps of a debut. The title track made the Top 20. Must have been very little competition that year. Note: both Mainstream reissues contain a bonus track, but you should pretty much be finished with your listening session before you get to it.
Rating                                                                          1

## Ted Nugent and the Amboy Dukes - Marriage On The Rocks/Rock Bottom   (Polydor '69)
Sounds like Ted lined up Scorpions to pen the name for this sprawling piece of Munsters Rock. For all Ted's talk about the evils of recreational chemicals, the man sure blew out of his heiny pret' near the most brain-battered, acid-soaked psychedelic cole slaw ever to be composed for guitar ensemble. This cleverly-monikered (that's called sarcasm) opus is a cross between Deep Purple's first three and a '69 Colosseum album I got for a buck three weeks ago, just threw on today, quickly and efficiently resulting in sweat-soaked implosion and crippling depression over 2/3 of my body. Where does a guy get this stuff? Man, I hate the sixties. The first as Ted Nugent And The Amboy Dukes, name changed in conjunction with the upgrade to Polydor.
Rating                                                                          0

## Ted Nugent And The Amboy Dukes - Tooth, Fang And Claw   (Discreet '74)
Ted slowly shakes the crusty inaction of the '60s, pushing forth into more song-based terrain on this first sorta modern Nuge record, which still sounds incredibly goofy, like an acid-casualty Pat Travers mixed with progressive tingeabilities, outside of the proud, sprawling outbacks that comprise Hibernation and The Great White Buffalo, not to mention the similarly mind-cooled Free Flight. Erstwhile, nothing that couldn't fit on a Cramps or James Brown record under the influence of buckets of moose blood and bags full of airplane glue. Just really moldy and unclean. Better recording than the newer Call Of The Wild.
Rating                                                                          4

## Ted Nugent And The Amboy Dukes - Call Of The Wild   (Discreet '74)
Alas a record that more than hints at the artillery barrage to come, Call Of The Wild still sits ages old, while a good 2/3 of the record comes off as a really bad collection of songs that might have graced Ted Nugent, most notable axe victims being the slightly Hendrix-like Cannon Balls and rauncher Pony Express.

Still, **Call Of The Wild** can't shake that depressing hippy sleaze of a man out of time, as painfully experienced on most of the stretchy, gooey side two. Quite amazing really, the transformation that would take place, given such an underground cluelessness and general lack of sparkle.
Rating                                                                          5

## Ted Nugent And The Amboy Dukes - "The Ultimate Collection"   (DCC '87)
Major wavy '60s psychedelia from a bunch of badly strung Detroit crazy men who may as well be the fledgling Alice Cooper band for all we know, or a past life of The Lyres. No less than 18 excruciating moments from the netherworld grace this collection from the Tedinator's deformative years better forgotten, namely '67, '68 etc., featuring huge monster smash hit (sarcasm again) Journey To The Centre Of The Mind. Kinda like the worst excesses of psychedelia driven by a guitar player who does not do drugs. Run away, Ted's old band was a sad joke.
Rating                                                                          0

## Ted Nugent - Ted Nugent   (Epic '75)
The liner notes from Deadly Tedly's major debut rave about how the midwest has been slammin' to the Nuge for eons. With albums like **Dr. Slingshot**, **Marriage On The Rocks/Rock Bottom**, and **Tooth, Fang And Claw** as cornerstones of the painful Amboy Dukes repertoire, the midwest must have had cowshit for brains. No . . . now, they have something to be proud of, as the Motor City Madman sheds his psychedelic snakeskin and backwoods hick in search of the fast, true and stinging power chord that fuels the flames of a finely written song. **Ted Nugent** rings bright and righteous, an early hard rock classic as American as the National Rifle Association, effortlessly capable and fluid traditional metal swinging with more than a psychological touch of the Wild West on such moonshine tales as the low slung Snakeskin Cowboys and Queen Of The Forest. Dovetailing such mountain tunes are more metallic gems like early OTT speedball Motor City Madhouse, the high-strung Where Have You Been All My Life, and legendary cruise missile Stormtroopin' (along with two mellow mistakes which we'll forgive), to comprise an airtight and seamless rock ride through only recently attempted terrains of hard rock Americana, a sound that combined metal, pop structures and the blues to spawn North America's first supergroups. The guitars are bang-on and so's Ted's undeniable personality, making **Ted Nugent** an early triumph of balls to the wall attitude over studio excess. The year's 1975, and although Kiss takes it to more wild, screaming fans, nobody lays down the groove hotter than Detroit's most famous predator and Boston's Toxic Twins, who together ruled the airwaves high above America's open air stadiums throughout the latter '70s.
Rating                                                                          8

## Ted Nugent - Free For All   (Epic '76)
Universally considered the whackmaster's most accomplished opus, **Free For All** was an early success of constructive rather than destructive hard rock, a uniquely American skill at this point in time, catapulting Ted to rock god status. The **Free For All** tour, Spokane, Washington was the first "big city" concert me and the buds ever saw, featuring a back-flipping, heavy-as-Ted Rex (Smith) and a confused Be Bop Deluxe as warm-ups, plus seas of psychotic, dope-smoking teenagers as edgy atmosphere, all conspiring to scare the shit out of three thirteen year olds plus dad from Smalltown, B.C. Suffice to say, Ted had us all (except my dad and a few of the security guards) in frenzied rapture, playing to his newly-acquired status as god of feedback, distortion, and other carnivorous axe antics; also quite capably defining himself as such

through his self-immortalizing, crowd-tantalizing, buffalo-murdalizing stage raps which is the choice treat of any Great Gonzo display. And **Free For All** was the perfectly brewed cauldron of switch-hitting, two-fisted rock'n'roll to bang off the boards of North America's hockey barns, yielding fast, slow, mid-pace, and experimental slabs of quasi-studio heavy rock, all reinforcing the teen dreem of party-time swillin'. Ted was considered a master of his chosen weapon more for riffing and attitude rather than for any purely technical reasons. He told us he was king, and we believed him. Even though he rarely let fly with truly awesome axe histrionics, his solos were always artful, bluesy, and full of great '70s clichés. You just knew he took pride in steering his coveted hollow body Gibson Byrdlands around those mountain roads night after night. More than anything, **Free For All** demonstrated Ted's art of the song with the classic Ted raps of the title cut, the *Stranglehold*-like slider *Writing On The Wall*, and more metallic wheelers like *Dog Eat Dog*, *Street Rats*, and *Hammerdown*. One wild thing about this record is that a hefty half of it features el paperweight Meat Loaf on vocals, evoking a southern, Molly Hatchet sort of feel. Nonetheless, **Free For All** is a groovy, kick ass 'n' redneck kinda album, with a well-conceived degree of variation and studio attentiveness causing warm accessibility despite its hard rockin' context. Grab a slice of history, kick back with a cool one, and turn it up, turn it up, make it louder 'n hell . . .

Rating       **9**

### Ted Nugent - Cat Scratch Fever    (Epic '77)

Worth it for the nifty gatefold cover alone, **Cat Scratch Fever** was another essential microchip in the formation of our adolescent nerve centers, featuring Ted's benchmark backbench of Cliff Davies on drums, Rob Grange on bass, and Derek St. Holmes on rhythm guitar and vocals. Ted's a walking, talking one man public relations storm by this point, the first heavy metal renaissance man cum caveman naturalist. **Cat Scratch** had its share of mean rock on it, including the title cut (one of the biggest radio hits about VD ever penned), *Wang Dang Sweet Poontang*, *Sweet Sally*, and *Out Of Control*; all the above rocking within a headspace not unlike rousing bouts of ZZ Top. Other than these, however, **Cat Scratch** was a fairly subdued, unassuming effort, suffering from somewhat flip metallic interpretations of boogie, metal-undermining sparseness, and a fairly mid-rangy recording. What the hell though, it's still a party, still four long-haired dudes going out on a limb, screwing the rules, overdoing it, and spitting it out in the grand tradition of the immutable entertainment ethic that gets tapped and shared all too seldom. Rock'n'roll with all the good-natured intent associated with players that are also true fans of old-time quality.

Rating       **8**

### Ted Nugent - Double Live Gonzo    (Epic '78)

A loud and proud testimony to a time with no worries, **Double Live Gonzo** features mondo-electric, classic line-up performances from '76 and '77 dates in B-cities, dusting off a couple of Ted's earlier nature hikes such as *Hibernation* and the large, looming and mythic *Great White Buffalo*, plus requisite cover of *Baby Please Don't Go*, and two previously unreleased, red-knuckle cruisers *Yank Me Crank Me* and *Gonzo*. Sort of an above average live album with average song selection, **Gonzo** nevertheless burns brightly in the blood of any headbanger in and around thirty years of age.

Rating       **6**

### Ted Nugent - Weekend Warriors    (Epic '78)

Another cool album cover and Ted's off chasing bear once more. **Weekend Warriors**, unfortunately brings to full fruition the thin, basic, toneless mix hinted at on **Cat Scratch Fever**, resulting in a general lack of

power to these equally heavy tunes. I dunno, not enough bass and not enough bass drum or something. Too much of this record bops along a bit too cheerily for status as metal, as witnessed on the plastic-headed *Need You Bad*, *I Got The Feelin'*, and the unremarkable title cut. However, three raging rockers, the lethal *Name Your Poison* and *Venom Soup* (the latter, a rare goth tonality for the Nuge), plus the speed metal *Cruisin'*, demonstrate that the problems with this album aren't due to philosophical shifts, just odd, overtly Southern-skewed song selection plus handicapped production. Classic of note: the no frills *Good Friends And A Bottle Of Wine*, a hard rocker buoyed by a warm, down-home riff and lyric. New addition to the family is Ted's second co-vocalist, Charlie Huhn, another in a long line demonstrating Ted's predilection for sidekicks with generically smooth, conformist voices, perhaps as foil to his own distinct singsongy twang.

Rating       **8**

### Ted Nugent - State Of Shock    (Epic '79)

**State Of Shock** is Ted's heaviest and most serious record, still infused with o'erflowing doses of party ethic, but sounding more complete, more uniformly rockin', and less likely to lapse into the novelty hit. Whereas on past efforts, Ted's low-slung boogie rockers might be tightened up and disinfected for radio, here they're left dirty and loose, as evidenced on the swooping title cut and the retro *It Doesn't Matter*, both simple but effective, both so totally Ted, philosophically speaking. Other heavier romps have that same sweat ethic and sleazy drive such as *Satisfied*, *Saddle Sore*, and flat-out metal classic *Snake Charmer*. Most caffeinated track of all however is intro cut *Paralyzed* which slams along real sinister-like beneath a power-surging wah-wah effect. All told, **State Of Shock** is ham-fisted combat-ready Gonzo madness, as a result, rocking with the down-home grime that brings the man's tales of simple values to life. Largely overlooked, this record demonstrates Ted's all-encompassing ability to emotionally span twenty years of American rock tradition, whilst sonically dishing it back within the context of metal, music's most powerful and inescapable language to date.

Rating       **9**

### Ted Nugent - Scream Dream    (Epic '80)

Ted's last wax to experience bountiful harvest displays a man in planetary alignment with the meaning of life, splitting it right down the middle, dishing one half record worth of caustic, iron-clad pounders, one half light-hearted novelty cartoons which usually take the form of manic, spinning low-cal, boogie rockers. Of the fiercisms, *Flesh & Blood* and the title cut are dripping chunks of quivering carcass on par with the weightiest and moodiest of Nuge numbers, and *Wango Tango* rides a loose, yappy garage riff to medium grade hit status, beefed by a rounded mix. All in all, an entertaining and colourful Ted project, yet one that takes the man further outside into parody of himself, treating the songwriting process with flip disregard. Full-bodied and caffeinated, but with an amused, self-satisfied disposition, **Scream Dream** still rules as one of Ted's more party-hard carnivals, squatting proudly over a submissive world as the definitive statement of Ted's head.

Rating       **9**

### Ted Nugent - Intensities In 10 Cities    (Epic '81)

Ted sez he wanted to call this *Ten Titties in Ten Cities*. Clever album title nonetheless, and clever album concept: a live record of ten previously unreleased rockers. Problem is, most of what clogs the sinuses on **Intensities** has that goofball novelty mentality to it, with titles like *Put Up Or Shut Up*, *My Love Is Like A Tire Iron*, and *The Flying Lip Lock*, although the album metallizes considerably, with all of side one (except for standard boogie throwaway *I Am A Predator*), cruising along like Ted's pressure points of old. Despite the general mania however, the songcraft has a hurried, loose, jamming feel which detracts from the gravity of the experience; too much pandering to the crowd, not enough blood-thirsty, lead-headed intent. And side two's mostly off-the-cuff crap. However, probably as the most telling measure of Ted's barometric pressure this time around, **Intensities** didn't sell, and nobody I know ever plays it, seeing it for the slap-it-down, head-it-out the door quickie that it is. Came with a Ted Nugent guitar pick.

Rating 5

## Ted Nugent - Nugent (Atlantic '82)

Predator Ted's palest piece finds our favorite cave dude dazed and confused after gorging himself with too much raw meat and nooky hide throughout the magical late '70s. Derek St. Holmes is back at the mike, Carmine Appice inevitably botches the percussive tasks, and Ted's writing is middling, laid-back, and juvenile, not to mention steeped in well-worn lyrical cliché and riffic predictability. Hard to explain, but this record and Ted's craft in general during these lost years has a sort of buffoon-ish, forced melodic Southern boogie feel to it, like he knows he's been toppled from the appropriateness of grand gestures, doomed to a life of noodly humility. In fact, **Nugent** pret' near bops along like some sort of updated '50s revivalist show with guitars, rarely descending into the precambrian life ooze of heaviness. No surprise that **Nugent** stands as one of Ted's least noticed records, humbly humming an ironic tune of optimism while Ted's green acres burn.

Rating 4

## Ted Nugent - Penetrator (Atlantic '84)

Churlish lead-off anthems *Tied Up In Love* and *Draw The Line* wash over my speakers in volcanic demonstration that Ted is hell-bent and heaven-sent on saving the world with layered and heroic rock lushness, pumping beneath the radio-sweet vocals of one Brian Howe, forming an impressive wall of ivories and axes. **Penetrator** barrels downhill from such lofty introductions, however, destroying side one with three puff-ass keyboard popsters. Side two comprises two of Ted's lite metal novelty toons, one cruncher with an awful chorus, one kinda ambitious ballad, plus one additional killer hard rocker in cover *Blame It On The Night*, which combined with the aforementioned tracks I and II, indicate a direction that could have made Ted a radio king, as embarrassing crazy uncle to the likes of Bryan Adams (who co-wrote *Draw The Line* with his bud Jim Vallance), given first, a recognition and second, some attention. In effect, **Little Miss Dangerous** is such a realization, although with a less conventionally mixed feel. In the final analysis, **Penetrator** disappoints as yet another vegetarian plate from a once bullet-biting gunslinger who years back built his spread on some of the baddest chunks of rock in the land.

Rating 5

## Ted Nugent - Little Miss Dangerous (Atlantic '86)

Bitchin' mohawk, Ted! The Nuge roars back with an updated, slammin' sound, even scoring a hit in the process with the slow, bass-funksterin' title cut. The biggest alteration on this record versus past projects is in the techy drum sound, essentially "man plays electronic drums", which actually translates as bright, current and savvy, given the uplifting celebration of life inherent amongst Ted's vignettes here, songs which feature the man's most OTT and harmonics-based axe attacks in ages, amidst some smooth croon-ability from co-vocalist Dave Amato, who immediately and artfully evokes images of Ted's first and most enduring vocalist, Derek St. Holmes. **Little Miss Dangerous** rocks quite heavily, albeit in a decidedly minimalist hard rock vein, as portrayed on kick-off tune *High Heels In Motion*, *Savage Dancer* and *When Your Body Talks*. Also along for the party are two speed metal numbers in the double bass *Crazy Ladies* and one of Ted's coolest builders ever, subversive closer *Painkiller*. I never though I'd say it, but this level of techy-ness is just the clatter and clang Ted needs to lend his latter day radio rockers the crack, fry, and sizzle to match the imagined energy in Ted's head.

Rating 7

## Ted Nugent - If You Can't Lick 'Em ... Lick 'Em (Atlantic '88)

Terrible Ted comes full circle, from first, the strange and subdued parodies that were **Nugent** and **Penetrator**, second, through the commercial dazzle of **Little Miss Dangerous**, back to an earnest attempt at re-creating the classic Nuge cruise of his first five '70s cornerstones. Writing-wise, it's the genuine buckskin, but in totality, it's off the rack, too-perfectly patterned, and too well-stitched. No, the attempt is made, but the blood, guts, sweat, and thrill of the kill seem to be side-stepped for an end product that is just too obviously factory-tailored. The drums are merely background snare and bass combinations when not wholly electronic, and bass guitar is almost non-audible. What remains are great old Ted structures executed with aseptic, auto-pilot precision, tightly wound, served up all substance, no style, under DLR-like manbeats-chest sloganeering. Still gotta like the new/old direction. All Ted needs now is to record under the influence of some good friends and a bottle of wine, because here he seems to be out of touch with the human simplicities of the life-affirmation that gave him personal strength and charisma throughout the vintage years.

Rating 6

## Ted Nugent - Spirit Of The Wild (Atlantic '95)

Well now the Whackmaster has truly earned his title Terrible Ted. Clearly (and very tragically for a twenty year fan like myself who bought **Ted Nugent** as a new release) out of touch with the rock world, Ted turds forth somewhat of a Damn Yankees record without so much keyboards and gloss. But the songs are all all stinkers in the hallowed Yankees tradition: toothless priss rockers, funtime sugary boogie trop, thumpless posturing, tired '80s production, weak vocals from Derek St. Holmes, hi skool humour, sad, sad, sad. Now it just remains to hear Ted hype this, destined to ring so hollow and embarrassing, I just wanna crawl. Songtitle sample: *Thighracious, Hot Or Cold, Kiss My Ass, Wrong Side Of Town*. Yep.

Rating 4

# O

## Obituary - Slowly We Rot (RC '89)

The perennially touring Obituary is the sound of vomit, pure and simple, a hulking mass of industrial level bleeding with vocals that sound like a spoiled troll throwing a tantrum. Thoroughly disgusting as it is, **Slowly We Rot** wins some accolades by default as its particular brand of apocalyptic radiated grindcore rarely degenerates into the specific thrash death metal polka beat that single-handedly wrecks bands like this. Harshly though not poorly recorded, the power is decipherable and the band gloriously despicable. Consider Obituary the hard black underbelly of Slayer (along with buds Morbid Angel and Nocturnus) and file under threat to national security.
Rating 5

## Obituary - Cause Of Death (Roadrunner '90)

Another deplorable stench of an album cover and we're off to the races, Obituary performing their go-dawful Death-like proto-thrash, well-constructed, well-mixed, doomy and drearily dissonant, somewhat akin to pre-**Arise** Sepultura. But it's John Tardy's harrowing sick mewlings that distinguish this mid-pack Florida freight train across a crowded, leather-shrouded room. Then there's the musical charade, slow smearing riffs one minute, blastbeats the next, but all sorta packed up like a nailbomb, giving Obituary its deserved way underground cache. Contains a cover of bad Celtic Frost dittie *Circle Of The Tyrants*.
Rating 7

## Obituary - The End Complete (Roadrunner '92)

Scott Burns looms at the horned altar once again, doing the usual good Lombardo-like things he does for drum sounds. But **The End Complete** has in retrospect been deemed this band's pooch, their hurried, uncreative, phoned-in slab without reason. Sounds pretty much the same to me, but yes, definitely no progression at all, maybe a little looser, more aimless and under-arranged. But hey, what do I care? As usual, wacky, nutty, out-there leads from Alan West.
Rating 6

## Obituary - World Demise (Roadrunner '94)

Continuing the trajectory from '92's modest commercial breakthrough (but creative bust) **The End Complete**, **World Demise** slows up, plowing the mine field with fat smeary riffs recalling less catchy Sepultura breaks, Scott Burns' production also leaning Sepultur-ish, capitalizing on Donald Tardy's inebriated drum madness. The mix is cool and the danger splatters, punctuated with vocals that are more discernible as simply horrific, hellish but human. **World Demise** has a reek of undiscipline, Obituary getting somewhat lost without the speed, but the record works as a sort of mood spin, a decidedly underground death metal buzz that almost has a psychedelic quality, a curmudgeoned mental bent of a band not letting up on opacity, while creating songs that swim around and sometimes drown. Mucous rock from one of death metal's best and most dedicated killing crew.
Rating 8

## Obliveon - From This Day Forward
### (Active/Music For Nations '90)

These blowhards are a minor Quebec sensation, what with their geometric progressive thrash labyrinths scooting off in all directions. An excellent watershed woodshed of late '80s ideas all crammed faceward with maniacal intent, **From This Day Forward** is a lusty bane for wannabe diddlers, and a gluttonous metal feast for the listener who is up to the challenge. But for pure headbang pleasure, seek elsewhere, this being an overserious monument to musicianship, wholly unconcerned with restraint. Well done for a genre quite dead and decomposed.
Rating 6

## Obliveon - Cybervoid (ASA/Cargo '96)

Coat, thicken and weigh down distressed old '80s prog-metal, and Obliveon's **Cybervoid** emerges. But this is a good thing, much of this record sounding like arch-Quebecois heroes Voivod at their best, **Cybervoid** reverberating with angled crunchtronics reminiscent of **The Outer Limits** sheened over with a smoked layer of grindcore. Sung partly in English, partly in French, Obliveon aim to please both the vibrant and insulated Quebec scene and the whole rest of the world, for the most part succeeding, the barked commands proving universal in taking metal to the frontlines. Bottom line: I found this creative and healthy, Obliveon wrapping math in song, chops in hook, and metal in a proposal for new legitimacy, the band learning, grooving and advancing in a tough competitive world, heads held high.
Rating 8

## The Obsessed - Lunar Womb (Noise '91)

Having arrived at The Obsessed through a much more modern record, I found **Lunar Womb** lacking in precociousness, preciousness, psychedelic swillage and Monster Magnetism. There's an element of trying too hard here, striving to rise above Sabbathism, clustering things up too much, stifling personality, the breathiness of '94's rarified airtracks missing. But that doesn't discount the fact that the agedness of this band leaks through like old paint smells, Wino having no problem convincing us that commercial concerns have wafted out the broken window like an unwelcome poltergeist on the Winds of Hawk.
Rating                                    7

## The Obsessed - The Church Within (Sony '94)

Distorting an analog axis somewherz between Kyuss, Monster Magnet and debut-era Masters Of Reality, The Obsessed seem to be winning the souls of those enamoured with all things aged. Vocalist (and guitarist) Wino possesses one of those storytelling voices that cloaks the band's quaking low cycles in a sort of isolated innocence. Oft-heard comparisons to Ozzy-era Sabbath are too contrite, for The Obsessed shovel way under, snapping metal's grizzled roots, caking their caveman sound in an electrocuted buzz straight out of psychedelia, takes left raw and unsoiled by modern contraptions. But versatility reigns, Wino taking us on a black and silver deep dive through multi-level decibel purifications, mining golden oldie riffs like few other acts can, even as they try with bandwagoneering frequency. Vacuum-suspended, but damnably delicious, **The Church Within** reeks of valiant pride in the purity of doom metal from all the ages.
Rating                                    8

## Obsession - Marshall Law (Metal Blade '84)

This one's an EP snagged during the ol' desperate days when I would try convince myself that Baron Rojo or possibly Rampage were the saviors of metal, and although he'd never admit it, partner in crime Fiver was known to buy Rods and Wild Dogs albums and like them. Repeatedly. Anyways, what Connecticut's Obsession dishes is fairly slick Priest-style metal (whatever that means) with a general wedging in of goth, speed, and techno slightly beyond the band's musical ear. This was about a **6** during the depression, but so was Mama's Boys. The band followed up **Marshall Law** with '86's **Scarred For Life** and '87's **Methods Of Madness**, before belter Mike Vescara split for Loudness.
Rating                                    4

## The Offspring - Ignition (Epitaph '92)

Like most who weren't on board before **Smash**, I heard this after the fact (I still have yet to hear older Green Day, not like I care). As expected, early Offspring is just boring old '90s punk played closer to the vest, less charisma, less novelty, more brisk, stiff, churning chording, albeit benefitting from Dexter's rarified vocal prowess. Strange, inappropriately classy artwork too, **Ignition** looking more like a Peter Gabriel record than the duncecap traffic jam that it so unremarkably is.
Rating                                    4

## Offspring - Smash (Epitaph '94)

Back in the old days this was called biker metal, Offspring rumbling along like Motörhead and Tank with way better vocals. And it's a smash hit, way past platinum in the U.S., following Green Day's **Dookie** (and maybe Bad Religion, NOFX and Rancid, who got pretty good billing at '96's (Metal)palooza) in a surprise revival of punk rock, straight up and simple. But **Smash** kicks, cranking more of a hardcore but disciplined sound with good production and as I mentioned, soar-

ing, spirited vocals from one Dexter Holland, who really makes this record fly wisely, making me forget that too many of the tunes go the same speed (old-style fast). It's a cool thing this new punk, somehow clearheaded and healthy yet sounding very much like an amalgamation of old California stuff crossed with early '80s metal from the U.K. Anyways, this one kills **Dookie**, because of its energy and headbanged hatred for those prissy college rock melodies. Fresh and worth the huge success it is attracting stateside.
Rating                                    7

## The Offspring - Ixnay On The Hombre (Sony '97)

Making the inevitable big label leap, Dexter Holland and posse re-crank their **Smash** success, windmilling it through twelve (plus *Disclaimer* and *Intermission*) dead-similar rants-with-a-difference. Dave Jerden produces, really injecting and suggesting the Jane's Addiction whenever things slow to a brisk gallop (*I Choose*), Dexter obliging like Perry. But the tall and short of it is that **Ixnay** simply reprises textbook '90s punk, most tracks raided by that same superfast drumbeat, as evidenced by braying lead single *All I Want*. And once more it is Dexter's voice which makes anyone care, in addition to surprisingly turbo-charged guitars, which do rapid-fire battle in layers befitting a metal behemoth. How interesting, you ask? Mildly to moderately, especially come *Amazed*, which marries Silverchair to Guns 'N Roses, signaling that these guys could be an exciting glam act, when that bandwagon swings round again. Oh, and there's one for the No Doubters, *Don't Pick It Up* causing heavenly visions of Gwen in short shirt.
Rating                                    7

## Old Man's Child - Born Of The Flickering
(Century Media '97)

Well-done and crispy-fried, this visceral, panoramic Norse-to-the-bone debut builds on what other fellow Norwegians have done before. Which is to say it's at the level of Cradle Of Filth, no further, no less, for better or worse. Not exactly a huge fan of this stuff, I can nevertheless celebrate the musicianship and the frantic blister of the thing. Also, like Cradle Of Filth, this sucker's getting the red carpet package-wise, which tends to underline the presentation of such vomit-blakk brutality. Released in conjunction with another four whiteface-cat-killers of similar ilk, Century Media perhaps challenging Osmose for honours as premier black metal label.
Rating                                    7

## Omen - Battle Cry (Banzai '85)

Omen's debut is a Maiden-ish, hangover on amphetamines, muddy, out of control, profuse with galloping riffs, progressive rock posturing, and talk of axemen, dragons, wenches, and last rites. If this was the last album on earth, I'd probably play it a few hundred times and after deciphering and assimilating it, begin to appreciate it. But with so much more professional speed and techno-goth out there speaking more directly to personal concerns, why would anybody except the band's moms take the time?
Rating                                    3

## Omen - Warning Of Danger (Banzai '85)

Omen's thrashier, more complicated, less musical, lower budget take on a sort of American-trying-to-sound-European goth just wears on the brain after a few painful minutes. Whereas a band of rabid wolves like Nasty Savage can pull this kind of material off by having their heads severed and spinning in the clouds and their feet firmly on the bass line, Omen sound affected and busy, and ultimately powerless, only finding black wind when shedding the trappings of their collective egos, which thankfully occurs more often

than on the debut. A blunt, learner's license version of Warlord.
Rating 4

## Omen - Nightmares (Metal Blade '87)
Omen remain American dudes caught up in the leather 'n' violence trappings to which so many of the second string axemen fall prey. Musically, it's still predictable Merlin rock that straddles techno and thrash, kinda like a less talented Helloween. This six track EP sounds like a lot of other cheap U.S. bludgeon plonk and offers nothing to motivate a judicious bloodletting. And the cover of AC/DC's Whole Lotta Rosie is both wildly inappropriate and less sonically smokin' than the original, if you can believe it.
Rating 3

## One Bad Pig - I Scream Sunday (Sony '91)
What to make of this bewildering slapdash of caustic funk and thrash riffs butted up against a sort of nutty evangelistic fervor? The whole tangle of signals spells fun, Hell and redemption, One Bad Pig kinda battering you black and blue into religion. There's even a Man In Black featuring Johnny Cash . . . just like U2! And exuberance is in tha house, the whole horned deal riding an octane high as it power punks its way through the teenage bible. It's almost as if major fun was whipped up by the Lord to infiltrate the mid-west's drop dead youth through the guise of a crack band of proto hooligans, 'cos these guys are a blast, kinda like a souped-up Terrorvision gone hardcore if not cardboard. Lots of songs about the evils of drugs, drink and ice cream, plus a slamdance called You're A Pagan. Groove forth and you shall be be saved.
Rating 7

## Only Living Witness - Prone Mortal Form
(Century Media '93)
We can pontificate back and forth on why this Boston quartet's music works wonders on the psyche. They do a bunch of things well, combining tuneful hardcore with a groove-oriented type of Sabbath grunge sporting clear vocals that split the difference between Ozzy and Life Of Agony. If it's metal or something that crosses into the heated end of Stone Temple Pilots terrain, that's for you to decide. But whatever the case, it sounds bitchin' in the car, despite its short 35 minute duration which will only get you to the liquor store and back. Strong songs is the thing, and Only Living Witness have that in spades, designing a sort of pure metal experience out of a quiltwork of influences that themselves, don't stray far from centre.
Rating 8

## Only Living Witness - Innocents (Century Media '96)
Three years since their first record, and seven since forming, Only Living Witness are back with ten more tunes of bashing crashing groove metal. Musically, it's similar to the last (Life Of Agony comparisons must persist), possibly a bit more raw and bravely simple, but lyrically, where the band always shines anyways, Jonah Jenkins is getting sharper, more concise and increasingly poetic, one line to the next being quite cryptic, but always provocative and intensely about real life matters. Recording values are a bit thicker, really feeding off of Eric Stevenson's freight train drumming, riffs rolling overtop like a tidal wave over Tokyo. Rock solid songs, even if the band is going to need a catalogue under its belt to really project a unique vision.
Rating 8

## Onslaught - Power From Hell (Under One Flag '85)
A rare British entry into the pointless ultra-speed snakepit, Onslaught are actually worse than average; somewhat forgiven, due to the age of this carnivore's prayer. Considered one of the death metal originals, **Power From Hell** attracted shards of public acceptance, moshing at least tightly and well-recorded in its mindless, unhinged blast. Vaguely similar to the amusing but inconsequential premier statement from Slayer.
Rating 3

## Onslaught - The Force (Under One Flag '86)
Exhibiting parallel growth to the mountainous Slayer, Onslaught looms more grandiose, offering lengthier lava flows of sinister death, matching Slayer sound for sound in all departments. However, I never liked early Slayer, and this is actually more imbued with the poverty crud factor than advanced, though uninviting science like **Hell Awaits**. Lacks the mission of the more highly evolved, which is usually the fate with tougher British fare. Still gives 'er to the point of cardiac amusement.
Rating 5

## Onslaught - In Search Of Sanity (London '89)
Steve Grimmett and The Ugliest Band In Rock Part II come headthrashin' back, still locking horns with the technological groundbreakers of the mid-'80s, content to re-write killer cornerstones like **Master Of Puppets** and **Spreading The Disease** ad infinitum. Trouble is, lyrically it's a sorry doom gloom raft of NDE trauma as per metal's creative edge circa more like the early '80s. So count yourself in, if technical '80s speed is your resin bag, 'cos Onslaught are literal retro monsters right down to their **Ride The Lightning** mix. Ruthlessly pro, but also commercially derivative, **In Search Of Sanity** arrives in torrid style, but alas, five years late.
Rating 7

## Opeth - Orchid (Candlelight '95)
And the splintering into subgenres continues unabated. There really are few unarguably trashy underground metal bands left these days, the vast majority signed to any sort of minimum deal, offering much in the way of creativity, production and validity. Case in point, Opeth fuses long post-Maiden/Fates Warning overtures with considerably unintelligible grind vocals. Riffs are fresh, constructs laborious and full of surprises (long acoustic and piano passages), and the whole thing spells purpose. I dunno, maybe my impatience with twelve minute songs was never resolved. Swedish with a big, frosty capital "S".
Rating 7

## The Organization - The Organization (Fringe '93)
The ultra-violent Death Angel carry forth under new moniker The Organization, after the departure of their lead singer, leaving guitarist Rob Cavestany to belt out the band's cooler '90s wisdoms. **The Organization** is not readily apparent as greatness, and maybe ultimately unapparent for many after numerous frustrating spins. Fact is, this is a toned-down Death Angel record, more melodic, greyer, less flashy, which often works and often doesn't. In a way, the band almost hard rockens their previous tech-thrash brilliance, trading one out-of-date genre for another, while obviously going for something timeless and above categorization. In the final analysis, the record meekly wins me over, based on my willingness to spin it, in turn based on this posse's fine reputation for intelligent metal. What results is a sort of loose Metallica of the '90s, trickier but no heavier, working with subtlety and shade, good clear vocals and smart refreshing lyrics. Sadly, this record didn't club me hard like I thought it would, but the musicality gives the record legs. I recommend level-headedly.
Rating 7

## The Organization - Savor The Flavor (Metal Blade '95)

The Org. is back after a characteristic absence, again oddly positioning themselves as some sort of catchy, hard rock, alternative, underground, above ground rock band. The sound here is rudimentary, melodic and "heavy" of a sort, often solid, often sour and confusing. There's even a punky Steely Dan cover to mix the brew weirdward. Strange one here. You want to grant the band smart veteran status, but the sum of the parts points more to a lost identity, or on a positive note, the lack of need for identity. Can't see the big sales following, as the non-committal approach will probably just alienate everyone. Middling with integrity intact.
Rating                                                      7

## Ozzy Osbourne - Blizzard Of Ozz (Jet '80)

Ozzy's debut was a tentative, somewhat lightweight step back into the limelight after his low-key split with long-time mates Black Sabbath, whose new throat, the diminutive Dio would have to endure a couple of years of bashing from the Oz man during the latter's on-stage raps. **Blizzard Of Ozz** embodies a push/pull heaviness; the very metallic guitar fireworks of new ill-fated wonderkid Randy Rhoads wrapped around song structures that are too often slow and lumbering yet not anti-melodically doom-laden in the tradition of great Sabbath monoliths. Even when courting depression, Satanism, insanity, pornography and hopelessness, there's a lack of sonic bite that undermines the perplexed lyrical anguish. I Don't Know, Crazy Train (both hits), and No Bone Movies are all too standard metal/HR fare musically, although some of the future malevolent innovation *does* rear its head on such depressing mood pieces as the much-maligned Suicide Solution (written as a veiled lament to Bon Scott) and Mr. Crowley, plus the evil apocalyptic visions of Revelation (Mother Earth). Ozzy's lyrics have always taken a backseat to his position as forked-tongued public enemy number 666 among the asthmatic, freaked-out paranoids of the religious right. This is unfortunate, for Ozzy is basically a very moral individual, more often lamenting the evils of mankind, rather than celebrating them or indeed even treating them with detached neutrality. The pain shines through on this quite thoughtful record, as Ozzy augments his sense of moral void in the world with genuine hurt at being a man misunderstood.
Rating                                                      8

## Ozzy Osbourne - Live E.P. (CBS '80)

This three track EP deserves mention here due only to the inclusion of an excellent vintage non-LP studio track, You Said It All, a slow to mid-tempo traditional metal piece with inherent hookiness. It is also worth mentioning that other Ozzy B-sides are generally worth collecting, the best of which is the aptly titled B Side, one of the man's choice early prowls.
Rating                                                      4

## Ozzy Osbourne - Diary Of A Madman (CBS '81)

Whereas **Blizzard Of Ozz** held back, **Diary Of A Madman** lets loose a drunken rock star cackling like a warlock all the way to the bank. Ozzy's second is a scorching blast of uncompromising noise propelled to new heights of energy by Rhoads' hair-raising, electrified and wondrously raw axework, the always dizzying percussive fury of Tommy Aldridge and the uncompromising high register production of Max Norman. Although a good half of **Diary Of A Madman** is less than flat-out metal—the single Flying High Again as throwback to debut-era sleepiness, Tonight and You Can't Kill Rock And Roll as essentially ballads, and the title track as a vampiric and progressive mix of shock rock stylings—the package in general emits wads of glorious sonic overkill due to the aforementioned personal contributions and the wall-of-sound histrionics of the

more metallic fare. And the metal doth rock. Believer and lead headsmasher Over The Mountain wrap two of Ozzy's most inspirational lyrics around truly sinister black holes of scientific riffery, Rhoads absolutely sizzling throughout. Little Dolls explores similar vintage Alice Cooper sentiments as the title track, and S.A.T.O. rides a faster, illuminating hard rock framework that continues the buoyant story-within-a-story that originated with the debut's Steal Away (The Night), living on through **Bark At The Moon**'s Slow Down. When all is said and done, **Diary Of A Madman** is a lasting classic that stands as the definitive showcase for Randy Rhoads, who shortly after would die in an on-tour fly-by prank gone very wrong, throwing the band into a tailspin (Bernie Tormé quickly came on board, only to quit after two weeks). SPCA note: Ozzy had no problem getting press during this heady but tragic heyday, having bitten the head off a dove at a label meeting (there's pictures), and doing similar damage to a bat on stage, after which the guy contracted rabies.
Rating                                                      10

## Ozzy Osbourne - Speak Of The Devil (CBS '82)

The coolest thing about this double live album of strictly Black Sabbath tunes is trying to break the code of the obscure language written on the front, back, and foldout of the cover. I'm not going to tell you what it says. Figure it out for yourselves, but the main message is a rambling heartfelt dedication to the deceased Randy Rhoads who here is replaced by Night Ranger's Brad Gillis who does a great job, yet is history by the time the next studio album rolls around. **Speak Of The Devil** is essentially the best Sabbath live album to date, slightly eclipsing Sab's own also excellent **Live Evil** which features Dio at the helm, kicking copious amounts of righteous butt due to a number of influences, including a hot recording, a possibly ripped performance by the madman himself, and of course Aldridge's most rhythmic percussive skills. **Speak Of The Devil** as a result ranks as one of the better live albums of all time, spewing forth virtually all of the great Sabbath commercial triumphs in supercharged fine form.
Rating                                                      8

## Ozzy Osbourne - Bark At The Moon (CBS '83)

Although no two Ozzy projects are alike to any great degree, **Bark At The Moon** and **Diary Of A Madman** is a pairing that seems apt for a couple of reasons. Both are stunning displays of metal acrobatics and versatility, featuring a formulaic similarity that promotes cut-for-cut comparisons: the scientific scorchers: Over The Mountain and Centre Of Eternity, the celebrations of rock'n'roll: Flying High Again and Rock'n'Roll Rebel, the collapsible ballads: Tonight and So Tired, the hopeful, bright hard rockers: S.A.T.O. and Slow Down, and the progressive haunted houses: Diary Of A Madman and Waiting For Darkness. No worries though, as this little critical exercise doesn't necessarily belittle the absolute genius of either feast, each brains-imbued composition burning brightly as a classic in its own right. **Bark At The Moon** features new, legally-blind axeman Jake E. Lee, whose pyrotechnics are equally mesmerizing as Rhoads', yet less readily identifiable as his own. The overall feel is tighter, more lush, and less ear-splitting or trebly production-wise. The songwriting also seems more fleshed-out, more seriously planned, which, due to Ozzy's ambitious standards, doesn't come off as better or worse, just different. The entire work is incredibly bright, Ozzy succeeding in every stylistic foray he attacks; and lyrically, **Bark At The Moon** is perhaps Ozzy's most focused diatribe on society's general hypocrisy and specific fixation on Ozzy's supposed toxic influence on today's youth. Major wailers include the Sabbath-like Now You See It (Now You Don't), the off-the-richter-

scale *Rock'n'Roll Rebel*, and the melodic, slightly Maiden-ish *Slow Down*. A superlative slab from a master of the genre, an under-rated serious musical force who too often attracts press attention only for his props and pigeons.
Rating                                                                 10

## Ozzy Osbourne - The Ultimate Sin   (CBS '86)

**The Ultimate Sin** is the failed Ozzy album, due mostly to the trashy, noisy, loose sound, the positively grungy guitars, plus shitty drumming from Randy Castillo. Per usual, Ozzy's lyric writing is better than most pretenders, injecting more soul, wit and, yes dudes, wisdom into his lyrics than most rockers bother with. The problem however is in the annoying garage mix of the album, the "who cares" attitude toward the outcome of the final product, as if it was recorded live off the floor in one take. I don't know, maybe it was, but it definitely suffers whatever the circumstances. Ozzy's was never a band that sounded over-produced, despite the obvious care taken with respect to execution. However, on **The Ultimate Sin**, there's one continuous drone throughout, no variety, no complexity in the arrangements, just one industrial-size hangover. Although there are a few strong tracks here, and some exceptionally smooth choruses, nothing really shakes the distortion off enough to kick. Strange departure, and I'm glad it was only a one off.
Rating                                                                  6

## Ozzy Osbourne/Randy Rhoads - Tribute   (CBS '87)

A sincere dedication to the deceased Randy Rhoads, killed in a plane accident March 19, 1982, this double live **Tribute** is loaded with Randy's searing axework, as it cuts a swath through *all* of **Blizzard Of Ozz**, a couple from **Diary Of A Madman**, and three Sabbath necessities of which we're all tiring, despite their spiritual magnificence. Packaging-wise, the tribute continues with lots of band and personal pics of Randy, a letter from Ozzy, and one from Randy's mom. Perhaps due to the fact that this was dominated by material from Ozzy's second worst record, it suffers in intensity compared to the all-Sabbath **Speak Of The Devil**, the latter also benefiting from one nerve-crushing recording. Also Ozzy's letter states that these are the *only* live recordings he has of Randy and him together, which is pretty surprising if true. Still, Ozzy proves once again his catalytic effect on good talent, as Randy and Aldridge put on one killer elite display of rhythm and riffery.
Rating                                                                  6

## Ozzy Osbourne - No Rest For The Wicked   (CBS '88)

Tighter than a tripwire veteran's survivalist compound and attacking with more sonic fury than a Manowar club date (believe me, I've been there and it ain't pretty), **No Rest For The Wicked** writes the one chapter of Ozzy's admirable catalogue that pulls out all the stops, rocking with such singular focus, that the heaviness of all previous outings pales in comparison. Ever the catalyst, Ozzy manages to whip yet a fourth (counting Brad Gillis) guitar wizard, Zakk Wylde, into a razor-edged frenzy that lends additional bite to Ozzy's already caustic society-deriding penmanship. Talk about a correction after The Ultimate Sinus blockage. This record shreds, yet in a '90s context, with an economy and clarity of sound, especially in Castillo's drumming which has an electronic, treated feel, yet retains its heads-down groovability. No mistake, **No Rest For The Wicked** is very laboriously produced, yet save for the lumbering *Fire In The Sky*, it never loses its considerable all-hell-let-loose bullet-spraying bludgeon. This is Ozzy's version of a no-nonsense, no-fun album, one that drives the point home, wasting little time trying to communicate or expose soul. The classics here are all exceedingly heavy riff rockers, such as

lead single and cool video *Miracle Man*, about Swaggart and his ilk, *Tattooed Dancer*, about bad chicks, and *Demon Alcohol*, about Ozzy's personal party companion. **No Rest For The Wicked** rides a singular controlled, well-produced drone throughout; a sonic onslaught of high quality riffery and this time only occasional, yet always arresting, melody; and most importantly, shows yet again Ozzy's obvious penchant for remaining cutting edge.
Rating                                                                  9

## Ozzy Osbourne - Just Say Ozzy   (CBS '90)

This strange stop-gap EP gathers wicked performances from one of Ozzy's best line-ups, Zakk, Geezer and Randy Castillo welding these cool Oz ditties to our foreheads but fine, awesome mix to boot from Andy Johns. Ozzy's liner notes get it right: this is a far superior version of *Shot In The Dark*. Rounding it out: *Sweet Leaf*, *War Pigs* (yawn) and four from **No Rest For The Wicked**, including masterpiece *Miracle Man*. Raging, dude.
Rating                                                                  8

## Ozzy Osbourne - No More Tears   (CBS '91)

Ozzy was always one of the more honest and perhaps fragile personalities operating among the upper echelons of metal. Originally titled Don't Blame Me, then Say Hello 2 Heaven, **No More Tears** seems to run more along a confessional, autobiographical tack, steering away from the lyrical and sonic electric storm of its predecessor for a more personal, subdued, less technical sound. On virgin spin, **No More Tears** sounds merely dull and basic, yet on repeated plays, which come willfully and often, tunes start to take on lives of their own, wrenching their way into one's head, gradually, insidiously, relentlessly. Structures tend towards slow and sparse, even unwieldy, given the chunks o' granite recording. Even lyrically, Ozzy seems blunted, lacking the colour of past efforts, laying down his thoughts in plainspeak, even though ironically, half of this was co-written with the usually ornate Lemmy. Yet all seems to coalesce into a more serious, more sincere work of gravity, veering away from pyrotechnics in search of hooks with long payback periods. A hard record to pin down, but one that just continues to reveal humanity, even freshness and optimism amongst tracks that lack the dazzle of so much of Ozzy's catalogue. Classics-to-be include the out-of-character heavies *Mr. Tinkertrain*, with its backed-off AC/DC riffery, and the title cut, a long, atmospheric number pumping along above a simple plodding bass line, sporting some hopelessly bleak melodic touches reminiscent of Ozzy's Sabbath daze. Cool video too. All in all, this record's really grown on me due to its gravity and gloom tones, no matter what the overt intensity level at hand. The recently and tentatively cleaned-up Ozzy continues to be a vital emotional force capable of fine quality, totally committed metal, yet word has it the record's tour was nothing to write home about, although tour document **Live & Loud** may correct these perceptions for some.
Rating                                                                  8

## Ozzy Osbourne - Live & Loud   (Epic '93)

The hand-clapping, lumpen troll we all love to check for percentage body fat is back where it all makes sense, the stage. **Live & Loud** is exactly that; a tornado of sound that finds Ozzy's band firing on all sixes (over two tours), pounding through an all-inclusive batch of classics, Zakk's killer axe swinging wildly, Ozzy vocalizing as if it's his last gasp. And the packaging roars too, black metal speaker grill case, 24 page book, a couple a' tattoos; all in all, thoughtful design work, lots to stare at while witnessing the majesty of one of metal's greats. One large and looming catalogue fired in the crucible

of the road. Long live. Also contains much ballyhoo'ed but luded Sabbath reunion tune *Black Sabbath*.
Rating      7

## Ozzy Osbourne - Ozzmosis   (Sony '95)

Metal's favorite battered old bird flies in full phoenix flame on this highly delayed/anticipated new sledge. *Ozzmosis* ushers in an Ozzy not averse to outside songwriting pros (Vallance, Hudson, the esteemed Mr. Kilminster), and the results are a success, especially on stormy passionate ballads like *I Just Want You* and *Old L.A. Tonight*. And despite there being a fair number of mellow, ballad-tipping tracks, the overall effect lacks cheese, each composition being well-written, a tad dark, and always with substance. No Scorpions or Crue drivel here, Ozzy being just too goshdarn talented a guy to screw up. Furthermore, production trickery is everywhere in an Aerosmith sort of way, making the results always entertaining from a fidelity standpoint, erasing one's temptation to count the riffs and lament the ponderous plough factor of the whole difficult experience. And the heavy tracks do sort of drag (a little down-grinded grunge influenced, cynically so I might add). Sum verdict: full of shade, nuance and that unstoppable Ozz charisma, even if I think he could have done it without the hired guns. Note I: Featured guitarist on the record is on-again-off-again friend Zakk Wylde. Steve Vai is featured on one track, but a good half-dozen were recorded and nixed. These, I for one, would like to hear. Joe Holmes joined post-release, and in March '97, left the band. Note II: saw the tour; great warm-up video of the Oz man spliced into all sorts of movie and documentary footage, after which Ozzy stumbled and bumbled about the place, giving it his all nonetheless, his young, combat-ready backing band (Joe Holmes, FNM's Mike Bordin and Suicidal Tendencies' Robert Trujillo) an amazing metal sight and sound fer sure. Note III: greatest hits album in the works, along with the massive Ozzfest tour, which will feature a reformed Black Sabbath, sans Bill Ward.
Rating      8

## Our Lady Peace - Naveed   (Sony '94)

Virtually unknown in their hometown, Toronto's OLP (hell, it could be ELP), climb right into the alterno-rock ring, major label and all, ready to address a fickle and perplexing marketplace with their brand of desperation expedition art grunge. Solid first single in *The Birdman*, but a general self-seriousness murks the waters along with a mix that muffles the guitars (which usually don't coagulate into power chords anyways). Lots of moody, important-sounding dynamics, and vocal work that is versatile but in love with its own sense of drama, make for a Tea Party-type reaction: it's either insanely god-like or a joke; the listener either believing in the band's fine literary skills and roaring rock'n'roll destiny, or smelling fake-ass pseudo art at every crease in the band's collective furrowed brow.
Rating      6

## Our Lady Peace - Clumsy   (Sony '97)

Record one went multi-platinum in Canada, and was a rare U.S. cracker for a Canucklehead band. I thought it poop, but **Clumsy** is quite dashing, the band really digging into their chops bag and smartening those arrangements. Not quite as exotic as comparative I Mother Earth, OLP stick to a song-based alt-pop-grunge with lots of dramatic spaces, the title track, *Automatic Flowers* and *Superman's Dead* reminding one of heavy (?) Oasis, while *Big Dumb Rocket* and *The Story Of 100 Aisles* sounding like inspired Stone Temple Pilot diversions. Still, it's hard to get a handle on this record, Raine's alternately passionate and fake passionate vibrato being the only truly trademark stamp on each of these try-harder tracks. Like the drumming, bigshot Arnold Lanni's production is earthy despite all the

surface detail. I'd give this race to I Mother Earth by a tuft of chin hair, because dammit, they sound like they're having more un-angsty fun.
Rating      7

## Outbreak - Master Stroke   (Pro Canada SDE '86)

Fairly accomplished debut of low-flying techno-goth from a bunch of Quebec dudes led into battle by a frontman who calls himself Kaïser Fist. Outbreak is the only band I know who has ever included Canon colour copies of themselves live, plus solicitations for career advice. Pretty tight package and decent recording for a self-done deal, **Master Stroke** fleshes out ideas expressed in the live show which features Nazi regalia, including prominently displayed swastikas and lots of black leather. Musically, as Kaïser accurately spells out for himself, the band mixes Priest and Metallica with liberal doses of early Maiden riffery and more liberal doses of Maiden twin lead work, albeit operating in a decidedly underground Euro-goth vein. A bit too much sonic wanking and depression for my tastes, these warriors could be contenders if they hang together long enough to forge their own sound. As far as **Master Stroke** goes, its songs are basically wax museum soundtracks.
Rating      5

## Outcrowd - Healer   (Blackout! '95)

**Healer** is yer basic, bashing fresh stack of knock 'em down alterna-punk from Joisey, distinguished by the fairly insistent buoyancy of the melody and mood, despite the garagey three-piece combat ethic. Vocals lean towards Chuck (the old guy) from Faith No More, Todd Morse's vocals competing vivaciously with lots of semi-tricky drumming (also vaguely FNM-ish), as arrangements do that whisper-to-roar thing found amongst a lot of like-minded noisy alternative goateed goats. But the high creativity does faintly recall Minutemen.
Rating      6

## Outlaw Blood - Outlaw Blood   (Atlantic '91)

Opening cut *Tower Of Love* melds Billy Idol and Kik Tracee with sly criminal intent, setting the stage for what hopefully becomes an artful and icy slice of corporate metal. Alas, results are mixed but hopeful of future bereavement. Heavily overproduced, which was the bane of so much big shot U.S. steel in the early '90s hair zone, **Outlaw Blood** bangs forth somewhat sparse and bluesy, lacking in almighty chordage, with a good third of the proceeds dipping below acceptable, sounding deflated and/or insincerely pop-infected, which could have worked had these boys been flaming artists with provocative thoughts on their minds. But they don't and intellectually stimulating they ain't. Still, Outlaw Blood do a sleazy enough job of their adopted craft, dressing up their non-threatening, radio-friendly fables of rock'n'roll life with nicely off-centre axe-ioms and flashes of vampiric finesse, possibly in the direction of L.A. Guns or Bang Tango, which seem similarly bent on crawling on their underbellies. Promising, which is rare in a competitive, professional genre that tends to bring the complete arsenal to the table from record one. Something slightly seedy, and barely eclectic going on here amidst the unsure stylistic shifts, if only that electric drum sound would go away.
Rating      6

## Overcome - Blessed Are The Persecuted
(Tooth & Nail '95)

Too funny, Tooth & Nail signing these Christian rock acts that crank unholy dins a little outside of what might be construed as allowable by most bible belters. Phoenix's Overcome sound like Obituary toned down to Testament, with a little skatecore thrown in to really perplex potential saved souls, the band retaining the

high school basketball team water boy look of its label mates Strongarm and Unashamed. So vocalist Jason Stinson barks out his sermons (not like you'd get them unless you can read), all the while his band lashing out with its death metal, anarcho-pink atonalities. But unlike Strongarm's really cogent punk/metal hybrid, this one's just average churning gloom despite its lily white message. One guy at 20, the rest in their teens.
Rating                                6

## Overdose - Tight Action   (Bonebreaker '85)

Thoroughly crippled by one of Axel Thubeauville's many mousy mixes, Overdose remains a non-issue even once you realize that, yes, that is the bass drum. Vocals are kinda thin and sent to the rear, on what would have been an alchemical iron feast given a Scratch recording and a Gravestone or Tox ethic to set the pile ablaze. In fact **Tight Action** is almost Oz-like in places, getting fully evil on various black patches. Too bad, but there's really quite a number of bands this Euro-horrific and iced, maybe too many to go around, no matter how punishingly mixed. Yet here it's only caustic potential gone distorted and sickly.
Rating                                5

## Overdose - Progress Of Decadence   (Futurist '95)

Overdose are Brazillian buds of Sepultura, growing in temporal conjunction, now six or so records deep, the band making their major U.S. play as Sepultura really catches fire, the Cavaleras even moving their organization to the metal hotbed of Phoenix. **Progress Of Decadence** (dumb thrash title) is as mature as one would figure, exquisitely mixed, good socially conscious lyrics, and lots of fresh power riffing. But something irks me about the overall sound, evoking the commercial, almost novelty side of Sepultura, lots of distracting Brazillian percussion and equally distracting Mexi-flavoured riffs. But really these are minor if not nagging complaints, the record really crammed full of expert, slow Slayer meets commercial Metallica type metal monsters. Verdict: easily enjoyable, heavy, Bay Area-style metal, if a tad too polished.
Rating                                7

## Overdose - Scars   (Fierce '96)

Olé! And Overdose mean it, taking their zesty Brazillian hardcore punch to enjoyable, even playful new realms, **Scars** really digging a lustful mosh while delivering messages of third world upheaval that should concern any white fatboy guarding his assets. Letting up not a speck on the rat-a-tat-tat equatorial percussive assault, Overdose coat the whole vaguely industrial, thrillingly rhythmic metal mash in an experimental ethic that matches doppelganger Sepultura head for bang. So even with this small U.S. track record of two albums, the band has won me over, tunes like School and the stop stutter burn rubber pummel of Out Of Control taking the listener on a razor edge hip-hop that is a fresh kick for urban sounds. Expertly recorded in Sao Paolo over a seven month period, **Scars** is a layered treat for a hardcore elite, stuffed and gorged with classy axework, multi-hued percussion and an unintentional naiveté that outstrips the chains of a derived past, Overdose speaking with a voice that is all their own and worth owning by you, Mr. Metalguy.
Rating                                9

## Overdrive - Metal Attack   (Planet '83)

Unfortunately, this rare NWOEuroHM LP doesn't remotely resemble the formidable and smothering Overdriven conquest of **Swords And Axes**. Although hints of depressing melody can be heard amongst the thin speed rockers here, the overall product is one of little consequence, with a cheap recording to boot. Stylistically, much faster, busier, and looser; and suicidally miles behind the band's aforementioned master-

ful opus, **Metal Attack** represents a sound worth developing although history took the band elsewhere. Cool album cover.
Rating                                5

## Overdrive - Swords And Axes   (Banzai '84)

No exaggeration whatsoever, but in the opinion of your obsessed author, **Swords And Axes** stands as the most desperately dark and concentrated slab of Euro sound ever etched in black. Said album is also the inspiration for the term "messed-up" you see hopefully responsibly placed throughout this book; messed-up being the leather soul of this album like no other. **Swords And Axes** comes welling up from the gut, pounding and attacking with detached sobriety in its tireless march towards self-inflicted anguish. Like the most hopeless alienations from Sabbath laid brooding against the most stirring and downright Aryan of Euro-melodic poisons, Overdrive delivers a subtle and poetic blackness beyond the most disturbing of literal black metalists, from the opening acoustic death knells of pummeling masterpiece Dream Away (I literally cannot say I like any one song in the world any better than this one) through the obliterating genius of Broken Hearted. In between, the insistent plod towards untold psychosis continues unabated. Side one of this is plainly one of the heaviest sides of metal ever recorded, in the dictionary sense of the word, leaden and grey, anchored with a merciless bottom-end. Simply four hopeless, messed-up classics out of four. Side two kicks off with a somewhat bad OTT instrumental reminiscent of **Metal Attack**, adding one more less-than-perfect fast one later on; yet, on the upside, two more ripped 'n' lethal paeans to pain in Living In Sin and the aforementioned album closer Broken Hearted. **Swords And Axes** clots the blood due to mind-numbing displays of depression from all facets of Overdrive's tragic sound, the dual axework, the lower-the-boom production, the crashing and dense percussion, and especially the heart-wrenching wails of throat Pelle Thuresson, a metal name if I ever heard one. This record manages to fly a flag of emotionless hate which rumbles with a precise opacity rarely experienced since early Sabbath. The tragedy is that few ever got to witness the carnage that is a **Swords And Axes** composition, Overdrive getting the same slim attention that every other lesser label outfit was awarded in the mid-'80's flood of releases. In Overdrive's case, it was probably from fear of potential Priest and Ozzy style suicide suits.
Rating                                10

## Overkill - Feel The Fire   (Megaforce '87)

Despite the bass- and treble-challenged production, one could tell Overkill were going to fling themselves at least into the middle tier of grueling tech-thrash acts, here showing their sense of humour in covering The Dead Boys' Sonic Reducer. A metal of a type that doesn't really exist anymore, many speak fondly of this exuberant but naive artifact of the Bay Area sound (even if the boys were from New York City). Guess you had to be there.
Rating                                5

## Overkill - Taking Over   (Atlantic '85)

A type of Bay Area bashing that combines muscle, grime and punk anarchy (moshability, more or less), Overkill suffers from Metallica delusions like no other fairly substantial act, although the overt poverty metal of **Feel The Fire** is gone. But I always lumped **Taking Over** with early Testament as largely redundant and too derivative for serious consideration. Chock crammed full of meaty riffs but, as per many ultra-heavy purveyors, too many to the point of distraction.
Rating                                5

## Overkill - Under The Influence (Atlantic '88)

Still caught in a punishing vortex of multiple riffs, Over-kill learn to mix up their velocities a bit, adjusting like a good pitcher in mid game. Still despite their mediocrity, Overkill are somewhat important, but I'm leaning towards both Testament and to a lesser extent Exodus for bludgeon rock, almost solely on the basis of vocals, Bobby "Blitz" Ellsworth's getting a mite yelpy, hysterical and enamoured with punk phrasings.
Rating **6**

## Overkill - The Years Of Decay (Megaforce '89)

A Terry Date production job doesn't do much to solve this record's lack of bottom end. And compounding things is the high and hysterical vocal performance of Ellsworth, whose trite, punky lyrics and speedy delivery take away the levity of all that good playing, axework that often previews the Pantera sound on **Cowboys From Hell**. I dunno, just tiring, the band scampering from one speedy track to the next. Thankfully, the last of the band's album covers unbecoming of their semi-star status.
Rating **6**

## Overkill - Horrorscope (Megaforce/Atlantic '91)

The first Overkill record I can halfways hack, **Horror-scope** brings back Terry Date who cranks up the levels, heavying up the band, while also getting a tight, sophisticated performance from all parties involved. Tunes are still fast, machine gun riffing it to the redline, but Ellsworth's vocals are both more operatic and growly, not to mention his lyrical material, which is stronger and darker. Novelty cover this time around is a power metal version of Edgar Winter's *Frankenstein*, sorta out of place among such fired-up rants. But the rest hangs frighteningly well, the band's chops a pleasure to behold.
Rating **7**

## Overkill - I Hear Black (Atlantic '93)

Overkill is moving far away from the second generation wolf pack, grinding up lesser, faltering bricks like Exodus in its path. **I Hear Black** is an insane blizzard of Sabbath melancholia grafted to Corrosion corrosion, making for a loose, edgy but ultra-modern release. Chock full o' grunting magnificence, **I Hear Black** puts Overkill at the fore of the brutali-metal sweepstakes, with the *Kashmir* meets Metallica of *World Of Hurt*, and the *Zero The Hero* meets Metal Church of the title cut, and the moshmeat discipline of closer *Just Like You*. Some of the most infectious ultra-heavy riffs this side of *Symphony*, this is one thrasher that moves with weight and groove, preferring to send truck-size power chords into traffic jams of slow-moving vehicles full of brains ready to explode with the imposed restraint. Hot caustic mix from Alex Perialis plus band, and great "mumbling crazy man" vocals from a vastly improved Ellsworth who uses more of his range to versatile effect. Blazing metal from yet another outfit that has learned to radiate beneath the shadows of the masters, Metallica.
Rating **8**

## Overkill - W.F.O. (Atlantic '94)

W.F.O. is the perfect companion piece to the head-stomp majesty that was **I Hear Black**. Now self-produced, the band has found a nice balance between caustic midrange penetration and Ellsworth's now cool, sneering admonishments. W.F.O. might be the more aggressive of the two, faster and more back to the roots (canal!), but both are absolutely cutting edge shards of futuro-thrash technology through the use of entirely traditional tooling. Not much more to say, Overkill being pretty much the best (tied with Testament) at pulling off this kind of metal wrestling match (no Overhill shots from me), Bay Area mayhem sent

sky-high via NYNY. Contains a hidden jam way, way up the counter, a piss-take of Sabbath psalm *Heaven And Hell*, which collapses into Priest's *Ripper* (both slapped down with only bass, drums and really hammered sounding vocals).
Rating **8**

## Overkill - Wrecking Your Neck Live (CMC/MCA '95)

An astounding live pack for the wrench to the head fan of this long-moshing bunch, **Wrecking Your Neck Live** comprises 22 tracks over two CDs, sampling every record, while offering no less than seven weighted coal cars from the last studio slab **W.F.O.** Recorded at the Agora Theatre in Cleveland, the sound is tough as nails, and more than adequate for a slamming night of working class metal, crammed down yer throats by veterans with chops to spare. A goodly supply of band pics, the obligatory backstage pass shots, what more do you need?
Rating **7**

## Overkill - The Killing Kind (CMC '95)

Overkill is just Overkill, a long-suffering band who continues to craft edgy, metal man's metal, fighting it out in the clubs, forever carving a place in history, destined to someday warrant a tribute album. **The Killing Kind** makes only minor adjustments, reconstituting with a punk thrash anger that is a return to their root canals of old. All the dime-on perfection is still manifest, but the band's self-production shakes the box vigorously, so a psycho deconstruction always seems just around the corner. It's a white-knuckle ride fer sure, destined to please fans while probably not gathering many new ones. Still (going on three records now), a band I praise but only sparingly play. Unfathomable, or I would have told you why by now.
Rating **8**

## Oz - Heavy Metal Heroes (Kraf '82)

Oz's premiere is a noisy little machine shop of amateurish retro-metal, the type of album that usually comes from strange, traditionally non-rock'n'roll countries, full of riffs that we've heard a hundred times before, played with a general lack of intensity or chops, kinda like early Krokus, or much French or Italian rock. Yet these guys are Swedes, not Yugoslavians. It's hard to believe **Heavy Metal Heroes** comes from the same sick minds that ripped through **Fire In The Brain** but I guess everybody's gotta start in the basement.
Rating **4**

## Oz - Fire In The Brain (Combat '84)

The adopted cartoon dogtags of Ape De Martini, Speedy Foxx, Jay C. Blade, Mark Ruffneck, and Spooky Wolff belie the fact that these Swedes are residents of metal's seedy black underside, and further belies the ominous metal rumbling of this album's cavernous, dead serious moral void. **Fire In The Brain** is a depressing, dark freight train of a record, a richly European and at the same time unclean work, which pounds relentlessly from the opening heaves of the brilliantly apocalyptic *Search Lights*, through the slow death trudge of *Black Candles*, to the violent concluding wails of the title track. I bought this at the same time as Witchfinder General's **Friends Of Hell** and together they performed a wicked one-two punch on my psyche. Although I've somewhat recovered, **Fire In The Brain** remains a dense, uncompromising wall of mayhem that gathers momentum and refuses to die without causing heaping slabs of pain in the process.
Rating **9**

## Oz - III Warning (Combat '84)

Whereas **Fire In The Brain** bludgeoned the senses mercilessly, **III Warning** merely annoys, with a ca-

cophonous, scurrying sound that muddies the riffs and further distorts Ape's much more desperate, strained, and less-in-tune vocals, which are appropriately mixed out the back door. The painful black metal teeth of the predecessor (and the vicious interim EP featuring the tenacious *Turn The Cross Upside Down*) are filed and capped to the point where Oz resembles no more than a dense, unwieldy Motörhead. Side one is markedly more savage, with driving dirty fables of anguish such as *Crucified*, *Runner*, and *Rock'n'Roll Widow*, yet side two is almost a total write-off, a headache-inducing din that is nearly indiscernible through the gutted grunge recording. The Oz that whipped **Fire In The Brain** is buried in this muck somewhere; and the overall emotive plane, although not overtly black metal, is still ragingly evil. Much of this could have been saved via a brighter, cleaner recording, but at least half is just written dumb, which no knob-twiddling could have salvaged. Note: next record was **Decibel Storm** in '86, followed by a break-up and reformation.
Rating                                                              5

## Oz - Roll The Dice   (Black Mark '91)

Through garage rock, Satanic mayhem, back to garage rock and now, a sort of greasy melodic metal, Oz have seen it all and impressed but a few. **Roll The Dice** finds ol' Ape finito, for new, more accessible throat Tapani Anshelm. Still the band's gritty axe attack carves some whopping Christmas turkey here, but the dim attempts at commercial hard rock can't wash off all that black soot accumulated over the band's sorry career. I mean, Oz does not exist to conjecture about boy meets girl relationships. Anyhow, this is an improvement on the last one, finding a sort of scowling Accept, indescribable nuances and sounds that nobody would be caught dead doing today. Bottoms up, rivetheads!
Rating                                                              7

# P

## Jimmy Page - Death Wish II: The Original Soundtrack (Atlantic '82)

Hey waddayawant? There's actually quite a bit of ol' Jimmy on here, the underemployed legend riffing nicely, soloing sublimely and adding much synth work that harkens unsurprisingly to the lush textures of **In Through The Out Door**. There are even a few **Outrider**-unquality vocals tracks (Chris Farlowe: yuck), and some fairly usual soundtracky stuff that nevertheless evokes Page's dark Kenneth Anger work. But really the joy is hearing the shambling, convoluted pimp-roll style of Page as he lurches into the '80s. And like I say, there's a lot of Pagey on this record.
Rating 6

## Jimmy Page - Outrider (Geffen '88)

Most agreed this was a pooch, recalling the thick, difficult gumbo of The Firm's twin cloggings. Page mixes conventional songs with horrible instrumentals here, everything sounding like heavy blues (or boring old virgin blues) made convoluted, like third-rate outtakes from the **In Through The Out Door** sessions, way below the out-takes that surfaced on **Coda**, but that same sort of slidey meandering of riff bulked-up for no reason, cold songs recorded bassy and warm. Jason Bonham does most of the drumming (playing like dad), Chris Farlowe most of the vocals (an odd, '70s pub rock voice, to be sure), and Plant does a poor guest vocal on The Only One. But hand it to Pagey, this is neither a collection of good rock songs, nor a riff showcase, or even a vehicle for guitar god solos. I mean, **Outrider**'s one reason I consider this guy overrated. **Death Wish II**, The Firm, Coverdale Page, and Page Plant are a few more.
Rating 4

## Jimmy Page & Robert Plant Unledded - No Quarter (Atlantic '94)

Well, yes our favorite aging minstrels have managed to overcome cynicism (theirs and ours), in making a batch of old fogie Zep tracks fresh again. Leaving Jonesy out of the equation, reportedly because it would feel too much like Zep with a missing wheel, Page and Plant have formed a surprisingly easy alliance, augmenting their slightly faded skills with a forceful backbench of musicians, most pronounced being deafening Bonham-style drum wizard Michael Lee, and the raft of non-western musicians that give this record its middle eastern/world music theme. Also deliberately planned was the strategy of picking many less trampled-under-foot Zep classics. So we get a lovingly loping *Nobody's Fault But Mine*, a mesmerizing *Friends*, a furious dervish-like *Gallow's Pole* and a bombastic gutting then reincarnation of *Kashmir*, perhaps the record's real title track. As I say, Page ain't much to write home about here, washing expressively if a tad ham-fisted over his weapon, and Plant has to adjust big-time given his waning range, but the idea, planning and team execution is all-Zep brilliance. The much-lauded new originals are a bit sketchy, more like mantras than real songs, but given this, they fit seamlessly into the exotic spicing of the record (which BTW is merely the live recorded documentation of the MTV Unplugged session performed by this army). So yes, these mythological patriarchs have reinforced the legend of a few more Led Zeppelin classics, painting with a richly textured brushstroke, a stable of songs as new age world music viables. And yes, to listen is good.
Rating 8

## Pain - Pain (Nuclear Blast '97)

Busy, busy bleeder of ears Peter Tagtgren (Hypocrisy, The Abyss) now has a foreboding solo vehicle to call his own, **Pain** being produced, written, and mixed by Tagtgren, who also masterfully plays all instruments on the short cyberdeath feast. I kinda like the ol' half hour rule when the music is so immediate and vital, a kind of ingratiate, infect, and peel on out mentality that stings like a sharp slap in the face. One thinks Nailbomb or Geezer Butler solo here, Tagtgren using electrics sparingly to rust-chill effect, lead track On Your Knees (Again) being a prime example of futuristic flourishes added to a groundswell of sorrowful, melodic-minded emotion. But our man still loves a drunken bash, so most tracks are clawed, pawed and clodded, lots of hypnotic, stiff grooves bolstered by crashing cymbals and insane ranting. Probably my favourite of the Abyss-Hypocrisy-Pain trinity, and not because of the '90s sounds, more because of the tidy, mainstream-tinted riffery and the contemplation carved from something so singular and solo-minded.
Rating 8

## Paingod - Paingod (Century Media '97)

Florida's Paingod have actually been treading the boards for nine years, under the moniker Raped Ape, a name which finally became too much of an albatross for this dead-serious hardcore groove metal outfit. The sounds enclosed are meaty, thick and bouncy, as good as, if no better than other fully capable players like Downset, Nothingface, I'M'L, Madball and Biohazard. Coupled with my general indifference to the genre, and the fact that this doesn't make discernable advances over the above, count me unimpressed.

Rating **6**

## Pandemonium - Heavy Metal Soldiers (Metal Blade '84)

What can I say? Ludicrously thirsty for new heavy wax, I trudged into Lyle's in Victoria for a fix. Here's what I found that day, and given the dearth of metal, it didn't sound half bad, until it hit me two or three years later that it was *all* bad. Refreshing to see a band that wasn't trying to paste you to the wall, but Pandemonium, to which the album cover would reinforce and attest, were not ready for prime time, rendering their primary metal dull, predictable and loose in execution. Basically betraying of its Alaskan isolation and age.

Rating **4**

## Pandemonium - Hole In The Sky (Metal Blade '85)

An obvious jerk-to-reality after the truly laughable debut that was **Heavy Metal Soldiers**, **Hole In The Sky** (no relation) has Alaska's Resch, Resch, Resch and Basch smoothing out their stiff delivery and stretching their middle-of-the-road craft towards an inclusion of groove-oriented party metal with their usual Shrapnel-like poverty-Priest, resulting in some warmth to the proceedings as per simple Van Halen, complex Crüe, or connectable Virgin Steele. Two unsightly blemishes: Trooper's *Boys In The Bright White Sports Car*, and yet another cut-rate album cover. Still, something nostalgically honest about this record which rocks confused, yet thoroughly in love with rock'n'roll.

Rating **6**

## Pantera - Metal Magic (Metal Magic '83)

In which a young bunch of Texans with stars in their eyes crank out an indie effort on par with much that surrounded it created by bigger wallets. Adequately mixed, crammed full of savvy metallic moves, equally built with metal and American-style hard rock. And everybody has talent, if not lack of restraint, **Metal Magic** immediately putting Pantera on the scouting list, albeit with miles to slog through the business before any real commercial success.

Rating **6**

## Pantera - Projects In The Jungle (Metal Magic '84)

Before the advent of Phil Anselmo, Pantera was a much tamer sort of animal. **Projects In The Jungle**, the band's second, demonstrates an early talent for riff, arrangement and soloing agility, sounding like an idea-rich version of Def Leppard's **On Through The Night**, due in large part to vocals that sound like a helium-hyped Joe Elliott. Ignoring the indie look, which manifests itself most embarrassing on the cheapo front cover, these are accomplished soundscapes for the era. A punter's gotta smile at the tactical brilliance already in full swing this far back. Even though they look like young pups, guitarist Diamond Darrell is already a kick-ass purveyor of metal magic, as is cannon man Vinnie Paul. It was cool then, we liked it then, and really, it holds up pretty well, but this is a band that no longer exists, Pantera making one of the most wolloping attitude shifts in metal to date (or is that Date), erasing this record's melody for the band's modern-day heaping piles of might. Conclusion: Pantera's early work was nothing to be ashamed of, even though they'd like us to forget it exists.

Rating **7**

## Pantera - Cowboys From Hell (Atlantic '90)

You know you've caved in a few brains when an unruly batch of our nation's teens run around vandalizing town and signing their handiwork "Cowboys From Hell", which happened right here in Ontario. Well, Pantera are truly worthy of the notoriety, having created about the Heaviest Metal one could possibly imagine, and that ain't just me sayin' it. Pantera's peers and competitors are now uttering the band's mighty name in hushed tones, because nothing anywhere on this earth sounds more like pure electricity, not even Slayer, although to be fair, Slayer is about the only force on equal with the sheer kill factor of the merciless machine that is Pantera. The essence of metal, purity, perfection . . . all superlatives apply, not to mention head-exploding, flesh-tearing and bone-breaking, as Terry Date sets the hydro station aflame with a mix that is all steel and gut, utilizing the gated drum effects pioneered on Metallica's . . . **And Justice For All** (and Peter Gabriel's third before that). Then the band takes over, Diamond Darrell blasting out the most inhumane and unholy of six string surgeries while Anselmo cracks open his head and hands you his brains. Wicked insanity to the bone, **Cowboys From Hell** forces a tension from all affronts, challenging mind and body to be hard, doing what the best of metals should, kicking you off your lazy ass.

Rating **9**

## Pantera - Vulgar Display Of Power (Atlantic '92)

Again, an avalanche of one frequency, metal so blindingly ideal, it lacks dynamic, lacks fullness, lacks anything but a piercing power, silence outside of the killer mid-level tones that emit black heat throughout this record's distressed duration. No vulgarity here, just new levels of perfection, compositions that strike and recoil, somehow, somewhere finding up-ratchet on its exploding predecessor, kicking off with a trio of terrors: *Mouth For War*, the vacuum cleaner riff to heave all Hoovers, *A New Level*, a statement delivering deafness with its bold challenge, and *Walk*, funk thrash for mastodons. Elsewhere, there's *Regular People (Conceit)* and *Fucking Hostile*, both strafed by the machine gun fire of Diamond Darrell's insane and commanding axe mechanics. **Vulgar Display Of Power** displays no emotion of any sort, resorting to pure animal reflex, cutting a swath of destruction with detached automated impulse. And like **Cowboys From Hell**, it is the frayed, fused then healed ends of ultimate Heft, defined by a sound that leaches all the pleasantries from its mix: toneless tone, nothing but the electric turned rabid. So take heed, the revolution is at hand. Mow down whatever you have to to obtain this opus of the Hyper-Extended gone ballistic. You'll never sleep quite the same ever again.

Rating **10**

## Pantera - Far Beyond Driven (Atlantic '94)

No disputing the fact that Pantera are the reigning beastmasters of sound in the '90s, **Far Beyond Driven** cementing their nuclear presence for all to witness in all its explosive, ludicrously heavy, smoke-filled glory. Saw the tour, Biohazard and Sepultura, both better than Pantera in specific areas (maybe lyrical maturity in both cases, and an odd personable charm in Sepultura's alone), backed-up with might and sledgehammer wit. But then Dimebag "pink goatee" Darrell and Co. emerged, just splitting the collective cranium like nothing I've ever seen, the band creating something so ugly, it could only be the product of truck-size crack-hoovering. Man, these guys are the flesh-eating virus of all sonic experiences, really probably the heaviest thing ever by almost every measure (excepting dumb ones like speed and noise). But it is towards this end that **Far Beyond Driven** has seen scattered criticism (amongst mountains of accolades in and outside the industry) for lack of song, substituting the ugly hookery of a *Cowboys From Hell* for extreme ambient and detached riffery, while Phil turns in an often borderline grindcore vocal, more of a complete stomach-driven scream than a true monster-mixed growl. But those exacto knife riffs are so death-defying, they whip these loosely-conceived pieces into songs that work more often than not, personal mental tattoos being the auditorium-size suicide funk of *5 Minutes Alone*, the apocalyptic bonescrape of *Use My Third Arm*, and that blessed black intro sequence to *Slaughtered*. True the long tracks wander and fatigue, but forget your carping. This is a masterpiece of sandblasted heft, mirroring a society drunk and ready to snap on adrenaline without food. Man, Phil's gotta find some stronger weed, because the fields he's mowing down daily don't seem to be working.

Rating                                                        10

## Pantera - The Great Southern Trendkill   (Atlantic '96)

All eyes on the Snake, as metal's crowning lords of leaching return with what is destined to be the second biggest commercial success for heavy metal in '96 (behind Metallica, ahead of Sepultura). And the band delivers in fine suvvern fashion, wetting and warming their sound in the swamps of gatorland, loosening that Pantera noose just a bit, writing some songs with staying power beyond mountainous riffs. The title track opens with a traditional thrash-out with war-cry, then collapsing into a signature groove, announcing that Pantera won't be radically changing their winning formula. But a few tracks here will really stick in the head like a forked twig, *War Nerve* with its aggressive stutter, the dangerous prog of *13 Steps To Nowhere*, and above all, the insanely lockable swing of *Living Through Me (Hell's Wrath)*, all framing what is a twistedly bluesy, Down-ish sort of experience. Lyrically Phil is more fragmented, tormented and apocalyptically amoral than usual, the man delivering his sick wisdoms in a new variety of characters with character. Other finessable touches: more layers, more drumming, more guitar voices . . . give me more! But the mellow wastecase places doth drag almost too bluesy, Pantera not really all that successful at these loitered experiments in mood. Minor carping though, for this is a creative triumph that invites with greater ease than past almost academic, acrobatic demonstrations. One tick less than 10 because there really are three-ish tracks that are either too harsh and unfocused or too luded. But of course, buy the damn thing.

Rating                                                         9

## Parade Of Losers - P.O.L.   (Giant '95)

I guess I just don't have a handle on '90s punk. The first Green Day rip-off band I halfways like, and everybody else slags them. Screw 'em all, 'cos these New Cretins On The Block have hooks, humour, production; a real mix-it-up batch of irreverent (if bandwagoned) anthems, even an alterna-cover of *White Punks On Dope*. Yeah, a total joke, what with titles like *Sux 2 B U*, *In Me I Trust*, *I Hate Myself*, *STD*, *Sick* and *Dirtbag*; but I'd much rather play this innocuous snowboard glue-sniff than duncecaps with supposed integrity like NOFX, No Use For A Name or even big daddies like Rancid or Bad Religion. But really, I'd rather not hear '90s punk at all. I wish it would just go away.

Rating                                                         7

## Paradise Lost - Lost Paradise   (Peaceville '90)

Man, I can see why people were telling me "don't go there" when I would enquire as to the nature of early Paradise Lost. For fact is, this debut record stinks to high heaven, evoking worse hells than Milton could ever have imagined. **Lost Paradise** is quite simply, a confused mishmash of dreary, doomy chord sequences, songs with no hope, bottom of the bucket Saint Vitus or Count Raven with thrash metal's disdain for craftsmanship and quality of mix, Holmes just phoning-in his sleepy-eyed grumble on these spectacularly boring half-compositions. No wonder this now suc-

cessful and highly interesting band is embarrassed by their past.

Rating                                                         4

## Paradise Lost - Gothic   (Peaceville '91)

This is the kind of record that could benefit from remixing or re-recording some day (hey, you never know; these guys are big shots), given the strength of many of the structures, all but botched by bad production and bad drumming. Even if the record is never fixed up, tracks like *Shattered* and *Rapture* would do well to show up on a live record some day, Paradise Lost finally grappling with a muse that will in the future deliver potent dungeon-brewed poison. Another **Gothic** distinction is its use of those witchy female vocals and orchestral arrangements we've all grown to love, even if they sounds stark and gimmicky, more wedged-in than blended. But Paradise Lost is nonetheless considered the pioneer of this idea, which has become widely used in the genre, all those dipsy violin and flute lessons little Helga took, paying off in ways daddy never imagined. In any event, fans of the band can have some fun with this one, but the debut, forgeddit.

Rating                                                         6

## Paradise Lost - Shades Of God   (Metal Blade '92)

**Shades Of God** represents a band chemistry still in flux, a sound still being forged. At this point, folks were at least paying attention, not sure how much of the band's ragged glory was planned and how much of it was a product of limitations. The upper crust artwork gave the signal that these Brits were going to places outside of the norm, even if they weren't quite ready yet. Songs are more complex here than future spins, perhaps the band still thinking they have something to prove. But the slightly brash production holds back the flow, more of a warm, bassy, sawed-off sound being needed to thicken the brew. But as I say, the signature sound is under full construction, and it's an exciting thing to watch, Holmes and the boys marrying death to doom with a charming disdain for cleaning up the rough edges.

Rating                                                         8

## Paradise Lost - Icon   (Music For Nations '93)

If Dio's Rainbow were stricken with **Manic Frustration**, if **The Skull** contracted the **Wolverine Blues**, if Cobain killed his band instead of himself and started hanging out with Eric Bloom, and if **Sabbath Bloody Sabbath** were to roll over in its grave, bolt up and inhale the '90s, **Icon** is the record that would rain down on thick punted heads like a wayward chunk of Soviet satellite. The grim demon spawn of dark British vibes from the early '80s, Paradise Lost, on this their fourth full album, carve a triumphant, apocalyptic scar on dark, dark metal, something I hesitate to call goth, and hesitate to call death or slow grind, a sound so rich in jet black perfection, one really can't point to '90s equivalents. Definite strains of my most complex visions of Sabbath, but also dare I say, psychic (not sonic) traces of The Cure, The Mission, Sisters Of Mercy, mere hints of the psychology these bands skirt, temporarily find (see The Cure's **The Head On The Door**) but never embrace, **Icon** in one fell swoop straining all the vile poison from years of non-metal Goth, then splashing it like acid all over their genius for doom metal drudgery. Heaving, sobbing guitars extract the souls of each tune with the steady-handed skill of Trouble, while Nick Holmes vocals reflect the new grind tendency to inflect humanity, shade, and an out-of-tune sort of chaos that heavies the mass like mercury in the blood, basically a more musical version of the Cathedral or Entombed school of thought, while not so far afield as My Dying Bride. Lyrics are thick with a particularly ancient and medieval rainbow of emo-

tion; eloquent tales painted in medium greys to dark black, the despicable deeds of man smothered under layers of slowing wattage, public service through power, soul cleansing through fervent prayer at the altar of Sabbath and that band's early disciples like Witchfinder General. Here's hoping Paradise Lost can finally get in on the commercial booty a limited few non-compromising metal acts are at least tasting (Pantera and Korn come to mind) in the wake of some big hard rock failures as of late, 'cos this is a band that has managed to sound fresh and 500 years old at the same time; serious, introspective, reflective, while laced with tantalizing but twisted heavy metal finery. A difficult, depression-celebrating experience, but one well worth the descent.
Rating                                                                    10

### Paradise Lost - Seal The Senses   (Music For Nations '94)
Only four tracks here, including two from **Icon** and an older live track, but the waves part for the stunning beauty of *Sweetness*, pretty much my favourite Paradise Lost song for ever amen. Seriously, this track is a masterpiece, shifting like the sands of time, from riff into gothic new wave, dripping poisonous melody that is all vampiric seduction, again, the band's crown jewel, and oddly enough, not included on **Draconian Times**, probably because it would have made all dozen tracks pale by comparison.
Rating                                                                    7

### Paradise Lost - The Last Time   (Music For Nations '95)
Media darlings Paradise Lost signal the impending arrival of their **Draconian Times** opus with this lavish four track EP, containing the dirt-dusted but catchy pre-single plus three that will not make the cut. *Walk Away* is a characteristic danse club macabre, a brisk, tuneful bit of fine grind too similar to title tune *The Last Time*. *Laid To Waste* and *Master Of Misrule* are a bit clunkier percussively, working that dynamic Paradise Lost schtick that has caught on with so many on the other side of the big pond.
Rating                                                                    7

### Paradise Lost - Draconian Times   (Music For Nations '95)
I've been delaying reviewing this record for months now, perplexed at whether I ride the tide of hysterical critical enthusiasm, or go with my gut and attempt articulation of my surprising and unexpected indifference. The hype for this record has been insane (like all hype), Kerrang! especially trumpeting Paradise Lost to the hills as the new Metallica. Months later, the record has still to break in America despite fall-in-line rave reviews, but sales are rumoured to be over one million in Europe, although murmurs that this is a flagrant, calculated falsehood are now making the rounds, 400,000 being offered as something closer to fact. But onto the music. **Draconian Times** is as expected, a fat, dirty, often very self-evident hybrid of increasingly traditional metal, mixed with grindcore, goth and whisper to roar dynamics. If this is the new Metallica, we're only talking about '93's lacklustre blockbuster, **Draconian Times** being simple to the point of lethargy, often crossing that line from tasteful constraint into plain. Still, no one can tug the gothic heartstrings like these boys, and when the music is reinforced by such elegant artwork, such hazy dark lyrics, and such hushed high praise from critics the world over, one can't help but lend an attentive, open ear. So I have, and am firmly enraptured by the emotion thriving within these squarely metallic, arrestingly morose tunes, even as I find myself rarely inclined to play the record, finding the band's "less is more" philosophy both a blessing and a curse. But as I say, they've captured those archaic Sabbath tones splendidly, Nick Holmes adding his uniquely out-of-tune Hetfield bark, a voice straddling suspensefully the precipice between singing and the

death metal growlies, as the guitar team of Aedy and Mackintosh pierce through their churning mud muck with those Sisters/Mission/Cult lead licks, adding that secondary new wave goth component to the prime goth of their metal. Epic vistas are attained (see *Once Solemn* and *Shadowkings*), and I stand dutifully impressed. But to knock it down a notch, my three or four favourite Paradise Lost numbers are not on this record. Hmm ...
Rating                                                                    8

### Parasite - Parasite   (Banzai '84)
Scandinavian Euro-depression with a blistering recording (from the always capable Sword Records), Parasite shows Gravestone-like promise on this four cut EP of Accept-ish generalities, a calling card that headbangs along tightly, while lacking range in the vocal department.
Rating                                                                    5

### Paw - Dragline   (A&M '93)
Proving that goodly grunge doesn't have to hail from the land of lumber, Paw padded into your living room after hasty conception, assemblage, the efficient woodshedding of a life of toons, and the quaffing of a few dozen cold beers before the proverbial bidding war that saw the band ink on with A&M. Totally worthy of your attention, **Dragline** is an instant sludge rock success; loose, stringy, in no hurry to follow rules, just stout power-riffing from under the porch, slack, almost careless vocals and hilariously inter-twined shafts of rootsy melody that sink like a big ol' chair much like the heady highs from old Soul Asylum. Thick pools of good tidings form around this record. But make no mistake: it pulverizes, although it's a kind of happy beating; total guitar savagery, with a powerful but rough-shod mix that slurs and swirls everything into a thick mashing glue, threatening to smother hooks that slip sanded-down through tunes almost unnoticed, bisecting Neil Young's amplified zone at its rustiest and lustiest. No point highlighting certain tracks, 'cos this is one sodbuster you just let rumble and ramble. Down-home wattage from the farm, evoking the smell of firecrackers the night before Halloween.
Rating                                                                    10

### Paw - Death To Traitors   (A&M '95)
That cover shot of stampeding horses was pretty much how I envisioned this band's wondrous debut. But **Death To Traitors** could only be a let-down, and it is, but not a disaster. The present record can be summed up quite accurately as a very similar spin, with a considerably mellower batch of songs, less of **Dragline**'s grit and blood, more of a straight-line roots rock record. And the critical community jumped all over its light touch, pining for those slash and burn power chords of old, finding this just unaggressive. I still absolutely cherish this band's sound and chemistry, not to mention their integrity in terms of not giving into the odd flip occurrence of heaviness as more commercially viable these days than safe melodies. More spaces, a bit of rehash (title track), and a whole mountain of heart, **Death To Traitors** still manages to scratch out a comforting homestead of its own, one with brisk fresh air, wide-open skies and earnest old rock values. It's a shame more people didn't get it.
Rating                                                                    8

### Pearl Jam - Ten   (Sony '91)
So what ultimately is the power of **Ten** that causes it to cling like a bulldog to the charts, not to mention its racking of sales dangerously close to the ten million mark and counting? Well it's probably something to do with its power to hold one's gaze. Not a particularly heavy record, nor particularly grungy, **Ten** (Named for NBA star Mookie Blaylock's number; Mookie Blaylock

being an early name of the band.) has almost become a flashpoint for Generation X'ers; shiftless, aimless and functionless, shaking on the edge of breakdown just like Eddie Vedder and his twisted smile, moving slowly and dream-like past the chains of circumstance of a world that seems to work only for others. Thus Pearl Jam somehow strikes a chord with a not so accessible album, one that's downright confused, loosely wound and noisy despite its hollow nature; by definition echoey. And the hits kept coming: *Even Flow*, *Alive*, *Jeremy*, all fairly hopeless, anything but alive, sounding sorry and uncomfortable amongst other chartables parading through the airwaves. All in all, despite its despondence, **Ten** shimmers with dynamic, intelligence and esoterica, all taking turns at centre stage in widening arcs of hypnotic swami-ness. The undisputed sales king of the Seattle set, **Ten**, like **Nevermind**, helped render terms like "alternative" near meaningless, proving the public's capacity for challenge, offering a fairly enigmatic and thorny experience, something alternately whispery and out of control, yet always sort of helpless. Probably the first Northwest rocker without any degree of shock value or flash, **Ten** just stops and thinks in a Seattle summer rain.

Rating        9

## Pearl Jam - Vs.   (Sony '93)

Probably my favorite recorded experience of all freakin' '93, **Vs.** was a masterpiece of pacing and all out wonderment; tune, tone, lyric and drum propelled forth with infernal and infinite purpose, establishing Pearl Jam as the biggest rock band in the world bar none, despite what scattered pockets of belly-achers in the press might begrudge them. Are they a retro '70s band, a sell-out, or true alternative champions? Hell, who cares when so much decade-straddling rock is just wound so beautifully? **Vs.** is simply an expertly eclectic mix of perfect songs, songs that skirt all sorts of genres like Zep acoustic (*Daughter*), like punk (*Go*), like heavy 'n' slack REM (*Glorified G*), and like, the most moving, spirit-cleansing choruses all year, *Rearviewmirror* and *Leash*. But above all, there is that sense of vanguard greatness, of music that is wrenched down on tape, blinding integrity carved so deeply (all this corporate rock talk slagging of the band by Cobain at the time baffles me, really), I just wanna bow and bellow "we're not worthy!" Rolling Stone made the interesting observation that the record is propelled most remarkably by Dave Abbruzzese's drums, and I'd have to agree, the boy almost left to his raw devices no matter the decibel level, always sounding live and boomy, again purposeful. And Eddie is again the captivating master of edge, especially on *Go* and the immense *Rearviewmirror*, where his sense of psychic scarring is both frightening and a balm on the sores of others. *Rats* and *W.M.A.* are kinda boring, although the latter sports a pretty cool lyrical theme, but the rest is swirling, sweaty, urgent and wise; rock divinely created in The Lonely Pocket, like a Zep record or like those dizzying U2 records from the '80s, unlike anything by the fake-ass alterno-rock scene of today. So maybe all that retro talk might apply, 'cos we have to dip way back to find the last truly amazing gathering of artists willing to work with the medium of rock music. Fine. So be it.

Rating        10

## Pearl Jam - Vitalogy   (Sony '94)

Well a lot of funky Pearl Jam news and thankfully not a lot of time has passed since the awesome **Vs.** experience that crowned 1993. We became glued to our radios for rumours of Eddie flipping out after Kurt Cobain's early checkout, valiant much-needed exposure of Ticketmaster's monopolistic pomposity (I think their "service" is a cruel joke at best), and the re-erection of The Wall, the one between the band and the press, who strangely seem to have upset the band by

over-praising them. Then out poops **Vitalogy**, the band's new record, at times rumoured to be called Life or just Pearl Jam, but alas **Vitalogy**, based on some quacky science from medical eras goneby. I bought the advance vinyl, the band turning champion of the undead format, penning lead single *Spin The Black Circle* (an annoying, sub-par thrashpunk tune) in celebration of all things not '90s. How's the music? Well, consider **Vitalogy** an unshaved, unshowered collection of **Vs.** out-takes, with true eeks-and-bleeps garbage thrown in in the form of sound segments between tracks that often aren't consequential enough to make up for the punishing interludes. The record's darker musically than **Vs.**, which is to say, less melodic and less enjoyable, although not really heavier, just nastier. Lyrically it's thicker and more fragged, thematically no more noble than its predecessor, but more subconscious, dreamy and cryptic. But all in all, I find it rushed, cantankerous and almost contemptuous of quality or value, coming to blazing levels of life only with side two's *Satan's Bed*, *Better Man* and the record's most spiritually uplifting pair of chords, *Corduroy*. The next level down, four or five tracks live and breathe unremarkably, but Pearl Jam all the same, tunes just wide-open and digestible enough to worm their way into your playlist over the coming months, because, hey, what else you got? This stuff's real and deliberate, even though it's kinda flip. Not a complete mess, but damn near half a mess, we are nevertheless lucky Pearl Jam make their music at all.

Rating        8

## Pearl Jam - No Code   (Sony '96)

With very little hype, the world's biggest band just hunkered the bunker and bashed out the sprawl of **No Code**, a record as alien yet comfortable as **Vitalogy**, but infused with a sort of excitement at all things homemade. There's a bunch of nature in this thing, a gritty Neil Youth, especially on the '60s luv of *Red Mosquito* and the obviously Crazy Horsed *Smile*. Twisted dabbles unto punk continue with *Lukin*, the Ramonesy *Mankind*, and the smart shocked *Habit*, while *Hail, Hail* is almost metal. Through all the heroics, there's still an opacity that will make real assimilation slow and arduous, Vedder and crew pretty much unconcerned with earnest social interaction at this point. I mean, without being weird, **No Code**'s lyrics speak of things, situations and emotions that are so inner circle, that the inevitable blank stares give the mosh an eerie overtone. I find this to be pretty much Pearl Jam's most enigmatic record, sort of lo-fi, but subtly arranged, grease-monkeyed but flown to the heights of artsy. So adding it up (this record begs a judicious note-taking), odd little tales are jarred straight by these garagey but mature, superstar punk numbers; experiments in liquid mood music and swami rock (especially sublime and beautiful first single *Who You Are*: influence courtesy Vedder's work with Nusrat Fateh Ali Khan) shoved into agitated wakefulness by powerful spontaneous (sounding) rants that work (but of course). And if that don't float it, there are two variations on the lullaby to send you back into the dream world these guys can own if they want. Innovative packaging features fold-out digi-pak format with a cardboard envelope containing varying collections of "snapshot" cards (lyrics on the back). We're all supposed to get in our PJs and trade them with the also-enlightened or something. Word has it they were a royal pain to assemble, having to be hand-collated into place. But hey, this is important work.

Rating        9

## Penance - The Road Less Travelled   (Rise Above '92)

Mike Smail's doom machine Penance were quite ahead of their time with this stretchy blubberfest, **The Road Less Travelled** being one of the early offerings from

Lee Dorrian's Rise Above label, Dorrian being a fan, even using Smail for some Cathedral work. And Smail being a drummer, the drums are crushingly loud and innovatively recorded, dominating the plodded chord patterns to the point of distraction. Still, this is almost psychedelic doom, given all the spacey spaces. Bottom line: vapoured vistas achieved.

Rating     6

## Penance - Parallel Corners   (Century Media '94)

Massive woofer-sodomizing bassquakes from Pennsylvania of all places, are now emanating forth in waves of ferry-sinking undulation. For ye repent ye hear, if you're hearing hasn't yet forsaken you forever. Penance rocks mightily enough to gather in black under the leaden wings of Cathedral, Lee Dorrian offering these total doom contenders much Sabbatherian guidance and rich tidings. Fact be, this record powderizes Cathedral as of late, storming them at their own game, growing this very current, slow turbine doom sound slightly ethereal and peaceville, somewhat like Entombed meets drugs but with less grind-gutted vocals. Picture Cathedral's breathtaking **Soul Sacrifice** EP with a voice plus an eccentric touch of The Obsessed and **The Skull**-era Trouble (some of this record backtracking in velocity a mite often for my liking). But man, I just eat this stuff up when it sidesteps boredom, which **Parallel Corners** does deviously, even the mellow moments wallowing in true psychedelic creepiness rather than monster rock cheese. Total gem of Birmingham pork-past-expiry metal, descended lovingly intact from Ozzy and his quad of sub-cycle hippy-slaying casualties.

Rating     9

## Pennywise - Full Circle   (Epitaph '97)

Pennywise are often billed as the next '90s punk band to break (along with Face To Face and Rancid). And their sound is sunny, high-octane and always strangely motivating, Jim and Co. racing through these short tales of hard-of-hearing heart with lots of drum rolls, strum rolls and diddly bass lines. Singing is often just that, the shouty stuff kept to a minimum, perhaps working against the band in retention of street credo. Too bad, 'cos this is just the kind of punk that is worth digesting, more positively energized than violently gutchecked. Pure, tightly -packed pop punk, no worries, no fat.

Rating     7

## Pentagram - Be Forewarned   (Fierce '95)

Recording very sporadically since their inception in 1971 (this is their first full-length since '87's **Day Of Reckoning**), Pentagram have miraculously entered the mid-'90s original line-up intact, like a doom behemothra cockroach that will not die. And that is this brooding act's forte, a sludgy underground doom metal that necessarily derives from Sabbath, driving through St. Vitus, The Obsessed, Trouble and Cathedral, into a sound that is somewhat a mini-trend these days. Pentagram ride the eccentricity line well, creaking and thumping towards the garagier end of this cloak and dagger genre; stiff pounding, good clear vocals, songs that dress up just far enough. The result: dirt, greaseball and bikechain for the the goth metal moat, low on awesome craft, high on attitude. All hail the apocalypse, for this blows stuff like Sleep and Count Raven out of the swamp.

Rating     8

## Perpetua - Irrational   (Pavement '96)

One hopes Argentina's Perpetua can follow Seputura's lead out of South America's pretty low-key metal scene, and break it big stateside. **Irrational** is a worthy first step, combining a death heft out of Sepultura's **Arise** era with cutting edge industrial scrapes, bumps and bruises, wrapping it all in a wall of uncompromising grime grind. Lyrically, it's typical South American political analysis, Perpetua railing against corruption in lizard-throated gasps of contusion, moving forward towards the millennium as a plausible competitor to similar well-positioned bands from frozen Scandinavian soils. Multi-shifting, mix-it-up death metal; better than decent, but a little too hardcore for my geriatric tastes.

Rating     7

## The Joe Perry Project - Let The Music Do The Talking   (CBS '80)

With Aerosmith on the rocks, Joe breaks up the Toxic Twins turbulent relationship, assembling this exceedingly buoyant debut project (to pay off his considerable debts), which essentially adds up to a stiffer Aerosmith record with a greater emphasis on both control and funkiness, yet still exuding tons of warmth and larger-than-life riffery. The album takes off in fine style with the stirring title track, which just flies groove-wise, cruising much smoother than the Aerosmith rendition would two years later. Other distinguished rockers include lustrous boogie stormer Conflict Of Interest and heroic metal cruncher Shooting Star. Threshold bar none however is side two's The Mist Is Rising, a hypnotic plodder with a sinister riff that just tears into a fat, elevated chorus, perpetuating this record's higher plane intensity. All is not devastation however, given a fair dose of off-the-cuff funk which although not particularly to my liking, fits nicely within the framework of Perry's mindscape re: Aerosmith skank such as Last Child and Sight For Sore Eyes. I always liked this record for its multi-paced dynamics and Perry's eccentric and hyper interpretations of the blues. On top of all the academics nonetheless, **Let The Music Do The Talking** is an effortlessly listenable good time. As fine and as connecting as any single Aerosmith record.

Rating     10

## The Joe Perry Project - I've Got The Rock'n'Rolls Again   (CBS '81)

Not content with making electrified solo versions of Aerosmith records, Perry switches gears, creating a righteous chaotic noise that rings in the ears weeks after disembarking. Whether slumming most heavily, or slinking around real bluesy-like, Perry and his assembled mechanics bang on everything in sight on this industrial onslaught, recorded not unlike Zep - **Presence**, although considerably more caffeinated and disheveled. Not that it'll level Dismember or anything, but this is one loud destructive jam. The four heaviest tunes, East Coast, West Coast, Soldier Of Fortune, South Station Blues, and the title track are absolute sweat-drenched heft rockers, especially the manic title wrench, a rumbling, thrashing metallic blues monster that is without reservation Perry's wildest romp. All in all, a thoroughly brash and grimy display of roots that creaks and groans with paid-per-dues authenticity. Miles from the sheen of the debut, but less brilliant riff-wise, **I've Got The Rock'n'Rolls Again** nevertheless packs its own formidable piece. Tidbit 1: ditzy sleaze booger Buzz Buzz was originally written and recorded by this record's bassist David Hull with his old band Dirty Angels. Tidbit 2: stiffed compared to the relative quarter million copy success of the debut.

Rating     8

## The Joe Perry Project - Once A Rocker Always A Rocker   (MCA '83)

In which Joe Perry engineers one of the most bizarre twists of r'n'r fate, assembling the weirdest looking band of funk dudes in search of an eclectic, almost intentionally chaotic, untuneful garage blues/metal mongrel. **Once A Rocker** is a confusing, unpalatable dose of skronk, full of epileptic, strained seizures like a random cutting room floor paste-up of Aerosmith's most Jagger-ed, failed experiments. For the most part, it's pretty interesting, at least on side one, and occasionally really decadent and sassy, as on the slippery *Black Velvet Pants* and the Johnny Thunders-style *Women In Chains*. Joe definitely shows his predilection for the convoluted funkiness that gave birth to so many famous Aerosmith riffs, but here it's just eccentric and difficult for difficult's sake. The nightclub album.

Rating                                                                4

### Persian Risk - Rise Up   (Metal Masters '86)

Looks much scuzzier than it is, but still Persian Risk are a grimy British variation on Dokken, a little more desperate and claustrophobic, and not so definable, looking pub-deep and speedy much more readily than Don's long-unplugged hair machine. Strong vocals, steady harmonies, but unfortunately the potential for ultra-cruise is considerably chopped at the kneecaps by the loud and over-exuberant drama, demonstrating that this band hasn't quite got the corporate Californian mindset they're after down pat. Classy album cover.

Rating                                                                5

### Pet Hate - The Bride Wore Red   (Heavy Metal '84)

Sort of out on their own in the early days of poverty metal, Pet Hate's sleazy street rock won some acclaim by avoiding the trappings and overall scurry of traditional shoot 'em up, leather and chains metal combos at the time. Their totally Hanoi Rocks feel showed promise, but never quite left the ground, due to a stiff, plodding song list, sabotaged by a blocky percussive performance over uni-speed marches, a situation that begins to sound nice and comfortable by side two's *The Party's Over* and a welcome cover of *Roll Away The Stone*, where Al does an uncanny Ian Hunter. In fact, side two's kind of a groundbreaker, revealing a risky band not without cool ideas, off on Mars with an oxygenated flat right next door to McCoy and Monroe. Production's a bit crunchy, and Al's vocals are mixed too far back, but otherwise a fresh albeit grimly low income stance that could have bore fruit had it left metal even more boldly and confidently.

Rating                                                                5

### Pet Hate - Bad Publicity   (Heavy Metal '84)

One of a scant few NWOBHM outfits that chased neither goth 'n' gloom nor prissy AOR, Pet Hate was after a stripped Kiss-type sound with shades of Hanoi Rocks, sort of a street scum version of plain guitar-driven rock, through this record and their more spontaneous predecessor, **The Bride Wore Red**. The proceeds don't really strike stride until the fourth toon, a cool 'n' luded cover of the Stones' *Street Fighting Man*. After that, the party begins to achieve that play-stupid-on-purpose nostalgia with Ace/Kiss glamster *She's Got The Action*, the poppier *Stale Lipstick*, and the steely-eyed *Wreck The Radio*. **Bad Publicity** might have succeeded given deeper, sludgier mix and more adventuresome, drunken performances from the individual dudes. But, the band would break up shortly after this second effort, lead guy, Alistair Terry (who once rented downstairs from me here in T.O.) moving on to a poppy solo album that **Kerrang!** gave 3 1/2 K's.

Rating                                                                4

### Phantom Blue - Built To Perform   (Geffen '93)

Man, or should I say, ladies, this thing smokes! Quite ignored at the time, this five-piece chick band is probably the best female band to have ever graced the world of heavy metal. Although the record-buying rabble was probably turned off by the sad (albeit tongue in cheek) fromage of the cover graphics, they ended up missing a heart-stopping festival of timeless

metal riffs, strong, passionate vocals, solos that would blow yer head off, and an octane-generatin' version of Lizzy's *Bad Reputation*. And them solos and riffs are quite astonishing really, both functions melding Dokken, Sykes, Schenker, and a host of wily metal greats; cutting clean and thoughtful the great songs on which they're intelligently draped. Indeed Marty Friedman and John Norum contribute here, although it's evidently Michelle Meldrum and Karen Kreutzer who churn the sweat, blood and sonics. All I can say is WOW, the girls know how to rock it with class.

Rating                                                                8

### Phantom Lord - Phantom Lord   (Pentagram '85)

German plonk with a cruddy mix but youthful Metallica-inspired (that was easy) exuberance. Can appreciate the vintage thrash unto OTT spiked mash and drooling titles like *Live Fast*, *Rock Hard*, *Mad Bash* and *Fight The Thunder*, but would never, ever, under any circumstances play it again.

Rating                                                                3

### Phantoms Of The Future - Call Of The Wild
(Sony Germany '95)

Man, sometimes I feel like a figure skating judge, lopping off a couple marks when a performer hasn't paid his or her dues yet. And this is one of those cases, **Call Of The Wild** being a perlexed and wonderful amalgam of sounds, unfairly diminished by the fact that I know nothing about its maker. This is all about creativity, Phantoms Of The Future creating a sky-high fidelity feast that combines everything from phat metal grooves to world music to Peter Gabriel to Faith No More and Saigon Kick, loaded up with innovations, brilliantly interwoven by producer Siggi Bemm. Sir Hannes Smith's vocals are an acquired taste, something almost Francis Dunnery-like but with ironic parody (!), like these guys are weary of 57 channels and nothing on, crammed full of culture and expunging it with a mix of cynicism and voracious appetite for more. Highly inventive, while each track's deck of invention is subjugated to a sturdy all-knowing sense of song.

Rating                                                                9

### Picture - Picture   (Backdoor '80)

An early purveyor of the swinging metal groove, Holland's Picture emerged on the scene as a viable big-beating metal act combining party power with a strongman's Teutonic core. Their disposition was ever so right, but the band wouldn't deliver the bacon 'til record #3, this debut clunking along loosely with foreign-sounding vocals and questionable production to boot.

Rating                                                                4

### Picture - Heavy Metal Ears   (Backdoor '81)

Not to be confused with the Canadian compilation of the same stupid name, **Heavy Metal Ears** is Picture's sophomore effort, plagued with much the same lack of focus and exposed separation of instrumentation that made the debut such a bush-league non-entity. Simply a band recording before its time. Occasionally enjoyable dual axe pyro, but betraying its lack of experience, Picture was nevertheless a puzzle piece integral to metal's early uh, picture.

Rating                                                                4

### Picture - Diamond Dreamer   (Backdoor '82)

A deafening hunk of shrapnel for the Year of our Lord 1982, **Diamond Dreamer** shines with surprise lustre, this from a bunch of Euro unknowns, aided by the woofer-blowing grandeur of producer Pete Hinton, who grafts heroic chunk-sized riffs to spacious percussive reclines and oddly Coverdale-like vocals. Hints of Accept, flatliner Priest, and vintage Scorpions combine for a purist metal feast evoking solid universal appeal.

A band that should have gone farther given their grasp of the traditional, decibel-drenched brainshake.
Rating **8**

## Picture - Eternal Dark (Backdoor '83)

Picture's heat-treated smoker ascends from the boiling depths, packing a malevolent punch as the unforgiven ones adopt a darker image and pulverizing aggression to match. Pete Hinton again cooks the sound, letting the low frequencies have their wanton way with our heavy metal ears on such cold, German-style artillery as *Make You Burn*, *Into The Underworld*, *Down And Out*, and personal fave *Griffons Guard The Gold*. Again the band does what they do best, chugging mid-tempo riffery, expertly maneuvered down the Autobahn of underground metal. Haulin' ass with class, and wholly deserving of punter respect, **Eternal Dark** is Picture in full splendor, cranking an attack reverent of metal's best of the late '70s and early '80s, for a proudly European updates on the updates.
Rating **8**

## Picture - Heavy Metal Ears (Phonogram '84)

Billed as a collection of the band's "greatest hits", **Heavy Metal Ears** is an ill-conceived North American marketing move on behalf of the band, serving only to confuse a potential Canadian fanbase who weren't really paying attention anyways. Side one is exactly half of **Eternal Dark**, while side two cherry picks from a dodgy, uneven past.
Rating **5**

## Picture - Traitor (Phonogram '85)

**Traitor**'s arrangements and general professionalism emulate **Eternal Dark**, but the riffs are dogs, giving birth to a litter of lacklustre songs that try to bridge too many styles: traces of scary goth, barroom metal, American hard rock, OTT, and even a murky funkiness as evidenced on *State Of Shock*. While Tony van den Bremer's production sounds muscular and expensive, it tends to cloud the issue on the better riffs, while pounding duds like *Loud 'n Proud* into the thumpa thumpa scrapheap, as the band tries to force a party topspin onto their rusty metallic hulk. Simply a ploy for commercial acceptance, but ultimately a futile one, as this band has proven themselves to be too hopelessly metal-encrusted to switch gears with so little forethought. And the boys still can't dress themselves, although the front cover at least brings them up a notch.
Rating **5**

## Piece Dogs - Exes For Eyes (Energy '92)

A bit of a gem, **Exes For Eyes** evoked a heavy, committed straight-faced metal somewhere between Skid Row, Anthrax, Love/Hate, Anthrax and The Organization, Piece Dogs enlisting the Perialas/Wacko Hunter team to beat us about the face, neck, head, arms and chest, while axe-exactor Mike Grimmett parlays a collection of tidy, t-riffic behemoths into the heady metal headbang zone. Check out *Who's Got It* and *Devil Dog* for the quality songcraft this unsung band was capable of, Piece Dogs dishing out a hi-fidelity serving of metal dude metal, street-wise in look, but professional stern to bow.
Rating **8**

## Pig - Sinsation (Nothing/Interscope '96)

Signed to Trent Reznor's vanity label, Pig slot nicely between NIN and Marilyn Manson, this vehicle for former KMFDMer often sounding like soundtrack music, often sounding like the scary, scratchy, morose trancebeats White Zombie and Marilyn have turned into radio and video fodder. I found myself intrigued by the sandpapered dreamscapes, and annoyed by the attempts at song, Watts just pulling the ol' menacing

psycho-ward man vs. machine whinery with which most other dudes in this format seem to identify all to readily. Lots of chopped up pig graphics and no lyrics. Tis a shame, since the vocals are well nigh incoherent, not to mention monotoned, over-treated and consequently tiring.
Rating **5**

## Pike - Lack Of Judgement (Black Mark '96)

Mathematically, this looks good, Pike grab-bagging diverse influences such as Pantera (well, more like Dianno's Killers), Meshuggah, Faith No More, Korn and Galactic Cowboys. But the end result is a loose, chaotic miasma of nothingness, Pike ultimately sounding like generalist grunge-delivered power metal. Other annoyances: buzzy bass, pointless weird jazzy passages and a snare drum tuned way too tight.
Rating **6**

## Piledriver - Metal Inquisition (Cobra '84)

More a business venture than a band, Piledriver was a management brainchild that enlisted one Gord Kirchin (soon to be ripped off despite his good work) for the role of "Pile Driver", lead throat for an extreme Toronto metal machine of the same name. Seen for the flagrant commercial scheme it was, the band was summarily laughed out of existence, but not before spawning two seminal OTT records in the vacant mid-'80s. This, the band's debut was surprisingly more studied than the cheezy cover art would suggest, being a rousing, drunken romp through inspired shock rock terrain, lyrically studded with black metal stupidity that is more or less excused for its suitability with the garagey metallic energy shaking the rafters. Fact is, **Metal Inquisition** kicks ass, driven by more than acceptable playing and production, with a general "level the place" sweat ethic that has the hired guns thrashing through putrid swamps of metal like thirst-crazed soldiers searching for a hidden still. Sure it's funny as hell, but after a few swigs of fortified elixir, it all begins to make sense.
Rating **7**

## Piledriver - Stay Ugly (Cobra '86)

More a heads-down blitzcake than the smelly debut, **Stay Ugly** is an abbreviated speed metal obliteration of all that breathes, as Kirchin growls above a moshable wall of waves that finds no less than five of only seven cuts (plus one intro) assuming near identical blur, each track demarcated by only minor variations in riff, and killer solo butcherings from lead axeman Bruizer Bernette, not to be confused with Carol Burnette or Fleetwood Mac guitarist Billy Burnette. A sustained frothing-at-the-mouth mania makes **Stay Ugly** an enjoyable debacle despite its unambitious samey-ness, although it's becoming readily apparent that if you weren't on board already, this won't make a fan of you now.
Rating **7**

## Pink Cream 69 - Change (Epic '95)

And **Change** they did, these quite popular and well-regarded Germans tossing the towel on three records of clean, good-natured pop metal and diving into crunchy, Seattle-ish power bulldozing, while still retaining their knack for addictive hook. Biggest leap forward is the addition of an American on vocals, a wise move after the defection of Andi Deris to a crowningly rejuvenated Helloween. Nice star quality to this as each track goes to charming places, from balladry to grunge while keeping it clear and simple. reminds me of funlovers Terrorvision from Britain, only heavier.
Rating **7**

## Pink Fairies - What A Bunch Of Sweeties (Polydor '72)

I actually groove crusty-eyed to this one at a higher elevation than the less rare **Kings Of Oblivion** record, **What A Bunch Of Sweeties** still shaking the vestiges of psychedelia, truly winged on a tab of Zappa, even though the guitars are turned up vaingloriously. The whole thing rolls like a big fat joint, electrics slaying the garage dragon, no brains, all burned-up and breaking the windows in some sort of metallic hootenany jamboree in the woods. Totally has no clue, which is kinda nice in these modern dog-days of perfection.
Rating                                              6

## Pink Fairies - Kings Of Oblivion (Polydor '73)

Rock journalists who attempt to fake their way through a knowledge of the noise that binds usually cite this power trio as one of the originals of metal, along with Blue Cheer, MC5, and The Stooges, none of which really meant to pursue metal or understood what the coolest sound in the world would require. Larry Wallis went on to serve time as a short-lived member of Motörhead, bringing with him the inconsequential *City Kids*; and Mick Farren is also mixed up with Lemmy somehow. In any event, **Kings Of Oblivion** (at least the band's second after **What A Bunch Of Sweeties**) is basically noise-clogged, hippy guitar rock that is more or less an unpainted, top-heavy vase to Hawkwind's spinning lump of collapsed clay. Punky, loose, and hopelessly underwater. Lone semi-nugget of wisdom: *Chambermaid*.
Rating                                              2

## The Pink Fairies - Kill 'Em & Eat 'Em (Demon '87)

Fourteen years hence, and they still can't sing, play or mix a presentable slab. Still sounds like Motörhead's first record, only with less rivet mash, and this time around, they're even more the novelty act, which is easy to buy, given the obvious lack of concern for quality. I'm probably missing the deeper relevance of The Pink Fairies here but who cares. They suck. More biscuits this time due to scant and fleeting traces of a grimy good time amidst a surprisingly late '70s punk feel. Plus more songs.
Rating                                              4

## Piper - Piper (A&M '76)

This early vehicle for Billy Squier was very much hyped as the next Kiss, much in the same manner as contemporaries Angel and Starz (Starz, Piper and Kiss were all Aucoin Management acts). Of course all got snappy logos! But Piper was much more the enigma, brewing a sort of overwrought emotion, reminiscent of some glam, some Queen and some Journey, in a way, previewing the poppier aspects of new wave circa the early '80s. A lot of depth here, in terms of arrangements, different guitar styles, and the band's five-fold vocal ability, making Piper one '70s "hard rock" act that stands up. Not exactly metal of any era, but tons of layered, very electric, very Sweet guitars. Heaviest tunes are the last on the record, *42nd Street* and *Can't Live With Ya/Can't Live Without Ya*. Worst: a cover of *The Last Time* by the Stones.
Rating                                              7

## Piper - Can't Wait (A&M '77)

. . . and like Starz with **Attention Shoppers!** in '78, Piper opt for soft rock, still delivering passion, loose and lush, while a fair dose mellower than the innocent exuberance of the debut, really sounding like prime Journey. And the packaging enforces this stratagem, photos portraying the band in embarrassingly feminine poses and postures. A guilty pop pleasure that goes a lot of brave places.
Rating                                              7

## Pist-On - Number One (Fierce '96)

Packed and sod-busted with distortion, this well-conceived debut from Brooklyn's Pist-On is a sort of hardcore, street-level slam with hooks and patient, whisper-to-roar vocals. Produced by Type O Negative's Josh Silver, **Number One** does indeed reflect the ponderous moods of Type O at times. But have no fear, these respites don't really last, as the band is more into churning power chords than funereal keyboards. Guitar tones are vast and many, and songs are simple enough to breathe and leave. There's even a death metal cover of The Smiths' *Shoplifters Of The World Unite* to keep one guessing.
Rating                                              7

## Pitch Shifter - Submit (Earache '92)

Even for its age, **Submit** is quite the hair-blazing piece of industrial metal, clanking like a Big Black Albini-smoke belching factory of heavy water sonics, these Nottingham nutcases marching onto Earache (after an ill-fated debut for Peaceville), ready to squalidly dirty fight with the gobbing likes of Fudge Tunnel and Godflesh. But the spoken croaken portion of the show is grindcore all the way, making sure no puff of the pollution gets above vibrating sub-cycle, the whole sinister burning mess roiling like a tank through a steel mill. A filmy, bad-mooded sort of appreciation wafts forth.
Rating                                              6

## Pitch Shifter - "desensitized" (Earache '93)

"desensitized" cages a sort of rumbling Ministry **Filth Pig** vibe with less electronics, more purpose; big, meaty walls of sound based on repetitious cavebanger riffs, roarcore vocals and predictable samples. But the attack's force seems blunted by a mix that is short on treble, all quirks and soundbites smothered, resulting in a pounding, ponderous tedium. Hey but still, a few more aggressive tracks like these might have looked mighty fine on NIN's **The Downward Spiral**. No more accessible than **Submit**, in fact miserably identical, but oddly pleasing in its grating charm.
Rating                                              6

## Pitch Shifter - The Remix War (Earache '94)

Earache is right, as Pitch Shifter take a few of their butt-ugly songs and do a sort of Mike Watt wrestling record, inviting a few of the band's fellow tour warriors to twist, renovate and enervate a few choice ditties. Seven cruddy cranks demonstrating the evil genius remix skills, bells and whistles of Gunshot, Biohazard, Therapy? and uh, Pitch Shifter themselves. Three versions of *Triad* and two of *Diable*. Truthfully, I'd wish this remix craze would just die.
Rating                                              4

## Pitch Shifter - Infotainment? (Earache '96)

It's been a long, slumbering wait for the new Pitch Shifter opus, and the day of reckoning has arrived, these UK decoys pumped and primed to assault our minds and bodies with political terrorism we'd all wish would just stay in the desert, the jungles or the inner city. The most shocking and refreshing thing about **Infotainment?**'s roiling, braying rock crunch is not its crowning cynicism, but its complex, smartly layered hip hop beats, an infotaining bed on which to stack newly engaging riffs, rants and poly-decibels, Pitch Shifter catapulting themselves into the forefront of industrial, finding a type of snobs-accepted accessibility, while still slobbering with thick punkmetal tar, nicotine and bile. Intellectual, anti-social metal dirtballs like *Underachiever* and *Phoenixology* are balanced with the new rhythms of tracks like *(We're Behaving Like) Insects* and *Whiteout*, all the while J.S. Clayden delivering messages of distrust and disgust with you and your stinking world that make you want to shape up or ship out everybody you loathe and all their relatives. Tracks 11 and 12 are samples designed for your sorry band to take, use, and abuse, just like Pitch Shifter has so many times before. This is also a philosophical statement, from this band known to call us all on our questionable morals.

Rating **8**

## Planet Hate - Mother Are You Mad?  (Energy '94)

Planet Hate seem poised to excel amongst the angry GenX bunch blowing through blustery moral enviro-core to strong effect. This cleverly packaged disc (see Danzig 4) rocks thickly with confidence, backing up a set of lyrics that is inspiring towards good, inspiring towards good literature. Shouty-face vocals from Michael Caronia lead the square-headed cause, as the band welts a rhythmic scar across inhospitable landscapes that court Biohazard, and maybe even M.O.D., yet with more love and hope than most bands of the bludgeon set. Cool act, and maybe one that can take metal into an alterna-responsible realm, bringing up the under-rear behind Megadeth. Catchy, moshy and heavy.

Rating **7**

## Robert Plant - Pictures At Eleven  (Swan Song/Atlantic '82)

Robert "Percy" Plant, fairly well-known crooner for the pop combo known as Led Zeppelin, returns to the fold in robust fashion, forced into a re-evaluation of his place on earth and his future contributions thereof, after the shocking demise of life-long friend John Bonham, and the necessary termination of the crazy-huge band they built. The resulting record, **Pictures At Eleven** is a fat feast of sounds that half the time sticks to glorious Zep-like machinations, and half the time strikes out, exploiting Plant's love of the new music around him, his tricky funk, his dramatic blues, and both his flip and serious forays into wholly new hybrids of expression. Along for all the explorations are bassist Paul Martinez, keyboardist Jezz Woodroffe, plus notable drummers Cozy Powell (who offers his usual blocky simplicity; see Slow Dancer) and Phil Collins (who adds shade and percussive wit, if there can be such a thing). But Plant's main trump card is guitarist Robbie Blunt, an old blues-steep warhorse (Michael Des Barres' Silverhead and others) who has become for this record the epitome of eastern influences mixed with traditional bluesy balladry, basically beating Page at Pagey's game. His solos are lush, exotic, worldly and eminently memorable (again, proceed to big Zep-style showstopper Slow Dancer, the delectable Like I've Never Been Gone and Moonlight In Samosa). I mean, this man's contribution here, dare I say, might be more substantial and impressionable than Page's on any one record. But not everything is a success on **Pictures At Eleven**, sometimes the drums overwhelming the thin, jammy arrangements, as on Worse Than Detroit, Pledge Pin and Mystery Title. Add to this a seriously brash, almost erroneous recording, and you've got a record that can be cold and clattery quite often. Still, just the right balance of fresh and traditional; building on Plant's and Zeppelin's strengths, while kicking up an eccentric dust.

Rating **8**

## Robert Plant - The Principle Of Moments
(Atlantic '83)

Alas, Robert Plant builds his blinding work of genius. A tantalizing showcase for the senses, **The Principle Of Moments** offers singular masterpiece after masterpiece, the band crafting each track with blunt, sparse tooling, leaving open vistas, shade, and exotic sights and sounds in its wondrous wake. Again Plant's lyrics are unremarkable really, or maybe just not showy, and his voice simply can't convincingly handle the high notes. But his singing is superb, using his tighter range

like a low tidal ebb, the man simply steering his pipes like a ship following shore lights. Again Robbie Blunt is easily half the show, all sinewy, crystal clear; eastern-flavoured runs, smooth, quiet but determined. Plus Phil Collins works a sublime brilliance that is his best performance on record as far as I'm concerned. I saw this album's tour. Collins was a monster live, maybe the best marriage of sheer enjoyability and technical expertise I'd ever witnessed in a concert setting. Also of note, Jethro Tull's Barriemore Barlow drums on Stranger Here . . . Than Over There plus the difficult and dark Wreckless Love, effortlessly matching the overall cohesive and restrained mood of Collins. And the record's unsurpassable quality was rewarded with commercial success, the gorgeous In The Mood (one of my favourite songs EVER; so smart and simple, it's hysterical) and mystical mantra-like romance Big Log scoring as major, well-deserving hits, while the fussy Egypto-funk of Other Arms and swimmingly swimming drums-as-lead ballad Thru' With The Two Step continue to be regular grist for classic rock radio now and probably forever. All in all, everything on this record just points to an intense distillation of your most magic and cherished, mellow Led Zeppelin moments, all tracks heavenly, becalmed or only edgy in a slight, active manner, Wreckless Love being about as noisy as it gets). There are no real rock songs here, much less metal, because everything seems a lush connected dreamscape, thinly draped on a skeleton borne of the world's greatest drums. The busy tracks softly rattle, and the mellow ones, well, like I say, are some of the most purely beautiful and emotionally mature songs to have ever been recorded. Simply stated, this record is one of my favourite four of all time, played hundreds of times, marveled at repeatedly.

Rating **10**

## Robert Plant - Shaken 'N Stirred  (Atlantic '85)

Perhaps too spooked by the intense perfection of **The Principle Of Moments**, Plant figures he'd lighten up, having experienced well enough irrational levels of hero worship with a band he used to work for. So he enters his nü wave phase, Plant as perpetually young satyr, student of songs on the edge, slayer of dinosaur rock. Even song tags are flip: Hip To Hoo, Kallalou Kallalou, Doo Doo A Do Do, most snap, crackle and popping along after bright tropical skies, tricky rhythms, bizarre sounds jumping out like monkeys on the road. The band is surprisingly intact from **Principle**, with one notable exception, Little Feat's Ritchie Hayward on drums, a sparkling soul who buoyantly matches Plant's lofty silliness throughout. Otherwise it's Woodroffe and Martinez who travel the furthest and loudest, synth and bass interplay providing zig zag direction, but the only direction Plant allows, Robbie Blunt relegated to chiming, colouring and generally flipping out on the edges. Toni Halliday is a perfect addition to the circus of sound, a snobby deadpan to Plant's new exploded expressionism. Funny how advance single Little By Little eases Plant's public into things, bridging the last record to this one, this minor hit being the most conventional song here, a light atmospheric musical movement on big drums. Here and elsewhere, there's tons of rhythmic experimenting, often sounding like latter-day Police which found Copeland snapping tracks to attention, Summers playing the English nutter, chirping hysterically over Copeland's jumpy bed. Gotta love Plant's courage and youthful vigor, even though **Shaken 'N Stirred** is a hard record to hold dear. Almost fragrant, gosh-darn wide ballad Sixes And Sevens closes the agitated show, linking this record to Plant's next.

Rating **8**

## Robert Plant - Now And Zen (Atlantic '88)

An entirely new band (young blood!), yet somehow Plant manages to retain much of **Shaken 'N Stirred**'s breezy, technical, unique cauldron of sounds. The big difference here though is in the songs, big, bold, beautiful songs that piece together artfully, recalling the cohesion and aristocratic elegance of **The Principle Of Moments**. The hits here are from opposite ends of the spectrum, *Tall Cool One* almost hard rocking (rare for solo Plant), chiming in with some playful Zep samples, contrasting *Ship Of Fools*, a traditional, unstoppable love letter, featuring velvety guitar work from Doug Boyle. Much of the record's upbeat, finding brisk pop (*Why*), futuristic funk (*Helen Of Troy*), and even rockabilly (*Billy's Revenge*), Plant ever the journeyman, positioning the listener among foreign, provoking sounds vigorously and often, laying down an education as he croons his characteristically clear and simple tales. Sum total: slick, thinking man's rock for and from the upper crust. Minor note: Jimmy Page contributes on two tracks, but he's deftly outperformed by Plant's new arsenal of young hotshots. Minor note #2: CD reissue includes horrid, INXS-ish bonus track.
Rating 9

## Robert Plant - Manic Nirvana (Atlantic '90)

Probably the only Plant record that is a bit gaudy, commercial and occasionally stupid, **Manic Nirvana** is mostly manic, very little peaceful nirvana. Let's try this play-by-play (I mean, this one's more a collection of songs than a unified statement anyways). Smash single *Hurting Kind* opens the show as Plant's heaviest track since *Slow Dancer*. But given the man's standards, it's kinda gimmicky, not everlasting and awfully rawk on. *Big Love* and *SSS&Q*, also both brash and heavy, also both suck. *I Cried* bafflingly breaks the trend, time-traveling back to Zep '73. Then the title track INXS's us back into jumpy loud rock, Plant cementing his new position as hard rock dance god, which he converts to success on the hip hop metal of *Tie Dye On The Highway*. *Your Ma Said You Cried In Your Sleep Last Night* is horrible, Plant's most annoying song, a disastrous hi-tech cover of an old, tired, idiotic blues tune. *Anniversary* is a thrilling march of a ballad, hard to describe, noisy, brash, but still comforting, collapsing into a righteous acoustic folk tune, which again is vintage Zep. Closing off this perplexed mountain of often synthetic noises: the most cacophonous track yet, *Watching You*, basically a tribal Peter Gabriel-type thingie, washed over with boldly strummed acoustic guitars. Like I say, a disjointed, overworked album, just that little bit too bells and whistles to be a tall cool one. I guess more like a fat cold one with a dumb album cover.
Rating 7

## Robert Plant - Fate Of Nations (Atlantic '93)

Awesome gothic Zep rocker *Calling To You* was this one's advance single, a dazed exotica with electric guitars droning through radios everywhere, and all ears were primed to see what Percy's next move would entail. Thankfully, he's left the trinkets, samples and screeches back in 1990, stripping it down for the close, fireside sound of this record's artsy tracks. And when sound fills the screen, as on *Down To The Sea*, it's back to Morocco (not a Pepsi commercial), Plant placing strategically on this record more of the middle eastern sounds his old band made famous, than on any past solo spread. The best tracks here are the pure shimmering popsters, characteristically cool and sly, notably *I Believe* and hit single *29 Palms*, both dark and inviting. His cover of *If I Were A Carpenter* even manages to fit this fold, sounding very retro unto hippie Zep, for that all important mythical twist. Three tracks towards the end totally stick out, but hey, you've probably moved

on by then anyways. Wise fer miles as usual, but for the first time in a long time, very solitary in tone.
Rating 9

## Po'Boy Swing - Lite & Sweet (Royalty '94)

So why not be a tad derivative, if the derivation be flowing from a band that refuses to give us what we want. And what I want is Faith No More's **The Real Thing** Part II. And what Long Island's Po'Boy Swing ships to the limited masses is a dangerous, live-ish crank of that illin' concept; tight snare, booming bassin', Mike Patton twang delivered with verve and funky desperation, courting the Chili Peppers at times but generally delivering the goods where FNM have absconded, something that skirts that silly EP the boys did after **Angel Dust**, come full-length and dormitory. I'd say it works where others have annoyed, these dudes having the persona and chops to pull it off. Maybe I'm in the mood for it, having not heard much funk metal in these days of excruciating and extreme death, but Po'Boy Swing do swing.
Rating 7

## Poison - Look What The Cat Dragged In (Capitol '86)

Poison were always the most shameless of teased glamsters, looking like healthy, upwardly-mobile hookers on this vacant little debut, which rides a sugar-coated teen dreem version of the Crüe, hyper helmsman Bret Michaels carrying a large part of the doppelgangbang with his natural Vince Neil twang when not copping Steven Tyler's rooster strut. The songs, or more accurately the hooks, which are the shakey legs this stuff's supposed to stand on, are just the wrong side of memorable, usually dragged down by boxy production and cheezy anthemic choruses, not to mention C.C.'s plain-jane axework. Very glam, all the way to the bank, even courting Hanoi Rocks at least in spirit, yet retaining a strong dumbness throughout which usually isn't even all that fun, 'cept maybe on *Talk Dirty To Me* and *#I Bad Boy*. Lone wolves in cheap clothing: the funky *Blame It On You* and the sub-radar title cruise. Not awful, just awfully silly, although the record's double platinum status is all serious.
Rating 5

## Poison - Open Up And Say ... Ahh! (Capitol '88)

More of the same hope and aspiration rock, with a honing of the band's inspirational party metal technique (or charade—it doesn't matter). Maybe it's just the beers talking, but this pile of poodle droppings works its glittery magic, at least to modest success. *Love On The Rocks*, *Nothin' But A Good Time*, *Look But You Can't Touch* ... it all rolls on down the highway (in love with Aerosmith) like a heroic tour video, for who but heroes would work in this business? As for my rating: you take a good look at this record's back cover. If you're still on board, then the wax inside may make your weekend. An astounding quadruple platinum when the ice cleared, a short one year after the cage creaked open.
Rating 7

## Poison - Flesh & Blood (Capitol '91)

One of those neon-headed bands you either buy into as saviours of your optimism, or discard as obnoxiously commercial chick rock. To me, the latter, finding such mantelpieces as *Unskinny Bop* and *Something To Believe In* offensive and counterproductive to any thoughts of future reputation. Nevertheless, Poison now finds themselves prone to reflection, in similar fashion to Crüe as of late, making for quizzling little tales of life's successes and disappointments. So at least the band reaches out, despite lacking a single original musical thought in their collective glamdomes. Hard to fault a guy with Bret Michaels' unbridled enthusiasm (diabetic to boot); I mean, some of it's got to rub off on you.

Worst damn thing about this record is that annoying slushy mix that's supposed to sound tough and embattled, but merely recalls nasal mucous. A **7** on the right kind of day.
Rating        **6**

## Poison - Swallow This Live   (Capitol '91)

An impossible instruction, with a painful horse pill like this loud and sprawling (2 CD, 100 minutes) testimony to just how bad this band can be. Poison were always a lite-weight take on Crüe, musically and psychologically, which gives them just about even odds in a battle of wits with an ant farm. I actually saw this tour live (free tickets), and I did come away mildly amused by the whole rock god charade the band swam in. Suffice to say, given the boyz' limited mental capacity, whatever the band was doing behind C.C.'s useless, ear-splitting axe solos doesn't translate well to plastic-pressed aluminum. Aside from lots of the aforementioned headcase's guitar solos, **Swallow This Live** displays ton's of Poison's mallo-puff Crüe, a few motivate-the-losers power ballads, four new studio cuts, and the band's latter-day attempts at getting a life by botching the blues. Poison is more or less testimony to what a band can get away with and still sell tons of records (thirteen million, as of Spring '91), as was Crüe, really, who nevertheless deserved the fear wrought against their skinny black souls from the parents of unruly rugrats experiencing deep dives in their grade averages. Poison on the other hand, no.
Rating        **4**

## Poison - Native Tongue   (Capitol '93)

An expertly pumped-up Bret Michaels leads Poison back into the rock'n'roll circus armed with new axe maestro Richie Kotzen and a full fourteen new cuts (plus intro) to make the undiscerning high school banger and bangerette twitch. **Native Tongue** is a lot more of the same, as the band progresses slowly with their rudimentary funky hard rock, unimaginatively exploring the tired ol' Crüe doing Aerosmith gesture, with some tasty sideline shadings from Kotzen which add southern flavour to the thing. The whole rainbow of artificial blues metal is represented here, from ballad, through hip shake and brisk boogie to a scant couple o' metal rockers, thus mildly teasing peroxide like *Body Talk*, *Stay Alive* and *Strike Up The Band*, and lead single *Stand*. No grand gestures here, Poison seems content to mine the same generic formula that's brought them success, making only minor improvements in delivery and slightly increased complexity of arrangement. Shuffle-off-to-the-liquor-store rock for beginners, and an acceptable chunk of background chatter for veterans.
Rating        **6**

## Chris Poland - Return To Metalopolis   (Enigma '90)

Axe-whiz Chris Poland was unceremoniously dumped from Megadeth during the pin-pricked turbulent years (when everyone should have been dumped), resurfacing here with his brother Mark on drums for a squarely metallic instrumental album (demo, resumé) that previews the progressive mastery the duo will display on '93's **Damn The Machine**. Actually released to a bit of fanfare at the time, this is the kind of no vocals record that is somewhat accessible, basically light-footed Megadeth, which breaks in with tasteful soloing where vocals might have been. Still bores the pants off me though. Pass and get **Damn The Machine**.
Rating        **5**

## Iggy Pop - The Idiot   (RCA '77)

One of Iggy's more critically-acclaimed statements, **The Idiot** finds David Bowie in full collaboration with Detroit's favorite firecracker, apparently rescuing the man from a drug-induced downward spiral. Bowie co-writes everything on this, lending his **Low/Heroes/Lodger**-style German decadence to the toxins, brewing a dense fog of jazzy, progressive, jilted rhythms high on tough technology and eclectic performance from esteemed fringe players. **The Idiot** is indeed dark and garish, lyrically provocative, destructive, fragmented, pumped with minimalist maximums and carnival-gone-wrong bad moods. There's no hard rock on this record outside of the vampiric *Funtime*, yet mindspheres are as damp and dour as one can take, and Iggy's vocals are pure genius; so comfortably sinister in a number of ranges. Most distressed of the lot would be the luded, deep-pocket classics *China Girl* (re-lived you know where) and the sprawling *Dum Dum Boys*, a fluid death trip through the comatose underbelly of town, which in fact could describe all of side two, one of the slowest, lowest half records on earth. One would consider this record an enemy of recovery, but in the world of art, such journeys often serve as exorcisms of personal demons. No denying, however, the power of this deflating trip through Iggy's Berlin years, which along with **Lust For Life**, would serve as the most dangerous duo of the man's checkered, often merely comical career.
Rating        **8**

## Iggy Pop - Lust For Life   (RCA '77)

The Idiot's soulmate, **Lust For Life** expands on the former's fish-lensed nightmare, adding greater levels of cacophony and urgency, spanning twisted cancerous pop, closer flirtations with hard rock, crashed psychedelia, and general wanton violence amongst its diversities. Hypnotic throughout, personal highlights include the title cut with its thundering drum intro, *The Passenger*, with its night-time unrealities, the swinging, almost fun *Success*, and the poisonous *Neighbourhood Threat*, yet another tune reworked by Bowie years later. Throughout **Lust For Life**, one of the wildest characteristics would have to be the loose and garage-blown instrumentation, rendered absolutely infected by Bowie's grimy and smothered recording, weaving a frayed threat of seediness that just sickens the lower abdomen, hindering attempts to penetrate the record's motivations. All in all, another desperate piece of wax from the trashed mindscapes of Pop and Bowie's particularly itchy Berlin.
Rating        **9**

## Iggy Pop And James Williamson - Kill City   (Bomp '77)

This slithering waif of a record matches yowl for yowl the most sordid, moisture-stained journeys in Iggy's languished lurch through life. Readily identifiable through forlorn belts of horn, tired honky tonk ivories and a sludgy though passable melding of guitar/bass/drums, **Kill City** is Iggy's real dirt, essentially the man's most underground and beaten record, shambled together with a set of complex influences harnessed with a focus on full loiter. Personal fave is the title track, which is also the heaviest and essentially most conventional rocker. Other magnetically-depraved invitations would include *Consolation Prizes*, and the addicto-depressive *Johanna*, two tunes that accurately evoke images of hopelessness under factory stacks. In many ways cohesive, serious, and for one rare moment, honest beyond novelty and props, **Kill City** is to be admired as a deflated hunk of art, yet it's really the self-degrading grime of the whole thing that prompts one to lay down and avoid the record like a dry lump of poison. No more a "one off" than 3/4 of the rest of Ig's catalogue, **Kill City** is nonetheless better left bleeding in the gutter, an artifact trapped between the cusps of time, an oily patch of sound wiggling in bad light.
Rating        **7**

## Iggy Pop - TV Eye, 1977 Live  (RCA '78)

Iggy rode the wastrel daze of punk as its grandfather, with two of his more cosmic and criminally insane records, **The Idiot** and **Lust For Life**, the wafting decadence of which made its way to this innocuous but frightful live document. Nightmarish Bowie influences riddle this record like a disease, especially on cuts from their collaborations like *Funtime* and the raped, freezin' and vacuum-packed *Sixteen*. The mix varies wildly, as must venue and date; non-LP slammer *I Got A Right*, *Lust For Life*, and *Nightclubbing* sounding like sucker punches from **Metallic K.O.** Best renditions are reserved for a fairly cogent update of *T.V. Eye* and a rhythmically bashable *I Wanna Be Your Dog*. Basically a hurried history piece highlighting the spent fragmentation of the man's catalogue and deteriorated mental state during the languished, vacuous period of Iggy's career. A difficult, edgy set of performances to say the least.
Rating                                                                 5

## Iggy Pop - New Values  (Arista '79)

Clear-headed and plain, Iggy's chemistry now shines through with charm. And here the man takes his simplest, most humble delivery through truly cool little rock toons, gathering hook, line and sinker, all his capacities into a bundle of pure, respectable, unclouded entertainment. Production at the hands of legendary **Raw Power** guitarist James Williamson, is bare-bones , comfortable and well, small, and performances are appropriately "there" and no further, making smart rockers like *Five Foot One*, *Billy Is A Runaway*, and the snakey title cut bristle with honesty, while chillier, more pop-based constructs like *How Do Ya Fix A Broken Part*, *Don't Look Down*, and *Tell Me A Story* benefit from nice bits of horns and honky tonk keyboards from Scott Thurston. **New Values**, above all else, is a highly personable, old-time, guitar-based rock'n'roll record, sent skewed to the fringes by one engagingly strange, well-traveled front man. And its best quality is that the record can be taken seriously as fun, staying clear of cheap laughs, preferring to rely on the genuine weird commentary that results from nonconventional thought patterns from a bunch of "been there" warriors.
Rating                                                                10

## Iggy Pop - Soldier   (Arista '80)

Best word to describe **Soldier** would be colourful  . . . urban colourful, noisy colourful, goofy colourful, chaotically colourful. **Soldier** is just one off-the-rails carnival of sight and sound, probably Iggy's most sweeping self-parody, shocking in amusing ways, so distressingly numbskull in its small ambitions, taking its rightful place as the product of a time-worn, intelligent, but self-deprecating charlatan of a punk. The heavier stuff, such as *I'm A Conservative*, *I Snub You*, and *Mr. Dynamite* are more guitar and drum atmospheres, lurching forward to trashcan conclusions about bad things, while crazier items such as *Loco Mosquito* and *Dog Food* just flop around on the rocks in clattered confusion. All silliness and psychosis live side by side, rendering **Soldier** a noise-inundated metropolis of extreme caricatures. Entertaining in a voyeuristic kind of way, but lacking the gravity of other Iggy projects due to disorienting collisions of bells, whistles, tics and pops.
Rating                                                                 8

## Iggy Pop - Party   (Arista '81)

Or at least Iggy's bent version of one, blending the '70s, the '60s and God knows what else in this strangely rock-historical piece of happy punk. Probably more akin to a **Soldier**-tinted **New Values**, but not like any single Pop disc, **Party** is a uniquely Iggy-ish goofball party favour, aiming for warmth but finding chummy embarrassment. Lots of simple melodic garage rock mixed with manic, hyperactive pop, **Party** does best when achieving cruise, such as on horn-honked kick-off *Pleasure*, *Shades*-alike romance *Pumpin' For Jill*, and personal fave *Sincerity*, which is soaked with just that. Yet the cover of *Sea Of Love* seems to capture the cheesy surfability of this record more than anything, a shmaltzy showtune feel, full of blaring horns and knowingly fake drama. Still, it's a fun record, fun in a resigned, sympathetic sort of way, fun when all hopes are dashed of ever getting to hang with the beautiful people, fun like the last ferris wheel ride before the apocalypse.
Rating                                                                 7

## Iggy Pop - Zombie Birdhouse   (Chrysalis '82)

Without a doubt, one of Iggy's more opaque and confusing moods, **Zombie Birdhouse** is also his most cerebral, garnering serious critical acclaim, yet not surprisingly, little commercial attention, given the record's tough, noisy eclecticism and strange, encoded discipline. Lyrically, Iggy exceeds his always high standards, offering greater insight and depth, and indeed sheer volume, **Zombie Birdhouse** comprising twelve caustic cuts that are more nightmarish mantras over which to place Pop's near poetic statements (note: *The Villagers*, *Life Of Work* and *Watching The News*). In some ways, this record approaches the more avant garde, mechanical landscapes of Bowie or Talking Heads, offering sophisticated instrumentation and arrangements in error, under a garage context, almost a misuse of high-brow elements. Iggy's out of tune and it really doesn't matter, as everybody else is busy being quiet, subversive madmen, undermining the whole pile anyways. Weird and slushy throughout, hard to listen to, but perversely artistic in its own paranoid corner, and simply likeable as a dangerous experiment.
Rating                                                                 7

## Iggy Pop - Blah - Blah - Blah   (A&M '86)

Sick of years on the sidelines, Iggy tries his hand at commercial gloss, albeit still quirky, eclectic commercial gloss, yet paving all avenues, however divergent, with a golden, scientific, well-charted and well-produced sheen. Save for the '50s cover of *Real Wild Child (Wild One)*, which Iggy turned into a dance hit and the biggest of three singles from the record, all else is either attributed to Pop/Jones or Pop/Bowie, the Thin White Duke also producing with high class, clinical aplomb. The verdict: mostly clattery, almost lush keyboard pop with heart and confident originality, plus two rockers, *Cry For Love* and the snakey 'n' stinging *Winners And Losers*. A confusing, confused mix of flotation devices, nevertheless commandeered with capable, time-worn wisdom, **Blah - Blah - Blah** attempts to lift Iggy from the streets to the drawing rooms of rock's elite, while achieving more like an exposé of the man's lack of fitness or desire to rub shoulders with the squeaky clean. In the process, Iggy tab   his craggy vocal chords more in the direction of ‾  , low-cycled croon on such wondrous ballads as ᷣ₋ation and *Shades*, a gem about honest love and fine sunglasses. A sell-out but a strangely comfortable and forgiving one.
Rating                                                                 7

## Iggy Pop - Instinct   (A&M '88)

Igford's lone obvious embracement of the tenets of metal proves that you can't force-feed rock'n'roll, even if aiming squarely at a fate that seems so just; in this case a return by a legend to his critically acclaimed, axe-bashing roots. Indeed, an album of metal from Iggy seems destined for classic status, yet on **Instinct**, one gets a watered-down construction and delivery from a soul-less band, newcomers to the fold nowhere near up to the task. Stumbling, rehashed riffs from the most brain-dead of American sources causes **Instinct** to fall flat on its toneless, humourless face, proving that Iggy's craft comes necessarily from free-form, high band-width manifestations of his fringe persona, rather than concerted placement within a defined style. No imagination here. Steve Jones does an even simpler job than on **Never Mind The Bullocks**, Seamus Beaghen's ivories are always out of place (by the very definition of metal, I might add), skinsman Paul Garisto is the ultimate squarehead, and Ig himself mumbles forth with less volume, less mania, all the while shakier and more out of tune than usual. Too flaccid, too slow, too perplexed, too stiff, and too stripped without the psychosis or grunge necessary to evoke the weakly intended images of Stoogemania, **Instinct** sleeps on such quizzlings as High On You, Tom Tom and the aptly titled first vid Cold Metal. Iggy finally gives us what we wanted, only to find that the man's many brilliant moments are all brilliant mistakes. Redeeming rockers: Easy Rider, Squarehead, and the righteous cover art courtesy of '60's poster legend Gary Grimshaw.

Rating                    5

## Iggy Pop - Brick By Brick   (Virgin '90)

As of late, Iggy's given us his failed rendition of the flat-out rock record, his successful foray into main-stream pop, and his usual host of goofball carnival rides. So now it's time for the desperate, fully realized artistic statement. And **Brick By Brick** does as good a job as possible in the post-innocence '90s, given that Ig's legendary status is long expired, and that the record reeks of big budget shadings from Waddy Wachtel, Kenny Aronoff, John Hiatt, Slash, Kate Pierson, David Lindley, and purile producer Don Was. Continually disoriented by Iggy's philosophical flip flops, I tend to encounter an Iggy project as merely his latest flavour, a buzz for a couple of months but that's it. In that sense, Iggy's going the way of Alice Cooper, Elvis Costello, Graham Parker, and John Hiatt (who contributes a tune here), the close familiarity of the band concept lost in a shuffle of studio guns with their own signatures or indeed instructions to offer no signature at all. Expensive help is not the Iggy way, and the end result is one of tough, acoustic and electric Pop-penned diatribes which ring hollow, embracing the very establishment it bristles against lyrically. The poison such as Butt Town, I Won't Crap Out, and the sprawling Neon Forest make up for the slop such as Moonlight Lady, The Undefeated and hit single Candy, yet still it's just a bunch of songs with a fairly famous ex-madman at the mike, too lovingly whipped into shape to carry the force of Iggy's highly moral, but bluntly graphic ravings.

Rating                    6

## Iggy Pop - American Caesar   (Virgin '93)

Again the chameleon turns, reversing the tables on the initially impressive but fast-fading **Brick By Brick**, cranking something here that shows maturity, integrity, guts, grime, but long stretches of discomfort akin to the skewered melodies and trashy deliveries of Tin Machine (see Mixin' The Colours, Plastic & Concrete and Caesar). And **American Caesar** is long alright, over 70 minutes worth of successful and failed Iggy compositions, rendered somewhat more valid due to the band feel of the record, Ig finally getting some sort of posse together, a band with which he is touring the record. And everything works its grease; acoustic tunes and garagey rockers (there is no other type here) alike all carving, honing and sharpening a wild diatribe on modern America, the record's lyrics probably the best of Iggy's career, eminently quotable, dramatic, chock full o' soundbites and skilful shock justice. But the music is jarring, sometimes unlikeable and as usual, all over the road, making for one of those spreads that could have used some editing and rearranging. Contains a refreshing re-do of Louie Louie with wry new words and sly new enunciations, perhaps best exhibit-

ing Iggy's increasingly versatile vocals, which are strong and purposeful throughout this elegant but thorny record. I want to say **8**, but there's probably a good six tracks that summarily repel, again recalling the brilliance and the horror of Tin Machine, a misunderstood band whose two studio records are each one half astonishing, one half ugly beyond reproach. I'm interested, Iggy slowly becoming somewhat the statesman **American Caesar** professes, a man who seems a lightning rod for the ills chewing away at a society too intelligent and culture-rich for our own good.

Rating                    7

## Iggy Pop - Naughty Little Doggie   (Virgin '96)

Well it's that turn of the wheel again, time for Iggy to shell some wisdoms about chicks and the state of the world. And as the manwolf's pre-release banter surmised, the record is more of a funtime shoot 'em up, simple low-slung rock and punk numbers with Igford's uniquely blunt verbal tooling, ten kaleido-toons at an acceptable forty minutes, three close and personal acoustic ballads, the rest, well-recorded garage rock. But it's that tight snare 'n' trebly recording that undermines the inherent heft of the tunes, faves like the almost Guns N' Rosy Keep On Believing and the rock'n'rollsy Heart Is Saved slammed out heavy but rendered paper thin. Only Pussy Walk (annoying and aimless riff with totally un-PC lyrics) and the watery psychedelia of Outta My Head don't make it as songs, the rest filling the space between the Stones, the Stooges and Foo Fighters adequately, if still marred by the blindingly shiny mix. But I'm sure most of this record will explode live. Much hookier than the last perplexion complexion, Iggy is back on track, if only he would drop the last vestiges of slickness and really be his own slimey greasy self.

Rating                    7

## Porch - Porch   (Mammoth/Prawn Song '94)

Porch. Love the name, but wanna run and hide when I hear their bruising, buckling, grizzly unbearable bass sound. No really, a somewhat cool, ultra-alternative act of terror here. Oddball titles, and even goofier funner, higher wackywerdz. And of course a nutty musical circus carries the tune, Wire, Jesus Lizard and Helmet all jostling and jousting to plug in and pollute at each's choicest sub-cycles. Leadhead heavy when the jazzgrunge din coagulates into advancing song as on Little White Cracker, Expectorant and Bum Holy, but wastrel as they come on the ambient insect itchable shambling tracks 'o pain. Gotta hand it to these aural ET's; their sound is special. However my enjoyment is not. Two thirds difficult for difficult's sake, but scads more interesting than your average **6**.

Rating                    6

## Porno For Pyros - Porno For Pyros   (Warner Bros. '93)

Unfortunately this record has sold well, vindicating Perry Farrell for this lazy, predictable piece of slacker grunge, a long-awaited record that merely takes the auto-pilot tendencies of **Ritual De Lo Habitual**'s tortuous last half and stretches them out for one noisy, cash-hungry yawn. All eyes were on Farrell to reinvent rock, to blow our minds, but alas our waif abstains, proving an unimagined creative void, as his assembled pharmaceutical beatniks flounder in default from jazzy chord to hiccup shuffle, with only a tenuous link to caring. Farrell's vocal signatures are exotic as usual, but his musical backing is a chaotic shambles, resulting in occasional emotional daggers between vast expanses of filler, rather than the reverse. Chilling first video with Cursed Female, a bleak and immoral look at the street, which by last squawk becomes a classic case of sight propping sound, video creating a life from spineless music, but too much of the rest is merely shock for shock's sake, and even there, only lyrically, Farrell convincing painting blood rag pictures of modern youth as despicable cockroach to be feared. As for the music: nothing's shocking.

Rating 6

## Porno For Pyros - Good God's Urge (Warner '96)

Perry Farrell continues to be an interesting guy, although sometimes it's easier to laugh at him these days than with him, enjoying a good chuckle as I peer into a guy who seems to (ahem) like his wine lately, which burbles and bubbles through this wiry wisp of a knave on all subjects hippie-presupposed and impossible. **Good's God Urge** does quite a bit better job of actually making music than the collapsed debut, Farrell and an esteemed coterie of sandal-hoppers arranging this mellow body-stone to the Steely hilt, even if writing is still a spontaneous overflow of kharma for these wiseacres. So it's all a conceptual psychedelic fruity tropical pop and twirl, even if irritating lead single *Tahitian Moon* reminds me a bit too much of *Whip It*, with that abrasive *Secret Agent Man* progression. But as I say, it's Farrell's Cali-fried Julian Cope compression that makes this such a refreshing pile of living through all the senses, **Good God's Urge** taking the listener, in a considerably less plugged state of mind, to those same exotic locales Jane's Addiction stayed at and stunk up. Truth be told, Perry's turning into Sting, becoming older, wiser, less braying and more reverence-worthy as time goes on, even if his wisdom points disturbingly to regression into childhood.

Rating 8

## Possessed - Beyond The Gates (Cobra '86)

A notch below thrash velocity-wise, however right in there vocally, California's Possessed might rise forth as soundtrack to your most psychotic of moods slamming real relentless and evil, reserved for the blackest and most hopeless of mindspaces. Wild, sinister riffs abound, and the title cut just might be the most sonically twisted chunk of doom I've ever witnessed, especially the last tortuous half. Per usual, awesome alien ideas, but too much, too soon, too crammed. Vinyl version came with a scary, expensive die-cut cover, sporting some bizarre sci fi demonics. Most reknowned for their guitarist Larry Lalonde, who would later resurface as axeman for wacky-ass bass fops Primus!

Rating 4

## Cozy Powell - Over The Top (Polydor '79)

I'm afraid I still don't understand this man. Powell's considered a second string great, getting his start with Jeff Beck and Rainbow, then bouncing around metal like a steely on the Kiss pinball machine, even being considered (briefly) as Bonham's successor in Led Zep. But as a (hack) drummer myself, I find the guy boring, unexpressive, unspectacular when he overplays, and wholly lacking in groove, losing on both technical skills and feel, leaving, uh, nothing, as evidenced on this old solo record which sounds like a bad drummer playing along with Magnum instrumentals, cheesy synthesized pomp rock (thank Don Airey), somewhat akin to the most dated, electronic-gizmo'ed kind of Jeff Beck. A tortuous listening experience, a type of washed-up prog without any chops, something as useful as Slayer unplugged. Reissued in Japan, proving those guys will reissue anything with stars on it.

Rating 0

## Cozy Powell - Sooner Or Later (Elite/Pickwick '91)

Cozy Powell gets the Elite reissue/compilation treatment here, almost as if he deserves it, which he doesn't. Anyhow, **Sooner Or Later** comprises some of his '81 and '83 soundcheck wanks (some with vocals), combining **Over The Top**'s synthesizer jazz pop with things that go rockier bump in the night (his drumming

is the sound of headaches), and more pseudo-classical aspirations that smoke a big joint. It's all a mess of tastelessness from the get go, kinda like soundtrack music for straight-to-video B movies. Get Bruford records if you want electric jazz rock with good drumming, will ya?

Rating 0

## Powerman 5000 - Mega!! Kung Fu Radio (SKG/MCA '97)

Powerman play a potent and piled-up type of rap metal, and that's a good thing in this case, this reworking of their indie debut **The Blood Splat Rating System** swingin' and rockin', crammed full of street culture, packed with samply sonics that keep the listener interested tune after dope tune. Picture Beck and Rob Zombie fronting the Peppers, Powerman combining frequencies much like Fishbone, but ones that work well together in definite metalness, explosive metalness at that. Hate the album cover, hate the title, and hate the look, but the sounds are very smart indeed, these Bostonians (lots of smart schools, geddit?), sucking on the same reality-dissolving pipe as nerdstar Beck, but with way better songs. Quite elegant, in a genre that is hard to get even close to right.

Rating 7

## The Power Trio From Hell - American Man (Reprise/Warner '93)

One of those weird, hard to rate records, **American Man** offers a bit of everything, all of it well done. So there's great groove metal (*Reach Out* is killer), heavier stuff, the odd ballad, some roots rock, a whole bowlful of great songs recorded proud and powerful by Eddie Kramer. For some reason I think of the Screamin' Cheetah Wheelies or even The Four Horsemen, this stand-alone chunk of rock generality having that same classic rock mystique, while being nowhere near as bluesy or funky as either; maybe more like the exuberant creativity of another stormy power trio, Collision. Solidly deserving of high grades, The Power Trio From Hell (great name, eh?), although flying in the face of an identity, seems to have approached each song like it would be its only or last, pouring a truckload of talent into every wildly divergent track.

Rating 8

## Powertrip - When Cut We Bleed (Public '83)

L.A. core that teeters on the edge of metal crossover, a distinction blurring more with each passing day, given that both bunkers have a lot to be pissed about in the '90s. Lots of fretfire and a surprisingly pumped mix constitute the upside of said blosh, but the usual brain-dead contempt for quality that reeks from the hardcore element stops this alkaloid oik quivering in its tracks as ineffectual and samey. Standard moshing cover of Iggy's *I Got A Right*.

Rating 4

## Praying Mantis - Time Tells No Lies (Arista '81)

An early NWOBHM entry which was essentially not ready for primetime, suffering from cheesy riffs, unraveling construction, vocal inadequacy and middling fence-sitting between sweetened American hard rock and grime-caked British metal. Contains a half decent cover of *All Day And All Of The Night* and little else that is of more than historical value. Later changed their name to Stratus. Bisecting the life of this band: Clive Burr, Paul Di'anno (this is also an incestuous story unto English Steel), Dennis Stratton and Bernie Shaw.

Rating 3

## Pretty Boy Floyd - Leather Boyz With Electric Toyz (MCA '89)

Another sickly slice of over-the-top, glamoid sonic pap that stakes an unconvincing claim 'twixt Crüe's funda-

mental stupidity and pop melodicism in search of a metallic upside-down cake for young chicks. Nothing kicks much ass here, or causes o'erflowing ventings of danger or chaos, rendering Pretty Boy Floyd a fairly vapid attempt at sleezoid star status. Per usual however, anything half decently recorded that doesn't take itself too seriously possesses some modicum of value and Floyd is no exception, having its unbecoming purpose way down the party-time playlist.
Rating                                                                  4

## Pretty Maids - Pretty Maids   (Par '83)

The Maids, along with perhaps Tokyo Blade and Heavy Pettin', were considered one of the more hopeful of NWOBHM acts, fleshing their decisively metallic six man assault with keyboard shadings and thoughtful melodies. Rivetheads had a soft spot for this 6 track EP (most notably good-time chugger Shelley The Maid), appreciating the traces of early Iron Maiden-like enthusiasm, punkiness, professionalism, and sense of purpose, despite the EP's noisy, but passably full-range recording. An impressive premiere; loose and human yet strong and veteran-like song-wise.
Rating                                                                  6

## Pretty Maids - Red, Hot And Heavy   (CBS '84)

Red, Hot And Heavy confirms that the Maids swell and swillin' debut was no fluke, this first full-length dishing up heroic goth-tinged rockers that span the horizons between speed metal, major groove chunks, and emotive hard rockers. All is attentively professional here, slamming along powerfully below Ronnie Atkins' Paul Di'anno-like growl. For an '84 premiere, from the U.K. no less, clichés are surprisingly few both lyrically and musically, although there's no mistaking the obvious Maiden influence, which is used fortunately more as home base for tidier, trickier, more accessible, but often fast gothic structures. Red, Hot And Heavy manages an accomplished and accessible groove despite its uncompromising metal stance, doling out the fast and true plus the odd trick such as a nice rendition of Lizzy's Little Darling. Sadly (but arguably), this early release would represent the highest level of human connection within the band's catalogue thus far, future releases striving for greater emphasis on technical prowess and melodrama.
Rating                                                                  8

## Pretty Maids - Future World   (CBS '87)

More royalty rock from a promising bunch of Brits, Future World kicks off with a killer title track which instantly recalls Yngwie as it races through goth soundscapes towards rousing conclusion. As the record unfolds, we get a deflating preponderance on dynamic synth-based melodic metal again à la Malmsteen or latter years Rainbow, with lead vocalist Ronnie Atkins singing voice sounding distractingly shakey when flipping the switch into growl, which becomes my main reason for dismissing the record. But despite such shortcomings, I'm also of the opinion that this sort of keyboard metal has failed the test of time, now years later sounding like a cliché used by British acts enamoured with America. And Pretty Maids play the part to the fullest, weaving an ornate goth tapestry on the butt-shakers and neck-snappers alike. Hard to say. Now that they haven't become big respectable rock stars, the missionary zeal of the whole well-conceived ploy seems sorta embarrassing.
Rating                                                                  6

## Pretty Maids - Lethal Heroes   (Epic/CBS '90)

Same sort of ghouly drooly spacey goofy album art, same kind of brisk, behind and buoyant Eurometal inside. And I really just care so little by this point, Pretty Maids really only remarkable for the fact that they are Brits slogging away at an American (or mainland European) corner of the genre. Produced by Roger Glover, not that it matters, Lethal Heroes sounds much like Eddie Kramer's job on Perfect World, or indeed any hair band record from the US. Elegant twin-attack soloing, which logically recalls laid-back Yngwie mixed with Lizzy.
Rating                                                                  6

## Prick - Prick   (Interscope '95)

Picture NIN's The Downward Spiral with a thorny pop edge, and you'll slide into the new wavey industrial crazyhead world of Kevin McMahon, whose shiny difficult record is produced by Mr. Reznor himself. Melody and songcraft prop this one into the listenable zone, even as all sorts of buzzing electro postures worm their way through most every track like some sort of millennial Pere Ubu feast meets multiplicit radio reception. McMahon's vocals are sweet and sour, entering dementia but keeping us unalienated just enough to thrust up hook. The hospitable, danceable face of bleak industrial.
Rating                                                                  7

## Pride & Glory - Pride & Glory   (Geffen '94)

Looks like Geffen is trying to carve a new but ancient taste sensation out of incorrigible Zakk, what with the fat contract and press push afforded this surprisingly authentic spread of southern rock. Yep, gone are the blazing pyrotechnics of Zakk's Ozzy days, instead, painstakingly accurate constructions of '70s suvvern rockers like Lynyrd Skynyrd, Allman Brothers, Black Oak Arkansas, and perhaps Blackfoot, gussied-up not too often-like with trudging metal blues chordage. Most surprising is Zakk's voice, which doesn't sound at all like his L.A. rocker looks, sorta cough-syrup Jim Dandy but less lunatic, again, Blackfoot's Ricky Medlocke springing to mind, low-down howling at its best. But like those '70s records, Pride & Glory is in no hurry to impress, for better or worse, leaving all flash for a reverent look at a somewhat lost and still fairly unexploited genre. This means lots of stuff too slow for my liking, too laid-back, and too jammy. But with so much studious redneck rock on which to feast, there's more than enough deermeat to go 'round. Very classy definitely, and believe it or not, fairly novel, given its absolute adherence to history, its total refusal to shine shiny like the '90s. Needs a lot of plays, believe me, but still, I'm very impressed with Wylde's grasp of something he was too young to witness first hand. Next move: vascillations between the Ozzy and Axl camps, finally resting upon delicate acoustic solo album Book Of Shadows for mid-'96.
Rating                                                                  8

## Primus - Sailing The Seas Of Cheese   (Interscope '91)

Call this the band's major label breakthrough, Primus somehow convincing pockets of the worlds that they matter, bespectacled slide-rule spectators grooving to the boys' spaghetti genius, their itchy jump and flee, their tales from the outside. "Accessible" specimens like Jerry Was A Race Car Driver and Tommy The Cat sort of work, making the record ever so slightly more songish than Pork Soda, even though there's a palpable air of panic here, more flopping around, more a staking of turf, not like anybody else has even rented here. You either geddit or you don't, which doesn't really much account for my middling grades.
Rating                                                                  6

## Primus - Pork Soda   (Interscope '93)

Ah yes Primus . . . surprise headliner of '93's Lollapalooza, San Francisco "power" trio, all the power going to the articulated bass octopus of leader Les Claypool, Geddy Lee disciple gone furiously pharmaceutical and futuristic. Pork Soda follows the critically-acclaimed Sailing The Seas Of Cheese, and to my surprise, is

a less entertaining, more ponderous chunk of nose funk, but essentially just too much of a one-of-a-kind, one trick pony thing. You either bathe in it or you don't, and I'm afeared I'm with the have-nots, only able to handle so much bass-as-lead structures; long, repetitive tracks featuring guitar only as aural white noise geometrics, drums as hip, fusion-tilted, soundcheck backbeat, vocals as nasal, nerdy, timid and mumbling (sorry, but Weird Al springs to mind), and Claypool's bass as party central, in my opinion, an instrument to be heard only when spoken to. Sure it's fresh and wondrous, but it wears out fast, after a quick chuckle at the equally eccentric lyrics (way greato character sketches), leaving the listener to surmise out loud "now just when am I expected to play this record? . . . huh? . . . answer me." Well, I can't, as much as I admire the concept, no other band attempting anything close to this odd egg. A lot of folks will tell you how fabulous Primus is, but how many repeatedly pop this one into their car deck? For spider-fingered bass monsters only, **Pork Soda**, amongst the band's mod era Warner releases, is the furthest afield from accessibility, the curmudgeon in the closet, the Trekky in the damp basement.
Rating　　　　　　　　　　　　　　　　　　6

## Primus - Tales From The Punchbowl　(Warner '95)

Les Claypool and his contortionist bass antics are back full flare on this latest rough ride. Claypool, killer percussionist Tim "Herb" Alexander and jazz skronkin' guitarist Larry "Ler" Lalonde have crafted, well, another Primus record, but with a twist, main advance being the record's much more opaque and enigmatic lyrics. Les still pulls from his punchbowl his assortment of oddball Americana, folks who are plain straight-up weird, out there, or eccentric as the hills, but then he buries their story in pungent poetics that mask meaning far more than on past biographies like *Tommy The Cat* or *The Pressman* or the hilarious *Nature Boy*. And more songs jump out and mosh through that up-front bass-as-lead chemistry that this band basically owns in modern music. *Wynona's Big Brown Beaver* is a veritable stage-diving funk-up, *Southbound Pachyderm* is a new atmospheric mystery vibe for the band, and *Over The Electric Grapevine* is simply an unforgettable trip into the unknown. There's still the annoying passages that make one surmise that this can only appeal to young bass wizards, but the overall package is one of immense creativity and originality, and for that alone, it might make sense to dive into the puchbowl headfirst. Wacky computer graphics throughout by Les and Ler. Update: drummer "Herb" now gone, Les taking the time to make a solo record, similar to Primus if not even more bizarre.
Rating　　　　　　　　　　　　　　　　　　8

## Prong - Beg To Differ　(CBS '90)

The atonal angles of Prong's fractured light tended to diffuse and confuse the critical community as to the band's allegiances. Were they metallizers, punks, hardcore anarchists or some urban splicing of all three, gone horribly wrong? I would guess the latter, as the boys cram the rhythmic audacity of Metallica full-frontal into M.O.D./S.O.D./Anthrax moshkenstein, all under a cloak of Rollins-like anger at a world not behaving as it should. **Beg To Differ** bore nourishing grist for many who were patient enough to disassemble and personalize the chaotic circuitry of ultra-riffs hereby encased. However, I never attended the camp, perhaps arriving at this record too late after the initial critical blessing. Packed full of innovative maneuvers, **Beg To Differ** shines within too minimalist and concentrated a framework, sounding like a chopped force with all the arrangements switched to purist neutral, making most of the wild ideas unimpressive in final effect. I just never got on board. Note: first major label

release, previous works being **Primitive Origins** and **Force Fed**.
Rating　　　　　　　　　　　　　　　　　　6

## Prong - Prove You Wrong　(Sony '91)

Spiraling with greater exploratory fanaticism into the bizarre, Prong bridge even greater gulfs within fringe metal camps, constructing a frenzied fire of riff artillery. One can hear (granted an uncontrolled imagination) Anacrusis, Faith No More, Mekong Delta, Overkill, Killing Joke, Soundgarden, and even Primus, as bass-fwapping becomes a foreground tool amidst the usual dry technical hair weave. **Prove You Wrong** thus becomes another academically solid pastiche of new age metal sensibilities, cranked home with a conservative palette of blasting boxy bass/guitar/drums. Fave raves would be the title track, with its sublime use of Zep's jangling *Celebration Day* riff, tribal rat salad *Irrelevant Thoughts*, and welcome straight ahead gut punch *Torn Between*. But wence again, a remarkable inundation of intellectual metal that I never play, no help to Tommy Victor's depressing vocal delivery. An 8 or 9 without the personal bias. Raging album cover.
Rating　　　　　　　　　　　　　　　　　　7

## Prong - Cleansing　(Sony '94)

Prong finally make that tactical adjustment that could see them stick it to the market, bringing in Terry Date to simplify and clarify and cleanse the band's often busy, overly divergent tunage. **Cleansing** rocks a little closer to Pantera, while not slurping overboard with the Texans' sense of power, keeping it tight, smaller and more underground and subversive. Tommy Victor's guitar sound rips through with added sting, and the songs are cooked groove-heavy and dynamic, although that tough, almost rappy assault is maintained. Victor doesn't like to be associate with that particular urban NYC sound, but it's definitely in there, Prong's violent percussivism recalling Biohazard at times. Only Prong's riffs now surpass most from the Big Apple, tending at least tentatively towards that gut-level crunch that rises in popularity each twisted day. And lyrically the band also picks it up, wrapping most of these twelve tunes around various "cleansing"-type story lines. All in all, major improvement, making Prong an ultra-metal competitor with which to be reckoned.
Rating　　　　　　　　　　　　　　　　　　8

## Prong - Rude Awakening　(Sony '96)

Pulling yet another adjustment, Prong forsake their Prongtera guise of '94, choosing to indulge in their Killing Joke connection, turning trendy and industrial, while lacking the songs to validate such a move. Lo and behold, **Rude Awakening** is only a minor improvement on Killing Joke's smeary, overproduced robotic churn, Victor, Raven and Parsons overloading each track with things from both metal and hard dance, pretty much every sound tried, true and relegated to the dustbin of datedness by bands both sides of the fence. But hey, it might work, this dive into a commercial medium, **Rude Awakening** being like a heavy Filter record, very '90s, very cold and sterile, very thud thud thudly. Pity really, as I had hoped these guys would up-ratchet into the top quartile of metal's second string. Note: even though Terry Date produces, it is Nine Inch Nails' Charlie Clauser whose stamp is all over the record, performing all the drum programming and keyboards. Great.
Rating　　　　　　　　　　　　　　　　　　6

## Pro-Pain - Foul Taste Of Freedom　(Energy '92)

Catchy in a perverted, urbanized way, this debut (after the name change from Crumbsuckers) is a dose more fun and slammable into one's memory banks than similar early fare from doppelganger Biohazard. Less the damp extreme visions of the follow-up, **Foul Taste**

**Of Freedom** employs a stripped moshcore sound, almost like really heavy mid-pace Anthrax or perhaps M.O.D. or D.R.I., vocalist Gary Meskil going for that enraged shout-spout that lands short of the equalizing non-vocal of grindcore.
Rating 6

### Pro-Pain - The Truth Hurts (Energy '94)
Butt-bruising urban-aggro metal from the scratchy surfaces of reality's blood-splattered pavements, **The Truth Hurts** places Pro-Pain top quartile of the rock dog pack successfully fusing death metal, hardcore and traditional mid '80s power metal. Vocals tend towards accessible grind like a strep-throated Phil Anselmo, while the band's lyrics paint putrid pictures of decaying America effectively, intelligently, boot to the temples. Leader Meskil seems furtively bent on projecting his message skilfully, whipping together a package that is well-executed, well-recorded if not rudimentally instrumentalized and arranged by Alex Perialas, also the knob guy on the debut. Perfectly proud, way darker, second record versus the ill-received **Foul Taste Of Freedom**. Play at risk of up-ratcheting your cynicism to dam-bursting levels. Note: the artwork displaying real crime scene photos had to be altered post-release due to obscenity issues.
Rating 7

### Pro-Pain - Contents Under Pressure (Energy '96)
Bio sez this combines aspects of the first two records, which is strangely accurate, **Contents Under Pressure** burning free with much cleaner, straight-line metal tunes, sorta what the Down album was after. So there's still an urbancore element (best exemplified in the insanely catchy Mercy Killings), but one thinks solid heavy metal first. The record's self-produced to communicate riff and rhythm with clear simplicity, like a warmer Pantera, but without the acrobatics. I hope this signals a return to heavy metal values, Pro-Pain obviously not concerned about the tag, offering very little alternative, although vocals still do a pirate bark similar to Clutch (which is fine by me). Really getting to dig this band.
Rating 8

### Psychotica - Psychotica (American '96)
Somewhat hyped like many American acts, one could say Psychotica live up to it, mixing Manson-esque shock rock with glam from two eras, the '70s stuff glittery in Bowie, Mott and T. Rex, and the '80s stuff neon-clad in Poison and perhaps more pointedly and sympathetically, Hanoi Rocks. Industrial, trip-hopped elements are balanced with good mellow tracks, multidimensional vocals and screechy, garagey guitars. Lots of covers (granted there are 18 tracks here), including a Marilyn-ish but plausible clank through Devo's Freedom Of Choice. Druggy like Jane's Addiction, and quite effective in its compression of junk culture into a tight ball of nerves.
Rating 7

### Puller - Sugarless (Tooth & Nail '96)
I thought I'd never hear another band like Paw, Puller twisting through that same, dang magical, heartland alternative thicket, no surprise given that Paw hail from Lawrence, Kansas, and Puller are part of the Oklahoma City scene that spawned Chainsaw Kittens, The Nixons, and For Love Not Lisa (their ex-singer, Mike Lewis, now fronts Puller). Much of what Puller gets up to begins with Green River/Nirvana-heavy grunge, lots of smart, smeared rhythms, really underground, formidably cool. The mix pulls back a bit for my liking, slouching along somewhat starved for treble, but much of this can be excused given the strong, anthemic melodies, and the riffs to keep said hooks from wilting

into any sort of sensitive zone. And any band that reminds me of Paw, well . . . you rule.
Rating 8

### Pulley - Esteem Driven Engine (Epitaph '96)
A shiny metal alloy between a bunch of seminal L.A. punk elements, Pulley is a minor punk supergroup as far as these things go (Ten Foot Pole, Face To Face, Scared Straight). It's fast, it's melodic, it's a sprightly collection of rollicking '90s punk. And what more can be said? Writing, riffs and arrangements are improving all the time, and Epitaph has quality standards (which they might not admit under duress), standards that make all of this deceptively hard-hitting music quite harmless.
Rating 6

### Puncture - Puncture (Century Media '94)
More Ministry and Front Line Assembly than Nine Inch Nails, Texas-based Puncture are yet another theoretically perfect, intense industrial metal experience. But to my mind, the band scores one out of three: crushing, molten riffs, rendered inoperable by synth drumming and highly treated, unintelligible cyberthrash vocals. They do well what they do, but sum total: this is a one trick pony.
Rating 5

### Purity - Built (Black Mark '97)
What happens when metalheaded Finnish sensibilities run head-long into the world of hard, smart Seattle grunge? Purity of course, a purity that is about as close to metal grunge gets, a purebred cross between commercial Alice in Chains and metallic STP, something akin to lost grunge hopefuls Gruntruck or My Sister's Machine. There's a uniformity of sound that sets these guys below the likes of Soundgarden. But hooks, riffs and timeshifts are still very fresh indeed, Purity being big on bombast, instant toe-tapability and vicious, deep-ground grooves. A bit too affected track after track by American angst, but still there are a ton of superfresh metal ideas afoot. Labelmate Quorthon is probably watching closely, given his similar aspirations towards a more alt. form of metal.
Rating 7

### Pushing Up Daisies - Wheedle (Cerebral '95)
Hot on the leather booties of fellow Montreal-ites Grim Skunk comes another scorched contender, Pushing Up Daisies smearing forth with a fortified street-smart slab o' grunge as per Alice in Chains with just a smattering of Monster Magnet to keep it crustified. **Wheedle** is indeed the real enchilada, a serious, well-structured record full of harmonies, hooks and heaviness, the '70s tall music therein almost making up for that entirely indie-dumb album cover (pencil crayon drawings are not to be tolerated, guys). Songs are sturdy and deliberate, damn close to an AiC circa the debut, but as I say, a little more under the porch; loose and echoey like mebbee Kyuss or mid-years Soundgarden. Vocals alone carry thick alterno-anthems like Mindset and Stumble into musclerock nirvana, indeed a good 3/4 of **Wheedle** tripping the metal fantastic, making P.U.D. a sludge factory on the belching rise.
Rating 8

### Pyogenesis - Waves Of Erotasia (Relativity '94)
A scant four tracks of enlightened death metal, **Waves Of Erotasia** rides a strange love of things old and decrepit as it vomitvox's its way through the greyest of gloomy suicidal goth grinds. Really evil and underground but arrestingly musical at the same time, **Waves** reminds one of formative Tiamat; hell, even modern Tiamat come closer Lost In Revery, a saddening ballad doom-crooned in normal voicings. Haunting and shimmeringly psycho-melodic, what with that goofy

viola and all, Pyogenesis ought to crawl above metal's cryogenic wormage with sidewinding ease.

Rating 8

## Pyogenesis - Sweet X-Rated Nothings (Relapse '95)

The excitement surrounding this band is because they are the first to forsake their death metal roots, but retain the genre's good habits, Pyogenesis moving into an uneasy but potentially bounteous realm of mordant melody. Others like Cemetary, Samael, Amorphis and Lake Of Tears are going here now, but Pyogenesis were one of the first, piling on both goth and old new wave influences, building onto their twisted frame, experiments that are still growly and harshly-recorded (too midrangey). **Sweet X-Rated Nothings** thusly proceeds, loping down this odd track, jammy with all sorts of jungley jugular metal soundscans, most divergent compositions linked by a lyrical thrust that is a sort of florid, fragile poetry oscillating between lust and love, pleasure and pain, intense emotions of unspeakable natures. Must be something in the water.

Rating 8

## Pyogenesis - Twinaleblood (Relapse '95)

And now the masterpiece floats full-flare into view, **Twinaleblood** forsoothing the somewhat rough-shod, confused quality of its predecessor for as cogent and cohesive a record that is possible under the sky-flying spacecore concept that is Pyogenesis. Fuse the frost of those low-chug, Sweden-borne riffs we all cherish, with an avalanche of creative timetravel timetables, and we all become one with this groovy rock combo enigma, a band that visits, anoints then steals Hawkwind through Nirvana, stuck in a blender of blustery death precepts from the far side. **Twinaleblood** is still most profoundly a bruising, blubbery, brooding piece of work heartily based in grindcore, but the ideas spark dance and fade like no other post-metal alien craft you've encountered. As you can see, describing and tagging becomes futile, so I'll stop now.

Rating 9

## Pyogenesis - Unpop (Nuclear Blast '96)

Now systematically purged of all metallic drama, Pyogenesis is merely an OK alternative band, churning an unstudied Nirvana pop with weird European overtones, sorta experimental, slowed-down Green Day with inflections unto XTC and Hawkwind. Man, looking back, it's been quite a tableturner, but for those seeing **Unpop** as a snapshot in time, nothing really all that remarkable will leap about. Sure there's an unsettled eccentricity to it, but it's now impossible to chart its origins, Pyogenesis just coming out odd but trendy. Hey, stranger things have happened. With a good break (and video, and choice of single: *Silver Experience*), these guys may finally get dinner. Note: label promo pack included a bottle of Pyogenesis body lotion!

Rating 8

## Q5 - Steel The Light   (Music For Nations '85)

Totally deserving of its rapid media buzz as up-and-comers, Q5 had the chops, the eye for dynamic and detail, and the general pro 'tude to win acclaim, mostly concentrated amongst U.K.'s **Kerrang!** set. **Steel The Light** was a proud, take-no-prisoners guitar rock album, an able contemporary to similar chest-beating from sister band TKO. Basically impressive for a project recorded in '84, **Steel The Light** wasted the melodic metal pack at the time, but suffers from personality vacuum (and lack of forgiveness on my part towards its follow-up) to make it a regular spin in the expert-studded '90s. But back then, it was cool to like Q5; groove-oriented man's metal, sweet and logical enough to pass in mixed company, therefore a cogent party choice during metal's transitional period in the mid '80s.

Rating                                           7

## Q5 - When The Mirror Cracks   (Mercury '86)

All the axe inventions in Floyd Rose's head don't amount to squat in my mind when records like this are made to document the man's creativity. And Q5 was such hot property one smartly-dressed record ago. Now, all axe-ioms are reduced to synth-ias as the Michelin Man at the ivories takes over in rank pollution o'er the guitar-bounding sound that for one vinyl statement, represented one of Washington state's more heady shots at the brass ring. **When The Mirror Cracks** is another sell-out to the imagined pop rock mountain of money, a shmaltzy, soap opera, yuppie scourge that heads into the obscurity books quickly and efficiently. The drummer is now credited with drums, drum programming, and percussion, which symbolizes the root cause of Q5's deep six, as the former rock 'n' roll boys become all too enamoured with the toys of Floyd and Floyd's techno-buddies. A dribbling wash of synth rock fit for pigs.

Rating                                           1

## Quartz - Deleted   (Jet '77)

A confounding outfit that gave us some of the most deadly metal of the NWOBHM, Quartz were always waiting in the wings, somewhat unhinged and unsure, this debut being no exception, representing a pastiche of eminently British rock stylings from Sabbath to Sweet through Supertramp, Heep and even Nightwing. **Deleted** (gutsy title, eh?) consequently makes for a mysterious, downward spiraling record, letting its

treasures reflect available light only through a thin crack in the door. Soaraway track is undoubtedly *Mainline Riders*, which bridges Sabbath to Angelwitch in reverent fashion, a killer doom metal saga, brooding, suicidal and a fitting tribute to the record's surprise producer Tony Iommi. Elsewhere it's a swirling mass of styles, many of them acoustic-based, most infused with rich harmonies of both vocals and guitars. Cream of the remainder would be creepy black metalizer *Devil's Brew*, the similarly gloom-shrouded *Around And Around* and meathook rocker *Pleasure Seekers*. Hypnotic and serious, but also disorientingly various, **Deleted** is a qualified underground gem, qualifier being your personal opinions on the above stated influences, and the confused sort of record that necessarily emerges. Came lovingly wrapped in a brown paper bag, no cardboard sleeve, just a brown paper bag.

Rating                                           9

## Quartz - Live   (Logo '80)

Immensely talented losers Quartz always had a twisted way of doing business, releasing four completely incompatible records during their short stint as seminal metal force, one being this useless, drink 'em, bash 'em live record as all-strategic Album II. Smooth move. The sorry stats: Seven cuts, three from **Deleted** (including a hyper version of the depressive *Around & Around*), two awful covers, and two non-studio self-penned ditties, *Belinda*, a dipshit metal boogie and *Count Dracula*, an acceptable pummel, crossing Sabbath with Sweet due to Mike Taylor's highly expressive voice. Everybody sounds hammered, especially the guy at the soundboard for this legendary performance at Digbeth Civic Hall.

Rating                                           3

## Quartz - Stand Up And Fight   (MCA '80)

A work of uncommon distinction that continues to blow my mind to this day, **Stand Up And Fight** was probably the most sure-footed and metallically expressive of NWOBHM albums, stomping all comers . . . Maiden, Tygers, Leppard, you name it. Fat drum-driven grooves, royal and intelligent riffs, bobbing bass lines, and swashbuckling vocals glide through a percolating, headphone-quality mix on a record that can do no wrong, save for one lurching pop rocker. Possessing all the hellish doom tones of the most foreboding of early black metallurgists with few of the overt references and none of the crap musicianship, **Stand Up And Fight** was heady wizardry to our small gathering of ragged jean jackets, taking us to intense, personal metalhead frontiers like no other record in recent history. Favorites would include the evilmelodic *Stoking Up The Fires Of Hell*, the rattling *Questions*, and the large Sabbath ooze of closer *Wildfire*, which re-wires *Megalomania*'s central riff, an act of sabotage I'm sure was exercised with deepest respect. Ultimately years later, **Stand Up And Fight** hasn't lost a shred of its largess, exalted for time everlasting by princely but haunting manipulation of hallowed heavy metal traditions. A fireball flung into the souls of a scattered few, rendering Quartz one of the greatest unsungs of the U.K. metal pack.

Rating       10

## Quartz - Against All Odds   (Heavy Metal '83)

Possessing a more poisonous sound (co-producer Robin George!) than masterpiece **Stand Up And Fight**, **Against All Odds** represents a band shrouded in misfortune. At least that's the way we saw it, what with grimier production values, new vocalist, new bassist, new smaller label, and a raft of paeans to pain that owe more to underground metal than the sky-straddling majesty of the band's crown jewel. **Against All Odds** aligned Quartz with a new, more desperate, more violent crowd, running neck and neck for the pulverization of our souls with the likes of Oz, Witchfynde, and Witchfinder General, not so overtly black metal, but just as weary and resigned to Hell with the crippling depression of *Hard Road*, *Tell Me Why* and *Avalon*. As the madness intensifies, the band descends into the Sab squalor for *Buried Alive*, *Love 'Em & Run* and final twitch before twilight (*It's) Hell, Livin' Without You*. But this is no down-the-gullet metalfest, much of the record in possession of lonely melodic goth tones, all the more creepy due to the cold and clanky recording. New vocalist Geoff Bate does the memory of Mike Taylor proud, steering the band through this hypnotic and tragic collection of variously accelerated dirges. Lifeless but beautiful. Sort of band member keyboardist Geoff Nicholls is the same guy silently propping all sorts of Sabbath albums, hence a second connection after Iommi's benefactorship.

Rating       8

## Quartz - Resurrection   (Neat Metal '96)

Regurgitation more like, this dodgy live collection from the late '70s sounding like so much pre-chewed food. No doubt about it, Quartz had a blubbery, Sabbath-like jam quality to their shows, but the track selection was an annoying mix of god-like heavy mechanics and child-like stupidity, this one showing little improvement over **Live**, most notable addition being racing metal mover *Born To Rock The Nation*. More songs sure, but maybe Neat should have scrounged around for a few tour tapes from when this band had a catalogue. I mean, it got pretty damn impressive.

Rating       5

## Queen - Queen   (Elektra '73)

Here I sit trembling at the thought of putting to words how I feel about the record that I've called my favorite of all time, period. **Queen** is a rock art masterpiece, a record that transcends time with its brilliant explorations of the rock idiom, taking the genre way beyond through song construction, lyric, exquisite chops, even production, which is magnificent, utilizing surging, swirling effects that transform the many sensuous sounds on this record into voices. **Queen** squeezes history into a compressed ball of wonder, letting it unravel a bright new way each time. The two flagship rockers are to my mind pure genius, *Keep Your Self Alive* and *Liar*, both monster hits, forever to be in rock radio rotation for their vitality and innovation, Brian May in touch with the kindest of muses who shades and shimmers his strings with magic dust allowing for a

rainbow of expressions from a mere quarter of this elegant collection of souls. Freddie Mercury is shining star of the quieter moments, most torrid being *Doing All Right* and *The Night Comes Down*, songs that are lovingly constructed, expertly steered through paradise, Mercury, May, Taylor and Deacon a force that glides through sound, despite what we hear of their very real difficulties in coming to consensus. And who can deny *Modern Times Rock'n'Roll*, hammering at the panic button, blitzing with brevity previewing the clamor that will be *Stone Cold Crazy* two records hence. There is nothing on this masterwerk that is less than heaven-sent, all corners of the **Queen** world worthy of stunned gaze, as the band makes infinitely full use of the studio time given the band to construct the ultimate opus (Queen was hired on as the "demo" band at London's Trident Studios, which basically meant free reign of the equipment when otherwise not in use). There's no way I can do justice to this record here or anywhere, each precious minute speaking volumes of rock'n'roll knowledge. The result: the shining gem of the rock experience. Note: the Hollywood Records reissue includes the previously unreleased acoustic romp *Mad The Swine*, an early take of *Keep Yourself Alive* and a remix of *Liar*, plus lyrics to everything. Probably the most valuable of the Hollywood re-releases.

Rating       10

## Queen - II   (Elektra '74)

Queen continue on their path of exploration, challenging us to rise above convention and indeed the band's own debut; earth, heaven, now new starry worlds where again time is a primordial soup where cultures through history intertwine, bringing with them their myths and legends, which become a reality as valid as actual past events. Queen **II** brings out the band's full arsenal, complex structures, the splendid keyboard work of Freddie Mercury, bright and almost inhuman vocal harmonies, all-seeing, all-knowing production that has an uncanny ability to smooth mellow passages, then explode into metal that is both regal and raucous, all in construction of a work whose logic can never be totally permeated and ingested. Indeed, **II** will always be Queen's lost record, the enigma to which the listener can return time and time again; the most conceptual and overwrought of a first class catalogue, yet always painted with a palette that is wholly the band's own, strenuously wide and exhaustive of colour but 100% Queen's. Joyful the sound. Hard to believe, but Queen's band members were still hard at their university studies and various day jobs as **II** hit the racks.

Rating       10

## Queen - Sheer Heart Attack   (Elektra '74)

Whereas Queen **II** reversed the tide on **Queen**, evoking something closer to one long, lush and divine Christmas carol, **Sheer Heart Attack** goes back to song, trading mitt-fulls of jewelry for distinctive and dearer gems. Thus *Brighton Rock*, with its dizzy head of steam evoking the memory of *Keep Yourself Alive*, effeminate hit single *Killer Queen*, maniacal metallizer *Stone Cold Crazy*, and nearly mortal chunk rocker *Now I'm Here*; all tracks that have altered my being for the better. But again, the sounds within are uniformly un-uniform in their breathless genius, the product of a four-way alchemy that is about as complex and subtle as any rock force out there, perhaps only Zeppelin as interesting in this regard, even though Queen's recorded output stomps Zep's under its glittery platforms. **Sheer Heart Attack**'s pleasures are many, and indeed, the record can be listened to on many levels, for lyric, for production, for arrangement, or most notably I think, the vast array of guitar sounds emanating from the presence of the mighty Brian May, my most fave axe mechanic on the globe, who inciden-

tally had to rush in at the end of this record's recording to add his parts, having only recently recovered from near fatal hepatitis. The last of Queen's most seriously god-like era, a string of three albums which are easily all within my fave 40 (and come to think of it, **A Night At The Opera** would probably slide in there at the end too). Fine childhood memory: mowing and watering the Glenmerry cemetery to the strains of the Queen catalogue blaring from the bedroom window of ultimate Queen fan Billy Weir, who seemed to log more hours with this band than I thought humanly possible until me, fifteen years later.
Rating            10

## Queen - A Night At The Opera    (Elektra '75)

Again long-time producer Roy Thomas Baker works his unparalleled magic, harnessing the unique talents of four wizards of song, sound and insight into a multi-tiered palace of glittering charms. But **A Night At The Opera** marks an even greater shift towards demarcated songcraft, offering jarring contrasts that spices the usual top-flight Queen affair with vignettes that are almost flippant: the folk of '39, the '20s-style picnic romp of Lazing On A Sunday Afternoon, Seaside Rendezvous, and Good Company, plus the psychedelic heavy rawk of Taylor's I'm In Love With My Car. There's also lucid pop like You're My Best Friend and lucid metal like May's lumbering and Zepp-ish Sweet Lady. But fave tracks would be the crystal clear progressive stun rock of Death On Two Legs (apparently about an unscrupulous ex-manager, although this was never overtly admitted), The Prophet Song and the immortal Bohemian Rhapsody, one of the largest rock classics of all time, an insane pastiche of all the Queen trickery to date, most notably the band's ethereal harmonies, a tune that is perhaps the album itself in compressed state. **A Night At The Opera** is ultimately the most effortlessly enjoyable Queen work to date, a record that takes itself less seriously, exposing the band more as court jesters than scheming cellar-dark Merlins. Many a fan's favorite Queen album, **A Night At The Opera** is indeed a shining classic, doing so many wonderful things so mercilessly well. But for the first time, the band wishes connection on a more human level, while simultaneously requesting that we learn their language to understand the story. It is indeed, worth the effort.
Rating            10

## Queen - A Day At The Races    (Elektra '76)

It takes my breath away to see how much Queen has accomplished in four short years of recording, a body of work that is without equal, continuing to grow in stature for at least an additional three years. Here, the band offers another fanciful collection of songs under another album title taken with permission from Groucho Marx and his movies. If only to feel some sort of orientation to mere reality, one can postulate that **A Day At The Races** bears similarity to its predecessor, matching up somewhat on a song to song basis, to the slight detriment of the present work. I never liked working crass rocker Tie Your Mother Down or Taylor's boring Drowse, but that's where my criticism ends. You Take My Breath Away and Teo Torriatte (Let Us Cling Together) (dedicated to the band's fanatical Japanese fan base) are breezy and dramatic piano ballads highlighting Mercury's purity of voice and ability as engaging storyteller. Biggest hit here was the heart-felt Somebody To Love; warm and moving, destined to be revived after Freddie's death as a quintessential Queen moment. Last highlight would be White Man, a grungy and vicious rocker (of course courtesy of May), containing heaps of May histrionics, a beautiful thing to witness. All in all, something of a down-notch in verve and vitality, as the band maybe encounters a lack of heart-

stopping forward impetus for the very first time. Still, almost a 10.
Rating            9

## Queen - News Of The World    (Elektra '77)

I can't help think of **News Of The World** as We Will Rock You and We Are The Champions plus a bunch of songs, what with getting bombarded by the chest-thumping duo at every damn hockey, baseball and football game I attend. But once past this considerably tall hurdle, **News Of The World** becomes yet another fine Queen album, one with a somewhat tougher hide, featuring the frenzied and mind-numbing metalliblast of Sheer Heart Attack, the oily pumproom guitar funk of Fight From The Inside and Get Down, Make Love, and the dirty literal blues of Sleeping On The Sidewalk. A sense of urban unfeeling characterizes this record, although the mix of feminine and masculine still wage war with each other. But the roughness prevails, making for uneven pacing and general fatigue that I didn't get from the last two, despite their similar sonic and psychological make-ups. Faves would have to be the sublime All Dead, All Dead and the celebratory It's Late with its soaring vocal harmonies and majestic May-isms come chorus time. Not a band known for cohesive albums (more like genius all over the map), **News Of The World** is perhaps the least cohesive thus far, less the immortal work of Art for its rawness and spontaneity. Still, it's just a joy to hear this band play no matter where the song is going. A shakey **9**.
Rating            9

## Queen - Jazz    (Elektra '78)

The zip, sizzle and bang are back in the Queen camp, as the boys plus Roy inject new frantic verve and elastic tempestuousness into a quirky maelstrom of Queen goodies, surprising the hell out of us with Mustapha, a sort of Arabic polka with may riffs careening in from the sides like an invasion from the Mongol hordes. **Jazz** features another classy album cover, cool studio shots and a cheeky poster of a bunch of buck-naked gals on ten speeds for the big bicycle race, a move that caused some controversy for the boys. But musically, there's no question this is Queen on full throttle, thirteen tracks buzzing around the ballroom talking and laughing with everyone. The really cool thing about **Jazz** is the intellectual quality of the heavy tracks. Whereas past rockers kicked royal ass then peeled out layin' rubber after stealing what's left of the beer, here they have no trouble rubbing shoulders with the most cerebral of Queen tracks, best examples being the almost Sabbathy Let Me Entertain You and the hyper Dead On Time, which utilizes that long-righteous Roger Taylor drum sound to the max. Elsewhere, there's a growing grasp of the pop idiom; simple, radio-destined ballads that further play on Mercury's, how shall we say . . . feminine side. There's buckets of LIFE here; energy without resorting to real metal on such tracks as Fat Bottomed Girls, If You Can't Beat Them and Don't Stop Me Now, which all pump along like party tunes despite their sly infusions of intricate Queen-isms. As the record blows out with the moody thump of More Of That Jazz, what we've witnessed is colourful creativity in bloom from a band possessing a seemingly endless supply of ideas (that's seemingly). For now, bask in the glow of some of the most sincere, bright and daring rock ever to flow from the minds of the genre's masters.
Rating            10

## Queen - Live Killers    (Elektra '79)

At the peak of their ethereal existence, Queen unleash the long-awaited live document, sampling seven of the most seriously god-like studio records ever constructed. What is lost in ground-breaking studio brilliance is made up for with blitz mentality, as rousingly evidenced with the flathead metallic delivery of opener We Will Rock You, a mere lumbering annoyance in its original state. Said anthem represents the frontier siege of this loose and frantic juggernaut, where medleys are formed, where compositions emit radically different tonalities from their original intents, and where the intensities are raised uniformly across the spectrum, transformed into the electrical storms that must rage when one owns probably 30 of the best 100 songs ever conceived. Yes, all is cloaked in cacophonous desperation here, a desperation borne of giants engaging battle with complex material; highly capable artists sent to tame the untameable. Swear to God, Sheer Heart Attack has got to be the heaviest song ever recorded, catapulted to its frenzy by artful and necessary manipulation of the studio, yet here it is still simply immense beyond words. I guess by show's close, nothing has been tamed, the material and the band both escaping the fray by the skin of their teeth; each bloodied but unbowed, tense and determined for the experience. Crucial document of a band far above its earthly confines.

Rating                                          8

## Queen - The Game   (Elektra '80)

Queen enter the '80s a transformed entity, coinciding with Freddie's full immersion into the cruising life of Berlin. And I can't help think that his intensifying gay lifestyle has something to do with Queen's confusing new direction. The Game was more the pop record than anything previous, rushed through the writing process, guitars turned way down, as the band explores rockabilly with big novelty hit Crazy Little Thing Called Love (a truly idiotic song), dance funk with even bigger smash Another One Bites The Dust (one of the most reviled songs in my personal universe, along with anything by the Barenaked Ladies) and the pointless Don't Try Suicide, which elicits exactly the opposite response when I hear it. Dragon Attack and Rock It (prime jive) rock moderately but elsewhere, it's a pretty tame affair, the band doing quite a fine job on Save Me and May's bittersweet Sail Away Sweet Sister. In conclusion, The Game is just too playful, turning Queen into a trend-following circus act, for which the band would be handsomely rewarded, the record being the band's biggest seller to date, not to mentioned the first not to be produced by Roy Thomas Baker.

Rating                                          7

## Queen - Flash Gordon Original Soundtrack Music By Queen   (Elektra '80)

Even me the megafan can't even get into this rip-off soundtrack, save for intense rocker The Hero, one of the band's heaviest compositions with a truly ripping May riff. Elsewhere it's just a bunch of effects plus smatterings of May's cool axework and Taylor's peculiar percussion. Oh yeah, and there's that annoying Flash's Theme that just drives me nuts. The movie stiffed.

Rating                                          3

## Queen - Hot Space   (Elektra '81)

Following the filthy success of The Game, on which Queen entered the mainstream through newfound dance sensibility and lowbrow composing, Hot Space delves further into the clubs Berlin-style, becoming minimalist, decadent, and decidedly camp; in a word disco. Yes, distressing as it sounds, the word disco describes side one accurately in its entirety. And so does the word gay. Here Queen offers about the least inviting raft of songs one could imagine; microscopic, synth-driven disco, lacking in melody, lyrical grist, even rhythm to some extent, leaving nothing Queen-like in its wake. One got grudgingly used to Queen's eye for novelty last time around, yet no one could predict that

Another One Bites The Dust could be a springboard for such absolutely flouncing, swishy disco puff. Anyways, enough already, because side two redeems itself somewhat with one May-dominated yet still tentative hard rocker, two lush acoustic ballads, and the fine duet with Bowie, Under Pressure. Sum total: Queen's lightest record. Still, despite traces of Queen beneath the bewildering priss, all is tonelessly recorded with some sort of striving for closeness and honesty; rattling under-dressed and under-achieved. Many consider Hot Space Queen's most disgraceful record, and I'm inclined to agree, wondering with the rest of the world what could be coursing through the band's newly vacant heads. The first of Queen's efforts that points to willful damage in quest of reversing the band's historical relevance.

Rating                                          6

## Queen - Greatest Hits   (EMI '81)

Selling a tall stack, Greatest Hits obviously had a gracious well from which to choose. No point getting too misty-eyed. There wasn't much to this thing, but it was cool that the songs were short (clipped?) enough to squeeze a bunch on, including that question mark of tracks, Flash. If ever there was a catalogue in which to roam giddily, it's Queen's. In a perfect world, there'd be no reason to sample so blasphemously.

Rating                                          7

## Queen - The Works   (Capitol '84)

Queen comes creeping back, offering lots more to confound and upset the old guard once again. A profusion of understated styles renders The Works another rag-tag collection of experiments, offering pure synth pop in lead single Radio Ga Ga, one huge piss-off to the fan base, yet nonetheless engagingly melodic, plus a few other like-wired techno-diddlers, Man On The Prowl, a dil rockabilly, a half-weaseled ballad here and there, and yes, a couple of gems. I Want To Break Free is a positively dandy little fable, while Hammer To Fall brings May back from exile for a smooth hard rock groove, buoyed by a magical, harmonious chorus and piercing, vintage May solo. Again, one spends so much time surmising as to the band's twisted motivations, attempting to crack the stand-offish enigma that gives rise to such weirdly mainstream records. One simple explanation (which the band doesn't mind laying plain in the odd interview), is that the guys really do pay close attention to public response to their work, caring a tad too much about hits and commercial success, perhaps willfully but misguidedly subterfuging their massive creative brilliance with these mixed mid-years grab bags. Likeable as a whole, but indeed, frustrating as any since Jazz brought the glory days to a close.

Rating                                          7

## Queen - A Kind Of Magic   (Capitol '86)

In the same manner in which BÖC's Fire Of Unknown Origin is somehow tainted by its connection to the Heavy Metal soundtrack, A Kind Of Magic suffers due to its affiliation with the movies Iron Eagle and Highlander. Not sure if that's justified, having seen neither film, but I do know this: Queen's worst or second worst record, flounces around disjointedly both sonically and lyrically. Most of it is either synthy and gay; unremarkably mellow like Elton John, exceptions being the three rockers, which are the market makers this time around, the May-laden tunes sent over the airwaves in identical fashion prior to each successive release so the press can tell us all how Queen has finally gone back to their roots, after which the unsuspecting but hopeful fan makes his purchase, discovering he has been cruelly tricked once again. This strategy has been artfully played out with all of the band's final four records, and I guess we'll never see it again due to Mercury's tragic demise. Here the metal is interesting enough as studio wizardry laying raw May's explosive solo work, but two of the three are lyrically naff medieval warrior stuff, totally out of character and a bit offensive for such an artistic juggernaut. No, on **A Kind Of Magic**, the life force is on idle, as an offensive commerciality seems to take control. Yet no one wins, as the record justifiably bombs (stateside, anyways).

Rating 6

## Queen - Live Magic   (Capitol '86)

This expertly constructed double live opus (almost dead identical to the posthumous **Live At Wembley '86**) rings in the truth that Queen was a brutally imposing live experience, Mercury in complete control while May is left to his gut-wrenching devices, destroying the place with his personal forms of high science. Song selection is adequate, given the band's declining stable of quality product from whence to choose. Negatives: a dull, auto-navigated version of Bohemian Rhapsody, the very inclusion at any energy level of Radio Ga Ga, A Kind Of Magic, and Another One Bites The Dust (here mercilessly extended), plus yet another run-through of We Will Rock You and We Are The Champions, which however halfways decent they might be, have been rendered tortuous due to never-ending association with sporting events. On the upside: heroic assaults on rare new rockers such as One Vision and Hammer To Fall, a beefed-up rendition of I Want To Break Free, and an embattled blaze of past glory with the well-carved but truncated Seven Seas Of Rhye, which gets introduced with an almost hostile "this is what you wanted, this is what you gonna get". Quite simply, this record is a pleasure to listen to, given its unavoidably unconventional panoramic ride through Queen's post-singular-genius highs and lows. Less to work with than **Live Killers**, but honest in its efforts to please. Recorded over three venues, with Wembley's show captured as a rousing although decidedly un-fancy full length concert video. More or less marks the pinnacle of Queen's concert domination, due to the first traces of Freddie's illness instigating the methodical and inevitable closing of the Queen shop.

Rating 7

## Queen - The Miracle   (Capitol '89)

We're to believe Freddie already knew about his illness well before the release of this album, but you wouldn't know it here, 'cos he's quite the party animal and general optimist. It doesn't make for the greatest of albums however, as most of the enthusiasm comes in the form of simple synthy structures while May frets around the edges. Two rockers total, one I Want It All a bit too greedy '80s for me, the other Was It All Worth It, a poignant life retrospective and predecessor to The Show Must Go On. But the rest of the record is just more failed ideas so distant from the Queen of old, making **The Miracle** a sort of storehouse of weird commerciality much like **A Kind Of Magic** or **The Works**, with less humanity than either despite the crackling popcorn energy of the thing, especially on the first four cuts of side two and Invisible Man which are all synth-rhythm propelled and strangely pleasing in a guilty manner. And horrors of all horrors, I actually like Breakthru, especially when the guitar revs in. I dunno, this seems to be a Queen that has to struggle to make a record we can grow to like, something you have to debate; a very different story from the days of **Sheer Heart Attack** or even **Jazz**, where one wouldn't dare dismiss the outcome. Here, a tropical fruity sort of experience. CD reissue includes the well-fitting real song Hang On In There, a sprightly synth thingie with cool guitar all over the end if it, Chinese Torture, which is 1:46 of well-composed guitar instrumental, and the extended, bells and whistles 12" version of Invisible Man.

Rating 7

## Queen - Innuendo   (Hollywood '91)

And so it comes to pass, Freddie Mercury, gravely ill for more than three years and stricken with AIDS for at least five at the time of this record's release, leaves this world still creatively vital, conducting the band's most seriously artistic work since Jazz. Not all need agree, but **Innuendo** is at minimum, dizzying in its various states, many potentially infuriating or at least unexciting for any number of listeners. But it is the studied artistic panache with which Queen and each genre tango that makes the record undeniably grand. Dispensing with unpleasantries, it is actually the heaviest here that disappoint, lead single Headlong and The Hitman skirting pedestrian and distasteful, the former musically, the latter lyrically. But the rest of the journey evokes both fragrant, sensual day and night, an elegance that can warm like the sun. as on I Can't Live With You, or cool one's thoughts under a chilling moon, so breathlessly portrayed on the painful I'm Going Slightly Mad. And at every ingenuous twist and turn, cascades of harmony vocals recall the magnificence of Queen's finer moments. **Innuendo** perpetuates the band's philosophy in the '80s that connection can be explored and established through simple structures, an idea that infuriated and lost many fans of the '70s brilliance. **Innuendo** tends to combine that same unadorned simplicity with a weary gravity and sobriety, creating uncomfortable, otherworldly atmospheres perhaps best exhibited on the majestic title track (a deliberate nod to Zeppelin), Ride The Wild Wind and the aforementioned I'm Going Slightly Mad. Ghosts resided over this record well before we even heard of Freddie's illness, so I can't say his death commands my view of the record, thinking exactly what I thought of it the day it came out. But one can't help take into account life's passage when confronted with the haunting conclusions of The Show Must Go On, a powerful dedication to the psyche of the entertainer, and one devastating emotional piece that rides the sturdy frame of Brian May's dependable chords and intricate conversational pathways towards an eloquent and tragic resignation that, for the consummate entertainer, all personal misfortune must be suppressed in subjugation to The Show.

Rating 9

## Queen - Made In Heaven   (EMI '95)

The last gasp for the world's most monumental band, **Made In Heaven** comprises outakes from just before Freddie Mercury's AIDs-related death in '91, as the band was finishing up their last true record, the breathless and melancholic **Innuendo**, well aware of Freddie's impending passing. But the morbidity of this record's context engulfs it in suffocating black, even if the sum total of the songs are a heady gospel revival of hysterical life affirmation. There are no heavy tunes on **Made In Heaven** (although May gets to blow with characteristic genius come solo time), only sunny, sick, piano-pounding torch songs from Mercury, a man obviously seeing a light that no others can detect. This really isn't a characteristic Queen album. It's quite tightly dedicated to not-so-great, lushly-produced, Elton-ian songs of exaggerated hope and love. My fave track is a full-band shine-the-light on May's previously released Too Much Love Will Kill You, sung torridly by Mercury. Elsewhere, it's a hot, intense, deathbed dialogue come churchfest; utterly failed or rock hard inspirational, with no middle ground, except maybe for someone like me, who can stand there stunned, unjudging of the songs, bathed in Queen's stellar production values and the regal elegance of Brian May. It's A Beautiful Day, Let Me Live, Mother Love, My Life Has

Been Saved, Heaven For Everyone . . . I think there's definitely a thread there, a thread that is echoed within the bombastic balladic celebration of the band's musical choices come this strange return of the dynamo called Freddie, rock's most essential entertainer.
Rating　　　　　　　　　　　　　　　　　　7

## Queensryche - Queensryche　(EMI '83)

Kicking off with Queen Of The Ryche, the four track Queensryche EP forcefully put this band of over-achievers at the fore of the parched and drifting metal scene, garnering acclaim both locally and among the Brits, Kerrang! trumpeting the band's Valhalla-high form of techno-metal to the hills. Unfortunately, Queensryche was the most metallic release the band would ever forge: three jab-and-thrust Maiden-influenced rockers plus The Lady Wore Black, a spooky acoustic/heavy ballad just to mix things up a bit, all four dominated by Geoff Tate's dog whistle vocals, establishing an elegant, chivalrous and dead-serious high-mindedness that is the foundation of the band's image to this day. No doubt an act prone to perfection.
Rating　　　　　　　　　　　　　　　　　　7

## Queensryche - The Warning　(EMI '84)

All eyes on the Great Northwest for the full-length debut of Queensryche, a band blessed with critic- and fan-level buzz, plus a major label contract, not to mention a case of self-importance that can sell any metal-starved punter on the theory that the messiah has arrived. The Warning was destined to disappoint, and it did, opening a faultline that exists to this day with the band, an overblown sense of drama that causes bloated song constructs and delays in the action. Of course Tate's pristine pipes and his band's Dungeons and Dragons chops lend themselves perfectly to such academically-inclined Manowar-isms, and Queensryche hesitate nary a bit in unraveling their fuzzy vision all over this curious record. Put in a personal light, I was such a committed devourer of metal in '84, that I tried and somewhat succeeded in taking The Warning as sanctimoniously as its creators, lead single Take Hold Of The Flame standing out as a personal anthem along with such thorny anthemic memorables from Heavy Load's Death Or Glory, Oz's Fire In The Brain and Schenker's Assault Attack. But no question—and all the borderline mental metalheads I hung with agreed—The Warning was rickety and un-focussed compared to the band's slammin' debut, and in total much less metallic and brisk, more dissipated and weak in the groove (witness the hiccup beats on Before The Storm and Warning). Too fancy, too slow to rile, and too polite when it does manage to let fly.
Rating　　　　　　　　　　　　　　　　　　7

## Queensryche - Rage For Order　(EMI '86)

Stealing a look that combines Culture Club, Adam Ant and Prince, Queensryche propose themselves the new fashionplates of the metal scene; the styled coiffures and flowing robes symbolizing a distancing from (and imagined elevation above) metal norms in similar fashion to kindred spirits Rush way back when they mattered. Rage For Order is The Warning with creative growth and added inspiration, less the metal record trapped between two worlds, more the progressive smorg of sounds, stringing suspended metal riffs over strange arrangements, thus Neue Regel and the excellent cover of Lisa Dal Bello's Gonna Get Close To You. But so much of Rage For Order moves slowly or not at all, experimental and difficult to less than stunning effect as on Chemical Youth (We Are Rebellion) and London, both weighted by tricks and sabotaged by Scott Rockenfield's always busy percussive non-grooves. Metallic fave: Walk In The Shadows. Esoteric Fave:

Screaming In Digital. A band fraught with baffling anti-climaxes. Proud, protracted and prissy.
Rating　　　　　　　　　　　　　　　　　　7

## Queensryche - Operation: mindcrime　(EMI '88)

Largely considered the Ryche's definitive statement, Operation: mindcrime is a laborious yet not over-bearing concept album (and full-length video), making up for the involved, heavy-handed storytelling with the band's most urgent, up-front metal since the Queensryche EP. DeGarmo and Wilton cook up some of their most threatening Maiden/Priest-inspired licks on such high class pounders as Revolution Calling, Speak, The Needle Lies and the surprisingly hostile Spreading The Disease, personal fave rave on the record. But Operation: mindcrime is a cool spin start to finish, finally adding cement foundation to the Queensryche crystal palace, at long last getting down and headbanging more than a few fireballs, over an odd electro-mix that causes only fleeting consternation. Side one walks all over side two (ten minute songs rarely impress), but never ye mind, this is a rare metallic tonic for the troops, from a band that often let the metal suffer as they tapped their complicated muse. Still, in the final analysis, Operation: mindcrime is somewhat stand-offish; emotionally dour due to the tale's scathing lamentations on society's degeneration, delivered with the band's usual unchecked flair for theatrics. But, alas it rocks.
Rating　　　　　　　　　　　　　　　　　　8

## Queensryche - Empire　(EMI '90)

And so Queensryche press onward and now upwards, making records, making videos, selling records (tons since mindcrime), critics giving them more truck, dedicated fans becoming more fervent, new ones, usually invited by Floydian mega-ballad Silent Lucidity or the fluid axe-ioms of Jet City Woman, arriving confused and inundated by ornament. Empire (thankfully not another concept record) is again thoughtful enough, richly textured, grand, and even a more mature and human work, but I'm still a wary participant at the palace ball. Same nagging complaint as always: this band takes forever to say whatever's on its mind. Some strange intangible respect grows within me for this band, as the always ambitious and sincere catalogue expands, but I wouldn't say lyrically and sonically these hard rock scientists are pushing the right buttons to make me a frequent participant at their aristocratic socials. A "trip", nevertheless.
Rating　　　　　　　　　　　　　　　　　　7

## Queensryche - Promised Land　(EMI '94)

Tate and Co. delve murkier into their fixation with all things epic, carving themselves what to my mind, is a pretty unappealing niche, as a sort of lightly metalized Pink Floyd, something akin to ol' Fish and Marillion, belaboured progressive balladry cloaked in morose fatigue. This is Queensryche's mellowest record by a long shot, fairly devoid of riffs or headbang structure, totally over-produced and overplayed at every crease in the Statement. And Geoff Tate's self-important vocal stylings are really starting to bug me, cheezy Roger Waters one moment, that patented dog whistle the next. Strange one, the band almost emulating the feel of mindcrime, but executing towards Empire's lavish soft rock directive. I'm personally bored by the whole big thick mess, and I ain't the only one. But I'm sure there are folks out there who will consider these twits the most cerebral guys in rock, simultaneously celebrating (with furrowed concept rock brow) the obvious craft of the thing. Grow up and smell the nineties; these guys are out to pasture.
Rating　　　　　　　　　　　　　　　　　　5

## Quicksand - Slip (PolyGram '93)

With **Nevermind** packaging and a high school metal shop sound somewhere between **Bleach** and Green River's **Rehab Doll** (throw in a little Fugazi and Helmet while you're at it), **Slip** does seemingly supercool things with a limited chops vocabulary. Whether New York's Quicksand has technical acumen is beside the point. Their effect is arrangement and loopy inversion of norms, a Sub Pop urge overkill to grow scruffy little metal rodents (all the while denigrating the form) with an imaginative use of clubs and trash cans. So creatively, Quicksand is neck deep, but such churlish, garage grunge imitation takes me North By Northwest with skeptical trepidation.
Rating                                                        6

## Quicksand - Manic Compression (Island '95)

Folks grooved to the raw percussive verve of Quicksand's **Slip** debut, finding an artful co-conspirator of Helmet, riffs that were built on pound and throb, vocals that belied a Tool-like slacker angst. But **Manic Compression** sadly suffers the follow-up blues, slouching too far into that boring verse/big pay-off chorus formula for my liking. Too many tracks flounder or loiter as we wait for the roar. The artwork rocks however, and the lyrics continue the succinct haiku-ness of the debut's Helmetschool origins. Still, the sum total is boring, like a heavy alterno-art statement rather than a punk record with jazz-tumored brains. Pass.
Rating                                                        6

## Quiet Riot - Metal Health (Pasha/CBS '83)

After simmering on the sidelines with a couple of dil pop metal records (which were the first germination of wunderkid Randy Rhodes, snatched up by Ozzy, then killed in a flying mishap), QR's official calling card arrives, a fully-realized metal wedgie, much like Ratt's **Out Of The Cellar** in terms of push and subsequent pull by legions of MTV-discovering fans. But that's where the comparatives end, **Metal Health** much more the dated party poop of the two, more in line with mid-to-late Twisted Sister. But outside of such lame candystore metal as oldie Slick Black Cadillac, Let's Get Crazy and bloody awful Slade (now that was a band of lugans!) cover-turned-mega-hit Cum On Feel The Noize, we rocked to the chops sophistication of the highly acclaimed players in the band (Sarzo, Cavazo, Banali), as they dished such professional fare as Breathless, Love's A Bitch and the anthem-of-anthems title track. Which sums up this competent though unremarkable chunk of early commerce metal: odious hits, anonymous filler, some trashy metal, and a few exceedingly enjoyable singalongs, even though all is somewhat poisoned by Kevin DuBrow's patronizing hands-on-hip poses and nerdy personality. A commercial success, and a band most general rock fans with at least an ounce of metal in them briefly took to heart as the next big thing, even though the record was fated to be the end of the line for the gravy train. Trademark distorto-mix by Spencer Proffer (see Kick Axe). Four times platinum by '86, with the ill-fated shadowband follow-up still managing a respectable single platinum status.
Rating                                                        6

## Quiet Riot - Condition Critical (CBS '84)

The beginning of the end for this inconsequential act finds the boys desperately trying to recreate the modest excitement of **Metal Health**, right down to ralphing up another excruciating Slade cover Mama Weer All Crazee Now, which actually became a hit, spoiling all conjecture on my part that the listening public possessed even a shred of intelligence. The record is actually quite guitar-toothsome, gaining some degree of lunging impetus, but Lady Fame has flown the coop.
Rating                                                        4

## Quiet Riot - QR III (CBS '86)

With the band floundering on the beachhead of DuBrow's pathetic rock star tragimentality, **QR III** becomes a predictable exercise in homogeneous erasure, offering a medico-mechanical collection of melodic synth metal, creating an irritating alloy of thunk rock with technology unleashed and unfeeling. DuBrow is mixed back in the woods somewhere, and bloody damn well that he is, 'cos he's got absolutely nothing to say or represent. Just forget it, go home, and fer chrissakes, get a new tailor.
Rating                                                        2

## Quiet Riot - Quiet Riot (CBS '88)

**Quiet Riot** is really quite extreme proof of how distant a band can get from what made them famous in the first place. With DuBrow finally pasted firmly on the highway to poseur Hell, one may have held hopes that such a veteran outfit might crash through their chains into new levels of showmanship with this record's acquisition of bluesy ex-Rough Cutt howler Paul Shortino. No way, José. This is easily the worst of QR abominations, full of embarrassing funk cack, coma-inducing ballads and fey attempts at teen-beat hard rock. And as one would expect, it's way overproduced, full of plastic technological clatter and general lack of all that rocks. Severely abysmal lounge metal lost in a sea of unreality, the potential re-definer can't elude the pull of the drainpipe. Gets my vote for the Rock And Roll Hall Of Shame.
Rating                                                        1

## Quiet Riot - Terrified (Moonstone '93)

Well I guess it ain't the worst. DuBrow is back, Cavazo's there, Banali, so the gang's all in. And the record they make is well, kinda thick, stiff hard rock with funny bits, bits that act like AC/DC in their defiance of growth, songs like Psycho City and Rude, Crude Mood making the last half of the CD a twisted sort of rock party that maybe even I might attend. Elsewhere there's too much thumpy bass, DuBrow yowls (Blackie Lawless would be proud) and plodding drums, although it is those structures that allow one to hear a fairly juiced Cavazo. Give 'em credit for flogging a dead goalie mask. I mean they're still a joke, but they'd still hit mid-pack if there were anything resembling a pack of bands playing this bubblecrud.
Rating                                                        6

## Quiet Riot - The Randy Rhodes Years (Parc/Rhino '93)

Talk about flogging, here's one of those actually quite useful compilations reviving tracks from the two expensive Japanese-only pre-**Metal Health** albums imaginatively monikered **Quiet Riot** and **Quiet Riot II**, and tracks that were more like shouldas, couldas and mightas. But it's actually a moderately interesting trip, liner notes by DuBrow setting up each pop metal dittie with self-deprecating humour, songs everywhere that are alternate versions, live, and even unreleased gems. The songs are of course total fromage, but of a sincere, pre-corruption style, sounding Slade-ish, Sweet-ish, Kiss-inflected and Dictators-loopy. Plus you get to hear lots of Rhodes wearing lotsa hats. Question: why does everybody except DuBrow look like exactly the same guy!?
Rating                                                        7

## The Quiet Room - Promo '95 (Room 15 '95)

Five songs comprising 24 minutes of mid-years Fates Warning elegance, **Promo '95** combines hurtin', feeling Geoff Tate-ish vocals with oblique riffing and a myriad of time signatures, resulting in a full, flowery

**359**

and pleasureable piece of prog, reminiscent of Tad Morose. Just enough cruise and crunch to make the melody (often pegged with judicious keyboards) sing with pride. I look forward to more. Big, six-piece band from Denver.
Rating 7

## The London Quireboys - A Little Bit Of What You Fancy (Parlophone '89)

These wily Brit simpletons were riding a wave as one of the forebearers of the '70s roots rock revival paying homage to Rod Stewart, The Faces and the like, the most notable major player being The Black Crowes, two faltering midcomers to the game being Cinderella and Poison, a couple of recent entries being Cry Of Love and Brother Cane. The songwriting is plain mallet-headed, and the general sound so shameless an imitation of pub rock with nary a reason to exist, 'cept mebbee that seven o'clock is as good a time as any to party. Fancy functions basically as "warm feeling" music for teenage wastecases looking for an equally stupid shoulder to ralph on. Rather than capture any magic associated with pedigree, this eventless turd rarely rises above a lost-years Mutt-ly Crüe ballad. Sad. Changed name to Quireboys for the oft-delayed Bitter Sweet & Twisted.
Rating 3

## The Quireboys - Bitter Sweet & Twisted
(Parlophone '92)

The little pub band that was supposed to but didn't, came boogieing (?) back with this deeper dive into the roots of British roots rock, getting less party-rockish, more folksy, and more lush on arrangements and instrumentation. But the timing was all wrong, the rolling ball had lost its mass, and the record did nothing. Not even a novelty cover of Brother Louie (reminding one of both L.A. Guns and Great White in all their marketing non-expertise), could ingratiate this band into the hearts of an America gone flannel. Still, you had to give The Quireboys kudos for exaggerating their exploration of the whole Humble Pie/Mott/Faces end of the bar.
Rating 6

## Quorthon - Album (Black Mark '94)

Quorthon of Bathory disfame comes up with a joyously accomplished mainstream heavy metal release recalling all sorts of '80s NWOBHM greats. Black metal's enigmatic originator considered this just something he had to do, a record of tunes he'd imagine himself listening to, a break from the exhaustive death metal experimentation of Bathory. Solid, almost intrinsically bluesy riffing (see Oh No No and Too Little Much Too Late) collides with tight, classy drumwork and crystal plain (although somewhat laid-back) vocals, all steeped in a thick, bassy mix that cloaks these timeless square-footed metal tunes in muscle-bound heaviness. Confidently worldly, absorbing a bit of Britain, Germany and the U.S. (via Sweden), Album blows away one's conception of where this record might have flamed. A hidden gem of '94's particularly low-profile releases, although you wouldn't know it given all the flak the man has received for going "commercial" (note: that's why he didn't call it Bathory).
Rating 8

## Quorthon - When Our Day Is Through (Black Mark '97)

Hard not to peer at this through poison metal eyes, Quorthon's past work as the infamous Bathory pretty much guaranteeing an inescapable twist to the guy's attempts at power pop. Yep, this is a Q that goes way beyond, into a type of metallic Beatles or XTC, or to put things in a more modern context, Smashing Pumpkins. These four tracks are a mere taster for the second Quorthon solo record, and judging from the man's state of mind, we're in for a liquid, languished, somewhat luded smear of sugary power chords, Quorthon singing with a low, patient croon that says British invasion for some reason. Standout track: I've Had It Coming My Way, which marries Nirvana to Aerosmith and the NWOBHM, the Q man ranting out a tale of alienation not without humour.
Rating 8

# R

## Racer X - Extreme Volume II: Live  (Shrapnel '92)

I believe this band's total output comprised two studio and two live records, this one being full of all sorts of reasons to be, beginning with personnel: frenetic fretmaster Paul Gilbert on guitar, one of his GIT students Bruce Bouillet on second guitar, Priest drummer Scott Travis, bassist John Alderete and awesome metal vocalist Jeff Martin, who sends these shiny metal space shuttles into the stratosphere. The guitarwork has got to be heard to be believed, as the band tears through tricky, vastly entertaining '80s metal originals like *Hammer Away*, *On The Loose* and in-the-pocket fave *Poison Eyes*. But there's also *Detroit Rock City*, an amplified, techni-fried *Moonage Daydream*, and last but not least, *Heart Of The Lion*, a stirring, very chartable, pop metal beauty previously unknown to me, credited to none other than G. Tipton, K.K. Downing and R. Halford, which of course Martin pierces with glorious, effortless Halford screams. I don't know, just a shoot 'em up pyrotechnic feast, celebrating all that was right with metal in the '80s, you know, actually dedicating some hours to learning your instrument. Anyways, it's probably culturally incorrect to like this leather and lace wankfest, but damn it if it doesn't make me wanna play Ratt records again.
Rating                                      **8**

## Rage - Out Of Control  (Carrere '81)

Hapless veterans of the Brit scene, Rage (formerly known as Nutz) play a sort of retro-'70s, hard-hitting blues metal, with all the detrimental effects thereof, and few of the benefits. Like much English music, Rage moves with an intensity-undermining simplicity that betrays naiveté as to present trends, many of which are potentially favourable additions to any band's repertoire. As a result, these guys have an old-fashioned, traditional approach, which evokes images of a heavier, more forward-massing Faces or Bad Company. The nostalgia is comforting, but not mind-altering. Urgent and feeling classic: *Out Of Control*.
Rating                                      **6**

## Rage - Nice 'N' Dirty  (Carrere '82)

Same blooz-driven chunder as with **Out Of Control**, only more blocky, modern, energetic, and commercially-pointed, **Nice 'N' Dirty** leans heavily on the beer-stained bar, trumpeting the cause of party metal as per AC/DC, yet stumbling in resigned stupor with its premature crashing of such clod-rockin' sweep-stakes, suffering terribly from an almost total void of songwriting skill. About as lowbrow and blue collar as humanly possible; generally listenable, but dull, dull, dull. Wizened vets who persist in the mistaken belief that they are in possession of the personal arsenal necessary in bringing charm to bare-bones rock (see Thunder).
Rating                                      **4**

## Rage - Execution Guaranteed  (Cobra '87)

Having been introduced to West Germany's Rage rather circuitously, I came to behold **Execution Guaranteed** after having enjoyed its three follow-ups, witnessing the full actualization of Peavey's fanatic metal alchemy. But fortunately Rage was a class act from day one, dishing its speed science with confidence and vitality here on such headbangers as *Down By Law* and fave *Hatred*. Cool band, with each of its four members in effortless control of his craft; German engineering at its finest, although songcraft rolls somewhat inconsistent.
Rating                                      **7**

## Rage - Perfect Man  (Maze '88)

More clean-burning speed metal than anything purely brutish, **Perfect Man** further focuses Rage's highly palatable iron man's metal, finding something like a power trio version of Priest's main technological feats **Sin After Sin** and **Stained Class** in full collide with Grave Digger's **Witch Hunter**. Peavey, Manni and Chris are three pillars of strength, firmly anchoring these energetic metalli-tales with their agile, rock hard chops. Each track shines on its own; thoughtfully layered, squarely attentive to metal-based melodies, European goth of a shiny, futuristic nature, bound tightly by disciplined patterns of rivet and riff. Let *Sinister Thinking* and *Round Trip* sink into your most hardened circuitry, and the majesty of this band's manic assault will be etched on your frontal lobes forever.
Rating                                      **9**

## Rage - Secrets In A Weird World  (Noise '89)

Over a raucous nuts and bolts mix that results in more chaos than on **Perfect Man**, Rage seems to turn up the burners, Peavey reaching the extremes of his vocal prowess, Manni sending riff upon pig iron riff through the speed metal incinerator, until a tangled pile of sonic agitation emerges. In effect heavier and darker than **Perfect Man**, **Secrets** offers moments where the extra tooth marks take us beyond its predecessor, cuts like *She* and *Distant Voices* becoming more soldierly and mission-bent under an uncompromising gothic veil. The record grinds out with a 9:00 epic in three parts, *Without A Trace*, closing on an ambitious if not progressive note, signally the fact that this is a band digging deeper into the psyche for an increasingly difficult metal experience. No question, this is the product of a formidably talented act, yet it's also a record that is more of a bitter pill compared to **Perfect Man**'s quick pay-offs.

Rating                                                                 8

## Rage - Reflections Of A Shadow   (Noise '90)

Rage continues to weave challenging tales of morality and might over a blistering display of killer capabilities, coming off as the more personable side of fellow speed thinkers Sabbat, Skyclad and Coroner, yet as time marches on, not by much. **Reflections Of A Shadow** expands on the mathematical possibilities of its direct predecessor, wedging a few too many change-ups between rafts of finely-smoked machine gun riffery. Personally, I find the dynamics refreshing, but the tonalities still too uniformly grave, as Rage overwhelms with cold steel, leaving emotion for the dogs. But **Reflections** is still a fine work, indisputable perfection of metal craft, dovetailed with lyrical concerns far above the slash 'n' pillage pack. Faves for me not surprisingly are the flatliners, *Waiting For The Moon* and *Nobody Knows*, which both get a hot beef injection of hard rock to go with the band's usual space age engineering. Newer product is highly revered, but I have yet to be blessed.

Rating                                                                 8

## Rage - Trapped!   (Noise '92)

Having unfortunately lost track of Rage over the last few years, I figured it was time once again to see what this smart, elegant, kickin' metallic band was up to. And **Trapped!** doth not disappoint, Manni's precision axe aggression providing the basis for this considerably accelerated piece of tuneful, technical thrash, a record not unlike early offerings in all its fastkill glory. Once again I like the breathy, personable numbers like *Questions*, *Take Me To The Water*, and the power chord headbang of *Beyond The Wall Of Sleep*, although it's fun puffin' stuff hearing Accept's *Fast As A Shark*, Accept songs I'm sure to start rearing their well-written heads on more metal storms in the coming years. Anyways, great stuff as usual. Support this band before they embrace the sweet slumbered night like bretheren Kreator and Coroner.

Rating                                                                 8

## Rage Against The Machine - Rage Against The Machine   (Sony '92)

Mucho hyped, and primed to live up to it, Rage Against The Machine instantly struck a promising hybrid of stripped-chasis metal, recalling heavy Red Hot Chili Peppers spiced with Sabbath, Zep and Masters Of Reality; lotsa bass licks, open spaces and rhythmic intensity arriving at Helmet or slammin' Sub Pop, while seething big-time all the time against a myriad of social inequalities. Real hip-hop counter-culture-like, with hyper rap vocals courtesy real live activist Zach de la Rocha, who spits lyrical signatures challenging the oppressed to arm themselves with a healthy dose of suspicion. A tough urban amalgam of styles; aggressive and weird. Yet I'm not altogether on board, finding it all just a little too multi-derivative. But definite integrity; a gang to watch closely, judging from their performances at Lollapalooza (despite that pain-in-the-ass, fifteen minutes of silence in protest of the PMRC).

Rating                                                                 7

## Rage Against The Machine - Evil Empire   (Sony '96)

And now four long years (and a presidential term) later, Rage Against The Machine takes aim at the **Evil Empire**, and probably just in time, the band's steadily increasing fanbase getting more and more cynical at suggestions the record would be just around the corner. But **Evil Empire**'s been worth the wait, Zack de la Rocha taking time to learn, study and live his revolutionary convictions, penning a record that is a bookish pantheon of political rock, all shot-gunned over riot-strewn streets by his most explosive of bands. Verily so, Tim Bob, Brad Wilk and Tom Morello slam down the iron gauntlet, creating wide thunder-reverberating vistas of rhythmic hopelessly hip-hopped-up metal, which now only hint at prime moments from Sabbath (bass lines) and Zep (*Vietnow*), the whole thing spreading fire like a Molotov cocktail. A big important record, if there's any hope in saving heavy metal from the suffocating clutches of history. Comes with a photo montage of suggested reading. One could do worse.

Rating                                                                 9

## Raging Slab - Slabbage/True Death   (Restless '91)

This CD scoops up a hearty meal of old, original Slab, the first eleven as **Slabbage** and the last four **True Death**. As imagined, the early fare is kinda trashy with a bad drummer and crudely fashioned songs, but the Foghatted boogie still reigns nicely. The aces are the **True Death** tracks though, all of them mighty fine and adequately mixed. Lots of slide, gnarly retro hooks and freaky funny lyrics. Contains a sludgy cover of the immortal *Earache My Eye*. At one hour, this one's definitely worth it for fans of home-made backwoods fixins'.

Rating                                                                 7

## Raging Slab - Raging Slab   (BMG '89)

Real fine part of making down-home old-style rock, feet firmly planted in the good earth, is that the trends of the day seem to have no effect. Raging Slab secure a major label deal, releasing this self-styled new start right in the thick of hair metal's golden age, and it still sounds like a summer-spelled cross between Savoy Brown and vintage '74 Aerosmith. Sure there's a palpable degree of tentative, self-conscious second-guessing here, the band constricting their previous raw tendencies, but this reserved pulse allows all those super slides to breathe. And the songs are spot-on perfectly homemade Americana rock. What more can you ask for? I dig this band.

Rating                                                                 8

## Raging Slab - Dynamite Monster Boogie Concert   (Def American '93)

Couldn't have tagged it better myself, thoroughly enjoying this one, reveling in the record's back-to-the-'70s excursions through Foghat via Skynyrd, albeit dishing more steaming plates of power chords than any kindred from that misbegotten era, arriving more or less at a user-friendly version of fellow Rick Rubin act Four Horsemen; more inviting in its sweetness, its use of dynamic, its versatility and hooks well away from hoodlum. Lots of slippery slidin' guitar, lotsa southern funk with its rust and generally . . . well, the title sez it all. Truth be told, I stayed clear of the band's previous work because I thought the gal was the lead singer, but she ain't. Greg Strzepka does the honours, and in fine bluesy fashion, whether rocking out, shuffling, or throwing a log on the fire for a quiet tale, as he does on banjo picker *So Help Me*. All in all, one friendly suvvern rocker, real American, real genuine. Recorded on the band's ranch in Pennsylvania.

Rating                                                                 8

## Raging Slab · Sing Monkey Sing (American '96)

Being the classic rock wing-nut that I am, Raging Slab's attempt at trading bellbottoms for big boots distresses me so, **Sing Monkey Sing** sticking out of the catalogue like a red-headed stepchild, all gangly and full of fuzzed signals. This is another one that sounds like its artwork, all ghoulish and dark, slightly acid-burned and Monster Magneto'ed. Sure the blues still move the wreckage, but it's more of an inky, icy black and blue, like a slow river, dead middle of winter, dead middle of night. So things move big and distorted, too many creepy sounds, too much stiff, bed-headed dissonance. Crossed wires fer sure, the Slab finding grunge, industrial, and '60s psychedelia duct-taped to their original worthier concept. An undeniable cool still persists, but said cool is no longer inclusive or positive, the band becoming exile outlaws, no longer willing to speak Skynyrd-style to the heart. Still, **Sing Monkey Sing** is a unique piece of work, the band remaining appreciably swamp-dogged to the point where nothing quite fits this snake-infested corner of rock'n'roll.
Rating 7

## Ragnarok · To Mend The Oaken Heart (Neat Metal '97)

I must admit I'm perplexed about this one, so much so, that any sort of committed reaction sits stunned and lumpen in my throat. Billed as pagan metal, U.K.'s Ragnarok are more like theatre (white facepaint included!), pacing their record with black metal thrash, folk, and timidly-attempted metal points in-between, sounding like a sillier demo-bound Skyclad, often thrashier, often closer to Jethro Tull. Of course, that's if you can ignore the rudimentary electronic drumming (shades of old Bathory) and the Filth-Cradled Butthead-having-a-fit vocal croak of lead story-weaver Deorth, who to be fair, uses his Gentle Giant warble more than his lizard-breath crank. But it's a heck of a read, not to mention severely Celtic and knotty, to the point of distracting one from the almost satiric, Manowar-ish tone of the music. Like they say, you'll laugh, you'll cry, you'll hurl . . .
Rating 7

## Rail · Arrival (Dynasty '81)

This Bellevue, Washington band, sporting a lead singer that looked too primly like Tommy Shaw of Styx, burst onto the scene with a plausible, well-produced record of clean hard rock, ranging from teeny-popper drip to the odd volcanic riff. We liked it at the time, the band being more or less local boys making noise in an era when metal was just recently becoming in vogue. Shortly thereafter, Rail won MTV's best new band contest plus the budget to produce their ill-fated **Rail** EP.
Rating 5

## Rail · Rail (EMI America '83)

The four track EP that resulted from MTV's gracious rating of Rail as best new band the year previous. More commercial, pansy and middling than the sum total of **Arrival**, Rail tended to brand the boys as non-believer lightweights, undermining all the work the band did to establish themselves as early heft rockers, a reputation that did not go unnoticed among punters in Britain, who were ravishingly hungry for anything American and even remotely metallic.
Rating 3

## Railway · Railway (Roadrunner '84)

Kinda entertaining German fare with a lite headbang to it, not unlike crossing AC/DC with **Metal Heart**-era Accept or **On Through The Night**-era Def Leppard, maybe creating a clear, headphone version of Krokus, albeit stuffed mostly with filler. Well-produced and simple with a weak Bon at the mike, **Railway** was always a mildly upbeat spin with some amusingly

skewed melodies amongst such Euro-tinged boogie woogers as Crazy, Dirty Boys, and Out To Kill. What the hell, have one for the road.
Rating 6

## Ritchie Blackmore's Rainbow · Ritchie Blackmore's Rainbow (Polydor '75)

What an anti-climactic way to bring a much-hyped new band into the world, band being the remnants of Elf, including a wicked little imp called Ronnie James Dio. Yea and verily, Ritchie betrays his creative vacuum that was much in evidence towards his last years with Purple, offering this boring, dated, diluted, and largely illogical smorg of guitar rock stylings, all inexpressively played over an inexpensive mix by Martin Birch. And it is this dulled production which ruins this already limp noodle of a record, although fledgling goth obelisks Man On The Silver Mountain and Sixteenth Century Greensleeves approach the worthiness of **Rising**, and achieve it in later live permutations. Elsewhere however, it's just droopy, funk-infected hard rock like Snake Charmer and Black Sheep Of The Family, and a general mix of tunage that leaves more questions than answers. Simply an extension of the failed experiment that was **Stormbringer** Ritchie's last with Deep Purple, not to mention an emulation of the Coverdale psyche.
Rating 5

## Rainbow · Rising (Polydor '76)

Proving to be a major second generation force, Rainbow lay waste to their inauspicious debut with this near masterpiece of medieval metal, a fortress six feet thick, built of chivalrous riffs that systematically evoke the cream of Purple's crop; slow ones, fast ones, fat ones, hard rockers and even funky ones. Fact is, this is the Blackmore statement most dominated by the man's chosen weapon, the largest guitar rock record from either Purple or Rainbow since **In Rock**. Stargazer and A Light In The Black, one languished and tidal, one frenetic and careening, are quintessential '70s bombast, comprising the whole second side of this gloomy cranker. Side one runs an admirable gamut of metal styles with the tasteful (and trademark) gothic of Tarot Woman, the bluesy chunk funk of Run With The Wolf, the forceful and swinging blues metal of Starstruck, and the warmest of what is essentially a haughty record, Do You Close Your Eyes. Dio's growl is in full control, providing a seamless duality to Blackmore who turns in one of his defining performances as axe alchemist of the ancients; both strong individuals leading a rousing charge above one of Cozy Powell's best percussive performances. A magical meeting of rock'n'roll wizards in pursuit of metallic mansions in the sky.
Rating 9

## Rainbow · On Stage (Polydor '77)

In typical Deep Purple fashion, Ritchie goes to Sominex City with a stultifyingly dull lineup of stretched proposals for a premature live album, just two records deep into his new career. Only side one offers any get up and go, with a preview of Kill The King (I wish more bands would do stuff like this, i.e. preview vs. review), a muscular Man On The Silver Mountain and a clipping Starstruck closing it out after a pointless blues called Blues. Side two: sixteen depressing minutes of Catch The Rainbow (remember Child In Time?). Side three: thirteen minutes of Mistreated, and side four, one half Sixteen(th?) Century Greensleeves, one half Still I'm Sad, which always reminded me of old folks tune The Lion Sleeps Tonight. Four sides of mostly instrumental wankery, eight cuts total, and only four iron fillets, make **On Stage** one droning, dull pile of pomp, proving that Rainbow are truly a product of the live jam ethic originating in the '60s and painfully perpetuated

by Zeppelin and Purple. A chance squandered in convincing fashion.
Rating                                                        4

## Rainbow - Long Live Rock'n'Roll (Polydor '78)

Another fine work from Rainbow's classic lineup, **Long Live Rock'n'Roll** is one of the seminal chapters in the gothic rock story, a testimony to metallic wisdom that demands respect. A great album cover (which we always compared to **Draw The Line**) reinforces the timeless feel of the pride inside. Like **Rising**, **Long Live Rock'n'Roll** features Blackmore and Dio weaving mysterious medieval textures through a number of directives, most artful being the traditional OTT speed of *Kill The King* (debuted on the previous year's live album), the *Wanton Song*-riffed *Lady Of The Lake*, and the clanking throb of *The Shed (Subtle)*. By this point, Rainbow had become a serious force, a band considered intelligent aristocrat of the form, exhibiting even greater bandwidth and versatility over a strangely appealing neutral mix, a blocky, mid-rangey sound that somehow adds to the feeling of age the record emits. Given its classical-based nuances (taken to almost Tullish extremes on *Gates Of Babylon*), **Long Live rock'n'roll** always had a cold, mystical aura surrounding it. Still, all the power to the band, as Rainbow increasingly becomes the torch-bearers and purest original purveyors of goth metal, truly influential in many of the NWOBHM greats, not to mention Yngwie Malmsteen and hosts of Euro-rockers. And given Rainbow's strong experimental streak, the sound rarely got oppressive or tiring, the band preferring to let classical music shade their compositions rather than define them.
Rating                                                        9

## Rainbow - Down To Earth (Polydor '79)

The meeting of intellects that is Ritchie Blackmore and Graham Bonnet bestow upon the world Rainbow's stellar statement, a record that brings to fruition the feudal warlord Rainbow persona, with none of the overtly distracting gothic imagery and previous tendency towards bare-bones production. Roger Glover weaves brilliant textures on **Down To Earth**, ecstatically juggling the talent dropped into his outstretched arms, boldest addition being lead vocalist Bonnet who once again proves catalyst to the stars, as Ritchie turns it up for some of his smoothest virtuoso masterpieces, such as *Eyes Of The World*, *Danger Zone* and the magnificent *Lost In Hollywood*, which weaves and bobs with sensual melody swirled in a brisk guitar-painted romp. Everybody's at their peak. Don Airey's keyboards are tasteful, reinforcing but never over-ruling the medieval feel, and Cozy Powell finds effortless groove, backing Ritchie's shining riff cathedrals. Glover adds bass and more importantly production, while Bonnet steers the lyrics towards universals, rising above metal trappings, adding a most croonful cruise to the high-minded affair. And elsewhere, there's a rousing but ambitious rendition of *Since You Been Gone*, and a mysterious balladic non-ballad in *Makin' Love*. Rainbow's pièce de resistance, forceful and majestic, sending nary a confusing signal or negative vibe. The first Rainbow, or for that matter Purple, capturing the core essence of Blackmore's potential, which only **Perfect Strangers** and **House Of Blue Light** have articulated since.
Rating                                                       10

## Rainbow - Difficult To Cure (PolyGram '81)

**Difficult To Cure** represents a deconstruction and drift of a once clear vision, a vision that peaked with **Down To Earth**, one unlikely record which took no pause for Rainbow's rising, despite the advent of a new vocalist (an extraordinary one to be sure). For whatever reason (does the word tyranny enter into it?), all that was chucked, ushering in the somewhat

fragile and incompatible persona of Joe Lynn Turner to articulate literally Blackmore's artistic palette. And some very real art lives, even if the overall upright British airs become shattered by the mainstream environment established by Turner's pin-up pipes, not to mention cotton candy rockers like Russ Ballard's *I Surrender*, piffle like *Magic*, the oddly hollow *Freedom Fighter* and two instrumentals. Enjoyable more as a sparing sampling of Blackmore's fluid riffing and snakey soloing qualities (best show being the unsung *No Release* and amateurish lead video *Can't Happen Here*), **Difficult To Cure** is more a smorgasbord of unimpressive American-style Rainbow ideas, an empty appetizer, somewhat undermined by Glover's compressed recording, which causes *Spotlight Kid*, the heaviest cut here, to collapse in panicky shambles. I don't know, chalk it up boredom or capitulation to Turner's radio rock tendencies, but this one's a bit of a dog.
Rating                                                        6

## Rainbow - Straight Between The Eyes (PolyGram '82)

After the slightly anemic guilty pleasure of **Difficult To Cure**, Rainbow pull a creative comeback of sorts, stomping politely back with a clever, self-assured collection of elegant rockers, the band's bells and whistles extravaganza as it were, the band's **Permanent Vacation**. Sporting one fabulously numbskull record jacket, **Straight Between The Eyes** is a colourful rock ride, peeling rubber outta the gates with *Death Alley Driver*, the Joe Lynn Turner version of *Highway Star*, one high octane pedal-to-the-metal scorcher that quickly snuffs out the strongest tonic on **Difficult To Cure**. Then it's on to *Stone Cold*, one of the band's largest career hits, again permeated by Essence d' Joe, who previews for us the Foreigner stylings of **Bent Out Of Shape** over sensuous Blackmore textures. From start to finish, the record's a roller coaster ride of aristo-rock stylings, most of them vigorously worked with an arsenal of micro detailing and technical mastery. The general tone is artful manipulation: a convincing hard rocker in *Power*, one of Ritchie's finger-twiddling riffs for *Rock Fever*, and a nod to **Down To Earth** with the spiraling gypsy goth of *Eyes Of Fire*. Entertaining for sure, but commercial and less than cohesive, both sentiments intended I'm sure, as the record lives more as a collection of mini-suites where formats are methodically and professionally covered off in compartmentalized, minutes-long exercises. A hard-working, eager to please record, respectable as craft, less so as art.
Rating                                                        8

## Rainbow - Bent Out Of Shape (PolyGram '83)

The confused signals that mark the Joe Lynn Turner era become one with beauty on this Rainbow swan song, a record captured in the muted greens and liquid optics of its cover art. Coming from a man purported to be ruled by ego, **Bent Out Of Shape** offers surprisingly occasional, light-footed but tasteful guitar shadings from Blackmore. And it is Turner's psyche that seems to surface and express its will on this very aristocratic, deeply elegant keyboard-based hard rock classic, a record both ornate and logically simple, decidedly un-metallic yet pulsing with somehow round, unstoppable motion. Much more cohesive than the heavier rawk show of **Straight Between The Eyes** or the gutless but salvageable **Difficult To Cure**, this last Rainbow project evokes images of a heavier but smoother and more melancholy Foreigner, letting melodies cook the brew to a steady simmer and silvery shimmer, as Turner places an artful if derivative croon over various explorations of night-shrouded restraint. Faves and perhaps metaphorical identifiers would include *Street Of Dreams*, a considerable hit for the band (with a naff video), and the slightly higher-strung *Stranded*, both cuts steeped in fluid guitar/keyboard interplay over unthreatening and enjoyable production values courtesy of Roger Glover. Elsewhere there's a bit of metal (see *Drinking With The Devil* and *Fire Dance*), but it is the subdued, fogged-in feel of the MOR types that really define this somewhat novel construction of a world with impeccable manners. Truly sensual and eminently more serious than any other piece of the Rainbow catalogue.

Rating      **9**

## Rainbow - Stranger In Us All   (RCA/BMG '95)

Sadly, Ritchie is locked in a rut, able to subjugate band members to his will, even if his will can't find the muse, the man's creative spirit chained to his guitar, his castle-weary riffs, and his quasi-mystical, painfully heavy metal lyrics. Unfortunately nobody is allowed to project here, John O'Reilly (ex Blue Öyster Cult) committing the first crime, mailing in a performance that is cloistered and afraid, further weakened by the record's boring, metal-lite production. Doogie White's vocals are similarly anemic, evoking the prissy strains of Joe Lynn Turner, flirting and flaunting his way through a set of lyrics that ruthlessly botch all of Rainbow's tired themes. The only joy here is wandering within Ritchie's always artful guitar solos, because all else (including his riffs) lightly perks along so air-headed and timid, nothing here even gets off the ground, despite a few decent Rainbow parodies wandering the moor. And that's the key sentiment wafting from this record: parody, **Stranger In Us All** just throwing out constrained, under-arranged versions of all sorts of things superficially expected of Rainbow.

Rating      **6**

## Rainbow Butt Monkeys - Letters From Chutney
(Mercury/Polydor '95)

A smash alt.rock success up here in frozen Canada, the Rainbow Butt Monkeys (I think people just like to say the name) dish forth a sort of ham-hocked funkgrunge, taking a few STP and AiC type boulder-riffs and giving them hip-swivel grooves of a reserved, mid-speed, senior citizen danceclub nature. Which is where sticky lead single *Circles* sits, suggesting a direction Dan Reed Network or Bootsauce might have driven to success. Scott's voice sounds a bit like Ozzy, which enforces one likening those steamy riffs unto Sabbath. File with Bush and Nixons as one of many metal flavours masquerading as alternative rock.

Rating      **6**

## Ram Jam - Ram Jam   (Epic '77)

A goofy buffalo burger of a platter, **Ram Jam** was the first of two infinitely different releases by this anonymous business arrangement, scoring a big lonely hit with Leadbelly's mind-expanding tribal stomp *Black Betty*, still a radio staple on more adventuresome classic rock airwaves. Erstwhere, all bumps and wheezes like some thudly and lead-headed cross between Skynyrd, Foghat and lesser-endowed agents of Americana such as Brownsville, The Godz, and The Boyzz. About as exciting as watching liquid paper coagulate, yet somehow so stupidly '70s, one can't help shakes one's head in embarrassed amusement. Turgid, funky, and sometimes wrongly complicated boogie rock throughout, **Ram Jam** jellyrolls tuneful and dumb, around fat wads of old-as-the-hills guitar charges, and vocal musings from at least a couple of sources, one that emits a low suvvern blues like a weed-slowed Billy Gibbons, and one that fits squarely twixt the growlies of Paul Stanley and Peter Criss. Twisty, muscle-bound and redneck as the cows, but definitely basking on the rocks under a coma-inducing mid-day slow-burn.

Rating      **6**

## Ram Jam - Portrait Of The Artist As A Young Ram
(Epic '78)

As if they'd been creating *exactly this sort of thing* for a hundred years, Ram Jam descend truly from nowhere with one of the classiest, wisest and modern metal albums to hit as of 1978. With one of the strangest lifelines in rock'n'roll, Ram Jam '78 has absolutely nothing in common with Ram Jam '77, sonically speaking. **Portrait Of The Artist** is such a caustic and capable work of power, propelled by classy percussion, rock-solid writing, wrapped 'round a strangely maddening mix, not to mention a comparatively early, razor-sharp knack for pushing the right metallic buttons at the right time amidst a near constant barrage of eardrum-piercing axe noise from Jimmy Santoro and the expert wailings of Myke Scavone. Truly ahead of its time, in a similar situation to that of Riot, Ram Jam loads **Portrait** with intrigue and raucous heft, dealing forth masterwerks of aggression such as *Just Like Me*, *Pretty Poison* (righteous chorus if there ever was), and *Runway Runaway*, among pure drinking fare like lead romp *Gone Wild*, and dynamic, regal assemblage *Turnpike*. Still a mystery to me and many other I'm sure, this record and its complex web of makers come truly from a void in the business, artistically sounding like no predecessor or contemporary, yet so squarely metallic, and not really strangely so at that. And even though the record's liner notes are detailed and complete, there's not a single name within the band, surrounding the band, or even among the "Thanks To's" that I've ever heard of at the time or since. And to add to the ambiguity, only one member gets in on the writing credits; co-writing six of ten here, the rest and vast majority of the credit going to "J. Strange", "T. Love", and "S. Goldman", the last also wearing the hat of Assistant Engineer. And, I don't know, but apparently the involvement of Kasenetz and Katz is highly relevant in some way due to their successes as producers of '60s bubble gum pop. But enough mystery, snag this awesome rock feast the minute it crosses your gaze. One killer '70s necessity fer sure; so heavily and loudly alone, lost in time but crashingly brilliant. Seek strenuously in hope that ye shall find.

Rating      **10**

## Ramones - Ramones   (Sire '76)

**Ramones**, the first American punk record, woke the world to a new way of doing business, and lit a fire to an exploding and angry N.Y.C. scene that would spend the next five years marrying art, noise, and social sickness with provocative results. The Ramones were the pure noise part of the equation, concocting a merciless guitar-driven drone of childish proportions, the ultimate three chord monster. And it all just barreled on, destroying conventional thoughts as to the seriousness of the music industry, offering a unique and unexplainable wall of good times, at one point fiercely metallic (*Havana Affair* and *Today Your Love, Tomorrow The World*), the next, surf rockin' with muscle (*Judy Is A Punk* and *Let's Dance*), underneath the flu-drenched low whines of lead bro Joey. Not the band's best record, but definitely their first, which means the first even remotely of its kind anywhere. A total nihilistic headbang in the stupidest sense of the word.

Rating      **7**

## Ramones - Leave Home   (Sire '77)

This is the kind of boppy Ramones shit that always bugged me. The year's 1965, and a quartet of flawless college whities are playing beach volleyball and doing that swimming thing with their arms while the strains of this record blare distortedly from a cheap radio. Yes, **Leaves Home** is essentially a heavy Beach Boys record, evidenced by the fact that *California Sun* covered here sounds *exactly* like everything else on the record, aside of the few metallically-skewed sections that are bound to tumble out when you while away your days exploring every mathematical combination of five fat, well-recorded chords. Choruses are annoying too, with a lot of those ditzy doo-wop moves, rendering structures more asinine and simpler than on any other Ramones platter, amounting to a series of brief novelty tunes, which nevertheless established the Ramones lingo, fleshing out the joke for those of us who were still a little disoriented after the debut. Looks real cool, but moshes harmless.

Rating      **4**

## Ramones - Rocket To Russia   (Sire '77)

For no other reason than the fact that I let it play, and let it play often, **Rocket To Russia** is my favorite of the earlier, no-frills Ramones records a disk that seems to take the livelier, more useful elements of **Leaves Home**'s beach sound while retaining the debut's metal weight. But really, one just "chooses" a representative Ramones record (or maybe two, three max), letting it become personal; **Rocket To Russia** being an adequate choice, many of its melodies being strong and memorable, most notably the unabashed gogo swing of *Sheena Is A Punk Rocker* and *Rockaway Beach*, plus the smokin' cover of *Surfin' Bird*, rendered loud and clear in trademark Ramones monotone. Plus the lyrics are a regular skate 'n' surfin', urban-crawlin', drug-ingestin' blast as the leathered ones desensitize their apocalyptic depravity with a disarming sense of humour (see the Dictators). Probably the quintessential document of the Ramones' purist era.

Rating      **8**

## Ramones - Road To Ruin   (Sire Est. '78)

More acoustic guitars than usual, more convincing stabs at metal, but mostly more of the same, **Road To Ruin** marks the first of many incremental tweakings to a rumbling train that rolls on through the subway system without a hope in hell of stopping. Not my chosen car, but urban, decadent, violent and above all, party-driven.

Rating      **5**

## Ramones - End Of The Century   (Sire '80)

The fact that **End Of The Century** is produced by the legendary Phil Spector is supposed to raise eyebrows of adulation on cue. NOT! Spector had his head up his ass as far as real rock'n'roll was concerned, being the knobman behind many an abysmal and powerless '60s hit, an era doomed to a dismal fourth of the four decades of rock so far. So what's he do to the immutable, untamable, untuneable Ramones? Well . . . predictably cloud 'em up to no artistic avail, end result being a soupy punk sound with gogo dancers, which is essentially what the Ramones were anyways. Only here it's more self-conscious and well, dippy, as if this romantic notion of the Ramones concept was the crux of the sound, banishing the band's crucial loud guitars to second stage. So all of side one turns down until the boys in black say "screw this", counter-striking with *Let's Go* at the end of the first half. Then side two surfs through the studio once again, absorbing every gizmo of clap-trap in the room. Dull, 'cos it lets in outsiders who are idiots when it comes to kicking ass.

Rating      **4**

## Ramones - Pleasant Dreams   (Sire '81)

One of the eminently more individual Ramones spreads, **Pleasant Dreams** coheres nicely in subtle homage to a '60s beach sound, which pumps smartly below the usual Ramones crust. Whereas **End Of The Century** represents the band's most committed exploration of mellow accouterments, **Pleasant Dreams** is most like pop, grimy power pop albeit, handled roughly within the realm of the band's guitar drone. Some of the boys' most infectious cuts flow from this record, such as *We Want The Airwaves*, *It's Not My Place*, and *Sitting In My Room*. Really jangly and jivey; melodically clever, yet "heavy" throughout, **Pleasant Dreams** to this day strikes me as one of the more mature, well-conceived chunks of Ramonia.

Rating      **8**

## Ramones - Subterranean Jungle   (Sire '83)

A tired hodgepodge of the band's leftover '60s hula hoops juxtaposed against three or so more metallic knives, including sustained meteor shower *Psycho Therapy* and the under-rated *Highest Trails Above*. Not much to do cartwheels over here as the band seems smothered in the Spector influence that made the last two albums such sonically different but philosophically similar nostalgia-based museum pieces. Here the Ramones are left live without a net, scrambling for direction, finding only noodly, TV commercial melodies. Unconvincing of anything and void of mission. Cool cover and appropriately apocalyptic video: *Time Has Come Today*.

Rating      **4**

## Ramones - Too Tough To Die   (Sire '84)

It's widely felt out there in wonderland that the Ramones as a concept was pretty nifty, yet as seriously fun dudes to listen to year after year . . . well . . . two or three platters, and you've pretty well tired of the idea. And as things got wimpier, campier, sappier, and dressier, many including myself, tuned out, looking for more challenging and progressing punk highs. Well the Flintstones are back and ready to tear a chunk of flesh from our collective backsides. And it's a case of one step back, two steps ahead, as this return to kicking Marshall ass is toughened for the urban battles of the new reality, armed with a boots-to-the-head bash of guitars brutishly recorded for maximum concussion. **Too Tough To Die** makes it more fun to like the Ramones than it ever was, 'cos things are increasingly muscular and dare I say deep, amidst the otherwise totally retro, time-warped visit with records I through III. Yeesh . . . the Ramones . . . a headphone band. It's true, things are so dang tight and rhythmically massive, it's a pleasure to take this one as a membrane-to-membrane direct hit. Things still get melodically undermining in places, detracting from the assault, but just when you're ready to turn your back, rounds of hot lead yank ya back to the fact that these guys are just getting more cantankerous with age. Two of the band's finest moments: the snakey *I'm Not Afraid Of Life* and the almost sophisticated *Daytime Dilemma (Dangers Of Love)*. Chill, man . . . the Ramones ain't half bad.

Rating      **7**

## Ramones - Animal Boy   (Sire '86)

All high-falutin' ambitions towards art have been systematically purged come the abusive punk snarl of **Animal Boy**, a record for all the urban n'er-do-wells, outcasts, and general goof-offs who love it loud and intrusive, yet simple enough for their impenetrable hammer heads. Again, all is muscular and perfectly primed for mosh warp one, from the aggressive blast of *Somebody Put Something In My Drink*, *Apeman Hop* and *Eat That Rat*, to the smoother glue of *My Brain Is Hanging Upside Down (Bonzo Goes To Bitburg)* and the retro *Mental Hell*. Well, come to think of it, it's all retro. What else are the Ramones capable of? Except a fine tuning to the point where all four corners of the leather-clad grimace accomplish their twisted goals. I don't know who does what in the band anymore, but I'm not too crazy with the craggy vocals used on mostly the thrashier numbers. Grating and counter-productive to say the least. Fave: the totally useless for any-

thing *Crummy Stuff*. Another strong record festering belligerently in rank tradition.
Rating 7

## Ramones - Mondo Bizarro (Warner Bros. '92)

Man, I don't know how many more Ramones albums I can get excited about. Well I do: none. 'Cos **Mondo Bizarro** is the usual Ramone hippodrone, packed full of aggressive three chord rock, devoid of musical embellishment, with an ever-improving attention to vocals, lyrics, and what both can do to tired old chord change-ups. So what's different? More punk in an almost English, heavy Damned-type direction; all rainy and depressing but fast. Sprinkle in a few melodic pop structures polluted with mallet-head metal guitar and you've got an all too unsurprising batch of weeks old hash brownies on which to fuel endless travels through the subway system of the nearest decaying urban nightmare near you.
Rating 5

## Ramones - Acid Eaters (Radioactive/MCA '94)

Betraying of age in a bad way, **Acid Eaters** finds our favourite leather steam monkeys covering popular but garagey classics from the late '60s, which is what the whole Ramones trip sounds like anyways. Best is first, with an oxygenated *Journey To The Center Of The Mind*. And *When I Was Young* is creepy and ambitiously arranged, with Dylan's *My Back Pages* an explosion of wonderment. But *Somebody To Love* and *Substitute* gotta hit the crapper, slappy. I dunno, it's an OK concept for '94, 'cos the tribute thing hadn't gotten out of hand yet, and I'd call a good third of this obscure. Plus it holds well, the Ramones exuding a cemented confidence gained from churning towards infinity, nary a collective deep thought within ten city blocks of the whole one-track trick.
Rating 6

## Ramones - Adios Amigos! (Radioactive/MCA '95)

Kinda kills the fun this band desperately needs to generate by naming your record **Adios Amigos!** and then not exactly dispelling rumours that the record's a swansong. But anyhow, **AA!**'s just another three chord Ramones mosh, I guess cutting out the fat of their experimental tracks, which might be why the record's so brief. All the talk about how "live" the recording went is neither here nor there, the production sounding the same as usual. The newest guy C.J. sings a bit which breaks up the monotony, *Scattergun* being of particularly hooky status. It ain't entirely out of the question that Joey and Co. can sell a stack of pancakes by taking their rightful place as punk's first family. That is, if there really was a new punk movement afoot. Update: third or fourth in stature on '96's Lollapalooza bill, depending on how you count.
Rating 6

## Rampage - Victims Of Rock (Hafenklang '81)

These depressing Germans struck a chord of personal anguish during the exciting and morally pummeling early days of the invasion, sounding and appearing like wondrous accidents, like a Jane or Eloy or Lucifer's Friend gone heavy without themselves or the fans noticing. **Victims Of Rock** looks cheap and confused, which is the translated brilliance of this rumbling and painful record, sonically speaking. A loud and trashy recording sets the scene for this ambitious though loosely-played piece of imperfect but emotionally destructive melodi-metal. Sounding more like life-embittered hippies, Rampage rocks cold and inviting, as distressingly witnessed on classic monolith *All The Lost Time* and relentless war cry *I Wanna Be Free*. The vocal chores are handled with erratic aplomb, often randomly ascending into swelling harmonies and quivering emotion. The axework is tortured, tasteful, and ever

so Teutonic; and all punishing frequencies work a grim magic, running together in some sort of rough, unhewn jam session, yet one based around higher than average quality song constructs. Like so many smothering German bands, these guys assault the centres responsible for optimism, managing foreboding overcast skies, which of course possess the extraordinary potential for the most impressive and intense of electrical storms.
Rating 8

## Rampage - Rampage (Fastlane '83)

Clueless church boy rock from the U.S. central south, possessing none of the componentry necessary to make big waves in corporate boardrooms let alone mall rat craniums. Keyboardy, lifeless, and mildly hard rocking with fine vocals from John Ehlert, who embraces blues signatures as per Lou Gramm, and even Charlie Huhn, Rampage is competent in all departments, yet nerdy and unaware of commercial metal's standards already in place in '83.
Rating 4

## Rancid - . . . And Out Come The Wolves (Epitaph '95)

Yeah, so big deal. It does sound superficially like The Clash, Rancid by association touted as a band that matters. And they did pass up the big label offers to stay street. But the problem is that punk musically speaking is dull, and was even quite dull in '78. There can't be much to it by rule, so Rancid just does the same inconsequential delivery of simple chugalug chords like its two lone bigger soul bro's Green Day and Offspring. They add that little reggae thing (which ain't new either), and they actually look like punks, leading the charge for mohawks into the millennium. And they have those maudlin, bloody but unbowed hero choruses. Add it all up, and you have an OK punk band. There will probably never be another good one, so if you need punk, I guess line up here. Just like the Ramones, third or fourth in stature on '96's Lollapalooza bill, depending on how you count!
Rating 6

## Rapid Tears - Cry For Mercy (Chameleon '84)

An early four track EP from Toronto that displays an act with a killer ear for poignant metallic melody, **Cry For Mercy** is the product of a band on the verge, buoyed by universally great reviews from the overseas press. Rapid Tears also hatched one full-length I vaguely remember as hideously recorded, schizophrenic but similarly studded with accomplished traditional alchemy as per Dio, Scorpions, Rainbow and early NWOBHM, but more specifically basic mid-years Priest.
Rating 5

## Ratt - Ratt (Time Coast '83)

In what will years later become frequent practice, Ratt scampers into view with a half album, concentrating on building buzz with a key few tunes well done. And by all accounts, the ploy worked, given the anticipation for and subsequent meteoric rise of **Out Of The Cellar**. Ratt comprises six scrappy Holly-rocks that pack a punch, a bar-bashing assault that in total headbangs thicker than the sterling debut, best cuts being *Sweet Cheater*, *U Got It*, and *Back For More*, the latter soon to be cleaned up and sent chart-bound on **Out Of The Cellar**. In general, sturdy and proud, gorged on deliberately-placed decibels, as Ratt heads off a potentially overpowering pretty boy image at the pass, decked in leathers 'n' loud. Check out Aero-cover-cover *Walkin' The Dog*. You'll get the point.
Rating 7

## Ratt - Out Of The Cellar  (Atlantic '84)

Just in time for the golden age of rock video, West Coast poutmasters Ratt were to be seen everywhere blowing picture tubes with eminently catchy lead single and video *Round And Round*. And onto the world stage they pranced, **Out Of The Cellar** selling briskly as America discovered a fresh, accomplished metal machine who went just the right speed, balancing control with princely power chords, a cavalier approach seemingly lost since the '70s, re-emphasizing the sentiment that if you *think* you're the king, you *are* the king. Everything is focused, all is correct, going down smoothly like fine wine, grooves commandeered with sly seduction and L.A. sheen by Bobby Blotzer's rhythmic sixth sense sent to headphone heaven by Beau Hill's full range mix. All in all, a clever update and exploitation of all the great '70s Americarockers, with a particular nod to the empire-building vibe of Van Halen. Faves: *Lack Of Communication* and *The Morning After*, both fine examples of Ratt's uncanny manipulation of hook come chorus time.
Rating 9

## Ratt - Invasion Of Your Privacy  (Atlantic '85)

Riff heaven abounds with lead single *You're In Love*, and it looks like showman Stephen Pearcy was going to lead new axe gods De Martini and Crosby, plus stadium-ready backbone Crouchier and Blotzer towards big limos, record II piggy-backing record I's powerful debut showing. But then something creeps into the brew, a type of sonic apathy, where grooves become ever so rutted and tedious, as tune after tune loses identity and exuberance, as if second record pressure has caused an easing of the throttle. Really, **Invasion** is **Cellar** II, without the peaks and valleys, just a sort of room temperature plateau, trying to avoid confrontation with more ornery species of carnivore or parasite. Pink prison walls and mauve album covers; definitely something in common there.
Rating 6

## Ratt - Dancing Undercover   (Atlantic '86)

After dropping the silver platter, Ratt are back fighting for scraps, cranking a little bit of street-level life into the chemical cocktail, driving the hyper *Body Talk* and fave rave *Looking For Love* to magical **Cellar** depths. All over **Dancing Undercover**, the band kicks, assisted by a more cantankerous mix this time, with even Pearcy getting more raw and rant out of his raggedy pipes. Other intrinsically Ratt-whipped jems would include lead single *Dance* and *It Doesn't Matter*, while *Take A Chance* does just that with a funkier riff, crafted by two of the slinkiest, low-strung guitars of the '80s. Cool record, exploring fully the heavier face of American hard rock. Well deserving of sustained attention.
Rating 8

## Ratt - Reach For The Sky   (Atlantic '88)

Another steamy intro track in the slash 'n' burnin' *City To City*, but what follows rides a low intelligence, teen beat theme with some of the band's poppier melodies infecting the thick Ratt critical mass. Make no mistake though, long-time producer Beau Hill keeps the Blotzer brew muscular and filled to the brim with axes, while the band weaves their usual quotient of capitalist, mood-enhancing melodies and quality change-ups throughout. Lost to the limelight, Ratt has steadily and methodically proven their mettle, unswerving in their ability to craft veritable bushels of hard rock that, by better combinations of timing, management push and luck, deserve to be hits by any fair measure. Maybe the glow is gone but the guts remain.
Rating 7

## Ratt - Detonator   (Atlantic '90)

It's a cruel world when you're no longer America's media darlings, and Ratt have known that sinking feeling for a long time now (despite everything to date going at least platinum, the debut at double). **Detonator** is the third relatively ignored rodent in a row, and is at least equal to the band's string of respectable records since **Out Of The Cellar**, the band's most magical shooting star. Desmond Child is in tha house, ostensibly to prop up the songs this time 'round, to no discernible improvement or degeneration of the core Ratt sound. Tracks like *Shame, Shame, Shame* and *Hard Time* kick smartly, while a simpler hard rock groove rolls through *Scratch That Itch* (my fave) and *Heads I Win, Tails You Lose*. But the Gene-like funky crap can use the door, as can sleep-walking ballad *Givin' Yourself Away*. One noticeable difference this time is that Pearcy's usually chest-thumping bellow seems thinner, quieter and unnecessarily treated. Overall though, Ratt still has something to offer, showing through restraint, their experience among corporate rockers. But I can't help but wish for a major re-thinking of the band's purpose.
Rating 7

## Ravage - Wrecking Ball   (Roadrunner '86)

Second rate American bludgeon, plodding bluntly the lines of Virgin Steele, Eric Steel, and the band's limited misconception of **British Steel**, with an operatic set of pipes like many an amusing mid-'80s castle builder. No real reason to ride along, unless you're buds of the band.
Rating 4

## Raven - Rock Until You Drop   (Neat '81)

An instantly likeable band of hapless punters, Raven quickly left behind this cheaply assembled but feisty debut for the whiplash grandeur of **Wiped Out**. Still, **Rock Until You Drop** is a gutsy record full of valuable punk metal booty, artillery like *For The Future*, *Tyrant Of The Airwaves*, and trench-wrestling opener *Hard Ride*, which work wunders slotting Raven somewherz between the marauding riffs of debut-era Tygers Of Pan Tang and the gutter grind of Tank, sort of a compact car version of Saxon with better ideas. With personal charisma right outta the blocks, built of John Gallagher's extreme vocal yelpings and a riff-mad love of mayhem, Raven were a unique Everyman sort of force, the quintessential NWOBHM power trio, working an endearing three-way creative bounty that emanated honesty and an enthusiasm to hit the stage blazing, whipping whatever size crowd that happens to show up into a headbanging feeding frenzy, all parties denim-clad buds out to lig a few pints. Well-written but scurried, scampered and sabotaged on its way to the pressing plant, lack of coinage no doubt the culprit. Neat/Roadrunner CD reissue adds three tracks: original hyper-tense versions of *Wiped Out*, *Crazy World* and *Inquisitor*, the latter provided in thick gluey demo tones for your archeological listening pleasure.
Rating 7

## Raven - Wiped Out   (Neat '82)

With iron-clad resolve, one humble, no-frills rock'n'roll power trio from jolly ol' cranks one of the most spectacular artifacts of the early NWOBHM, a record smeared with energy, chops, and loosely-harnessed anarchy, Wacko and the brothers Gallagher sending a thundering wake-up call to all thirsty metalheads who live to mosh in earnest. Massive improvements abound, as previous cracks in the sound are filled in by low frequency throbs and a general urge to assemble weight with speed, all points of the triangle hell-bent on being heard amongst the carnage. Lots of aural inundation, but the layers heroically gel, sent to fortify another strong batch of speedy OTT smokers.

**Wiped Out** was repeatedly pasted to our circuits during the mid-'80s, becoming the record we proudly unleashed on unbelievers (usually snobby jazz guys) to represent the cutting edge of metal, a hard sell given Raven's crazed and almost haphazard approach and disdain for subtlety, resulting in a record of punk-inspired high science, brilliance without pomp, hair-raising velocities without concern for clean. Personal anthems (lethal with caffeine or gin) would include the brooding *Star War* and hostess with the mostest *Hold Back The Fire*, probably fave neuron fryer of the whole Raven panorama, the Gut of the metal experience as we know it. Enough underdog amperage to rumble the bones of any unruly denim-clad hoodlum. This time 'round, the Neat/Roadrunner CD reissue adds another three tracks, the **Crash, Bang, Wallop** EP, comprising the title track, *Rock Hard* and *Run Them Down*, all loopy, nattery and Raven to the loving core.
Rating 9

## Raven - All For One (Megaforce '83)

The magnet opus, the big noise, the leadfoot, the stupenating, cannonating Classic. All superlatives converge on this Powerhouse of Metal, an orderly mass of truck-size power riffs laid down with bone-breaking precision, as Raven cements the brains of unbelievers with the pulverization production murdalization of Double Trouble. Bass (courtesy Mark Gallagher) blobbed way up front, guitars stomping the world with inhuman chords, and Wacko pummeling cave walls miles below the substrata combine for a thick heaviness of groove rarely matched and arguably never exceeded, as blood can't help but synchronize with the tidal flow of riff and rhythm. No shit rivetheads, I can't help but envisage that swords of truth like *Take Control*, *Run Silent Run Deep* and *Take It Away* must have influenced Mustaine in some covert or maybe overt fashion in eventually finding *Symphony Of Destruction*, a song I feel is one of the most philosophically important in metal in the '90s, as purity of power through simplicity. **All For One** has four or five lesser symphonies, and unbelievable ripplings of brawn throughout all of its dense hide. Man, the level of tragedy in all this just pops vessels in my head though when I think that after one fine live thrashing, all creativity will vaporize with such finality. Forget the future. It hurts too damn much. Let the plate in your head shift with the tectonic plates under your boots as you crank **All For One** 'til all quakes in cosmic metallic synchro-swell. Both gut-wrenching throbs will unmistakably become one as you witness the majesty of power chords at their most primordial.
Rating 10

## Raven - Break The Chain (Banzai '83)

Taking deep drags on the infinite wattage that enthroned **All For One**, Raven clash skulls with Udo Dirkschneider (one half of Double Trouble) to produce one ferocious package of cuts comprising this six track EP, flagshipped by rowdy-beyond-words single *Break The Chain* and far and away the most manic, sabre-toothed *Born To Be Wild* ever commandeered. Friggin' hilarious as Udo and John Gallagher trade belts and canine frothings above the only truly *heavy* version of this tired old '60s tune I've ever witnessed. Elsewhere four more non-LPers (until the CD reissues): *Wiped Out* is vintage **Wiped Out**, *Rock Hard* flounders, *Inquisitor* annihilates in this redone version, and to close out the invasion, *The Ballad Of Marshall Stack* stomps off with the prize, staging a thieving, thumping display of cinder block rock, one "ballad" that could easily sink criminally-altered torsos with anything on **All For One**.
Rating 9

## Raven - Live At The Inferno (Banzai '84)

One full-length studio classic, one rip-roarin' EP, and now one dangerous live document, closing out the second and last of two spectacular golden eras in the Raven saga. **Live At The Inferno** samples from all three studio albums to date, while also offering **All For One**-style technical updates on a few rarities, *Crazy World*, *Crash Bang Wallop*, and long-lost first single for the band *Let It Rip*. But really the metallic pleasure is in experiencing booming versions of early bashers like *Star War*, *Fire Power* and *Hell Patrol*. Obviously a natural at the live act (at least technically), it's sad to see that so much talent would shortly become suppressed for good. One of the better live albums, especially given the vehement statement denying any use of overdubs.
Rating 7

## Raven - Stay Hard (Atlantic '85)

Almost as if scared to death at the thought of following **All For One**, Raven, in what I can only imagine as total and shameless capitulation to clueless label bosses, tries a Twisted Sister-style cartoon rock record, the aural equivalent of their ridiculous stage wear, a sort of sports/sci-fi hybrid of tackiness, like a store-bought Hallowe'en costume in the fifteen dollar range. Anyhoo, see **The Pack Is Back** for more personal anguish on the part of this sorry critic, and meet me back at **The Inferno** once yer done.
Rating 4

## Raven - The Pack Is Back (Atlantic '86)

I don't want to go into agonized depths again the extent to which staggeringly inept marketing trampled this band's hopes and more importantly, its creativity. Suffice to say, come about '85, Raven looked simply embarrassing, like fools climbing into metal Elviswear, constructing compositions far below previous sophistication levels, which once bestowed upon this wretched earth **All For One**, a titanic ground-breaking opus; one of the hugest metal records ever smoked. **The Pack Is Back** sadly displays for the mercilessly second time, a trio of amazing talents ordered by their label to come up with something prechewed; being forced, with disastrous consequences, to write variously hard rock, variously simplistic metal as per Crüe or Twisted Sister, while possessing no idea how to be idiots on purpose. It's the worst example of rock'n'roll whoring I can recall; further spikes to the heart coming with the inclusion of novelty cover *Gimme Some Lovin'*, one of the most irritating tunes ever penned, and the unbelievable presence of "The Uptown Horns." The case of Raven inspires about the most venom I can swell up with respect to the business side of rock'n'roll, utterly undressing a legendary and prolific union of minds. And of course the whole sorry ruse was a commercial failure, fans of a once proud power trio battalion knowing contrived when they see it.
Rating 5

## Raven - Mad (Atlantic '86)

Just as Raven realize what lugans they've been, one finds the band has returned to uncompromising metal with their creative faculties and grasp of heaviness erased. Five tracks sabotaged by sub-par self-production and in indescribable loss of metallic sense, writing riffs that act like joke OTT, sounding like a hybrid between punk and techno-metal, spiced with juvenile little blurts and wangs which purposefully break the flow and kill the groove. And the boyz still haven't completely shaken the kiddie rock spewtations of the last two ill pills, with *How Did Ya Get So Crazy* and *Seen It On The T.V.* (you get the picture). Weird, but the revival Raven seems bent on has an all new host of problems. Discomforting and sad, like watching someone lose their mind.

Rating     4

## Raven - Life's A Bitch   (Atlantic '87)

The rejuvenated Raven kicks off generously enough with the speedy but disciplined *The Savage And The Hungry*, yet as much as the band grunts and pushes, they still sound jumpy, nervous and impatient, with lots of stops, starts, blur tempos, over-riffing and most importantly, bizarre, atonal melodies (see *Never Forgive* and *On The Wings Of An Eagle* for a demo of all five). But the title cut rocks with levity (until the chorus), as does *Juggernaut*, and *You're A Liar* is magnificent, recalling the staying power of *Hold Back The Fire*. However, as all winds out in tortuous earache-my-eye status, **Life's A Bitch** is impossible to warm to, sounding like a cold, tricky, technical exercise in metal-based physics, self-produced in unexpressive fashion, which combines with the untrackable twiddling in construction of a record that sounds like it's been erroneously spun on 45.

Rating     6

## Raven - Nothing Exceeds Like Excess   (Relativity '88)

Faster, higher, to a plane only dogs can appreciate. That seems to be the central tenet here. Everybody's far up the proverbial fretboard, including John's voice and the new guy's bass drums, which sound like toms, thanks to another self-produced effort. And increasingly eccentric, hysterical riffs reinforce the *Over the Over The Top* (into the wading pool) feel of a record I can't enjoy, for the personal conclusion that Raven has become a ranting parody of a speed ethic long ago transformed into the Megadeths, Anthrax's, Testaments and even Ministry's of this wicked world. I'm still interested and hopeful that this proven noise-making consortium can locate their marbles, perhaps reaching back and recapturing the low cycle rumble that made **All For One** such a richter wrecker. If the band would crane up and take an objective look at the modern world, they just may discover that cutting edge today is merely an extension of the band's own early triumphs. Nothing like fickle fate to screw with peoples' minds.

Rating     4

## Raven - Glow   ('94)

Man, something definitely got really lost along the way, Raven still going for those quirky structures with no pay-off, oblique and dissonant jazz-style chords and vocals that sound off-keyish but I guess really aren't. Still can't believe the Raven still flies, but the task at hand is to tell you that **Glow** improves by getting less hysterical, tunes like *Altar* and complex opener *Watch You Drown* riding a cool metallic wave unlike much of the panicky rest. Included: an obscure Lizzy cover in *The Rocker*, personifying Raven's inability to pick music we want to hear, there really being twenty better choices that I might have really wanted to make my own. Fact is, this is another anemic 1986 record from Raven. **All For One** boys! . . . one for all of us . . . SOON!

Rating     6

## Razor - Violent Restitution   (Fringe '88)

The continued existence of this band year after year defied all logic. Cranking untuneful wads of hostile thrash-cum-death over tons of records since '84 including—and the following list may not be perfect, but you get the idea—**Armed And Dangerous, Executioner's Song, Evil Invaders, Malicious Intent, Custom Killing, Violent Restitution, Shotgun Justice,** and **Open Hostility**, these cantankerous (actually very soft spoken) Canadian merchants of adrenaline doom see no end to their mission of torture. Ineptly moshing blurs I've experienced previous to this one just sent me screaming for the exits, yet with **Violent Restitution**, I can at least see how somebody could dig this bludgeon, which for once is adequately recorded, and adequately varied with the riffs that kill. Still tons of frash, but this time around, cool tempo de-winds and caustic grindcore infest the corpse like so many leather-winged beetles. Lyrically the band lays it on thick with angry politico-punk assaults and standard axe butcher tales. And one of the worst strings of album covers ever scratched together. Pretty funny stuff, but overall, I just don't wanna know.

Rating     4

## Razor - Exhumed   (Fringe '94)

Leader Dave Carlo finally packs it in after years of frustration cranking his form of intense '80s thrash. Towards this end, Carlo and Fringe have assembled this 38 track, two disc retro package, sampling tracks from all seven records (plus a debut EP) in chronological mayhemic order. Carlo believes his band to be hand-to-hand with Slayer and no one else, virtually alone in the world, curmudgeonly sticking to his pistol-whipped love of speed. And indeed, for fans of the genre, Razor's last few records expressed that defiance with insistent rejection of growth, a philosophy that bellowed "you punters either stick with us or leave!" Many rivetheads did move on, but a small legion around the world turned Razor into modest legends. As Carlo states, his happiness lies within his own satisfaction of where the band went, and his bitterness lies with his feeling that the band was woefully underexposed. Yes near the end, Razor was as good at this very specific type of metal as any, but it's the genre itself that was starting to smell. And therein lies my total indifference to the band's legacy.

Rating     6

## Reckless - Heart Of Steel   (Quality '85)

Open and clanky hard rock from the Great White North; too stripped and exposed, lumbering plain and painful, betraying its trail-blazing status with respect to melodic hard rock, a genre not yet fashionable, and more importantly, not yet handled by any outfit capable of showing how it should be done. Listenable due to a couple of sticky choruses on *Hot 'N' Ready* and *Drivin' You Mad*, **Heart Of Steel** is the brainchild of lead axeman and character Steve Madden who's taken this band through a lot of changes prior to this record, including a stint with a female lead singer, before settling with ex-Witchkiller throat Doug Adams.

Rating     4

## Red Dawn - Red Dawn   (Now & Then '94)

Prolific AOR label Now & Then can keep making these sorts of perfection hair metal records forever, and I'm sure greedy pockets of sweet-tooths worldwide will be glad to make the effort worthwhile. Red Dawn is a minor superstar band for the puzzling genre, sporting David Rosenthal, Chuck Burgi and Greg Smith (all travelled guys, biggest overlapping duties including Rainbow and Blue Oyster Cult), plus a vocalist in Larry Baud who's a dead ringer for Graham Bonnet. But that's where the fun ends, this piffly piece of dated pop metal doing all things AOR adequately, while offering nothing new. High grades for craft and axework (Tristan Avakian), but the songs are limp.

Rating     5

## Vernon Reid - Mistaken Identity   (Sony '96)

After the perplexed run of semi-successes that was the Living Colour catalogue, the band called it a day, guitarist Vernon Reid returning with this accessible, largely instrumental solo record. **Mistaken Identity** borrows heavily from many Living Colour conventions, adding healthy doses of hip hop and sampling, all revolved around fairly accepted guitar god instrumental record structures. Which is where the accessibility comes in, Reid keeping it light, zesty and un-academic throughout, injecting humour and pop culture weirdness amongst his still quite metallic riffing. Of limited appeal fer sure, but as instrumental guitar rock goes, Reid hasn't flipped out nearly as much as I'd expected him to, robustly cranking along like an inner city Satriani. Don't let the jazz talk fool you. This is merely entertaining guitar-driven hip hop, any jazz inflections left arcanely buried within guitar patterns alone, versus spreading to other instruments or overall song structure.

Rating    6

## Reign - Exit Clause   (Mausoleum '95)

One of those bands without glaring faults that just doesn't satisfy, U.K.'s Reign are a sort of beyond power metal machine, kinda like commercial death metal or if generalist Bay Area stuff got slower and stiffer (wait a second, it has!). Second record after a '94 debut called **Embrace**, not like I care, finding this chunky, rhythmically proud chuck of bog-blasted granite frustratingly close to remarkable, but somehow simultaneously dated.

Rating    6

## The Rejects - Quiet Storm   (Heavy Metal '84)

Heavy Metal Records continues to skirt the issue, signing acts from the logic-thwarting fringes; in this case, an ex poverty punk band that obviously lacks any understanding of metal. **Quiet Storm** adopts flashy metal graphics, hiding a sorry case of mistaken identity; a record that offers nothing more than generic ruff rock, touching on non-committal reference points like The Stones, The Who . . . you get the picture. Plus the mix sucks, and the vocals sleep on the vine, betraying this project as a shameless leap to a bandwagon that will only reward those who believed through the lean years (well, the occasional poor sod anyways).

Rating    2

## Release - End Of The Light   (Century Media '95)

Big, brooding, but above all, sublime and artful, Release's debut **End Of The Light** shines with astounding fresh arrangements, of all things unforgivingly greyish metal, somehow delivering the pig seductively appetizing. Imagine progressive death metal simplified and stressing song, rife with pause and open architecture. This is where Release lives, the band showing wisdom through patience, sounding underground but not overbearing, a sort of serene, weed-whacked Sabbath, Hawkwind with both chops and brains, or mebbee Coroner/Death/Rage cracked open and suntanning. I'll get back to you.

Rating    8

## Renegade - Rock'n'Roll Crazy   (Allied Artists '83)

Club-level partypop metal with yelpy vocals sunk by a real cheezy late '70s nerdvibe. Strangely innocent, which works to the band's advantage, kinda like a humble Def Leppard wannabe or heavy Piper or Babys, or sumthin' Canuck insulated. Kind marks for simple sincerity, whatever that means.

Rating    5

## Replicants - Replicants   (Zoo/BMG '96)

An aptly-titled (a tribute in itself) covers album by members of Tool and Failure, **Replicants** adds a cluttery but sublime layer of heroin rust to a wildly divergent batch of songs which time-travel kitschy culture from three decades. It doesn't really play like a covers record though, because even a staggeringly knowledgeable rock historian like myself doesn't recognize a good half the tracks (i.e. obscure tunes from Marc Bolan, Lennon, Missing Persons, Gary Numan and Pink Floyd). And even recognizable numbers get a highly

personalized stamp, rendered fat, bashing and alterno-cool (emulating the chic and current Chicago sound), tunes like The Cars' *Just What I Needed*, Neil Young's *Cinnamon Girl* and Steely Dan's *Dirty Work* rumbling like Melvins on a Disneyworld train, while McCartney's *Silly Love Songs* gets stretched, mangled and summarily discarded. So what ultimately emerges (at least for me), is an academic, Wire-like, loose, eccentric and spacey slog through time, prog for the millennium, free drugs for the hip during happy hour.

Rating    7

## Respect - Despair   (Black Mark '95)

Don't know what it is (or what the hell they're saying, given that about a third of it's in French), but **Despair** is a pretty cool spin, with influences from all over the place, hardcore, thrash, Pantera, progressive, even '80s Deep Purple, all melding quite successfully throughout this enigmatic record. And typical of metal bands from off the beaten track markets, it sounds totally strange, not preconceived like say Tad Morose might be (in a good way), more like someone's metal collection fell off a truck and recoagulated. Fairly shouty vocals throughout are really the only harsh thing about this pleasurable pastiche of styles, a blend demonstrated amply by lead track *Mort D'Esprit*, which switches streams a few times to no ill effect. Various different keyboard sounds sometimes intrude and clash like something straight out of Rick Wakeman's flowing white hair, robes and dry ice, but generally things are kept to a relevant, '90s metal level. Quality stuff, if a bit wonky and confused. The band's second in six years.

Rating    7

## Reverend - Reverend   (Caroline '89)

Metal Church's David Wayne shoots his guns of revenge with a strapping new band, something darker, more carnal and seething-red compared to Church's ever-widening metal elite. The **Reverend** EP is a scant four tracks long, yet arguably the band's finest percentage-wise, after two full-length studio behemoths (+ one live) as of '93. Apocalyptic and basic, **Reverend** is also heavy as a hundred year old furnace, with an edge as sharp as the split from the Church. Real discernible underground snarl to this one, a no-holds-barred pile of metal ugliness to be sure.

Rating    8

## Reverend - World Won't Miss You   (Charisma '90)

With a considerable gaggle of onlookers giving a damn, Reverend hatch their first full-scope plot, re-plastering the walls of mosh palaces everywhere with their hectic, claustrophobic, black and blue bludgeon. **World Won't Miss You** wins points for aggression, while losing a few for its squared-off, pared-down tooling, a relentless wave of metallic pounding that is ever so slightly too uniform in expression to make this a classic. Maybe a bit too Anthrax or Exodus, in other words, echoes of derivation, all crammed down yer gullet with an anti-social punk boot that just won't quit. Still, a riotous, survivalist display of purple rage, creating a grimy, off-putting atmosphere. Unbridled respect, but wary ingestion, with a blistering cover of Sab's *Hand Of Doom*, serving as metaphor for both repulsion and attraction, given my similar cold aspersions assigned to **Paranoid**.

Rating    7

## Reverend - Play God   (Charisma '91)

Down to one mean-looking four piece, Reverend bulge their often mosh-level sound to envelope new chops-driven creativity. Riffs demonstrate a new sinister intricacy, and the overall effect is more intense in terms of monumental, almost artistic despair versus its predecessor's street violence. Outside of CCR's *For-*

leather mayhem, yet more lyrically limited, stuck with the genre's metal themes while sonically ever re-inventing themselves, biding time until hopefully something like **Countdown To Extinction** falls out and knocks the metal community on its ass. Wayne's voice is a fortified cry to battle, a necessity if he is to be heard and respected above the mechanics, the perfect foil to Brian Korban's punishing doom licks. Spacious record, almost risky and exposed in the spirit of Alice in Chains' eloquent **Dirt**, with its dynamics between slow and fast, killer drone and suicidal balladic, but alas ultimately, something still over-cranked and hard to choke down.

Rating **8**

### Rex - Rex   (Columbia '76)

1976. **Free For All** tour, Spokane Washington. A trio of bands: Terrible Ted, a bewildered-looking Be Bop Deluxe, and Rex, featuring Rex Smith (yes, the Rex Smith) backflipping all over the stage. They rocked, and we ran to the local wax dispensary to scoop up **Rex**, the debut album, which became both tour document and solid hard rocker for us, an eminently American guitar party not unlike **Starz** or **Violation**. So affably '70s, Rex is an amalgamation of pre-savvy riffs, some boogie-based with slide (Feeling Better), some like Ted (Violent Playground and Trouble), some spooky (Ten Seconds Of Love and Dead End Kids), all high school guitar rawk as if there was any other kind coming from the good ol' US of A in the mid '70s. Rex Smith is a ringer for Michael Lee Smith from Starz. Are they brothers, or did I dream it? I may have heard something to that effect once but my mind's been scarred by too much school. Alas, my memory fails me. In any event, **Rex** is that kind of animal, packed with cool '70s clichés; rounded-off guitars and a blended, tame sort of recording from Ed Leonetti (see Angel). Talent? Art? Not the prerogative here, just soupy warm '70s Amerimetal. Nostalgia, nothing else.

Rating **7**

### Rex - Where Do We Go From Here?   (Columbia '77)

Angel wore white. Starz and Kiss wore black. Rex never had a look, which somehow undermined their metalness in an era where hard rock and costumes were one, image (and requisite platform boots) being an unselfconscious part of the circus. On **Where Do We Go From Here?**, Rex pull their distancing act, scattering north and south, offering three cuts as heavy or heavier than the debut (Do Me, 7 Come 11, and Running Wild) and more than a few stickier and poppier, perhaps predicting Rex's brief teen beat future. Liked it less at the time for its overall lower metal quotient (14-year-old's idea of sellout), yet surprise, Rex II ages better than Rex I, being busier, more challenging, more colourful and I guess more melodramatic than the debut, the sense of greater chaos making for a deeper sort of '70s spin. Faves for the Hoople-ish hope: You're Never Too Old To Rock & Roll and the title track, which poses the question with traces of wisdom and earnest yearning for an answer.

Rating **8**

### Rhino Bucket - Rhino Bucket   (Reprise '90)

Surprise! AC/DC clones that carry truck with the critics. And why not? We never did get a faithful follow-up to **Highway To Hell**, although **Back In Black** was just-fine-thank-you in its place. **Rhino Bucket** does Bon-era AC/DC in fine denim fashion, nary an impurity, impunity or grunge chord within earshot. So kick back and drift back, close your lids and harken th' time when all you worried about was lining up an honest, reliable bootlegger. Got no life of their own, that much is obvious, and the proceedings are at times a little light 'n' airy, but all in all, you'll achieve that time and place for which you pine, along with buddies who swear up

and down, things were better when they probably sucked. Ten for ten percentage-wise, but of course watery in its premise.

Rating **7**

### Rhino Bucket - Get Used To It   (Reprise '92)

Truly more of the same, rutting the Bucket as a gimmick band, this time around actually offering weaker versions of the band's patented AC/DC knock-offs. Maybe the recent addition of Simon Wright on drums might give these boys a boost, but with the demise of party metal, Rhino Bucket's prospects don't look good.

Rating **6**

### Rhino Bucket - Pain   (Moonstone '94)

I'm copping to these guys now that there's little of this sort of sparse-arse party metal left, Rhino Bucket ringing with a sort of clarity Kix and Dirty Looks ain't got. And landsakes maties, Mad Maggie and What'd You Expect are as good as anything on AC/DC's lactose intolerant **Ballbreaker** opus, Rhino Bucket a close and comfortable approximate of something that shimmers into view only fleetingly. So we've come full circle, arriving in a world gone alt., perplexed, surprised and pleased that bands like Rhino Bucket still exist. Emphatically will not change the face of rock'n'roll, which emphatically is the point.

Rating **7**

### Riggs - Riggs   (Warner Bros. '82)

Cheap, rough-cut, demo-quality hard rock from one Jerry Riggs who experienced fleeting fame for Radar Rider, his riffic little number on the **Heavy Metal** soundtrack album, a toon much more awake than anything here. You have been warned.

Rating **1**

### Righteous Pigs - Stress Related   (Nuclear Blast '90)

Funny how fairly hostile and technical thrash takes on a whole new punked-up meaning when you have a jokey name. But fact is, this is just another Nuclear Blast or Earache-style body slam, Righteous Pigs moshing and stage-diving their way through competent but ugly blindcore, lapsing in and out of blasted drum fury just to keep it fresh and dynamic, not that it really worked.

Rating **4**

### Rio - Sex Crimes   (Music For Nations '86)

Britain's Rio rides a clanky, unruly mix through party metal territory sounding sort of like Highway Chile's questionable **Rockarama** with a chunk of Heavy Pettin' thrown in for general lively upswing. Major transgression: submissive guitars contrasting loud, intrusive, machine-like drums. But hell, the songs are solid and scraggly at least in some of the right places. In possession of at least an inkling of British melodic glory.

Rating **5**

### Riot - Rock City   (Fire Sign '77)

Fairly amazing little record for a '70s indie release, **Rock City** had the acumen to put Ted on the ropes (at least in terms of sheer volume) and walk all over Kiss (**Love Gun**, yeah right!), offering a hot flash of Starz/Legs Diamond/Teaze-style hard rock, astonishingly ready for prime time. Sporting one of the better metal recordings circa '77, **Rock City** proves that big bucks and label know-how aren't the only pathways to knowledge, and the clean-burning duo of lead throat Guy Speranza and axeman Mark Reale have the songs to make full use of the shiny mix, Desperation, Warrior, Overdrive and Hearts Of Fire taking us on a summer excursion through the big city, top down, sparks a flyin'. A pleasant surprise from the cheapies bin at Magic Mushrooms in good ol' Spokane Wash.

Rating **7**

lead throat Guy Speranza and axeman Mark Reale have the songs to make full use of the shiny mix, *Desperation*, *Warrior*, *Overdrive* and *Hearts Of Fire* taking us on a summer excursion through the big city, top down, sparks a flyin'. A pleasant surprise from the cheapies bin at Magic Mushrooms in good ol' Spokane Wash.
Rating 7

## Riot - Narita (Attic '79)

Already this was our band, a solid metal force with a surprisingly confident although somewhat squared-off debut. Boom. **Narita** arrives, and NYC's Riot have entered the hallowed zone, cementing more bricks into the band's mighty wall of riffs while shedding all vestiges of club rock rust. Speranza commands your attention as the boys dish up some sky-high voltage on classics like *49er*, *Kick Down The Walls*, *Do It Up* and the adrenalized *Road Racin'* (which we managed to mangle along with *Outlaw* during our brief existence as bar band extraordinaire, Torque), a pacemaker of sheer force and beauty that hints at incinerations to come with **Fire Down Under**. Riot for us were martyrs for metal, so damn good at it, yet commercially ignored, despite the American ease of their licks, the inviting vibe, the expert helmsmanship of Speranza. One of the unsungs fer sure, and I would bet a major influence on a lot of the luckier name tags today.
Rating 9

## Riot - Fire Down Under (Elektra '81)

With one of the most abhorrent band mascots in history casting its icy stare from the front of this red-hot firebrand, Riot submit their volcanic masterpiece, a molten collection of pure, face-melting American stadium metal, *Swords And Tequila* leading the charge, the liquid electrocution of *Flashbacks* taking us out back to be shot, come journey's end. One power chord sandwich after another, **Fire Down Under** is an intensification of **Narita**'s basic premise, a little of this, a little of that, this time more urgent and carnivorous. Thus Tomahawk warhead *Outlaw*, the vicious ambitious *Don't Hold Back*, the miles-high *Altar Of The King* and the merciless title track, which manages to clip *Road Racin'* in a flaming photo finish. Again, it's sad to think that Riot became more of a hotbed for ideas and inspiration for others than a commercial success in their own right, **Fire Down Under** being such a classy work of the brightest, shiniest of steels, all spitting power lines, peak meter sustain, crisp ringing cymbals and that voice. A most valuable American rock experience.
Rating 10

## Riot - Restless Breed (Elektra '82)

With a heartfelt thanks and wishes of good luck all around, Riot bid farewell to Guy Speranza. Not sure what went down there. Maybe like us spectators, he was mentally worn by such a quality act going hungry. In any event, **Restless Breed** marks the entrance of golden-tressed Rhett Forrester who steers the embattled band in a bluesy, southern direction, only a few baby steps away from their flat-headed riff-mad core, but unmistakably affected by a new, gunslinging dynamic, lyrically evident on *Hard Lovin' Man* (the record's coolest riff), *CIA*, *Loanshark* and *Violent Crimes*, and musically so, on Eric Burdon cover *When I Was Young*, *Dream Away*, the understated title track, and especially the Skynyrd-driven *Showdown*, surprisingly the band's first ballad. Definitely a lesser record than **Fire Down Under**, **Restless Breed** rambles kinda tentative and reflective, as if a relaxed summation of tiring roads taken. Pluses and minuses though, as both the poppier and thrashier elements suffer from a loose mix, and the moody, almost Whitesnake-like numbers roll with weary new pride and additional depth, per-

haps the result of fresh blood with less obvious, less easily assimilated influences.
Rating 8

## Riot - Born In America (Quality '83)

The second and last Riot act to feature the six-gun pipes of Rhett Forrester blows the doors open for a major rock show, a cantankerous display of U.S. Grade A beef. Forrester's influences become more a part of the Riot fold here, or vice versa as the redneck becomes Reale on such head-spinning chewing tobacco as *You Burn In Me*, *Wings Of Fire* and personal fave *Running From The Law*, one mutha of a backwoods barnstormer. Whereas **Restless Breed** sounded unsure with its somewhat hasty hybrid, **Born In America** kicks ass, totally focused on bashing, booming and colliding in a brash lawless world, evoking, yes, Lizzy's **Thunder And Lightning**, both records galloping desperados waging their own personal battles far from politics of life in the rock mainstream. Warm in the gut like firewater.
Rating 9

## Riot - Thundersteel (CBS '88)

Alas Riot roams no more, whilst leader Mark Reale walks off with the name, enlisting gleaming new machines to send his unit into hyperspace. **Thundersteel** employs the services of robot-precise speed metal merchants, turning Riot into a 78 RPM maelstrom of traditional OTT, sorta like a red, white and blue Helloween, complete with a yelper higher than Speranza, and ear-piercing staccato bombardments from all corners of the instrumental fortress. Major bite, but crammed with too much science and not enough blood, sweat and tears, **Thundersteel** has Reale punishing the world. Damn rights, we deserve it. So it's not exactly Riot, and it's a bit conceptually dated (see Shrapnel and Metal Blade circa '85), but a panzer division by any other name is still a body-bagging flesh-eating machine. Recommended for their head-shredding qualities: *Bloodstreets* and *Run For Your Life*.
Rating 7

## Riot - The Privilege Of Power (CBS '90)

Fine German engineering permeates the Riot camp yet again, as the band blinds us with science while this time fusing a vengeful but inspired metal muse to the outer hulk of the careening contraption. **The Privilege Of Power** devastates with the most frenzied of metals, while inundating the listener between tracks with samplings from our brain-dead TV society. Also embellishing the show are sporadic blasts of horns, well-placed collisions of brass with brash, lending an eccentric ear to a much more filling feast than the fleeting atom-splitter that was **Thundersteel**. Here the most elegant pieces are the poppy, dynamic numbers like *Runaway*, *Maryanne* and *Little Miss Death*, although the bulldozing *Metal Soldiers* would have to be the crowning event, collapsing a history as wide as Priest, Accept, Metal Church and the real Riot into an apocalyptic dime-sized black cube hovering at knee-level under the perpetual energy of a million power chords layered through time. Oh were it not for the caca-cacophony of Reale's OTT excursions, I'd be singing the praises of this record to the thinning ozone. Dispensing with my curmudgeonly grumbles however, **Privilege** is a buzzing creative romp, sent all the more skyward by Tony Moore's clarion calls, forcing Reale to his acrobatic extremes. Spiritual when at a speed we want to comprehend.
Rating 8

## Riot - Riot Live (Metal Blade '93)

Capturing the band in their just slightly pre-perfection glory, **Riot Live** documents a rockin' blaze through England, 1980 (half at the Hammersmith, half at the venerable Monsters Of Rock festival at Donnington), just after the release of record #2 **Narita**. The sound is more than adequate and the song selection an even split between the band's pair of records, also offering a rip-roarin' cover of *Train Kept A Rollin'* (i.e. the *Honey Hush* version practiced and perfected by Foghat) and doofus-rock original *Back On The Non-Stop*, one of the band's few embarrassments. Full groovin' glory for us old fogies, Speranza making sure we all remember. Added bonus: the lyrics to all (well, maybe that ain't a bonus).

Rating                                                                7

## Riot - Nightbreaker  (Rising Sun '94)

Mark Reale, keeps of the flame, delighting a small but rabid legion of fans, especially in Japan, the earthquake zone that essentially made this record possible. This is one of those intrinsically metal experiences, loaded with European melodies, nothing like old Riot, a bit like Yngwie meets Annihilator meets Deep Purple meets Vicious Rumors. Indeed Riot covers *Burn* here exquisitely. Vocals tend towards any number of nimble, acrobatic metal throats, Glenn Hughes (who also covers *Burn* in '94!), Joe Lynn Turner, and any of Malmsteen's belters, the perfect complement to the steel-hearted fury of the band's predictable and proud of it riffs and solos. Indeed, very little sounds American here, except maybe Coverdaled blues thump *Medicine Man* and straight-line riff rocker *Magic Maker*. So ultimately, there's something for all metal alloys and allies, and if you don't believe that, check in with the last track, a remake of Speranza-era Riot chestnut *Outlaw*. Logical overall pervading complaint: grave lack of identity, something Riot has suffered since Rhett Forrester left.

Rating                                                                7

## Riot - The Brethren Of The Long House  (Rising Sun '96)

Mark Reale continues to craft elitist metal, here building a belabored concept record based on the American Indians and their battles with the white man. And listening to **The Brethren**, one can't help think classic Rainbow and classic Yngwie, solos oscillating between '80s goth and frightening evocations of Thin Lizzy. Once more the whole thing seems very much tuned for Japanese consumption, Reale working with a team of competent yet emotionally cold, chopsy players, vocalist Mike DiMeo perhaps rising above, somewhat suited for these very noble structures. And perpetuating the Lizzy links, a nicely dovetailed version of Gary Moore's *Out In The Fields* rocks valiantly, by familiarity alone becoming a personal centerpiece of the record. Collector's note: this "limited edition" version contains a second full-length **Live In Japan** CD, which visits all eras of Riot's alarmingly long career within one levelling mix. Glad to see Reale persevering with his Savatage-heady ambitions.

Rating                                                                8

## Ritual - I Give  (Lautir '94)

Ontario's Ritual slice their own piece of the '90s metal pie with this chunk of rhythmic groove metal, **I Give** featuring six tracks (plus intro) that breathe openly, exploring the space between Metallica and Pantera, adding a mellower and moodier prog ethic, which doesn't overstay its welcome. Sean Harley's vocals may inflect too closely to Hetfield's, but it's a style that suits the stinging, exact crunch rock enclosed, Ritual mixing simplicity with an underground Bay Area ethic, gruffness meets tune and texture. Timely and expertly crafted semi-electro mix, solid lyrics, various un-hysterical speeds . . . **I Give** competently addresses a purist corner of the genre which seems to truck on despite the demise of hair bands and the domination of hard alternative. Only complaint, brevity obviously,

and a discernible tentativeness, the band maybe dating itself with its no-hurry, conservative approach.

Rating                                                                7

## Ritual - Hate  (Vespa '96)

Sean Harley and crew are back, having established ties with Harem Scarem's Harry Hess and his hobby label Vespa. And **Hate** is a capable, assured piece of purist metal for sure, sounding a tad more guttural and tribal, now the band evoking a cross between Metallica and Anthrax, with a bit of slow, hooky grunge thrown in. So structures are mammoth and traditional, the recording thick and meaty, arrangement succinct and effective. Closes with one of the better covers of Jimbo's *Break On Through* I've heard, kind of a sawed-off full metal jacket version, benefiting nicely by Hess' full-bodied mix. Still dated, but as good as any playing straight-faced power metal.

Rating                                                                7

## Riverdogs - Riverdogs  (CBS '90)

Justifiably ignored during its brief shelf-life, this "power" trio featuring the amazing frets of Vivian Campbell (proud of Dio, disgraced of Def Leppard) strung over a fake-ass blues metal pose, a sound that wafts more hairspray than deep south. Rob Lamothe's vocals manage a sort of Bad Co./Coverdale pedigree, but the writing is middling. Sure 1990 is before this stuff went out of style, but boy, does it sound average now. Viv moves onto the even worse Shadow King, a brief stint with Whitesnake, and finally guitarless gutless wonders Def Leppard.

Rating                                                                5

## Riverdogs - Bone  (Dream Circle '93)

Nick Brophy replaces Viv on guitar and the whole concept gets more bluesy, easy listening, and strangely integritous. Tracks on **Bone** cruise low-pocket and mellow again in a rich Whitesnake vein, strong melodies, veteran skills, total disregard for fashion. So like, thumbs up on the deliberate nature of the record, but like, thumbs down on an unremarkable decision that makes me see Thunder.

Rating                                                                6

## RKL - Riches To Rags  (Epitaph '94)

Hot label Epitaph seem bent on finding more fast melodic punk bands who can play, RKL fitting the bill, while being perhaps too punky and furiously speedy for any sort of mass consumption. Sterling recording, tight delivery, awesome rhythm section, 'cept they only have one rhythm: loudfastrulesskatepunk. Which is why I don't like it, besides the unique but off-putting pipes of growler/mooner Jason Sears. This ain't no Green Day.

Rating                                                                4

## Rock City Angels - Young Man's Blues  (Geffen '88)

A veritable feast for fans of grungy barroom rock'n'roll, **Young Man's Blues** is three sides + 1 tune (a duplicate) long, totaling fifteen different cuts of sleazy, shoot 'em up roots metal, looking like G'NR but sounding like a host of vanilla biker rockers, i.e. Junkyard, Sea Hags, Outlaw Blood, Hangmen, Little Caesar or Circus Of Power. Never warmed up to it in a big way, despite my intrigue with the ambitious format. Good choruses and the odd move outside of the box, but roots rock has a ton of rules, and most of the time they have to be followed or it just ain't showing respect for the past. I like the fringe stuff though, like *Beyond Babylon*, *South Of The Border* and *Rough 'N' Tumble*, not to mention the fact that this record sorta came and went with nary a ripple despite Geffen obviously caring. Even a bit of Hanoi Rocks in there. Not without some daring and credibility.

Rating                                                                6

**Rocket From The Crypt - Circa: Now**   (Cargo '92)

Armed with a wagon-full of nursery rhymes for the wasted, San Diego's Rocket From The Crypt crank home a sort of sneering but tuneful punk metal hybrid with slight affectations towards Nirvana in terms of disarming melody amongst rave. Simple, plain-jangly produced but full of interesting quirks and blooms, Circa: Now still rides a bit cute for me, with sporadic but intrusive sax, and an overall college giddiness. Faves: *Don't Darlene*, and *Killy Kill* which smokes like a classic mid-years X send-up, geared and primed for no less than **Under The Big Black Sun**. A band distinguished with one of the best album names ever, for this one's predecessor: **Paint As A Fragrance**.

Rating                                                    6

**Rocket From The Crypt - Scream, Dracula, Scream!**
(Interscope/MCA '95)

Wow, talk about finding one's special purpose. Only one other record has sounded as deliciously pop chartable heavy as this resoundingly infectious record as of late, and that would be Everclear's brilliant **Sparkle And Fade**, pretty much my fave rave of all '95. Behind that, one would have to point (reverently this time) to Nirvana and late '80s Soul Asylum to find such electrocuted verve, Rocket From The Crypt cramming these windmill punk metal pop sculptures with horns, symphonic textures, even tubular bells, sounding like Springsteen, The Clash, Aerosmith and Kiss dogpiling in the Dairy Queen parking lot. But the crux of the matter is that time-honoured tradition of heroic guitar trading battle moves with big boisterous singalonging, a trait Hüsker Dü had in devotionally religiously inspirational spades (opening war cry *Middle* might remind you of *New Day Rising*). Deserves to ride Everclear's comet tail to sweat-flyin' proto-punk glory.

Rating                                                    9

**Rockhead - Rockhead**   (Capitol '92)

**Rockhead**'s about what you would expect from the great mediocritizer of Metal Legends, Bob Rock, producer to the stars, rockhound in his own right with early pop punksters The Payolas and later permutation Rock And Hyde. I've always found his effect on bands questionable, turning them ever so slightly towards a mainstream blandness. And this basically Canadian corporate hard rock record bears out those tendencies, with the added advantage of being borne of a mind that is no amateur. Lead single *Bed Of Roses* offends me greatly, being yer basic Dan Gallagher's **Video Hits**-type PG13 sock hop. But surprisingly, the lighter moments bear the most experimentation, rounded out with good vocals, various speed and intensity levels, and full instrumentation. I was prepared to shitcan this commercial piffle all the way back to Vancouver (the second greatest city on earth after Nelson, B.C.), but *Bed Of Roses* and a couple of other pissy attempts at volume are the worst this record can muster. Really, I'm surprised at the depth of variety here when things tone down, where strong melodies and damn inspired vocals from Steve Jack steal the show. Could have been worse, couldn't have really been much better given the shaky premise. A mainstream sound that's had its day.

Rating                                                    6

**Paul Rodgers - Cut Loose**   (Atlantic '83)

Just a cursory mention for this stodgy kind of guy and his post-Bad Co. work. You can go read my reviews of The Firm if you dare, but you won't find anything on the man's turgid Muddy Waters tribute or horrible incarnation as The Law. However, this solo gesture is a harmless and amiable enough rounder, sounding like the failed ends of Bad Co. or a low-key collection of Firm songs, fave being the contemplative *Live In Peace*.

Horrible cover art, but kinda respectable as a project 'cos Rodgers plays all the instruments.

Rating                                                    5

**The Rods - The Rods**   (Arista '81)

The butt of all our inside HM jokes going on a decade now, The Rods were unlikely purveyors of an intrinsically suburban poverty metal, and not all that shabby sounding, more like surrounded by an aura of insurmountable loser tendencies, evoked with a bang by one of the silliest band names in rock. Fact is, **The Rods** kicked ass for '81, and we couldn't care less. The band delivers the goods and we all laugh. Strange. Really the band's second record after limited edition indie **Rock Hard**.

Rating                                                    4

**The Rods - Wild Dogs**   (Arista '82)

Wot th' Hell, ya gotta like one Rods record, and for me, this is it, wrapped in one "bitchin'" record cover and chock full of some versatile street metal as Rock Feinstein (the guy's from Elf, if you can believe it!) and the greasy ones blast their way through America's heartland in search of fast food and faster women. So why does **Wild Dogs** do it for me? . . . because there was still hope.

Rating                                                    7

**The Rods - In The Raw**   (Shrapnel '83)

Now the decline, as the grizzled, rock pig trio identify themselves as combat punters once and for all, resigned to the moshpits of the purely metallic. **In The Raw** kicks and hums appropriately, as the enthusiasm for commercial success seems to have waned (evidenced for me by the dweeby cover art).

Rating                                                    6

**The Rods - Let Them Eat Metal**   (Combat '84)

Sorry dudes, but the show has packed up and left town, as creativity has flamed, flickered and died, as things get louder and more hysterical. Call off the dogs. Get Thor on the phone.

Rating                                                    4

**Rod Sacred - Rod Sacred**   (New Ent. '85)

Shades of Vanadium all over again, as Italy's Rod Sacred (huh?) thoroughly botch their English lyrics, bestowing on us raging titles like *Don't Fear The Rain*, *Will Of Living* and *Lonly Between Mass Of Puppets*, which has nothing to do with going to a Metallica concert by yourself. La musica? Gutted U.S.-style poverty metal, like any number of deluded Shrapnel or Combat casualties.

Rating                                                    4

**Rogue Male - First Visit**   (Elektra '85)

Somehow this crusty British grease-chain got hyped as important back in '85, even though it slogged on with no regard for playing, production, adequate song skills or vocal ability. **First Visit** was timid Motörhead with hints of Krokus after their first beer, and to be perfectly honest, probably a goofy enough rivethead rocker after *your* first beer. Anyways, somebody had to duke it out with the likes of Tysondog, Battleaxe and Avenger.

Rating                                                    4

**Henry Rollins - Hot Animal Machine**   (Texas Hotel '87)

Sort of a weird crease in the Rollins repertoire: this one's a kind of solo album on an obscure label, strange line-up with a few English guys (plus Chris Haskett), recorded in much-joked-about England. That might account for the Motörheaded mix and requisite rollicking bass chubby that permeates the tracks of this lively pile of punk tunes that finds the Dolls, Stooges and Dead Boys put through Hank's psycho lyrical shredder. Real noisy, real nutty and real raw, which strangely is

quite unlike Black Flag or other Rollins stuff, **Hot Animal Machine** has about the same jammy dissonant noise quotient versus forward massing songs as on most other Rollins assaults, only, uhhh, different!
Rating                                                                                  6

## Rollins Band - Hard Volume   (Fringe '89)

Still not sure whether Rollins Band is an improvement on Black Flag, finding only scant additional nuance to the blast of grit. Musically, the current band has more guts, chops, anger and flexibility, but nevertheless create with the same disdain for structure, economy or accessibility, which usually hurts the cause, as the listener exists perplexed then comatose, then neck-deep in plush casket velvet at the lengthy, crashed Sab-like crawls despite the presence of *that voice* which jars the nerves to an excited, on-guard attentiveness. Fact is **Hard Volume** shakes with Henry's rock-hard will, as the man plasters his traumatized words to a tough, unfeeling wall of psychedelic garage metal that can't live up to the pressure. And in that darkened spirit, Rollins Band serves no more a purpose than Black Flag did as caustic backdrop to the Rollins rant, a violent, morally spent machine that takes time to inhale as well as exhale. When it converges on song, it's truly gut-churning, but when it diffuses into some beat generation slant on punk jazz or other forms of wandered noise (Rollins listens to Coltrane), it merely wastes your time and space, surprising given Rollins' disgust for wasted time. I mean, side two of this may as well be Killdozer meets live Grateful Dead, stretched but chaffing like an iron pig, as the band succeeds in creating ugly atmosphere, but little in the way of music that one would want to confront.
Rating                                                                                  5

## Rollins Band - The End Of Silence   (Imago '92)

Henry Rollins' java-boiled red eye comes shot, pumped and primed to meet the world's gaze on this major label debut, the band's first truly ambitious and first properly recorded release. Fraught by the Rubinesque mixing pots of Andy Wallace, Hank's band never sounded so focused and at war with its unhewn, jazzy, Iommi-riffed and Lemmy-bassed mongrel stagger. Progressive, off-kilter and still somewhat built on neurotic patterns, **The End Of Silence** is no easy contraption to disassemble. As usual, the best tracks are the most cohesive and connectable, like premiere single/video *Low Self Opinion*, hip, sin-draped slasher *Tearing*, evil-metal cruiser *You Didn't Need* (the best Sabbath tune since *Johnny Blade*), and *Another Life*, which again conjures Iommi and maybe an eccentric and delimited Trouble. Yet unfortunately, there's the usual raft of confusion; long, grinding jams based on the most fragile and barren of premises, coagulating into five tracks that are over seven minutes long without a whole lot going on inside them, sounding as grim and heart-wrenchingly tedious as one could imagine. On the upside, drugged and epidemic like tortured early Sabbath; on the downside, like *Funhouse*-era Stooges or Hawkwind. So again, Rollins is banged-up, caffeinated like an enraged horse, but prone to bouts of stupor where he loses me to more inundating terrain on similar mindscapes. Although, let's face it, there's really no one quite as ripped 'n' flayed as Henry Rollins on Black Sabbath Day. If you dig the lyrics, get the man's books, starting with **Art To Choke Hearts & Pissing In The Gene Pool** (now two books in one) or **Black Coffee Blues**.
Rating                                                                                  8

## Rollins Band - Weight   (BMG '94)

Henry Rollins has spent wisely his long sojourn from recorded Rollins Band, burning into America's consciousness through his jolting books and his spoken word tours plus associated recordings. Throw in a movie (he's a cop), his ever-widening 2.13.61 publishing co., and you've got the first full-throttle renaissance punk, capably pummeled hard through the steely guidance of Tony Iommi and Juan Valdez. But Rollins Band was always more the enigma, all fuzzy, refracted, hard to get working in concerted directions. **Weight** presents another sliding floor, Rollins doping his anti-metallic metal with an engaging chem lab of black musics, borrowing from rap, funk, jazz and blues, not to mention the loopy explorations of moshing new-agers like Fishbone and 24-7 Spyz. Always willing to smack his inner metalhead across the jaw, Rollins undermines and underloops his base instinct to rock out with a deep understanding of what can be hip and somewhat icy at once, bloating forth with jagged, meandering riffs that bow to a pulverizing art groove. But he'd be the first to credit his cookin' band, an extremely happenin' rhythm section (Sim Cain and Melvin Gibbs), who fuel a firestorm of percussive contusion beneath the difficult, cantankerous scrap heap that is guitarist Chris Haskett, a human snake, miserable descendant of curmudgeonly Black Flag axeman Greg Ginn, but with triple the IQ. All told: quite the pounding but engaging feast; tons of integrity thrust faceward by artpunks disguised as cavemen.
Rating                                                                                  8

## Rollins Band - Come in And Burn   (MCA '97)

I can't get over the hump of not having lyrics to this thing, becoming afraid to review something I'm not sure I can digest without reading. Henry and his dour bunch haven't changed too much, still itchily twisting through their considerably unique metal-on-hip-hop-bed rock. Chris Haskett has found more accessible textures to add to his anti-social, non-evident wank patterns, evoking a Tool or Handsome at times. And as usual, Haskett is called in to burn at the end of a low bush-bass lope Rollins meditation, the band becoming the master of whisper-to-roar, even if the results are just too obscure, jazzy and r+b-ish for alternative rawk tastes. Gotta hand it to 'em, a pattern has been established over the last three records, a pattern that evidences work ethic, maximum, even snobby cool, but a strange off-kilter chemistry that is of epicurean taste. Without a doubt, an excellent read (maybe I'm the only guy still totally interested in Rollins' writings), but Henry has been doin' too much Gang Of Four, and not enough Thin Lizzy.
Rating                                                                                  8

## Rose Tattoo - Rock 'n Roll Outlaw   (Mirage '80)

A tolerable hybrid of Angel City and Krokus (both bands different chips off the AC/DC block) yet with a boozier, more hopeless bar-room slog to it, not to mention the presence of an evil looking little bald man on lead throat. Fun but brutish.
Rating                                                                                  6

## Rose Tattoo - Assault And Battery   (Mirage '81)

Angry Anderson's collection of rogues takes a turn for the worse with this wimpy romp through pop-inflected scum rock. Less the rusty AC/DC headbang of the debut, here the band gets light and ditzy, with backward melodies and a lack of seriousness, as if whacked in the head with the realization that they just ain't going to cut it.
Rating                                                                                  5

## Rose Tattoo - Scarred For Life   (Mirage '82)

More seriously polluted butt rock from one mean looking bunch of bar stools. Getting eccentric now with a sort of scurrilous punk minuteness. Weird band, and one only their murders could love.
Rating                                                                                  5

## Rosicrucian - No Cause For Celebration
(Black Mark '94)

One of those unslottable records that occurs when European bands opt for a technical '80s thrash like the Bay Area boys. I mean it's usually a swing-hammered good time, and Sweden's Rosicrucian do it up just fine, injecting an unpredictable loopiness into their reality-stretching songs. Gruff, but not grind vocals, face-melting production, and a burning raft of lyrics that are a wordy trip worth tumbling. Influences soaked-up and spit back with a twist of lemon.

Rating 8

## Uli Jon Roth - Earthquake ('79, Griffin '95)

In the harsh light of the '90s, it becomes bracing once again to hear the Hendrix-fluid strains of renegade Scorpions guitarist Uli Jon Roth, the man who brought all those exotic mid-eastern, Spanishy sounds to classics like **Virgin Killer** and **Taken By Force**. Here Roth indulges his love of Hendrix' full spectrum and all things psychedelically spiritual (*Lilac* finds ultimate wisdom in the humble flower), while also exposing his interest in Japanese culture. The soloing is restrained and magnificent, but the songs are pretentious (see the ten minute title track). Still, taken as a guitar showcase, the record pleases, despite the slight distraction of Roth's wheezy vocals.

Rating 6

## Uli Jon Roth - Fire Wind ('80, Griffin '95)

**Fire Wind** extends Roth's talents into the realm of more world-relevant songs, even as his vocals get more scattery, eccentric and distracting. But the man's fluid, thoughtful guitar patterns abound, **Fire Wind** exhibiting greater exploration into springier heavy stuff and more soulful acoustic tracks. Just a joy to follow once solo time arrives, it's easy to see why Yngwie finds Roth such an inspiration (his band moniker Rising Force is named for **Earthquake**'s cover painting), Roth displaying those same quick, classical-based runs while sounding more studious of melodic structure and all-round planning. Another bombastic album closer in the ten minute, four part *Hiroshima*. Cool couple of albums in quick succession; jazzy, tight, adequately to well-recorded, but somehow raw and electric. Gotta be a little twisted, serious and retro to like Uli's Germanic sound, but hey, the curmudgeon in me is be-hooved to speak.

Rating 7

## Uli Jon Roth - Beyond The Astral Skies
(EMI '84, Griffin '95)

Well some time has passed, and Uli is back, back in the clouds that is, leaping straight into the stratosphere for a new bunch of space toons that slipstream any thoughts of getting with the times. Yea and verily, Uli has notched back on the raw rock and layered up a stack of lush prog metal tunes with all sorts of sounds and more importantly, singers galore! Any time a vocal takes place, it's fortified with bizarre harmonies of both the male and female ilk. But the coolest vocal move is the inclusion of Michael Flechsich, who I'm pretty sure is the guy from bro Zeno Roth's record (my copy has no liner notes). His high science is a refreshing addition to Uli's ethereal song stylings, which this time around sound damn near to spunky Hawkwind or Hillage, a sound and speak surrendered to the world of spiritual sci-fi magick, as Uli fills up every track with questionable nods to esoterica. But forget for a sec the talk of weird; the guitar work is enough of a draw to make this a staggering monolith to inspiration, as the whole smear just defies logic descending into loopiness.

Rating 7

## David Lee Roth - Crazy From The Heat (Warner '85)

Recorded just before the split with Van Halen, this novelty EP finds Dave diving headlong into the croonin' lounge lizard persona hinted at on lighter Halen moments. It's really awful, hatching the hits *California Girls* and *Just A Gigilo* in the process of exposing western society's fast food-poisoned stupidity.

Rating 0

## David Lee Roth - Eat 'Em And Smile (Warner Bros. '86)

Dave continues his quest to define particularly American hard rock excess on this his first "serious" personal statement since Van Halen, hiring a band that overplays proudly in each of their chosen fields, making this a metal musician's record that sacrifices song excruciatingly and often, with constant termite-infested diddling filling every minute space from messengers Bissonette, Sheehan and especially Vai, who is always forgetting to play the riff. What results are great party anthems full of annoying distractions, great timeless cheer like *Shyboy*, *Bump And Grind* and lead hit *Yankee Rose*, overtreated with disdain, smothered by flurries of fast notes from all angles. Never ye mind, however, because after a million plays or so, it becomes easier to enjoy for Dave's wide smile and obvious love of his job. As with all his stuff to date, there's way too much huckster-minded time-wasters 'n' juvenile party tricks, Roth ignoring substance and bottom end for fanciful noisemaking. But cutting through the drabble, I find the record a joy to spin over and over again for that undeniable Roth link with the good times of summer. Still, after the abominable **Crazy From The Heat**, you'd think Dave would be just itching to get down to business in a more concerted way. **Eat 'Em And Smile** shows that he's really in no hurry.

Rating 7

## David Lee Roth - Skyscraper (Warner Bros. '88)

On Dave's least critically successful foray to date, the man circumlocutes breeze metal; lite swirling, complex and blowing in the wind, and it's an ozone-maddening fringe phenomenon worth sidling up to fer sure. **Skyscraper** (a clever title, and if you don't get it, forget it), is Dave's very coolest piece of ornate amusement. Vai's still a dork, but given everyone else's complete surrender to this orbital piece of new age hard rock, Evil Stevie fits right in with his histrionic hernias of liteness of being. This is Dave so deep into his Self and it's all a great view, playable twistedly time again, from the galactic title cut, through low cal rocker *Knucklebones*, down—way down—to masterpiece of the world, *Hina*, an epic worthy of the most choicest minute in the lives of Van Halen, a sonata so conceptually crucial to the very vortex of the band's blessed being, I can't believe Ed was of no consequence in it's ethereal making, *Hina* being a classic of *Diver Down* incandescence, and without a doubt Dave's crowning glory, but I over digress. Taken as a weird, goofy, but imposing whole, **Skyscraper** does wonderful things, just kickin' slyly with that Dave swingability. Whereas **Eat 'Em And Smile** is kind of blunt, and **A Little Ain't Enough** is just rehash, **Skyscraper** wedges briefly and soars, sparks a' flying as all points spin uncontrollably onwards to a display of brash excess without recess or indeed, regard for gut substance. To crash to conclusion: magnificent although no one in their right mind would think so. Note: both **Skyscraper** and **Eat 'Em And Smile** managed a respectable platinum.

Rating 8

## David Lee Roth - A Little Ain't Enough
(Warner Bros. '91)

Dave's the coolest, no question, even if the wax wobbles in quest of living up to the raps. And this time around it's no different, again bringing a similar, if not evolving, set of faults to the fore, again offering just enough to sink one's teeth into, but at nowhere near the true integrity levels of his former pop music combo. In fact, that's the central problem here; the novelty tunes (this time a little more disguised as legitimate rock songs) serve no purpose other than to feed the image: stripper tunes for the king of sound-bites. And even when Dave delivers the bacon on rockers such as the slippery *Lady Luck*, the smokin' *Baby's On Fire*, the loopy *Drop In The Bucket* (a cheap version of *Walk This Way*), and the nicely connectable *A Lil' Ain't Enough* (intro cut, intro single), it's vapidly commercial and safely rendered, sensible shoes off at the door, which granted is usually the way to go with a stable full of hot musicians. Don't get me wrong, it's not a bad record; in fact it's full of intricacies like Dave's days of old, except that song-wise it's just so damn juvenile and expected. And this from a man personally known for taking risks with his life. It's of interest to note that **A Little Ain't Enough** was one of '91's commercial disappointments, as was its tour, which I thought was undeniably infectious, even though the man actually trotted out more VH tunes than DLR by a slim margin. Final verdict: an acceptable but predictable third self-parody, not without both technical finesse and hummability.

Rating 7

## David Lee Roth - Your Filthy Little Mouth
(Reprise '94)

Early leak of this record's title led us to believe DLR was going to come back with more of the same, but alas the man has basically quit rock, carving himself a new (doomed) personality as Vegas Guy. So on the heels of more-of-the-same single *She's My Machine*, a slippery average rocker (and very deceptive as a single), came the odd-looking record. What a horrible, horrible surprise. After the first three duff, but "heavy" tracks come eleven scattered confused novelty tunes, visiting with tantamount cheese and no powerchords, slow blues, fast blues, dressy r+b, reggae, jazz, lite boogie, the new country duet with Travis Tritt, the Willie Nelson cover of *Night Life*, all polluted full of crap by the mainstream production non-talents of Nile Rodgers. Universally panned when it came out, I couldn't bring my shaking hands to write a word on it until now. I just could not believe how low Dave had sunk. Now my rage has subsided, because one would think there's gotta be a chance the man will return to rock. Yes? No? Who the hell knows. Please Ed, take him back! August '96: Of course, the unimaginable has happened, Dave tentatively back in Van Halen for at least one new tune, slated for the band's greatest hits spread.

Rating 2

## Rotting Christ - Triarchy Of The Last Lovers
(Century Media '96)

This is the third full-length for Greece's top death metallions, **Triarchy** finding the band paring back to a trio after experimenting with a full-time pianist. Pretty traditional if not psychedelic stuff lyrically (it's English, and not black metal in the least), even if the evil graphics blaspheme big time. But the music is a cool mix of melody and abrasive death, sorta symphonic and Maiden-ish in emotional tone, but Swedish in execution. Main point: don't denigrate the fact that the band's Greek. Rotting Christ are a veteran creative force, doing very cool things with metal extremes, most notably harmony leads that are the utmost in elegance. Classic: *One With The Forest*.

Rating 7

## Rough Cutt - Rough Cutt (Warner Bros. '85)

Upon deeper inspection, Rough Cutt is somewhat of a minor enigma, offering elusive originality, despite its by-the-book California metal look, lyrical grist, and unintelligent album covers. Not that it's any screamin' hell, but these guys do show some promise with their particular bombast, an often slow rockslide of blunt dynamics, more like worlds in collision as witnessed on *Black Widow* and *Kids Will Rock*, with occasional forays into speedier structures, mellow rock, and fat melodic choruses. Heroic individual performances by veteran producer Tom Allom and muscle-beach vocalist Paul Shortino.

Rating 5

## Rough Cutt - Wants You! (Warner Bros. '86)

The good news is that this long-lost non-success will most likely cross your path demanding a less than princely sum, a price it will most likely be worth. The bad news is that it's still no righteous masterpiece, definitely created within the realms of dunce-like American trenches metal, despite its digressions. Stepped-up in terms of the life force, **Wants You!** is surprisingly mellow, surprisingly often. In fact, after the full throttle romp of *Rock The USA*, all of side one pumps propped on simple unadorned bass lines and other forms of quiet passages amidst metallic descensions. Again, strange band, who obviously has no reservations about offering liberal swatches of subdued emotion, one would imagine, to create a highlighting effect for its considerably massive metallic periods. As a result, a lot of holding back both speed-wise and riff-wise, usually to pleasing dramatic effect. Shortino onto Quiet Riot and a '94 solo album called **Back On Track**.

Rating 6

## Rough Cutt - Live (DeROCK '96)

Billed as a bit of a recalling card, proving in semi-convinced fashion that this Crue-ish thud metal act mattered, **Live** relives an era when men wore scarves and white pants, and Paul Shortino belted out rust-belt anthems to the trailer-parked minions. **Live** works a spell, mainly in its jarring, kicked across the room lack of context, swilling it up somewhat on level with Twisted Sister's recent **Live At Hammersmith** set. But no idea if this is an accurate representation of the band now or ten years back, lone new studio track *House Of Pain* doing nothing to bring these likeable dough-brains much more recent and reticent than say, Widowmaker, despite a looped little Porno For Pyros harmonica solo.

Rating 6

## Rough Diamond - Rough Diamond (Island '77)

As bad as his second and third solo records, **Rough Diamond** is David Byron's first post-Heep baby steps, a full band concept whose only other notable member is axe veteran Clem Clemson from Colosseum and Humble Pie. As expected it's a pointless conglomeration of hard rock, funk, jazzy arrangement, blues, ballads, r+b, all erratically delivered. Once more, think Ian Gillan Band's **Scarabus**, both records just general snobby rock, supposedly exhibiting some sort of subtle touch. Became Champion after Byron wandered off.

Rating 3

## Rough Silk - Circle Of Pain . . . Or: The Secret Lies Of Timekeeping (Massacre '96)

So good they hadda name it twice? Maybe, if you like big, serious German pomp, which I'd say generally I do. This is the band's third record, and sounds quite confidently like a cross between Queensryche, Helloween, Morgana Lefay and contrived Rainbow. Heaps o' production, castle-bound keyboards and vocals that would kick some life into Yngwie's band. Basically high quality prog-metal worthy of some attention.

Rating 8

## Roxx Gang - Things You've Never Done Before
(Virgin '88)

Major glam look on these boys, big hair, quality western footwear, but not much else, as this tolerable debut fist-pumper hums along much more behaved than its talk would suggest. Not all that bad, just a tad stiff and hugely geeky, walking right down the middle of a well-worn path through Sleazetown, California. Thudly and self-evident, **Things You've Never Done Before** is what it is: a record for young, unsophisticated metal fans, mixing equal parts Leps, Poison, Crüe and Ratt to no great effect. Skirts a **6**.
Rating                                                                     5

## Roxx Gang - The Voodoo You Love   (Perris '95)

Defying all logic (but what's logical about being a metalhead?), Roxx Gang haven't changed a scintilla, belching up the same turgid party metal they've always belched, a little Hanoi Rocks, a lot of Poison, if anything, less upscale than the only other Roxx Gang record I've had the privilege of hearing from seven years back. But the main problem would be Kevin Steele's raspy, out-of-tune vocals, pegging these guys as limited of potential (he writes everything too, which means he isn't exactly expendable). Kinda like the Quireboys but with more fast food and less history. And that look; what, are you joking?
Rating                                                                     6

## Roxy Blue - Want Some?   (Geffen '92)

Geffen's last concerted stab at hairspray metal, Roxy Blue do it up right if you give a damn, except maybe for that ridiculous album cover, sheesh! Picture L.A. Guns adrenalized with a shot of rambunction circa Love/Hate, Spread Eagle and the one-take heavies from later GN'R, and you're pretty much on board for this band's guitars, cars and bars party, a record textured and tenderized at the capable hands of Mike Clink, the guy perhaps a little too good at his job, able to phone in these performances at will. Pulls out all the stops come final track *Main Attraction*, but like I say, after perusing the cover art, you probably don't care.
Rating                                                                     7

## The Royal Court Of China - The Royal Court Of China   (A&M '87)

On the strength of the present wax, Nashville's The Royal Court Of China as a band wouldn't rate mention in this book, the record being more of a swampy roots rocker; nice barroom feel like The Del Lords. Startling transformation to **Geared & Primed** to say the least. Here, basically all ballads, with the occasional hard rock skeleton, without appropriate guitar effect adjustment to make a full changeover.
Rating                                                                     5

## The Royal Court Of China - Geared & Primed
(A&M '89)

Confusion evaporates as The Royal Court Of China greedily pluck power chords from the sky and turn honky tonk bar rock into sleazy L.A. club rock, title track leading the charge into a record that bulks the band's roots tendencies into something approaching the blazing heat of Kings Of The Sun. Great voice on that Joe Blanton guy: Billy Idol sings Chris Isaak and John Doe; torrid, throaty Elvis smoke over chunky, resonant rhythms that don't commit to any one style. The result: roots metal by way of roots, rather than an always contrived vice versa. And like Kings Of The Sun, raw, booming drums blast the bacon on home, sent through the grinder by Vic Maile's bronco-bustin' production. A charming slab from one of the unsung.
Rating                                                                     7

## Rubber Snake - Rubber Snake   (ACD '95)

A rare gem amongst all the poxy trop (fake British talk) released these days, this very indie LP/EP from Toronto-based 'n' Windsor-bred rock dogs Rubber Snake rides an electric exotica similar to only two acts I can think of, I Love You and Liquid Jesus, both forsaken but not forgotten. Maybe a slight Pearl Jam vibe (via Zeppelin, especially come *Candy Coated*), as expressionist guitars and complex Bono-inflecting vocals bubble up with warm divinity, each track paradoxically drifting with purpose, like a strategically psychedelic mission of music. Bum packaging here, way too little info and no lyrics, but the well-produced pride inside speaks volumes. If soupy, slippery unslottable hard alternative be your brew, this'll do ya fine.
Rating                                                                     7

## The Runaways - The Runaways   (Phonogram '76)

With this first of thankfully few all-girl heavy metal groups, paparazzi-love-ins were an inevitable and mercilessly frequent occurrence with the foxy five back in the gushable '70s. A brutally fragrant rock combo, The Runaways nevertheless spawned future brutal rock combos—and the female rock thing in general culminating in Alanis M.—through the velveteen careers of Cherie Currie (most famous for her squalid biography), plus Lita Ford and Joan Jett (both most celebrated for their wank-city rock and slur). In any event, this debut is understandably the worst of the band's four platters evoking Suzi Quatro on **Happy Days** or **Laverne & Shirley** or whatever the hell that was. Basically a trumped-up ploy by sleaze-about-town Kim Fowley, sued by the band in '94 for unpaid royalties.
Rating                                                                     3

## The Runaways - Queens Of Noise   (Phonogram '77)

More of the same with added crunch, less the whiff of novelty, and a general doomed play for serious consideration among stadia ilk, **Queens Of Noise** ran the gamut from guitar-bolstered starlet rock to U.S. metal worthy of Kiss, Starz or luke-cool Nuge. In other werdz, dumb as a bag of hammers, but loud as one too, with a fresh commercial jizz factor of blunted tuneful chuggery.
Rating                                                                     6

## The Runaways - Live In Japan   (Phonogram '77)

Boisterous renditions of early marmalade from the ultimate sho-biz leatherettes, **Live In Japan** continues a venerable '70s tradition of well . . . live in Japan, bringing the carnival to a none too liberated or sophisticated Oriental throng, bent on watching a few tall 'merican metal queens get the place hot and sweaty. The '70s win again! . . . but where did they get those guitars in children's sizes?
Rating                                                                     4

## The Runaways - Waitin' For The Night   (Phonogram '77)

Cherry Bomb having been detonated (onto a solo stiff with **Beauty's Only Skin Deep**), the glitter team is now four, minus a frontwoman, leaning downright cerebral as they go for that technically adept netherworld full of ambitious dynamic and sweeping postures as if they were Aerosmithohgivemeabreak. Yea and verily, **Waitin' For The Night** offers the band's purest, most impressive riffwork, and also its most ponderous experiments in soft rock, turning the wax into an up/down sort of affair, half fully baked, everywhere and nowhere at once. Final vinyl verdict: **Queens Of Noise** above the rest, for sheer '70s hilarity.
Rating                                                                     6

## The Runaways - Young And Fast   (Allegiance '85)

Circus manager Kim Fowley stumbles back into the chick band biz, finding five more gals to call The Run-

aways, having no qualms listing them as vocalists with 23 guys listed as "The Musicians", leading one to believe these chicks ain't touring. And the music is miserably amusing, a sort of helium doo-wop pop punk metal (like GoGo's on crack, or early Madonna meets post-washed-up Twisted Sister), truly a convincing but puerile parody of the original Runaways who were just a shade more serious than this. Almost a children's record. Weird. No, insipid.
Rating **0**

## Running Wild - Gates Of Purgatory (Noise '84)
Cheap German plonk with a one plan attack that picks the right plan, but leaves the brains at home, going chugga chugga 'til the winged hornets of Hades come home to roost on their alcohol-addled metalheads. Raised a few eyebrows at the time because the recording was so damn clean, despite the dulled samey-ness of the riffs.
Rating **4**

## Running Wild - Branded And Exiled (Noise '85)
An improvement in listenability due to simple growth and maturity. Records after this one, especially **Under Jolly Roger** established the band as a viable source of pounding metal. Still, a squared-off, riff-dependent act not above ridicule.
Rating **5**

## Running Wild - Port Royal (Noise '88)
Growth by the gallon jugs, as Running Wild steer towards Grave Digger and even Helloween, teching up their old trundleness with Maiden-derived gallop riffs and precision dime turns. And through it all, the band's humour remains, weaving through the record their pirate imagery, although you gotta read the lyrics to get it, Rock 'n' Rolf's high reg vocals mixed weakly. Unabashed, old-style metal with a black vein of Germanity. Faves: *Uaschitschun* and *Blown To Kingdom Come*, which achieve lusty Accept-like realms.
Rating **7**

## Rush - Rush (Mercury '74)
Well, way back in '74, Toronto's own Rush started down the long pathway of life a very different animal than it is today. In fact **Rush**, the debut is the only statement of the entire spacious catalogue not to court the band's patented progressive, drums-and-wires alchemy, due to the absence of Neil Peart's lyrical and percussive labyrinths, his chair here warmed by yer basic rock 'n' glitter skinsman John Rutsey. Too bad, because **Rush** was a take charge sort of record, all squealing guitars and that startling Geddy Lee shriek, a deformed wail thought humanly improbable, albeit one that occasionally looked to Plant for Ooh Yeahs. Zitheads loved the record, a rare Canuck platter combining power chords and a plethora of rawk moves, in its scattered, almost psychedelic datedness, not slavishly imitating any one contemporary riffmeister, largest lunkheads being lead track *Finding My Way*, Sab swinger *What You're Doing*, and closing classic *Working Man*, all built of shlocky, stadium-dreamable patterns that predicted glory to come. Elsewhere, the warm and fuzzy *In The Mood* aided and abetted the cause, providing one of the band's early concert wake-up calls. All in all, a fortified first taste, which demanded a love it/hate it response due to its bravado and above all, *that voice*.
Rating **7**

## Rush - Fly By Night (Anthem '75)
With the acquisition of all-around fusspot Neil Peart, Rush took on a drastically different shape, different realms, *Beneath, Between, & Behind By-Tor & The Snow Dog* in *Rivendell* and other fantastical locales, hatching convoluted metallic journeys to other planes, places where each pillar of this bubbling-under trio could play the hell out of his chosen weapon, making seemingly straight-forward ditties like *Fly By Night* and *Best I Can* sound like the equipment bus in full roll down an embankment. Yes, an invigorating new band is born, tons of modest complexity, all wrought with standard guitar, bass, drums, and vocals, brought to the fore in state-of-the-art technicolour by producer-for-life Terry Brown. Of course, cynics smirked at the pomposity of it all, but teenage punters the tundra over found these new cerebralites perfect complements to a life of jean jackets, zits and oily hair. Instead of smoking a joint and staring at the tube, future big hairs (and not so big hairs) were lighting up and getting calluses learning the bass, or sore wrists figuring out their favourite Peart fill. Rush tacitly proposed a mission. Rush made you want to work at it. Rush were the professors, asking us to conveniently forget our one-dimensional definitions of heaviness, providing new possibilities for basic rock'n'roll instrumentation, all set to lyrics that seemed pretty deep to any young pup raised on Kiss.
Rating **7**

## Rush - Caress Of Steel (Mercury '75)
Rush continue on their laser trajectory inward and outward, carving the foundations for a legendary progressive metal identity, lyrics on more intense flights of fantasy, unraveling with side one closer *The Necromancer*, rolling right through a most fanciful side two, which finds the band dog-paddling through **Tales From Topographic Oceans**, loving every nanosecond of their new responsibility as wand-waving conjurers, ethereal cryptics who rock. Elsewhere one flagship rocker, *Bastille Day* and one new *Fly By Night*, *Lakeside Park*, combine human connection with the band's inherent technological chill, for better or worse. By this point, most critics had pretty well made up their minds that Rush was about as ridiculous a proposition as ever was, a cruel joke, marginal rock'n'roll aspiring to classic literature. Whatever your level of acceptance, it was hard to deny that this was a band serious about craft, which in my opinion is one of the most reliable pathways towards art. Questionable results here however, as all seems plagued by both dislocation and thin-ness of mix. More an exercise in forging the band's vision than the vision achieved. One of the creepier and murkier Rush works due in no small part to the cover art.
Rating **6**

## Rush - 2112 (Mercury '76)
One half concept album, one half the usual eclectic display of steel and silk, **2112** is Rush's first truly confident work, a record tall and elegant, completely at peace with the band's inflated mission. Side one, *2112*, offers a **1984**-type future vision where music is outlawed by The Federation, and the hero of our story finds and learns to play an old guitar, proceeding to reflect on the nature of music and its relationship to society. Mildly amusing, but most of us were more enthralled by the majesty of the record's high-minded rockers: *The Temples Of Syrinx, A Passage To Bangkok*, and *Something For Nothing*, all fueling the theory that Rush could be kings of the heap if they'd only focus on muscle. But the combined whole was necessary to lend Rush its particular aura as creators of a new sub-genre, challenging writers parading their chops. You were either on board their sci-fi trip or not, wholly and reverently committed, or throwing up at the mere sight of a beak-nosed Canuck pretending to make full use of a double bass. 2112 really did it for me however, Peart, Lee and Lifeson all rendered quite shiny and extreme by Terry Brown's most muscle-bound mix to date; versatile drum sound, munchy power chords, Geddy's mangled pipes set to full stun, and of course,

instrumental extravagance par excellence or repugnance depending on your Rushness. Fond memory: **2112**'s radio debut on Spokane's KREM-FM, the record afforded a level of respect usually reserved for royalty.
Rating 8

## Rush - All The World's A Stage (Mercury '76)

Notable more for the splendidly opulent four sides of great songs the band has been able to amass, **All The World's A Stage** was a mighty fine, grandly rocking affair, well-paced with a hodgepodge of techy songs comprising side one, prog rock excursions for sides two and three, finally blazing outta the place with the debut's three most bludgeoning cuts on side four. And all divergent styles gain consistency due to the liquidity of a single live mix, a sound that bulks up what in original form, were pretty tame and self-conscious deliveries. Also great packaging with its innovative triple fold out plastered with live shots, highlighting a unique band on the way through the roof.
Rating 8

## Rush - A Farewell To Kings (Anthem '77)

Rush enter their hyper-verbose golden years, fingers a' flyin' all over the fretboards, fist flurries to tom toms as small as dimes, leaving this earth for the halls of academia. Horrified when I first slapped it on the ol' Hitachi HT-354, furtively in search of metal in the conventional sense as any 14 year old would be, I later learned to respect and even enjoy this record's challenges, fave being the almost song-like title track and the almost kickin' but totally cyborged *Cygnus X1*. Biggest claim to fame however was huge single *Closer To The Heart*, a fairly regular piece of human embroidery that simply stood way to the left of the band's usual thematic haughtiness. Again, love it or hate it, Rush was an independent force, looking for classical-level compositional extravagance using instrumentation much preferred to the euphonium or piccolo flute (although Peart was not averse to the odd triangle). And whether you scoffed at the suggestion that Peart could hold a candle to Bruford, Gadd or Keltner, he did have a damn fine sounding kit, in addition to being the master of the dressy drum fill. The reward: lots of first places in **Modern Drummer**'s annual reader polls. Pretentious or truly artistic, **A Farewell To Kings** wove a formidable tapestry of tunage into a bright, enjoyable hard rock celebration of chops, on occasion, delving into terrain more reminiscent of Jethro Tull, yet always cognizant of buoyancy across the emotional spectrum. Aspirations to grandeur to be sure, an on many levels, it's mission accomplished, although a record this flashy cannot avoid falling short on certain planes. For the most part however, it's a welcome offering of more and mostest.
Rating 9

## Rush - Rush Through Time (Mercury '77)

Merely a nice collectable, this is a Dutch, single vinyl compilation of Rush, ahem, through time, spanning **Fly By Night** through **A Farewell To Kings**. With eleven tracks, it's kinda compressed, but these things aren't for playing anyways.
Rating 7

## Rush - Hemispheres (Anthem '78)

All balderdash and beauty, total trop and tremendousness, **Hemispheres** is the ultimate Paris runway of infinitely-faceted guitar licks, maze-like bass patterns and mega-drums unrestrained, a budding hard rocker's dream, unlocking the treasure chest to finger flights of fancy, an exercise in limber digitalis, wayward literary undiscipline and mystical wattage in the here and now. I won't even get into *Hemispheres*, the title track comprising all of side one. Suffice to say it's an obtuse aural explosion infuriating the band's detractors with renewed vigor: direct resplendent descendant of *Xanadu* with all the same power-trio-gone-mad mechanics. Side two is where this record really lives, kicking off with *Circumstances*, one of the band's classic hyperboles of optical heaviness, Peart all hiccups and furtiveness as Lee and Lifeson lay down the tale of the ideal. Next is *Trees*, a union tune sandwiching like plywood power chords, the progressive and the sublimely melodic. Finally *La Villa Strangiato*, a highly informative instrumental that is the essence of total unbridled verve, caring nary an iota for the inevitable disbelief of a world briefly distorted by punk. Hard to believe, but I see a certain raw, intellectual anarchy, here let loose in the hands of players, rather than bullshitters. Fact is, when I try to dis the boys, I can't help but noticing that **Hemispheres** stands up a heap taller than anything by the Dead Boys or the Angry Samoans. Hard work, no matter how misdirected, will always result in some sort of permanence.
Rating 10

## Rush - Permanent Waves (Anthem '80)

One of very few golden era Rush records that doesn't gaze unto itself for identity, **Permanent Waves** almost feels like an EP of **Hemispheres** out-takes. Hints of briskness and brightness to come dwell within the electrically-charged grooves, but much of this is a sort of watershed of clever ideas juxtaposed with little forethought, *Jacob's Ladder* and *Natural Science* bordering on aimless wankery. But lead track *The Spirit Of Radio* was a splendid and successful smash single, like a ballet of fireflies performing before a vigilant row of Marshalls. Track two, *Freewill*, has also become a classic rock radio staple, showcasing the band's tightness amidst early examples of Lifeson's shift from reliance on riff to a melodic, cascading sort of guitar style. To me **Permanent Waves** marks a pause or a stop-gap between its two regal predecessors and the vigorous pyrotechnics of **Moving Pictures**, a record widely considered the band's best. Here, Rush hones its cold bright alloy, progressing by inches rather than leaps and bounds.
Rating 8

## Rush - Moving Pictures (Anthem '81)

Considered by most to be the definitive Rush document, **Moving Pictures** pleased punter and musician alike (even winning over a few critics), sparkling with a new electric zip and maturity of song, despite its so obvious love of strutting showmanship, more rockstars-in-training studying and dissecting this one over any other Rush opus. **Moving Pictures** is memorable for its fresh hit singles, the percussive, dive-bombing majesty of *Tom Sawyer*, and the almost human, melodic dynamics of *Red Barchetta* and *Limelight*, both so intrinsically Rush, the band's trio of distinctive and independent sounds percolating along happily towards a single vision, achieving pop despite pyro, finally exploiting the pastiche of sonics the band has owned for years. Elsewhere, there's *YYZ* (Toronto Airport's call numbers), the band's second best instrumental after *La Villa Strangiato*, although some prefer this one's metallics and conciseness. And that's just side one. Side two offers stretchier pieces that still embody that perfect three-way blend, albeit with a few more heavier riffs; power chords arranged like French cuisine, turning **Moving Pictures** into what it is, the most energetic and guitar-dominated from Rush since the oddball debut. And so it goes: infectious vitality and a love of chops-driven composition win the day, most observers conceding that this was a creative force with a very distinctive and enthusiastic mission.
Rating 10

## Rush - Exit . . . Stage Left (Anthem '81)

The ultimate historical artifact to a self-styled grandeur that exploited all the finery and pomp of progressive rock within a metallic context. The dizzying selection of hippy math herein enclosed touches on all the high points of Rush's metal-for-musicians era, kicking off with the heroic *The Spirit Of Radio*, pacing and racing its way past such alchemical highs as *Red Barchetta*, *Free Will*, and *Tom Sawyer* through to the pyrotechnical finale afforded by instrumental *La Villa Strangiato*. Rush managed major communion with the massive throngs amongst the jean jacket set harbouring aspirations towards musical, literary, or otherwise ethereal pursuits by delivering a self-righteous sound no adult had a right to put down, for any reason other than differing tastes. It was a display of flash and substance to be proud of, fueling the creative fires of many a teen dreamer including myself with respect to the drums. **Exit . . . Stage Left** documents Rush's most overtly pretentious period splendidly, a body of work almost equally loved, ridiculed, respected and reviled among music fans everywhere. Simply put, I bought into it and still do with the passing years.

Rating                                                           7

## Rush - Signals (Anthem '82)

After closing the books on Rush's magicianly musician phase with a ripping live album, the band returns with a sort of resolute calm, a detached composure which finds all corners of the Rush machine turned down, Geddy's shriek gone forever, Peart and Lifeson both enriched with creamy, pastel sounds, swirled into a seamless whole with elegant, under-stated synth washes. **Signals** is the first of a most-hated directive in the Rush saga, the introduction to the band's vastly inferior second decade as a recording entity. But hell, I think it's a great record, the last classic Rush album despite the total band makeover. **Signals** is the work of a trio who now fashion themselves mature artists versus mature craftsmen, preferring to let their formidable skills emanate from the compositions rather than leap. Peart and Lee retain their instrumental grandeur, while it is Lifeson who is most altered, relegated to a role of colour and shade, fortifying engaging rhythms rather than defining with riff. And the rhythms are diverse, Peart expanding on his angular and mutated tech reggae (via Stewart Copeland) catalogue with *Digital Man*, catchy hit single *New World Man* and most notably *The Weapon*, all clever progressions from **Moving Pictures'** *Vital Signs*. But personal highlights would be openers *Subdivisions* and *The Analog Kid*, both sublime rockers smoothly propelled by production values that are cool and elegant, and the magnificent *Losing It*, a rich and tragic tale lamenting the fading of one's glory years. All in all, I consider **Signals** the most intelligent Rush record; wise, dynamic, fresh and so expertly blended, sadly the last with so many successful songs. Solid, self-assured art.

Rating                                                          10

## Rush - Grace Under Pressure (Anthem '84)

Breathe deeply of *Distant Early Warning*'s stirring chorus, because that's the last time—eight years and still counting—you'll ever hear Rush rocking out. **Grace Under Pressure** expands on Rush's new-found preference for busy texture over rock groove, creating fussy electric reggae robotics, an interesting hybrid but a tiring one, the band augmenting the clatter with an increasing palette of synth skronks and electric drums, not to mention an increasingly eccentric approach to the role of the guitar in the band. **Grace Under Pressure** represents an artsy Rush in full flare (even the group shot is by Karsh), a band asking its fan base to grow where they're going, while much of the record doesn't go anywhere all that commendable, sabotaged by anxious beats and fuzzy logic. Still, a sort of academi-

cally satisfying listen, but pleasurable, no. A detectably dirtier mix than on the smooth-as-silk **Signals**, but worse music.

Rating                                                           7

## Rush - Power Windows (Anthem '85)

**Grace Under Pressure** marked the last time I ever really cared what Rush was up to. So I heard **Power Windows** only when it wasn't *my* dollars at stake, only when it became convenient. Bit o' life to *The Big Money* and *Manhattan Project*, but Peart's drum set sounds horrible, as does Peart, who's given up passion for algebra. I guess you'd call these exotic rhythms or world beats, but I'd call them a depressing waste of time. Synthetic hogwash.

Rating                                                           4

## Rush - Hold Your Fire (Anthem '87)

Like '80s Queen, the pre-release hype was always the same: the band is back to their roots and kickin' . . . and it always turned out to be a cruel joke. Must admit, the album graphics are always dashing. But **Hold Your Fire** is quite possibly the biggest Rush dump ever; the most synths, the stoopidest beats, Lifeson lifeless, producer Peter "Cetera" Collins, no small part of the problem. Twisted smiles all around as the Canadian press looks for something positive to say about our quickly tarnishing national treasure.

Rating                                                           2

## Rush - A Show Of Hands (Anthem '89)

Pan to cover: geometric automatons, one at the drums, one on guitar, and one on the goddam *keyboards*, surrounded by a swath of pristine white. Yep, this is Rush Alive! in the late '80s, hockey barns filled with headbangers re-living **2112** and **Moving Pictures**, and for that matter, **All The World's A Stage** in their dope-smoked cranial cavities while the professors weave through such rip-roarin' ho-downs as *Marathon*, *Mission*, *Mystic Rhythms*, and the captivating *Time Stands Still* up on the operating table. Like, what the hell *is* this? Bridge to Spock? Hell I don't know. A recipe for a snooze at the library, that's what. I hope the band's much vaunted video distraction was in full kaleidoscopic view during these snobby affairs, because watching Alex string one thin, painful, chiming rock'n'roll mistake after another over virtually unattached Peart patterns from Legoland (exclusively constructed from a vast array of novelty cymbals, woodblocks, and things attached to wires) is more textbook schooling than one should be subjected to at a goddam rock concert. Yep, this is highbrow rock at its most viral, gnarled and sabotaged, stiffly identical to the appropriate studio renditions from whence these "live" pieces annoyingly originated. Highlights: the throbbing *Subdivisions* and the dynamic *Distant Early Warning*, one of the last moments where Rush rocked, if only during the chorus, the remainder of the tune pretty much as three-legged as the rest of the band's last ten years. All in the name of intellect. A typically butchered Canadian reaction to the discovery of brains.

Rating                                                           3

## Rush - Presto (Anthem '89)

More itchy agit-pop from the dish-panned hands of Lifeson, Lee and Peart, **Presto** was a rousing commercial success for the band, but you'd never know it, Rush for all intents and purposes falling from the collective consciousness of rock'n'roll, long past their usefulness, crafting obscure curio shop rock; clueless, deflated and dribbling, with occasional popcorn rhythms reinforced by the band's usual astonishing weightlessness. Two "hits": *Show Don't Tell* and *Superconductor*, both over-

dressed and under-armed; skittery mouse rock worthy of your most profound loathing.
Rating                                          3

## Rush - Roll The Bones   (Anthem '91)

Rush's lot in life continues to baffle, as I'm increasingly convinced that with each successive dismal, offensive release, the band's continuing and ever-widening acceptance by virtually everybody must amount to no less than a conspiracy of mass mindlessness. Have no fear. Despite the accolades, Rush's latest is again, as countless times before, no cause for rejoice, as the serious ones continue unabated with their powerless fret-diddling, their tinkly, popping percussive ballet, and simply erroneous arrangements that neither rise nor descend to anything much, merely plodding forth in tribal, angular, jazzy, waves of bad guitarwork and intrusive synth washes. **Roll The Bones** again looks good on the racks, fooling the hopeful once more that the band might have traces of adrenaline still influencing their wintery, dour psyches toward some sort of life. Subject matter this time around is fate, destiny, man's purpose etc., and lyrically Peart is just as slightly above average as he's been for the last eight records or so, showing no sign of waking up from his tiring gravity. Geddy's vocals are as unexpressive as ever; a boring voice rendered even more robotic and sleepy since he put his wild metallic banshee to rest along with any remaining vestiges of youthful purpose. And he still destroys every shot at putting together a good rock tune with too many bass notes too high up the register (also an affliction of Steve Harris). Final nail on the fate of Rush's latest highbrow attempt at reaching the lowbrows comes via the misguided nimble fingers of Alex Lifeson, who again refuses to attach riff to power chord, playing *around* everything within earshot, rarely addressing his duty to carry the mass. One of the biggest, failed, and mercilessly played-out experiments in modern rock, Lifeson swishes ever on, chiming and jangling his way into the books of fretful impotence. And had the band not colluded to come up with the ultimate overplayed statement on anemic frailty, Rupert Hines alone would have sent it crying home to mommy, offering forth a decidedly middling, unarousing wimp mix that sounds like his name. Dreadful, tuneless, powerless, illogical, and so sadly aimless, Rush drags us to the till each and every relentlessly unfolding year, exploiting our dimming remembrances of past glory, only to bestow upon its battered and ultimately submissive fan base, flashy, well-dressed arrangements of uniformly-shaped, and expertly-bronzed poodle turds.
Rating                                          3

## Rush - Counterparts   (Anthem '93)

Watching the volcanic chords of *Stick It Out* flow from my speakers like boiling back bacon grease summarily brought a tear to my eye, raising my hopes that Lifeson was forsaking his sonic vegetarianism, reaffirming his inherent nature as bush-roaming mammal. Well, yes and no, Rush's arcane, impotent melodies still pockmark this latest grand gesture, but rhythms are bolstered, hooks stronger, and stacks of chords are delivered intermittently albeit with some regularity. Really, not a large departure in tone, but discernibly more lubrication, biggest improvement being the flow of Peart's beats, although lyrically it's still the sermon on the mount. Lifeson retains his eccentric but vast vocabulary, with the usual emphasis on Howe/Hackett/Holdsworth-style art solos, U2 chimings, and ethereal non-obvious phrasings, but Peart snaps the show into a semblance of attention towards forward mass, "rock song" pasted firmly to his over-active forehead this time. Same ol' anemic '80s Rush: *Speed Of Love*. Stirring new '90s Rush (I hope): *Animate*.
Rating                                          7

## Rush - Test For Echo   (Anthem '96)

Mauve over, Rush has another record ready, Test For Pulse, I mean **Test For Echo** reversing the jets on the moderately sparkly **Counterparts** opus, comfortably refitting Rush amongst the has-beens of creativity. So what we get is somewherez between the band's worst record and fourth worst, a dreary mess of fragile guitar, bass and doldrums, o'ertop which Lee deadpans some of Peart's most juvenile and pretentious lyrics yet, cute and snobbed beyond belief, songs about dog time, Internet love and the various meanings of "driving" and the concept of "half", mucking forth in compositional collapse, cheap pun punching metaphor, trite observation chafing cliché. Yeah, Rush doesn't show off instrumentally anymore, but they make sure arrangements confuse the pants off their Trek-face fanbase, cramming in boring riffs and unaggressive rigging in quick succession much like Maiden, editing nothing out, just like Zappa. But of course there's no real metal. Anytime Lifeson plays, he's halfways to unplugged, browning-out all heartless attempts at guitar rock so we can uh, hear the words. Dead identical to yer **Roll The Bones** or **Presto**, Rush prove themselves surprisingly and stupidly consistent since '87 in creating smothered, toneless production values that accomplish the dubious math of making Rush a power trio of equal sixths: one half the band they once were and twice the annoyance.
Rating                                          5

# S

## Sabbat - History Of A Time To Come (Maze '88)

Not for the faint of heart, Sabbat were (and continue to be despite the defection of leader Martin Walkyier) a brutal shock of thought-provoking thrash, an expulsion of sinful sonics; surging power like a smothering Rage or Grave Digger or Voivod, at this point still led by one twisted poet, Walkyier himself. No bones about it, **History Of A Time To Come** is something of a masochistic pleasure, sending black waves on the backs of distressed and savage doom chords, all the while Walkyier barking his vomity belch. Which all makes for a spiteful, ugly record but one so independent and committed (both types) to the most grating of European metals, you just gotta crack a smile for a world that would grow this stuff. Thrashy but worthy of your fear and respect, which should be evident from the freakshow cover.

Rating 7

## Sabbat - The Mourning After (Noise '91)

Our fave UK deaf depressives get it on with an American singer after the cakewalk by an artistically frustrated Martin Walkyier to form the much superior Skyclad. But this was always Andy Sneap's vehicle anyways, here the guitarist coming up dry and unemotional perhaps exposing the real talent in the band as the departed troll up front. The record's still downright vicious, but the stiff riffs seem lost in a distorto-maze of goth-heap possibilities; too intrusive, too often, too pointless. And vocalist Ritchie Desmond's operatic warblings sound a bit Manowar for the quasi-wise metal enclosed. Solid graphics, smart lyrics, but too little musicality, bulk without carrying handles, grouchy buzz without beauty. The band called it quits shortly thereafter, never even getting the record toured.

Rating 5

## Sacred Reich - Ignorance (Metal Blade '87)

Name and graphics spelled hardcore seizure for this Phoenix, Arizona band, but underneath the cogent politics was a bunch of long-haired metallions, pumping proficient thrash, capably recorded by label honcho Brian Slagel, quite pioneering for its time, building onto a Slayer-bred beast a loose-bolted mosh that would become popular years later. Shoot 'em up musicianship drunkenly arranged for maximum anarchy.

Rating 6

## Sacred Reich - The American Way (Metal Bade/Enigma '90)

Another short record (after the even shorter **Surf Nicaraugua** EP), and Phil Rind is back in style roaring out the politics of responsibility, even ending the record with *31 Flavours* an admonishment to those who close their minds to other forms of music. Great production on this one (Bill Metoyer and Sacred Reich), the band's twin guitars on full flare, electrified and power-surged, driving solid, power metal songs that continue a deliberate jack-boot stomp away from thrashmosh. Faves would be the title track and eco-chugger *Crimes Against Humanity*, but Jason and Wiley come up with all sorts of slamming riffs, turning this 35-minute hard reality feast tuneful and professional. The last before the band's fruitless major label experience.

Rating 7

## Sacred Reich - Independent (Hollywood '93)

Soaking up the frontier-bending vibes of modern ultra-purists like Pantera and Corrosion Of Conformity (both late to the form), Sacred Reich leap groin-tearing bounds above previous output, which was yer basic headplate thrash. Here, riffs are caustic and intense, mega-extreme in fine fashion under vocals that are a touch too much like the corroded pipes of Phil Anselmo. But the metal rules, even hatching intermittent globs of Sab, if still a bit squared-off and punky. A definite contender, raised from the skate malls by a willingness to learn, not to mention the buzzsaw aural terrain carved up by the one and only Dave Jerden.

Rating 8

## Sacred Reich - Heal (Metal Blade '95)

Hell's bells, I thought **Independent** was a menacing chunk of iron, but evidently long-time fan and band alike got that familiar itch for shorter, sharper shockers. So **Heal** (the band's fourth), delivers the rapid-fire brevity, each angry composition arriving stripped to the basics, but produced tight as a drum (back to their old producer), evoking Pantera to Souls At Zero to DRI, with a dash of punk irreverence to keep it to the core. Totally urban, totally metal, **Heal** is the product of one of those bands you had to adopt early and cheer on through the peaks and valleys. Potent stuff, but a little too much the sum of its influences, or a mix of too many sounds that through reversal, might have been influenced by these guys years back. Basically, the slight return to hardcore roots seems to have shoved them

back into a crowded pack. I mean, major spirit and fiery leads, but there's just so much out there right now.
Rating 7

## Sacrifice - Torment In Fire (Diabolic Force '85)

Plainly stupored thrash mayhem with no redeeming qualities of which to speak, further sent to the depths with a drum-dominated recording not unlike early Exciter, with third-rate Slayer-like divebomber solos and sin-draped riffs buried in the muck. Vein-popping torture from Toronto.
Rating 4

## Sacrifice - Forward To Termination (Diabolic Force '87)

Because they're artistically brave and extreme Canadian boys, I've actually had to endure the video for Re-animation on Canada's intrepid video station a gazillion times while waiting for more useful visual caffeine. No change from the useless vacuum that was **Torment In Fire**. If I saw any reason to like this kind of blastcore, I might compliment the drumming and the overall intense aural effect; but to me, this turgid black goo all sounds the same. Above average for the curmudgeonly genre, but I'm too stressed already to be tuning in.
Rating 6

## Sacrilege - Turn Back Trilobite (Metal Blade '89)

Sullen goth tones snake their way through this difficult prog metal minefield, recalling all the heavy moments from Fates Warning, or even perhaps old legends Warlord, Sacrilege's sound being quite dated. Over the churning miasma soar female vocals from Lynda Simpson, occasionally flat, always melodramatic like any poodle-head guy would be under the circumstances. Nifty richter scale rating for each song, kinda like Kerrang's Koncert reviews. But of no lasting significance.
Rating 4

## Sad Iron - Total Damnation (Est. '83)

. . . subtitled Sadder Than They Wanna Be, **Total Damnation** is all crab and crust, sounding as imagineless and distantly body-bagged as Soviet rock, clawing towards death metal, bringing home only a chafing itch fixed by any three dollar, over the counter ointment. Crafted in the early days of the decibel revolution, when much could be forgiven.
Rating 2

## S.A.D.O. - "Shout!" (Noise '84)

Judging from the band pics on the back, it looks like a S.A.D.O. show is a multi-disciplinary affair with lots of nudity, bondage and live sex acts, which have nothing in common whatsoever with the band's dark and curious metal alchemy, mixing keyboard hard rock à la Viva (never mind), AC/DC rock and deadly perfect German amphetamine metal, for some reason bringing to mind **Virgin Killer** and **Taken By Force**; vintage Teutonic chaos, sin-steeped metal grown in dark, mainland European isolation. Thus Rubber Bondage, instrumental Rage, and the whacked-out brilliance of Run Baby Run, a song that just spoils my mood in indescribable ways. No shit, S.A.D.O. possesses German metal, which flashes its perfection sparingly but with unforgettable results. Ten minutes of this up-and-down, boundaryless record are like that, finding Scorpions, Accept, and Grave Digger gravity, albeit of a more dank and chilling nature. Depressing, emotionally-confused, thus sparingly ingested. Most days it just wouldn't make sense.
Rating 8

## S.A.D.O. - Dirty Fantasy (Noise '88)

More of a rivethead burger than '84's sinister but mesmerizing cold fish **"Shout!"**, **Dirty Fantasy** displays a band hot to ride the Accept express, building

infectious rockers out of meaty riffs and solid-as-oak bass lines. And S.A.D.O. are worthy of the shot if I wasn't so creeped out by **"Shout"**! André Cook's vocals are as copious as before, infusing **Dirty Fantasy** with edge and a touch of slydog mischief, while the band scoops out basic headbanging fare with caustic vigor. Main problem: uniformity, the band stuck on certain specific grooves, lacking in any desire to roll the dice. I think they call it "playing it safe."
Rating 7

## Sadwings - Lonely Hero (Criminal Response '85)

Another drowned and dreary, pork-fisted slab of depression metal, **Lonely Hero** chugs heavily in the usual Euro-goth Ebony manner, leaving nothing to warm up to amongst its Swedish chill so adeptly portrayed on its cover. The drums have that treated, low-reg thud to them, while lead throat Tony Ekfeldt is mixed way back, possibly due to the English-as-second-language thing, or maybe his flat monotone. One of many bands in this icy vein, which fortunately demands fairly high minimum standards. Sad and lonely.
Rating 4

## Saigon - One Must Die (Criminal Response '85)

Same Swedish blight as with labelmates Sadwings, only Saigon pound it on home fat and throbbing, opting for top-heavy metallic marches, below the excellent Euro pierce of winter-throated Anders Ahlund. Reminds one more of Torch and Gravestone in its relentless gravity and ultra-seriousness in terms of its tunnel-visioned cause. Another classic flesh-dissolving Ebony mix. Love it loud or leave it alone.
Rating 7

## Saigon Kick - Saigon Kick (Atlantic '91)

One of the more pleasantly perplexing acts to emerge from the edges of hairness, Florida's Saigon Kick weave the most amazing textures into their deceptively straight-forward hard rock sound, finding time and space for exotic eastern melodies, Cheap Trick-isms, Sweet-like vocal harmonies, thrash, trash, ugliness and beauty. What emerges is a tropical cocktail unavoidably fresh, causing justified buzz for this band whose break apparently came from paying a club to let them play instead of the slated act, knowing that Skid Row was amongst the crowd, resulting in rave reviews from Baz and the boys. Known for indulging in the odd party treat, Saigon Kick are proof that a little mental recreation goes a long way in the creation of art, this debut packed full of exquisite tales in so many shades and colours. Personal fave is undoubtedly infectious lead single What You Say, while other exceedingly likeable tunes would be popster Suzy and lush ballad Come Take Me Now, sort of a precursor to breakthrough hit Love Is On The Way. And to complete the enigmatic presentation of this record, all this complexity of purpose is brought to fruition through a grimy and echoey type live mix, not particularly bad, just very stage, especially in the midrangey guitar sound, giving the impression that all this high-mindedness is not altogether planned, more like a heaven-sent accident.
Rating 9

## Saigon Kick - The Lizard (Atlantic '92)

More of a sharpening up of emotions expressed on the debut, **The Lizard** seems to get grimier on the rockers, and more fragrant on the ballads, over a mix that possesses the same echoey stage presence as the debut, yet with fuller range. Big deceptive hit scored with Love Is On The Way, a breathtaking ballad with a strong harmony chorus, while Feel The Same Way also found its Way onto radio, propelled by equally perfect harmonies. Saw the band in concert (backing up Extreme), and I must say, they were pretty rock'n'roll looking in their leathers, able to crank an almost Crüe-

looking in their leathers, able to crank an almost Crüe-ish grind at times (i.e. opening chords to *The Lizard* and *Hostile Youth*), proving their mettle in the world of metal. Place Saigon Kick between Warrior Soul and Enuff Z'nuff, but place them higher, as the personae of the band just seems to shift like a mirage, making for a top-flight cerebral experience that headbangs at the same time. Cosmic, slack and cutting edge all in one, Saigon Kick gets me every time.
Rating                                              10

## Saigon Kick - Water   (Third Stone '93)

Big, bold, beautiful changes abound in the Saigon camp, as dangerous vocalist Matt Kramer gets the boot (along with a switch on bass), rendering the band a power trio, completely dominated by guitarist Jason Bieler, who now adds lead vocals to his guitar, production and songwriting chores. What results is a lush, pharmaceutical, new age sort of spin, a record much more experimental and exploratory than the band's previous two grunt rockers. **Water** makes full use of the band's patented harmonies, missing nary a beat with the ouster of Matt, swirling into view as something daring indeed, finding The Beatles more often than anything metallic, even smatterings of Prince-style electronics, odd tribal beats, and Floyd for the '90s atmospherics. Faves would be surprise sweets *I Love You* and *On And On*, while *One Step Closer* and *Torture* are more or less left alone to provide the guitar crunch, amidst a sensuous display of courage. Full marks for the guts to say what's on his mind, the integrity to break all rock'n'roll rules, but all in all, a shade less successful than the robust hybrids of old. Respect, nevertheless. Awesome packaging, awesome lyrics.
Rating                                               8

## Saigon Kick - Devil In The Details   (CMC '95)

AOR expert and buddy Mike Drew can't stop raving about this band and record, and for a bunch of years I too have been a Saigon Kick supporter of unhealthy proportions. But I'm finding this newer, less raw and more fancy-pants direction just a bit too quaint, precious and bourgeois. Maybe it's my recent stress-hammered years of logging too much Swedish death metal, but I find myself turning back this cup of java 'cos there's too much sugar. Jason's explosive musical and lyrical creativity worked best when more than half of what was going on could make Motley Crue's nasty rhythm section blush. As the Mensa campfire ballads begin to take over, Saigon Kick begins to sound too smart for its own good, wanting greedily to keep its hand in the worlds of metal, prog rock, pop and alternative at the same time. Sure we're to think, it's all just music, man, the best on the planet, and to be sure, Jason is a craftsman and artist par excellence. It's just that the noises he wants to make are getting a bit art school, and the rare times he's rocking out (i.e. *Killing Ground* and *Flesh And Bone*), it's just a rehash of earlier Saigon riffs.
Rating                                               7

## The Saints - (I'm) Stranded   (Sire '77)

Australia's first and only sand-blasting adrenaline punkers, The Saints today remain one of my favorite artistic forces although only their first two of at least seven records were heavy; later efforts rollicking richly with celtic aplomb, fragrantly enhanced with strings, horns, and lyrical magnificence from soaring mastermind Chris Bailey. But back to the trenches for the sonic brainshake that is the legendary **(I'm) Stranded**, which slams out of control like a psychotic, too far gone crippling the Ramones crossed with the desperate power surge of The Damned, sent deep into the garage among rats as big as dogs. The recording ain't so much bad as ill-willed; truly awful but somehow hellishly justified under the hopeless circumstances.

And for once, a band actually does sound like **Fun House**, **Raw Power** and **Kick Out The Jams**; glued to the basement under intense black light, and demolished in white noise resignation of long, polluted hangovers to come. Thoroughly imploded, historically tantamount, and heavy as shit for '70s punk.
Rating                                               8

## The Saints - Eternally Yours   (Sire '78)

Wisdom leaks in down under as The Saints find illustrious alloys of punk and the elevated riffery of metal, whilst simultaneously letting us in on the lush sounds to come (i.e. acoustic guitars on *Memories Are Made Of This* and *A Minor Aversion*, and horns on *Know Your Product*). But the weenie roasters are of a more belligerent nature, toons like *No, Your Product* doing a great job of The Dictators, while *This Perfect Day* documents a dark, messy 24 hours indeed, heaps of angry guitars dueling with the rodental punk snarl of Chris Bailey. But the overall impression I glean from this record is one of smarts and experience, **Eternally Yours** rising above the work of its predecessor in construction of a well-rounded, nicely-paced guitar rock opus, lots of successful and nostalgic forays into the incestuousness of the rock idiom, all mucked-up with greaseball licks and thick fuzzy production values. The last slash 'n' burnstormer from The Saints, although what followed was equally enjoyable, albeit closer to The Church than Lords Of The New Church or Metal Church.
Rating                                               9

## Saints & Sinners - Saints & Sinners   (Aquarius '92)

Perpetuating a trend towards long band names, Saints & Sinners are yet another un-needed entry into the flawless corporate rock sweepstakes, led by Rick Hughes, a kick-ass set of pipes who cut his teeth with respectable but disbanded Montreal act Sword. Unfortunately, **Saints & Sinners** leans towards the more sleep-inducing side of chick metal, often funky, tentative and light-headed, always too slick, only saving grace being Hughes and the occasional **Slave To The Grind** stylings of axedude Stephane Dufour. But just too tired and predictable (except for *Kashmir*-ic epic *Frankenstein* clocking in at an unnecessary 9:57), with no less than three ballads out of ten cuts. Sorry, but this one's merely a gathering of poor quality songs.
Rating                                               4

## Saint Vitus - C.O.D.   (Hellhound '92)

Mid-level, mid-grade . . . everything about this band is mid, Ain't Vitus just mashing their potatoes through this acceptable but never crucial mid-years record. **C.O.D.** (as in Care of the Delete Bin) just bashes like all else in the vast and snoozy Saint Vitus catalogue, simplex doom to the fore, face to the floor, all discerning Sabbath fans to the door. Vague Hawkwind whiff to the thing, but the intellect or eccentric get-about just ain't in the room.
Rating                                               6

## Saint Vitus - V   (Roadrunner '94)

Through umpteen dirgy records straddling the '80s, Wino and his doom-dull Saints gouged a niche as the garagey, not all that proficient homage to Black Sabbath, the indie tribute, the sorry mash of slow sounds. This reissue of a 1990 record documents a career that has now transformed into The Obsessed, a slightly more elevated version of the same, both bands made chilly by Wino's hollow, warlocked vocals and very creepy outlook on life. Cool, old-style mix, but the preponderance towards slow and simple spells Black boredom, as witnessed on the truly sleepy *Patra* (*Petra*). A bit of a laughing stock back in the mid-80s, **V** tells us that there was something to that hippy hybrid into doom. With solid songs, Saint Vitus could have achieved the stellar success levels of Trouble. That's called sarcasm.

Rating **6**

## Saint Vitus - Die Healing (Hellhound '95)

Always mining the dregs of Sabbath riffs passed up as scrap by smarter second gen doomsters, St. Vitus have finally packed up their tarnished crucifixes. This last sound chomp churns out more of the band's patented slow, high-school simple, and painfully obvious blubber rock. Still confused about what these doofs were doin'. I guess they've backhandedly inspired modern turgidoom, but have they ever kicked our ass like Trouble? Ah, no. Still, a minor joy to hear castle-clear vocals like this, and the werds are effective through unflash. Perceptive blanket generalization: Saint Vitus never had the songs.

Rating **6**

## Steve Salas Colorcode - Steve Salas Colorcode
(Island '90)

Weak and slick compared to the band's whomping '94 release, this debut for terrifyingly rhythmic guitar god Steve Salas rides too close to guys like Dan Reed Network, more light and funky, almost like heavy Chili Peppers at times. I dunno, the whole project has that twee, hair band prettiness to it, leaving me cold and suspicious of the band's artistic freedom or lack thereof in the making of this record. But the soloing is a rollercoaster ride, flashy, buoyant carnival madness that makes this miles more fun than any instrumental axewank from the guy's peers.

Rating **5**

## Steve Salas Colorcode - Back From The Living
(Pavement/Zoo '95)

Best known as hot lickin' axeman to stars like George Clinton, Rod Stewart, Terence Trent D'Arby, Sass Jordan and Buddy Miles, Salas did what many an esteemed and ignored technical guitar player has done, take his product direct to Japan, where chops and all-round caring often lead straight to increased sales. Well, after several records with Asia-only release, his '94 **Back From The Living** culinary delight has seen reissue here through Pavement. And a joy it is to behold, one of the most musically buoyant permutations of that Hendrix thang in a long while. If you've been disappointed in Lenny Kravitz, then come over here, because this is essentially a record full of those heavier Kravitz moments, all those great singles that totally misrepresent the rest of any snoozy Kravitz full-length. You know them well. Slinky, hard funk rhythms (thanks to all-pro bassist T.M. Stevens and drummer Brian Tichy), effortless guitar-drenched melodies, and Salas' sly R+B vocal stylings combine for something enjoyable as hard rock, as well as a rock lesson steeped in three or four daunting traditions. faves: *Start Again* (offered both studio and live), and *God I'm Going Down*, both inspirational suntanned summer rockers ill-timed with fall release to usher in an inevitably cold, bitter winter.

Rating **8**

## Salty Dog - Every Dog Has Its Day (Geffen '90)

Sauntering into town packing one bitchin' retro tale in the rousing *Come Along*, Salty Dog were one of the most interesting '70s throwbacks in a long while, more headbang boogie woogie than the historical ways and means of Black Crowes with a wonderfully loose bass drum sound and a set of pipes in Jimmi Bleacher that recalls the best of early Plant, other old Zep comparatives coming fast and furious in the clanking blues structures and general Bonham hamfisting by skinsman Khurt Maier. Everything sounds pleasantly aged on this record in faithful reverence of past legends, most notably Foghat circa **Fool For The City**; lotsa slide

guitar, boogie power chords and all things slouchy and slack, contemporary soul brothers being acts like Raging Slab and Four Horsemen. Polished and souped-up like an old Mustang, ready for the resurgence of that lost and ridiculed decade, Salty Dog could have easily become darlings of the new traditionalists out there. I mean, Steve Miller still sells out his shows. It can't be that hard.

Rating **8**

## Salvador Dream - Ur (Warner '94)

I'm on the fence with this one. Vancouver's Salvador Dream have concocted a sound that slows up and de-complicates Helmet for a sort of lackadaisical Sons Of Freedom, an apt comparative given the shared hometown. Tight snare, (seemingly) long dreamy tunes, and many references to Zep-style *Kashmir* riffs (hence **Ur**?), all rolling on under a vocal that sounds a bit like Elvis Costello, and a lot like someone else I can't place at the moment, Graham Parker or someone, I dunno. So fairly cool, definitely hip to '94's selling genres, but also a bit too languid.

Rating **7**

## Samael - Blood Ritual (Century Media '92)

Oddly enough, early Samael was much slicker than the raw bleeding exhibited on later flares, **Blood Ritual** sounding somewhat like Celtic Frost, what with its unflashy (mostly slow) riffs conservatively recorded, even its cover art and booklet being quite advanced for the band's yet unproven track record. Refreshingly level-headed, but level-headed to the point of apathy and boredom, no help from Vorphalack's grinded up vocal spewages straight from the charnel house (just wanted to use that word).

Rating **5**

## Samael - Ceremony Of Opposites (Century Media '92)

Awesome grindcore forged in the white-hot spirit of mid-years Entombed, **Ceremony Of Opposites** should find Samael denting crossover heads, although vocals are still traditionally belched in bile from the lower intestine. Extra special bite and toughness rises from the midrange-heavy mix (a much more radical sound than the almost relaxed debut), while lyrics drive right to the stake of Norwegian-style black metal (coming to a correctional facility near you). Real evil and dark, introducing Paradise Lost-style atmospherics courtesy new keyboardist Rodolphe H. for that convincing goth ornament. Crushing, heinous and freaky.

Rating **8**

## Samael - Rebellion (Century Media '95)

Samael continue to scratch and claw themselves above the death metal vermin with which they compete, on this EP offering their best song yet, evil genius epic *Rebellion*, a blood-poisoned cover of Alice Cooper dirge *I Love The Dead*, a couple of classy remakes of earlier material, and two tracks (one hidden at the end) of spooky, ambient, unworld music. It all points to big apocalyptic changes in the future, as Samael begin to find more doom and traditional and plain loopiness to bolster their curved death metal backbone. 36 minutes of madness, again bone-bruisingly recorded by Sorychta and Bemm at Woodhouse in Germany.

Rating **7**

## Samael - Passage (Century Media '96)

Sparkling and alone in the world of orchestral death metal (orchestral by way of deceptive layered keyboards), Samael have entered a rarified realm indeed. Brothers Vorph and Xy have fine-tuned their duties, really for the first time weaving deeply all those chivalrous keyboard arcings and drum programming (apparently these aren't live drums, but you'd never know it: the drum parts are convincing and absolutely stunning) into an aristocratic attack that just might take this band beyond the likes of Amorphis, Cemetary and Gorefest in providing the rich cream of extreme metal. Favourites are openers *Rain, Shining Kingdom* and closer *A Man In Your Head*, which whip into a frosty froth, expert moves from grindcore through traditional NWOBHM ideas, all slathered with the history-rich moves of Deep Purple. So what results is a masterpiece that is gothic on at least four levels: the '70s, the '80s, the '90s and gothic new wave, Samael having no problem touching each imposing composition with electronics far from metal, before sending many of these rippers through prog terrain, always cognizant of elegance and the sturdy rules of song. Not merely the next tweak in this young band's sound, **Passage** really marks a leap beyond the trappings of death into a spacier realm (*Jupiterian Vibe, Moonskin, Born Under Saturn*), Samael no doubt keeping an eye on the dozen or so other creative death metal forces that have made this shift. An astonishing and stirring pageant of heavy, heavy music.

Rating     10

## Samain - Vibrations Of Doom    (Roadrunner '84)

Samain drove a sort of uptight, uneventful take on Accept, the in-vogue, fast-rising local boys at the time. Coming closest to **Balls To The Wall**, with engaging twin rhythm riffery, a hearty mix, and groove-oriented cement-like, mid-pace structures, **Vibrations** gets undercut by lack of imagination, the usual butchering of the English language (e.g. *The Metal Breaks The Senses*), and generally flat, toneless vocals. A veritable verminous scad of this stuff festered up all over the racks throughout the '80s, and just as quickly, almost all of it faded with a month's buzz at most.

Rating     6

## Richie Sambora - Stranger In This Town

(PolyGram '91)

Bon Jovi axeman Richie Sambora delivers a tasty, low-key pop blues effort here, reinforced by the guy's surprisingly soulful lead vocals and of course, his fluid Satriani/Clapton phrasings (Mr. Slowhand even guests on one track). But the record can't escape its stifling commercial context, nobody from Bon Jovi Inc. really expected to be anything other than turgidly mainstream at heart. In fact, this might be the most middle American appearance of fiercely wise bass legend Tony Levin, who I'm sure is on board as a fairly indifferent hired gun (how can you take this seriously after Crimson?). Still, this record's got every Bon Jovi bonbon beat in terms of integrity and maturity. But adventuresome it ain't, just rolling like a lush, plush carpet of layered blues and ballads, exuding a certain kind of taste that money calls into question. Y'know, Grammy-type stuff.

Rating     5

## Samson - Survivors    (Laser '79)

And so it begins, one long exercise in futility, injustice and the hapless Tapped life of rock'n'roll rogues. **Survivors** is Samson's squeaky debut, a pub rock affair with a little bit of hard-edge blues, some funky Gillan-style hard rock (Colin Towns and John McCoy are both featured here, neither as an official band member, although McCoy co-writes all but one tune on the record), and a couple of drip ballads. Most (and maybe all) the vocals are courtesy of Paul Samson, although Bruce Bruce is listed as an additional set of pipes. I'll pay the musical chairs no mind, because the record ain't worth a dime, being badly mixed, written, played . . . pretty much nothing worth hooting over, except maybe lead track *It's Not As Easy As It Seems*. Simply nowhere ready to cut wax, while entering the fray at an opportune time.

Rating     4

## Samson - Head On    (Grand Slamm '80)

Proving themselves a band with both ideas and spark, Samson bounce back with a record that sadly wilts due to loose execution and junky mixing (nice drum sound, mates!), despite a robust performance from future star Bruce Dickinson and some hooky riffs and arrangements from one talented Paul Samson. Still just a shoot 'em up, bash 'em out bunch of garage rockers that remind me more of co-underdogs Fist than anything worthy of rescuing from the underground. Preferential ditties: *Take It Like A Man* and *Hammerhead*, kicking in after an intro called *Thunderburst*, which is identical to Maiden's *The Ides Of March* (Who actually gets credit for it? Ask someone who cares.). Anyways, a record that if re-played and re-mixed here in the '90s, would be a damn fine affair indeed.

Rating     6

## Samson - Shock Tactics    (Grand Slamm '81)

Tapping into a focused primal energy previously alien to the band, Samson hatch their classic, a record drunk with aggression, one on which everyone performs their duty with a life and death urgency. Stomping to centre stage with a kick-ass cover of Russ Ballard's *Riding With The Angels*, **Shock Tactics** proceeds to level the place with a grimy, street-level, full frontal attack. Sadly Bruce Bruce's swansong with the band, Dickinson makes **Shock Tactics** course with the stuff of life, the perfect complement to Paul Samson's blistering but traditional metal riffery. There's something so British and so pure about this record, a screeching performance that's loud and proud without being flashy, delivering the goods without yapping about it; versatile, fully ready for glory and expecting carnage in its wake. And the flames are a' fryin', smokin' ten foot TNT on dull pounders like *Blood Lust* and *Earth Mother*, while revving it up for driving anthems like *Go To Hell*, *Bright Lights* and *Grime Crime*. I dunno, the record just lasts, year after year making my car deck with its perfect chemistry of trash and class, the band on a mission, unfortunately dealt the blow of the man at the mike leaving for greener pastures. Can't say he didn't give Samson 100% though, but that's business.

Rating     10

## Samson - Before The Storm    (Polydor '82)

With Dickinson departed for more ghoulish and obscene stacks of cash, Samson pulls what I would consider a CLM (career limiting move) in hiring Nicky Moore for lead mike duties. It's a sad commentary on the world, but looks unfortunately count for something in the world of rock'n'roll—that's no surprise I'm sure—and this man, despite his soulful pipes, is a Tad wide of girth, especially for the central role of frontman. You've heard my opinion, and I mean the man no ill will, 'cos I love the guy's voice. Anyhoo, **Before The Storm** is a stirring record, taking full advantage of Moore's versatility, depth and southern rock inflections, making exquisite hybrids of beauties like *Danger Zone, Life On The Run* and *Losing My Grip*, all richly recorded and harkening back to a large AC/DC groove, making fresh meat of tradition. The record's crowning moment however comes with *Test Of Time*, my fave Samson song with the mostest, riding a killer chug riff with combustible authority and an urge to wreck large buildings. Overall, a well-paced affair that isn't afraid of melody, mix and subtle assimilation of somewhat eccentric American traditions. Intelligent control and restraint, not to mention tasteful licks from a man not without a trace of Dave Lindley's work-is-pleasure ethic coursing through his nimble fingers.

Rating     8

## Samson - Don't Get Mad - Get Even    (Polydor '84)

Record II for the Nicky Moore configuration finds the band bulking up along with the big man for some of the

most warlike and simultaneously hooky Paul Samson patterns of the band's dodgy career, hatching grand divebombers like *Love Hungry*, *Burning Up* and the headbanger simplicity of *Into The Valley*. **Don't Get Mad - Get Even** marks a sort of creative watershed for the band, matching stride-for-stride, and often exceeding **Shock Tactics** for riffs, if a little downwind in terms of enthusiasm, with Moore's southern bite mellowing the tone compared to Bruce Dickinson's OTT mania. But Paul Samson is as fluidly enjoyable as on any other release, riffing then embellishing with a self-esteem that points as much to street hardiness as the aristocratic echelons to which his playing belongs; the jean jacket at the black tie event as it were, exhibiting more manners, more depth and more human perspective than the egos crowding the ordeurves (sorry, not in my dictionary). As a record, this one's more sure of itself than its predecessor, sporting a general evenness and no ballads, basically **Animal Magnetism** versus **Blackout**, both records near equals, one better on the percentages, the other containing more standout tracks.
Rating                                        8

## Samson - Live At Reading '81   (Grand Slamm '90)

Aah, this was a band of nutters firing on all sixes, Bruce Dickinson performing from the gut, in front of a batch of songs that distilled an exciting era in British metal to its essentials. Recorded shortly after the release of **Shock Tactics** (and remixed in '90 by Chris Tsangarides), this was to be Bruce's last concert with his old buds, Paul Samson wanting to take the band in a bluesier direction than Bruce could handle. But of course all sorts of **Shock Tactics** anthems were present and ready for battle, *Earth Mother*, *Bright Lights* and *Riding With The Angels* all sounding particularly alive. Also includes an interview with Bruce reminiscing about his Samson days, including some funny stuff about leather-masked "legend" Thunderstick doing little to communicate except grunting, and his wish to have a cage built around his drum kit, something that actually happened for this gig. Ends off with previously unreleased simpleton rocker *Gravy Train*, closing one door and opening another . . .
Rating                                        7

## Samson - Refugee   (Communique '90)

Must confess, I have no idea what Samson's been up to in the six years previous to this vigorous reworking of NWOBHM values, but **Refugee** makes me want to find out, the immutable, inscrutable Paul Samson blazing his way through another fine collection of tunes rendered crackling and crisp for the '90s, with a suitably acrobatic and clear-headed set of pipes at the mike in Peter Scallan. **Refugee** is almost Lizzy-ish in terms of heart, even evoking shades of Schenker's **Assault Attack**, enveloped in champion chops and victorious melodies, splitting it down the middle between hard rock and metal, both imbued with Brit-style keyboards and the best type of techy drum sound. Preferred tracks would be percolating opener *Good To See You* and marauding rockers *Love This Time* and *The Silver Screen*, but the whole thing hangs together surprisingly well, main complaint being the overall politeness and squeaky clean quality of the total package. Still, it's always a joy just to hear Paul Samson's traditional and expressive metal magic.
Rating                                        7

## Paul Samson - Joint Forces   (Rondor '86)

Truly disappointing "solo" effort from one classy axeman, who here enlists his old band anyways for a surprisingly rickety, cheap sounding batch of third-rate rockers, sounding much older than 1986, and well below the mid-to-high polish for which Samson is renowned. Nicky Moore sounds wasted and the whole

sorry mess just rattles along behind him, Paul rarely even offering those well-composed solos he seemed capable of just unleashing at will. Horrid production provides the final rusty nail. Knee-jerk is to proclaim that Paul lacks leadership skills, but since everybody came along for the project anyways, one can imagine this a Samson record the band politely let Paul run solo with. Just guessing, but there's no mistaking that trucksize stumble.
Rating                                        4

## Sam Thunder - Manoevres   (Bullet Est. '85)

My lone picture disc. Bush-league melodic hard rock with hopelessly out-of-tune vocals, and keyboards that sound like a well-equipped kitchen. Don't feel too bad about trashing this record, 'cause the band looks like they were still in high school when they assembled this personal artistic statement, which hopefully means they've learned to play or moved on to day jobs.
Rating                                        3

## Sanctuary - Refuge Denied   (CBS '87)

Another Bay Area-style ultra-sledge, Sanctuary race their volcanic chops through rousing mathematical permutations of the Big Four or Five or Six, whatever. American techno-goth of the highest order, **Refuge Denied** does the genre justice for '87, while epic and overblown for the more groove- and payoff-oriented '90s (see Overkill, Exodus or Megadeth). Vocalist Warrel Dane's a gas, taking Virgin Steele's David Defeis to new hysterics. The man's a shriekhawk from Hell. Overall, a supercool disc for purists, but I rarely spin it, perhaps somewhat distracted by its odd time signatures, not to mention broken flow when courting 4/4. Cool cover of *White Rabbit*; really one of only a handful of successful metalizings of '60s tunage (along with Raven's *Born To be Wild*, that is).
Rating                                        7

## Sanctuary - Into The Mirror Black   (CBS '90)

He with the Hair and witchy bellow is back and kickin' bright white gothic apocalypto-vision with strapping new tech feast **Into The Mirror Black**. '90's offering possesses more edge, more danger, and heaps more bite in Dane's vocals, while the band nets out their grooves with a determination that flies lower to the ground. Fave track would be *Taste Revenge*, but the whole thing gathers at least a modicum of combat verve, at least somewhat reversing the frilly flourishes of the debut. Still, for fans of this self-important ego-driven American genre only. Well scratch that, I'm not big on the genre, but I can handle large piles of **Into The Mirror Black**. A metamorphosis into grittier but similar complication metal act Nevermore ensues.
Rating                                        8

## Santers - Shot Down In Flames   (Ready '81)

Santers shone briefly as an early '80s power trio from Ontario, comprising Rick Santers on guitar and vocals, brother Mark on drums, and Rick Lazaroff on bass. From record one, the sound was scrubbed clean, tight, well-recorded, and somewhat detrimentally aseptic. Structures were fairly simple, firmly rooted in '70s no-frills hard rock metal, sort of like a more transparent and lucid version of Coney Hatch, especially with respect to Mark's crystal but plaintive vocal delivery. **Shot Down In Flames** suffers from uneventful songcraft more than anything, the band sleepwalking through a good half of this with a sort of paint-by-numbers safeness. Major exception comes crashing through with the weighty low register title track, a moving tribute to Bon Scott, built of a soulful riff, sincere sadness and sophisticated control. One of the choice compositions of the Santers catalogue.
Rating                                        6

## Santers - Mayday (Ready '82)

Nice trip back into clinical Canadian guitar rock. The goods: alternative, pre-cooked versions of the awesome *Mistreatin' Heart* and the dipsy *Still I Am*, plus a couple of well-mixed live tracks bracketing a longish guitar wank from brother Rick. Good value EP from the good value boys.
Rating 6

## Santers - Racing Time (Ready '82)

Don't know how much buzz Santers attracted in their native T.O. at the time, but in any event, from the isolated reaches of Trail, B.C., things looked on the upswing with this improved product extension of the debut. **Racing Time** is a strangely joyous and conversely sorrowful Canadian hard rock enigma, one of the most winter-evoking records in my particular psychological skewing, capturing the spirit of cooperation and isolation of an accomplished, well-constructed hard rock band of regular guys amidst the affectations of a corrupt business. The overall feel is unadorned, ringing clear and true, whether courting metal, in the professional speed-rocking title cut, the uncharacteristically gothic (Canadavanillagoth) *Road To Morocco*, or the record's real forté, poignantly constructed melodic rockers such as the magnificent *Mistreatin' Heart* (previewed on the 4 track **Mayday** EP), the morose *Mystical Eyes*, or personal fave *Winter Freeze*, an emotional jewel which pulsed and pumped insidiously to the depths of my brain in successful carving of a permanent home. Effortlessly entertaining, **Racing Time** enthusiastically and humbly taps the great '70s HM clichés that shaped our minds, and indeed those of the metal generations recording today, clichés that reflect respect for melody, logic, and quality recording values. Sadly, **Racing Time**'s subdued beauty was never to be repeated as the band would call it quits after the depressing, uncommitted **Guitar Alley**.
Rating 9

## Santers - Guitar Alley (Ready '84)

Maybe it was a progressively jaded view of the business, or maybe the creativity-destroying presence of Rik Emmett who weakly produces the record; whatever the sordid reasoning, **Guitar Alley** smacks of a band in decline before its taste of fame; forcing and ultimately botching the trademark stadium sound that flowed so smoothly on the wings of **Racing Time**. Here similar moving melodic pounders self-destruct, descending into ineffectual choruses, rather than ascending to emotive climaxes, dragging potentially enjoyable, hook-laden anthems into failed barroom mediocrity, albeit well-recorded mediocrity. Overall, one senses that recurring Canadian tendency towards denial of competitive pressures, an ignorance of the necessity to forge ahead and take risks. **Guitar Alley** ultimately parallels the career conclusions of Coney Hatch, representing a band losing its sense of exuberance and fun. And once a hard rock band becomes saddled with a sense of defeat, nobody wants to be around for the ride down. **Guitar Alley** is such a shade; one rife with pregnant pauses, lyrical re-hashes, and emotional dysfunction. All one needs to hear is the ludicrously plain walk-through of Free's classic *All Right Now* to realize the heart of Santers has decisively imploded. Rick went on to join Triumph's touring band, and brother Mark wound up playing with Coney Hatch's Carl Dixon. '96: Rick is back with a low-key, barely plugged solo record.
Rating 5

## Saracen - Heroes, Saints And Fools (Nudeus '81)

Cloud-headed one chord wonders who worship to no avail at the ornate altar of jumpier prog rock, Saracen were trying to be a guitar-directed Marillion or Pallas or IQ or GTR or sumthin', yet couldn't play their way out of a wet paper bag, smelling more like quasi-cerebral Demon. Scary music school stuff really, and I'm glad it's all over. Record #2: '84's **Change Of Heart**.
Rating 2

## Saraya - Saraya (PolyGram '89)

As in Sandi Saraya, vocalist of the female persuasion who asserts herself o'er top vampy party rock in the miserable tradition of Allanah Myles, The Headpins, Toronto, Joan Jett, Lita Ford, plus mostly clueless spinny chick Lee Aaron. Earns a 1 for about 45 fragmented seconds of Rainbow-like melodies and three arguably metallic numbers. Album two, **When The Blackbird Sings** came out Fall '91 and you won't be disadvantaged in the least by not seeing it here.
Rating 1

## Satan - Court In The Act (Neat '83)

Before the metamorphosis into the much-improved Blind Fury in '84 (with new vocalist Lou Taylor), Satan were an early and even influential techno-goth outfit, rife with ideas and British gloom, yet limited by the vocal range of the controversial Brian Ross and the sucked-dead production characteristic of much early Neat product. As a result, **Court In The Act** fits the bill as admired, advanced for its era, but snuffed by its delivery, translating as a low-priced cross between Maiden and Angelwitch, buzzing and dour, underground and proud, cheap and distorted. Like I said, huge strides would be made as the band would trash its weak black metal premise and really let fry with **Out Of Reach**. Neat Metal reissue contains (uneventful) bonus tracks, but good graphics and info.
Rating 4

## Satanatras - Eight Ate Hate (Raw Energy '94)

Yeah that's right, these are the guys with the Toronto Maple Leafs logo and the snappy punk sound that recalls The Pixies hangin' with Sugar, DOA and even The Dictators. Catchy ratchety stuff, with intelligent tosses and turns throughout and a general grinding, critic's poppunk groove which is plain undeniable at times. Could cash in on this '90s punk rock wave hitting exactly two bands at the moment, but we'll have to see.
Rating 7

## Joe Satriani - Not Of This Earth (Relativity '86)

It took this early homespun wankfest for me to really appreciate the scope of Satriani's skills, fave thingie of his whole catalogue being the title track, which features a fierce, distorted Holdsworthian barrage. The rest comprises fairly uncluttered showcases, drums sounding canned, but if real, at least staying out of the way. *The Enigmatic* is another fave, fusing Fripp to Belew for heaps of off-the-wall melody inversion. Quite peaceful and non-metal, which is how I like my instrumentals, thank you.
Rating 7

## Joe Satriani - Surfing With The Alien
(Relativity/CBS '88)

Pretty much the benchmark and breakthrough record for instrumental guitar rock, **Surfing With The Alien** finds Satch serving it up straight and almost hair bandbound. I guess you gotta treat this stuff academically, watching where the guy takes his weapon, here, there, up, down, quickly, with feeling, kind of a study in creativity, a purer version of music, for better or worse. Of course Joe's one of the better proponents of making instrumental music interesting (given his many dimensions and light-hearted delivery), but under most circumstances (to me anyways), this stuff's mere background music, unless I've got the inclination

to really block off time. Gotta hand it to him though; this was actually a bit of a commercial success.
Rating 5

## Joe Satriani - The Extremist (Relativity '92)

Many six string students are big fans of Joe's fluid, bluesy, and imaginative crunch rock but hell, I personally don't go for instrumental music; metal or non-metal, because when it comes right down to it, it's a cop-out, offering little risk, emotional exposure, or staying power. Here Satriani blows through hard rock, funk metal, nice acoustic passages, all with his above-par flare for the riff, but without words, it's sleep city. Bent far into another dimension, I'll throw on Peter Gabriel's **Passion** or one of Eno's ambient trips (far preferring **Films** to **Airports** or **Apollo**). But instrumental metal . . . why?
Rating 2

## Joe Satriani - Time Machine (Relativity '93)

If you're going to do some Joe, may as well do too much. So this double CD retrospective obliges, offering over 140 minutes of Satriani from many era as the title suggests. Some of the grab-bag goodies include the curly-maned one's out-of-print **Joe Satriani EP**, three new tracks with Stu Hamm and Jonathan Mover, an entire live CD, instructive liner notes and a big prosaic story on the guy's career path thus far. Kind of jarring hearing all this shred next to the man's more sublime and arty fare, but still a heck of a package.
Rating 7

## Joe Satriani - Joe Satriani (Relativity/Sony '95)

Many fans think this is crap, which I think totally misses the point, the whole concept being what verges on crap. But Satriani's got to reinvent himself if he deems it necessary to press on with his no vocals dead horse. So this stylish record strives to be dynamic, delving deeper into funk and blues of every nature, Satch bringing along his usual formidable batch of players for what amounts (in my opinionated opinion) to sound-check or movie music. Lots of pressure-cooked drum-work (from bashing to brushes), and Satch noodles of every ilk, from whisper to roar, like I care or somethin'.
Rating 6

## Satyricon - Nemesis Divina (Century Media '97)

Like Norse bretheren Old Man's Child, this third record from Satyricon is getting truly elegant packaging, including a 20 page booklet. And the sounds inside support the attention (if black metal turns your tail), **Nemesis Divina** being as blistering, sinister, sad and expertly assembled as they get. One cool thing about this is that despite the inhuman arrangements, all instruments sound real, very little window-dressing in the drum department, and few effects on the guitars. But alas, this is still way-extreme music, nothing in the way of groove (as if these bands care), and thrashed beyond the back shed. And it's funny how Maiden of all bands, is proving to be the melodic touchstone of the new deathsters, that is when anything that can construed as melody flits in and out of the fleshfire. Note: listen for the drawn sword.
Rating 7

## Savage - Loose 'n Lethal (Ebony '83)

It was a wicked day in Metaldom, B.C., best bud Fiver and I returning from one of our vinyl expeditions in Spokane, snapping up Savatage's **Sirens** and Savage's **Loose 'n Lethal** at the same time. While **Sirens** scorched a mile-wide patch of lush B.C. forest as it ripped through the border crossing at Waneta, **Loose 'n Lethal** wasn't far behind, once home, leaping out of the Toops' Bose 901's with astonishing heat and power. **Loose 'n Lethal** is the perfect two-fisted descriptive for the charged grooves inside this molten mutha, a British debut that makes astounding use of a bristling Ebony mix, with vocals, riffs, percussive might and synergistic delivery that builds the most massive of metal walls. For me, **Loose 'n Lethal** captured the core soul of metal, in crushing manner similar to Witchfinder General's **Death Penalty**, Diamond Head's **Lightning To The Nations**, Grim Reaper's **See You In Hell** and even Saxon's **Power & The Glory**; in effect a toxic blend of all four, the best of Britain at the turn of the decade. Once strapped under the phones, the record works best as one electrocuted smear, although particularly Valhalla-size riffs strafe *Cry Wolf*, *Ain't No Fit Place* and *On The Rocks*, riffs battered home by the vengeful cannons of power drummer Mark Brown, who can take large credit for this record's alcoholic sound and fury. Heavy metal magic from the New Wave Of British Heavy Metal. Update: nicely reissued by Neat Metal in '96, adding a few crustified and ancient bonus tracks.
Rating 10

## Savage - Hyperactive (Zebra '85)

Major expectations accompanied the release of this follow-up to the head-shredder that was **Loose 'n' Lethal**, one of the premiere releases of the early '80s British invasion. Alas, all that remains come record II is the debut's dense wall, this time built around a fairly aimless, unobtrusive, and less equipped core army. Hard to pinpoint the downfall of this record, but for starters let's take the self-assembled recording, which clouds the delivery with an over-treated, clunky drum sound, while retaining the garage-ablaze guitar/bass fusion of old, resulting in a separation of philosophy: vocals and strings still fighting it out on the streets, drums fussing around in some expensive studio. Also at fault: loss of focus, with occasional forays into Hard Rock, which in Savage's case means misplaced melody and misplaced complication. What made the debut such a gloriously horrid wash of ill feelings was the band's perfect chemistry for aggression. Fills just fell off a cliff. Here the sound essentially remains the same, but the songcraft makes feeble attempts at "growth" towards the commercial; true, half-hearted and only occasional, but enough to blow the continuity. Still wired, but less the sustained flood of pain.
Rating 6

## Savage - Holy Wars (Neat Metal '95)

Don't count me an expert on where these guys have been sleeping for the past decade, but I was there at the beginning soaking up every power chord, and I'm glad they're back. It is so cool hearing a great NWOBHM act like Savage, steadfastedly recapturing those heady, exciting years, **Holy Wars** absolutely electrified with raw, electric grooves. Ripping leads abound, alternately sailing over and piercing through the mountain-size riffs, as vocalist Chris Bradley performs his patented smeary slur, recalling vintage Joe Elliott circa **On Through The Night** (yeah, he was once good) or Sean Harris of Diamond Head. Soaring tracks are everywhere, especially *Anthem*, *How?*, delicate Zeppish ballad *Suffer The Children*, and *Fashion By Force*, which musically quotes part of Lizzy's *Thunder And Lightning*. The boys even re-do debut quick trick *Let It Loose*, the band maybe recognizing the fact that that first Savage record was a diamond in the rough. Hard to describe, just roiling, raw and scorched onto tape, like if UFO got really drunk (never!) and kicked out a full record of one-take pedal to the metal. Such an odd, astonishing leap back into time.
Rating 9

## Savage - Babylon (Neat Metal '97)

Let's start up with a trivia note: Metallica's early demo tapes included covers of classic Savage stomps *Let It Loose* and *Dirty Money*, the band enthusiastically adding that these songs helped get them their first deal. Yes, praise came from all corners, the band existing from '83 to '85, then reforming for '95 for the awesome retro-metal of **Holy Wars**. Well, glad to hear it wasn't a one-off, '97 starting off gangbusters with **Babylon**, another brilliantly "old-sounding" slice of NWOBHM madness, sorta like heavy UFO and Lizzy as roughshod demo-mashers. Hard to nail this great band's sound. Picture Van Halen as yobbish limeys, hotcracked with confidence somewhere circa **Fair Warning**, Savage fully volatile and spontaneous, yet purveyors of fairly brisk, technical metal, like Eddie's most metallic masterwerks piled in a beer-soaked mess. Inspired, inspiring metal, **Babylon** proves that the legendary chemistry of this band was and is no fluke.

Rating          **9**

## Savage Grace - Master Of Disguise   (Important '84)

Early and laughable American techno-speed thrash that gets high octane ratings for sincerity and vocal overkill. However, a tin can recording and general trashiness doom this violent excursion as old and hokey rather than ahead of its time. Kicks off with an intro called *Lion's Roar*, a shameless lifting of Maiden's *The Ides Of March*, which then heaves way to the unkempt ones' version of an up-the-ante **Killers**, a sound in vogue at the time, with nary an ounce of personality, talent or restraint.

Rating          **3**

## Savage - Sirens   (Par '83)

Shattering our despondence at heavy metal's slow side-drift of the mid '80s, Florida's Savatage dropped their debut warhead, the unprecedented **Sirens**. How one record could squeeze so much bone-rattling fury out of neutral soundwaves is beyond science, **Sirens** impassively chomping down and shaking the daylights out of the poseurs and pretenders attempting the craft of heavy metal. Indie release, no pictures, no lyrics, no press . . . only a debut record (let that sink in) of epic importance, serving as a second tier milestone in metal's evolution, three first tier spikes being **In Rock** and **Master Of Reality** at the turn of the '70s, **Sad Wings Of Destiny** in '76 and **Ride The Lightning** in '84. **Sirens** is eminently crucial in the progression of metal, yet rather than creating new worlds as did all of the above, it perfects a long and treasured tradition that began with Sabbath and Priest, turning a downright frightening metallic gaze towards creation of the ultimate gothic pulverizer. And **Sirens** is such a work of awe and admiration, bolstered by punishing production values, slashing full-range guitar histrionics, throbbing bottom end and searing vocal work from mike master Jon Oliva; sum total being the essence of metal rendered blinding with state-of-the-art tooling. *Holocaust, I Believe, On The Run, Living For The Night* . . . every last piece (save for throwaway closer *Out On The Streets*) blasts with infinite knowledge and conviction on how to construct towering cathedrals within the genre. Black as night, white hot, hard as diamonds, and again, shaking the very core of metal's thickest ideals, **Sirens** is a furious inundation of harnessed energy, personifying volumes of metal wisdom, demonstrating dead-serious gravity in the pursuit of art for the sturdy of heart. One of those works that you thought could only be imagined. CD reissue includes two extra badly recorded tracks, sub-par ballad *Lady In Disguise* and sub-par rocker *The Message*, plus that "kids in sewer" cover art that was almost immediately adopted after the initial indie press run on vinyl.

Rating          **10**

## Savatage - Power Of The Night   (Atlantic '85)

**Sirens** was the first record in a ton of years to instantly cause upheaval in my hierarchy of favorites . . . best band . . . best album . . . best vocalist . . . best production . . . best debut album . . . our rock lists were in turmoil! A fierce classic. Thus the very existence of record II was enough to blow our minds, raising a wary guard in the face of imminent let-down. **Power Of The Night** summarily trounces such doubts, drowning them in crazy, maniacal laughter, doing **Sirens** proud despite the signals from record's dangerously "heavy metal" cover art, big label release and ever so slightly more accessible aura. Can't praise this bad-ass posse enough, cranking track after track of exactly what I love to hear from traditional metal: barely controlled fury, major chiseled axe, heated power and mountainous skill. To be fair, there was no way **Power Of The Night** would rival the shock factor, the surprise, the mystique and isolated genius of **Sirens**, and it doesn't. What it does do is blaze with the debut's metal acumen, a slightly shifted, more bang-thy-head form of state-of-the-art, building perfect riff-smoked beasts like *Unusual, Necrophilia, Fountain Of Youth* and *Skull Session*, all conceptually capable of fleshing out **Sirens** in another pre-surprise space and time. Major richter scale workout. Ten glorious numbers: one ballad, nine chilling flights of hard rock insanity. A metalhead's paradise.

Rating          **10**

## Savatage - The Dungeons Are Calling   (Combat '85)

After a somewhat less alien but equally staggering sophomore effort, Savatage blow yer mind with a return to their most foreboding of metal muses, climbing back inside **Sirens'** frightening dreamscape for an insane dose of teeth-rattling wattage. Armed with six lengthy tracks falling just short of full LP status, Savatage reclaim their lunatic metal vision on such vintage poison as *By The Grace Of The Witch, Midas Night* and *City Beneath The Surface*. What more can I say? Pounding concrete goth, sterling sore production, and vocal vengeance from the man himself, Jon Oliva work their patented terror, as the band delivers the goods in the fine spirit of its missionary predecessors, Sabbath and Priest at their creative peaks. Genius metal dementia sent straight to the temples, loud, blistered and true. CD reissue includes (deja vu?) two badly recorded extra tracks, sub-par ballad *Fighting For Your Love* and sub-par live out-take *Sirens*.

Rating          **10**

## Savatage - Fight For The Rock   (Atlantic '86)

Four cheezy words such sobering talents would never utter without a gun to their heads, **Fight For The Rock** is a sad commentary on the business end of the music industry, an ill-conceived attempt to drag Savatage mainstream. The record's half-hearted commercial primping becomes painfully evident everywhere: the band shots, the cover jingoism, the painful novelty covers (*Wishing Well* (huh?) and the record-ruining *Day After Day*), the silly balladeering (*Out On The Streets*, suitably rehashing the worst track on **Sirens**), and some wide-lapelled coke freak's idea of a salable recording, Doc Wacholz's drumming cannons reduced to cans of soup. However, the suppression isn't total, the boys being let loose, albeit in somewhat bitter and tainted fashion on rockers *The Edge Of Midnight, Hyde, She's Only Rock 'N Roll* (nice title, remember the gun to the head?), and sinister closer *Red Light Paradise*, the only tune here untouched in total by the eternal struggle between art and money. A spoiled record not without metallic crunch; infected with an inept commercial rock strategy (see Raven and Saxon) and a sickly recording. Hey, we all gotta eat.

Rating          **7**

## Savatage - Hall Of The Mountain King   (Atlantic '87)

Nice ring to it, eh? After ridding their bodies of the poison that gave birth to **Fight For The Rock**, Savatage raise the ire of my justice centres with their

Savatage raise the ire of my justice centres with their fourth indispensable work of genius in a career only five records high, again to no avail: practically zero press or sales, despite unanimous praise from metal purists the world over. It cuts me up, even more so with the lukewarm response to follow-up **Streets: A Rock Opera** and everything thereafter. Anyhow, **Hall Of The Mountain King** will quickly have you thinking **Fight For The Rock** never scarred the landscape, building on the sinister pleasures of **The Dungeons Are Calling**; more ornately riffed than **Power Of The Night**, more gothically distressed, more medieval and grandly fiendish, blasting such wizard's brew as *Beyond The Doors Of The Dark*, *Legions*, the onward marching title track, and traditional lone OTTer *White Witch* (direct descendant of *Rage*, *Washed Out* and *The Whip*). And guess what, cloaked believers? No ballads (although we do get two instrumental intros), demonstrating a Savatage hell-bent for stormy weather, pounding out a return to the underground, albeit a trip slightly less focused and vigorous. A killer act all the way. Somebody send them money!
Rating                                          **9**

## Savatage - Gutter Ballet  (Atlantic '89)

And one can only scratch one's head, Savatage following a raging return to form with this record of grand, fanciful gestures, way overboard on mood, woefully inadequate in terms of getting down to business. More of a serious work that simply has less concern for power chords than a preconceived sell-out, **Gutter Ballet** suffers from a Queensryche-like tendency towards the cinematic. A curious record, even a fine one, where a profusion of epic balladeering recalls Queen (see *Hounds*, *When The Crowds Are Gone*, and the stirring title track). Yet I find it hard to accept Savatage in this role, preferring the rockers of which there are arguably only five amongst eleven cuts, with even a couple of these being more like high fancy flights than gutter lowballs. By record's end one applauds a depth equal to past masterwerks, even the discovery of the band's most thoughtful piano-based stuff to date, stepping beyond ballad into unique story-telling textures. But then one conjectures, "Where's the beef?" Fact is, this record should have been maybe twice as long, with another, oh, eleven or so, face-melters, making the transition to the theatrical less shocking to the senses. The loss of a great band, or the metamorphosis into something worth expanded respect? All I know for sure is that my internal headbanger cowers in wait.
Rating                                          **7**

## Savatage - Streets: A Rock Opera  (Atlantic '91)

**Streets** is the record that initiated Savatage's deep dive into bombast, indeed after the initial shock, many in retrospect calling this one of the greatest metal concept albums of all time (although **Operation: mindcrime** usually wins these polls). The story is what one might expect as a first stab (i.e. write about what you know), Savatage telling a tale of rock'n'roll, drugs, and redemption similar to that of Blackie Lawless' **The Crimson Idol**. But as with my opinion of most of these records, I find the bombast almost always lapsing into dreariness, all these fat, vaguely Alice Cooper-ish piano ballads clogging my energy centres, causing me to reach for something a little easier, like, uh Kiss (just kidding, I never play Kiss anymore). So count me amongst the deeply forlorn, Savatage beginning life as criminally perfect metal, now courting and somewhat achieving a perfection of a different kind, this rock opera realm in their minds at least, delivering them to the hallowed halls of music's upper class. Oh how wrong they be.
Rating                                          **7**

## Savatage - Edge Of Thorns  (Atlantic '93)

With legendary howler Jon Oliva stepping away from the mike, basically fed up with Savatage's thankless ten year grind (but back stomping heads with Doctor Butcher), **Edge Of Thorns** signals a new beginning, with Oliva still very much part of the team, co-writing and co-producing (plus tinkling the ivories) while new throat Zach Stevens translates his visions in a decidedly old 'tage vein. The new record marks a raucous return from the poor showing afforded '91's **Streets: A Rock Opera**, adding new spark, bite and spontaneous combustion on such startling shredders as *Damien*, *Degrees Of Sanity* and fave *Lights Out*. Still, there's something lacking in the faithful Savatage sound here in the '90s, an odd adherence to a goth past that is all but buried by the cutting edge acts of today, the "alternative" metal set. Tunes still soak in that murk, taking long intros to build, sometimes never shaking the shackles of the band's mellow tendencies. Cool band nevertheless, with not all that Heeping much to say, but mountains of thirsty power riffs with which to speak their piece. More of an operating institution with a corner on a fading genre.
Rating                                          **7**

## Savatage - Handful Of Rain  (Atlantic '94)

Adding Testament's Alex Skolnick after the untimely demise of Chris Oliva hasn't altered this band's inexplicable trajectory into further fascination with power pomp, accomplished, progressive light/heavy balladry, but balladry all the same. Argue if you may, but even the power chorders here are constructed in no hurry like ballads (i.e. *Handful Of Rain* and *Chance*). Upsetting and confusing some, gathering a new core of fans but losing many, Savatage might as well jump right into that prog metal ring (and scoop that fanatical Japanese praise of all things pomped) so we rivet-minded old school 'tagers can move on and mosh. Ten tracks: six softies, two in the middle and two metal machines (remember metal?).
Rating                                          **5**

## Savatage - Dead Winter Dead  (Atlantic '95)

This is the kind of record that turns a band into a global entity, a massive, theatrical piece that tackles world problems, in this case, Savatage creating an entire record based on the war in the former Yugoslavia. What I mean by global entity, is that records like this seem to sell in small, steady amounts in every market that buys music, the Internet and its legion of knowledgeable music fans helping the cause immensely. Scorpions also traveled this road, with its Berlin Wall attentions (*Winds Of Change* etc.), paving the way for hard rock acts with large, dramatic ambitions to be heard from the U.S. to Japan, to all over Europe, to Australia. I had to finally give up the ghost for the old Savatage to appreciate this record for what it was, give up the anger at softer, softer songs for four records in a row, coming to view this simply as a great piece of theatre, elegant, expressive, guitar-driven story-telling of the highest order, as usual, with much of the stage afforded liberal use of piano (c/o patriarchal shadow member Jon Oliva), clear, uncluttered vocal passages, and big purposeful drumming. Probably one of the most forceful concept records going, not so much sad as it might have been, but imposing. Obligatory 'tage personnel shuffles: Alex Skolnick replaced by Chris Caffery and Al Pitrelli, long-time drummer Steve Wacholz by Jeff Plate.
Rating                                          **8**

## Saxon - Saxon  (Carrere '79)

A pre-consciousness record from a foggy, ill-conceived band, **Saxon** doesn't recognize the NWOBHM of which it will become such an integral part. Meekly recorded and timid in execution, this debut was to fade quickly into the woodwork once the take-no-prisoners crunch that was **Wheels Of Steel** revved onto stage central. Better left unheard.

Rating 4

## Saxon - Wheels Of Steel (Carrere '80)

If retrospect be kind, **Wheels Of Steel** was a qualified classic, putting Saxon on the map (It's their fault they later drove off it.), cranking an early biker metal drone, a scuzzy jean-jacket-with-patches NWOBHM rock ride, one of really two or three of the movement's building bricks, which I just happened to acquire as an import along with another seminal wedge, Maiden's debut, the very same day. **Wheels Of Steel** was Motörhead with better riffs, better vocals—not great on either count; let's not get carried away—marginally cleaner mix, but an accomplished chugfest of distorted wattage nevertheless, a record on a mission, willing to take responsibility as spokesvinyl for legions of English punters with a thirst for regular metal guys who are comfortable with their persecuted lot. So **Wheels Of Steel** motors along, riffs performing their toil over steady one note bass lines, most carnivorous displays being *Motorcycle Man*, *Freeway Mad* and early blueprint for speed *Machine Gun*, the record's "tour de force" if one must be named, although the title cut is the "anthem", also somewhat insidious and effective. Zero ballads, which is another fairly new thing for hard rock. Anyways, raise one to Biff and the boys, will ya?

Rating 8

## Saxon - Denim And Leather (Carrere '81)

A curiously vacant, airhead sort of record from a band at the peak of their success, **Denim And Leather** highlights the band's progressively feeble song skills while gaining points for conviction, and this time, a strong recording, leaving its greasechain sound at the side of the highway. On the whole, boppier and sillier than **Wheels Of Steel**, but still catchy. Plus as I say, history (my version of it anyways) is on Saxon's side. Favorite badges of courage: *And The Bands Played On* and *Princess Of The Night*, although the fraternal lyrics to *Play It Loud* and *Denim And Leather* also bring tears to my headbang eyes. The redneck Saxon record, spiced with just a hint of Skynyrd.

Rating 7

## Saxon - Strong Arm Of The Law (Carrere '82)

Proving my nagging personal theory that the aggression of **Wheels Of Steel** represented the band operating at the upper end of their potential, **Strong Arm Of The Law** and **Denim And Leather** prove an anemic two-step anti-climax indeed, quite featureless, starting with their dodgy cover arts. It's not so much that **Wheels** was such a monumental feat, or that **Strong Arm** is such a pooch, it's just that there's zero forward movement, the band sporting an un-nerving share of nerdy riffs, as on the title cut, *Sixth Form Girls* and especially *Taking Your Chances*. Still the gritty street nature of the sound is back; stripped, basic and enthusiastic delivery of metal in an exciting new era. *Dallas 1 PM* is a solid enough tune, and the rest, well . . . it sounds comfortable and nostalgic if never remarkable, built for the stage I guess, while definitely betraying Saxon's lack of ideas, evidenced perhaps most convincingly in the rehash quality of speedballs *Heavy Metal Thunder* and *20,000 Ft.* I like this record more now than I did at the time, believe it or not (Hell, I was even in the "Saxon Militia Guard"), 'cos I'm kinder towards my roots. But let's face it: Saxon was getting left in the dust.

Rating 7

## Saxon - The Eagle Has Landed (Trigon/EMI '82)

Recorded at the band's bloody 'ell British peak, **The Eagle Has Landed** found Saxon with a dear little franchise, punting it out with blue collar NWOBHM grit and determination. The acceptable but rudimentary production values do indeed make you feel like you're right there in the crowd, even if most the time you wish you could be sitting at home having a pint. Anyhow, the record meekly but persistently makes the case that Biff et al. had strung together a modicum of good bangers and mash, *Wheels Of Steel* always shivering me timbers, even in this mud-caked state.

Rating 6

## Saxon - Power & The Glory (Carrere '83)

Come on, admit it, none of us thought Saxon had it in them to crank a princely feast like this, and really, in their previous configuration, maybe they didn't. But I would guess new ass-kickin' drummer Nigel Glocker and a new mad-eyed approach to production have conspired to push Saxon onto feverish plateaus, spawning one furious assault of caustic mayhem. **Power & The Glory** rages heavily, and I couldn't be more pleased, everybody working a metal magic that is the embodiment of the NWOBHM's ideals. The mix is almost Ebony, sizzling hot, buzzing, gutted guitars, piercing solos and violent brash percussion, while by some miracle, the band's songwriting is dead serious, no dough-brained wimp riffs, just power and glory, despite mellow/heavy dynamics evident in *Nightmare*, *The Eagle Has Landed* and the stirring *Midas Touch*. But perhaps as metaphor to what makes this record great, my favorite would be *Watching The Sky*, which would have been weak given **Strong Arm Of The Law** production and delivery values, while here it just smokes, soaring with major *Life*, large thanks to Glocker's raucous fills. And there's the rub: despite everything being vastly improved, it's really the crucible in which it's all fired, the frenzied chaos of the delivery. Elsewhere, blazing metal such as *Warrior* and the title cut reinforce the disturbingly manic new side to the band, a band sparked to unbelievable heights, crystallized for me at a Spokane show where Saxon, sandwiched between Fastway and Maiden, kicked off their set with *Power & The Glory*, Biff entirely in white, belting it out in front of an awesome wall of guitars, loud and sonically accurate to this record's white hot mix. One of my more memorable concert experiences.

Rating 10

## Saxon - Crusader (Carrere '84)

Maybe the boys were just as surprised as I was that their sweat and blood fireball **Power & The Glory** didn't perpetuate their upward commercial mobility. But for whatever reason, it's a second total paradigm shift this time around for a romp through a low-cal, kinder, gentler metal stressing arrangement, open architecture and brains, that is to say a vigorous workout of what limited grey matter they could muster. Some call **Crusader** a failure, a bald-faced commercial maneuver, but I always found it refreshing if more than occasionally flawed. Sure the recording's downright distracting, but it's a well-conceived experiment (reaching peak with pleasurable lead single *Sailing To America*). Not altogether unenjoyable, despite a wanker cover of Sweet's *Set Me Free*.

Rating 6

## Saxon - Innocence Is No Excuse (Capitol '85)

Indeed it ain't. And anyways, Saxon is eons past innocence, evoking more so doddering, old age ineptness on this rule-book headbanging fare, a uniformly heavy cinder block, which falls flat on its fat head, due to ridiculous cliché posturing painfully exposed in titles like *Rockin' Again*, *Call Of The Wild*, *Back On The Streets*, *Devil Rides Out* and *Rock'n'Roll Gypsy*. And that's just side one. Lo and behold, Saxon tries, returning full-steam to the bastions of metal, without an idea in their dust-clouded heads. Need I go into side two . . . *Gonna Shout . . . Everybody Up . . . Raise Some Hell . . .* not

bloody likely. Escapes total obsolescence due to halfways buoyant rhythms plus halfways vindictive riffery on about half of it. What's that .. one eighth the band they were on **Power & The Glory**? You just don't wanna know.
Rating 4

## Saxon - Rock The Nations (Capitol '86)
A little more full-bodied production-wise, and less overtly metallic and by-the-book construction-wise, **Rock The Nations** breathes with a little more exposed life; more reason to be than the last, while still suffering from coasting on one's scant laurels, and a preponderance of songs hollering about how loud they are. More personable, but still, the drudgery of the whole Saxon concept by this point drags down any possible positive effects of the individual statements.
Rating 5

## Saxon - Destiny (EMI '88)
The band so much as admits **Destiny** was an exercise in pandering to American tastes, the record piling on all the production goop it can find, also delving into hair band metal harmonies all over the place. So Saxon find themselves either churning sluggish parodies on metal, or trying to be Great White, or worse, Chris Cross, whose *Ride Like The Wind* is turgidly and miserably covered and trotted out as **Destiny**'s first track. Probably one of the band's better cover arts, clean and not at all built of cheese, but man, the music inside stinks.
Rating 4

## Saxon - Solid Ball Of Rock (Virgin '90)
Rightly relegated to import-only status, Saxon propose to live out their sorry career upholding the flag of simple, '80s-style street metal, a little of everything, pret' near nothing that works, save for the **Balls To The Wall**-ish title track. Just dumbo-eared riffs everywhere, and Biff still writes like Biff.
Rating 4

## Saxon - Greatest Hits Live! (Castle '90)
**The Eagle Has Landed** at least had a point. Not sure if that's the case with this Spinal Tapped revival tent that mixes glory years Biff with stiffs from the vapid middle years. At 75 minutes, it's almost too much of a dissipated, much less relevant thing, the band's fairly unremarkable riff skills becoming exposed for critical slaughter. But durn it all if *Wheels Of Steel* and *Motorcycle Man* just get better and better, this perennially gig-torn band able to chew up and burn rubber with whatever material they've been fortunate or unfortunate to own.
Rating 6

## Saxon - Forever Free (Virgin '92)
The bite is back, as Saxon carve their best riffs in years, headbangin' hairballs like *Get Down n Dirty*, serious metalizers like *Hole In The Sky* and *One Step Away*, and even an odd reclining cover of *Just Wanna Make Love To You* all tipping the scales with an abstract sort of enthusiasm, perhaps best exemplified by the surgical steely guitar solos which serve to add juice to the band's very traditional songwriting tendencies. Limited rock vocabulary to be sure, but brainshaking with a new aggression, the wheel keeps on turning for Saxon, perennial road warriors, tireless *Grind*-ers, and ambassadors of a sound most others would pretty much like to forget.
Rating 7

## Saxon - The Best Of Saxon (Griffin '94)
This would fit in the category of slap-dash, **The Best Of Saxon** being an illogical jumble of tunes, with only a two page essay and no pictures. But as a Saxon taster it's worth it, given its 72-minute scope, the inclusion of many classics, a few live tunes, and very little from the odious late '80s records. No attempt has been made to place the tracks in chronological order, so one is hit with *Ride Like The Wind* and *Crusader* early, which then fold into a watery track from the debut record. But heck, raise a shotglass anyways, will ya?
Rating 6

## Saxon - Dogs Of War (CBH/Virgin '95)
Second solid album in a row for these NWOBHM stalwarts, **Dogs Of War** most often cruising like vintage Krokus meets vintage Saxon meets average Accept, a bit bang my head, but mixed for combat, and delivered with a mission. No ballads, and only a handful that spill out of biker metal into a tough street-minded hard rockiness. Vocal harmonies, solos, and generally sturdy choruses prop up most tracks (faves: non-Nuge-cover *The Great White Buffalo* and spirited closer *Yesterday's Gone*), and the whole thing rolls on home, fueled as usual by drummer Glockler, dated on purpose, played with purpose. I'd rate it higher, but at the close of the day, it's a damn hard piece of work revisiting the past with real style.
Rating 7

## Scanner - Hypertrace (Noise '88)
Speedy Spock rock from planets unknown (well, Germany), **Hypertrace** is a dated chunk of capable sci fi goth metal, stacked high with ice cube trays of Scandinavian metal moves. Classy, Accept-tinged work that ages poorly due to its goofy inter-stellar concept record concerns. Sophomore: '90's **Terminal Earth**.
Rating 5

## Scarecrow - A Touch Of Madness (Pavement '95)
Record two for these Long Island straight-ahead wrench-metal men, Scarecrow in possession of an east coast sound that harkens back to many he-man metal conventions, full of crunchy fireworks, sort of like if Van Halen were a street gang from Brooklyn. Which accounts for quite a hefty sound, full of deep-dish grooves, excellent traditional pyro from TJ Jordan, and mature, powerful vocals from leader John Blaze. One thinks Widowmaker with more ideas, both bands lumbering down thick, post-grunge and back to metal again pathways. Sounds like a really cool Y&T record in the **Earthshaker** vein, which is fine medicine by me.
Rating 7

## Scary Mother - Tai Laeo (Mushroom '94)
Don't know squat about these guys, but a furtive letter-by-letter analysis of the liner notes have me guessing that this is an Australian band on a small Australian label. In any event, Scary Mother's sound is a heavy progressive grunge (!), those ethereal keyboards and tough, biting rhythms taking it to the FNM zone, while Andrew Gillespie's vocals are a smokey, throaty low Coverdale with a strange drawly accent, like he's got a sock in his mouth, an acquired taste but one worth acquiring (mmm, socks!). So to capture, tag and release this one to the wild, call it an inventive, heavier Pearl Jam unto Soundgarden, but fraught with interesting non-American eccentricities (unlike Silverchair).
Rating 7

## Scatterbrain - Here Comes Trouble (In Effect '90)
*Earache My Eye* sums it up all too clearly. For a split second, one marvels at the stop-on-a-dime lane changes, but then one quickly arrives unfazed and later disgusted at the parody rock spewed by this gathering of funk metal clowns. A few hollow guffaws but that's about it.
Rating 2

## Scatterbrain - Scamboogery (Elektra '91)

The whole Scatterbrain concept makes me wretch; the derivative funk metal bandwagoneering, Tommy Christ's useless rapping, and the illogical maze of numb skatecore riffery. But mostly it's the not-even-funny total preoccupation with comedy rock. And that's the rub, it's not even funny, sorta like PG 13 bathroom humour, which makes **Scamboogery** not much more than a loud version of Weird Al Yankovic. *Grandma's House Of Babes*? Come on.

Rating     3

## The Michael Schenker Group - The Michael Schenker Group (Chrysalis '80)

Schenker's premiere after his mysterious split with UFO (which apparently included intense examination of various religions, a visit with the Moonies, and a few attempts at drying out), is an extremely tasteful yet claustrophobic display of commercial Euro-metal, featuring the smooth vox of Gary Barden, the oddly recorded and eclectically delivered percussive wizardry of the non-metallic-minded Simon Phillips, and the pre-Yngwie, pre-Vandenberg pomp of the Teutonic fret igniter himself. The feel is somewhat clumsy, close and rushed, versus the monolithic command and wide open spaces of UFO's heavier side, but the overall songcraft is under-stated and proud, fusing heavy AOR and metal seamlessly in fine '70s fashion. More a nostalgic memory with a nice "studio project" smell to it than a groundbreaking democratic effort, featuring interesting but not overly powerful production by the skilled and thoughtful Roger Glover. The record's best track *Lost Horizons*, would be reverently covered twelve years later by doom merchants Memento Mori.

Rating     7

## Michael Schenker Group - MSG (Chrysalis '81)

Like the debut, but even more so, **MSG** suffers from ham-fisted delivery, plus a strange, fogged-up, blocky recording, evidently botched then unilaterally OK'ed by the full-of-himself Ron Nevison, the man who handled UFO's own **Light's Out**, **Obsession** and **Strangers In The Night**. Riffs thud, but rarely groove, due in no small part to the influence of Cozy Powell's blunt, and oddly boring drumming style. Overall, **MSG** is a heavier, more aggressive attack than the ponderous and uptight debut, yet also choppier and funkier, never taking wing. Per usual, choruses usually ease up with an increased melodicism, exuding an aristocratic air to the proceeds, especially on heartfelt rockers *But I Want More* and *On And On*. Another fine record featuring Schenker's basic but enjoyable riffery and fluid, classically influenced solo licks, which all too often get second billing to the pound of the drums.

Rating     7

## Michael Schenker Group - One Night At Budokan (Chrysalis '81)

I guess all fret-burners are allowed premature live product; witness Rainbow, Alcatrazz, Ozzy (yeah, he counts), and Ted, who all cranked one out, one to three albums deep into their respective "actuals." MSG, after two records, corked this double which, surprise, is composed of tunes from said first two (which means you get almost the whole damn collection), plus UFO II's standard race-through of *Doctor, Doctor*. Nothing new, nothing risky, no real reason to get excited, although the band apparently kicks in the flesh. Did very well as an import before this quasi-domestic release.

Rating     4

## The Michael Schenker Group -Assault Attack (Chrysalis '82)

MSG become wholly transformed into a wickedly intelligent sonic maelstrom due to magnificently skilled performances on all fronts. Schenker is the most turned up of his career, Rory Gallagher skinsman Ted McKenna sounds like he's been forging metal for a hundred years, and even Chris Glen's basswork manages central threading in well-positioned doses, speaking eloquently of the undeniable art that occurs when British vets attain synergy. Last and most tremendously moving is the torrential vocal presence of Graham Bonnet, who rips through these confident dazzlers with an exuberant and controlled ferocity we've come to experience from the man's few chunks of recorded history. All is understated, smoothly controlled, and artfully arranged for maximum emotional impact on this masterpiece which gains further enhancement from Martin Birch's crystal clear mix, letting all facets of the **Assault Attack** identity shine and punch through on each's own level. Foremost crown jewel would be six minute opus *Desert Song*, one of the most amazing mountains of sculptured steel ever forged; gothic, dark, bright and blinding; driven and borne of the moors (or should I say Moors). Other shafts of starlight include the maze-like structures of the hypnotic title cut, the galloping riffery of *Samurai*, and the large metallic, bass-driven rhythmic juggernaut of *Broken Promises*. **Assault Attack** will undoubtedly remain forever Schenker's highest achievement, rendered stainlessly divine through Bonnet's unique and staggering track record as catalyst for genius. One of the finest examples of rock royalty ever anointed, and a proud necessity of any metal collection.

Rating     10

## Michael Schenker Group - BBC Radio One Live In Concert (Windsong '82)

This MSG addition to a long line of BBC's high quality concert series (this one reissued by Griffin in '95) is notable for the fact that vocal chores are covered by Gary Barden, called up on 48 hours notice after the ouster of Graham Bonnet from the band. It seems that two nights before this esteemed Reading gig, Bonnet was being his usual firecracker self, fighting drunk on stage with Schenker. After a crack about the guy hidden behind the amps handling rhythm guitar chores (and playing the solos "the German can't do"), Bonnet was wrestled off by Schenker's manager. So Barden was called back to do this high-powered showcase, the band dropping two of the three **Assault Attack** tunes, leaving only *Rock You To The Ground*, which Barden calls *Heavy Blues*, also taking liberty with a few of the lyrics. The performance is average to good, fault really lying with the boxy tunes, which Ted McKenna doesn't manage to revive. And of course, Barden isn't on his best, cringing his way through the falsetto on *Attack Of The Mad Axeman*. With adequate sound, as is always the case on these fine live documents, BBC caps an eventful year which saw Schenker considering signing on with Ozzy, Whitesnake and possibly Aerosmith.

Rating     6

## Michael Schenker Group - Built To Destroy (Chrysalis '83)

This record nearly destroyed *me*, as constant, demonic and despondent siren song to one of the most depressing years in my almost exclusively untraumatic life. Barden's back at the mike, sacrificing his soulful croon to some of MSG's most tortuously acrid and melancholy melodirockers ever to bear the name. All sounds defeated and tired on this confusing but enigmatic record. The production is halfways back to the worn, basic bluntness of MSG I and II (apparently needing complete remixing at one point), and McKenna's flame

that scorched **Assault Attack** to a smoldering crisp is reduced to a somber cold flicker. The metal, the hard rock, and the balladry all sound like death warmed over, downtrodden, bluesy, washed-up, no deposit, no return, for the most part accidentally. It's kind of confusing, but I experience major push/pull, love/hate tendencies with most of this clouded work, most notably and for no good reason, *Systems Failing*, *Red Sky*, minor hit *Rock My Nights Away*, and the downright manic depressive *Rock Will Never Die*. **Built To Destroy** is a strangely doomed record that permanently scarred my mind with its convincing melodic drowning and deceptively naive, elusive evil. No obvious signs of damage, but pieces of my psyche are shut down forever. Cool album cover on which Schenker smashes his axe over the windshield of a Mercedes, a "stalemate" which apparently took about fifteen swings to resolve, amidst amused interrogations from the local boys in blue.
Rating                                                          10

## McAuley Schenker Group - Perfect Timing
(Capitol '87)
This latest reincarnation of a tragic and doomed career finds the mad axeman teaming up with some anonymous no-talent vocalist/writer plus other assorted yes men in quest of commercial acceptance, finding only misery and deserved disrespect amongst the vast hordes of more fired-up, more mischievous, more versatile bands competing in the tough melodic hard rock marketplace. All the usual descriptives apply: anthemic, clean, well-recorded, well-played, and as much life as a Fripp/Eno instrumental concert backed by juggling mimes. No soul left, no idea where to go, and Robin McAuley is truly offensive as a frontman (recalling Sammy Hagar). One shaft of hope: on the rare occasion when the machine revs the red line, Schenker displays distinct traces of increasing technical sophistication to match his advancing years. McAuley would later downplay this record as over-produced, light on guitars, also citing the fact that he was still getting to know Schenker, having only been in the band three months.
Rating                                                           4

## McAuley Schenker Group - Save Yourself  (Capitol '89)
Considered to be a concerted return to guitar rock after the keyboard-polluted pansiness of **Perfect Timing**, **Save Yourself** does leak minor increases of raw meat mix-wise and considerably larger doses of Schenker's patented axework. Still the general songcraft has all but abandoned the '70s gothicism of earlier works, leaning too heavily on California sun tan rock and grandiose melodic love-ins, despite the discernible steel-toed step in the right direction. Maybe the flying V will soar once more, but for now, given **Save Yourself** plus the middling Contraband project (on which Schenker painfully teams up with a myriad of other losers for no apparent reason than to take donations), the amps lie silent. Suggestion: one of the majors ought to concentrate some of these impressive talents and send 'em all on an extended tour of the world's trouble spots. I can see it now. Lifeson, Vai and Palmer, plus their back up band The McAuley Hagar Emmett Trio, shot down over Bosnia's no-fly zone.
Rating                                                           5

## Michael Schenker - Anthology  (Chrysalis '91)
Just the facts, given that we all know the legacy Schenker has cut over essentially two decades worth of axe mechanics. This two CD set (reissued by Griffin in '94), features one CD of UFO hits (all pretty much the expected tracks), one of Schenker, ahem, highlights, mostly stirring anthems that are at minimum equals to the UFO classics included (barring the watery McAuley Schenker tunes of course). One cool thing,

the CD booklet contains lyrics to the whole she-bang. Otherwise, just a bunch of songs, and not really the ones that might have showcased Schenker, the guitarist.
Rating                                                           7

## MSG - "Unplugged" Live  (EMI Japan '92)
As McAuley's liner notes explain, **MSG** was already finished when they decided to do this dodgy record, hiring on Shark Island's Spencer Sercombe to fill out the sound, doing four UFO tracks and a bunch of recent MSG tunes in the ever cash-inable unplugged format. McAuley called it a cheesy idea, but then they really ended up enjoying it. Guess what Robin? It can still be a cheesy idea. And crushingly boring too.
Rating                                                           4

## Schenker McAuley - MSG  (Capitol '92)
**Built To Destroy** way back in '83 was the last time the European in Schenker outweighed the man's AOR tendencies. And things haven't switched back yet, as this confusingly titled record sticks with the California rock, the backing band of Jeff Pilson and James Kottak keeping it firmly hard rock-based, but still too synthetic. **MSG** breaks down thusly: eleven tracks total, four ballads which all suck, the rest pretty much party rock of various intensities, McAuley's vocals being fairly commanding and versatile, but even the most stirring tracks like *Paradise*, *Crazy* and *Invincible* lacking the weight of nostalgia bred of a vast Germanic vocabulary. The soul is gone, even though this is a considerable heavy record, featuring tons of Schenker and arrangements that stick to the facts at hand. All in all, middling, AOR somehow more the realm of the young.
Rating                                                           6

## Michael Schenker - Thank You  (Positive Energy '93)
**Thank You** is one of those records that should probably remain unrated (note: my **7** grade has often come to mean that; see **Anthology**!), being an entirely acoustic album, all tracks tied together by the same guitar sound, often easy listening-type solo/melodies over a bed of strumming, also tied together by song titles like *Peace*, *Harmony*, *Love And Kindness*, *Joy*, *Truth*, and *Open And Willing*. The record is designed as a thank you to people from all facets of Schenker's life, including the fans, with most of the booklet used to thank dozens of people individually. And the way it is meant to thank is in a purifying, religious way, Schenker peppering the graphics with references on how he has basically seen the light or resolved his religious questing. The soft, delicate music enclosed is meant to project this and spread it around, Schenker calling it "the beginning of a new chapter in my life", even though he would be back shortly kicking up dust with UFO. One vocals track, which is consistent with this theme of shedding the cumbrances of the material world.
Rating                                                           7

## School Of Violence - We The People . . . ?  (Death '88)
Paper-thin on axes, and almost erroneous production-wise, S.O.V. do little to make up for being chopped at the knees, wielding the blunted combination of Karl Agell's toneless growl, M. S. Evans' convoluted nowhere beats, and Stegmo Von Heintz' predictable riff waffles. Sort of a bloshing death metal drone with a T.S.O.L. agenda for rebellion against those who hold the keys. Major tensile fatigue. Metal Blade's track record becomes less impressive every day.
Rating                                                           1

## Schubert - Toilet Songs  (Mausoleum '95)
A modest title for such an upper class record, **Toilet Songs** (the band's fourth since **the 5th** (!) in 1990) combining the ultimate heft of powerful European

metal with the flowing royal robes of Queen and the '90s keyboard-laden atmospherics of Faith No More. And it is perhaps the latter to which these Austrian nutters nod most deeply, not FNM's funk, but their most metal of metals, Schubert cranking the jets on their stun guitars while icing the cake with keys, dynamic use of space, and off-the-wall lyrics that slyly undermine the pompous metal of their whole arresting groove. Best thing I can say is that this is an extremely fresh and mischievous record, delivered by veterans who obviously know their way around the studio, able to add light industrial touches without losing their fabulous songs. Faves for their deep-dish grooves: *Reflections Of The Past* and *Better Splatter*, the latter splatter combining a slippery hoover of a riff with a hair-raising vocal that has to be heard to be believed.

Rating                                                          9

## Scorpions - Lonesome Crow  (Bomb '72)

I guess if you want to exhibit maximum growth, start from nothing. And here it is, a record that's worse than nothing, worse than Wheel Of Fortune, worse than a sharp stick in the eye, a downright suicidal old shoe of a '60s trip, festered in German isolation then gutted open like an unspectacular lake trout with a few wayward stun chords from Black Sabbath - **Black Sabbath**. Nothing but turgid strips of landfill. Not really behind the times, but under them.

Rating                                                          0

## Scorpions - Fly To The Rainbow  (RCA '74)

Here the jackboots with destiny take their first baby über-steps into the house of guitars, crafting what can loosely be described as rock songs, yet something closer to progressive garage rock, whatever that means. But the boys can play, and the boys care about frontiers, while their budding genius gets misguided into the same astral void as the baffling debut. **Fly To The Rainbow** is ultimately remembered (when recalled at all) for one song: *Speedy's Coming* (pre-cursor to *Ten Seconds To Love*?), the first of the band's many fine metallic signatures, this one more of a basic *Louie Louie*-riffed (yet nicely executed) hard rocker; tuneful, well-vocalized, and forever a concert favourite.

Rating                                                          3

## Scorpions - In Trance  (RCA '75)

With *Dark Lady* crashing full-tilt into your living room, one quickly snaps to a realization that Scorpions is going to be a big part of the future of metal. Crammed with vocal and soloing overkill, almost like a heavy Queen track, this opening mindstorm is the band's call to arms, even if the sum total of **In Trance** results in no more than a hung jury. No, sadly, we the spectators of the loudest German revolution in 35 years would have to wait one more record, **In Trance** often drooping into melloid prog rock melancholia and '60s psychedelic fuzz, amongst the four breath-taking guerrilla bursts of blinding perfection: *Dark Lady*, *Top Of The Bill*, Sab-style sleeper *Living And Dying*, and manic rat's nest *Robot Man*. Klaus Meine is already the consummate voice (I still think he looks like Dio), dual guitars are set to rip, and the rhythm section is forged in Teutonic fire. But friends, this interplanetary alignment rules the heavens on less than half this record, so when I snap my fingers . . . move on.

Rating                                                          5

## Scorpions - Virgin Killer  (RCA '76)

The first of a string of monster records from the one and only Scorps hits brutal in its blunt metal wisdom, culled from a slow awakening from a psychotronic fog into the bruising alchemical highs of a metallic skyscape. Scorpions were just enigmatic and foreign enough to lack obvious influences. Scorpions *were* influences, songs like *Catch Your Train*, *Hell-Cat* and

most notably the screaming, demonic *Virgin Killer* having no real precedent in style and tone. *Virgin Killer*, the song, fried most anything to date just by looking at it, scarred to indescribable hideousness by relentless Meine shrieks and slashing, dive-bombing guitar work from emerging twin gods Ulrich Roth and Rudy Schenker. Arguably the most metallic track anywhere as of 1976. Elsewhere, more power chords arranged almost playfully on the melodic *Backstage Queen* and the hot-licked *Hell-Cat*, while vestiges of a melancholy past remain on *In Your Park* and *Crying Days*, both more capable of tugging the heartstrings as intended than similar hokey gloom from previous efforts. Above all, *Virgin Killer* is probably the first palatable example of German metallic angst. Axes wail in pain like nowhere previously visited as Scorpions become rock'n'roll spokesmen for the whole West German nation, an eminently important metal hotbed, more influential creatively than commercially, yet one that spawned many of the most soul-bruising guitar anthems of the '80s. One of the first records I remember getting as a new release. Man, how time flies.

Rating                                                          8

## Scorpions - Taken By Force  (RCA '78)

The mighty Scorps seem to enter a new phase with **Taken By Force**, throwing their weight around with more authority, like the six string shooters they have now become. **Virgin Killer** seems the last of a band frozen in the headlights, unsure while exhibiting a rough, unpredictable class. Here, it's full steam ahead, as the band taps its magic wand (more like twenty pounds of lead pipe) on a variety of exquisite Germanic barnstormers. *Steamrock Fever* has the stage written all over it, as does *Virgin Killer* rival *He's A Woman - She's A Man*, while *We'll Burn The Sky*, *I've Got To Be Free*, *The Riot Of Your Time* and the elegant but devastating *The Sails Of Charon* (one of *the* metal masterworks of the '70s, period.) explore dark caverns with engaging mysterious melodies only the Scorps and Priest seemed capable of conjuring throughout the '70s and early '80s. **Taken By Force** just soared with confidence no matter what complex web of emotions it was trying to evoke, moving with an unstoppable and somewhat isolated sense of mission throughout its muscular but sympathetic rock ride. Cool to the touch but art nevertheless; truly the last of the Scorps' isolated era.

Rating                                                          9

## Scorpions - Tokyo Tapes  (RCA '78)

The double live **Tokyo Tapes** reinforces the rock hard truth that Scorpions were quietly becoming one of the top five metal acts of the late '70s and early '80s. Japan gets the amplified ones on the cusp of their pre-commercial creative peak, pumped and primed as they metalize their way through eighteen vastly different pieces of guitar-drenched German fare, most of which shake the airwaves with some of the most innovative riffs sowing the seeds of the new metal resurgence. Combat-ready recording, savvy drumming from Herman Rarebell, and quality platform boots lead the charge, blazing through almost all the heavies to date (glaring exception: *Virgin Killer*) plus two power chord newies *All Night Long* and *Suspender Love*. Scorpions deliver.

Rating                                                          7

## Scorpions - Lovedrive  (PolyGram '79)

Our dead-serious band of metal lords begins to lighten up a little, seeking a bit of crowd connection with its first arsenal of summer-ready, car deck rockers, not to mention the record's amusing (and oh so European) bubblegum-on-breast cover art. More like an earnest assault on America, **Lovedrive** is dominated by thick, state-of-the-art, yet accessible headbangers, leading with the warm hard rock chug of *Loving You Sunday*

**399**

*Morning,* moving through swooping OTT'er *Another Piece Of Meat, Can't Get Enough* and the classic and cerebral (well, musically anyways) title track. But unfortunately, **Lovedrive** is the band's biggest study in contrast to date, kicking über-ass one minute and playing dead the next, as the band stumbles upon what will become a predictable and embarrassing fixation, the "power ballad" (more on this disconcerting turn of events later). So you can't just huck on the record and pump your fist to the glory of might. But so what. That's what cassette decks are for: editing, which will net you a good 20+ minutes of superlative metal, delivered by a top-flight band who has looked around and realized the responsibility they shoulder. Because besides Priest, who else in metal was this studious about craft?

Rating      8

## Scorpions - Animal Magnetism    (PolyGram '80)

Scorpions come bounding back with their fattest, most enjoyable album ever, **Animal Magnetism** cutting out all continental eccentricity for a sturdy total of eight rockers and one ballad. A long-delayed round of applause, after which this baby gets snapped into the ol' car deck for an all-seasons extended play. **Animal Magnetism** is basically the first of all of the band's output to this day that concentrates on melody, removing much of the multi-riffery and ornate exploration of previous metallic moments. What results is great stadium rock, an engaging mix of metal ethic with hard rock, nothing elegant and prissy, just stout-of-heart hooks, best examples being *Make It Real, Hold Me Tight* and *Falling In Love,* while *Don't Make No Promises (Your Body Can't Keep)* moves slow then swift and sure, *The Zoo* stomps and chomps its way as a surprise hit, and the title cut suspends an old-days goth riff over a heat-dulled atmosphere, kind of like staring at a raw egg in a glass. For the first time, the band can be justified as tunesmiths, spreading their axework smoothly and simply over a number of chartable numbers, rather than striking in the night then hiding. Ultimately this is the first Scorps slab that forgets entirely its Germany, rock'n'rolling for the fun of it, heavily, heavenly and evenly; less the dark intellectual exercise of old, more the guitars a' howlin' party in the streets. Almost as much a high school staple for us as **Back In Black**, and that's saying a ton.

Rating      10

## Scorpions - Blackout    (PolyGram '82)

Putting aside how sick we all got of *No One Like You* and *You Give Me All I Need,* one would have to admit that this was Scorpions' best record, marking the pinnacle of their career (although maybe not in sheer numbers), combining the technical flash of old with the song skills of **Animal Magnetism,** all wrapped in the band's best of many excellent Dieter Dierks production jobs. Proving to be reigning masters of both shimmering hard rock and artful metal, Scorpions mix it up but good, sparked with the liveliest of performances, most inspiring being the spitting guitar alchemy of Matthias Jabs and old warhorse Rudy Schenker who whip out lick after lick of pure fire; tasteful, shining, and always squarely metallic. Again, only one totally committed ballad (I'll raise a frothy brown one to that), and the rest is planetarily-aligned Scorps, faves being the artful metalizers *Dynamite, China White,* and *Blackout* all demonstrating the band's continual penchant for constructing the best, crystal-blue riffs in rock. Elsewhere, it's hard rock that sneaks up on you and gives you a big hook and a hug, like the aforementioned ingratiating smash singles, sliding into radio land like a thief in the night. Fave sleeper *Arizona.* Pair with **Animal Magnetism** as the final two from the Scorps' golden years.

Rating      10

## Scorpions - Love At First Sting    (PolyGram '84)

All hard rock and less, rather than hard rock and more, and it's a curious push/pull pain I'm feeling at the creative demise of Scorpions. The band's grasp of reality seemed to be slipping here, yet who am I to argue with the huge numbers being rung up at the till? **Love At First Sting** was a fresh sort of alloy, mostly lite hard rocking like the hits from **Blackout,** yet with a little more percolating zip and no less melody. And I liked it damn it, although the boys' previous killer instinct was noticeably absent, even from pensive speed rockers *Coming Home* and *The Same Thrill,* which both sport sub-standard central premises, rendering the record's two heaviest tracks the least impressive, rare for this band indeed, and a sure signal of a metal band's drying creative well. Simple but boastful of hook is the operative here, *Bad Boys Running Wild,* lead single *Rock You Like A Hurricane* and major hit *Big City Nights* (have you ever heard three stoopider song titles?) working despite the rivethead in me wishing they didn't exist. Sleepers: *As Soon As The Good Times Roll* and *Crossfire,* one a poignant metal reggae (well not really), and one a poignant metal march (really). And of course there's smash snooze *Still Loving You,* one of a string of dull, unimaginative power ballads (get out them lighters!), causing this band to be heralded as kings of the genre, spewing an obligatory one or two for time eternal much to my excrutiation. 'Nuff said. All Scorpions power ballads are an embarrassment to metal; lame, predictable, worthy of Spinal Tap-inspired ridicule. This band doesn't exists to have feelings. It exists to strafe our circuitry with immense German riffs sent drilled into our bleeding ears from unrepentant, screeching rows of Marshalls. End of story. However the kinder, gentler Scorpions is a salvageable proposition; pleasant, which in my old age is just fine.

Rating      7

## Scorpions - World Wide Live    (PolyGram '85)

Definitely the last good live album these increasingly pathetic ex-legends will ever make, **World Wide Live** is a double dose of the band blowing through tracks from three smokin' records (**Lovedrive, Animal Magnetism, Blackout**), and one middling but grudgingly OK one (**Love At First Sting**). Only two disastrous power ballads, lots of live shots, and the obligatory roll call of everybody involved with the band. Straight renditions, but hey, these are pretty amazing songs (ahh, when these guys had material!).

Rating      6

## Scorpions - Savage Amusement    (PolyGram '88)

You know a band's in a constipated bind when it can't even come up with a decent album title or cover. Much to my chagrin, Scorps are going the way of Maiden and as with Maiden, I have no idea why. Just an unexplainable inability to stay vital. Old bands should ideally mature with their old fans so that hopefully while picking up newer ones, they can be like Aerosmith and move eight million units, or like Deep Purple, at least deserve to. Simply put, the art ought to advance with the wisdom gained with age. **Savage Amusement** is a marginally heavier slab than the immensely successful **Love At First Sting,** but it's a record on auto-pilot, cranking average hard rock, average metal and a strange stiffness caused in no small part by dull production. It tries, but predictably, with a vacant fist-pumping action while holding back all over the place as it furtively seeks for the next lead single. Zero mystery, as even its polite predecessor embodied more risk amongst its commercial pandering. Here it's just sideways drift without any sense of mission spewing more pointless song concepts with titles like *Don't Stop At The Top, Rhythm Of Love, Passion Rules The Game, We Let It Rock . . . You Let It Roll* (Now what the hell does that mean?), *Love On The Run . . .* you get the picture.

Don't even crack the cellophane. You just know what's inside. You just know what you're going to hear: something like the fluttering then dull thud of a big velvet curtain coming down on Klaus' chroming dome, and I say that with utmost respect for the man's past accomplishments.
Rating 5

## Scorpions - Crazy World (PolyGram '90)
Again a record that tries, but this time in an environment where fewer and fewer are listening with any excitement, allowing for some semblance of being able to work in peace and quiet. But to no avail, as the band fails to wake up and realize their deficit. Another dumb record title (with Spinal Tap lyrics to match) and another plodding commercial mix and things don't look too good. Outside of the surprisingly with-it *Who's To Blame*, the **Balls To The Walls**-ish *Don't Believe Her* and the lunkhead title cut, chalk this one up to an act that's lost its competitive edge. Yet with the reunification of Germany and cultural sod-busting in Eastern Europe and the former Soviet Union, The Scorps may be preoccupied with mining their immense success far away from more fickle, more sophisticated western ears. Indeed, sad as it may be for the Euros, a veritable landslide of American acts have been running roughshod through the minefields of metal for years now, challenging our faculties, all but erasing the memory of British and German bands that gave us so many good times in the early '80s.
Rating 5

## Scorpions - Face The Heat (PolyGram '93)
So the usual hype applies, and the usual dread follows, the hapless Scorps Org. preparing to do battle with a world that's leapt well over their balding domes. So great, right? . . . after the band's biggest seller to date, why think anything might need fixing? So they don't, talking about how raw and rocking this exciting new album is going to be . . . then hiring Bruce Fairbairn to produce it. Brilliant. Well, the writing has picked up at least, after the three insipid power ballads, there being adequate "spontaneous" rock to go around, a vast plethora of good licks (amongst few good riffs), and the odd melody exhibiting depth, witnessed on *Hate To Be Nice* and *Unholy Alliance*. Erstwhile, *Nightmare Avenue* (the usual dil lyrics), and lead single *Alien Nation* spread chords like so much artery-clogging butter, making me despondent at an act that just has no idea. New bass player after fights over money, as if they don't have enough.
Rating 4

## Scorpions - Live Bites (PolyGram '95)
An insipid live set (with another ridiculous title that sounds like a breakfast cereal) featuring this most global of bands phoning in their "hands across Berlin" anthems that have wrecked this band for the last decade. Closes with a lurching, upchucked trio of new studio tracks, one an all-thumbs pop metal turd, the other two, big horrible, brains-void, barely conscious power ballads (how the friggin' hell did you guess?).
Rating 4

## Scorpions - Pure Instinct (eastwest '96)
Pure bollocks, more like it. Not sure what is cruising through this long-reclining band's collective uber-domes to make such a strangely un-Scorpions-like record. For **Pure Instinct** sucks, which is expected at this late date, Scorpions long squandering any reputation they had built for vital music. But it sucks in a more pleasing manner than for example **Face The Heat**. There's a maturity and bravery here in going for such simple, pop-based lite metal, a sound that owes as much to the Beatles, Byrds and Bon Jovi than anything bruising. There are a six pack of new ways to be

mellow here for the band, Klaus and crew thankfully burying their awful big balladeering, replacing it with acoustic strumming at various speeds, and only stingy use of background power chording, and pretty much no riffs or impressive displays of axecraft anywhere. It's almost like they can't stand the racket anymore, and have looked for new ways to make upbeat rock, finding a general, quite unremarkable sound, but one with less cheese than the last couple of embarrassments, some nice, almost intelligent ideas (*Time Will Call Your Name*) but virtually no metal. My disgust has been replaced by a fairly detached sense of confusion, and perhaps a new understanding of where bands can go with age.
Rating 6

## The Scream - Let It Scream (Holywood '91)
Known for being the band that exposed the talents of leonine pipist John Corabi, (first seen with Racer X, soon to defect to Motley Crue), The Scream were highly touted as the next GN'R, skanking deliberate enough in their strip mall Naz/Zep/Aerosmith-pickin', heart-stompin' drawl to turn insider heads westward in rock starry anticipation. **Let It Scream** covers it all, surprisingly not too metal-faced as it big leaguers down Hollyrock Blvd., hook in hand, axe across its back, all eyes on the contents smouldering inside. Honky tonkin' with amps, vamped and primed, **Let It Scream** acts the winner, which is more than half the battle. Party metal that makes you reach for that damnation-defining last brown soldier, nothing more, but nothing less. Guitarist Bruce Bouillet also a Racer X alumni, as second banana to guitarist Paul Gilbert, who was one of Bruce's instructors at GIT.
Rating 7

## Screamer - Target: Earth (New Renaissance '88)
Organizations like this, whether anybody ever gets to hear them or not, fill the void Queensryche left somewherz between the **Queensryche** EP and **The Warning** to wax longwindedly on the fate of mankind while their sound evaporated into soupy mirages of prog metal. Lead screamer Bill Carter is a dead ringer for Geoff Tate, but it's the scientific maelstrom behind him that craps all over the last Queensryche from a height of several miles (at least in terms of grind). Scientific in construct, but slightly loosened however in terms of execution, Screamer isn't the final word on high-level Amerigoth. It'll take more of a budget to equal the palaces of say Forbidden or Sanctuary. Promising but still a bit cumbersome and serious, which is often the case with difficult metal.
Rating 7

## Screamin' Cheetah Wheelies - Screamin' Cheetah Wheelies (Atlantic '93)
Roughly parked in the camp of all those southern retro-rockers, SCW's forte-niche would be their tightly exhilarating funk rhythm prowess, evidenced most clearly on lead single *Shakin' The Blues*, while second big hit *Ride The Tide* confounds with a case of the Counting Crows. And after swimming through a long, ambitious record of kickin' southern rock and Skynyrdian balladry (*Sister Mercy* rules!), I'd have to say the record endears, while a sort of crass commerciality nags in the background that all is not so truly artistic here. Yes, my faves are those lush, well-protected and projected acoustic numbers, the rockers sounding just too carefully executed for classic rock radio and its rednecked demographic (of which I generally consider myself a part). Classy record, but maybe a bit too polished for us squinty-eyed rock cynics.
Rating 7

## The Screamin' Cheetah Wheelies - Magnolia
(Warner '96)

Perhaps taking vague direction from the death of metal, the Wheelies cut it back to the root, looking to Drivin N' Cryin', Hootie, Dave Matthews and the Spin Doctors for their strong r+b undercurrent. So the record is a success artistically, the band delivering their usual rhythmic rhythm guitar textures, touched in the head by strategically placed retro keyboards, hints of the south, hints of the Dead all welling into a shaggy, almost late '60s sort of Humble Pie with EWF or Lighthouse or Chicago or Joe Cocker influences (huh?). But in bottom-line terms, this is a much more laid-back, swampy piece of work than the debut, although perhaps this lends the record more history-straddled depth. I for one, am displeased.
Rating 5

## The Screaming Jets - All For One (Mercury '91)

Can't get too excited, 'cos all I pine for when I hear this is another record from the magnificent Kings Of The Sun, The Screaming Jets definitely sounding derivative of their Australian brothers, although less bluesy, less studied and more Aussie eccentric, shades of old rockin' Midnight Oil spoiling the flow. Enthusiastic (another caffeine-headed drummer with a tight snare), leaning towards Angel City at times with their straight-ahead pub riffery, but I dunno, maybe I'm just not in the mood.
Rating 6

## Scum - Mother Nature (Black Mark '94)

Most of Black Mark's stuff these days is pretty cool, but Finland's Scum (change the name!) rises above the pack, spreading like crop poison an ever so slightly industrial form of death metal which mixes equal parts lethargic doom, traditional power metal and grindcore to heady results. The lyrics are quite the trip too, stenching to the high sky, but making a dent on the imagination centres that can't be pounded out. Could do without the straight-line gargle vocals, but the music leaves enough spaces so it still works. Contains a stomach-churning slow brood through House Of The Rising Sun.
Rating 7

## Scum - Purple Dreams & Magic Poems (Black Mark '95)

Couldn't ask for more here, Scum deepening their explorations of traditional metal, filling each of these eight impressionable tunes with grooves for northern miles, approaching the searing forward march of bands like Sentenced and Entombed. Askola's vocals are still unrepentantly grinded, although traces of dynamic drip from the mix, rising to meet the killer metal splayed all over this fierce and memorable release. And Scum's lyrics (again, change that name!) are vivid and fantastic to the point of dizzying, pictures of ancient Scandinavian mythological themes flashing like flashbulbs in the head, intelligently left unpegged to specific tales, entirely within inviting realms of fantasy and pageantry. Massive imposing metal that carries with it the potential to crossover.
Rating 9

## Sea Hags - Sea Hags (Chrysalis '89)

Call it roots metal, blues metal, California sleeze, boogie woogie, whatever you want. Fact is it's predictable and simple on purpose, along the lines of Hangmen, Tattoo Rodeo, Junkyard and even Poison, reaching back to the New York Dolls for sneer linkage through the '70s into the '50s and '60s, as the beat, tired and true slog rock it from bar to bar in a never-ending tribute to futility. Open hanging chords, low slung Keef solos and a lot of shufflin' and twangin', but unless you're the type that can listen to the same trad structures rehashed over and over through the mounting decades of your pathetic life, this one will pass like a whimper in the night.
Rating 4

## Seance - Saltrubbed Eyes (Black Mark '93)

Bestial, malignant frost-burn thrash with a compressed, almost punk recording, the divinely monikered **Saltrubbed Eyes** pits Sweden's Seance as a potentially successful portrayer of the putrid and deliciously disharmonic. So call this one a success of extremity, but too monotonous in tone for my liking. Tumultous and gutted, but unloved.
Rating 6

## Season To Risk - Season To Risk (Sony '93)

Wide-open, buzzing and rattling, **Season To Risk** is a unique type of '90s hard music, dreamy while real electric and live-like, lots of atonal tribal structures windmilling into power chord breaks and choruses. But still difficult and brainy, in a cantankerous noise direction, bits of Helmet, Nirvana, The Big F and Therapy?, but the wrong bits, all belaboured and butting heads, tinny tiny snare, crashes, shouts and feedback, caterwauling over nothing. Hookless, heartness, but not headless, Season To Risk call Kansas home and their favorite colour is grey.
Rating 6

## 2nd Heat - Shreddervision (Rock The Nation '94)

These Germans are almost the Nitro of the '90s, deluging the rockhead with a flood of metal sounds from many worlds. Lavishly packaged, well-endowed, pinched and over-tightened, **Shreddervision** is first and foremost a heavy AOR record, slammed faceward by a ton of Euro-goth flavourings, and yes, shredly soloing, controlled prog at many speeds, and least desireably, a clattery, electronic, noisy drum sound, made all the more irritating by the tricky OTT patterns throughout. So think hysterical, off-the-rails Gamma Ray with a wry AOR fetish. Too much, all the time, but admirable for its craft. Note: **Shreddervision** began life as a successful indie cassette, Rock The Nation essentially taking said product and releasing it as the band's debut record. Lyrics: way beneath the musical presentation; imagine Scorpions doing porn.
Rating 7

## Section 315 - Drop Dead (Sin Klub '94)

For those rivet-minded riffdomes waiting for the new Corrosion of Conformity but making do with Biohazard, Prong and Crowbar, Section 315 just might be the ale that cures your anticipatory pain. Hailing from Pittsburg, Section 315 whip together a dense, sub-strata bass throb, riffs way down low and groovegodly, vocals barking out harsh realities of the street in finer form than Biohazard but right up similarly dark crosscore alleys. Cap with an awe-inspiring mix, and you're left with a professional, pounding slow-to-mid tempo sledge that should not remain indie for much longer, given the timeliness of this thick, brutal sub-genre of "hard music".
Rating 7

## Section 315 - Section 315 (Sin Klub '96)

Section 315 return and retain, hatching this self-titled 35 minute shortie. No real advance occurs, just more bleeding hunk of flesh metal, propelled by power-packed slam drums and coagulated riffing straight from the street. Chunka kunja.
Rating 7

## Seduce - Too Much, Ain't Enough (IRS '88)

A Detroit power trio sounds like the right beer now, putting the Motor back in the City with this rowdy wedge of Amerimetal, harkening back to Y&T's buzzard-breathed classic **Earthshaker**. **Too Much, Ain't Enough** ain't nuthin' special, but it does what it does with integrity, bangin' offa the bricks, pumping through a brash and battered mix such hooky grinders as *Any Time Or Place*, *Crash Landing* and *Empty Arms*. The usual problem is one of sidling up to a record in such contextual isolation as this, me as a listener knowing of no other Seduce output, and indeed, never having seen a column inch of press on the band. Why should this matter? I dunno, something to do with loser quotient. I'll get back to you.

Rating       **7**

## Seducer - 'Eads Down - See You At The End
(Stud '86)

A real swell display of combat metal from a British trio of streetheads psychically and economically linked to the liggin' spirits of Tank, Chateaux, and Wolfsbane. **'Eads Down** is U.K. Steel tried and true, storming the gates of the NWOBHM in greedy, frenzied plunder of both its science and trench code of boozery that created cult heroes of the most down-trodden of pub rockers. Brewed into this thoroughly authentic and engaging slab of meat are veins-full of Germanic speed, punk griminess, and magnetic vocal acrobatics from one Chris Hunt, whose berating tongue-lashings reign upon high with those of Savatage's immortal Jon Oliva. Like an un-cut, un-clean, and un-shaven race through Europe's angriest of riffs, **'Eads Down** is hopelessly in too much of a hurry to let its tales of betrayal simmer into self-importance. Basically a no bullshit, no pretensions, "life is a game" slammer; hastily but proudly assembled for all the right rock'n'roll reasons.

Rating       **8**

## Seelenwinter - If Soul Turns Into Flesh   (Massacre '96)

Seelenwinter are a snobby, serious and quite frankly interesting act, evoking the very German vibe of Scorpions '76 (check out *Only A Few Words*) or Lucifer's Friend. A new, possible direction for metal, these kinds of crossover conundrums potentially ooze creativity, Seelenwinter fitting the description perfectly, sounding like a cross between Amorphis, Type O Negative and Golden Earring! Spooky, without really trying.

Rating       **7**

## Senser - Stacked Up   (A&M '94)

Welcome to the new agey world of world music influence, most specifically the worlds of hip hop, metal, London intelligence and American gang violence. Yeah, Senser look like Dexy's Midnight Runners or The Pogues but they rap like Rage Against The Machine, albeit more into that acid house hip hop stuff (you can tell I really know what I'm talking about) than the power chords. But despite the lofty loopiness butting up proudly against the large percussive lope of the thing, I'm mesmerized into a sort of swaying boredom, as I am with all dance music, a genre devoid of structure, melody and reason to be, I swear it's true. The floaty female vox of Kerstin Haigh are a nice highbrow touch, but no, this one's just too damn urban and light at the same time.

Rating       **6**

## Sentenced - North From Here   (Century Media '93)

From the black bubbling perma-frosted mindscapes of Finland's Sentenced comes a greatly improved second record. **North From Here** is a dizzying blast of technical death metal propelled by freak drum patterns and an overall tendency to disorient under a chilling presentation of vague but intensely hateful lyrics damn hard to read in the CD booklet. Almost Voivod-ian or Floridian in its off-the-wall eccentricity, **North From Here** makes up for its difficultness with foreign Finnish drear quotient. But still too "speedy" and grind vocal-

ized for my tastes, despite marveling at its flaming creativity and pitch blackness.

Rating       **7**

## Sentenced - Amok   (Century Media '94)

If **North From Here** mixed hyperchaos prog tendencies with standard Eurodeath, **Amok** trades up to Rush, Queensryche and moreso, your deepest experience of vintage Maiden, stringing melodic harmony structures that startle butted-up against the band's committed death scrape. **Amok** thus delivers divinely, offering a sensuous array of conventional metal flourishes cloaked in a current grind cache that adds lead to the water. The grenade-in-adenoid vocals remain, and lyrics still freeze with their Scandinavian themes, but Vesa Ranta's commanding drum skills now look solidly to groove, while guitar melodies ring rich and exceedingly underground integritized, yet of a different earth, one besotted by the rainy riffs of Quartz, Witchfynde, Diamond Head, Angel Witch, debut-era Maiden and the whole **Metal For Muthas** ilk. So defying all description really, **Amok** somehow evokes the progressive more with tone and psychological isolation (**Animals** vs. **Fragile**?), laying the listener on a bed of silky and timeless riffery, paradoxically creating epic vibes with unlaboured hook-laced songs. Soaring, captivating and so musical despite its cryogenic chill, **Amok** is a refreshing addition to the evolution of underground metal taking place at Century Media, pure genre-bending genius rubbing cold, blue shoulderblades with the likes of Tiamat, a wash of classic old metal from the magic years lightly dusted with the grime of grind.

Rating       **9**

## Sentenced - Love & Death   (Century Media '95)

Twenty-one minutes of sheer metal gorgeosity, **Love & Death** is a joy to behold, the perfect potent mix between the bruising production values and gruff vox of the new death, and the sobering melody of gothic metal '80s-style. Tracks (a scant agonizing five) rock and roll like a freight train through the underground, straddling dark metal integrity and unadulterated enjoyment; sleazy, evil and driven through the heart of metal's motives. Damn close to my favorite band right now (**Amok** was killer), Sentenced is positioned perfectly to excel along with the impressive raft of fellow Swedes redefining heavy music this very minute. Includes a cover of *White Wedding*, cheesy choice, scrapingly well done as usual. But the four originals are amazing granite monoliths of groove.

Rating       **10**

## Sentenced - Down   (Century Media '96)

Last month's "the record Metallica should have made" was Dearly Beheaded's **Temptation**. This month it's **Down** from Finnish "suicide" rockers Sentenced, a young band of wise metal gurus destined to become at least middle-tier masters. Grand metal grooves are everywhere, Sentenced finding a way to pack all the best components of legendary metal into something stirring, elegant and grey-sky European. **Down**'s tones are magnificent, tracks like *Bleed* and *Ode To the End* blending blessed Maiden and punchy Paradise Lost in timeless fashion, pulling the heartstrings on a frosty Finnish eve, perfect with that mug of sacrificial apple cider. New vocalist (with appropriate Hetfielded aspirations), but thank the heavens, same old top-notch Sentenced.

Rating       **9**

## Sepultura - Morbid Visions   (Cogumelo/Shark '86)

Beginning their ascent from the pits of over-the-top thrash poverty, Brazil's Sepultura were pretty much the height of inaccessible blastbeat boredom, badly recorded, badly barked by Max, but fairly tight, if you can even bring yourself to care. Horribly maimed music, way beyond the band's stated influences (Celtic Frost, Venom, Bathory, Dead Kennedys), Sepultura were in fact one of the earlier bands to champion the cause of extreme thrash, which has spread like a virus ever since. Note the similarity to the name of Celtic Frost's debut **Morbid Tales**. Not really the debut, having made a split record with Overdose in '85 called **Bestial Devastation**.

Rating 0

## Sepultura - Schizophrenia  (Cogumelo/Roadrunner '87)

To much Brazillian coffee (or something stronger) for Max, 15-year-old Igor and crew, as Sepultura toils to perfect blindcore, in some sort of mano y mano cockfight to prove that the heaviest bad-ass sounds around come from south of the equator. But even this early, Sepultura practices, hones, and sharpens the breaks, solos, percussive chaos, and oddly pleasing repetitive structures that lent the band such uniqueness on **Arise** and **Chaos A.D.** And the recording ain't half bad (it's all bad; just kidding). Remastered (along with **Morbid Visions**) in '90 with bonus track, a re-recording of *Troops Of Doom*. Next question is why?

Rating 4

## Sepultura - Beneath The Remains  (Roadracer '89)

Pretty much this endearing band's first of a formidable trio of glory-shrouded chugging behemoths, **Beneath The Remains** contains roughly the same change-ups and velocities of early to mid-years Slayer, way less wall-of-sound blastbeats than early terrifying Sepultura vaccinations, more unique, blood-boiling groove. And when racing (as these nutters often still do), they've managed to make it dynamic and listenable, due to increasingly razor-sharp execution. But hey, it's getting there, **Beneath The Remains** even seen in the red rash of history, as a bit of a **Reign In Blood**, a sentimental crowd favorite due to its being the paradigm shift between the brainshaked, less than working class lunkheads of old, and the power-drenched metal leviathans of the band's good fortune in the '90s.

Rating 7

## Sepultura - Arise  (MCA '91)

The record that would light the blue flame under this charismatic bunch of Brazil nuts, **Arise** goes way beyond its tacky album cover (and way beyond the band's previous trashfests) into an ignited mosh that set the stage for the success of **Chaos A.D.** The move to Phoenix and subsequent U.S. connections has intensified Sepultura's awesome chemistry, flinging the band into one inspired headbang, still illogical and rough, but potently so, soaking the best elements of early Metallica, mid-years Slayer and early thrash in a big bottle of tequila, spitting forth with a tribal venom only the Cavalera crew seem to understand. Quite the warehouse of riffs, piled high and hypnotic, always bashing, always just lo-fi enough to sound so incredibly street, **Arise** is a classic of well, as I said, a certain metal chemistry. To note: many long-time fans consider this the band's crowning achievement.

Rating 9

## Sepultura - Chaos A.D.  (Epic/Roadrunner '93)

Sepultura's big statement flares with that same edgy metal madness that made Death Angel's **Frolic Through The Park** such a dangerous record. After a long and scabby career thus far, the band is finally making major shock waves, within the industry (peers love 'em), and on the streets. The live show is just insane, an oddly human display of moshing machinery, songs with heart, big black bursting metal heart, thumping through the ugly vocals of Max Cavalera, a man who projects persona and pace, strength of song to the fore. **Chaos A.D.** is a rough-hewn affair, really

carving deep impressions with its first four tracks (especially *Territory*, y'know "war for territorrrraaaayyyy!"), while offering maniacal slam oases with the likes of *Manifest* and *Biotech Is Godzilla*, exploded segments that represent an unbridled punk undiscipline, riffs out of control, unmanageable and therefore left unmanaged. All the while Cavalera barks out the plight of his native Brazil and oppressed peoples everywhere, making the whole cosmic carnivorous stack of chords a lightning rod of shame as well as an exercise in uncut metal nuttiness (see untitled track 13). But really, my greatest praise defers to the playability of the record, me logging a good hundred spins the month I got it, the record serving as an inviting bridge between the thrash underground and the thrash mainstream. And the record's fusion of moral messaging with raving drunken assemblage further reeled me in, the balancing act between sonic pummeling and positivity stressing a new responsibility within the band matching their newly elevated status. The most exhilarating headbang of the year, aided and abetted by a brash and stinging mix at the hands of Andy Wallace.

Rating 10

## Sepultura - Roots  (Attic/MCA '95)

Thrash champions and all-around cool guys Sepultura have carved a sonic masterpiece with this all-important follow-up to their global break-through **Chaos A.D.** (1.5 million copies worldwide, 300,000 in the U.S.). **Roots** is an amazing piece of futuristic hardcore metal, a record that miraculously doesn't need to resort to cheap industrial ploys to carve a new world sound. In fact, its innovations come from the old world, Max, Igor and crew recording a vast array of sounds, instruments, passages, full musical pieces and timeless life experiences with the Xavante tribe deep in the Amazon rain forest. Hence the title **Roots**, the band writing a triumphantly heavy record revolving around their roots as Brazillians, the deeper roots of the tribe they broke bread with, and importantly, their roots as lovers of loud, extreme metal, restless kids following slavishly their thrash heroes from the early '80s, bands like Hellhammer, Celtic Frost and Venom. **Roots** melds two main influences. First is the band's recent, groove-focused slower music, their massive stone-carved, down-tuned patterns rendered frenzied by Igor's always heavy, cymbal-crashing madness, speed be damned, chops increasing in skull-crushing leaps and bounds. Second is their home-country's roots music, the sounds of the Xavante tribe, which are interwoven quite seamlessly as intros, outros, breaks, instrumental pieces, and as part of each track's furious percussion attack. Thus the aural mindbend of *Ratamahatta* (sung mainly in Portuguese), the infinite mountain man catchiness of *Roots Bloody Roots* (a lyrical nod to Sabbath there, of course), and the insane, almost urban hiphop hardcore of *Lookaway*, which features both Mike Patton and Korn's Jonathan Davis. And there's another influence on this record, the dressed-up but somehow old-fashioned recording values of Korn's highly unique first album, Max admitting as much in interviews. Another noticeable change: Max's vocals have found evil new voices, screaming harshly like Phil Anselmo, or low-whispering like Mike Patton (*Breed Apart* does both). I might as well cut it off there (so I can go listen to this damn heavy, damn mesmerizing record some more!). Suffice to say, this is an incredibly intense, and somehow highly listenable master work from a band with miles of heart and even more brains. Sets the bar disconcertingly high for the return of Metallica.

Rating 10

## Serenity - Breathing Demons  (Holy Records '96)

This band's a mystery to me, but a fairly pleasant one, sounding like wayward Obsessed with leaden heart;

doomy and homespun, uncontrived and squarely untalented. Which makes for a ragged enough piece of embroodery, **Breathing Demons'** uniformly sorrowed tones creating a place that is classic cheap NWOBHM, the band capturing the wobbles Witchfinder General possessed into the grave, and Quartz suffered from early on. Crack-a-smile song titles: *Inside Of I*, *10 Snakes* and *Darker With My Eyes Open*.

Rating      8

## Serpent - In The Garden Of Serpent
(Radiation/Nuclear Blast '96)

Serpent features Lars, ex of Entombed and Therion, and Piotr from Therion (plus three) indulging in a shared propensity of doom; clean vocals (like low '70, '71 Ozzy), gargantuan quicksand riffs, and melted production, conspiring to perch on the eccentric, less accessible ledge of the genre, closer to Sleep, Count Raven and The Obsessed than the stellar overdrive of Cathedral and Trouble, or the alt. sounds of Kyuss or Fu Manchu. Which is to say it sounds older and more European than most, like something a deleted NWOBHM band might have conjured. Funny though, now that there's a dozen doom bands like this, I seem unimpressed with increasing frequency, needing the dire eccentricity of a Paul Chain to perk interest once more. Stuck right between the genre's elite, and the dreary and way too derivative.

Rating      7

## Sevenchurch - Bleak Insight    (Noise '93)

Bleak indeed, Sevenchurch rising from the Yorkshire moors to deliver soaked and sneezing six songs and 71 minutes of morose retro doom metal, retro in that it's more Mercy, Candlemass and Count Raven than the supercharged sounds of Cathedral or Trouble. There's a definite NWOBHM uh, bleakness to this that makes you think things can only grind to a comatose halt, this five-piece finding success in evoking ancient rot. Which I'd say is its downfall, me as listener finding it hard to take the layers of irony seriously. But this is a genre which I find forbidden and delicious, so grades be kind.

Rating      7

## Sex Love & Money - Era    (Rockworld '94)

This longish seven track EP rocked my world forthrightly, with its swaggering slow-burn grooves propelling an expert metal sound that I can only describe vaguely as My Sister's Machine or Alice in Chains meets Deep Purple or Skid Row circa '95. Strong, complicated songs with power, melody and brains, this band ought to lose the cumbersome moniker and stay in the business, for their sound rules. Classics: *Here & Now* and *Elephant Skin*, which points a poignant and viable direction for bands like Dio or UFO in the '90s. I have no idea what that means.

Rating      8

## The Sex Pistols - Never Mind The Bullocks Here's The Sex Pistols    (Warner Bros. '77)

The Pistols were the ultimate ruse, the ultimate rock'n'roll swindle, four crumpled pieces of street trash who couldn't play and couldn't care less, manipulated by a snake of a manager after nothing but the band's few dollars and ours; a total joke elevated to cultural icons. But barring the sordid hi-jinx and critical pontification as to the band's sociological significance, beyond all the clap-trap about how Johnny Rotten, Sid Vicious, Paul Cook and Steve Jones conspired to shake up a bloated rock aristocracy, sits one jolt of a record, a ten-story-tall monument to kicking ass. The reason **Bullocks** is so remarkable is how it approximates a desperate, toxic sort of metal with those great crashing cymbals, those rolling rock riffs and those bracing, profane beratements from the shock of spiked red hair hanging like a booger from the mikestand. **Bullocks**

had stirring big beats, grooves that caused beer drinking with gusto, quaffing like there was no tomorrow, eliciting bold destructive action, unlike the tinny, scampering and often dreary sounds coming from the band's pissy English contemporaries. **Bullocks** is simply a great metal record without guitar solos. That's the way we saw it as kids, and years after punk's anti-climactic fizzle, that's the best way to experience it today. That's why my faves are the unsung darker rockers like *Bodies*, *Problems* and *New York*, rather than the notorious mega anti-hits like *God Save The King*, *Anarchy In The U.K.* or *Pretty Vacant*, which all possess something approaching melody despite their legendary and defining punk protests. What a rousing bash of a record though, stuffed full of the best type of (heartily multi-tracked) power chords, locked on a mission hellbent from the gutters of London. I suppose in context the Pistols were a scary proposition, really quite nasty boys threatening our hard-won assets, but now it all rings like an empty threat, perhaps the band's biggest contribution being its catalytic effect on the next generation of rock stars, many of today's metal heroes heeding the call to get out and play, even if not quite ready. Heroic and frenzied, **Bullocks** will forever remain a classic, defining the punk era through volatility and that ultimate of rock swindles, the force-feeding of metal to punks, while preaching the demise of the dinosaurs that wrote their riffs. Rumour has it that Chris Spedding did most of the record's guitar tracks.

Rating      10

## The Sex Pistols - The Great Rock'n'Roll Swindle
(Virgin '79)

Yea, we all know the naughty Sex Pistols only stumbled into synch for one gruesome Punk opus, but if you're looking for useful product beyond the essential **Bullocks** and all the re-packaged hoopla, look no further than this gem-studded double kaleidoscope, for indeed, **The Great Rock'n'Roll Swindle** is *almost* considered the band's only other real record. Granted, one spin and it's obviously a pretty vacant, wise-ass construct, loosely deemed a soundtrack to the film of the same name, and aptly titled for approximately half its contents. The bad news: all sorts of orchestrated, non-rock joke content; juvenile little comedy tunes, many of which the band were of little or no part. The good news: the wastrels' own non-**Bullocks** compositions, *Belsen Was A Gas* and the excellent *I Wanna Be Me* (previously available as a French 12" B-side), *Silly Thing*, sung by Paul Cook and the Sid single *My Way/Something Else*, Steve Jones' N.Y. Dollsy *Lonely Boy*, and the rousing *No One Is Innocent*, hollered by Ronald Biggs. In betwixt . . . a lot of live covers and the title cut, another righteous Pistols original, horridly sung by an unworthy battalion of auditioning Rotten replacements. Playing **Swindle** start to finish would drive any clear-thinking wanker nuts, what with all the funny English accents and guffawing classical interludes, but there's more than ample material for one fairly solid slab of Pistols. Glaring omissions: almost expert B-sides *Satellite* and *Did You No Wrong*.

Rating      6

## Sex Pistols - Filthy Lucre Live    (EMI '96)

So the Sex Pistols have returned, and now that they have some experience, surprise, surprise, they can more than hold their own as a live act. **Filthy Lucre Live** was recorded early on in the band's "we're only in it for the money" tour, the band tearing up London quite smartly, Rotten announcing that they're "fat, forty and back" before launching into welcome rarity *Did You No Wrong*. Like I say, the boys have benefitted greatly by keeping their hands in the sewer of rock'n'roll (to varying extents), Rotten showing the most growth by braying quite commandingly through these tracks in fine, media-is-the-message PiL fashion.

Plus Jones and original bassist Matlock prove to be capable enough anchors, Cook also doing exactly what he did nineteen years back, I'm sure this record finding a bit of suit-suited doctoring along the way (just like **Bollocks**). So all in all, quite a surprisingly sizzled and grizzled live show, much fireworks storming the stage, featuring a nasty selection of songs, including B-side masterpiece *Satellite*, sort of album track *Submission*, and fierce intro tune *Bodies*. Hats off, 'cos I thought these guys would suck. This album proves differently.
Rating **8**

### Shadow King - Shadow King   (Atlantic '91)
Retreat y'all, except for indiscriminate lovers of all things AOR, and collectors of '80s bigshots. Yes indeedy, Shadow King was one semi-supergroup that fired nothing but blanks, this quartet's significant duo being none other than blazing Dio and Def Leppard guitarist Vivian Campbell, and Foreigner's consummate entertainer Lou Gramm. But the goods are a simpering, almost silent batch of simplistic AOR, Viv absolutely bound and gagged, putting in the most inane of performances (perhaps predicting his future with the braindead Leppard organization), just squared-off chording, competing with dribbling keyboard washes. Not exactly released with much fanfare, then fading gruesomely quick, **Shadow King** will always be a bit of a collector's item, and if some value is to be gleaned from the thing, it would be in Gramm's fairly up-front and impassioned vocals. But all in all, this was a creative and commercial joke. What were they thinking?
Rating **4**

### Shake The Faith - America The Violent
(Alfa Burnette '94)
Sounds like the Gunners doing punk covers, 'cept this ain't them and it's mostly originals (check out the band's hyper version of the Kinks' *Destroyer*). So lots of cussing and ranting and carrying on, the presence of both Axl and Slash being very much felt, scratch-paper vocals and freight-train guitar licks colliding and congealing with deep-grooved Matt-style drum bashing and a very Guns production job. Maybe a little Love/Hate here, Spread Eagle there, but this is very much a sleaze metal that crosses into punk simplicity, served up by the best Guns N' Roses cover band I've ever heard. In fact, these guys could make their records for them, leaving the millionaire mopheads ample time to argue.
Rating **6**

### Shakin' Street - Vampire Rock   (CBS '78)
As artistically important as Fanny and The Runaways for female hard rock (uh, I guess), Shakin' Street were an all-guy band with a gal named Fabienne Shine yelping out an exuberant vocal o'ertop the band's tuneful punky metal blast. Sorta like New York Dolls, Patti Smith, Ted Nugent and Riot at yer clambake. Title track *Vampire Rock* smokes, and obscure Stones cover *Yesterday's Papers* ain't half bad either.
Rating **6**

### Shakin' Street - Shakin' Street   (CBS '80)
BÖC puppeteer Sandy Pearlman enters the scene, in an attempt to recreate the street vibe he so deftly accomplished with the Dictators and The Clash, taking Shakin' Street punk with a pop underflow, guitars cranked like **Raw Power**, but songs lightly sugared like Blondie. A warmer record results, doing all that was right with haggard and sleepless '70s rock. And the Dictators thing is definitely happnin', Ross The Boss handling lead guitar, Pearlman producing with gritty urgency. Shine snarls, and the band belts it out. Would have made a tidy little return as an Iggy project.
Rating **7**

### Shark Island - Law Of The Order   (CBS '89)
One of those corporate metal bands I wanna like, but come away unimpressed by the lack of actual substance beyond the acceptable style, Shark Island strike me as a mellower version of Ratt when they got lazy towards the late '80s. Main problem is the songcraft, which lacks aggression, going for dynamics which get lost in the overly busy, unexpressive, drum-heavy mix. Merely one of many would-be Slaughters, Wingers and Warrants, so far lacking the killer instinct to cut through the clutter, or the urge to cascade the room with its emotional will.
Rating **4**

### Dave Sharman - 1990   (Noise/BMG '90)
Not sure what to say about this pleasant and versatile instrumental semi-shred from high class German (?) axeman Dave Sharman. The man is definitely smooth, his runs evoking Holdsworth, Yngwie, Morse and even prog like Marillion. Rumour has it Sharman has worked with Gillan in recent years, but other than that, his name draws a blank. Look for the guy with the checkered guitars.
Rating **6**

### Dave Sharman & Graphic - Here 'N' Now
(Bleeding Hearts '94)
Sharman takes flight with this full band record, featuring ten tracks, seven with vocals. The sound is classic technical, heavy, Eurostyle AOR, Sharman really quite inventive with his breaks and solos, the band able to switch from high-minded metal to thoughtful acoustic in a heartbeat, esteemed Lizzy producer Kit Woolven capturing each guy's skills in hi fidelity suspension, a bit cold overall, albeit evoking the good qualities of bands like Blue Murder, Europe and White Lion.
Rating **7**

### Sharp Nine - Untimed   (Mausoleum/BMG '95)
Not quite sure what to make of this Swedish (Gothenburg scene) grunge act's debut, which convolutedly has hit Canadian shores via Mausoleum, BMG, then EMI, more than a year and a half after the record was recorded. Sharp Nine outgrunge countrymen Mental Hippie Blood by digging way into the Soundgarden for a slow and slower power smear expanse, tune after possibly progressively boring tune. But it all howls forth real artistic life, sincerely getting at the crux of Cornell and crew at their psychedelic best, vocalist Jesper Starander just leaning on those horizonal, horizontal notes fer miles, his band gathering a textural gritty bluster that delivers the record into synergy, the listener entering into a power-boot trance by record's end. So I guess it works, part because of the band's wide rhythmic blast, part because of its (ironic by this point in grunge's rinse cycle) lack of commerciality, satisfied to keep the grooves deep, depressed and down, offering little in the way of pop hooks to send it chartable.
Rating **7**

### Shaw Blades - Hallucination   (Warner '95)
Tommy Shaw from Styx and Jack Blades of Night Ranger together defined AOR from two decades, and when they work together in a third, the results are a heady success indeed. **Hallucination** finds the boys reaching between all the gloss, keyboards, and party rock lyrics that killed the genre, pulling out a bouquet of very likeable influences, blending them into a record of campfire intimacy, plush hooks recorded well, emphasizing foremost the resplendent sounds of voice and acoustic guitar, while retaining the AOR ethic of attention to detail, and sterling sharp recording values. And I hum along in earnest, finding the record a new, clear-headed, and most importantly grounded piece of

music for pleasure, knowing and rejecting the reviled power ballad for songs that skirt The Beatles, CSN, southern rock, Mellencamp, roots music, country and all the good habits of AOR. What results is a record that vibrates, pops and sparks with hit potential if not for the blackballing of personalities like Shaw and Blades (and Hootie sells eleven million!), the record overwhelmed with good tidings, sincere in its ambitious assemblage, and built for enjoyment of the most basic kind. An oasis among so many sick metal bands, many of which I don't hesitate to support by the dozens in very different moods from the one in which I write this.
Rating 8

## Sheavy - Blue Sky Mind (Dallas Tarr '96)
Hard to believe, but St. John's, Newfoundland has a bit of a doom metal movement going, After Forever and now Sheavy trundling down a loose bolts road to Sabbatherian madness, rattling a few fillings in the process. Sheavy are definitely on the crusty, 'shroom-serviced side of the genre, more like a volatile Obsessed or Count Raven, despite their Kyuss meets Midnight Oil record moniker. Negatives: muffled recording starving for treble, although this might have been on purpose. Positives: Steve's vocals out-Ozzy Ozzy unto Witchfinder General. Very cool. And Ren's drumming is spot-on, especially come double bass showcase *Cosmic Overdrive*. Eight tracks listed, eight bonus tracks to be discovered. Recommended for all archival trolls trawling for sounds of old.
Rating 8

## Sheer Terror - Love Songs For The Unloved (MCA '95)
Quite beyond Offspring and Green Day, these street urchins are more like an east coast version of Rancid, maybe more hardcore and just as dirt-face pedigreed. The whole major label dance is of course, because of a couple of punk successes, so it's nice and weird to see this grim bash bunch get to this point, on a supposed following built of three indie releases and a decade of squalor. But punk and this band both have a ceiling of **6** points far as I'm concerned, given the dimwit rant and churn at hand. Nice but fleeting metal moments, the band lapsing into the M.O.D. zone here and there. Y'know, there's integrity and there's bad music, and never the twain shall meet. C'ya.
Rating 5

## Shihad - Killjoy (CBM/Noise '95)
Magnetic, hummably frenetic, smoke and mirrors alt.metal, **Killjoy** saw fairly deliberate label push from adopted home Futurist, and for good reason, Shihad in possession of a slammin' amp-buzzed star quality that can turn them shekel-prolific if they continue their trajectory. Fave is twangy kick-off track *You Again*, which collapses the rest of the record into a sort of groove-delicious, vaguely danceable kind of headbang, the record as a whole sounding rough of edge, commercially indifferent (see Sponge), and firecracker entertaining. Worth pursuing.
Rating 8

## Shogun - 31 Days (Jet '87)
Wildly idiotic cover art hides what is superficially a professional commercial hard rock vehicle for ex-Tokyo Blade rockers Marsh, Wrighton and Pierce. Basically soap opera rock, poodle rock, whatever, featuring elegant axe solos, odious synth work and prissy songs. Totally competent, just boring and way out of style.
Rating 5

## Shooting Gallery - Shooting Gallery (PolyGram '92)
Urban bad boys Andy McCoy and Dave Tregunna seem to find squalor wherever they roam, their next semi-random vehicle Shooting Gallery aptly named, brushing the spiritual void of the fallen Johnny Thunders and his crash 'n' burn past with the New York Dolls, **Raw Power**-era Stooges and even Altamont-era Stones. Vocalist Billy G. Bang! (drummer Paul Garisto rounds out the line-up) has a distinct and pleasurable nasal whine that gives this record its unique timbre, as it slips and slides through dark CBGB/Kansas City sleaze terrain, grimy and dark without really wanting to be; simply unable to wash the stuff off. **Shooting Gallery**'s distinct feel is one of fallen stars long from their glory days. Don't get me wrong, I wish the band well, it's just that the sound has that sort of dark desperation, like it's been bruised and battered by years in sleazy dives. Paced quite nicely, **Shooting Gallery** is dominated by bashable punky dark horses like *I Mess Around, House Of Ecstacy* and lead rant *Restless*, while letting up for the haunting *Magic*, Van Morrison's *Brown Eyed Girl* and yet another remake of Hanoi Rocks' *Don't Never Leave Me*. Overall, the record finds and strangles its underground roots, knocking off long-comatose legends of the pre-punk era, providing a tentative thread to unsung gutter rockers as they remained virtually unchanged through the '50s, '60s, '70s and '80s, later scumbags feeding off the remains of earlier ones, the present '90s scumbags perhaps serving as wormfood for disheveled, self-abusing longhairs in the next decade. The more things change the more they stay the same, or something like that.
Rating 9

## Shotgun Messiah - Shotgun Messiah (Relativity '89)
This universally panned debut is surprise, not all that bad, combining zingy glam metal with shred and detectable spontaneity. But still, it's slick poodle rock, and not nearly top tier at that. Peppered with unpredictable arrangements in a sea of predictable biz moves, **Shotgun Messiah** deserved at least a little more than its ignored status. Not unloved amongst guitar players.
Rating 6

## Shotgun Messiah - Second Coming (Relativity '91)
As per usual with solid product that's well-assembled and shipped enthusiastically to the masses, **Second Coming** kicks off with a careenable statement of business, but backs off drastically after said premiere cut. No improvement over the debut, the obvious high levels of sheen here failing to make up for the lack of excitement or edge. Sounds sort of like bad Lynch Mob or bad Skid Row; heavy, but pandering and predictable, and rigid instrumentally, wary of any possible strayings into spontaneity or art. It's too bad, because maybe ten years ago this may have sounded state-of-the-art for skidder metal, but with acts like Guns N' Roses, Kik Tracee, Bulletboys, and God forbid, the awe-inspiring kings of the heap Love/Hate, bringing emotions and class musicianship to this genre as it was dying, still fairly slick bands like Shotgun Messiah, Lillian Axe and Sweet F.A. sounded plain and already dead, even for the early '90s. More than a few dipshit ballads, bad funk metal, lyrics that try too hard to shock, plus a gamey cover of *Babylon* combine to make **Second Coming** soulless and contrived; spinning tires of a well-oiled machine with nowhere to go.
Rating 4

## Shotgun Messiah - I Want More (Relativity '92)
After exciting nobody with a perturbably corporate sophomore longplay, Shotgun Messiah try to demonstrate playfulness or something with this confusing lil' EP comprising two originals and three predictable, laid-up fer dead covers. As the Brits might surmise, I quite fancy the title track, nice pop single that one, and the acoustic *Nobody's Home* chords with a somewhat

compelling tension. Verdict: humble ambitions achieved.
Rating        **6**

### Shotgun Messiah - Violent New Breed    (Relativity '93)

Retreating and regrouping, our favorite kicked-around Scandinavians storm back with what can only be called a sell-out of welcome but dodgy proportions. **Violent New Breed** slams all those bad California experiences in the dustbin of life, for an arguably convincing industrial metal assault, lots of tinkling, crackling samples behind distorto-vox and insistent, consistent axe mechanics. *Sex* and maybe the title track are the only even remotely chartable numbers, the rest pounding into Ministry terrain, with the unfortunate baggage of a Hollyrock past. But even though it's an obvious play for alternative acceptance, you can't dis the band for trying, many of their cohorts sticking to their bubbleguns, refusing to accept the tide of forceful hard music taking over the genre. I dunno, I find it quite convincing and listenable, for few others dare this sort of transition. A metal case study.
Rating        **7**

### Shout - In Your Face    (Music For Nations '89)

Here's Shout: burst-out-laughing shiny uniforms, blazing guitar heroics from leader Ken Tamplin, vocals that inflect between Coverdale and Triumph's Gil Moore, and a general pop metal sheen that is adequately allowable if this stuff didn't get blown out of the pond by grunge one year later. Alex Masi, Marty Friedman and Randy Hansen (plus three other "Shreadkings") show up for the title track and the whole thing just party bops along, despite the record's lightly addressed Christian metal leanings.
Rating        **5**

### Shy - Brave The Storm    (RCA '85)

Just a thinner, more nuts-in-a-vice version of a sound that would add more axes and urgency with the coming years. The most key-and-synth-woven of the lot, but remarkably advanced technologically and technically speaking for such early pap.
Rating        **3**

### Shy - Excess All Areas    (RCA '87)

**Kerrang!**-endorsed (and encouraged) AOR wimphem with hopes of greater hoopla and a reality of anonymous poverty. Just depressing in its forced and painful interplay between steel and cotton candy. A lot of "moody" ornate pieces, frilly and in love with its own drama, with a music school sort of aspiration. Verdict: I moderately like the rockers, but the ballads snooze.
Rating        **4**

### Shy England - Misspent Youth    (MCA '90)

These boys have come miles since the Stryper-ish accouterments liberally applied to **Brave The Storm**, opting for a more rough 'n'ready, rock-heavy and anthemic, yet still key-laced version of U.K.-comes-to-L.A. swagger. Excellent helium-vox from Tony Mills grace this admirably rowdy but over-produced shot at the big time. That's about it. Simple, hooky pop metal that falls this side of the listenability spectrum due to layers of respectable muscle. One strange phenomenon with this record—and I may be reading into things somewhat unjustifiably given that Shy are veterans—**Misspent Youth** seems to use higher grade, early '80s trickery in terms of chord shifts and break decisions (vs. particularly '90s postures) that lend it just that trace of history, a tendency that may also just be a part of the band's British psychological make-up. Or maybe it's just fake analysis on my part. Highlights: lead cut *Give It All You Got* and the Dokken-ish *Never Trust*

*A Stranger*. At long last, Shy isn't looking down their aristocratic noses at their potential fan base.
Rating        **6**

### Silverchair - Frogstomp    (Sony '95)

The story's trampled and stomped by now: three moptop high school teens from Australia take Down Under by storm, vaulting to number one by giving the country its first grunge band, a 100% derivative blend of Pearl Jam and Alice in Chains. I love Eddie Vedder's voice and more importantly what he does with it, but it really bugs me when someone copies the manlegend so slavishly. Strike one. Strike two: the songs are slow, boring, in a word sluggish, slopped by a rough and tumble recording that doesn't do the band's lack of chops any favours. If grunge is dead (which I don't buy. I think it's big players have just been dormant for a year and a half), why is there such a label schmooze around this bunch? Oh yeah, strike three is that I'm a bitter and jaded Seattle follower from the Green River days.
Rating        **6**

### Silverchair - Freak Show    (Sony '97)

Man, this is exactly how I reviewed the last Silverchair album. I just played it over and over, often as a background throb, just waiting for something to leap out and impress. And it never did. Unlike the other Nirvana cover band Bush, Silverchair just plod along, delivering their mean median average, churning out obvious, predictable and simple grunge lobsters that wilt within minutes of shuffling off. Lead single *Abuse Me* has a hint of addictive melody, but after that, man this just all swims together, despite better than average lyrics. Eighteen year olds, ha ha, tour with their dads, ha ha, buys 45 guitars ha ha, but, one would hope half a rule might be broken somewhere. I mean, there's even a "reflective" violin and cello dirge. Possible youth card advantages aren't even considered, any potential fresh spark, naiveté, silliness or raging hormones muted for a contrived air of destructive, mopey GenXperience. Man, I can't even get angry, which is really depressing.
Rating        **5**

### Silver Mountain - Shakin' Brains    (Metal Blade '84)

Known for their early association with the lordly and leaping Yngwie monster, Silver Mountain were fierce guitar moguls in their own right by this time under the capable tutelage of Jonas Hansson, who also unwisely tackles lead vocal chores. **Shakin' Brains** is a somewhat hurried slab of classical music-based metal, that is to say goth of the more ornate, less doom-laden nature: more castle than dungeon. **Shakin' Brains** scurries in its interesting Deep Purple meets frostbite keyboard/axe hybrid, crammed full of interesting ideas that are handled a might roughly, faves being *Spring Maiden* and the difficult *Keep On Keepin' On*. A bit too loose for my liking. Follow-up **Universe** would become the elegant realization of the band's aims.
Rating        **7**

### Silver Mountain - Universe    (Roadrunner '85)

With **Universe**, Sweden's Silver Mountain has developed into one of the premiere Euro goth acts, mixing keyboards and icy melodies with the extremely sorrowful Yngwie stylings of axeman Jonas Hansson whose swirling double helix magnificence comes to full head on the solos straddling sinister lead cut *Shakin' Brains* and Rainbow demon *Why*. New vocalist Christer Mentzer isn't a huge stretch more nimble than Hansson, but the overall effect, combined with the record's flawless execution, is one of chilling Euro royalty, rendering **Universe** one of those near perfect but poisonous releases, the type best worshipped from a distance. A veritable cathedral of classical riffs recorded in a sort of edgy, apocalyptic panic (that's a compliment), **Universe** is an acquired metal taste, sadly ineffectual on most punters stateside.

Rating     8

## Simple Aggression - Formulations In Black
(Leviathan '93)

There's something cool about this young Cincinnati/Kentucky band that is hard to pin, Simple Aggression cannily combining a wealth of influences based on the general mechanic's metal of Metallica and Anthrax, then springing to life from there. So on top of the tight, sharply produced bed of riffs, we get animated enthusiasm straight outa Gwar and Biohazard, the flip funk of the Chili Peppers, and the bulldozing, shouty underground charm of Clutch, even though they came later. Cover art might remind you of Savatage's **Sirens** (the kids in sewer version, not the blue one).

Rating     7

## Simple Aggression - Gravity   (Leviathan '96)

It's rare to see a band do a stylistic about-face and still make a good record, Simple Aggresson doing just that: one classy, fairly straight-faced metal debut and now this visceral, menacing, percussive, vaguely Soundgarden-like follow-up. Biggest change here has been the addition of vocalist Eric Johns from another solid Leviathan act Full Circle, who complements the stone-carved Seattle-ish power chording perfectly with his shrieky Cornell-emotive wail. Top it all off with a great drumming performance and recording, and what you get is a bruising yet tuneful record of technically adept, grunge-inflected metal. Faves, oddly enough, are the last two tunes on the CD *Lifeguard* and *Why?*, which are tribal whirlwinds of riffage, demonstrating these guys have what it takes to straddle heavy genres of the '90s without barely breaking a sweat.

Rating     8

## Sinister - Hate   (Nuclear Blast '95)

Total sonic annihilation marks this putrid purveyor of extreme brain-blasting death. And as a result you gotta applaud these Dutch thrashers' disdain for success, 'cos there's a limit as to what kind of cretin would buy this mess. Amazingly, **Hate** is the band's third (after '92's **Cross The Styx** and '93's **Diabolical Summoning**), and just does not veer from the path of total destruction. Consequently, it sucks. Ghoulish, sculpture-like cover art by Wes Benscoter, who did Slayer's **Divine Intervention**.

Rating     0

## Sinner - Fast Decision   (Scratch '83)

Good ol' **Fast Decision** (the band's second) actually logged a lot of air time in the early days of the Panzer invasion, gliding along on a wave of melodic cum metallic holler fodder that made for an accessible but still evil spray of shrapnel. Like a vastly superior Ethel The Frog, Sinner rocked smartly for the time with classy cruises like *Runnin' Wild*, *Magic* and *Trouble Boys*, proving good feelings don't necessarily have to follow guoad intentions. Well-recorded, slightly naive, but studied and committed, **Fast Decision** rode a Teutonic trail of ice, impressing on our brains heavily for a good two years during those exciting early days in the forge.

Rating     7

## Sinner - Danger Zone   (Viper '84)

The unfinished and unsure ballet of steel that was **Fast Decision** drops a few octaves in slow and pounding pursuit of growls and boulderisms on this loudly recorded chugfest that enters terrain trampled by Gravestone and Grave Digger, even evoking an Accept in a most Neanderthal and drunken state. Like a pit bull that shakes its prey into brain-bruised catatonia, **Danger Zone** slams in deep commitment to the traditional headbang. Definitely a drinking record, one which

relies on riff for its sole effect, a concept which ices the veins exquisitely after the first six pack. At least three more records followed.

Rating     7

## Sir Lord Baltimore - Kingdom Come   (PolyGram '70)

One of the grimey grails of metal's ancient years, Sir Lord Baltimore were an unruly bunch of Brooklyners whose distinction is considerable heaviness circa '70, the year metal was invented in a big way (Sab, Heep, Purple, Zep **IV**). Couldn't really include these guys in the Hallowed Hall of the Metal Grill, the band owing more to Hendrix and crusty older Zep (and Yardbirds), than the truly new visions of metal emanating from the likes of Deep Purple's **In Rock**. But still, you gotta give this trio a Marshall stack of pancakes, at least for their loopy upratchet on Hendrix, making better songs more zesty Italian than Jimi's often melted psychedelia. I mean there's almost art hidden in these damp basement grooves, a sort of open architecture disdain for logic, while guitars keep up their end of the deal, gut-punching the listener, preparing him for the inevitable arrival of say, **Master Of Reality** next year.

Rating     7

## Sir Lord Baltimore - Sir Lord Baltimore   (PolyGram '71)

. . . and also give 'em credit for remaining heavy buckets on this second and last record, Louis Dambra bringing in brother Joey to expand the line-up to four, the guy actually making a difference, filling out the sound a bit, or at least lubricating the band's creativity. Still, when the pink smoke clears, a laughable kind of cryogenic Spinal Tap emerges (see *Caesar LXXI* and ten minute Heep meets Mothers Of Invention monster *Man From Manhattan*), the guys performing like mad scientists with weapons bigger than they bargained for. Sounds like they're having a right royal romp though, despite those tortured 1971 guitars and tube amps, making a record that is ultimately spacier, fuzzier and wiggier than the debut. Note: both records reissued on one 1994 CD. Note II: for similar caveman rock, see Bang.

Rating     6

## Sisters Of Mercy - Vision Thing   (Est. '90)

The first less than tentative hard rock record from Britain's ridiculed vampire rockers (and thus the only platter I've reviewed), **Vision Thing** swells forth into almost human terrain with dancy goth rockers like *Detonation Boulevard* and the hypnotic title cut, replete with signature simpleton beats and low-cycle sinisterisms from Andrew Eldritch's outside view of life. Elsewhere, dead acoustic rock and killer Killing Joke-type science such as the uniformly evil *Ribbons* and *Doctor Jeep*, the latter less so KJ, but equally cave-grown. Still, with a dismal track record, driven stake through the heart with the painful washout of **Floodland**, it's going to take a little more raw adherence to the tenets of metal for these hollow men to live up to their fairly frightening imagery. And it's not like I don't get the point. Fact is, the old stuff died on the vine, sucked dry by cheesy instrumentation and chopped-at-the-ankles production values. Time to kick ass, 'cos even still, this is too thin, laid back, atmospheric, and stiff in its ongoing failing insistence on mixing scary rock with dance grooves. Sort of exaggerated, affected, but warmed-over early Cult.

Rating     5

## Six Feet Under - Six Feet Under   (Europa Film '83)

No, not a power trio from Australia, but weird looking Swedes with a keyboardist, and at least one Deep Purple shirt . . . looks promising. Well after the opening keyboard honkings lifted wholesale from Mr. Jon Lord, all thoughts evaporate in terms of Purple pageantry. Yea and verily, **Six Feet Under** is kinda cheapo 'n' crusty melodimetal, and not at all whipped and stinging

by the colds of the impenetrable Scandinavian mind-sphere found on elsewhere, erstwhile classics. Some scintillating arrangements that could have been **Machine Head**-ers on another planet, but said artisms are few and far between. Mostly, it's poverty-level slap-dashes more characteristic of the American underclass.
Rating 4

### Six Feet Under - Haunted (Metal Blade '95)
Somewhat of a death metal supergroup (and not the above Swede inconsequentials), Six Feet Under features ex-Death and Obituary guys plus Cannibal Corpse's world champion of filth, Chris Barnes on vocals. The record sounds like Barnes is starved for an ever so slightly more commercial vehicle, slowing it down, apparently caring more about song, and cleaning up the lyrics. To my tortured ears, **Haunted** is somewhat scrapingly enjoyable, totally death in production, a constant mid-to-slow churn of guitars, but overall, just too much like an average of seven or ten bands, a leveling of various death sensibilities, definitely not fresh in any way. Produced by label guru Brian Slagel.
Rating 6

### Six Feet Under - Alive And Dead (Metal Blade '96)
America's supergroup scabs of death return with this 23 minute curio, pointing to possible new sublime, relaxed, melodic directions for the band. **Alive And Dead** contains four well-recorded live tracks from **Haunted**, a straight, if death-vocalized cover of Judas Priest's *Grinder*, and two new tracks *Insect* and *Drowning*, which are both downright pleasant in an ammonia-drinking sort of way, both simple, hypnotic, kinda similar to the catchiest tones from Napalm Death's **Diatribes** spread. One's a description of a bug-ridden corpse, the other a description of a drowned corpse. Consistency!
Rating 6

### Six Point Six - Fallen Angel (Hot Blood '84)
Disappointingly garage-like for Europroduct, saddled with a shit-can recording to match, **Fallen Angel** could have benefited greatly from the thunderous technical settings that usually accompany such Euro despondence. As it stands, merely dimestore melodic metal, blown skyward by at least ten other near-identical Rambo combos.
Rating 4

### 16 - Drop Out (Theologian '96)
Drop kick this one between the doom goalposts of Kyuss, Trouble, Eyehategod, Pitch Shifter, Helmet and Crowbar, and you've picked up three hard-won points from this blubbering, bruising assemblage of hypnotic noise overdrivers from sunny California. **Drop Out** is only the band's second full-length, but a scary level of rude kill skill already pours like buckets of boiling tar from the record's ten tall tales. Vocals are agonizing but discernible, more hardcore punk than anything from death, although they are quite electro-treated, blunting the hair-raising lyrical hellscapes so you gotta read 'em to fry. The operative word here is bass, both the weapon and the frequency, the band usually moving slowly but frantically, if that's possible, tracks like *Trigger Happy* and *Sniper* building walls of sticky mud that nevertheless show heft and even whispery thin strands of melody (again, very much like Kyuss). Pretty extreme overall, sorta like something Earache or Dwell would put out. Prepare for a pummeling.
Rating 8

### Six Was Nine - . . . a single senseless word
(Par Excellence '94)
An indie that should have been a major, this record from Montreal is a swinging, groovy, slick melodic

metal album somewhere between King's X or Saigon Kick and more strictly AOR-ish fare, albeit AOR of a heavier nature. Produced by Frank Marino with way wider, more enjoyable range than any of his own twenty or so records, **. . . a single senseless word** triumphs in two distinct ways: the cutting, disciplined, often funky guitarwork, and above all, the major league vocal acrobatics of Frank Raposo, who balances his skill with measured drama. Sweet, sweet record, despite the high degree of electric energy.
Rating 8

### Skid Row - Skid Row (Atlantic '89)
All the elements were in place here for making waves, as a bunch of Jersey wharf rats enlist the services of Peterborough-raised, ex-Madame X vocalist Sebastian "Baz" Bach, whose good looks, kickin' vocals and metal-'til-death will to conquer, combine to push Skid Row in your face. **Skid Row**, the debut was yer basic well-executed corporate metal feast, commercial with just enough middle finger to haul us off to the party. And the record just took off, led by generation disintegration examination *Youth Gone Wild* (for that all important well-timed alignment with the Gunners), then *18 And Life* (ditto), then *I Remember You*, the latter two being your basic, grimy, lighter-flicking power ballads, songs unrepresentative of the rest of the acceptable Ratt 'n' roll throughout (rendered somewhat soupy by an overdone Double Trouble mix). Really, it's Baz who carries this record, roaring from his razor-thin frame on pointy boots, raising the average to something worth reckoning. Never mind the carping though, 'cos come record II, the Skidders will be stomping this tentative debut into a thin mash, wiping that superior smirk right off your face.
Rating 7

### Skid Row - Slave To The Grind (Atlantic '91)
Baz and the boyz are back, fangs dripping, mentally decked in leather and chains for a murdalization of your concept that Skid Row might be predictable lightweights. **Slave To The Grind** smokes most feverishly, the band proving their mettle, their self-worth, their guts, in flashing their collective finger at the poseurs and blue-suited soldiers expecting *18 And Life* Part II. A wolloping up-ratchet to be sure, as Snake, Bolan, Hill, Affuso and Bach let their punk snarl fester through a bone-grinding collection of power chord classics like lead single *Monkey Business*, *The Threat*, *Psycho Love*, the harrowing title track and bulldozing fave *Riot Act*, all evoking society in flames, anarchy, a world ruled by skidders, most compositions street-scorched with fat, feral, funky grooves, like Aerosmith hitting rock bottom. Even the "ballads" demand respect (and concern), all taking you to dark unsettling places where reflection collides with worry. Whereas the skid in **Skid Row** represented a slide into compromise, here it's an arresting and disturbed slippage into a world sicker than the rock'n'roll grime from whence the band came, one just as morally void, but one with money. Up the hammers for this one, the band proving themselves ballsy risk-takers, metalheads with principles, mental cases with a dim and defiant view of the business. The result: a record that bites, jaws snapping at the whole stinking mess outside your window, Baz in fine, head-shredding form, Snake 'n' Hill's dual axework devouring of the weak and timid, and Wagener's production tough, urban and urgent. A surprising and welcome jolt to the system.
Rating 9

### Skid Row - B-Sides Ourselves (Atlantic '92)
This five track cast-off EP (still don't know where the title came from, but I'll ride along) relives the roots of rockers our age in typical **Wayne's World** fashion. The rundown: a little ancient history in Hendrix's *Little*

Wing (first single and video), some kiddie rock in C'mon And Love Me from Kiss, some homage to Baz's Ontario origins with Rush's What You're Doing, a sample from the heavier side of punk (it was all just messy metal anyways, right?) with the Ramones' Psycho Therapy, and some wollop from the year Priest brought us whipped and screamin' into the modern world with **Hell Bent For Leather's** Delivering The Goods, here handled live in duet with Baz's hero, Halford himself. Really, besides the obscure, high quality Priest and Rush tunes, who cares? It could have been a lot more imaginative, knowing the vast catalogue of obscure old metal you just know these guys worship. Performance: stripped, garagey, wicked but headphone-rated, and it's cool seeing that we're all fans when it comes right down to it. But sorry dudes, at $9.99 for a five track EP of covers, count me elsewhere.
Rating                                                    6

## Skid Row - Subhuman Race   (Atlantic '95)

Baz and the boys remake themselves into a smoke-belching, low-cycle machine of mammoth proportions, carving into those '90s influences (much like the under-rated **Motley Crue** album did) for a thundercloud of mid and slow pocket complexity, absorbing the best elements of grunge into their over-the-top love of all things metal. Sebastian Bach's performance is probably the shining jewel of this ambitious no-bull spread of power chords, the man growling with forceful aggression in reverence of his hero Rob Halford, Baz adopting Halford's healthy work ethic and belief in the potential of a vocal to steer tracks skyward through diversity. Above all, the band remains street-savvy, hatching unarguably one ballad (the rich, oddly textured Breakin' Down), arguably up to three max, all tracks that are more prog triumphs with quiet bits than anything formula. And that prog ethic burns right on through the rockers too, many tracks experimenting in that old Sab/Zep II style of heavy, tribal drums with bass exploding through the construct, pret' near everything on here guttural and complicated, and '90s-relevant to boot. In a fickle metal marketplace, I have no idea how this will sell, but it won't be the fault of the record, although I'm not sure this spread does much to distant the band from scuzzball arena rock culture.
Rating                                                    9

## Skin Yard - 1000 Smiling Knuckles   (Cruz '91)

Jack Endino and Cruz Records were sort of fringe precursors to the Sub Pop phenomenon, Jack being an influential producer dude, Cruz cranking a bunch of early grungers from around the states, bands considered the first faint heartbeats of the Northwest sound. Skin Yard is Jack's baby, a band of which he is of course producer, plus guitarist and key hombre. On vocals: "Ben," who will move on to Gruntruck, whose latest **Push** is produced by Endino. But enough already . . . what is this **1000 Smiling Knuckles** stuff about anyways? Well, it's blueprint Seattle grunge, tribal, spacey and pharmaceutically schlocking, if not a little over-dramatic, like an underground and less accessible version of Gruntruck or the more Sab-based side of early Soundgarden. Pretty grey psychologically speaking, which is a bit of an annoyance given that the overall tone is an expected amalgam of old Sub Pop anti-sentiments, which bothers me because it isn't all that fresh or pioneering, missing the true point of the creative ethic that blew all those bands skyward at the beginning of the movement. Maybe I'm wrong, 1991 being only barely post-explosion (not to mention the existence of earlier Skin Yards), but I've always found it hard accepting grunge acts outside my worshipped five or six. Maybe it's the snobbery of my advancing years

spoiling the brew once again, but I find this an exploitation of other people's work.
Rating                                                    7

## Skrew - Burning In Water, Drowning In Flame
(Metal Blade '92)

Having heard this record after Skrew's other wired contraptions, I was pleasantly surprised to hear how snapped to the '90s it is. There's a uniformity to the sounds that might actually help the thing if they were sonics with a scrap of warmth. But Skrew make up for their monotoned scrape with a wealth of songstyles, following the James Bonded Charlemagne for example. As with **Dusted**, there's a palpable metal hue to this thing, Skrew essentially writing like metalheads and then transforming things through a battalion of machines. Not my bag, really. Contains an unrecognizable cover of Sympathy For The Devil, somehow adding a Metallica riff then sticking it into an electrical socket for a full frizz.
Rating                                                    7

## Skrew - Dusted   (Metal Blade '94)

On record two, Skrew hone their monstrous industrial metal sound, basically achieving Ministry scrape-scapes, really carving into their turns, establishing themselves as one of the better contenders in this narrow genre. But this is more guitar heavy than industrial, more like serious White Zombie, right down to the fairly horrific Pinhead-style head/hand on the cover art. I can see quaffing a few to this one, bobbing to those layers, squeaks, shrieks and pops that weld the riffs in a sonic hairweave of death. With all these near perfect exercises in rock rolling by, one wonders what the bands who have spent the last couple years on the sidelines (Ministry, Metallica, Slayer, Tool, RATM) are going to do to chop all these eager newcomers at the knees. For now, let Skrew have their say.
Rating                                                    7

## Skrew - Shadow Of Doubt   (Metal Blade '96)

Texan tendon-snappers Skrew are back with their biggest, boldest, catchiest record yet, and to say it sounds like White Zombie doesn't really do it justice. Oh, it does, but it's also almost as good as Zombie's latest, finding those same rich deposits of apocalyptic groove (see Black Eye) while going places beyond into a sort of dazed, NIN psycho-delia (which diminishes it for me). And lyrically it's a harsher, more cynical pound, evoking Pitch Shifter and various up-scale death metal acts in its imagery. But all in all, call this a rousing success in the world of industrial metal, leader Adam Grossman and Co. (including Overkill's Bobby Gustafson on guitar) slowly and methodically carving themselves a reputation as a major player. Why the dull 7's? Just not my bag.
Rating                                                    7

## Skyclad - Wayward Sons Of Mother Earth   (BMG '91)

Martin Walkyier has ruthlessly honed his craft over the years, culminating in this space age maze of techno-metal, an overwhelming conflagration of speed-goth in doomtime, enlisting the razor-athletic services of Satan/Blind Fury's Steve Ramsay and Graeme English. The result: one wicked gathering of rogues in earnest lust with the medieval. Walkyier's bountiful lyrics poetically carve the world with the sword of morality, attacking corruption, greed, the fade of religion, the pillage of the environment, and the evils of war, while his band strafes the airwaves with apocalyptic adhesions, turning their twisted chops on a society buckling in the wind. Overall, **Wayward Sons** evokes the woven hope and despair of Trouble, fleshing out the Chicago band's vision with additional history, colour and character; mankind and his manufactured folly as strutting peacock, doomed despite self-importance.

And the instrumented portion of the package speaks almost entirely of this doom; fast, panicky but clinical, insane and isolated from warmth or interaction. A disturbing but refreshing dose of reality and the inevitable fantasy world that must follow. Favorites: *The Widdershins Jig* (yes, a heavy metal jig), *Our Dying Island*, which breaks into a brain-bruising groove come chorus time, and closer *Terminus*, a progressive freak-out about nuclear annihilation.

Rating     **8**

## Skyclad - A Burnt Offering For The Bone Idol
(Noise '92)

Brisk, spirited and pagan-thrashing (yow!), this second Skyclad statement hones the band's provocative and interesting philosophy and sound into shape. For sooth, this might be the band's most expertly assembled and technical medieval banquet, songs moving along nicely, tracks like the vicious delicious *Salt Of The Earth* and the more exotic and sensual *King Stone Round* comprising two ends of an exceedingly gothic feel, yet both keeping disciplined towards song. Then there's the Celtic knotwork, the costumes and those always quixotic poetic lyrics, working to weld the vision into one of the most exciting rock presentations we have today. But it all gets chucked for one of the band's most swingin' tunes, *The Declaration Of Indifference*, the closest thing to punchy, fire-breathing Accept Skyclad will ever admit. This band is just so cool, it's scary.

Rating     **9**

## Skyclad - Jonah's Ark  (Noise '93)

As ambitious and florid as any Skyclad spread, **Jonah's Ark** just might go overboard in the progressive sweepstakes, too much violin, too many changes and too many cold sour moments. *Thinking Allowed* however is a classic, rousing rocker (after a long Spinal Tap intro), a smart tale about the positive effects of speaking one's mind and mulling over matters, something at which Walkyier is the Man. But I can't help view **Jonah's Ark** as a sort of metalman Tull album, very icy and medieval and darkly tuned. Great album cover though, by the band's new artist.

Rating     **7**

## Skyclad - Prince Of The Poverty Line  (Noise '94)

At long last, the incomparable Palace Skyclad, thrash thinktank of Martin Walkyier, make their U.S. debut after three pulverizing full-length wedges, once more fusing philosophy and technically intense metal at sincerity levels that should send others scurrying to check their mettle. Much erudite talk of the environment has made way for a devastating (but at times over-punned) treatise on the crumbling state of Britain and its downtrodden, Walkyier spitting his venom over a full band attack laced with the wandering new agey strains of Cath Howell's violin and keyboard delicacies. The band's velocities are tempered nicely here, as experiments in rhythm, shade and bracing melody elevate the record to regal levels, constructions on high, fave being the muscular Accept-able strut of *A Bellyful Of Emptiness*, plus of course Lizzy's inspired *Emerald*, here kind of defiled by the violin work, although an interesting experiment nevertheless. Such a meaty record, deep musically as well as lyrically, **Prince Of The Poverty Line** is the king of seriously aristocratic British records in the '90s, not ashamed of quality, not ashamed of extensive planning, thick with distressed heart-scraping metal, yet also thick with human insight. Welcome Walkyier stateside and give his record your undivided attention.

Rating     **10**

## Skyclad - The Silent Whales Of Lunar Sea  (Noise '95)

The king of puns, Martin Walkyier pulls probably the biggest in album title history (well, tied with Public Enemy and Smashing Pumpkins), for a record that is equally grand, belaboured, fantastical and progressive. The refreshing thing about this remarkable band right now, is that they successfully combine the work ethic of progressive pomp with the raw edge of underground metal. **Silent Whales** oddly pumps up in both departments, more huge structures, better integration of violin and a more eccentric, uncommercial goth metal tarnish, arriving at a thrash metal trashing of Jethro Tull. And it's an awe-inspiring experience, many ways more creative than its predecessor, while less immediately gratifying. Bonus: Walkyier's lyrics, which gain focus, wit and insight with every fine record (five studio at this point). Note: like **Prince Of The Poverty Line**, this one saw European release many months before distribution in North America. Missing in action: '95's **Irrational Anthems**.

Rating     **9**

## Slam St. Joan - Saved By Grace  (Heart & Soul '93)

More of a glammy L.A. Guns thang than the similar hair rock tendencies posed by Chicago labelmates Sphinx, Slam St. Joan party it up but more plainly, really dipping back to 1986 for their sound, which is something we shouldn't necessarily begrudge. Fact is, if big label 'n' latex hard rock is your scene, you'll find it done well here. It's the relevance you might find missing, not to mention that '90s whinegrime to which we've become accustomed.

Rating     **6**

## Slammer - The Work Of Idle Hands . . .  (Warner '89)

Fans of the Bay Area thrash scene will grow to love this versatile and studied British techno-feast, but I ain't a fan, finding this too atonal and laboured; too many riffs, too much shouting, too much double time. Well-assembled but hyper.

Rating     **5**

## Slash Puppet - Slash Puppet  (Fringe '93)

File with pre-grunge Slik Toxik and Sven Gali as tough, commercial, Ontario street metal, slightly better than (old) Slik, less toothy than (old) Sven, although chrome dome Mif has pipes for unpaved miles. Definite above average hooks here, but this sound is kinda dead, especially for new acts (i.e. G'NR and Kiss can basically do whatever they want at this point). Six accomplished renderings of fairly uneventful party toons.

Rating     **5**

## Slash's Snakepit - It's Five O'clock Somewhere
(Geffen '95)

Let me get that part over with where the critic says this is the best Gunners solo record yet, which maybe it grudgingly is, I dunno. Better than Gilby and Duff, but not as warm and purely likeable as Izzy, Slash's fillgap (while his band burns) sounds the most like a Guns record, which makes sense given that many of these tracks were petulantly refused by Axl for the next GN'R. Still, this sleaze metal thing is getting tiresome, Slash not doing much more with it than any mere mortal would. Jellyfish's Eric Dover is your basic strip-mall singer, fine, even robust for the genre, but the genre itself being dead. Won't go into specific tracks. Let's just say all the bases are covered, I mean all of them, and the overall effect is unclean and unkind like scumbag metal is supposed to be, the record populated with slimebags, rip-off artists, losers and all-round jerks. With all the bad blood around the Guns camp, it's hard to get happy about a Slash record. Bad timing, but the only timing Slash could get.

Rating     **6**

## Slaughter - Bite Back  (DJM/Phonogram '80)

This particular Slaughter is a considerably cleaned-up, well-behaved and pop punk metalized version of ghastly early punk bashers Slaughter And The Dogs, a band known mainly from the seminal **Live At The Roxy** showcase from '77 or so. Here Eddie Garrity and the droogies aren't sure whether they're a metal band or a getting-skinny-tie new wave casualty. And we're all better for it, 'cos fact is, this is a punchy, well-recorded guitar rocker, somewhere between the Boomtown Rats debut, The Dictators, The Lurkers and heavy David Johansen, label honchos no doubt trying to make these bozos palatable for U.S. tastes. Idea: just re-release it as is, now. It's better than 90% of '90s punk.

Rating      7

## Slaughter - Strappado    (Diabolic Force '87)

Heinous thrashcore from T.O.'s frash guru Bob Sadzak; explosively mixed, in rank possession of a guitar sound that sends chisels to the frontal lobes, 'neath the predicted frash vocal equivalent of a forty year smoker screaming through Ajax and roadsalt. Better than average but still totally unlistenable. Had to change their name to "Strappado" to avoid confusion with the leonine popsters from south of the border, although the moniker Slaughter does more accurate vigil right here. An early fave of many big thrashers, including Sepultura's Max Cavalera.

Rating      4

## Slaughter - Stick It To Ya    (Chrysalis '90)

The Mark and Dana show was a money machine from word go, or at least became so with a few breaks and a bit of time-worn wisdom from deals gone by. Loose, ego-driven, hysterically-recorded, and god-awfully American, **Stick It To Ya** became The Buzz, fueled by the Zep-ish pomposity of Fly To The Angels (a tune that ostensibly drove some guy in Texas to confess to double murder. America: gotta love it.), and a gaggle of cruisin' anthems to add just enough meat and potatoes to cross the thin line into respectability. And the rockers are what keep this cleverly chaotic traveling show exciting, tunes like Eye To Eye, Up All Night and Mad About You ramming home the basic frequencies of makin' it in the big city. Really, besides a take-notice set of pipes, and a strange one-take sort of vibrance, Slaughter makes it on enthusiasm and willingness to pander alone, preferring to call it "doing it for the fans" than anything with negative connotations. And it's all written into the grooves. While it may just offend, striking some as another Warrant, **Stick It To Ya** has personality, verve, and a ton of hooks that simply stick it to ya, hummably imprinting the brain into comfortable familiarity This is one you like because of the success story, not in spite of it. CD adds two throwaways: an acoustic Fly To The Angels and a little Halen bumf called Wingin' It.

Rating      8

## Slaughter - Stick It Live    (Chrysalis '90)

The shrill ones with a dream take their hair band bombast to Nashville, Knoxville and Atlanta, recording these five tracks live and lovingly overblown. The goods: Burning Bridges, Eye To Eye, Fly To The Angels, Up All Night and Loaded Gun, taking one back to a simpler, giddy time in hard music. If everybody just played Slaughter, there would be no war.

Rating      6

## Slaughter - The Wild Life    (EMI '92)

Despite hoots of derision from the metal community at large, I was a supporter of **Stick It To Ya**, tanning in the rays of its gracious but faint-hearted energy. And despite press-directed comments from the band as to their enormous "growth" since their lucky premiere, **The Wild Life** is a virtual knock-off of **Stick It To Ya**, interchangeable on every facet, and if anything, more saccharine, melodramatic, light-footed, and willing to shed the trappings of heavy metal forever. Which is fine, because even though there's little progression here, Slaughter's debut, like many debuts today, was a fully realized state of mind, and **The Wild Life** continues to reveal the band's obvious comfort as fast-rising, business-oriented rock stars, emitting an extremely gun-shy but loose party rock sound that struts proudly and spaciously while courting the more melodic, chick-driven side of guitar rock. Definitely not out to change the world, and even a little cowardly in the face of challenges from Kik Tracee, Bullet Boys and of course Skid Row, and more recent concurrent releases like the shattering second from Love/Hate and a raft of cerebral, boundary-expanding statements from Seattle, **The Wild Life** nevertheless swaggers bold and American, carrying its own all-encompassing guilty charm despite its overt reliance on convention, offering overflowing levels of pomp, countered with a strange, "one take" spontaneity, evidenced by a raw, open architecture delivery, where axe solos often lash out loudly with no undercurrent of rhythm guitar, a technique often used by Van Halen. Having seen the band's energy levels live (free tickets), I more or less have grown to like the idea of Slaughter, and as a somewhat committed fan, more of the same, and in this panoramic quantity (63 minutes worth), is fine by me. But if something bothered you about Slaughter's blinding, bolder-than-brash commercialism, Mark's shrill pipes, or the overall bombast without ballast, this one won't win you over, but for starters, you may be surprised with the inherent soul of the ballads, especially the stirring Times They Change and more pedestrian pleasure Days Gone By, which transforms into a flurry of shameful Queen tricks by tune's end. A cruisin' with the top down album fer sure, and one that will grow on me as the mercury rises this summer. Opened the Billboard charts at #8, but faded pretty fast.

Rating      9

## Slaughter - Fear No Evil    (CMC '95)

One hopes this dreamer's band can escape the fate befallen their party metal cohorts, **Fear No Evil** a capable follow-up to the shiny, ambitious **Wild Life** sophomore three years back, a record that was a disappointment at platinum, in light of the debut's quick double platinum status. Indie niche label CMC now has their biggest signing, and it will be interesting to see if Slaughter can make all involved at least a modest chunk of change. **Fear No Evil** is a smarmy, mischievous rehash of a sound that was always bright, loose and irreverent, glam rock spontaneity personified, like the '80s were just the coolest thing. The eclectic, raw mix is the same (if a little less trebly), and Mark's twangy pipes are on target. No big changes and I'm glad, same number and silly style of ballads, balanced against summer rockers that are so pop savvy, ya gotta smile. Less perfumed by the smell of money, but ragingly (perhaps foolishly?) self-confident all the same, **Fear No Evil** upholds just barely the standards that Slaughter has established for themselves. Low mark reflects lack of progress, lack of "mission".

Rating      7

## Slave Master - Under The Six    (Black Arc/Ryko '94)

As mentioned in my review of Hardware's **Third Eye Open**, I seem to recall that Black Arc was an imprint created to promote black artists. And like Hardware, Slave Master is a groovy piece of black music-affected hard rock, Only in this case, the sound leans towards urbancore and rap, much closer to Living Colour, quite ahead of its time, more of a '96er than a '92er fer sure. Production even leans towards Vernon Reid and Co., Bill Laswell adopting that boomy, restless barn mix with tight snare that is an acquired taste but one worth acquiring.

Rating      6

## Slayer - Show No Mercy   (Metal Blade '83)

As much as I never became a big booster of this band really until '86's unfathomable **Reign In Blood**, Slayer were a pivotal band in the advancement of metal. **Show No Mercy** scared the bejesus out of everybody, being the first totally Satanic wedge of metal stateside, rivaling the likes of Venom for sheer disgust and over-kill. What's more, the record co-starred with Metallica's seminal **Kill 'Em All** in defining state-of-the-art speed metal, fusing chops, ambition and studio skills to previous examples of thrash (again, Venom), resulting in cutting edge OTT, ultra, speed, black . . . you name it, while inspiring new rafts of hellions to expand the limits of metal, finding progressive metal, more extreme versions of thrash (i.e. Bathory, Possessed) and the emergence of grindcore, today's most prolific metal minefield. **Show No Mercy** was simply outrageous, almost like Kiss all over again, adding dizzying mathematical speed, blazing chaotic guitar solos, upside down crosses and pentagrams to the smoke, leather and soon-to-be-dropped eyeshadow. Still, I always found the record stiff and one dimensional, never being a big fan of speed metal, here laid down in stifling arrangements, translated by an OK mix technically speaking, but one not to my personal preference, particularly with respect to snare sound. Still, any record that begs the question, "What are these guys on?", deserves full recognition for waking up the neighbours like they've never been before.
Rating   6

## Slayer - Haunting The Chapel   (Metal Blade '84)

This six track EP (three new studio, three from the debut, live) demonstrates the fact that there's a bit more thrash bang wallop in the thick Slayer hide than we once thought, stretching it out over a spontaneous race to the red hot gates of Satan's domain. Riffs are more punishing, preferring to release a few dog-sized rats than hundreds of carnivorous mini mice. Even the lyrics are beginning to sharpen the tongue, as the band gets deeper within their sin and deeper within their chaos, working full tilt to maintain their justified billing as the world's heaviest band. Dave Lombardo's patented double bass barrage gets full workout here, particularly death-defying on the EP's title track. Strange, but both the new trashy studio sound and the live expulsion are more enjoyable than the debut's aseptic feel. Maybe Venom was onto something with their anti-recording. That's maybe.
Rating   6

## Slayer - Live Undead   (Metal Blade '84)

A fairly inconsequential purging of Slayer's past, as the hallowed harpies tear a strip off seven oldies at 23 minutes (almost as long as some of their real records!), my version being a remastered CD, no real improvement soundwise on the original festered scar. Initial shock to Slayer's credit: thrash hasn't really gone much beyond this in the dozen years since.
Rating   5

## Slayer - Hell Awaits   (Metal Blade '85)

**Hell Awaits** takes Slayer's first incarnation about as far as it can go, creating the thickest wall of sound that speed metal hath wrought to date. Painfully true to their no compromise maxim, Slayer decides to blow its OTT wad, creating their most flambés; long, accelerated bludgeons that just don't let up, making **Hell Awaits** an almost progressive gorefest, something outside of music, totally unlovable and cardiac, but worthy of respect as Araya, King, Hanneman and Lombardo cremate the crowd without pause for consequence. Lyrically the band is well into their shift towards plain vile, mixing their slew of Satanic sewage with buckets of blood and body parts, searching the thesaurus for all the shock spitable at 120 MPH. As a

listening experience however, **Hell Awaits** is too unintelligible, polka-monstered, and pioneeringly blast-beated for my sensibilities, wholly lacking in power groove, an element of which the band will soon become reigning masters.
Rating   7

## Slayer - Reign In Blood   (Def Jam '86)

**Reign In Blood**, the first of three Slayer assaults closing down the '80s, produces near impossible levels of mania, as Slayer discovers the seething energy of the power groove, mixing their very best fast stuff with tortuously beatific mid pace mindmelts. Even Araya's vocals reach new extremes, rising to the challenge of the flesh-frying conflagration at hand. Many a deranged punter considers this record Slayer's masterpiece, caught writhing in pain on the cusp of the band's most apocalyptic thrash and their most bone-crunching gut punches, both exposed and bleeding on *Angel Of Death*, *Criminally Insane*, the record's climactic Jekyl and Hyde epic *Raining Blood*. And the point is well taken, **Reign In Blood** arguably being the band's most infectious and excitable project, even if its follow-up packs greater gravity. No question, the grinding passages of this record capture the essence of preposterously heavy metal with merciless perfection, but it's the thrash stuff that seems the most improved, becoming full rants, Araya just belting out his poison, solos approaching Greg Ginn-like anti-musicality; a truly OTT hatred of all things timid. And it would all probably implode, had Rick Rubin not given the band his most volcanic of production jobs, turning Lombardo into the powerhouse from hell we all knew he was. When the smoke clears, Slayer walks tall from the rubble, breaking its own record, remaining the heaviest band on earth.
Rating   9

## Slayer - South Of Heaven   (Geffen '88)

Another pleasant album cover hides what I feel is the weightiest record of all time, possibly the purest expression of heavy metal to strafe the airwaves. **South Of Heaven** is an insane construct of pummeling power riffs, nary a moment slipping out of the jet stream of Sheer Force One. No shit, every time I experience this awesome black hole of hate, I come very close to actual heart palpitations, the gravity of Lombardo's relentless pound drawing all tidal tendencies into a vortex of his own lockstep, building some of the largest beats in existence on such cranium crushers as *Behind The Crooked Cross* and *Mandatory Suicide*. The very blood-stained crux of death metal, **South Of Heaven** is a torrential downpour of what made **Reign In Blood** such a hurtful piece of machinery. It seems Slayer alone can pull off such psychotic overdrives, making no apologies for their lyrical hideousness, knowing full well such verbal slaying is merely the spoken equivalent of the careening death howls emerging bubbled and festered from the instrumental invasion. These are the kinds of riffs you dream about then can't remember the next morning, progressions so demonic, you just gotta crack a smile. I don't know, what more can I say. Slayer is in sole possession of a sound that is about as violent as music gets, and with each record more people become attuned to the band's legacy. Unstoppable cover: Priest's *Dissident Aggressor*.
Rating   10

## Slayer - Seasons In the Abyss   (Def American '90)

Considered by many to be a cross between **Reign In Blood**'s hyper aggression and **South Of Heaven**'s two ton riffery, you just know **Seasons** isn't going to be that much of a departure or progression. Well, more of the same is just fine by me, **Seasons** indeed cranking with greater clatter and contusion this time over a somewhat brasher mix from the totally bitchin'

Rubin/Wallace team. Solos are more slicing, Lombardo's high hat seems a little more open, and a detectable thrash ethic permeates the band's poison gases as if to say all is not right with the world, and Slayer still slays, lacerating its own arteries in the process. The Slatanic headshred lives on, energy levels so far beyond what most people dare to confront. No wonder Slayer was the band of choice among soldiers during Operation Desert Storm, both worlds being equally suffocating under choking walls of black smoke.

Rating                                                                    9

## Slayer - Decade Of Aggression    (Def American '91)

Alas and only apparently, it becomes time to document properly a career of evil par excellence, a nerve-shattering blight of speed and eventual gravity that would become the standard against all else would whither (until Pantera of course). **Decade** offers a rash of time-leaping thrash, but in ultimatum, offers no reason to be studied, other than the usual head-scratching as to the obvious super-human abilities of a band able to pull off such insane material live. Let's face it, Slayer is a studio experience foremost, actually an intensifying progression of experiences, making the earlier numbers here sound panic-stricken against the welts of modern day Araya. Simply redundant however, and even more so given the existence of **Live Undead**.

Rating                                                                    6

## Slayer - Divine Intervention    (American '94)

Slayer embody the bluest flame of metal; you know it, they know it. The band sits (loiters) dear to the hearts of all beholden to the heaviest fringes of recorded music, smoking a doobie, boob-tubing the freakshow that is America, while pretenders struggle to articulate their own interpretations of the most massive of metals. And surprise, surprise . . . many have succeeded in matching Slayer's skull-powdering standards, while the kings of thrash have languished complaining about drummers. Well, **Divine Intervention** arrives, harkening back to the looser thrash electricity of **Reign In Blood**, very little change, and little change needed really, even new skinsman Paul Bostaph doing Lombardo to a T. But the propensity for short (30 minute) albums continues inexcusably in this CD age (buddies with Mellencamp?), Slayer giving us their usual abbreviated display of prime blood-dripped techno-thrash, only discernible difference being more aggression. But y'know the coolest thing going here? With all the smokin' records as of late, nobody has really trampled the Slayer turf, either successfully or unsuccessfully, giving rise to this record as 100% body-blow fresh, only unadvancing in the face of the Slayer catalogue to date. So the bottom line is: you need this record. It'll at least kick you off the couch as Slayer gets ready to get back on theirs, at least 'til public opinion once again drags their lazy asses back into the studio. Rating reflects disgust with brevity.

Rating                                                                    8

## Slayer - Undisputed Attitude    (American '96)

The long-discussed Slayer punk covers EP is at hand, this esteemed clan of closet hardcore degenerates finally getting to pay respects to the short shocked blasts of noises that were the germination of Slayer's particularly virulent form of speed metal. Scarcely half an hour long (what else is new with Slayer?), **Undisputed Attitude** displays this band's astonishing punk acumen, totally improving on the originals, most of which are quite obscure. Fleshing out the uniformly fangs-dripping blitz are a couple of Hanneman-penned punk project tracks from '84/'85, a nice mid-chug change of pace in a rewrite of *I Wanna Be Your Dog*, and one new Slayer tune, slap-bang crashfest *Gemini*, which with a sanitization, could have come from Metallica's **Load**, what with all that real singing and floun-

dering about, as it stands, a frightening, unkempt baglady of a song, really quite amazing. Heck of a mental mosh all told, but punk as a rule is pretty stale stuff, Slayer making sure they've found the most "up yours" ditties imaginable.

Rating                                                                    7

## Sledgehammer - Blood On Their Hands
(Illuminated '84)

Argle bargle of the highest order, Sledgehammer were a ball of corny-coloured confusion on par with other no-names like Brocas Helm, Saracen, Demon and Ethel The Frog. Rumbling and rickety, nowhere to run, nowhere to hide, you get the picture, sorta dense and unsure whether they're prog metal, bar metal, biker metal or head metal. One kind word: imaginative.

Rating                                                                    4

## Sleep - Sleep's Holy Mountain    (Earache '92)

A "sleeper" of '92, Sleep's Sab-crustified debut didn't really get recognized 'til late '93, and even now is somewhat looked upon as a new arrival. The record's underground hype is somewhat justified for non-obvious reasons, reasons to do with isolated, spontaneous, lack of concern for final product, **Sleep's Holy Mountain** bashing its way through a very deliberate Sabbath-rectified demon demo dirge, similar to Cathedral, The Obsessed, even Monster Magnet, given the record's hurry-up and flounder pharmaceutical offense. And this is why it works. The recording ain't great, and professionalism isn't anywhere within this San Jose band's vocabulary, but hey . . . what better way to get to the char-blackened crux of **Vol 4** or **Master Of Reality**, than to ignore every influence beyond 1972? So lean it towards Hawkwind or early St. Vitus for a closer three-eyed gaze. Major caveman bashfest, major basement bassquake.

Rating                                                                    7

## Sleeze Beez - Powertool    (Atlantic '92)

A modicum of buzz existed up and down neon-bathed boulevards for the Beez, and certainly **Powertool** delivered what any respectable spandex rockdog would have wanted in all hiz/herz deluded glory. Big, glossy corporate AOR in all speeds, the odd ballad, guitar fireworks, and vocals that grate like Kik Tracee/Bang Tango one minute, then gloop it up with the multi-tracked harmonies of Def Leppard the next. But in retro, this breaks every brick of cheese that built the house of Hard Rock. Dumb double entendres, airhead party piffle, fun but empty, slightly heavier than most this shamelessly commercial. And nobody quite jumped for joy at its release. One of a handful of European bands that managed to erase any sense of class their pedigree might have presupposed.

Rating                                                                    5

## Slik Toxik - Doin' The Nasty    (Capitol '91)

Too obviously a serious band, too seriously preoccupied on making big bucks, Slik Toxik are one of few industry buzzes from Toronto's unimpressive metal scene. Love the look, the slimy moniker, and Nick Walsh's feisty pipes, but great ambition is no substitute for solid songwriting, **Doin' The Nasty** sounding ultimately like a hundred other lame and calculated California-style slabs. I sincerely hope Slik's career path grows to resemble Skid Row's thus far: one pandering and safe premiere then bang! . . . revenge, because **Doin' The Nasty** is just that, annoyingly commercial and anonymous, so fashionably planned in its well-produced sleaziness, there's nary an ounce of danger anywhere, save for lead vid *Helluvatime*'s oddly eccentric verse riff and the majesty of the record's instrumental finale. So scared of leaving anything out, Slik covers all bases like a good business should: a swearing tune (for the press), a "worn" bluesy ballad or two, lots

of funk metal like *Blood Money* and *Marionette* (Aerosmith is very much in vogue), *Cherry Bomb*, which is the millionth pointless 'n' gutless party boogie this year, more fuzzy, listless "groove" metal than is necessary, and some dynamics pieces all driven by poor riffs and no direction. All points of the compass combine towards a full display of well-arranged air, 'neath abysmal "controversial" X-rated lyrics to match, slapped together with de rigeur loose street logic by non-band member Dave Mercel. Too loose and full of holes like any not-ready-for-prime-time bar band, Slik Toxik is just too eager to please the boss, per the usual course of action with starstruck Canadian acts. Still, they do a million things right, but here, chalk it up to weak, predictable songs, which could change quickly for a band three years young. I dunno, kinda annoying overall, 'cos you just *know* it's Canadian.
Rating                                                    5

### Slik Toxik - Irrelevant   (A&M/Strawberry '94)

After their superfluous, dated and doomed debut, a Motley debacle concerning a borrowed and crumpled limo, and the unceremonious ouster from Capitol (see Pistols cover *EMI*), Slik Toxik get with the program, transforming themselves into a low chug juggernaut. Darker, deeper and bent on poised ball control, Toxik '94 is a worthy behemoth, Nick Walsh spitting through *I Wanna Gun* and *Fashioned After None* like a brooding star. Sure it's a little fashionably My Sister Alice's Machine In Chains, but the riffs often crunch 'n' munch righteously, and the mellow ones (although too numerous) earn their space with logic, easing dirge-like into such a resoundingly more angry spread. Plus a pro job at the board, and obvious hard work by the band make this a welcome, toothsome comeback. I wanna say **8**, but there might be four to five tracks that try too trendily hard to please, edging the record towards the second bandwagon-jumper in two records, begging the question: why should we believe these guys? Skid Row and Sven Gali comparisons rightly persisted, until the band had had enough, throwing in the towel in '95.
Rating                                                    7

### Slow - Against The Glass   (Zulu '85)

One of the coolest bands that never got to be, Vancouver's Slow self-destructed after a bout of indecent exposure at a prestigious Expo '86 gig. Brought to its flaming glory by Zulu's "in store" indie label, **Against The Glass** broke out with all guns blazing, tearing a strip off The Stooges in cardiac fashion, skirting the darkness with equal doses of heavy Bauhaus and a stiff shot of The Damned. A band who smoked the north and paved the way for the glaze-eyed mastiff that was Sub Pop, Slow broke the rules with their cancerous brand of garage punk that reached way back for its horns, its bastardized dealings with metal, and its death-cold melodrama. All is coked-up and disintegrating as each unique package of chaos carves out its territory of random anger. Greasiest of the lot would be *Have Not Been The Same*, which drags with a psychedelic exhaustion until the walls crash down come chorus time, and *Bad Man*, who conjures up the most wickedly chopped intro to his tale of moral disintegration. As this tragically stunted 6 track EP creaks to a close, one is left exhausted at the possibilities of greatness in this ground-breaking assembly of souls. Sadly, just a shaft of rock-hard integrity shattered at birth.
Rating                                                    9

### Smack - On You   (Viper '85)

Critics' attempts to define this Finnish band's sound in '85-'86 come across as amazingly accurate descriptions of the Sub Pop sound circa '88-'90. Smack are basically that; a pre-Sub Pop, Sub Pop band, from the primary metallic structures through Claude's classic 'merican snarl, right down to the band's unkempt,

stringy-haired poverty dude slouch. Without a doubt, a pretty hip record, and one that stood near to alone at the time in its pursuit of retro-garage metal. Trouble is, I rarely play it, due to a pervading samey-ness and lack of a Sub Pop element of surprise or psychosurge beneath the skin: i.e. a lot of guitars slung low, but few wild riffs; a lot of chuggin' down the middle, but nothing manic or depressive. One I'll probably always admire, but never desire to internalize.
Rating                                                    6

### Smack - Rattlesnake Bite   (Pink Dust '86)

Improvements abound here, although more serious shortcomings still fester deep. Claude's vox are sounding more like Stiv Bators, which is cool by me. Variety is up, and so is psychosis and grunge, but the songs still don't chew into one's neck or let us know if these urchins have any chops. Actually more luded than **On You**, perhaps even more mentally Sub Pop à la Green River or Mother Love Bone yet without the psychological skewing. Highlights: none, just an even, mildly engaging quality to all of it.
Rating                                                    6

### Small Ball Paul - You In Flames   (Thirsty Ear '94)

A solid alterno-rock offering not without charisma, **You In Flames** touches many bases, at times with exquisite tunefulness as on full-chord chargers *Like Swallows* and *Drip*, despite overdone J Mascis impersonations. But all too often the band goes for those artsy bass-driven mantras, like a less forceful Quicksand or Helmet. Nice, youthful college band tinge to the thing, like Smashing Pumpkins or more sensitive Nirvana something, these guys at least write sturdy songs, which should put them in good standing with all the hard alternative stuff swimming around in our over-addled music circuits.
Rating                                                    7

### The Smalls - Waste And Tragedy   (Cargo '95)

An amazing lost gem of Canuck rock, The Smalls hail from Taber, Alberta, not exactly a hotbed of the visceral, potent alt.metal The Smalls are steering. There's an undeniable stooped, relaxed cool about this record, most of **Waste And Tragedy** in fact sounding like heavy metal Meat Puppets, spiced with a slice of snapped-disciplined Jesus Lizard and NoMeansNo, all sent through a tight metal grinder, explosive but controlled like a Megadeth record! Highly innovative, textured, but firmly planted in metallic song structure, if that makes any sense, The Smalls dang near one of the most interesting bands I've heard in the past two years, driven by riffs that fuse the cerebral to the metallic with freshness way beyond the best of grunge. The criminal part is that this was such an indie thing, you'll probably never see it. Wot th' hell, I'll break with tradition and provide you with an address: Box 4375 Taber Alberta, T1G 2C8 (hopefully it's still active, or uh, call Cargo). And no, I don't know anybody in the band. It's just a fabulous mystery all 'round!
Rating                                                    9

### Smashed Gladys - Social Intercourse   (Elektra '88)

Glam glam glam with a poodle rock snare that goes for miles. Raspy female vocals strung o'er a sort of late '80s Kiss meets early Poison bubblegum metal. Thin layer of dirt like L.A. Guns, but no.
Rating                                                    2

### Smashing Pumpkins - Gish   (Caroline '91)

As Billy has quite cheekily observed, his Pumpkins were one of the first grunge bands. But not the first, Seattle still beating him to the punch on many fronts. However, **Gish** is good quality Nor'west music via Chicago, sounding a bit like a smudged Mother Love Bone or My Sister's Machine, lots of steamy Aero-de-

416

rived riffs rendered dirty and dangerous. And you gotta love those long-haired hippie shots, which do funny things with time, if you think about it. The macho-dishing stops occasionally for a ludespool, really messing with one's attempts to set volume levels. But of course, it all works fantabulously with 20/20 hindsight, don't it? Fact is, this is cleaner and less eccentric than the follow-up, even though it was one of those fish in the barrel nothing records for a mid-size label. One could tell Billy really cared, resulting in a record that is no amateur wank, one worth owning beyond affiliation with infinite stardom.
Rating                                                    7

## Smashing Pumpkins - Siamese Dream   (Virgin '93)

Finally trucking on back after '91's well-received **Gish**, Smashing Pumpkins play their sublime trump card with this major label premiere, a record that marries all the best elements of college band pop to a sobbing cataclysm of grunge riffs, surpassing fellow likeable Chicago band Urge Overkill, as choice guitar band from the midwest. **Siamese Dream** is a sneering, almost delicate but strangely anti-social pile of guitar goo, careening this way and that, rocking out, luding down, not unlike a less enraged version of Nirvana (**Nevermind**-era songs with **In Utero** crapsmanship). As much as these guys (plus one gal) hate being trendy, they are (and will become the definition), and there's nothing wrong with that, **Siamese Dream** being a nice wash of sounds, quite often mellow, but quite often jet-engined with a particularly Sab sort of guitar sound, even when trying to look sensitive. Headliners at '94's Lollapalooza. Pretty weak closer if you ask me, but oh so prophetic.
Rating                                                    7

## Smashing Pumpkins - Pisces Iscariot   (Virgin '95)

Corgan and his assembled freaks are a perfect marriage between low-fi and caring, laziness and creative explosion. So it's no surprise the band has such a surfeit of b-sides, out-takes and rarities, **Pisces Iscariot** definitely satisfying in its (actually the label's) aim to satiate a growing legion of fans until the next hard-won opus emerges. If it was a good idea for Nirvana, it should work here. Lots of tell-all notes detail the origins of each track, but what emerges is an admiration for Corgan's obsession to write songs, play songs, all over the rock idiom, to be a timeless tireless fan of much, addressing all domains with his skinny cool.
Rating                                                    7

## The Smashing Pumpkins - Mellon Collie And The Infinite Sadness   (Virgin '95)

Like this record's fabulously unapologetic title, The Smashing Pumpkins return like a brandished sword, spilling onto the salted earth a cornucopia of intense, personal visions that will baffle for years. First off, I'm a sucker for double albums, rarely taking the snooty view that a good editor would have whittled this down to a single. And with **Mellon Collie**, Corgan defies that editor, is already that editor, and has read those editors through **Physical Graffiti**, **Tusk**, **The River**, and break-my-head classic of them all, **London Calling**. So even though I don't agree with Corgan sequencing seven drippy, Bowie, Princey, bluesy, quiet thingies at the end of disc #2, I can't say the band has lapsed unarguably into filler anywhere on this strident, brave, relentlessly creative disc. **Mellon Collie** is a world unto itself, if you can accept Corgan's pencil-necked voice, the only record you need this year, spanning an expert, unique and viciously futuristic Sabbath through so many shades of Bowie, T. Rex and most things Nirvana ever did. Talk about a deep record, the hits thus far (*Zero, Bullet With Butterfly Wings* and *1979*) going many fiercely competitive '90s places, inviting us all to chomp into this gluttonous feast, at which time

we will find heavier 21st century grunge, delicate, looped and psychedelic 1974 soft rock, and a zoomy time-travel to all points in between, dark horse of a winner being the band's rhythm section and attendant warm, retro recording, which conspire to bracket these 28 individual flowers in a garden that can be enjoyed for years. No surprise that this record has racked up sales of six million, Smashing Pumpkins building a tower impossibly tall, a statement few bands have the energy or nutritional intake to topple. An accomplishment that almost repels with its hipness, **Mellon Collie** forces folks from all camps to gather and celebrate our similarities, despite our snobby guarding of our own micro-cultures. Tired ol' update story: Touring keyboardist Jonathan Melvoin OD'ed and died while doing heroin with drummer Jimmy Chamberlain in their hotel room in New York. Jimmy was turfed, Billy got pick-me-up advice from Gene Simmons, and the band juggered on. Jimmy is now working with Sebastian Bach in The Last Hard Men. Meanwhile, the Pumpkins released a nifty singles collection (in a vintage 45 RPM box). Expensive, not all that many songs by Pumpkin standards, but a cool cover of Alice Cooper's *Clones*.
Rating                                                   10

## Snail - All Channels Are Open . . . .   (Big Deal '94)

Five slurpy tracks of alterna-acid punk with melodies, verve and no verve, from a trio who definitely have fun chemicals on the brain. A whole record by these guys would be a slovenly pleasure I'm sure, possibly studded with a couple o' hits to turn Snail into surprise stars or sumthin'. Or maybe I'm just dreamy, but this is pretty cushy guitar goof pop worthy of your looksee. Hawkwind meets Nirvana in the lo-fi zone.
Rating                                                    7

## Snake - New Light   (Cain Est. '85)

Opening cut *Day Of Solution* quietly remarks that one day there will be less "foreign" groups and more German ones in the metal mags, a day when we'll sort the good from the bad. Maybe so, but Snake won't be there, 'cept maybe as roadies, their brand of powerless, southern rock-affected metal suffering from garage separation and a general clanky, chaotic oldness (can't find a year on it) that makes it more an unusual curio than an alloy to believe in. Too bad though, 'cos I could see a thoroughly re-performed, re-mixed version of this record becoming an embraceable "regular rocker" on my table in the same offhand way that the first Bodine has wended its way into my field of assimilation.
Rating                                                    5

## Snake Nation - Snake Nation   (Caroline '89)

Possibly the early germination of the present enigmatic, stigmatic Corrosion Of Conformity sound, Snake Nation is a power trio of which two-thirds is one-half of present-day COC, namely Woody Weatherman and Mike Dean. This record's got some legs even though it's a pretty cranky, loose and underground type of proto-grunge, stuck between Melvins, Soundgarden and Eyehategod. But it definitely recalls the subversive, volatile and spontaneous metal of COC now, who are quickly becoming one of my favourite bands. Nice to hear the trend line, although this is quite raw, oily and punked-out. A minor collectible anyways.
Rating                                                    6

## S.O.D. - Speak English Or Die   ('85)

A calamitous collaboration between early 'thrax dude Dan Lilker, Anthrax-like core meddler Billy Milano of M.O.D. and M.O.D.-like morality peddlers Anthrax themselves, Stormtroopers of Death is a whole heap of jarring fun, one or two minutes at a time, sometimes less, consisting of a long string of loudfast riff jokes including *Anti-Procrastination Song*, *What's That Noise?*, *The Ballad Of Jimi Hendrix*, *Milk* and *Chromatic Death*, the latter pair of which appeared re-encrusted on **Attack Of The Killer B's**. A true novelty record, but full of those great Anthrax dentist drills that made the band such a rush early on. Also indicative of the band's pre-fashion tendency to crossover into skatecore. AC's only conceivable predecessor.

Rating 6

## Sodom - Obsessed By Cruelty (Steamhammer '86)

Which about sums up this preposterous Teutonic thrash trio consisting of guys named Angel Ripper, Witchhunter and Destructor, competing steroidically to see who can create the largest meltatious wad of continuous, vile monodrone.

Rating 0

## Sodom - Persecution Mania (Steamhammer '87)

Stay the course. Still impossible, highly stressful thrashers lost at breakneck speed, actively repelling all reason to exist.

Rating 0

## Sodom - Agent Orange (Steamhammer '89)

Two slow ones. The rest . . . everybody polka! Classy fold-out artwork, wildly inappropriate for such useless crap. What a joke. Gives metal a bad name, steering away potential converts in droves.

Rating 0

## Sodom - Masquerade In Blood (Steamhammer '95)

Mr. Ed Balog really took me to task for my Sodom grades first time around, yet I stand by my earlier impressions, feeling exonerated somewhat by this band's blubbery adherence to delete bin thrash years later. But the title track kinda backswitches like Napalm Death as of late, and *Fields Of Honour* is a cogent enough Motörhead rip-off. Still a grating mess, but Sodom's ten-year-old sound is starting to sound so out, it's in! Missing (but not missing, if you get my drift): '88's **Mortal Way Of Life**, '90s's **Ausgebombt**, '91's **Better Off Dead** and '93's **Tapping The Vein**.

Rating 4

## Soho 69 - Scatterbrain (Hypnotic '93)

Reliable Canuck rocker Andy Curran (Coney Hatch, then a solo record) is back with his latest band concept Soho 69, an admirable brew of streethooks and broken hearts, Andy's '90s take on his favorite album of all time, Aerosmith's **Rocks**. Yea and verily, the Aerocompares are front and centre what with lots of rumbling drums, horns, harmonicas and vocals that achieve Steve like crazy, especially on *No More Promises* and touching glam ballad *Kiss My Boots*, the record's finest track. However, the dumbo blues of *Burn The House Down* just irritates me, standard beer commercial rock we hear all too often out of our native bands, and anything called *Voodoo Serpentine* doesn't even get off the ground, inane lyrically in a big way. And leave the scary *Kashmir* riff on *Stone Keeps On Rolling* to The Tea Party or sumthin'. But all in all, I like this one. Sure it's commercial, but it achieves its barroom ruckus well, especially on fast-tracker *Hippie Homicide* and the soaring bass-driven chorus of the title toon. The overall approach is loud and boomy, definitely influenced by the leader being the band bassist, and the pacing works, despite maybe too much of the material doing that blues metal thing that rarely sounds real.

Rating 7

## Soilent Green - Pussysoul (Dwell '94)

Soilent Green belch a sort of way underground thrash that incorporates a dose of punk and a lot of grind. That said, the evil bunch somehow make it musical in a truly ugly way, their methodology made even more putrid

by the fact that vocals approach that really hideous Norwegian/Obituary mewling sickness that can derail a wolverine's naturally optimistic disposition at fifty paces. Alas however, too much battered and dazed riffing going nowhere for the sake of inverting musicality. Count me repelled, reduced to tears, and somewhat confused.

Rating 5

## Solitude Aeturnus - Into The Depths Of Sorrow (Roadracer '91)

Writing this sort of well-assembled prog metal when it was so horribly out of fashion (things haven't improved much, but at least minds are open), earned these brooding battalions accolades amongst the metal press at the time. But as with all their records, it's the slow manic depressive drone of the thing that makes me run off and play the Bullet Boys. So you can't fault the massive musical movements here really. It's just me, I guess.

Rating 6

## Solitude Aeturnus - Beyond The Crimson Horizon (Roadracer '92)

Doomslab II for this Texas leviathan finds the band gaining focus, hatching a progressive excursion that is almost as close to early Fates Warning as it is to the new Sabbath-derived doom metal. Well-executed and soaringly sung (band trump card: vocalist Robert Lowe), **Crimson Horizon** is one grey-toned chunk of bombast from start to finish, which to my mind gets a little tiring. One thinks Candlemass, impatiently, but then again certain passages are not unlike old, cold Trouble.

Rating 6

## Solitude Aeturnus - Through The Darkest Hour (Pavement '94)

Solitude Aeturnus venture overseas to record this label-switched third, using Paul Johnston of Cathedral fame as producer. And the results are improved, heavier, more majestic, even if the band's meandering goth grooves may not be your cup of tea. Which is the crux of my experience with this widely appreciated band. I lose interest when it gets this spacey, depressing and belaboured, equating this with atmospheric downer doom like Memento Mori. Draws a blank, for the same reason so much mid-'80s medieval metal left me cold and damp.

Rating 7

## Solitude Aeturnus - Downfall (Pavement/BMG '96)

Styled somewhat as an "up yours" to the denigrators of true metal, **Downfall** belligerently courts '80s prog, sounding not unlike Trouble crossed with old Fates Warning. And many are liking this morose, yet somehow more accessible direction. Lyrically there's lots of psychological thrills, the werewolf track (*Midnight Dreams*) being particularly insightful, turned Cathedral-ish by a nice film excerpt intro. *Elysium* is quite the freaker too, just a bunch of guitar noise with a harrowing, old Alice Cooper-ized psycho vocal turned thespian. All in all, this is still mopey stuff, but the overall effect of dank metallic chill is most definitely achieved, Solitude Aeturnus taking the listener on a vivid trip into mysterium, commercial aspirations be damned.

Rating 7

## Solus - Slave Of Mind (SkinMask '96)

Fully studied and operational death metal from Toronto, Solus make a bee-line for crushing and obscure and just stay there, combining the looped possibility of Voivod, Grave, and Death with a gnashed teeth urgency, most complex tracks here driven by Darrell Dumas' jazzmetal percussion perfection into zones of rusted extremes. It all makes for a grim, dynamic

pummel, this four-piece quite sure of what makes grindcore tick, sending it all through a unique mash of riffs, dozens of influences subjugated then leaked like sewer water. Will Korbut's vocals straddle the line between treated rote grind and more organic human anguish, turning what could have been a pain into craven metal euphoria, or something like that. Progressive, evil, and almost completely void of blastbeats, which is just fine by me.
Rating                                                     8

## Sons Of Freedom - Sons Of Freedom   (Slash '88)
A single swinging light bulb: the perfect metaphor for the Sons' crystalline rhythms, and the band's only live prop to date. This massive debut record springs from the android mindspheres of Jim Newton and the three Dons (Harrison, Short and Binns), who comprise what is pretty much my favorite Canadian band ever. Vancouver's Sons Of Freedom carved a fresh deadly sound that is hard to nail and impossible to shake, an intense, bass-driven bludgeon that thrives on repetition and intensification over time, words being secondary to the tortuous throb (check out the lyrics to intro stomp *Super Cool Wagon*), a throb that parks its ass and spreads. A record that is a strange and psychologically harrowing expedition indeed, **Sons Of Freedom** wins through dynamic, holding back then cresting (witness *Mona Lisa*'s hyper close), creating a backdrop of craggy, rock solid uncertainty, a path tried, true and chartable, yet totally unpursued anywhere in the annals of rock. In fact the only comparative I can think of would be the *spirit* or the *essence* of Nirvana's **Bleach**, yet not really its sound. Riffs just drone on, unbending, unapologetic, over and over and over like Chinese water torture, until will is broken and submission complete. Classics are everywhere: *Is It Love* tattooed with a discordant stun riff that becomes imprinted indelibly on one's frontal lobes, *Dead Dog On The Highway*, a rubber band that stretches to infinity, end of story, and *This Is Tao*, something like a sublime drift onto an open ocean oil slick. All compositions work a similar sort of hypnosis, each at its own speed and texture, all courting disaster and inevitable chaos that arrives calmly with resigned expectation. Tragically ignored, even though I'm positive the Sons' surroundsound could have struck it big given some exposure. Where were the majors?
Rating                                                    10

## Sons Of Freedom - Gump   (Chrysalis '91)
After one of the most paralyzing debuts of all time, the Sons tour their faces off (saw 'em six times) then vacate the place leaving only ringing ears and stunned vacant stares. Then alas, comes the sideways lope of **Gump**, a dire disappointment I've come to enjoy. **Gump** is the accessible pop face of the Sons' killer sound, main point after the initial shock being that it is still very much the Sons' patented distorto-bass minimalism, despite the wacky, nutty and fabulous courting of pop foibles that overlies the underlying urge to implode skulls through volcanic rumbles. But lead track *You're No Good* buys none of this, being **Gump**'s pit viper, a riffmonster perfectly in tune with the debut's catatonic mystique, all massive rhythms and strategic shelling, one of the band's righteous invasions. However *Dreamgirl* (two versions on this short album: shame on you, guys) and *Call Me* are downright dancefloored, whereas other constructs like *Circle Circle*, *Jesus And Jim*, and cryogenic ballad *I Can See* are just so cut and dried, filleted and gutted, their sturdy frames contain nothing but bloody, still beating hearts. Some of these tracks have been played for ages (*USA Long Distance*), and judging from the lull before and (so far) after **Gump**, not to mention the record's brevity, frankly I'm worried about the Sons' lack of productivity, reminding me of Slayer's admission of just how hard they found it putting together records. Here, one feels the stress of having to

live up to one's critical billing, as the boys make a record that is so laid bare and fragile (or void) of arrangement, that you wonder how it doesn't starve to death. But **Gump**'s a weird little contraption ya just gotta love for its simple bruising quality despite songs that are almost melodic, almost friendly. **Gump** definitely lands itself in that "misunderstood" category, a work that marries a band that is a rhythm section first and foremost, to songs that try to do the four or five things songs are supposed to do, a very different strategy than first time around. However, a band this nuts (and even with the scads of wild alternative acts everywhere, nobody's duplicated the Sons' particular bite) can't help but elicit gawks and dropped jaws, no matter the commercial suggestions **Gump** embodies. A landmark sound hopefully not forgotten, even if the Sons eventually ended up throwing in the towel in blank frustration
Rating                                                     9

## Sons Of Freedom - Tex   (Divine '95)
Basscrape the boombox and hide the corrosives, the Sons are back and blue, stun guitars in hand, tentatively willing to give us the fickle public another kick at a rock combo that five years back was Canada's most original chunk of amplified custard pie, this nation's hippest rock citizens, really our greatest band. Forget that **Tex** is demos and b-sides shit, this record being fortified, fresh-stung Sons, cavernous bass, explicitly-carved grooves and in reality, 10/16 as new or newer than their **Gump** swanhowl, all of it as cleanly produced as the band's other earthquaking material, even if most of **Tex** is considered "demo". And it's hellaciously more pummel-precious to boot, Jim's suave, sometimes on-key croon lacing black sheets of alcohollow apathy over a rhythm section that is shuddering astonishment. Walking, talking Cool, although it does bother me that the more impressively denting pieces are the tracks from the late '80s.
Rating                                                     9

## Sons Of Otis - Spacejumbofudge   (Hypnotic '96)
If Monster Magnet and Kyuss just didn't seem to go far enough for you, carve into the fudge that is this bud-luvin' Toronto trio's gruesome debut. **Spacejumbo-fudge** takes gluey, chewy drug metal past songs into a type of bulldozed ambient, for indeed there are no printed lyrics, and what passed for vocals (a sort of phase-shifted, backwardsy, sub-audible mumble), just seem to drift into the boiling oil and then drift on out, no plan, no point. Indeed after a few dirges from a place Wyndorf or Hawkwind wouldn't dare go, comes track six, *Big Muff*, which is ten minutes of quiet guitar sound effects, right in the middle of the record, just to trip you out as the acid kicks in. It's cool that this kind of caved-in post-Sabbath psycho-rock exists, but this may just go too far, sub-quaking into terrain that is uncommercial by almost any measure. Love them drums though, which are a formidable woofer test at even moderate volume levels. Afraid to say I respect the lack of compromise, but I'll probably reach for Fu Manchu (released the same month), when in this kind of turgid metal melt. I mean, it's practically instrumental, and by nature, not too actively instrumental at that. Note: debut EP called **Paid To Suffer** released in '92. Even dirtier.
Rating                                                     6

## Soothsayer - Have A Good Time   (New Renaissance '90)
Quebec's always been a hotbed of thrash, making it and buying it with alarming frequency, also apparently all over Sony's Earache product with appreciable gusto. Soothsayer fit the bill, adding a sense of humour, good production, and multiple speeds to a trashy vibe

I basically find worthless. Good at their monstrous game.

Rating 5

## Sortilège - Metamorphosis (Banzai '84)

May as well be from France, because it don't sound like anything from previously explored metal planets. Indeed, **Metamorphosis** was an awe-inspiring feast, movingly rhythmic and forward thrusting despite scattered jarrings of odd time signatures and other tricky quick changes. Just zero humour, zero diversion from purity, and zero feelings of any constructive type, **Metamorphosis** freezes the listener in an ever-darkening vortex, wound tightly around the twin cave sounds of axemen Dem and Dumont. Emotionally, this record surfaces no farther than the legendary **Sad Wings Of Destiny**, looming equally archaic, desperate, wickedly intelligent and mad; rife with the same time-defying universalities as the Sabbath before and the Maiden to follow. Tragic in that the follow-up seemed the work of a band dispossessed and scrambling, **Metamorphosis** wells up with sorrow through a combination of poisonous, metallic glides such as *Majesty*, frightful, down-trodden dirges like *Delirium Of A Madman*, and killer progressive maelstroms like *Cyclopes Of The Lake*. And through it all, performances simply swirl, from the bleeding, operatic pipes of Christian Augustin, through the slamming science of percussionist extraordinaire Bob Snake, who gets more than a little help from his soundman. A masterpiece of classical metal, painstakingly made effortless, in the grand tradition of serious art.

Rating 10

## Sortilège - Hero's Tears (Steamhammer '85)

Curious release is this one; which barely resembles the rhythmic storm that was the vaulted and slamming **Metamorphosis**. **Hero's Tears** shakes this popular French band's penchant for old Priest-style alchemy, watering it down to a loose and tinny shell of a power that once cried with violent alienation. Christian Augustin's first class wail is still in place, but structures get too sloppy and gothic, possessing nary the shake of **Metamorphosis'** singular drive. Almost like the difference between good Queensryche and bad Queensryche. Disappointing, because this was one French band that seemed to bring unique qualities to the table that one might easily chalk up to their foreignness. All in all, too lumbering, ponderous and clattery production-wise, all of the above faults evidenced quite depressingly on side two's *Fight The Dragon*, a dulled maze of aimless proportions. Mere dimestore goth surprisingly often, with no help from the production acumen afforded its predecessor.

Rating 5

## Soul Asylum - Say What You Will . . . (Twin Tone '84)

Minneapolis' scruff rockers Soul Asylum crashed onto the scene plaid-clad and angry with this nine cut, 25 minute mini-album, punk-proudly produced by like-minded local Bob Mould. More a strange, noise-making guitar band than punk or hardcore or new wave or metal, Soul Asylum carved a tough street-level sonic chaos similar to that of mid to late Dü or early Replacements, less defined than the former, more so than the latter. **Say What You Will** . . . shakes and shimmies rudely with who-gives-a-shit abandon, stumbling through eccentric noisefests that skirt jazz, lounge, country, metal and hardcore, while retaining control of their burning ship, sticking to their beat-up axes despite supposed requirements of the style ceremoniously butchered. Mostly farm team versions of stupendous and blazing **Made To Be Broken** and **While You Were Out** actualities, **Say What You Will**

. . . is still a belligerent mess, perfect for that chemical confusion between Mexican beers four and six.

Rating 7

## Soul Asylum - Made To Be Broken (Twin Tone '86)

Get it? It's a record. Again produced by Bob Mould, **Made To Be Broken** is Soul Asylum's closest relation to Hüsker Dü, sonically set by Bob and accommodatingly written by front Soul Dave Pirner. Melodic power punk throughout, this album displays the band's greater depth, wrapping its white noise around aggressive but progressive rock structures, coolest being country-tinged directives both blast-off (title cut), and reflectively subtle (*Never Really Been*). To the band's righteous credit, **Made To Be Broken** marks the point where the boys begin to edge away from their heavy competition, Hüsker Dü, whose samey brilliance is nevertheless still brilliance, and The Replacements, again all 10's in my books, but getting a touch melodramatic. Of the three, Soul Asylum just continues to give 'er flat out no matter how tricky the terrain gets; here most obvious on killer contusions like *Growing Pain* and awesome metallic apocalypse *Don't It*. Throughout, it's just guts all over the floor, as the band just storms through the wild mid-west, creating their own searing marriage of crashed chaos and scientific discipline in their wake. Soul Asylum is what happens when the cerebral but vicious from the fringes embrace the tools of metal while discarding the neanderthal mindsets that often come with those raised within the metal framework, a situation which spawned many an enigma in the early '90s.

Rating 10

## Soul Asylum - Time's Incinerator (Twin Tone '86)

Deathly against the cassette format, I nevertheless had no hesitation in snafu-ing this cassette-only compilation of twenty short 'n' wasted snappers from Soul Asylum's goofball past. Comprising mostly punky one-offs, amusing covers, and the odd interview from '81-'86, **Time's Incinerator** is mostly an imploded shambles of chaotic wisecracking punk akin to The Replacements' **Sorry Ma, Forgot To Take Out The Trash**. I mean geez, judging from this, they were once practically the same band. The liner notes qualify the proceeds stating that "this is more where the band is coming from than where the band is going", and how true it is, 'cos fact is, from record one, Soul Asylum assumed a position of quality, despite their chosen field of waste-case mayhem. As a result, this sounds pretty slapped down in comparison to official product, but it's still a good time, being for the most part adequately recorded and full of flipped-out punk splatter. Highlights: the three **Made To Be Broken** out-takes (naturally so, being the newest romps), plus '81's Ramonesy *Nowhere To Go*.

Rating 6

## Soul Asylum - While You Were Out (Twin Tone '86)

If **Hang Time** represents Soul Asylum's most accessibly metallic moment, **While You Were Out** is surely the most violent, careening through brutal punk landscapes with a ferocious growl like no other Asylum project. Again, fairly Dü-like in terms of buoyant, absolutely wondrous riff patterns, but again, there's more of a sense of exploration and adventure than with the Hüskers' particular winning formula. Opening cut *Freaks* swells to a deafening roar, reminding me of my concerns for my hearing while being mercilessly mowed down at one of the band's outpouring of emotional brilliance at triple figure decibel readings. And the cardiac mayhem continues unabated, with *Carry On* right through this rousing caustic feast of distortion and introspective power. At this point, a mischievous, more ambitious version of Hüsker Dü, not content with the backseat, boiling with greater intensity as it speeds from one slashing riff to the next. The perfect alloy of attitude and axes looking for the deepest truths within rock'n'roll's soul, just like Aerosmith and the Stones before.

Rating 10

## Soul Asylum - Clam Dip And Other Delights
(Twin Tone '88)

A fully amazing gut-level six track EP by one of the coolest bands in the world, **Clam Dip** is a pounding stop gap between ethereal slams. Perhaps taking cue from **Pleased To Meet Me**'s and **London Calling**'s faithful revitalizations of Elvis album covers, Soul Asylum does them both one better with this side-splittingly accurate lifting of Herb Alpert's Tijuana Brass' **Whipped Cream And Other Delights**, which I just had to buy as **Clam Dip**'s hilarious companion piece. But the groovy punk metal is anything but a copy of Herb's suave love tunes, crunching largely on metal classics *Artificial Heart* and one of the band's most awesome dinosaurs *Just Plain Evil*. Elsewhere, we get bluegrass stomp *P-9*, pop punkster *Chains*, metalized funker *Take It To The Root* (four years old at this point), and melodi-cruiser *Secret No More*. Rolling rough-shod over a crackling strong mix, **Clam Dip** is just more variously skewed muscle rock brilliance from the most righteous of the Minneapolis big three. Note: in a strange twist of fate, Alpert would become the band's ultimate boss with their ill-advised move to A&M.

Rating 9

## Soul Asylum - Hang Time   (A&M '88)

Soul Asylum's grandest work, **Hang Time**, caught flak for being a bit too clever and professional. Nothing wrong with that in my books, as this record absolutely pounds despite the cool axe showmanship and surprise arrangements. **Hang Time** kicks off with one of the band's most burning hunks of steel, *Down On Up To Me*, continuing to bleed all over the monitors on such wildly riffic strangulations as *Ode* and album closer *Heavy Rotation*, a whipped feast that builds to a breakneck harmony demonstrating the band's singular ability to write the most heroic of guitar rocks. Elsewhere, three or four glorious Dü-like jet streams, *Marionette*, an English kinda thing similar to *Victoria* by The Kinks, and *Twiddly Dee*, an acoustic sorta jig into the band's regularly plundered countrified bag of tricks, all recorded with a loving live grit by Lenny Kaye and Ed Stasium, who show an immediate understanding of the Asylum's huge and mythic spinning whipsaw.

Rating 10

## Soul Asylum - And The Horse They Rode In On
(A&M '90)

If the stage is one half of a band's persona, Soul Asylum haven't lost their edge. I caught the T.O. leg of this record's tour and it was one of the loudest, cleanest six-string love-ins I've ever been subjected to; the band veritably crushing the crowd with massively heroic renditions from all corners of their esteemed career, finally blowing out the place with a killer accelerated tear through ZZ Top's *Move Me On Down The Line*. Having been wrecked by the band's on-stage power somewhat softened my disappointment at the band's newly close, softened, simplified, yet still completely guitar-based sound. First off, this record is plain incredible despite the axiom shift, which takes the band more towards the loud humanity of heavier mid-years Replacements, than was evident on the tough-as-nails metallicisms of **Hang Time**. And for the first time, I don't like the mix, primarily the blocky snare sound, also finding the instrumental separation too pronounced for the new-found, less busy, garage sensibility. Almost as if the band is downplaying their greatness, compositions are understated, undergunned, and even more various than on past efforts

which swung wildly yet somehow ended up back in the same mosh pits. Here, a new seriousness, a subdued glimpse at getting older, maybe wiser or just more jaded, seems to be causing a shift to commerciality, either voluntarily or by force. *Easy Street*, *Veil Of Tears* and especially *Grounded* and Murphy's *Gullible's Travels* represent a new mellowness which I guess can be more welcome than reviled depending on your reasons for visiting the Asylum. Thoroughly appreciating this record, I for one would still rather blast **Hang Time** or this album's *All The King's Friends* through my phones, but then again **Give 'Em Enough Rope** was my favorite Clash album.

Rating 9

## Soul Asylum - Grave Dancers Union   (Sony '92)

The last breathing bastion of the Minneapolis sound comes ambling back, despite a continuing lack of commercial recognition from a public not used to such honesty in art. **Grave Dancers Union** offers greater urgency, ominous clouding, and mud through a mid-rangy mix, while Pirner steers the ship into heroic guitar rock, even more pointedly close to The Replacements than its predecessor, an album philosophically close to this one, yet comparatively lacking in mission. Yup, from one angle, this is a magnificent Placemats record, but for all its neck and neck observations with Westerberg, Soul Asylum keeps its intellectual lead with greater musical chops, imagination and daring, with such open-minded rockers as lead cut *Somebody To Shove* and the old-feel *Get On Out*. And balancing the larger proportion of acoustic rock comes thud rockers like *April Fool* and the sinister *99%*, both iced with squirming Pirner vocals that keep the Asylum sounding eccentric and dark. As I grow out of "intellectual" college-type rock and generally all things sensitive (contrary to what at 20, we thought would occur), I'm enjoying the fact that Soul Asylum escapes such a doomed tag, which taints probably a good 150 records in my collection picked up in my university years. Rockers rule, and despite the gobs of melody on **Grave Dancers Union**, Soul Asylum mentally mental mental rockers to the core. Update: After rare lukewarm critical response for the band, **Grave Dancer's Union** has gone platinum, blowing away its predecessor's sales fifteen fold and just gaining steam. Soul Asylum is the new pop sensation.

Rating 9

## Soul Asylum - Insomniac's Dream   (Sony '94)

Now that Pirner and his shaggy locks are the voice and follicles of a generation, one can almost understand such a strange "sell-out" sort of thing like a crass Unplugged project. But really, the man and the band are leaning acoustic anyways, so these fine fireside renditions are in the pocket and comfy warm, despite that opportunistic waftation of cash-in permeating the jam session. Six tracks, 22 minutes, kinda why? Why is 'cos they're awesome songwriters. Highlight: *Stranger* from the crusty debut.

Rating 7

## Soul Asylum - Let Your Dim Light Shine   (Sony '95)

Once the big hype machine cranked, the fairly discerning throngs of Soul Asylum fans began to harbour suspicions. And suspicions were confirmed once the record corporately slimed into view, Pirner indulging wholesale in his softer side, his roots rock Jayhawk, his Victoria Williams feminine side, perhaps that trip to the Grammys with Winona snuffing the last bit of punk the guy had left. This band's shattering shafts of truth were always many, but they occured and announced because there was a considerable amount of noise from which to break and daisy-dance. Well, **Dim Light** is all daisies and fragrant meadows of chewy grass, bottom line: too mellow, melodramatic, radio-friendly and just

plain over-ingratiating, from the Soul sell-out of *Misery*, to the bewildering bad taste of *String Of Pearls*, even the album cover reviving and coddling the same money greens of the band's break-thru predecessor. I dunno, just way too much of what I always liked about these guys, caving in the whole concept to something churlish, exposing Pirner as actually not that smart after all. And just as fast as Soul Asylum became stars, fans smelled a stinker, turning the record into a comparitive stiff, even Wynona dropping ol' Dave like a hot potato.
Rating                                                                 7

## Soulhat - Good To Be Gone  (Sony '94)

Mixing big fat rolling rock metal funksters with droopy quiet jams, Austin's Soulhat show promise with their unwieldy retro, yet leave me unmoved, given the vast array of crankin' tunes out there to be had. Sadly it often comes to that: too many sounds, not enough time, little things like not printing the lyrics obscuring my view of the band's thoughts, hindering my attempts to get to know the band. And thus, this one will probably fade in my memory banks, despite the goodly quantity of big rhythmic '70s metal (via short-haired, professional alterno-rock-looking guys) all over this, sorta crossing grunge with the Black Crowes, with vocals that sound like World Party's Karl Wallinger. Kinda hippy, kinda psychedelic, definitely "alternative", but not meandering too far from excitement, **Good To Be Gone** could have used a minor tightening up, although on another day, I just might have really glued myself to this one. Update: that annoying *Bone Crusher* tune's become a hit.
Rating                                                                 7

## Soul Kitchen - Soul Kitchen  (Giant '92)

Soul Kitchen manages to cross the line from commercial sleaze metal into something with a little more integrity, something closer to roots rock or southern rock. Singer Jeff Wilson sounds like Janis Joplin half the time (I actually had to check that it was a guy), and the band seems to be content playing third-rate Black Crowes, which is much preferred to (and less common than) third-rate Poison or Slaughter. Of course they look pretty much like Slaughter, but let's excuse that and briefly revel in this hopelessly synthetic, shiny bright rendition of Skynyrd for the '90s (pause, hum along). OK, move on, I didn't really buy it either.
Rating                                                                 6

## Soulquake System - Angry By Nature Ugly By Choice  (Black Mark '96)

Soulquake System deliver a grim, serious, squared-off, smarmy artcore that borrows equal parts Meshuggah and hardcore punk (especially those annoying vocals). Into the brew are chucked screaming and writhing, riffs of stark metallic beauty, even if songs seem to be secondary. So what emerges is a very successful exercise in new metal thinking, but a prototype all the same, perhaps the only constant being a Biohazardous rap metal pound that lopes down the middle of the band's challenging ideas. As is usual with Black Mark signings, a high level of quality is achieved (drummer Henrik Bergstrom is wicked), but the final braying contraption leaves me both impressed and cold.
Rating                                                                 7

## Souls At Zero - Souls At Zero  (Energy '93)

Formerly Wrathchild America, Souls At Zero take a hot grunge injection between the temples, scorching off a couple of heads o' hair in the Stone Temple Process. And where Souls At Zero arrives is at a techno-thrash sound between Corrosion Of Conformity's subterranean Sabbath sobs and Pantera's precision marksmanship, with a greasy Seattle burger thrown in for good measure, to go along with the new, clever band moniker. At this point it's a hell of a spread,

almost too much to absorb, mega-tight playing purposely loosened, complexity dragged through the gutter, cutting edge but over-extended '90s metal comprising a record that is almost too long for its own good, masking identity in a myriad of hyper-tense riffs. **Souls At Zero** is one of those labour-intensive spins to which pleasure matches effort, gain for gain. But unlike other difficult, opaque records like, say **Space In Your Face** from Galactic Cowboys, your efforts may end with a realization that this is too angular, too squarely metallic, too uniformly stressful, too freeze-dried with a nervous, '90s kind of gloom. Swing that hammer, break those rocks.
Rating                                                                 7

## Souls At Zero - six-t-six  (Energy '94)

Short (22 minute) six track stopgap EP that nevertheless offers good value, given that none of the tracks are on the band's two albums ('cept *Hardline* here in demo form). Still, something bugs me about this act, something vaguely sell-out-ish with those street-level Pantera/Metallica riffs and requisite angsty vocals. Spirited cover of *I Against I* by fellow DC-area rasta thrashers Bad Brains.
Rating                                                                 6

## Souls At Zero - A Taste For The Perverse  (Energy '95)

These guys always served up the meat raw and quiver-fleshed when they were Wrathchild. Then the name change came, and the boys got copiously urban metal grunge short-shorn angry. Well, record II's arrived and SAZ aim once again for that rhythmic stop/go metal niche relentlessly pummeled by Helmet, Biohazard, Pro-Pain, Killers and Prong. Given the high quality of this creative corner of our beloved hard music realm, SAZ stand as equals but no higher, adding a bracing, Pantera-esque hooveraxe sound to their aggro-slam, while sounding much like an average of these bands vocally. Nevertheless, if pounding alternative is your poison, this is a fine example of such urban angst.
Rating                                                                 7

## Soul Tattoo - Transcend  (Socan '94)

Weirdly engaging, this one, a record with a butt-ugly cover, and some of the best psychedelically tainted lyrics I've seen in awhile, establishing Ottawa's Soul Tattoo as one of those acts in a vacuum, insulated from influences, definitely invoking the term underground. Hard to pin **Transcend**. Suffice to say it's a sort of smeary rhythmic grunge, but fairly upbeat while dirty, thick and funky with slap bass and smatters of horns, plus odd, warbly vocals from one Matt Minter. I think of bands like Last Crack or I Love You or more so Liquid Jesus, although this one ain't quite as mesmerizing as either three, while aspiring to those band's sincere and vital creativity levels just the same. Foggy, intelligent stuff. fave: soul-crazy ballad *Breath*.
Rating                                                                 7

## Sound Barrier - Speed Of Light  (Metal Blade '86)

Distinguishable for two reasons: 1) Sound Barrier were headbangers of the negro persuasion; purely committed to metal, a kick-ass precursor to the scant number of black rockers even to this day years later; 2) the band really had their chops together, not to mention songwriting skills; real contenders for big success, if not for the unjust novelty element afforded their skin colour. However, **Speed Of Light** can't entirely shake the shackles of '80s cliché and general "heavier than thou" ego flash amidst trash, yet it was easily top quartile at the time, sounding like a hot Virgin Steele, Priest or a pumped Q5, fast and techy, but too obsessed with the trappings of '80s metallic baggage. Too bad, Sound Barrier was definitely a band ahead of their time. Missing: '83's **Total Control** and '84's **Born To Rock**.
Rating                                                                 6

## Soundgarden - Screaming Life (Sub Pop '87)

A critically crucial piece of the Seattle sound puzzle, Soundgarden's **Screaming Life** EP became a floating platform on which to hang descriptives out to dry, as a small gathering of onlookers squirmed to grasp and articulate these enigmatic rumblings staggering out from under the rain-filled thunderheads of Seattle. **Screaming Life** is a volatile mixture of Zeppelin, Sabbath, garage rock and art rock, twisted into an undisciplined, lurching mess of dementia, like a scrapyard dance of whirling fenders. Chris Cornell does his best to keep the vocal portion of the show as ambiguous as the jagged slashing from the agonized guitars and irregular drum patterns, howling above complicated noise mantras that alternately rock out and lapse into coma. The beauty that falls out is one of turgid, messy vegetation, like a jungle (Nietzsche's jungle), alive with both motion and stillness. My fave Soundgarden slab until **Badmotorfinger**, for its sludgy desperation and consistency (easier to manage granted, over only six tracks). Still, the most daring and creative of early grunge rock documents. CD reisssue includes '88's **Fopp** EP: Mudhoney-dewed imp rocker *Kingdom Of Come*, Green River's *Swallow My Pride*, the stiff title track, and a double-length *Fopp (Dub)*. More sub par than Sub Pop.
Rating                                    9

## Soundgarden - Ultramega OK (SST '88)

Soundgarden creep out to the edges of town for another machine head powwow, honing their wormy craft, achieving mass nirvana in a number of rusted cages, again heaping tangles of old metal, old punk and new punk sent through a psycho-delic grinder. Fave raves are the adrenalizers like *Flower*, *All Your Lies* and *Head Injury*, all drastic plastic classics that break all the house rules, blurring musical distinctions like gasoline on a Picasso. Soundgarden were quickly becoming the quintessential Seattle force, everywhere weirdos with heavy artillery and no instructions, ready to crash its car to create random new sculptures of steel. Ultimately **Ultramega OK** resonates as an animal untamed, in no particular hurry to leave its kill. Join in the feast.
Rating                                    9

## Soundgarden - Louder Than Love (A&M '89)

**Louder Than Love** gleans the wondrous eccentricities from out of the Soundgarden stew for a rubber hammer of a sound that finds the band paralyzed in the headlights of their darkest Sabbath/Zep permutations. What wafts from the big black cylinder is an evil smog that slows the processing centres of instrumentalist and spectator alike, rendering the record curmudgeonly and weathered. The swamp swami of the colourful Soundgarden story thus far, **Louder Than Love** is the storehouse of riffs, the scrapheap of big stone-carved guitars, a uniform and loping hippodrone that threatens to cover Cornell's snakey sermons in dust and rubble. Zep without the blues, contorted and char-broiled, becomes Sabbath, and **Louder Than Love** is Soundgarden without the blues for the first time, in essence a limiting record despite its daunting rhythmic explorations, one that plays too close to the vest, too tight and faithful to external perceptions of what the band should be, and too damn slow! A record restrained, **Louder Than Love** is both brains and brawn, while not nearly enough bite or bile.
Rating                                    7

## Soundgarden - Badmotorfinger (A&M '91)

The baddest of the bad are back in control of the bridge, S.S. Soundgarden off to new three-eyed worlds, propelled by new energies which cast off the same clouds of poisonous black exhaust fumes which soiled the skies around the lethargic **Louder Than**

**Love**. Only now, messengers Cornell, Thayil, Cameron and Shepherd burn with a new urgency, carving riffs into the minds of onlookers rather than letting them wiggle around like tadpoles in acid-laced pickle jars. Standout exercises include *Rusty Cage* (which makes me think *Toys In The Attic* for some strange reason) and deathly lead single *Jesus Christ Pose*, the band's most laser-like blazeking, where everything swirls with architect-directed scientific mega-rhythms, Thayil's riffs exposing the dark, horned side of New Age. Everything is tight and silvery on **Badmotorfinger**, but the band's incestuous bass-stratified chaos remains intact, the boys' Generation X interpretations of old Iommi thought patterns leaking through the wreckage, slowing compositions to a dull but persistent thud, infected with the usual array of shredded time signatures. Like **Louder Than Love**, there's almost too much to assimilate, but here you want to eat, even if it means throwing up later. Cleaner than chief rival **Dirt**, but only because of the twinge of hope in Cornell's chords, and the band's artsy intelligence.
Rating                                    9

## Soundgarden - Superunknown (A&M '94)

Seattle's brightest and most esteemed rock combo triumph by chilling, relaxing, stretching and caring less about snazzy structure, more about shambling their gluey mess in the spirit of inverted metal madness. It is a beautiful thing, this swampy sculpture of peaks and valleys, a Seattle sounder full of wicked weirdness, darkness revealed and most invitingly, lush, memorable melody, come a trio of smash singles in *Fell On Black Days*, *Black Hole Sun* and classic fer life *The Day I Tried To Live*. Cornell's vocals are the most versatile and gifted on the planet, welling from a bluesy croon to his patented cheetah cry often repeatedly within the same song, while Kim Thayil chimes and bangs right along with his healthy work ethic and credo, one which requires him to constantly re-work ways of being heavy. *Spoonman* was a strange first choice for single, kind of a basher, but seriously, who hasn't had this one stuck to the roof of their mouth for days? Other rockers are equally catchy, while working within tough time signatures and ironically elastic instrumental slashings. But then *Superunknown* just buzzes along, while *Kickstand* shortens up for a rare galloping punk romp. Sure there's dull melted filler, but these leaden respites work towards highlighting all the great songs scattered throughout the sprawl. And that's really the rub. This one works for its flaws and its unabashed fallibility, amazingly mature hooks rising from the usual Sabbath-on-valium mud, an incredible array of freaky stylies flopping like an exuberant fish on the decks of your sorry life. The ultimate tribute is this: the record is crammed with integrity, and the record just will not leave your thoughts, indeed in practice, making repeated assaults on the charts, sinking, rising, sticking, addicting. Probably the most glowingly revered band in hard music these days, questionable live gigs excepted.
Rating                                   10

## Soundgarden - Down On The Upside (A&M '96)

Don't like the Zeppish title or the cover art, but that's where the creative coasting ends, Soundgarden returning with another fantabulously baffling set of permutations on what rock can be. Pre-release buzz spoke of how the band had to self-produce because nobody wanted to put their name to such a dirty caterwaul of crumbled distortion. Well, the record sounds fine, if a little more Bonham-distressed than **Superunknown**, a bit more bashed in the noggin with bass machine heads, defiant but decipherable all the same. The first thing one notices about the record is that despite its breath-taking ambition (sixteen tracks

**423**

of heavy work), the band's big, beautiful balladry that formed a trinity of hits last time around is conspicuously extinguished, save for droopy Oasis-like loser *Blow Up The Outside World*, half-hearted attempt at low volume *Boot Camp* and bluesy screwy trick gungster *Zero Chance*, none of which even try to break into overt melody. Dissecting the record (and man, these guys don't deserve it), low points would have to be the three long, garagey blues contraptions, the new thudly production combining with the band's belligerent anti-social side to form these noisy descents into unpleasantry. But lead single *Pretty Noose* is formidably infectious, as is the podunk (*Hot Dog!*) punk of *Ty Cobb*. Lone Kim Thayil sculpture (lyrics and music) *Never The Machine Forever* is predictably a supercool crunch rocker, however drummer Matt Cameron steals the show, turning in one awesome progressive rhythm, as he does to a lesser extent on three or four other tracks here, the band as a whole in genius convoluted grunge mode for much of this long, extremely smart, musically tricky record (destined to be the smartest smash hit album in years; since **Superunknown** to be exact). Even the punk this time around sports white-knuckle chord changes that graft Mudhoney to King Crimson like no other org. could ever hope to attain. I suspect any derogatory grumblings one might have heard about this record derive from the fact that there is just so much creative grist to digest, Cornell and crew avalanching the listener with a challenge to join them at the frontlines, even as they become more eccentric, visceral, confusing and noisy. Total respect must flow.
Rating　9

### Southgang - Group Therapy　(Charisma '92)
Essentially sassy, southern party metal from Atlanta, **Group Therapy** evokes an equally vivacious, somewhat bluesier and nuttier version of Slaughter, leaning Motley, leaning towards Junkyard, leaning heavily on the bar for a couple of quick firewaters before last call. Hatched just before the demise of poodle rock, this one fizzled but quick, no fault of the decent enough heavy AOR enclosed. One can't really say unequivocably that Southgang's all-American fare is better done elsewhere. The problem is that the genre has been driven into the ground by way too many bands that are roughly this band's equal.
Rating　6

### Spade Ghetto Destruction - Spade Ghetto Destruction　(BMG '94)
Spade Ghetto Destruction ride a jiving jolt of slow-burning gangsta metal, a sound that becomes fairly unique, given the low weighty hum of most tracks enclosed. Down-pocket compared to Body Count or Rage Against The Machine or even Living Colour, this one's closer to Rollins' latest, open, bass-exposed and stroll funky, almost jammy and nicely ancient sounding. Lyrics bark out hard-won wisdoms of South Central L.A., with greater introspection than other rapcore shock artists, even more hope, making this one warmer, and not just because of those big ol' drums and guitars. A bit angular and lacking in melody, SGD is a bit of an elephantine trash-about, but if that gluey groovy gangsta type thing characteristic of Rollins' *Disconnect* or *Liar* is your malt liquor, then by all means pack this piece.
Rating　7

### Spartan Warrior - Steel n' Chains　(Guardian '83)
One speed, one chord blunders from deep beneath the British pub circuit who sustain a machine-like mediocre dragonslayer drone throughout our stay, but offer nothing to rescue said slab from cash-in city. Kennel rock.
Rating　3

### Spartan Warrior - Spartan Warrior　(Roadrunner '84)
Stealing and subsequently botching riffs from everywhere, the Warrior and their whiny lead throat walk us through another bang-by-numbers chunk that captures a trace of Euro-suicide à la Gravestone but still gets relegated to the scrap heap of one-time spinners.
Rating　4

### Speedball - Do Unto Others Then Split　(Energy '95)
Crunchy street-heated scuz metal like this existed ten years ago, but the passage of time has added a sly hipness to dirtball biker rock, and these guys turn up the party with no apologies needed. A bit o' grunge, punk, a hint of psychobilly and lots of Detroit drag-racing heritage go into the making of **Do Unto Others**, a record that leaps from track to abrasive track with the conquer factor of old Ted Nugent. I guess it's dangerously close to deleted stuff like Dangerous Toys, Junkyard and Sea Hags, yet the record somehow stands fresh and defiant, due to the fact that few bands want to be in this ring. Hey, someone's gotta eat huge steaks, drink tall ones and belch competitively. Well, like, this is the soundtrack album.
Rating　7

### Speedball - Drive Like Hell　(Energy '96)
Covertly but with volume, Speedball are making the shift from lusty biker metal to potent long-haired punk, this head-bashing EP peeling out, beercans a' flyin', four new dragstrip-ready originals collapsing into three live tracks for a 24 minute romp through Detroit ways of thinking. Hard music categories become blurred in an alcoholic haze, the band burning the blues, you better for it, or at least wide awake. I like this band.
Rating　8

### Sphinx - Test　(Heart & Soul '94)
Sphinx deliver a sort of flawless hard rock metal that combines Saigon Kick's searing sense of melody with standard Hollyrock poses. Strung o'ertop is a vaguely Christian metal message that is watered to the point of being merely nice, polite werdz that just fade out of any sort of distinction. In 1988 this might have really excelled, but today it's just another frustratingly good enough **7**, crowded out by records with more magnetism; more the fault of too many recorded ass-kickin' revelations than any glaring faults with **Test**. Full-bodied production, robust vocals and hooky choruses—so why will I be tucking it safely out of mind? Maybe I've just bought into the hype about the death of good ol' American hard rock. Maybe you shouldn't.
Rating　7

### Spider - Rock'n'Roll Gypsies　(RCA '82)
Lead cut *A.W.O.L.* winds 'em up as a thoroughly detailed knock-off of Status Quo, a tag these liggin' Brits would never shake as if they would ever want to. And indeed, the boogie mechanix just roll right on through this small, ineffectual but amused dedication, on the upside resembling filler from **On The Level** or **Hello!**, down through more sickly material like the pale *Part Of The Legend* and *What You're Doin' To Me*. But not only is it all second-string Quo, it's also all so bored and uniform to an extent Quo never was until their stifled latter years. Love the concept, but the execution is about as lacklustre as could be proposed.
Rating　4

### Spider - Rough Justice　(A&M '84)
**Rough Justice** stays the course meekly carved on '82's **Rock'n'Roll Gypsies**, with only ever so slight digressions into non-boogie mindspheres. Still, who cares, 'cos there's zero progress in terms of chops or personal assertion, and the recording, despite production by the illustrious Chris Tsangarides, is still

toneless and disinterested. Plus the boys still look like Spinal Tap or Slade. The sorry verdict: scads of featureless, numbskullian barroom boogie as per Quo's more thick-headed ideas, with the odd romp such as *You Make Me Offers (I Can't Refuse)* showing avenues hopefully to be pursued at a later date.
Rating **5**

## Spinal Tap - Break Like The Wind (MCA '92)

A cutting room floor splicefest of feisty Alice Cooper-type uptakes sent careening through a blended average of the '60s, '70s, and only brief smatterings of Spinal Tap's best imitators from the '80s (i.e. Scorpions). Sure, **This Is Spinal Tap** rates as legendary video, but the necessity to drape this much-vaunted in-joke with gooey doses of metallic parody leaves the "reunion" record no more than the mere novelty it was intended. Glimpses of old rock, psychedelia, Stonesy metal (*Bitch School*) and even Manowar, with the loquacious *The Majesty Of Rock* stud the landspheres inhabited by these most telling studs, in a successful fumbling of goof rock styles, sort of like Saxon past expiry date. An ultimately vast and empty array of confused signals featuring all sorts of esteemed rock guests as lost as the concept.
Rating **4**

## Spiritual Beggars - Another Way To Shine
(Peach/Music For Nations '96)

Yet another crazy creative neo-retrometal (?) act (featuring Michael Amott, ex-Carcass), this one doing something entirely different from the others, digging into a torrid power trio jam that sounds like a fantastical, slightly psychedelic hybrid between Trouble and Collision. I'll take a step back as you absorb that in all its heavy, heavy meaning. This is one amazing, oddly funky, Sabbath-leaden record, the band wending its colour-burst way through accessible yet extremely retro numbers like the totally Troubled *Magic Spell* and *Blind Mountain*, the Deep Purple-meets-Obsessed large dirge of *Picking From The Box*, and slamming closer *Past The Sounds Of Whispers*, strutting with the authority of twenty record veterans. Indeed the band thanks Uli Jon Roth and Frank Marino for inspiration, and both of their Hendrix-derived hefts are evident here, many of the sure-footed doom patterns linked with slinky roller-coastered '60s funk axe-slashings, the band wrapping it all in disciplined, detailed songs that eradicate the eccentric occasional meandering boredom of Sleep, Count Raven, The Obsessed, Monster Magnet, and Kyuss, even though there are only nine tracks here totaling fifty minutes. But what an inspiring, ludicrously groovy fifty minutes they are. Peace, man.
Rating **9**

## Splatterpunk - this infinite god . . . (Diabolic Force '92)

A surprisingly non-thrash offering from Brian Taylor and his punishing Toronto-bred Diabolic Force label, **this infinite god . . .** kicks in a Bay Area frame of mind, with excellent Hetfield-inflected vocals and an atonal riff arsenal that on the less impressive end, recalls Overkill, Testament and Exodus; on the raucous front, vintage Metallica (*Nemesis, Vicious Circle*), Slayer (all the pointless breaks) and even preachy Pantera (see *Something Wicked*). Still, as with much ultra-heavy product, too many riffs, too many slow builds and a general OTT mentality that tire irons the mind long before journey's end. A welcome blast of disciplined mega-metal unfortunately mired amongst a ton of similarly professional acts.
Rating **7**

## Sponge - Rotting Pinata (Sony '94)

A rumbling sort of rough-hewn alt. rocker that was slow out of the gates but now doing brisk sales, **Rotting Pinata** finds Sponge doing battle in the same esteemed rings as Everclear, Bush, Seven Mary Three and a host of other commercially accepted hard alternative songsmiths. I like the way this record sort of works its way into a frenzy from long periods of contemplation, really sounding anti-commercial, establishing a crazy cool of no particular inclination to impress. What used to thrill me about about old Replacements is altered but in place for the '90s here, shady, shambling tracks like *Giants* and the freight train title tune breaking into inspiring, life-affirming choruses, slowly and subversively hooking the listener, moving him one track at a time into the whole record. The whole thing just sounds sparked and spontaneous in a good way (and there are a lot of bad ways to be this way).
Rating **8**

## Sponge - Wax Ecstatic (Sony '96)

Ah yes, this volatile, deserved buzz band called Sponge. After shifting a million pieces of **Rotting Pinata**, these self-professed hillbilly glam merchants (don't call us grunge), were actually considering making this a concept record about drag queens, hence the two tracks with that term in their monikers. What finally emerges however is a clearly bonkers, considerably anti-commercial piece of rough-chinned power alt., a record somewhere between the breezy funpuss of Collective Soul, and the dark and druggy paranoia of Manic Street Preachers. Of course the first single will have none of this, *Wax Ecstatic* being a firm and clever punk metal hairball with a chainsaw guitar signature. No doubt about it though, the record has a certain star quality, like this is alternative rock's Black Crowes, appropriately perched on a dam-busting second record with Ame(o)rica-straddling vignettes that exhibit an ugly beautiful droop. Or to run with a whole other stack of categorical pancakes, you really can start with a base of grunge, Sponge then proceeding to slather on eccentric Commonwealth toppings from Aussie Midnight Oil to Irish Therapy?, like I say postcarding many U.S. states and then going western culture global. Weird stuff, each track being a curmudgeoned sculpture you wanna check out a few times before wrinkling your nose, most wrinkles never coming.
Rating **8**

## Spread Eagle - Spread Eagle (MCA '90)

One of the more promising sleaze metal acts of the early '90s, Spread Eagle sits guzzling beers squarely between G'NR and Skid Row circa **Slave To The Grind** (with a dram of Love/Hate for good measure), in rank possession of one toxic guitar sound, all Live Free Or Die, hair blowin' in the wind distortion, and an uproarious set of pipes in Ray West. Kick-off track *Broken City*, scruff punk raver *Scratch Like A Cat* and sizzler *Switchblade Serenade* lead the charge, in construction of a brain-crushing battering ram notched with street kills, a mad-eyed mongrel that shreds the hide off the sweaty underclass of metal. A record of honest dishevelment that prompts bewilderment at why we put up with the poseur politeness of corporate metallers like Crüe, Cinderella and Poison when there's more urgent sounds busting to break out. Sadly, Record II didn't do much for these east coasters, and their deal was toasted. But they deserve your ears.
Rating **7**

## Spread Eagle - Open To The Public (MCA '92)

Missing nary a beat, **Open To The Public** picks up where these Bostonian heirs to Aerosmith left off, cruising into town with a stoked and primed collection of sassy metal highballs, all blessed with the Axl-steeped pipes of Ray West and the Joe Perry on crack leads of Paul DiBartolo. Faves are the high science funk metal of *Preacher Man, Rhythm Machine* and the *King Of The Dogs*. Two mellow tracks keep it interesting

**425**

(*Fade Away* and *Faith*), again perhaps emphasizing the Aerosmith influences of this talent-heavy act. Unjustly ignored, Spread Eagle was never the beneficiary of bad words amongst the small circle of metalheads that ever got to hear them. Just shows, success ain't always about talent, but you knew that.

Rating      **8**

### Sprinkler - More Boy, Less Friend   (Sub Pop '92)

Prompting desperate and inevitable requests for more Sub and less Pop, Sprinkler's **More Boy, Less Friend** comes bookended with healthy blasts of slur foam in lead *Wide Zero* and last *Landlord*. In betwixt, further brooding brews of wimpy bandwagonesque college-boy sludge that dooms it up between heavy Cure and off-shelf Cult; mostly luded grunge battered with high note riffs, sparse power chords, and a general simpering eye to sell-out. Paint-by-numbers Sub Pop which goes to show that imitation can even happen to the incomparable and indescribable (for it remains that there is no definitive Seattle sound). Oregon's Sprinkler made sure the one word song titles were in full and shameless supply; check this unbroken stream: *Blind, Ulcer, Doyle, Flood, Sandbox* . . . Weird, but I think of all imitations, this kind sickens me the most. Sorry, can't do 'er.

Rating      **4**

### Spudmonsters - Moment Of Truth   (Massacre '96)

Record #3 for these Cleveland tire-irons, **Moment Of Truth** keeps the band's somewhat loose brand of urban hardcore dangerously punky, especially the vocals, which are an aggravated bark that might be called an acquired taste. Riffs are often belligerent towards melody, making this a committed piece of firebrand skate music. I for one lament the '80s convention of it all, preferring a Downset or Biohazardous sense of polish.

Rating      **5**

### Squadron - Fatal Strike   (Heart & Soul '88)

Pretty solid power goth here, Squadron sucking up all the levity of those magick early years of the NWOBHM, banging off a manhandlin' no frills Maiden vibe with a guttural Hoover built of sturdy production values and a sense of adventure. Shame it's a six track EP.

Rating      **7**

### Billy Squier - The Tale Of The Tape   (Capitol '80)

A l'il bit heavier and brash than the sickly puppy sweet cover art would lead you to believe, **The Tale Of The Tape** is really a new Piper record, the exact same loose-fitted guitar rock, nothing particular 1980 about it. Billy's Choir even revives *Who's Your Boyfriend* from **Piper**, and gives us an early version of *The Stroke* in *The Big Beat*, while *You Should Be High, Love* fuses the same hockey barn steamroll to Led Zep, Squier feeding on Plant's phrasings hook, line and sinker. Squier's particular forté, past, present and future: delicate pop melodrama with shaggy dog rock arrangements, pure, simple and purely playable. Guitars by Bruce Kulick.

Rating      **7**

### Billy Squier - Don't Say No   (Capitol '81)

Our boy Billy breaks it big with his first Mack-produced pioneering dance metal record, **Don't Say No** spawning Squier's biggest hit *The Stroke*, with no less than squashed disco *My Kinda Love*, catchy pop metal cheesecake *In The Dark*, and beefy anthem *Lonely Is The Night* also making the radio rounds. I swear it's that collapsed drum sound that makes these dirty Perry-meets-Petty guitar rockers project as novel, although Squier's theatrical Robert Plant yang I suppose deserves some credit. Whatever the case, **Don't Say No** hooks the listener without obvious reason like many a

hit record (Foreigner fits that bill), pushing melody and edge-of-chaos verve first above an itchy trashy sort of rhythm bed. *Too Daze Gone* sounds suspiciously like a sick-with-flu *Living After Midnight*. Doesn't this guy just have the worst album covers?

Rating      **8**

### Billy Squier - Emotions In Motion   (Capitol '82)

No surprise that much of this sounds like the scant few heavy tunes on Queen's **Hot Space**, given the distinctive brashy sassy drum sound of producer Mack on both records and this one's bold predecessor. So **Emotions In Motion** (cover painting of our cover boy by Andy Warhol) tries to be a sort of heavy-handed, low-grinding dance record, perhaps best exemplified by booty-shakin' lead single *Everybody Wants You*. Mack gets the funk out too, introducing a new minimalist element to Squier on *Learn How To Live*, and much of the rest covers the usual Squier bases with a hint more eclecticism and that compressed Mack sound, a sound that is distracting but attractive in small doses. Less the whack on the head than **Don't Say No**, but philosophically similar.

Rating      **6**

### Billy Squier - Signs Of Life   (Capitol '84)

What was stiff but charmingly ragged on **Emotions In Motion** is merely stiff here, as Squier teams with Meatloaf-ed wonder Jim Steinman, turning this into a sort of hard rock Cars record, turning on the guitars then muting them down, converting their delivery into something delicate and slight, kind of a foppish dance sound. Well at least there's a thrilling guitar solo courtesy of Brian May on *(Another) 1984*, a sort of progressive synth-metal track that diverges from the dismal norm. Otherwise, can't get too excited about this entirely synthetic dash for the cash.

Rating      **4**

### Billy Squier - Enough Is Enough   (Capitol '86)

This time around it is anal retentive producer Peter Collins that cleans Squier's sound up to the point of making him dangerously AOR (that *All We Have To Give* ballad is a stinker). Queen trivia point #2: Freddie Mercury adds co-vocals to perplexed Queenie mishmash *Love Is The Hero*, also co-writing another, *Lady With A Tenor Sax*. But as I say, too slick, given that Squier arrives fairly slick and sickly sweet (say that one fast!) by nature. The fancy pants drumming and percolating synths just detract from what is best treated as a rock'n'roll party, kickin' it freestyle with basic back-up. A bit darker and moodier than the poppy **Signs Of Life**, but man, so manufactured.

Rating      **5**

### Billy Squier - Tell The Truth   (Capitol '93)

Easily the man's most dramatic, heart-on-sleeve crusade of melody, **Tell The Truth** finds Squier digging deep for his hard rock, his hook and his place in a new age. It is easy to see why he is a bud and sometime working partner of Queen. Squier has no problem matching the verve of '80s-era Queen the rare times they hard rocked, evoking Freddie's effusive, from-the-gut singing and sense of the entertainer, his band matching the edgy chaos of heavy arrangements played raw, especially the drums, which bash, swing and cymbal-destruct throughout the rockers (lead single *Angry*) to splendid, panoramic ballad *Break Down*, the record's most stirring track, a marriage of finesse and power made in heaven. Everything's very electrified, even as it sits squarely but complicatedly in Squier's unique, Beatles-tinged pop metal (see Lenny Kravitz' singles). Elsewhere in this cultivated garden: *Shocked Straight* revives The Clash's *Should I Stay Or Should I Go*, *Mind-Machine* is a smeary, almost maudlin sweetheart with a frantic, melodic chorus, and *Lovin' You Ain't So Hard*

features some very Zep-like acoustic guitar under a characteristically surrendered Squier vocal. A very loving and lush sort of hard rock, breathing with humanity, **Tell The Truth** find's Squier making that successful transition from his past, vaguely frat-boy commercial hard rock to a similar sound filled with soul.
Rating                                    8

### Billy Squier - In Concert  (King Biscuit Flower Hour '96)

Squier's enjoying a plateau right about this time (March 26, 1983), buoyed by two hit records packed with easy concert executionables like *Everybody Wants You*, *In The Dark* and *The Stroke*. And things are fine here, sound quality well up to snuff, renditions quite rocky, Squier's voice occasionally strained and slurry but acceptably on course. Weird moments: a derivative hammer-on solo, a *Too Daze Gone* which is reclined and barsy, and the crowd participation bit during *The Stroke*.
Rating                                    6

### Stabbing Westward - Wither Blister Burn + Peel  (Sony '96)

These angsty L.A. futuro-noiseniks have covertly built a reputation as industrial metallers with brains to spare, buzzing above the pack, the industry and critics at least paying some attention to their particular deck of innovations. Still not a huge fan, I nevertheless respect the grafting of Christopher Hall's bedheaded breathy croon onto layers of psychedelic, electronically-enhanced metal, lending the band's sound a foppish Britishness, a de rigueur laid-back slouch despite the noise, a star quality that is unconcerned with impressing. So it's a spacey, raved sort of industrial afoot, more confessional, luded Trent than the buzzseek and destroy of Ministry, Skrew, Front Line Assembly or Monster Voodoo Machine. And for this reason, my attention span gets spoon-pushed into the soup then soggy, much more captivated by the undeniably raw humanity of Alice in Chains, when visiting metal of this velocity and tone. Just kills the concurrently released **Filth Pig** from Ministry though, but what doesn't?
Rating                                    6

### Stainless Steel - Stainless Steel  (Bonebreaker '85)

The usually gothic, traditional German fare with a dose of the amateur, grimy, and headbangin', Stainless Steel are a pretty amusing parody of metal, something that would hit the spot at just the perfect juncture of a classic metal piss-up, but otherwise pops along a bit too hokey, like countless low IQ Euro-rockers. Axel Thubeauville's mix is acceptably trench-warfaring, but the general skills of the band are just too inflexible, heightened by the flat and unrestrained performance of the man at the mike. Got to hand it to the German mindscape though. Even their worst metallic sons doth rock with iron conviction. Beautiful Teutonia: *Lost Games*.
Rating                                    5

### Stampede - Hurricane Town  (Polydor '83)

I somehow always wished more for these NWOBHMelodicametallers, finding hidden ambition beneath this crusty Leppard wannabe and the band's earlier and even clankier **Official Bootleg**. Stampede's claim to fame was their hot young guitarist Laurence Archer, whose lovingly Moore-ish, Sykes-ish flourishes landed him a gig in Lynott's doomed Grand Slam project (Mark Stanway, keyboardist here also got involved). Simply not ready to record, Stampede however gunked up more like a toneless Black Rose than a shaken and stirred Heavy Pettin', somewhat dragged downward by the vocals of Laurence's stepfather Rueben Archer. Long lost in time and long lost at the time anyways, it's sinful beauty nevertheless to hear Archer's archetypal fills and mod metallic Lizzy solos.

Entering the annals of sought-out Lizzy-related collectibles.
Rating                                    5

### Stanford Prison Experiment - The Gato Hunch  (True North/MCA '95)

Purveyors of a punk whip that echoes the angular arrangements of Quicksand through Rage Against The Machine, Stanford Prison Experiment have scored a smart, stinging direct hit, layering their elusive alterno-jazz metal lessons over rocking punk metal structures. And there's the rub: songs, big cymbal-crashing songs (see *You're The Vulgarian*, *El Nuevo*, and *The Accomplice*), which is why this more fun than either hip but cold Quicksand album. Mario Jimenez' vocals combine SoCal punk with Elvis Costello and Bob Mould, inciting a white riot like punk '77, managing to glue the listener in rapt attention with his vexatious tirades. Ends with a half hour lecture excerpt (*Class War: The Attack On Working People*) from Noam Chomsky, the modern world's most famous philosopher. Bristling, electric, but neither too thrashy nor too convoluted and artsy.
Rating                                    8

### Starfighters - Starfighters  (Arista '81)

Alarmingly early for a band to be emulating AC/DC (well, I guess there's also Angel City), Starfighters' debut does a loose, new wavier version of their heroes, not on purpose but probably just from lack of funds, although Tony Platt is in producing. The result is something like middling Krokus although pub rockers from the Stiff camp also come to mind (and then quickly leave). So what. It's cool to have stuff like this collecting cobwebs in the ol' collection.
Rating                                    6

### Starfighters - In-Flight Movie  (Quality '83)

This simple, unassuming hard rock record circulated mightily throughout most of the dollar bins in North America, and fortunately one ended up in my hands, as, all in all, **In-Flight Movie** is a fairly warm and affable AC/DC-ish bar crawl, featuring a rough 'n' capable Bon Scott/Rod Stewart-style throat at the helm, overall sounding bigger and harder to move than the affable debut. But still, **In-Flight Movie** is marred by the earlier record's over-simplicity, adding this predilection for slow structures and build-ups long on payback, essentially emulating the worst one half of any given AC/DC record. Overall however, tuneful, punchy, and fairly consistent in its unambitious chosen direction. And the main AC/DC connection? Guitarist Stevie Young is a relative of Malcolm and Angus, who no doubt got their mixer bud Tony Platt on board to produce the record. AC/DC also pegged Starfighters for back-up slot on their UK tour.
Rating                                    6

### Starz - Starz  (Capitol '76)

Big goopy '70s hype on for Michael Lee Smith and his Kiss-able Starz, and **Starz** the debut delivers that moist, warm **Ted Nugent/Free For All/Destroyer**-style American metal to the masses. Jack Douglas production, Bill Aucoin management, Capitol Records . . . the future's so bright I gotta wear shades. What could go wrong? Nothing for now, **Starz** being a truly likeable feast of burger-and-fries power chords. Hummables include lead single *She's Just A Fallen Angel* and *Live Wire*, while heftier numbers like *Detroit Girls*, *Now I Can* and minor dinosaur *Boys In Action* gummed up the pinch rollers in the ol' underdash on many a steamy night's cruise. Just fun, summertime rock'n'roll, marketed heavily as state-of-the-art American hard rock (that crown really belonging to Aerosmith, whose pivotal **Rocks** was undeniably the best record of the year). Still, **Starz** is an album that wears well with the

years, representing the dreams and aspirations of one of rock'n'roll's friendlier, more relaxed eras.
Rating 7

## Starz - Violation (Capitol '77)
**Violation** finds Starz really coming into their own, brandishing a well-adjusted confidence that allows them breathing room to experiment. From this spirit comes opening track *Cherry Baby*, a breezy pop cocktail which should have been a smash, and scary ballad *Is That A Street Light Or The Moon?* Elsewhere, interesting inflections spice up the band's traditional, boxy chord structures, making classic summer rockers like *All Night Long* and *Rock Six Times* sweeter and more chick-chartable than on first inspection. The two biggest guitar raves are of an almost novelty nature, *Subway Terror* being an early slasher tune and *Violation*, yer basic rebellion rocker with a Big Brother/1984 twist. And in between, there's all sorts of sticky guitar postures (not to mention twirly moustaches), making Starz the mature side of Kiss, but definitely less credible than Aerosmith or even Ted.
Rating 8

## Starz - Attention Shoppers! (Capitol '78)
Hard to imagine the depression I encountered as I spun **Attention Shoppers!** for the very first time—*starting with side two!* Me: Right on, man . . . *X-Ray Spex*, speed rocker, one of the band's coolest tunes . . . what's this? *Good Ale We Seek*, an almost progressive rocker, sorta like *Golden Age Of Leather* . . . I'm liking this . . . hmmm . . . then like a descent into a dark cloud of gloom, no less than *seven* wimp rockers to finish out the sorry mess. Pop, blues, ballad, bubblegum . . . the whole odious shmooz, dead after two tracks. Major downer. And to boot, it bombed, doing no one any good whatsoever. I should have known something was up with the cutesy band photo on the back. Oh well, if retrospect be kind, . . . just another wrinkle in the wayward journey that was the '70s.
Rating 4

## Starz - Coliseum Rock (Capitol '78)
After the embarrassing disaster that was **Attention Shoppers!**, Starz attempt a return to their harmless style of power chord rock, only to find out that once you abandon the metal muse, she becomes icy and aloof when you want her back. More or less the band's heaviest album, that didn't stop an increasingly complex me from noticing **Coliseum Rock**'s lifeless delivery, worst performance being drummer Joe Dube, although to be fair this sounds like more of a collaborative decision by band and producer to keep it totally white, clean and neat. No soul here, no creative spirit, sending potential barnburners like *Don't Stop Now*, *It's A Riot* and *Where Will It End* off for a little milk and cookies. A couple o' cases of beer might have made the difference here, but as it stands: one uptight, constipated record. After break-up (which occured only after touring this record for an exhaustive two years), Michael Lee Smith and Richie Ranno briefly carried the Starz torch with NWOUSHM upstart Hellcats.
Rating 6

## Starz - Live In America (Violation '83)
This slapped together non-official piece of Starz poop comes designed to satiate those dim, scant cravings some might have for live Starz, a band based on commercial guitar-wanked cheese, lovingly whipped dairy fresh for a brief, fun-packed year or so, year being 1977. Here we get a short, badly sequenced, weakly captured walk-on, dominated by a drop-bored-dead ten minute *Pull The Plug*, and a drop-bored-comatose ten minute version of *Boys In Action* (drum solo attached).
Rating 4

## Starz - Live In Action (Metal Blade '89)
Examining this with my review copy of **Live In America** sitting 3,000 miles across the country, I can't tell for sure if one half of this much longer pastiche of two live sets is duplicate material. Anyhow, this Brian Slagel-assembled fourteen track retro sorta celebrates Slagel re-issuing the entire Starz catalogue. Half the tracks here are from a live radio show, and half are from a rare, unreleased Capitol promo. The radio tracks are a joke, badly recorded and surprisingly sloppy, especially with respect to Dube's drumming, which always was a limiting factor for these guys. The rest however, is fairly tight and well-produced, the band competently working their way through such groovy banana seat tunes as *Rock Six Times*, *Subway Terror*, *X-Ray Spex* and pop hit *Cherry Baby*. At an hour plus, good value for the Starz fan.
Rating 7

## Status Quo - Dog Of Two Head (Pye '71)
Stuck quivering like a fork between a poncy past and blue-jean boogie mania, **Dog Of Two Head** shuffles out with (surprise) mewling boogie riff-rock recorded badly like a '60s record, sort of fledgling **Piledriver** without the zen-like discipline. So maybe this is like intense Stones or somethin', *Midnight Rambler* done trashy and in love with electrics. Sorta constructed like self-actualized Quo but still babies at their game.
Rating 4

## Status Quo - Piledriver (A&M '72)
**Piledriver**, aided quite capably by **Razamanaz**, **Sabbath Bloody Sabbath**, **Kiss**, and **Toys In The Attic**, was one of the first records that showed us major heft was lurking around the corner from our CCR and Three Dog Night collections. By today's standards, **Piledriver** is no screamin' iron feast, but nevertheless, the record stands the test of time splendidly, offering more textural depth beyond metal that we ever cared to explore back in the mid-'70s. **Piledriver** was Quo's fifth album, and the first for a major label, rocking proudly as one of the esteemed statesmen of hard blues records, rendering three unique and classic twists on traditional Americana in the mantra-like mono-metal of *O Baby*, the thoroughly weird, buoyant boogie of *Paper Plane*, and the epic drive of *Big Fat Mama*, an ambitious, independent cruiser, one of Quo's proudest moments. Elsewhere, *Don't Waste My Time* offers up a warm, stout-of-heart, traditional Quo stomper, *Roadhouse Blues* offers little except appropriateness, while *All The Reasons* brings it down a bit for one of the band's more emotive, mellower moments. All in all, a classy, accomplished record that shines new light in a number of areas, rendering itself an enigma, despite its status as the first of the band's golden era. An authentic and enjoyable work of vintage blues metal.
Rating 9

## Status Quo - Golden Hour Of Status Quo
(Golden Hour '73)
This isn't an actual Quo studio project per sé, but it's the only taste of pre-**Dog Of Two Head** product I've ever had to endure, reviewed here to represent ancient Quo, which sucks through and through as far as I know (see Mark I Deep Purple). Early Quo was a band like any other '60s joke, dated, dour, confused, badly-recorded, and wholly without ideas, basically the equivalent career origins of any '70s outfit, metal or otherwise, with roots stretching back to the trend-conscious '60s. As was usually the case, the band begat its career as machines that were fed tunes to play, and

nice suits to wear, a strategy that actually worked, as the band seemed to get bigger with each successive release. Because of **Golden Hour**, I've never bothered to check in to three of the four albums from which these dil boogie popsters originate, said platters being **Picturesque Matchstickable Messages From The Status Quo**, **Spare Parts**, and **Ma Kelly's Greasy Spoon** (review of **Dog Of Two Head** following). Not saying I haven't missed a few classics somewhere, but I sincerely doubt it.
Rating                                                                    I

## Status Quo · Hello! (A&M '73)

Lead cut *Roll Over Lay Down* accelerates the boulder set in motion through **Piledriver**'s *Don't Waste My Time* and *Roadhouse Blues*, laying the foundation for **Hello!**'s dope smokin', long-haired lumberjack-jacketed, working man's grind, and in general, the monolithic heat-forged barroom boogie the band would inject into their collective arteries, never to be wholly expelled, going on 25 years now. Quo's unparalleled mastery of the most righteous, kick-butt boogie grooves, which flashed across the fields on *Big Fat Mama*, again reaches full smoke here with *Blue Eyed Lady*, *Caroline* and the insistent trudge of *Forty-Five Hundred Times*. When Quo hits its stride, there's really nothing that can match it for blue collar, four-wheel-drive, save for AC/DC, both bands being cut from the same barroom grime, love of simplicity, and reverence of rockers dead and buried. **Hello!**, although not the band's hottest record, is Quo's most representative, bristling with heads-down boogie, hillbilly understatements, and unadorned sincerity. Smokey steam engine rock worthy of your inspection.
Rating                                                                    8

## Status Quo · Quo (A&M '74)

**Quo** is Status Quo's formidable masterpiece, and quite possibly the most moving blues metal album of all time, a British record that soundly crushes the aspirations of all Southern rockers with the hopes of someday creating that first perfect, quintessentially American marriage of blues and hard rock. Skynyrd had the heart, ZZ Top had the finesse, and Foghat were the best at making us all forget our troubles, but it takes the mighty **Quo** to forge it all into one devastating weapon, adding a measured dose of futility to make it really cry the blues. **Quo** is the soundtrack for genuine red-blooded recreation, for sitting on the porch, surrounded by weeds, in the middle of nowhere, with a rifle on your lap, smoking dope, waiting for something to move. It's got the most backwoods, fog-locked, no-influences resonance of any blues rock record to ever really let fly, even when riding the most kick-ass high-NRG boogie slams caged to wax, as gloriously evidenced on the ferociously tall *Back Water*, *Just Take Me*, *Slow Train*, and classic metal highball *Drifting Away*. Something just smokes redwoods about this fiercely proud record from start to finish, despite some deep-seated mellow moments and successful attempts at less adorned, light-hearted boogie. All segues by sundown into a time-weary violence, making **Quo** a major masterwerk of sonic earthtones. Best experienced in an alcoholic haze, utterly and ecstatically alone.
Rating                                                                    10

## Status Quo · On The Level (Capitol '75)

The mighty ones ease up on the diesel fuel a bit, rendering their lead-headed boogie images in shorter, more bubbly, quick-paced fashion. Two crackling classics emerge, in adrenaline duo *Little Lady* and *Down, Down*, while Quo shows effortless brilliance in storming Chuck Berry's *Bye Bye Johnny* like nobody's done before. After the amps cool, what remains is another time-honoured romp through the muscular possibilities of boogie, a language bred boiling in the blood of

these basically regular, approachable guys, likeable longhairs infused with a particularly specialized mission from the muse.
Rating                                                                    8

## Status Quo · Status Quo (Capitol '76)

The boys in blue drive their battered black Cadillac into town one last time on this final chapter of the band's ultra-octane era, spilling their dense thrashaboogie tool kit onto vinyl in construction of another handful of Quo classics. Largest blaze of all comes with *Is There A Better Way*, Quo's most metallic body-blow, and most heaping rendition of Quo with a rocket up its ass. Other soon-to-be staples of a vintage Quo diet come with *Rain*, *That's A Fact* and *Mystery Song*, rendering half this album ardently respectful, while the rest is still decent boogie rock, upbeat but traditional, so eminently Quo and so warmly constructed by a band so obviously in love with their liggin' lot in life. Known as **Blue For You** in England, said version also featuring different cover art from the nifty die-cut American release.
Rating                                                                    8

## Status Quo · Live (Phonogram '77)

The blooz never really learned to lift off and emanate power until the chundering Quo locked horns with boogie, transforming an apparently dead icon into daylight-taming blocks of granite. **Live** is the rock'n'roll equivalent of the monster truck pull, and is about as thick-blooded American as it gets; deeply traditional, gutsy, and authentic, all slammed in our faces, steaming and strong by a bunch of jean-clad Brits on ramp in Glasgow. **Live** recalls many of Quo's more powerful statements and sends 'em chugging home with major authority and sweat. **Live** turns the band into a loose, smothering wall of sound, with appropriately distant vocals and echoey resonance. High octane flashes include the tight-fisted sonic destroyer *Is There A Better Way*, *Little Lady*, and the band's monolith of blues rock pain *Forty-Five Hundred Times*. One of the more heroic, trench-rockin', World War II kinda live assaults committed to vinyl, from a band who rarely bothered to bring the show stateside.
Rating                                                                    7

## Status Quo · Rockin' All Over The World (Capitol '77)

**Rockin' All Over The World** represents a shift from dense, legendary, riffic, hard rock variations on boogie metal to the more uptight and buoyant experiments in pop that have progressively and relentlessly obsessed the band on each successive release. Due to **Rockin'** being poised on the cusp of this transition, the marriage of dirty metallic blues and more succinct communicative structures is frequent heady magic, on such cuts as the Bo Diddley shuffling *Let's Ride*, the severely grooving literal boogie *Hard Time*, the backwoods hobo *Dirty Water*, and one of the band's most manic, sustained and kickin' night drivers ever, *Too Far Gone*, an ambitious, ever-widening gyre, which simply unwinds like a flaming ball of wire, whipped into frenzy by combined strokes of horns, hot axework, wicked arrangements, and wise, level-headed vocals from Quo's second voice in command. But alas, when all spins down, **Rockin' All Over The World** remains a patchwork of diverse motives and questionable emotive planes, the boys seemingly becoming restless with their well-carved, hot-blooded history lessons in search of new terrain. Discernibly distant from past gems, but nevertheless studded with a good half album of extremely classy Quo cruisers.
Rating                                                                    7

## Status Quo - If You Can't Stand The Heat
(Phonogram '78)

In one of the oddest neurotic fixations witnessed in rock, Status Quo descend full stride into its newborn career as boogie riff archivists; as purely fans, or more like over-extended fanatics, versus serious rock artists, joining Queen, Nazareth, Sweet and Foghat as rock cornerstones gone eccentric or simply seriously confused. Quo has become the overseas version of the Lyres, faithfully reworking obscure tonalities from the '50s and '60s amidst its waxing and waning traditional boogie ethic. I'm almost embarrassed to like this regressive, wholly but illogically naive sound. Sure it's cheesy and completely vacuum-sealed in a simpler time, but it's also up-front, honest and accessible, which is about all one can expect from pop, whatever its origin. The first Quo with absolutely nothing approaching metal.

Rating 6

## Status Quo - Now Hear This (Riva '80)

And still more, tight, wee and harmless boogie arrangements which have long since quieted the guns, opting for repeated annoying flicks in the forehead, sort of like Chinese water torture, except that you don't necessarily want it to stop. Something about Now Hear This speaks with a greater trace of grit than the similar records surrounding it, although the band still sounds declawed, forever locked in some higher, power pop register. Individual tracks rise above the endless mathematics, most notably the elegantly simple, acoustic-driven lead cut Living On An Island, and funky album closer Breaking Away. My soft spot for this particular latter-day Quo dreck stems from the fact that this is one of the first of the era I acquired, allowing for mellowing and continued assimilation with the passing years. Without a doubt, age, history and tradition are all terms that sit well with anything Quo does, and whether or not the band's slavish belabouring of a point goes down with you at all, there's something of the scholar floating through these halls.

Rating 6

## Status Quo - Just Supposin' (Phonogram '80)

The Ramones of pop boogie just keep washing 'em ashore. And like The Ramones catalogue, all is interchangeable with '80s Quo, a bopping and plainly silly hybrid of relentless boogie beats and the melodic golden nuggets studding beach music 45's and other uncomplicated musics of the '60s. Nothing on Just Supposin' causes any commotion except perhaps the almost nostalgically heavy strains of The Wild Ones and total driver Coming And Going. Quo's attempts at new directions always seem to subscribe to a very safe, constrained framework, rendering most challenges as momentary novelty or sonic shading, rather than confident strides into new territory. Still, a pointless hoot, courtesy of a gang of base hillbillies, who probably couldn't care less if they ever mature.

Rating 5

## Status Quo - Fresh Quota (PRT '81)

I know I dredge the memory of the formidable Spinal Tap fairly often throughout this book, but I swear, Quo becomes the Tappers circa the Summer of Love and Bad Music on this ridiculous EP billed as "The Six previously unreleased Status Quo Tracks". Horrid, powerless, pointless (and anything but fresh), not to mention the sorry fact that there's only one Quo-penned track amongst the stoner blues loosely contained here. Consider this fair warning: lay down and avoid at any price.

Rating 1

## Status Quo - Never Too Late (Phonogram '81)

Probably the least consistent in terms of groove pay-off, Never Too Late suffers from busy-ness and jangly production values, while nevertheless driving the band's usual point (or lack of one) home with merciless waves of dime store woogie. Given that Quo doesn't get an ounce of press stateside, I've never heard any explanation of Quo's thinking, and I have no idea whether this stuff still sells for the band in its traditionally strong British market. But it just keeps coming, year after year after . . .

Rating 5

## Status Quo - 1982 (Phonogram '82)

Similar shortcomings to '81's dead identical Never Too Late with respect to production, 1982 is perhaps even more sickly and thin tune-wise, sporting unabashed pop bounce, naked harmonies, and general clownish underachieving. Jolt to the past from one cool, yet ironically synth-laced Quo retro-rocker, album closer Big Man, but nary a low rumble elsewhere. The strange ride continues.

Rating 4

## Status Quo - At The N.E.C. (Phonogram '82)

A well-recorded live throwaway with the sole distinction of being a gig attended by Chuck and Di, if you can believe Royalty bangin' along to such prehistoric scruff boogie. Only side two delves into recent history while side one reaches way back for great run-throughs of Caroline and Little Lady, and a flaccid take on Backwater. Ten basically coasting cuts; no big deal.

Rating 6

## Status Quo - In The Army Now (Phonogram '86)

Status Quo continues to curmudgeon themselves into old age with their endless explorations of pop cum boogie possibilities, cotton candy glossings of the age-old heartbeat of rock'n'roll. Time marches on, and five albums into the '80s, Quo is unswervingly hellbent on examining every last permutation of the seemingly unexplorable. It's such a joke, but also such a well-crafted and bewildering occupation, the most revealing of human imperfection and willful laziness in pronounced refusal of ambition, that equates Quo to the lowest but most heartening of lowbrows. Dave Edmunds, who also produces this record, spices the proceedings with tight, bopping clusters of horns and synths, perhaps lending importance more as philosophical pivot, as In The Army Now reflects the man's affability, history, and sense of insignificance amidst the grand twirl of the world. I've long since left the frustration stage at Quo's baffling career contour, and now simply hum along. I don't know, what else can you do? Spiritual high: Ian Hunter's Speechless.

Rating 7

## Status Quo - Ain't Complaining (Phonogram '88)

Way too over-produced, keyboardy and just plain busy, Quo is finally showing traces of mutating past boogie bop, however the direction is even more vile, given that the enclosed generic key-pop is far from the band's forté, and far from virgin territory, stylistically speaking. Yea and verily, the boogie licks only serve as weak premises, or even more faintly, sly insertions, around which acoustic guitars, synths, and big snappy '90s drums bound right in and take over. It's almost new-wavey, and definitely cute, retaining the novelty, bubble-headed feel of all latter-day Quo, evoking innocuous fun, which ain't all bad 'cept for the fact that these guys had an exceedingly more vital mission when they first slammed ashore back in '72. Missing in action: '89's Perfect Timing and '91's Rock 'Til You Drop.

Rating 5

## Status Quo - B-Sides & Rarities (Castle '90)

For archivists only, **B-Sides & Rarities** is pretty much the same dreary, insipid, opportunistic '60s pop as is found on **Golden Hour**, only this one really digs deep for the rarities. In fact, the first eight tracks are by the band's pre-Quo incarnations Spectres and Traffic Jam. Only later into this 24 song monument to bad taste does the band stumble into a morphed, somnambulent form of booger rawk. Yeesh, what garbage.
Rating                                                                   1

## Status Quo - Rocking All Over The Years
(PolyGram '90)

Proving the insane popularity of ol' Quo in Europe, this 22 track "best of" racked up seven million in sales. Surveying all the years (if a little scant on the '70s), **Rocking** documents the three incarnations of the Quo, beginning with natty '60s flyboys, progressing to grease monkey boogers, and finally to the fun-luvin' history profs the boys have operated as through the '80s. All the hits, all the glory, tuneful as all get out.
Rating                                                                   7

## Status Quo - Don't Stop (PolyGram '96)

Management thought it an interesting lark to make the Quo's 30th anniversary record a percolating covers show, so that's what happened. I interviewed Francis about it a year later, and he expressed mixed emotions about the thing, figuring the big 30 maybe should have been marked by a splendid originals record, along the lines of the man's fave Quo record of the modern era, '94's **Thirsty Work**, which I ain't heard and subsequently ain't reviewed. But methinks he's being hard on himself, because despite the silliness of Quo enthusiastically pogo boogieing through things like *Fun, Fun, Fun, Get Back, Safety Dance* and *The Future's So Bright (I Gotta Wear Shades)*, one finds oneself getting euphorically silly right next to 'em. Some of these tunes were boogie to begin with (*Get Out Of Denver* works instantly), but the ones that aren't, benefit from the light-hearted treatment that only Quo would ever dream to design. A bold move, and quite Gary Glittery daft, wouldn't you say? Nevertheless, given the stature of these guys, it's nice to see them jockey up to the dunk tank.
Rating                                                                   7

## Steel Angel - . . . and the angels were made of steel. (Devil's '85)

Razor-sharp medieval metal unfortunately from France, Steel Angel do an acceptable job of metaphysical Priest, coming forth with tons of classical riffs. And the France thing ain't a glaring stumbler, except one can't miss the stiffness vocally, making the record at least a bit painful and lyrically cliché, although I'm not really sure if the operatic "Pat Montero" is necessarily French. Too many stops and starts, landing . . . **and the angels** too squarely with the inanities of goth. Ambitious but a bit grimy and foreign.
Rating                                                                   5

## Steelbreed - Expect No Mercy (Mausoleum Est. '85)

Smash 'em, bash 'em Mausoleum-type cannon fodder bent from the trenches and ready as hell, sandblasted into our heart and souls with lead-intended conviction and Tank-like abandon. Wallish and squalled, heads down and almost moshable, Steelbreed do the best with a Mausoleum shit mix, clamoring to destroy like a much improved Killer or Warfare. Includes an absolutely comic and grim plastering of the Stones' *Paint It Black*, which luckily emerges from the ashes as nowhere near the same song.
Rating                                                                   7

## Steeler - Steeler (Shrapnel '83)

Put a young Ron Keel in the same room with a young Yngwie Malmsteen and you've got a band lucky to get one record out. And here it is, Malmsteen's American intro, a rambunctious barroom rocker representing close to the best of the Shrapnel stable. Keel's yer basic lunkhead, and Yngwie is obviously wedged into a role, playing reel stoopid on this cross between dil Amerimetal and stadium hard rock, an adequately recorded, adequately paced piece of pie, flagshipped by lead single *Cold Day In Hell* and kick booty hellraiser *Hot On Your Heels*. Steeler proved to be no more than a stepping stone for its two main stars, Yngwie getting to blather on come solo time, even though his riffs here are an embarrassment to the man's good name. Served its purpose for band and listener alike.
Rating                                                                   6

## Steeler - Steeler (Earthshaker '84)

Passing on this really dumb looking record would be a mistake, given its redeeming wastecase delivery of truly Accept-like Teutonia. No, it ain't the Mighty Ones, but it does shred with desperate conviction, like a not so cerebrally-endowed Tank, fusing Accept with top-flight Saxon; the former's Euroblight on exquisitely-riffed *Hydrophobia*, and the latter's speed metal wall on *Gonna Find Some Place In Hell*, as if apartments are hard to come by. A hugely committed drinking record fer sure, when nothing but the most hopeless and heads-down will do. At least one other called **Undercover Animal**.
Rating                                                                   7

## Steelheart - Steelheart (MCA '91)

A visually and sonically clueless mishmash of updated soft metal and surprisingly toneless early '80s metal makes this a two-faced release of bewilderment that I would never buy so neither should you. Until these NYC big-haired bod rockers find out why they want, stick it out on the sidelines. Sounds Canadian.
Rating                                                                   3

## Steelheart - Tangled In Reins (MCA '92)

Still the very embodiment of poodle rock metal in every exhaustive manner, Steelheart are an AOR lover's dream, and a nightmare to everyone else. Big leonine roars, big production, cutting but predictable axe postures, dumb sexist lyrics. Really annoying in most every department, this is the crux of why this kind of rock should be and has been burned at the stake.
Rating                                                                   3

## Steel Vengeance - Call Off The Dogs (Black Dragon '85)

I was rather impressed with this gutsy, grimy slice of power metal from this uncompromising set of bashers from Michigan. Steel Vengeance possess a loud type of history-steeped combat readiness, given their nostalgic fusion of Priest with early violent rockers like Onslaught and Nuclear Assault. Definitely beer-drinking mayhem, lovingly distorted, melted and crammed down yer throat.
Rating                                                                   7

## Steel Vengeance - Second Offense (Black Dragon '86)

The butthead wardrobe modeled on the back of **Second Offense** was probably enough to slash potential sales by a third, and unfortunately for the band, those dollars were probably spent better elsewhere, **Second Offense** rocking somewhat disjointedly in comparison to the smokin' debut. Take more average riffs (and simply *more* riffs), mix in illogical writing, loose execution and a recording that buries Scott Carlson's expressive wail, and you've pretty well got this disappointing follow-up nailed. Songs whither on the vine, dying a slow, garage-bound death as if inspiration and

**431**

motivation were left cold and alone in the service bay. Still such a *heavy metal* band in word, deed, red leather and fishnet, you just gotta laugh.

Rating     **5**

## Steel Vengeance - Prisoners   (Giant '88)

New look, new label, same curious American Euroblast from the underbelly, and really no advancement, as the boys look within and even further under rock for their uncompromising grime goth. Carlson's still mixed echoey and too far back, and playing is still loose, creaky, and anti-climactic. Stuck in a rut is about all I can say, wondering under what mood other than exploration will I ever play this. Rowdy then botched, kickin' then ponderous, but always noisy, lost and so cheap in its aspirations, **Prisoners** is a push/pull proposition of committed goth, rendered this side of hellraising for its love of the headbang. Note: this is the band's fourth record (third being **Never Lettin' Go**), leader Michael Wickstrom having to change a couple members after their second, due to drug hassles.

Rating     **6**

## Stellar Dweller - Hiwattrauma   (Bear/Cargo '95)

Montreal's Stellar Dweller further perpetuate the favorable image of Montreal as a city above a sound, a conundrum of weirdly darn good bands beyond description. The present task at hand mebbee crosses Mudhoney with Pavement, gussied up grease with slouch and loiter, fully guitar-bent, sweet and sour, grungy and artsy. Songs are slow and sloppy, thick and backwashed, but there's a nice variety, propelling the fab mess into the entertainment zone despite those laid too far back vocals. Swell toon monikers: *Kitchen Ideas*, *Cheater Theater*, *Washing Raccoon And The Karma Wheel*, and *Jess Took You Late*. Sludgy but purposeful; call this one good if not truly leaping out for your attention.

Rating     **6**

## John Kay & Steppenwolf - Rise & Shine
(I.R.S./MCA '90)

Just throwing this in here to open a can of worms, really. Some might conjecture that Steppenwolf mighta been an early heavy metal band, what with their sort of hard for the '60s sound, and more notably their bad-ass biker looks. Well, their *Born To Be Wild* has of course been made into a signature hard rock anthem through various cover versions and their semi-successes as hits. And *Magic Carpet Ride* is a considerably catchy metal calypso. But on the strength of the full albums, forget it: raw, psychedelic, bluesy drug blubber at its most-dated. Yet, I figured I'd throw in this horrible reunion era slab, because of course, every rough '60s act that reforms gets a l'il heavier, Steppenwolf included. So the "goods": awful, Ronnie Hawkins/Long John Baldry/Joe Cocker-style hard hitting blues rock, adding counter-intuitive techy drums-and-mix, '80s guitar hero solos, chimey Night Ranger keyboards, and Kay's smokey vocals. Possibly the worst songwriting I've ever heard.

Rating     **0**

## Steve Stevens - Atomic Playboys   (Warner '89)

No doubt expecting to capitalize on everyone's ooh and aahing over his Billy Idol video "performance", Steve gets a record of his own. And everybody just hated it, Atomic Playboys pulling every cock rock move in the black book; way too many layers of gunk, songs courting every moronic style known to hair, he even an obligatory cover of Sweet's *Action*. Nice look, guys. One smokey, smokin' acoustic instrumental, and *Action* has spirit, but the rest, flush it. Produced (to bury the reputation of of heavy metal forever) by Beau Hill, aided and misguided by a raft of bigwigs that includes Ted Templeman, Kasim Sulton and Anton Fig. 'Nuff said.

Rating     **1**

## STG - No Longer Human   (Rotten '93)

Punk-infested industrial from the dark and unamusing side, **No Longer Human** finds this quartet of loathsome urchins at least grooving briskly on exactly half the numbers. Scratchy vocal rants range from fuzzy political views to various tirades on religion, while the band thumps in belligerent grey shades. Alas though, heard it all before (insert Ministry, NIN references here), and it just wears me out. No real riffs, no real versatility, no longer valid, given the gains made by industrial in '94.

Rating     **4**

## Stone - Stone   (Mechanic/MCA '88)

Here's one of those long-lost records that is a veritable gem in the rough, Finland's Stone in possession of one wolloping guitar sound, and a batch of songs that projects that sound so relentlessly forward, you gotta rock. It's too bad these traditional power metalists have a propensity for thrash, because their truly perfect sound works best on mid-groove numbers like *No Commands* and *Eat Your Pride*, the band's riffs recalling a heady mix of Torch, Accept and Overdrive, three bands that just know metal, no explanations needed. Pretty cool, self-deprecating lyrics too, sorta like Suicidal Tendencies meets Anvil (thought you'd never see those two bands compared eh?). Solid, thick, opaque, just like, uh, stone.

Rating     **8**

## Stone Fury - Burns Like A Star   (MCA '84)

Driven to moderate levels of publicity by '84's general vacuum in the melodic HR field, early Lenny Wolf vehicle Stone Fury whipped together this scattered piece of commercial axe candy everybody wished was heavier. Still, the sugary side of the record was raw enough, and more lumbering metallic tracks like *Mamas Love* and *Tease* stood out as accomplished American fare with a Zep edge (oh oh). Best of all is the disarmingly simple title track which builds quietly in minor epic fashion: an intelligent blend of caress and might. Wolf sounds great, if not melodramatic, but the overall effect is something like a band of rising stars on a mission, although this was to be the end of that particular bent as the follow-up tooled down beyond repair.

Rating     **6**

## Stone Fury - Let Them Talk   (MCA '86)

Down to a duo, Stone Fury abdicate any critical acclaim they may have expanded on given a more guitar-oriented course, by discovering synth technology and studio abuse beyond The Cars or Toto (indeed Wolf hated both the production and the producer). No longer anywhere near a hard rock band, packaging, sonic puff and for that matter, album title, all point to a marketing ploy of Wolf and Bruce Gowdy as teen heart throbs, sorta like a band that would guest star on **90210** or the soaps or maybe some cop show. A sad disintegration and loss, even if we got Kingdom Come out of the sorry mess. Earns a 1 for the obvious long hours put into recording this offense, likely arranged by armies of non-musician sound techs.

Rating     **1**

## Stone Temple Pilots - Core   (Atlantic '92)

One hopes Stone Temple Pilots could have existed without the influence of Alice in Chains and Soundgarden, but then again, one never knows. Core is a Sub Pop record to the core, but a good 'un; heavy, lumbering like a Washington State sawmill, and well-paced, if not technically wild-eyed like its obvious big brothers.

The main derivative is Weiland, a cool enough throat, yet one genetically equipped like Layne Staley with stylistic aspirations towards Chris Cornell and Eddie Vedder. The music kicks, carrying a much more sturdy (stiff?) beat than most Sub Poppers, more flattening, smeared power chords and a simpler, to-the-groove blast ethic, as evidenced on the creamery butter of *Crackerman* and anti-date-rape anthem *Sex Type Thing*. Lots to like and lots to warm to, as it lops off the eccentricities of grungers for a no fat boilermaker of wastecase metal; something new age and polluted at once; Generation X'ers at play 'cos there's no work. A shakey **8**, for its Tad shameless Northwest aspirations, even if the band is quick to downplay such connections. But hey, **Core** turned out to be the biggest commercial success for early grunge since Pearl Jam's *Ten*.

Rating                                                    8

## Stone Temple Pilots - Purple   (Atlantic '94)

**Core**'s clean and clingy, almost irritatingly well-assembled grunge-by-numbers makes way for a heartening and self-assured dirtrockride, almost foggy but so grown old by comparison. **Purple** is STP's **Superunknown**, not altogether as wastey, experimental, charming or genius, but still burned-up, power-packed and cavernous, hot and hazy, and well . . . damn confident, all that clone stuff just sliding off Weiland and Co.'s back like so many Seattle raindrops. And speaking of the pixie-lidded one, his voice and more importantly his vocal melodies, make **Purple**'s fat, bashing and simple songs soar ever so mighty, swimmingly fetching examples being *Pretty Penny* and toon of the year, *Interstate Love Song*, Weiland somehow for the first time really acting like a team captain, adding a couple of new sounds to his perfect grunge delivery. Despite tons of folk wanting to see STP fall flat on their rich rock star faces, one can't deny that the band has handled their pressures with class and aplomb, writing their way out of a jam, manhandling the fickle muse of the '90s, and stealing her songbooks. So the jingle writers have blossomed on that difficult second record (see secret last track) with more insanely hooky jingles, shambling but smart assemblages that recognize the moving target that is the street-smart marketplace these days, walking that line between clear-thinking and cryptic, too weird and formulaic, realistic and shocking. The verdict: Stone Temple Pilots crank it just right, giving us wide and wicked tunes we couldn't be ashamed to assimilate. Congratulations are in order.

Rating                                                    9

## Stone Temple Pilots - Tiny Music . . . Songs From The Vatican Gift Shop   (Atlantic '96)

If Weiland's drug-addled disappearing acts haven't confused you yet, perhaps another hide-and-seek game with record and songtitles might provide a spot of fun. Once you figure out what to call everything, STP's new one will provide some sock-hop and solace, the band elevating their lyrical acumen, while finding farther-flung extremes on which to musically chew. In a way, this is merely another quite great Stone Temple Pilots record, sandwiching some big spreadable chords (many smartly Pagey), between smart burst of pop-craft until the muscles responsible for meaningful swaying begin to twitch in one's weary mass. Favourites are the proto-STP sweet sexual grind of *Trippin' On A Hole In A Paper Heart*, and the Beatle-esque *Lady Picture Show*, easily the band's second stickiest chorus since *Interstate Love Song*. But I find the dopey lulls almost record-destroying, causing me to want to resequence this thing, desperately wanting the band to keep itself and me up, optimistic and entertained, a sentiment made difficult when thinking of the nasty AiC parallels (Staley and Weiland both heavy into heroin) happening to this median, averaged, bell-curved fine-

by-me grunge staple. I keep thinking about Blind Melon's **Soup**, and that's not a good thing, casting a pall over this bursting and then recoiling, whirlwind of sensual sonics. Still a necessary, useful band, but that upward and forward mass has been stalled.

Rating                                                    8

## The Stooges - The Stooges   (Elektra '69)

Welcome The Stooges . . . the world's worst band, and the world's most explosive and craziest, and it all started with something more like a whimper, from a haphazard collection of chemical-ingesting Detroit reptilian cretins who could barely hold their weapons let alone play them. The Stooges would become a major influence on all sorts of motley punks, new wavers and metalheads, lead Stooge Iggy (aka James Osterberg) bent on self-destruction of his sinewy physique (not enough food, too much dope), and the band bent on destruction of music, like that warning against home-taping. **The Stooges** had *1969* and *No Fun*, rollicking but futuristically accurate laments on being punk, slack, x'ed out, defining an angst that wouldn't really sneak outside of The Stooges' freakshow until the Pistols' barked No Future in '77. And **The Stooges** had *I Wanna Be Your Dog* and *Not Right*, loose, chaotic belly-rumbles approaching metal, squirming out of the rust belt to do somewhat disheveled battle with the shockwaves reverberating in from the U.K. Yeah, **The Stooges** is a smelly pile of garbage, the seamy side of the hippy phenomenon, a collision of noise that falls out when mental processes fail, or more likely were never operative in the first place. Hence . . . The Stooges. Sure I wasn't witness at the time, but even from my distant perspective, this record still sounds exciting and dangerous, degenerate and toxic, despite its scarred and punctured hide. Desperate stuff, that just spreads like a virus through the rock underbelly.

Rating                                                    7

## The Stooges - Fun House   (Elektra '70)

The zit on the face of rock that was The Stooges just got uglier with the harsh electric fuzztones of **Fun House**. Iggy is uncageable, logic centres torched, as the drastic disaster zone that is his band (Scott Ashton, Ron Ashton and Dave Alexander) tears up the carpet with the unholiest of howls, all the while agitated sax work scarring the still-cooling rough surfaces like cigarette burns on flesh. **Fun House** is out of control, songs bashed into place missing most of their rivets, indeed *Dirt*, *Fun House* and the surrendered white noise of *L.A. Blues*, barely even trying to shake the shakes. Thus **Fun House** cranks notorious throughout its drug-crazed trashing, a record that screeches to a stop but was never finished, sounds piled onto a bonfire, left to burn while Iggy picks away at his twisted torso, roaring out tales of the street, visions of squalor society would rather not have to deal with. Shaggier and more horrific than **The Stooges**, **Fun House** exposed a band who emanated apocalypse, at least damn sure they were going down, expending moderate but ill-skilled effort to try drag a few buddies into the trash heap to keep them company.

Rating                                                    8

## Iggy And The Stooges - Raw Power   (CBS '73)

Then along comes the Ig classic, **Raw Power**, a statement disastrous and ferocious at once, the peptic ulcer of rock'n'roll, arguably the nastiest, dirtiest record scratched to date, butt-ugly, caved-in, and stunted in so many elegant directions at once. Legendary album cover, legendary Munsters-style logo, squalid back cover shots, and a chilling raft of tunes that expose a band way beyond sleep or showering, raising the curtain with *Search And Destroy*, again challenging our comfort level like only The Stooges ever could, all jagged slashing power chords from new axe-zombie

**433**

James Williamson, while all drowns in a pit of body parts, production being too proud a word for what passes for sound quality here, a reek courtesy the bloody stumps of David Bowie and the Ig himself. Words are hushed then howled, mumbled then roared, making for a seedy excursion through loud rock perversion, demons, booze and pills wafting through each empty shell like a snakey blue cocktail of exhaust fumes. Every tune does its own sordid little dance, most disturbed being *Penetration* (punctured and deflated), and *I Need Somebody* (to shovel the dirt back in), while *Raw Power* might be what would crawl out of an Aerosmith that was all drugs, no talent. Finally, *Death Trip* takes us out, reinforcing the insipid but violent power chords of *Search And Destroy*, galloping three-legged on to disaster, bleached solos barb-wired to its husk as Iggy rants and babbles real totally out of it like. 100% raw power, heavy on the raw, crustified and asphyxiated on the power. Frankenstein lives.
Rating 10

## Iggy And The Stooges - Metallic K.O.  (Skydog '76)

Billed as "the last ever Iggy and the Stooges show", **Metallic K.O.** is an amusing and depraved batch of mostly previously unreleased Iggy ditties, brutally recorded but a laugh riot all the same, lots of swearing, stage raps that harken to a great Vegas future for the Ig, and a boozy, barrelhouse roll to the agonized finish, thanks to Scott Thurston's honky tonk ivories. The fun picks up on side two with *Rich Bitch* and *Cock In My Pocket*, finally ending it all with the Igmonster's unique take on *Louie Louie*, preceded by an on-stage tuning session while Iggy gets pelted by eggs. Through the clouds of dust, smoke, and crowd-launched projectiles, you can tell this was a band that by journey's end, did find its own gruesome pocket, and Iggy was definitely a bomb ready to explode at any moment. What a mess.
Rating 5

## Storm - Storm  (MCA '79)

If you can even remotely take the concept of chicks singing on hard rock albums seriously, you might appreciate this ancient, immediately deleted, poppy HR and occasionally metallic effort for its upbeat delivery, interesting, unique arrangements, traces of Queen, and bizarre, long-lost studio trickery. Basically for technical archivists only.
Rating 4

## Stormbringer - Stormbringer  (Madrigal-France Est. '85)

Sporting French, Swiss and German connections, let's just call this one frosty Euro and call it a day. Stormbringer relish the frilly interplay between keyboard and guitar, spicing these classical pop hard rock numbers with enough fine axe to turn them ever so slightly metal. Good production except for the stiff drum sound (and performance, I guess), with typical princely vocals from David Baretto. Alas, not rockin' enough for this genre, Stormbringer are too intent on pulling the hot babes instead of the punters. Hey if it works for you, go for it.
Rating 6

## St. Paradise - St. Paradise  (Warner Bros. '79)

Line up: Ted Nugent's Derek St. Holmes and Rob Grange plus Montrose/Heart guy Denny Carmassi on drums, a supergroup of sorts especially in '79. Hated the record at the time because it pales in heaviness to Ted, but now can appreciate it for its (aimless) combination of softer guitar rock, Lynyrd Skynyrd southern pickings and muscle pop metal circa Rick Derringer. All are in evidence on Tedly cover *Live It Up*, silly '70s rocker *Jesse James* and brooding mini-epic *Beside The*

Sea. A bit subdued but a nice guitarish piece of a great rock decade nevertheless.
Rating 7

## Izzy Stradlin And The Ju Ju Hounds - Izzy Stradlin And The Ju Ju Hounds  (Geffen '92)

Word has it Izzy left GN'R for a combination of personal priorities and musical differences, both necessarily linked, because to communicate the low-slung roots rock he envisions as his calling, Izzy feels that he has to play intimate venues, live a simple life and shed the hype of a star quality that was rapidly becoming insane, unnecessary and unhealthy for the music. The **Ju Ju Hounds** record walks that kind of talk; rambling, shambling, honky tonkin' blues rock with all sorts of '50s/'60s/'70s influences from boogie rock through folk rock through Foghat and the Stones. Main complaint: an empty, simple and commercial feel to much of the proceedings which is fine on such remarkable grooves as lead single *Shuffle It All*, but destructive to the three or four here which are ten-times-derived blue collar rockers like a ton of American or Canadian radio hits. An oft-repeated comparative that bears citing here: Izzy is the second incarnation of Keef and his X-pensive Winos, both guitarists exploring their traditional blues bases under appropriate low-glitz circumstances, Richards a true descendant of early rock, Stradlin more a descendant of the '60s and '70s students: Townsend, Page, Perry, and Keith himself. And therein lies a nagging shortcoming. As a third generation working with superior technology, it becomes easy to clean it up *too much*, the arrangements lacking for grit. Ju Ju Hounds does that to some extent, resulting in a record that is comfortable, enjoyable but not everlasting, sounding smooth and welcome but lacking in depth. No love/hate relationship here, just a like, then fade.
Rating 7

## Strappado - Fatal Judgement  (Strappado '92)

Somewhat of a thrash institution for Canada, Bob Sadzak and Strappado (formerly Slaughter), influenced many an act locally and internationally with their blazing thrash skills, only Razor (and sorta Anvil) carrying more of a legacy amongst extreme rivetheads. This indie captures the band in full flare, combining the best of the '80s with the skill-level and production demands of the '90s, under a vocal performance that recalls the shout style of most of the Annihilator vocalists. Basically neck and snapping neck with the best of the Bay Area sound, **Fatal Judgement** carves the deepest of headbang grooves (love them harmony axes) despite its love of mayhem metal, exhibiting growth well beyond the band's scruffy, street origins.
Rating 7

## Strapping Young Lad - Heavy As A Really Heavy Thing  (Century Media '95)

Strapping Young Lad is the wildchild of 23-year-old Devin Townsend, a wicked imp of a multi-talent, who's played with The Wildhearts, Frontline Assembly, Geezer Butler and most noticeably, Vai, filling in as oddball lead singer. Here the mad professor hatches an exuberant, creative and fairly unlistenable wall of industrial sonics, basically abstaining from vocal chores for a textbook industrial stressgrind. The overall vibe is one of hyper manic fun, lots of plot twists, mucho bent sound sculpture, nine futuristic music prototypes, with few you would wanna drive home unless ultra-caustic cyborg metal is your floated, bloated boat. Picture Stan Ridgeway, Andy Prieboy, or Klark Kent gone heavy as a really heavy thing, and you're in Devin's playspace. Too much.
Rating 6

**Strapping Young Lad - City**  (Century Media '97)

He's still a real wild child at 24 years flung, manic-about-town Devin Townsend finally finding the time and space to work on another masterpiece of impermeable science. It takes hard training and hot-wiring to get to the level where SYL can be listened to for enjoyment, Devin and Co. (which now includes Death/Dark Angel drummer Gene Hoglan) layering as much as buddy Steve Vai, but layering with Townsend's usual raft of corrosive, caustic unlistenables rather than Vai's springy rock god conventions. Call it Brutal Truth meets Cheap Trick, I dunno. All I know is that I kinda like it, and full-on find it fascinating in a fearful factory sort of way. Bottom line: the boy is talented, intelligent, and exploratory of emotional, melodic rainbows, even if his choice vocabulary is white noisy, assaultive techno-thrash. He cannot be ignored.

Rating  **7**

**Strawman - Strawman**  (Power And Industry '95)

This CD is just one part of the artistic collective that is Strawman, a consortium of musicians, poets, film folk and photographers that execute live, a multi-media show that is a sort of bare bones, punk-induced rock theatre. But the CD is the crucial gesture, and strangely enough recalls the same positives and negatives of a similar sounding band, Warrior Soul. The highs: an expressive, arresting vocalist and vivid, intelligent lyrics. The lows: weak, overly corporate and safe production, coupled with low-key hard rock songs, not heavily committed when rocking, slightly too cluttery when mellow; guitar riffs meek and pedestrian, with solos that are astonishingly tasteful and varied (Note: these are also The Tragically Hip's problems to a T, 'cept their solos ain't any good either). Imagine the simplified prog metal of today's Queensryche hangin' with the edgy explorations of Jane's Addiction, then sheen it over with a bit o' '70s and '80s big hair metal (I guess Alice Cooper in both cases), and yer close (I sez humbly!). Refreshingly literary hard rock, even if the rock is frustratingly constrained, **Strawman** is visually and lyrically way ahead of its music.

Rating  **6**

**Streetfighter - Shoot You Down!**  (Venus '84)

One of the few supremely German records that falls short of the kill factor, **Shoot You Down!** rides a smooth, accessible, but frail HR/metal sound like mid-intensity Scorpions, rendered clean and professional through the expansive Double Trouble production team. The results are weak and predictable, even leaning towards the non-committal Krokus at times. And the short hair doesn't help the cause. Neither do the broken English lyrics.

Rating  **4**

**Stressball - Stressball**  (Pavement '93)

You can neatly add these wrench-heads to the batch of blue Nola bruises including Crowbar, Eyehategod, Down, Tungsten and a little band called Pantera, Stressball positioned most like Crowbar, blobulous simple riffs dominating fore and backgrounds. Steven Gaille's vocals are a bit of a distraction though, caught somewhere between grind, hardcore and AC, cutting through the cleanly recorded backbreak perhaps too hysterically. Hey but guess what? Too little happening, causing something not unlike boredom, like being caught in a long line-up at the bank. Ultimately, it all seems about the guitar sound, to the detriment of other departments.

Rating  **6**

**Strike - Strike**  (Banzai '84)

Swedish six track. Boring, syrupy sweet, melodic AOR, albeit kind of raw and Kiss-like (especially re: vocal comparisons to Paul Stanley), featuring shafts of Teutonia and some blended mechanics. Half a skewed and dishearteningly rocking success. Fave: *Loose Trigger*.

Rating  **4**

**Strike - Strike**  (C.O.M.A. '84)

Large and heroic Northwest cock rock plasma complete with Halen solos, Halen Attitude and even Halen obtusions, Strike conjures images of geographic soulmates TKO by injecting wanton brashness and undisciplined frags which is part of the band's sleazy coolness. Definitely vicious and desperate, riff-torn and fluidly scattered, these guys could have been stadia gods given a coddled shot at the brass ring.

Rating  **7**

**Strip Mind - What's In Your Mouth**  (Sire '93)

Strip Mind evoke a sort of dangerous, pisstank punk metal hybrid, into the crudities of life, into energy and a sense of chaos but stuck squarely in the realm of metal. Kinda thrashy, alternative, funken and drunken all at once, this one stiffed on the street, despite deserving more. Lots of sex, lots of robust vocal belting, this one's out there on a limb, fairly alone and proud of its place.

Rating  **7**

**Strongarm - Strongarm**  (Tooth & Nail '95)

Definitely what I like to see, Florida's Strongarm taking hardcore higher, mixing in Biohazard and Pantera grooves with their punk integrity, even a touch of prog, given the bright, busy drumming. Lyrics are of a veiled, Christian nature, more about strength and hope than anything preachy, still a strange combination, this angriest of musics and vocal styles chafing against the savvy '90s street-riot metal enclosed (see Krishna-core dudes Shelter). But I guess that's the plan really, to get a positive message into the pit with kids too cool to be seen with Petra, Stryper or even DC Talk, something I pretty much agree with doing. Very vivid, classy artwork throughout by the aptly-named Bruce Heavin. Other doctrine-aligned, sonically similar acts on the label: Overcome and Unashamed, all three bands also oddly enough going for that short-haired pipsqueak in loose clothing look.

Rating  **7**

**Stryper - Soldiers Under Command**  (Enigma '85)

Don't the buzzing bees for Jesus look simply fetching all decked out in front of their black and yellow tactical recreational vehicle! If you've stopped laughing now . . . the review: state-of-the-craft melodic metal for the year of our Lord '85 AD, **Soldiers Under Command** comprises all sorts of prancing riffery including three annoying-as-Bon Jehovah ballads, closing the sorry mass off with an unfathomable rendition of *Battle Hymn Of The Republic*. Michael Sweet's sheep-like bleat spills blood all over these uptight, curfew rockers on the way to making Sweet, his hairspray and his well-behaved band the most famous bible belters on God's green. Oh by the way, for the record, Stryper wasn't ripping off Quiet Riot with the stripes thing, having dressed themselves in such engaging manner since '80 as Roxx Regime. Michael just wants to make that clear.

Rating  **3**

**Stryper - The Yellow And Black Attack**  (Enigma '86)

Same fluid and fiery axework from the Peavey pulpit, but still nothing riffically innovative. Just more melodic chuggers and anthemic choruses to the Entity upstairs, strangely finding a way to graft Yngwie to the Crüe, creating a sweatless din not unlike bad Y&T. The most feminine band pics I've ever seen, and that includes my Kate Bush, Heart and Poison collections.

Rating  **3**

## Stryper - To Hell With The Devil   (Enigma '86)

Clarifying the ambiguous phrasing of the Crüe's smokin' **Shout At The Devil** (yeah, right), Stryper turn it up a notch with the hellacious, Trouble-infected strains of the title track, convincing, menacing ragefests *The Way* and *More Than A Man*, and a marginally improved "live feel" recording. But *Calling On You* is one brutal single. Visions of Ned Flanders' kids, fer sure. All in all, a solid five minutes of axework by Satan. Went platinum.
Rating                                                        4

## Stryper - In God We Trust   (Enigma '88)

Back to weak, anemic Sunday school metal, this time invaded by smatterings of tinkling synths. Oddly dependent on riff alone, like these guys are amateurs or something.
Rating                                                        3

## Stryper - Against The Law   (Enigma '90)

Christian scientists with nothing better to do will debate this for years, but lo and beholden to the One, Stryper have shed their Godly mantle, opting for more secular lyrical grist (judging from this, they've got a lot of catching up to do) and in the case of half the band at least, a downright Damien-like approach to personal grooming. Like I say, they've got a long way to go if they wanna rock and roll. Without the bibles and bee suits, Stryper's just another polished, professional rawk band looking for an audience. You'd think with all the practice, this band would excel once horizons became expanded, yet really, **Against The Law** is a pretty lame expression of funky metal bombast, like a collection of dressy Kiss songs or at best, fancy pants Dokken, peppered with a couple of powerless OTTers à la modern Van Halen or DLR. Lost in the shuffle, no prayer for the dying, skewered in the harsh light of novelty.
Rating                                                        4

## Stryper - Can't Stop The Rock: The Stryper Collection 1984-1991   (Hollywood '91)

The reigning Rockers For God have always had their chops down despite looking like big-haired bees for much of their born again existence, and this compilation proves that despite their smiley disposition the desire to stay current (note last record's beards) should preserve or at least slow the erosion of their fan base. Two new sermons here: *Believe*, a tears-swelling-up-in-the-eyes grand sweep that does its duty, and the title track, a calamitous blues thrasher, again stressing a techy melodi-crunch know-how that diminishes the silliness surrounding the Sweet ones. Packaging includes lyrics, a useful band profile for those who care, and a full discography including singles.
Rating                                                        5

## Stuck Mojo - Snappin' Necks   (Century Media '95)

High hopes were in store for this marriage of assaultive rap and smoke-choked mastodon riffs, and modestly brisk sales have countered the fact that some of the reviews have been less than enthusiastic, lamenting this extreme metal label branching out, more than the music enclosed. **Snappin' Necks** might be my favourite record thus far in a genre I find cold, layering the vocals with electronics, and lacing the production with lots of cut (as Vinnie from Pantera might say). So the combination of urbancore deliveries with death metal mixes turns this well away from other rap metal acts, most of which use fairly conventional production values. But as I say, the whole idea turns me off, so I have to resort to my version of neutrality . . .
Rating                                                        7

## Stuck Mojo - Pigwalk   (Century Media '96)

Back fairly quickly from their critically panned debut, Atlanta's Stuck Mojo really turn up the vitriol, **Pigwalk** being one slab o' rhythm, heat-swelled and seriously heavy, really about the best record I can think of from this assaultive genre. And it's no surprise that a certain "oomph!' is achieved, given production courtesy of Devin Townsend (*Down Breeding* is all SYL) and Meshuggah knobsmith Daniel Bergstrand. The record's kept interesting with a Fishboned sort of playfulness, most notable on *The Sermon, Inside My Head* and *Despise*. What results is a slambamfest with pace, dynamic and a crushing sense of groove. Dig it, kiddies, 'cos this band is wide awake and lowdown-tuned for destruction.
Rating                                                        8

## Joe Stump - Night Of The Living Shred   (Leviathan '94)

This totally revered axe god doubles as #1 rock guitar prof at Boston's revered Berklee College Of Music. And it's easy to see why, given his monster grasp of everything from blues through funk to hair band shred to Yngwie shred, making this one of the more enjoyable instrumental resumé records at the heavier end of the spectrum. Noodly as all get out, which is the point, but also very musical, especially all the Malmsteeny stuff, as if I know what I'm talking about. Record #2 after a debut called **Guitar Dominance**.
Rating                                                        6

## Joe Stump - Supersonic Shred Machine   (Leviathan '96)

Stump and his mighty power trio continue to make visceral, harmonic, enjoyable instrumental ultra-shred, grabbing and vigorously shaking the golden boughs of all those neo-classical influences we all love, namely the real classical guys like Beethoven, Mozart and Paganini (everybody namedrops devilboy), plus modern arpeggio gods like Yngwie and Ritchie Blackmore, who gets a tune dedication here. So if you love those castle-grey flights of axe-mad fantasia, this record's way beyond any one Yngwie showcase. Except of course, showcase pretty much sums up its reason to be. Elucidating track-by-track notes from Stump, which makes all the more sense, seeing that he's starting to look more like Jeff Waters. ludicrous tech fave: *The Need For Speed*; pounding groove fave: *Wrecking Machine*.
Rating                                                        6

## Subhumans - Incorrect Thoughts   (Est. '80)

Vancouver punk contemporaries of DOA, the Subhumans kicked ass of a more metallic, almost Rollins-directed nature with classics like *Slave To My Dick* and stun-gunner *Death To The Sickoids*. This well-carved full length is somewhat of a collector's item now, and rightfully so, being both rare and a rare professional punk accomplishment, steeped more in beer-soaked teen anarchy than anything seriously political, no matter how embarrassingly half-heartedly they tried. Goofy, but slapped down with spontaneity, and a parallel lack of hope of ever achieving anything but.
Rating                                                        7

## Subhumans - Pissed Off . . . With Good Reason!   (Essential Noise '96)

You couldn't ask for a better reissue, **Pissed Off** taking probably the best Canadian punk album ever, remastering it and adding as many more rarities and live tracks, plus a long and amusing band history. With 24 tracks, this is obviously and forever the definitive statement on the band, spanning their Bob Rock-(when he was a punk)-produced debut **Incorrect Thoughts**, the band's singles, the manic self-titled EP from '79, assorted aged live squalls, and some crusty, badly-recorded, reunion live nuggets from Edmonton circa '95. Some of the excitement and danger has faded, but as

document to Vancouver's punk scene, this stands head and shoulders above all.
Rating 8

## Sudden Impact - Split Personality (Diabolical Force '88)

Looks like a thrasher, but rocks convincingly like a mid-to-fast doom metal scraper with only hints of crossover, most exposed in the conversational holler fodder, which kind of, y'know, talks in short phrases, rarely exuding melody; the vocal equivalent of the record's profuse death-like minor-chorded riffs. One of those expressionless, though nevertheless caustically mixed, bestial riff feasts that switches aimlessly from one gothic cradle of damnation to another, in resigned, tumbling uniformity; a bit of Slayer here, a bit of Celtic Frost there, with traces of Black Flag, all illogically mapped and over-crammed with badly-timed speed shifts and riff acrobatics.
Rating 4

## Suffocation - Pierced From Within
### (The All Blacks B.V./Attic '95)

Is it just me or is traditional thrash metal getting more listenable without altering its goals? Suffocation's latest stays extremely loyal to its death underpinnings, no commerciality here, save for maybe a tinge of Bay Area thrash, given the many change-ups, blastbeats unto bruising chunk grooves, and perfect production from Florida's reigning production behemoth Scott Burns. Killer for the form, and yet another act along with Deicide and Morbid Angel refusing to get more musical to please the next level of rivethead. Low grade reflects the fact that this next level includes me.
Rating 6

## Sugar - Copper Blue (Rykodisc '92)

After two day and night solo records, Mould emerges from his depression to form Hüsker Two, Sugar in most every way dead similar: a power trio cranking smeary, hugely electrified pop songs, songs deftly hooky and exhilarating due to the prolific songskills of Mould, a man who claims to own a backlog of over 200 ditties. But the band, however safely similar it might be to the legendary Minneapolaroids adds a bit of Pixies if anything (see Good Idea), and perhaps a greater propensity for straight rockin' pop (albeit adding more boldly strummed acoustic guitars), lopping off the extremities of say one-third of each Hüsker trip. Sum total: bright and well done, if nothing new and a bit twee.
Rating 7

## Sugar - Beaster (Rykodisc '93)

After a wishy-washy first track, the **Beaster** EP kicks into high gear with the ignitable Tilted, a quick-footed guitar popster that is one of the more rousing, Clash-able moments of the dear, affected Sugar catalogue to this point. Hell, there's even a ripping guitar solo! Then more deafening wall o' Sugar, as Bob generally breaks out like a kingpin metalllan, screeching and screaming over a loud but brief bunch of Sugar in yer gastank. Hard to say much more. If you liked Bob's old band, you'll like his new one, that is if you aren't feeling duped by getting a carbon copy.
Rating 7

## Sugar - File Under: Easy Listening (Rykodisc '94)

Don't know why, but critics panned this one, perhaps more frustrated with Mould's dogged, determined guitars-to-eleven sameyness than the inherent quality of the songs. But hey, I think lead track Gift is the best Sugar track ever, that stop/go jet engine riff being one of the most infectious I've ever heard, crashing and bashing like a freight train off the rails. The rest of F.U.E.L. oscillates amongst the usual Mould wisdoms, hooks, and velocities the band can implement so well,

more than half the record fundamentally light pop tunes smothered in amplified windmill chords. And of course it works heady magic. We've known that since about 1984.
Rating 8

## Sugar - Besides (Rykodisc '95)

Taking advantage of Mouldy's insane songwriting obsession, Rykodisc gathers up a few of the couple hundred compositions laying around for your listening pleasure. But these are leftovers for a purpose, most sounding scattered and weakly mixed compared to the official product. Rykodisc is spot-on with the packaging as usual, printing lyrics to the whole undulating pool of electrics. I guess the good thing one could say about this is that the more ragged-ass the live tracks (see Anyone; a total of seven of the 17 tunes are live), the more Sugar sounds like the Hüskers, which Sugar may as well be anyway. Post-note: in '96, Bob put the band to rest and made another curmudgeonly solo album.
Rating 7

## Sugartooth - Sugartooth (Geffen '94)

Slippery sabgrunge in no particular commercial hurry, Sugartooth lean towards the psychedelic vibe of Monster Magnet or The Obsessed, clamped hard and hardcore with a dose of ol' Biohazard or old Prong. This is pretty loose stuff, live and soupy, truly to the slack end of power, like those hazy Soundgarden tracks between masterpieces. But the slurring journey gathers steam, inching towards artistically valid as the swirling chordage sucks you into its vortex. Question though: can your short attention span gear down to these cycles? Can you spare the time or effort? For my part, too many more urgent records crowd this one out.
Rating 7

## Suicidal Tendencies - Join The Army (Caroline '87)

Well everybody's gotta have roots, and those of ST are relentlessly hardcore, as this quintessential skate band immediately establishes themselves as eloquent lightning rods of suburban alienation. Too bad the music lacks imagination, **Join The Army** being standard zitfaced mosh metal, with nary a break in the teen-rebellious distortion. Don't sweat it, the band grows up but fast.
Rating 4

## Suicidal Tendencies - How Will I Laugh Tomorrow When I Can't Even Smile Today (CBS '88)

The Suicidal skate punks of the mid '80s die a quick, pavement-scraping death on this rumbling ascent to bad mutha-hood, establishing a proud legacy of red meat smothered in provocation to action. Muir begins to carve a new manifesto, storming the chain link gates with lead track Trip At The Brain, a head-exploding tirade announcing a journey that begins and ends with non-stop intellectual and physical frenzy. Much of the rest of the album serves to clarify Muir's vision while Rocky George takes tentative steps through somewhat foreign terrain, finding himself one length back of the Anthraxes, Metallicas and Megadeths of this world in terms of metal actualization. The infectious grooves are few and far between, due to a lingering mosh ethic in both riff and Muir's often flat shout-style vocals, not to mention Mark Dodson's unexpressive, midrange-dominated mix, most notable in the claustrophobic drum sound. Love the concept, but the execution betrays lack of experience.
Rating 7

## Suicidal Tendencies - Controlled By Hatred/Feel Like Shit . . . Deja Vu (CBS '89)

Horrible graphics, totally confusing title, and a weird, unexplained selection of tracks. Hey! Welcome! Be-

cause try as it may, this package (sort of a split double EP comprising nine slammin' tunes) can't hide all these great new Suicidal tracks, plus a couple of versions of *How Will I Laugh Tomorrow*, the second being unplugged and damn cool. Heavy in the vein of the band's not so commercially successful hybrid of chunky speed metal and hardcore, fave raves would be *Controlled By Hatred* and *Choosing My Own Way Of Life*, one slow and bulbous, the other grooved to the hilt. Elsewhere, some pretty harsh punk, but all in all, this is a full LP of material that is essential to the Muir mystique. Pity about the artwork.
Rating                                                                7

## Suicidal Tendencies - Lights . . . Camera . . . Revolution   (CBS '90)

**Lights . . . Camera . . . Revolution** turned out to be a disappointment for the boys in ST, as a fickle and talent-inundated metal community smelled drift, finding the band a trace complacent in this virtual re-telling of its predecessor. The record up-intensifies in a number of areas, even though its core sound is similarly atonal and square, thanks to another unfeeling job at the knobs from Dodson. Lead track *You Can't Bring Me Down* swings a shovel at *Trip At The Brain*, scoring a direct hit, teeth a' flyin', while elsewhere the metal is more committed and the funk more breathable, thus more tracks that stand above the brutal brainshake, case in point being *Lovely* and *Go 'N Breakdown*, both injecting that humorous but deceptive defense posture, Muir as psychological disaster pummeled into confusion by society. But I dunno . . . I can't get really excited about this record. The intensity is there, but it never deviates, tearing a strip off our complacency with a hysterical but monotoned mosh; sonic blitz without mercy, smothering the emotional intensity of Muir's ravings under an arguably contrived but undeniably derivative speed metal precept. What remains as I clear the wattage from my ears is a philosophy in search of a soundtrack, a sonic bed as unique and invigorating as the message.
Rating                                                                7

## Suicidal Tendencies - The Art Of Rebellion   (Sony '92)

Suicidal at long last rescue from the pound a dastardly cur of a muse unfathomable, erratic and ultimately unshakable as the divergent voices comprising the band. **The Art Of Rebellion** brings to boil a cauldron overflowing with years of preparation and formulation. And producer Peter Collins provides the kerosene, finally cultivating a soundgarden over which this frustrated and ultra-talented force can shower its rays of cloaked optimism, a landscape where riffs charge the air, where drums cannonate with reverb, and where Mike's mike is loud and clear, thematically razor-sharp, class "A" Muir to the bitter end. **The Art Of Rebellion** is above all, a pleasure to hear, which is half the battle with ST's tough-hided fusions of punk and metal. Good recording, exacting sonic surgery from lickmen Rocky George and Mike Clark, and a mellower, more expressive tone from Mad Mike. So it's the dynamic of the different alloys that makes this record slide down so easily, oscillating between punk detonation, tricky funk (leaning both black and Latino), and daring acoustic arrangements (please proceed to single *Monopoly Of Sorrow*). An often exotic soundtrack to the workings of Muir's mind, **The Art Of Rebellion** climbs and dives regularly as the caffeine flows freely, providing a black stream of catapulted energy throughout all the twists and turns the band has learned to negotiate so well. So as Helmet would say: strap it on! Believe me, we could all use the jolt.
Rating                                                                9

## Suicidal Tendencies - Still Cyco After All These Years   (Sony '93)

On **Cyco**, Mike and the band returns to their rant 'n' roll roots—literally, remixing their first record (plus a few), and seeing what we think. Will we take to a sharp blast of skatepunk like ten years have never passed us by, or will we cry foul? Neither as far as I'm concerned, 'cos a) I was warned, and subsequently didn't buy the disc thinking it was a new raft of studio gems and b) the record works in a caffeinated blurrock sort of way. Healthy supercharge to the core, although faves would be the '90s stuff (which sounds written to fit the '83 porridge-like mosh surrounding it): *War Inside My Head* and *Don't Give Me Your Nothin'*, both cyclones of thorny, carbon-dated metal. Still, it's kinda sleazy not announcing on the cover that this is regurgitated ST. But hopefully those duped will not revolt, the band proving that they were indeed at least three or four years ahead of their time (but not six or seven).
Rating                                                                6

## Suicidal Tendencies - Suicidal For Life   (Sony '94)

Mike Muir stands howling in the wind tunnel towards conspiracy-level obscurity by this sorry point, continuing to launch fine hard music product, inexplicably selling zero, when all seems so relevant and right with the Suicidal doctrine, something Rollins seems to expound with much more direct impact, and power to him. Muir seems to want to spit in the collective face of the business here, lacing profanity through the very songtitles of the record's first half. But things rock, with a much more guttural urgency than was the case with **The Art Of Rebellion**, a masterpiece the band is wont to call a mistake in interviews these days. Here, direction is somewhat listless, but individual songs combobulate with tall class, the band not really growing their sound, simply composing solid tracks with what they know. Consider **Suicidal For Life** as something akin to Suicidal circa '88-'90 with a better recording and eye towards rhythmic kill factor, but above all consider it a tough-as-nails pillar of strength; tight, aggressive and pumped full of positive energy. Salute!
Rating                                                                8

## The Suicide Commandos - Make A Record   (Blank '78)

The Suicide Commandos prove that the Twin Cities had even more to offer than Hüsker Dü, Soul Asylum, and the Placemats. **Make A Record** is mouse-like but manic vintage punk that qualifies for my hallowed tome here due to its Buzzcocks-like fever, nibbling axes, and Clash-like percussive energy. Kinda like a real heavy XTC, the Commandos rip through short an' speedy ditties such as *Shock Appeal*, *Mosquito Crucifixion*, and the rat-domiciled *Semi-Smart*. Although **Make A Record** stands virtually alone in American punk in terms of mixing heady Wire-like art with guitar bashing, it ain't gonna win any points for emotive depth, strained way too high reg and disjointed, small in its methods, and tinny in its mix, especially with respect to the really tight snare. Kinda cool, but wee and buzzing like a bug.
Rating                                                                7

## The Suicide Twins - Silver Missiles And Nightingales   (Lick '86)

This elegantly packaged little rarity is yer basic stumbling and stoned unplugged record from Hanoi Rocks duo Andy McCoy and "Nasty Superstar" aka Nasty Suicide. I wanted to like it, but it's just so dour, dank, drugged and coffin-crawled like Johnny Thunders, the squalor eventually wins and the attempt at delicate turns to thoughts of deathly slumber. The record can be quite lush at times, adding all sorts of shady percussive layers, but the doper blues and bluegrass, coupled with the creaky vocal work (the Twins are simple both billed as guitars and vocals) just turns it morbid and one

dimensional as the grim show grinds on. Has its place, I guess.
Rating 6

## Sun - Jam House Wah (6un '93)

Sun crank a sort of industrial metal din, low on technology, high on guitars and acoustic drums. So what's so industrial about it? Basically the drum mix, the three-legged beats and the claustrophobic writing, which leans tribal and irritating, kinda like a dance party in a busy underground parking garage. But the most distracting element of this record is its lyrical and vocal delivery, both incestuously sabotaging each other due to the singer's broken English (the band and indeed every detail of the project is German). So the vocalist kinda screams everything, botching idiom and emphasis as he bleats along, trying valiantly not to be found out. Plus isolation-minded covers from Hendrix and Bob Dylan don't help the cause. Of course, it's finely engineered, but I can't get on board, finding this a combination of flawed, and simply not to my liking, Sun reminding me of Seattle in collision with British goth bands like Killing Joke, The Mission and Sisters Of Mercy, a hybrid getting tiring real fast.
Rating 4

## Sun Red Sun - Sun Red Sun (Sun Red Sun '95)

Finally this dead sea scroll of the bootleg world sees proper release, Sun Red Sun, of course being the final recordings of vocal legend Ray Gillen, who died of AIDS after two spectacular records with Badlands. This short, eight song, album features Gillen on four tracks, with Ray West and Al Romano splitting vocal duties on the final four. But the record hangs together well, being more of a technical, straight power metal display than what Ray gave us with Badlands, no small part due to Romano's fret-fire, sent reeling by the all-star rhythm section off AiC's Mike Starr and Rainbow's Bobby Rondinelli. For an indie release, this is well-stocked with lots of photos (Ray not looking too well), full lyrics, and full credits so you know what was going down with this promising act. Totally professional, if still somewhat lacking in identity, this would have really blossomed into a killer album if death hadn't interfered.
Rating 7

## Supersuckers - The Songs All Sound The Same
(Empty '92)

Gutted and glorious grungemania from Seattle, these unsung Supersuckers combine the pot-boiling rant of Mudhoney with 4/4 punk, even covering the Dead Boys' What Love Is here. Lots of drunken groove to this band, really capturing the chaos of the scene, the bar band madness, the crazy purity of the Sub Pop sound. Only complaint: discernibly less clever than all their bigger, brighter peers, Supersuckers really loving the garage and just givin' 'er with no thought to consequences. Ends with a distorto-version of Nazareth's Razamanaz, ending the record in fab fashion with a thrashed-up one-note wind up that lasts 25 minutes. And it's pretty much funny (well, maddening) for the whole damn near half hour of it. Apparently Burnin' Up is a Madonna cover.
Rating 7

## Supersuckers - Sacriligeous (Sub Pop '95)

Easy to see why folks swear by this crashed and burning Seattle posse, Supersuckers honing their spirited punk grunge into songs of hooky persuasion, All the while Eddie Spaghetti's ragged vocals doing what Dave Pirner used to do, in fact the band as a whole windmilling like the vital, vociferous Soul Asylum of ten years ago. Scattered throughout the band's raging guitar cruise are smatterings of cowpunk, heavy metal and big, pitcher-swillin' harmonies, mixing gloriously with

this top-flight example of what '90s punk could be. Critiqueing this in the dead middle of a Toronto winter kinda flies in the face of the hot summer sounds all over this witty, low-slung record, tunes like Born With A Tail, 19th Most Powerful Woman In Rock and paean to greatness Ozzy just kicking sadder wiser grunge in the butt. Produced by stinkbomb on stick legs, Paul Leary.
Rating 8

## Sven Gali - Sven Gali (BMG '92)

Through circuitous and often finger-burning pathways, Hamilton, Ontario's Sven Gali managed to rise above their amateur business moves, arriving at major label status in fine fashion with this slashing chunk of aggressive hardrockmetal. Skid Row comparisons are inevitable, especially with the Baz-like enthusiasm of David Wanless on throat, who does an excellent job of announcing this band's presence to the world. Musically speaking, Sven Gali is a hard rock version of Slave To The Grind, nowhere near the blandness of Skid Row, and miles more pounding and pro than the pablum comprising T.O. peers Slik Toxik's similar era debut Doin' The Nasty. Almost a missing link between the Skid's first two really. Not to belabour the point, but such comparisons (which might also include mid-years Priest) are no detraction from Sven Gali's overall loud effect. This is a mean, corporate release, sporting such nice touches as well-planned "triple" structures (i.e. verse, chorus I, chorus II), and rude boy rockers like Freakz, plus a trio of curiously similar speedsters in Stiff Competition, 25 Hours A Day, and Here Today, Gone Tomorrow. Not crazy about the choice of Under The Influence as lead vid/single, but minor complaint on an acceptable Attitude rocker from Steeltown, with an added kick in the ass from a treble-and-bass-intensive mix. Twelve cuts, two and a half ballads, Little or no fat.
Rating 7

## Sven Gali - In Wire (BMG '95)

No way Hamilton's Sven Gali were going to stand still and get strafed by a public gone esoteric in their heaviness, here the band using their own scant dabblings in psychedelia (found sparingly on their shiny debut), as a platform into a sharper-tasting version of I Mother Earth meets Skid Row circa 1995 (Sven Gali somehow tied to the advances of Baz and the boys, if only in my addled mind), Jane's Addicted vocals meet soupy, dreamy heaviness throughout this fairly provocative record, a disc risky in its own way as a departure far afield for the boys. Multi-dimensional and sometimes damn near impermeable, In Wire makes a serious play for credibility, one you should attend with open ear, a record leap-frogging inevitable comparatives Slik Toxik and their also fine but not quite so fine Irrelevant sophomore. Slammed in Canada, but released months later in the U.S., not without exuberant praise, and uh, dismal sales, just like Sloan.
Rating 8

## Swallow - Swallow (Sub Pop Est' 88)

One kickin' early Sub Popper that owes more to unabashed bashing punk than most grunge rockers with their assimilations of early metal, Swallow is a moshing sort of guitar romp, featuring "Rod" on vocals, who out-slouches Mark Arm in spotty spots. Full song listing: Zoo, Foetus, Coffin, Guts, Hard, Cold, BSA, Trim. Nice and simple for a record that's simple but not all that nice, but not all that serious either. Definitely a garage rocker, reeking of pre-"scene" lack of concern for potential stardom. Sorta like if Iggy's Kill City was a metal album.
Rating 8

## The Sweet - The Sweet (Bell '73)

Already veterans of rock'n'roll prostitution at its most manipulative, Sweet got down to business and found

themselves surprisingly adept merchants of metal. And **The Sweet**'s full of it, early simple axe-rock mixing glam novelty and pulsating electric guitar on such candy rock classics as *Little Willy*, *Wig Wam Bam* and *Hellraiser*, three tracks nearly identical in their gushing sock-hop feel (appropriately all Chapman/Chinn creations), bluntly carrying forth the trademark sound that would transform itself into *Ballroom Blitz* and finally *Action*. And it gets ugly too, with more sinister-type metal like *Man From Mecca* and *Need A Lot Of Lovin'*, proving that The Sweet were right in the thick of the metal revolution wrought upon our hides from overseas. Nonetheless, **The Sweet** still sounds dated and kinda grey, nowhere near as sophisticated as the follow-up product that would briefly but astoundingly captivate America in the coming two years.
Rating **5**

## Sweet - Desolation Boulevard  (Capitol '75)

Who can forget such roller-rink hits as *Ballroom Blitz* and *Fox On The Run*? Nobody with a heart, that's for sure, **Desolation Boulevard** winning over a generation of platform-booted rockheads and screaming chicks alike, zooming up the charts across the western world with prizes for all. **Desolation Boulevard** and its follow-up *Give Us A Wink* formed Sweet's golden era, both records showcasing an astonishingly strong raft of songs, sacrificing no hook as Andy Scott burns up the fretboards (especially come solo time), establishing himself as one of the unsung axe heroes of the '70s. Bashful and endearing pop rock such as *The 6-Teens*, *A.C.D.C.*, and aforementioned bonanza *Fox On The Run* do battle with state-of-the-art megametal like *No You Don't*, *Sweet F.A.*, *Into The Night* and the much-covered *Set Me Free* on this record that is essentially the stateside version of the U.K.'s **Sweet Fanny Adams** with a few swapped tracks. Essentially, **Desolation Boulevard** is a collection of songs on a mission, each unique and unto itself, each a flagship cut, classy whatever its exploration. And vocally . . . hey, this is Sweet talking, Connolly and Priest both torrid in their respective duties, Mick Tucker rounding out the performance on drums, again, one of the unsungs of his chosen weapon. A classic of the '70s, with its surprising sense of accomplishment in a number of fields, **Desolation Boulevard** is one of those rare works where everything just seems to go right, good feelings all around, excitement at every crease. An essential piece of rock history, and hot performances to boot.
Rating **10**

## Sweet - Strung Up  (RCA '75)

Perpetuating the reality that the minds of Sweet were impervious to marketing logic, this double import comprises one record live, one record studio compilation, which together trot out a few more heretofore hidden metal highballs. The live half shows Sweet, the kick-ass, loose, irreverent rock pigs, gorging themselves on some of their early stompers, including weighty Sab/Zep ode, *Burning/Someone Else Will*, plus a spirited blaze-through of *Hellraiser*. The studio half is basically genre-bender **Desolation Boulevard** with a few key substitutions such as the band's most high-minded construct, bad boy alter-ego of *Bohemian Rhapsody*, *Action*, plus two meaty rockers, *Miss Demeanour* and all-out street-heater *Burn On The Flame*, one of the band's finest buried gems, second among B-sides only to metaphysical smoker *Medusa*. For knowledge-seeking Sweet tooths only. Perhaps in response to criticism of the band's lack of autonomy, the cover graphics by Petagno portray ironic caricatures of the band pulling their own strings.
Rating **6**

## Sweet - Give Us A Wink  (Capitol '76)

Probably the band's most intelligent and cohesive work, **Give Us A Wink** finds the band expertly walking the line between pomp and songcraft, like late '70s Queen. *Action* is the pièce de resistance, pretty well my most treasured Sweet track with its swirling riffery and daring breaks brewing a sensuous career retrospective in under four minutes. And the metal on the record is widely divergent, speedy, slow, down the middle, all studded with meaty Scott soloing and a general resonance that is thick and surging, taking the only vestige worth keeping from the glam years and applying it to a batch of compositions that go to many dangerous places (see the grungy, almost Zepp-ish *Cockroach*) returning laden with riches. Despite its roller-coaster ride through cool rock styles, **Give Us A Wink** always feels professional, Sweet in capable control, ever-knowing of the destination, which as with many of the best '70s lab technicians, is someplace completely new, a land built of solid, even traditional songs that combined, make a record that is fresh, enigmatic and capable of many moods. Faves outside of *Action*: *White Mice* and *Keep It In*, both metal highballs confidently ahead of their time.
Rating **10**

## Sweet - Off The Record  (Capitol '77)

Using one's imagination, it is possible to consider this a golden-era Sweet release, full of rumbling guitars, heaven-sent harmonies and elegant flashbacks to the '60s. Yet the over-riding feel is one of pop fragmentation, as the band loses its desperate, exploratory edge. **Off The Record**'s a weird one, in that many of its components harken back to the band's guitar-driven bubble gum hits, noticeably nostalgic on *Fever Of Love*, *Live For Today* and the amusingly Cooper-ish *Stairway To The Stars*. Drilled and maniacally out-of-place is Sabbath-style collision *Windy City*, which closes side one with a bang, driven deep into memory banks by an ethereal but pummeling chorus and parallel verse riff. And that ain't the end of the steel, as the choppy *Hard Times* bristles with devil-ish axe decisions, and closer *She Gimme Lovin* races with a nice phase-shifted insistence. Great vintage constructs mixed with simple fun from a classic set of musical brains, yet somehow it all feels so deserted and lost, as a pervading sense of the band's decline can't help but influence the impact of the album. Shouldn't happen but it does. Dammit though, if Andy Scott ain't one of the most talented guitarists to ever walk the planet.
Rating **8**

## Sweet - Level Headed  (Capitol '77)

The first record of the great inexplicable slide into what? . . . amusement with new technologies, catatonic apathy . . . who can say for sure? In any event, **Level Headed** entirely lacks Rock, slushing along with tons of synths, acoustic drudge and self-defeated song ideas, rising to froth only with vibrant, Queen-pranced popster *Love Is Like Oxygen*, one of an increasingly rare flow of U.S. hits for this ass-backwards band of near geniuses. A sorry chunk of anonymity from a band lacking the desire and psychological fortitude to experiment properly at this point in their peaks and valleys career.
Rating **5**

## Sweet - Cut Above The Rest  (Capitol '79)

Sweet continues its tragic aimlessness in quest of the heady magic that turned puppet popsters into influential legends. With one of the strangest career paths ever, it's no wonder the years had taken their physical, emotional and creative toll by this point. On **Cut Above The Rest**, the original lineup (apparently minus Connolly) retains its angelic harmonies, and trademark axework as per brethren Queen and Lizzy, while exploring acoustic and synth-laced pop of a more melancholy nature, simultaneously far-reaching and stumbling. Overall feel is one of a well-crafted, angst-ridden and dated '70s pop record, steeped in decadent fatigue. Most interesting compositions would be minor hit *Discophony*, an overblown piece of symphonic rock reminiscent of early Tubes, standing as Sweet's somewhat novel attack on disco, *Play All Night*, a standard lowbrow Sweet stomp, and the melodious and close acoustic *Eye Games*, the band's unadorned denigration of the bar scene. Entertaining as a bad but accessible record by a once proud force for change.

Rating 6

## Sweet - VI (Capitol '80)

Clip-clopping lite-hearted power pop from a rapidly sinking ship of Neros, twiddling knobs in expensive studios as their creativity crashes in flames. **VI** is one long, failed experiment in puffed up party fare, mixing acoustic and electric guitar work with horribly cheesy '70s synth tricks throughout exclusively market-minded tunes that never shake the pervading smell of burn-out. Again, you sorta want to own it 'cos it's Sweet, but that's all.

Rating 4

## Sweet - The Best Of (Capitol '92)

These sixteen tracks comprise an artfully picked collection that tells a story. Of course given the enigmatic quality of this band, every fan would have their own, wildly divergent set of faves. But this one does an amazing job of weaving all those wasted years together with songs that all essentially conform to Sweet's three or four brilliant characteristics. Quite a feat, given the often unwise mood swings with which the music was battered over the nutty, fruity years represented. Hard to screw up the early years (and this doesn't), but a fetching job is done with the hazy lazy daze, the inclusion of *Lost Angels*, *Stairway To The Stars*, *Fever Of Love* and *Love Is Like Oxygen* turning the show into a sugary sockhop far beyond what Cheap Trick (or 10cc!) could ever spark. Liner note tidbit: by 1976, Sweet had sold 26 million records (. . . and by 1980, that total had surpassed 26,002,101. Just kidding). Reaper's update: Brian Connolly, dead at 52, February 10, 1997; liver disease, after years of pounding back pints with the best of them.

Rating 8

## Andy Scott's Sweet - Andy Scott's Sweet (SPV '92)

Not the sad disaster one might assume, ASS try awfully hard to please on this guitar-based stab at party metal. Soar-away moment by far is a downright Quo-table version of Angel City's classic *Am I Ever Gonna See Your Face Again*. Of course, not in the least reminiscent of the unattainable Sweet, but well-constructed nonetheless, albeit uneven of style; somewhat stiff but brazenly mixed, as is usually the case with commercial metal from Britain. Faves: manly boogie *Marshall Stack* and thumpy Big Brother bruiser *Red Tape*.

Rating 6

## Sweet Pain - Sweet Pain (Combat '85)

Basic glam buttheads with a preference for whale tails, fat tires, and rearview garterbelts, in the fine tradition of lost '70s phenomena everywhere, most notably The Dictators, Kiss and Starz, who are covered here with a fumbled, off-key version of *Subway Terror*. All crashing, juvenile eight cuts here exist in rank dedication to all that was an uproarious laugh about hard rock in the '70s. Riffs are simple and goofy, like heavy Dictators, yet so obviously existing for the sole purpose of pulling chicks; and vocal chores are treated with a whiny, class clown rebellion towards actually learning anything. Really pretty funny, and probably meant to be. *I Get My Kicks, Down On The Boulevard, Knock Your Socks Off* . . . you get the drift.

Rating 6

## Sweet Savage - Killing Time (Neat Metal '96)

An interesting metal curio, **Killing Time** is a Neat release of a debut album by early '80s Belfast act known for being Vivian Campbell's first recording band. The music enclosed is quite convincing, much like debut-era Def Lep crossed with faster Riot or Tygers Of Pan Tang, riffs afire, although vocals tend toward flat. Supposedly four Sweet Savage tunes, reworked, made their way onto Dio's tall classic **Holy Diver** (along with Viv of course), none of them included here, *Straight Through The Heart* being the most visible for the originator, having been released as a Sweet Savage single in '81.

Rating 7

## Sweet Water - Sweet Water (Atlantic '93)

The long-anticipated debut from Seattle's Sweet Water shows its preparation with a sound that like all from the land of the misused grunge tag, mixes a number of commendable elements, into a new and old type of rock experience. Sweet Water's central strength is the fluid and forceful axework of Dudley Taft (lead) and Rick Credo (rhythm), although I guess it's Taft I'm most impressed with, being drawn to what are "leads", impressive, strangely traditional metal solos, fills and otherwise shadings, which lend the project an upscale air. First (and only) comparative that comes to mind is Mother Love Bone, Adam Czeisler's vocals possessing Wood's sometimes over-affecting sense of drama, and Sweet Water's product mix finding Bone's dynamic but wayward juxtapositions of spacey quietness and funky metal squalor. But **Sweet Water** is above all, a fine guitar album of many colours, rich in melody, versatile in the most positive sense, almost effortlessly likeable in a mainstream manner, easily crossover-able if adequately misunderstood by the masses. Something puts this in the same frame of mind as Afghan Whigs, Nudeswirl, Liquid Jesus and The Big F for me, fringe-dwelling (no help to the creepy band shot on the back), down-wound, melodiously assembled and meticulously mixed. Well worth the wait, and in no particular hurry once parked.

Rating 8

## Sweet Water - Superfriends (Atlantic '95)

Count Sweet Water as another already weird and unslottable band diving headlong into alternative, the boys cutting their hair and simplifying their deliveries into nice power chord churns ranging from grunge lite to a brisk '90s punk. But it's hard to hide the fact that Sweet Water have roots in a brainy, provocative corner of Seattle grunge, so there's some artful riffing here, not to mention (gasp) guitar solos, amongst all the sing-songy hard alternative storming the gates. I dunno, liked the first one better, but these guys still wipe the floor with most of the no-talents out there. Faves: *Superstar* and *Win*, which have choruses to die for. All told, stout of heart, rich with melody and luscious production, but well, precious.

Rating 8

## Sword - Metalized (Aquarius '86)

Sword were an under-rated metal act from Montreal, whose main claim to continuance is much inferior outfit Saints & Sinners, featuring Sword vocalist Rick Hughes. Oddly plain but effective, **Metalized** evokes a band that knows what it's doing, with a simple, even greasy delivery, yet nuance of veteran skills. No prissy Canadian hard rocker, **Metalized** is pure crunch, all chugging power chords and might, sounding like no other band and a thousand other bands at once, maybe like early Metal Church meets middle Priest, yet more with the former's clashing chaos. And Hughes does a killer job at the mike, sending such anthems as F.T.W., Stoned Again and Stuck In Rock into clubbing, sweatdog metaldom. No matter what ridicule one could shower upon mid '80s metal, not to mention most rock from Canada, Sword was above it as far as I'm concerned, being a solid, no bullshit type band. Too bad about Saints & Sinners.

Rating 7

## Sword - Sweet Dreams   (Aquarius '88)

Gone is the clattery, drum-dominated delivery of the debut, for a sound that capitalizes on the band's muscle-bound guitar thump. **Sweet Dreams** opens with a flagrant Zep stomper, proceeding on with more of its purist pub metal, again somewhat a contradiction in terms, but not really for those who remember the emphasis on the technical that turned headbanger club dates into workshops for denim dreamers. Thus Sword's oeuvre and legacy is a sort of soldierly trudge that combined the missionary zeal of isolated '70s hard rockers with the shameless fireworks of the '80s. A modest piece of history's puzzle, yet a band with lots of which to be proud, not the least being their purity of purpose.

Rating 8

## Sykes - Out Of My Tree   (PolyGram '95)

Curly-maned guitar legend John Sykes returns with this unwieldy, Japan-only release, a lavish pack of thundering, often blues-based tunes that showcase tastefully the man's proto-metal riffs and solos. Along for the ride are rock journeymen Marco Mendoza on bass and Tommy O'Steen on drums. Of course the record is slick, well-executed and layered up nicely, but the songs demonstrate the lukewarm mix of heavy funk, blues of various sizes and speeds, and AOR crap (If You Ever Need Love), that caused such indifference to Blue Murder's **Nothin' But Trouble**. Strangely, four or five tunes sound like covers (but none are), oddest one being the '90s melodic punk of I Don't Wanna Live My Life Like You, which starts with the ol' "Wakey, wakey!", which I'm sure he borrowed from The Damned or Tank (later in the track, he quotes the Beatles). But other seemingly lax or middling ventures show the band as more of a textured machine, Do Or Die and morose ballad I Don't Believe In Anything exuding the band's star pedigree within normalish, unflashy structures. I think gone forever is Sykes as flash rockin' metal machine. But even as this record's cauldron of styles might elicit vacant stares, the playing and arranging is top-notch. The lyrics suck.

Rating 7

## Syre - It Ain't Pretty Being Easy   (A&M '89)

Party-down, pretty boy, pop metal from Canada with all the right moves and painstaking attention to detail to make a serious shot at stardom, Syre keep it fun, buoyant, and fully in motion throughout these sweetly hard rockin' portrayals of life with no worries. Fully ditzy, almost glam in disposition, Syre have one thing on their minds, becoming non-stop, rock'n'rollin' teen stars, and the enthusiasm shows. If I were more accepting of this rock genre, I might rate this release more highly, but for now, I like my cake with a bit more edge and craziness, not to mention leanings towards the metallic. Vocals bring back memories of Rick Santers.

Rating 5

## Tad - Inhaler (Mechanic '93)

Sit Tad on the same Seattle sofa as Melvins, both bands grunge originals that are only now seeing much recognition after lots of greasy, smelly anti-records. Tad is by far the more musical bunch, **Inhaler** pounding with a fine, accessible heavy grunge force, big Tad Doyle and co. wrapping together tight rhythmic boulders of cool turgidness, squarely heavy metal hooks with that doomy Northwest raindance we've all grown to envy. Solid tunes, deep grooves and skewed melodies make Tad a fairly professional slice o' grunge, which is quite surprising given the band's cheapo past. But I'm still not a huge rockin' fan, the record (perhaps unfairly on my part) sort of second guessing a sound that strangely enough, Tad helped bluster into worldwide view. Not sounding like any other band really, just a patchwork of a very down bunch.

Rating                                                                7

## Tad - Live Alien Broadcasts (Futurist '94)

This splintered blockhead of a record was a contractual obligation deal, produced with disdain, recorded live at Bad Animals studios. Weird, but you can't fault Tad's particularly black and blue intrinsically grunge rant. It's almost always better than Melvins, and their recording, well, let's just say my woofers are quaking in their sockets. Vicious rhythms are the band's forté, but once past marveling in that particular black-winded space, one instantly forgets Mr. Doyle's songs, which might be why Tad hasn't broken through the yellow-brown ice of the grunge underpack.

Rating                                                                6

## Tad - Infrared Ridinghood (eastwest '95)

And the injustice of Tad not succeeding big wears on like a flat ball-bearing, this latest exquisitely titled feat of bass, melody and arch-grunge groove doing little at the box office, despite the wisdoms enclosed. **Infrared** bops with a bit more of a pop sheen, all the while the band still building their cathedrals of chop-blocking rhythm, songs waaay down in the pocket like the most demented of Seattle denizens. Oh, and there's lots more bazooka-brilliant titles: *Ictus, Bullhorn, Thistle Suit, Emotional Cockroach, Bludge, Tool Marks, Mystery Copter*; pretty bloody nifty stuff, if anybody can shake that morose (see below) feeling that the catalogue is getting too big with no results of which to speak.

Rating                                                                8

## Tad Morose - Leaving The Past Behind (Black Mark '93)

After milling around the scene since '91 (with a different singer), Tad Morose made one lone demo tape (new singer Krille now in place), then got signed by Black Mark, adding Frippe on keyboards, hatching this debut which went on to receive underground accolades the world over, especially in Japan. And for good reason, the band's full-on pomp rock already fully realized, perhaps blending a more conservative progressive with a more conservative metal, slick as all get out, but less the creative whirlwind of future, more committed spreads. Lyrically, the band is well on the way to examining spiritual questions, each track's character cloaked in palpable desperation, surmising universal yearnings, a welcome approach given all the angst-ridden crap out there in both the worlds of metal and alternative. If you like new Tad Morose, you'll like old Tad Morose. They are largely the same good thing.

Rating                                                                7

## Tad Morose - Sender Of Thoughts (Black Mark '95)

Thought you'd never see another flavour in the much-maligned, already splintered genre of heavy metal? Well, think again, 'cos Swede cerebrals Tad Morose have put a new twist on progressive metal, combining the self-evident priss of Queensryche and the over-rated Dream Theater with heavier Marillion, IQ and atmospheric death. Most surprising is the almost hair band vox of Kristian Andren, which somehow place this squarely at odds with everything out there right now. Demonstrating moreso a recognition and internalization of new slow doom, Tad Morose choose to dedicate themselves completely to an open architecture art rock, and let the death leak out insidiously, through dreamy lyrical themes and unobtrusive but dirty guitar work, axes tethered for the most part, but part of the band's snobby palette all the same. Oddly enough, this is close to what Magnum and Nightwing were getting at all those years ago; new doomy emotions but similar well-tailored complication and tone, prone to cause occasional to frequent boredom unless prog metal doth really turn you on (personally, I love prog and metal, but rarely prog metal). But I think this kills Dream Theater, if that means anything. Perfectly fitting cover of Rainbow's *Gates Of Babylon*, a helluva choice if I ever seen one.

Rating                                                                7

## Tad Morose - Paradigma (Black Mark '95)

In the banana seat days of Kiss, this would almost be deemed a full album, **Paradigma** being close to half an hour long, featuring five tracks clocking around five and six minutes each. Songs here bulk up here, getting heavier and lower register, the band's castle-grey keyboard strains buttressed by very chunky riffing and an ever so slightly more distraught and dynamic vocal presentation (i.e. they're becoming more like uber-twins Morgana Lefay). A tad more immediate and just as morose, this points to a direction Dream Theater, Fates Warning or even Rainbow might have gone, if each were willing to get heavier. Exaggeratedly gothic, and subsequently, a great escape from time into timelessness.
Rating　　　　　　　　　　　　　　　　8

## Tad Morose - A Mended Rhyme (Black Mark '97)

I grow weary at finding new things to say about Tad Morose (remember the Eskimos and their thirty words for snow?), this polished band of castle rockers coming back often and confidently, sure to have another German hit record, even if America gives them the cold shoulder. The new one's recorded a bit more conservatively, even if keyboards and techno touches fill the gaps. Consider it far left of Nevermore, and near left of Iced Earth. As usual, Urban Breed's vocals are torridly metal in the classical sense, but the progressive cramming begins to overload after awhile. So not thrilled at the sameyness of it all, even though I can see revisiting the catalogue ten years down the road and finally deciphering, mastering, compartmentalizing, opinionizing, emotionalizing and taking to heart the proud legacy Tad Morose is building. Comes back to my theory (slowly being realized), that toil and subsequent quality western culture can sell consistent (small or large) quantities for hundreds of years. I'd put these guys among the possibles for Jetson-car-downloading in May, 2112.
Rating　　　　　　　　　　　　　　　　8

## Tai Pan - Slow Death (Shark '95)

This Axel Thubeauville-produced project (glad to see he's still in the biz) combines the big cliff-dwelling riffs of Metallica's uneventful **Metallica** album, and the trimmed-down progressive goth of many fellow European acts (these guys are German) of the mid-'90s. So consider it a doomier, much heavier direction Fates Warning could have taken, or a more accessible, speedier Solitude Aeturnus, sorta doom and gloom, sorta back to traditional postures from the '80s, with a caffeinated dose of '90s Bay Area thrash. Swanky look to the thing too, with lengthy, morally anguished lyrics (what else is new?). Classy, but too grey and "Heavy Metal" for me at this arc in my personality.
Rating　　　　　　　　　　　　　　　　7

## Talas - Talas (Evenfall '79)

Talas' independent debut (with a scant pressing of 15,000 copies) is pretty much spangled, hokey hard rock, as can be expected from a power trio from the '70s. Billy's already wiggling his fingers but songs just flounder in a sea of irritating cluelessness, courting mewling hard rock, pop and even a cover of Stop! In The Name Of Love, a composition I truly loathe on par with Gimme Some Lovin' and Mony, Mony. But yes, a just-fine-thanks mix complimented with clarity and humour raise this vintage toy from the muck. Thus, really not all that hard to tolerate.
Rating　　　　　　　　　　　　　　　　4

## Talas - Sink Your Teeth Into That (Relativity '82)

Ladies and gentlemen, Talas: metal's most verbose and effluent bass wizard Billy Sheehan and his first recording band. This second effort sports pretty pedestrian songwriting glazed with loose, junky production; bass mixed way up front, which in my opinion only works if the instrument is approached with restraint and a healthy bottom-end work ethic, both which Sheehan lacks. **Sink Your Teeth Into That** is more or less a vehicle for Sheehan's bass histrionics, and although he doesn't really ego out with solos, instrumentals, and covers of old classical tunes, the quality of the songs, already poor, is further sabotaged by the garage delivery. Pretty amateur, low budget metal like a lot of the American stuff at the time, **Sink Your Teeth** could have benefited from Sheehan spending a little more time on songcraft as opposed to his legendary long hours of bass practice. Personal speed rocker Shy Boy eventually resurfaced on David Lee Roth's first solo LP.
Rating　　　　　　　　　　　　　　　　5

## Talas - Live Speed On Ice (Important '83)

No big improvement here, as Bill takes his completely new band to vinyl, after only twelve gigs together, as rebellion against the over-treated, overplanned state of modern rock'n'roll. After planning then abandoning a next Talas move, Billy weighs his many outside options, marking time first with UFO and Diamond Dave, then assembling his present, lacklustre, but improving and commercially well-off outfit Mr. Big. Maybe that was the ultimate point of these two resumes anyway. In respect to the grooves herein enclosed however, who cares, **Sink Your Teeth Into That** sounded live anyways, and thus is the only even remotely useful Talas product.
Rating　　　　　　　　　　　　　　　　3

## Talon - Neutralized (Bacilus '84)

German bang-thy-heads hyper on alchemical treble and unruly supremacist emotion, Talon tread the trundled path of Black Forest demonizers with reckless aplomb, wincing desperately close to speed and biker forms of the genre, and not altogether original riffs of Teutonia. All in all, gut-satisfying although not ground-breaking.
Rating　　　　　　　　　　　　　　　　7

## Tamplin and Friends - An Axe To Grind (Intense '90)

Ken Tamplin is yer basic well-studied AOR shredsmith with strong Christian beliefs, beginning life with white rockers Shout, now making glossy AOR numbers under his uh, Christian name. So this one's what one might expect, heliummy harmonies, lots of tasty guitar, keyboards, melodic party rock and occasional inspirational, devotional lyrics. Chuck Wright and Ken Mary from House Of Lords are along for the ride, and by record's end, what has transpired is a pretty dull commercial hard rocker with academic axe overtones, probably more suited to success amongst the videotape and tablature set than Poison fans.
Rating　　　　　　　　　　　　　　　　5

## Ken Tamplin - Soul Survivor (Intense '91)

Even though this is more of a homemade solo effort (Tamplin is credited as drummer, but it's a machine), **Soul Survivor** escapes the shackles of having to make the big rawk record, getting a touch bluesier, more playful and even poppier to positive effect. Tamplin's got a nice, resonating voice and a heck of a touch come acoustic vibe (see Midnight 'n Peru), turning this personal project just that touch more entertaining and human. Always buoyant, always positive.
Rating　　　　　　　　　　　　　　　　6

## Tangiers - Four Winds (Atco '89)

Riddled with surprisingly bad quality keyboard blues metal, **Four Winds** received a more than fair amount of corporate bend-over. But next to the stiff competition out there, this sounds naive and amateurish, locked in a less urgent state of being, achieving all the embarrassing features of retro, soaked up and spit out by '85 or so. Followed up with **Stranded** in '91.

Rating 2

## Tank - Filth Hounds Of Hades (Attic '82)

A smokin', party-with-your-buds debut skidmark from the British band often considered the poor man's Motörhead. And Motörhead elements abound, Eddie Clarke producing, Algy Ward's guttural croak resembling Lemmy's, and the patented distorto-bass buzz ringing loud, proud, front and centre. Comparing both greasechains however, Tank records have a higher percentage of classic toons due to more innovative riff-writing, more diddling, more *trying*. So **Filth Hounds** is full of memorable pre-grunge rockers that range from all-out thrash (early '80s style) to mean-spirited mid-pace rockers with strong melodic choruses, all topped with lyrics that can best be described as colourful. Don't let the odd use of melody fool you, Algy and the boys spew the most pleasantly putrid of chaos metal brews all the way, which unfortunately tended to reveal itself in the band's uniformly horrible live shows, which among U.K. punters earned the band no greater than joke status. Prime killers: *Blood, Guts And Beer*, *T.W.D.A.M.O.*, and *(He Fell In Love With A) Stormtrooper*.

Rating 8

## Tank - Power Of The Hunter (Kamaflage '82)

Another great blast of biker metal classics, **Power Of The Hunter** clangs together the same dastardly elements as the first. We get four or five speed rockers (which tend to be the weakest tracks), while the balance gives us such sweat ethic swillers as *Walking Barefoot Over Glass*, *Used Leather (Hanging Loose)*, and *Set Your Back On Fire*, all powered by inspired riffs and knee-slapping lyrics. And one of the better tunes (rendered heavy as hell of course), is *Crazy Horses* by those toothy Osmonds. I guess I've rated the first couple of Tanks highly because although I really get into only about half of each record, the boys' knock 'em down attitude is inspiring as all get out, with each record's four or five best ditties absolutely life-affirming to the extreme. Kinda like early, out-of-control Megadeth on nothing more stimulating than warm beer.

Rating 9

## Tank - This Means War (Music For Nations '83)

Moving from short punk metal attacks to longer, more topographically-varied battlefields, **This Means War** rides an epic, panoramic war theme throughout. It's still edge-of-chaos, down 'n' dirty garage metal, but things are not the same in the bunker of mosh. On the upside, there's a higher proportion of tunes based around memorable classic metal riffs; on the downside, less toons that stand out as much as the attitude adjusters on the first couple 'o slimebuckets. Additionally, **This Means War**'s lyrics are more conventionally metal, lacking the eccentricity and humour afforded by the band's previous joke status. Still, a rowdy album that wears better over time, this is the stuff beer bellies are made of.

Rating 9

## Tank - Honour & Blood (Attic '84)

**Honour & Blood** tries to emulate the critically-acclaimed **This Means War** with the same 3-on-side-one, 4-on-side-two format, offering less monumental tracks than on either of the last three. But it's still a heroic effort, sending 'em to the mosh pits half-baked, untested but true. *The War Drags Ever On* (lead cut) is a ringer for *Just Like Something From Hell* (lead cut, last album) which is fine by me, and the title track is somewhat of a new modern style for the band. But much of the rest lacks zip, perhaps reflecting a growing despondence at continued lack of commercial success. A heavy air of rehash.

Rating 7

## Tank - Tank (GWR '89)

Similar to the **Honour & Blood**, but with a fatter, more treated, and self-consciously weighty sound, **Tank** leans toward epic structures and a serious, if somewhat clichéd, sound. The worst of Tank albums while still solid, **Tank** also sports Algy's most painfully strained vocals, as if he's slowly losing his range from too much bodily abuse. As a result, he's mixed way back. All in all, a frustrating release in that Tank is exhibiting little progress, which would be fine if the riffs were on par with their previous substantial array of smokin' tunes. But they aren't, causing more valleys than peaks, and a dull fade into the liggin', retirin' section of NWOBHM history.

Rating 6

## Tankard - The Morning After (Noise '88)

The album cover's definitely the best part of this German thrashpanzer punkfest, a record that crackles and buckles as it rips along bent on destruction of the band's bad reputation. Competent and not without the odd black leather guffaw. One of many.

Rating 4

## Tattoo Rodeo - Rode Hard—Put Away Wet (Atlantic '91)

The purchase of said CD (mercifully for a scant $6) lulled me from my sense of security that a debut in the '90s universally gets delivered with more than just minimum talent but with some germination of fresh magic. Wrong, and I should have known better 'cos this ain't the first time. Tattoo Rodeo load their talentless carcasses onto an anthrax-infested cow doped with so much synthetic sleezoid blues medication that after it staggers to centre ring spewing forth a few idiotic clichés about wild women, drugs, and booze, said rounder just flops down and lies there like the pointless exercise in sell-out metal that it is. And little slidey acoustic intros? Hell this record's got seven of 'em. And along for the ride comes one of those "commanding" blues voices that is supposed to roar out wisdoms of the road, yet here you don't believe a damn word of it. In the GN'R, Faster Pussycat, Cats In Boots (via Crüe, Aerosmith, and the Stones) corner of the genre, one looks for an infectedness that ages the toons like hard booze. When it's real, it's a trip, when it's a rip-off, little enjoyable can be salvaged from the deal.

Rating 0

## Tattoo Rodeo - Skin (Mausoleum/EMI '95)

Of course being less inundated with swampdog metal makes all the difference, Tattoo Rodeo now sounding at least slightly fresh compared to all the jangly punk lo-fi rattling the windows the world over. Skin rdeems this band by not buckling to such pressures, if anything getting even bluesier, thicker and less plastic-tracked, closer to Zeppelin, Skynyrd, and unfortunately Thunder. Faves: all the downwound, kiln-fired mellow ones (egad! where's that rocking chair?), which take me halfways (Brother Cane) to all the way (Black Crowes). Either I've grown soft and piney for pine cone rock, or this band has made deliberate shifts in focus. Probably both.

Rating 7

## The Tea Party - Splendor Solis (EMI '93)

This one definitely falls within that category of accept forthrightly or reject in disgust. The debut from this Windsor band crafts an excellent cathedral of sounds that on the downside derives too evidently from acoustic, middle-eastern Zeppelin musically, and Jim Morrison vocally. And that's it really. Very puffed up

and self-important, The Tea Party invite you to grant them that importance or laugh in their face. Many are saying yes to the band's big boomy exotic tones, while remaining iffy on those too cool vocals, a low morose "look at me" sound that makes me want to say "lighten up." Surprisingly mellow, in a forward rocking context, **Splendor Solis** is strangely similar to Plant and Page's **No Quarter**, really enamoured with all that heady Egypto-cruise stuff, brushing a tad close to the masters, who on **No Quarter** even push it a bit far. I don't know, I'm in the reject camp, which can possibly be chalked up to my age, being under the impression that rock guys five or so years my junior can't know it all at their age. And believe me, this band acts like they Know It All.
Rating                                                          6

## The Tea Party - The Edges Of Twilight   (EMI '95)
Everybody's gonna say the same thing about this 'cos it's so obvious and blindly true: this is the record we could only hope for from Page/Plant; a total Zep/eastern music hybrid that is really quite fabulously well textured and conceived. But it helps being a classic rock junkie to accept and subsequently embrace what this almost too serious band of Montreal-via-Windsor white males is trying to achieve. De-limelighted greatly are the Jim Morrison-flirtatious vocals, but pumped up is the epic, "Quiet: Masterpiece In Progress" self-actualized ethereal vibe of leader Jeff Martin's culture-straddling spiritual quest. And really, for all of this towering record, The Tea Party pull off the gargantuan task, almost important-topping the Crowes' **Amorica** in a whole different world, one with loose fitting sheets and turbans. **The Edges Of Twilight** boasts about 30 different instruments, 25 of them weird and used often. Aside from the pastoral quiet acoustic tracks, there's a dose of Bonham bash blues, and quite splendidly, killer flash rockers like *Fire In The Head*, *Sister Awake* and fave classic *The Bazaar*, Moroccan hooks so deep you can smell 'em. Production is exquisite, and it's amazing how those instruments gel into something emotionally and arguably sonically "heavy". Serious as all levity, and truly striving for mastery when it isn't hip, this one's in an exotic world of its own, Martin opening himself up for scathing but lazy criticism for what is only the gravest of sincere intentions, intentions focused on this marriage of world music and heaviness, a marriage that screams a certain classic rock band. Honestly, I have visions of Page/Plant just coming in real conspiracy like, and signing up the band to write and play all their material, Percy wailing away in the limelight, Page invited to add a bit of guitar. Only problem is: The Tea Party ain't going to be anybody's backing band given their meteoric rise all over the planet thus far, with only the fickle U.S. to address formally.
Rating                                                          9

## The Tea Party - Alhambra   (EMI '96)
Well we've finally crossed that line where those of us without CD-ROM may not be qualified to review a rock CD. For The Tea Party has hatched this exotic, quixotic EP that is more multi-media than it is conventional audio music. There's a ton of video/audio here, including full videos, live performances, a lesson on the world instruments used by the band, discography, lyrics and bio stuff. Like I say, way more than the audio, which is pretty much the Page Plant record, the band going increasingly Eastern all over acoustic versions of their Zeppish rock tunes. Closing it out: a mushy, unfocused remix of *Sister Awake*, much less forceful than the version from the band's full-length masterpiece (Yes, it is.). The low-down: Jeff Martin is quite enamoured with techno, and has been threatening to take the band in that direction.
Rating                                                          7

## Teaze - Teaze   ('76)
Unarguably the heaviest offering from this promising Windsor, Ontario (thus Detroit-influenced) band that went nowhere due to dil management and simple dumb luck. **Teaze** dishes with intensity some pretty expressive, meathead rock, at a time when there weren't many bands with loud guitars, outside of a half dozen triumphant stadium draws. Very rare, and apparently hastily-assembled, but worth it for historical value, not to mention the solidity of the record, reminding one of early Legs Diamond, Moxy, or Kiss on brain food. A verbacious bevy of nostalgic talk about how they're gonna blow the doors off tonight. Hey, no argument here.
Rating                                                          7

## Teaze - On The Loose   (Aquarius '78)
Teaze's sophomore effort, marked by a move to Montreal, leans both ways compared to the debut, belting damn metallic tunes one minute and more boppy popcorn rock the next, with not much in between. Another piss-off of '70s lack of focus, as everybody tried to figure out if it was the loud guitars or the quiet ones that sold records (answer: both sold records but usually not on the same album). Teaze fell victim to this oft-repeated confusion with the launch and subsequent success of the light-livered *Sweet Misery* as single, while elsewhere we got starry-eyed, "modern" riff rock in the chopping, lusty title track, the even heavier *Ready To Move*, and monster mood-chug *Lady Killer*. Kick-off track: a cover of Vanda and Young's *Gonna Have A Good Time Tonight* as if I have a clue and/or care who Vanda and Young are outside of their association with AC/DC.
Rating                                                          7

## Teaze - Tour Of Japan   (Aquarius '78)
When there's no coin at home, go East, where the appetite for Western metal seems insatiable. On this album, you'd think these guys were the ultimate heavy metal juggernaut of the western world, even though this was the band's first show outside of Canada and first as a headliner. Good time rock'n'roll and a nice look at a past with considerably more breathing space and elbow room for the world's metallic types.
Rating                                                          5

## Teaze - One Night Stands   (Aquarius '79)
This innocuous shuffle plus the slightly less bent follow-up **Body Shots** (both produced by the unremarkable Myles Goodwyn) sealed Teaze's doom, as one of those strange cases similar to Nazareth, Foghat, Starz, Angel, and Status Quo, bands that started life both hard rockin' and talented, on the verge of breaking the bank, who then soundly abandoned any promise of God-like wax in the making, opting for corporately motivated general journeyman rock that nobody could mistake for art. Baffling. Less an internal breakdown, Teaze (and these other casualties of what could have been) seem to be examples of marketing gone wrong, combined with a not altogether surprising greed factor. (Slight disclaimer: I do have a soft spot for recent Status Quo, and who can totally fault the legendary Angel?) Anyway, Teaze's offerings took the form of embarrassing teeny bopper rock, sappy ballads, and the odd bit of uninspired hard stuff, the latter more so here than on **Body Shots**. Couldn't be interpreted by anybody as anything other than infantile and regressed, the band trying to cash in too quickly on a rising U.S. buzz.
Rating                                                          4

## Teaze - Body Shots   (Aquarius '80)
Lo and befallen, **Body Shots** is an exploded foray into all sorts of bad directions, including axe-based pop, new waveyness, sorry Huey Lewis-style r+b, ballads, (all of which is essentially washed-up April Wine. Al-

though risky in an admirable way, this record coincided with the loss of a promising and promised U.S. record deal. And Teaze was no more six months late, closing the books on an isolated case of Great North Hope. Flown apart, into what or where I have no idea.
Rating 2

## Teenage Head - Teenage Head (IGM '79)
Only this debut by these Frankie Venom-misled Hamilton, Ontario boyz (now old men) deserves mention here, as subsequent efforts descended into a morass of rockabilly, psychobilly, engineering student rock, and general boozy self-parody. **Teenage Head** had an overt New York Dolls complex image-wise, sounding like a stripped and flat-out Dolls, a low quality Fallen Angels or an early Hanoi Rocks, but sillier, more like a heavy Dead Milkmen. All told, the record's about one third heavy, with comedy rock and throwbacks to the '50s making up the balance. Rare as hell. Countless albums since this went straight to the delete bins. Second fave: '96's **Head Disorder**, which finds these wizened rock slugs diving straight into '90s punk hooks, totally legitimately, given that they've been making drinkable punk rock for years.
Rating 4

## Teeze - Teeze (SMC '85)
Pennsylvania neon glam dressed like Twisted Sister at their worst, sounding like average Crue, somewherz between their debut and **Shout At The Devil**, right down to Luis Rivera's bratty nasal twang. Sports an extremely embarrassing front cover band shot with costumes I can't even begin to describe. Loose, cheap and so inextricably linked to 1985, probably the year with the biggest avalanche of scrap metal.
Rating 5

## Temple Of The Dog - Temple Of The Dog (A&M '91)
Lead siren of Soundgarden Chris Cornell and assorted kharmic bro's, (most notably two Mother Love Bone, then Pearl Jam dudes) coalesce to erect a chugging, heaving, heartfelt freight train of a temple to dead Bone vocalist Andrew Wood, victim of a heroin overdose in '90. The sleeve notes give a brief and honest intro to the proceedings here, and the confident and barren strains of the sonic terrain bear out the sentiment that **Temple** is a somber family gathering, a trip dense with gravity, cloaked in a remembrance of a surreal and heady world intruded upon by reality; a fine collection of individual songs, yet at the same time drifts like a loopy jam, a crafted swirl of simple unadorned art and bitter humanity. **Temple Of The Dog** doesn't ram a tire iron in your face as might be expected from such an uncompromising grunge alloy, although a cold Sonic Youth-like depravity shakes nearly every cut. Foremost eulogy on the disc manifests itself as **Say Hello 2 Heaven**, a liquid piece of the moon if there ever was. Steamiest rockers: the Sabbath/funk monsters **Your Savior** and **Pushin Forward Back**, although it's injustice to say anything on this really rocks, as even the heavy ones are so insidiously controlled by both Cornell's unusually sober voice and the skeletal production which breathes and clanks among the even-flow of the music like a nicotine-stained lung. No, the heavy ones are just uncomfortable stirrings within the overall deep and bluesy oceans of the whole. In essence, **Temple Of The Dog** houses one of the heaviest psychological mindscapes of latter-day Sub Pop, managing to bludgeon and infect without the sonic and lyrical overkill of much of the label's second half. Experienced somewhat of a resurgence over a year later by the relaunch of the exquisite **Hunger Strike**.
Rating 9

## Terrorizer - World Downfall (Earache '89)
Bestial arch-mayhem from the transitional days of 200 MPH thrash. This one's of historical value, being a pre-cursor to Morbid Angel, featuring death poster-boy David Vincent and drummer Pete Sandoval, along with the proto-grind voice of Oscar Garcia, axe merchant Jesse Pintado (onto Napalm Death) and producer Scott Burns, who gets a photo here, looking nothing like the Satan-pasted troll one might expect. Ruthlessly extreme, caustic, bile-soaked holler fodder for the fed-up.
Rating 2

## Terrorvision - My House (EMI '93)
Just a little (and I do mean little: three tracks, eight minutes) pre-debut teaser from cool white U.K. funksters called Terrorvision. But hey, it kicks, does backflips, and sizzles, with hot vox from mikester Tony Wright. The title track rides an infectious, ragtag swing, definitely worthy of radio play; **Coming Up** is slammin' barrel-headed riff metal, and **Teu Dunce** a subdued blues shuffle like the Chili Peppers fooling around, and that's all she wrote. I'm sold. Low grade reflects poor value for the buck.
Rating 7

## Terrorvision - Formaldehyde (EMI '93)
Terrorvision take the leap wide-eyed and laughing into a hooky power chord zone that only the Wildhearts can claim to share, both bands sizzling and sparkling with electric rock while coming across as sugary Cheap Tricksters that just wanna have fun. And **Formaldehyde** is an admirable first step, offering all sorts of variations on pop metal, except that is, for all the American ones that killed the genre. Faves would be the tracks with more wallop (**Problem Solved** or **American TV**), even though each successive tune vibrates with verve, whether courting metal, pop, new wave, punk or tender balladry. All in all, a bublegum beauty with loud guitars everywhere you leap.
Rating 8

## Terrorvision - How To Make Friends And Influence People (EMI '94)
More of the same, and once again, totally ignored, **How To Make Friends** just might offer too many baffled sides to this Rubik's Cube of a band. Losing that unifying raw sheen that infected its way through the debut, this one just does everything too well, from lush, orchestrated ballads like **Some People Say** to the speed metal of **What The Doctor Ordered**, both going farther to extremes than anything from **Formaldehyde**. Count me still on board though, just sock-hopping to these light, good-mooded Cheap Tricks, sum total stretched dangerously close to the limit, well past easy pigeon-holing, but grounded firmly in good songs. Warning: maybe a bit meek and mild for some.
Rating 8

## Tesla - Mechanical Resonance (Geffen '86)
Yes, the hype on Sacramento's Tesla was justified to some extent, the band leaping onto the airwaves of their beloved radio with this lengthy, professional truckload of good time metal. For '86, this debut was well-fleshed and confident, yet under the microscope, weak compositionally, rising to wells of Leppard and Y&T mass on the crunchier digs, but wallowing all too often in lackadaisical lite metal, ranging from boppy hard rock to funkiness and gruesome ballads, all a bit too chart-focused with cliché predictability. Still, if you culled your faves from this and '89's similar offering, you'd be blessed with some large melody American-style from grit-piped Jeff Keith and his assembled aspirers. Yeah, it's safe and even a little sleepy, which hasn't escaped critical notice, most oft heard adjective

being "boring", yet Tesla's sound is also more or less correct and crowd-pleasing for the genre.

Rating 6

## Tesla - The Great Radio Controversy (Geffen '89)

Tesla (named for the *real* inventor of radio), are considered by some to be heroes of honesty, purveyors of a universal hard rock sound, the kind of larger than life rock dudes that can get away with an acoustic live album two records into their careers. Others can't stand 'em, lumping them in with all bands considered in bed with the business. This, Tesla's second, clocking at close to an hour, rides a bluesy, low-pocket hard rock/metal sound with fat anthemic choruses and other throwbacks to the '70s. Ambitious, detailed and tight, Tesla offers a fair feast for the dollar, perhaps deserving their quicker than average fame, which had at least positioned them tops of a second string (before the platform collapsed into Nirvana). Complaints: safeness, lack of identity, and an over-use of slow structures. Heavier than you might think given the band's playful image, but so far little that reaches out and fires the soul.

Rating 7

## Tesla - Five Man Acoustical Jam (Geffen '90)

Talk about pre-empting the Unplugged trend in a big way, the good-time boys in Tesla strumming forth with this 67 minute buffet of soft rock classics and disarmed Tesla originals. The whole acoustic thing was a bit of a haphazard, piecemeal development, germinating from some brief radio recordings to a few full-blown shows squeezed in on the band's tour in support of **The Great Radio Controversy**. Then a Boston radio station turned tapes of *Signs* (y'know the ol' hippy song by The Five Man Electrical Band) into a big hit, and a record was born, documenting a July '90 show in Philadelphia. So like I say, there's a bunch of Tesla tracks turned folksy and Jeff Keith screechy, plus old chestnuts from the idealistic '60s such as *We Can Work It Out*, *Truckin'*, *Lodi*, and *Mother's Little Helper*. And it all gels well, Tesla always embodying that down-home intimacy that would make this sort of campfire concert work.

Rating 7

## Tesla - Psychotic Supper (Geffen '91)

It's damn easy to be swept along in the tides of Tesla's unbridled enthusiasm. Their's is a band that takes themselves seriously, demanding listeners to take them seriously, creating full, heroic, energetic records that rather than blow you away with state of the nation complexities, prefer to work studiously and emotionally within a hard rock framework, which expands to include truly kickin' metal, chunk funk, down through more populist melloid connector candy fit for hockey barn lighter rituals. Past all the labeling, which incidentally the warmest cut on this record, *Call It What You Want*, addresses, **Psychotic Supper** is one huge rock show, expertly woven in slick commercial fashion, and I mean that as a compliment. Tesla is a combination of talent who undoubtedly want to be kings (see Slaughter), spending each successive release as a learning process toward that end. And this record brings their work to fruition, as the sweat ethic comes full steam for this testimony to California rock greatness. Throughout **Psychotic Supper**, all is effortless class. The Hannon/Skeoch guitar weaves are simply brill, surprises are smooth, seamless, and after awhile expected, and Keith's vocals are soulful and commanding, rendering top-of-the-line flights like second video *Edison's Medicine*, strident eulogy for Leppard's Steve Clark *Song And Emotion*, and vintage Lep-style tank *Freedom Slaves*, proud and lofty. All works capable navigation here, rockers and quiet introspections alike (of which there are essentially two out of twelve cuts).

Above all the platitudes, however, Tesla is merely one of my adopted faves of corporate metal, connecting with authenticity all over the spectrum, making this one of California metal's formidable passion plays.

Rating 9

## Tesla - Bust A Nut (MCA '94)

If anybody can keep the flame of smooth and drinkable, big budget hard rock alive, it's Tesla, a band who somehow can rock and not rock so commercially, while evoking serious mutterings in the direction of integrity, class and maybe even timelessness. **Bust A Nut**, finds the band brewing their usual long and winding road of big hair styles; succinctly put, taking Def Leppard's cavalier **High 'n' Dry** into the late '90s, intelligence, modern work levels and all, running proudly the torch of the Leps early triumphs, while the real Leps continue forth with some of the most abysmal records in the annals of guitar (?) rock. Throw in Zeppelin and Aerosmith, after which Tesla weaves smartly their own messages of hope, their own understated licks, all produced with immaculate chuggery under the increasingly rough, rolling vocals of Jeff Keith. Outside of crass novelty Melanie cover *Games People Play*, the record hangs well, faves being the morose *Shine Away*, *Try So Hard* and *Wonderful World*, all three personifying the record as a whole with their studied, dynamic tones, main dif from **Psychotic Supper** being this one's level gravity, fewer party rockers, more world weariness. But still, Tesla strikes me as one of the last strong creative forces in this war-torn genre. Hopefully the buying public will agree and let them live!

Rating 8

## Tesla - Time's Makin' Changes: The Best Of Tesla
(Geffen/MCA '95)

Through all the hairband-bashing of the '90s thus far, Tesla is one act that has quietly escaped the slagging and snickering. Not exactly on upward trajectory sales-wise, the boyz have remained a guilty pleasure of rock scribes and a fiercely loyal chunk of the buying public, due to the band's sense of groundedness, passion, and their adherence to stadium rock standards without the dated and dating elements. Tunes are about, well, song and emotion, just everyday life stuff, massively constructed, hooky and heavy; and as I've said many times before, everything Def Leppard could have been, the blossomed culmination of the Leps very real potential, just as they became the world's least talented band after '84's **Pyromania**. The record at hand culls all sorts of golden Tesla moments from five not unsuccessful records, four painstakingly large studio albums, plus their celebrated live acoustic set, adding lots of pics and liner notes to put it all in context. One can see the transition from the overly glitzy through the sharper, more poignant songwriting of **Psychotic Supper** (*Edison's Medicine*, *Song & Emotion*; the latter the only tune I know eulogizing Lep's guitarist Steve Clark, until Lep did one themselves) and the vastly under-rated **Bust A Nut** from last year. Only one new track adorns the 75 minute set, *Steppin' Over*, which is classic Tesla all the way, loving ballad-like passages to majestic riffery executed with seamless, dynamic delivery, causing justified anticipation that this band won't give up the ghost. Maybe you want this, I don't know, but my recommendation is snag the last two studio feasts. The highly held "heads" of suntanned rock'n'roll.

Rating 7

## Testament - The Legacy (Atlantic '87)

A violent debut from an act that comes out swinging, **The Legacy** is intelligent speed metal seasoned with a healthy wollop of thrashmosh, making for an experience that is bludgeoning, yet as far as I'm concerned, frantic and forgettable. Testament has definitely been

through the ringer through these last few years, what with the **Souls Of Black** debacle and something of a critical comeback with **The Ritual**, but I've just never been on board, much like my experience with Overkill (until **I Hear Black**) or Exodus. Main reason: imitation of a sound left in the '80s. Half-saved by careening, drunken production values.
Rating 4

## Testament - The New Order (Megaforce/Atlantic '88)

Trashy-on-purpose highly engineered thrash that makes no advancements on the debut, marred by too many in that California hardcore-inspired shout-and-reply zone, fast OTT beats that collapse briefly into Metallica grooves time and time again, then leap back out until we all can predict the next wave. Glaring exception: the band's low grumbling cover of Aerosmith's *Nobody's Fault*, that band's heaviest metal, appropriate choice for committed rivetheads and earthdogs like Testament.
Rating 5

## Testament - Practice What You Preach
(Megaforce/Atlantic '89)

Same workforce, same producer (Alex Perialas), same kinda botched, bass-less drum sound (maybe worse), but the band has gotten more raw, sweating it out in the moshpits, sounding hurried, spontaneous mostly in a bad way, picking riffs from the dumpster outside the studio in which Metallica made **Master Of Puppets**. Hilarious really, how so alike the careers of Testament and Overkill progressed (or didn't if you talk numbers), both arriving at a really smokin' truckload of crunch at roughly the same time in the mid-'90s, yet still undermining their heaviness with wiseguy speed at the turn of the decade.
Rating 5

## Testament - Souls Of Black (Megaforce/Atlantic '90)

I've never seen a record released to such bad press, the band itself even underwhelmed. Forsooth, **Souls Of Black** is a more of the same type spin, but the songs are B-grade at best, reason being that its release was a hasty, rushed and otherwise slapped together thing, pushed out to coincide with the band heading out on the European Clash Of The Titans tour, which included Megadeth, Suicidal Tendencies and Slayer. The lost Testament document.
Rating 4

## Testament - The Ritual (Atlantic '92)

As with many organizations of this ilk, the big whomping tower of impenetrable steel comes delivered with a classy album cover and a new producer, here Tony Platt leading the band away from their scrappy, kicked underdog status into large, molten metal riffs that are the epitome of class. So **The Ritual** sounds like old, bold Sabbath with the studied knowledge of Priest, made hip with a '90s scrape that leads Chuck Billy and crew towards the volatility of a Corrosion Of Conformity. Flamethrowers are everywhere; the thumping drives of *As The Seasons Grey* and *Electric Crown*, almost Accept-like in their heart-pumping headbangs, and guess what? There isn't a single fast song on the entire record, something that would inevitably disgust a large legion of old, scowling, know-it-all fans (but not the groove-lover like me). Absolutely craven of power, **The Ritual** is a manual for muscle-bound recording skills, all the while Billy's Hetfield-like delivery rendered measured and serious in tone, Skolnick's riffs dense, devouring and spread over the width and length of this record like a heavy velvet shroud.
Rating 9

## Testament - Return To The Apocalyptic City
(Atlantic '93)

One deafening half hour of prime-time thrash Americana, this violent little EP finds the band sounding less like a Bay Area institution, more like a bad moon brew between hardcore and death. Of course **The Ritual** tracks are my faves, but really, the experience as a whole shows what a kickin' live machine these guys can be.
Rating 7

## Testament - Low (Atlantic '94)

After waxing and waning for a few years, Testament seem to be back on trouble's track with a couple of line-up changes, key addition being vet James Murphy on guitar, and a mid-process switch to Dave Jerden as producer. **Low** comes out swinging, with a more frantic, cram-it-all-in work ethic; caffeinated, high-flying, but with an element of the loose and rickety. Lots of lightning quick fills (mostly axe and drum, but even bass) string together catchy thrash-tinted Bay Area tech rockers, best being the magnificent title track, manic double-timer *Ride*, and deeply carved mid-pacer *All I Could Bleed*. Something urgent and underground about this one, almost punky and subversive while still being much about chops. Still, an easy listening piece of ultra-professional hardcore, Chuck's vocals sounding wise and pissed at once, world-weary I guess. Fans should eat it up (being much more manic than **The Ritual**), while many may find themselves edging it aside for more demarcatable acts like Slayer or Megadeth. I for one can't fault the record in any way, while still lamenting the band's lack of a clear, discernible persona. Cold steel or living breathing genius: you decide.
Rating 8

## Theatre Of Tragedy - Theatre Of Tragedy
(Massacre Est. '95)

Funereal death melodies mixing gruff grind vox and angelic chick vox to acceptable and intricate effect, maybe more substantially than The Gathering, if less catchy and calm; busier and more arranged than My Dying Bride, if less soberingly frightful. Sad, sad, vampiric metal, cut for whom or what reptile life form, I'm scared to ask. Humanity continues its relentless slither towards the apocalypse.
Rating 6

## Thee Hypnotics - the very crystal speed machine
(American '94)

**the very crystal speed machine** becomes wry irony applied here, to what amounts to a very solid, blues metal jamfest, emphasis on blues as old as 1972. The Black Crowes connection becomes very relevant as the record shambles on, digging something Crowes-like but simpler and more playful like Humble Pie, Savoy Brown, heavier Ian Hunter, or **Exile**-era Stones. Legitimate honky tonk ballads get butted up against a few time-wasters (wank-off instrumentals and a couple o' lethargic and literal bluesers), but the balance rides a rousing Bonham-blasted metallic groove that is every bit as authentic, loose, live and desperate as any in the tricky retro-rock stable. Blows away Brother Cane or Cry Of Love because it doesn't care.
Rating 7

## Therapy? - Nurse (A&M '92)

Irish grungsters causing quite a stir stateside, Therapy? grind it up real hyper and high strung like Helmet, while harkening back to U.K. stun punksters like Gang Of Four and even Magazine to some extent. But rather than falling apart, **Nurse** keeps it snappy and tight, lotsa energy, diverse guitar tonalities, which quite often scrape degenerately over grazing bass lines, finding something akin to Sons Of Freedom. Not sure where I stand, **Nurse** being a bit the wrong side of artsy, but the future looks bright.

Rating 6

## Therapy? - Troublegum  (A&M '94)

Less the scrapyard of electrics obscuring **Nurse**, **Troublegum** gets closer to the core of power punk, eyeball to hooks of a vastly different era from today's hard alternative music, that of early British punksters like Buzzcocks or even the Stranglers or in a modern sense, maybe Midnight Oil. And therein lies my alienation with this sort of record, feeling a bit cold with these stripped melodies. Even though each track wells with its own integrity, I'm not altogether on board, finding the whole thing a bit juvenile, like a college band that tries to be sweet and sour at once, depressed, violent but sensitive. Not sure where this one fits, because it's definitely far from grunge (which you'd never guess from the songtitles), more like dirty, aggressive power pop, like the dark side of Urge Overkill, a band who definitely seem to have a niche carved in the vast rainbow of guitar rock.

Rating 7

## Therapy? - Infernal Love  (A&M '95)

If Therapy?'s eccentric crank has bugged you (like a goateed mosquito on heroin) so far, this one won't change things, the band still after a decidedly obstinate, grimy, hyper-semi-noise. A perplexed hybrid for sure, **Infernal Love** throws in metal, punk, reggae, alt, Bolan, Bowie and snobby art rock, the band watching the whole thing rattle about, ultimately kicking out a pained, wincing heavy new wave, a Stranglers-infected clank that sounds nothing like popular conceptions of alt.grunge. Therapy?'s ace in the hole (if you grant them one at all) would have to be their sturdy songwriting ethic, the thorniness of their vaguely hard, unclean modern rock being almost secondary to their stressful, involved lyrics. I mean, that sums up my semi-fan status right there, granting the band respect, indulging a quick spin and a cursory read, but ultimately passing on their annoying, plainly noisy, turned-up pop junkclunk. In comparison to past efforts: a dissipated anti-climax of the band's power chord potential.

Rating 6

## Therion - Lepaca Kliffoth  (Nuclear Blast '95)

This fifth record in seven years from Sweden's Therion (formerly Mega-Therion in tribute to heroes Celtic Frost) finds the band eminently listenable and almost traditionally metal at times, crafting an old-style black metal that is ultimately cranked through the grinder of new Scandinavian death tones. But Christofer Johnsson is a pretty wild guy lyrically (not that you can tell from listening in), delving deeply and intelligently into all sorts of weird historical evils from various religions for the belched portion of his show. But **Lepaca** also shows his predilection to let instrumental passages roll on and on if he likes the riff, filling in the sound with female caterwauls and healthy bits of keyboards. One of the more listenable and calmly executed scourges of the Swedish death scene. The third of three U.S. releases, after '94's **Symphony Masses: Ho Draken Ho Megas**, and previous pock mark **Out Of Darkness**.

Rating 7

## Therion - Theli  (Nuclear Blast '96)

Getting weirder all the time, Therion dive more twistedly and cancerously into the world of evil classical music. Such wicked church sounds seem to have triumphed over metal, turning this into an art rock swirl, far beyond chick-sang goth or violins or all that getting-tired pile of depresso espresso. The term apocalyptic has never fit so well, only this is less the hooves of the Horsemen, than the Second Coming of Jesus, calm, arms outstretched above a deliriously panicked populace. Powerful sounds for a powerful event.

Rating 8

## Thessalonian Dope Gods - Urban Witchcraft  (Sin Klub '94)

Ohio's TDG carve a damp and chilly, but pleasantly freaky landscape of industrial scrapes, slithers and scratches on this their full-length debut. Influences range from Nine Inch Nails to punk to metal to hip-hop, plus a whole community of electronic bands I never learned about. Loads of trippy samples collide with treated vox over solid constructs with hook and funk, both increasingly rare these days in industrial. Faves: cacophonous mess Gerald Needs Flesh and the brutal Ministry metal of I Say Goodbye. Ends with a straight-faced classical piece.

Rating 7

## Thin Lizzy - Thin Lizzy  (Decca '71)

**Thin Lizzy** marks the fervent flashpoint of one of the most distinguished, timeless and endearing contributions to rock'n'roll with which the world will ever be blessed. Thin Lizzy was a fortress of crashing, fallible artisans beyond compare. Throughout their enigmatic career, they gave us masterpiece after masterpiece drawing from a variety of inspirations, from traditional Irish music to ahead-of-their-time scorching rockers, much of it soulfully delivered via the famous Lizzy harmony guitar sound. These early compositions are astonishingly well written, very Irish, very heartfelt, drawing mainly from bluesy, non-metal influences (including famous Irish son Van Morrison), delivering close, timeless experimentation from Day One, unlike many of its bandwagon-jumping contemporaries. **Thin Lizzy** is one involved folk record, brimming with worldly tales of man's contemplations, delivered with steady belief in the healing spirit of song. And musically, when brought to the fore (as on Look What The Wind Blew In and Return Of The Farmer's Son), Downey already kicks, at total ease with Lizzy's unconventional early percussive patterns. Much more confounding than its follow-up, **Thin Lizzy** elegantly displays a studied professor of folklore at his fount of wisdom, fusing lyrical traditions with sounds both new and old. And the rest was history. Note: the CD version of **Thin Lizzy** tacks on the rare four track **New Day** EP, recorded and released a mere month and a half after the release of the full-length.

Rating 8

## Thin Lizzy - Shades Of A Blue Orphanage  (Decca '72)

Grand and intimate at once, **Shades Of A Blue Orphanage** (Orphanage being an earlier incarnation of Lizzy) builds on Lynott's clarity across spectrums, his mesmerizing ability and sheer desire to weave engaging tales. Here one finds songs further harkening back to Phil's folk acoustic past; smooth, textured pieces such as Buffalo Gal, the haunting and fragile Brought Down, and the almost flamenco Chatting Today, plus early complicated rocker Baby Face, a preview of engineering feats to come. Still some '60s-directed progressive psychedelia and even dil rockabilly break the intrinsic Lizzy flow as is to be expected on such fledgling, early '70s outings. When all is said and done, **Shades** is one of those records that sits isolated, hopeful and radiant in the power of music; in the general timelessness of honest work, and so strangely un-old sounding, perhaps due to an embracing of traditions that will never lose relevance.

Rating 7

450

## Thin Lizzy - Vagabonds Of The Western World
(London '73)

Lizzy's third LP continues with a forging of the band's sound under a variety of stylistic auspices. The title track and *Gonna Creep Up On You* are early metal classics, infused with fringe dynamics, while *Little Girl In Bloom* displays Phil Lynott's complex mastery of balladeering, a self-built philosophy that mixes Irish soul, historic traditional machismo à la Romeo or Don Juan, and a firm grasp of hero mythology in general, seasoned with a deep respect for American blues and motown traditions. And tasteful, historically reverent musicianship heightens the delivery of these tunes, Lizzy being borne of an ethic where chops came first. **Vagabonds** gets the lowest rating of all the Lizzys, due to about four tracks which seem either simple and out-of-character, or dated, bearing scant few traces of the high class Lizzy imprint. But per usual, an arresting charisma permeates, making **Vagabonds** a must-own, despite its sonic whiff of acid casualty, both in its crusty sound quality, and style-searching waywardness.
Rating                                                      6

## Thin Lizzy - Nightlife   (Vertigo '74)

In some indescribable way, **Nightlife** (or arguably **Fighting**) would be the last of the dated, somewhat uncommunicative, unconfident era of Thin Lizzy. **Nightlife** is probably the least guitar-driven Thin Lizzy work, stylistically all over the map, as the band tries to do it all in quest of universality, or more likely, the smash single that will keep their fragile dream alive. *Showdown*, *Philomena*, and *Nightlife* have bluesy R+B feels, Lynott once more giving nod to his fixation with things American. *Sha La La* shreds scientifically, and *Banshee*, an instrumental clocking in at 1:25, offers one of the most fluid and emotive examples of Lizzy guitar harmony ever sliding down sundown. This tune with its '40s cowboy naiveté, romanticism and natural calm, captures the tranquillity of the desert like nothing else in r'n'r this side of ZZ Top's blues tour de force **Tejas**. Aside from the odd gem however, a fair bit of the record strays too distant from the Lizzy heart and soul, into more overtly black musics, Phil often searching for ways to pay homage to his racial heritage. Still, more enigmatic, sincere, and philosophically complex than much else out there at the time, although the destructive love of the rock'n'roll lifestyle often overshadowed the band's love of art.
Rating                                                      6

## Thin Lizzy - Fighting   (Vertigo '75)

Lizzy really hit their stride with this soulful, stirring hard rock classic, which again finds the band exuding warmth and charm in a number of styles. *Suicide* and *Ballad Of A Hard Man* are hard-drinking metal, *Fighting My Way Back*, *King's Vengeance* and Bob Seger's *Rosalie* (Lizzy toured with Seger and became friends) are blushing examples of the band's melodic, occasionally jazz-shaded guitar alchemy, much of the rest being rich, pensive, subdued and dark, yet hopeful. Philosophically, **Fighting** is dedicated to tales of outlaws and outcasts, past and current, spun on a fairly grandiose, history-encompassing, tragic scale. This, Lizzy's fifth, is also the first collection on which Robertson and Gorham's fluid guitar harmonies would become such an integral texture of the Lizzy sound, woven into the very fabric of the arrangements. Legendary, heart-wrenching music.
Rating                                                      9

## Thin Lizzy - Jailbreak   (Mercury '76)

Full of Lizzy firsts and lasts, **Jailbreak** was the most commercially successful Lizzy album, containing old arena standbys *Cowboy Song* and the band's biggest hit ever, *The Boys Are Back In Town*. **Jailbreak** is also blessed with some of Lizzy's meanest, sharpest metal to date with the highly strung *Emerald*, cruiser *Warrior* and the classic, marauding title track. And for the first time, the rockers are the emotive and melodically memorable compositions, a magical, flipped-over achievement which will occur often over the remainder of the lush Lizzy catalogue. **Jailbreak** would also be Lizzy's last album where eclecticism outweighs the cohesive signals, although overt attempts to portray the band conceptually as an outlaw posse or street gang made the lyrics read more like a loose concept album. Of course, with Lizzy, the overall songcraft, however varied, downplays any ill effects of such ups and downs. Hereon in, however, the albums would become much more singular in intent, focusing on the band's considerable arsenal of guitarists, underscoring the melodies of Phil's rich and powerful stories.
Rating                                                      9

## Thin Lizzy - Johnny The Fox   (Vertigo '76)

Again, loosely a concept album, **Johnny The Fox** is Thin Lizzy's first confident masterpiece; a rich and textural tragic work of melodic metal. Lyrically soulful and melancholy, **Johnny The Fox** examines the personal anguish resulting from moral dilemma, while twin guitars sadly howl at the moon within the framework of some of the smoothest hard rock riffs ever conceived. Although all performances are classy and distinctive, Downey's drumming deserves special mention for his tasteful fills and obvious skill for creating an effortless and comfortable groove, expertly balancing nuance and controlled muscle. **Johnny The Fox** seamlessly links the timelessness of stories of old—fairy tales, fables, old west tales, tales of ancient battles, and circus imagery—with the trampled hopes of the fallen (or rockers about to fall) who wander our aging cities, offering both a sympathetic and panoramic viewpoint on the history of man's ambitions. Classics include minor hit *Don't Believe A Word* (originally a slow ballad as per Moore's solo rendition), the misnomered tribal-metallic *Boogie Woogie Dance*, and gorgeously poured ballad, *Old Flame*, gushing harmony guitars brightly afire. Trivia note: Iron Maiden does a wicked cover of *Massacre*.
Rating                                                     10

## Thin Lizzy - The Rocker (1971-1974)   (London '77)

This compilation put out by the London Collector Series people looks at Lizzy's formative years: '71-'74. It deserves mention (and your cash) due to the inclusion of five tunes not available on LP, including surprise novelty hit *Whiskey In The Jar*. Two of them, *Black Boys On The Corner* and *Sitamoia* are surprisingly inspired, complex metal tunes; worth the price of the package alone. The other stuff is pretty good too, and because the older albums are hard to find, this disc may be your best available early-days fix.
Rating                                                      7

## Thin Lizzy - Bad Reputation   (Mercury '77)

Yet a third stroke of genius in two short years, **Bad Reputation** relies on the strength of individual songs rather than an overall theme or sound for its genius status, containing emotional, subdued Lizzy guitar rockers such as the meaty melodic *Soldier Of Fortune*, *Southbound* and *Dear Lord*, with their countrified balladeering, balanced by inspired and mean metal classics in the percussive/progressive title cut (Downey's showcase) and the unique twisting high lead riffs of *Opium Trail*. Elsewhere, R+B departure *Dancing In The Moonlight* was a minor hit for Phil and the boys, featuring some straight-faced sax work and jazzy, nimble-fingered axe work. Thematically the album resembles **Fighting** but is more confessional, reflecting and spiritual, again examining the temptations of various moral and physical poisons of "the old town", Phil document-

ing in wax his downward slide, while rocking smartly and technically as if the skills of the street and the skills of the studio were meant to be one. And in some rare, rock'n'roll instances, in lives dedicated to the craft, the two are inseparable.
Rating     10

## Thin Lizzy - Live And Dangerous   (Mercury '78)

To me, most live albums serve little purpose, but this one does the concept bracing service by supercharging some of the old guitar-based tunes that were a bit stiff, dated, or under-dressed on studio vinyl, compositions such as *Cowboy Song*, *Massacre*, *Don't Believe A Word* and *Sha La La* bulked-up nicely as Phil and the boys slam it on home like the great touring machine they've become, despite major chemical frostings before many an important gig. We also get a short and snappy, straight-forward speed rocker called *Are You Ready* previously released only as a B-side, a tune the band never considered album-quality material. All in all, a good shot of energy to some great '70s classics, with tasty percussive magic from Downey. Integrity in full swing, and a major success as a calling card for the band, commercially. Tops many a critic's lists of favorite live sets.
Rating     8

## Thin Lizzy - Black Rose   (Warner Bros. '79)

Another charmed Lizzy release, **Black Rose** continues with the familiar mix of styles: ballads, hard rockers, metal, and the odd surprise (naughty funkster *S&M*). Two Lizzy classics emerge, minor hit *Waiting For An Alibi* and heartfelt confessional rocker *Got To Give It Up*, both tunes propelled by strangely un-nailable, complex chord structures which tend to highlight the Lizzy other-worldliness, even when creating the intense spaces and pregnant pauses on which these two tracks feed. Title tune *Roisin Dubh (Black Rose) A Rock Legend* finds Lynott confronting his Irish heritage directly giving cameos to great Irish figures from the past within the context of an obscure Gaelic poem, amidst rumbling axe updates of centuries-old melodies. Just another seemingly effortless and timeless classic by a clearly superior band, writing on a plane more in league with fine literature than anything as base as rock'n'roll. Well into their addictions by this point (including heroin), the band still could spin a yarn, despite their frustrating lack of success in cracking the American market.
Rating     10

## Thin Lizzy - Chinatown   (Mercury '80)

**Chinatown** is the only Lizzy album that even hints at being contrived or self-consciously compiled, indeed the band fairly fragmented and despondent about its future during the record's conception. Although comprising some spirited tunes in the uplifting *We Will Be Strong* and *Having A Good Time*, plus tidy speed rocker *Sugar Blues*, the record sounds cold, lacking the usual Lizzy charm and ethereal, no hurry delivery. Lyrically and thematically, the songs seem forced and all too topical, as if for the first time, they didn't really cry out to be written. Even though there are no obvious lemon shrimp on **Chinatown**, the overall level of quality is below Lizzy's soulful standards. Lynott seems for once, not to have thrown himself, body and soul, into his composition chores, rendering **Chinatown** a detached Lizzy; a Lizzy at work rather than play, perhaps the band's **Presence**. And Snowy White, more a studied session man, would soon be making waves about his appropriateness for such a posse well off the rails.
Rating     8

## Thin Lizzy - Killers Live   (Vertigo '81)

This live six track EP (not to be confused with Queen's **Live Killers**!) relives a batch of recent great Lizzy rockers which here sound pretty well equally tight to the studio versions. Highlights include *Bad Reputation*, *Opium Trail*, and *Got To Give It Up*. Quite a collectible among Lizzy lunatics, however not nearly as rare as the Funky Junction Deep Purple tribute record from '72, the Holy Grail of all Lizzy collectibles. Good Luck!
Rating     7

## Thin Lizzy - Renegade   (Vertigo '81)

**Renegade** is Thin Lizzy's premier tour de force, an absolute masterpiece of deeply soulful and richly textured hard rock. The production is superb, while Scott Gorham and Snowy White weave some of their most vivid guitar tapestries on the title cut (the closing minutes are magnificent), *The Pressure Will Blow*, and confessional opus *It's Getting Dangerous*. Maybe I'm being psyched out by the cover art, but this album sounds so royal, so professional, so state-of-the-art, as if there was some grinning self-knowledge in the process of creating it; that it could mark the summit, the end of an era of quality British hard rock. But there's also an overall somberness, a blanket of melancholy which puts this brand of metal in commercially dubious territory. On **Renegade**, the returns are not cheap and immediate, as the album's fullness and maturity tend to emerge only when played repeatedly in the spirit of concept status. Taken as a whole, this LP offers the most poetic look into the complex soul of a band rocked by drug addiction, a band that never shied away from the examination of mankind and life's fallings from grace. Reverently assembled and legendary in its scope.
Rating     10

## Thin Lizzy - Thunder And Lightning   (Vertigo '83)

**Thunder And Lightning** was to be Thin Lizzy's semi-unintentional swan song. But that's all whiskey under the bridge, as Phil Lynott died January 4th, 1986 at the age of 36, of what was reported to be a massive physical shutdown due to years of drug and alcohol abuse (Note: For an excellent examination of the genius of Phil Lynott, see a chapter dedicated to him in Eamon Dunphy's thoughtful U2 book **Unforgettable Fire**, not to mention of course, Mark Putterford's **Philip Lynott - The Rocker**, one of the best rock books you'll ever encounter). More of a battle cry from the Four Horsemen of the Apocalypse than a work of aging legends, this last Lizzy statement sees the esteemed gathering lashing out with their most violent metal onslaught ever. The production is gritty, loud, and mercilessly throbbing with midrange; anything but the smooth fluidity of old; and almost all of the cuts feature blistering guitar pyrotechnics, including my favorite guitar solo of all time on *Baby Please Don't Go*, from the largest assembled but stumbling battalion of past Lizzy axemen. A caustic yet still melodic Lizzy scorcher with the emphasis on scorcher. Outside of the title track, which is a bit uninspired and self-evident (i.e. it could have been written by any great metal band), *The Sun Goes Down*, which is a hypnotic quiet mood piece, and *Bad Habits*, which is a high spirited barroom rocker (at least our pathetic bar band thought so), the balance of the album is classic shoot 'em up metal—Lizzy style. Dense but characteristically willing to speak to the heart, **Thunder And Lightning** is full of Lizzy greats of a more aggressive, raucous nature; melodic but muscular mayhem such as *Cold Sweat*, *Holy War*, *This Is The One*, and *Heart Attack* rumbling in direct contrast to the melodic richness from the last such as *Renegade*, *Leave This Town*, and *Angel Of Death*, the latter still weighty numbers, yet nowhere near as desperate and cold. As the sun goes down, **Thunder And Lightning** delivers an uncompromising, wall-of-sound epitaph, closing the books on one of the finest. Tis a crying shame, Phil enthusiastic for the first time in years about some sort of future, quite enamoured with his latest wunder axeman John Sykes. However all was not to be, due to a tragic death for a self-confessed rogue. Sadly missed.

Rating            **10**

## Thin Lizzy - Life  (Vertigo '83)

Lizzy's second and last double live extravaganza creates a city of guitars, and as with most cities, even those who breath the life of the place day after day can be left feeling cold and alone. And the ultimate irony of this large, blocky, stiffly-produced feast (Phil was left to his sorry, production devices) is that the appreciative throngs and the echoing rock chambers of the world from whence this record draws its tenuous life, tend to cloak the still quite heroic but struggling performances in a sort of anonymous loneliness of crowds, a dense throbbing din; nevertheless amply recorded yet smothered in power, all parties in battle with the glories of metal. And every last Lizzy axe slinger shows up somewhere . . . such awesome talent dazed and confused, I just wanna cry. With a heartfelt and raging *Got To Give It Up*, a smooth and familiar *Boys Are Back In Town*, and a pulverizing everything else, **Life** certainly raises agonized mountains of soul for painful voyeuristic plunder, but in the end it becomes just that: painful, as one longs for the stirring context of these classic pieces as psychological dramas integral to the blinding studio records from where they so vitally bloomed. **Life**, and the torn and frayed live rock'n'roll experience in particular, somehow just seems to drag Lizzy's material into the muck of public view . . . too temptingly close to the evils of the road which caused a tragic parting.

Rating            **7**

## Thin Lizzy - BBC Radio One: Live In Concert
(Windsong '92)

Documenting Lizzy's last British concert of their farewell tour in 1983, **BBC** is a poignant but strangely hurried sort of affair. Lizzy's commercial success had been on slow wane ever since **Jailbreak** way back in '76. Through a string of classic, increasingly sophisticated records, the public lost attention, culminating in one final caustic celebration, '83's **Thunder And Lightning**. Here the sentiment, sorrow and sense of loss is so thick you can cut it with a knife, as Phil steers his ballsiest guitarist ever, John Sykes through faster versions (I mean check out *The Cowboy Song*) of heady hits and hard modern rockers. Phil's vocal performance is his best ever, his most versatile, and his most sadly world-worn, as the man watches and hears one of the world's warmest rock experiences blaze out in a storm of glory, less devotion in quantity, the fans that are left picking up the slack with ever-growing admiration. Adequate mix, better and worse in some ways than **Life**. Rock heroics beyond compare. U.S. label Griffin added this one to their Radio One reissue series in '95, standing proud along similar high quality rockers from Travers, Schenker, UFO and others.

Rating            **8**

## Thin Lizzy - The Peel Sessions  (BBC '94)

Expecting one of those crappy, scrappy little EPs, I was pleasantly surprised to find this fifteen track studio-quality opus, documenting this great and hallowed rock institution. Lizzy recorded some 41 songs over eleven sessions for John Peel's radio show. Evidently, the bands got to give it a couple of gos, but were essentially captured live in studio. So here we get extremely faithful, yet raw versions of Lizzy classics spanning '72 through '77. The best gizmo about this is that the early stuff like *Little Darling, Little Girl In Bloom* and *Vagabonds Of The Western World* are actually of higher quality than the originals. Otherwise, it's played pretty straight, although *That Woman's Gonna Break Your Heart* gets a pretty sparky treatment, and Phil's vocals stretch out a tad more here and there. Packag-

ing-wise, where this thing might have really shined, it's pretty inconsequential: a nice little tribute by Peel, two shots of Phil and that's it. Still, for the Lizzy starved like me, if you're gonna play these songs over and over again, why not make it these alterno-takes for awhile? Rating reflects minimal contribution to the Lizzy portfolio, but thanks anyways.

Rating            **7**

## Thin Lizzy - Wild One: The Very Best Of Thin Lizzy
(Mercury '96)

As Stuart Bailie's elegant and concise liner notes attest, the influence of Thin Lizzy insidiously but reverently winds its way through all genres of rock, including alternative. So in conjunction with the remastering and rereleasing of much of the Lizzy catalogue, PolyGram has deemed it fit to hatch yet another hits package. It's always great to be reminded of Lizzy's creative power, but this is pretty much unnecessary for established fans, offering nothing new, except for a leap over to the Gary Moore catalogue for a couple pints. But by all means, I hope **Wild One** acts as a calling card, introducing new generations to Phil's daunting pageantry of song. Verdict on the tracks? Weak around the middle (tracks 8 to 12), but strong start and finish.

Rating            **8**

## Thorn - Bitter Potion  (Roadrunner '95)

It's not just the lush fractal graphics that made me think of Killing Joke here, Thorn's elegant industrial goth metal recalling that pioneering band's stiff, futuristic castle tones. Yea and verily, this trio has some slick moves, filling their not all that heavy compositions with all sorts of exotic, Egypto flavourings, carving a hi-tech feast for the ears that remains grounded in real instruments, despite its hip dance directives. Still, very depressing and plodding unto the batcave (not to mentioned anaesthetized), which limits playability by well-adjusted human specimens like myself.

Rating            **7**

## Thought Industry - Mods Carve The Pig
(Metal Blade '93)

Hearing this after the band's '95 assault, I was pretty much braced for the avalanche of soundful ideas I was about to encounter. And fact is, this sophomore (debut was **Songs For Insects**, also '93), is perhaps even more disjointed and frayed than **Outer Space**, combining greater jabs at ferocious precocious punk like NoMeansNo and Jesus Lizard, to go with its crazy Beefheart/Zappa moving floor (maybe throw in a little Gang Of Four, XTC and Anacrusis for good measure!). Appropriately, we get a Dali painting for the cover, the literature enclosed sounding like a psychedelic compact combine mulching acid trips and extra-terrestrial excursions. Bottom line: killer progressive punk, not afraid to show its metal teeth. Pretty well unique in recorded music. No, seriously.

Rating            **8**

## Thought Industry - Outer Space Is Just A Martini Away  (Metal Blade '95)

This perplexed enigma of a record caught me just at the right time, the last few months being spent bathing in King Crimson's **Thrak** opus and generally revisiting old progressive rock including unhealthy servings of Brian Eno. And where does Thought Industry fit in all this? Well, they sorta look like Pere Ubu and Captain Beefheart's band, or an old and jaded beatnik combo from 1959, take yer pick; and sound like, I don't know, a cross between new King Crimson, old King Crimson, Wire, Pixies, new punk, aggro-grunge and Swedish heavy metal. You're right. I'm confused, but these guys live to confuse. Which is a good approach to embrace, Thought Industry serving up an exotic blend of intel-

lectual noises, most of them quite power-chorded, all of them provocation to rethinking musical boundaries. But don't worry, it's not all hippy math, as hooks abound at a much greater rate than on its predecessor. Enough talk though, 'cos you just know this band cringes at their reviews, be they positron or negatron. Count this old prog rocker enthused.
Rating **8**

## Thrall - Chemical Wedding (Alternative Tentacles '96)
To carry the Alternative Tentacles brand name, a band pretty much has to have bucketloads of acerbic wit, a sound capable of breaking society into little, ungovernable bits, and a gnawing urge to action that ties stomach knots in prospective listeners. Well, this bunch does all that and more, former God Bullies vocalist Mike Hard and crew hacking out a record that sounds like Jesus Lizard, Killdozer and NoMeansNo playing at a terrorist fundraiser. But the thing's so nicely coated in the discipline of smart, alternative metal (I guess Soundgarden is pretty much the only band in that genre), that you find yourself actually enjoying Hard's David Yow-like howling. Lyrics are a slap too, pointing at our pathetic other-worldly aspirations, then proposing that the plate is about to be licked clean.
Rating **8**

## Thrasher - Thrasher (Combat/Banzai '85)
**Thrasher** was a Carl Canedy-produced one-off by El Boffo himself plus assorted both coast music half-somebodies, and is actually pretty good, doing an adequate, grounded job of Priest/Accept-style change-ups (grimacingly blue collar, mind you) while sounding like a basement swillfest in the process. Still, I never liked all-star jams, and there are no stars here (and thankfully no ego-filled performances), unless you count as stars guys like Kenny Aaronson, Billy Sheehan, Mars Cowling (all bassists!), and Brad Sinsel, guys I consider worthy contributors, or at least stars to a curmudgeoned few.
Rating **5**

## 311 - 311 (Capricorn/Sony '95)
Starts out like a cookie-cutter of heavy Red Hot Chili Peppers, but then hip-hops out, becoming something more akin to the Peppers without the qualifier. Long-winded, unashamedly derivative and pretty good if you like funky rap metal and can live with the slavish imitation. Unfortunately, I'm nowhere near interested enough to try.
Rating **4**

## Throbbin Hoods - Ambush (A&M '94)
Beerpunkarolla from Toronto strangely slammin' with a case of The Cramps, NoMeansNo and DOA, Throbbin Hoods is a dose of the fast, liquored-up and the not so pretty, with guffaw lyrics straight from the party circuit of your local university. But the mix is chunky enough, vocals versatile, and song concepts varied and magnetic in a juvenile sort of way. Fun, stupid, and ultimately disposable.
Rating **6**

## Thrust - Fist Held High (Metal Blade '84)
One of the countless low budget speed metal albums released in the U.S. about this time, **Fist Held High** come off as sincere, kinda drunk and not without engaging twists and turns. The delivery is proud, the playing loose and aggressive. A boozin' album fer sure, so magically linked to an exciting era in metal five years previous.
Rating **6**

## Thud - Life & Death (Fifth Column '92)
Overgrown blobs of guitar cement bound their merry way through this sludgy, grungy doom-kopf of a record. Sorta death metal, sorta clubland punk, Thud pound with suicidal simplicity, taking me nowhere fast. Five years back, one might have held this as somewhat competitive with the earliest of Seattle quakings, but in '92, just too ordinary.
Rating **5**

## Thunder - Back Street Symphony (EMI '90)
As is almost always the case when Brits attempt rootsy hard rock, Thunder tends to rely on simplicity, space, and strong melodies rather than the energy, ambitious arrangements, and playing dexterity of their American counterparts. Nope, this is pork-fisted monolithic hard rock; British, and as a result somehow less communicative and hokey, delivered by a band obviously not used to the competitive pressures of the L.A. scene. Propelled by strong vocals that recall Rod Stewart, Plant, and Paul Rodgers, plus admirably weighty production, this metallic version of the lame London Quireboys delivers a pretty decent party, a loud 'n' proud brew of HR, blues 'n' boogie metal, fast stuff and surprisingly soulful mellow stuff. Nothing much new, which I guess is the point, but also nothing much overly corrective of past earwax. On the upside, however, Thunder come off as attitudinally sassy like Whitesnake and convincingly sincere in terms of the band's grasp of stolen British rootsiness. This one could grow on me over time but I doubt it. Interesting career path, as this album had been re-launched with new graphics a year later, a strategy that worked at least a trace of magic with a couple of diverged singles.
Rating **6**

## Thunder - Laughing On Judgement Day (EMI '92)
Still bent on expertly sidestepping the fall of this sort of classic rock sound, Thunder search for a high road that digs deeper into the blues, velvet-packing their sense of self with an aristocratic air, clutching greedily at all sorts of Zep psychic anchors, which then filter through a myriad of also distant derivatives, biggest tendency still being Whitesnake, only more insidiously this time out. All is clean, innocent and efficient burning, built with a self-assured defiance at anything new. Well, despite such pontification, I'm not a big booster, but I do prefer Thunder to similarly directed (but blusier) bloozbutter like Tangiers, early Tora Tora or Tattoo Rodeo. For those who just don't wanna know the future. A nimble sidestep of the critical slaughter afforded other big hair hard rockers.
Rating **6**

## Thunder - Behind Closed Doors (EMI '95)
Unfathomably back comes Thunder, new questionable graphics in tow, and more of that safe arena metal held in check. **Behind Closed Doors** adds another six or so clichés, a bit of horns, some Egypto-Zep and lots more Bad Company as the boys party metal it up, again pulling non-moves that almost work if you're British. No hurry, no worries big-haired hard rock professionally steered towards that hidden segment repeatedly cramming the classic rock. As usual, the ballads are above average, the rockers, average.
Rating **6**

## Thunderfoot - Southern Discomfort (Perris '95)
I can't resist calling this gracious southern feast a cross between Thunder and Blackfoot, 'cos that's the truth, Thunderfoot (featuring Kevin Fowler, ex of Dangerous Toys) doing a helluva lotta great things with southern metal, evoking the integrity of Lynyrd Skynyrd more than the fake blooz of Cinderella, more grits than cheez, but touching regularly on facets from both worlds, roots rock and corporate metal. All the clichés

are here and I'm lapping it up, Thunderfoot making me forget Jackyl but fast, helped maybe unfairly by the fact that this is in essence an indie; i.e. strange seeing this kind of music on the small but ambitious Perris Records (run at fast pace by Tom Mathers). In 1992 I might have passed this one up, but now with such a dearth of old values rock'n'roll, a big bottle of **Southern Discomfort** sounds just fine.

Rating　　　　　　　　　　　　　　　　　　　8

## Johnny Thunders & The Heartbreakers -L.A.M.F. Revisited　(Jungle '84)

Thunders was a horrendously death-warmed NY junkie to the end, OD-ing on life itself a long time ago, stumbling blindly through a post-Dolls fifteen years of low-key notoriety before his ultimate physical demise at the turn of the '90s. Along the way, Johnny and his various hangers-on were captured on wax occasionally and sporadically, often live, never too prepared. **L.A.M.F. Revisited** is one of the best; one of the man's few studio efforts, featuring mostly great punky NY Doll-style originals, rocking heroically, tragically, loosely, and reverently of a complex past like the Dolls, like Hanoi Rocks, like a time-worn piece of trash. Also recommended: '78's **So Alone**, for much the same body-bagged reasons, a record that was reissued in '92 with four extra tracks.

Rating　　　　　　　　　　　　　　　　　　　8

## Thundertrain - Teenage Suicide　(Est '78)

**Teenage Suicide** is a white vinyl indie from Boston which I picked up in '79 or so, because at the time, one simply bought without question anything that looked this heavy, having a vaguely DMZ-ish dirt to its black and white packaging. The wax inside is basically high school hard rock similar to early Kix (early like *before* the first album). Wish I still had it, 'cos I'll probably never see it again.

Rating　　　　　　　　　　　　　　　　　　　5

## Tiamat - The Astral Sleep　(Century Media '91)

The Astral Sleep is somewhat of a bastard sister to Unleashed's **Where No Life Dwells** debut, both recorded by the team of Sorychta and Bemm in Dortmund, Germany, both packaged similarly, indeed both going to the same fantastical, surprisingly mature lyrical realms. But this one isn't exactly a debut, the band putting out a low-key, rougher, less philosophically Tiamatian record called **Sumerian Cry** first. And this one is a more experimental, indeed more courageous piece of work, mixing death metal, doom and mellow bits in almost equal doses. Which is to say it's very similar to **Clouds**, and not much behind in maturity. Elegant extreme music for those pensive, poison hours of the soul.

Rating　　　　　　　　　　　　　　　　　　　7

## Tiamat - Clouds　(Century Media '92)

Record #3 for the blackened ones finds Tiamat raising eyebrows with their deliciously mellower form of death, establishing themselves at the fore of the gloom bunch slowing down and going more than occasionally unplugged. Classy stuff squirming on the cusp of death metal and death dirge, **Clouds** is crammed full of intricate little flourishes that keep the sanctified slog interesting, fave tracks being *Forever Burning Flames* and *The Scapegoat*, both chilling tales scraped forth by grindcore vocals lurching into a sorry state of dimly tuneful humanity. A fine quiet doom record, but not the fully conflagrating jewel that is **Wildhoney**.

Rating　　　　　　　　　　　　　　　　　　　8

## Tiamat - Wildhoney　(Century Media '94)

One new discernible trend in metal these days is a tendency towards atmospheric, moody and decidedly non-metal approaches to the form. Paradise Lost and My Dying Bride characterize the beautifying of death metal. Even Queensryche, The Cult, and especially Danzig all put out records in '94 surgically extracting the guitar for explorations into the unknown. Tiamat's exciting foray perhaps matches most closely the Danzig experience, both bands departing from riff-heavy demonics into realms that evoke a quieter inner chill, replacing sound for a fear borne of silence and peace, too much room to think, too much thought resulting in truckloads of damp, wilted depression. Johan Edlund has created a brooding monster with **Wildhoney**, diving headlong into a form of death metal Pink Floyd that is executed panoramically, resigned guitar melodies intertwining funereal keyboards, vocals dual personifying between spoken catatonia and accessible grind dementia, all dragged like a slain mountain man through the muddy moors of Nordic fantasy hells. Progressive, conceptual pieces for the cool of night, **Wildhoney** works its magic like an elixir, slowing the brain then removing it from throbbing reality for a silent, suspended air voyage over mystery hill and dale, Edlund constructing a cathedral of confident sounds, solid and assured as ancient history. Not too many acts could pull off this sort of transition. Tiamat does, through conviction and the abandonment of half measures (of which **Clouds** might arguably be considered). For reality be, the band has left only fleeting traces of conventional heaviness here, and even these louder moments are integrated for full hypnotic impact, the record just unrolling like a plush one hundred mile carpet. So avast ye, enough swarming praise, abscond heavily, suck it back and sink away.

Rating　　　　　　　　　　　　　　　　　　　10

## Tin Drum - Cool, Calm & Collected　(Spy '92)

An innocuous little release that actually made the main racks at HMV, **Cool, Calm & Collected** is a Scandinavian corporate hard rock spread in the prissy vein of Fate, TNT and **Eye To Eye**-era 220V; aseptic, melodic and driven by a techy drum sound and tons of precision axe work. Zero attack though, as Tin Drum betray an dated tin ear towards required competitive levels in the '90s.

Rating　　　　　　　　　　　　　　　　　　　5

## Glenn Tipton - Baptizm Of Fire　(Atlantic '97)

My opinion runs along the lines of most others on this, and that is one of acceptance and little more. Tipton has hatched a pleasureable enough effort, and what's more, it's useful to all, the record comprising ten vocals tracks and only one instrumental, Tipton himself singing the whole thing as well as anybody could. But there is a strange '80s malaise to the thing, reminding one too much of mid-to-upper Priest, and even more so, recent Accept. I dunno, the thing's just too steeped in melodrama, which a thorough reading of the lyrics will prove unwarranted. A clinic in solid record-making fer sure, and a minefield of flowing, breathy Tipton solos, a bounty of which at least will make this fine, fine wine for students of the guitar. Note: big shots everywhere: Robert Trujillo, C.J. de Villar, Shannon Larkin (well, a little shot anyways), Billy Sheehan, Cozy Powell, Don Airey and even John Entwistle, enforcing the datedness effect.

Rating　　　　　　　　　　　　　　　　　　　7

## TKO - Let It Roll　(Infinity '79)

The long-lost loser debut from the Brad Sinsel-led Washington state band, **Let It Roll** is a nutty little gem demonstrating how different brains were in the '70s. Not even trying to be metal, the record contains a few jangling, studio-harnessed hard rock tunes with decent pop hooks but not much else, approximating The Cars crossed with mebbee Ted or Derringer. Actually fairly catchy, but very naive and consequently nostalgically funny, coming just before an era in which the band

might have more forcefully asserted itself as a hard rock bunch (as opposed to mildly belligerent alternatives to the Eagles or Styx). Warmest moments: *Come A Day* and *Gutterboy*.
Rating **7**

## TKO - In Your Face   (Music For Nations '84)
The reason **Let It Roll** is reviewed in this book is that TKO re-emerge on this body-blow, five years later, as a deliberate, soaring metal band, **In Your Face** being anachronistic, true-blue, stadium-style metallic hard rock with doses of delightful devilry from Diamond Dave. Basically Operation Desert Storm with long hair. Full of anthemic, chest-thumping metal propelled by the strength of Sinsel's vocals and imposing persona, **In Your Face** draws heavily from the same emotional well as Van Halen, Whitesnake, Dokken, Terrible Ted, and Bon Jovi, while heavier than all of the above. A good summer-with-the-top-down party album, with curiously loud production values, that in retrospect, the band dismissed as less than satisfying. Also features two ex-Culprit dudes in bassist Scott Earl and axe-god Kjartan Kristoffersen, who were somewherz abouts the 20th and 21st members of the band at this point. Inspired cock rock, actually praised on many continents, yet bought only by a lucky few.
Rating **8**

## TKO - Below The Belt   (Roadrunner '86)
**Below The Belt** woefully attempts to emulate the knock 'em down swagger of **In Your Face** but fails due to going-through-the-motions songwriting, overwrought clichés, and an irritating mix that lacks power by abusing it; somehow leaving guitar, bass, and drums sounding separated from each other, entombed in heat-blistered mud, giving it anything but a live feel. Seriously, this record is ruined by the production, which is totally dominated by clanky, boulder-like, machine-tooled drums, which make it difficult breathing for all else who might want to be heard. Nevertheless, not nearly the kick-ass approach of **In Your Face** in many departments, **Below The Belt** is a dim reflection of its predecessor and an absolute disgrace butted-up against Sinsel's '92 comeback **War Babies**.
Rating **5**

## T.N.T. - Deflorator   (SL '84)
Not the same band as the somewhat successful Norway pretty boys, this version of the glorified firecracker is a German scourge who churn a truly convincing type of Euro-distressed AC/DC for about half this oddly-titled poverty rocker, while offering slow, boring stuff for half II (Krokus with headier highs, stoopider lows). Buy used for a couple bucks; otherwise pass.
Rating **6**

## TNT - Knights Of The New Thunder   (PolyGram '84)
Squeaky clean production, operatic vocals, and downright scientific guitar pyro in a decidedly European pop-metal style, TNT mix heavy tech-metal with pop and balladeering to come up with a misguided Norse version of L.A. glam. Ronni Le Tekro's axe work is ultra-Malmsteen-ish; hilariously overblown, cutting, clean and crisply produced. Could have made a lot of money in America. Tip: pass on the Viking suits (on loan from Heavy Load and Faithful Breath?), and deep six the on-stage long ship.
Rating **7**

## TNT - Tell No Tales   (PolyGram '87)
Man, that Tony Harnell's got a girlie voice, his piercing pipes almost distracting from the band's increasingly pop metal sheen. Le Tekro is as death-defyingly acrobatic as usual (check out ludicrously speedy short solo *Sapphire*), but the songs really straddle two worlds,

European heaviness and pan-world AOR. A rare case of an '80s band actually going downhill. Clear as a chiming bell at dawn, but too light and tuneful for the pyro rock sounds emanating from both voice and instrument.
Rating **6**

## TNT - Intuition   (PolyGram '84)
Not sure how they've done it, but TNT have retained their overwrought melodies, while shifting from a sort of tongue-in-cheek hair band metal to something more sober and up-market, a type of pomp rock that almost evokes the slight goth-tones of Deep Purple or Rainbow in the '80s, no surprise given the two talents soaring overtop of this misunderstood band. Very tasty stuff, mellow but of a higher station in life (see the eloquent *Tonight I'm Falling* and almost gospel-size ballad *End Of The Line*), Harnell's way sky-high voice somewhat more suited to this aristocratic-on-purpose type of music.
Rating **7**

## Token Entry - The Weight Of The World
(Roadrunner '90)
Token Entry go after one of my favorite "what if?'s", said surmise being "what if the Red Hot Chili Peppers stuck to the power chord trajectory flirted on **The Uplift Mofo Party Plan**?" Well, they might have made a record like this, kinda rappy, fwappy, funky and generally guitar-based. But loser quotient seeps into my judgment centres, as I ultimately choose to dismiss this as low budget copycat fare . . . pogo funk metal for skate brats, only dim inklings of the Peppers' raging "music as sweaty sex machine" manifesto, fit to grace the delete bins, but maybe fit to spin the rounds at another time in another place.
Rating **5**

## Tokyo Blade - Midnight Rendezvous   (Banzai '84)
A vital, spirited debut from these hopeful NWOBHM rockers, **Midnight Rendezvous** touches on many classic '70s and '80s styles from Priest and Maiden to Ozzy, while also making nod to motivational cock rock from America. Good headbangin' metal with enough licks, solos, inter-song variation, and roughness to make it interesting, but also just naive, cliché, and bush-league enough to keep it from really standing out. Could use some selective editing, as tunes seem to drone on a shade longer than necessary. But give it an extra point for sincerity which the follow-up lacks; ambition in the same vivacious frame of mind as Pretty Maids. Pushes **7** simply 'cos we really got into it back in the old days. Before record II, vocalist Alan Marsh would be replaced by Vic Wright, due to the former's case of stage nerves.
Rating **6**

## Tokyo Blade - Night Of The Blade   (Banzai '84)
Less punky and insistent, leaning more towards an anthemic Def Leppard sickly meow (but much heavier), **Night Of The Blade** stands equally varied and interesting as the debut, yet just a notch below arresting idea-wise. Make-it-big production (complete with deep snare) and more melodramatic vocals grace this ambitious but oddly spontaneous effort, while the whole thing falls short on enthusiasm, the band suffering painfully from cash panic.
Rating **6**

## Tokyo Blade - Blackhearts And Jaded Spades
(Banzai '86)
Throughout records I and II, the Blade emulated classic British metal; wide-eyed as fans, wielding an urge to rule the world. On **Blackhearts**, they cross the sea in search of a loose 'n' dirty Mötley Crüe-ish brew (stratospheric leaps above Crüe musicality I might add)

crossed with the grooves of heavy Dokken, winding up with a British version of L.A. Guns. Rousing flamethrowers here such as *Dirty Faced Angels* and *Always* do battle with dil power ballads and Van Halen joke posturing, suicide if you're short and you dress like samurais. Further annoyance: lyrics that are yer basic dough-headed macho trash talkin' about how cool the bods in the band are. Thanks be to America for spooking Euro-hopefuls into this sort of confused submission.
Rating                                                                                           5

## Tokyo Blade - The Cave Sessions (Est. '86)
Trashy but proud, this French four track EP features in total: *Monkeys Blood, School House Is Burnin', Shadows Of Insanity* and *Jezzabell*. Not sure which tracks ever showed up where otherwise, except that a cleaner version of *Monkeys Blood* doth occur on **Blackhearts**. Solid, edgy trash metal to the core, with *Shadows Of Insanity* low-cruising with an Yngwie-ish Maiden riff that ya gotta love with all yer heart. Likeable, sincere and street.
Rating                                                                                           6

## Tool - Opiate (BMG '92)
The **Opiate** EP was Tool's calling card to alternative Nirvana, these sharp, shocking tattoo'ed freight-trained songs announcing a not-altogether-new sound, but more a honing of grunge instincts. Six tracks, mixing live and studio, all pretty characteristic of what would show teeth on the full-length **Undertow** (which eventually went platinum).
Rating                                                                                           6

## Tool - Undertow (BMG '93)
Building on a buzz generated by the band's **Opiate** EP, L.A.'s Tool send forth **Undertow**, a record that drags all onlookers under and into a thorny terrain of a truly underground sort of grunge, no shine, no beauty, just layers and layers of paralyzing (and alternately-tuned) Sabbath-In-Chains mondo-riffs, trundling ever on laconic and venomous, distinguished by the foppish then mighty schizo-vocals of Maynard James Keenan, and the twisty percussive creativity of Adam Jones, whose drums are forged in fire, rendered white hot and sterling crisp. But while **Undertow** has a no-sell-out, no-hurry sort of integrity with its pure-as-sin meditations on all things Loud, tunes tend to drone on; large beasties lumbering through miles of mud rivers rendered thick and destructive through the power of torrential rain. **Undertow** creates such a world, thus is no mere collection of sounds, more of an effect, like an intensification and brutalization of Soundgarden's **Louder Than Love**, darker, murkier and damn near perfect for the more suicidal of the slack set, which may explain why the band was considered the act to see at Lollapalooza '93, headlining the second stage and subsequently scaring the bejesus out of all those who gazed in. Samey and wastey but bludgeoning, until the last third of the record, which consists of throwaway dirge *Flood* and *Disgustipated*, which is all sound effects and talking, finally buzzing out in eight minutes of some kind of ringing sound. 20+ minutes of a 69 minute disc squandered; not pretty but excusable.
Rating                                                                                           7

## Tool - Aenima (Zoo/BMG '96)
And finally in advance of the millennium, Maynard and his assembled malhavocs return with a new, whisper-to-roar springroll of evil, **Aenima** picking up where the platinum **Undertow** left us headbanged in the lurch. **Aenima** certainly exhibits a slow brew and stew, Tool building an almost progressive sort of rolling alt.metal (Rollins and Pitch Shifter crossed with the latest Prong or Killing Joke comes to mind), the band still pummeling relentlessly but texturing their meat

with quizzical electronic touches and sorry respites of angled sounds. The artwork is the most disturbed I've ever seen, culminating in the groovy 3-D eyetrip of the front cover. Too bad the lyrics aren't included, because they would have helped demarcate and deliberate the tracks of this fairly opaque, anti-social work of profound nightmarishness. Succinct verdict versus its predecessor: less raw, more ambitious, more trippy.
Rating                                                                                           8

## Toranaga - Bastard Ballads (Peaceville '88)
This may have stood out in England, but compared to the metric ton of Bay-style thrash acts all over the U.S., **Bastard Ballads** is pretty average, despite the fresh and musical riffs, which are snuffed under busy arrangements and a rotten drum mix. Six ambitious, longish but junketty tracks; promising but justly buried under years of advancing steel.
Rating                                                                                           4

## Tora Tora - Surprise Attack (A&M '89)
One of the countless, inherently American metal hopefuls aiming to be the next Dokken, Poison, Guns N' Roses or Crüe, a batch of bands still selling in thick wads up until about '93. **Surprise Attack** attempts depth and history via slick roots metal, succeeding instead in creating fake blues on such tunes as annoying minor hit *Walkin' Shoes* and other assorted worn-out, soul-less rockers, Tora Tora putting forth few ideas that haven't been lifted wholesale from the MTVAOR book of poses. Uneventful and offensively commercial-minded, this kind of painfully transparent stuff eventually killed hard rock as anything but a larf.
Rating                                                                                           3

## Tora Tora - Wild America (A&M '92)
Memphis boys Tora Tora slurp in a shot of adrenaline, toughening their blues metal focus into something approaching Spread Eagle, heavier riffs, bluesier blues, more commanding delivery. One of the best at bluesy hair band metal (if you care; I certainly don't), biggest ace being Plant-leaning vocalist Anthony Corder. Like it a fair dose, but would have been happier if it was a Great White record. Faves: lush and languished roots ballad *Nowhere To Go But Down*, and menacing closer *City Of Kings*.
Rating                                                                                           7

## Torch - Fireraiser (Mausoleum Est '81)
Bloody 'ell, Torch rocks. This five track EP marks the debut of a killer band of raucous Germans that spit out two LPs then disappeared, at least to these Western eyes, although rumour has they were back in search of plunder in '91. Torch is a perfectly brutal example of the deafening power metal that can be forged from simple, truck-sized riffs and an urge to snap necks through brain-shaking vibration alone. Magic breathes within this volatile mix of talent, attitude and production like some sort of early, confused form of the virus affecting Dave, Glenn and Phil. Aggressive twin guitar riffing, powerhouse drumming, and a crazed OTT metalhead frontman in the incomparable Dan Dark solidify the sonic cyclone. Frightening anarchy, laced with capable self-enforced order. Buy it all.
Rating                                                                                           9

## Torch - Torch (Tandan Est '82)
A masterpiece of heads-down, to-the-quick Teutonic power metal, **Torch** comprises basically ten scorchers out of ten tracks, nary a wasted moment and not a pansy pause in the mayhem, obliterating the idea that you have to play complicated to deliver level, menacing, serious metal. I mean, it can work wonders when everybody in the organization does their job like they own the joint. So **Torch** rolls forth like a tank, OTT in diamond-toothed attitude, but artfully controlled mu-

**457**

sically, just so heavily guitar-laden, and so ridiculously intent on creating a driving groove that couldn't slow down if it so wished (see Diamond Head). And the production is perfectly and brilliantly forged in fire, kicked into gear by the manic drumming which itself is bolstered by boisterous use of cymbals. Titles such as *Warlock*, *Rage Age*, and *Beyond The Threshold Of Pain* do sufficiently rough justice to the essence of the Torch philosophy. *Rage Age* indeed.

Rating     10

## Torch - Electrikiss    (Sword '84)

**Electrikiss** is still so evidently the product of the one and only blunderbuss known as Torch, yet the band is markedly slower on this departure versus the debut's willful axe slashings; more jarring thud than cruise, threatening to be smothered under a dull, merciless critical mass of ponderous percussion. Torch's electrocuted sound is still stripped to essentials, wollopingly loud and poundedly cannon-like, yet there's more space, more mood, even some overt melody (sorta like the sullen tones of 220 Volt). Nine desperate shards and again not a wasted moment anywhere, although parts of this record trudge so dangerously slow and power-packed, it risks grinding to a halt. **Electrikiss** may not slay your command centres on first rotation, but after a few plays, the Germanic genius of the thing will just pound you in the head relentlessly, Torch being so ludicrously one of metal's best studies in bent focus and delivery. Let's hope they re-surface and pummel a few posers in the process. Hey, it's tradition.

Rating     10

## Bernie Tormé - Turn Out The Lights    (Kamaflage '82)

This hapless, bed-headed guitarist has toiled with a number of British bands, most notable being Gillan. His solo albums have a post-punk wasted 'n' jaded mentality, but musically seem to wander through various well-traveled hard rock territories, resulting in only a handful of quality vignettes, best here being the wicked *Lies* and infectious popster *Possession*. Tormé sports a subtle sense of humour, sorta like Ray Davies meet Johnny Thunders, but the albums as a whole remain patchy, and the man ever so charmingly can't sing his way out of a wet paper bag.

Rating     4

## Bernie Tormé - Electric Gypsies    (Attic '83)

A punky, snarling delivery of variously spirited, variously tired hard rock. However, *Wild West* is a classic raver, one of the most intense fusions stuck quivering and dive-bombing between new wave and heavy metal ever penned. **Electric Gypsies** is adequately consistent stylistically, evoking an exotic, glam-hammed Hanoi Rocks, smearing forth with a squalid paid-my-dues feel, much more intense in comparison to last year's awkward **Turn Out The Lights**. Tormé's guitar work isn't exactly earth-shattering, but it does have a garagey sort of integrity, bending the man's delusions of grandeur toward gritty, economic and noisy riffing, doing an adequate job of smothering the rest of the band's watery performances in their tracks.

Rating     6

## Totenmond - Lichtbringer    (Massacre '96)

An embittered debut darkcore offering, **Lichtbringer** might remind one of Mindrot or It Is I, seeping into the mud like a salted slug. Call it doom, call it coagulated punk, call it truly disturbed. Warning: sung in German, as if you would notice.

Rating     5

## Touched - Back Alley Vices    (Ebony '84)

The barreling nuclear boom box of Ebony's Darryl Johnston is cranked full bore on this far-gone mutation of the brilliant Savage, an album that kicks off inexplicably with a horrendously loud epic cum power ballad. The razor numbness of the production adds a wasted insistence to **Back Alley Vices** which, despite fairly traditional non-threatening structures, makes the difference between convincing and brain-dead (i.e. Mausoleum). And the presence of a shrieker along the fine line of Steve Grimmett or Chateaux's Krys Mason doesn't hurt either. Hopelessly Brit/Euro poverty metal with probably the most extreme of Ebony recordings, Touched kicks and destroys considerably, given their limited weaponry.

Rating     6

## Touched - Death Row    (Ebony '86)

Touched pull a Tysondog or a Chariot here, letting fly on the throttle and wrecking the place with a scurrying, boozy, manic but unsure battery which undermines the gravity of previous work. Kinda scruffy and stupid, slurred and evil, but almost defeated, I'd say the band was going for something like spontaneity, not realizing that their lot in life is encrusted with more than enough raw grit already.

Rating     5

## Tox - Prince Of Darkness    (Camel '85)

Something ghoulish this way comes in the form of one odd hybrid of Germanic underworld despair and simple groove rock as per loose 'n' juicy American power chorders. No shit, Tox is a wild trip, sort of like an awfully Swedish and suicidal Accept or sumthin', all pounding echoey drum patterns and pregnant pauses, which more often than not, harken the blues through an unrecognizable guise of Gothic mass. Wickedly clever and wildly manipulative of restraint and innovative melodic progressions, the badly titled **Prince Of Darkness** is one of those hot lost oddities of the '80s, cranking wondrously throughout its strange, underground warmth. Classy, unpredictable and emotionally distressing.

Rating     7

## Toxic Reasons - Independence    (Century Media Est. '82)

Recording since '81, still touring on the backs of eight, count 'em eight full-lengths, Toxic Reasons aided and abetted the cancerous growth of U.S. hardcore. But their curious sound owed as much to bad-brained Brits from '77 (i.e. Eater, Adverts, The Clash) than anything American and skatish. The boys at Century Media found this seamy punk debut snarl worthy enough to reissue (along with a strange stable of other goonies), and I can see how the record might have been the virtuous acne-scarred bane of many a midwest metaller's existence, sounding much like anything fifteen and high on glue. But sorry, I wasn't there regionally, and the vibe remains alien to me. As good as much of that old spitoon-addled dreck, most of which doesn't hold up, unless case in point was of course "your band."

Rating     5

## Trance - Breakout    (Rockport '82)

Pained, brooding, darkly melodic and traditionally German, Trance is similar to 220V, Overdrive, and maybe the emotional essence of Accept re: **Balls To The Wall**, pumping Teutonically beneath Lothar Antoni's fine metal shriek, which resembles the throats behind Trouble and Nazareth. **Breakout** is excellent, depressing mood metal, quite heavy, and quite melodic but decidedly European. Lyrically the band laments the world's moral emptiness throughout all strata, preaching a sort of compassionate anarchy, tortuously exposing such a solution's ultimate failure, along the same lines as Trouble, but not nearly with the same isolated anguish, dedication and loosely Christian lessons. Very stirring music with a hint of the enigmatic.

Rating     8

## Trance - Power Infusion (Rockport '83)

Similar to the debut, and identically loud production-wise, **Power Infusion** is most markedly a better collection of songs. Classics abound, such as *Heavy Metal Queen*, *Glasshouse*, and *Shock Power*, songs that stirred our blood with visions of Valhalla. A perfect, two-fisted metal combination binds much of this: twin guitars, brash but powerful production, banshee vocals, and the German knack for mixing melody with mayhem. Concentrating on faster, upbeat tunes here, Trance deliver the mystique of a metal band with something philosophically complex and emotionally deep to offer, set to a pace well below panic, but vigorous all the same. Intensely Euro and intensely tragic, looking to dominate with psychology as well as muscle.
Rating                                                                 9

## Trance - Victory (Rockport '85)

Again more darkly rich, intrinsically German metal, **Victory** works the same war-torn territory as **Power Infusion** but with a trace less vitality and punch, in effect delving deeper into depression, angst and lack of open air; claustrophobic and top-heavy, despite advances in exploration. A solid album, but so similar to the first two, there's not much more to ramble on about. Warning: all three at once may lead to depression at the situation that is your sorry life.
Rating                                                                 7

## Trans-Siberian Orchestra - Christmas Eve And Other Stories (Lava/Atlantic '96)

Taking on greater and greater challenges, Savatage and 'tage producer Paul O'Neill have created their ultimate masterpiece, this expanded band family project essentially re-writing and rejuvenating a vast array of Christmas tones and tomes in splendid, respectful fashion. Make no mistake, this is a Christmas record, combining many carols with classical works and Slavic folk pieces, weaving a complicated fabric combining the Christmas story with slices of modern life from New York to Bosnia. O'Neill figures highly in the writing credits, as does Jon Oliva and pianist Robert Kinkel. So it's no surprise that the keyboard work is front and centre. But the overall feel is of recent Savatage; sporadic axe-metallic fire, triumphant builds, theatrical brilliance, and an abundance of gorgeous peaceful acoustic guitars all combining for a unique and worthy pastiche of Christmas emotions. A variety of vocalists further elevates the proceedings, making this a true Christmas pageant barely resembling a rock record, moreso built like a big-budget theatrical production. Great work, folks.
Rating                                                                 9

## Trapeze - Hot Wire (Warner Bros. '74)

Just a quick token review for a band of hopeful Limeys a few seniors have said I ought to include in this book. I disagree, but this succinct mention is in order, Trapeze at one time featuring Glenn Hughes, and on this record including Mel Galley and (mediocre) Judas Priest drummer Dave Holland. When heavy, they sounded like dusty ol' Humble Pie, Savoy Brown or Bad Co. Otherwise, it's a kind of yukky funky r+b not unlike early Whitesnake/Coverdale solo. Over-rated, but then again, this isn't considered their best.
Rating                                                                 4

## Trash - Watch Out (Est '84)

The fact that this band's Euro helmsman can't even enunciate the word does little to diminish the fact that lead cut *Vicious* is the most smokin' rendition of a Lou Reed-penned dittie ever carved. And the album in general manages infectious rowdiness, coursing through the veins somewhere akin to Highway Chile and AC/DC, with a bit of Bodine thrown in for attitudinal ballsiness and apt comparison in terms of barsy, bluesy brew. And the vocals rock too, traveling the same frequencies as Klaus Meine, albeit less trained and tuneful. **Watch Out** kicks with more abandon than its lumbering follow-up, even when grabbing a chair and pulling up for a quiet chat, proving that so-called maturity can rob a band of their innocent charm and mobility. Trash was one of the few European bands that proved capable of inebriation rock, although unfortunately, the buzz wore off before flaming into full groove.
Rating                                                                 7

## Trash - Burnin' Rock (Atlantic '85)

On **Burnin' Rock**, Trash recycles itself into a big beat, fat-stringed European band shooting for a cross between bluesy AC/DC and L.A. sleaze. As a result of this admirable mix and with the help of a powerful recording, **Burnin' Rock** at least partially aspires towards its swingin' predecessor, while falling short due to average riffs and a predilection for slow metal. They got the big hair, though. So there's no good reason why they couldn't have been contenders.
Rating                                                                 5

## Pat Travers - Pat Travers (Polydor '76)

A humble, almost countrified debut from a mind that will give us some classic guitar rockers over the coming years, **Pat Travers** is chock full o' blue collar blues and old boogie woogie-based stuff designed or chosen to showcase Travers' traditional r'n'r licks. Four of nine tracks are muscled-up covers, with only the brilliant *Makes No Difference* hinting at future genius, driven by angled, precisely-placed riffs dancing over an insistent marching beat. Ultimately this debut is an opportunity surrendered to its maker's influences, and a large part of why I used to confuse Travers, Thorogood and Trower, way before I was paying attention.
Rating                                                                 4

## Pat Travers - Makin' Magic (Polydor '77)

Travers' second effort offers more of the debut's sassy, down-home rock 'n' blues, while beginning to stretch out in terms of funk and overall songwriting prowess. The band's rhythmic jazziness and percussive chops shine on tunes such as the way-cool syncopated title track, not to mention '70s-style funk metal classic (as opposed to Faith No More's '90s spin on the genre) *Hooked On Music*, one of the band's most heat-stroked live rabble rousers. Y'know, Pat Travers best stuff would sound great on mid-years Aerosmith albums. Maybe Sony's forever young, thirty million dollar signing oughta carve a tribute album to Canada's most smokin' native son, or at least a live EP or somethin'. Or maybe Extreme will do it now that no one's listening to their own songs.
Rating                                                                 6

## Pat Travers - Putting It Straight (Polydor '77)

Travers finds and locks on his forté, becoming intricate, jazzy, and uncannily funky all within a hard rock context, doing that highbrow intellectual '70s guitarist thing; king of a certain twangy, artsy level of wattage. *Gettin' Betta* ranks with *Hooked On Music* and *Go All Night* as Travers' tastiest funk grooves, and blazing lead calling card *Life In London* demos the band cruisin' like speed rockers with doctorates in maglev train technology. Amongst all the high wire riffery, Travers sounds cocksure of himself, philosophically resolved and solid, as he leads a crack band through this universally enjoyable musician's music, pushing the envelope of guitar rock in shining and shimmering manner, far above the murky likes of contemporaries Frank Marino and Robin Trower, while peaking in parallel with American soul bro Rick Derringer. Ultimately **Putting It Straight** is the Travers record most like a "solo"

album, and most academic in execution, no small credit to the automatic Smooth of future Maiden-basher Nicko McBain.
Rating 8

## Pat Travers - Heat In The Street (Polydor '78)

Heavier, more confident and even smug compared to the man's '77 classmaster flash, **Heat In The Street** combines great playing with a will to celebrate life and summer fun, fun, fun, the record oozing with some of the most loud 'n' proud guitar-hero rock reminiscent of, but more intelligent than Ted Nugent, while less metallic but more seriously aristocratic and squeaky scrubbed than Van Halen. Go All Night and Heat In The Street are simply brilliant, agile lube-rockers, propelled by the labyrinthical rhythmic sixth sense of drumming legend Tommy Aldridge, a perfect complement to Travers and his penchant for odd time signatures and jazzoid surprises. Exceedingly talented '90s wunderkids Extreme hit the nail on the head when they paid homage to Travers in **Pornograffitti**'s thank you list "for getting the FUNK OUT for years." It just goes to show that as Pat continues his tragic drift into obscurity (commencing with **School Of Hard Knocks**), he can stand assured that his place in history is firmly acknowledged, Travers spellbinding the rock world as the original wizard of the funk spin that was such an important part of hard rock in the early '90s. One of the most appropriately-titled records ever, **Heat In The Street** breathes in the heady fumes of summer in the city, and slams 'em back all coked and zingin' through the razor-tuned amplification of the Travers heated brew.
Rating 10

## Pat Travers - Go For What You Know (Polydor '79)

Pretty much my favourite live album of all eternity (tied with X's **Live at the Whiskey A Go-Go on the Fabulous Sunset Strip**). Funky, jazzy, metallic and scorched to the touch, Travers and his effortlessly brilliant band rip through a set of rhythmic low riders that capture the best qualities of live summer rock'n'roll festivals of the '70s. Yet at the same time, this is musician's music, spiced with enchanting fills and swanky technical wizardry, Travers feeding us a mixture of music lesson and booty-shake at the same time. Most live albums simply consist of worse recordings of studio tunes that were never intended to hang out together. **Go For What You Know** is a furious kick in the head with respect to such traditional and almost universal shortcomings, slapping side-by-side, like-minded molten Travers twisters delivered with the man's canny mix of technical genius, unbelievable sense of rhythm, and delirious abandon. No cajones, this red hot opus delivers the crown jewels of the considerable Travers repertoire with a dizzy violent agility that strikes at the molten core of quality stadium rock from an era and a feel that is lost forever, the combination of the compositions taking on a synergy of its own as Travers basks in the blinding sun of his glory days.
Rating 10

## Pat Travers - Crash And Burn (Polydor '80)

**Crash And Burn** finds Travers once more working within a variety of contexts which for the first time, on the cool and tasty title track and Bob Marley's Is This Love, include chunky, axe-steeped reggae. Rock radio staple Snortin' Whiskey (conspicuously absent from the airwaves in these politically correct times) and the angular Can't Be Right, although the lone metal offerings, do the genre proud justice, offering hot, rhythmic, solid rock riffs laced with Travers' inspired guitar melodies; two of the man's best amplified meals. Superb production (which has been the case on every album since and including **Heat In The Street**), brings these versatile compositions alive, while offering a thread of consistency to what is an extremely exploratory record. You can't help thinking, however, that Travers is confusing his fans. I'm sure he would have become a commercial giant had he kept writing in the heavier vein. Of course, challenging rock's frontiers also has its merits. After all, it worked for Zeppelin and Queen.
Rating 8

## Pat Travers - Radio Active (Polydor '81)

Here Travers changes gears, going for more of a stripped-down, melodic hard rock sound on such personality-rich gems as My Life Is On The Line, I Can Love You and Feelin' In Love. The hopefully monikered **Radio Active** is almost warmly naive; humble in comparison to previously grandiose gestures, striving for a closeness between entertainer and listener that begins with the finesse of a pop caress. Travers' fluid, jazzy guitar inflections are still evident, but secondary to the personal, simple songwriting. One may deem **Radio Active** one of the least ambitious, least arranged records of the Pat Travers catalogue. However, it is this cozy vulnerability, the simplicity and enthusiasm of emotion that make it just that much more appealing. Sort of reminds me of why I listen to Rick Derringer.
Rating 9

## Pat Travers - Black Pearl (Polydor '82)

**Black Pearl** is the Travers Band grand opus, combining the teeming, rhythmic virtuosity of the '77-'80 albums with the emotive melodic songcraft of **Radio Active**. The mix is brilliant, resonating like oak, and the playing so tasteful, so confident, that **Black Pearl** tacitly and without much commercial success, stands as one of those few and far between quality benchmarks in rock'n'roll, like Lizzy's **Renegade**, exuding manners and prefered breeding without acting snobby. Opener I La La La Love You is simply a hard rock tour de force containing an album's worth of ideas, while still sounding cohesive, on the pleasurable side of overblown. Stand Up and Bob Marley's Misty Morning radiate sincerity and tropical warmth, fused with a guitar sheen that is rich and full, comfortable and jazzy. Only Rockin' and Beethoven's The Fifth are not overtly dovetailed into the good tidings, the former being an all-thumbs **School**-quality thudmonster, the latter being another dumb classical cover (blame Blackmore). The shimmering remainder however, is smooth and timeless hard rock, perhaps reminiscent of '77-'81 Thin Lizzy, UFO, or reunion-era Deep Purple. An under-rated gem of huge ambitions.
Rating 10

## Pat Travers - Hot Shot (Polydor '84)

Pat Travers' heaviest album, **Hot Shots** comprises mostly uneventful metal spiced with brilliant melodic hard rock, with little else in between. In one sense, Travers is abandoning his loftier goals of previous efforts for simple, American stadium-style rock. This may confuse less fans, even if the quality of the metal on this is nowhere close to the elegant, intricate and textural heavy material from past glories. But, hell, it's still a lot of fun; surfing like Diamond David Lee Roth, a wave made of sheer heart. The title track is the lone, acceptably complex, high quality steel plate, but the memorable fun-in-the-sun stuff everywhere else makes up for the no frills writing. In The Heat Of The Night, Tonight, and Night Into Day (!) are simply gorgeous popsters Hagar wishes he could conjure, dripping with hooky choruses and tidy cruising beats. But like I say, the metal plods, sounding like the uninspired lounge act rockers that loiter the halls of **School Of Hard Knocks**. Sum total: a three quarter horse.
Rating 8

## Pat Travers - School Of Hard Knocks (Episode '90)

Pat's first in years sounds fragmented, chaotic and uncharacteristically tired, the songwriting almost exclusively clichéd, too L.A. rawk, too automatically "product", pretty much the only inspirational rocker being lead track *The Fight Goes On*, a heady bluster of riff and melody that tugs at the heart strings while rocking with Travers' celebrated sense of rhythm. But a definite disappointment overall. Travers, rumoured to be a victim of years of substance abuse and egomania (and he *is* looking a bit puffy), seems ill-prepared for a new record, **School Of Hard Knocks** being a shambling, fragmented and soulless offering butted up against his past accomplishments. Essentially the last before an anti-climactic retirement, the man returning in '92 with a guitar-themed album comprising mostly blues covers.
Rating    4

## Pat Travers - Boom Boom (Castle '91)

Long after Travers' inspired star has crested, the man is still capable of whipping a show white hot, this time accompanied by long-time war horse Mars Cowling, independent tunesmith Jerry Riggs, and drummer Scott Zymowski, the line-up for Pat's last, fairly dull studio project. But this U.K. only double vinyl soundstorm does much of what **Go For What You Know** did, 'cept maybe that Pat's vocals are a mite out of tune at times. Lots of classics, plus *I La La La Love You*, plus better tracks from **School Of Hard Knocks** scorch very warm to burning, Zymowski and Cowling fusing into a rhythmic fury recalling those shows of old. Plus the mix is just fine, this spread quite unbelievably a club gig, recorded at the Diamond in Toronto. Highlights: *Life In London* and as usual *Stevie*.
Rating    8

## Pat Travers - Blues Tracks (Blues Bureau '92)

Hey hepcats, this could have been duller than it is, given the dreary line-up of blooz covers, as besotted Pat enters his Floridian purist phase far from home, home being hotfunk '70s metal in Canada. No buds, this one surprises as Shrapnel's offshoot Blues Bureau reaches back into pappy's house for those amps that go to 11. Fortunately, **Blues Tracks** sounds as electric and rhythmic as Foghat or Pat of old. Unfortunately the record comprises nine covers over ten tracks, with ZZ's *Just Got Paid* blazing the way, opener *Memory Pain* almost as stoked. But fortunately again, the record is a hard rockin' affair, lots of drums, vocals, power chord sandwiches and high-pitched barroom axe solos sizzling in the pan through a squarely metallic mix. But unfortunately the whole concept of the blues is only fuzzily creative, objectively dull and predictable in structure, just low on work ethic from a handful of angles (although something unspeakably bizarre happens to *I Can't Quit You*). So in a nutshell: loud but slack.
Rating    6

## Pat Travers - Just A Touch (Blues Bureau '93)

On **Just A Touch**, Pat lightens that feel, really approaching the blues like water and silk versus the steely stomp of his performance on **Blues Tracks**. So progressively and logically, this is a more artful, less obvious blues approach to comfortable, low-slung tracks that flow from Pat's own pen. Granted there's a fair amount of slinky, Stevie Ray-style r+b here, but all in all, the compositions are less pinnable, although Pat's playing is still immutably Pat, quite traditional, derived of Clapton but in love with volume, the flashman from the '70s dishing up the heroics. Summarily, these two records are a pleasant surprise, because Pat seems to appreciate the value of a good sturdy song through

which he filters his newly bluesy muse. Not my cup of muddy water, but a bang-up job all the same.
Rating    7

## Pat Travers - BBC Radio 1 Live In Concert (Griffin '94)

I do believe Travers' **Go For What You Know** is one of the best live records of all time. No, really. Travers, Pat Thrall, Mars Cowling and maybe most potently drummer Tommy Aldridge were a live venue rock monster at the turn of the '80s, criss-crossing America as lethal backing band to metal's then current greats, many forced into gut-check mode as Travers cleaned up on said headliners night after night. So it's no surprise this 1980 Reading set (plus four tracks from '77) is a shining stud in the BBC Radio One reissue series. Highlights that weren't on '79's **Go For What You Know** include tech hotrod *Life In London* and most importantly, gorgeous metal duo *Your Love Can't Be Right* and *Snortin' Whiskey* from the then-current **Crash And Burn** opus, an otherwise surprisingly non-heavy masterpiece. Performances sizzle, and rhythms, although complicated, flow effortlessly like summer rock memories, and the whole spread is paced beautifully, documenting a crack unit firing on all sixes. Sadly, this Reading show was to be the last performance of this ludicrously high-octane line-up.
Rating    9

## Treat - Scratch And Bite (Mercury '85)

Poor quality songwriting dooms this Dutch band's attempt at teeny bopper metal stardom. Pop metal without the chops, ideas or attitude necessary to pull off material in this difficult genre. Needs grease.
Rating    3

## Treat - Dreamhunter (Mercury '87)

Not sure what transpired between records, but I don't much care either, Treat being a toweringly dull high school-level AOR blight, stiff-thumping drums driving these dopey keyboard and harmonies ditties to now-heresville. Bush league Europe meets Night Ranger without the players, or mebbee Dokken ballads and popsters without Lynch.
Rating    4

## Tredegar - Tredegar (Aries (UK) '86)

Evidently somebody must have been thinking big thoughts for this aristocratically British five-piece, which includes Tony Bourge and Ray Phillips from Budgie and a lead mike who looks like Paul Stanley. It's a weird one, gatefold sleeve, silver embossed cover, a strange and dreamy back cover shot, and song monikers like *Duma*, *Richard III* and *Battle Of Bosworth*. But skipping past the surface curiosities, **Tredegar** is a heroic guitar trip, expertly assembled and heavily dominated by a considerably more metallic Tony Bourge than was the case with the legendary explorations of Budgie. Progressive, grand, but immediate, **Tredegar** manages to rumble brash and loud throughout this decidedly British minor opus of goth sweeps, indeed colliding with Budgie's **Power Supply** in places more earthly, an album of which Bourge was no part. A bit on the unwieldy side with its self-seriousness, multi-layered arrangements, synth shadings, crashing cymbals, and distant vistas, but nevertheless strangely scrappy in its over-riding confidence. A very limited edition CD exists (press run: 500; different from **Ex Budgie** reviewed below) comprising this record and an unreleased full album from '91.
Rating    7

## Tredegar - Ex Budgie (VSC/Sabre Dance '92)

This confusing little collectable is a limited edition, Budgie fan club item, put out in a 45 sleeve, all 500 copies signed by Ray Phillips. Liner notes are some-

what elucidating, except for the double numbering of tracks. Tunes enclosed are out-takes from Tredegar (pronounced tre-DEE-ger) in various incarnations, including selections with female vocalist Trixie Thorne. Then there's pre-Tredegar bands Titus Oats and Freez, the sum total defining Ray Phillips' meandering, uneventful trip from '78 right up until '91, the latter showcasing tunes that Ray has brought into his current band, Six Ton Budgie, which was Budgie's original moniker. The music all sounds like bad **Power Supply**, scrappy OTT, spooky goth, some melodramatic soft bits, pretty rivet-headed and amateur, proving that the actual Tredegar album was really a hard-won triumph of a bunch of guys operating at their peaks.
Rating      4

**Tribal Stomp - Tribal Stomp**    (Limit '96)
With I Mother Earth going a tad alternative, it's up to bands like Tribal Stomp, Fear Disorder and Gutsonic to fly the flag of slamming, rhythm-dense alt.metal Toronto-style, each possessors of an accomplished, modern deep-groove mosh that could place them in good stead vis-a-vis taking metal into the millennium. Riffs, percussive attack and grunge-inflected vocals work a menacing brew here, although the production is a bit muddy and low on treble, not disastrous, but just enough to cause early fatigue. All in all though, a complex and thoughtful stack of tracks that need not bow to any of the many competitors out there, even if it might get lost in the shuffle.
Rating      7

**T-Ride - T-Ride**    (Hollywood '92)
A fresh injection to the metal scene, **T-Ride** was a sensuous visit to a new world, a merry-go-round of sounds that evokes an ornate, technical update on the spirit of Queen, while lyrically stalking Tubes terrain, a sort of colourful look at situations both real and celluloid. Even a bit of Stan Ridgeway, Andy Prieboy and Dan Reed Network to it; a definite love of technological tinkering, like some fiendish ham radio enthusiast or computer hack. Layers of electro beats, electronic drums and electronically-treated drums (courtesy Eric Valentine) tribally collide with machine gun strafings from guitarist Jeff Tyson and the spiral wails of lead vocalist and bassist Dan Airie. And out falls a beautiful alchemy, a downright charming sound that reaches full gush with throbbing ballad You And Your Friend, an absolute gazelle that deserved to be a worldwide hit. Heaven-sent. But whence the Queen comparatives? For starters the embracing of technology with equally convincing footholds in strength of song and belief in plenty o' guitar. But mainly it's the ethereal and heart-stopping vocal harmonies liberally draped over most everything on this unique project. And the record turns heads on a dime, finding a groove, then next stop creating a new one, all bob, weave and punch; my kinda dance record, sprinkling in all sorts of sonic popcorn that is nourishment to my ears. A band with something bright, stylish and intelligent to say. I welcome more.
Rating      9

**Triumph - Triumph**    (Attic '76)
One of Canada's smelliest musical embarrassments, Triumph had one redeeming factor about their clod-brain heads. They were "metal" when few other bands knew distortion, which is the only reason they ever went anywhere (oh . . . and because Rik Emmett is such a nice young man). **Triumph** is bar band metal recorded well, devoid of any real originality and delivered aseptically behind the thin and boring vocals of the aforementioned Mister Rogers of rock. Loud enough to stick out, also benefiting from our love of power trios, Triumph would become the cheesiest thing on your radio going on twenty years now.
Rating      5

**Triumph - Rock'n'Roll Machine**    (Attic '77)
Triumph's second adds a bit of flash, chops, diversity, prompting a realization that the band won't be able to cut it with their lame nods to Rush, BTO, Hendrix and Zeppelin. Only marginally improved, sporting the speed rockin' title track and other slightly more ambitious undertakings, **Rock'n'Roll Machine** also contains a thoroughly pointless cover of Joe Walsh's Rocky Mountain Way. The innocently smug Triumph record, one that struggles to a semblance of six string pride.
Rating      5

**Triumph - Just A Game**    (Attic '79)
Canada's biggest rock'n'roll snicker wastes no time commencing their AOR formula slide into whoredom with this cynical, lazyboy rock, only half redeeming itself on the shakey-butt slut metal of American Girls and the bombastic progressive morass of hit power ballad Lay It On The Line. A record that evokes the worst 10% of The Eagles crossed with the worst 5% of BTO. Gatefold contains smashingly accurate Rush poses and a board game motif that leaks a bit of humour.
Rating      4

**Triumph - Progressions Of Power**    (Attic '80)
In conjunction with **Allied Forces**, **Progressions Of Power** is one of two decent Triumph records, semi-focused statements where the band's philosophy coalesces into a Canuck shtick that is both idiotic and amiable, sorta like SCTV or a saunter through the Hockey Hall Of Fame. The formula goo is out in full force yet **Progressions** is an adequate laugh at our mediocre, non-threatening Canadian psyche. You know they mean well. Most convincing blue collar beer commercial on the album: I Live For The Weekend, whilst I Can Survive rehashes Lay It On The Line to luke-warm enjoyment levels.
Rating      6

**Triumph - Allied Forces**    (Attic '81)
Believe it or not, this is one of two Triumph turds I can halfways tolerate, as it contains two of the more uplifting morale pieces Triumph is noted for amongst losers the world over. Magic Power and Fight The Good Fight are so shamelessly overblown, they actually do manage to serve the encouraging, bright purpose for which they were written (to help extra-stupid twelve year olds). And the rest of the album is either hooky (on the verge of sap) hard rock metal or just decently tuneful, dumb, hosehead hard rock. I mean, Triumph served only one perhaps two narrowly defined functions with any skill, and **Allied Forces** seems to spend its dime attending to these areas; areas denoted by the presence of shlocky, melodic laser-inundated stadium-ness, mixed with delusions of greatness and Canadian sympathy for the underdog.
Rating      6

**Triumph - Never Surrender**    (Attic '83)
**Never Surrender** finds Triumph's pomp and circus pants in its full, "poor man's Rush" glory. Of all the wanker albums after the band discovered that they could sell their virtuoso act to most bad musicians under sixteen, this is the most indulgent, and consequently the most entertaining in an embarrassing, guilty pleasure way; wannabe hapless Rush posturing, just this side of infantile. Or maybe I was just in a receptive mood when I first heard it, being the holiday season and all. Fave of this sort of mountain-size guilt: World Of Fantasy.
Rating      5

## Triumph - Thunder Seven (MCA '84)

The inaugural blight in a long line of dreadful formula stadium rock albums from the utterly limp Triumph, the most predictable band of cash-in Canadians in rock. Originally titled Turn Of The Wheel, if you care.
Rating **1**

## Triumph - Stages (MCA '85)

Not that Triumph ever did anything well, but **Stages** does do a good job of highlighting that guitar and drum hero thang that evoked comparisons with Rush, Rush themselves being often irritating, fellow Canuck rockers who nevertheless had a ton of pretty cool ideas throughout the years (excuse me, early years). **Stages** focuses on the inspirational, almost born-again Triumph tack which is at least the band's strong suit, demonstrating that even complete lugans can attain their dreams. Triumph's method: throw lots of money at your "blinding light show" and always headline. Note: two studio tracks were included on **Stages**: *Empty Inside* and the sorta heavy *Mind Games*, which featured Max Webster drummer Gary McCracken replacing an injured Gil Moore.
Rating **4**

## Triumph - The Sport Of Kings (MCA '86)

One of Triumph's least cheesy album covers comes wrapped around one of Rik's most annoying piles of sitcom caca, as the band starts feeling label heat to produce singles. Inspires the most intense of hatreds soaring to red levels with the catalogue of one Bryan Adams.
Rating **0**

## Triumph - Surveillance (MCA '87)

Combined with the last, Triumph has the distinction of spewing two of the most offensive records ever produced with a straight face, in any genre of music. How any self-respecting musician could ever get so far with so much stupidity with respect to basic rules of taste is beyond me. Well, not really. I keep forgetting the Canadian music industry's canny grasp of Soviet economics, where if potatoes are being produced, potatoes is what you get. Power struggles within the band begin to erode the viability of carrying on.
Rating **0**

## Triumph - Edge Of Excess ('92)

After a long and pleasant departure from the scene, and more importantly, the departure of smilin', sincere Rik, Mike and Gil are back with new axeman, Phil X, who burns the fretboards up and down this, the heaviest Triumph release to date. Still, the band is plagued by a boringness, characterized by Gil's turgid vocals and an obliviousness to modern songwriting's quality levels. And lyrucks? This one could duke it out with Jeff Healy and Sammy Hagar and still lose. Heavy, but in a hysterically predictable and clattery sell-out sort of way, Triumph may be back, but they're still Triumph, the clueless.
Rating **2**

## Triumph - In Concert (King Biscuit Flower Hour '96)

Capturing the band at their inspired height, **In Concert** finds the band relatively ripping up Cleveland in '81 with their patented Canuck fromage. The booklet essay tells the story of the band's signing to RCA, in which Triumph had gathered the moxie to book and subsequently sell-out hometown Maple Leaf Gardens. Eleven A&R heads saw the show and read the stinking reviews the next morning, all passing on the band. The RCA guy, who was late for his morning flight, left in the afternoon, reading a later edition of the paper which carried a rave review. The rest is history. Anyways, **In Concert** is a rousing enough representation of this

pointless band, lots of heavier, unsung rockers and hit power ballads, a real concert sound with requisite good drums and bad guitars, added bonus of Rik Emmett being a little off key.
Rating **6**

## Trixter - Trixter (MCA '90)

Trixter are basically hair band metal's version of Silverchair (well, there was also Bad 4 Good), the band being dismissed for their young ages, even if the recorded grooves sounded like every other hard rock band at the time. And this is regular stuff, really, just hooky hard rock primed for the charts, not altogether dressy, just a mix/mean/median of a million acts at the time, offering weekend fare for miles, ballads for the gals. And hey, it kinda sold.
Rating **5**

## Trixter - Under Covers (Backstreet Est. '91)

Those brats in Trixter are back making mischief with this covers EP, each track put through a nice, tight, hyper commercial metal combine; good versions, OK songs. The menu: *Pump It Up, 50 Ways To Leave Your Lover* (in both shuffle version and unplugged), *Terrible Lie, Take The Long Way Home, Dirty Deeds Done Dirt Cheap, Revolution,* and *Fight For Your Right To Party* (done live and nasty). Funny and fun . . . once.
Rating **5**

## Trixter - Hear! (MCA '92)

Dealt a jealous bit of criticism with the whole "Trix is for kids" accusations back with the band's successful pop metal debut in '90, this young Jersey quartet have moved it along quite nicely, offering some wider, White Lion-type melodic hard rock with tons of variety and rich vocal work. Hell, even the ballads are above par, demonstrating a band who'd rather fight than lay down resigned to a not so admirable reputation as juvenile, not so delinquent rock stars. **Hear!** rounds the bases of corporate metal: funky metal, standard ballads, tricky ballads, party boogie, metallic blues, and candy-coated groove rock. But it's all tempered with considerable class, nothing ear-shattering, simply a general feeling of being on a mission towards credibility (à la Winger and Warrant), offering solid penmanship and fully-fleshed ideas. Promising, and certainly within the top half of the commercial metal genre.
Rating **6**

## Trouble - Trouble (Metal Blade '84)

And so it was born, the thickest, most tortuous chords in metal, sobbing cataclysmic riffs that shook the ground from six feet under, sent drowned and bloated with Love from **Master Of Reality** and **Vol 4** through the mediums that comprise Chicago's legendary Trouble. **Trouble** the debut (also known as **Psalm 9**) is one hell-bent slab of Christian vindictiveness; God portrayed as destructor of all things evil, of which there are a multitude infesting this record. One part despairing religious cleansing, one part ecstatic Christian suicide, **Trouble** is a resolute steamroll over souls, kicking into battering ram overture for chuggers like *Assassin* and the eminently precious *Bastards Will Pay*, but mostly enveloping a flagellated mankind in waves of meltaious wattage, so bent on communicating with nothing human, pummeling with the most desperate and subconscious of Iommi-inspired cries for help as Eric Wagner variously croaks and harangues sinners into the bright flames of God's forgiveness. Truly something alone in loud contemplation of itself.
Rating **9**

## Trouble - The Skull (Metal Blade '85)

Trouble come pounding back with a record destined to become their thickest, most dream-like and drowsy of a catalogue marked by brilliance from day one. **The**

**463**

**Skull** is almost the eccentric crazy relative, slipping into a lethargic thrash through shuddering fatigue. Still a marvelous nightmare to behold, there's something overly loose and panic-stricken about this record, which takes over a dirge like *The Wish* (clocking in at 11:35) and the masochistic title track, making the listener thirst for a roaring headbang. Strange, but I think the illness lies in the drum sound and general percussive performance which is overly busy at times. Of the formidable Trouble repertoire, **The Skull** will forever reign as the most buried and lost unto itself, most inwardly cancerous, maybe the most frightening.
Rating                                                                 8

## Trouble - Run To The Light   (Metal Blade '87)

If Trouble's previous grave warnings haven't sent you full sprint towards the light, this one ought to scorch your heels. **Run To The Light** marks a new cohesion to the merciful Trouble onslaught of word and deed. A new producer sends a megaton shiver through the limbs of new drummer Dennis Lesh, who conspires with messengers Bruce Franklin, Rick Wartell, new bassist Ron Holzner and the indomitable Eric Wagner to construct cathedrals of lead that leach poison to those who dare pray. Still much of **Run To The Light** evokes the sorrowful sludge of **The Skull**, in places searing the flesh with awesome unstoppable momentum (witness *The Misery Shows*), while in others freezing appendages in stone, rendering all caked in hopelessly weighted despondence. A band so beyond gothic into genetic instinct, Trouble is above any sort of dissection and denigration, above the law, sent with The Law to infiltrate and cast out; a brain terrain over which to bridge time, space and the beaming shield of divinity. Enter at your own risk and resist its controlling grasp (i.e. counter briskly with Van Halen, preferably *Dance The Night Away*, *Beautiful Girls*, or *Jump*).
Rating                                                                 9

## Trouble - Trouble   (Def American '90)

The world in which Trouble toils tirelessly has no weather, no expression and no sound save for dark religious rumblings emanating in agony's waves, an agony forged from moral codes lost for a hundred years. **Trouble** is the horrified look around, not so much an examination of society in ashes, but a lament at intrusion into a twice-removed dream world, shocked by invasions from mere lucidity. Eric Wagner is far beyond and beneath the concrete within himself and others, his world stage occupied by the liquidity of pure soul forced to flow through the waves of pain, love, hate and redemption that comprise the stench of Earth, in search of benevolent arrival back in the world of dreams. **Trouble** is the band's most devastating and stark utterance to date, rendered basic, carnal and spiritually uncomplicated by the love and respect of studio force Rick Rubin and his signature Def mix. Through clouds of misunderstanding and subsequent tragic understanding, the band pile in gleaming heaps, their most decadent, stinging and anguished riffs to date, metal beyond the mind's eye, metal aimed at blood. Thus the molecular Sabbath of *At The End Of My Daze*, thus *The Wolf*, thus *The Misery Shows (Act II)*, a never-ending cry from seas of red velvet lining the infinite coffin. And woe to be, thus *R.I.P.* and *Heaven On My Mind*, a twisted pair of thorny caffeine pounders that demonstrate Trouble's insane vortextual heaviness, power chords as high as K2, life experience unimaginable; leaden and weary beyond reality into a haze of retro ecstasy. Blistering and pure, Trouble has assumed both the actuality and potentiality of vintage Sabbath, roaming far beyond in creation of their own kingdoms in the shifting uninhabitable sands of souls in torment. Yet I'm convinced Trouble would have occurred without Sabbath. Too much truth to be a derivation. I only compare. Both bands were right.

**Trouble**, the record is the clearest glimpse through this storm Sabbath also braved, and the view is spectacular and sad.
Rating                                                                10

## Trouble - Manic Frustration   (Def American '92)

Named for Trouble's frenzied and lucid observations of a sick world, the words **Manic Frustration** evoke the nervous itch that drives this record into heady metal dementia. Whereas **Trouble** and indeed **Run To The Light** portrayed the band smothered in steel wool gauze, hazy dream states of life on the other side, **Manic Frustration** catches the band enveloped in ringing, scratching, flesh-tearing tension between matter and psychic vapors, heavy as the end of the world but blistered through burnt wiring again by Rick Rubin, this time brilliantly out of character. There is no better record anywhere on the third stone from the sun's scorched terrain, maybe different ones lent the same importance, but none greater. Trouble continues to burrow into dark angles of the pathetic human psyche and its ungrateful motivations, scooping us all into its gleaming craw for an uneasy and undeserved trip into the cyclone of God. Whereas **Trouble** ached, **Manic Frustration** is a sharp, nerve-rattling pain, forced into hysterical currents as it fights the critical mass of its being. When the wattage of its waves can be subjugated, one becomes enveloped in exquisite metal perfection, the white core of a devilishly black sound, constructed of '60s idealism (psychotic cultish idealism gone wrong) in full collision with the dense reality-wedged axe slashings of Wartell and Franklin here and now. By embracing time and its resonances, this is a record above time; its only tenuous link being its insane sonic concreteness of being, its cascading insistence on moving mountains. Nothing less. Thrashing through twisted bed sheets in an airtight chamber suspended and blanketed by God's wrath, Trouble's legendary manipulation of music continues with blinding force completely outside of recognition, as if even the most blessed are too scared to confront the light. Thus zero press despite tacit reverence amongst metal's major pioneers. As Earth lies broken, over-turned and leaking fuel in the ditches of Extermination Day, **Manic Frustration** will no doubt be chosen as God's final 8-track selection, droning while draining the battery in continuous loop as the twisted wreck (it is written the Armageddon will drive a '72 GMC longbox) rusts and returns vigilantly to dust. Small comfort, licked by the flames of Trouble's deceiving hope.
Rating                                                                10

## Trouble - Plastic Green Head   (Music For Nations '95)

Lofted from their American Records deal (a mutual parting), Trouble found quick acceptance in Europe, releasing this albums months ahead of time there before Century Media snapped them up stateside. **Plastic Green Head** (an awkward title designed to evoke both war and drugs) was self-produced and self-financed by the band before any record deal took shape, Adams and crew confident something would transpire, creating another hurtful sledge of psychedelic-inspired anachronistic doom, well up the Trouble pathways of metal heaven. **Plastic Green Head** is unfortunately a "more of the same" type spin, getting the show off to a rousing start with the carving title track, then offering the usual thick, maybe bluesier and more tentative cauldron of hell-fried flambés, including covers of The Monkees' *Porpoise Song* and The Beatles' *Tomorrow Never Know*, amongst such rumbling tumblers as *Opium Eater* and the hypnotic *Another Day*. If I sound less enthused, it might be the familiarity of it all, not to mention the record's excellent but ordinary recording, a bit of a cold sound after the two odd mixes of its two predecessors. Still one of the best bands on the planet,

but I'd have to call **Plastic Green Head** my third favourite Trouble record.
Rating                                                                9

### Robin Trower - Twice Removed From Yesterday
(Chrysalis '73)

Early, post-Procol Harum Trower (he left in '71; this is his debut) noodled in rudimentary jammy structures, which just by accident flopped from its hysterically Hendrix blues state into a sort of filmy, 1969 stadium rock (*Man Of The World, I Can't Stand It*), and bouts of psychedelic seizure (the title trip). But most of the time it just wallowed and hollowed in acid blues (*Daydream, Ballerina*), much like this toaster's album cover.
Rating                                                                5

### Robin Trower - Bridge Of Sighs   (Chrysalis '74)

**Bridge Of Sighs** lifts off with the classic adrenaline Hendrix of *Day Of The Eagle*, one of Trower's master monoliths. But then things dissipate into the usual bongwater blues, peppered with lively bits of Santana-like sanity. Still it's the expressive, bendy guitar meat that one comes here for, the sonorous vocals of Jimmy Dewar (ex-Stone The Crows) the perfect foil for the antiquey freaky sounds enclosed. Like any generation that just doesn't want to know, I find myself more inclined to listen to this than the original, squeezing just that little bit more relevance out of the only minutely less-dated production and song-skills. Over a million copies sold. At least a couple missing in action: '75's **For Earth Below** and '78's **Caravan To Midnight**.
Rating                                                                6

### Robin Trower - Live!   (Chrysalis '75)

Recorded less than a week after the performance used for the **BBC One** set, **Live!** contains pretty much the same tracks, non-**BBC**-ers being rumble-tumbler *Too Rolling Stoned* and the snare-rattling, desert-swelled blooz of *I Can't Wait Much Longer*. Very brash, electric and '70s-agitated, the perfect canvas on which to splay Trower's time-suspended, crazy-man soloing verbosity. Sounds like a whole pile of craft and chemistry, the likes of which is rare amongst today's lo-fi loafers.
Rating                                                                6

### Robin Trower - In City Dreams   (Chrysalis '77)

Perhaps Trower's purely funkiest record, **In City Dreams** makes a languished, austere lolligag through a complex hybrid of American musics. Obtuse, snobby but at the same time comfortable, Trower's rhythm section almost projects more than Trower, Bill Lordan's session-ish, electric prog drumming and Rustee Allen's slap-bass defining this record like no other. Fave without a doubt would be melodic r+b beauty *Sweet Wine Of Love*, which connects on an emotional level, something lacking with the rest of this academic but worthy record. Easy to see why Trower is of limited appeal, the man really off in a humid netherworld of slow-drip exotics only few will truly care to visit.
Rating                                                                7

### Robin Trower - Victims Of The Fury   (Chrysalis '80)

Trower's stuff always skirted the edges of metal, in similar fashion to Frank Marino and Mahogany Rush, due largely to both bands' obsessions with Hendrix. Both outfits, out of 10+ records each, could fill a double album with their respective metallic moments. Mahogany Rush's record, however would knock the stuffing out of Trower's as Robin is more the purist, more the bluesman, and less the energetic messenger of pain, preferring to stomp a wah wah than a distortion pedal. We'll not dwell too heavily on the man, 'cos unless you're a guitarist, an ardent follower of axemen or a lover of electric blues, Trower'll leave you cold and confused. In any event, **Victims Of The Fury** is one of his least muddy, most direct and enthusiastic efforts,

sporting a good four rockers and some choice axisms that get way down low, fusing with funky bass lines and soulful, syrupy vocals from James Dewar. Fave raves: *Mad House* and *Jack And Jill*. Closest companion records: **B.L.T.** and **Back It Up**.
Rating                                                                7

### Robin Trower - B.L.T.   (Chrysalis '81)

More like a beefy, ballsy Clapton show, **B.L.T.** (Jack Bruce, Bill Lordan and Trower) burrows deeper under Trower's vast understanding of amplified blues, finding a pride inside that orbits Hendrix with a strong dose of Bad Company and of course, Cream. Loads of integrity; an unsung craftsman who deserves your respect.
Rating                                                                7

### Robin Trower - Passion   (GNP Crescendo '87)

My collection probably peaked with a chart-topping six or eight Trower albums to my possession in the early '80s, however, after shedding them all, I'm slowly gathering them back when the price is right, because if yer gonna collect music, why not get stuff with quality? The case at hand: more bluesy hard rock from an axedude whose over-riding sound is Jimi all the way, yet whose bluesiness falls between the downright boring Eric Clapton and the downright soulful Billy Gibbons. Nothing much heavy on this perfectly asleep record, one that evokes a techy stiffness not found elsewhere in the dreamy Trower catalogue. Only feature of note: Davey Pattison on vocals, one of the smoothest and most accomplished blues throats in the biz, a man who cuts a memorable swath through Gamma's three records, a trio of fantasticals every fan of the guitar should own.
Rating                                                                5

### Robin Trower - Take What You Need   (Atlantic '88)

Neil Norman improves on his muffled production job on **Passion**, adding treble but still leaving the dirt, which all chafes against the valiant attempts of fusing dated, synthy keyboards (the way Foreigner uses them), with the two-fisted blues attack of Trower and Pattison. So a little brighter and more basic, even funkier with lots of that rainy, rumbling axework we've all grown to admire, if not passionately embrace.
Rating                                                                6

### Robin Trower - In The Line Of Fire   (Atlantic '90)

Trower continues to produce vaguely/potentially commercial blues rock that kinda straddles Clapton, Gary Moore and Bad Company, infected with too much production from the '80s. But through it all once again, it's a joy to behold the smokey, soulful vocals of Davey Pattison trading licks with an understated, simple and piercing Trower. Songs are generally what you might deem self-defeating; maudlin then glitzy, the tired side of AOR, although there are low intensity rockers and croonable blooz tunes riddling the record doable. One for the old rockers on their rockers, just like me. Warning: not really heavy enough to be in this book, but wot the hell, us metal guys like our guitarists.
Rating                                                                6

### Robin Trower - BBC Radio 1 Live In Concert
(Griffin '95)

Again the BBC people (then Windsong, then Griffin), do the right thing, catching a band at their peak, Trower's nasty trio captured live just after record #3, **For Earth Below**, in all its glory, mixing grind and fluidity like any number of '70s blues combos, with the added weapon of Trower's articulated matriculation. As good a recording as any of the early studio LPs, this one really brings out the drums and cymbals of newly-installed

skinsman Bill Lordan. A must for lovers of ancient funky excursions into the heart of guitar.
Rating 7

## Robin Trower - In Concert (King Biscuit Flower Hour '96)

As usual, the King Biscuit gang do a fine job, bringing us this '77 gig from New Haven Connecticut, the band's catalogue ever-growing, efficiently touching every base of American blues. Show features James Dewar as vocalist only, Rustee Allen taking over on bass, turning the band into a wicked little four piece. Liner note tidbit: James Dewar has since become confined to a wheelchair, after suffering a stroke in 1987. Somehow a little looser sounding (especially those bashing drums) than the '75 sets, and not exactly better for it . . .
Rating 6

## Trust - Repression (CBS '80)

These guys have the unfortunate distinction of being the most widely known French metal band, pretty famous in their homeland. And still they suck, sounding like a regressed AC/DC (they were good friends with Bon Scott, who was slated at the time of his death, to translate the record's lyrics into English for them), mixed with boppy power punk. And I guess it's supposed to be hip to know who they are as even Anthrax covered them. Lots of albums, this I believe the first to come out in both French and English versions. None that I've heard worth owning, French hard rock being about the most pathetic music on the planet anyways.
Rating 1

## TSOL - Revenge (Enigma '86)

Punk, drugs, the gutter and vague political notions pretty well sum up my limited knowledge or impression of the True Sounds Of Liberty, a band I've always lumped with New Model Army and Social Distortion for no good reason, the latter of which I've yet to hear. TSOL embody a kind of morose Cult-ness, a vaguely tribal, basic quality that is too tightly wound for punk, although the vocals tend to ratch out fairly often. Lyrically, I think these guys get credited with too much deepness due to their slippery persona. In essence, they're basically scruffy outsiders with the same sordid tales to tell as everybody else, although with these guys, one gets the feeling they like to wallow in the grime and the perversity of it all, or at least accept it as their inevitable habitat. Revenge kicks, yet it's more a kick of the walking, soul-less dead. Faves include opener No Time and speedy closer Everybody's A Cop. Repels as much as it attracts.
Rating 6

## TSOL - Hit And Run (Enigma '87)

The boys from the abandoned strip malls of L.A. look a ton more metal on this one; leather-decked 'n' leering, ready for a brawl. And the formula remains the same: doom metal and hard rock laced with punk, occasional country, blues, and acoustic touches which lean towards the dirge, sort of like a really confused, gutbucket Cinderella or Faster Pussycat nursing a death wish. A couple of extra too simple toons and anti-cohesive dynamic shifts make this less steady than Revenge; although, always wanting to assign more wisdom to the comparatively newer product, one might be tempted to attribute this one with more finesse. More mature maybe by definition, but less entertaining as the structures hang lazier and more predictable, begging the obvious questions: does this band have any idea who they are, where they come from, and who they want to be when we're finally ready to listen?
Rating 5

## Tsunami - Tsunami (Enigma '83)

One of those bands that you figured just went out and did their thing in a vacuum of their own creation, Tsunami was often compared to Y&T which is somewhat valid, this disc resembling the wall-of-sound feel and overall heaviness of Earthshaker; also similar vocals to Meniketti (before he was neutered). A fairly accomplished debut and damn near excellent for the time, Tsunami sports solid, traditional, heavy AOR riffing, a liberal, frantic mix and even a scary goth tune. Scored a minor hit with bombastic but convincing muscle ballad Runaround.
Rating 6

## TT Quick - TT Quick (Megaforce '84)

One of the few fledgling U.S. outfits that shook the universal grandeur of various '70s metal cornerstones, in creation of a muscular drive to sonic domination, this five track did an adequate smoke through pounding chug riffs, faster low-flying OTT moments, and even a cover of Fortunate Son. Emerged as one of the hopefuls, borne of an ingestion of all that came before it, and an iron will to improve upon the past, entirely and almost self-righteously from the trenches.
Rating 7

## TT Quick - Metal Of Honour (Island '86)

TT Quick's debut EP over-flowed with well-harnessed tunnel-chops, demonstrating that these strong arms of the law were serious about what they crammed furtively between our ears. Metal Of Honour builds on the initial buzz with a sound that resembles a Virgin Steele forced into hand-to-bayonet combat for survival. The axework is searing, the vocals kick-ass, and the songcraft varied, making this a rowdy trip through high-octane landscapes of early '80s chops metal. There's an almost cocky sort of elderly detachment to this band similar to Montreal's Sword or even Riot, that somehow puts them outside the business, where all three bands unfortunately stayed. Hard not to appreciate in terms of road-embattled professionalism. Still, a one-dimensional studs 'n' leathers mentality leaves this in cramped company with countless combos of closed mind and pudging body, bands that either extricate themselves from the usual metal-for-metal's-sake trappings, or get buried as relics of styles past.
Rating 7

## Tuff - Religious Fix (Mausoleum '95)

I have no problem locating this with the "haves" of heavy AOR, rather than the "have nots", Tuff blending together the grim street elements of Alice Cooper, Guns 'N Roses and Hanoi Rocks with the high production acumen required of hair band metal. So there's a touch of sassy glam here (I Like What I See is almost Cheap Trick, and certainly Enuff Z'nuff), and a dose of blues twang there (right to the source with hard-done-by cover Sixteen Tons). As a result, the record paces itself well, putting this long-suffering (nine years, two records) California act in good stead as viable melodic hard rocker in the mid-'90s, an era where so far, pickins' have been mighty slim, although surprisingly few bands have thrown in the towel completely. Not quite the effervescent shine of Tyketto or Lillian Axe, but still a believable rock package in their beseiged, street metal sandbox.
Rating 7

## Tungsten - 183.85 (Pavement '93)

Tungsten's officially just a two-piece, drummer Mark Talamo and lead metal-luvin' madman Al Hodge. The band hails from that swampy, ugly New Orleans scene that has spawned Crowbar, Eyehategod, Down and a little farther flung, COC and Pantera. Call this one

Crowbar with better songs, big smelly tire-burning metal that sits between characteristic Nola dirt and the chopping rhythms of urban metal merchants like Biohazard or Prong. But the coolest thing is the general "spurned lover" theme to the thing, 185.85 (tungsten's chemical number) being a non-stop barrage of ranting bile around a male-female relationship that crashes in flames. Arrangements are a little sparse, but a perfectly slight sense of melody barrel-rolls through the thing, making shards of wishful dismemberment like Born XY and Just Fades Away as memorable as they are brief. Closes with a cover of Forged In Fire (Anvil is one of Hodge's faves), which interleafs perfectly with the pig-iron rumble of the man's spiteful originals. Geez, I'd say this pretty much closes the door on a reconciliation.
Rating                                                8

**Turbo - Dead End**   (Under One Flag '90)
Underscoring Under One Flag's penchant for technically well-versed "thrash" acts (there's really no term for this stuff, but Bay Area thrash will have to do), Turbo's **Dead End** grinds forth with brisk spot-on stun riffs, a bit lost in the '80s, but kinda like a new Anvil, y'know driven, committed, and so in lust with metal. Doesn't mean I give a damn, but if that hammering Frisco-style power metal be your tea, then this won't necessarily disappoint.
Rating                                                5

**Turmoil - From Bleeding Hands**   (Century Media '96)
Noisy, boysy and seething with anger, Pennsylvania's Turmoil have been in existence since '92, touring with similar crash-wollop punk machines as Madball, Earth Crisis, Snapcase, Shelter and Killing Time. This first gets graphics that are more lavish than the production values, which are a grueling mid-ranged kind of affair, turgidizing these deathly hardcore tracks of admonishment, vaguely straight-edge tales of reprisal that wear the temples to a bloody mash by record's end. I dunno, I guess I'm not screwed up enough to relate.
Rating                                                5

**Twelfth Hour - Die Screaming**   (Second Sun '94)
**Die Screaming** rides a dangerous doomgrunge hoodrock vibe through the dead of destructo-club night, fueled by the multi-tonal vocal prowess of one Jason. Thunderous drum sound too, melding nicely with the percussive heft of lead and bass, which snake heavily and occasionally psycho-delically through each retro-thunk-chunking track. Mix an ounce of Jane's Addiction, a pinch of Alice In Chains, a dram of Johnny Thunders, and a case of Kyuss and call me in the morning. Subversive, throbbing, and Toronto-based to boot.
Rating                                                7

**21 Guns - Salute**   (BMG '92)
This semi-lauded commercial pomp rock pageant features the return of Thin Lizzy axeman Scott Gorham, whose thick and meaty riffery is scattered sparingly over the length of **Salute**. His band is also up to the slick quotient demanded of such a rich affair (drummer Mike Sturgis did time with Wishbone Ash, Asia and Aha), especially vocalist Thomas La Verdi who even if he looks a bit twee in the bellboy costume, is one of those classic AOR voices. Yet even as it's a pleasure to hear Gorham, the few rockers that there are disappoint, lacking real spice (kinda like Sykes), dying a death from too much tech.
Rating                                                6

**Twisted Sister - Ruff Cutts**   (Secret '82)
**Ruff Cutts'** liner notes talk about how this EP is intended to be a mucho-requested taster from a band whose fan club already claims 15,000 members, quite a feat for a group without a record. Anyways, four cuts, including a kickin', raw version of Under The Blade plus a less insane take on What You Don't Know. Finishing off: Leader Of The Pack and a pretty sleepy Shoot 'Em Down.
Rating                                                5

**Twisted Sister - Under The Blade**   (Secret '82)
Motormouth Dee Snider and his N.Y. contingent cook up a debut brew that makes Twisted Sister sound like the headliners they rapidly became. The cross-dressing image Twisted Sister adopted was dead relevant to the band's philosophy, prompting the obligatory glam, Kiss n' Alice comparisons which are also apt in terms of party mentality and camp horror ambiguity. And TS stretches the ambiguity further as tough guys with a sense of humour; tough guys undermining macho precepts, literally by strapping on dresses. Of course, all this would get a little out of hand if the music didn't deliver, and **Under The Blade** delivers in spades, sporting mostly ultra-powerful, razor-edged speed rockers such as Run For Your Life and Sin After Sin, which cut to the chase with exuberance and veteran skill. Other styles include slow boredom boogie (Day Of The Rocker) and party-time hard rock (Bad Boys Of Rock'n'Roll and Shoot 'Em Down), a direction that would eventually overwhelm the band and eat its brains. Overall however, **Under The Blade** is dead serious despite the garish imagery, a good 4/5 of it rocking with hellacious clout, attitude and clever economy. Unfortunately it's pretty well all downhill after this. Trivia note: basic tracks of the record were bedded in some barn deep in the English countryside, which reportedly contributed to the "good vibe" of the record. Production by Pete Way.
Rating                                                8

**Twisted Sister - You Can't Stop Rock'n'Roll**
(Atlantic '83)
The band's brash, committedly metal production values are gone, as Twisted Sister become even simpler, more stripped sonically speaking, more AC/DC-ish in philosophy, replete with major space, squared-off kick-boot rhythms, and hanging immobile chords. The songs however are strong, most of the record ringing quite heavy if not sparse, shallow but hook-laden in a metal context. Containing fewer all-out speed ravers than the dastardly debut, **You Can't Stop Rock'n'Roll** achieves a consistent, controlled, mid-pace kind of momentum start to finish. Quality Sister for senior citizens, including the first of many signature self-affirming anthems in stomper I Am (I'm Me).
Rating                                                7

**Twisted Sister - Stay Hungry**   (Atlantic '84)
Here comes success, as Twisted Sister become a short lived household name, propelled to fame by bubblegum MTV anthems We're Not Gonna Take It and I Wanna Rock, both lusty football romps bellowed forthrightly by guys in make-up and pink spandex. Heavier and simultaneously more teeny-bopped than its level-headed predecessor, **Stay Hungry** marks the shift to where make-up, costumes, hair, comic book horror, and video stardom begin to jumble together, overshadowing, infiltrating and polluting the spirit of the band's admittedly lunch-bucketed music. But there are some judiciously heavy rockers here such as Burn In Hell, SMF, and The Beast, albeit all plagued by deliveries that are so simplified, so basic, that there just isn't enough going on to hold one's interest for more than a couple o' capitalistic spins. Call it kinda fun but kinda stoopid and dismally over-produced.
Rating                                                6

## Twisted Sister - Come Out And Play (Atlantic '85)

A new list of faults emerges as the SMF Sister is blown out of the water, crew left to drown in a sea of over-commercialized sensationalism. Not only is **Come Out And Play** still too drop-dead plain, but now the recording is worse. Plus the more metallic tunes are dreadful (almost like bad Crüe circa **Theatre of Pain**), while the pandering to the five-to-ten year old age bracket gets right out of hand with lunch box crud like *Be Chrool To Your Scuel* and *Leader Of The Pack*. We also get formulaic Triumph-like power ballads about believing in yourself, which, when all is said and done, is Dee's most lasting conceptual contribution to humanity I guess, given that his Widowmaker project was such a crock. But as for **Come Out And Play**, this is cartoon metal at its commercial worst, Twisted Sister as flubbed parody of itself.

Rating                                                                   3

## Twisted Sister - Love Is For Suckers (Atlantic '87)

**Love Is For Suckers**' back cover prophetically features a TS logo sucker languishing in the gutter. Well suck on more positively catatonic kiddie metal as per the last album. Twisted Sister always tried to write economically but here they try to write even dumber and more mentally scattered than their usual wet bag of hammers. It's almost as if they are actively unlearning or erasing their musicality and their technical skills. Or more like some marketing suit with a tire-size beer gut has smoked too much crack, getting it in his head to attempt connection beyond the band's secured fan base of five-to-ten year old white males, to include a new one of fours, threes and terrible twos, band as unwilling circus clowns, puppets of the whole sorry ruse. The end of a fun-filled flash in the pan.

Rating                                                                   4

## Twisted Sister - Live At Hammersmith (CMC '94)

Everybody say hi Dee ho, it's 198-fo, the biggest brashest year in the shlocky rock career of Twisted Sister. Having just hatched **Stay Hungry**, Dee was indeed talking proud, boasting the victory of New York's "most colourful" rock combo of the day. Hell, this is a pretty decent live thang, taking the listener back freezer-packed to the time when metal ruled. Good recording, and Dee's quite the (trash) talker, roaring to the SMFs as much as he is fronting his good simple band, packing in most every frontman cliché in the book. As a bonus we get two covers from '79, proving that the boys had their road legs but early. *Shoot 'Em Down* sounds extra fine, as does the extremely fast version of *Under The Blade*.

Rating                                                                   7

## 24-7 Spyz - Gumbo Millenium ('90)

I don't know what all the hype is about with these guys. I'm sure a lot of it's the usual novelty of seeing black guys play hard rock. Anyway, **Gumbo Millenium** is so frustratingly schizophrenic, mixing in equal doses bad funk, tired blues, irritating sampling, rap elements, and untuneful thrash metal like the worst of Bad Brains grab-bags. Close to completely unlistenable. As a roadmap, turn left at Living Colour's **Time's Up**, strip Fishbone's Caddy of its jazzy chrome, drop a tab, and you're halfway there.

Rating                                                                   4

## 24-7 Spyz - This Is ... 24-7 Spyz! (eastwest '91)

OB (that's Original Bodycount to you) swell up with more epileptic Living Colour, displaying a metal logic on this 20 minute five track EP that is more digestible than on the harrowing **Gumbo Millenium**. I have major respect for this band, in the same way I like Fishbone, for their black rock vocals, poetic lyrics, and funk and rap injections, while staying well away from pure rap or R+B which are often over-produced and

under-played. Here we get a progressive marriage of all of the above with ultra-heavy riffery and a cleverly-commandeered Zappa-esque chaos. Commendable and for the first time, effortlessly enjoyable.

Rating                                                                   7

## 220 Volt - 220 Volt (CBS '83)

A highly respectable band from the early Euro invasion, 220 Volt struck a chord of metalhead despair with their sizzling renditions of galloping medieval metal, too mature for the D'n'D imagery of the genre, preferring to lament the deterioration of morality and loss of love over proud Teutonic power chords sturdy as oaks, resembling no band in particular, tapping their very own richly-adorned but bitter cold muse, an ice queen with emotional pain in her memories and furious buzzing riffs on her bloody hands. Music like this will always hold up because it avoids trends, creating its own distinct palette with a genre often attempted but usually turned into cartoons. And those guitars just crush.

Rating                                                                   8

## 220 Volt - Power Games (CBS '84)

On heroic trajectory from **220 Volt**, **Power Games** continues to hone the band's unearthly grasp of searing metallic melody, blasting into view with galloping riff maiden *Firefall*, one of the boyz' finest crystals. Elsewhere, the tragic Teutonic despair continues, on the fiery wings of pulverizing, forward massing Euromonsters commandeered by Jocke Lundholm's clear-headed vocal prowess, a pained man fronting a bruising band. The wall of misery pervades most everything here, but breaks into crashing rock for the Zepp-ish *Child Or Beast* and the mechanical hard rock interplay of *Don't Go*. Large, lordly and loud, evoking a majesty not unlike Trouble via Accept.

Rating                                                                   9

## 220 Volt - Mind Over Muscle (CBS '85)

Icy and brilliant as the tundra they evoke, 220 Volt's first two monoliths were fairly identical in their wall of sound attack, both drenched in thick, buzzing dual axework. Here the band adds a new creative vigor to their class, building from their core sound, an expansive and versatile work, mining the same vein but bringing to the surface gleaming jewels such as the energetic *Electric Messengers*, the **Balls To The Walls**-ish *Power Games*, the killer elite of *Secret Dance (Xymania)*, which is kinda like a frazzled update on Rainbow's somewhat delicate *Gates Of Babylon*, and the sustained clip of *Touch Of Fire*. Insane class frosted with flame now pervades the palace walls, 220 Volt establishing themselves as the ultimate goth metal machine, balancing signature melancholia with universal lyrical matter, and a spaceship full of stellar riffs, sending wave after wave of great song ideas. One lost beauty worth the search.

Rating                                                                  10

## 220 Volt - Eye To Eye (CBS '89)

With a truckload of hair and make-up consultants at beckons call, label bosses toil in vain to turn 220 Volt into standard stateside 110, hoping for the latest pin-up babes, with an air-tight hard rock beat and clear-minded delivery, erasing all the scratch, tension and despair from the band's sound. Too bad the experiment didn't work financially, 'cos I kinda like the new sound, the band seizing the role with conviction, proving themselves to be versatile professionals in the process. **Eye To Eye** is punchy, rhythmic, well-played and well-accented, still completely guitar-driven but definitely infused with Bon Jovial hard rock melodrama and maple-sweet melodies to match. It's a shame really, because **Eye To Eye** has what it takes to excel in the genre; hooks, energy, sparkling musicianship, and total tightness due in no small part to the financial

discipline inspired by big dude Max Norman twiddling the knobs. Possibly on the heavy side for hit metal, it's likely **Eye To Eye** merely lost fans who smelled sell-out, while neglecting to garner any new ones for any number of reasons, I'm sure many beyond the band's control.
Rating 7

### Tyga Myra - Deliverance (Ebony '86)
A yowling Ebony migraine positioned deep in the basement of castle-black mindspheres. Actually less goth than inebriated 'n' heavy hard rock, too racked with English ineptitude to join the ranks of the head-bending, although basic riffs tend to kill as on combat rocker *Never Givin' Up* and pummeling closer *Future Vision*. Adding it all up, probably as many records have been wrecked by the Ebony sound as elevated, although to be fair, this was a self-produced effort, only obsessed with the legacy.
Rating 4

### Tygers of Pan Tang - Wild Cat (MCA '80)
**Wild Cat** is the raucous, street-treated debut from one of the NWOBHM originals, a band who never made the same record twice, slapping forth this charming little pre-Tank bucket, ricocheting like an errant bullet; punky, loud, loose-bolted, and heavy, fun for all and all for one. Of note, it's the lone Tygers album to feature Jess Cox on vocals. Granted the guy ain't no Dio or Halford, lacking a real singer's range causing the boy to lapse often into a strained, conversational style. But I dig his voice, his hearty metal growl, lending this album guts and grime. Scrappy, headbangin' metal at its most unloved and neglected, **Wild Cat** is a chaotic noisemaker steeped in the integrity of a Motörhead or Tank, but with better riffs than either; lusty, unpretentious rock'n'roll, most definitely one of the early magic moments of the British invasion, and one of the very first releases we sought-out after furiously combing those bewitching issues of **Sounds** and **Melody Maker** from '79, trumpeting the new power surge-ables from all over jolly ol'. A stupendous drinking record of long-haired biker metal, featuring enduring carnivores *Euthanasia* and *Badger Badger*, amongst a general barrage that refuses to let up, give in or move over.
Rating 9

### Tygers of Pan Tang - Spellbound (MCA '81)
On their all-important sophomore, Tygers opts for a serious, upscale sound, adding a credible metal technician at the mike to wail forth standard tough guy metal lyrics, which are alas and alack, too unsurprising to work, the band's songwriting reverting to bland formula metal, lacking the chaotic, torn and frayed blitz of the debut. And of course it wouldn't be a serious play for superstardom without the obligatory radio rockers, of which there are at least three. But neither the production nor the chops are up to serious contention for state-of-the-art metal, Tygers being a band that sounded best dirt-poor and under pressure, here their Judas Priesty aspirations betraying the band as liggers and punters before their prime. In time, maybe they could have pulled it off, but one more kick at the metal cat and they'd be hanging up those working man's riffs for a deep dive into confused AOR.
Rating 7

### Tygers of Pan Tang - Crazy Nights (MCA '81)
Taking fiery cue from its album cover, **Crazy Nights** is the most confident, aggressive and heaviest Tygers of them all. The production makes your ears bleed. Loud, and oddly distorted, it's a perfect mix for the records simplistic riff-machines, which gather copious weight compared to the powerless speed rockers loitering the streets of **Spellbound**, or indeed even the punky flamethrowers of the debut. A good 80% of **Crazy Nights** is top-notch British arena fare, capturing the sparked, live mayhem of the debut while simultaneously making a convincing play for serious metal contention with a palpable renewed levity of purpose. And Jon Deverill sounds in complete control of the ship, growing into his role as prima donna and entertainer, vocalist of an elite class. Unfortunately it didn't work at the bank, and next time out, the boys abandon heavy metal in search of some needed cash.
Rating 9

### Tygers of Pan Tang - The Cage (MCA '82)
Tygers surprise wholesale on this shift to pop metal, engineered by neat freak Peter Collins who would one day encourage and enlarge Rush's weaknesses on **Hold Your Fire**. Clocking in at under thirty minutes, **The Cage** contains nary a single heavy rocker. However, despite its sell-out nature, I fell for the record in spades, feeding off its hope and energy and excitement at trying something new. Great hooks are everywhere, buttressed by a swagger straight outta David Lee Roth, delivered with a rich and unsure British twist, Deverill in full possession of the dramatic sense to pull it off. Highlights include a smokin' version of oldie *Love Potion No. 9* and the innovative, subdued atmospherics of both *Making Tracks* and *Tides*, odd book-ender tunes which point to fresh vistas this band might have explored further. Ultimately, **The Cage** caused widespread revolt among Tygers' old guard and for all the clatter, it didn't pick up many fans from the AOR end of town. Nevertheless, **The Cage** was a refreshing, positive example of wimp metal, making no apologies for its romancing of style over substance.
Rating 9

### Tygers of Pan Tang - The Wreck-Age
(Music For Nations '85)
**The Wreck-Age** works the same Night Ranger/Bon Jovi light metal angle as was attempted with **The Cage**, but sadly the will to become stars seems to have waned. Even though superficially it's the same sweet sounds, **The Wreckage's** ten limp wrists whine and whimper, all paling one-to-one versus any of the ten confident teen anthems shaking **The Cage**. The record's forced and awkward hooks surpass the limits of good taste and the noisy, plodding production drags each defeated track even further into the muck. Finished it without a record deal to their name, and it shows.
Rating 2

### Tygers of Pan Tang - Burning In The Shade
(Zebra '87)
See above review for **The Wreck-Age**, then file with Samson, Saxon, Raven and Twisted Sister as marketing gone so very wrong. Once great, now losers on the watery wane. Time to re-think the whole thing, or pack it in.
Rating 2

### Tyketto - Don't Come Easy (Geffen '91)
Funny business this AOR stuff (or maybe it's just like any other), there being a bunch of accepted bands, bands considered worthy by serious students of the form (note: for an excellent Net-zine on the genre, see SFK). Tyketto is one of these, crossing that perplexing AOR line into sincerity, sidestepping all those formidable landmines marked sell-out, cheese, wimprock, poseur etc. **Don't Come Easy** features the vocal talents of Danny Vaughn, who served a brief stint with one of my fave under-rated acts Waysted, singing on '87's **Save Your Prayers**. Here, his new band is like a mellower Tesla, not afraid to go acoustic often, not afraid to shower their sound with lush, dramatic melodies, almost White Metal in disposition. So I guess what

makes this rise above the fray is the lack of really flat-out contrived commerciality, much of this being so AOR, it couldn't possibly make it. And Tyketto never really did, although like I say, they have the respect of many a pomp rock fanatic.

Rating 7

## Tyketto - Strength In Numbers (Music For Nations '94)

This time 'round, the band thickens up the drum sound and exploits to a greater degree Brooke St. James' surgical '80s hard rock funk, all the while Vaughn belting out his vocals with flair, bolstered by hook-enhancing harmonies. But the band's product mix remains intact, Tyketto proving themselves no bandwagon-jumpers, again the ballads being this band's brighter good feeling moments, personal highlight being *The End Of The Summer Days*, which comes enlivened by some tasty, blues-based soloing. Ultimately, Tyketto's the kind of guilty, guilty pleasure that makes you wish hair bands still ruled the roost. Obligatory "band in ripped jeans leans against wall covered in graffitti" back cover. I guess some clichés are better left dead.

Rating 8

## Tyketto - Shine (Music For Nations '95)

Tyketto have blossomed into what is probably the premiere pop metal act of these mean times, **Shine** taking the listener to sunny, boisterous vistas, combining compositions slashed and liberated by surgical steel power chords, with softer, heartening moments built of clear acoustic guitar for miles, all produced with crisp perfection. And somehow, Tyketto manages to wrap in one wondrous package, all the best points of Zeppelin, Whitesnake, Tesla and Journey, creating a hard rock feast that just sings with pride. Oddly enough, the cornerstones of this bright, optimistic record are lead track *Jamie* and *Get Me There*, both wistful, beautiful ballads, with *Jamie* exploding into big, almost southern rock chording come chorus time. *Long Cold Winter* does the Journey stripper boogie, complete with amazing, heartfelt vocal acrobatics from new guy Steve Augeri (Danny Vaughn to Flesh & Blood), while *Let It Go* finds a smooth, retro-groove, driven into memory banks with a gorgeous, Humble Pie-faced dual lead lick. Just a hard record to put down really, Tyketto bounding out of the gates with that necessary confidence required to do commercial (I guess that would be anti-commercial, nowadays) hard rock in today's market.

Rating 10

## Type O Negative - Slow, Deep And Hard
(Roadrunner/Attic '91)

Folks gravitate towards this band for many reasons. Number one, Pete Steele's really tall, has big arms, and is a cranky sort of right wing hardliner, so he'll hurt you if you don't support capitalism and buy his record. Number two, he's probably a vampire. Number three, Type O Negative (sludged together from NYCHC rockers Carnivore), is a very unpredictable, critically lead-poisoned gathering of the damned, pretty much unconcerned with logic and thereby shifting units. So right off the bat, *Unsuccessfully Coping With The Natural Beauty Of Infidelity* lurches and stops and thrashadooms in industrially-rusted circles, confounding, arty, if not all that pleasant. And there's twelve minutes of it. Then the rest does the same thing, lengthy, flamethrowing songs of callous NYC nihilism red-knuckling it forlornly, fraught full-up with irritating buzz guitar, either violently impatient or in paralyzed stupor, tracks drowned in aimless doom or uneventfully smearing out urban hardcore chords. So call it an interesting, even unique concoction of failing chemistries, theoretically irresistible but grinding and irritable in execution.

Rating 5

## Type O Negative - Origin Of The Feces (Roadrunner '92)

One hulking "live" record that exposes just how grim Type O in the flesh can be, this 1991 Brighton Beach, Brooklyn occurence is a fascinating and sad example of the band's one-mood, two-sound gutterswill. A bunch of songs from the debut (covertly renamed) and God knows from what rock the rest emerged (well *Hey Pete* is *Hey Joe* Lestat-ified). The surprise success of **Bloody Kisses** caused this to be re-released without the sphincter and turds packaging, adding the band's mercury-poisoned slow-drip version Sabbath's *Paranoid* (with a bit of *Iron Man* thrown in).

Rating 5

## Type O Negative - Bloody Kisses (Roadrunner '93)

Green and black attack number three for New York's favourite sick depression rockers broke slowly and steadily on the blackened heinie of exhaustive touring, Pete gulping new fuel for his wavering, xenophobic hatred of mankind. **Bloody Kisses** is the band's first really actualized, hurdle-smashing record, combining plush but noisy thrash riffs with increased doses of gothic new wave, lots of gloomy effects, long builds and cacophonies of many types, most notably drums that boom like hearts plucked and eaten. Long, soul-frying record fer sure; forceful, vengeful, man-kills-woman lyrics, Steele attracting all sorts of derision for his many controversial attitudes, not like he cares in the least. Rough and unhewn like earlier confounding compounds, **Bloody Kisses** at least cuts a swath through the studio that slurps up a dumptruck of exquisitely evil ideas, the band henceforth slapping them down in such cool, anti-commercial fashion, that the subsequent commerciality of it all is just that much more of a lark. Bottom line though: Pete's still heaps more fun in print (lyrics, interviews and hopefully a book someday?) than Type O Negative is on record, all of this band's core half dozen characteristics chafing against my personal musical tastes. So my **7** is both theoretical and based on high praise from critics I respect.

Rating 7

## Type O Negative - October Rust (Roadrunner '96)

The enigma flickers then fires up, Steele and his assembled street bats continuing to batter and transform their noisy symphonic machine into a type of twisted ballad muncher. **October Rust** offers more tales of love, death and blood spilled in pleasure, only this time lovely layers envelope all, and the metallic is rarely witnessed. And when it is, it's smothered in so much of that cheap fuzz that you just gotta laugh. This is a realm, not a record, a place of remarkable ugliness, the true soundtrack to the vampire craze currently jolting the nation, Pete celebrating all things black, red, rusted and lime green in that characteristic wrenched, operatic howl. But like I say, this is without a doubt the band's most musical, deathly and tame scratching post all at once, making for a softened rock frostfire like no other. An effect has been fantastically achieved, even if the hollowed trunk harbouring Steele's talismens is in secret-spilling decay. Contains a dead-of-nightclubbing cover of Neil Young's *Cinnamon Girl*. Now the hellish business of touring begins anew, Pete warning us at the close of the record, adding that he hopes the record wasn't too disappointing!

Rating 8

## Tyran Pace - Eye To Eye (Scratch '84)

Tyran Pace is another example of a hilariously Euro-skulled blight on mankind that without major mobility manages considerable wallop due to killer delivery, heads-down, no-shit groove, and powerful recording (here another scorcher from Scratch). **Eye To Eye** admirably approximates high octane versions of Priest's simplified mid-years' product, i.e. less technical

**British Steel** crossed with pissed-up renditions from **Point Of Entry**, scurrying along like leather-swathed rats below the soaring wails of a dead ringer for Halfie himself. And if that ain't enough, the whole thing is messed-up, naive and backwoods like the most reclusive of deadpan Euro-alchemists, replete with stirring, depressive choruses, fat chugging riffs, and poetic evil. And that's basically it, a hopelessly German version of hammered-up mid-years Priest. Touch the night, drink a barrel of you're worst poison and submit.
Rating        8

## Tyran Pace - Long Live Metal   (Banzai '85)
Looks like these boys have been hangin' with Helloween and Grave Digger, soaking up scads of technoflash, adrenalin and general nastiness in the process. Gone are the rough Priestisms of **Eye To Eye**. Front and centre comes wall of sound intensity, fortunately still focused on the mid-pace spectrum, heavy as hell, Euro as hell, but . . . well . . . slick, more cautious, and more complicated. And **Long Live Metal** suffers because of it. Ralf Scheepers vox are higher up the scale, and if we must bring up JP again—and why the hell not—this record is heavier in the way **Defenders Of The Faith** was: written heavier, yet delivered like a bloated cash cow. The drumming merely thuds; a lot of bass, cavernous snare, and little in the way of cymbals, high hat or spontaneous outburst. **Long Live Metal**, although by no means dead in the water, is deceived by its own cleverness, undermined by its seriousness, and somewhat crushed under its own weight.
Rating        7

## Tysondog - Beware Of The Dog   (Banzai '84)
Well, can't say they didn't warn us. Scruffy mutt metal from Newcastle, shooting feebly but proudly at Priest, yet achieving a grimy din, sorta like Tank with less talent, or like the first Jaguar (remember them?). Roughly recorded and executed, and generally badly written, but they try hard like Fist. Production by Cronos who curiously shortly thereafter slagged the band soundly. Deeply righteous NWOBpovertyM slammer: *Dog Soldiers*.
Rating        4

## Tysondog - Crimes Of Insanity   (Neat '86)
After an obligatory OTT kick-off, **Crimes Of Insanity** settles into a massive controlled chaos, adding layer upon layer of cement in creation of an eminently more imposing sound than the pleasantly amusing debut. Trouble is, although Tysondog have evolved into a competent and serious metal act, they've lost their sense of place, their goof-off charm, here rocking noisy and fast and blocky, basically stiff like a cut-rate American leather band, erecting a wall of clatter to prove how extremely frayed they can be. Gives me a dull headache.
Rating        2

## Tyton - Mind Over Metal   (Restless '87)
Dense California-via-Texas nobodies with a not-so-ultra ultraheavy sound, pockets of groove and goth, occasional HR melodies, and too many riffs like buzzing, bespectacled well-educated flies. Pretty classy and well recorded, given the ruff 'n' tumble look.
Rating        6

# U

## U.D.O. - Animal House (RCA '87)

With "music and words by Accept and Deaffy" and madman Udo Dirkschneider at the mike, **Animal House** is more or less the follow-up to **Russian Roulette**, possessing the same mix of speed and chunky groove, adding soccer holler choruses fer miles. Yet I still find **Animal House** a bit of a letdown, low on standout tracks and somewhat stiffly recorded. Totally pro and really on a dead-on tangent from Accept, there's nevertheless something safe and predictable about this that made me file it without letting it steep. Compared with four or five tracks on **Russian Roulette** that I would define as classics, here it's more like a scant one or two, fave being the boisterous Blutto-inspirational title track. And the rest: 1/3 high-grade, 1/3 acceptable, 1/3 cold metal filler.

Rating                                               6

## U.D.O. - Mean Machine (RCA '88)

Another stack of juiced Accept-able explorations, **Mean Machine** once more comes up long on merciless metal, short on memorable melodies, as Udo's mostly new band romps through a pile of riff rockers that are beginning to sound like rehashes from Accept's glory days, all speeds represented, the writing merely phoned in. Not impressed, although I feel I should be, this record being fastidiously assembled and ferocious in its own Teutonic way. But where's the art?

Rating                                               7

## U.D.O. - Faceless World (RCA '90)

Something more urgent, lean and atmospheric about this one, a record courting advancement, U.D.O. abstaining from beating us over the head like some sort of self-conscious up-notching of Accept. Riffs are more imaginative yet less boasting, and even though the drums are still way too coldly rendered, there's an increased emotion to the tunes, which lyrically have expanded more into societal universals than badgering platitudes on kicking ass. Nice hard rock touches, strong choruses, and tons of technical skill make this a totally viable act in the traditional German manner (Gamma Ray?). Finally, the humanity and variety of Accept fly once again, to the point where one could say U.D.O. *is* Accept, reconstituted; up-dated if not really improved upon.

Rating                                               8

## U.D.O. - Time Bomb (RCA '91)

Striking similarity here with Priest's **Painkiller**, U.D.O. really storming back with a fast, powerful, heat-seeking metal man's metal, replete with searing and arcane divebomber guitar solos at every yank of the chain. Faves would be the ones that let up a bit and assume the power groove like only Udo and Accept can, tracks like *Back In Pain* and *Kick In The Face* headbanging, neck-snapping and otherwise flowing like silvery beer. Turning into a respectable little catalogue, no one record really sucking, lots of demonstrative uber-metal for you cringing sheep. 1992: Udo gives it up and rejoins his old buddies for **Objection Overruled**, followed so far by **Death Row** and **Predator**.

Rating                                               8

## UFO - 1 (Nova '70)

Forget calling this glued blob of lethargy a UFO record, and that goes for **Flying** and **Live** while you're at it. I is the melted offspring of psychedelic cavemen with a stomach flu, out on wah-wah trips through dim-witted gunk, UFO's career path mirroring that of Scorpions, neither having a clue what they were doing early on, loitering through their first painful vinyl disasters in a dense fog. I oozes gobs of comatose blues, bass-heavy, and incorrectly recorded in its woofer-fwapping distortion. Everything that was wrong with '60s music is here wiggling in naive pointlessness . . . dated, sedated, class dismissed. Like I say, you'd be wise to pass on UFO's first half decade or so, and pick it up around **Force It**. Highlight: the liner notes, which remark how "a couple of months ago (the band was) still having some difficulty co-ordinating. Now we consider them to be together enough for us to release a first album." Having people listen to it is another story.

Rating                                               1

## UFO - 2 Flying (Nova '71)

Four messed-up more babies from the motherland climb deeper into the womb, taking their pointless hippy jams on longer, mind-frosting trips into what they deem "space rock", and what those in the know (me) would deem lobotomy rock. Now I know what it's like to be locked out of the space shuttle in mute, oxygen-depleting disarray.

Rating                                               0

## UFO - Live (Nova '72)

Thereby closing the chapter on excruciating sloth, demarcating the headless blues wanderings of UFO '60s-style, from the rising creative phoenix that sees its first flicker with '74's interesting **Phenomenon**. **Live** is one side covers of over-rated and over-plundered blues rock tunes, one side UFO's contribution to an OD on downers. Lay down and avoid.

Rating 0

## UFO - Phenomenon (Chrysalis '74)

**Phenomenon** marks UFO's giant, crusty-eyed awakening to the rock possibilities of the real world. New label, new guitarist in pioneering, Euro-gothic legend Michael Schenker (brother of Scorpions' Rudy), who replaces the clueless Mick Bolton, thereby completing the classic UFO line-up of Mogg, Parker, Way, Schenker. **Phenomenon**'s metallic persona is limited to three or four tracks depending on your acceptance level. Two became forever carved in the Axe-Slinger's Hall of Flame; *Rock Bottom*, one proud and eminently British metal opus, a careening and complex speed rocker which shortly thereafter became the central UFO statement, and *Doctor, Doctor*, a soulfully-riffed cruiser that broke ground as an early Euro-style hard rock precursor to Scorpions, Accept and eventually Yngwie. Elsewhere on **Phenomenon**, we find Mogg's voice maturing o'er top rich and melodic blues, plus acoustic-based twists on the new music, soundly offsetting the sludgy, literal plow-throughs of old. Aside from the aforementioned bruisers, little on this really showed legs, causing **Phenomenon** to be forever seen as a bridge between the band's past and future; indeed, in some respects, a debut album.

Rating 6

## UFO - Force It (Chrysalis '75)

The unassuming charm that was UFO is in full swing on this, the first full stride of the band's classic era. **Force It** drives UFO into full commitment to the power chord, dedicating a full three quarters of the album to metal, or that sweet alloy of keyboard rock and metal that would define the trademark sound of the band's most enduring pieces. Mid-years UFO delivers me to the same emotional terrain as mid-years Lizzy does, yet not at such an artistically intense level. Both bands wove arresting tales of the street, wrestling with and taming the monster that was heavy metal, infusing the beast with wit, subtlety, and British aristocratic class. Personally, I find Lizzy to be more magical, soulful, and consistent on an inter- and intra-album basis, yet UFO creates its own inviting world, shaded with a touch of roughness, immaturity and naiveté that made their best half-dozen records an important part of my past. Schenker steers a lusty ship through such early classics as staccato chugger *Let It Roll*, Sab cruncher *Mother Mary*, and funk rockers *Dance Your Life Away* and *This Kid's*. My only complaint with **Force It** is its bluntness, thanks to its unexpressive, cinder block recording, made all the more obvious by a detectable flatness of delivery. Under the microscope, this record always raises a smile, yet I find I reach for it less often than, say, **No Place To Run**, **Mechanix** or even **Obsession**, due to a detached density, age, and lack of connection with the listener. In any event, minor faults on a fairly important flagship of fledgling British hard rock.

Rating 8

## UFO - No Heavy Petting (Chrysalis '76)

An artistic improvement over **Force It**, yet stepping back from metal to court exploration with presumptions of greatness, **No Heavy Petting** is really the first brightly imposing UFO jewel, a record where the metal and the ornate both punch through to emotional highs, exuding confidence and control amidst elevated

**474**

levels of respect. There's still an alchemical tension here, as new alloys are forged as per the brilliant, deeply European axe-burning ivories of *Can You Roll Her* and the rumbling, ground-breaking keyboard hard rock of *Highway Lady*. Elsewhere we have bestowed upon our hides more earthly beraterents such as monster-riffed staple *Natural Thing*, algebraically-riffed snakecharmer *Reasons Love*, and snakey-riffed blues opus *On With The Action*. Overall, UFO display an awesome ability to cascade floods of stirring guitar and keyboard shadings within the spirit of agile exploration, all sent low-cruising above a crisp, mountainous terrain via the band's first, crystal clear recording. **No Heavy Petting** embraces it all, becoming comfortable at once with a number of sentiments, defining class by virtue of its timelessness, its lack of dated '70s elements which could have made this merely a magnificent museum piece. Highly alien and urgent.

Rating 9

## UFO - Lights Out (Chrysalis '77)

Often considered UFO's most magical release; in effect, the record where the band becomes itself, **Lights Out** ironically soars and dives through the most diverse personas of any single UFO project, evoking an opacity through puzzling independence and elusive identity. Throughout the record, we find welcome melodramas; larger than life smotherings of humanity, whether constructing overwhelming walls of sound, as per the seminal and imposing title track, or lacing delicate keyboard patterns through granite-like lumberings as per *Love To Love*, a future showstopper of magical proportion. Superficially, this is one of the more melodic of UFO rounders, still surprisingly guitar-based, but only truly metallic on *Light's Out* and the ponderous *Electric Phase*. The rest intersperses the band's patented hard rock with looming moody balladry, again demonstrating that UFO is professionally and steadfastly resolute with life as enigmatic moving target. Much like **No Heavy Petting** in its raw clarity, yet farther out among Martian landscapes. Inappropriate cover: *Alone Again Or*, also inappropriately retooled by The Damned.

Rating 9

## UFO - Obsession (Chrysalis '78)

**Obsession** seems to occupy centre spot in a triumvirate of technical, high-minded UFO records, preceded by the almost lush **Lights Out**, followed by the morose and powerful **No Place To Run**. **Obsession** was a "winter" record for us as teen pups, freezing our asses off blasting booming rockers like *Pack It Up* and *Hot 'n' Ready* on the car deck on the way to raquetball sessions at Cominco Arena. And it's hard to shake the chill, rendering the record an aseptically professional, melancholy, yet finely crafted and memorable display of keyboard metal. One irritable feature of this one, despite its ambitions, is its brash, live-feel production, which undercuts the thudly possibilities of the six tracks of essentially nine that make this the heaviest unidentified flying object since **Force It**. Another difference: an almost total lack of the band's connecting, warm hard rock; opting for either metal or swirling piano balladry. In any event, a less than thoroughly satisfying, uncommunicative effort, sporting fewer god-like structures or grooves than on previous gems, a record admired from afar but rarely played as of late. Wild artwork by the spacey gang at Hipgnosis.

Rating 8

## UFO - Strangers In The Night (Chrysalis '79)

There's damn good reason this double assault is considered by critics all over the world to be one of the premiere live monuments ever erected; reason being the downright, vicious, battle-torn and bloodied renditions of UFO's largest monoliths, including *Light's*

Out, *Rock Bottom* (11:02), *Doctor, Doctor*, and personal fave *Only You Can Rock Me*. Boiling-hot production and heroic performances fuel these power-packed reacquaintances with history, spanning pressure points from the past five years, some of which received fairly conservative treatment in their original settings. **Strangers In The Night** soundly snapped back to reality a following that was drifting. Ultimately raucous and intuitive, **Strangers** documents performances that could only be whipped clear and stinging by strong-willed, abuse-pounded veterans fighting for their lives. Marks the exit of integral axeman Michael Schenker.

Rating                                                                 8

## UFO - No Place To Run   (Chrysalis '80)

The *serious* masterpiece arrives, hauling with it new, ex-Lone Star fret manager Paul Chapman, in construction of a record that rumbles with brooding introspection, again whether rocking or creating ominous mood, managing maximum impact through determined advance. Whether or not you think this is UFO's best record, **No Place To Run** *is* the best of the band's ambitious, painstakingly focused era. All coheres as usual, the metal segueing into quiet bass or piano-driven confessionals, which in turn blur artfully into the few but welcome hard, pop metal hybrids. Simply a superior collection and arrangement of human vistas, revealing a never-ending, unfolding complexity of influences. The metal (most notably heroic cruiser *Lettin' Go* and the fiercely wired title track), just roar with intent, while *Youngblood* and *Money, Money* spin two of the band's more stirring yet humble American-style hard rockers. Most artistically formidable however, are two of the darkest numbers, subtle icescape *Gone In The Night* and stopped-then-stomping monolith *Anyday*, both of which resume the muted majesty of the band's sonic dynamics last heard on *Love To Love*. Huge and moving, raw yet meticulous, and again, universal in its stride.

Rating                                                                10

## UFO - The Wild The Willing And The Innocent
(Chrysalis '81)

Perhaps UFO's most Lizzy-ish release, **The Wild The Willing And The Innocent** is also the band's most confident with minimum effort, a record on which the band consciously try to pare it down to savage basics. Almost entirely hard rock or metal, and almost always on the more metallic side of both formats, this record cries out most desperately of the pains associated with street life, backed by some of the band's fattest backbeats and monster cable riff work. Further clarity of translation is achieved through the appropriately warm, huge, and rumbling recording, which is one of the fullest of the band's long list of sometimes eclectic mixes. The most electrocuted headbangs such as *Chains Chains*, *Long Gone*, and *Makin Moves* do the genre proud justice, heaving large blocks of concrete below Mogg's heart-torn cries of conviction. Buoyant hard rockers *Lonely Heart* and the title track roll with further street bravado, while the moody *It's Killing Me* strikes a chord of resigned depression on par with some of Lynott's most moving confessions. UFO constructed many a great record, but **The Wild The Willing And The Innocent** is definitely the flaming phoenix of the spread, if not a bit cool and detached, pounding with considerable might, yet exuding accessibility with perhaps the band's most decipherable and least obscure collection of songs, still retaining that same quiet sense of doom that threads the fragile nature of the band's panoramic street lore.

Rating                                                                10

## UFO - Mechanix   (Chrysalis '82)

Time and momentum are mercilessly working against Mogg's wasted rogues on this one, a record that sounds like a collection of loose ends, a roughly-assembled mix of second string scrappers that nevertheless punch into your woofers through sheer sweat and determination. **Mechanix** is stripped-down, souped-up, and almost garagey in its exposed delivery, sporting a dull, toneless-but-tough, drive-it-home production, which adds to the grit of these combative tracks. **Mechanix** is all heart and pride, and very little flash or even brains, as metal highballs like *The Writer*, *We Belong To The Night*, *Doing It All For You*, and personal rave *Dreaming* just smoke and chug with heads-down conviction; the hard rock also getting back to basics, most emotive being lite metal minor hit *Let It Rain*. Great songs, great choruses, yet somewhat strangely lackadaisical, **Mechanix** may attract derision due to its detectable self-parody (perhaps evidenced by hokey cover *Somethin' Else*). Yet slowly and methodically, the record assembles hard-fought scraps of respect with each successive listen. Really, a band still in control of their craft, despite internal dissolution.

Rating                                                                 9

## UFO - Making Contact   (Chrysalis '83)

Unfortunately, few discerning fans were paying attention to UFO by this point, at least stateside, as perhaps the stories concerning in-fighting and drugs were starting to erode the confidence and fun associated with such a high-flying dynasty. **Making Contact**, however, upheld the band's noble standards, maintaining one of UFO's most complex, sustained and ambitious deliveries throughout, amidst their fullest of many eclectic production jobs. The sophisticated, traditional axework of Paul Chapman provides major anchor for the many hot riff-rockers studding this record. The lion's share of **Making Contact**, including *Diesel In The Dust*, *When It's Time To Rock*, *The Way The Wild Wind Blows*, *All Over You*, *No Getaway*, and *Push, It's Love*, are all weighty metallic crunchers, many quite technical, with gorgeous trademark UFO choruses infusing the tracks with that reassuring depth that keeps us coming back to these English institutions. Of the remaining tracks, we get one power ballad, plus two simply acceptable UFO hard rockers, carried nimbly through silky landscapes via the capable keys of Neil Carter. **Making Contact** proved that UFO was still a vital, very human, but judiciously axe-laden force among the dwindling ranks of the old guard, and in retrospect, one of the most euphoric based on the recorded evidence at the time. I view this record as the band's last, really, capping off an illustrious career of some of the most sumptuous, rich, and comfortable hard rock ever to flow freely. In a world gone mad, it's my ultimate pleasure to kick back and remember the spirit that consumed our youth listening to UFO's grand old hard rock. Fortunately, such authentic sounds are preserved for all to discover at their own pace.

Rating                                                                 9

## UFO - Misdemeanor   (Chrysalis '86)

On **Misdemeanor**, UFO becomes a fragile shell of what they once were, sadly losing that band feel with its latest round of line-up alterations. Nothing on this possesses the quality, spontaneity or sweat of past triumphs. The production is way too glossed, offering liberal intrusions of trendy synths and electronic drums. And despite **Misdemeanor**'s obvious lack of guts, it's more the depressing nature of the whole UFO saga that brings this down. Mogg isn't a strong enough personality to lead on his own, and his backing band (outside of other long-time UFO-er Paul Raymond), are anything but equals, rendering our latest incarnation more a tribute band than anything fresh and assertive in and of itself. If **Misdemeanor** really hauled off

**475**

and lowered the boom, we might be swinging otherwise, but in reality, this is nothing more than candyassed, keyboard-destroyed radio fluff of a most whorish nature, with more than its fair share of dreaded power ballads and grandiose whining. UFO is one case where cryin' in yer beer about the good ol' days is about all we're left with.

Rating                                                              3

### UFO - Ain't Misbehavin'  (FM '88)

Basically Phil Mogg's voice in front of a professional but dreary hard rock band, this six-track EP offers nothing dangerous, while nevertheless emitting a somewhat more adventuresome, upbeat melodimetal version of '86's sickly **Misdemeanor**. **Ain't Misbehavin'** is well-conceived enough (UFO superficially at least, don't make lemons), even approximating real metal on three of six here, wailing on **Misdemeanor's** wimp-like demeanor. Not enough however, to erase that pale aura of a fragmented band far past decline, and it ain't even a full-length album, leaving one to hope Mogg would just hang it up. If UFO is in fact an entity outside its members, that entity indeed feels raped.

Rating                                                              4

### UFO - The Best Of The Rest  (Chrysalis '88)

Of course who gives a damn about a compilation, but I'd have to call this one a rousing success at picking the biggest, brightest tracks from UFO's best era, namely the four records from '80 to '83, while stretching to '86 by including with bad judgment, turds from **Misdemeanor**. One shakes one's short or long-shorn locks at how exalted this band was, and could be again. Seventeen almost perfect tunes demonstrating an alchemy of potent fiery guitars and sinewy keyboard lines that had a big hand in creating the pop metal that ruled the '80s. Lift some suds to the sods and crank the jets on the hot tub that is UFO. Go skiing first so you deserve the double soak.

Rating                                                              9

### UFO - High Stakes & Dangerous Men  (Razor '92)

Now well into their dim existence as bumbling has-beens whose orbits cross and sometimes lock, UFO were back after years of loitering, the ever-present Mogg, Pete Way, Clive Edwards and near legendary young guitarist Laurence Archer set to do battle in the '90s. First thing they do is raise the white flag, this light-headed puddle of piddle being nothing but a mewling AOR platter, biggest travesty being the gagging of Archer, a rare talent who blazed his way through records by Stampede, finally ending up in Phil Lynott's Grand Slam (see review for a discussion of this guy's melodic genius). But the songwriting here is a joke (kinda like Bad Co. in the '80s or Nazareth in the '90s), Edwards' stiff, auto-pilot drumming and producer Kit Woolven's unimaginative, blocky mix conspiring to make this elegantly-titled hopeful a guitarless weakapotamus, 'cept for maybe a few big Foreigner chords gap-tooth smiling every second tune. Lowly summation: faceless power pop with no brains.

Rating                                                              4

### UFO - Radio One Live In Concert  (Griffin '95)

UFO's '79 double live **Strangers In The Night** is often cited as one of the top live metal records of all time, so it's no wonder this one from '80 kicks copious butt. **Radio One** (one of many in a series from Griffin, which includes live Lizzy, Schenker and Travers showcases) captures the band divinely smokin', new guitarist Paul Chapman seriously humming, touring what is damn near my favorite UFO disc, **No Place To Run**. The sound quality is astonishing, and the heft inspiring, as the band kicks off with a fiercely powerful rendition of *Lettin' Go*, crashing into the metal majesty of *No Place To Run*, other rarities including the sweet pop of

Cherry plus amphetamined blues standard *Mystery Train*. Tacked on the end are the band's three biggest anthems (plus little heard blues cover *Built For Comfort*), live from '74, again eerily well-mixed. An incredible live album: mondo track picks, superb sound and a lusty performance. **Strangers In The Night** has just been nudged from its pedestal.

Rating                                                              9

### UFO - Heaven's Gate (Live)  (Griffin '95)

This phoned-in '86 live set's a bit of a pooch, if only for the fact that it's mostly tracks from cheesy priss metal lowpoint **Misdemeanor**. But really, the band is even a bit on the dodgy side (this is a rare Atomik Tommy M live performance), arranging tracks full of holes, culminating in a dreadful dead run through *Only You Can Rock Me* and an extended too long *Doctor Doctor*, all else being non-hits, including 7/10 of the **Misdemeanor** abomination. Not the greatest packaging either, which I guess ain't really the point of these timetravels. Of course, it's really all the strangers and ill will that must sink this coasting version of the band. And where there's "no place to run", like recorded live, it's hard to hide the unraveling nature of the beast. The eccentric partner of the Griffin reissues.

Rating                                                              5

### UFO - Lights Out In Tokyo - Live  (Griffin '95)

On what is one of four servings of live UFO released in quick succession by reissue label Griffin (this one originally Razor Records '93), the band blows free through the usual collection of old hits, plus tracks from the dreadful **High Stakes & Dangerous Men** studio offering. But good news accompanies that fact, given that esteemed axeman Laurence Archer is on board, driving all tracks to new heights, putting his thoughtful spin on solos throughout this well-recorded, magical live record (albeit a record damaged by those dull **High Stakes** tunes). Another twist: lyrics to everything on the record, giving us a rare glimpse into Mogg and gang's fairly idiotic wordskills (the transcriber also includes all the inter-song banter, Mogg mainly calling out the titles and yelling 'Keep on rockin'!'). Still, the blistering mix props up even the tepid tracks, and the rest matches the heights of the other fine live documents that have haphazardly surfaced throughout the band's chequered past.

Rating                                                              7

### UFO - Parker's Birthday  (Griffin '95)

This boot-quality, Griffin semi-official re-release will be quite a shock to those used to UFO as a formidable, destroy-all-comers live machine, **Parker's Birthday** most likely one of those fabled drunken thrashabouts we've read about in Kerrang!, my fave line-up slurring its way through a collapsed set of hits "Live In Texas: 21.3.79." Quite "interesting" renditions of *Love To Love* and *Rock Bottom*, to say the least, Mogg barely comprehensible, Andy Parker perhaps well into that birthday celebration. An amusing, astonishingly inept pile of UFOlogy to be sure, but serious listening, ah, no.

Rating                                                              5

### UFO - Walk On Water  (Zero '95)

Well, the elusive Mr. Schenker is back in the fold (apparently for about a million bucks), re-establishing UFO's best volatile, slapstick, drug-addled, classic, heaven-sent line-up, all major players tentatively grouped for what is truly a comeback album from cryogenia. It has taken Japanese enthusiasm to put this together, so it's only appropriate that the last track on the album, *Message For Japan*, is an ol' hi-ho to the land of the re-assembled bums. Onto the music. Other than snappy remakes of *Doctor, Doctor* and *Light's Out*, **Walk On Water** is a stirring new collection of thankfully typical UFO rockers, spanning medium-grade riff rock (*Darker Days*) through gorgeous pop metal (*Stopped By A Bullet (Of Love)*) to *Dreams Of Summer*, a nice rip-off of *Love To Love*, all laced with rambunctious Mogg vocals, exquisite solos from Schenker, and production that is crystal elite and muscle-beached. Tracks build on the bridges, rising to intensities that one might not expect, best illustration of this being *A Self Made Man*, which has Schenker blazing trails of unexpected creativity three times over and up as the track winds out. Not an earth-shattering stompback, but easily, way too easily, the best since **Making Contact** a dozen years back. And all in all, a damn fine, truly enjoyable record and recording; an elegant balance between heaviness and lush melody, like the cream of the UFO crop. Note: during the band's subsequent well-received U.S. tour, first Andy Parker left (replaced by Simon Wright) and then Michael Schenker vamooshed, reportedly due to arguments over who if anybody should be on the wagon. Boys will be boys. Latest twist has Schenker replaced by John Norum, although the band now can't use the UFO name which is half-owned by Schenker.

Rating    **8**

**Ugly Kid Joe - As Ugly As They Wanna Be**   (Polydor '92)
The skates most bodaciously rule! . . . judging from the fast track on which these churlish imps cruised, buzzed and beaming, pretty surprised about the whole thing. Ugly Kid Joe, perhaps as metaphor for the band's hasty career so far, chose their moniker in response to a gig (later ki-boshed) which the band had secured with local faves Pretty Boy Floyd. On this introductory EP (a hip marketing format these days), UKJ blow through some agile, hoppin', clean thrashin' funk metal (witness the naughty Disney tale), their big, loveable novelty popster *Everything About You*, and a faithful version of the immortal *Sweet Leaf*. Accomplished and energetic stuff from a band who claimed to be nowherz ready, **As Ugly As They Wanna Be** skirted the current funk metal trend perhaps a tad too closely, lapsing into well-trodden rap better left to Scatterbrain, who I can't stomach despite their oh so clever bounciness. Twenty-five minutes of upswing and follow-through.

Rating    **7**

**Ugly Kid Joe - America's Least Wanted**   (PolyGram '92)
Ultimately empty calories from squirmy Whitfield Crane and boys, **America's Least Wanted** spends too much time exploiting the band's success thus far and not enough time delivering the goods. With too many cute mellow ones like *Busy Bee* and *Mr. Recordman*, not to mention ingratiating hitcover *Cats In The Cradle*, **America's Least Wanted** reads like a dumb sitcom, rife with guffawing novelty simpletoons that only occasionally offer an innovative chorus here, riff there. It's all too calculated to sell pancakes, never really hanging together as a record, with each idea sounding just too damn plain, assembled around lacklustre riffs that sound like stripped pop versions of mid-speed Anthrax or M.O.D. Then there's "Pat" from Saturday Night Live, recycled inclusions of *Everything About You* and *Madman* . . . a hang loose buncha songs for twelve-year-olds, ditties only a brain cell away from Saturday morning cartoons. Tried to like it, then I realized, like popcorn, it was all air.

Rating    **5**

**Ugly Kid Joe - Menace To Sobriety**   (PolyGram '95)
Recorded in "cozy house" location fashion like the Chili Peppers' **Bloodsugarsexmagik** and **Weight** by Rollins Band, **Menace To Sobriety** pretty much lives up to its moniker, a relaxed process that saw the killing of many brain cells inside this fun lovin' band of buds. The Ugly sound has changed in ways one might expect, being a fair dose dirtier, down-tuned and grungified, with more screaming on the part of Boy Whit, but the

results are rock hard and resolute. The songs just take it to the next level, for example *C.U.S.T.* being miles trickier and miles smarter than anything this three and four and five times novelty band had been capable of in their goofy successful past. Conclusion: a play for legitimacy, many tracks beating a stormy, passionate path into the '90s. But hold on a minute, you folks didn't buy it, proving that it'll probably take a couple more stiff shots like this to erase those brat rock images. High **7**, mateys.

Rating    **7**

**Ugly Kid Joe - Motel California**   (Castle '96)
Sure cool to see these trad metal bands soldiering on, even if it means a step off the major label merry-go-round. **Motel California** is less of a grindy, greasy affair than the unjustly ignored, also smartly monikered **Menace To Sobriety**, more of a combo platter of **Subhuman Race** Skid Row heft and large funk metal moves. And I realize that probably doesn't sound so inviting, but UKJ put their usual playful spin on things, and Whit is a passionate vocalist, especially come moving melodic rockers (ballads?: more bad connotations!) *Would You Like To Be There* and *Undertow*. No reason this can't please a discerning but thin layer of the rock populace, which I'm sure both Castle and band projections have projected is of limited but modestly viable size. Risky, but who knows?

Rating    **7**

**Uglystick - Uglystick**   (Pavement '95)
Scraping fairly mesmerizable grunge grit outa Oklahoma, Uglystick slice smatterings of Tool into a sound that is wide-open and spontaneous, closer to the cavernous, elastic grooves of Rollins than the snap-to-it ethic of Helmet. Plus the lyrics beat Helmet at their own game, while drummer David Brown inflects metalli-jazz beat crazy throughout the sinewy structures. Sure it's slambang shoutrock, causing one to utter that hated word "angst". But these guys do it up real dangerous and uncareful, collisions to the fore, commercialism be damned.

Rating    **7**

**U.K. Subs - Another Kind Of Blues**   (RCA '79)
Can't say I cozy up to this nasty little record too often, due to its grimy and diseased, plainly cranky disposition. Harper, Garratt & Co. do too adequate a job recreating the earliest of punk sounds, spewing forth hyperactively, choosing the back-mixed, thickly-accented, soccer bellow as verbal weapon of choice, and appropriately cheap, crash 'n' burn production to bring the barrage of noises to the fore. Influences occasionally leak from the amps (including The Vibrators, early Saints, and **Machine Gun Etiquette**-era Damned), but the driving force would have to be the sordid *idea* of punk, with all its imperfections, depressed and violent boredom, and driving rain wilting the mohawks of the homeless. Stylistically, the record fulminates with chaos in and of itself, using its simple and raw guitar/bass/drums format to get variously vicious and spontaneously childish and poppy. Blackest calling card: *Crash Course*, in which Harper pulls off a fairly convincing Ian Hunter impression.

Rating    **7**

**U.K. Subs - Live Kicks**   (Stiff '80)
This 45 RPM live LP comprises thirteen minor moshes, mostly from **Another Kind Of Blues**. Recorded at the legendary Roxy in '77, **Live Kicks** fails to rejuvenate even an ounce of the notorious punk rumble that made the aforementioned studio wax such a sustained and chundering blight. Parallel record: The Damned's - **Live Shepperton 1980**, which suffers from a similar tin-man guitar mix.

Rating    **2**

**U.K. Subs - Endangered Species** (NEMS '82)
Go figure. Side one of this slams with savage poverty pollution while side two invents scrapyard new wave, not unlike The Cars or Gary Numan forced to ply their trade with rusty garbage can lids and leftover crane parts. Exceedingly bleak and thoroughly punk in a coal-dustedly English manner, **Endangered Species** won't win any awards for human connection, but it does stand defiant, door-crashing the '80s in pursuit of a '77 punk ethic, however valuable that may or may not be.
Rating                                                                5

**Ulver - The Madrigal Of Night** (Century Media '97)
Eschewing the polish job going on with many black metallers these days, record #3 for Norway's Ulver sets the world back and drop-kicked a couple years, Lo and Lucifer-bound, **The Madrigal Of Night**'s eight soundscans, itch with high-treble guitar, tick-pop drumming and mixed back 'n' muddy vocals. But if you care to navigate these inky waters, a concept album awaits, each song entitled Wolf & something ( i.e. Wolf & Fear, Wolf & Passion, Wolf & Destiny etc.), the band exploring lycanthropy in Norwegian folklore. A good library book would do the trick with less ear damage.
Rating                                                                4

**Unanimated - In The Forest Of The Dreaming Dead** (Necropolis/Pavement '94)
A crappy recording and muddy, textbook grind vocals mar this otherwise effective, very Swedish mystical death metal rounder, which sounds like raw, unactualized At The Gates, courting speed precision and those diddly high guitar melodies that are supposed to inspire a full gallop through polar plains. And then there's welcome flourishes of various keyboard textures over the manic din, placing these grim rivetheads squarely amongst those pinnably ethnic frost-tones that sound so Scandinavian, stirring western blood so well. A perfect basecamp for future greatness, once the band tones down the death, cleans up, and expands horizons, like anybody from the underground selling any records these days.
Rating                                                                6

**Unashamed - Reflection** (Tooth & Nail '95)
They look like punks (more accurately skinheads) and come from Orange County, but Unashamed are best described as a Christian death metal act, fusing grindcore, even Norwegian and Swedish influences, and maybe Helmet, to a decidedly Christian message, much like two other Tooth & Nail acts, Strongarm and Overcome. Pretty evil-sounding stuff, often slow and dissonant as vocalist Jeff scowls like the Goatlord through these twisted metal sculptures. **Reflection** wafts the same blue-ish fumes as early Trouble, Unashamed's brand of Christianity full of torment and black depression, a pleading unto religion based on desperation, amplified a thousand times when heard versus read. When the smoke clears, I don't know if **Reflection** works its real purpose, and that's infusing young stage-dived minds with the Word of Christ. The sonic assault is just too scary, too aligned with metal of a jet black Satan-luvin' nature.
Rating                                                                7

**Uncle Crunchie - Uncle Crunchie** (Watch/MCA '97)
Never did I think middle Ontario could produce groovin' sounds like this, Uncle Crunchie combining grunge with funk metal, a sort of thicker, stoopider Korn, crossed (all too often) with Iggy-dumb garage rock and auto-pilot punk turned for a lark. My original enthusiasm has waned a bit, based mostly on the back half of the record doing a rudimentary, somewhat juvenile wilt, the Crunchers grabbing a simple riff and

shaking it doggedly for too long. But the premise is mighty fine, the band tapping into the frat-gonad excitement of Chuck-era Faith No More, again a sound pretty rare for dull ol' Canuckleheadland.
Rating                                                                7

**Uncle Sam - Letters From London** (Skellar '90)
Hard to pin this band's influences, which coagulate on opaque sounds ranging from The Stooges, Sex Pistols, The Cramps, Teenage Head and Motley Crüe, creating a hungover heavy metal din that is unique and strangely enjoyable despite the blocky thumpa thumpa beat on which almost every wise-ass tune is based. Totally underground and hard to handle, but kinda proud and visionary. It's the vision however that is fuzzy and not altogether sane.
Rating                                                                6

**Under Neath What - "What Is It"** (Atco '89)
Creepy garage-abilly metal, claustrophobic and admirable in concept, but simply lacklustre in delivery, with vocals mixed deep into the cellar, and riffs rust-bucketting by simple, dull, and old as the hills. Reminding me of an axed-up version of Love And Rockets, this British three-piece tries valiantly to add colour with vibrant songtitles like Eggs, Bacon, Coffee And Suicide, Bad Karma Chameleon, Their Heads Exploded, and Firebomb Telecom, attempting to be the next U.K. pop sensation or sumthin'. Result? Rainy, depressed and too luded to carry the novel approach. Slushy production values.
Rating                                                                4

**United - No IQ** (Metal Blade '96)
Japanese veteran thrashers United make their stateside debut with this crushing, violently-mixed slab of power metal. **No IQ** (the band's third full-length in ten years) judiciously uses blastbeats to set up forearm smashing riffs (see Hit Me (One More Card) and Words In Disguise), sounding like a pained Sepultura, primetime Metallica or raw, inebriated Pantera; in other words, face-ripping '90s metal. And the riffs are fresh and intoxicating (you'd thought they'd all been written?), especially on Kill Yourself For Business, which just soars like your most impressioned NWOBHM memories, crossing into early Anthrax terrain, the band I'm sure benefiting from being based in Japan, away from direct influence from trends. Spontaneous, fired-up and raucous, United's final ace is the expressive vocal work of Yoshiaki Furui, which balance grit and clarity, kind of a cleaner James Hetfield, his style not at all prone to the Eastern eccentricities that sunk Japanese bands in the past. Clean-burning metal magnificence.
Rating                                                                8

**Unleashed - Where No Life Dwells** (Century Media '91)
Even back in the dark ages of '91, Unleashed were churning a shocking blast of death that was slightly ahead of its time, this debut finding the same gutted glorious depths as early Edge Of Sanity, Cemetery and Entombed. And I ain't the only one saying it, many critics picking Unleashed from the pack, the band possessors of a noticeable spark, an engaging and personable star quality, even though they dish a seemingly not unusual pile of crashed and burned death. So give it a chance, pick up on those riffs, the drums, the sound quality, all the while remembering that this is 1991. Produced and mixed by the terror team of Waldemar Sorychta and Siggi Bemm, which can't hurt.
Rating                                                                6

**Unleashed - Shadows In The Deep** (Century Media '92)
And so the band soldiers on, on this their longest record at forty minutes (!), Johnny, Tomas, Fredrik and Anders discovering that galloping mosh that makes later albums such a lusty rusted bucket 'o metal hijinx.

You just gotta like these guys, who are fast becoming the Wildhearts or Wolfsbane of tundra-blasted Viking death. The sound's a little thicker this time, and the attack more palpable, Johnny not letting up one iota on his throat-ripping rendition of Unleashed's tales from the deep. But they lighten it up with a sweet cover of Venom's *Countess Bathory*. Ain't that nice?

Rating 7

## Unleashed - Across The Open Sea (Century Media '93)

If the opening strains of *To Asgaard We Fly* don't sound like the thundering hoofs of the Four Horsemen (OK, we're mixing mythologies here, but so do they), then you're already dead. Unleashed have ridden into the thick of battle here, with their most jarring and violent record yet, rendered moreso by the sparse mid-tempo crush of the thing (see headbanging neck-snapper *The One Insane*). Again it's the cannonading drums that propel the monster, the band self-producing this time with a merciless mix of bottom-end and faceflung mid-range. Contains a lovingly turgid and garagey shoot 'em up through Priest's *Breaking The Law*, perhaps personifying the band's slow but deliberate shift away from death towards metal. A gin and tonic sort of band, the elixir chilled for easy guzzling, preferably downed in a snowy blizzard around a blazing northern bonfire.

Rating 8

## Unleashed - Live In Vienna '93 (Century Media '93)

Almost sounds like this was pushed out to thwart an enterprising bootlegger. But the world is better for it, Unleashed doing what they do best punching out a rollicking batch of their concise, black and blue anthems, closing the show with their shabby, heroic *Breaking The Law*. Long record with lots of songs, which is a change of pace for these briefsters, all coagulating to demonstrate how inspiring this band can be. *Into Glory Ride* indeed. Thor be proud!

Rating 7

## Unleashed - Victory (Century Media '95)

If one can call any sort of Scandinavian metal terrors a party band, this is it. Unleashed have cranked four catchy, fast-paced grind spreads, each getting chuggier, thicker and darn well funner than the last. Sure there's the odd blastbeat, but most of *Victory* (and there's only an inexcusable 33 minutes of it) is that drinkable drinking man's death circa Sepultura or Entombed, total underground mayhem with heart. Sticking to their no-frills howitzers is what this band does best, and *Victory* continues that fine mosh-head tradition. Champion Unleashed, and you will suffer no ills (except maybe a bad hangover).

Rating 8

## Unleashed - Eastern Blood Hail To Poland
(Century Media '97)

The bio calls 'em the AC/DC of death metal, but one could also call them the Manowar, tirelessly fighting for the cause, their particular cause being a self-defined kingdom, oddly dated, oddly personable, oddly unique. This second live album heightens that "one for all" fuzzy feeling, Unleashed whipping through 21 tracks over 78 minutes, a few repeaters included. It's a bit strange listening to a scrappy couple of death metal gigs recorded in Poland, but consider it a ham radio transmission by the ultimate hams. Highlight from promotional material: "They're Vikings! Vikings are in, man!!"

Rating 7

## Unorthodox - Balance Of Power (Noise '95)

This D.C. power trio waxes astonishingly musical on this solid-as-hell debut, combining hardcore with The Obsessed and traditional heavy metal. All told, entertaining from start to finish, if not too much of all things too soon. Hooky, molten, and entirely outside time and influences that are obvious, this is one of those records that sounds destined for travel-tune status: no crazee praise, but lots of level-headed respect of the band's obvious chops and experience. Chalk this one up to yet another Noise act that really drives deep into all sorts of early '80s influences very few remember. Weird but not all that weird.

Rating 7

## Unwritten Law - Blue Room (Red Eye '94)

This indie debut has actually seen re-release by Sony, simultaneous with the newer **Oz Factor**, fueled by sales of 10,000 in and around the band's SoCal home-base. I actually like **Blue Room** more, given a greater degree of integrity, personality, rougher vocals and a slightly brasher mix. But '90s punk is still '90s punk; simply dull by design, the last refuge of the great unwashed and the uncreative.

Rating 5

## Unwritten Law - Oz Factor (Sony '96)

I guess this kind of thing is the Beach Boys for the '90s, Unwritten Law making extensive ties with the surf and skate community in their native Southern California, blasting out a sweet happy-pappy blend of speedy punk and accessible harmonies, just like Offspring and Bad Religion. Which is no surprise, given that Greg Graffin produces, also dragging the band out on tour as Bad Religion's support act. Man, how many ways can you write a melodic punk song? Sugary breakfast cereal, which I guess is what a certain demographic will eat every day if so instructed. Fave feature: the first twenty seconds, which is a direct lift from Sabbath's *War Pigs*.

Rating 4

## Uriah Heep - Uriah Heep (Mercury '70)

Amusingly deemed **Very 'Eavy, Very 'Umble** in their homeland (alert: best track on the U.S. record *Bird Of Prey* is swapped for a ballad on **Very 'Eavy**, which eventually shows up on the U.K. version of **Salisbury**), Uriah Heep's debut is the weak partner in the trio of early '70s metal records which I consider the true originators of the genre, the other two being **In Rock** and **Paranoid**. Weak partner, because it's the least whompingly heavy, yet included because it's every bit the innovator, o'erflowing with bombast, fire-breathing guitars, and eerie goth emotion that finally steered aggressive rock away from the blues and/or psychedelia into molten new terrain. And the pronouncement couldn't have been much more mentally devastating than opening classic *Gypsy*, a sinners' march par excellence, one of the most regal marriages of crunching organ and power chords ever forged in fire, one that strangely enough melts in a nuclear flash the two ground-breaking camps of Sabbath and Purple through superior production. Elsewhere, original riff-rockers like *Walking In Your Shadow* and *Real Turned On* further shape the future of the World's Greatest Music. But the real chemistry is reserved for *Bird Of Prey*, arguably the band's most raging work of genius, a searing blend of glowing Byron operatics and sinister metal craftsmanship which previewed Heep's progressive metal side splendidly. Stunning for so many reasons (including recording range, which is surprising given its age), **Uriah Heep** suffers only from sporadic psychedelic footwork, which even still is snapped into place by the disciplined exploitation of power that is the new majesty called heavy metal. Dark, brooding and medieval, **Uriah Heep** is dead serious and not without chill, making it a wary and ultimately occasional play after its original taming. But from many angles, in the true multi-dimensional sense of the word, **Uriah Heep** is a classic.

Rating 9

## Uriah Heep - Salisbury  (Mercury '70)

Whoa! Somebody must have slipped something recreational into the creative trough from which this band
was slurping, 'cos **Salisbury** reverses the crunch of
Uriah Heep for a deep dive into Floydian psychedelia
under a production globule that glues the whole thing
trebleless but bassy to the sinister underbelly of the
now distant and ridiculed Summer Of Love. Alternately slow, mellow, lazy and heavy, **Salisbury** is always spacey and miles under moss and muck, leaking
minor enjoyment from the Sabbath-like strains of *Time
To Live* and *Simon The Bullet Freak* before collapsing into
a colossal pile of crap with the title turd, a '60s prog
rock nightmare complete with braying horns and lofty
goals that just make me want to wretch in my sleep.
**Salisbury**, if not for the records that followed, would
have made **Uriah Heep** an accident of genius, for this
record is a 100% authentic document of '60s drug
culture, British-style, pure and simple, defying logic
when seen in temporal space between Heeps I and III.
Tie it to your dog and let them both run around
outside.
Rating                                            4

## Uriah Heep - Look At Yourself  (Mercury '71)

As jarring an about-face as was **Salisbury**, **Look At
Yourself** sees the band back on a bombastic path to
progressive metal Shangrila, this time producer Gerry
Bron setting the pageantry afire, the opening title track
setting the stage, rollicking forth with tons of guitars,
tons of Byron and tons of glazing keyboard labyrinths
from Ken Hensley, who is so prominent here, he
quickly establishes his mark as the definition of the
band's sound, out-leaping Jon Lord's contribution to
chief rivals Deep Purple. Vestiges of the acid rock that
diluted **Salisbury** remain, tainting *I Wanna Be Free* and
ten minute epic *July Morning*, but the healthy doses of
killer metal mash such threatening colours to a pulp.
Thus on the wings of one punishing woofer-chomping
mix come three new classics, on which Byron is nothing less than superb. *Tears In My Eyes* opens side two
with glorious weighty chords, which transform into
one of the monster grooves of the early '70s. Next
there's *Shadows Of Grief*, eight minutes and forty seconds of hellish cathedral rock, soaring and spiraling
under the bone-crunching twin attack of Box and
Hensley while Byron sings for his life. Finally (after
anonymous Floydian respite *What Should Be Done*),
there's soon-to-be concert fave *Love Machine*, which
is pure lunatic power metal of the highest order. When
all lurches to a halt, **Look At Yourself** is ultimately a
record of awesome textures, a record strafed with
wanton but healthy over-wanking from all musical and
vocal angles, gleaning the most presentable elements
of psychedelic experimentation and firing them solid in
the harsh crucible of heavy metal. Whether one as-
cribes genius to this process or not, one can't deny the
pounding elegance that Heep hath wrought upon the
world. Be thankful.
Rating                                            10

## Uriah Heep - Demons And Wizards  (Mercury '72)

The first of two signature Heep releases (further demarcated by similar Roger Dean graphics), **Demons
And Wizards** again marries belting Hensley organ
washes, Mick Box's bulldozing riffery, and Byron's
saintly vocal prowess in search of mystical frontiers.
Rounding out the band's most memorable line-up is
new bassist Gary Thain (a New Zealander) and new
drummer Lee Kerslake (worked with Hensley in The
Gods and Toe Fat) whose combined killer sense of
metal rhythm would become a worthy addition to the
unique Heep pastiche. **Demons And Wizards** is a
spooky sort of record, somehow ancient and alchemical with its huge gothic anchors, as the band lumbers
on in a lyrical otherworldly fog, over pounding, "old

world metal" structures, letting up on the medieval
emotive reigns only for rollicking party rocker *All My
Life* and perhaps the most recognizable Heep tune
ever, *Easy Livin'*, a metalfest directly descended from
the panzer encroachment of *Love Machine*. All in all, a
fiercely alone, contemplative sort of record, existing in
a hazy flux on the more mystical side of early heavy
metal, as Heep hang on to a psychedelic past for dear
life. Other noteworthy hit: *The Wizard*, which was
co-written by Hensley and Marke Clarke, briefly the
band's bassist.
Rating                                            10

## Uriah Heep - The Magician's Birthday  (Mercury '72)

With the band at perhaps its greatest critical and commercial peak, Heep embark on their eeriest psychedelic trip since **Salisbury**, with heavy rock and mellow
moments alike building on the mystical terrain of **Demons And Wizards**, sounding less accessible and in
total, much less metallic, only *Spider Woman*, *Sweet
Lorraine*, and truly distressing plodder *Sunrise* fully embracing metal or hard rock principles. What results is
an anguished, spacey trip, culminating in the band's
most harrowing, nightmarish epic of them all, the ten
minute title cut, a multi-part oddity combining Beatles-
like psychedelic sound effects, chilling fade-ins and
fade-outs, and a hypnotic recurring riff, almost warm
despite its creepy environs. A somewhat disjointed
record results, more the victim of two-tiered thinking,
rocking bashingly in close quarters with two or three
whispery reflective numbers. But **The Magician's
Birthday** is yet another colourful, mystical journey
nevertheless, like a sleepless night combing the forbidden texts in the dusty basement of some huge, maze-
like library. Shades of Al Bouchard and his elaborate,
unreleased *Imaginos* extension: Hensley wrote a
longer version of **The Magician's Birthday** story
which remains shelved to this day.
Rating                                            7

## Uriah Heep - Live  (Mercury '73)

Marred only by the ridiculous, wildly inappropriate and
counter-productive '50s rock'n'roll medley closing out
the record, **Live** couldn't have been stacked much
better. Not only is this double opus crammed to the
brim with the band's more pulverizing pieces like *Easy
Livin'*, *Tears In My Eyes*, and *Love Machine*, but we get a
history of the band, detailed personal bios, a bunch of
amusing news clippings, and a photo booklet, not to
mention a full-bodied Gerry Bron mix, and inspired
personal performances from the band itself. All in all,
a near perfect document of a band of rock pigs striking
while the iron is hot.
Rating                                            8

## Uriah Heep - Sweet Freedom  (Warner Bros. '73)

And so begins the long, puzzling slide, as the band
begins to drift seemingly involuntarily from the formula
that brought them filthy lucre. All the hypnotic elements remain intact: Byron's elegant vocals, Hensley's
droning organ grind, Box's punishing Sweet-like solos
and Sabbathy metal chords, and Kerslake's powerful,
booming drums, but here they're all wrapped around
songs that are leaving the realms of fog-shrouded
alternate realities, songs with oddly eccentric melodies
and sort of predictable rock'n'roll patterns that can't
absorb the bombastic shock of such flamboyant players. The instrumentation is superb and confident, almost fanciful, yet resigned and disciplined, clipped to
fit the new approach, a sort of rambling, distant thunder which spells an unprecedented melancholy in the
band; less mysterious, more plain old depressed and
languished in a sea of rock'n'roll burnout. I'm still in
awe at the fevered gathering of sounds that is this band,
despite the odd songwriting, but the cohesive conceptual panoramic feel is gone, and come to think of it,

maybe it should be, as rock begins to distance itself from the '60s. Lone mind-bender: *Pilgrim*, which immediately evokes *Gypsy*, as Byron embarks on yet another heroic quest for truth. Remastered Castle reissue includes essential metal hammer *Sunshine*, a pointless radio edit, and a stretchy alterno-take on *Seven Stars*, plus a beautifully done CD booklet which includes essay, press clippings and notes from Box and Hensley.

Rating                                                                 8

## Uriah Heep - Wonderworld   (Warner Bros. '74)

Conceptually vacant, **Wonderworld** is a mere collection of hair-brained schemes, lacking even the instrumental trademark that loosely held together its predecessor, coasting from uncomfortable style to style, under one of Bron's least expressive mixes. But like a bolt out of the blue comes *Suicidal Man*, a pounding classic of metal mayhem built of a complex despairing melody in full collision with a merciless riff. But once back on earth, it's a pretty odious affair, polluted by new and gravely unwelcome funk experimentation like *We Got We* and prancy party pop like *Something Or Nothing* (uh, soon to be a concert fave). Just abominable. Last record for bassist Gary Thain, fired from the band February '75, dead from drugs by the end of the year. Castle reissue includes another killer rarity in *What Can I Do*, a long version of *Dreams* and a pair of live tracks from '74 (plus of course, awesome and meticulous liner notes).

Rating                                                                 5

## Uriah Heep - Return To Fantasy   (Warner Bros. '75)

Now completely adrift without a trace of spark (save for the album cover), Heep seem doomed to slog on automatic, not caring whether they're a pixies 'n' fairies band or a bar-room boogie band (in retrospect, Hensley thinks this record sucks). Even the recording's a soupy mess, dominated by blaring but thin organ wonks and sloppy drumming rendered brash and trebly. And Byron, perhaps signifying his waning lifeforce, sounds distant and unsure as he bellows over bad Kansas crossed with ELP crossed with The Who crossed with your worst memories of Deep Purple's **Stormbringer**. Once firmly floated in other realms but able to see, Heep are now trying to be regular guys, and all seems fuzzy to the point of nausea. Fave track: the title tune, a sort of sullen prog rock hyper-shuffle; weird rhythm, but chemistry still ablaze. Castle reissue includes the usual slew of booklet nuggets, two heavy B-side beauties in *Shout It Out* and *The Time Will Come*, a heavier (and better) version of *Beautiful Dream* and a radio edit.

Rating                                                                 5

## Uriah Heep - High And Mighty   (Bronze '76)

Set to bloom with the majesty of *One Way Or Another* (vocals courtesy of John Wetton), **High And Mighty** looks promising indeed. But after said rhythmic opus, Heep are back to the left-fer-dead rock star noodlings that have become their sorry, decrepit state. Off chasing some sort of muse nobody outside the band could begin to understand (except maybe Nazareth), Heep confound with a myriad of soupy styles which proceed to make disastrous use of the band's flickering talents, especially Byron's vocals and related harmonies, sounding out of control, perhaps mirroring Byron's spiral descent into alcoholism and eventually death. As an album, totally effeminate, illogical and/or overblown. What a joke, and judging from the song credits, it looks like it's Hensley's fault. After Byron's '76 firing, rumour has it Ian Hunter almost joined as the band's new vocalist.

Rating                                                                 5

## Uriah Heep - Firefly   (Bronze '77)

Alas now, even Byron is toast, so the deconstruction of a once great collective intensifies in earnest. With John Lawton now at the mike of one of the rock world's most tarnished reputations (and Trevor Bolder in on bass), maybe things will change, for musically, the band has nowhere to go but up. Well, the recording's better and the boys are tight, but their energies are still logic-defying in their misdirection, as if the band is trying to throw the game and couldn't care less if anybody notices, offering a mixed bag of scroungy, comatose blues ballads, nerdy party rockers and "scary" prog rock abortions that try in vain to recall the magic of old, sounding more like the third-rate Jethro Tull Heep were earlier wrongly accused of being. Weird, unexplainable, tragic.

Rating                                                                 1

## Uriah Heep - Innocent Victim   (Warner Bros. '77)

Funky, bluesy hard rock with crazy man renditions of Heep vocal harmonies, **Innocent Victim** begins life as a heavy album cover, then disintegrating into Coverdale filler Hell, crossed with the peaceful easy feelings of '70s California recliner rock. Quick, I'm gonna hurl. Surprise hit: *Free Me*, later covered by Lucifer's Friend.

Rating                                                                 2

## Uriah Heep - Fallen Angel   (Chrysalis '78)

Kicking off with another lame, prancy boogie tune, it might sound like **Fallen Angel** is going to be another progressively worse Heep tragedy. But surprise, there's some smart and tidy rock'n'roll in them thar hills, not a lot but some, such as *Falling In Love* and *Woman Of The Night*, both straight-forward cruisers with choice guitar blends. And elsewhere, it's almost as if the creepy Heep of **Demons And Wizards** is rearing its head, as on *I'm Alive*, Lawton sounding somewhat like Byron in places. But don't worry, it all unravels by side two, culminating in the stupefyingly dull title track to wind things down. No worries, the fans all left the building five years ago.

Rating                                                                 3

## Uriah Heep - Conquest   (Bronze '80)

Uriah Heep continues its tragic descent as enigma gone embryonic with this long-lost record that never got released over here and never reared its head too often in the import bins, both for good reason. **Conquest** is 100% failure, and not of an experimental nature, just horribly maimed songwriting of a very pedestrian and hard-to-please nature, somewhat rocky, but not in the least heavy. Only laughable traces of Heep trademarks are present, shining dimly among the sparse harmonies, subdued keyboards, and depressingly third-rate gothicisms that intrude mercilessly and often. **Conquest** is the lone Heepster to feature the vampy, melodramatic vocal overstylings of John Sloman (ex-Lone Star), whose chords resemble those of Glenn Hughes, and whose pained delivery overstates the lack of any weight on this record, which features another notable journeyman, Chris Slade who drums on AC/DC's **The Razor's Edge** plus a million other records. **Conquest** is a jumbled mass of influences including Heep itself, Supertramp, Boston, old Whitesnake, and a host of other non-committal entities; hell, even David Byron as solo mistake. Ultimately just sad (as Ross Perot would say), delivered loosely, despondently, as if bent on self-destruction. Very painful, very humble, **Conquest** would be the last for Ken Hensley, the man many figure was the beating creative heart of the band. A short, official break-up of the band ensued.

Rating                                                                 1

## Uriah Heep - Abominog (PolyGram '82)

Mick Box reinvents the crashed Heep, trashing his entire band except Lee Kerslake in acquisition of a similarly mixed portfolio of well-traveled rock veterans, and the result is something beautiful to behold indeed. Possibly *the* soundtrack to my awesome year in Nelson, B.C., **Abominog** is crammed with personal nostalgic value. But attempting an objective look, I can fully ascertain that the record slays on its own, fortifying a collection of tough, aggressive, hooky hard rock originals with exciting but warm and fuzzy covers like Russ Ballard's rousing *On The Rebound* and D.B. Cooper's celluloid *Prisoner*. Elsewhere, new lead vocalist Peter Goalby (Hensley's original choice for use on **Conquest**) leads the wizened ones on invigorating, harmonizing romps through molten metallic terrain that evokes the magic of the NWOBHM, tinged with the peak Byron years. The conversion of mellow and axe-slashing moments alike into a sort of brash white heat makes **Abominog** an intelligent, well-paced record from start to blazeout, each song standing on its own as a vibrant re-tooling of its specific genre, all accentuated by an urgent, stinging mix, wise use of dynamic and honking keyboards (John Sinclair) over what amounts to a decisively strong foundation of melodic metal. Although it's a travesty to dissect this royal righteous slab, I had to claim favorites. Killer metal dramas like opener *Too Scared To Run* and *Think It Over* would stand out, both tapping into a sense of history no mere upstart could claim. Generally however, take **Abominog** in its entirety, a heroic statement of rich legacy, too beautiful to let die. Note: a whopping 17 of 18 tunes originally recorded for the record were scrapped, the band struggling with this new heavier but slicker direction. Apparently a few copies of these sessions still exist within the clutches of various band members.
Rating　　　　　　　　　　　　　　　　10

## Uriah Heep - Head First (PolyGram '83)

Establishing a surprise semblance of continuity, **Head First** finds the same line-up ripping through similarly street-ready but aristocratic hard rock tales as its predecessor, while losing a trace of **Abominog**'s combat tendency. Goalby again leads the charge, turning Heep into a massive improvement on Foreigner at its best, with his lively Lou Gramm signatures, perfect for the anthemic bangers which, as often as on **Abominog**, come courtesy of established songwriting institutions, thus *Love Is Blind*, *Lonely Nights* and *Stay On Top*. But side two is all Heep, one intro, one pooch, three killer tracks: *Straight Through The Heart*, one of the band's strong key-shaded melody rockers, *Red Lights*, a speedy professional metalfest, and closer *Weekend Warriors*, a purely heroic, galloping rocker demonstrating Heep's versatility around a admirable aggressive gut rock core. Grand and capable in largely the same vein as its predecessor, **Head First** again finds wily British veterans making their collective history accessible to new audiences, in the tradition of other reputable dynasties as UFO and Lizzy. The result: **Head First** swirls vibrant and young, while possessing the undercurrent of a record steered by old pros. Sadly, at least stateside, nobody was listening save for a handful of faithful. And who can blame the masses, Heep never really in possession of such pronounced identity until now. Note: '84 marked the collapse of Heep's old label Bronze, the band losing a stack of cash in the process.
Rating　　　　　　　　　　　　　　　　8

## Uriah Heep - Equator (CBS '85)

Despite essentially the same line-up, Heep's newfound lustre begins to fade, as the band's previously tight, survivalist sound somehow unravels, with a trebly mix too generous with keyboards and electronic drum effects, which diminish the solid guitar foundation of the record's two fine predecessors. With Heep's label switch to CBS, essential band producer Ashley Howe was shunted aside for label choice Tony Platt, who proceeded to spend over a hundred grand wrecking the record's sound. But I hesitate to blame it on this, 'cos the band themselves write every tune, and the overall effect is twice or thrice anti-climactic, clattery and cliché, as the band tries to emulate a party metal atmosphere without many deep hooks. Overall however, I can imagine this record really kickin' with less fancy layering of technologies (Fairlight, Synclavier etc.), because beneath the claptrap, **Equator** is actually a marginally heavier record. I don't know . . . somehow it just lacks the humanity, the drive and the guts of the **Abominog** or **Head First**, seemingly adrift in disillusion at a career marked mostly by frustration. Anyway, for whatever reason, I rarely play it, situating it lost in time, obscure and the product of yet another blue period for the Heep. Exit vocalist Peter Goalby, on good terms, his voice basically packing it in due to wear. Also of note, David Byron dies this year, on February 28th.
Rating　　　　　　　　　　　　　　　　6

## Uriah Heep - Live In Moscow (Legacy '88)

Heep dish it up to 180,000 rock-starved fans over ten days in Moscow, lighting a welcome fire in a career that had gone cold. Here the Bernie Shaw/Phil Lanzon-era band tear through radically different arrangements of Heep classics like *Bird Of Prey* and *The Wizard* while offering faithful versions of stormy **Abominog** tracks like *Too Scared To Run* and *That's The Way That It Is*. The recording's good as is the vocal performance. Heck, it's all kind of inspiring. Heck, I think I'm going on a Heep kick! Three otherwise unreleased Lanzon/Shaw-era tracks, *Pacific Highway*, *Corina* and *Mr. Majestic*, the latter a perky, feel-good type of pop rocker that captures the hands-around-the-world purpose of this particular live gig.
Rating　　　　　　　　　　　　　　　　7

## Uriah Heep - Raging Silence (Enigma '89)

Mick Box and Uriah Heep perk up their punchy, keyboard-fortified hard rock, Here Bernie Shaw's pipes (which cross previous mike Peter Goalby with Bruce Dickinson) up-intensify, offering a spirited and simply louder performance. But again, the songwriting is a bit naff if not perkier, exposing a certain behind-the-times isolation, making the record borderline exhilarating, borderline forgettable; in total energetic and accessible, but limited in its usefulness in a world gone grunge. Which is a shame, because I'm sure if this had somehow become a hit, the addition of winner mystique would have ingratiated it well into my psyche. But its commercial failure, and the feeling that through the late '70s and '80s, the band was no more than a nametag unit with a questionable track record, makes **Raging Silence** no more than a melodramatic yet fun, heavy Foreigner sort of release by no one in particular. Closes off with an acceptable cover of Argent's *Hold Your Head Up* and a muddy live blaze through *Look At Yourself*, further fragmenting potential focus, betraying evidence of a creative well gone dry. Still, **Raging Silence** might hook you slowly and solidly (approximating that push/pull you might feel with Joe Lynn Turner-era Rainbow), and really, *Blood Red Roses* is a fine single, written by last singer Peter Goalby I might add. The '94 Griffin reissue deletes both the live *Look At Yourself* and the printed lyrics.
Rating　　　　　　　　　　　　　　　　7

## Uriah Heep - Still 'Eavy Still Proud (Griffin '90)

Slapdash sort of retro this one, combining four smoking live tracks with odd studio choices from inconsequential records like **Wonderland** and **Innocent Victim**. Highlights would be the undifferent remix of

Blood Red Roses and The Other Side Of Midnight from the superfine **Head First**. But it's the wollopingly recorded live tunes that make this one sorta worth it, eclipsing the performances on **Live In Moscow**, best take being the monstrous plow-over of Gypsy.
Rating                                                                 5

## Uriah Heep - Different World   (Legacy '91)

I was extremely surprised when I saw this '94 reissue from Griffin, because indeed, it was the first time I'd ever heard of the damn thing. But alas, I was underwhelmed, finding the stiff delivery of forced pop funk metal grimacingly lame, under-delivered and under-vocalized by new guy Bernie Shaw who quite simply howls splendidly like a wolf all over **Raging Silence** and **Live In Moscow** (Victoria, B.C.'s Shaw comes to the band via Paris, Grand Prix, Praying Mantis and Stratus). Heavy but watery, this one's almost like third-rate Whitesnake circa the early '80s, sorta guitar-laden but polluted with cheez keys. Tentative, unconfident, and the bad kind of raw.
Rating                                                                 5

## Uriah Heep - Rarities From The Bronze Age

(Sequel '91)

One of the very best compilations I've ever laid ears on, **Rarities** is a 78 minute tour de force of powerful Heep tracks, 21 in all, a handful of radio edits, otherwise a killer display of surprisingly excellent B-sides from all eras of the band. Faves are four amazing organ-grinding, metalizing tunes from way back ('72 to '75), Why, Sunshine, What Can I Do, Shout It Out and Time Will Come, all serious Heep stresspoints, full-up with all the glories we've come to love from this band. Later up the disc, there's various interesting and fully realized tracks from my second favourite Heep era ('82 to '83), including a vastly different version of Think It Over with John Sloman on vocals. But if all this top-notch Heep wasn't enough, this thing is loaded with pictures, full band line-up documentation, an essay on the band, and an exhaustive track-by-track explanation of everything included on the album; trivia galore. Worth it for Sunshine and Shout It Out alone, two of the thickest, beefiest things to ever sludge out of this band. What a record.
Rating                                                                 9

## Uriah Heep - The Lansdowne Tapes   (Viceroy '94)

Exaggeratedly for collectors only, this well-meaning pile of trash gathers tunes from basically two sources. Half the stuff is dreary '60s drivel from pre-Heep band Spice (with nothing from The Gods or Toe Fat), essentially Heep just before their first album and a name change. Tunes are pseudo-jazzy, way too long, stoned, and five years behind the times, easy. The other half documents unreleased Heep demos and experiments from '70 and '71, including a couple alternate versions of tunes that happened (the radio edit of Look At Yourself painfully shows up everything else on this). Nothing heavy (save for that fascinating radio edit), nothing even remotely modern, even while 3/4 of the official Heep output at the time undeniably was. But even though the music's deep sixville, Viceroy half makes up for it with the extensive liner notes, track explanations, detailed history and rare photos. Plus it helps when note writer Corich directs one to particularly nice vocal or guitar or keyboard passages. Otherwise, you'd never notice through your disgust/rage/boredom.
Rating                                                                 3

## Uriah Heep - Sea Of Light   (Steamhammer '95)

I can only think of one comeback record that bristles with so much new life, and that would be UFO's **Walk On Water**. Heep definitely give Mogg's sprogs a run for their money, assembling this lavish, palatial record of pomp metal perfection, a record that is exhaustively and expertly detailed, from the gorgeous Roger Dean cover art, through the snapped-tight songwriting, to the superstar production job. Signifying the band's 25th anniversary, and the first record since the insipid **Different World** four years back, **Sea Of Light** kicks off with a bang, Against All Odds snapping the listener back to the heady days of **Look At Yourself**, the song marking that perfect alchemy of metal, prog rock, Hammond organ and guitars, Mick Box ripping off one amazing, fluid and musical axe solo. Heep '96 is a veritable goldmine for the classic rock fan, ranging in styles, while retaining focus through production and performance. Vocalist Bernie Shaw is fantastic, treating each song like theatre, whether it's the almost pop Whitesnake blues of Sweet Sugar or the panoramic elegance of ballads like Dream On or personal album fave, Love In Silence, both tracks taking the sublime surrender of keyboardy Styx, upping the relevance factor and adding the discipline that flows from Trevor Rabin through modern-day Yes (this really does sound like a heavy Yes album). Elsewhere, the rock doth flow, evidenced by the hot-stepping, veteran-hooky groove metal of Fear Of Falling and the melodic stadium swagger and lyrical optimism of Spirit Of Freedom, the record lyrically as a whole, cohering in an almost ecstatic, hippie-days celebration of love. A very self-actualized record, deleting the eccentricities of all those failed records by the band, retaining no less than the prog, the arrangements, the balladry, the metal, and the successful hard rock sheen of **Abominog** and **Head First**, somehow wrapping it all in a package that confidently recaptures that tenuous alchemical mix the band pioneered so many years ago.
Rating                                                                10

## Uriah Heep - A Time Of Revelation   (Castle '96)

A splendid companion piece to the excellent single album Heep reissues Castle has been assembling, **A Time Of Revelation** is a four CD mammoth featuring all the hits plus twenty previously unreleased tracks and versions. The cool thing is that there's no overlap in the rare stuff (so far), Castle doing a sort of second sweep of the vaults to make this groovy box quite the treat, although few of these new tunes really endear. In addition, all of the album tracks are remastered, really exposing how great these songs were. Then there's a massive 60 page booklet, with full track explanation, discography and band personnel inventory (lots of changes with these guys). Of course what most of us talk about is the travesty of spelling the band's name "Heap" on the spine of the thing, showing that no matter how much you proofread, rainbow demons and typesetting wizards will play. But the booklet's the real gem here, stuffed with band and memorabilia shots (and also more typos!), laying out in concise chronological terms the story of this rollercoaster phenom. Nice construction too, that hardcover book set-up (like The Police's **Message In A Box**), i.e. all one piece, discs nicely inset into the front and back covers, booklet stitched into the middle. Food for thought: listen to Valley Of The Kings and then Ozzy's Fire In The Sky, then note the presence of John Sinclair and Bob Daisley in the credits of both songs. Hmmm . . .
Rating                                                                 8

# V

## Steve Vai - Flexable (Akashic '88)

Logically so, Steve's first solo album finds the man blurting out a bazaar of sounds, a creative juggernaut finally getting to speak his hyper mind. And the proceedings are (also logically so), the most Zappa-like of all his rollercoaster solo works, indeed much of this imaginable as Zappa concepts unaltered, funny flip vocal parts hopping over inverted humorous shreds. Lyrics are equally amusing, as are Steve's comments track by track. I don't know. I feel I had this guy pegged wrong all these years. I mean, I still don't like what he's done to heavy rock records by big balding stars, but when he's left to his own zany nutbutter devices, the crazy professor comes through, letting his axe speak a colourful language that sees the stupid fun amongst all the posturing of the music business.
Rating 7

## Steve Vai - Passion And Warfare (Relativity '90)

Probably the instrumental shredwank to end all wanks, **Passion And Warfare** is full of Steve's subtle humour, a lingering derivation from Zappa what with the little spoken bits of commentary peppering the sometimes Satriani-like rapid wonk melodies. I stand by my guns that Vai's chosen pathways leave me cold, towering exception being his work on **Sex & Religion**. This one seems to be fired in the crucible of bad, big hair intentions, and the over-the-edge craziness of **Sex** or indeed **Flexable** or **Alien** are nowhere to be found.
Rating 5

## Vai - Sex & Religion (Relativity '93)

Stevie Vai makes what I consider his first truly earnest play for band respectability with this provocative, alternative-looking sprawl of zany chops rock. That doesn't mean it doesn't flare with Vai's offbeat humour, **Sex & Religion** sounding like Paul Shaeffer (spelling?) and his CBS Orchestra's soundbite rock meets David Lee Roth, lots of jazzy, Zappa-prog shadings over convoluted metal tunes, all spiced with vocals from Devin Townsend that divebomb, caterwaul and otherwise challenge the technical razzledazzle from Vai, bassist T. M. Stevens and drum chum from the old Zappa days, Terry Bozzio. Pretty grandiose but knowingly, which works so intelligently, rendered uniquely philosophical with large religious themes juxtaposed against amusing spoken sections. I mean, that title track is simply brilliant, massive Queen-like cathedrals of sound balanced against a truly insightful essay on religion's hang-ups

with sex. Big Stuff, cannily over-played, over-arranged and over-produced. Frank would be proud.
Rating 8

## Steve Vai - Alien Love Secrets (Sony '95)

I actually interviewed the pyro-whiz himself about this one, Steve saying that this EP was more or less a collection of flat-out "simple" guitar tunes that was to come out AFTER the half vocals/half instrumental full-length on which he was toiling away. I ain't gonna try to fool ya, this is for guitar fans only really, just mega-soloing instrumental ravefests that nevertheless find Vai expanding his vocabulary past his patented fret-fire '80s hairband diddling into something often very melodic and low-reg lush (shades of Nuno here). Released in conjunction with a bare-bones video performance of the EP's seven tracks.
Rating 5

## Steve Vai - Fire Garden (Sony '96)

Ol' overload Stevie has provided another vast morass of surfeit and surface texture, laying on the discerning and up-to-challenge rock aficionado 74 minutes of playing and parlaying, half of it instrumental, half sung, stung and written by Steve in total tantrum. The man becomes and blossoms sublime through sensory avalanche, warning us in print that "being as dense as it is, this CD may best be experienced by devouring it in pieces," going on to suggest that "those with a strong constitution may dare to consume it as it is. Dig in . . . ". Which captures the man's sparkly spark, his inverted metal irony, his culture shock walk. Phase I (the instrumental half) is like too much chocolate. But Phase 2 moodswings wildly, from the Nuno-funk of *Little Alligator*, to the slippery balladic jungle madness of *All About Eve*, to the Prince crunch of *Aching Hunger*, to the Queenie bash of *Damn You*. One feels the effect of 300-channel satellite TV by wit's end, but one also feels refreshed by a creative dressing-down. A weird, colour-inundated man fer sure, L'il Stevie is as irrepressible as his alter-ego Devin Townsend, and **Fire Garden** proves that a rock record can be the best stick-poke to a quiet lie-down.
Rating 7

## Vain - No Respect (Island '89)

This band of wastrels looks and sounds like they spend way too much time in the bars inhaling smoke and recreational beverages, approximating good quality Crüecraft delivered by the half-dead Crüe of the

485

doped-up middle years; sorta what **Too Fast For Love** might have sounded like on the **Theatre Of Pain** tour. Decent melodies, decent arrangements, lazy execution. Lead vox Davey Vain does a convincingly pained rendition of the stung by love, stung by the street, prima donna. You really haven't missed much if this one slipped by you in '89 as it did with me. No real peaks and valleys, just a steady drone of live 'n' loose no-frills bar slop, bangin' the line between hard rock and heavy metal.

Rating  7

## Vanadium - Metal Rock  (Durium '82)

Something that never ceases to amaze me. You would think these European bands (in this case Italian), who are taking the effort to learn to play, grow their hair, write songs, spend money on equipment and promotion, and eventually put out a record, would have the brains to search out at least one lone English tourist to take ten minutes to correct spelling, grammar, and yes, even botched idiom throughout their valiant attempts at English lyrics. Hell, Scorpions has been a multi-million dollar industry for years and *still* no one seems to bother to even glance through their dipshit witticisms (i.e. **Best Of Rockers 'n' Ballads**, *Rock You Like A Hurricane*, *When The Smoke Is Going Down*, **Lovedrive**). One would think the record exec types who consider these bands meal tickets might notice just how idiotic it all sounds. Totally inexcusable, but nobody said there were any brains in this business. How bad does it get? How's "Bad times and bad things everybody listen to the radio/ it's hard to settle look all fall down/ we are ready we are strong hey men drow along/ to day and to night will he everything all right". I applaud the ambition to go after other markets but dammit, bring something to the table or stay in Italy.

Rating  3

## Vanadium - Race With The Devil  (Durium '83)

Musically, Vanadium are after an admirable Deep Purple/early Heep nostalgia but fall way short on songcraft, sounding for all their effort, like bad Saxon with keyboards. Although really no better than the last in this respect, **Race With The Devil** asserts itself with snappier production, musicianship and general confidence, while still riddled with strange Euro-izations of metal clichés both musically and lyrically, that is, when you can make sense of the wincingly painful werds of wizdumb Vanadium struggle to articulate.

Rating  4

## Vanadium - Game Over  (Durium '84)

**Game Over** possesses the most impressionable bevy of tracks of all Vanadium discs, but it's still sheet metal percentage-wise, highlights including *Pretty Heartbreaker*, and the scorching *Streets of Danger*. No question, these guys show heavy-duty promise, achieving a highly respectable sound, with roaring vocals, but major work needs to be done in the riff-writing and lyrical departments, i.e. general catch-up ball to world standards, as is the case with almost all bands outside the British, North American, German, or Scandinavian metal mainstream. The Heep histrionics are palpable though, making one really wish these boys would come along.

Rating  4

## Vandenberg - Vandenberg  (Atco '82)

Vandenberg is one of the classic unsung bands from the past to which this book is dedicated, an under-rated giant talent that shone brilliantly for three albums then fragmented into oblivion. This debut had adequate PR push behind it, gaining momentum due to Van Halen comparisons borne of similarities between bandnames (source thereof being each's resident guitar hero), similar patch and t-shirt ready logo, and indeed similar

brash but versatile and hook-laden American hard rock (even though Vandenberg is of Dutch descent). With such a marketing base working towards considerable radio buzz, the fluid, classical axe work of Adrian Vandenberg, the ahead-of-the-beat natural percussion mania of Jos Zoomer, and most importantly, the confident, emotive and soaring vocal croonings of Bert Heerink, formed an effortless alloy which swaggered its way through an album of tasteful, mature European hard rock, American party favours, slowish Van Halen camp pieces, early OTT, and heavy-handed but convincing balladry as in *Wait* and *Burning Heart*, both of which became minor hits. This very personable record exudes magic on all fronts, breezily working its melodies and harmonies through the entire spectrum of fine '70s metal traditions. More spontaneous and edgy than the dead-smooth follow-ups, **Vandenberg** captured the excitement of a confident but grounded upstart on the verge of stardom. But more importantly, this rich and textured record gave us a lot of good teen-years memories, and we extend a hearty thanks to Adrian and the boys for bestowing upon us the choice Vandenberg sound.

Rating  10

## Vandenberg - Heading For A Storm  (Atco '83)

**Heading For A Storm**, brilliant as it is, may just have been the marketing gaffe that confused enough fans of the debut to send sales into a tailspin. The record's a shiny second effort, painstakingly produced and overworked, most noticeable in the overuse of trendy electronic percussion. And more importantly, the overall composition of the record is considerably closer to melodic hard rock than the arresting, shoot-'em-up, Euro hard rock/metal hybrid of the debut. The shift causes no lapse however in creative genius, as A. Vandenberg proves himself a full-blown guitar virtuoso, uniquely blending Yngwie-inspired classical music-based fluidity with unabashed hard rock, composing and resolving within a much more intelligent and human context than that of Malmsteen's one track moat. Throughout **Heading For A Storm** (which incidentally features nifty cover art by Adrian himself), riffs are fat, stirring, and deeply European, choruses full-blooded, flawless, and warm, and arrangements thoughtful and complex, yet intrinsically enjoyable. Outside of artful speed rockers *This Is War*, *Waiting For The Night*, and top-notch ballad *Different Worlds*, the entire album oscillates nimbly between sumptuous Euro-metal and equally sumptuous hard rock, so seamless in the changeovers that the distinctions begin to fade, laying bare the universal, effortless, and insistent exuberance within the grooves. So alas, **Heading For A Storm** yields a surprisingly different Vandenberg from the debut, but one no less riveting, diverting attention from its tidiness and lessened vitality with an avalanche of professional postures.

Rating  10

## Vandenberg - Alibi  (Atco '85)

Another cool painting by Adrian himself adorns the front cover of this third Vandenberg treat, the magnificent last offering from one of the '80s' most influential AOR bands. Save for a long instrumental and two less than perfect mellow pieces, **Alibi** would coast to an easy 10 in my books. What remains however, is gorgeous and decorative Eurorock similar to, although slightly heavier than the sum total of **Heading For A Storm**. Best of the lot are lead-off tune *All The Way*, which somehow manages to surpass the intense life force of **Storm**'s *Friday Night*, and *Dressed To Kill*, a metallic anthem driven by a vicious but elegant and intricate Vandenberg riff. The rest of the album consists mainly of slow to mid-pace fare, classy, atmospheric, and inspired as the best from say, UFO. **Alibi** stands forever in time as an intelligent and ambitious swan-

song, of a sound sadly missing in the '90s. Years later, Adrian Vandenberg would resurface, caught in Whitesnake's revolving door of guitar gods, spilled inside then summarily spilled back out, heard briefly with a sense of tragedy in the knowledge that his considerable talents and leadership abilities were greatly under-utilized.
Rating                                                                9

## Van Halen - Van Halen  (Warner Bros. '78)

Without a shred of doubt, Van Halen's bold premiere is a cornerstones of any metal collection. **Van Halen** (the record so vital they hadda name it twice), bristles with confidence and electrocuted energy, showcasing one of rock's biggest new guitar heroes in Eddie Van Halen, king of the hammer-ons, a crack rhythm section in brother Alex Van Halen and Michael Anthony, and an unstoppable showman in Diamond David Lee Roth. **Van Halen** is no less than a thrilling stylistic tour of the hard rock universe. We get blistering flat-out scorchers in futuristic metal like Atomic Punk, Ain't Talkin' 'Bout Love, On Fire, and I'm The One, dynamic, rhythmic party rockers in Runnin' With The Devil and Jamie's Cryin', the first of the band's bang-up covers in The Kinks' You Really Got Me, the first loungey lizard joke tune in Ice Cream Man, and of course Eruption, the most famous guitar solo of all time, that rite of passage for many an aspiring teen axeman. There's all kinds of well-written, professional metal on here, diversely spotting the energy spectrum, an approach which belies an enigmatic greatness that so many legendary rock'n'rollers such as Zeppelin, Lizzy, Queen, and Deep Purple, all share. Hats off to Gene Simmons, who apparently "discovered" the band and put his good name to the project, and to Ted Templeman, who produces with sweltering, gut-wrenching brilliance, lots of electricity and friction dogpiling this Holy Grail of records. Of course, one of the most fiery and most spacious, gracious and bodacious debuts of all time, justly rewarded as one of the best-selling records of the catalogue, officially certified six times platinum as of '89, with only 1984 exceeding its pace.
Rating                                                               10

## Van Halen - II  (Warner Bros. '79)

Whereas Van Halen's debut was simply an awesome rock album, VH - **II** moves daringly towards establishing an identifiable Van Halen sound; a rough, hurried, garagey, live-feel din that would figure most prominently here, on **Women And Children First**, and on **1984**. Eddie's fluid "heavy metal Allan Holdsworth" stylings ramp all over this dangerous record, affording us the first complete exposure of the eccentric wizard at work, including his somewhat annoying practice of soloing without rhythm guitar backtracking. In the spirit of most enigmatic bands, **II** sounds nothing like the debut, due in no small part to the production and loose, jammin' quality of the playing, also because songs tend to stand on their own, discouraging direct track-for-track comparisons. So underscoring the variety enclosed, we get mega-riff rockers like D.O.A.. Light Up The Sky, and Somebody Get Me A Doctor, uncommunicative dense bass-throbbers like Bottoms Up! and Outta Love Again, and the first in-earnest good-time, top-down summer anthems in Beautiful Girls and Dance The Night Away, both toons registering as Creamsicle-melting classics, forever to be imprinted in the consciousness of classic rock radio. **II** found Van Halen well on their way to superstardom, in much the same manner as another brash, confident band a few years earlier, Led Zeppelin, both acts bristling with excitement, creating a buzz built of chemistry colliding with chops, the public early on, allowing rough, hasty experimentation, deferring to

the wisdom of the quartet at hand, despite their collective youths. The rest as they say, was history.
Rating                                                               10

## Van Halen - Women And Children First
(Warner Bros. '80)

**Women And Children First** finds the gifted ones delving further into wall-of-sound raggedness, getting both more seriously noisy and more polished at the same time. On the Pere Ubu-ish industrial clatter front, we get the frantic, aptly-titled blur Loss Of Control, guitar-jammin' obelisk Everybody Wants Some, Sabbatherian blues stomper Fools, and fleeting, kick-ass, speed metaller Romeo's Delight. On the clinically scrubbed front we get melodic but throbbing classic And The Cradle Will Rock . . ., demonstrating Eddie's aptitude for creating clever melody from diverse instrumental layering, plus Take Your Whiskey Home, a menacing bluegrass tune zipped through the idiom of metal, a cocky hit single which features Diamond Dave in full control of his vices. And of course it's all wickedly edgy, smartly spontaneous stuff, accentuated by the distinct contributions of large individual personalities, not the least of which is Alex's manic crash-as-ride-cymbal percussive hurricane. All in all, a rip roaring, rhythmically complex metal feast played with steadfast integrity and belief in the indescribable but stressful, white-knuckle Van Halen process, fragmentation to choice, four-part creative jungles reassembling for a din unlike any other.
Rating                                                               10

## Van Halen - Fair Warning  (Warner Bros. '81)

One of the more arresting things about Van Halen has got to be the band's bravery and nonchalance in the process of record-making; never afraid to try new things and try them often. Generally speaking, **Fair Warning** is not overly different from the sum total of past efforts, but per usual, particular tunes shine as new, cutting edge Van Halen classics, best of which include the unsung One Foot Out The Door, a quick in/quick out speed rocker built around a sort of wild guitar/synth tonality, Unchained, a straight-ahead riff rocker, and Mean Street, an ambitious rhythmic tornado that features one of the fiercest guitar intros laid to vinyl. **Fair Warning** to my mind, is one of those lost albums you never really get a handle on; half-studded with obvious dazzlers, half-studded with unassuming gems that reveal their lustre only after repeated plays, due less to overt brilliance, more to subtle nuance and instrumental shadings often brought to the fore only through the magic of headphones. A detectable sense of drift exists, but with these guys, it's more like genius lounging on the rocks, scooping up gold coins between tides.
Rating                                                               10

## Van Halen - Diver Down  (Warner Bros. '82)

| Side One | |
| --- | --- |
| Cover | 3:02 |
| Real Van Halen song | 3:28 |
| Guitar fluff | 1:20 |
| Joke Van Halen song | 3:25 |
| Guitar fluff | 1:39 |
| Joke cover | 2:53 |
| | |
| Side Two | |
| Cover | 3:43 |
| Guitar fluff | 0:42 |
| Real Van Halen song | 3:47 |
| Joke cover | 2:44 |
| Real Van Halen song | 3:18 |
| Joke cover | 1:03 |

Dismal verdict: 11:33 of genuine, new Van Halen. Pretty ambitious, eh kids? Despite the scam-job however, **Diver Down** is chock-full of good times, an intense sampling of summer on the upswing, despite the season only lasting a week. Of the covers, *Dancing In The Streets* becomes lifted via a unique guitar effect throb throughout, while the Kinks' *Where Have All The Good Times Gone* and Roy Orbison's *Pretty Woman* get Van Halen's scrappy version of red carpet consideration, the stamp of irreverent reverence, a lusty four-part tear, done once but done right. Of the scant few useful originals, *Little Guitars* is a melodic and rhythmic tour de force, one of Van Halen's brightest moments, apparently played on one of Eddie's miniature axes (hence the title), and *The Full Bug* is vintage camp boogie, again featuring Eddie working well away from the obvious. Grudgingly speaking, despite the band's lack of concern for delivering value, what there is of **Diver Down** pleases with a big slap on the back, delivering a lively, butt-shaking good time, probably the most accurate celebration of the affable, off-the-cuff attitude that is the cornerstone of the band's non-stop party machine, a life-view which includes for all to see, a lovable degree of laziness.
Rating      8

## Van Halen - 1984    (Warner Bros. '83)

Another decidedly unambitious exercise in brevity, showcasing eight compositions clocking in at scarcely half an hour, **1984** sounds slapped together, for the first time derogatorily spontaneous and live; especially annoying given Eddie's continued practice of taking solos without dropping in a backing rhythm track. Nevertheless, despite the hurried approach, **1984** is bold and cutting edge, not to mention the band's most gargantuan and lasting of many commercial successes, sporting such superior hits as the cheery Diamond Dave-autobiographical *Jump*, the moody, keyboard-powered *I'll Wait*, plus such inferior massive hits as the sloppy *Panama* and speed lark *Hot For Teacher*. And the fun doesn't stop there. **1984** offers no less than four more dangerous, volatile Van Halen rockers in the blustery *Girl Gone Bad* (my fave), tidy speed boogie *Top Jimmy*, melodic funkster *Drop Dead Legs* and the purely metallic, swooping and slippery *House Of Pain*, a tune from the original demo given to Gene Simmons back when the band was label shopping. In general, **1984** delivers an acceptable array of rough and raw, well-written Van Halen, much of it featuring Eddie's new-found keyboard experimentation which at times can become whole riffs as in *Jump* and *I'll Wait*, putting Ed in company with Brian May and Jimmy Page (at least on **In Through The Out Door**) as legendary axemen who seem to have taken leave of their considerable talents for synth-diddling. Unfortunately **1984** would turn out to be Diamond Dave's swansong, for all intents and purposes, closing the books on an American institution, post-Dave Van Halen lacking the fire and fun that put this band so impressionably on the map.
Rating      8

## Van Halen - 5150    (Warner Bros. '86)

David Lee Roth out, Sammy Hagar in, causing insurmountable problems that seem to loom larger as time wears on. Musically, 5150 is fairly tepid, deflated Van Halen (although mostly written and recorded before Sam arrived); scarcely half the record spirited and/or melodically heavy and/or well-written. Lone classic is the tuneful and complex *Why Can't This Be Love*, a gem of a hot nightz rocker, begging for Dave to turn it legendary. Other celebrations include the aptly-titled *Summer Nights*, bluesy singalong *Inside*, and the percussive sheen of "*5150*", the latter being the name of Eddie's home studio. The rest: mediocre to inexcusable: ailing corporate ballads (*Love Walks In*), powerless

OTT just like Dave gone solo (*Get Up*), and stumbling wanks (*Best Of Both Worlds*). As usual, Alex's drumming is a chaotic blast furnace of percussion; a wall of oddly-recorded noise, crashing cymbals, funny toms, "brown" snare sound, and hi-tech double bass drums. Strange, but even as is, this album might have worked with Roth at the helm. As it stands, however, **5150** is marred by Van Hagar's painful merger between two diametrically opposed camps, despite what are very common influences behind a shared fifteen years of rock as a career. Slick album cover.
Rating      6

## Van Halen - OU812    (Warner Bros. '88)

**OU812** is supposed to be the auspicious return to down 'n' dirty rawk after the keyboard-laced morass of 5150. But even though it's marginally more axe-heavy, it's still over-produced and actually more commonplace. And I still can't take Sammy Hagar seriously as lead vocalist. His voice is too distinct, for better or worse, as the Red Rocker, and most importantly, the DLR act just doesn't jive with his clean-cut generic rocker past. He just ain't a frontman no matter how he shakes his bad hairdo or how many dumb red maternity suits fill his closets. And lyrically, Hagar sounds plain locker-room foul-mouthed, getting off at the expense of the chicks, laughing at women like the fratboys expect him to. Diamond Dave laughs at life and everybody grappling to tame it, including himself. And Hagar's just dying to be accepted, bending way over for the cheap laughs at every corner. Like any great rock'n'roll, it's all in the delivery. You got it or you don't, and even though Hagar is in possession of a fine set of pipes, and is a nice guy to boot, he's still a bit out of his element. In any event, Alex, as usual, is a drum dynamo, and there's more blazing Eddie licks than one wax previous. Faves would include hi-tech, mystical speed-metal classic *Mine All Mine*, Zep-ish retro riff-rocker *A.F.U. (Naturally Wired)*, and dumb stomper *Sucker In A 3 Piece*. And what sucks on this? All the rest. Overall verdict: cynical corporate rock. It's damn unfortunate, but no matter how you slice it, the philosophical soul and warmth of this band evaporated when David Lee Roth packed it in. They should have closed shop and gone home. Now it stands that Roth is an emotional force looking for a band and Van Halen is a crack band looking for emotional force. The reunion would surely save the world, or at least cheer everybody up for a couple weeks.
Rating      6

## Van Halen - For Unlawful Carnal Knowledge
(Warner Bros. '91)

The non-awaited follow-up to the second Van Hagar wimpfest confounds all cynics who thought Halen was dead in the water. F.U.C.K. (title derived from the band's disgust at the whole Tipper Gore censorship issue) finds the band still dicking around with life and acting annoyingly juvenile. You'd think legends like this would grow up. In fact most do. Yet Van Halen is content to be a dynasty of high school bathroom humour. But, once past the dumb lyrics however (not to mention Hagar's embarrassing fashion sense), the band backs it up with a vengeance, commanding renewed respect among those looking for red-hot riffery. Much of F.U.C.K. throbs with the bottom-end, wall-of-sound mania of our man Alex, who keeps the proceedings buoyant throughout, leaving Eddie in many instances to colour the dominant melodies beneath Sammy's attitude and cheesy sex raps. This is the case with *Pleasure Dome* and brilliant lead single *Poundcake*, which along with two or three others here, evoke a heroic Zeppelin quality (producer Andy Johns was also the man behind Zep - **IV**), a dance with the extremes, yielding brutally rhythmic yet melodic log jams. There's really only one keyboard tune on this, and really nothing mellow (except for the naff instrumental), which makes for a substantial wail throughout, and besides the dopey funk-rock of *Spanked*, the entire album is chock-full of good or great hard rock and metal; American music an intricate and chops-laden cut above the radio norm, which of course is expected from such legendary players. **For Unlawful Carnal Knowledge** is ultimately a kick-ass return to power for Van Halen, while still not a classic creative juicer on par with timeless releases from the band's Dave era. Halen in the '90s bears the all too similar shortcomings of Halen of the latter '80s, mainly lack of lyrical growth, yet the act has become markedly more serious, heavy, and authentic. A lot of folks still want Diamond Dave back however, and after recently seeing Mr. Showboat live, I can't help think he'd dive right in. Although the man put on a show of pure sweat and spirit, he *did* play more VH than DLR by a count of 7 to 5, give or take. But it ain't going to happen, and y'know it's OK, 'cause Hagar is starting to build his own legacy, and you can't deny the man's vocal prowess. For now, consider **F.U.C.K.** a mixed triumph of rhythm over rhyme, mud over melody, a valiant effort given the power tools available. Ground-breaking (and deservedly award-winning) video: *Right Now*.

Rating      8

## Van Halen - Live: Right here, right now

(Warner Bros. '93)

Really folks, with a large corporate juggernaut like Van Halen, how much mystery and intrigue can there be here? Answer: none, outside of the clever cover art, as the boys tear through a predictable but graciously long set of Sammy-era Ameri-rockers, plus a scant few DLR anthems, butchered (*Ain't Talkin' 'Bout Love* being particularly Sam-scarred) for whatever reasons, two being range incompatibility and fun factor. Totally inane raps from Sammy, bracing, new-agey adventure from Eddie's guitarspeak, and a Fripp-ish bass solo from Mikey work their +/- imprint towards making this yer basic studied live romp, studio quality execution and sizzling electric mix with screaming crowd sounds, which is fine, Van Halen's particular chemical high being an inclusion of All, musician snootiness no part of this likeable band's vocabulary, as the sun-sweltered Fresno festival fries on into the early eve. I dunno, go ahead, but I'll make my own car tape.

Rating      6

## Van Halen - Balance    (Warner '95)

A palpable "who cares" attitude awaited the release of **Balance**, a record much less pre-hyped than the bristling **F.U.C.K.** project from '91. And I can see why. **Balance** pulls all sorts of non-starters, Eddie's trendy new grunge look, some chanting monks, and a general luke-warm creativity causing one to wonder: what has this band been doing for the past three years? Monster rock cheeseball writin', that's what. Sure the first single is catchy enough, a somewhat emotionally dark tale with a nice Halen retro thump, solid melodic chorus, one of the only interesting lyrics on the record, a true hit. But the ballads are miserable, *Can't Stop Lovin' You* being the worst, just a perky peroxide, dil, dullard delete-bin ditty that no one should support. Then there's a fantabulously hideous piano pomp pooper called *Not Enough*, something this band used to manage and *be* the times not *behind* the times, this clunker further marring the fragile Hagar-era reputation that's ten years old and still not resolved. Balancing the bad mellow however, is a sensuous Zep-style acoustic composition called *Take Me Back (Deja Vu)*; right guys: classic rock not not has-been rock. But the louder tracks drift like afterthoughts, riffless jams relying on rhythm to carry the tune, *Big Fat Money* ripping off *Teenage Nervous Breakdown* on auto-pilot, *Aftershock* just hanging, Eddie filling time, ching-chiming around,

loitering as does most of his performances here. Still as always, it's a thrill to hear this rhythm section, and a record this big, by players so individually distinct. But sorry, **Balance** only cares about half the time, on an objective level comprising four soft rock tracks, five rock tunes with vocals, and three instrumentals. Main travesty in all this soup is this: the rockers are mostly wasted opportunities with aimless solos and the stoopidest lyrics I've ever heard from a major label act.

Rating      5

## Van Halen - Best Of Volume I    (Warner '96)

So a quick run-down of the Diamond Dave fiasco. Ed kicks Sammy out because he says that sober, he is able to see that Hagar is both a bad lyricist and a compulsive liar. Dave is brought back, sort of, the manlegend brought in and apparently tried out on many, many songs, only to betray the fact that his range is shot. Plus there's this episode of Dave flipping out about the *Me Wise Magic* video, and his limelight-hogging escapade at the MTV Music Awards. In any event, who knows what's true? Dave counters with the supposition that he was strung along and tricked, and that the band was auditioning or even had chosen another singer before Dave was single-handedly reviving the band's reputation through a mere two songs of pure uh, magic. So word is out that Eric Martin might be in, but then Gary Cherone gets the gig (yawn). Which is where we stand as I write. The cash-grab at hand sports another bad Halen cover and title, wrapped around all the predictables, a nice discography, and three non-LP tracks. This trio of gems is the record's only reason to exist. *Humans Being* (from the **Twister** soundtrack) beats the pants off of anything on that horrible **Balance** record. Of the two Dave tracks, *Can't Get This Stuff No More* is merely good, and *Me Wise Magic* is brilliant, deep-grooved, heavy, enigmatic and stuffed with personality. Dave: you rule.

Rating      6

## Vardis - 100MPH    (Logo '80)

This bumbling power trio was a ground-floor NWOBHM outfit, approximating a roughed-up, low-budget Motörhead from the '50s, or a heavier but not very talented version of Status Quo, a comparison Vardis would be proud to accept, having graciously called one of their albums **Quo Vardis**. **100MPH** is actually live, "guaranteed no overdubs", and probably due to the play-to-survive intensity of the live experience, is one of their heaviest outings, mixing boogie woogie with metal the way Quo themselves managed so capably in days of old. Lead dude Steve Zodiac looks sorta like Edgar Winter. Too plain jane to rule the world, but parts of this rock smartly like a pedigreed Ramones. Entering the lower register of moshdom comfortably: *Situation Negative*, *Let's Go*, and *If I Were King*.

Rating      6

## Vardis - This World's Insane    (Logo '81)

**This World's Insane** is less the flat-out careening bar-room booger compared to the band's live debut, foolin' around with melodic variations of traditional r'n'r which would make it interesting, listenable and nostalgic, if not for the surprisingly sickly-to-the-point-of-mistaken recording for this the band's first studio record. A likeable bunch of dented heads with no talent, it all flies out the window if the mix smells as much as this. Includes a spaceship ride on Hawkwind's *Silver Machine*.

Rating      5

## Vardis - Quo Vardis    (Logo '81)

All the more the hootenany for its obvious disdain for the tenets of metal, **Quo Vardis** does a smooth boogie polyester hip-swivel, raising smiles all around the room, courting risk of ridicule at every corner, and coming off humble and fresh despite its ancient, low-budget placement in metal's shabby back books. Despite the confusing signals and the purportedly bad live gigs, Vardis assumes a semi-serious levity in the construction of decidedly flip song ideas. And despite your strong or weak opinions on the band's inconsequence (and many there are), the man can sing, and the man can wrap a bluesy solo around a bashful riff, betraying his sense of folly and history at the same time. Maybe a wee chapter, but a chapter nevertheless, for there was nothing quite like Vardis and their slavish though low faculty focus on the love of Quo. Faves: the gushy acoustic *To Be With You* and the no-ambitions *Where There's Mods There's Rockers*. rock'n'roll with heart but no money.

Rating                                                        7

### Vardis - The Lion's Share   (Razor '83)

A pointless mishmash of previously released studio and live stuff plus other questionable newies. I had a soft spot for this band because they were just so doomed from day one; so mercilessly panned by the critics, and so stung by the business side of life. But hey, nothing wrong with Steve Zodiac's smiling bleat and the spirit in which the moshable boogie histrionics blast forth in relentless succession. Back with **Vigilante** in '86.

Rating                                                        5

### Varga - Prototype   (BMG '93)

Hamilton's Varga have taken some flak for haphazard stylistic changes over past releases, here on their major debut doin' it again, incorporating trendy new samples with a decidedly cleaner, more groovin' sound. Well, barring past discretions, **Prototype** kicks ass, sounding confident and cruising, definitely the product of somewhat seasoned rock dogs from Hamilton. Fact is, few bands are touching this sort of hybrid, something more 80-20 metal to industrial quotient versus Ministry's perhaps 60-40. The record breaks out strong (maybe too strong), my fave tracks being the first three of the spread, *Unconscience*, *Greed* and *Bring The Hammer Down* all extraordinary heft-tunes, probably the crystal crunch of what Halford might have wanted to achieve with Fight. Elsewhere lead single *Freeze Don't Move* is a little cheezy with its opportunistic rap, and *Self-Proclaimed Messiah* is too '80s, something Maiden might do. But the record's strengths triumph, Joey and crew playing up a storm while pounding the metallic hot buttons; killer grooves, sterling production and ideas all over. Main complaint: lyrics, which sound dated; scant few good topics, tolerable execution but nothing great including their minor attempts at humour (Annihilator or Anthrax-style at best). But all in all, Varga carve a cool niche with their catchy '90s megametal, the band perhaps Canada's greatest hope for a hard music stadium draw on scale with Pantera or Metallica. Well, one can hope.

Rating                                                        7

### Varga - Oxygen   (BMG '95)

Getting the gears for bandwagon jumping here in Canuckland à la Sven Gali, the now crashed Slik Toxik, and I Mother Earth, Hamilton's Varga have nevertheless completed their transition from chops-driven thrash band to that love 'em hate 'em '90s sound. **Oxygen** is a tricky, technologically daunting hybrid of down-tuned Sabbatherian/Alice in Chains riffs, and industrial production values, which include bullhorny and rappy vocals here and there, plus de rigeur hip hop beats. The whole ambitious shmeer is chock full of ideas, but I still come away a little cynical, not able to put aside all the angst and just enjoy, even if the end result has been a really heavy, pounding, marauding record, well-recorded and dressed to the nines. Take

this review as a description not a judgment, because I'm still on the fence.

Rating                                                        7

### Various Artists - Airheads: Music From The Original Motion Picture   (Fox '94)

Far and away highlight of this excuse to jumble a bunch of collectible tracks together would be smokin' new bludgeonator *Feed The Gods* from White Zombie, a definitely massive direction indicator for the over-cartooned surprise breakthru band of '93. Elsewhere Ice-T and Whitfield Crane cameo on a fine Motörhead track and Anthrax does a Smiths' song. No biggie otherwise, what with the inclusion of 4 Non Blondes (butchering obscure Van Halen track *I'm The One*), plus Primus and Candlebox obscuring the focus. Closes out with one of my fave Ramones tracks *We Want The Airwaves*, which is essentially the plot of the movie.

Rating                                                        6

### Various Artists - The Beavis And Butt-Head Experience   (Geffen/MTV '93)

Plays just like an episode of the (huh-huh) "show", only there's a truck-load full of solid metal rarities here (although two of the best, Megadeth's *99 Ways To Die* and Aerosmith's *Deuces Are Wild* have since shown up on full-lengths). Other coolios include a scary urban metal hip-hop by Anthrax, a Primus face-paster, the Chili Peppers' crashy thrashy *Search And Destroy* cover, and most valuable player, *I Am Hell* from White Zombie, a massive piledriver up to the band's high "throwaway" standards. In betwixt are segues and other (huh-huh) pearls of wisdom from our fave bards of the apocalyptic stoner-chuckle, making this a comedy album, a metal record, a desert topping and a floor polish.

Rating                                                        7

### Various Artists - Bill & Ted's Bogus Journey: Music From The Motion Picture   (Interscope '91)

A surprising little soundtrack highlighting a number of as-of-yet non-LP tracks by a lot of artistically and/or commercially hot acts before hard rock hit the crapper. The notables: Slaughter's slippery **Stick It To Ya**-style rocker *Shout It Out*, an above-par tune from Winger, Kiss' overblown but arithmetically uncharacteristic ballad to rock (and sort of a cover) *God Gave Rock And Roll To You II*, Megadeth's evil *Go To Hell*, *Tommy The Cat*, a rappin', bass-fwappin' alien from Primus (who toured with U2, an then Rush), and King's X's *Junior's Gone Wild*, a heavy, almost doom-laden ladle, here serving large bluesy chord feasts 'neath fairly extreme vocals for the mighty X. Negatives: the usual predictable no-name stuff, the presence of Steve Vai, and *The Perfect Crime*, a formulaic disappointment from Faith No More. Time will tell how much of this material ever makes it to records by the respective artists, but as it stands, this is one of the most robust soundtracks ever, save for **Last Action Hero**. Plus lyrics to the whole she-bang.

Rating                                                        7

### Various Artists - Black Night: Deep Purple Tribute According To New York   (Revolver '96)

Purists may stand aghast at this irreverent, relevant, phresh and phun deconstruction and funkconjunction of a bunch of Purple classics. For circus master T.M. Stevens has assembled a chops-flown gaggle of New York funk rockers to pay this most entertaining of tributes. Notables include Joe Lynn Turner, Al Pitrelli, Vinnie Moore, Will Calhoun, Richie Kotzen, Cory Glover, Stevie Salas, T.M. Stevens (who does the liners notes and produces), and Tony Harnell, all parties combining for Living Colour-type arrangements with the slick and steely production found on other Purple tributes. Main drummer Will Calhoun gets the most rope, givin' it up with a coterie of thwappin' bassists, turning each track eminently funky, *Child In Time* even transformed into a reggae. Fun is kept foremost, various folks piping in with enthusiastic little comments here and there, the whole thing culminating with a truly silly rap roll call led by Stevens. Radically altered renditions, but isn't this what you'd rather have?

Rating 7

## Various Artists - The Crow: Music From The Original Motion Picture (Warner '94)

Brisk sales for yet another star-studded soundtrack album, this one (for the movie starring Brandon Lee in which the actor was accidentally killed on set filming a shooting scene) shmoozing together an illustrious pack of Generation X favorites like Stone Temple Pilots, Pantera, Rollins Band, Violent Femmes, Nine Inch Nails, The Cure and Helmet. But really, the record's kinda limp, for the most part lethargic and depressing (see Rollins' irritating *Ghostrider* and STP's uneventful *Big Empty*). As usual, count on Pantera to wake everybody up, here ripping through Poison Idea's punk-basic *The Badge*, Helmet also propping up the catatonia with *Milktoast*. A curio but that's it, **The Crow** nowhere near deserving the sales it's attracting. Good to see awesome Toronto diva Jane Siberry getting around though.

Rating 6

## Various Artists - Demon Knight: Music From And Inspired By The Motion Picture (Atlantic '95)

The theme here might be hammerhead rockers gone off their rocker, as we get a batch of uncharacteristic tracks by heavy metal's new elite shoring up this **Tales From The Crypt** concept movie. Sure, *Beaten* by Biohazard is quintessential, hip-hop-stompin' Biohazard, and the Melvins spoil music like only they can with *Instant Larry*, but elsewhere, weirdness is afoot. Machine Head, Megadeth and Rollins Band offer weirdly laid-back, almost funky bluesy metal constructs, while Sepultura does a punk full-on mosh with *Policia*. And Ministry . . . well, let's just say they've got a lot of soul-searching to do before releasing that much ballyhoo'ed follow-up to **Psalm 69**. Kinda jammy and wastey like **The Crow** soundtrack, but on the upside, not all that commercial.

Rating 7

## Various Artists - Dragon Attack: A Tribute To Queen (DeRock '97)

By now you're probably getting used to these gather-all-ye-legends tribute records, most of them coming from hot new upstart DeRock. The sterling performances here are just too numerous to mention, although track selection is a little pedestrian. But like I say, a bunch of heavyweights turn many tracks downright thrilling, especially a nasty, downtowned *Sheer Heart Attack*, and Robin McAuley doing *I Want It All*, sounding the most like Freddie of the bunch. On the downside, the much lauded Lemmy/Nugent tagteam on *Tie Your Mother Down* is a fizzle, and *Another One Bites The Dust* is horrible music no matter who shows up. But tops of the lot: Yngwie tearing a strip off *Keep Yourself Alive*, and John Bush adding a warm twang to my fave Queenie track of all time, *It's Late*. Straight-played and of uniformly high quality, **Dragon Attack** contains few creative shocks, making for a pleasant and reverent visit to this most gravely important of rock institutions.

Rating 8

## Various Artists - For A Fistful Of Yens!

(Century Media '94)

Like the bio sez: 20 bands, 33 punk bop ditties spanning 70 minutes of stage-flop careers I ain't never heard of. These are the kinds of bands all those '90s punk

rockers might cite as influences, or vital contemporaries depending on which era you slice. Some catchy Green Offspring here, if the non-stop pogo jangle doesn't drive you silly by spread's end. Reminds me of "regional" punk from the early '80s, which I gather some of it is.

Rating 6

## Various Artists - Hard To Believe (C/Z Est. '91)

Subtitled "A Kiss Covers Compilation", **Hard To Believe** comprises fifteen covers by hip underground bands who, if they aren't technically Sub Pop, are fairly ensconced in that space philosophically with C/Z. Who wouldn't want to hear Skin Yard slog through *Snowblind*, or Melvins similarly corrode *God Of Thunder*, or Chemical People zip through *Rip It Out*, or the great Nirvana train wreck *Do You Love Me*? I for one would, but probably only once. Grim fact is, Kiss actually did a better job of most of these ditzy ditties, despite the time period in which they were first trotted out. No, **Hard To Believe** is the sludgy cool bunch yearning for drunken one-off irreverence, resulting in inept, badly-recorded, automatic run-throughs, sorta like, (although not as bad as) when annoying pensive pixies REM displayed their lack of musicality and balls botching *Toys In The Attic*. Hottest rendering: Smelly Tongues' *Parasite*.

Rating 5

## Various Artists - Heavy Metal: Music from The Motion Picture (Elektra '81)

The disappointing dope-smokin' celluloid from the frustrating sci-fi comic book of the same name just had to sport some rockin' tunes come soundtrack time. But all in all, this double record's a predictable, corporate bonehead compilation, originally slated to be all Blue Öyster Cult, then whittled down gradually to one song when the politics of the whole thing took over. However, a few gems emerge, including two non-LP'ers from Cheap Trick, warm lite rocker *Reach Out* and loopy, debut-style mongrel *I Must Be Dreamin'*, plus one previously unreleased Nazareth tune, *Crazy (A Suitable Case For Treatment)*, sort of a solid bluesy metallic thingy. Aside of those, and maybe Riggs' *Radar Rider* and Hagar The Terrible's *Heavy Metal*, not much else to get excited about.

Rating 5

## Various Artists - Heavy Metal Monsters (Cambra '85)

I mention this double Brit compilation due only to the inclusion of a few hilarious offbeat tunes from happy-go-losers Sledgehammer and Nightwing, especially the former's *Over The Top 1914*. The rest is Sabbath, Priest, Nazareth, etc. No big deal.

Rating 3

## Various Artists - Howard Stern Private Parts: The Album (Warner '97)

Trust our man Howard to keep us in stitches on his soundtrack record, the Yobbo of All Media alternating new and classic old music with chuckly knuckly snippets from his hit movie. But the effect is fleeting. Musically, there's Porno For Pyros' surprise hit *Hard Charger*, which sounds like naive art. Elsewhere there's average and tiring new music from Rob Zombie and Marilyn Manson, and an electrified doom version of Status Quo's *Pictures Of Matchstick Men* by a snarly Ozzy and unhumourous Type O Negative. Things really hit the crapper with Green Day's faithful walk through The Kinks' *Tired Of Waiting For You*. Crammed on the end, a disappointing assortment of grossly overplayed smashes by Cheap Trick, Deadly Tedly, Deep Purple and AC/DC (yawn!). So a bit for all, and not a lot of anything for one. But it does make a splendid taster for the movie, which is a scream.

Rating 5

## Various Artists - In Memory Of Celtic Frost
(Dwell '96)

Crawling out from various rock formations the world over, death's current domain have seen fit to pay tribute to one of black metal's major pioneers. And from the Giger-inspired cover art, through the excellent, detailed band history by Tomas Pascual, to the individual band bios, this is a pretty professional l'il pile of hate. Who the bands are is insignificant, most versions sticking to the clanky dank crux of who the Frosties were. What is kind of cool is noticing the difference in death songwriting these days, as the record takes you back to dark, grey simplistic patterns that often hook better than the speed, ambient and carnal crust of these bands' original material. Bigger bands included would be Opeth, Grave and notorious Norse hellions of Viking metal Enslaved, Emperor, and grandharpies of them all, Mayhem. A bruising, drilled and thrilled blast of sullen, sonic anti-serenity. Or something like that.

Rating 7

## Various Artists - In The Name Of Satan: A Tribute To Venom (Est. '94)

On this appropriately cellar-deep, underground, unnoticed and unloved tribute record, a burning raft of nighthowlers pay tribute to the originators of filthy black metal. And the record shows how much more extreme and stressed metal has become, many of these acts already known for sounding butt-uglier than Venom ever did. Heavy as a ten ton sledge, the record nevertheless offers little in the way of explanations. Crowning performer: the esteemed Skyclad.

Rating 6

## Various Artists - The Jerky Boys: Music From And Inspired By The Motion Picture (Atlantic '95)

Having constructed the two rip-roaringest, side-splittingest comedy records of the '90s, our fave fone terrorists make the transition to celluloid, requisite soundtrack cashgrab in tow, tough guy. Scattery, watery, pop punky, rappy and quite pointless, this slapdash nevertheless manages one gem in a sprightly, horns-a-poppin', Superfly version of Are You Gonna Go My Way, vocals courtesy of the so-far-out-he's-in Tom Jones. Elsewhere, Helmet's out-to-pasture Symptom Of The Universe wilts next to Sepultura's recent rendition, and the world is blessed with a lesson in old Green Day circa Kerplunk (sounds fun 'n' fluffy like famous Green Day). And that's all she wrote, fruitcake, or do we have to come down there and straighten you out?! Pass on it, ya Jerky!

Rating 5

## Various Artists - Johnny Mnemonic: Music From The Motion Picture (Sony '95)

Like the movie, this snobby soundtrack record comes off cold, technical, confusing and damning of the future. The bands here are the cutting edge of hard industrial, the newer second-string bands that in '95, are treated with as much awe as Internet providers and animation gurus, yet are rarely chosen for pleasurable play. So we get frustrating, vaguely itchy acts like Stabbing Westward, Cop Shoot Cop, KMFDM and God Lives Underwater, while Helmet and Rollins Band (Hank R's in the movie) are chosen to be exactly that same sort of irritating experience from the more traditional end of things. So what you get is a bunch of clanking, sullen noise purported to be the hip future of music, just like

the movie is supposed to make you fresh to the millennium. Both fail as entertainment.

Rating 5

## Various Artists - Judgment Night: Music From The Motion Picture (Epic '93)

My kinda rap! Big bone-crushing guitars in full collision with some of the nation's biggest rappers, in construction of a soundtrack record that is destined to last longer than the flick from whence it spills. Given that urban hardcore and rap are the bad boys of rock these days and given that both are enjoying a resurgence, this project functions as something vital and aggressive to behold, a glimpse at a future to come, underground cultures doubling over, under a twinned oral and sonic assault beratements from all barrels, as Helmet & House of Pain blaze through Just Another Victim, as Slayer & Ice T slash it up for Disorder and as Mudhoney & Sir Mix-A-Lot monster mash through Freak Momma. A tonic for the troops indeed, caustic, cutting and in your face to an extent rap could never accomplish without metal's might. On the lighter side, things slide into soup with Fallin' from Teenage Fanclub and De La Soul plus I Love You Mary Jane from Sonic Youth and chart-topping pot hoppers, Cypress Hill, making for an eccentric and jumpy chunk of metal funk that kicks. Bring the noise.

Rating 8

## Various Artists - Kiss My Ass (PolyGram '94)

Eminently less dangerous than C/Z's elusive Hard To Believe Kiss Tribute from '91 (featuring all sorts of fringe and future grunge stars), Kiss My Ass seemingly samples the entire musical spectrum, with an eclectic mix of household names and no names, haphazardly assembled under the puppeteering guidance of Gene himself. But they shoulda made this disposable like those cameras, because after one curious examination, I can't think of any reason to return, simply being reminded of how sick I am of these lite-weight compositions to which I grew up and grooved. The setlist sticks unimaginatively to over-plundered hits from way back (nothing newer than 1977), but most renditions veer off crazily (some into mere silliness), faves being Dinosaur Jr.'s sweetly turgid Goin' Blind, Lenny Kravitz' retro-funky Deuce and Extreme's cyber-funky Strutter. Garth Brooks and the Lemonheads on the other hand should be arrested for loitering. Like any joke, once is enough. Trust me.

Rating 5

## Various Artists - Last Action Hero: Music From The Original Motion Picture (Columbia '93)

The Terminator proves his most excellent taste in tunage here, the best soundtrack album since Bill and Ted II. Check out what's in tha house: What The Hell Have I and A Little Bitter, two killer acid rockers from Alice in Chains, Angry Again, a volcano-riffed mid-pacer from Megadeth, AC/DC's catchy radio hit Big Gun, one huge epic scorchfest from Anthrax, and a goth-tinged early '80s-style rocker from Tesla. Sure there's some commercial pap (man, Def Leppard are dummies), but it's worth the wade, what with the cutting edge of the industry circa '93 rising gloriously to the challenge with their lovingly burnt offerings.

Rating 7

## Various Artists - Live And Heavy (NEMS '81)

Grab your big ol' easychair and trash the thing whilst British compilation Live And Heavy fills it to the brim with a bunch of mostly (all?) previously released classics brought officially live (and unofficially doctored to various degrees) into your hovel of a home. Some of these tracks are widely available (e.g. UFO's Light's Out, Purple's Smoke On The Water), but I don't personally own (until now heh heh), Nazareth's *Razamanaz* from the Hammersmith Odeon, or Sabbath doing *Paranoid* in '73, or Rainbow doing *All Night Long* at Castle Donnington '80, or Gillan's frantic *Unchain Your Brain* from 1981. So I'm in Limey metal heaven here, y'unnerstand. Sleeve includes one live shot per headbangin' track.

Rating **8**

## Various Artists - Lost Highway Soundtrack
(Nothing/Interscope '97)

It's been a time elsewhere for weirdo movie maker David Lynch. So the guy comes back with his strangest yet, enlisting the services of king of all media Trent Reznor to create soundwaves to match Lynch's cinematic vision. The result is a morass of Tarantino-like road movie dribs and drabs, many traditional, many bolstered by electrics, these pieces then punctuated by fresh music from some of rock's shiniest luminaries. But these tracks are mostly sorta limp, one from the Pumpkins and two from Marilyn Manson sounding undercooked and undercoked. The much lauded Nine Inch Nails offering *The Perfect Drug* is pretty trippy, especially that wobbly manic drum riff, not to mention the absinthe-swilling video. But the best stuff are the two Rammstein tracks, which are both jagged, Ministry-like metal with German lyrics, sorta Hogan's Heroes meets Rob Zombie. Sum total: OK but no more, as a type of ambient, background experience. Perfect image: the back cover portraying a guy driving at night, radio probably on but not really listening.

Rating **6**

## Various Artists - Metal For Muthas  (EMI '80)

Pretty bad various album overall, but historically valid due to the inclusion of some ground zero Iron Maiden renditions of *Sanctuary* and *Wrathchild* (un-featuring soon-gone axeman Tony Parsons) and prehistoric Angelwitch behemoth *Baphomet*, a bleak, careening mud stomp through smoke-choked Hell, one of the band's roughest rides. Aside from these fossils and Ethel The Frog's nifty *Fight Back*, little else stands out, and indeed, some of it's got nothing to do with metal, betraying the fact that this release was so early, it actually pre-dates the actual concept of the coming British metal resurgence.

Rating **6**

## Various Artists - Metal For Muthas Volume II
(EMI Est. '81)

Big improvement over the disjointed and pre-understanding **Metal For Muthas**. Unfortunately none of these bands went anywhere, making this an unsuccessful attempt at garnering exposure. Coolest of the lot is Trespass, who offer forth the blistering *One Of These Days* and *Stormchild*. This band exemplifies the mystery and magic of early Brit gutter metal in the great tradition of Angelwitch, Savage and early Grim Reaper. Sadly missed. Other gems include Red Alert's punky *Open Heart* and Dark Star's melodic goth classic *Lady Of Mars*. **Metal For Muthas Volume II** embodied the excitement of the NWOBHM in its formative years and stands as one various album worth owning due to the obscurity and depth of the tunes enclosed.

Rating **7**

## Various Artists - Metal Killers Kollection Volume II
(The Collector Series '86)

One of those chaotic European dealies that contrasts old and new, Euro and North American, monster and obscure, for whatever ultimate purpose I don't know. For me, it tends to highlight how classic Raven and Accept really were, butted against all comers from any era. Most refreshing items: Teaze's *Boys Nite Out*, Hell's Belles kickin' *Wastin' Away*, a ferocious live ver-

sion of *Tragedy* from Hanoi Rocks, and Starz' fun-in-the-sun *Rock Six Times*. Personable band photos.

Rating **6**

## Various Artists - Metallic Storm  (Ebony '82)

Ebony was a wrenchingly rowdy metal label, and anything from house producer Darryl Johnston promises to at minimum, melt the flesh from one's face. So **Metallic Storm**'s got some stirring NWOBHM stuff sporting that trademark, messed-up Ebony crustytone sound courtesy of a surprising slew of no names. Contains an early take on Mercyful Fate's *Black Funeral* and a whole pile of bitchin' band names like Tarot Sutra, Wikkyd Vikker and Pentapus. God bless.

Rating **5**

## Various Artists - Metal Massacre 4  (Metal Blade '83)

As I write, I am amazed I'm hearing a CD reissue of this thing. Surely there must be better stuff in the vaults (although after the latest rash of reissues, they must be cleaned out but good). Anyways, 4 is just more of the same blue collar Maiden bullshit, except for *The Last Judgement*, a lost Trouble track that is trashy, brilliant and nuts.

Rating **4**

## Various Artists - Metal Massacre VI  (Metal Blade '85)

More rust belt brutecore from the crank 'em out folks at Metal Blade. Unlike many other compilations, it looks like very few of these are destined to become collectors items over time, given that there ain't too many acts here that have become limo-lounging rock stars. File under exuberant and in love with the metalness of the mid-'80s. Biggest fish: Nasty Savage, Dark Angel and The Obsessed.

Rating **5**

## Various Artists - Metal Massacre VII  (Metal Blade '85)

Yet another from a long line of putrid Brian Slagel various projects (which, granted, brought Metallica to vinyl for the first time), tire-iron #7 punishes the listener with all kinds of laughable U.S. metal with shite production. Cuts of note include Krank's *Rented Heat* and the choice driving riffery of Mad Man's *Backstabber*. Generally studded with garbage, turning this worse than average as a various album, although hats off to Slagel for keeping the flame alive, slab after slab.

Rating **3**

## Various Artists - Metal Militia: A Tribute To Metallica  (Black Sun '94)

Pretty funny that this underground homage to the masters picks such old tracks. Funny that is, until you listen to this a week after **Load**, realizing how good Metallica once, and how smarmy they've now become. Anyhow, **Metal Militia** showcases twelve largely unknown acts doing innovative things with amazing classics, Luciferion speeding up *Fight Fire With Fire* (even at original speed, the fastest song on the record), Pagandon slowing *Battery* to a rap metal groove, and Idiot's Rule turning *For Whom The Bell Tolls* into a female-vocaled power ballad. Elsewhere it's mostly a death-metalized, grindcored conversion, always well-recorded, and hey, really quite entertaining for the rabid fan (count me in). Cover mimics **Kill 'Em All** with what looks like a plastic hammer busting a jam jar.

Rating **7**

## Various Artists - Nativity In Black - A Tribute To Black Sabbath  (Columbia '94)

This blown chunk of electric Hell sends that **Kiss My Ass** tribute whimpering home to Pete The Cat but fast and feline, the project's masterminds lining up a killer clan of Sab worshippers for quite possibly the finest

one of these gizmos to date. Whether you'll care much after about a week is another story, but on that first initial spin with trembling, curious fingers, one will find mostly raving lunatized send-ups of our favorite Wicked Worldmen. Negatives first: 1,000 Homo DJs' *Supernaut* (uncreative industrial), Ozzy and Therapy?'s *Iron Man* (embarrassing to both parties), and Ugly Kid Joe's *N.I.B.* (both dull and old). Positives: most the rest, especially Bruce Dickinson and Godspeed's *Sabbath Bloody Sabbath* (daring choice well-executed), COC's *Lord Of This World* (where did that six pack go?), and of course White Zombie's nutty butt-crushing *Children Of The Grave* (so, so heavy; samples included!). Twelve well-paced tracks, still a little obvious in tune choice, but a few surprises just the same (thanks, Biohazard). Grave omissions? *Dirty Women* by L7, *Hole In The Sky* by Last Crack, *Children Of The Sea* by The Waterboys, *Over And Over* (pick either AC/DC or Ramones), *Sweet Leaf* by The Screaming Trees, *Disturbing The Priest* by Fight, and *In For The Kill* by Budgie. Otherwise, hey . . . B.S., we love it!
Rating     8

## Various Artists - New Electric Warriors   (Est. '81)
Don't remember much about this pioneering various record as I traded it away eons ago. What I do recall is its bevy of of to-the-quick barroom metal highballs by an array of no-name entertainment combos from the first days of the illustrious NWOBHM, with easily five or six attention-grabbing scorchers. Totally worth owning for historical reasons.
Rating     6

## Various Artists - New York Metal-84   (Rockcity '84)
Highlights: Takashi's Kiss-like *Live To Rock*, Teazer's chuggin' *Day Zero* and Jack Starr's cheesy *Guitar War '84* axe killer solo. Only band to crawl out of these brutal trenches: Overkill who offer *Feel The Fire*. Album "art": metal vixen with rivethead in handcuffs, chains, and diapers.
Rating     4

## Various Artists - Nordic Metal: A Tribute To Euronymous   (Necropolis '95)
If you care about the church-burning Norwegian black metal scene at all (at minimum, it's a pretty fascinating story), then this is an excellent place to get a survey of the bands involved. This compilation is a tribute to the originator of the scene Euronymous (murdered by rival Count Grishnackh), who along with "Typhon" was the force behind trying to put together a compilation on the scene in the first place. So Typhon has finally completed the project, culling the listenable and the unlistenable, the ambient and the grindcored, the slow and the insanely speedy, emerging with a record that is more entertaining than any one Norse scourge could ever be, halfways cool because of all the variety. But the best part of this is the 24 page booklet with essays on the scene, the man, the beliefs, short quotes, lots of photos and detailed bios on all the facepainted freaks involved. Like I say, quite the little history lesson into this wild, wild corner of metal. Bands included: Abruptum, Mayhem, Dissection, Emperor, Mysticum, Marduk, Thorns, Ophthalamia, Enslaved, Arcturus and Mortiis.
Rating     6

## Various Artists - 100% Pure Metal Sampler
(Roadrunner '84)
Roadrunner was the least discriminating of the small labels during the mid-'80s signing frenzy, and this low-priced compilation painfully highlights the label's ineptness. Although the Euro-tech Mad Max, the legendary Mercyful Fate, semi-moshers Jaguar, and cementheads Blackout somehow stumbled their way into the Roadrunner fold, the rest of this record displays some of the

trop that would be forever doomed to obscurity, hogswallow such as Battleaxe, Dark Heart, Spartan Warrior and Samain making me chortle heartily at what metal used to be. Useless label with useless ears.
Rating     3

## Various Artists - Righteous Metal II   (K-tel '91)
While the unchosen are out getting swilled and smoking choice recreational herbs, the White Metal vanguard must be at home welding their acts, judging by this purely pro piece of pulpit rock. Sure it's '91 product and thus expected to be slick, but this is pleasantly scientific, packed with techno-speed, impressive goth, fresh ideas, and crowning mixes. Godly highlights include Jet Circus' rappin' *Victory Dance*, Novella's *Do We Just Surrender*, Believer's *Nonpoint* and especially X-Sinner's *Livin' On The Edge*. Hard to take with any semblance of gravity, but still, not as clueless as one might expect, given Christian metal's hysterical image.
Rating     6

## Various Artists - Singles: Original Motion Picture Soundtrack   (Warner Bros. '92)
Saw the flick, liked it, wish I lived in Seattle. Anyways, enough bitchin', the soundtrack rules, but I gotta say, the biggest thing this does for me is reinforce my growing respect for Soundgarden. Mudhoney may be the true gut of the Seattle sound, but Soundgarden is its brain. Here they torch the house with *Birth Ritual*, a carousing cruncher soaking up the spirit of **Master Of Reality**, releasing any demons still unexpunged after the band's cover of *Into The Void*. Elsewhere, some well-worn Paul Westerberg (the 'mats rule!), two disappointing offerings from Pearl Jam, a haunting acoustic from Chris Cornell, Alice in Chains' half-cool *Would?* and a not surprisingly crusty Mudhoney earache called *Overblown* which could have just as easily been called Overtowed or Under Town. Rounding it out: The Lovemongers, Mother Love Bone, Hendrix, seminal Northwest underdogs Screaming Trees, and an infectious bass mantra from Smashing Pumpkins.
Rating     7

## Various Artists - Smoke On The Water: A Tribute
(Shrapnel '94)
This tribute trend has got a hold of Shrapnel, who release this simultaneously with one studying Cream, a band you won't find in this heavier than dairy products tome. **Smoke** is almost like a re-recording of some of Purple's best tracks, as a jaded and traveled backing band of Deen Castronova, Jens Johansson, Todd Jensen and Russ Parrish support various guitar and vocal perfectionists bent on utmost realism. In many ways, these are improvements on the originals, better grooves, recordings and astonishingly better ways at being Gillan by virtually all ten vocalists. Besides the unavoidable hits, **Smoke** includes some welcome choices, *Speed King*, *Stormbringer*, *Rat Bat Blue* and *Fireball* all being fine but often overlooked heft-rockers. The theme here is metal technicians who perhaps had their greatest moments in the '80s, guys like Winger, Yngwie, Glenn Hughes, Dokken, Paul Gilbert, who you know will do a solid and sincere, if not adventurous job. Retro but technologically flawless production from Mike Varney.
Rating     7

## Various Artists - Sonic Obliteration Vol. 1
(Utopian Vision '95)
Toronto writer, metal expert, Slav brother and now Black Mark label exec for North America Ed Balog has put together this vast compilation under his own imprint, in his never-ending quest to spread the word on underground metal. So **Sonic Obliteration** cranks out a stunning thirty tracks by 27 bands from all over

the world, delivering thrash to death to traditional, much of it with interesting industrial leanings. Contact addresses are provided, photos for pretty much everyone, and even a whole swack of lyrics. The perfect shopping guide for labels looking for fresh meat, which I guess is in tune with Balog's quest to galvanize the world in massive metal tones. Hail!

Rating 7

## Various Artists - Sonic Obliteration Vol. 2
(Black Mark '97)

From high upon the offices of Black Mark North America, metal mobster Ed Balog surveys a metal scene crashed in flames, picking the crushers from the dogpile and giving them some much-needed exposure. Thus the second of his uncompromising, futuristic compilations is born, giving us such manic mechanic metal as promising Toronto bands Jaww and Solus, plus others from this frozen land and beyond. All tunes are punishing, angular, but methodical, in true metaphoric extension of Balog's own foreboding persona (just kidding. After all, Ed runs the Cranberries and Spice Girls fan clubs in Canada, also providing back-up vocals for long-time galpal Toni Braxton).

Rating 7

## Various Artists - Spacewalk: A Salute To Ace Frehley (DeRock '96)

Pretty bizarre dontcha think? Whatever. I mean what we have here is a considerable gathering of metal stars oggling their great white hope (little skill, big star), playing a level-headed, exquisitely recorded (in L.A. and New York) collection of Ace solo and Ace Kiss tracks, nicely done but who cares? Some names: Marty Friedman, Gilby Clarke, Scott Travis, Scott Ian, Ron Young, Jeff Watson, Jason McMaster, Snake Sabo, Seb Bach, Tracii Guns, John Norum, Bruce Bouillet, Dimebag Darrell and Vinnie Paul. One of three Kiss tribute albums in this book, and probably the least imaginative and most enjoyable.

Rating 7

## Various Artists - A Tribute To Judas Priest, Legends Of Metal (Century Media '96)

This is quite the stellar line-up linin' up to pay their respects to one of the most important bands in metal. But even though 3/4 of the bands play it quite straight (including the usually fruitcaked Devin Townsend), Testament (Rapid Fire), U.D.O. (Metal Gods) and Mercyful Fate (The Ripper) put smile-cracking personal stamps on the material, especially King Diamond, who gives us one of his most majestic vocal performances ever. The record's worth it for this lusty track alone, Fate demonstrating that they carry the Priest flame brighter and higher than all others. Second bonus: photos of all bands, full discography, and lyrics to everything.

Rating 7

## Various Artists - U.S. Metal (Shrapnel '81)

Something called Chumbi kicks off with a nuts-in-a-vice title track that will commence a long raft of showcase records assembled by Shrapnel boss Mister Mike Varney, a series that serves more as testimony to failed ambitions, most bands featured going nowhere fast. Best here are No Time by Gilles-Meblin Assault and Rockin' Disease by Toyz, with marks going to Shrapnel loafabouts The Rods for the best mix, not surprising, Feinstein and crew being the lone heavyweights on this surprisingly "with it" early NWOUSHM document.

Rating 3

## Various Artists - U.S. Metal Vol. III (Shrapnel '83)

More Stryper meets Ethel The Frog as Varney continues to trumpet the cause of six-string charity cases across the wide and baffled U.S. of A. Mixes are again acceptable as we get a handful of future LP makers like Hawaii, Wild Dogs, and again The Rods, who offer one of their better monoliths in Hot City. Seriously, no real improvement on the raft that comprised the first U.S. Metal two years back.

Rating 3

## Various Artists - U.S. Metal Vol. IV (Shrapnel '84)

Highlights here include early Keel, TKO, more Wild Dogs, goth gallop Dark Sun from Scanner, and the almost Helstar-crossed high-reg chaos of Aggressor's Predator. Still, it's '84, and all in all, it's a jumbled but well-meaning pile of cack, although some of these tracks would definitely sit well in the context of a uni-bandito'ed full-length studio project.

Rating 4

## Various Artists - Violent World: A Tribute To The Misfits (Caroline '97)

With punk riding high for no good reason, it was inevitable that someone would dredge the memory of Glenn Danzig's old band The Misfits. So the maroons reformed (sans Mighty Mite), and Caroline gathered the '90s benefactors of the Misfits' schtick to pay tribute. Funny how the material used is both unremarkable as, and indistinguishable from the fodder used to make Epitaph wealthy in '96, bands like Pennywise, Snapcase, Goldfinger, NOFX and Sick Of It All gathered to noise-make to no discernible advantage. Braying, uneventful material remains just that, when braying, uneventful bands are asked to interpret. Fourteen songs, thirty minutes (wasted). Tip for morons: there is indeed such a thing as interesting, dynamic punk: it's called heavy metal.

Rating 4

## Various Artists - Wayne's World: Music From The Motion Picture (Warner '92)

Once past oggling at the CD case in rapt curiosity at the pre-release of Sabbath's Time Machine, the soundtrack to our Life becomes just another scattered Hollyrock collection of signals. Painful covers of Ballroom Blitz and less so Rock Candy, some twangy Cinderella and amusingly, Gary Wright's lazy '70s hit Dream Weaver. The movie was a scream, really, damn near the original blueprint for our teen years, but the soundtrack is nowhere as party-focused as to what Wayne and Garth would really have assembled themselves. Hats off, though for propelling Bohemian Rhapsody vigorously chart-bound once again, the famous, dead-perfect car scene being at least 1/4 responsible for the latest re-examination of Queen's blinding brilliance.

Rating 4

## Various Artists - Wayne's World 2: Music From The Motion Picture (Warner '93)

Another high impact cinematic experience, but another way too corporate soundtrack, a bunch of nostalgic old hits, new up and comers, plus two live Aerosmith tracks, and Robert Plant doing a fresh Louie, Louie. Get Beavis And Butt-head instead.

Rating 4

## Various Artists - Working Man (Magna Carta '96)

Magna Carta and DeRock are the undisputed champions of classy tribute records. But Magna Carta is strictly progressive, giving us a truly godly Yes tribute, plus ones for Floyd, Genesis and Tull. This one swirled in controversy, Rush not wanting to see release because of their (unwarranted) opinion that a tribute means you're washed up (actually, Test For Echo enforces that argument more lustily). Working Man is as clean, clear and crisp as Rush would have done themselves, Magna Carta enlisting solid chops-hair-band-types to do the deed, guys like Eric Martin, John Petrucci, Billy

Sheehan, Jake E. Lee, Mark Slaughter, Dean Castronovo, Fates Warning, and Canuckers Baz and Jamie Labrie assembling in makeshift collectives to equal Rush's faculties and in many cases, exceed them. So it's thoroughly progged nicely, like a remastered, intensively detailed and layered upgrade on the originals. No real surprises (these songs hardly allow interpretation), but that warm, fuzzy tribute feeling is indeed felt, said glow brightened by the pair of intelligent, lauditory essays included for Trekstalgia effect.

Rating                                                                 7

## Vendetta - Vendetta   (Epic '82)

Not to be confused with the German obliteratos of the same name, Vendetta was an early American outfit led by Nikki Buzz, now (or at least nine years ago), of M80. This was a solid though not outstanding, well-recorded, straight-forward riff-rocker, kind of like a Coney Hatch record; simple, weighty, immobile and middling. Wish I had it now but I kinda doubt I'll ever see it again. (Note: A month after first writing this, I did see it again, for three bucks, and I didn't buy it). Original grade: **5**.

Rating                                                                 4

## Vendetta - Go And Live ... Stay And Die
(Maze Music '88)

Extremely tight, vaguely Slayer-ish German power metal with strained shout-vocals mixed a ways back, **Go And Live ...** is full of long, dense metallic opuses that just slowly pummel the energy out of the listener. Too many fast ones bordering on thrash, too many riffs, and too much to handle. So heavy it's funny, typical of Maze's roster of thick, chopsy bands with at least a minimum degree of talent.

Rating                                                                 4

## Vengeance - Vengeance   (CBS '84)

A proud and menacing slab of Attitude metal from Holland poised to kick ass worldwide, **Vengeance** is stacked and full of liquored-up abandon on this loud cranker of corporately potential proportions. Can't help thinking of fellow CBS hopefuls Pretty Maids, who possess that same riffic and reverent enthusiasm for accessible decibels; that infectious drive to win larger audiences while remaining true to their Saxon/Priest/Dio-type roots; most notably Saxon, whose crown jewel **Power & The Glory** rides the same high strung heroics as this sustained "live feel" smoker, not to mention the fact that vocalist Leon Goewie is a dead ringer for Biff. Much more "of the earth", street wise, and inebriated than the only other Vengeance I've sampled, '88's white, neat and clean **Take It Or Leave It**. Missing in action: their second, **We Have Ways Of Making You Rock**, and their fourth, **Arabia**.

Rating                                                                 7

## Vengeance - Take It Or Leave It   (CBS '88)

This Dutch entry into the no-mistakes sweepstakes rocks with surprising impotence and lack of direction, reversing the jets on the slurring heroic wonder that was the '84 debut. Stumbling blindly between heavier HR and metal, Vengeance seems the corporate dream; Tight, technically adept and hooky, the band nevertheless suffers from its America fixation, trying desperately to capture the essence of heavier commerce metal, finding instead mediocrity borne of its fear to sleaze and take risks. Wholly lacking in the killer instinct (the band admitting to being desperate for a hit), **Take It Or Leave It** is quietly swept to the rear by the vast legions of uglier, hungrier, take-charge wannabes on the beat, bands that shove themselves in our faces, know they've got five minutes to make an impression, and burst their vessels taking their shot. Here, the band's sound becomes mere, fey and stiff, like a tech-

nical version of commercial Priest, stunted by an electronic and lifeless mix and rigid writing, proving that there is such thing as selling out. To be fair, **Take It Or Leave It** does occasionally find Accept (see the panzer-driven **Hear Me Out** and slow daze **Women In The World**), but the sum total is merely clinical and lacklustre.

Rating                                                                 6

## Venom - Welcome To Hell   (Banzai '81)

The putrid initial burnt offering from the accounting firm of Lant, Dunn and Bray reeled 'em in by openly knock, knock, knockin' on Beelzebub's forked gate. Once inside, Venom invents a new phenomenon: the garage coven. Sloppy drumming, anti-Christ vocal mutterings, and horrid mixes to conceal said shortcomings are the order of the slobbery sabbath. No denying that Venom, talentless as a wet bag of hammers that they were, had a prime part in the invention of both black metal and thrash, although thrash more in the sense of mental obliteration rather than speed. To messed-up limey earthdogs, Venom was the ultimate flag of anarchy and hate, the legendary live shows being the ultimate amorphous mass of confused rebellion on any given Friday night (well maybe not that often: the expense of the Venom presentation made gigs rare and legendary). To the English, Venom was their own sinister Kiss abortion gone very wrong, the annihilation of sound—and swear to God, many a leather-clad mutant claimed to like their music. **Welcome To Hell**'s got a certain fabulously stupid forward impetus to it, despite the sub-bootleg quality recording, and Cronos quickly establishes himself as the most annoying voice in rock. Not the band's most listenable product of on-purpose filth, yet a record of historical metal relevance on par with the Sex Pistols effect on punk (well, not quite).

Rating                                                                 5

## Venom - Black Metal   (Banzai '82)

An album many a masochist consider the most quintessential Venom swillage, **Black Metal** is muddier and more lyrically Satanic than the debut, also somehow unleashing Mantas' axe genius, which rears its head infrequently and briefly throughout this awful but hilarious sonic hole. A few individual "compositions" climb from the muck, most notably stumble-frash anti-anthem Leave Me In Hell, the driving riffery of Don't Burn The Witch, and one of Venom's most scorching and twisted marks on mankind, Countess Bathory, an enduring classic of Baphomet vomit. When you've given up on life, there's Venom and Venom alone, which is perhaps the only reason for this agonizing carcass of noise to exist, for it was widely believed in metal circles that Venom is your only friend after you've downed that twentieth and damnation deciding brew.

Rating                                                                 7

## Venom - At War With Satan   (Banzai '84)

Inna Godda Da Vidda for Satanists! At last the epic battle between good and evil is re-fought. The noise and stench is overpowering and guess what? Nobody wins! After the title track subterfuging the entire first side at a merciless 19:52, who could absorb any more mercury poisoning? Well, Venom oblige like a rabid pharmacist, with six additional slabs of garbage dump filth; most horrific and pervertedly pleasurable of course being decipherable mid-pacers Cry Wolf and Stand Up And Be Counted. Actually, **At War With Satan** is one of the better Venom albums, if looking deep within the sewers of rock is your idea of party-time. The recording is almost tolerable in a filmy, hungover manner of speaking, and the choice of anti-songcraft, including the consistently sick and wonderful At War With Satan, is fairly high percentage. A loveable mess of sludge, this,

Venom's third abortion, signs off with a neck-snapping slugfest aptly titled *AAAARGHHHH* which again presents our favourite lepers enjoying the last wheezing cackles as they fumble through your wallets.

Rating      **7**

## Venom - Canadian Assault   (Banzai '85)

Finally, a band that sounds as good on a live record as in the studio. Of course with Lant, Dunn, and Bray, that's because the studio albums sound as if they're recorded with a dictaphone in the nosebleed section of your local hockey barn. **Canadian Assault** comprises three new studio tunes, plus three live scars, further driving home the point that in fact it makes no difference. Sounds like three or four layered tracks of out-of-tune guitar in trademark "vacuum cleaner with drums" fashion. Highlights: *7 Gates Of Hell* and the wistful, suspended *Warhead*.

Rating      **4**

## Venom - Possessed   (Banzai '85)

Providing more of the same thrash swill as on the last couple slabs, with a similar intense disdain for sound quality, **Possessed** is a perverted mess of tangled cables, rusted-out oil drums, and industrial toxins, a blunt instrument with which to punish fan and cynic alike, while simultaneously transforming fans into cynics. Sickeningly black metal, with indiscernible riffs further clouded by basslines seemingly slapped down in another key, most of it sounds like my blow dryer. Yet again, when the drunken goofs slow down in search of groove, more times than not a grotesque riff swells forth causing glorious blood-boiling havoc, such as enjoyed on *Harmony Dies*, *Suffer Not The Children*, and two of Venom's most righteous paint-strippers ever, *Flytrap* and *Hellchild*. **Possessed** was alcohol-induced (or at least inducing) proof that after four albums, Venom still couldn't care less about production or progression, that in fact, the death of music was their aim all along. And guess what? People noticed, the rabble finally revolting in minor fashion, slowing the band's previously unchecked commercial and critical forward mass.

Rating      **5**

## Venom - Calm Before The Storm   (Filmtrax '87)

**Calm Before The Storm**, originally dubbed Deadline, is the first of what so far total four "modern era" Venom projects, that is to say records few and far between temporally, lacking in much marketing hoopla or interest from a previously abused legion of earthdogs. Gone is the blatant black metal imagery. In fact, my copy lacks imagery period, sporting a dumb black and white cover, no lyrics, and no pics of the band, which has Mantas replaced by two new possessors of the same inferior equipment. The production, vocals, and loose 'n' pissed delivery is age-old diseased Venom. But there *is* a bit more variety stylistically, even hints of melody in some of the choruses such as those almost rescuing *Under A Spell* and *Beauty And The Beast*, although the attempts sound terrible, nobody spending even five minutes learning the harmonies. Cronos is as grating as ever with his tortured troll routine, and also as usual, the odd obliterating riff cokes up the proceedings as on—you guessed it—the mid-pacers such as *Black Xmas*, *The Chanting Of The Priests*, and the almost ambitious title toon. In short, another mudfest à la early Venom in every way except for the down-playing of previous overt Satanism and the preponderance this time of more chunky mid-paced trashabilly.

Rating      **7**

## Venom - Prime Evil   (Under One Flag '89)

Venom perform an about face for '89 with their first almost-clean and fer-sure powerful bottom end ever. **Prime Evil** opens with fax machine tones offering the first clues that Venom has decided to adopt new technologies. Much of the demented songcraft resembles Venom of old, yet without a doubt, this is the band's most smoked collection of songs. About half the OTT sucks, still being the eternal simplified thrash fare for which Venom is notorious. But speedcore aside, **Prime Evil** is a dense and bludgeoning document of black thought; expressing frenzy, power, and chaos in ways the Venom philosophy always succeeded in doing, and the recorded product did not. And the force is further amplified by the vocals which are more dead-serious and angry than ever (note: sounds like Cronos; sleeve sez it's "The Demolition Man"). Fave slabs are the psychotic portrayal of Sabbath's already drilled and insane *Megalomania*, taking on new opacity due to Mantas' legendary cement-caked guitar sound, *Blackened Are The Priests*, an almost progressive hymn of evil that exploits the riff-mutating genius of madman Mantas, and the title tune, a heaping monolith of pain not unlike slow Angel Witch. Venom comprises four guys on **Prime Evil** as on its predecessor, but makes noise like ten as they often have. Yet for once in their sick catalogue, they're all playing the same song. Apparently at this point, Mantas is increasingly extricating himself from the band, wishing to remain involved with recording only.

Rating      **8**

## Venom - Temples Of Ice   (Under One Flag '91)

Back in the olden golden days, they used to call this thrash, but since the rise of ludicrously intensified grind and death, we have to revert to old tags like OTT, most of **Temples Of Ice** scurrying along, boozed-up and bent on reliving past messy crashes. Indeed, the band sounds like they're operating on hurry-up offence, riffing almost punk-like (well, Tank-like then) throughout this wizened old coot of a thrasher, reviving proud and scuzzy British traditions, including bad album covers with cheezy Zapf Chancery typestyles. Even the lyrics revert to an era where sci-fi monsters, bad girls and Hell did the dogpile, making Venom the likeable joke they always were. Weightless but chaotic, truly in psychic synch with Venom's age-old "death to all braincells" credo. Contains an appropriately off-the-rails version of Purple's *Speed King*.

Rating      **7**

## Venom - The Waste Lands   (Under One Flag '92)

I know it's a dreary way to peg a CD, but **The Waste Lands** is basically yer crooked cross between **Temples Of Ice** and **Prime Evil**: trashy, shoot 'em up speed metal with a darker, murkier, lurkier mix; of the blackened trinity, **Prime Evil** still ruining the day, despite some very strong, almost noble tracks here. But have ye fear, **The Waste Lands** is still a creepy crank, an ill wind blowing through the '90s, curmudgeoned and obstinate, wallowing in mud and low budget pride of ownership. There's still some anti-life in these black leather Munsters, despite another totally counter-productive album cover. Foist ye a hearty draft, for the unrepentant and undying destructors of music.

Rating      **7**

## Venom - Skeletons In The Closet   (Griffin '94)

In the true spirit of an odds and sods collection, **Skeletons** offers no exact LP tracks, scoring a bunch of bassy, boomy sludgy remixes and about four previously unreleased tracks depending on how you count 'em. Interspersed are tour intro tapes and radio ad snippets, making this a crazy-ass mish-mash of smells and sounds. Of the four inebriated new ones (*Dead On Arrival*, *Hounds Of Hell*, *Bitch Bitch*, and *Sadist*), *Bitch Bitch* is probably the clearest-thinking, although who's counting? In total, a very bludgeoning, bass-heavy version of Lucifer's favorite clowns.

Rating      **6**

## Venom - In Memorium: The Best Of Venom
(Griffin '95)

**In Memorium** is probably the best Venom compilation to scorch the earth, given its most official status, featuring five pages of essays by Malcolm Dome and Greg Moffitt, a few pictures and track-by-track liner notes by Abbadon himself. So trust the perverted good taste of Griffin to secure and reissue this, sort of an evil twin to the **Skeletons In The Closet** CD released in '94, which overlaps this one by about a third, not recognizing remixes. Choice potatoes of the present release: those first three fateful demo tracks from 1980 (I've had better results with one mic recording on a ghetto blaster in the middle of my parents' rec room), the non-LP semi-hits (huh?) *Warhead* and *Manitou*, a few of the cornerstones of the Venom legacy in *Black Metal*, *Welcome To Hell* and *Countess Bathory* (bashed out live), two unreleased tracks from the *Calm Before The Storm* sessions (I really can't see Venom having "sessions"), and a couple of newer (i.e. '91), unreleased numbers in *If You Wanna War* and *Surgery*. All the previously unreleased tracks are fun, fun, fun, harkening back to metal circa 1982, cruddy Venom mix and all; belching, boiling troll vocals intact, offering forbidden tales of woe, as only Venom can imagine. A worthy addition to the Venom virus clogging your collection, given the vault-cleaning.
Rating 7

## Joey Vera - A Thousand Faces (Metal Blade '94)

After the break-up of Armored Saint, bassist Joey Vera goes it alone with this normal, vocals album, a hard one to pin, given its plainly stated hard rockers, acoustic structures, and introspective, occasionally religious themes. One quickly thinks a G-rated version of the Gunners' solos mixed with a sort of Ted Nugent guitar bravado, very solo and alone sounding, commercial although at the same time committing various forms of commercial suicide. Very light on the touch, **A Thousand Faces** attracts a sort of admiration but no wild and leaping praise, rounding the '80s metal purist bases with a cold intellectual loftiness, while keeping arrangements simple, but production up-scale. Fave would be the somewhat Jimmy Page-ish *Song Of Doubt*, with its Lou Reed-style intro and subsequent smooth vocal delivery. While this most likely satisfies Vera's creative urges, I can't see it selling too many pancakes, outside of the scant gathering of Saint-heads that might want to peer into the man's sincere and moral thought processes.
Rating 6

## Verity - Interrupted Journey (Compleat '84)

**Interrupted Journey** is a warm, unassuming, hard-edged but unheavy rock'n'roller which variously evokes images of Foghat, Foreigner, Russ Ballard, Derringer, even Mama's Boys at times. Ex-Argent dude John Verity and his wily band of veterans have come up with a warmed vibration that combines commercial American hard rock with wizened British defeat. It's the kind of stuff that sounds a bit too naive and retro to make it big, but can still grab attention with great harmonies, hooky choruses, and punchy playing. The most convincing tunes are the heavy ones such as *Rescue Me*, *Are You Ready For This*, and *Chippin' Away At The Stone*, but it pretty well all works. An unpretentious charmer.
Rating 8

## Veto - Veto (Scratch Est. '86)

No denying that Scratch product virtually all crashes and crunches with that amazing Germanic numbness and soulcraft we've all grown to love and fear. Like Gravestone, Veto pounds fast and pounds slow, with successful forays into Scorpions-like hard rock. Man alive though, the first thing one always notices with this particular rich vein of ore is the overwhelming power afforded by a Scratch recording, which just cooks the componentry of metal to a blistering potency of a level rarely survived. Veto do the sound proud, although Liebhäuser's voice would really rock the house given a bit more abandon at the high end as per rousing album closer *Join The Band*. Scratch proves itself to be one of the most solid and consistent recording organizations of the mid '80s once more, scaring the dead heavily with this hair-raising German attack. Vital and destructive of the soul.
Rating 7

## The Vibrators - Pure Mania (CBS '77)

As previously mentioned, I just gotta pay homage to a handful of original punk bands in this book because, sonically speaking, punk was just bad metal. **Pure Mania** was the first punk album I ever bought and it is definitely that: bad metal. Tight and tiny, hilariously British gangland punk rife with soccer chants, **Pure Mania** is a slightly heavier but much less important version of The Clash's ground-breaking debut, released in and around the same time. The Vibes actually sounded like a metal version of Nick Lowe, suspiciously poppy, as if punk was a bandwagon to milk for what it was worth. A controversial name and some chaotic wardrobe choices and it was off to The Roxy. Grimy little metal tunes like *Into The Future . . .* , *Yeah, Yeah, Yeah*, *No Heart*, *Petrol*, and *Wrecked On You* owe more to some strange hybrid of The Ramones, The Pink Fairies, and power pop than to actual punk sentiments making this a unique and likeable guitar oddity from rock's past. Confused? So are The Vibrators.
Rating 7

## The Vibrators - V2 (CBS '78)

**V2** marks a more accomplished and varied approach to The Vibrators' unique-by-default brand of power pop/punk/metal, sounding more like mid-period, medium-quality Damned. Still very English and overcast, but tight and buoyant, **V2** offers fleshed-out ideas on such simple guitar rockers as *Wake Up*, *Destroy*, and *Pure Mania*, and more metallic noiseniks like *War Zone*, *Nazi Baby* and tribal dirge *Troops Of Tomorrow*. I don't want to mislead as to the heaviness of this thing. Indeed, any half-on-the-ball metalhead knows to be wary while mining for pre-'80 ore, especially punk, if heaviness is an important factor. Suffice to say that much of **V2** is mere unabashed, bar-wipe power pop, even if it can be considered weighty for punk in '78, despite its clean sound. Definitely versatile and interesting, well-recorded melodic punk with life and the weight of experience; darker than the debut but more ambitious.
Rating 7

## The Vibrators - Alaska 127 (RAM '84)

More a sludgy English mess of guitar-edged avant garde vs. the flat-out pogo punk of the first two, **Alaska 127** sounds like a sneering version of The Jam, or even XTC, yet with a boozy, druggy film à la Johnny Thunders or Knox side-project Fallen Angels; very rainy, industrial, and British and not very tuneful or open. Highlights include *Amphetamine Blue*, which was also on **Fallen Angels**, and *MX America*, *Punish Me With Kisses*, and *Jesus Always Lets You Down* which could have been. Kinda sleazy, grungy, crappy, disheveled but cool.
Rating 5

## Vicious Rumors - Soldiers Of The Night (Shrapnel '85)

As an inspiring triumph of talent over marketing, Frisco's Vicious Rumors (in my opinion a glammy, unrepresentative band moniker) was one act that survived the mid-'80s fallout, reputation intact. Debut **Soldiers Of The Night** is pre-signature vocalist Carl Albert, but the potent guitar fury of Vinnie Moore and founder Geoff Thorpe is already a force, melding stoked twin leads, crushing Accept-capable riffery, and a sense of electrified energy throughout this ultimately dated, but in context, top-flight underground poundcake. Temptation unto **7**, but too many Shrapnel-silly fast ones of exactly the same scampered, shout and reply ilk. Blame Exciter. Global warning: I'm probably harder on mid-'80s thrash than is deserved.

Rating 5

## Vicious Rumors - Vicious Rumors (Atlantic '90)

Hell, I probably like this one more than the follow-up, Carl Albert's vocal performance being one of his best, a dirtier, more muscular version of Geoff Tate's theatrical passion, as his band blows through chunky, focused, accessible power metal, that obviously limits saleability in the age of hair band proliferation. Again, one thinks Metal Church here, which places the band plagued as down-the-middle metalheads, prototypical headbangers. Mark McGee and Geoff Thorpe put on a helluva guitar show, recalling those great Scorpions, Priest and Dio breaks of old, just a touch of European engineering, lots of American brute force. But inane trop like *Hellraiser*'s gotta go.

Rating 6

## Vicious Rumors - Welcome To The Ball (Atlantic '91)

A kind of cult following exists for this band, much like any deserved following due to underlying undeniable quality inherent in the band's presentation. Call these guys a slightly more dated version of the majestic Metal Church; tight, tuneful power metal leaning Goth-ward, cheese-ward, and a little mid-'80s. Vocalist Carl Albert (sadly deceased in '95) leads with a total take-charge attitude, sounding like a blend of the Church's two throats, and the axework is Heavy Metal with a capital Hammer. Many a knowledgeable metalhead's favorite unfamous band.

Rating 6

## Vicious Rumors - Word Of Mouth (GTM '94)

By sticking to their guns, Vicious Rumors have become a working class champion of traditional, gothic power metal, for better or worse, many critics heaping praise upon the band with each record, then quietly admitting that their amour was short-lived and really not all that intense. **Word Of Mouth** makes only passing nods to the '90s, sounding fairly guttural, slower, more depressed and dirtier in spots, reminding me of other only slight modernizations made by bands like Flotsam And Jetsam and Testament. Relegated to indie status after an unceremonious dumping by Atlantic (GTM stands for Geoff Thorpe Management), with Thorpe contracting then beating carpal tunnel syndrome, not to mention suffering from the death of torrid throat Carl Albert, Vicious Rumors is a dedicated band on the ropes. The fact that this is their strongest, most song-stressed record is a bitter pill indeed. Oddly enough, with post-release tours of Japan and Europe, Thorpe figures this has been their best year yet business-wise, even without a deal. The D.I.Y. ethic still lives.

Rating 7

## Vicious Rumors - Something Burning (Massacre '96)

Geoff Thorpe has taken Vicious Rumors far away from its '80s ego metal roots, **Something Burning** being the manlegend's grungiest, most down-tuned, vocal-swallowed record yet. But what a lusty marriage of riff and sludge it is, tracks like *Out Of My Misery*, *Concentration* and *Perpetual* carving grooves as big, brown and sun-baked as the Grand Canyon. Slamming with sweaty pride start to finish, this is a starkly stripped Vicious Rumors, sod-busting along with the driving force of killer (*Killers*?), stonewalled guitar sonics, Thorpe bringing only a small basket of '80s ideas into

a stirring pile of buzzing inebriation, extremely down in the muck and loving it. Pretty much the most pummelled yet useful VR collection, of a catalogue that is generally high concept to begin with.

Rating 8

## Victor - Victor (Anthem '96)

Enter the dark, toiling, perturbed waters of Victor, the surprising solo band and record from Rush's Alex Lifeson, who decided to test himself rather than languish, during one of Rush's longest breaks, called due to a birth in the Lee family. The man has assembled a record that uses as its base, his usual watery guitar sound and attendant production values found on most of the watery Rush records from the '80s. But that, and the odd convoluted riff that sounds like heavy extreme Rush, is where the links to his snobby band end. **Victor** lashes out with snakey, disturbing patterns that somehow find a way of fusing this Rush-ness to slamming '90s conventions and the loopiness of both '70s and '80s King Crimson, finding both Belew and Fripp amongst Lifeson's versatile guitar voicings. The lyrics (Lifeson's first since *Making Memories* on **Fly By Night**!) are amazingly vital, charting the twisted, often tortured course of relationships, love into sex into hate and back again. Vocals are handled by himself, Edwin from I Mother Earth and Dalbello, sending the whole quite fascinating avalanche of sounds scattered into polar-dark, hard progressive realms. Guitar is somewhat muddily mixed in with all the other mooshed together sounds, much as it is with Rush, lending a real team feel to the sinister proceedings. Call this the suppressed, murderous tendencies lurking behind Rush, as if the heaviest compositions from **Counterparts** had descended into a life of fatalistic chaos. Quite the head trip. Mind nuggets: one track features Alex's wife and friend yapping (Alex yelling shut-up!), one guest-stars Les Claypool on bass, and the title track is a W.H. Auden poem put to music.

Rating 8

## Victory - Hungry Hearts (Metal Masters '87)

Ironically, **Hungry Hearts** tends to sound more big league, over-produced and less honest than the newer **Culture Killed The Native**. Herman Frank reveals here that he must have been subverting his commercial L.A.-ish tendencies in both Accept and his short-lived but fine Hazzard project. Who knows, maybe his eye to the bottom line could have someday made Accept the megastars they deserved to be. In any event, **Hungry Hearts** is one of those albums that once dissected, looks pretty good; confident, brash and professional, but without depth or staying power, working only on the level of superficial quality. Features generic and washed-up belter Charlie Huhn whose best days were spent with Terrible Ted.

Rating 5

## Victory - That's Live (Rampage '88)

Still a boot in the butt to see Charlie Huhn scratching out a living, and this record don't even sound live, but it don't sound like living either. Four from **Hungry Hearts**, and none from the newer **Culture**, so it adds to my collection just fine, although I still scratch my head at owning three Victory albums. Recorded in Hamburg.

Rating 6

## Victory - Culture Killed The Native (Rampage '89)

Quite low-down and weighty compared to **Hungry Hearts** but still melodic and completely American sounding, **Culture** is a strong, cock-sure rocker fueled by a powerful recording and swinging grooves that connect, reminding me somewhat of 220V's latter-day radio-friendly direction. Still, a bit aseptic and middling for what's supposed to be dangerous music. Better vocals than most stuff like this and the best impression of an L.A. sound (for better and mostly worse) by guys with funny German names.

Rating     6

## Victory - Temples Of Gold   (BMG '91)

Increasingly highly strung, Victory in the '90s is too quick to embrace technology, resulting in a trebly record, itchy with static electricity. In fact, the mix of metal, melodic hard rock and pop goth lends **Temples Of Gold** a feel reminiscent of early Def Leppard (both solo and harmony vocals included), with tight, clattery production values found all over hair band records. Really, this band has foregone carving an identity, opting for a sawed-off California rock sound with only vaguely European leanings, titles like *Backseat Rider*, *Hell And Back* and *Rock The Neighbours* doing little to dispel the rawk dog drear of the faltering Victory concept.

Rating     6

## Victory - You Bought It, You Name It   (BMG Germany '92)

Up. up and away, Victory's sound getting more stratospheric and edgy, now evoking a weezy '80s metal Tesla, zipping along quite briskly, squarely placed in metal versus the poser hard rock flirtations of previous spins. So solos, riffs and vocals are still of utmost elegance, even if the sum total is a bit on the theatrical side. Faves: *God Of Sound* and *Fool* which are regal cathedrals of clean-burning classical-based metal. Still, don't count me as much of a fan, finding the production too thin, slick and manufactured to support the weighty melodrama of the thing.

Rating     7

## Vinnie Vincent Invasion - Vinnie Vincent Invasion
(Chrysalis '86)

As a soloist, ex-Kisser Vinnie Vincent (born Vincent Cusano) is a hyper and edgy metalloid version of Eddie Van Halen. But as a tunesmith, he's a dull amalgam of standard issue pop rock, straight-ahead hard rock mixed with metal, kinda like Kiss only with more layers like Ace. But possessing less soulful integrity than Ace, the Invasion become merely a generic L.A. glam band, with smooth, pretty-boy vocals that don't help counter the sheen, courtesy ex-Journey guy Robert Fleischman. Vinnie's a screamin' axe warrior, but the man definitely needs to work among other strong personalities to create cohesive, meaningful product. After much internal bickering and a poorly-received follow-up (which Vinnie himself publicly slags), the Invasion blew apart, giving birth to '90s instant heroes Slaughter, of which Vinnie himself is emphatically no part.

Rating     4

## Vinnie Vincent Invasion - All Systems Go
(Chrysalis '88)

An ill-fated release featuring Dana Strum and Mark Slaughter (half of what would become Slaughter), **All Systems Go** is a spirited, sometimes complex and sometimes prissy hard rock romp that could have easily been a Slaughter album, given more personality, projection and less soupy, swimming layers of sound, clouding what are in reality, simple visions. Four mellow, ballad-type drippers, however, steer the record close to girly-man status. The fashion theme today? Lots of coloured beads hanging from fringy leather.

Rating     6

## Virgin Steele - Virgin Steele   (V.S. '82)

The much-hyped debut from these vaguely Manowarish (image-wise, anyways) east coast rockers was surprisingly tight and well-conceived for independent NWOUSHM product. Yet polish is never a substitute for good songs (unless perhaps you're Lenny Kravitz),

and DeFeis and his warriors shoot blanks all over this record, letting their blue collar sense of cheese waft through each track until we all burst out laughing. Ultimately, **Virgin Steele** comprises one part partytime hard rock, one part he-man metal, lone hooterama being the kick-ass title tune. Sounded pretty good at the time, but of course we were desperate.

Rating     4

## Virgin Steele - II Guardians Of TheFlame
(Mongrel Horde '83)

Mine eyes are hazed over with the forgetfulness of things past and passed on this one, 'cept that it combined the raw exuberance of record one with a scant trace of skill and accessibility. The band's most focused.

Rating     6

## Virgin Steele - Burn The Sun   (Maze Est. '84)

David Defeis lamb-like trill (honed from hours in awe at Angel's Frank Dimino) is back on this much cleaner, more melodic disc (Virgin Steely Dan?), coming off as clichéd and unwieldy, lacking in the riff and production departments, sounding echoey and overblown. Almost nothing riveting enough to make you want to play it a second time, **Burn The Sun** suffers from pre-stardom burnout and loss of purely artistic intentions in forced pursuit of sensitivity. Girlfriend trouble?

Rating     3

## Virgin Steele - Noble Savage   (Cobra '85)

I really tried to like this album, David Defeis striking me as such a psychotic, fiercely independent megalomaniac, but besides two bitchin' Zep-quality, Egyptiantinged epics in the title smorg and *The Angel Of Light*, plus a couple of other less distinct headbang-type pleasures, the rest is pedestrian macho metal and worse. **Noble Savage** is blanketed with a sort of over-grandness and false power that far surpasses the riff quality, resulting in a disc that seems to cruise on two disjointed emotive planes, like a Manowar manifesto without the obliteration and apocalyptic deafness. Nevertheless, **Noble Savage** is the best-strategized, best-produced Virgin Steele project, the first without the pathetic low budget album art and effort to match.

Rating     5

## Virus - Force Recon   (Metalworks '88)

Street-level Slayer bordering on thrash, or more accurately, loose diseased death. Some of this just blazes: witness the Voivod-ian title-creaker and protracted riff inventory *No Return*, both twisted and massively evil, and bang-on with their dead-eye deliveries. Scorching dirt-metal when skulking at discernible speeds, flown-apart mosh bullshit when accelerated.

Rating     5

## Vision Of Disorder - Vision Of Disorder
(Roadrunner '97)

One of a raft of urban hardcore band that goes the distance, due to dangerous, city-burnin' production, rough and tumble writing, and muscle-man riffs unto groove. Big things are expected, and a bit of label push hasn't hurt in furthering the band's cause. I'm in the middle (I interviewed the guys, and they were quite thoughtful about it all), with many of my writer buds tossing off a "who cares?"

Rating     7

## Viva - Dealers Of The Night   (Dureco Benelux '82)

**Dealers** hits the mark with less consistency versus its lusty follow-up, but man, what a cool band, at least in concept. Paganini's major snarl kicks these Euroblunders into Black Forest swilldom, rendering Viva one of the most intrinsically German bands self-bent on ever-

widening downward spirals to rock obscurity. Perhaps too greedy in its intent on offering balladry, stripper tunes, and about three other forms of rare AC/DC diversity. But also wildly off on a truly rock hoggin' jackboot joyride, ya just gotta buy into it.
Rating      7

## Viva - What The Hell Is Going On   (Est. '83)

Viva was a deeply European-hearted, hard rock band, whose claim to fame was Michael Schenker's sister on keyboards (who thankfully didn't sing). Throughout their brief catalogue, Viva either pooped out doltish, failed metal typical of French or Italian bands, or truly magical, hard rock classics like this record's divine *What Next*, *Little Rock Tonight* and hard-to-believe scorcher *Break Out*, three tunes I practically wore out during the NWOBHM years. And the vocals of rock rat Marc Paganini were a metallic force all their own, even more an accomplishment given the obvious fact that English is not this belter's first language. Tragically hit or miss, when Viva was on, they fused melody and raucousness so poetically, invoking the energy of AC/DC and the stout-of-heart Eurotones of Accept, Scorpions, Highway Chile, and even fellow oddities S.A.D.O. Brilliant and more savvy to world trends than **Dealers**, but unfortunately equally patchy.
Rating      7

## Voivod - War And Pain   (Metal Blade '84)

Beats the hell outta me why, but Quebec has always been fertile ground for death, thrash and grind, Voivod being one of the original wiseacres, ensconced in billowy green clouds of hemp from the fine PQ countryside. Always somewhat the enigma, Snake, Piggy, Blacky and Away ralphed into view with this intense technicolour yawn of overdriven chaos. Only Voivod (and of course Bathory) in the few years following Venom revelled in such cacophony, cranking major amphetamine sludge, occasionally hinting at their sciborg proto-thrash agenda to come, while usually just piling on the barbed wire until it all resembles a thieving heap of twisted pain. One of those records you feel proud to be able to hack.
Rating      5

## Voivod - RRRÖÖÖAAARRR   (Noise '86)

Now well on their way out of their minds, Voivod thrash and crash through a new set of insane train wrecks. Line up the album covers, and you've pretty much seen the mechanihell in which Away crouches seething. it's a loudfastrules death grip with a point; point being stay the hell away. A second badge of courage from Montreal's alien monsters who seem to have crawled further into the recesses of their underground hovels, bong-headed and thirsty for wattage.
Rating      4

## Voivod - Killing Technology   (Cobra '87)

Off to Berlin for recording, which doesn't make a damn bit of difference for the trashcan shit-canning at the boards afforded the Din from Hatross. An evolution is at hand however as Piggy's chords become more dissonant and foreign, and Away finds a singing voice beneath his still prevalent Ajax gouge. Much like the contrived **Shout At The Devil** and **At War With Satan** linguistic conundrums, **Killing Technology** may denote technology that kills or the destruction of technology. Here Voivod destroys technology that kills, getting an earbleeder from both sides. Marginal upswing on the mix, and *Ravenous Medicine* is a dribbling lunatic of a song. Three records deep in electrocution, one can only shake one's head at such a commercial death wish, ascribing an obligatory dose of respect at weirdos so committed to their . . . art.
Rating      5

## Voivod - Nothingface   (MCA '89)

The video for the righteous Syd-era Pink Floyd cover pretty much sums up Voivod's dissonant new sound, a swirling cagey, upside-under maze of jarring chords; in short a sound for which I have no love. Voivod has strangled the much maligned spirit of progressive rock, giving it a doom metal twist that approximates a grungy metalized Cure, a scurrying rat-like gnawing with ugly jazz tentacles and illogical pathways. Noble enough in concept, kind of botched in execution, as the loose-knit arrangements are left to bleed under a power-starved mix ruined by too much treble and a midrangey Lemmy bass sound. A freakshow with good lyrics, but totally depressing and junky. Highly-acclaimed the world over but lost on me.
Rating      7

## Voivod - Angel Rat   (MCA '91)

Voivod continue to plow new worlds with their nightmarish sci-fi bulldozer, this time noted detail man Terry Brown (Rush, appropriately) fixing the band's previous sound problems (except for that gutted bass), in construction of another challenging, almost painful record only a little less traumatic and grey than **Nothingface**. Best track here is again the lead video (an increasingly deceptive marketing practice that has caused me a pile of wasted dollars lately, **Angel Rat** included). Of course we're talking about *Clouds In My House*, an arresting, shambling tale of weirdness with a mesmerizing melodic vocal. As with **Nothingface**, it's not hard to appreciate the panoramic exploratory nature of Voivod's mindset, however uninviting and distressed it may be, despite the total misinformation in the music press that this is a commercial sell-out (albeit an artistically successful one). I don't know, it's just too rainy and gothic or something, like a deserted merry-go-round in an electrical storm. It just makes me want to go live in a cave, in which case my coffee maker would be useless.
Rating      7

## Voivod - The Outer Limits   (MCA '93)

Feeling cold and alone calling this Voivod's best record, given that the band's rivethead legions of fans seem to unanimously call for harsher times. I on the other hand rejoice the (for once) near perfect production values, the calm vocals, and the tight execution of these visceral, lightly, lovingly sci-fi themes, finding a polite Victorian ring to these mysterious tales, something akin to H.P. Lovecraft. And the stark, '50s-retro 3-D packaging reinforces the step back to a simpler, more mannered time. For once the band's nervous, atonal tributaries are a pleasure to travel, bulked-up without all that trashy treble and falling-apart deliveries, lending an aristocratic air to the proceedings. Fave tracks are *The Lost Machine* and seventeen minute non-stop art metal opus *Jack Luminous*, which shows what geniuses Voivod are when they craft song for a living. An intellectual escape no one else could have created.
Rating      10

## Voivod - Negatron   (Hypnotic '95)

**Negatron** is a very different record than the strident prog metal strains of **The Outer Limits**, and for good reason: the Quebecers have a new bassist and vocalist in Toronto's Eric Forrest. What results is a vicious return to the thrashy bark and aggressive production values of Voivod records from the '80s. But the songs remain dissonantly chorded, brooding, and blinded by science fiction and friction. **Negatron**'s neurotic edges make for a rough, clattery ride (lotsa drums here!), but the essential Voivod chemistry of challenging frontiers remains, the band taking rubbery recreational chemicals to the stiff world of technical metal with predictably loopy results. **The Outer Limits** is still my favorite Voivodian experience, but this would

**501**

be second, which is quite high testimony, given the very crucial line-up change, one that many thought should have sunk the band. Shoulda came with lyrics, but drummer Michael Langevin's kitschy computer art provides some degree of consolation. Bombed in Canada, but did acceptable business in the U.S. and Europe.

Rating     **8**

### Von Groove - Von Groove    (Chrysalis '92)

Big boisterous hair band metal with blowin' free power chords that evoke Dokken, indeed Lynch and Deadly Don himself coming to mind. Recording (in Toronto) right at the end of the roughly six year reign of melodic hard rock, poodle metal, AOR, MOR, MRM (new European term: melodic rock metal), Von Groove does a good job of the genre, filling the tank with bashing exuberance and songs that remain simple in nature, guitarist Mladen's pyro used sparingly but effectively.

Rating     **6**

# W

## Wallop - Metallic Alps  (Bonebreaker "85)

Any guy who thanks his gal for "being a good wife and drum roadie" can't be all bad, eh? Well, anyways, this is one of those signature chunks of raw from Bonebreaker and Axel Thubeauville, that revels in frosty Germany. And really a few of these types of records are stirring, worthy metal of a type that is forever gone. This one's merely average (just too loose and live), and song titles like *Stealthy World*, *Idols Die Too*, *Lack Of Power* and *Matallize* don't lend much gravity to the cause. But as usual, the axework fuses Accept and Yngwie to old Priest; breaks, leads, fills and riffs all quintessentially good metal practice, unlike the trash coming from American indie acts at the time.
Rating                                    **6**

## War Babies - War Babies  (Sony '92)

At long last, Seattle's Brad Sinsel plots his return with a band and record borne of sheer grit and determination. **War Babies** is a commercial rock record with major depth, getting well under the skin of its deceptively straight-forward compositions. Comparisons have been made to Aerosmith and of course, TKO, both camps evident in War Babies' brand of pistol-packing blues metal. Yet it seems like every track, be it ballad or rocker, is written with a strength of song that could conceivably turn tune to anthem, anthem to hit. The overall feel is one of defiant timelessness, combining the American best of the '70s, and the American-influenced best of the mid-'80s with '90s-style urgency to give it your best shot now. Thus lead vid and single *Hang Me Up*, personal fave *Killing Time* and second vid *Blue Tomorrow* (yet another dedication to Andrew Wood) all go places intense and struggling, Sinsel assembling a crack band to make his presence felt. Through a stubborn but brilliant and battle-worn re-working of traditional riffs, traditional lyrical concerns, and traditional recording processes, **War Babies** triumphs, the emotional wreckage of a rock'n'roll lifetime bleeding from Sinsel's vocals, driving the performances of the marksmen at his side. Tough as nails.
Rating                                    **10**

## Bill Ward - Ward One: Along The Way  (Chameleon '90)

Bill Ward proves here and now that he was forebodingly more than just the manic, cymbal-bashing skinsman behind the legendary Black Sabbath, he was a necessary writhing shard of the band's maligned soul. The man's surprising first solo album is a plush psycho-logical rollercoaster ride into the man at hand. Heavy and serious, full of intricate arrangements, voice sampling, and textured keyboards, **Ward One** is best portrayed as a metalized version of Pink Floyd, slashing through similar dark and inhospitable landscapes as **Animals** and **The Wall**. Even though the record sports an all-star cast of players (including Ozzy on two tracks), **Ward One** sounds singularly unique and high-minded, due to Ward's literary ambitions on these cathedral-like works, not to mention the exotic and weird quality of the songcraft. It's only a guess, but after hearing **Ward One** and hearing Tony Iommi's ghost and goblin parodies of Sabbath in the '90s, it sounds like Ward (or Ward plus a pile of unpredictable chemicals) was the hidden genius, or at least a large part of the inspiration, behind such brilliant ether-worldly classics from Sab's productive and maddening middle years. In any event, **Ward One: Along the Way** seems to flow fluidly from that same tormented mindspace. Enigmatic thinking man's metal from a force all too easily dismissed as merely a drummer for a legendary band.
Rating                                    **9**

## Warfare - Pure Filth  (Banzai '84)

Venom contributes and Tank's Algy Ward produces; but call it closer to Venom, these punk metal crossover disasters rumbling like a lower-end, alcoholic Cronos and crew (how snake-faced low can you get?), while Algy infects the sound with the loose bolts work non-ethic for which Tank was infamous. Sloppy, tepid, tuneless garage evilmetal with soccer match shout-and-bray, **Pure Filth** got press for its cover of Frankie Goes to Hollywood's *Two Tribes*, if you can believe it. Proud to have never heard the original but this sounds sorta like *Countess Bathory*. Overall, Warfare's almost seminally grungoid mayhem can handily amuse if you're easily amused, even as their tiring sound becomes paltry and unshocking with age and growing sonic desensitization to extremes.
Rating                                    **5**

## Warfare - Metal Anarchy  (Neat '85)

Soothing classical opens Warfare's second laughing, burning trashpile, segueing into *Electric Mayhem*, the bitter march of *Warfare* and on, into the deepening filth. But Evo and buds even attempt an epic, *Wrecked Society* galloping like prime Tank, while Evo punk croaks his tale of degeneration. As usual there's storming NWOBHM riffs stumbling around in there beneath

the muck, but the speedy Damned Motörhead thrashiness usually drowns them out. Yobbo limey pollution you kinda wanna keep.
Rating      6

## Warfare - Metal Fuckin' Mayhem    (Neat '86)

Perennial non-tourers Evo, Gunner and new thick-stringer Slaughter press on grimly, recording with added bite (kinda like chewing on rocks), white-knuckling it through a raucous record that is ultimately 3/4 bad ol' clanging thrash circa Venom's bashiest early '80s blatherings. In fact Evo's old bud Cronos contributes the bass tracks here, seeing the terrible trio through the sacking of old bassist Falken, and the results are the turgidly expected, Warfare carrying the torch as second fan band in command to a sound no one else wants to touch. Uh, nice album cover. Looks real fine next to Destruction's **Release From Agony**. Trivia note: three records, produced in succession by Algy Ward, Lemmy, and Cronos.
Rating      6

## Warlord - Deliver Us    (Metal Blade '83)

A classy debut EP from a clan of wizards who always seemed to be on the fringe of the business, **Deliver Us** is reminiscent of early Queensryche or Fate's Warning; varied, complex and self-gratifyingly grandiose. The guitar production and skillset admirably recall Randy Rhoads as per **Diary Of A Madman**, but the drumming is careening and overblown past the point of good taste, diminishing the power of the grooves and the ominous riffery with excessive fills and double bass work. The songs however are quite sturdy melodically, even if the lyrics are a bit too melodramatically concerned with witchcraft (which comes off best when treated with an OTT sense of humour). An ambitious but ridiculously self-important debut that nevertheless does cross that line between parody and arresting imagery.
Rating      7

## Warlord - And The Canons Of Destruction Have Begun . . .    (Banzai '84)

Strangely enough, Warlord's debut full-length is this live "soundtrack" album to the video of the same name. I don't think their flick was as big as **Jurassic Park** or **Batman**, and I don't recall the boys getting the nod at the Academy Awards. Four of six from **Deliver Us** are featured here along with other similarly convoluted dragon-slaying pageants. Unfortunately, Warlord in the studio tended to overplay like some black metal/Yes monster, and you know what happens when we get to "stretch out" live. A lot of the drumming is so overdone, it doesn't even get back to the beat on time, as Thunder Child looks for the resolution of that great Peart fill in the sky. And sloppy is the last thing this band would ever want to be called. However despite the egos, the craftsmanship is high bandwidth, D'n'D imagery, and debutante aspirations aside.
Rating      6

## Warlord - Thy Kingdom Come    (Metal Blade '86)

Included here as a public service announcement more than anything, **Thy Kingdom Come** is a compilation of past frilly circumlocution, further displaying the fact that these guys may be a decent band, but their recording career is a tangle of confusion. Verdict: get the debut EP.
Rating      6

## Warlord U.K. - Maximum Carnage
(eastwest/Nuclear Blast '96)

Perched wallowing and spreading between flogged-to-death metal and Bay Area power frash, **Maximum Carnage** manages to miss on both counts, the band

more or less on the slow boat back to the '80s. So there's walls o' plenty, blastbeats, OTT and grooves, but a turgid confusion melts the record stiff, cloistered and unfresh, until it slips through the cracks made by more creative, forward and free-thinking metal forces.
Rating      5

## War Machine - Unknown Soldier    (Neat '86)

Seriously distressed power drive with a female frontwoman. And damn it if this ain't a waste of a rumbling, proud Grim Reaper of a band, a steely 'n' evil bundle of black emotion that could have been special. Man, what were these guys thinking? A sinister and chiseled, almost progressive **9** without the female vocals.
Rating      4

## Warning - Warning    (Est '82)

Beware . . . said record's enunciated in French, the language of love, which greatly diminishes its value for us speakers of God's own tongue. Otherwise it's a barn-stormer. Accomplished, rowdy but tight, blessed with glorious, face-melting production and shrieking vocals, **Warning** mixes Judas Priest-like coliseum chops with a slice of blue collar AC/DC-inspired headbanging. A hearty **9** if it weren't for the French vocals, plain and simple. Fierce and wondrously top-flight like vintage Highway Chile.
Rating      6

## Warning - Métamorphose    (EMI '84)

I think I missed a second record called **Second Warning** in there somewhere. Anyhow, this sucker's a bit of a letdown after the zesty kill factor of the debut, being a bit ploddish or hectically OTT, missing the middle grooves so eloquently addressed on **Warning**, while also turning those electro-drums up too loud. Still 100% in French, which draws a blank on me. Inspired guitar work.
Rating      5

## Warpigs - Stay Cool    (Howling Bull '91)

Best damn Japanese band I'll ever hear, Warpigs look basically like Death Angel which gets them past hurdle one. Hurdle two: no prissy Yngwie impressions. Hurdle three: vocals, which here are friggin' hilarious (and English I should point out), sorta like a grindcore growl mixed with laryngitis neglected for months. No shit, this record's a scream. a total underground blast, thundering along with a booming mix and economically ultra-heavy riffing, sorta like S.O.D. but more musical. First Japanese band with a sense of alcohol to it, and these guys definitely smoke the evil bud. Sorta thrash in spirit and deed, but just a howling, no prisoners, thud metal brew, from rise to setting sun.
Rating      7

## Warrant - The Enforcer    (Noise '85)

Not the puff-asses from Poofter's Froth, this considerably blacker incarnation is a generic German speed metal bunch with a bad drummer and occasional midpace teeth as on the bitchin' Cowards Or Martyrs. Actually not as bad as it could have been given the usual heavier-than-thou concept and the tired period from which it hails.
Rating:      4

## Warrant - Dirty Rotten Filthy Stinking Rich
(CBS '89)

Now there's a band that puts their mouth where their money hopefully will be some day, Warrant emerging from the pack, quietly building a following through no overt talent of their own. 'Cos this debut record's nothing to get your pink California rock cowboy boots all worked up over, surprisingly meek and cadaverously produced, very tight, abbreviated and dull

throughout. Just another silly-looking band of gypsies at this point, no killer instinct, most likely because they haven't killed anything yet.
Rating 4

## Warrant - Cherry Pie   (CBS '90)

Probably the defining poodle metal record by the defining poodle metal pack, Warrant's second was a big cheesecakey hit, all teased and tousled, kicking off with *Cherry Pie*, which along with its video would become the favorite kicking post of the alternative nation, yelling sexism, like they'd never heard of Van Halen before. Second track *Uncle Tom's Cabin* kinda redeems the record with its tasty acoustic intro and marauding metal riff, becoming a fan fave in the process. But then it's back into the teen beat pages, for a raft of perky cute songs that are almost as watery and weak as any Bon Jovi pimple, although Jani Lane's powerful pipes blow away Mr. B. Jovi's wheezy multi-tracked croak any day of the week. Brightly, even vivaciously produced by Beau Hill; big, animated improvement over the debut.
Rating 6

## Warrant - Dog Eat Dog   (Sony '92)

Being enough in the know to stay well enough away, my previous encounters with this much reviled success story fortunately didn't include parting with my cash. Luck has it again, as a free walk through the dog patch became the order of the day, thus there I pounced for a look in at the new, improved, kick version of these former poseurs. Well-positioned with the bubbling-under set of shoo biz acts such as Slaughter and Tesla, Warrant brew up a muscular piece of work which fleshes out strong ideas to serious fruition. **Dog Eat Dog** (monikered for both Ted and the band's impression of the industry) is a welcome dose of leather, tattoos and thirsty guitars, still more than occasionally "groove rock"-directed as per dismally flaccid single *Cherry Pie*, but also a good piece frameworked like an ambitious thoughtful metalwerk, as witnessed on lead siren *Machine Gun*, the catchy *Hollywood (So Far So Good)*, and strident mood piece *April 2031*. As with Tesla, this pivotal juncture burns with an urge to be heard and seen as a critical success, perhaps prompting the trip away from the commercial signals of L.A. to Florida for recording. Still liberally patterned with pop finesse, balladry, and production largesse, **Dog Eat Dog** is long enough to rock, about on par with a batch of finer Y&T moments, early Leppard directives, or, yes, Tesla's **Psychotic Supper,** all champions of quality "general" rock. No question, rebellion towards critical slagging, and a desire to gain more discerning fans (read: guys) was firmly at the fore throughout the construction of this fine release. And all visual and sonic cues point towards a tougher stance in the future, an image more in tune with the band's live shows. More growl than woof, and well away from Warrant's chick-driven past.
Rating 7

## Warrant - Ultraphobic   (CMC '95)

Warrant continue to make inroads with their brainy arrangements, bringing the creativity of '90s alternative metal into their comfy bed borne of big budget '80s hard rock, subtly and synergystically fusing the two into something viable, if for many unremarkable. What results is a conservative, less exotic version of King's X, songs still very much corporate rock-based, yet laced with really smart riffs and complicated melodies, an album which succeeds for any who will excuse the band's dated past. Jani Lane is back in the fold (after the band crashed in flames following the under-rated **Dog Eat Dog**'s poor showing), crooning like his letter-perfect self, while harmonies emphasize most breaks and choruses, the band exhibiting a work ethic that just might bring back '80s metal after all the stultifying laziness crapped out in music over the last few years. Less bite than the mid metal of **Dog Eat Dog**, but more forethought, **Ultraphobic** (in conjunction with Slaughter's **Fear No Evil**) carries the biggest potential for the '80s hair band experiment that is the CMC stable of artists. It is of note that the band's first two records sold 2.5 million copies each. These guys have been places.
Rating 7

## Warrant - The Best Of Warrant   (Legacy/Sony '96)

Laugh if you must earthlings, but Warrant have a bit of a catalogue going now, certainly their latest records worthy of some attention. This comp lines up all those moderate hits, also offering a historical essay, a likeable Cheap Tricky b-side called *Thin Disguise*, an acoustic version of *I See Red*, and the band's dressy uptake on Queen's *We Will Rock You*. Quite a shocking sound all in all, here in the combat zone, but persnicketty rawk all the same.
Rating 6

## Warrant - Belly To Belly Volume One   (CMC/BMG '96)

It isn't so much that this is a bad record, it's just that it's a bit of a re-do of its quite fantabulous predecessor **Ultraphobic**. Benchmark careerists Slaughter were guilty of the same thing, as was Dio, each act delivering, but not knocking their listenership on their ass. The problem here is dissipation, a kind of washed-out, take-your-time sort of miasma, Pearl Jammy drums lurching into open spots that feel and smell like the bus station. And that convoluted title? What's with that? Warrant '96? It's pretty much the same quite viable game as warrant '95. 'Cept Jani Lane is mixed a bit timidly, and nobody explodes come chorus-time, even though the writing is still strong and harmonies still warm the cockles. It's just that moldy patch of psychedelia, that upturned nose at commerciality that, well, turns my nose to more immediate hair metal like Tyketto. I guess when irony visits in complex groupings, your basic rock guys kinda wig out and search furtively and obsessively for the non-obvious. Stick to the pudding. It's always been rich and satisfying.
Rating 7

## Warrior - Fighting For The Earth   (10 '85)

Strangley universal in an '80s way, like Malice, a body shop clangin' take on **British Steel**, or even Saxon's more buoyant anthems, **Fighting For The Earth** carries the class of a contender, shooting rays of disciplined metal at all speeds. Very American but uncompromising with a sort of push/pull commercialism, the record revs heavily on side one, but loses its edge come side two with a casebook ballad and experimental closer. But hell, for low expectations, mid-'80s output, Warrior (also known as USA Warrior) were doing something proud and just, hauling along a worthy nostalgic reverence for times only recently gone by. A bit melodramatic with all that talk of how their souls are evidently burning. Original grade: **7**.
Rating 6

## The Warriors - The Warriors   (Attic '84)

Unfortunately, my warning will come too late for a lot of you who had bought this occasionally Euro-tinged and Kiss-like candy-ass fluff out of sheer boredom at lack of good product in '84. For those of you who missed this, or saw through the ridiculous attempt at Manowar-ish imagery on the back cover, The Warriors are a Yugoslavian melodic hard rock outfit who were boated over, dressed up, and paraded as competents within a no-risk framework. Very manipulated, very commercially offending.
Rating 3

## Warrior Soul - Last Decade Dead Century (Geffen '90)

Warrior Soul aren't a band, they're a city state unto themselves, one always on the verge of riot, strafed by sporadic looting, ready to boil over. And that's why each progressive record is better than the last: increasing mayhem, increasing fire and spit. Thus **Last Decade Dead Century** is an impressive world to gaze glaze-eyed at from a secured hill, but I wouldn't wanna live there. Band mastermind Kory Clarke has already honed his venomous vision: exposing the very real and active evils promulgated by the U.S. government, the disintegration of society, the hopeless cesspool that is America. And Clarke's vocals form one hair-raising battle cry. But despite the arresting panoramic concept that Warrior Soul carves, this ambitious debut finds the band stiff in delivery, tunes somewhat immobile, tightly packed around sub-standard, repetitious riffs, riffs designed for hypnotic interplay with Kory's expressive enunciations, yet riffs and plain jane drum beats (almost dance, but way slow) which sabotage song mass, dragging the whole thing into grey depression. Simple rock for exciting and challenging concepts, a sound that evokes the heavier thumpings of The Cult circa **Love** or loud Midnight Oil from ten years back crossed with the spirit of old U2. But heavier than all that, got it? Way cool junior, but I'm sorry, the music is a mite dull. Unsung anthem for the slacker generation: The Losers.
Rating 6

## Warrior Soul - Drugs, God And The New Republic (Geffen '91)

**Drugs, God And The New Republic** kicks off in fine fashion, dredging the memory of Ian Curtis, Kory Clarke's mentor and a bracing commentator on the stink of earth, a thin waif of a man who wore his convictions around his neck. Interzone is one of Joy Division's most raging, rock and rolling tracks, setting the tone for Clarke's latest scathing attack on the Bush administration and its devastating effects on the nation's angry and expendable youth, a whole layer of society found to be redundant, unnecessary and even harmful to an elusive economic recovery. Warrior Soul II cranks up the heat: more variety, more intensity, better songs all around, including the first classic, The Wasteland, which discovers a punk rock vein from which the band will learn to mine their most kickin' statements come record III. Alas, the muse is still far ahead of the music though, Clarke making for a paint-stripping read, while the band still walks stiff and understated, no thanks to Geoff Workman's techy drum mix. By this point Clarke's ravings against the workings of government would take on the hysteria of conspiracy theories, as the man's bitterness begins to erode his hopes for his own band's fortunes, causing a sort of veiled spite at a society that will not buy his records (see Adrian Belew). Chalk it up to a case of shooting the messenger.
Rating 8

## Warrior Soul - Salutations From The Ghetto Nation (Geffen '92)

Profound rage spills from the waves on this, Warrior Soul's wildest wilding to date, getting right down to the business of condemning the business with Love Destruction, a tune whose characteristic laid-back riff is punctuated with brilliant metallic solos from guitarist John Ricco, while Clarke up-ratchets to a sustained roar throughout. **Salutations** injects a new level of aggression to match Clarke's infinite capacity for the negative. Now when a premise is weak (i.e. Blown, Shine Like It and The Fallen), the delivery picks up the slack. And when the premise is rock hard, tempered in the steely reality of punk, Warrior Soul are a force with which to be reckoned, all the baggage of unrealized goals spewing into the streets like heavy water

over rats. Thus Punk And Belligerent, Ass Kickin and I Love You, three similar slash and burns that get right to the point, point being there is no point to anything. Here's hoping David Geffen comes to view Warrior Soul as one of the jewels of the Geffen organization that it is, a band of substance if not sales, an act to retain for integrity's sake. Sure Clarke's bracing levels of depression may go beyond reality, but it's a trip more people should book. Just make sure you buy a return ticket.
Rating 8

## Warrior Soul - Chill Pill (Geffen '93)

Truck-size disappointment, as el Paranoid wordwizard takes a turn deeply into the germy characteristics that threatened to bury past releases. On **Chill Pill**, the newly hippy-encased one gets drippy droney and psychedelic, really only I Want Some and Shock Um Down pulling out the punk scabbard for a let-fly smokefeast. Things variously move slowly or aimlessly or not at all, almost as if Kory has given up trying to sell, flopping down in a big ol' kaleidoscopic chair, the defeated artist. It's too bad, but this band's problem has always been an ordinariness of Kory's backing soundtrack, vocals, lyrics and mantelpiece man being the whole show, the only show, the captivating show (see The Tragically Hip, but not in my damn book). A psychic soulstorm nevertheless, but one that finds pessimism at prospect at its lowest ebb.
Rating 6

## Warrior Soul - The Space Age Playboys (Music For Nations '94)

Eschewing the soupdroop of **Chill Pill**, Kory cranks it up for a bunch of shorter faster songbursts, exactly what I've always wished, 'cept the riffs are still dull. I don't geddit. The man speaks of punk and its virtues, yet he records record after record so clean with snappy snare like some sort of Mellencamp record, and to this day, he can't see that his problems lie with those thoroughly unremarkable smear riffs. This record rocks, and it has no bite whatsoever, although I'm still captivated by the force at the mike. Really, guy, it's time for a solo album. Fire that band, please.
Rating 7

## Warrior Soul - Odds And Ends (Futurist '96)

Back cover sez it all: "8, 16, & 24 track recordings from the band that fought America, fought the System . . . And ultimately lost." But what that doesn't get across is the fact that 15 of 17 tracks are '94 and newer, recorded over three pessimistic, bitter sessions with little sleep. Fortunately for the most part, this is the fast, manic, venomous version of the band, not really any more raw than usual, but perhaps more cantankerous. Okay, granted, a good third droops in both energy and sound quality ("Recordings C", in Kory's handwritten liner notes), but let's not forget we have 74 minutes worth of Soul conviction here. Less of a record due to its lack of cohesion, but no barrel-scraper, as these projects often are. If anything, it demonstrates how prolific the band was, and how passionately they kept creating despite being snuffed by label (and let's face it, public) indifference.
Rating 7

## Wartime - Fast Food For Thought (Chrysalis '90)

Funky, industrial rap from the fire-and-water team of Andrew Weiss and Henry Rollins, **Fast Food For Thought** is for bass thugs only, essentially being Weiss' show, while Rollins lays distantly mixed and heavily treated raps over stomping distorto-bass patterns to no artistic avail. Six tracks, 27 minutes of droning gobs of throbbing slouch funk, lots of scary samples, boring as hell, and somehow managing to cover Grateful Dead's Franklin's Tower, if you can believe it. Given

Rollins' dissing of Weiss for weakness, laziness, and rock star tantrums in his book **Now Watch Him Die**, it's hard to believe they would do a side project together but here it is. Not my cup of java.
Rating                                                                  3

## W.A.S.P. - W.A.S.P.   (Capitol '84)

Coming off a bit too much as a shock-for-shock's-sake commercial ploy; a violent, overblown '80s-excessive version of riffless Kiss, Blackie Lawless and his tattooed hateboys play slightly-above-average, '70s-style "hanging chord" metal, which ever so slightly smacks of going through the paces, in futile quest of acceptance by the learned. I'm not crazy about Blackie's melodramatic rawk vocals or the production, specifically the over-treated and electro-distorted drum sound (see **Skid Row**, Quiet Riot, and Priest's **Defenders Of The Faith**). Three or four butt-shaking, anthemic rockers prop the thing up (*The Flame, I Wanna Be Somebody* and *On Your Knees*), but ultimately the whole project smacks of filthy lucre.
Rating                                                                  5

## W.A.S.P. - The Last Command   (Capitol '85)

Blackie and his over-indulging goons chug along menacingly on this X-rated little improvement on the brain-dead Crüe. Lean 'n' mean, toothsome machine-gunners like *Ballcrusher* and *Jack Action* lead the attack on the markedly better side one, while side two's *Blind In Texas* takes a corrupt li'l side trip into redneck territory. Anything but a huge fan, I nevertheless like the increasingly dynamic life-affirming, life-wrecking drive of this album coupled with Blackie's urge to infect in the name of show biz. Lots of press, because the pictures sold magazines.
Rating                                                                  6

## W.A.S.P. - Inside The Electric Circus   (Capitol '86)

Same ol' Blackie Lawless bullshit, which even at its worst, has more texture and heart than the Crüe. Maybe slightly more simplified and hard rock-based than previous aggressive stings, **Circus** has the distinction of recranking Heep's *Easy Livin'*, a considerably classy choice of covers, which also serves to expose Blackie's age. Blackie in retrospect considered this record a failure, a crossroads riddled with self-doubt and a disproportionate amount of personal lows. Perhaps the guy is finally growing up, no?
Rating                                                                  5

## W.A.S.P. - Live . . . In The Raw   (Capitol '87)

The best thing about this mayhemic foray into corporate metal's got to be the packaging, which no-hold-barred offers us photo testimony to the most overblown, disgusting, violent, morally perverse, yet smugly conceived, big business stage show in rock, complete with blood, raw meat, and chicks in confined compromising positions. Rather than make Blackie look degenerate, however, it only caused critics to bring attention to the marketing aspects of Blackie's particular brand of sellout, dismissing the whole codpiece circus as another Wendy O. Williams or Adam and the Ants (remember them?). W.A.S.P.'s show is in fact detrimental to their attempted sonic effect, for truthfully, "anthem" is not a ridiculous utterance for many of Blackie's moments, especially as his status grows as rock outsider. No, for genuine terror, visit the otherworldy landscapes of Sabbath, Danzig, Chameleons U.K., Trouble, and Witchfinder General. Pretty violent swing for a live album though.
Rating                                                                  5

## W.A.S.P. - The Headless Children   (Capitol '89)

Picture **The Crimson Idol** without the concept, and you've pretty much summed up this serious play for down-the-middle metal acceptance. Officially down to

a three-piece, the boys work in Ken Hensley for a truly Heep-ish title track, while generally rumbling through a batch of brash street rockers with messages of foreboding for those tempted to stray. But that drum-dominated and dumb-combobulated mix from Hell buries enjoyment for me, Blackie's shrill vulture calls not helping the brew. Still, this one's more of a success, individual tales that tone down the theatrical crap for a look at a bruised and mentally shredded bunch of leather-clad warriors. Of course, once Blackie gets over this Who fixation, we'll all be better off (*The Real Me*: come on). The W.A.S.P. record for those who don't like W.A.S.P. Hollow, damp and alone, integrity intact. Note: this is the band's biggest seller thus far, clocking in at over two million pancakes worldwide, with most others apparently skirting the 1.8m zone.
Rating                                                                  7

## W.A.S.P. - The Crimson Idol   (Capitol '92)

Our man Blackie, somewhat misunderstood as a one-track, bacchanalian oaf, can't be entirely excused for his critically-ignored status, rising to notoriety as commander of the ultimate rock'n'roll butcher shop. On **The Crimson Idol**, we find our surprisingly pensive hero attempting to reverse the red tide, with an ambitious, ridiculously labour-intensive concept only inches above commoner proportions, a fragile glass palace in which to wrestle with mid-life crisis under a haze of recreational pharmaceuticals. Merely a predictable semi-fiction of a rocker's rise and fall (with better than average attention to societal cause and effect), **The Crimson Idol** is a piece to be admired, for its complex, convincing web of pity and self-pity if nothing else. Yet sadly, this expansive, blathering, panic-stricken yowl is no mean listen, oscillating jarringly between blubbery, dark ballads with long builds and oddly drum-dominated metal over-productions with *tortuously* long builds, infested with noise, vacantly low on creative riffs, a problem that has plagued W.A.S.P. from opening day. Sorry man, but as much as Blackie quite eloquently rails against the sleaze of the industry, upholding his ever-waning flame of morality amongst his chosen subculture, this, his apparent defining work seems to lack the creative resonance the painstaking process so obviously should have nurtured. Chalk up another unenjoyable, even hurtful failure in the concept album department, for **The Crimson Idol** either hushes one to sleep, or batters one awake, with none of the joys of either state.
Rating                                                                  6

## W.A.S.P. - First Blood . . . Last Cuts   (Capitol '93)

A compilation of very recent and very old, **First Blood** does little to motivate the fan to buy, offering a few pointless remixes (*Blind In Texas* mebbee sounds better), and I guess a representative sampling of the band's anthemic, Jack-swilling hits. Blackie told us that this was straight contractual obligation, nothing more, also re-marking that the first time he saw the sub-standard artwork used, was when he saw it in a store, the original packaging supposed to include a novel folding booklet that revealed different eras of the band, depending on what order it was folded in.
Rating                                                                  5

## W.A.S.P. - Still Not Black Enough   (Victor '95)

Well, you probably already know if you are a fan of ol' hag Blackie by now, his noisy mishmash of glam rock influences, his Alice Cooper and Who melodrama, all put through a California metal shredder built in the '80s, a disintegrator and reconstructor of guitar rock's weighty history, until all sounds brash and drum-dominated. This one's a lot like **The Crimson Idol** without the concept, a little bit of all of Blackie's tiring and raggedly tired styles, all crooned echoey or shrieked with heart, the whole mess of confused but traditional

**507**

sounds ringing true with heart, whether you like it or not. So count me respecting but once again, beaten into shutting the door by that midrange mix and those over-extended drum fills. Covers of *Somebody To Love* (I really hate that song) and *Tie Your Mother Down* (brilliant band, strangely and uncharacteristically vacant song). Blackie now considers this album one of his least favourites of the catalogue, not bad, but destined to be "lost in the shuffle".

Rating 6

## W.A.S.P. - K.F.D. (Castle '97)

Hell, we got the scoop from Blackie and Chris over lunch, and none of us really hear what Blackie sez is the most intense W.A.S.P. album ever. But you gotta hand it to him for making big changes, barb-wiring the whole thing with industrial caustics and increasingly clattery production, the effects of classic rock rat Chris Holmes not really all that present, but sure to come to the fore when the downright horrific stage show blows through your town (as it was descibed to me, I can't see too many promoters allowing it). Blackie adds all sorts of effects to his vocals, synthesizes the guitars, and crams every moment of the thing with electro and acoustic tom fills, all traits that bothered me about W.A.S.P. brought to the fore. True, the thing's pretty dark and impenetrable, but does this translate to enjoyment? Not quite for me, although true W.A.S.P. fans might find it all deliciously evil, what with all the swearing, vampiric vocal work, and scary instrumental respites. I just can't get past the drums or the production to even try.

Rating 6

## Watchtower - Control And Resistance (Noise '89)

Somewhat considered an important record somewhere in the middle of progressive metal's evolution, **Control And Resistance** is somewhat a precursor to Cynic's **Focus**, both records about the most dizzyingly complicated, technical, music school metal ever produced. A total quick change blur of stops and starts, with almost funny helium vocals from Alan Tecchio, and Holdsworth-ian (see Meshuggah) axework from Ron Jarzombek. Short-lived legend.

Rating 6

## Waysted - Vices (Chrysalis '83)

UFO's Pete Way puts his heart of ale on the line, fronting a crackling, dangerous band stuffed with sizzle, sleaze, and a brilliant grasp of the power shuffle. This strident, rumbling debut is chock-crammed with down 'n' dirty lumbering hard rock/metal extraordinaire, plowed like a train with integrity and loose, apocalyptic professionalism. Way drags co-ex-UFO-er Paul Raymond on this booze 'n' blooze, cokehead cruise along with the esteemed, bed-headed, Jack Daniels-schooled "Fin" on mike duties, one frontman way out on the edge of Desperado Town in terms of honest, biting hard rock pain. **Vices** is choice '70s loud and proud attitude metal, swelling with slurring, swirling fatman production, ideal for this kind of barroom brawl. Pete Way, in one fell swoop manages to focus more bellyfire and spark onto his debut than UFO was ever capable of in 20 years. Don't get me wrong, UFO was legendary hall of fame material (that's was), but **Vices** actually possesses more of a certain urgency than any single UFO disc cared to court. Would have been pure bliss if not for the cover of Jefferson Airplane Starship Enterprise whatever's *Somebody To Love*. Useless song, no matter how renovated and enervated.

Rating 10

## Waysted - Waysted (Music For Nations '84)

Another rowdy, faith-restoring chunk of fist, this five track EP rocks with the same fighting intensity as **Vices**, while shifting to a tighter, stripped-down sound; Kiss this time as opposed to Aerosmith. *Hurt So Good*

steps to the fore, offering a warm melodic hard rock, one of the band's more surprising larger-than-life areas of success, here penning a classic coursing with soul and ever-spiraling emotion. The remainder of **Waysted** offers excellent, to-the-point '70s hard rockers; tight, street level grit, that in its metropolitan total comprises the perfect soundtrack for cleanin' out the carbons on the old car deck.

Rating 8

## Waysted - The Good The Bad The Waysted (Music For Nations '85)

More line-up changes mark this direct progression from the tough-as-bullets **Waysted** EP. And we're graced with another grand and gregarious, Stonesy, melodic hard rocker in *Heaven Tonight*, a breathless composition that displays the desperate depths of this band's soul. **The Good The Bad The Waysted** quite plainly cranks more of the same six-guns-blazing garage rock, which is magnificently fine by me, even if a few tracks do smack of filler, most notably traces of too literal (read: lazy) boogie woogie, such as *Dead On Your Legs* and Chuck Berry's *Around And Around*. The torrid remainder however is dead serious, lean 'n' mean bad-boy retro-metal, slapped together with a hard-edged no-time-to-practice approach, powered for the last time by Fin's excellent growl. But long gone are the days when Pete could be seen careening around London in his Jag, steering wheel in one hand, brandy bottle in the other. Ten years later Way's involved in a worthy UFO reunion record, and **The Good The Bad The Waysted** has been reissued by Griffin, adding the entire **Waysted** EP plus octane rocker *Ball And Chain*.

Rating 8

## Waysted - Save Your Prayers (Capitol '87)

**Save Your Prayers** represents one of those personnel changes that makes a big predictable difference for the worse. The new guy (future Tyketto boy Danny Vaughn) is a good singer; competent and self-assured, but his voice lacks the world-weary charm of Fin's, chafing against the embattled feel of the Waysted psyche. And the music makes a parallel shift uptown. If the old stuff was Ted Nugent meets Tank, this one is Ted meets Journey; clean, slick, accomplished, and yes even surprisingly heavy and occasionally fire-bellied. Yet somehow it just lacks the spontaneity and time-honoured battery of old. And it's a good enough hard rock album, full of well-placed bells and whistles and adequate power, it's just that it's got nothing to do with Waysted anymore, and that's a crying shame.

Rating 7

## Weezer - Pinkerton (Geffen/MCA '96)

Listening to Weezer is like groovin' in the front row of Cheap Trick's triumphant Budokan invasion. There's lots of sugar, lots of spice, and lots of howling, backfed guitars doing battle with battered crash cymbals, a white-knuckle ride in white suits. And the din is quite glorious, these so-called nerd rockers siphoning the purest Pavement, Nirvana and Kiss gases, supertoking the classics, creating perhaps the sweetest mosh to hit your candy-ass town. It's almost as if the Beatles witnessed Poison in all their earsplit C.C. Devillian 1990 glory, divorced their ugly wives, plugged in and turbo-metalized the **White Album**. Pure distorto-heaven of the creamiest order. Lopped off a couple grades for brevity. Legal note: Pinkerton Security is officially bummed at the band, who have informed the fake cops that Pinkerton is a character in Madame Butterfly.

Rating 8

## Helen Wheels Band - Post Modern Living (Real American Est. '84)

Helen of course is the rock poetess who has contributed half a dozen or so lyrics to the Blue Öyster Cult,

including the classic *Tattoo Vampire*. Her own recorded output was sporadic to say the least, always professional, but pegged to the times in which they occured. An early flexi-disc and 45 were more seedy punk metallic in nature, reminding one of solo Johansen or the Dictators, while this six-track EP combined a manic and speedy punk energy with influences like Patti Smith (Helen is quite a fan) and the Talking Heads. It is also of note that Helen's one-time boyfriend Al Bouchard contributes in terms of drumming, production and even writing, Al and Deb (now fronting The Brain Surgeons) still very much close friends with Helen, who has now moved on to running her own publishing company.
Rating                                                         7

### Michael White - Michael White    (Atlantic '87)

After seven years as the king of Zep tribute bands, Michael White gets his shot at drippy teen stardom, with this flagrant, corporate AOR escapade like many attempted by Atlantic (and CBS) at the time. But try as they might, the suits can't hide White's innovative licks, riffs, arrangements and melodies, tracks like *Fantasy* (great Euro-tinged chorus), *Matriarch* (Bonham-boisterous Zep) and *Dirty Dancer* (Jon Lordy Purple) rising above, while *Psychometry* is the record's classic Zep-mathematical epic, full of all sorts of prog-Egyptian excursions, tapping into a wealth of years evoking Percy, Pagey and Co. But all in all, too keyboardy and commercial, producer Mack passing on the eccentric sonic trickery that made selected Queens and Squiers so brashy sassy.
Rating                                                         5

### Michael White - The White    (Griffin Est. '93)

A heck of a history lesson into the incestuous nature of blues-based rock'n'roll, Michael White returns in house of mirrors fashion to his Led Zep tribute concept, **The White** demonstrating in a bunch of ways how it's all borrowed and blue. So we get half a house of originals that either sound like Zep or its influences, covers by Zep's influences (and one by a contemporary in Alex Harvey's *Swampsnake* that sounds like an oldie), a straight, live and fairly flat Zep copy in *Whole Lotta Love*, and a genius, slow-brew power-groove through *Communication Breakdown*, the record's best track. So it all hangs well, fused by consistent Zep recording trickery (i.e Pagey's watery guitar sound and Bonham's loose-headed bass drum sound), making this a time-travel that is smooth and drinkable, even if twelve originals might have made for record with more gravity.
Rating                                                         7

### Michael White - Plays The Music Of Led Zeppelin
(Griffin '95)

Sounds great and all, but I'm not sure I get the point of making carbon-copy versions of fourteen different Zep tunes, except to impress curators, art restorers, coroners, historians and others who might take the challenge of recreating and documenting something that has already happened. And as an academic study, it is pretty cool, White meticulously commanding detailed, dead-perfect performances and an array of recording techniques that mimics all the strange, not great sounds Zeppelin would get. Faves are the open-air feel of *Kashmir*, the lusty, actually better vocal performance afforded *Nobody's Fault But Mine*, and the modern production fixing *Communication Breakdown*, but as I say, something like **Encomium** would get first dibs by me for purpose of playability, and above that, the freakin' originals if logic counts for anything.
Rating                                                         6

### White Flag - Wild Kingdom    (Positive Force '87)

Raging hormone new wavey punk à la early Replacements and more pissed-off carnivores like Hell's Kitchen and Necros, paying psyched-up homage to its (and our) roots, lending vicious spark to BOC's *Hot Rails To Hell* and The Saints' *Demolition Girl*, while getting all teenage on Cheap Trick's *He's A Whore* and *Deuce* from Kiss. The originals are more like traditional punk face blasts, leaking melody like Hüsker Dü, recorded with an approximation of Dü's surroundsound buzz. Proves that punk improved vastly seven or eight years after its demise, soaking up gobs of power during its appointment with the grave.
Rating                                                         6

### White Lion - Pride    (Atlantic '87)

I always looked on White Lion with fondness as a band who played to their strengths, no matter how unpopular they may be with serious music fans. This wasn't a heavy band making pin-up rock then defending it by saying how ass-kickin' they were live. White Lion worked like Guiffria and Night Ranger of old and Slaughter and Tyketto of late. White Lion *like* and *admire* pretty rock songs. They take it *seriously*. They *like* melody and elegance and music that attracts chicks, and they probably listen to it on their own time. Thus **Pride** doesn't pretend, it just is. And speaking of Night Ranger, **Pride** is in effect a Brad Gillis (and even Eddie Van Halen) sort of show, Vito Bratta providing an engaging, starstruck texture throughout the record, nimbly picking his way through Mike Tramp's perfumed vocal garden. Why the respect? Again, honesty, plus the fact that **Pride** is technically proficient and challenging wimp rock, a kind of highbrow study of the form, unlike early Poison or Bon Jovi which are plain dumb. Here there's layers of guitar fireworks, pleasing melodrama, harmonies, lots of ornamental goodies, not to mention the odd pistol packer which when they occur, are always top-notch.
Rating                                                         8

### White Lion - Big Game    (Atlantic '89)

Arrangements become more lush, melodies more Jersey, and the whole concept that much brighter and sterling crisp. White Lion's is a boisterous fat-hearted sound, a sound about making it, a sound built for that big stage under a hundred tiny lights, again bringing to mind Slaughter and Tesla, who both emit joyful waves of optimism as they zig zag across the country dreaming. White Lion is the intelligent side of that good vibe, less the rawk dogs with their nice clothes, acoustic guitars, and shameless pop sense. But it's always Bratta's polite metal pyro that keeps the more rivetheaded glued to the phones. Preferred anthems here would be lead track *Goin' Home Tonight*, thoughtful cool character *Cry For Freedom*, Roth-style OTTer *Let's Get Crazy* and headbanger *If My Mind Is Evil*. Yet **Big Game** is such a well-paced effort, it becomes a sort of concept record in totality, that concept being sensitivity, happiness, pleasure, honesty . . . and overall good will through the thoroughly maligned vehicle of commercial pop metal. Not an all too credible career path to say the least, although **Pride** went platinum, and this one gold. Not bad.
Rating                                                         9

### White Lion - Mane Attraction    (Atlantic '91)

Maybe it's just me, but I'm finding a trace of battle weariness here, **Mane Attraction** being an ambitious and lengthy work, yet one that lacks the enthusiasm of greater things to come, the buoyancy that made **Big Game** such a tall tale. Thicker and less spontaneous, **Mane Attraction** stomps out to centre stage with an 8:09 lead cut, *Lights And Thunder*, which seems to exemplify the band's implosion; a fine track, yet one that seems to rework past glories rather than forge

ahead. Faves are *Farewell To You* and single *Broken Heart*, both characteristic teen dreamers that rival the sweetness of Enuff Znuff. I dunno, maybe my enthusiasm has been affected by the way business hassles destroyed this band, as I search for the sound of defeat in Mike Tramp's vocals. An interesting chapter in the history of rock'n'roll, when all was said and done, White Lion managed to bridge metal and pop in a manner that was acceptable to both camps. A hearty ale to the boys.
Rating                                                                    8

## David Coverdale's Whitesnake - Snakebite
(United Artists '78)
Coverdale's first official slab o' Whitesnake rides the same almost confusing, behind-the-times mix of failed blues and funk ideas that just irritated with incestuous hokeyness on the man's previous two solo albums. Liking the whole concept of Whitesnake, I can warm up to about half of this, with a kind of twisted, academic smile on my face. Best rockin' glimpse of the future: the previously released *Breakdown*, which shuffles muscle in the tradition of Heep's *Love Machine*. Note: side one derives from actual Whitesnake sessions from '78 featuring production by Martin Birch. Side two is a mix of dead similar "solo" tunage recorded a year earlier with Roger Glover at the board. Boozy, balmy and sincere of purpose.
Rating                                                                    5

## Whitesnake - Trouble   (Geffen '78)
This follow-up to **Snakebite** is similarly arcane, bluesy and misguided, exposing a band or at least a mind that isn't sure if it's hard rock, heavy metal, r+b, funk or the Beatles (with their muscle funk version of *Day Tripper*: yawn). **Trouble** reminds me of **Stormbringer** in its loss fer direction, however one constant does emerge from the mix, the undeniable personal strength of Coverdale's belief in his abilities. Classic early speed rocker: *Take Me With You*.
Rating                                                                    4

## Whitesnake - Lovehunter   (Geffen '79)
Coverdale slowly begins to bestow his presence on the real world with this his first modern era, mostly heavy record, which roughly follows the formula of **Ready An' Willing**, offering a bit o' blues, some metal and some of his old, nerdy backwoods material. Trouble is (to quote Sword), the songcraft is light years away from the aristocratic charm portrayed on his next opus. Heavy, dense, and slightly uncommunicative, **Lovehunter** stands as a further mapping-out of Coverdale's blues metal voyage but comes off as slow and depressing.
Rating                                                                    5

## Whitesnake - Ready An' Willing   (Mirage '80)
**Ready An' Willing** is one of the great, British bluesy metal albums of all time. Coverdale's self confidence is unmistakable, as he leads his crack band of understated lounge lizards through low-down-mean, but silky-smooth mid-pacers such as the title cut, *Sweet Talker*, and one sheer classic of artful manipulation in *Fool For Your Loving*. Inspirations seem to span Bad Company, Stones, Skynyrd, Faces and maybe even more off-the-cuff Status Quo from the late '70s. The production is crystal clear, and really, despite the complexity of Coverdale's roots, this is his first record with real focus, coming off as some sort of voodoo brew of hot blues and metal licks, boogie woogie, a dose of '70s funk and a whole lot of David Lee Roth. Effortless, enjoyable, and destined to enter the rock mainstream through the backdoor.
Rating                                                                    8

## Whitesnake - Live . . . In The Heart Of The City
(Mirage '80)
This totally unnecessary live afterthought demonstrates that our resident Brit super ego suffers the same ailment as his old band: the bizarre opinion that we metal fans really like the blues. Nevertheless, besides the hellaciously boring title track and the even more excruciating 11:00 rendition of *Love Hunter* (a piece of shit Gene Simmons would be proud of), the remaining half of **Live** offers forth some of Coverdale's prouder moments in such early cock rock classics as *Sweet Talker*, *Fool For Your Loving* and pacemaker *Take Me With You*. Too little too late. Proceed to the studio albums.
Rating                                                                    4

## Whitesnake - Come An' Get It   (Mirage '81)
A bit of a style shift here as Whitesnake becomes simpler, boppier, less serious artistes, the album resembling more the stripped-down power chord hard rockers of **Slide It In** than the soulful and historical variations of **Ready An' Willing**. And of course, it doesn't work as well as either. Whereas on **Slide It In** the production, adherence to taste, and control raised the entertainment value, here the band is still uncomfortable with arena rock, the butt-shaking collection of dumbo metal so obviously their first kick at the cat. As a result, **Come An' Get It** sends forth a mildly amusing fluff, maybe even more than 50% toe-tappable, however lacking in anything that approaches the ten or twelve absolute barnstormers Coverdale and the boys have done over the course of the fantabulous '80s.
Rating                                                                    7

## Whitesnake - Saints & Sinners   (Geffen '82)
More upbeat, bluesy, boogerwooger metal in the same vein as **Come An' Get It**, *Saints & Sinners* has the band on productive idle. *Here I Go Again* and *Crying In The Rain* from this get replayed and beefed up for '87's hit album **Whitesnake**, but besides these two soulful departures, plus sustained and kickin' classic *Youngblood* which swaggers with as much pride as *Fool For Your Lovin'*, the rest is standard camp Vegas Elvis macho metal, undermining in its low cal delivery. Still, a lot of meaningless fun, good for a jogging tape. One of the harder Whitesnake records to come by, me settling for a picture disc version.
Rating                                                                    7

## Whitesnake - Slide It In   (Geffen '84)
The first 'snake to hit it big commercially (although more a set-up for a much larger windfall), **Slide It In** takes the band's previous simple, somewhat corny hard rawk approach and gleans the naivety out of it, venturing full stride into the '80s. Martin Birch produces **Slide It In** with robust forethought, firmly propelling the album, designing it for every ludicrously overloaded Alpine system cruising the midwest behind the dash of Camaros and Mustangs built for speed. Tight, punchy metal with surprisingly discreet drumming from loud man Cozy Powell, this stripped-to-the-basics disc features such summer rockers as the hefty, driving title track, the stop/start Zepp-isms of *Slow An' Easy* and the melodic and brooding *Love Ain't No Stranger*, the record's deserving smash hit. However, Dave can't shake the Bad Company-like tendency to write like a meathead, offering three or four duff ones, highlighting the fact that Whitesnake hasn't tried to make a fully serious album since **Ready An' Willing**.
Rating                                                                    8

## Whitesnake - Whitesnake   (Geffen '87)
The unambitious, unsurprising, but headstrong tough guy hard rock of **Slide It In** gives way to one of the most wollopingly power-drenched recordings ever,

while the songwriting itself is both heavier and lighter. On the light side, *Here I Go Again* is (still) Stonesy/Bad Co. blue collar fare, and *Is This Love* is a pathetic and cynical give-me-money power ballad. On the heavy side, *Bad Boys* kicks ass as a fast rocker slowed by the formidable weight of the recording, and the updated *Crying In The Rain* howls the blues under the juggernaut riffs of musical chairs hitman John Sykes. But the real story here is *Still Of The Night*, the grand opus of the entire Whitesnake catalogue, a metal tour de force wrapping a brilliant riff around inspired breaks and a climactic and melodically complex finale. At the time, Robert Plant seemed to thrive on the mileage he got with his David Coverversion shtick and accusations of every other band on earth for ripping off Zep, which is basically a crock. Granted *Still Of The Night* has Zep touches. It stops and starts like *Black Dog*, has a psychedelic breather like *Whole Lotta Love*, and Dave's vocals do inflect like Percy's early yelps back when he had his range. However, this is the only 6:38 in the entire 'snake repertoire where Zep even crosses Coverdale's mind. Earth to Plant. step down from the pulpit, and quit letting the press and your spin doctors lead your life. Alas, *Still Of The Night* is highly inspired work and screw the superficial and insignificant Zeppisms. In regard to the album as a whole, call it patchy: one half profoundly on fire, and one half sellout, featuring formidable power albeit in scant, checkered supply. Originally titled (tongue firmly in cheek), Pull It Out, Clean It Off, and Slide It In Again. Went on to sell over ten million copies worldwide, six mil in the U.S. Yow.
Rating 7

## Whitesnake - Slip Of The Tongue (Geffen '89)

More hi-tech and nimble, but also more metallic more often than the last, **Slip Of The Tongue** follows up full of flash and big world savvy. This is due no doubt to the replacement of crunch merchant John Sykes with count 'em two guitar gods, tastefully classical/metal Euro-virtuoso Adrian Vandenberg (whose old band was decidedly better than Whitesnake), and overplaying shred-jokester Steve Vai, who tried his best to wreck both David Lee Roth's band and Alcatrazz. Fortunately, Coverdale keeps Vai in check (although Coverdale later will admit to failure in this regard) and tunes such as the title track, *Kittens Got Claws*, and *Wings Of The Storm* zip along nicely while retaining their power. However, two more useless power ballads in *Now You're Gone* and *The Deeper The Love* betray the fact that Whitesnake is now cranking out what for the most part amount to soulless formula metal albums, basically abandoning their metal roots for an "updated" mature techno-flash. Although **Slip Of The Tongue** is the band's most serious album since **Ready An' Willing**, it loses its integrity on such commercially cynical points, racing to its finale with a sense that nobody had much fun putting the project together. Ambitious, but after the initial hoopla, not of lasting importance, its double platinum status being a letdown after the heady commercial highs of its predecessor. Note: it is rumoured that most of the riff and rhythm work on this record is by the uncredited Sykes, Vai brought in late to add solos and other bits, but the band retaining most of Sykes' bedtracks.
Rating 7

## Whitesnake - Greatest Hits (Geffen '94)

**Greatest Hits** keeps it tight, visiting the three Whitesnake records that have a clue. So the monster metalizers are here, the beer-swillers and the blathering ballads. You know 'em well. But thankfully, this is a hits pack that tries harder, so the liner notes are studded with little jewels of wisdom (sample: **Whitesnake** took three years due to a career-threatening sinus illness Coverdale incurred). Also: three all-new tracks:

*Looking For Love* (a large brooding blues ballad), *You're Gonna Break My Heart Again* (a thick, wrench-faced hard rocker), and *Sweet Lady Luck* (a fastback featuring fiery Vai leads): all tracks modern and worthy, if not earth-shattering.
Rating 7

## White Spirit - White Spirit (MCA '80)

This major NWOBHM hopeful comes up with an admirable retro-keyboard metal album highly reminiscent of Deep Purple's **Machine Head** vibe, notable in the guitar/keyboard mix and interplay, and the tightness and economy of songcraft, if not the quality of the songwriting. One of those serious long-lost British jems that in theory commands respect but in practice doesn't hit my table too often, I think due to the naivety of the songs and the ever so slight sub-par feel of the arrangements. Even though one can hear hints of *Highway Star*, *Never Before*, *Smoke On The Water*, *Smooth Dancer*, not to mention early Heep and Lizzy (smatterings of subdued dual guitar harmonies), the main feel is cheezy Magnum. Resident future rock star. Janick Gers, making this somewhat collectible. On that note, **White Spirit** received a '92 Japanese re-issue, which added three bonus tracks *Suffragettes*, *Back To The Grind* and *Cheetah*, only the latter scooting along metal-wise, all three kinda pomp rock dreary.
Rating 6

## White Trash - White Trash (Elektra '91)

Forget funk metal, man. These New York dudes take a sleaze metal image into direct collision with hard-edged funk; that's right, close to sincere funk, no matter how disgusted purists might be with the attempt. Hearing the single, I pegged these guys for one of the early GN'R rip-offs complete with a whiny junior Axl at the helm, albeit with a more personal, funky slant on life. Well forget that noise, 'cos all else on this, and I do mean all, delves even further into funk structures and its tools of communication, such as fwappin' bass, horns (three of seven members are credited as The Badass Horns), and heavy doses of ol' Superfly wah wah breaks. However much I now believe these guys are serious, I still don't approve; not being moved by funk unless it's forged in fire beyond recognition under steaming slabs of vengeful Flying V's. Could be mega, however, given the esteemed technical and managerial talent at the band's disposal.
Rating 4

## White Wolf - Standing Alone (RCA '84)

Canadian boys who never seemed to jump right into the metal sweepstakes, White Wolf roll out (with no particular enthusiasm or engaging tale to tell) simple melodic hard rock/metal, about the quality and heaviness of Helix's **No Rest For The Wicked**. A few bright hooks, but naive and uncommitted to the cause.
Rating 4

## White Wolf - Endangered Species (RCA '86)

Less the retro-mash of '70s rock styles portrayed on the debut, **Endangered Species** combines liberal use of electronic drums and other studio trickery for a more punchy, updated sound. Musically, the band leans more to potentially cash-generating hard rock and does a pretty decent job of it, despite its isolation quotient. Pushes **5**.
Rating 4

## White Zombie - La Sexorcisto: Devil Music Vol. 1 (Geffen '92)

Hey, it's like, O.K. if you've outgrown the road movie mentality, 'cos White Zombie lay it all on so opaque and properly hardcore that all the lyrical nonsense and sampling can be rightly seen as so much desert dust on the way to a newly confounding alter-metallic Slayer

on the path to Corrosion. White Zombie's widely panned career to date gets major distance as the boys (and girls) discover for the first time mobility, chops, and a hellish carnival of personas that works for them alone. The technicolor comic look sounds like what we want: a wisely distant affirmation that NYC has finally just blown its manhole covers, like it's become safe and acceptable behaviour to lose the whole code of conduct, and indeed the ability to use language in anything but dizzy storms of colour. Fact is, this is White Zombie's first hip record, a sun-baked purposeful trudge through shiftless but atmospherically disturbing Slayermetal. And when it winds up and courts an odd funk, as with lead vid and surprise dance hit *Thunder Kiss '65*, it's a rhythmic blast. No wonder most the record is a slashing variant of the theme, 'cos this is alternative hyperspace at its best. **La Sexorcisto** just sits fused like one big bad ride, basically unbreakable and uninterruptible to the cave strains of Rob Zombie's perfectly untuneful adenoidal scrape. Almost too much like a movie, and almost too stupid, but so chopped with love and almost rap-like angles it simply and splendidly rocks on its own humble piece of planet.
Rating                                                                 7

## White Zombie - Astro-Creep 2000   (Geffen '95)

I was always luke-warm to the kaleido-kulture concept of White Zombie, but starting with **Sexorcisto**, really slam-banged to their tunes. **Astro-Creep 2000** doesn't alter these sentiments, offering more psycho-rama bongwater gibberish while striking some of the danghappiest alloys of hip-hop, industrial and overbearing metal this side of B-movie Hell. As Rob Z. explained to me one interview, the record is "more" in every direction it goes, more industrial here, more groovy there, more sampled over here, and ten times heavier all over, all the while Rob caterwauling in that curmudgeonly eccentric rant we've all grown to know as The Truth. But there are other vocal performances, and some really killer hepcat rockers, fave being *Super-Charger Heaven* which is what I hope Deadly Ted Nugent's new one approaches in old-style metal exuberance. Truly entertaining, and less stiff than **Sexorcisto**, **Astro-Creep** finds the Zombies nudging green elbows with Monster Magnet in the trippy metal sweepstakes, leaving Green Jelly for Hawkwind, Zombie still the mightiest, nuttiest noise factors of the two, Wyndorf and crew more the creeps in the cellar.
Rating                                                                 8

## White Zombie - Supersexy Swingin' Sounds
(Geffen/MCA '96)

After being stuck in the washing machine that is White Zombie live, I wasn't all that enthused at listening to extra spicy versions of the band's already brain-barraging caustic collages. And once inside, my eyes rolled predictably, here various mixmasters reducing acceptably hungry tunes to uh, zombies, most tracks just nodding like sunrise at the rave, achieving that tranced numb that is hot caca these days. I guess when Unplugged is out of the question, you go pocket-protector rewired until the Trekkies show up and fill the place. However, intelligent conversations are nowhere to be had. Raid the bar, and drink voraciously to make other people more interesting! Heck, given a few cocktails, even that rasta-headed culture implosion that is Rob Z. might raise a few of those mumbles to communicative levels. Artwork: naked '60s chicks everywhere, getting the band into lukewarm bathwater for about five minutes.
Rating                                                                 5

## Brad Whitford / Derek St. Holmes -Whitford / St. Holmes   (CBS '81)

As in Aerosmith's Brad Whitford and Ted Nugent's co-vocalist Derek St. Holmes, who step forth timidly

with this time-worn piece of flu-like hard rock, evoking images of a kinder, gentler, sillier time, or a heavier and trickier Bad Company. Sounds like old Kiss crossed with third-rate Nuge, except when it truly takes flight with the insistent *Action* and the street-heated *Mystery Girl*, the latter, dare I say, a classic of deleted fossil rock. Malletheads without a malicious bone in their bodies making noises we can all live with, without the threat of having to think. Evidently Whitford wanted to turn this into a full-fledged band, including tours and more records, but Ted called St. Holmes up with a juicy contract Derek couldn't pass up. Well the world was really no better for it, that's for sure.
Rating                                                                 5

## Widowmaker - Blood & Bullets   (BMG '92)

Dee Snider returns with his version of Twisted Sister for the '90s, the early '90s that is . . . like 1989. Which is of course the problem, this sort of no-bones, no-blood, no-bark corporate metal, no matter how no-frills, being dead in the water. Yes in 1989, this might have worked, successfully reminiscing about all things Twisted, while eradicating the kiddie rock props, and getting tougher in terms of subject matter and riff, while the production stays thick and cloddish. Verily so, nobody liked this record when it shuffled into view, **Blood & Bullets** offering nothing remarkable, just big plodding power chord party toons, poodle rock clichés to the foreground, thinking fans of the '90s to the exits. Lazy and out-of-touch.
Rating                                                                 5

## Widowmaker - Stand By For Pain   (CMC '94)

CMC (Cheese Metal Cemetery to the non-believers) picked up Dee Snider's second attempt at making Widowmaker an act with which to reckon. And try as he may, with those pounding, down-tuned grooves, there's something missing here, causing this to sound contrived, manufactured rather than received from the leather-studded muse of metal. Parallel record: Stephen Pearcy's second Arcade spread, again a record with no obvious crap components, just somehow nothing fresh, tuning into '90s low and slow tones with no understanding of why they're there.
Rating                                                                 6

## Wig Hat - This Came Out Of Me   (Futurist '93)

Wig Hat slam through a sort of neckbrace grungepunk that harkens back to heavier NY Dolls and Johnny Thunders, sense of humour and sense of desperate squalor combining in a dark damp club deep in the embattled heart of the city. Ditties wing by pretty fast, so don't blink, although the odd house of cards wallows in grey, garage sludginess. Kinda cool, with a vocalist that sounds like Mudhoney's Mark Arm. Basically Detroit rock from Brooklyn.
Rating                                                                 6

## Wild - Wild 1   (Columbia '88)

Wild (two guys, just like Milli Vanilli) combine The Cult's gothic nightpunk look and **Love**-era melodicism, cranking out tunes that evoke heavy Billy Idol complete with electronic percussion, sneer vocals, and overt mindfulness of groove. Also sounds like Charlie Sexton's first album. Too loose and amateurish to rock with any weight, **Wild 1** is a forgettable dash-for-cash from two guys looking to be some kind of groove messiah crossover phenomenon.
Rating                                                                 4

## Wild Dogs - Wild Dogs   (Shrapnel '83)

Hells of all hells, a poor man's Rods! Yep Wild Dogs take that same rehash of '70s Lenny and Squiggy clichés, turning the show into a parody of parodies in the same brash, insensitive manner that their poverty-stricken labelmates did. One of those bands you just

can't fault in too many ways, but you never would seriously listen to. Well-rounded recording for early Shrapnel but for some vague reason I just don't care.
Rating 4

## Wild Dogs - Man's Best Friend (Shrapnel '84)

Mike Varney's pack of mangy mutts is back with a slight improvement in intensity, tightness and recording, plus a hilarious album cover showing the blood-splattered aftermath of a playful wrestling session between man and man's best friend. Vocalist and Rob "Lifer" Halford-lookalike Matthew T. is in strong form as he leads his competent but unexciting band through yet more garage Priest-style retro rock. Said album pushes **6** except for the fact that there's something ridiculous about the Wild Dogs concept, causing me never to take their particular brand of American poverty metal seriously.
Rating 5

## Wildfire - Brute Force And Ignorance
(Mausoleum Est. '83)

Wildfire were an ambitious traditional metal NWOBHM band led by golden-throat Paul Mario Day, ex of More, a band which took a flying leap into the realms of major heftic brilliance upon his departure with **Blood And Thunder**. This premiere gesture contains excellent, hooky, complex metal such as the god-like *Another Daymare* and *Violator*, yet for the most part consists of fairly naive-sounding, loose bolts rock; kinda rough-shod, disjointed and powerless. Still the flash points of brilliance are hard to ignore, making **Brute Force And Ignorance** frustratingly inconsistent, with hopes of what could be. Some great arrangements, innovative riffs, Lizzy-ish soloing but also a fair bit of bar band songcraft. Shows thoughtful strategy not without promise, but a lot of rust to lose in the process.
Rating 6

## Wildfire - Summer Lightning (Mausoleum Est. '84)

Wildfire's second album continues with the classy, intricate but spontaneous riff rock of the debut, albeit with stronger, better-planned songs. **Summer Lightning** rides an eminently British mix of riveting, traditional heavy metal in *The Key*, *Gun Runner*, and *Screaming In The Night*, and not so successful melodic hard rock in *Nothing Lasts Forever* and *Fight Fire With Fire*. One general problem with this band is that given the imagination and inherent hookability, the recording and indeed the playing have an ever so slight low budget, rushed feel, which is really no surprise for Mausoleum output, which is why the metal hauls ass and the AOR sounds like a Dokken demo. Still, **Summer Lightning** is one of those quality discs that can be home-spun start to finish without boredom, due to its unanticipated twists and turns. A devastating force in the making, whose mandate ran out when the money was all gone.
Rating 8

## Wildhearts - Earth vs The Wildhearts
(Warner Music '94)

Early Wildhearts was a fantastical burst of colour and flavour of a whole different chewy design than the stripped godly hookery of **p.h.u.q.** No kablooey, **Earth vs The Wildhearts** almost tries harder, offering bigger riffs, faster funner hooks (hey, *Caffeine Bomb* even sounds like Status Quo), and just verve for endless joy-riding miles. It really is amazing to watch, hear and devour the big choruses, the Cheap Tricks and the anthemic power of this band. And it's cool to witness them in their comparatively complicated hard rock phase, combining the ecstatic cream of Californy rock with Mott, Slade, Stones and all things British and jovial.

An absolutely top-flight, top-down summer booz crooz record.
Rating 9

## The Wildhearts - Caffeine Bomb (Warner Music UK '94)

In typical convoluted, make-a-buck, singles-crazy UK fashion, The Wildhearts create this four cartoon EP that every dedicated fan must buy. **Caffeine Bomb** comprises the brash, punk metallic title track (available on **Earth Vs**), another similar punk bash, plus two of the band's irresistible pop metal banana splits in *And The Bullshit Goes On* plus personal fave *Girlfriend Clothes*, proving the exhilarating melodic madness of these fab streetniks.
Rating 6

## Wildhearts - p.h.u.q. (Warner Music UK '95)

These U.K. unslottables have been getting Europress for ages, yet here across the pond, we've been left in the dark as to the allure of the canny pop metal crankcases called the Wildhearts. Well no more, as **p.h.u.q.** arrives, less smarmy and quaint than homeboys Terrorvision and miles more interesting than similarly hooky Chicago sensation Urge Overkill. Simply slaughtering guitarish airhead alternative like Matthew Sweet, Juliana Hatfield and Pavement with good solid songwriting, production, chops, and good old fashion giving a damn (remember self-respect as a band? remember caring?), Wildhearts lacquer a metal sheen over the trendiest of sounds, spilling over with arresting, Clash-hearted hard rock anthems at every twist, bop and shimmy, palpably more hypnotic and simple than past records, deeper into the crux of the band's purpose. Sorta like yer favourite thirteen Hanoi Rocks songs played by Cheap Trick after listening to AC/DC all day. *Nita Nitro* and *V-Day* could break this band like Nirvana.
Rating 9

## The Wildhearts - I Wanna Go Where The People Go
(Warner Music UK '95)

An EP of a much higher quality than **Caffeine Bomb**, this latest is mocked-up to look like a stamped passport, again offering four tracks with three being non-album raves. And they are all shining beacons of fun, fun, fun, *Shandy Bang* being one of those stop/starters with spaces, *Can't Do Right For Being Wrong*, a party to be celebrated, and *Give The Girl A Gun*, a "building" track laced with bagpipes and one of those hooks that sticks fer days.
Rating 8

## The Wildhearts - Fishing For Luckies
(Warner Music UK '96)

Not exactly a new record per sé, **Fishing For Luckies** was a fanclub-only release, this version dropping two tracks from said record and adding six. And given the (genius) uniformity of the band's spark and fire sound anyway, an airtight cohesion reigns. So it's a slam-bang batch of rainbow trout we have here, even if tunes lean towards the heavier, more technically worked-up end of the Wildhearts repetoire. Fave would be the rambunctious but almost progressively-involved *Do The Channel Bop*, but it's all immaterial, each track woven with at least a couple or three hook-heavy riffs, making the record almost conceptual in its sugary power chord flow. Zesty, piquant fun 'o plenty, but what else did you expect from the U.K.'s best kept secret?
Rating 8

## Wild Horses - Wild Horses (EMI '80)

With Lizzy careening in drunken disarray, resident lunatic pugilist Brian Robertson piles on with equally difficult excuse for human being Jimmy Bain for a little jamming outside the limelight. Along for the haphazard ride are Neil Carter and Clive Edwards, and what occurs is a simple pub rock record, fairly unflashy, strained and naive in just about every way. Only one co-write with Phil here, *Flyaway*, a decent ballad amongst a lot of Bain/Robertson exercises in humility, surprising, because at the time, the Lizzy org. was pooling their tunes, and picking them out as needed for whatever project was at hand. Good doses of dumb guitar (re: Bad Co.?) make this a less thoughtful record than its follow-up, but more importantly, both records are decisively rare. Hard rocky to the point of pop, Wild Horses were fortunately put down after a couple of dozy kicks.

Rating     **6**

## Wild Horses - Stand Your Ground   (EMI '81)

Lizzy spawned a stable of fine, intelligent guitarists, Brian Robertson being perhaps the definitive contributor. Here Robo collaborates with veteran Jimmy Bain (who handles lead vocal chores as well as his trademark bass), plus assorted other old pros in the pursuit of craftsmanship, a work ethic which fortunately always seems to be engrained in collusions between members of the British rock aristocracy. **Stand Your Ground**, the band's second, delivers much of what one could hope for, offering tight, highly strung melodic hard rockers amidst other much less metallic yet equally soulful vignettes in a fragile but Lizzy-ish vein, revealing taste and finesse without busy-ness or pretension. Robertson and John Lockton hold no reservations about smoothly dishing forth harmony axework, and lyrically, the proceedings are kept simple and human, hopeful and heartfelt. Although a good portion of this record rocks at a fair clip, absolutely nothing gets full-bodied or muscular, preferring nimble mobility, revealing links between the core HR sound and appreciation of jazz, and more conventional rock structures rather than leanings towards metal. Coolest cuts include riff rocker *The Axe*, smooth rider *Miami Justice* and the tricky *I'll Give You Love*. **Stand Your Ground** benefits from its project-like feel and its commitment to simple, emotional quality in preference to complication, offering forth a nice collection of Thin Lizzy-style rock, appropriately so, as Robertson was always one of the briskly beating hearts of the Lizzy sound. Shortcomings: thin sound quality and occasional frailty in terms of vocal ability.

Rating     **7**

## Wild Horses - Bareback   (Atlantic '91)

Man, I cashed in so many discs that attempt this sort of sonic hipshake through Hollywood metal, and it's really a fine and sometimes illogical line between the guilty pleasures (Tesla, Kik Tracee, Slaughter, Enuff Znuff, White Lion, Tyketto, Love/Hate) and the vile (Poison, old Warrant, Danger Danger). Wild Horses (one half of which is Rick Stier and James Kottak, ex of Kingdom Come) does the genre more than half proud, offering overblown portions of gloss and dynamics, while lacking the humanity, uniqueness, and/or fringe eccentricity of corporate metal's best. Such must be expected early in a band's career, especially in such a commercially focused market, where everything's gotta be perfect, technically speaking; and here it most definitely is. The guitars pierce the skies like the purest of electric buzzes, and the mix is one wild party of heat-swollen clarity. Performances are mighty fine too, leaving only the songs, which are not as original or energy-sustained as one would expect from the such an impressive sound machine, lumbering too often with a weighted-down effect, relying too much on chunky rhythm versus forward mass. More than acceptable, **Bareback** could grow on me, joining ranks with the shining mood enhancers mentioned in hushed tones above. Surprisingly enough, personal faves would have to include the exploratory Stevie Wonder cover *Tell Me Something Good*, and slippery Whites-

nake-style ballad *Matter Of The Heart*. No matter what the shortcomings, there's no denying the band's total professionalism and enthusiasm.

Rating     **6**

## Wild 'T' And The Spirit - Givin Blood   (Warner Bros. '93)

Robust funk metal from T.O. in the fine tradition of bands wide-eyed and wondrous at another fine tradition, Jimi Hendrix. Wild 'T', Nazeem Lakey and Danny Bilan create a sparkling derivation that started with Frank Marino, Pat Travers and Randy California, touches the lives of King's X and Vernon Reid's Living Colour, and really commands the floor with the likes of The Eric Gales Band. But Wild 'T' (who got called down to lend some axe to Bowie's **Black Tie** joke) has more pep, more ideas, more mobility, not to mention a penchant for a louder sort of affair, really letting fly on closer *Lovesick Woman*, which also features a nice Zep *Rock And Roll* drum intro. Very solid, very rhythmic, **Givin Blood** is a chunk of funk rock that rises above. U.S. release on Thermometer Sound Surface swaps a bunch of tracks.

Rating     **7**

## Will And The Kill - Will And The Kill   (MCA '88)

Standard hard rock fare with a touch of the twang from Will, brother of Charlie, now in Arc Angels. Over-produced by legend and personal hero Joe Ely, who puts a roots-rock-via-Austin boot to the proceedings, like a heavier, teen-rated version of his own **Dig All Night**. Although Joe also co-writes a good half of this mega-glossed Texas twister, perhaps his biggest contribution to the Will concept is Joe's regular guitarist, and current Mellencamp sidekick, David Grissom, who chimes and shapes his expressive weaponry often and colourfully throughout. Interesting, and deeper than brother Charlie's wanderings as of late, Will benefits greatly from his friends in high places.

Rating     **6**

## Winger - Winger   (Atlantic '88)

Experiencing somewhat of an identity crisis with their fortified '93 release **Pull**, Winger seem to be caught with their chosen genre on the wane. But back in the beginning, there was **Winger** the platinum-selling debut for band leader Kip Winger, Paul Taylor, Reb Beach and ex-Dixie Dregs percussive genius Rod Morgenstein. Over-produced by Beau Hill (turgid drum sound), **Winger** picks up on Ratt's high precision California riffery for a slick but muscle-bound hard rock sound not without technical flourishes, culminating in a polished reconstruction of *Purple Haze* to close out the record. So there's definitely Ratt, considerable doses of Dokken, plus White Lion and Tesla all influencing the Winger proposition, getting the band nowhere with critics, although hooks are in abundant supply, along with intelligent arrangements, making for something much more substantial than high school metalizers like Poison; something almost European in tone. As might be predicted however, totally unnecessary.

Rating     **6**

## Winger - II: In The Heart Of The Young   (Atlantic '90)

I lost patience with Winger come record II, the band lapsing into an avalanche of synthetic sounds, glossing it up higher than the CN Tower, leaving nothing to human feel, hands and heart. I guess 1990 or thereabouts was the peak of poodle metal, and on this mirror to society, it shows. The wait unto **Pull** will work small wonders.

Rating     **5**

## Winger - Pull   (Atlantic '93)

Strip me of my press badge, but dammit, Winger is summarily bitchin', bottom line. Whether you like this

sort of well-arranged, melodramatic epic metal, you can't deny it's well done, evoking the best of Tesla gone a tad progressive, self-inflated, ambitious and ambidextrous. But that don't mean I'm rating through the roof, **Pull** being a record I'd pull under many a circumstance for livlier, more attackive fare. There's still too much Leppard and too much hair, as Winger deliberately and knowingly stays steadfast in the realm of hi gloss hard dross, rejecting the lo-fi ethic of the '90s. Very, very, very good exercise in corporate shmooze metal, assigning the band an inverted backdoor integrity that is valid in its own right. Again very much like Tesla.
Rating　　　　　　　　　　　　　　　　　　　7

### Wipers - Land Of The Lost　(Est. '81)
Before there was a Sub Pop scene, the Northwest claimed unhewn bands like Screaming Trees, Melvins, and Wipers, precursors fusing punk, psychedelia, and grunge guitars to no artistic avail, and no commercial success. **Land Of The Lost** is basically a U.K. Subs record; turgid garage punk; pre-ambition, pre-brains, tripping along like a fluid-clogged Ramones. Punky, dreary and forgettable for its audacity to think it can impress solely on college band crankiness.
Rating　　　　　　　　　　　　　　　　　　　3

### Wipers - Follow Blind　(Est. '83)
Been records before it, been records since, as **Follow Blind** grinds merely another tough, dreamy cog in the strange Wipers machine. Here the band is wholly transformed from its pogo predictability into a sort of heavier Cure, wallowing in dank caves built of strumming bass, echoey, weasel-toned vocals, and loosely-instrumented sparseness, embracing the chill of Joy Division by third dirge. Never metal, and on the present disc, under half heavy in any sense of the term, putting Wipers in this book just feels right, as there's something looming in fierce potentiality amidst the torn and frayed loitering of the new direction. And the drowning pre-Sub Pop meltations reverberating from the core of this record deserve recognition. Lost in time; indeed violently detached from it. Plain talk: may bore you to tears.
Rating　　　　　　　　　　　　　　　　　　　4

### Wireless - No Static　(Anthem '80)
Wireless were an early Canadian hard rock band that plugged in and left without much stir. On the same small label as band buds Rush and Max Webster, this clever third effort was produced by Geddy Lee, while its predecessor **Positively Human, Relatively Sane** was produced by Max's Mike Tilka. By no means heavy metal, **No Static** nevertheless contains some great nostalgic '70s style guitar rock, tight and slightly progressive, studio-focused, reminiscent of early Max, although not as brilliantly off-centre. I don't think you'll ever see any of these for more than three bucks so pick 'em up and add 'em to your wax museum. Note: the debut, **Wireless** sucks.
Rating　　　　　　　　　　　　　　　　　　　6

### Witchcross - Fit For Fight　(Roadrunner '84)
One of the jewels in '84's contract-free-for-all rough, and a critically-acclaimed slab to boot. These Danes whip up a generous melodic slab of appreciably heavy Euro-metal, full of stirring hooks, in the process spawning one masterpiece of evil in *Face Of A Clown* driven by scientifically twisted riffwork, and innovative drumming reminiscent of **Metal Church**'s title cut. Alex Savage's emotive vocals and respectable range further enhance the quality of these variously intricate flash rockers and straight ahead tragi-goth highballers. Although the recording is a bit pedestrian and low on treble, it hasn't stopped me from spinning this hypnotically in my most cancerous of lead-poisoned moods, 'long side the immortal Quartz, Highway Chile, and

Heavy Load. Classy and memorable, **Fit For Fight** captures the magic of NWOBHM demonstrating a general shaping and exploratory zeal of a revitalized music.
Rating　　　　　　　　　　　　　　　　　　　8

### Witchfinder General - Death Penalty　(Heavy Metal '82)
The debut overdose from the one and only ultra-doom merchants (from where else but the outer fringes of Birmingham) serves up a loose and inebriated display of dark psychotic black metal wholly lifted, but brilliantly so, from Black Sabbath's early warfare. Although **Death Penalty** is rough, raucously recorded, and bluntly lacking in chops, the sledges within display a blood-soaked melancholy so downright sincere and unpleasant that one detects these guys may be kidding. *Death Penalty* and *Witchfinder General* rival the best of dirges from the **Friends Of Hell** opus, and with a hint of the mighty Diamond Head in the delivery, this band is creaks and groans like no Americans could ever be. Features one of the trademark naked chicks 'n' violence album covers courtesy of Heavy Metal Records' owner Paul Birch, legendary rock pig extraordinaire.
Rating　　　　　　　　　　　　　　　　　　　10

### Witchfinder General - Friends Of Hell　(Heavy Metal '83)
More brilliantly-conceived early Sabbath globrock which goes beyond Iommi into the depths to escape the imitation band tag, **Friends Of Hell** mixes **Master Of Reality**-quality songcraft with the messed-up headspace of **Black Sabbath** and the chug groove wollop of **Mob Rules**, differing from the band's hair-raising premiere in that the playing is wound a bit tighter and the songs are a notch more logically gutted. **Friends Of Hell** is brutally stark and depressing; lumbering in drunken, volcanic immature stupor, while Zeeb Parkes' vocals, wholly possessed by the spirit of strung-out, early-days Ozzy, bleat out sentiments of shattered innocence such as *Love on Smack*, *Last Chance*, *Requiem For Youth* and suicidal acoustic wake, *I Lost You*. Only the Generals, Trouble, and now Cathedral have managed to tap the tormented attics of the early Sab psyche, each evoking more whiffs of chemical sleep than **Technical Ecstacy** played backwards at Jim Jones' retirement party. Souls in quest of a reversal of self-inflicted misfortune.
Rating　　　　　　　　　　　　　　　　　　　10

### Witchfynde - Give 'Em Hell　(Rondelet '80)
This unsolved mystery of a debut marks the beginning of a confusing and confused chapter in the NWOBHM sweepstakes, not to mention the first serious incarnation of black metal ever. Even though **Give 'Em Hell**'s cover is about as black metal as is demonically possible, lyrically, the band is only occasionally in Satan's camp, and never as approvers of his counselling. Musically, **Give 'Em Hell** approaches the warm and melodic (see *Gettin' Heavy* and *Leaving Nadir*), amidst other more traditional riff-maps of Lower Purgatory. Steve Bridges' vocal shriek marks a perfect fit, but the production slithers a bit cheap and midrange-y, causing undermined signals in self importance. All of side one is pretty well eclectic and nifty, whereas side two, comprising only three cuts, is 50/50 at best, causing Manowar-like percentages. **Give 'Em Hell** is definitely heavier than the mucho strange follow-up, and is quite uniformly standard '70s style HR or HM, demonstrating that the boys have their heads roughly turned full twist to straight ahead, eyes on the future. Overall, possibly because of its obscurity and backwater oddity, this album carries a dark and uncommunicative sheen that establishes the Witchfynde mystique, if only momentarily.
Rating　　　　　　　　　　　　　　　　　　　8

## Witchfynde - Stagefright (Rondelet '80)

The sophomore blakwax from these amateurish but likeable NWOBHM originals looks real cool, real heavy, real sinister but is, alas, an understated screwball of a release. Talk about confusing. The packaging is dead serious black metal whereas the songs are schizo, cheap, even chummy. We get shamelessly embarrassing numbers Spinal Tap would be proud of such as *Doing The Right Thing* and *Would Not Be Seen Dead In Heaven*, yet conversely, two manic, gloriously overblown metal scorchers, *Stage Fright* and *Wake Up Screaming*, that heave and creak with huge blasts of black wind; easily the band's most obvious symphonies of genius. In between we get solid Euro-HR such as *Moon Magic* and *In The Stars*, and a bouncy, harmless but warm little number, *Big Deal*, about being the lowliest of bar bands. Very strange, endearing, bumbling, but the best Witchfynde of all, due to music that is humble and true, making no attempt to hide the personalities behind props. An enigmatic English oddity.
Rating                                                      8

## Witchfynde - Cloak And Dagger (Expulsion '83)

This giant leap into the modern era finds the Witchfynde boys losing their quirks for a more uniform updated Halloweenie roast which comes off as less sincere but more metallic and rockin', although in terms of concept, the band was rumoured to have spent many hours in research of the black metal subject matter addressed, much to the detriments of their other musicianly responsibilities. Great cover too. Alas, Witchfynde's career woes intensified with this professional but commercial record, the label deeming it so fit to offer zero financial support, dooming the band in the process.
Rating                                                      6

## Witchfynde - Lords Of Sin (Mausoleum '84)

Not that they could ever write consistently anyways, poor man's King Diamond, Luther Beltz and his conspirators come up with a sludgy, dark, British record of fairly standard HR metal that hints at past exquisite blackness but usually just gets by with lazy, hanging chords and metal clichés. For the former, witness the Maiden-ish melody of quicky *Wall Of Death* and the slow but insistent *Conspiracy*. For annoying complacence, witness the tried and untrue riffery of *Scarlet Lady* and *Hall Of Mirrors*, the latter of which could be a heavy Angel City cut without the black wrapping paper. Per usual, Witchfynde has no idea about what kind of band they want to be, coming off here as both musical and lyrical moderates. All in all, file this decent upon inspection but rarely played.
Rating                                                      5

## Witchkiller - Day Of The Saxons (Metal Blade '84)

This Ottawa band's five track EP shows a leather and studs band with ideas, even inventive melodies, working with standard '70s and early '80s metal in a decidedly Judas Priest vein (in fact the band covered loads of Priest and Maiden live). *Beg For Mercy*, *Penance For Past Sins*, and the title track are hook-laden metal tunes that don't compromise on heaviness. Promising stuff from a long-defunct band with scads more cool originals to their pen that could have made this a scorching full-length LP.
Rating                                                      6

## Wolf - Edge Of The World (Mausoleum '84)

Another disposable jetsam from a raft of average-to-bad bands from the grimy Mausoleum label, Wolf goes after an admirable trad metal sound but fails due to lack of songcraft and old-fashioned practice. Sounded pretty good amongst '84's other drabble, but pales badly in these lightning-fast, competitive times. And it

doesn't help that most of the tunes were two or three years old by the time the record was assembled.
Rating                                                      3

## Wolfsbane - Live Fast, Die Fast (Def American '89)

A bit of an odd project for Rick Rubin and his megaton masters, Wolfsbane were a scrappy British posse that possess the uncanny destiny to revive and update the low income underbelly of the NWOBHM, bands like Fist, Chateaux, Grim Reaper, Savage, Samson, Tygers Of Pan Tang and Witchfynde, who were undeniably pure of heart in their respective corners of the genre. Rubin cages the band's pesky rat-like sound, inspires, then carves his initials into some devastatingly loud and edgy guitar solos, all the while preserving the band's British underdog persona, its traditional '70s approach to OTT, its misplaced tunefulness, its numerous grimy attempts at melodic hard rock, and its high-strung punkiness. What results is a warm and communicative, yet truly axe-heavy slab of skidder metal, worthy of the myriad of influences it slaps on the back. Sounds like one raucous, beer-soaked soccer holler which is fine by me.
Rating                                                      8

## Wolfsbane - I Like It Hot (Def American '90)

Description: way cool 12" EP pressed on red vinyl, gatefold jacket with lots of band shots. Commemorates a stab at a commercial hit with the likeable *I Like It Hot*, while tacking on three live tracks recorded at the '89 Rip convention in L.A.: *Limo*, *Loco*, and *Manhunt*, three usual Wolfsbane confusions that demonstrate the band's weird street metal hybrid.
Rating                                                      6

## Wolfsbane - All Hell's Breaking Loose Down At Little Kathy Wilson's Place (Def American '90)

Big long title for this short sod-bustin' EP that comprises six tracks and 23 minutes of ruff and ready Wolfsbane originals, none of which are on any of the three studio slabs. The mood is a little more party action this time, less frantic but still alive and spontaneous like crazy. Faves are emotional near ballad *Hey Babe* and moody metal closer *Kathy Wilson*. Elsewhere there's pop metal, speed, mid-paced stuff, the usual good judgment shown by this very believable band. Produced, and I use the term loosely, by Brendan O'Brien.
Rating                                                      8

## Wolfsbane - Down Fall The Good Guys (Def American '91)

Blaze and his assembled falling down punters continue to hone their odd and folksy pint-lifter metal, Brendan O'Brien again taking the reigns, shifting the guys ever so slightly upscale. So what burns out of the woofers is an eccentric English hard rock, courting AOR, the NWOBHM, southern rock and minor speed metal, all slapped together with an exuberant smack, like all parties are barely being held in check. Main difference here is the attention to detail, choice rootsy rockers like *Broken Doll* and *Twice As Mean* (there's some Billy Gibbons in this one!) taking all of the above and adding Van Halen, all the while Blaze showing incredible pre-destination with his Bruce Dickinson impressions (circa Samson, mind you). Pretty spirited stuff all in all, Wolfsbane giving old Blighty their very own potent, potential arena rockers, who, also like Maiden, manage to exude star quality while remaining grounded amongst the   rivetheads who afforded them their fame. Closes out with Wolsbane's very own *Hot Dog*, *Dead At Last*.
Rating                                                      8

## Wolfsbane - Wolfsbane (Castle '94)

The last gasp before Blaze Bayley would vamoosh to make a dreadful Iron Maiden record, **Wolfsbane** begins life as an austere graphic concept, all black and white and artsy fartsy. But have no fear, the band is still firing rounds of cantankerous competent metal, tunes like *Wings* and accelerated torch-rocker *Lifestyles Of The Broke And Obscure* announcing and trumpeting the Wolfsbane cause with deafening heroic tones. Fact is, it gets harder to handle that these guys are no more, especially given the horrid stinking mess that is **The X Factor**. It's rare to find a band with this much personality (Wildhearts come close), and furthermore it's a damn pleasure to hear such a volatile, spirited mix of hook and heft. The Wolfsbane magic is still defined by this marriage of riff and mischief, and really little has changed over the years, except that this is the band's best collection of songs, the boys bloodied and un-bowed, belting it out like they already know it's their last swift boot at the music establishment. Again, it's time to raise a pint to one of rock's unheralded little franchises. Cheers.

Rating     9

## Wolvz - Down & Dirty   (Grudge '89)

Wolvz (stupid name) are a noisy, stripped-down gang of backstreet rockers, presumably from Pennsylvania, who straddle the line between mean hard rock and good simple metal. Nuthin' too fancy here, just cred-ible, well-recorded chug rockers that sound like Dok-ken before showering. A problem with samey-ness here, with a lot of hanging chords, and formulaic mel-loid first verse, heavy-all-else structures, but also a lot of lusty drinkin' dreck amidst the un-stirred redneck drone.

Rating     6

## Mark Wood - Voodoo Violince   (Guitar Recordings '91)

"There are no guitars on this record" screams the liner notes, as Juilliard renegade Mark Wood showcases his weapon, very, very electric violin. But sadly, **Voodoo Violince** plays like a product demo, almost exclusively the domain of instrumentals, although extremely intri-cate while hummable ones, heavy prog rock with melody. Mark provides humourous and illuminating comments on each track, displaying a sense of play you might not find with a guitar demagog, and the man mixes his freaky styleys well. The best approximation of a metalized Yes or U.K. I think I've ever heard, Wood finding Steve Howe's vocabulary on those damn ma-chines of his effortlessly. Perhaps insultingly low-ish **6** grade reflects personal disdain for instrumental music unless its barely audible bongwater designed for floaty horizontal mushmindtravel.

Rating     6

## Wood - Against The Grain   (Guitar Recordings '94)

Tool, Wool, Wood . . . all the same, right? Wrong, 'cos this posse is the domain of one Mark Wood, the world's first heavy metal violinist (Yngwie might cite Paganini), who caused many a furrowed brow with his more academic **Voodoo Violince** debut. Wood also bides his time constructing space-age violins for other Wood-bes to stroke, a craft that will probably eclipse this rock star fixation as the years pass. **Against The Grain** is more of a furious power funk metal rock band record, layered loud and aggressive by real players (sorta what we all want David Lee Roth to get back to). You wouldn't really pick out the violin-ness here (un-less you were a guitarist), Wood evoking a fluid but more muscular Steve Vai here, the inherent smooth-ness of the violin making for intriguing pathways. A bit tainted by Wood's slightly poodle-rocking past, but mod-angsty enough to matter in the '90s. Vocals on most tracks.

Rating     6

## Wool - Budspawn   (London '92)

Wool hail from the bass-scape school of alternative heaviness, dumping a sort of Helmet meets Therapy? meets Nirvana rhythm din, while leaning a bit shattered and angled towards Fugazi, given guitars that occasion-ally smell very off-putting indeed. But the songs are strong, desperate and pained, spiced with dynamics and blank generation musings, delivered tightly but not so second-guessed. Six tracks, 26 minutes. I look for-ward to more.

Rating     7

## Wool - Box Set   (London '94)

Feeling somewhat bitter about the poor showing of this full-length debut (bad label match?), Wool oughta look within to their boring, artgrunge record itself. Parallel with Quicksand's sorry follow-up as low pay off riffs, percussive non-starters and here, simple punk mixed with simple pop to no avail.

Rating     6

## World Of Silence - Window Of Heaven   (Black Mark '97)

Indicative of metal's merging with progressive, this new Swedish act goes far beyond the likes of prog metallers like Fates Warning and Dream Theater into fully committed art rock. And even though the first thing that might come to mind is Marillion, given that this is Sweden '97, and the label is Black Mark, those electric guitars are never far behind. What results is a perfect, potent mix between keyboards, piano, and heavy guitar textures, over a bass and drums bed that carries with precision, the band's odd time signatures. Even vocals are normal, conventional, understated singing, no dog whistle operatics or pitbull growls anywhere. Bottom line: I'm a nutty prog freak, and I welcome the label's endorsement of something that takes this next step away from their prog metallers Tad Morose and Morgana Lefay, striving to lighten up a genre that is beginning to fill to capacity.

Rating     8

## World War III - World War III   (Est. '87)

Ultra-heavy fodder which is generally too thrash to say much useful. Slows down about one third of the time at which point it achieves gristle nirvana (like when Exciter or Slayer hit their stride). Otherwise too noisy.

Rating     4

## Wrath - Nothing To Fear   (Est. '87)

See reviews for Dark Angel and World War III, as all is murky and interchangeable under such pig-ironed crusts. Only difference here is that Wrath's ultra-heavy mercuric veins slow down more often, roughly at Slayer's late '80s levels. However, lyrical and riffic ideas are woefully few and far between.

Rating     4

## Wrath - Fit Of Anger   (Medusa '88)

An additional serving of nebulous faceless power metal that in '88, is a presidential term in office too late. Good album cover though, unfortunately wrapping a record that could only be loved as a new release, by buddies of the band, or by hometown fans; not so much incom-petent, just an absolutely unimpressive grab bag of technical Bay Area dosh, econo-debut-style.

Rating     4

## Wraith - Schizophrenia   (Neat Metal '97)

As is typical of many Neat Metal signings, Wraith have a bit of a haphazard past, releasing two records since their inception in '88, their second, **Riot** seeing re-working and re-release in '95, their first **Danger Call-ing**, seeing re-release in '96 (Japan only), and now this convincing, sublimely melodic new record for '97. The present record is a curious but instantly likable alloy of

hard-hitting AOR and somewhat pleasingly trashy production values. Songs possess a sort of under-stated
languish, interesting, drama-filled arrangements colliding with layers of guitars and full-on traditional metal
vocals. The record's drum sound seems to be gutted
by choice, allowing other frequencies to over-ride with
a strange surging effect (think Queen, Vandenberg or
lost legends T-Ride). Quite a remarkable happenstance
(even if it may be an accident). All in all, give this one
two thumbs up for vocals, arrangements, strong choruses and this strangely satisfying street vibe that has
no business being there.
Rating                                                    8

## Wrathchild - Stakk Attakk   (Heavy Metal '84)
Poor quality glam metal; bad songwriting and kinda
schizo stylistically. These girlie-guys got a lot of hype in
Britain, even though they were the laughing stock of
their NWOBHM contemporaries and other industry
insiders. Unfortunately Wrathchild didn't have the
ideas to back-up the buzz they briefly inspired, following this one up with the un-loved **Trash Queens** in '85
and at least one other, **The Biz Suxx** from '88, both
of which I've lost no sleep over never hearing.
Rating                                                    3

## Wrathchild America - Climbin' The Walls
(Atlantic '89)
This one attracted a modicum of attention for this
Virginia-based band of crazy magicians, because it was
the product of good players embracing both raw and
light-hearted arrangements, sort of laughing at the
melodrama metal sometimes gets caught up in, chops
pointing the finger at the silliness of ego-driven thrashers. I dunno, this somehow held more integrity than
the alternative angst and anger of the band's mid-'90s
incarnation.
Rating                                                    7

## Wrathchild America - 3-D   (Atlantic '91)
A band almost too smart and centred for their own
good, Wrathchild America (the America added to
counter confusion with the fright-coiffed UK abomination) cranked a sort of mischievous mosh; technically
high concept tunes put through a punk blender, sort of
Bay Area thrash meets California hardcore, the latter
more in spirit than deed. And it ended up confusing,
sorta funny, satirical, heavy but undercut by the raw
display of elements best refined (this one more eccentric than **Climbin' The Walls** to be sure). In any event,
the band's music and lyrics made you think, straddling
genres and philosophies despite the oil and water mix.
Later changed their name to current moniker Souls At
Zero, in an attempt to stay or get with the '90s. And
the sound remains somewhat the same, if a little Pantera greasier. Strange act, somehow hard to get close
to.
Rating                                                    7

## WW III - WW III   (Hollywood '90)
Vinny Appice and Jimmy Bain overdo it a bit, enlisting
Viv Campbell-inspired guitarist Tracy G (no relation to
Kenny G) and Satani-growler Mandy Lion, in construction of a bad-ass 'n' blackened experience a touch too
caustic and lethal for mass consumption in pre-death
1990. Cracks a smile with the purists though, evoking
fanged images of **Mob Rules**, **Born Again** and **The
Last In Line** sent to the rockpile of insanity. Appice is
the consummate percussion fiend, thumping **WW III**
into submission under the borderline grindcore vocals
of Lion, which somewhat detract from the proud
clubbing carried out by his backing trio. Slow, thick and
tortuous, **WW III** is a modern day Sab fleshfry with a
curious corporate spin, a kind of hip garish glitz, like a
vampire biker cruising the Hollywood hills, like taking
a drag on his chopper's tailpipe: black exhaust in the
lungs and a major rumble in the brain.
Rating                                                    8

## Zakk Wylde - Book Of Shadows   (Geffen/MCA '96)
After flirting with unnatural extensions of Pride & Glory
(possible work with Ozzy or Axl Rose's axis of G'NR),
the prolific Zakk embarks on a natural one, essentially
constructing an unplugged, declawed and contemplative version of his earlier solo excursion. **Book Of
Shadows** is a lush, soulful piece of acoustic roots
music, Wylde's vocals realing coming into their own,
sounding like a fixed, de-eccentric take on Jim Dandy
or Greg Allman. Fave would be *What You're Look'n For*,
which gathers it all together for a campfire
CSN/Skynyrd/Dead type hybrid, perfect for classic
rock radio, viable as anything by say, Tom Petty, Zakk
really demonstrating an appropriateness for this kind
of music, one which may not be afforded the guy given
his screeching rock past. *Too Numb To Cry* delves even
further with its orchestration and piano, taking Wylde
on a creepy tour of all sorts of '70s balladeers. Strange
little record, and so successfully retro and ironically
infinite, it ain't funny.
Rating                                                    8

# XYZ

## X-Cops - You Have The Right To Remain Silent . . .
### (Metal Blade '95)

Well, lookee here, looks like those boys in Gwar have cleaned up their festered rash and become boys in blue. But these redneck renegade cops are corrupt as a three dollar bill, and love to cuss, swear, carry on and inflict pain. And somehow between writing parking tickets and stealing contraband, this precinct have become tight-thrashing, death metal pigs, intensifying beyond their Gwar-ish past (and present: Gwar is still a going concern), constructing a white-knuckle metal that betters each and all Gwar pimples. But man, is it crude, rude and bathroom-humour funny, which means X-Cops are probably no more than a one-event spin, an enjoyed check-me-out, then quick to the racks, more like a movie or theatre production than something you'll play repeatedly. If chuckles is your goal, you can't expect much beyond a brief visit.
Rating **7**

## X-Sinner - Get It   (Pakaderm '89)

For once a set of corroded pipes in love with AC/DC that isn't so much Bon Scott but Brian Johnson, X-Sinner's David Robbins leads a blunt, swinging, and subtley White Metal band of ragtag rockers through this solid batch of party metal that's miles above similar fare from Johnny Crash, Junkyard and Hangmen, more shoulder to shoulder with Rhino Bucket and The Four Horsemen. Hell, a lot of it rises to heavy Crüe circa **Shout At The Devil** (witness trench rockers *No Way* and *Walking Evil*). Yet these are Christian rockers, although that knowledge comes as much from the band's inclusion on a White Metal compilation I review here, and from the fairly downplayed fear of Hellfire warnings throughout this flat-out, often old Def Leppard-ish affair. With all the killer records blasted into town in 1992 (the best year in metal for some time), it's easy for strong but unremarkable rockers like this to get File 13, without too much sense of loss. Like many of my 7's, **Get It** will only mean higher marks to you if you are a serious craver of the stylistic direction at hand; in this instance chunky, headbangin', no frills, no ballads rock'n'rolling. If that's the case, **Get It**.
Rating **7**

## Xysma - Lotto   (Relapse '97)

Xysma are an underfrost band of zany Finn nutballs bent on reshaping modern rock in their warped image. Eleven years long in the tooth at this point, the band has three previous full-lengths under their belts, along with a reputation for rough-shod indie rock insanity somewhat akin to the likes of Melvins, Butthole Surfers or Clutch. **Lotto** sports a bevy of great alternative metal crunchers, barked out like pirates, recorded sorta trashed, gutted and left to dry on purpose. There's something strong, defiant and individual about this band that captures the danger of grunge from '88, or Ministry circa **Psalm 69**, shaggy lead vocalist Joanitor in particular commanding the attention of those wondering whether he'll jump and go splat. But enough circumlocution. What we basically have here is charismatic, psychedelic, funky, grunge metal with spicy samply bits. And it is worth the visit, despite that garage-level recording.
Rating **8**

## XYZ - XYZ   (Enigma '89)

XYZ's glossed-up debut package was justifiably dragged past the gauntlet as a Dokken knock-off, teeming with hot Dokkenisms structurally, vocally, and riffically; and of course, Don himself quite capably produces, also acting as general mentor to this particular set of perms. I dunno . . . the boys sound fairly intelligent in interviews, pretty clear-headed in terms of what they want to do, but this debut (and evidently follow-up **Hungry**, by all accounts) just lack killer instinct, fading into the back-drop amongst lots of stiff competition. XYZ romps through all phase shifts of the Dokken swing, nimbly and convincingly, albeit with loiterous preponderance on the slow 'n' easy, hatching four mellow cuts out of ten and lots of hanging atmospherics on the remaining six boulders. Easily a "good" LA record, just how necessary is another question.
Rating **6**

## Yesterday And Today - Yesterday And Today
### (London '76)

Y&T's inauspicious debut was little more than tolerable, laughable barwipe metal but hey . . . who was doing much better in '76? Ultimately the more record stands the test of time, sounding tired and aged but in a pleasurable way, kinda like kick-ass Bad Company with brains; gritty, dense, but just fine for a bellyful of bad draft in a boomy B-city nightclub. High marks for Leonard Haze's helluva percussion display, fueling the band's raucous, to-the-quick unpretentious songcraft. Spiritual grandpa to fellow, farther south Californians **Van Halen**, Y&T were for many years the perennially gigging pride of San Francisco, this first record ushering

**519**

in a new phase for arena-style hard rock across America.

Rating 7

## Yesterday And Today - Struck Down (London '78)

**Struck Down** is Y&T's second and last of the band's short-lived proto-metal sound, the two forming a vinyl duo that features regular rockers in the humidity of the clubs, an echoey, live-off-the-floor wallop that is the precursor to Van Halen's cymbal-crashing chaos. Similar to the debut in age and weariness, **Struck Down** leans heavier and more serious, as evidenced on slow Zepmetal stunner *Dreams Of Egypt* and the drowning blisterblues of the distressing title track, both marked by eerie vocals from a Dave Meniketti on fire. Torrid, early thumping, oddly recorded (i.e. spontaneous and cavern-tested in the spirit of Van Halen - **II** or Zep - **Presence**), **Struck Down** holds its place in history with pride, a grand old record that enriches with age, revealing dense rhythmic layers play after play.

Rating 8

## Y&T - Earthshaker (A&M '81)

Y&T's third bone-cruncher (and first of a new, post-NWOBHM sound, also first with the abbreviated moniker) is a deafening juggernaut of mostly fast or semi-fast metal with just the odd bit of latter-day Y&T bop rock to keep one hand in the mainstream. But **Earthshaker** is without a doubt the heaviest, noisiest Y&T cranker, full of good old-fashioned '70s-style cock rock; groove tunes *Hungry For Rock*, quickster *Squeeze*, melodic power ballad *Rescue Me* and excellent pocket rocker *Dirty Girl*, all combining to build this one for the stage. So call **Earthshaker** Y&T's giant street-wise leap into the real world, ceremoniously trampling most of the metal pretenders at the time, while attaining new levels of showmanship for the arena battles ahead. Wide-open with possibilities.

Rating 8

## Y&T - Black Tiger (A&M '82)

Less the aural blast of **Earthshaker**, more the smooth cruise of **Mean Streak** (though more caked with raw, unkempt wattage), **Black Tiger** is for the most part another fine chapter in the funtime catalogue of Meniketti and his second-string Halens. Anvil-headed anthems this time would include *Black Tiger* (a quick-to-rile bush-whacking beast similar to *Meanstreak*), jackboot stomper *Hell Or High Water*, melodic fast-picking kicker *Forever*, and *Don't Wanna Lose*, Y&T's very best melodic luv rocker, whip-creamed onto wax for your coo-ing pleasure. Only major gaff: *Barroom Boogie*, an inexplicably dipshit throwaway, sorta like a one-take stripper tune. All-told, **Black Tiger** is another warm-hearted guitar celebration, featuring weighty production values by Max Norman (taking the band to Britain for recording), plus Leonard Haze's trademark rhythmic sixth sense at the skins.

Rating 8

## Y&T - Mean Streak (A&M '83)

**Mean Streak** would have to be Y&T's fiercest, tastiest slab of choice U.S. hard rock brilliance; successful due to a combination of classic hard rock hooks and the smooth power of Chris Tsangarides' excellent gluey production. **Mean Streak** is the ultimate Van Halen companion, all California melodrama and American swagger; summer tunes with a capital Partaaay. We get screamin' metal with the maraudable title toon and *Hang 'Em High*, *Forever*-like harmonic drive in *Midnight In Tokyo*, and the band's second best melodic rocker in *Lonely Side Of Town*, all intoxicated with a heady exuberance tanned by the sun's rays. And it all manages to rock with the band's celebrated percussive resonance, culminating in Y&T's most focused and self-assured album to date. A car stereo classic, reflecting the band's

status as minor heroes of the punter set, on both sides of the Atlantic.

Rating 9

## Y&T - In Rock We Trust (A&M '84)

The first of many records from Y&T marred by song dry-up, **In Rock We Trust** sounds tired, lacking the upward confident mobility of previous works, the overall collection smacking of formula composition: a drib of metal, a drab of chick rock, traces of chewy mellow bits, some mild experimentation, and a lot of unfounded posturing peppered throughout what is mostly clunky unsuccessfully anthemic clodrock. Also one of the few Y&T spins without a performance that plays splendidly off the unique attributes of the recording. Contains at least one hair band gem in metallic minor hit *Don't Stop Runnin'*, a fist-pumping rabble rouser to be sure.

Rating 4

## Y&T - Down For The Count (A&M '85)

More writer's block stuff similar to the last finds Y&T runnin' out of steam, headin' for disaster and in dire need of some slurping quaffs from the fountain of youth. And the back cover photo shows it. Dumb front cover too, with one of those stupid metal monsters we used to see adorning poodle rock records in the mid '80s. Y&T are becoming Krokus.

Rating 4

## Y&T - Open Fire (A&M '85)

Y&T's obligatory live album isn't exactly the best collection of tunes that could have been chosen (at least it ain't as bad as Zep or Purple), sporting the studio *Summertime Girls* for that extra off-season hit action, and seven live tracks which include bad newie *Go For The Throat*, the juvenile *Barroom Boogie* and boring, Triumph-ready power ballad *I Believe In You*. The remainder however rawks, (especially *Open Fire*), and the band's delivery is spirited, fueled by a robust **Mean Streak**-style recording. Makes me think of parallel decliners Great White or again, Krokus.

Rating 4

## Y&T - Contagious (Geffen '87)

The horror . . . the horror. **Contagious** is the worst of offensive corporate abortions. Geffen has ruined this band. From the fancy new haircuts, artsy photo shoots and femmy clothes, to the hopelessly overblown production values and Meniketti's perfect therefore blatantly sickening Sammy Hagar impressions, no words could possibly convey the contrived trash that hath been pressed onto this innocent piece of vinyl. The cynical commercial garbage passed off as songs are the worst of Warrant/ Poison/ Bon Jovi-style outtakes spewing forth with unbelievably predictable riffs, die-laughing anthemic choruses, and a most annoying blocky drum sound which manages to serve one useful purpose, that of drowning out the soap-operatic songs enclosed. A sordid and disgraceful manipulation of a once relevant band, in desperate pursuit of sales. personnel note: Heart and soul drummer Leonard Haze replaced by Jimmy Degrasso.

Rating 0

## Y&T - Ten (Geffen '90)

More vanilla papology, like the new competitive levels of the '90s never buzzed over Y&T's curly manes, **Ten** is a dissipated mess of sounds you've heard a million times. Sad situation here, a band scraped of life, indeed even Meniketti sounding like a wheezy shell of what he once was, a man tired of the games, tired of watching his ocean recliner float on by. There is no inkling of the old Y&T spark left here, **Ten** being one of those anonymous California rockers that any band could have written (or had handed to them by their label bosses). Avoid and move on. Personnel notes: guitarist Joey Alves replaced by Stef Burns, and original producer none other than Ronnie Montrose replaced after four months work.

Rating 1

### Y&T - Yesterday & Today Live (Metal Blade '91)

Stomping all over that **Open Fire** piece of piffle, this farewell concert does vaingloriously what Meniketti professes it to do, that is reminisce about a career that worked a little magic, a little mayhem, and a little bit of disappointment near the end. Only the boyz in the band can tell you whether Y&T were a success or not, although their status as local heroes and a fairly respected act in Europe and Japan is undisputed. Whatever the case, this well-meaning, well-assembled slab offers a host of Y&T chestnuts, including non-**Open Fire** classics like *Meanstreak, Don't Stop Runnin'* and *Black Tiger* along with some surprising oldies like *Hurricane, Squeeze* and *Struck Down* all given the band's grind-'em-out heat treatment, good recording, solid playing, rock'n'roll. Also, wait for it, the obligatory backstage pass shots, and an appreciative essay from Brian Brinkerhoff. Stirring heavy stuff, no coincidence that it's weighted towards old stock Y&T.

Rating 8

### Y&T - Musically Incorrect (Music For Nations '95)

Meniketti and his persevering warriors are back with their give the people what they want record, cutting the pop crap of the last few, delivering guitars a plenty but with questionable ethics. **Musically Incorrect's** stupid, often playful rock songs run the gamut from funk metal, blues metal, party metal and old Y&T semi-technicality skirting all points inbetween, sum total of the package sounding like smart Kiss. So idiotic Crue-cut cartoons like *Cold Day In Hell* get Buttheaded-up next to a fast, fierce, political number like *I've Got My Own*. And amongst the metal miasma, Hendrix rears his head, as do the Beatles, Stevie Ray Vaughn, the band even redoing old **Struck Down** number *I'm Lost*. Definitely heeding those fan requests to shut up and play yer guitar, Meniketti has forgotten to first decide his compositional context, delivering what is an acceptable survey of metal and hard rock styles, but not a record that attacks with one vision.

Rating 6

### Yosh - Metaphors (Black Mark '96)

Pretty spiffy debut for this Belgian traditional thrash outfit, Yosh ironically time-traveling to the middle '80s, packing back with them a bunch of cool '90s ideas perhaps best exemplified by mainstreamish Swedish death like Sentenced, and Bay are-inspired fare like Dearly Beheaded and Machine Head. What spits out the other end is a level-headed but speedy record of newly-minted songs, sort of a cross between new and old Voivod (or old Maiden and old Metallica) crossed with a whole hacking cough of mid-America speedsters from '86, but way better y'understand? No easy task describing this convolutedly retro record as new stuff but it somehow gets there, simply by soaking up volumes of metal under the bridge, and pulling bodies that are still breathing ashore.

Rating 8

### Zar - Live Your Life Forever (Hurricane '90)

One of those strange bands that never got any press, Germany's Zar churned through a sort of heavy-lidded gothic hard rock, 220V without the songs, main ace being aging Heep/Lucifer's Friend pipester John Lawton on vocals, his voice still one of the best in the biz. General impression though: dated, '80s metal with a brash, W.A.S.P.-like mix, nice guitar licks but just too out-of-touch, even if I usually like bands that show '80s roots that are strictly European. Logo rips off Starz.

Rating 5

### Zar - From Welcome . . . To Goodbye (Solid Rock '93)

Vastly improved, Zar is now a five piece, with only two original members, including the addition of Thommy Bloch on vocals, Lawton only appearing on one track. But this is kickin' man, Zar creating a seething, electrocuted elegance, towering but crushingly recorded melodic metal, now oddly enough evoking the very best of the influential 220V. The lyrics are still poor English from non-Anglos, but you just don't care given the stirring Euro-metal enclosed. Bloch's vocals are vaguely in the Lawton camp, while leaning more towards Gamma Ray/Helloween, clear-cutting operatic Halfordian joy from start to finish. Thirteen tracks of stout-hearted groove, including two instrumentals and a cover of Hendrix's *Angel.* Pure magical metal enjoyment.

Rating 8

### Zaxas - Zaxas (Noise '95)

Noise signings Zaxas follow fellow Noisers Lost Breed into a celebration of metal that isn't supposed to be hip these days. Zaxas' influences are two-fold, split right down the middle, musically evoking a blustery simplified grind version of Metal Church or Virgin Steele while vocalist Dale Anthony recalls Geoff Tate, adding shade, humanity and drama, really stealing the show with his metallian purity. Strange brew, a tuneful garagey din, melodic, yet not really at all prog except in drama, over which this Dale character Dio's his sacred heart at the Metal Church, driving a stake right through the '80s, hoping there's enough of us who will get it. Thick, rough and oh so sentimental of the daze when metal men thought they could construct the ultimate master cathedral.

Rating 7

### Zebra - Zebra (Atlantic '83)

Formerly a Zeppelin cover band, these suvvern-based proto-AOR-ists leapt onto the scene with this almost prog-ish hard rock shiner, combining Journey, Styx and of course Zep, arriving at something like The Babys. But *Who's Behind The Door?* was a pretty big hit, with its elegant Page-like acoustic guitar, epic-leaning lyrics and vocals, and ivory stairway unto finale. Just a great song, very purifying. Bluesy metal opener *Tell Me What You Want* was a secondary hit, while the rest of the record rounded the pomp rock bases, all the while Randy Jackson flipping into his distracting, affected falsetto, a very strange vocal technique indeed. But all in all, just a whole ton of good, detail-rich playing, visiting seven or eight forms of pop-based guitar rock.

Rating 8

### Zebra - No Tellin' Lies (Atlantic '84)

Jack Douglas is back to recreate the silken values of the band's debut, and for the most part, this is a direct continuation, semi-hit *Bears* reliving the plush, fragrant, hippy recline of *Who's Behind The Door?*, although with less prog commitment. Elsewhere, it's the same strange grab bag of poppy, almost glam-ish hard rock, visiting arcane '60s melodies at times, really quite marred by Jackson's helium-level, falsetto vocals. Like I say, this is a strange band, nobody sounding quite like them, their prog-inflected bombast over normal songs sounding maybe like heavy Triumph at times. Anyhow, the decline sets in, America perhaps done with the novelty component of Jackson's vocals, and pretty much satisfied with one record that sounds this way.

Rating 6

## Zebra - 3.V   (Atlantic '86)

Main difference this time around is that Douglas' creamy stir of power trio sounds is gone, the band self-producing this one, going for a brasher, more drum-dominated sound, again recalling Gil Moore and Triumph. The songs ride that same forced mix of big, passionate ballads and hard rockers filled in by good playing, Jackson's guitar solos being particularly sweet. I dunno, New England, Giuffria, Night Ranger, throw 'em all in the same boat, given Zebra's similar sublime melodies wafting in from all sorts of places. Many an AOR fan's guilty pleasure, that's for sure, but not really mine.
Rating                                                5

## Zed Yago - Pilgrimage   (BMG '89)

Big boisterous Teutonic metal like a slow-moving Accept, mid-years Priest or surprisingly, L.A. tunesmiths Malice. Oh and of course, fine female vocal work from something called Jutta. Catchy, bottom-heavy and well-Euro-ized, these folks give Doro a run for her money.
Rating                                                6

## Zeno - Zeno   (EMI '86)

One of those unassuming, understated records, seemingly lost in the shuffle, **Zeno** thrills and spills with rich aplomb and buoyancy in a decidedly European pop metal vein, sorta like Silver Mountain meets Night Ranger, Guiffria or White Lion. Led by guitarist Zeno Roth (younger bro of early Scorpions axeman Ulrich Roth), Zeno constructs high-flying, exuberant melodimetal; well-recorded, well-vocalized, and well-endowed with tasteful keyboards and fluid studio-precise axe mathematics. Titles like *Eastern Sun*, *Heart On The Wing*, *Don't Tell The Wind*, *Circles Of Dawn*, and *Sent By Heaven* accent the ethereal nature of the band's hopeful sound (and a spirituality similar to Ulrich's post-Scorps records). Personal fave, however, would be the exquisitely-riffed *Signs On The Sky*, featuring a deeply spirited vocal performance and general washes of warmth and well wishes. And I wish I could tell you more, but I have one of those promo copies with no inner sleeve, which must be where all the band info is kept. Suffice to say though, if you ever find this one, and are amenable to intelligent, inspirational lite metal, abscond heavily. **Zeno**'s well worth it for the fine studio skills alone.
Rating                                                8

## Zero Nine - Blank Verse   (Web '82)

Closest approximation would be White Spirit for this early piece of keyboard metal for Finland, produced in **Machine Head**-purple by the one and only Ian Gillan, who does a nicely traditional job at the knobs with a still disjointed and unsure retro-unit. I liked **Blank Verse** at first spin but now find it pale and amateur in comparison with the more high-minded White Spirit, really the only other band in this derivative genre, marked by constant but tasteful Jon Lord-style keyboard honkings. Sounds its nationality, and its age or older, due to its floundering, vacuum-produced approach, unconcerned at present trends, unpossessed with any urgency or central philosophy.
Rating                                                4

## Zodiac Mindwarp And The Love Reaction - High Priestess Of Love   (Arista '88)

Zodiac was probably the most obvious proponent of the "high fashion biker" trend that briefly permeated British metal in the late '80s. With a colourful sound to match, Zodiac were like an exuberant though derivative take on The Cult circa **Electric**, all imported hard rock power chords, trash-talkin' and danceable grooves attached to fancy song titles. Fun enough, but the overblown marketing always detracted from the experience. Hot mix.
Rating                                                6

## ZZ Top - ZZ Top's First Album   (Warner Bros. '71)

Blues for rockers plain and simple, ZZ Top emerged from the plains of Texas with a large redneck stew that owed lots to ages-old black music via hard-edged Anglos like Clapton, Beck and Page, bringing with it just a trace of England's psychedelic jam ethic while celebrating the band's unique Texas-via-Memphis traditions with hearty love of the road. Billy Gibbons is instantly miles above his peers, offering versatility, ballsiness and immense reverence to the past all at once, strung purposefully over a grinding rhythm section, adding vocal signatures that croon expertly in complement with his deft and diggable guitar textures. All here just melds into a singular vision to deal blues with bite, aided in the cause with a robust recording that breathes with bottom end and longing gaze at purple sundowns. Understandably the least known of the ZZ catalogue, the only one indeed without real hits.
Rating                                                7

## ZZ Top - Rio Grande Mud   (Warner Bros. '72)

As the opening chords to *Francine* float through the air like fine, fine, homegrown, it becomes apparent that our Texas heroes would be infusing more rock into the roll, here looking to the Stones, adding voltage to their solid blues base, following with *Just Got Paid*, a killer hard rock hybrid that is solely of their own legendary construction, all buoyant bass line, predatory riffing and venomous slide. Elsewhere, it's back to the debut for various electric blues explorations, improving on the past with creative rule-breaking, something in short supply in traditional music. Another reason to respect this band's early output (as if more were necessary): complete reliance on originals, knee-deep in a genre which usually defaults to a predictable stable of old stand-bys three or four times per record. The last of the band's two "brown period" album.
Rating                                                7

## ZZ Top - Tres Hombres   (Warner Bros. '73)

Hold on to those pearly white ten gallons, 'cos here comes ZZ Top on full throttle, cranking their undisputed masterwork, a record where every single tune was a hit to some degree, all ten still making the rounds on classic rock radio the world over. **Tres Hombres** is a trés powerful blues rock record, one of my four faves of the genre, right up there with Status Quo's **Quo**, Foghat's **Fool For The City**, and ZZ's own **Tejas**, this being the low-down bluesiest of the bunch, perhaps the least accidental. It's high times all around, as the boys whip out their brightest licks, whether on cruise control straddling a straight patch of freeway with *Beer Drinkers & Hell Raisers*, *Move Me On Down The Line* and the immortal *La Grange*, or getting funky and insane for *Master Of Sparks* or *Precious And Grace*, the latter one of my fave ZZ tales, featuring one of Billy's weightiest riffs sandwiched between a combined rhythmic heatwave from Dusty Hill and Frank "Rube" Beard at their most buzzardly. Throw in a dash of gospel and some funky fur-coat-in-a-Cadillac r + b, and **Tres Hombres** cooks and sweats like no other twangfest. Damn near the best southern rock'n'roll showdown ever, branding ZZ Top the masters of the most Budweiser of rocks.
Rating                                               10

## ZZ Top - Fandango!   (Warner Bros. '75)

Basically two half albums, **Fandango!** found ZZ Top at the heady peak of their career, being both rich and respected, commercially successful and loved by guitar magazines. Side one I've always considered a throwaway: a live smear of covers and originals that may have

well been covers for all their imagination, all themati- cally linked for their bash 'em out, spontaneous old time rock'n'roll lack of quality. Just a big boogie woogie mess as far as I'm concerned, but probably as close as we'll get to authentic live ZZ Top, given the band's current lack of authenticity. Side two is another story, one of blinding genius, as we get something more akin to **Tres Hombres**: side three, six red hot peppers, preferred cut being elegant lead track *Nasty Dogs And Funky Kings*, one bad mutha that should have been tarred, feathered and dragged through town for crimes against the lone star state. And of course there's *Tush*, that most famous of scruffy little boogie shuffles, prob- ably the most worn out barroom rocker of all time. Elsewhere, one of Frank Beard's rhythmic dust storms sends *Heard It On The X* through the rafters while *Balinese* recalls the good time swingshift of *Francine* and *Move Me On Down The Line*. A thoroughly lovable half order of down-home cooking, leaving Terry Tape- worm howling for more; more which would eventually come in the form of a down-ratchet to something more exotic, but equally scorched by the desert heat.
Rating 7

## ZZ Top - Tejas (Warner Bros. '76)

**Tejas** takes ZZ Top on mesmerizing flights of fancy, captivating the listener with off-road tales of the wild west, set to the most sensual evocations of desert flora and fauna, sprouting in violets, moody blues, sundown yellows and muted scarlets from Billy Gibbons' ever- expanding six string palette. And cohorts Dusty Hill and Frank Beard are right on cue, Beard turning in a singular percussive performance, brilliantly understated, fi- nesse rendered elusive through one of the most inter- esting recordings I've ever experienced, capturing the essence of the word "traps", punctuated by a ploipy bass drum that sounds like the head is barely screwed secure. And it is within this engaging feel that the band's arresting compositions sprinkle their magic dust. Vari- ous insidious shuffles form the sonic theme, *Arrested For Driving While Blind*, *Snappy Kakkie*, and *Enjoy And Get It On*, all driven but sensitively so, silently gliding above the brush while Gibbons gives his best textural commentary of his career, using all sorts of old time effects in construction of what is easily the most clever ZZ Top album ever, complex but completely micro- scopic. Every song on this work of blues genius re- writes the book on traditional sounds, forming almost untraceable liaisons between country, bluegrass, boogie woogie, hillbilly, jazz, southern rock, biker rock, funk, r+b, hippies, rednecks, and the patented riffs of ZZ Top's wholly-owned brand of heavy rock. After all the pointless conjecture, what remains is a record that treads lightly through a rich treasure trove of tradi- tional musics reaching back a hundred years and more. Bite into it and taste the sound of history being deli- cately retooled.
Rating 10

## ZZ Top - Degüello (Warner Bros. '79)

ZZ Top quietly turn the corner, becoming somewhat the novelty act, albeit still a smokin' one. **Degüello** retains some of the closeness of **Tejas**, almost an acoustic feel, with even-keel structural heavyweights like *Lowdown In The Streets* and *Cheap Sunglasses* rolling off the tongue like a jam session without amps, Gibbons again tasteful and expressive, blowing more wattage into his solos than his riffs here, evoking a one-take version of Steely Dan or something. The songs suit the bill perfectly, lacking in lyrical weight, simply looking for a good time. We get two lazyboy boogies in *She Loves My Automobile* and *Hi Fi Mama*, even a couple of covers, in construction of a record that breathes con- fidence, even allowing the boys with beards to show- case their rudimentary (and completely brand new) sax chops as "the lone wolf horns." Always considered

a bit of a mental lightweight, the power of **Degüello** is in the touch, the dynamic and low-key control of material that is more a vehicle for three unique players than great art. Very bright and lively, bouncing along with a relaxed chuckle increasingly the terrain of the band as their legendary status becomes more assured.
Rating 8

## ZZ Top - El Loco (Warner Bros. '81)

I always considered this ZZ Top's Steely Dan record, for its plush studio recline; smooth and versatile, lay- ered with sensual solos and sly humour. **El Loco** is perhaps the band's most "high class" record, ironically packed with novelty tunes as it creates a virtually unplugged sort of boogie, case in point being *Ten Foot Pole* and big hit *Pearl Necklace* which both thump along almost invisibly. But my fave would have to be elegant ballad *It's So Hard* which has Gibbons drifting forth with his most magical and understated solo since *Asleep In The Desert*, a sound which splendidly characterizes the record's drowsy heatwave, whether the band be kickin' butt or kickin' back. An eclectic record from an eclectic band, **El Loco** is an intelligent grab bag of tricks, from a trio actively ridiculing their intelligence, sprinkling double entendres that divert attention from the record's breezy sonic design. In retrospect, one can see the inclination towards the all-out dancetrack madness that would define **Eliminator**, at least in toons like *Tube Snake Boogie*, which despite its spiritual proximity to the sparse arrangements of **Degüello**, gets red carpet treatment from the record's technical department. A fun collection of tales which neverthe- less has its haughty elements, recalling Zappa's irrev- erent marriages of chuckles and chops.
Rating 8

## ZZ Top - Eliminator (Warner Bros. '83)

With a snap of the fingers, ZZ Top discover their thang, their particular marketing special purpose, long beards, hot rods and hi-tech computer rock, in con- struction of the band's **Let's Dance**, both records burning off the complexity from eclectic pasts in cele- bration of cutting edge clubbing. A truly novel idea (at least this once), **Eliminator** is a hybrid of techno and trucker, the space age cowboy for the plastic-plated '80s. **Eliminator** was an interesting sort of shock to the system, as the rigid dance grooves became the recipients of more heavy metal guitar than on the last three records combined, tallest rockers being *Bad Girl* and *I Got The Six*, two kickin' cruisers that fit seamlessly with more accessible fare like *Gimme All Your Lovin*, *Sharp Dressed Man* and *Legs*, all monster hits with hugely influential videos to match. Shallow, empty piffle to be sure, but **Eliminator** fits the guilty pleasure tag, sounding so open, clear, restrained and almost atmos- pheric (*TV Dinners*), nary a challenging moment to be imagined, except maybe as an academic exercise in studio technique. But talk about breaking the bank, spitting like an instant teller no less than five smash singles, delivered with a sort of cartoonish fun factor into the arms of a public ready to boogie without the history lessons. A risky reconstitution of a worthy institution, ZZ Top alas finds new ways to confound and in many cases, enrage. Officially six times platinum by '87.
Rating 7

## ZZ Top - Afterburner (Warner Bros. '85)

I'm sure that even the most vigilant ZZ Top fan couldn't help but feel a trace of disgust with the band's work ethic, shoe-gazing back after two years off with this pale imitation of **Eliminator**. I've managed to grudg- ingly accept **Afterburner**'s dead identical hi-tech boogie, which makes for your basic inoffensive, unob- trusive, unchallenging road tape. Too bad it's all down- hill after the popcorn sizzle of lead track *Sleeping Bag*, although it's more of a meandering, suburban jellyroll rather than a pressure drop to disaster. The whole world cried foul and rightly so, ZZ Top just abandoning their studied blues integrity in search of hot rods and hot bods, twice now, this time with an unsightly lack of vision. The worst of the triptych so far, but as I say, mildly pleasant.

Rating      6

## ZZ Top - The ZZ Top Six Pack    (Warner Bros. '87)

For all its self-congratulations, **Six Pack** is tilted more towards annoyance and omission than the great archival necessity that it claims to be. First of all, I applaud the concept of getting six ZZ Top studio albums on CD in one fell swoop, if mainly for the fact that the price of the package would undoubtedly be less than that of the sum of its parts. With **Degüello** already out on CD, **Six Pack** gives us remixed versions of records 1,2,3,4,5 and 7. Herein lies my first complaint. I love what producer Bill Ham has done to the band's "brown" albums, but **Tejas**, to my mind, is summarily butchered, eradicating the record's wonderfully modest drum sound for a dance club electro-shock more in line with the band's robotic bytehead persona on **Eliminator**, **Afterburner** and **Recycler**, thereby not only botching life in the '80s, but going back and meddling with a legendary past. Tacky move, guys. Same thing with **Tres Hombres**, which granted, was pretty badly mixed in its original state. Elsewhere, no real gripes sound-wise, but I would have liked the packaging to include a little more data on the band other than four special interest stories which don't shed much light on the trio itself. How about a little career retro or chronology, or lyrics, or full cover graphics of the included albums (i.e. backs, sleeves, gatefolds etc.)? After all, who can resist that yummy Mexican meal wafting from the mid-section of **Tres Hombres**? Mmm good. Anyways, it's obviously not my baby, so who am I to complain? Last comment: if you consider yourself a big fan, your collection isn't really complete and accurate unless you've acquired **Tejas** on original vinyl. Nuff said.

Rating      7

## ZZ Top - Recycler    (Warner Bros. '90)

After the meek retread that was **Afterburner**, ZZ Top stroll back five long years later with what is supposed to be a return to roots. But that must have been something the band was instructed to tell journalists, because **Recycler** is just **Eliminator** III, what with the likes of *Concrete And Steel* and *Doubleback* and *Burger Man* being spineless returns to the well that was so bountiful seven years back. No question, **Recycler** at least breaks a sweat when compared with **Afterburner**, truly getting down on *Lovething* and the perhaps too similar *Tell It*, turning the record a tad schizoid, as humans and machines are left to duke it out on the shop floor. The verdict: a stiff, predictable record not without its attempts toward recapturing some of the band's considerable, and considerably long-lost, magic. With so many years between records, ZZ Top will always manage to elicit a goodly level of curiosity. Still, without some sort of progress and creativity, the bearded ones may someday find their fanbase eroding, or at minimum getting stoopider. Maybe they care, maybe they don't.

Rating      7

## ZZ Top - Greatest Hits    (Warner Bros '92)

As much as I hate to admit it, it really is time for another hits package for these perennial blue (and red) collar legends. Drawing heavily from the band's last three (yes, three) interchangeable techno-boogie sell-outs, **Greatest Hits** is real testimony to the potential of video marketing, ZZ Top being perhaps the biggest beneficiary of the MTV revolution, offering story

threads that anchored our attention throughout those early years of knock 'em dead graphics. Outside of a couple of newies (Elvis cover *Viva Las Vegas* and the sparse but likeable *Gun Love*) which both maintain the band's electro-metal penchant for kickin' boogie ass with the likes of Prince, all else is dead predictable, even re-releasing *Tush* and *La Grange*, both of which took space on the last hits package. Basically a double album-length bushwhack through a decade of classic rock radio.

Rating      6

## ZZ Top - Antenna    (BMG '94)

Tone-Taste-Tenacity. Yep, that about sums up ZZ Top's hollow, ringing, resoundin' body rock comprising **Antenna**, a record of elegant boogie metal wrapped in those formidable '90s tech beats that I guess we just better all get used to. Despite Frank Beard's love of gadgetry, **Antenna** still manages to sound sparse, academic and reverent of the old rock to which it is dedicated, tasty sounds drifting from Mexican radio, gut instinct blues rock first immortalized through *Heard It On The X*, basically the concept song of this whole record. Sure some stuff here is **Afterburner** filler (lead single of all things, *Pincushion*), and other tracks are just too low slung and atmospheric (*Breakaway* and *Fuzzbox Voodoo*), but chucking all this song and lyric stuff (words: they don't care), ain't it just the most doggone pleasurable thing to listen to that guitar? Yes it is, Billy's guitar truly howling like a six string thing of beauty, making all else irrelevant, solo and riff charging the air like lightning. I mean, just strap on the phones and listen to this brushfire burn! So many colours, so hot and smoky, sidewinding in unison with a voice that gets gruffer every gulch. And overall, the record achieves a true hard rock, hiding fierce twisters like *World Of Swirl*, *PCH* and *Antenna Head* which just strafe with bundles of blues metal knowledge let fly. No, this record isn't **Tres Hombres** all over again as some may pronounce. It's obvious ZZ Top really doesn't know how to go back. But **Antenna** is its own hi-tech train wreck of a success, nobody else able or willing to challenge this sort of uber-electro boogie monster, which gets more ornery with each passing semester of bionics.

Rating      8

## ZZ Top - One Foot In The Blues    (Warner '94)

Nice twist on the greatest hits concept (for a band that has two hits albums already), **One Foot In The Blues** brings together a healthy sample of the band's bluesiest, tastiest down-home swamp babies, seventeen (all previously released) songs of hurt, pride and truckery. Excellent liner notes by Bill Bentley enhance the concept, which also gains credence through the modest but cozy packaging of the thing. All eras are visited, but of course the new stuff pales in sincerity with all that electronic claptrap, even if Gibbons is still soulful as the good earth, unswerving in his delivery of the twangiest tangiest licks in the suvvern rock genre. Hell, I bet he's my favorite blues guitarist period.

Rating      8

## ZZ Top - Rhythmeen    (BMG '96)

Well, I guess that pathetic lip-synch through *Legs* and *Sharp Dressed Man* during the '96 Super Bowl did little to revive ZZ Top's flagging career. Man, that sucked. Oh well, consolation can be had, given this thoroughly pleasureable re-run of '94's **Antenna**. So it's not exactly pumped full of creativity, so what? Like **Antenna**, one comes for the crisp, stellar bandwidth production, a futuro-bed of rhythm over which Billy Gibbons roars, cries and whispers six-string tales, expertly assembling a veritable clinic in accessible blues rock. Like I've said before, that ZZ Top bio I read really tainted my impression of these guys as buddies or God forbid, equals. But

if Gibbons is the only one who wants to work his thang,
so be it. I'll be first in line to buy it.
Rating                                        8

# APPENDIX 1: Glossary of Terms

Reading this section first might be somewhat helpful in understanding the reviews in this book, if only to be able to extrapolate from all the colour commentary just what kind of record you're reading about on a very basic level. I've often read reviews in magazines that went a page and a half, at the end of which you still have no idea if the thing was a country rock album or a hard rock album, and yeah . . . it matters. A few well-chosen categorical tags never hurt anyone if used with a sense of responsibility. As a result, I try to use the following terms quite carefully, with qualification if necessary. However sometimes the real meaning depends much upon the context or the comparisons at hand. Hey, it's only money.

**AOR** - That nebulous low-slung, hair-band guitar fluff that makes you want to drink coolers, put on a nice shirt and chase women, rather than drink beers, dress in black and defile a graveyard. Largely an American phenomenon, pioneered by bands like Aerosmith, Kiss, Ted and even stretchin' it, Journey, Styx and Loverboy, AOR is above all melodic, hooky generically structured, and overtly concerned with luv, sex, or hair styles. Almost always involves bright colours, the Big Beat, rock poses, stadiums, attitude, partying, the flag, and overt attention being paid to looks. For our purposes, often interchangeable with the term hard rock, which itself can also be used by music illiterates as a generic term for heavy metal. Note: a bunch of my older reviews abbreviate hard rock as HR; heavy metal as HM. Bigger proponents of the form these days: Bon Jovi, Def Leppard, and to a lesser extent Poison, Cinderella, Slaughter, Warrant, Tyketto, Lillian Axe and Danger Danger. Excellent net-zine on the genre: SFK.

**Alternative** - Aah yes, that new loaded term that used to mean something, and has now become synonymous with the mainstream. I still think it means something, vaguely put, music and lyrics with strange, non-conservative ideas, even if it sells like Smashing Pumpkins or Pearl Jam. But without entering the debate, let's just say that in terms of the descriptive tag you will see throughout this book, it might mean post-grunge, lo-fi-ish, '90s-punk-metal-ish, slightly rappy, slightly hardcore, slightly jangly . . . a whole bunch of things. And I guess the idea of blurring distinctions or crossing boundaries comes to mind. In any event, I think the term still means something outside of the commercial aspect of record sales, still being descriptive of a sound and lyrical presentation that is left of centre. Let's leave it at that.

**Bay Area Sound** - Speedy but technically adept metal sound, pioneered by Exodus, Testament, Death Angel, Vicious Rumours, (NY's) Overkill, Megadeth and Metallica. Now refers to any fast, powerful, well-executed metal; slight thrash or punk edge allowed.

**Black Metal** - A term arguably brought to fruition by Venom although most likely only clarified by the evil trio. Refers to Satanic metal, in its most extreme form, actually celebrating evil, denouncing Christianity, and blaspheming its traditions. In its less extreme form, merely using such goings on as lyrical grist, as mood altering and as image-making, neither condoning or denouncing Satanism. Both forms usually use copious amounts of blood, guts, crosses, skulls, black leather, smoke plus the odd nun. Examples of the former are Mercyful Fate, Venom, Morbid Angel, Deicide, Danzig (maybe), early Slayer, early Bathory and more recently, the Norwegian scene, who have even taken to murder and burning churches. Examples of the latter include Witchfinder General, Witchfynde, Quartz, Ozzy, and latter-day Slayer. Most inhabitants of either camp don't take it too seriously, most being concerned more with the horror and power imagery, and the attendant marketing potential. The flipside: white metal or Christian Rock; most famous example being Stryper, one listenable example being Mass, only brilliant example

being Trouble, who worship at the Church of Suicidal Christianity. Usually a scarier proposition than black metal.

**Blastbeats** - Super-fast drumming that began with the thrash scene, now let loose in genres like grindcore, death metal, and the new black metal. In my opinion quite pointless, sounding neither fast nor powerful, the whole idea lapsing into double time which has no groove, which I guess is why I use the term polka-beat a fair bit. Sounds like this: tick, tick, tick, tick . . .

**Death Metal** - Pretty much interchangeable with grindcore. Black metal topics are game, but really the idea is gore, blood, body parts, Cannibal Corpse being pretty much the far-flung reaches of the idea. Other signatures: blastbeats, grindcore vocals, down-tuning, doom chords.

**Down-tuning** - Don't really know the technical mechanics of this, but the idea is to tune the guitars lower (I've heard D and C# bandied about), so the resulting riffs are heavier, more rumbling, dense, scarier, strings flapping and vibrating from their loose-ness. Used a lot these days to evoke the grand masters of the idea, Sabbath, and all sorts of sounds now considered grungy, doomy or deathly.

**Euro-Metal** - The Euro sound is something most associated with Danish, Swedish, or German metal; that deep, emotive, stirring, mysterious, melodic tone that on the heavier side results in goth-metal and on the lighter side, Euro-hard rock. Examples of bands who possess the Euro soul, yet use it in radically different ways, include Scorpions, Accept, Heavy Load, 220V, Gravestone, Picture, Sabbat, and Rage. A little cheezy and out of date in the '90s, just like AOR, which intertwines with Euro sentiments quite readily.

**Extreme Metal** - Can be defined as the far-flung, exploded edges of thrash as per crappy Norwegian bands or non-musical, industrial-based sounds like distortion and other white noise as per Japanese audio terrorists like Merzbow. Can also be used to describe garbagey doomy death grunge stuff like Eyehategod and even Brutal Truth. Fairly self-evident. If it's not music by most measures, you might kindly and simply call it extreme. Ironically, the term symphonic death metal describes what many would call extreme (and even unlistenable).

**Goth Metal** - As in Gothic. The dungeons and dragons, medieval, classical, Valhalla-bound, doom, minor chord sound and lyrical imagery most prevalent early on in Rainbow, selected Sabbath, selected Priest, Dio and Maiden; later on in Yngwie Malmsteen, Savatage and Mercyful Fate; and later still with Cemetary, My Dying Bride and Paradise Lost. Lyrically speaking, goth's mostly a European thing, rife with castles, dragons, vampires, wizards, warlords, and other Black Forest apparitions. Sonically speaking, goth is richly dark and Euro sounding, with much pilfering of classical music styles especially with respect to guitar solos, very little patience for the blues, hard rock, or indeed anything American and upbeat. Usually quite technologically impressive and often progressive. Wears thin after a few albums due to its depressing and self-serious tones. When goth edges towards extreme, it becomes doom or death.

**Groove** - Hard one to pin down. Groove refers to that magical drive, that Big Beat, that energetic jet stream that some tunes (usually the "mid-pace" ones), have that stirs the soul and makes one want to jam with the boys, headbang, drink beers, or simply get up and belt out a few riffs on the ol' air guitar. AC/DC are the grandfathers of groove. Maiden and Dio often have it. Aerosmith's *Draw The Line* (perhaps the hottest groove ever), *Sick As A Dog*, *Adam's Apple*, and *Permanent Vacation* have it in spades, as does more monolithic stuff like Deep Purple's *Smooth Dancer*, *Highway Star*, *Gettin' Tighter*, *King Of Dreams* and *Hard Lovin' Woman*. Accept are masters at it. Check out *Restless And Wild*, *Aiming High*, *Man Enough To Cry*, and *Bound To Fail*. Mustaine and Trouble co-owned it in the early '90s, now deathier bands like Entombed, Dismember and Dearly Beheaded taking up the cause, with their more pronounced, grindy groove. In terms of genres, most notably the hard rockers (Dokken, Ratt, Slaughter, Poison, Tesla) cling, with mixed success, to the party groove as their fire down under, their reason to be. In simple terms, the groove is what powers metal far beyond the capabilities of other types of music, this deep magical spark that works best with a metallic framework. It is this very essence of the best metal that makes it the proudest, most righteously ass-kickin' form of music ever invented. When it's turned on, nothing can touch metal for sheer power.

**Grunge** - A fresh, intelligent marriage of punk and metal that erupted out of Seattle in the late '80s with bands like Nirvana, Green River, Screaming Trees, Tad, Soundgarden, Mudhoney, Mother Love Bone, Swallow, Fluid, Melvins and Wipers. Has since branched out to other cites and other sounds, Pearl Jam and Stone Temple Pilots perhaps the most mainstream proponents of the form. Grunge is a big part of anything that bridges metal to alternative these days, indeed grunge being the original type of music to receive the alternative tag in all its controversial force.

**Hardcore** - As in hardcore punk. Refers to thrash and/or speed punk often associated with skinheads, anarchy, racism, slam dancing, and skateboards. In the late '80s, the lines between hardcore and thrash metal became blurred with bands such as—in punk to metal order—The Descendants, Corrosion Of Conformity, D.R.I., Suicidal Tendencies, and Anthrax, inciting other accusatory but complimentary tags such as "crossover". Lyrics aside, hardcore always was thrash and vice versa, yet in the '90s, the activism, anger, and moral outrage of hardcore seems to have infiltrated right through to state-of-the-art bands like Biohazard, Pro-Pain and Pantera.

**Heavy Metal** - Pages can be written on this one, yet as it pertains to the actual album reviews, heavy metal can be defined as 1) the umbrella term for all aggressive fuzz-pedaled guitar rock, i.e. loosely all the music in this book: Aerosmith is heavy metal, R.E.M. is not, or 2) and most importantly for understanding of the reviews herein, roughly half the music in this book: Machine Head is Heavy Metal, Aerosmith is not. This is crucial to understanding what the hell I'm talking about here, as I often refer to a band as hard rock, but not heavy metal. Metal leans more towards minor chords, doom, violence, lack of communicative melody, and often speed. Hard rock is generally an American deal, featuring optimism, guys that look like chicks,

guys that talk almost exclusively about chicks, and guys that write songs that even their girlfriends might like. To completely drive home this distinction, here are some elucidations. Heavy Metal: Black Sabbath, Metallica, Anthrax, Pantera, Slayer, Judas Priest, Ozzy. Hard Rock: Dokken, Angel City, White Lion, Slaughter, Poison, Aerosmith, Van Halen, Kiss. In between: W.A.S.P., UFO, Deep Purple, AC/DC, Whitesnake. Confused yet?

**Industrial** - Music that has adopted computer technology as its driving force. Began life as electronic psychedelia in the '70s, then synth pop in the '80s, and now goes a few ways: psychedelic, dance-oriented and most useful for our purposes, industrial metal. Industrial metal includes bands like Ministry, Nine Inch Nails, White Zombie, Skrew, Bile, Filter, Prick etc.

**NWOBHM** - as in New Wave Of British Heavy Metal. Refers to, as one would guess, the resurgence of metal that originated in jolly ol' England in 1979-80 with such bands as Iron Maiden, Saxon, Motörhead, Angel Witch, Samson, Tygers Of Pan Tang, Quartz, later including Chateaux, Savage, Witchfinder General, Fist, and a raft of others. The NWOBHM brought respectability and renewed vigor back to the metal scene after the transformation of punk, spawning huge underground swellings in Europe and stateside that continue unabated to this day. Musically, I often refer to the magic of the NWOBHM. This refers largely to the fact that marketing competence and its respective cynicism was nowhere to be found amongst these exuberant, inspired and largely naive first outings. A certain integrity seems to surround even the most poverty-stricken of NWOBHM combos, resulting in nostalgic feelings for those who came of age with Eddie.

**OTT** - As in Over The Top. Possibly derived from Motörhead. Generally means manic, indulgent, past the threshold. In the '70s, Rainbow's *Kill The King* was OTT. As metal got heavier in the early '80s, OTT became to refer specifically to songs or bands that exhibited a wall of sound, most often characterized by blinding speed and machine gun-like double bass drums; thrash, or speed metal as it were. Early OTT: Accept's *Fast As A Shark*. Modern OTT: almost anything fast by Slayer, approximately half the grindcore and thrash genres, and even Priest's *Leather Rebel*, although incidentally, Priest as a band would not be considered OTT. Although the most common use of the term refers to ultra-heavy, usually fast uncompromising metal, we often refer to OTT guitar solos and vocals, which one could probably ascertain means no compromise, inherently metallic, all hell let loose, attitudinally explosive, and one would have ascertained correctly. Emotively speaking OTT is anything ultra-indulgent, trashcanned to the hills, the more the better, seek and destroy.

**Pop Metal** - The lighter, more playfully AOR-ish, "G" rated version of melodic hard rock, targeted at chicks under sweet sixteen. Just that much less metallic, and that much more high school. An almost indiscernible shift to a more elegant and satin-laced American hard rock. I guess Def Leppard and Bon Jovi rule this roost.

**Power Metal** - Describes really heavy bands that are neither predominately speed, thrash, or necessarily OTT; bands like Metallica, Testament, Sanctuary, Slayer, Anthrax, Trouble, Megadeth, Memento Mori, Pantera, Machine Head, Dearly Beheaded, Sentenced or even Priest. Most power metal bands pride themselves on their playing ability and can lean towards progressive at times. Most techno-metal bands are also power metal and vice-versa, but there are exceptions. Trouble, Candlemass, Cathedral and Entombed are ultra-heavy but not particularly techno (more like "retro" or "retro-Sab", which is another story altogether). Queensryche, Alcatrazz, and Yngwie are techno but not power metal. In the context of the following reviews, then, power metal means dense and considerably heavy, the most pummeling and truly weighty of metallic alloys.

**Progressive Metal** - The marriage between progressive rock and heavy metal, pioneered by Rush and then '80s bands like Queensryche and Fate's Warning. Experiencing a resurgence due to the success of Dream Theater, bands like Morgana Lefay, Tad Morose, Iced Earth, Cynic and Blind Guardian taking up the flag, scattering to different corners of the subset. Generally results in lots of over-playing, egomaniacal displays of chops, superfluous indulgence, long songs, fantasy-based lyrics and operatic singing.

**Punk** - Well, first there's the late '70s stuff from Britain and small pockets of America (Pistols, Damned, Adverts, Ramones, Dead Boys, Saints, Clash, Eater etc.). Next came US hardcore like Dead Kennedys, Black Flag, Descendants. And now there's the new smoother '90s pop-punk of So-Cal success stories like Green Day, Offspring, Rancid, Bad Religion etc., more joining the ranks worldwide every day, much to my chagrin. The music: boring, fast, simple heavy metal, usually by mall-rat-types too lazy to learn their craft. Lyrics: either above average political stuff or moronic teen twaddle.

**Retro Metal** - Could refer to bands that harken back to Sabbath (Cathedral, Paul Chain, Serpent), while more often referring to bands that go for old, blues-based sounds, often including a penchant for vintage recording equipment. Could also refer to bands with specific retro tendencies, i.e. sounding like AC/DC or Aerosmith or Zeppelin. One half of retro bands are also Roots Metal.

**Roots Metal** - The metallic or hard rock form of roots rock, which embodies the qualities most associated with southern rock, a bit of the blues, country, boogie woogie, and general cowboy, redneck, or blue collar overtones. Roots rock's name derives from the fact that this is where early rock, i.e. '50's rock, originated. Roots rockers include bands like The Del Lords, John Cougar Mellencamp, Springsteen, Bad Company or in a more southerly direction, Skynyrd or Molly Hatchet. Roots metal, which is essentially heavier roots rock, includes Junkyard, Dangerous Toys, Salty Dog, Cats In Boots, Company Of Wolves, Havana Black, Four Horsemen, Brother Cane, Cry Of Love, Jackyl and latter-day Cinderella and Poison. You pretty well have to be American to be considered roots rock, although The Tragically Hip, Blue Rodeo, Tom Cochrane, and Britain's Thunder make feeble attempts at legitimacy. Although it would seem that the Stones or Status Quo would fit the bill, they don't represent the jingoistic ideals of good ol' traditional boys. Roots rockers gotta love America, forever mourn its demise, and/or demonstrate the fact that their own excessive drinking and womanizing is in fact the cause of its demise.

**Speed Metal** - exactly what it says and nothing more. Loosely the same as OTT without the attitudinal connotations. Speed metal can either be done thrash or techno, that is with reckless abandon, or scientific precision, yet it is very often thrash because most intelligent bands quickly see the limiting aesthetics of constantly playing at 78 RPM, and move on to ultra-heavy, groove or techno forms of metal. Metallica, Megadeth and Slayer went this route. Anthrax did the opposite for a couple of records, until seeing the light with **Sound Of White Noise**.

**Techno Metal** - Refers to metal with major chops, at least technically speaking, with some or all of the following: hard to play, wildly intricate and profuse riffs and solos, odd time signatures, long songs, complicated arrangements, no sensitivity for restraint, and huge egos. Runs the gamut from very tasteful (Alcatrazz, Megadeth, Galactic Cowboys, Helloween, Blind Guardian, Pantera) to tasteless (Fate's Warning, Flotsam & Jetsam, Dream Theater maybe Souls At Zero). Can often be ultra-heavy, as with Metallica's **. . . And Justice For All**, most Bay area-style bands and hyper-technicians like Death, Coroner and At The Gates. Almost always brightly, heavily, expensively, or otherwise well-produced. Earliest incarnation: Rush, which is an example of the more progressive aspects of the term, as opposed to an artist like Yngwie who mixes axe wizardry with the most agonizing of Euro hard rocks to create his particularly castle-black heavy metal. Both are techno, (a term which has nothing to do with synthesizers), as are newer labyrinthicals like borderline traditional metalheads like Iced Earth or Nevermore.

**Thrash** - A term often used incorrectly to refer to anything ultra-heavy or speed. Thrash, in the sense that it is used in this book, possesses the following qualities: 1) thrash runs the gamut from actively black metal, to less extreme black metal to violence and nothing much else. It's never about man-woman relationships or getting in touch with one's feminine side. 2) thrash is almost always high speed, for usually more than half the record at hand, with drum parts characterized by snare on one and three at triple-time, that quite un-tuneful and ultimately un-heavy overdone blastbeat that gives more of a doubled-up effect than speed (witness most of Slayer - **Hell Awaits**, and almost all of the grindcore genre these days, including Deicide and Cannibal Corpse). 3) thrash is usually played badly, loosely and frenzied on purpose "to prove a point". 4) thrash is usually sung badly "to prove a point", the characteristic vocal choice being vomit-like growls from hell, either recorded out the back door of the studio, phase-shifted and down the street, or so in-your-face it causes a stroke. 5) thrash is often recorded badly (i.e. Venom, Possessed, Bathory, Brutality) "to prove a point". And the point thrash bands are trying to make is that they are the blackest of uglies, in a world that is ugly, full of people that would sooner put a bullet in your head than look at you. Sonically speaking, thrashers consider themselves a sick mirror of a sick planet, the new brutal honesty, kinda like rappers in the '90s and punkers in the late '70s.

**Traditional Metal** - As time rolls on, this term has less to do with the '70s, and more to do with the '80s, describing bands with heavy, technical, gothic, progressive elements, vaguely bracketed by Priest, Dio, Maiden, Slayer, Accept and perhaps Helloween.

**Urbancore** - The particularly street-wise, combat-style hardcore that fuses hardcore punk, power metal and rap (either vocally, thematically or both). Examples: Downset, Prong, Pro-Pain, Biohazard, L.U.N.G.S., Manhole, and Stuck Mojo.

**Viking Metal** - A term invented to describe the growing preoccupation of Scandinavian death bands away from Christian themes towards more nationalistic themes, themes from their own early history. Manowar is an American anomaly of the genre, Bathory practically invented it in the '80s with respect to its current form, and bands like Mayhem, Darkthrone, Amorphis and Unleashed carry the northern flag into the '90s.

# APPENDIX 2: Rock Lists

Me 'n' the buds used to make these lists all the time, probably at least twice a year since we were fourteen, hammering out categories, filling 'em in, comparing, then going to great lengths to convince each other how uninformed the other guy was. Later on it thinned out a bit, as we would meet up back in Trail at Christmas, back from respective universities or jobs, reacquaint ourselves with what each other was listening to and where our heads were at, in the process drinking a lot of beer, hard stuff or coffee. Take this with a grain of salt. Obviously it's a gross simplification of something I take very seriously. You'll note how little many of these rankings have changed over the years, proving basically that I'm getting entrenched and set in my ways as lifeblood wanes. So without further ado, here's the 33 year old version, frozen respectfully in time, of what we've for years been affectionately calling Rock Lists.

## A. BANDS

### Best Band
Qualifier: Must have a track record, i.e. three albums or more. Why? It's more of a challenge to make a string of good albums than just one.

1. Thin Lizzy
2. Aerosmith
3. Queen
4. Blue Öyster Cult
5. UFO
6. Trouble
7. Black Sabbath
8. Gillan
9. Dio
10. Sepultura

### Best New Band
Qualifier: Major label debut album 1993 or newer.

1. Everclear
2. The Tea Party
3. Spiritual Beggars
4. Doctor Butcher
5. Meshuggah
6. Rocket From The Crypt
7. Sentenced
8. Clutch
9. Dearly Beheaded
10. Mourning Sign

### Most Consistent Band

1. Aerosmith
2. Trouble
3. King's X
4. Ozzy Osbourne
5. Pantera

### Brilliant But Inconsistent

1. Queen
2. Deep Purple
3. Status Quo
4. Uriah Heep
5. ZZ Top

### Best Comeback
Qualifier: Previous has-been status eradicated by renewed vigor (may be a recent comeback or one in the past).

1. Aerosmith ('87)
2. AC/DC ('95)
3. Ozzy Osbourne ('95)
4. Deep Purple ('84)
5. Black Sabbath ('80)

### Worst Comeback
Qualifier: Previous status hacked to pieces by a commercial (but not always creative) stiff.

1. Iron Maiden
2. Black Sabbath
3. Megadeth
4. Motley Crue
5. Skid Row

## B. WAX

### Best Album
Qualifier: You can appreciate the agony I went through trying to limit this to 25 (now 50, *that* I could manage). But here goes. I've tried to rank them, but consider the following list more like a pointless exercise, a two or three-tiered tangle of ties, leaving out a good 30 or so other releases that might make the list on any given day. For a more plenteous and perhaps more revealing smorg of life's necessities, see my lists of 9's and 10's in Appendix 3.

1. Queen - Queen
2. Black Sabbath - Sabotage
3. Thin Lizzy - Renegade
4. The Dictators - Bloodbrothers
5. Accept - Balls To The Wall
6. Trouble - Manic Frustration
7. Blue Öyster Cult - Cultösaurus Erectus
8. Megadeth - Countdown To Extinction
9. Led Zeppelin - Physical Graffiti
10. Love/Hate - Wasted In America
11. Sepultura - Roots
12. Pantera - Far Beyond Driven
13. Gillan - Mr. Universe
14. Alcatrazz - No Parole From Rock 'n' Roll
15. Everclear - Sparkle And Fade
16. Metallica - Ride The Lightning
17. Judas Priest - Stained Class
18. King's X - Ear Candy
20. The Clash - Give 'Em Enough Rope
21. Raven - All For One
22. Danzig - 4
23. Black Sabbath - Born Again
24. Rainbow - Down To Earth
25. Deep Purple - Purpendicular

### Best Debut Album

1. Queen - Queen
2. Alcatrazz - No Parole From Rock 'n' Roll
3. Kick Axe - Vices
4. Badlands - Badlands
5. Torch - Torch
6. Gamma - I
7. Savatage - Sirens
8. Nirvana - Bleach
9. Machine Head - Burn My Eyes
10. Collision - Collision
11. Van Halen - Van Halen

12. Sons Of Freedom - Sons Of Freedom
13. War Babies - War Babies
14. Green River - Rehab Doll
15. Montrose - Montrose

### Best New Album
Qualifier: 1993 or newer.

1. Pearl Jam - Vs.
2. Everclear - Sparkle And Fade
3. Sepultura - Roots
4. Danzig - 4
5. Deep Purple - Purpendicular
6. The Tea Party - The Edges Of Twilight
7. Soundgarden - Superunknown
8. King's X - Ear Candy
9. Nirvana - In Utero
10. Uriah Heep - Sea Of Light

### Best Live Album
1. Pat Travers - Go For What You Know
2. Blue Öyster Cult - On Your Feet Or On Your Knees
3. Black Sabbath - Live Evil
4. Judas Priest - Unleashed In The East
5. UFO - BBC Radio One Live In Concert

### Best Non-Metal Album
Qualifier: See Best Album for an explanation of how obviously impossible this task is. I'm just doing it to pay homage to some great tunes I otherwise would be ignoring.

1. Waterboys - This Is The Sea
2. Robert Plant - The Principle Of Moments
3. Adrian Belew - Twang Bar King
4. The Church - Starfish
5. Pete Townshend - All The Best Cowboys Have Chinese Eyes
6. The Bears - Rise And Shine
7. Waterboys - A Pagan Place
8. Peter Gabriel - Security
9. Meat Puppets - Huevos
10. 54-40 - Show Me
11. Eno - Another Green World
12. Grateful Dead - Terrapin Station
13. The Clash - London Calling
14. Minutemen - Double Nickels On The Dime
15. X - See How We Are
16. Meat Puppets - Up On The Sun
17. Yes - Close To The Edge
18. The Chameleons - Strange Times
19. Philip Lynott - The Philip Lynott Album
20. Graham Parker - The Up Escalator
21. XTC - Skylarking
22. Mike Watt - Ballhog Or Tugboat?
23. The Replacements - Pleased To Meet Me
24. King Crimson - Beat
25. Warren Zevon - Bad Luck Streak In Dancing School

### Best Canadian Album
Hey .. what do you want? It's my homeland! Note: I'm combining metal and non-metal here, which to me means including 54-40. Frightening how there's nothing much new here, eh?

1. 54-40 - Show Me
2. Kim Mitchell - Akimbo Alogo
3. Kick Axe - Vices
4. Sons Of Freedom - Sons Of Freedom
5. 54-40 - 54-40
6. NoMeansNo - Wrong
7. Max Webster - A Million Vacations
8. Rush - A Farewell To Kings
9. The Tea Party - The Edges Of Twilight
10. Pat Travers - Heat In The Street

### Best Concept Album

1. Rush - 2112
2. Queensryche - Operation: mindcrime
3. Cemetary - Sundown
4. Amorphis - Elegy
5. Blue Öyster Cult - Imaginos

### Best Grunge Album
Hey . . . I can't get enough!

1. Mudhoney - Superfuzz Bigmuff
2. Nirvana - Bleach
3. Green River - Rehab Doll
4. Pear Jam - Vs.
5. Alice In Chains - Dirt
6. Paw - Dragline
7. Green River - Dry As A Bone
8. Soundgarden - Screaming Life EP
9. Nirvana - Nevermind
10. Temple Of The Dog - Temple Of The Dog

### Best Post-Sabbath Doom Album

1. Trouble - Manic Frustration
2. Trouble - Trouble
3. Kyuss - Blues For The Red Sun
4. Cathedral - The Carnival Bizarre
5. Penance - Parallel Corners

## C. PERSONNEL

### Best Vocals
Qualifier: Going for a combination of hottest God-given chords and ability and class with which they are brandished.

1. Steven Tyler
2. Rob Halford
3. Bon Scott
4. Freddie Mercury
5. Phil Lynott
6. George Criston (Kick Axe)
7. Graham Bonnet
8. Phil Anselmo
9. Frank Dimino (Angel)
10. Glenn Danzig

### Best Guitarist
Qualifier: Best all around axe-meister here, i.e. classy, technically smokin', exuding effortless mastery of both riff and solo duties, or at least god-like domination in one or the other.

1. Brian May
2. Ritchie Blackmore
3. Jake E. Lee
4. Adrian Vandenberg
5. Brian Robertson
6. Michael Schenker
7. Angus Young
8. Tony Iommi
9. Billy Gibbons
10. Kim Mitchell

### Best Soloist

Qualifier: I've created this category to pay particular homage to the dudes that have come up with the most mentally imprintable fret-burning solo breaks.

1. Brian May
2. Ritchie Blackmore
3. Kim Mitchell
4. Billy Gibbons
5. Thin Lizzy's arsenal of magicians

### Best Drummer

1. John Bonham
2. Tommy Aldridge
3. Vinnie Paul
4. Dave Grohl
5. Alex Van Halen

### Best Bassist

1. John Paul Jones
2. Michael Anthony
3. John Deacon
4. Phil Lynott
5. Geddy Lee

### Best Keyboardist

1. Jon Lord
2. Ken Hensley
3. Allen Lanier
4. Greg Giuffria
5. David Rosenthal

### Most Over-Rated Performer

Qualifier: Included to cast particular scorn upon those who are treated as gods for whatever reason and don't deserve it, or those that abuse or squander their technical proficiency. Otherwise known as the Eric Clapton Award.

1. Eric Clapton (guitar)
2. Alex Lifeson (guitar)
3. Eddie Van Halen (guitar)
4. Billy Sheehan (bass)
5. Cozy Powell (drums)
6. Steve Harris (bass)
7. Jimmy Page (guitar)
8. Courtney Love (all departments)
9. Carmine Appice (drums)
10. Sonic Youth (am I missing something?)

### Best Showman

Qualifier: The dude responsible for keeping one awake or downright hypnotized at the much-over-rated live experience.

1. David Lee Roth
2. Freddie Mercury
3. Steven Tyler
4. Iggy Pop
5. Phil Anselmo

### Best Producer

Qualifier: Don't actually know what a producer really does, but I've always considered it the guy responsible for the recording.

1. Rick Rubin
2. Matt Wallace
3. Roy Thomas Baker
4. Jack Endino
5. Terry Date

## D. EVERYTHING ELSE

### The Origins Of Heavy Metal

According to various experts on the subject, and me.

1. **In Rock**, **Uriah Heep**, and **Paranoid**
2. *Helter Skelter*
3. The Kinks' *All Day And All Of The Night* and *You Really Got Me*
4. Buddy Guy, Vanilla Fudge, The Byrds and/or alchemy (according to Sandy Pearlman)
5. Led Zeppelin's *Communication Breakdown*
6. Blue Cheer, MC5, The Stooges
7. "Heavy metal thunder!" from Steppenwolf's *Born To Be Wild*
8. Jimi Hendrix, Cream, Yardbirds
9. old blues guys
10. Venom!

### Best Lyrics

1. Blue Öyster Cult
2. Max Webster
3. Thin Lizzy
4. Clutch
5. King's X

### Best Album Covers

1. Blue Öyster Cult
2. Motörhead
3. Uriah Heep
4. Budgie
5. Hawkwind

### Worst Album Covers

1. AC/DC
2. Foreigner
3. Aerosmith
4. Cannibal Corpse
5. Judas Priest

### Most Influential Band

Qualifier: Bands that have had the greatest impact on the growth of metal.

1. Black Sabbath
2. Judas Priest
3. Metallica
4. Kiss
5. Deep Purple
6. Venom
7. Iggy And The Stooges
8. Nirvana
9. The Beatles
10. Aerosmith

# APPENDIX 3: 9's and 10's: The Desert Island LP's

The following list summarizes the records I believe are the best heavy metal, hard rock and its adjacent offshoots have to offer, the few hundred works of wattage that I would deem essential nourishment stranded on the proverbial desert island, with nothing but a spear, case of beer, and 300 solid watts of hi-fidelity home entertainment electronics. I've included both 9's and 10's because 10's alone would be no life at all. An asterisk (*) denotes a 10 for that added trace of recognition blazing perfection deserves. For the record, there are approximately 249 10's and 246 9's.

## A

Accept - Restless & Wild*
Accept - Balls To The Wall*
Accept - Metal Heart
AC/DC - Let There Be Rock*
AC/DC - Powerage*
AC/DC - Highway To Hell*
AC/DC - Back In Black*
AC/DC - Flick Of The Switch*
Aerosmith - Get Your Wings*
Aerosmith - Toys In The Attic
Aerosmith - Rocks*
Aerosmith - Draw The Line
Aerosmith - Night In The Ruts
Aerosmith - Pump*
Aerosmith - Livin' On The Edge (ep)*
Aerosmith - Get A Grip
Aerosmith - Nine Lives
Agony Column - God, Guns & Guts
Agony Column - Brave Words & Bloody Knuckles*
Alcatrazz - No Parole From Rock 'n' Roll*
Alcatrazz - Disturbing The Peace*
Alice in Chains - Face Lift
Alice in Chains - Dirt*
Alice in Chains - Alice in Chains*
Amorphis - Elegy
Angel - Angel*
Angel - Helluva Band*
Angel City - Face To Face*
Angel City - Darkroom*
Angel City - Two Minute Warning*
Angel Witch - Angel Witch*
Anthrax - Spreading The Disease*
Anthrax - Sound Of White Noise*
Anvil - Metal On Metal
Anvil - Forged In Fire

## B

Badlands - Badlands*
Badlands - Voodoo Highway*
The Big F - The Big F*
Black Crowes - The Southern Harmony And Musical Companion*
Black Crowes - Amorica.
Black Crowes - Three Snakes And One Charm
Blackfoot - Siogo
Black Sabbath - Master Of Reality*
Black Sabbath - Vol 4*
Black Sabbath - Sabbath Bloody Sabbath*
Black Sabbath - Sabotage*
Black Sabbath - Technical Ecstacy*
Black Sabbath - Never Say Die
Black Sabbath - Heaven And Hell*
Black Sabbath - Mob Rules*
Black Sabbath - Born Again*
Black Sabbath - The Eternal Idol*
Blue Öyster Cult - Secret Treaties*
Blue Öyster Cult - Agents Of Fortune*
Blue Öyster Cult - Spectres*
Blue Öyster Cult - Mirrors*
Blue Öyster Cult - Cultösaurus Erectus*
Blue Öyster Cult - Fire Of Unknown Origin
Budgie - In For The Kill
Budgie - Bandolier*
Budgie - If I Were Brittania I'd Waive The Rules

Budgie - Impeckable
Budgie - Deliver Us From Evil*
Bulletboys - Freakshow
Bulletboys - Za-Za

## C

Carcass - Swansong*
Cathedral - Soul Sacrifice (ep)
Cathedral - The Ethereal Mirror
Cathedral - Cosmic Requiem
Cathedral - The Carnival Bizarre
Celtic Frost - Vanity/Nemesis
Cemetary - Sundown
Cemetary - Last Confessions
Chateaux - Chained And Desperate
Cheap Trick - Cheap Trick
Chum - Dead To The World
The Clash - The Clash*
The Clash - Give 'Em Enough Rope*
Clutch - Clutch
Collision - Collision*
Collision - Coarse
Alice Cooper - Billion Dollar Babies
Coroner - Mental Vortex
Corporal Punishment - Stonefield Of A Lifetime
Corrosion Of Conformity - Blind
Corrosion Of Conformity - Deliverance*
Corrosion Of Conformity - Wiseblood
The Cult - Electric

## D

The Damned - Damned Damned Damned
The Damned - Music For Pleasure*
The Damned - Machine Gun Etiquette*
Danzig - II Lucifuge
Danzig - 4*
The Dead Boys - Young, Loud And Snotty*
Dearly Beheaded - Temptation
Death Angel - Act III
Deep Purple - In Rock*
Deep Purple - Fireball
Deep Purple - Machine Head
Deep Purple - Perfect Strangers*
Deep Purple - House Of Blue Light*
Deep Purple - Purpendicular*
Derringer - Sweet Evil*
Derringer - If I Weren't So Romantic I'd Shoot You
Diamond Head - Lightning to The Nations*
Diamond Head - Borrowed Time
Bruce Dickinson - Skunkworks
The Dictators - Go Girl Crazy!
The Dictators - Manifest Destiny*
The Dictators - Bloodbrothers*
Dio - Holy Diver*
Dio - The Last In Line*
Dio - Dream Evil
Divine Sin - Winterland
DMZ - DMZ*
Down - Nola
Doctor Butcher - Doctor Butcher*
Drivin' N' Cryin' - Whisper Tames The Lion
Drivin' N' Cryin' - Mystery Road

## E

Edge Of Sanity - Purgatory Afterglow
Entombed - Clandestine
Entombed - Wolverine Blues*
Entombed - Entombed
Enuff Z'nuff - Strength
Enuff Z'nuff - Animals With Human Intelligence
Europe - Europe*
Everclear - Sparkle And Fade
Extreme - II Pornograffitti
Extreme - III Sides To Every Story*

## F

Faith No More - Introduce Yourself*
Faith No More - The Real Thing*
Faith No More - Angel Dust
Faith No More - King For A Day
Fastway - Fastway*
Fear Factory - Demanufacture
Fist - Fleet Street
Foghat - Fool For The City*
Four Horsemen - Gettin' Pretty Good At Barely Gettin' By

## G

Galactic Cowboys - Space In Your Face*
Galactic Cowboys - Machine Fish
Gamma - 1*
Gamma - 2*
Gamma Ray - Sigh No More
Gillan - Mr. Universe*
Gillan - Glory Road
Gillan - Double Trouble*
Gillan - Magic*
Glory Bell's Band - Dressed In Black
Gorefest - Soul Survivor
Grave Digger - Heavy Metal Breakdown
Green River - Dry As A Bone (ep)*
Green River - Rehab Doll*
Grim Reaper - See You In Hell*
Guns N' Roses - Use Your Illusion I*
Guns N' Roses - Use Your Illusion II*

## H

Hall Aflame - Guaranteed Forever
Handsome - Handsome
Hanoi Rocks - Self Destruction Blues
Hanoi Rocks - Two Steps From The Move
Heavy Load - Metal Conquest (ep)
Heavy Load - Death Or Glory*
Helmet - Meantime
Helmet - Betty
Highway Chile - Storybook Heroes*
Highway Chile - For The Wild And Lonely (ep)*
Holocaust - The Nightcomers*
Hüsker Dü - New Day Rising*
Hüsker Dü - Flip Your Wig
Hüsker Dü - Candy Apple Grey*
Hüsker Dü - Warehouse: Songs And Stories*

## I

I Love You - All Of Us
In Flames - The Jester Race
Iron Maiden - Killers
Iron Maiden - Piece Of Mind*
Iron Maiden - Powerslave

## J

Jag Panzer - Ample Destruction
Jane's Addiction - Nothing's Shocking*
Jane's Addiction - Ritual De Lo Habitual
Jesus Christ - Jesus Christ
Judas Priest - Sad Wings Of Destiny*
Judas Priest - Sin After Sin*
Judas Priest - Stained Class*
Judas Priest - Hell Bent For Leather*
Judas Priest - Unleashed In The East
Judas Priest - British Steel
Judas Priest - Painkiller

## K

Karma To Burn - Karma To Burn
Kick Axe - Vices*
Kik Tracee - No Rules
Kik Tracee - Field Trip (ep)*
Kings Of The Sun - Full Frontal Attack
King's X - Out Of The Silent Planet
King's X - Gretchen Goes To Nebraska*
King's X - Faith Hope Love*
King's X - King's X
King's X - Dogman
King's X - Ear Candy*
Korn - Life Is Peachy
Kyuss - Blues For The Red Sun
Kyuss - Sky Valley

## L

Lake Of Tears - Headstones
Lake Of Tears - A Crimson Cosmos*
Last Crack - Sinister Funkhouse #17
Last Crack - Burning Time*
Led Zeppelin - III*
Led Zeppelin - Physical Graffiti*
Led Zeppelin - In Through The Out Door*
Lillian Axe - Psychoschizophrenia
Liquid Jesus - Pour In The Sky
Living Colour - Vivid
Love/Hate - Blackout In The Red Room*
Love/Hate - Wasted In America*
Love/Hate - Let's Rumble
Philip Lynott - Solo In Soho
Philip Lynott - The Philip Lynott Album*

## M

Machine Head - Burn My Eyes
Yngwie J. Malmsteen's Rising Force - Marching Out*
Manic Street Preachers - Gold Against The Soul
Manic Street Preachers - The Holy Bible
Manowar - Hail To England*
Manowar - Fighting The World
Manowar - The Triumph Of Steel
Manowar - Louder Than Hell
Masters Of Reality - Masters Of Reality*
Masters Of Reality - Sunrise On The Sufferbus
Max Webster - Max Webster*
Max Webster - High Class In Borrowed Shoes*
Max Webster - Mutiny Up My Sleeve
Max Webster - A Million Vacation*
Max Webster - Universal Juveniles
Megadeth - Rust In Peace*
Megadeth - Countdown To Extinction*
Megadeth - Cryptic Writings
Melvins - Stag
Memento Mori - Rhymes Of Lunacy
Mercyful Fate - Melissa
Mercyful Fate - Don't Break The Oath*
Mercyful fate - Into The Unknown
Meshuggah - None
Meshuggah - Destroy Erase Improve*
Metal Church - The Human Factor*
Metal Church - Hanging In The Balance
Metallica - Kill 'Em All
Metallica - Ride The Lightning*
Metallica - Master Of Puppets*
Metallica - . . . And Justice For All
Michelin Slave - Poised To Meet The Maker
Ministry - Psalm 69
Kim Mitchell - Kim Mitchell (ep)*
Kim Mitchell - Akimbo Alogo
Montrose - Montrose*
More - Blood & Thunder*

Morgana Lefay - Knowing Just As I
Mötley Crüe - Too Fast For Love*
Motley Crue - Generation Swine
Motörhead - Overkill
Motörhead - Ace Of Spades*
Motörhead - Another Perfect Day
Motörhead - Bastards*
Motörhead - Sacrifice
Motörhead - Overnight Sensation
Mourning Sign - Mourning Sign
Mudhoney - Superfuzz Bigmuff (ep)*
My Dying Bride - The Angel And The Dark River
My Dying Bride - Like Gods Of The Sun

## N

Nasty Savage - Nasty Savage
Nasty Savage - Abstract Reality (ep)
Nevermore - The Politics Of Ecstasy
New York Dolls - New York Dolls*
New York Dolls - Too Much Too Soon*
Nine Inch Nails - The Downward Spiral
Nirvana - Bleach*
Nirvana - Nevermind*
Nirvana - In Utero*
NoMeansNo - Wrong*
NoMeansNo - The Worldhood Of The World (as such)
Non-Fiction - In The Know
Notorious - Notorious*
Nudeswirl - Nudeswirl
Ted Nugent - Free For All
Ted Nugent - State Of Shock
Ted Nugent - Scream Dream

## O

Ozzy Osbourne - Diary Of A Madman*
Ozzy Osbourne - Bark At The Moon*
Ozzy Osbourne - No Rest For The Wicked
Ozzy Osbourne - No More Tears
Overdose - Scars
Overdrive - Swords And Axes*
Oz - Fire In The Brain

## P

Pantera - Cowboys From Hell*
Pantera - Vulgar Display Of Power*
Pantera - Far Beyond Driven*
Pantera - The Great Southern Trendkill
Paradise Lost - Icon*
Paw - Dragline*
Pearl Jam - Ten
Pearl Jam - Vs.*
Pearl Jam - No Code
Penance - Parallel Corners
The Joe Perry Project - Let The Music Do The Talking*
Phantoms Of The Future - Call Of The Wild
Robert Plant - The Principle Of Moments*
Robert Plant - Now And Zen
Robert Plant - Fate Of Nations
Iggy Pop - Lust For Life
Iggy Pop - New Values*
Pyogenesis - Twinaleblood

## Q

Quartz - Deleted
Quartz - Stand Up And Fight*
Queen - Queen*
Queen - II*
Queen - Sheer Heart Attack*
Queen - A Night At The Opera*
Queen - A Day At The Races
Queen - News Of The World
Queen - Jazz*
Queen - Innuendo

## R

Rage - Perfect Man
Rage Against The Machine - Evil Empire
Rainbow - Rising
Rainbow - Long Live Rock 'n' Roll
Rainbow - Down To Earth*
Rainbow - Bent Out Of Shape
Ram Jam - Portrait Of The Artist As A Young Ram*
Ratt - Out Of The Cellar
Raven - Wiped Out
Raven - All For One*
Raven - Break The Chain (ep)
Riot - Narita
Riot - Fire Down Under*
Riot - Born In America
Rocket From The Crypt - Scream, Dracula, Scream!
Rush - 2112
Rush - A Farewell To Kings
Rush - Hemispheres*
Rush - Moving Pictures*
Rush - Signals*

## S

Saigon Kick - Saigon Kick
Saigon Kick - The Lizard*
The Saints - Eternally Yours
Samael - Passage*
Samson - Shock Tactics*
Santers - Racing Time
Savage - Loose 'n' Lethal*
Savage - Holy Wars
Savage - Babylon
Savatage - Sirens*
Savatage - Power Of The Night*
Savatage - The Dungeons Are Calling (ep)*
Savatage - Hall Of The Mountain King
Saxon - Power And The Glory*
The Michael Schenker Group - Assault Attack*
Michael Schenker Group - Built To Destroy*
Schubert - Toilet Songs
Scorpions - Taken By Force
Scorpions - Animal Magnetism*
Scorpions - Blackout*
Scum - Purple Dreams & Magic Poems
Sentenced - Amok
Sentenced - Love & Death (ep)*
Sentenced - Down
Sepultura - Arise
Sepultura - Chaos A.D.*
Sepultura - Roots*
The Sex Pistols - Never Mind The Bollocks Here's The Sex Pistols*
Shooting Gallery - Shooting Gallery
Skid Row - Slave To The Grind
Skid Row - Subhuman Race
Skyclad - A Burnt Offering For The Bone Idol
Skyclad - Prince Of The Poverty Line*
Skyclad - The Silent Whales Of Lunar Sea
Slaughter - The Wild Life
Slayer - Reign In Blood
Slayer - South Of Heaven*
Slayer - Seasons In The Abyss
Slow - Against The Glass (ep)
The Smalls - Waste And Tragedy
Smashing Pumpkins - Mellon Collie And The Infinite Sadness*
Sons Of Freedom - Sons Of Freedom*
Sons Of Freedom - Gump
Sons Of Freedom - Tex
Sortilège - Metamorphosis*
Soul Asylum - Made To Be Broken*
Soul Asylum - While You Were Out*
Soul Asylum - Clam Dip And Other Delights (ep)
Soul Asylum - Hang Time*
Soul Asylum - And The Horse They Rode In On

Soul Asylum - Grave Dancers Union
Soundgarden - Screaming Life (ep)
Soundgarden - Ultramega OK
Soundgarden - Badmotorfinger
Soundgarden - Superunknown*
Soundgarden - Down On The Upside
Spiritual Beggars - Another Way To Shine
Status Quo - Piledriver
Status Quo - Quo*
Stone Temple Pilots - Purple
Iggy And The Stooges - Raw Power*
Suicidal Tendencies - The Art Of Rebellion
Sweet - Desolation Boulevard*
Sweet - Give Us A Wink*

# T

Tank - Power Of The Hunter
Tank - This Means War
The Tea Party - The Edges Of Twilight
Temple Of The Dog - Temple Of The Dog
Tesla - Psychotic Supper
Testament - The Ritual
Thin Lizzy - Fighting
Thin Lizzy - Jailbreak
Thin Lizzy - Johnny The Fox*
Thin Lizzy - Bad Reputation*
Thin Lizzy - Black Rose*
Thin Lizzy - Renegade*
Thin Lizzy - Thunder And Lightning*
Tiamat - Wildhoney*
Torch - Fireraiser (ep)
Torch - Torch*
Torch - Electrikiss*
Trance - Power Infusion
Pat Travers - Heat In The Street*
Pat Travers - Go For What You Know*
Pat Travers - Radio Active
Pat Travers - Black Pearl*
Pat Travers - BBC Radio 1 Live In Concert
T-Ride - T-Ride
Trouble - Trouble
Trouble - Run To The Light
Trouble Trouble*
Trouble - Manic Frustration*
Trouble - Plastic Green Head
220 Volt - Power Games
220 Volt - Mind Over Muscle*
Tygers Of Pan Tang - Wild Cat

Tygers Of Pan Tang - Crazy Nights
Tygers Of Pan Tang - The Cage
Tyketto - Shine*

# U

UFO - No Heavy Petting
UFO - Lights Out
UFO - No Place To Run*
UFO - The Wild The Willing And The Innocent*
UFO - Mechanix
UFO - Making Contact
UFO - The Best Of The Rest
UFO - Radio One Live In Concert
Uriah Heep - Uriah Heep
Uriah Heep - Look At Yourself*
Uriah Heep - Demons And Wizards*
Uriah Heep - Abominog*
Uriah Heep - Rarities From The Bronze Age
Uriah Heep - Sea Of Light*

# V

Vandenberg - Vandenberg*
Vandenberg - Heading For A Storm*
Vandenberg - Alibi
Van Halen - Van Halen*
Van Halen - II*
Van Halen - Women And Children First*
Van Halen - Fair Warning*
Voivod - The Outer Limits*

# W

War Babies - War Babies*
Bill Ward - Ward One: Along The Way
Waysted - Vices*
White Lion - Big Game
Wildhearts - Earth vs The Wildhearts
Wildhearts - p.h.u.q.
Witchfinder General - Death Penalty*
Witchfinder General - Friends Of Hell*
Wolfsbane - Wolfsbane

# X, Y, Z

Y&T - Mean Streak
ZZ Top - Tres Hombres*
ZZ Top - Tejas*

# APPENDIX 4: Non-Metal: A Bunch of Cool Bands.

Believe it or not, your hallowed author listens to stuff other than headbangin' fare. Occasionally anyways. This is my list of rock combos I find important for vast reams of reasons that would take at least another book to explain. Given that you peruse this book out of a shared appreciation for heavy metal and hard rock, I'm not going to rail on, even though I feel a name-check is in order. And even if I consider these artists as creative, important and essential as Lizzy, BÖC, Gillan or Pantera, they ain't heavy. I'm well aware that I've review records in this book that are not strictly metal (i.e. crossover new wave stuff, completely mellow albums from generally heavy bands, early hard rock pioneers, new alternative rock). But suffice to say most of what made the cut has more than the usual amount of loud guitars, essentially what counts for inclusion in this esteemed volume.

So take this list as a personal indulgence, thanking these bands for what they've done to my way of thinking. But explore at your own risk. Rather than brush-stroke any of these bands with ratings (which would be a monumental and ultimately ludicrous task), I nevertheless couldn't resist adding my critical two-cents worth by bolding the names of bands I consider most musically brilliant, philosophically complex, enigmatic, highly entertaining, or on occasion heavier and more dangerous than any metal band could hope to be. Sometimes its all of the above. It's no exaggeration whatsoever in saying some of these bands have dented my head as heavily as great literature, changing my psychological brew forever. I have drifted asleep literally hundreds of times to compilation tapes I've made of The Grateful Dead, The Church, Little Feat, and Joe Ely, and under circumstances such as the quiet time before nodding off, it's hard not to become enthralled. I hope you can find the exploratory zeal to seek the collective wisdoms to be found amongst the following artists. They promise to reveal avenues never imagined.

Dave Alvin
Phil Alvin
The Allman Brothers Band
Eric Ambel
Atlanta Rhythm Section
The Babys
**The Bears**
Adrian Belew
Big Audio Dynamite
Blues Traveller
Billy Bragg
Bram Tchaikovsky
**Kate Bush**
John Cale
Camper van Beethoven
Captain Beefheart
**The Chameleons U.K.**
The Church
The Clash
Elvis Costello
Terence Trent D'Arby
The db's
**The Del-Lords**
Dinosaur Jr
**John Doe**
Joe Ely
Eno
The Explorers
54-40
Donald Fagen
**Firehose**
Fishbone
Robert Fripp
**Peter Gabriel**
Gang of Four
**Jerry Garcia Band**
Golden Earring
Golden Palaminos
**The Grateful Dead**
Great Plains
Roy Harper
Hum
Ian Hunter
Robert Hunter
Joe Jackson
The Jam
Jason and the Scorchers
David Johansen
Klark Kent
Steven Kilbey
**King Crimson**
The Knitters
Ed Kuepper

**David Lindley**
Little Feat
Gary Lucas
The Lucy Show
Lynyrd Skynyrd
Magazine
**The Meat Puppets**
John Cougar Mellencamp
Midnight Oil
**The Minutemen**
The Motors
Mott the Hoople
Bob Mould
New Riders Of The Purple Sage
No Dice
The Northern Pikes
The Outlaws
**Graham Parker**
The Payolas
Penguin Cafe Orchestra
Pere Ubu
Phish
The Pixies
The Police
REM
The Records
Red Hot Chili Peppers
**The Replacements**
Keith Richards
Jonathan Richman
**The Saints**
Sonic Youth
Chris Squire
Steely Dan
The Sun and the Moon
Roger Taylor
David Thomas
**Pete Townshend**
The Tubes
U2
**Violent Femmes**
Tom Waits
Joe Walsh
**The Waterboys**
Paul Westerberg
Chris Whitley
World Party
**X**
XTC
Yes
Neil Young
Frank Zappa
Warren Zevon

## ABOUT THE AUTHOR

Born: Castlegar, B.C., 1963.
Raised: Trail, B.C.
B.A. English, University Of Victoria, 1984.
M.B.A. Marketing, McMaster University, 1987.
In sales with Xerox, 2 1/2 years.
Co-owner of The Perfect Page (desktop
publishing and print-broking) with Neil Deas,
Sept. '89 to the present.
Married Beth Sept. '90; no kids yet.

# Hot Wacks

**Hot Wacks XV**
*$22.95 US*
*($24.95 Canada)*

**Hot Wacks Supp. 1**
*$12.95 ($14.95)*

**Hot Wacks Supp. 2**
*$14.95 ($16.95)*

**Hot Wacks Supp. 3**
*$15.95 ($16.95)*

**Hot Wacks Supp. 4**
*$17.95 ($19.95)*

**Hot Wacks Supp. 5**
*$17.95 ($19.95)*

# Hot Wacks

**Hot Wacks books** are bootleg CD & record rating guides and discographies than can save you money. For the past 20 years, **Hot Wacks books** have been indispensable tools for the bootleg collector. You'll find bootleg listings with song titles, matrix numbers, recording sources, sound quality and specific comments for artists ranging from Aerosmith to Frank Zappa, arranged alphabetically by the artists' names, making this a complete and easy-to-use guide.

**Hot Wacks Book: XV** *Master guide, over 800 pages (1992)*
ISBN 0-9698080-3-8 (paperback)  $22.95 ($24.95)
**Hot Wacks Book: Supplement 1** *(1993)*
ISBN 0-9698080-4-6 (paperback)  $12.95 ($14.95)
**Hot Wacks Book: Supplement 2** *(1994)*
ISBN 0-9698080-0-2 (paperback)  $14.95 ($16.95)
**Hot Wacks Book: Supplement 3** *(1995)*
ISBN 0-9698080-2-X (paperback)  $15.95 ($16.95)
**Hot Wacks Book: Supplement 4** *(1996)*
ISBN 0-9698080-5-4 (paperback)  $17.95 ($19.95)
**Hot Wacks Book: Supplement 5** *(1997)*
ISBN 0-9698080-8-9 (paperback)  $17.95 ($19.95)

# THE MAKING OF...

The Making Of...72 Pages,
Color covers, Packed with facts, over **20,000** words,
each packaged in it's own **Jewel Box** and all for only
$7.95 US or $9.95 Canadian

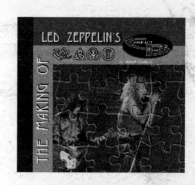

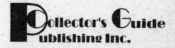

## CENTURY MEDIA RECORDS Presents: The Collector's Guide To Heavy Metal - CD Sampler

Reference for CD on opposite page:
1. TIAMAT "Cold Seed" (taken from *A Deeper Kind Of Slumber* CD, avail. August '97)
2. SENTENCED "Noose" (taken from *Down* CD)
3. ICED EARTH "The Hunter" (taken from *The Dark Saga* CD)
4. SAMAEL "Rain" (taken from *Passage* CD)
5. SUNDOWN "19" (taken from *Design 19* CD)
6. NEVERMORE "This Sacrament" (taken from *The Politics Of Ecstasy* CD)
7. THE GATHERING "In Motion #1" (taken from *Mandylion* CD)
8. MOONSPELL "Opium" (taken from *Irreligious* CD)
9. STRAPPING YOUNG LAD "Underneath The Waves" (taken from *City* CD)
10. MY OWN VICTIM "Unjustified" (taken from *No Voice, No Rights, No Freedom* CD)
11. SKINLAB "Race Of Hate" (taken from *Bound, Gagged & Blindfolded* CD)
12. STUCK MOJO "Twisted" (taken from *Pigwalk* CD)
13. MORGOTH "This Fantastic Decade" (taken from *Feel Sorry For The Fanatic* CD)
14. MERAUDER "Mirror Shows Black" (taken from *Master Killer* CD)
15. CHUM "Stepping On Cracks" (taken from *Dead To The World* CD)
16. TROUBLE "The Eye" (taken from *Plastic Green Head* CD)
17. GRAVE "Lovesong" (taken from *Hating Life* CD)
18. SENTENCED "Nepenthe" (taken from *Amok* CD)
19. TIAMAT "Visionaire" (taken from *Wildhoney* CD)

*Editor's Note:*
*Picking a single CD's worth of tracks to represent the future flame of metal is pretty much an impossibility. But of all the labels and their stables, Century Media is the undisputed king, this book having been crammed with more 8's, and 9's, and 10's bearing that venerable name, long before the idea of a sampler ever arose. If anything, the following metal sledges should convince nay-sayers that metal bears many flavours, both lyrically and musically, that craftsmanship is revered, and that the heavy institutions of the '90s ain't no trip down memory lane! As the mighty fall, falter or simply go away, bands like these have been quietly building catalogues to be respected. So dive right in and witness what myself and many of my rock scribe buds have figured represent hard music's soaring creative hopes . . . Salut!*
*Martin Popoff*

Thanks for the kind words, Martin, and we couldn't be more honored to be part of this esteemed and invaluable guide for the heavy metal connoisseur . As you'll hear from the CD we've supplied you with, Century Media is dedicated to bringing you some of the best and brightest groups in the ever-changing world of metal today. Every band on the compilation may not be your particular cup of tea, but we won't dispute the fact that our roster is quite a diverse one that attempts to conquer the close-mindedness that continually threatens to drive this great form of music deep into the underground. We therefore ask that you listen to these songs at least twice before making any real judgment, as many of these bands avoid immediate hooks and verse-chorus-verse arrangements in favor of something more adventurous yet with greater reward and a lasting impact.

Hopefully you agree. Regardless of where you live, you should be able to find (or order) these titles at your local record retailer, but in lieu of that you can always order them directly from us. Each of the CD's mentioned above are full-length titles, and are available for $10 each plus shipping/handling dependent upon where you happen to be situated. Just call our toll-free number listed below with any major credit card, or write your order on a separate sheet of paper along with your name and address, and mail or fax it to us along with a Money Order or Personal Check payable in US Dollars (no Canadian personal checks, sorry) or well-concealed US currency, using the information listed below. Shipping/handling rates are: Within the USA - $2.50 for the 1st item, 75 cents for each additional item; Canada/Mexico add $3.50 for the 1st item; $1.00 each additional item; Central/South America add $6.00 for the 1st item, $2.00 for each additional item; Rest of world add $8.00 for the 1st item, $3.00 for each additional item. Even if you don't plan to order, just contact us and request our free catalog, loaded with over 150 titles, all available at equally great prices. We sincerely hope you enjoy the music on this disc, and that we hear from each of you. Regards,

Century Media Records

E-mail: mail@centurymedia.com
Fax #: (1) 310-574-7414

For orders, send to: Century Media Mail Order
1453-A 14th St. #324
Santa Monica, CA 90404, USA
Toll-free orders within the USA: 1-800-250-4600
Worldwide orders & inquiries: (1) 310-574-7400, ext. 116